THE
DOCTRINE
OF GOD

A THEOLOGY OF LORDSHIP

A SERIES BY JOHN M. FRAME

Also available in the series:

The Doctrine of the Knowledge of God

THE
DOCTRINE
OF GOD

JOHN M. FRAME

P&R PUBLISHING
P.O. BOX 817 • PHILLIPSBURG • NEW JERSEY 08865-0817

Library of Congress Cataloging-in-Publication Data

Frame, John M., 1939–
    The doctrine of God / John M. Frame.
        p. cm. — (A theology of lordship)
    Includes bibliographical references (p.) and indexes.
    ISBN 0-87552-263-7
    1. God.   I. Title.   II. Series.

    BT103 .F73   2002
    231—dc21   2001059110

To Justin

"For my thoughts are not your thoughts,
    neither are your ways my ways,"
                                    declares the LORD.
"As the heavens are higher than the earth,
    so are my ways higher than your ways
    and my thoughts than your thoughts." (Isa. 55:8–9)

For this is what the high and lofty One says—
    he who lives forever, whose name is holy:
"I live in a high and holy place,
    but also with him who is contrite and lowly in spirit,
to revive the spirit of the lowly
    and to revive the heart of the contrite." (Isa. 57:15)

Oh, the depth of the riches of the wisdom and knowledge of God!
    How unsearchable his judgments,
    and his paths beyond tracing out!
"Who has known the mind of the Lord?
    Or who has been his counselor?"
"Who has ever given to God,
    that God should repay him?"
For from him and through him and to him are all things.
    To him be the glory forever! Amen. (Rom. 11:33–36)

Worthy is the Lamb, who was slain,
to receive power and wealth and wisdom and strength
and honor and glory and praise! (Rev. 5:12)

Why can't I see God; Is he watching me?
Is he somewhere out in space, or is he here with me?
I am just a child; teach me from his word;
Then I'll go and tell to all the great things I have heard.

Teach me while my heart is tender;
Tell me all that I should know,
And even through the years I will remember,
No matter where I go.*

* "Why Can't I See God?" From *Songs on the Westminster Catechism* by Judy Rogers, used by permission. www.judyrogers.com © Judy Rogers, 1991.

Contents

PART FIVE: BIBLICAL DESCRIPTIONS OF GOD

PART SIX: THE TRIUNE GOD

Analytical Outline

Preface

I am now returning to my Theology of Lordship series, fifteen years after the publication of its first installment, *The Doctrine of the Knowledge of God*.[1] First, let me thank all of you who encouraged me to continue, despite many interruptions! I'm sorry to have kept you waiting so long, but I do believe that in God's providence these intervening years have helped me to make this a better book than it otherwise would have been.

I have spent these years researching and focusing my thoughts, as well as doing other writing that has helped me to put the doctrine of God into a broader perspective. My *Medical Ethics*[2] and my *Perspectives on the Word of God*[3] were originally series of lectures in which I was able to explain and develop my three-perspective approach in application to specific issues and with a broader range of readers in mind.

My *Evangelical Reunion*[4] and my two books on worship, *Worship in Spirit and Truth*[5] and *Contemporary Worship Music: A Biblical Defense*,[6] were responses to church controversies—responses that, in these situations, I felt really couldn't wait. But though my studies of worship were forced on me by circumstances, I must regard those circumstances as providential. Nothing has been more helpful to my understanding of God's nature and work than my study of what it means to worship him according to Scripture.

And, of course, 1995 was the one hundredth anniversary of Cornelius Van Til's birth. I had long planned to pay homage to him in that year, and my rereading of his work yielded my *Apologetics to the Glory of God*[7] and *Cornelius Van Til: An Analysis of His Thought*.[8] I have always seen the Theology of Lordship series as in large part an attempt to apply Van Til's insights, and so I am very glad that I was able to give him some thorough attention before writing the present volume.

---

1. Phillipsburg, N.J.: P&R Publishing, 1987. Beginning in chapter 1, I shall refer to my books as shown in the list of abbreviations that follows this preface.
2. Phillipsburg, N.J.: P&R Publishing, 1988.
3. Eugene, Ore.: Wipf and Stock, 1999; originally published by P&R Publishing, 1990.
4. Grand Rapids: Baker, 1991. Now out of print.
5. Phillipsburg, N.J.: P&R Publishing, 1996.
6. Phillipsburg, N.J.: P&R Publishing, 1997.
7. Phillipsburg, N.J.: P&R Publishing, 1994.
8. Phillipsburg, N.J.: P&R Publishing, 1995.

But I'm very happy to be back on track now with this series, and I hope that, after this book, *The Doctrine of the Word of God* and *The Doctrine of the Christian Life* will follow in fairly rapid succession—well, with perhaps a few minor interruptions. *The Doctrine of God* is the second volume to appear, but the third in the series as I envision it. The completed series will be on the doctrines of (1) the Word of God, (2) the knowledge of God, (3) God, and (4) the Christian life. The principle of this organization is that we meet God in his Word, a meeting that gives us knowledge, which enables us to describe him as God, which enables us to live for him. Of course, in my view this is not a rigid, temporal sequence. Each of these presupposes and enriches the other three, and each can be described from the perspective of the others. Careful readers will notice that each of these books discusses the subjects of the other three in summary fashion, so that the books differ more in emphasis and perspective than in sharply distinguishable subject matter. So the series itself has a perspectival structure, though each book can, I think, be understood by someone who hasn't read the others.

I envision these books as seminary-level texts that will be helpful to pastors and also to lay Christians who have done some college-level study.

Again, I want to thank all of those who have helped me to think through these matters, including my negative critics. As I approach this particular subject, I feel especially indebted to my teachers and colleagues, living and departed, who have taught the doctrine of God: Cornelius Van Til, John Murray, Edwin H. Palmer, D. Clair Davis, Norman Shepherd, Vern S. Poythress, and Sinclair Ferguson. Thanks also to Doug Swagerty, who produced an excellent edition of my lecture notes, a crucial step in getting my thoughts into some meaningful order; Carla Meberg, who helped me with proofreading on a volunteer basis; Steve Hays, Jim Jordan, and Vern Poythress, who sent me their usual thorough and insightful reviews of the book; the faculty and trustees of Westminster Theological Seminary in California, for giving me a leave of absence to complete the book; my students in the Doctrine of God and Man course at Westminster, who studied and discussed my manuscript, making many useful suggestions; the people at Reformed Theological Seminary, who welcomed me to my new position and encouraged me much through a difficult time in my life. Thanks also to James W. Scott, who edited this volume, and to P&R Publishing for their great patience with me.

Abbreviations of
Frequently Cited Titles

I will refer to classical sources merely by title (or abbreviation). These can be found in a variety of editions, some of which I have listed in the bibliography.

AGG	John M. Frame, *Apologetics to the Glory of God* (Phillipsburg, N.J.: P&R Publishing, 1994)
ChD	Karl Barth, *Church Dogmatics* (Edinburgh: T. and T. Clark, 1936–60)
CVT	John M. Frame, *Cornelius Van Til: An Analysis of His Thought* (Phillipsburg, N.J.: P&R Publishing, 1995)
DBI	Leland Ryken, James C. Wilhoit, and Tremper Longman III, *Dictionary of Biblical Imagery* (Downers Grove, Ill.: InterVarsity Press, 1998)
DG	Herman Bavinck, *The Doctrine of God* (Grand Rapids: Baker, 1951)
DKG	John M. Frame, *The Doctrine of the Knowledge of God* (Phillipsburg, N.J.: P&R Publishing, 1987)
Institutes	John Calvin, *Institutes of the Christian Religion*, ed. John T. McNeill, trans. Ford Lewis Battles, The Library of Christian Classics (Philadelphia: Westminster Press, 1960)
JETS	*Journal of the Evangelical Theological Society*
RD	Heinrich Heppe, *Reformed Dogmatics* (Grand Rapids: Baker, 1950, 1978)
SCG	Thomas Aquinas, *Summa contra gentiles*
ST	Thomas Aquinas, *Summa theologiae*
WCF	Westminster Confession of Faith
WLC	Westminster Larger Catechism
WSC	Westminster Shorter Catechism
WTJ	*Westminster Theological Journal*

CHAPTER 1

Introduction

There is nothing more important than knowing God. Consider these Scripture passages:

> "Let not the wise man boast of his wisdom
>   or the strong man boast of his strength
>   or the rich man boast of his riches,
> but let him who boasts boast about this:
>   that he understands and knows me,
> that I am the LORD, who exercises kindness,
>   justice and righteousness on earth,
>   for in these I delight,"
> declares the LORD. (Jer. 9:23–24)

> Now this is eternal life: that they may know you, the only true God, and Jesus Christ, whom you have sent. (John 17:3)

But we live in an age in which the knowledge of God is rare. Many speak glibly about their belief in some god or other. But most would not even claim to know the true God, the God of the Bible. We know of so many people, of whom the psalmist's words are true:

> In his pride the wicked does not seek him;
>   in all his thoughts there is no room for God. (Ps. 10:4; cf. Rom. 3:11)

A large percentage of people today would say that they believe in God, but they rarely give him a thought, and they routinely make their decisions as

1

if he didn't exist. So "the fool says in his *heart*, 'There is no God' " (Ps. 14:1), whatever else he may say with his lips. Modern culture becomes more and more secular, pressing even to remove expressions of Christian faith from the public square. Abortion becomes a constitutional right. Criticisms of naturalistic evolution are excluded from public discussion because they are "religious."[1] Opinion makers and the mass media regard as hopelessly outdated the views that sex belongs only within marriage, that homosexuality is wicked, and that marriage is for life.

Alongside this idolatry of the secular, there are elements of modern society that are becoming more open to various old and new spiritualities, to views and practices dismissed by traditional Christianity as superstitions: crystals, occult healing, channeling, and mysticisms of various sorts.[2] The irony is that while society becomes more tolerant of these things, it becomes less tolerant of biblical Christianity. Although the opinion makers tell us that there are "many paths to God," they exclude the Christian path because it claims to be exclusive. The interesting fact is that both those who idolize secularity and those who promote alternative spiritualities agree in rejecting the God of Scripture. Only he is of sufficient weight for them to recognize as their enemy. So they are eager to shut him out of the cultural dialogue, to replace him with almost any alternative.

This cultural drift often captivates Christians as well. David Wells speaks vividly of the "weightlessness of God" in many churches today.[3] Churches and individual Christians devoted to the service of God often govern their lives by the standards of modern secular culture, rather than by the Word of God. They hear and speak about God, often with enthusiasm, but he makes little real difference to them. But how can it be that the Lord of heaven and earth makes no difference?

The doctrine of God, therefore, is not only important for its own sake, as Scripture teaches us, but also particularly important in our own time, as people routinely neglect its vast implications. Our message to the world must emphasize that God is real, and that he will not be trifled with. He

---

1. See especially Phillip Johnson, *Reason in the Balance* (Downers Grove, Ill.: InterVarsity Press, 1995) for a critique of this compartmentalization.

2. See the books of Peter Jones, *The Gnostic Empire Strikes Back* (Phillipsburg, N.J.: P&R Publishing, 1992), and *Spirit Wars* (Escondido, Calif.: Main Entry Editions, 1997).

3. David F. Wells, *God in the Wasteland* (Grand Rapids: Eerdmans, 1994), 88–117. I have expressed some differences with Wells's critique of modern evangelicals in my *Contemporary Worship Music: A Biblical Defense* (Phillipsburg, N.J.: P&R Publishing, 1997), 175–201, a discussion also published in *WTJ* 59 (1997): 269–318, with responses by Wells and Richard Muller, and a further response from me. But I have profited greatly from his observations.

is the almighty, majestic Lord of heaven and earth, and he demands our most passionate love and obedience.

THE DOCTRINE OF GOD IN HISTORY

Theology helps us to formulate that message, applying the biblical teaching about God to us and to our time.[4] The doctrine of God is one of the traditional "loci" of systematic theology, such as the doctrine of Scripture, the doctrine of man, the doctrine of Christ, and so on.

However, the doctrine of God is different from other loci in significant respects. For one thing, the church has reflected on the doctrine of God largely in dialogue with Greek philosophy and ancient Gnosticism. Early Christian theologians did disagree with the Greeks on significant points, and they were strong opponents of Gnosticism. Occasionally they agreed with some Greek philosophers, but when they did, they usually cited biblical reasons for doing so. It is wrong, therefore, to find in these early theologians a wholesale capitulation to non-Christian thought. Nevertheless, there were some compromises, as we shall see.

And, more obviously, this philosophical discussion had a profound effect on the vocabulary and style of Christian teaching concerning God. Terms like *being, substance, attribute, accident, essence, necessity,* and *intellect* came to dominate the Christian discussions of God, even though they are absent from Scripture. It isn't wrong to use extrabiblical language to formulate theology. The very nature of theology is to take the language of Scripture and put it into other language, so that we can better understand the Bible and apply it to issues not explicitly mentioned there. But the rather pervasive use of Greek philosophical language had significant effects on the substantive content of theology, and it impeded the church's understanding and use of the actual ways in which the Bible speaks of God.

The Protestant Reformers purged much of the philosophical language from the doctrine of salvation. Pre-Reformation theologians and post-Reformation Roman Catholics tended to see grace almost as a material substance that flowed from God through the church's sacraments to the people. The Reformers saw it, rather, in highly personal terms. In Protestantism, grace is God's personal attitude of favor to those who deserve his wrath, received not by the sacraments *ex opere operato,* but by faith (personal trust). Luther's rediscovery of the gospel (salvation by grace alone, through faith

---

4. For the concept of theology as application, see *DKG,* 81–85.

alone, in Christ alone) led to a drastic restructuring of the doctrines of sin and salvation.

But the Reformers did not revise the doctrine of God nearly as drastically as they revised the doctrine of salvation.[5] Luther and Calvin themselves said relatively little about God's nature or attributes or the Trinity. Rather, they basically accepted the formulations of their medieval predecessors. The great emphasis of their work was not on "theology proper" (the doctrine of God), but on God's saving grace in Christ.

It is interesting in this connection to compare the *Summa contra gentiles* of Thomas Aquinas (1225–74) with John Calvin's *Institutes of the Christian Religion.* Aquinas's *Summa* is written in four "books," dealing with God, creation, providence, and salvation. Present-day theologians usually treat creation and providence under the general category of the doctrine of God. On this understanding, the *Summa* gives three-fourths of its attention (actually more, in terms of pages) to the doctrine of God, and only one-fourth to the rest of the loci, comprising what we consider to be the heart of the gospel. And, in fact, Aquinas discusses the Trinity in book 4, so that much of that book, also, deals with the doctrine of God.[6]

Aquinas's treatment of the doctrine of God is greatly influenced by the Greek philosopher Aristotle and by pseudo-Dionysius, a virtual Neoplatonist. This philosophical emphasis, together with a method of making very fine distinctions, is what defines the term *scholastic* as it is applied to many medieval theologians.

Calvin's *Institutes* is also divided into four books, but very differently. They are entitled "The Knowledge of God the Creator," "The Knowledge of God the Redeemer in Christ . . . ," "The Way in Which We Receive the Grace of Christ . . . ," and "The External Means or Aids by Which God Invites Us. . . ." Of these four parts, only the first focuses on the subjects normally associated with the doctrine of God. That first part, however, deals with many other things as well. Chapters 1–9 deal with our knowledge of God through creation and Scripture. Chapters 15–18 discuss the creation of man in God's image. Only chapters 10–14 deal with the traditional subjects of theology proper. And in those chapters the main emphasis is on distinguishing the true God from the false. Chapter 13 deals with the Trinity. Calvin discusses election in book 3,

---

5. Otto Weber says, "Since the Reformation showed little interest in the traditional doctrine of God, it survived the fiery ordeal of the Reformation's reworking of all tradition far more unscathed than was really good." See his *Foundations of Dogmatics* (Grand Rapids: Eerdmans, 1981), 1:397.

6. Aquinas's *Summa theologiae* has a greater emphasis on grace than his *Summa contra gentiles,* as might be expected from its purpose. But the doctrine of God receives a far greater emphasis there, too (covering perhaps half the treatise), than in most Protestant theologies.

in the context of salvation, rather than in a general survey of God's decrees or actions. The *Institutes* contains no survey of divine attributes, no discussion of such matters as the relation of God's essence to his existence, no elaborate proofs for God's existence. The subject of proof comes up briefly in chapter 8, where Calvin mentions many evidences internal to Scripture, but presents no philosophical arguments for God's existence.

There is, therefore, a huge difference between Aquinas and Calvin in how they handle the doctrine of God. Calvin's treatment is quite minimal, compared to the emphasis of almost any pre-Reformation theologian. And Calvin's *Institutes* shows virtually no overt dependence on philosophy, which is pervasive in Aquinas.

Calvin's interest was not in developing an academically respectable system of thought, but "to show the applicability of the great doctrines to everyday life."[7]

Calvin's successors, such as Beza and Turretin, did take a great interest in the doctrine of God. But in their treatments there is very little that is distinctively Reformed. For the most part, the post-Reformation theologians followed, in this particular locus, the medieval models of Aquinas and others. Their doctrine of God, like that of Aquinas, is quite Aristotelian and much inclined to multiply distinctions. For this reason, they are often called "Protestant scholastics."

Since the eighteenth century, however, most Protestant theologians have been critical of both medieval and post-Reformation scholasticism. It has been argued that scholasticism was a kind of nitpicking venture, unnecessarily focusing on minutiae. Furthermore, it has been characterized as speculative and philosophical, rather than biblical. Finally, its teaching has been said to be largely irrelevant to the practical Christian life. My own judgment is that these criticisms are vastly overstated, but there is at least some truth in each of them.

What were the alternatives to scholasticism? Part of the appeal of theological liberalism, from the late seventeenth century to the present, has been its claim to offer alternatives to the scholastic approach. The liberal solution was to base theology on human experience, feelings, history, or ethics, rather than upon Scripture. This approach did appear to end the focus on minutiae, although readers of books like Schleiermacher's *The Christian Faith*[8] will wonder if the liberal effort didn't merely substitute one

7. Christopher B. Kaiser, *The Doctrine of God: A Historical Survey* (Westchester, Ill.: Crossway Books, 1982), 99. Theology as application! Kaiser also points out that the subtitle of Calvin's *Institutes* in the first edition was *summa pietatis*, an interesting contrast to Aquinas's *ST* and *SCG*.

8. Friedrich Schleiermacher, *The Christian Faith* (Edinburgh: T. and T. Clark, 1956).

set of minutiae for another. Liberalism did not in fact break the bond between theology and secular philosophy. Rather, it was far more bound to secular philosophy than was scholasticism. It did not make theology more practical, either. Its reduction of Christian truth to mere scholarly opinion actually made its claims quite irrelevant to those who were seeking the knowledge of God. Say what we may, there is a vast gulf between mere scholarly opinion and the knowledge of the living God.

Kierkegaard, Barth, and others sought to free Christian theology from any sort of philosophical system, although they actually substituted one philosophical view for another, with no increase in relevance. Existential, liberation, and process theologians accepted the assistance of philosophy—relying not on Plato or Aristotle, but rather on Heidegger, Marx, and Whitehead, respectively. And, unlike the scholastics, they arrived at views of God drastically different from the teachings of Scripture. Denying the sovereign God of the Bible is too large a price to pay to escape the relatively minor problems of scholasticism.

Such denials of God's sovereignty have even appeared in evangelical circles. One is the recent movement toward an "open view of God."[9] According to this view, God is temporal and lacks exhaustive knowledge of the future, being unsure of the free choices of human beings.

Orthodox Protestants[10] have also tried to escape from scholasticism in various ways. Pietists, Anabaptists, and later charismatics placed more emphasis on the inner life and less on the intellect. Some American fundamentalists tried to reduce the doctrines worthy of serious defense to a small number.

In Reformed circles, there have been various antischolastic strategies. Some have thought it important to vary the order of topics—for example, to deal with election, as Calvin did, under soteriology, rather than under theology proper.[11] Although varying the order of topics may occasionally have value in bringing out fresh perspectives and neglected relationships between doctrines, such modifications cannot make a great deal of differ-

---

9. For example, see Clark Pinnock et al., *The Openness of God* (Downers Grove, Ill.: InterVarsity Press, 1994); Richard Rice, *God's Foreknowledge and Man's Free Will* (Minneapolis: Bethany House, 1985); John Sanders, *The God Who Risks* (Downers Grove, Ill.: InterVarsity Press, 1998). I criticize this position in my *No Other God* (Phillipsburg, N.J.: P&R Publishing, 2001) and elsewhere in this present volume.

10. I define an "orthodox" Protestant as one who accepts the supreme authority of Scripture and who accepts one or more of the classic Protestant confessions as biblically sound. In my view, the deviations of the open theists from these standards exclude them from Christian orthodoxy.

11. This was one of the disputes between Moise Amyraut (1596–1664) and the more "scholastic" successors of Calvin. See Brian Armstrong, *Calvinism and the Amyraut Heresy* (Madison, Wis.: University of Wisconsin Press, 1969), and my review in *WTJ* 34 (1972): 186–92, published as appendix I in this volume.

ence in the problems associated with scholasticism. If a doctrine of election is scholastic in the worst sense, it won't help matters to move it, otherwise unchanged, from one locus to another.

It is important to see election, as Calvin did, as the fount of our salvation. But it is also important to see it, as Calvin also did, as an aspect of
God's eternal plan. Moving election to the locus of soteriology makes it
easier to express the former aspect of its meaning, but then one must go a
bit out of one's way to express the latter aspect. This is why locus shifting
is usually not very helpful. If it be said that this kind of approach is needed
to reproduce the emphasis of Scripture, I would reply that the work of theology is not to reproduce the emphasis of Scripture (to do that precisely
would require the theologian merely to quote the Bible from Genesis to
Revelation), but to apply Scripture to the needs of people.[12] Usually, such
a pastoral form of theology requires us to maintain something close to the
balance of doctrinal emphases in Scripture. But sometimes it involves giving attention to matters that are not heavily emphasized in Scripture, but
which have taken on particular importance for people today. Furthermore,
Scripture is not arranged in loci at all, but relates doctrines to one other
in a multitude of ways. Thus, it is often hard to determine from Scripture
under which locus a particular doctrine belongs.

Herman Dooyeweerd thought that the antidote to scholasticism was to
abandon Greek philosophy and to replace it with a specifically Christian
philosophy,[13] namely his own, which would then legitimately determine
the scope, and, to some extent, the subject matter, of theology. But others
have found in Dooyeweerd's approach a philosophical imperialism without a clear biblical warrant for its claims,[14] and therefore without any compelling reason to be accepted as the philosophy of Christianity.[15]

Others have thought that the methods of systematic theology must be
controlled by the methods of "biblical theology" or "redemptive history."[16]

12. See *DKG*, 81–85.

13. Herman Dooyeweerd, *In the Twilight of Western Thought* (Philadelphia: Presbyterian
and Reformed, 1960), esp. pp. 113–72.

14. E.g., John Frame, *The Amsterdam Philosophy: A Preliminary Critique* (Phillipsburg, N.J.:
Harmony Press, n.d.). Also see my *CVT*, 371–86.

15. For an attempt to formulate Reformed theology in accord with Dooyeweerd's general philosophical outlook, see Gordon J. Spykman, *Reformational Theology: A New Paradigm for Doing Dogmatics* (Grand Rapids: Eerdmans, 1992).

16. See, for example, Richard B. Gaffin, "Contemporary Hermeneutics," *WTJ* 31 (1969):
129–44; id., "Geerhardus Vos and the Interpretation of Paul," in *Jerusalem and Athens*, ed.
E. R. Geehan (Nutley, N.J.: Presbyterian and Reformed, 1971), 228–37; id., "Systematic
Theology and Biblical Theology," in *The New Testament Student and Theology*, ed. John H.
Skilton (Nutley, N.J.: Presbyterian and Reformed, 1976), 32–50.

On this view, theology should emphasize the narrative of Scripture, as it follows a divinely ordained path from Creation to Cross to consummation. I agree that systematic theology should be more aware of the history of redemption, and I will seek to do that in this book by emphasizing the covenant lordship of God. However, we should not allow this emphasis to eclipse other aspects of biblical truth, such as God's eternal (and therefore suprahistorical) nature, his law, his wisdom, and his involvement in the believer's subjectivity.[17] I support a greater influence of biblical theology upon systematics, but to say that biblical theology (as opposed to other theological methods) should "control" systematics is an overstatement. Systematics should be controlled by everything in God's word.

Still others have sought to overcome scholasticism by adopting various "controlling motifs," such as the feeling of absolute dependence (Schleiermacher), the fatherhood of God (Harnack), the Word of God (Barth), the divine-human personal encounter (Brunner), existential self-understanding (Bultmann), the new Being (Tillich), the language event (Ebeling), holy history (Cullmann), theological imagination (Kaufman), hope (Moltmann), liberation (Gutierrez and many others), the experience of women in a patriarchal setting (Elizabeth Johnson and other feminists), history (Pannenberg), community (Grenz), and the openness of God (Pinnock). These motifs form the central concepts by which the theologian expounds (and in some cases rejects!) the teaching of Scripture as he sees it. Often, theologians advertise these motifs as the central emphases of Scripture, and they claim that if we do theology according to a particular motif, we will thereby follow the emphasis of Scripture and escape the speculation and irrelevance of scholasticism.

I have no objection to theologians writing books on divine fatherhood, the Word of God, or the other topics noted above. We can usefully view the whole Bible from each of these (and other) points of view. But I do object when these are pitted against one another, or when a theologian claims (explicitly or implicitly) that his is the only way to formulate biblical doctrine. And of course I protest vehemently when the motif becomes a filter for rejecting portions of Scripture itself (e.g., 1 Tim. 2:9–15, with its "patriarchalism"). As for the attempt to reproduce the emphasis of Scripture through these motifs, I am as skeptical here as I was with the earlier forms of antischolasticism.

Cornelius Van Til was also an opponent of scholasticism, particularly of its

---

17. For more on these issues, see *DKG*, 207–12. Here too, as with the question of locus shifting, the issue of maintaining "the emphasis of Scripture" arises. I would reply to that here as I did above.

dependence upon Greek philosophy.[18] He never defined his alternative to scholasticism in any summary way, but it was essentially a renewed emphasis on *sola Scriptura*. He insisted that we recognize the profound antithesis between Scripture and unbelieving philosophy, and that we accept the teachings of Scripture as our presupposition in theology, as in all other areas of thought and life. Scripture alone has the final say; all our thought should be brought captive to the self-attesting Christ of Scripture (cf. 2 Cor. 10:5).

Van Til was also convinced in his heart and soul that the confessions of the Reformed faith were thoroughly in accord with Scripture, though he did take exception to parts of the Westminster Confession's teaching on the Sabbath. So, in practice, his presupposition was not only Scripture by itself, but also the Reformed faith as the definitive exposition of Scripture. I too am enthusiastic about Reformed theology, but I am convinced that we need to draw a sharper distinction between the Reformed confessions and the Scriptures than Van Til did, for the sake of the very principle (*sola Scriptura*) that was so important to him. According to the Reformed faith itself, we must be able to reform all the traditions of the church (including the confessions) according to the Word of God.[19]

A RESPONSE TO SCHOLASTICISM

Sola Scriptura Versus Philosophical Imperialism and Traditionalism

As I have indicated, my own response to scholasticism is less critical than the responses of those noted above. In my view, the Protestant scholastics differed from Luther and Calvin mainly in that the former were seeking to develop academically rigorous theological systems, while Luther and Calvin saw the main task of theology as pastoral and polemical. Attempting to understand biblical doctrines thoroughly and systematically is a worthy project, and I don't object at all to the post-Reformation effort to make fine distinctions and explore minutiae. These discussions are not for everybody, but

18. See *CVT*, 241–68, 339–52.
19. See my "In Defense of Something Close to Biblicism," *WTJ* 59 (1997): 269–318, also published as appendix 2 in my *Contemporary Worship Music*. I have developed my critique of traditionalism also in a debate with D. G. Hart, *The Regulative Principle of Worship: Scripture, Tradition, and Culture* (Glenside, Pa.: Westminster Campus Bookstore, 1998). The WCF itself says, "All synods or councils, since the Apostles' times, whether general or particular, may err; and many have erred. Therefore they are not to be made the rule of faith, or practice; but to be used as a help in both" (31.4).

they are helpful in some situations. Nevertheless, it is true that the Protestant scholastics were generally too uncritical of the Greek philosophers and of the Medieval systems. Therefore, particularly on the subject of the doctrine of God, their thought was not always firmly grounded in Scripture. Furthermore, their theological writings, though intellectually impressive, do not always speak to the practical concerns of contemporary believers.

So my resolve in this book is first of all to maintain *sola Scriptura*. I seek here above all to present what Scripture says about God, applying that teaching, of course, to the questions of our time. I am not trying to write both a biblical study and a history of doctrine. The focus will always be on Scripture, though of course I will often refer to older and contemporary sources in formulating the relevant questions and in exploring possible answers. The history of doctrine is important and valuable, but, granted *sola Scriptura*, it is not in itself a sufficient or independent source of truth.

As I have indicated in my writings on biblicism and tradition,[20] there is a tendency among some leading evangelical thinkers today to base theological judgments on tradition, rather than directly on Scripture. I don't deny the value of traditions, confessions, or historical study. But to make them ultimately normative is to violate the sufficiency of Scripture as God's word. In most cases, the arguments used constitute genetic fallacies: something is good because it comes from a good tradition, or bad because it comes from a bad one. Thus, traditionalism weakens the cogency of theological argument.

Sola Scriptura, therefore, will guard us against bad speculation[21] and philosophical imperialism. The point is not that philosophical terminology or argument is always bad, but rather that such terminology and argument must be tested by Scripture.

In using Scripture, my focus will not be primarily on the minute exegesis of individual texts, but on the major themes of Scripture, those teachings repeated over and over again in the canon's glorious redundancy. I offer the following reasons: (1) It has often been said that no doctrine should be based on a single text, and I agree, not because single texts lack authority, but because the church has wisely refused to give official sanction to ideas based on only one text. (2) I doubt that after two thousand years of Bible study in the Christian church, any new exegetical discov-

---

20. See the preceding note.

21. There is, I think, a good kind of speculation. That is to let our minds consider the range of possibilities that Scripture leaves open. That exercise increases our understanding of Scripture, because it helps us to see the precise location of the biblical boundaries of thought.

eries will warrant serious doctrinal change. (3) In the present theological ✗
situation, our main problem is not that of exegeting obscure texts, but
rather the strange inability or reluctance of many to see what is big and
bold and obvious.

I shall, then, include many references to biblical texts on particular subjects. Often, I shall just give the reference without comment, or quote the
passage so that readers can see it for themselves. This approach may expose me to the charge of prooftexting, but see my defense of proof texts in
DKG.[22] I have thought about each passage cited and have taken its context (actually, its contexts)[23] into account. I cite so many passages to indicate the pervasiveness of these doctrines throughout the Bible, even
though there is not room to discuss each one.

COVENANT LORDSHIP AND THE CENTRAL MESSAGE OF THE BIBLE

As for the criticism that the scholastic doctrines of God are to some extent irrelevant to the Christian life, we must remind ourselves that God is
the supremely relevant one. Without him, nothing else could exist or function. Without him, there could be no meaning in life. Perhaps the scholastics still have much to teach us about what is truly relevant, as opposed to
our typical modern preoccupations.

Nevertheless, one can ask significant questions about various specific assertions in the traditional doctrine of God. For example, is God supratemporal, is his goodness necessary or voluntary, and are his essence and existence
identical? I believe these questions can be answered, but the answers are not
obvious, and the scholastic theologians did not answer them persuasively. ✓

Another way to look at this is to ask how these assertions are relevant ✓
to the gospel, the good news of salvation, the main theme of Scripture. It
is not difficult to expound other loci as parts of the gospel: the doctrine of
Scripture describes the authoritative source of the good news; the doctrine
of man describes the desperate situation from which we need to be saved;
the doctrine of Christ describes the Savior; the doctrine of salvation describes his saving work for us; the doctrine of the last days describes the
completion of that work. But how is the simplicity of God related to our
salvation? Why is it important to salvation to define the nature of divine
omnipotence? Can God make a stone so large that he cannot lift it? Why
should we have any interest in answering that question? Compared with

22. P. 197.
23. See *DKG*, 169–70, 194–214.

the other loci of systematic theology, the doctrine of God often seems like a collection of intellectual games.

Sola Scriptura will help us here too. We know that all of Scripture is about salvation, about Jesus (Luke 24:27; John 5:39; Rom. 15:4; 2 Tim. 3:15–16). If the doctrine of divine simplicity, say, is a biblical doctrine, then we can be sure that it will have some connection with salvation, and we should seek until we find it, as I will try to do in this volume. But if the doctrine is not biblical, it should be rejected.

In making such judgments, it may be helpful for us to make use of some central motifs, not as exclusive ways of conceiving of God, but as ways of keeping our eyes focused on the gospel. Being finite, we cannot look at everything in the Bible at once. We have to start somewhere, and it is best that our starting point be a matter of some fundamental importance.

The central motif of this book (in accordance with the general theme of the series) is that God is Lord of the covenant. Since God chose the name Lord (or Yahweh, from the Hebrew *yahweh*) for himself, since it is found thousands of times in Scripture, and since it is at the heart of the fundamental confession of faith of God's people (Deut. 6:4–5; Rom. 10:9), it would seem to be a promising starting point. Covenant lordship does not exclude other basic biblical themes, such as hope or community, or even liberation. Rather, it includes these other themes and helps us see how they are related. The concept of covenant, as I understand it, incorporates many diverse elements, so that it provides a key for us to understand how the other themes fit into the overall biblical story. And it often liberates us from the temptation to set one theme against another, even to affirm one and deny another, for in the covenant these apparently diverse concepts and themes display a wonderful unity.[24]

So I will try to show how all of the acts, attributes, and personal distinctions that Scripture attributes to God are expressions of his lordship. God reveals all of these to us so that "you will know that I am the LORD your God" (Ex. 6:7).[25] This emphasis on the lordship of God (and particularly of Christ) will focus our attention on the main biblical message of salvation without ignoring or denying the large amount of biblical teaching on the nature and acts of God.

---

24. See my article, "Covenant and the Unity of Scripture," available at the Third Millennium Web site, www.thirdmill.org.

25. This is a pervasive theme in Scripture. In Exodus alone, see 7:5, 17; 8:10, 22; 9:14, 29–30; 10:2; 14:4, 18; 16:12. God does what he does so that we may know that he is the Lord.

Engagement with Recent Philosophy and Theology

I mentioned that some responses to scholasticism (especially in recent years) compromise biblical teachings. I will need to look at some of those, in the interest of theology as application, and by way of contrast with the biblical teaching. I shall look at some of the recent philosophical and theological treatments of the doctrine of God, particularly those that have endorsed open theism.[26]

The proper response to the challenge of open theism is not to compromise biblical teachings, but to press them all the more forcefully (yet graciously). My intention is not to mitigate in the slightest the biblical (and traditional Reformed) doctrine of divine sovereignty, but rather to expand it into areas of concern to the open theists. For example, the open theists have raised the question of how an atemporal God could know items of temporal experience, such as "the present time." They have contended that to answer that question we need to eliminate the doctrine of divine atemporality. I shall argue, however (in chaps. 24–25), that God is both atemporal and present at every time, both transcendent over time and immanent in it, so that he sees the world from a supratemporal perspective and also from every temporal perspective. So the answer to the problem, in my view, is not to regard God as less sovereign, but as more so, ruling time both from above and from below.

These discussions of the current scene will not take up much space in the book. But I hope they will clarify my position by showing us how not to respond to scholasticism.

Changes in the Order of Topics to Facilitate Communication

I will also be dealing with some of the subheadings of the doctrine of God in an unconventional order. As I said earlier, I do not believe it makes much substantive theological difference what doctrine comes first and what comes second. But it can make some pedagogical difference.

26. There has been a renaissance of Christian philosophy over the last thirty years, led by people like Alvin Plantinga, William Alston, and Nicholas Wolterstorff. This development is exciting to me. When I studied philosophy from 1957 to 1961, one would have been laughed out of the classroom for suggesting that the biblical God might help in the solution of philosophical problems. But today many well-respected philosophers urge the philosophical relevance of the biblical, theistic worldview. Unfortunately, these thinkers tend to hold Arminian views of free will and limit biblical inerrancy. Some have given support to open theism.

Reformed theologies traditionally begin by discussing God's nature before his acts of creation, providence, and redemption, and they traditionally deal with the "incommunicable" attributes (such as eternity and simplicity) before the "communicable" attributes (such as wisdom, knowledge, justice, and love).[27]

I will invert some of these traditional sequences in this book, for three reasons:

1. There is a biblical pattern of reasoning by which God's nature is discerned in his acts. The traditional order makes it difficult to describe this pattern. Thus, I shall discuss God's acts before his attributes.

2. The traditional order is best for those with some philosophical training and interests, who find it helpful to proceed from the abstract to the concrete, the eternal to the temporal, and so on. There was a time when we could assume that seminarians and pastors had this sort of philosophical training and interest, but that time is past. In general, I shall proceed from history to eternity, from the ethical to the metaphysical, from the communicable to the incommunicable. That, I think, will make the overall argument more intelligible and interesting to contemporary readers.

3. In Scripture, the ethical qualities of God (such as love, justice, and mercy) are no less fundamental than his metaphysical qualities (such as eternity, immensity, and simplicity). Indeed, the passages that come closest to defining God speak of him in ethical terms (Ex. 33:19; 34:6; 1 John 4:8). This point will be easier to make in a somewhat changed order of topics: first the ethical attributes, and then the others.

My intention here is not to develop a "theology from below," as some contemporary writers understand that phrase.[28] That language indicates a plan of starting with a religiously neutral analysis of the history of Israel and Jesus, in the hope that from that analysis we can derive our Christian theological convictions about God and Christ. On the contrary, my methodology will be governed by God's revelation in Scripture and will thus be "theology from above," in the usual understanding of that phrase.[29] But Scripture does speak of this world as well as the next, of earth as well as heaven. A good teacher often starts with the present focus of his students' attention and moves from there to teach them what they don't know. So Scripture often begins with earthly things to teach us heavenly things. Ac-

---

27. I shall later indicate some reservations about the distinction between "incommunicable" and "communicable."

28. See, for example, Wolfhart Pannenberg, "Christology from Below," in his *Jesus: God and Man* (Philadelphia: Westminster Press, 1968), 34–35.

29. Remember, though, my point in *DKG* that one cannot understand Scripture without understanding the world to which it applies. See *DKG*, 66–69, 73–75.

cordingly, this book will be a theology from above that sometimes, with biblical precedent, and without any pretense of religious neutrality,[30] begins pedagogically with what is from below.

THE STRUCTURE OF THIS VOLUME

I shall begin with a general study of the covenant lordship of God. *Lord* is, first of all, a proper name, and therefore the Lord is personal. But he is unique among persons. Our appropriate response to the Lord is reverent awe and worship. In this attitude, we recognize a person who is holy: incomparably great and wonderful, majestic, exalted, and transcendent. This holy being stands in a special relationship to us: he is the head of the covenant.

So the Lord is, first of all, a holy person, our covenant Lord. But further study reveals more specific connotations of the term *Lord*. As in *DKG*, I shall refer to these lordship attributes as control, authority, and presence, and I shall spend some time expounding them. As in *DKG*, the three lordship attributes will generate a number of triadic distinctions,[31] preparing us for the discussion of the Trinity toward the end.[32]

The Lord in Scripture reveals himself in three ways: by a narrative of his

30. In the final analysis, Christians can only reason as Christians. Every thought must be brought captive to Christ (2 Cor. 10:5); there is no neutrality. I have discussed this point often in earlier books. See also my response to Richard Muller in "In Defense of Something Close to Biblicism."

31. Readers should make up their own minds as to how seriously they should take all these triads. I vacillate in my own thinking about them. Sometimes I think that I have uncovered a deep layer of Trinitarian meaning in the Scriptures; at other times I think I have merely hit upon a useful pedagogical device. And there are times when I think even less of the scheme—as a kind of mental crutch, or at worst a procrustean bed for theological formulations. Certainly I am trying to avoid the worst kind of schematic thinking, in which the main motive is to make the scheme work, even at the expense of exegetical cogency. But the triads nevertheless continue to appeal to me as somehow appropriate to the biblical story, and so I continue to use them.

32. I disagree with Paul Jewett's contention that "to discuss the nature and attributes of God before the doctrine of the Trinity, as has been traditionally done, leaves one open to a natural theology whose subject is just God in the general sense rather than the God who is the proper subject of all Christian theology—namely, the God who is revealed in Christ the Son through the Holy Spirit" (*God, Creation, and Revelation* [Grand Rapids: Eerdmans, 1991], 342–43). Compare the even more extreme language of Jürgen Moltmann in *The Trinity and the Kingdom* (San Francisco: HarperCollins, 1991), 17. In a systematic theology, every part should presuppose every other, so that it does not much matter what is discussed first. Further, it is not wrong to talk about God without explicit reflection on the Trinitarian distinctions. To condemn such a way of speaking is to condemn most of the Old Testament.

acts, by authoritative descriptions of his nature, and by revealing something of his inner life through the Trinitarian persons. These correspond respectively to the lordship attributes of control, authority, and presence.

The narrative of God's actions can be further subdivided into narratives of creation, decree, and redemption. God's authoritative descriptions include images, attributes, and names. And God's inner life consists of a communion among Father, Son, and Holy Spirit. Each of these concepts will have further subdivisions. The attributes of God will be distinguished as those of goodness, those of knowledge, and those of power.

So the following outline indicates the main divisions of the book. The triadic structure may help the reader to conceptualize the overall biblical doctrine of God. But the content within the structure is, of course, far more important.

   I. The Lord
     A. Initial Observations
       1. A Person
       2. Holy
       3. Head of the Covenant
     B. Lordship Attributes
       1. Control
       2. Authority
       3. Presence

  II. Some Problem Areas
     A. Human Responsibility and Freedom
     B. The Problem of Evil

 III. A Philosophy of Lordship
     A. Ethics
     B. Epistemology
     C. Metaphysics

 IV. The Narrative of God's Actions
     A. God's Working in Creation
       1. Miracle
       2. Providence
       3. Creation *ex Nihilo*
     B. God's Eternal Decree

This outline does not correspond precisely to the chapter divisions, to the length of the discussions, or to the order of topics. For some of the categories, there will be more than one chapter, because of the relatively large number of issues to be discussed. In other cases, more than one of the above divisions may be included in a chapter. I will not devote a specific section of the book to redemption (IV, C), since that topic is usually discussed under loci other than the doctrine of God. But this volume will be more concerned with redemption than are most traditional treatments of the doctrine of God, because of its emphasis on God's covenant lordship.

PART ONE

YAHWEH THE LORD

CHAPTER 2

The Lord

The first thing, and in one sense the only thing, we need to know about God is that he is Lord. Surely no name, no description of God, is more central to Scripture than this.

THE CENTRALITY OF LORDSHIP

When God met Moses in the burning bush and announced that he would deliver his people from slavery in Egypt, Moses asked his name. Then God replied, "I AM WHO I AM. This is what you are to say to the Israelites: 'I AM has sent me to you' " (Ex. 3:14).

In verse 15, the name becomes *yahweh*, which sounds in Hebrew like a form of the verb *to be*:

> God also said to Moses, "Say to the Israelites, 'The LORD [*yahweh*],[1] the God of your fathers—the God of Abraham, the God of Isaac and the God of Jacob—has sent me to you.' This is my name forever, the name by which I am to be remembered from generation to generation."

So *the* name of God, the name by which he wants his people especially to remember him forever, is Yahweh or Lord.

---

1. For the justification for translating the Hebrew word *yahweh* as "Lord" and thereafter identifying the two terms, see chapter 3.

The Shema of Deuteronomy 6:4–5 is the most famous confession of faith in the Old Testament:

> Hear, O Israel: The LORD our God, the LORD is one. Love the LORD your God with all your heart and with all your soul and with all your strength.

This is a confession of lordship: that Yahweh, the Lord, is the one and only true God, and that therefore he deserves all of our love and allegiance.

Over and over, we are told that God performs his mighty deeds so that people "will know that I am the LORD" (Ex. 14:4; cf. 6:7; 7:5, 17; 8:22; 10:2; 14:18; 16:6, 12; 29:46; 31:13; Deut. 4:35; 29:6; 1 Kings 8:43, 60; 18:37; 20:13, 28; 2 Kings 19:19; Ps. 83:18; Isa. 37:20;[2] Jer. 16:21; 24:7; Ezek. 6:7, 10, 13, 14; 7:4, 9, 27; 11:10, etc.), or so that "my name might be proclaimed in all the earth" (Ex. 9:16; Rom. 9:17). We find "name" and "Lord" throughout the Scriptures, in contexts central to God's nature, dignity, and relationship with his people. "Lord" is found in the New International Version of the Bible 7,484 times, mostly referring to God or to Christ.

The name Lord is as central to the message of the New Testament as it is to the Old Testament. Remarkably, in the New Testament the word *kyrios*, meaning "Lord," which translates *yahweh* in the Greek translation of the Old Testament, is regularly applied to Jesus. If the Shema summarizes, in a way, the message of the Old Testament by teaching that *yahweh* is Lord, so the confession "Jesus is Lord" (Rom. 10:9; 1 Cor. 12:3; Phil. 2:11; cf. John 20:28; Acts 2:36) summarizes the message of the New Testament.[3]

At a time when theologies are regularly built around central motifs like history, hope, love, reconciliation, and liberation, it is a bit surprising that so few of them focus on the concept of divine lordship.[4] In view of the centrality of lordship in Scripture's own doctrine of God, and specifically in its Christology, it would seem to be an obvious choice as a central motif for a theological discussion.

It is even more surprising that people writing about the biblical God

---

2. See also the "I am he" passages, in which the name *yahweh* is prominent. God will act so that Israel and the nations will know that "I am he": Deut. 32:39; Isa. 41:4; 43:10, 13, etc. In John, the words often translated "I am he" are simply "I am" (John 8:24, 28; 9:9; 18:5–6, 8), identifying Jesus as Yahweh.

3. In Paul's writings, "Lord" (*kyrios* in Greek) regularly refers to Jesus rather than to God the Father.

4. A rare exception in the twentieth century is the theology of Karl Barth, for whom divine revelation is always a revelation of God's lordship. See his *ChD*, 1.1.339–83 and many other places. My understanding of divine lordship is rather different from his, however. See *CVT*, 353–69.

would actually oppose or deny the biblical concept of lordship. Jürgen
Moltmann, for example, opposes what he considers to be nominalist views
of divine freedom and power:

> In this language freedom means Lordship, power and possession.
> It is this interpretation of freedom as power and Lordship over pos-
> sessions which is being theologically employed if we assume as our
> starting point that God reveals himself as 'God the Lord'. Then
> 'God's liberty' means his sovereignty, and his power of disposal over
> his property—creation—and his servants—men and women.[5]

As we shall see, it is certainly true on the biblical view (as on what Moltmann calls "nominalist" views) that God's lordship entails power and possession. But to eliminate these concepts, with the title Lord, is to abandon
something at the heart of the biblical message.

Similarly, Elizabeth Johnson says:

> The theistic God is modeled on the pattern of an earthly absolute
> monarch, a metaphor so prevalent that most often it is simply
> taken for granted. As a king rules over his subjects, so God the Lord
> has dominion over his creatures, a view which, in Sallie McFague's
> analysis, is intrinsically hierarchical whether the divine reign be
> accomplished through dominance or benevolence.[6]

She inveighs often against the ideas of "power-over," dominance, and the
like being applied to God. These are patriarchal and hierarchical, she says,
and as such have no place in her feminist doctrine of God. But the bottom
line is that Johnson simply does not like the biblical concept of divine lordship.[7]

In a more subtle way, Clark Pinnock contrasts the model of God as an
"aloof monarch" (unchangeable, etc.) with that of God as a "caring parent with qualities of love and responsiveness."[8] He encourages us to choose

5. Jürgen Moltmann, *The Trinity and the Kingdom* (San Francisco: HarperCollins, 1981),
56. He alludes to Barth's slogan that "God reveals Himself as the Lord."
6. Elizabeth Johnson, *She Who Is* (New York: Crossroad Publishing, 1996), 20.
7. What other reason is there for denying God's dominion? Johnson and McFague do
not present any evidence from the natural world, and their citations from Scripture are highly
selective. But surely it is irresponsible for a writer to determine the nature of God merely
by consulting his or her likes and dislikes, and those of his or her constituency. In this volume, I will discuss such views from time to time. But I find it hard to take seriously views
that are based only on subjective preferences.
8. Clark Pinnock, "Systematic Theology," in *The Openness of God*, by Clark Pinnock et
al. (Downers Grove, Ill.: InterVarsity Press, 1994), 103.

between these models, which, he thinks, "are the most influential that people commonly carry around in their minds."[9] Well, what about the model of a monarch who is not aloof at all, who is also a caring parent, and who is both loving and unchanging? Surely that more complex model is a better reflection of the thinking of most Bible believers than either Pinnock's caricature of Calvinism or his own version of open theism. But notice here how the idea of God as "monarch" (king or Lord) comes out sounding negative, even if we set aside the word "aloof." Once again, we find contemporary theologians playing down God's lordship.

Certainly the biblical Lord is not just any ruler. It would be wrong for us to expound God's lordship merely by appealing to extrabiblical models of kingship, rule, dominion, and so on. God is different in many ways from an oppressive patriarch, a Roman emperor, a feudal lord, or a European king. But the basic concepts of hierarchy, rule, and power are intrinsic to the lordship of God. To oppose the rule of God is to oppose his lordship altogether.

I am also rather perplexed about the recent controversy in evangelical circles over "lordship salvation."[10] As we have seen, the lordship of Jesus is absolutely fundamental to the preaching of the gospel in the New Testament. It is inconceivable that anyone could respond appropriately to that gospel without confessing *ex animo* that Jesus is Lord. To acknowledge the lordship of Christ is not, of course, to be sinlessly perfect or flawless in one's discipleship. Scripture teaches plainly that sincere believers do sin; they act inconsistently with their profession. But if that profession is genuine, it will motivate them more and more to turn from sin and to seek Jesus' righteousness.

So the lordship of God turns out to be controversial in modern theology! A theologian might not think he was taking any risks by expounding the biblical doctrine of God in terms of lordship, but in the present theological climate this approach will not go unchallenged. Lordship does not at all fit the model being urged upon us by feminist and other liberation theologians, nor does it fit the model of process theologians, for whom God's influence on us is always "persuasive," rather than "coercive." Nor is it con-

9. Ibid.

10. For the arguments, see John MacArthur, *The Gospel According to Jesus* (Grand Rapids: Zondervan, 1988), favoring lordship salvation. On the other side, see Zane C. Hodges, *Absolutely Free! A Biblical Reply to Lordship Salvation* (Grand Rapids: Zondervan, 1989). It is certainly true that God justifies us (declares us righteous) apart from works, and therefore apart from our service to Christ as Lord. But salvation is not only justification, but sanctification as well. Sanctification, too, is a work of God. But it always presumes a regenerate heart, pledged to serve Christ.

sistent with open theism, process theology, or theological pluralism. From one perspective, however, this fact is not surprising. The very nature of liberal theology, for the past three hundred years, has been to assert human autonomy. The liberal theologian wants to avoid at all costs the notion that he belongs to someone else, that he must think according to someone else's standards, that he must obey someone else without question. He may be willing to use the term *Lord*, but the biblical doctrine of God's lordship is inimical to his most fundamental instincts. In this respect, liberation theology and the other modern theologies are not new.

But these positions are, at this point, fundamentally anti-Christian. The central message of Scripture is that God is Lord.

YAHWEH: THE NAME OF A PERSON

So it is important for us to determine the meaning of divine lordship. I shall try later to determine some of the meaning of the mysterious language in Exodus 3. First, however, we should observe the obvious: Yahweh, or Lord, is a personal name, a proper name. This is not to deny that it may also connote various levels of theological meaning. Names in the ancient Near East typically connote as well as denote. But, first and foremost, Yahweh is the name of a person.

In Exodus 3, God speaks and acts. He commits himself to deliver Israel. He promises redemption and threatens judgment. He empowers Moses and Aaron to accomplish his purposes. He is not, therefore, an impersonal force to be manipulated by human ingenuity. He has his own purposes, his own standards, his own delights and hatreds. He loves the people of Israel and seeks their love and obedience. He acts on his own initiative, rather than merely responding to events.

Each of us relates to him as one person to another. Rather than taking him for granted, as we do with impersonal things and forces, we must always take his concerns into account, responding to him in repentance, love, thanksgiving, and worship.

Scripture rarely if ever uses the word *person* to describe God, or even to refer to the Father, the Son, or the Holy Spirit. But, like *Trinity*, *person* is an extrabiblical word that is very nearly unavoidable for us. It is the word in our vocabulary that applies to beings who speak, act intentionally, and so on. The biblical term *living* reinforces this picture. God is the living God, over against all the nonliving gods of the nations. (See, e.g., Deut. 5:26; Josh. 3:10; 1 Sam. 17:26, 36; 2 Kings 19:4, 16; Pss. 42:2; 84:2; Jer. 10:10; Matt. 16:16; 26:63; Acts 14:15; Rom. 9:26.) Oaths in Scripture frequently begin with "as surely as the LORD lives" (as in Judg. 8:19; Ruth 3:13; 1 Sam. 14:45).[11]

Certainly the God of the Bible is much greater than any finite person. That very greatness tempts us to think of him as impersonal, for we have been taught that the great natural forces that govern the universe are impersonal. (But have we forgotten that God makes his angels winds and fire [Heb. 1:7]?)[12] God is, to be sure, the greatest of all forces or principles. But if we ask Scripture whether in the final analysis God is personal or impersonal, the answer must surely be that he is personal.[13] We move away from Scripture's pervasive emphasis if, with Paul Tillich, we deny that God is "a" person, and affirm only "that God is the ground of everything personal and that he carries within himself the ontological power of personality."[14] An impersonal principle could fit the terms of Tillich's formula.

Thus we learn something very important about the biblical worldview. In Scripture, the personal is greater than the impersonal. The impersonal things and forces in this world are created and directed by a personal God. According to naturalistic thought, all persons in the world are the product of impersonal forces, and they can best be understood by reducing them to impersonal bits of matter and energy, or by making them aspects of an impersonal oneness. In these views, persons are reducible to the impersonal. But in the biblical view, the impersonal reduces to the personal. Matter, energy, motion, time, and space are under the rule of a personal Lord. All the wonderful things that we find in personality—intelligence, compassion, creativity, love, justice—are not ephemeral data, doomed to be snuffed out in cosmic calamity; rather, they are aspects of what is most permanent, most ultimate. They are what the universe is really all about.

Only in biblical religion is there an absolute principle that is personal.

11. Paul K. Jewett points out that anthropomorphic references to God in terms of body parts should be understood as confirmations of his personal character. See *God, Creation, and Revelation* (Grand Rapids: Eerdmans, 1991), 187.

12. In one of the first philosophy courses I took at college, the professor asked his students to judge between two hypotheses: (1) the rustling of the leaves in the tree outside is caused by wind; (2) the rustling is caused by angels. Being a logical positivist, he expected us to conclude that only the first hypothesis deserved serious consideration, for the second hypothesis was scientifically unverifiable. As a Christian, I responded differently. And since that time I have always wondered if there were angels in that tree making the wind blow, or even rattling the leaves themselves.

13. I shall discuss later how God's personal nature relates to the three persons of the Trinity. I see no contradiction between saying that God is by nature personal and that he exists in three persons.

14. Paul Tillich, *Systematic Theology* (Chicago: University of Chicago Press, 1951), 1:245.

Other religions have personal gods, but those gods are not absolute.[15] Other religions and philosophies (Hinduism, Aristotle, Spinoza, Hegel) have absolute principles, but those principles are impersonal.[16] Islam believes in an unknowable God who can (inconsistently) be described in personal terms; the extent to which Allah is personal is due to Mohammed's original respect for "the book" (the Jewish/Christian Scriptures) and to the Arab polytheism described in the Hadith. Other sects also hold to some level of personality in God, because of the influence of the Bible upon their founders. But groups like the Mormons and the Jehovah's Witnesses, like the Muslims, are inconsistent in their confession of God's absolute personality.

YAHWEH, THE HOLY ONE

The second obvious thing that can be said about the name Yahweh is that it is the name of a profoundly holy being. Although he is a person, he is unique among persons. We are not to meet him as an ordinary friend or enemy, but as one who is radically different from us, before whom we bow in reverent awe and adoration.

When Yahweh speaks to Moses from within the burning bush, we read:

> "Do not come any closer," God said. "Take off your sandals, for the place where you are standing is holy ground." Then he said, "I am the God of your father, the God of Abraham, the God of Isaac and the God of Jacob." At this, Moses hid his face, because he was afraid to look at God. (Ex. 3:5–6)

The ground is "holy," not because there is something special or dangerous about it as such, but because Yahweh is there, the supremely holy one. God's messenger is to stand back, to remove his shoes in respect. He is afraid to look at the face of God.

When redeemed Israel meets with God at Mount Sinai, the whole mountain is holy ground (Ex. 19:23). The people must draw back; anyone who touches the mountain must be put to death (vv. 12–13).

---

15. Sometimes polytheistic religions supplement their personal (but finite) gods with an impersonal absolute, such as the Greek "fate." See Carl F. H. Henry, *Remaking the Modern Mind* (Grand Rapids: Eerdmans, 1948), 175–97.

16. There is, nevertheless, a tendency in such religions and philosophies to refer to the impersonal absolute in personal terms, inconsistent though that may be. In the view of Carl F. H. Henry, that "reflects an intuitive awareness of a personal deity." See Henry, *God, Revelation and Authority* (Waco, Tex.: Word Books, 1982), 5:143.

Centuries later, when the prophet Isaiah meets the Lord in the temple, the seraphs call to one another, "Holy, holy, holy is the LORD Almighty; the whole earth is full of his glory" (Isa. 6:3).[17] Perhaps it is this experience that motivates him to speak regularly of God as "the holy one of Israel" (e.g., 1:4; 5:19; 10:20; 12:6; 17:7). In the New Testament, Jesus is regularly called holy (e.g., Luke 1:35; 4:34; Acts 2:27; 3:14), as is, of course, the Holy Spirit.

Holiness, then, is God's capacity and right to arouse our reverent awe and wonder. It is his uniqueness (Ex. 15:11; 1 Sam. 2:2), his transcendence. It is his majesty, for the holy God is like a great king, whom we dare not treat like other persons. Indeed, God's holiness impels us to worship in his presence.

Because we are sinners as well as creatures, God stands over against us, not only as transcendent, but as ethically pure. It is particularly as sinners that we fear to enter God's holy presence. When Isaiah heard the seraphs cry "Holy, holy, holy," he immediately remembered his own sin:

> "Woe to me!" I cried. "I am ruined! For I am a man of unclean lips, and I live among a people of unclean lips, and my eyes have seen the King, the LORD Almighty." (Isa. 6:5)

And before he could hear God's call to prophesy, a seraph laid a live coal on his lips, symbolically communicating God's forgiveness.

So holiness is ethical as well as metaphysical. The Lord's holiness transcends us, not only as creatures, but especially as sinners.

Thus the holy Lord tells us to back away. But, amazingly, he also draws us to himself and makes us holy as well. Israel becomes his "holy nation" (Ex. 19:6; 22:31). They must be holy "because I, the LORD your God, am holy" (Lev. 19:1; cf. 1 Peter 1:16). They participate in a holy assembly (Ex. 12:16), keep a holy day (16:23), sacrifice at a holy place (26:33), through a holy priest, wearing holy garments (31:10), anointed with holy oil (30:25).[18] They learn God's will through "the Holy Scriptures" (Rom. 1:2; 2 Tim. 3:15). Christian believers are "saints," holy ones (Rom. 1:7; 1 Cor. 1:2).

Israel's holiness, like God's, involves both separation and moral purity. They are separated from all the other nations as God's special people (Deut. 7:1–6), and they are to image God's ethical perfection (Lev. 19:1).

---

17. In the Bible, holiness is the only divine attribute proclaimed in threefold repetition.
18. And God's promise is that one day they will cook in holy pots (Zech. 14:20–21).

God's holiness, then, which initially seems so forbidding and judgmental, is the means of our salvation. God draws us to his presence, making us his friends. Those drawn into God's circle are holy, in contrast to the profane world. So in Hosea 11:9, God's holiness is the basis for his mercy:

> I will not carry out my fierce anger,
>   nor will I turn and devastate Ephraim.
> For I am God, and not man—
>   the Holy One among you.
> I will not come in wrath.[19]

Speaking in Psalm 22:1–5, the Messiah invokes God's holiness as the reason why God should deliver him:

> My God, my God, why have you forsaken me?
>   Why are you so far from saving me,
>   so far from the words of my groaning?
> O my God, I cry out by day, but you do not answer,
>   by night, and am not silent.
> Yet you are enthroned as the Holy One;
>   you are the praise of Israel.
> In you our fathers put their trust;
>   they trusted and you delivered them.
> They cried to you and were saved;
>   in you they trusted and were not disappointed.

As the Holy One, God has for centuries delivered his people from death and destruction. There must be a reason why this Holy One has now forsaken the psalmist.

Holiness, then, is a very rich concept. It speaks of God's transcendence and separation from finite and sinful creatures. But it also speaks of how God draws them to himself, making them holy. Holiness marks God's transcendence, but also his immanence, his presence to redeem us. He is not only "the Holy One," but "the Holy One among us," "the Holy One of Israel." And both as transcendence and immanence, judgment and salvation, law and gospel, God's holiness drives us to worship him. Yahweh is the Lord who moves us to worship him with reverence and awe (Heb. 12:28).

---

19. Compare other passages in which God's holiness is redemptive: Isa. 41:14; 43:3, 14; 49:7.

LORDSHIP AS COVENANT HEADSHIP

From our discussion of holiness, it is evident that divine lordship is a relationship between God and his creatures. His holiness exalts him above them, but it also draws them near to him, as he consecrates them to himself. Obviously, where you have a lord, you must have servants or vassals. In that sense, lordship describes a relationship. This is my third "obvious" observation, and I would like in this section to describe that relationship in general terms.

Some might think that the relational character of lordship disqualifies it as a central theological motif. Shouldn't we rather begin with God's aseity or eternity, describing God as he is in himself, apart from any relationships with creatures? To put it more provocatively, isn't my approach a "relationship-theology," even a typically modern "me-theology"—one that focuses on ourselves, rather than on God?

I reply: (1) Lord is the central name of God in the biblical revelation. To criticize the centrality of lordship is to criticize Scripture itself. (2) All of our thought about God, even about his aseity or eternity, should be qualified by our status as covenant servants of God. We never escape the status of servants, even when we are studying theology. Aseity and eternity do, certainly, characterize God even as he would be if he hadn't created anything. But even as we think about these things, we must do so as servants, subject to the Lord. For us, therefore, God's lordship is in one sense prior to his aseity or eternity. (3) The use of lordship as a central theological motif does not compromise the transcendence of God, the radical difference between the Creator and the creature. We have already emphasized divine transcendence in our discussion of holiness. Indeed, divine lordship itself, as we shall see, implies God's independence of, and sovereignty over, the created world. (4) Even John Calvin recognized the inseparability between the knowledge of God and the knowledge of ourselves. And he said he did not know which came first.[20]

We should here seek to define, in general terms, the relationship between the Lord and his people. The best way to describe that relationship, in my view, is as a covenant. In the covenant between God and Israel, the Lord selects a people from among all the nations of the earth to be his own (see, e.g., Deut. 4:37–38; 7:6–8; 10:15). He is the Lord, and they are his servants. He redeems them from their bondage in Egypt and demands their obedience to his law; so the covenant includes both grace and law. In the fear-

---

20. *Institutes*, 1.1.1–3. This observation is the root of the perspectival epistemology expounded in *DKG*.

some holiness of the Mount Sinai meeting, God says to them through Moses:

> Now if you obey me fully and keep my covenant, then out of all nations you will be my treasured possession. Although the whole earth is mine, you will be for me a kingdom of priests and a holy nation. (Ex. 19:5–6)

In Exodus 20:1–17, God speaks to Israel the words that we usually call the Ten Commandments or the Decalogue. Meredith G. Kline has analyzed this passage as a "suzerainty treaty" between God and Israel.[21]

Examples of suzerainty treaties have been found in the ancient Hittite culture. In this literary form, a great king (a suzerain) formulates a treaty with a lesser king (a vassal). The great king is the author. He sets the terms of the relationship. The document regularly includes certain elements: (1) the name of the great king, identifying him as the author of the document: "I am king such-and-such"; (2) an historical prologue, in which the great king tells the vassal what benefits he has brought the vassal in the past; (3) the stipulations, or laws that the vassal is expected to obey in gratefulness for the great king's past beneficence (often divided into a general command to love or be exclusively loyal to the suzerain and particular commands indicating the ways in which this loyalty was to be expressed); (4) the sanctions, or blessings for obedience and curses for disobedience; and (5) continuity, or provisions for public reading of the treaty, royal succession, adjudication of disputes, etc.

Kline finds that the Decalogue follows this treaty pattern fairly closely. First, God gives his name: "I am the LORD your God." Again, the mysterious name Yahweh, or Lord, appears. Then the Lord proclaims his past blessing on Israel, identifying himself as the one "who brought you out of Egypt, out of the land of slavery." After this, God utters the commandments themselves. The first commandment (perhaps the first four) requires exclusive loyalty to God and repudiation of all other would-be gods. The other commandments spell out the implications of this commitment. There are sanctions embedded in the commands (rather than relegated to a specific section, as often in the secular treaties), as in verses 5–6, 7b, and 12b. There is no specific continuity section in the Decalogue, but at the end of Deuteronomy there are provisions for the public teaching of God's law (31:9–13), for maintaining the covenant after Moses' death, and for dealing with rebellion (vv. 14–29). Kline also analyzes the book of Deuteronomy as a suzerainty treaty in form.

21. Meredith G. Kline, *The Structure of Biblical Authority* (Grand Rapids: Eerdmans, 1972).

The written treaty is crucial to the relationship, both in the extrabiblical treaties and in the biblical covenants. To violate the treaty is to violate the covenant. Copies of the treaty were to be placed in the sanctuar-
ies of the gods of the suzerain and the vassal and brought out for regular
public reading.

Israel's covenant was first heard by the people assembled around Mount
Sinai from the mouth of God himself. But the people were frightened by
the voice of God. They were no doubt fearful of judgment because of their
sin (as was Isaiah in later times). They asked Moses to speak with God as
their representative, so that they would not have to hear the voice of God
directly. God gave Moses tablets of stone "with the law and commands I
have written for their instruction" (Ex. 24:12). The biblical narrative stresses
the divine authorship of this document. Exodus 31:18 refers to "the two
tablets of the Testimony, the tablets of stone inscribed by the finger of God."
Exodus 32:16 says, "The tablets were the work of God; the writing was the
writing of God, engraved on the tablets." When Moses brought the tablets
down the mountain, he saw the people worshiping a golden calf, and he
threw the tablets down in anger, breaking them. God, however, replaced
them: "The Lord said to Moses, 'Chisel out two stone tablets like the first
ones, and I will write on them the words that were on the first tablets'" (34:1).

Note here the sustained emphasis on the Lord's authorship of the written covenant document—a datum of tremendous importance in our current discussion of the nature of Scripture. It is also significant that, like the
secular suzerainty treaties, the written covenant was put in the holiest
place in Israel, beside the ark of the covenant, as a witness against Israel
(Deut. 31:26).[22] It is, literally, *holy* writing, *holy* Scripture.

On almost any page of Deuteronomy, there are admonitions to keep all
the laws, statutes, commandments, testimonies, and words of the Lord. In
that eloquent redundancy, we are directed to make all of our decisions according to that written word, never adding to it or subtracting from it (4:2;
12:32),[23] never turning to the right or to the left. In Psalm 19, that written law is said to be "perfect, reviving the soul" (v. 7). In Psalm 119, nearly
every verse testifies to the greatness of God's laws, commands, and decrees.
Again, the reference is not to something God uttered in a private revelation or mystical encounter. The reference is to God's written word.

So the covenant between Yahweh and Israel, like the present govern-

---

22. As Edmund Clowney points out in the pamphlet *Another Foundation* (Philadelphia:
Presbyterian and Reformed, 1965), the written word is not here man's witness concerning
God, as liberal theology would have it, but God's witness against man.

23. *Sola Scriptura!*

ment of the United States of America, has a written constitution. Israel's relationship to God was not to be governed by the people's imaginations, or by religious wisdom, or by scholarship, or by oral tradition, but by a written word, authored by the Lord.[24]

So Yahweh is the covenant head of Israel. But, in various ways, the model of the Mosaic covenant illumines God's relationship to all his creatures, not only to Israel. In the creation narrative of Genesis 1, God defeats darkness and divides waters, as he did in Egypt.[25] His powerful word commands new creatures to come into being, and they obey. At the end of his creative labor, he makes a holy place for himself and mankind. He treats all the creatures, including man, as his covenant servants.

Then, in Genesis 6–9, God judges the wickedness of men by sending a flood, but graciously delivers Noah and his family, as he would later deliver Israel through the waters of the Red Sea. In Genesis 8:20–9:17, God establishes a covenant with Noah and with "all flesh," that he will never again destroy the earth in a flood.

Thus, all God's creatures are, in a sense, his covenant servants. Human beings are disobedient servants, subject to the covenant curse. Only some receive special grace (God's unmerited favor) to inherit the covenant blessings. But all people, indeed all creatures, are subject to God's covenant lordship.

If people do receive divine grace to live in glory forever with God, they receive it on the basis of another covenant, the "new covenant" in Jesus Christ. Jeremiah speaks of a covenant in which God will put his law in the hearts of his people (31:33). This is the covenant sealed by Jesus' blood (1 Cor. 11:25). Jesus is Lord, Yahweh come in the flesh, to achieve the final victory over sin and death, of which the Exodus from Egypt was only a picture. As with Yahweh under the old covenant, we are to love Jesus, and if we love him, we will keep his commandments (John 14:15, 21, 23). And since the Spirit teaches his apostles all truth (John 14:26; 15:26; 16:13), we should obey their written words (1 Cor. 14:37) as we continue to obey the Scriptures of the old covenant (Matt. 5:17–20; Luke 16:31; John 5:39, 47; 10:35; Rom. 15:4; 2 Tim. 3:16; 2 Peter 1:19–21).[26]

24. In this chapter, I have emphasized that the written word of God is divine law. But, as I will point out in The Doctrine of the Word of God, there are many other aspects to the word of the Lord. It is not only law, but also gospel, promise, an expression of love, wisdom, and questioning. In all these ways as well, the written word expresses the authority of the great king.

25. Compare Meredith G. Kline, Images of the Spirit (Grand Rapids: Baker, 1980).

26. No doubt there is much more to be said on the subject of biblical authority. I hope to expand this argument at length in The Doctrine of the Word of God.

In the new covenant, God reaches out to all nations, not only to Israel (Matt. 28:19–20). Indeed, that has been his purpose in all the covenants, throughout the history of redemption. God's covenant with Israel is specifically with them, but they are to be his witnesses to all nations, for in Abraham all the nations of the earth are to be blessed (Gen. 12:3). Indeed, even in the Old Testament, God's covenant love has a universal reference. His "unfailing love" in Psalm 36:5, 7 is his *hesed*, his covenant love, a term often used of his special relationship with Israel. But the range of God's *hesed* here is universal: "O LORD, you preserve both man and beast" (v. 6), and "both high and low among men find refuge in the shadow of your wings" (v. 7). It is therefore God's covenant that provides the blessings of common grace, the kindness of God to all his creatures.[27]

So God's covenant lordship is not limited to Israel. His kingship is over all the nations, over all the earth (Ps. 47:7–9). Of course, it takes different forms and has different consequences for different kinds of creatures: inanimate, animate, plants, animals, covenant keepers, covenant breakers, Israel, the nations, and so on. But covenant lordship is a relationship between God and the whole creation as his servants, and all our thinking about God should take place within that relationship.

There are other important ways in which Scripture describes the relationship between God and his people. One is the marriage figure: he is the groom, and we the bride (Ezek. 16:1–63; Hos. 1:2–11; 3:1–5; Eph. 5:25–33; Rev. 19:7–9). But marriage is a kind of covenant in Scripture (Ezek. 16:8, 59–62; Mal. 2:14). Another figure is that of sonship: God is the Father, and we are his adopted sons and daughters (Matt. 12:50; Rom. 8:14–17; Gal. 4:6; Eph. 1:5). But we are sons and daughters of God because Christ is our Lord. Since we belong to the Son, we are in God's family. God has given us to his Son (John 17:2, 6), and it is the Spirit of the Son in us who enables us to cry "Abba, Father" (Rom. 8:15; Gal. 4:6).

Of course, even our relationship to Christ is not merely that of covenant servants. He calls us his friends (John 15:13–15). And Paul at one point speaks of servanthood as the status of Old Testament believers, something less than fully mature sonship (Gal. 4:1–7). Yet Jesus says that even on the Last Day, God will address us as servants (Matt. 25:21), and Paul, too, continues to refer to himself as a *doulos*, "bondslave" (Rom. 1:1; cf. 14:4; Gal. 1:10; 2 Tim. 2:24; Titus 1:1). James and Jude, who were most likely literal half brothers of Christ, also call themselves servants of Christ (James 1:1;

---

27. Thanks to my colleague, Mark Futato, for some of these thoughts. Of course, I take full responsibility for their formulations.

Jude 1:1), as do Peter and John, two of the disciples closest to him (2 Peter 1:1; Rev. 1:1).

Paul does use the slave/son contrast as a metaphor to indicate the new maturity and freedom we have in Christ, but it would be wrong to import the negative connotations of servanthood in Galatians 4 into every other biblical context where the term is found. In many other passages, Paul does not deny, but rather affirms, that we are now servants of Christ. And a servant of God is one who is in covenant with him.[28]

So the simple, obvious point I wish to make in this section is this: the name Lord names the head of a covenant. His essential relationship to us is that of a great king who has delivered us from death and calls us to serve him by obeying his written word.

---

28. Sonship, too, is by way of covenant, since (1) it is by adoption, and (2) it exists by virtue of our covenant relationship with Christ as Lord.

CHAPTER 3

The Lordship Attributes: Control

We have seen that the Lord is a profoundly holy person who creates a covenant relationship with his creatures. This is the basic truth we learn when God reveals himself to Moses as the Lord. But I promised earlier that I would look more carefully at the strange names of God presented in Exodus 3:14–15: I AM WHO I AM, I AM, and *yahweh*.

This passage of Scripture, where God reveals his name to Moses, is certainly mysterious. The Hebrew phrase translated "I AM WHO I AM" (*'ehyeh 'asher 'ehyeh*) can be interpreted in many ways. The verb *'ehyeh* can be rendered into English in either the present or the future tense. Various writers have also found various nuances in *'ehyeh*, such as "be present," "be now," or even "become." The relative pronoun *'asher* has been rendered "who," "what," "that," or "because." The permutations of these readings suggest a large number of grammatically possible interpretations of the phrase.

The name *yahweh* is also mysterious. Since it appears in verse 15, which immediately follows verse 14, we get the impression that it stands in place of the formula "I AM WHO I AM." The name seems to be related to the Hebrew verb meaning "to be," whether by etymology or by mere resemblance, but that relationship remains obscure. Its pronunciation is problematic, too. At an early point in the transmission of the Bible, the Jews decided that God's name was too holy to be uttered, and so they replaced it in Scripture reading with *'adonay*, which means "Lord." Because the vowel points of *'adonay* were superimposed on the consonants of the sacred name in the Hebrew text, we cannot be sure what the original vowels were, but most

36

scholars have settled on *yahweh* as the original Hebrew word. The older English name Jehovah (used, for example, in the American Standard Version of 1901) follows the Hebrew text as it literally appears, combining the consonants of *yahweh* with the vowels of *'adonay*.

Certainly the translation "Lord" is appropriate for God's name, since (1) the Jews read *'adonay* for *yahweh*, (2) the Septuagint (the early translation of the Old Testament into Greek), often quoted in the New Testament, uniformly uses *kyrios*, meaning "Lord," for *yahweh*, and (3) the New Testament writers also follow this pattern regularly.[1] To say this is not to prejudice the meaning of the term *Lord* or the term *yahweh*, but merely to stipulate their equivalence. The meaning of this pair of terms must be derived from the Bible, not from our general cultural impressions of what kingship or lordship must be like. So we shall treat *yahweh* and *Lord* as equivalent, even though that equivalence in itself leaves open most questions about their meanings.

RECENT AND TRADITIONAL VIEWS OF EXODUS 3:14

Some have contended that in Exodus 3:14 God refuses to answer Moses' question—as if he were saying, "Don't ask my name! I will be what I will be, and I will keep my nature to myself."[2] But God tells Moses to present I AM to the Israelites as a name, and in the next verse it becomes a proper name (Yahweh) that, as we shall see, is profoundly meaningful. Certainly God did not provide the kind of answer Moses was likely expecting, and certainly the answer leaves much unrevealed. But we cannot conclude that the name I AM reveals nothing at all.

Others have maintained that God's intention is to reveal his incomprehensibility: he is telling Moses that no name in human language is appropriate for him. Helmut Thielicke expresses this view dialectically: the name is "wrapped in a final inappropriateness, so that God escapes and transcends it."[3] But Scripture never treats the name Yahweh as even slightly inappropriate as a designation of God. Rather, God keeps reminding us of

---

1. The main difference between these terms is that *'adon* (a form related to *'adonay*), *kyrios*, and *lord* can refer to men in some contexts, but *yahweh* can refer only to God. Therefore, I identify *yahweh* with the terms meaning "Lord" only when they refer to God.

2. On these alternatives, see Carl F. H. Henry, *God, Revelation and Authority* (Waco, Tex.: Word Books, 1976), 2:213–23; Helmut Thielicke, *The Evangelical Faith* (Grand Rapids: Eerdmans, 1977), 2:109–10.

3. Thielicke, *The Evangelical Faith*, 110.

the appropriateness of his name. He is the Lord, and human beings must reckon with that fact. (See Ex. 15:3; Lev. 18:2, 4–6, 21, 30; 19:3–37; Ps. 83:18; Isa. 42:8; 43:11; 45:5–8, 18; 47:4; 48:1–2; 49:26; Hos. 12:5, and many other passages where God reminds us that Yahweh is who he really and truly is.) As we saw earlier, God performs mighty acts so that people will know that he is Yahweh.

Karl Barth combines this idea with the previous one:

> That the revelation of the name (Exod. 3:13f.) is in fact, in content, a refusal of any name . . . is significant enough; for the revealed name itself by its wording is to recall also and precisely the hiddenness of the revealed God. But still under this name, which itself and as such expresses His mystery, God *does* reveal himself to his people.[4]

Thielicke also mentions the view of Kraus, that the name reveals nothing of God's present nature, but amounts to a promise of future revelation:

> Everything is left "open," as H. J. Kraus says. [Yahweh] himself will make it plain in the future who he is and will be.[5]

These alternatives, however, fail for the same reasons that Thielicke's own view fails.

Thomas Aquinas understood this passage as teaching that God is Being: "I am he who is."[6] In his view, therefore, "Being itself" is the "most proper name for God."[7] From this name, Aquinas derives a number of philosophical assertions about God's nature, setting the course for later generations of Thomists and other scholastics. Étienne Gilson comments:

> No hint of metaphysics, but God speaks, *causa finita est,* and Exodus lays down the principle from which henceforth the whole of Christian philosophy will be suspended. From this moment it is understood that the proper name of God is Being and that . . . this name denotes his very essence.[8]

---

4. *ChD,* 1.1.365. Carl Henry observes, "This passage so shuttles between mysticism and meaning that it erodes the intelligibility of God's name and suspends the rational significance of the name in mid-air" (*God, Revelation and Authority,* 2:180).

5. Thielicke, *The Evangelical Faith,* 109.

6. The Septuagint translation *egō eimi ho ōn,* "I am the one who is," encourages this interpretation, but it is hard to justify this reading from the Hebrew text.

7. *ST,* 1.13.11.

8. Gilson, *The Spirit of Medieval Philosophy* (New York: Charles Scribner's Sons, 1940), 51. He adds in a later note (p. 433), "Of course we do not maintain that the text of Exo-

But it is hard to reconcile this interpretation with the context, in which God was promising to deliver Israel from Egypt. In that situation, why would God have given to Moses a metaphysical definition of himself? And if God had intended to give such a definition, why didn't he do so more clearly? Furthermore, how would the knowledge that God is "Being" have encouraged the Israelites to expect divine deliverance? To ask these questions is not to deny that God's name has metaphysical implications, and we shall consider those at a later point. Nonetheless, metaphysics is implicit, rather than explicit, in Exodus 3—and, as we shall see, it is rather different from the metaphysics that Aquinas and Gilson propose.

It is possible that the passage stresses the being of God by way of contrast to the nonbeing of the false gods of Egypt and the other nations. God is the one who "is," as opposed to those gods who are not. But the fact that Yahweh is real rather than unreal is insufficient to ground the metaphysical arguments of Aquinas and Gilson. And there are ideas other than mere reality that expound the meaning of the name Yahweh in Scripture. Yahweh demonstrates his reality by his words and actions. In the great contrast between Yahweh and Baal in 1 Kings 18, Yahweh is the one who "answers by fire" (v. 24). And in Exodus, Yahweh defeats the gods of Egypt by his mighty deliverance (Ex. 12:12). The name Yahweh not only distinguishes the reality of God from the unreality of the false gods, but also tells us something about that real God.

The more recent consensus is that in Exodus 3:14 God is saying, in effect, "I will be present (to deliver you)."[9] This interpretation sometimes takes the verb in the sense of "be present."[10] Other writers take the whole phrase as a variant of the "self-presentation formula"[11] in which God promises to deliver or judge, so that people will know that he is Lord. Often this

---

dus is a revealed metaphysical definition of God; but if there is no metaphysic *in* Exodus there is nevertheless a metaphysic *of* Exodus."

9. See Martin Buber, *The Kingship of God* (London: Allen and Unwin, 1967), 105; Walther Eichrodt, *Theology of the Old Testament* (London: SCM Press, 1961), 1:190; Christopher B. Kaiser, *The Doctrine of God* (Westchester, Ill.: Crossway, 1982), 21–22; Gerhard Von Rad, *Old Testament Theology* (Edinburgh: Oliver and Boyd, 1962), 1:180; Theodorus Vriezen, *An Outline of Old Testament Theology* (Oxford: Blackwell, 1970), 179–80. E. J. Young surveys the similar views of Holwerda, Noth, and Plasteras in "The Call of Moses II," *WTJ* 30 (1967): 1–24.

10. Hans Küng, *Does God Exist?* (Garden City, N.Y.: Doubleday, 1980), 621–22, arguing in effect that the present tense of the expression *I* AM entails presence here and now.

11. Henry, *God, Revelation and Authority*, 2:151. But if "I AM" is a shortened form of the self-presentation formula, we must then ask the meaning of "Lord" (*yahweh*) in that formula itself. So this identification only pushes the problem of determining the meaning of *yahweh* back one step.

redemptive interpretation relates verse 14 to verse 12, where the Lord says, "I will be (*'ehyeh*) with you."

Much biblical data favors this interpretation. Henry points out that similar "to be" language is found in Revelation 1:4, 8; 4:8; 11:17,[12] in contexts dealing with God's presence and coming. A number of passages tell us that God comes to the aid of his people for the sake of his name: Psalms 23:3; 25:11; 143:11; Jeremiah 14:7; Isaiah 48:9. He is "the LORD, who rescued you" (Ex. 18:10), the Lord "who brought you out of Egypt, out of the land of slavery" (Ex. 20:2). Through Isaiah, God reminds the people over and over, particularly in chapters 40–49, that it is he, Yahweh, who saves them and judges their enemies. Clearly, Yahweh is the redemptive name of God. Yahweh is the Savior, the Redeemer (Isa. 43:3, 11; 44:6, 24; 48:17; 49:7, 26).

PASSAGES EXPOUNDING THE NAME YAHWEH

The consensus view, in which the divine name refers to God's redemptive promise, is true as far as it goes. But I suspect that there is more to be said—that the Hebrew name *yahweh* is not merely a synonym of *savior, deliverer,* or *redeemer*.[13] If "savior" exhausted the meaning of *yahweh,* then "Yahweh is savior" would be a mere tautology. But his salvation is such wonderful good news, in part, because of all the other things he is known to be.

Further, we should remember that the consensus arose in the context of the strongly antimetaphysical spirit of modern theology. The influences of Kant and existentialism have led some theologians to resist, not only the scholastic metaphysics of Aristotle and Thomas Aquinas, but any attempt to describe God's nature, even though Scripture itself does not at all hesitate to describe him. We also saw in chapter 2 that there is some resistance in recent theology to the concept of God as a king or ruler—a prejudice that may have led to exegetical imbalance. We should ask, therefore, if *yahweh* also includes elements of control and authority, for example, as well as redemptive presence.

Accordingly, I shall seek a broader framework within which the redemptive connotation of the divine name will be a part of the whole. I will conclude that divine lordship can be more fully described by the three concepts of control, authority, and presence. I shall call these the lordship at-

---

12. Notice also the satanic parody in Rev. 17:11.

13. E. J. Young, in "The Call of Moses II," argues that Ex. 3:14–15 teaches some things about the metaphysical nature of God that are relevant to Israel's deliverance. God is not *becoming,* but being, *a se*; however, he is not the static being of Aristotle.

tributes. The three lordship attributes are "perspectivally related";[14] that is, each one is involved in the other two. None of them can be rightly understood, except as inseparably related to the others. So redemption necessarily involves God's control and authority, as well as his presence.

I will not pay further attention to etymology[15] or much more attention to the grammar of the *'ehyeh* phrases, about which little more can be said. My method, rather, will be to look at Exodus 3:13–15 in relation to other biblical passages, particularly those where the name Yahweh (or I AM) is prominent, in order to determine the contexts and implications of the name. These passages include:

1. Exodus 6:1–8, in which God contrasts his revelation to Abraham under the name *'el shadday* with his revelation to Moses under the name *yahweh*.

2. Exodus 20:1–17, the original covenant document in which Yahweh proclaims himself as Israel's great king.

3. Exodus 33:19 and 34:6, in the context of Moses' desire for a fuller revelation of God's name.

4. The "I am he" (*'ani hu'*) passages: Deuteronomy 32:39–40; Isaiah 41:4; 43:10–13, 25;[16] 44:6; 46:3–4; 48:12; 51:12. In these passages, both the pronoun *I* and the name *yahweh* are prominently mentioned, so that the words "I am he" seem to reflect the expression "I AM" in Exodus 3:14.

5. Other Old Testament passages that seem to have as one major purpose the exposition of *yahweh*: Psalm 135:13; Isaiah 26:4–8; Hosea 12:4–9; 13:4; Malachi 3:6.

6. Jesus' "I am" statements in the gospel of John. These have predicates (e.g., "I am the bread of life") in 6:48; 8:12; 9:5; 10:7, 14; 11:25; 14:6; 15:1, 5, but not in 4:26; 8:24, 28, 58; 13:19; 18:5–8.[17] Note that in 18:5–8 the soldiers "drew back and fell to the ground" when Jesus said "I am." John 8:58 is an especially impressive appropriation of the divine name. There Jesus says to the Jews, "Before Abraham was born, I am!" It is remarkable that all these "I am" statements refer to Jesus, rather than to God the Father. This datum is very important for the doctrine of the deity of Christ

---

14. *DKG*, 62–75, 89–90, 191–94, 200–204, 206–12, 235.

15. Etymology, of course, can tell us only the history of a word (and not much of that in the case of *yahweh*), not its meaning at the time of an actual use. To discern the latter, we must look at other uses that are comparable. I believe that the basic meaning of *yahweh* remains constant throughout the biblical period (although its connotations are enriched with the progress of revelation), so all biblical data are open to consideration.

16. Here and in 51:12, the Septuagint reads *egō eimi, egō eimi* ("I am, I am").

17. The English texts usually insert "he" in these passages, to read "I am he." That is not necessarily wrong, but it somewhat obscures the allusion to Ex. 3:14.

(see chap. 28). Christ is not just God in some general sense, but actually the covenant Lord, Yahweh.[18]

7. Other passages that speak of God, where the verb *to be* is prominent: Revelation 1:4, 8; 4:8; 11:17; 16:5. (See also the equivalent use of "first and last," "beginning and end," and "alpha and omega" in Isa. 41:4; 44:6; 48:12; Rev. 1:8, 11, 17; 2:8; 21:6; 22:13.)

THE COVENANTAL TRIAD

We shall also be looking again at the nature of the covenant of which Yahweh is the head. The triad of control, authority, and presence can be seen in the five-point suzerainty treaty that I described in chapter 2. After the name of the covenant Lord comes the historical prologue, in which the Lord proclaims his mighty deliverance of the vassal. Here he confirms that he is qualified to be the Lord and is established as the Lord by his great display of power in the past. He therefore sets the terms of the covenant, unilaterally imposing them on the vassal, for he is in control of the relationship and of all factors relevant to it. He is fully competent to impose his will and impose sanctions for the vassal's behavior. This is what I call the lordship attribute of control.

After the historical prologue come the stipulations of the law (with, as we have seen, the law of love as a central element). The Lord claims authority to command, and he expects obedience. This is the lordship attribute of authority.

Then follow the sanctions, in which the Lord promises that he will not be an absentee ruler, but will be present with the vassal to bring blessings for obedience and curses for disobedience. He will thus be regularly involved in the ongoing life of his covenant people. This is the lordship attribute of presence in blessing and judgment, which I will abbreviate as "presence." The covenant form continues to emphasize this presence as it concludes with an emphasis on continuity: the relationship between Lord and vassal will continue for generation after generation.[19]

18. I am inclined to see allusions to Ex. 3:14 also in the Synoptic Gospels and Acts: Matt. 14:27; Mark 14:62; Luke 24:39; Acts 9:5; 22:9; 26:15. This usage is not as obvious or as pervasive in the Synoptics as in John, but in these books, too, it typically appears in contexts where Jesus' nature becomes startlingly apparent.

19. I continue to expound the covenant in three points, even though I do see some merit in the "five point covenant form," expounded by Ray Sutton in *That You May Prosper* (Tyler, Tex.: Institute for Christian Economics, 1987) and employed by other writers, such as David Chilton, James Jordan, and Gary North. I take the first point of the suzerainty treaty

YAHWEH THE CONTROLLER

But we need to look at much more biblical evidence, first for the attribute of control. In the book of Exodus, on behalf of his enslaved people, Yahweh deals a crushing defeat to the most powerful totalitarian government of the day. Not only does he defeat Pharaoh and his army, but he invokes all the forces of nature to bring plagues on the Egyptians and to deliver his own people. He defeats Egypt and its gods (Ex. 12:12; 15:11: 18:11), thus showing himself to be Lord of heaven and earth.

God knows that

> the king of Egypt will not let you go unless a mighty hand compels him. So I will stretch out my hand and strike the Egyptians with all the wonders that I will perform among them. After that, he will let you go. (Ex. 3:19–20)

So God's "hand," "wonders," and "mighty acts" are a repeated emphasis of the Exodus narrative (as in, e.g., 4:21; 6:1, 6; 7:3–5). In Exodus 6:2–5, God relates the giving of the name *yahweh* to his powerful deliverance. After this deliverance, the Lord says:

> Then you will know that I am the LORD [*yahweh*] your God, who brought you out from under the yoke of the Egyptians. And I will bring you to the land I swore with uplifted hand to give to Abraham, to Isaac and to Jacob. I will give it to you as a possession. I am the LORD [*yahweh*]. (Ex. 6:7–8)

So in the Decalogue, the covenant document that defines Yahweh's relationship with Israel, the historical prologue follows the giving of the divine name, identifying him: "I am the LORD your God, who brought you out of Egypt, out of the land of slavery" (Ex. 20:2). The Lord is the one who controls all the forces of nature and history to deliver his people and thus to fulfill his covenant promise.

---

form to be a general announcement, the consequences of which are elaborated in the rest of the treaty, not a provision on the same level as the others. Similarly, I take the fifth point as continuing the whole treaty into the future, rather than adding content of another kind to it. But that's a close call. I could be persuaded otherwise. Perhaps my real problem is that some of the five-point applications of this structure seem to me to be a bit far-fetched. No doubt some will say the same thing about my three-point scheme. But my cognitive rest at the moment is sufficient for only three points, not five (*DKG*, 152–62). As to the substantive points about God's lordship, I affirm everything that they do. Their emphasis on transcendence (first point) and succession (fifth) are certainly legitimate, and I deal with them under other headings. So we differ in perspective and structure, rather than theological substance.

This emphasis on the Lord's sovereign rule can also be found in the mysterious terms of Exodus 3:14. However we choose to translate "I AM WHO I AM," the phrase certainly reflects God's sovereignty. Consider the possible renderings:

- I am what I am.
- I am who I am.
- I will be what I will be.
- I am because I am.
- I will be because I will be.
- I cause to be what I cause to be.
- I am present is what I am.
- I am the one who is.

These sentences have different meanings, of course, and some of them can be interpreted in a variety of ways. But all of them certainly stress God's sovereignty. They indicate that Yahweh is very different from us, determining his own nature, or his choices, or even his own being, without any dependence on us.

Geerhardus Vos[20] notes that there is an important parallel between the name "I AM WHO I AM" in Exodus 3:14 and Exodus 33:19, where God says to Moses:

> I will cause all my goodness to pass in front of you, and I will proclaim my name, the LORD [yahweh], in your presence. I will have mercy on whom I will have mercy, and I will have compassion on whom I will have compassion.

The connection between the first and second parts of this verse is difficult: how does the proclamation of God's name (which doesn't actually take place until 34:6–7) relate to the sentence about God's mercy and compassion? Is it that Moses must receive God's sovereign mercy in order to behold, even in a partial way, the theophany? Or is the second sentence itself a preliminary exposition of the divine name? In any case, it is part of a larger narrative in which, by vision, act, and word, God gives to Moses a fuller understanding of his lordship.

Vos points out that the second sentence is grammatically parallel to the name revealed in Exodus 3:14. In both cases, verbs are repeated ('ehyeh, "to be," in 3:14; hanan and raham in 33:19), and in both cases the repetitions are connected with the relative pronoun 'asher.[21] The parallel can be seen if we present the phrases thus:

---

20. Geerhardus Vos, *Biblical Theology* (Grand Rapids: Eerdmans, 1948), 129–34.

21. In 33:19, the particle 'et precedes 'asher, since 'asher functions as a direct object. That, of course, is different from its role in 3:14.

- I am *'asher* I am.
- I will have mercy *'et-'asher* I will have mercy.
- I will have compassion *'et-'asher* I will have compassion.

All the verbs in these sentences are Hebrew imperfects, which can be translated into English in the present or future tenses. Vos suspects that here is at least an allusion to Exodus 3:14. If so, this strengthens our contention that Exodus 3:14 emphasizes divine sovereignty in God's being, decisions, and actions.

The *'ani hu'* ("I am he") passages also stress God's sovereignty in redemption:

> See now that I myself am He!
>> There is no god besides me.
> I put to death and I bring to life,
>> I have wounded and I will heal,
>> and no one can deliver out of my hand. (Deut. 32:39)

> Who has done this [stirring up an eastern warrior to conquer
>> nations] and carried it through,
>> calling forth the generations from the beginning?
> I, the LORD [*yahweh*]—with the first of them
>> and with the last—I am he. (Isa. 41:4)

> "I, even I, am the LORD,
>> and apart from me there is no savior.
> I have revealed and saved and proclaimed—
>> I, and not some foreign god among you.
> You are my witnesses," declares the LORD, "that I am God.
>> Yes, and from ancient days I am he.
> No one can deliver out of my hand.
>> When I act, who can reverse it?" (Isa. 43:11–13)

In these passages, the pronoun *I* is prominent, bringing a message of divine monergism in salvation and judgment. *He* puts to death and makes alive; *he* brings judgment and mercy. Rulers and warriors are but tools in his hand. From that hand no one else can deliver, nor can anyone reverse his actions.

So Yahweh controls the entire course of nature and history for his own KEY glory and to accomplish his own purposes.

The same conclusion follows from the biblical affirmation that Yahweh is king. We saw in chapter 2 that Yahweh is the head of his covenant, indeed of various covenants that ultimately include all his creatures. In those covenants, he is the great king; everyone and everything else is his vassal, his servant. So he sovereignly issues commands in Genesis 1, and even things that do not exist obey him, by springing into being. Thus, the Psalms bring praise:

> The LORD [*yahweh*] reigns, he is robed in majesty;
>> the LORD is robed in majesty
>> and is armed with strength. (Ps. 93:1)

(Cf. Pss. 97:1 and 99:1; also Pss. 2; 47; 96:10–13.) Notice that the kingship of Yahweh is not only over Israel, but also over all the nations of the earth.

Yahweh, then, is the sovereign, the Lord over all his creatures.

CHAPTER 4

God's Control:
Its Efficacy and Universality

We have seen that one of the major connotations of God's name Yahweh is that he is king, the one who rules the whole creation, controlling the whole course of nature and history. Before we look at the other two lordship attributes, we need to explore some theological implications of this one. The nature of divine sovereignty has been one of the most discussed issues in the history of theology, and we cannot bypass those issues here. For this discussion, we shall have to go beyond the question of the meaning of the divine name and look at the broader range of biblical data. In this chapter, I shall present biblical teaching that indicates the efficacy and universality of God's control over the world.

THE EFFICACY OF GOD'S CONTROL

To say that God's controlling power is efficacious is simply to say that it always accomplishes its purpose. God never fails to accomplish what he sets out to do. Creatures may oppose him, to be sure, but they cannot prevail. For his own reasons, he has chosen to delay the fulfillment of his intentions for the end of history, and to bring about those intentions through a complicated historical sequence of events. In that sequence, his purposes appear sometimes to suffer defeat, sometimes to achieve victory. But, as we shall see later in our discussion of the problem of evil, each apparent defeat actually makes his eventual victory all the more glorious. The cross of Jesus is, of course, the chief example of this principle.

Nothing is too hard for God (Jer. 32:27); nothing seems marvelous to him (Zech. 8:6); with him nothing is impossible (Gen. 18:14; Matt. 19:26; Luke 1:37). So his purposes will always prevail. Against Assyria, he says:

> "Surely, as I have planned, so it will be,
>   and as I have purposed, so it will stand.
> I will crush the Assyrian. . . ."
> This is the plan determined for the whole world;
>   this is the hand stretched out over all nations.
> For the LORD Almighty has purposed, and who can thwart him?
>   His hand is stretched out, and who can turn it back? (Isa.
>   14:24–27; cf. Job 42:2; Jer. 23:20)

When God expresses his eternal purposes in words, through his prophets, those prophecies will surely come to pass (Deut. 18:21–22; Isa. 31:2).[1] God sometimes represents his word as his active agent that inevitably accomplishes his bidding:

> [As the rain waters the earth,] so is my word that goes out from my
>   mouth:
>   It will not return to me empty,
> but will accomplish what I desire
>   and achieve the purpose for which I sent it. (Isa. 55:11; cf. Zech. 1:6)

So the wise teacher reminds us:

> There is no wisdom, no insight, no plan
>   that can succeed against the LORD. (Prov. 21:30; cf. 16:9; 19:21)

Scripture speaks often of God's purpose in terms of "what pleases him" or "his good pleasure." God's pleasure will surely be realized:

> I say: My purpose will stand,
>   and I will do all that I please. (Isa. 46:10)

> All the peoples of the earth
>   are regarded as nothing.
> He does as he pleases
>   with the powers of heaven
>   and the peoples of the earth.
> No one can hold back his hand
>   or say to him: "What have you done?" (Dan. 4:35)

---

1. Not every prophecy in Scripture is an expression of God's eternal purpose. Some prophecies indicate what God will do in various *possible* situations. Sometimes, therefore,

> At that time Jesus said, "I praise you, Father, Lord of heaven and earth, because you have hidden these things from the wise and learned, and revealed them to little children. Yes, Father, for this was your good pleasure." (Matt. 11:25–26)

> In love he predestined us to be adopted as his sons through Jesus Christ, in accordance with his pleasure and will. (Eph. 1:4–5; cf. v. 9)[2]

To illustrate the efficacy of God's purposes in our lives, Scripture uses the image of the potter and the clay (Isa. 29:16; 45:9; 64:8; Jer. 18:1–10; Rom. 9:19–24). As easily as the potter molds his clay, making one vessel for one purpose and another vessel for another purpose, so God deals with people. His purpose will prevail, and the clay has no right to complain to the potter about it.

The general efficacy of God's purpose forms the background for the Reformed doctrine of irresistible grace. As we mentioned earlier, sinners do resist God's purposes; indeed, that is a significant theme in Scripture (Isa. 65:12; Matt. 23:37–39; Luke 7:30; Acts 7:51; Eph. 4:30; 1 Thess. 5:19; Heb. 4:2; 12:25). But the point of the doctrine is that their resistance does not succeed against the Lord. When God intends to bring someone to faith in Christ, he cannot fail, although for his own reasons he may choose to wrestle with a person for a long time before achieving that purpose.[3] We shall see later in this chapter that God's election always precedes, and is the source of, our response of faith. And we shall also see that God calls sinners effectually into fellowship with him. We shall have to discuss further the nature of human resistance in our later consideration of creaturely responsibility and freedom.

But Scripture regularly teaches that when God elects, calls, and regen-

---

he announces judgment, but "relents" when people repent: see Jer. 18:5–10. I shall discuss this issue again in connection with God's unchangeability. See also Richard Pratt, "Prophecy and Historical Contingency," at www.thirdmill.org.

2. There are also in Scripture, to be sure, many examples of creatures who displease God by disobeying his commands and thereby failing to measure up to his standards. Here the traditional Reformed distinction between God's decretive and preceptive wills (or, here, pleasures) is important. God always accomplishes what he ordains to happen, but he does not always ordain that his precepts, his standards, will be followed. In other words, he is sometimes pleased to ordain his own displeasure, as when he ordains the sinful actions of human beings (see later in this chapter for examples, and my longer discussion of God's will in chap. 23).

3. There are also situations where people who appear to be elect turn away from God and prove themselves not to be among his people. There are also cases where God chooses someone without the intention of giving him the full benefits of salvation. Judas is one example (John 6:70), as is national Israel, which, because of unbelief, lost its special status as God's elect nation.

erates someone in Christ, through the Spirit, that work accomplishes his
saving purpose. When God gives his people a new heart, it is certain that
"they will follow my decrees and be careful to keep my laws" (Ezek. 11:20;
cf. 36:26–27). When God gives new life (John 5:21), we cannot send it
back to him. Jesus said, "All that the Father gives me will come to me" (John
6:37). If God foreknows someone (i.e., befriends him, as we shall see below), he will certainly predestine him to be conformed to the likeness of
Christ, to be called, to be justified, and to be glorified in heaven (Rom.
8:29–30). "God has mercy on whom he wants to have mercy, and he hardens whom he wants to harden" (Rom. 9:18; cf. Ex. 33:19). Believers can
say, "God did not appoint us to suffer wrath but to receive salvation through
our Lord Jesus Christ" (1 Thess. 5:9). The psalmist adds:

> Blessed are those you choose
>   and bring near to live in your courts!
> We are filled with the good things of your house,
>   of your holy temple. (Ps. 65:4)

Like his word, therefore, God's grace will never return to him void.
    We can summarize the biblical teaching about the efficacy of God's
rule in the following passages, which speak for themselves:

> But the plans of the LORD stand firm forever,
>   the purposes of his heart through all generations. (Ps. 33:11)

> Our God is in heaven;
>   he does whatever pleases him. (Ps. 115:3)

> The LORD does whatever pleases him,
>   in the heavens and on the earth,
>   in the seas and all their depths. (Ps. 135:6)

> No one can deliver out of my hand.
>   When I act, who can reverse it? (Isa. 43:13)

> These are the words of him who is holy and true, who holds the
> key of David. What he opens no one can shut, and what he shuts
> no one can open. (Rev. 3:7)

UNIVERSALITY: THE NATURAL WORLD

    The rest of this chapter will deal with the universality of God's effica-
cious control. I shall try to show that God exercises such control over every-

thing that happens in the world. First we shall consider God's rule over the events of the natural world.

The natural world, first of all, is God's creation. Scripture emphasizes that frequently (Gen. 1:1–31; Ex. 20:11; Pss. 33:6, 9; 95:3–5; 146:5–6; Jer. 10:12; 51:15–16; Acts 17:24; Col. 1:16). He has made it according to his own wisdom, his own plan. He knows it inside and out and has planned all the laws and principles by which it operates.

The biblical writers do not hesitate to ascribe the events of the natural world directly to God:

> You care for the land and water it;
>   you enrich it abundantly.
> The streams of God are filled with water
>   to provide the people with grain,
>   for so you have ordained it.
> You drench its furrows
>   and level its ridges;
> you soften it with showers
>   and bless its crops.
> You crown the year with your bounty,
>   and your carts overflow with abundance. (Ps. 65:9–11)

> The Lord does whatever pleases him,
>   in the heavens and on the earth,
>   in the seas and all their depths.
> He makes clouds rise from the ends of the earth;
>   he sends lightning with the rain
>   and brings out the wind from his storehouses. (Ps. 135:6–7)

> He sends his command to the earth;
>   his word runs swiftly.
> He spreads the snow like wool
>   and scatters the frost like ashes.
> He hurls down his hail like pebbles.
>   Who can withstand his icy blast?
> He sends his word and melts them;
>   he stirs up his breezes, and the waters flow. (Ps. 147:15–18)

(Cf. Gen. 8:22; Job 38–40; Pss. 104:10–30; 107:23–32; 145:15–16; 147:8–9; 148:8; Jer. 5:22; 10:13; 31:35; Jonah 4:6–7; Nah. 1:3; Acts 14:17.) Notice the monergism in these statements: these are things that God does, because they please him. He does not merely allow them to happen; rather, he makes them happen. *God* waters the land. *God* drenches the furrows. *God* makes the clouds rise. *God* thunders (Jer. 10:13). *God* makes it snow or rain. *God* sends the frost and the ice, and then, when he pleases, he melts it. As he created all things by his word, so he sends his command, his word, to govern the events of nature.[4]

Even those events that appear to be most random are under God's sovereign control. "The lot is cast into the lap, but its every decision is from the LORD" (Prov. 16:33). Throw dice or draw straws; God controls the result. He decides the numbers to be drawn in the lottery. Indeed, in some cases he reveals his will through the drawing of lots (Jonah 1:7; Acts 1:23–26).[5] What we call "accidents" come from the Lord (Ex. 21:13; Judg. 9:53; 1 Kings 22:34).

Scripture also teaches the sovereignty of God by showing his purposeful discrimination in natural events. Before bringing Israel out of Egypt, God brings plagues on the Egyptians; so Israel has known Yahweh as the Lord of nature. In Exodus 9:13–26, he brings a terrible hailstorm upon the Egyptians, but leaves one area untouched, the land of Goshen, where the Israelites lived. God is the one who gives rain to one town and withholds it from another (Amos 4:7). He sends prosperity and he sends famine (Gen. 41:32).

Jesus emphasizes that this divine control extends to the smallest details. He teaches us that our heavenly Father not only makes the sun rise and sends rain (Matt. 5:45), but also feeds the birds (6:26),[6] clothes the lilies (6:28–30), accounts for the falling of the sparrows, and numbers the hairs on our head (10:29–30; Luke 12:4–7). And he demonstrates his unity with the Father by calming the sea at his own command (Matt. 8:23–27; Mark 4:35–39; Luke 8:22–25).

So the biblical view of the natural world is intensely personalistic. Natural events come from God, the personal Lord. He also employs angels and

---

4. Open theist John Sanders says that according to these passages God brings about some but not all weather phenomena. See my reply in *No Other God* (Phillipsburg, N.J.: P&R Publishing, 2001), 89–95. The sheer number of biblical passages refutes Sanders's position. And these passages clearly speak of weather in general terms rather than in this or that specific instance.

5. I am not advising Christians today to ascertain God's will by lot. In the case of Jonah, I think it was wrong for the sailors to try to find the culprit by lot, although they were, of course, desperate, and ultimately they expelled Jonah, not because of the lot, but because of his own confession of sin against God. As for the apostles in Acts 1, I assume that Joseph and Matthias were so alike in their qualifications that the lot was the only way to choose. Nevertheless, in both passages God uses the lot to reveal his will. Certainly Acts 1:24–26 represents the apparently random decision as God's answer to prayer.

6. Of course, he feeds the lions, too (Ps. 104:21), and sometimes shuts their mouths (Dan. 6:22).

human beings to do his work in the world. But the idea that there is some impersonal mechanism called "nature" or "natural law" that governs the universe is absent from the Bible. So is the notion of an ultimate "randomness," as postulated by some exponents of quantum mechanics.[7] Now obviously there are such things as natural forces, like gravity and electricity. Scripture indeed mentions the natural forces of the weather. But it is plain that in the view of the biblical writers any impersonal objects or forces are only secondary causes of the course of nature. Behind them, as behind the rain and the hail, behind even the apparent randomness of events, stands the personal God, who controls all things by his powerful word.

HUMAN HISTORY

Scripture doesn't tell us about God's work in nature merely to satisfy our curiosity. Rather, as always, God in his Word intends to teach us about our- *AND PRIMARILY ABOUT GOD* selves. God made us from dust (Gen. 2:7), and so we are a part of nature and dependent on the rain, the sunshine, the crops, and the animals. Without the cooperation of the "lower creation," we could not exist. When Jesus talks about God providing for the sparrows and lilies, it is part of an *a fortiori* argument: *how much more* does he care for you? We are "worth more than many sparrows" (Matt. 10:31).

Nor could we exist without a vast accumulation of apparently random events. We all owe our existence to the combination of one sperm and one egg, out of a vast number of possible combinations, and to equally improbable combinations that produced each of our parents and our ancestors back to Adam. And consider how many natural events enabled each of our ancestors to survive to maturity and reproduce. All of these things, plus the improbable events of our own life experience, have made us what we are.

So if God controls all the events of nature, then certainly he also controls the course of our own life. And we do not need to infer that conclusion from the preceding discussion; rather, Scripture teaches it explicitly. The apostle Paul tells the Athenian philosophers: "From one man [God] made every nation of men, that they should inhabit the whole earth; and he determined the times set for them and the exact places where they should live" (Acts 17:26).

7. Quantum mechanics may demonstrate a randomness in the finite world, that is, events without finite causes. But it can never demonstrate that those events have no causation at all, that is, that they are independent even of God's determination.

God is King, not only over Israel, but over all the nations, over all the earth (Pss. 45:6–12; 47:1–9; 95:3; cf. Gen. 18:25). He governs the events of human history for his purposes. So the psalmist says:

> The Lord foils the plans of the nations;
>   he thwarts the purposes of the peoples.
> But the plans of the Lord stand firm forever,
>   the purposes of his heart through all generations. (Ps. 33:10–11)

Consider some of the ways in which God governs the great events of history. We are familiar with the story of Joseph, who is betrayed by his brothers and sold into slavery in Egypt, but later is elevated to a position of prominence. God uses him as the means to preserve his family in Egypt, where they become a great nation. The Genesis narrative ascribes all these events to the Lord.

Joseph interprets Pharaoh's two dreams as indicating seven prosperous years, followed by seven years of famine. Joseph denies that he has any innate ability to interpret dreams: "I cannot do it, but God will give Pharaoh the answer he desires" (Gen. 41:16). God is not only the interpreter of the dream, but also its subject. Joseph says, "God has shown Pharaoh what he is about to do . . . and God will do it soon" (vv. 28, 32). It is God who will bring prosperity and then famine.

Even the betrayal of Joseph by his brothers is the Lord's work. When he reveals his identity to his brothers, Joseph says:

> And now, do not be distressed and do not be angry with yourselves for selling me here, because it was to save lives that God sent me ahead of you. For two years now there has been famine in the land, and for the next five years there will not be plowing and reaping. But God sent me ahead of you to preserve for you a remnant on earth and to save your lives by a great deliverance.
>
> So then, it was not you who sent me here, but God. He made me father to Pharaoh, lord of his entire household and ruler of all Egypt. (Gen. 45:5–8)

Later he adds:

> You intended to harm me, but God intended it for good to accomplish what is now being done, the saving of many lives. (50:20)

Again and again, it is God who brings about each event, good or evil, for his own good purposes. He does not merely allow Joseph to be sent into Egypt; rather, he himself sends him, though certainly the treacherous brothers are responsible. Throughout the Scriptures, God stands behind each great historical event.

As we have seen, it is Yahweh who brings the people out of Egypt by his strong arm. Then he puts terror into the hearts of Israel's enemies as his people take their inheritance in the Promised Land (Ex. 23:27; Deut. 2:25; cf. Gen. 35:5). After Joshua's conquests, God's hand is evident:

> The LORD gave them rest on every side, just as he had sworn to their forefathers. Not one of their enemies withstood them; the LORD handed all their enemies over to them. Not one of all the LORD's good promises to the house of Israel failed; every one was fulfilled. (Josh. 21:44–45)

Later, the nations seek to destroy God's people. The nations are gathered against Israel, says the Lord:

> But they do not know
>   the thoughts of the LORD;
> they do not understand his plan. (Mic. 4:12)

Israel is often at war, but God decides who will prevail:

> The horse is made ready for the day of battle,
>   but victory rests with the LORD. (Prov. 21:31)

God promises to give victory to Israel, as she is faithful to him. He tells Israel to allow liberal exemptions from military service, for he can win with many or few (Deut. 20:1–15; Judg. 7:1–8; 1 Sam. 14:6). The outcome is always in the Lord's hands (Deut. 3:22; Josh. 24:11; 1 Sam. 17:47; 2 Chron. 20:15; Zech. 4:6). But he will also bring defeat on Israel to show his displeasure with her disobedience (Josh. 7:11–12).

Indeed, God's people prove unfaithful to the covenant. So Yahweh raises up the Assyrian power to judge his people in the northern kingdom. The Assyrians do not intend to do God's bidding, but they do it, for their own reasons, after which God judges their sins as well (Isa. 10:5–12; 14:24–25; 37:26). Isaiah's prophecy about Assyria concludes:

> This is the plan determined for the whole world;
>   this is the hand stretched out over all nations.
> For the LORD Almighty has purposed, and who can thwart him?
>   His hand is stretched out, and who can turn it back? (Isa. 14:26–27)[8]

---

8. Compare the prophecy of Cyrus, below.

Similarly, God raises up the Babylonians, who conquer the southern kingdom and lead the people into exile (Hab. 1:6–11).

So God sends his people into exile, using the Assyrians and the Babylonians as his tools, but he will restore them again (Jer. 29:11–14). He will stir up the Medes, in turn, to destroy Babylon (Jer. 51:11). He "sets up kings and deposes them" (Dan. 2:21). The chastened Nebuchadnezzar concludes:

> [God's] dominion is an eternal dominion;
>   his kingdom endures from generation to generation.
> All the peoples of the earth
>   are regarded as nothing.
> He does as he pleases
>   with the powers of heaven
>   and the peoples of the earth.
> No one can hold back his hand
>   or say to him: "What have you done?" (Dan. 4:34–35)

But there is more. The Persian Empire supplants the Babylonian, and God chooses Cyrus, the Persian ruler, as his instrument to bring Israel back to the land of promise (Isa. 44:28; 45:1–13). On the conservative understanding of the chronology implied by the biblical text, God through Isaiah calls Cyrus by name, centuries before Cyrus is born. Then, through the edict of this pagan king (Ezra 1:2–4), God ends Israel's exile. Their return is at every point the work of God:

> [God] says of Cyrus, "He is my shepherd
>   and will accomplish all that I please;
>   he will say of Jerusalem, 'Let it be rebuilt,'
>   and of the temple, 'Let its foundations be laid.' " (Isa. 44:28)

Cyrus is a free agent, and doubtless he makes up his own mind for his own reasons to let Jerusalem be rebuilt. But God says here that Cyrus was doing God's good pleasure, and that Cyrus would certainly make the decision God predicted long before. The book of Ezra tells us that "the LORD moved the heart of Cyrus" (1:1) to order the return of Israel from exile (cf. 2 Chron. 36:22, and later, Ezra 6:22 [in regard to Darius] and 7:27 [in regard to Artaxerxes]). Note also how the Lord repeatedly says "I will" in Jeremiah's prophecy of restoration (30:4–24).

Thus, God sets the stage for the central point of human history. It is to restored Israel that God grants the visit of his Son Jesus:

> But when the time had fully come,[9] God sent his Son, born of a
> woman, born under law, to redeem those under law, that we might
> receive the full rights of sons. (Gal. 4:4–5)

Again, God brings everything about. Jesus' conception is supernatural.
Everything he does fulfills prophecy.[10] He does everything in obedience to
his Father's will.[11]

But he is betrayed:

> This man was handed over to you by God's set purpose and fore-
> knowledge; and you, with the help of wicked men, put him to death
> by nailing him to the cross. But God raised him from the dead, free-
> ing him from the agony of death, because it was impossible for death
> to keep its hold on him. (Acts 2:23–24; cf. 3:18; 4:27–28; 13:27)

Judas makes a personal decision to betray Jesus, for which he is fully responsible. Nevertheless, the betrayal of Jesus takes place "as it has been
decreed" (Luke 22:22; cf. Matt. 26:24; Mark 14:21). God's purpose stands
behind Jesus' betrayal and death. He intends it to be an atoning sacrifice for our sins (Mark 10:45; Rom. 3:25; 1 John 4:10), recalling his words
to Isaiah:

> "I, even I, am the LORD,
>   and apart from me there is no savior.
> I have revealed and saved and proclaimed—
>   I, and not some foreign god among you.
> You are my witnesses," declares the LORD, "that I am God.
>   Yes, and from ancient days I am he.
> No one can deliver out of my hand.
>   When I act, who can reverse it?" (43:11–13)

> "I, even I, am he who blots out
>   your transgressions, for my own sake,
>   and remembers your sins no more." (43:25)

The gospel of John teaches that Jesus' death happened at a particular
"time" determined by the Father (2:4; 7:6, 30, 44; 8:20; 12:23, 27; 13:1;

---

9. God announces the timing of the Messiah's coming centuries before it happens, in
Dan. 9:25–27. Notice also Dan. 11, where an angel tells Daniel in advance a number of future political developments. Here is another remarkable indication of God's sovereignty
over centuries of historical developments, both in Israel and in the pagan nations.

10. This is a pervasive theme in Matt.: 1:22; 2:15; 3:3; 4:14; 16:21, etc. See also Luke
12:31–33; Acts 13:29.

11. This is a major theme in John: 4:34; 5:30; 6:38; 7:16–18, etc.

16:21; 17:1). Before that appointed time, nobody could kill Jesus (7:30, 44), though they wanted to do so. He died only at the time planned by the Father.

It was God's act that raised Jesus from the dead. It was God in Christ who by the power of the Holy Spirit sent the new Christian church to proclaim Jesus' name throughout the earth (Matt. 28:19–20; Acts 1:8). And it was God who ordained that few Jews and many Gentiles would believe (Rom. 9–11). God also told Paul, the apostle to the Gentiles, that he would have to suffer for the sake of Jesus (Acts 9:16, 23) and that the Jews in Jerusalem would bind him and hand him over to the Romans (21:10–11).

It is God who has planned the day and hour of Jesus' return in glory (Matt. 24:36). Jesus will come in his sovereign power and glory (1 Thess. 4:16). Jesus himself is Lord, as we shall see, and salvation is his work, as it is the Father's. In the book of Revelation, the twenty-four elders sing to Jesus, the Lamb in the center of the throne:

> You are worthy to take the scroll
>   and to open its seals,
> because you were slain,
>   and with your blood you purchased men for God
>   from every tribe and language and people and nation.
> You have made them to be a kingdom and priests to serve our God,
>   and they will reign on the earth. (5:9–10)

Overwhelmed by his vision of God's plan of salvation, Paul responds:

> Oh, the depth of the riches of the wisdom and knowledge of God!
>   How unsearchable his judgments,
>   and his paths beyond tracing out!
> "Who has known the mind of the Lord?
>   Or who has been his counselor?"
> "Who has ever given to God,
>   that God should repay him?"
> For from him and through him and to him are all things.
>   To him be the glory forever! Amen. (Rom. 11:33–36)

Through the centuries of redemptive history, everything has come from God. He has planned and done it all. He has not merely set boundaries for creaturely action, but has actually made everything happen.

Thus, God rules the whole course of human history. Scripture, of course, focuses on the great events of redemptive history: God's election of Israel, and the incarnation, death, resurrection, ascension, and return of Jesus. But for these great events to take place, God has to be in control of all the nations—Egypt, Babylon, Assyria, and Persia, as well as Israel. Indeed, his mighty deeds prove him to be no less than King over all the earth.

INDIVIDUAL HUMAN LIVES

But God does not control only the course of nature and the great events of history. As we have seen, he is also concerned with details. So we find in Scripture that God controls the course of each human life. How could it be otherwise? God controls all natural events in detail, even including apparently random events. He controls the history of nations and of human salvation. But these, in turn, govern to a large extent the events of our daily lives. Conversely, if God does not control a vast number of individual human lives, it is hard to imagine how he would be able to control the great developments of history.

In fact, Scripture teaches explicitly that God controls the course of our individual lives. That control begins before we are conceived. God says to Jeremiah,

> Before I formed you in the womb I knew you,
>> before you were born I set you apart;
>> I appointed you as a prophet to the nations. (Jer. 1:5)

Is Jeremiah an exception to the general rule, because he is God's prophet, or does God know us all before conception? If God knew Jeremiah before his conception, then he must have arranged for each of Jeremiah's ancestors to be born, and then Jeremiah himself. So God is in control of all the "accidents" of history to create the precise person he seeks to employ as his prophet.[12] God's foreknowledge of one individual implies comprehensive control over the entire human family. Paul says of all believers that God "chose us in [Christ] before the creation of the world" (Eph. 1:4).

So the whole history of human procreation is under God's control, as he acts intentionally to bring about the conception of each one of us (Gen. 4:1, 25; 18:13–14; 25:21; 29:31–30:2; 30:17, 23–24; Deut. 10:22; Ruth

---

12. The same must be said of Cyrus, discussed earlier. Also, according to 1 Kings 13:1–3, an unnamed prophet told wicked King Jeroboam that a son of David named Josiah would kill his idolatrous priests. As with Cyrus, the prophet mentioned Josiah by name, and his activities, long before his birth (1 Kings 13:1–3).

4:13; Pss. 113:9; 127:3–5). And of course God is also active after each child's conception, as he is formed in the womb:

> For you created my inmost being;
>   you knit me together in my mother's womb.
> I praise you because I am fearfully and wonderfully made;
>   your works are wonderful,
>   I know that full well.
> My frame was not hidden from you
>   when I was made in the secret place.
> When I was woven together in the depths of the earth,
>   your eyes saw my unformed body.
> All the days ordained for me
>   were written in your book
>   before one of them came to be. (Ps. 139:13–16)

So we owe our very existence as human beings to God's gift of life. Furthermore, we are who we are as individuals by God's providence. Modern science continues to discover more and more things about us that arise because of our genetic makeup, through the incredibly complex programming of the DNA code.[13] How could anything but a person account for such information technology within every living cell? God is that person, and by controlling our genetic makeup and gestation, he makes us to be the physical beings we are, before we are even born.[14]

After birth, too, the events of our lives are in God's hands. Exodus 21:12–13, a law concerning the taking of life, reads:

> Anyone who strikes a man and kills him shall surely be put to death. However, if he does not do it intentionally, but God lets it happen, he is to flee to a place I will designate.

Here the law ascribes what we would call "accidental" loss of life to the agency of God. Naomi, the mother-in-law of Ruth, sees the hand of God in the death of her two sons:

---

13. I do not believe, however, that the genetic code accounts for everything we are. There are complex relationships between body and spirit.

14. Compare Paul's statement in 1 Cor. 12:18, "But in fact God has arranged the parts in the body, every one of them, just as he wanted them to be," with 15:35–41, where we are told that God gives to every creature precisely the kind of body he wants it to have. If someone wants to make an issue of the fact that these passages mention bodies, but not minds, see the next section. But recall at this point that there is a close relationship (in my view, not an identity) between mind and brain. Injury to the brain often impairs thinking.

No, my daughters. It is more bitter for me than for you, because the LORD's hand has gone out against me! (Ruth 1:13)

In her prayer, Hannah, the mother of Samuel, recognizes the hand of God:

The LORD brings death and makes alive;
  he brings down to the grave and raises up.
The LORD sends poverty and wealth;
  he humbles and he exalts. (1 Sam. 2:6–7)

The psalmist recognizes the work of God:

If the LORD delights in a man's way,
  he makes his steps firm;
though he stumble, he will not fall,
  for the LORD upholds him with his hand. (Ps. 37:23–24)

So God plans the course of our lives: our birth, our death, and whether we prosper or not.

The differences between us—our relatively different natural and spiritual abilities—come from God (Rom. 12:3–6; 1 Cor. 4:7; 12:4–6).

James offers this wisdom about the planning of our lives:

Now listen, you who say, "Today or tomorrow we will go to this or that city, spend a year there, carry on business and make money." Why, you do not even know what will happen tomorrow. What is your life? You are a mist that appears for a little while and then vanishes. Instead, you ought to say, "If it is the Lord's will, we will live and do this or that." As it is, you boast and brag. All such boasting is evil. (James 4:13–16)[15]

Clearly, for James, all the events of our lives are in God's hands. Whatever we do depends on God's willing it to happen.

HUMAN DECISIONS

We now approach a more controversial area, that of human decisions. Does God bring about our decisions? Some of them? Any of them? In a later chapter, I shall discuss the nature of human responsibility and freedom,

---

So if God controls the brain, he thereby controls much of our thinking function as well. The rest, of course, he also controls, but by other means.

15. For a negative example, see Jesus' parable of the rich fool in Luke 12:13–21. Cf. also Jer. 10:23, "I know, O LORD, that a man's life is not his own; it is not for man to direct his steps."

which are genuine and important. But here we must face the fact that our decisions are not independent of God, and therefore that our definition of freedom must somehow be consistent with God's sovereignty over the human will.

In our survey of the history of redemption, we saw that God brought about the free decisions of certain people, such as Joseph's brothers (Gen. 45:5–8), Cyrus (Isa. 44:28), and Judas (Luke 22:22; Acts 2:23–24; 3:18; 4:27–28; 13:27). So we should not be prejudiced by the unbiblical, but popular notion that God never foreordains our free decisions.

Furthermore, we have seen that God ordains the events of nature and the events of our daily life. How can such pervasive divine involvement in our life not profoundly influence our decisions? It is God who has made us, inside and out. To make us who we are, he must control our heredity. So he has given us the parents we have, and their parents, and their parents. And to give us our parents, God had to control many of their free decisions (such as the free decisions of Jeremiah's parents to marry) and those of their parents, grandparents, etc. Moreover, we have seen that God has placed us in our environment, in the situations that require us to make decisions. He decides how long we shall live and who brings about our successes and failures, even though such events usually depend on our free decisions, in addition to outside factors.

Negatively, God's purposes exclude many free decisions that would otherwise be possible. Since God had planned to bring Joseph to Egypt, his brothers were, in an important sense, not free to kill him, although at one point they planned to do so. Nor could Goliath have killed David, nor could Jeremiah have died in the womb.[16] Nor could the Roman soldiers have broken Jesus' legs when he hung on the cross, for God's prophets had declared otherwise.

But, over and above these inferences,[17] Scripture teaches directly that God brings about our free decisions. He does not foreordain merely what happens to us, as we have seen, but also what we choose to do.

The root of human decision is the *heart*. Jesus says,

---

16. See Gordon H. Clark, *Predestination in the Old Testament* (Phillipsburg, N.J.: Presbyterian and Reformed, 1978), 5–6.

17. Another inference may be made on the basis of God's exhaustive knowledge of the future. If God knows our free decisions before we are born, then certainly we are not the ultimate source of them. However, many today deny God's exhaustive foreknowledge, including process theologians and open theists. So I will argue the matter in chapter 22. If that argument is cogent, then God knows our free decisions from eternity, and since he is the only being who exists in eternity past, he must be the cause of those decisions.

No good tree bears bad fruit, nor does a bad tree bear good fruit. Each tree is recognized by its own fruit. People do not pick figs from thornbushes, or grapes from briers. The good man brings good things out of the good stored up in his heart, and the evil man brings evil things out of the evil stored up in his heart. For out of the overflow of his heart his mouth speaks. (Luke 6:43–45)

A thornbush cannot bear figs, because that would be contrary to its very nature. So the heart is the center of human life, our fundamental nature and character. But that heart is under God's control: "The king's heart is in the hand of the LORD; he directs it like a watercourse wherever he pleases" (Prov. 21:1). Certainly this is what God did with Cyrus, as we have seen. It is also what he did with the pharaoh of the Exodus (Rom. 9:17; cf. Ex. 9:16; 14:4), as we shall see in the next section.[18]

God directs the heart, not only of kings, but of all people (Ps. 33:15). So he controls the decisions, not only of Pharaoh, but also of the Egyptian people, giving them a favorable disposition toward Israel (Ex. 12:36). Scripture underscores that this change was the Lord's work, for it mentions that God had predicted it in his meeting with Moses at the burning bush (3:21–22).

God not only forms the purposes of our heart, but also decides the steps we will take to carry our those purposes:

> In his heart a man plans his course,
> 　but the LORD determines his steps. (Prov. 16:9; cf. 16:1; 19:21)

According to many Scripture passages, God controls our free decisions and attitudes, often predicting those decisions far in advance. He declared that when the Israelites went up to Jerusalem for the annual feasts, the enemy nations would not covet their land (Ex. 34:24). God was saying that he would control the minds and hearts of these pagan peoples so that they will not cause trouble for Israel at those times.

When Gideon led his tiny army against the Midianite camp, "the LORD caused the men throughout the camp to turn on each other with their swords" (Judg. 7:22). During the Exile, God "caused" a chief Babylonian official "to show favor and sympathy to Daniel" (Dan. 1:9). After the Exile, the Lord "filled [Israel] with joy by changing the attitude of the king of Assyria" (Ezra 6:22).

The soldiers at Jesus' crucifixion freely decided not to tear Jesus' garment, but instead to cast lots for it. But God had foreordained this decision:

18. See also 1 Sam. 10:9 on Saul, and 1 Kings 3:12 on Solomon.

This happened that the scripture might be fulfilled which said,
"They divided my garments among them
  and cast lots for my clothing." (John 19:24, quoting Ps. 22:18;
    cf. John 19:31–37)

John's point is not only that God knew in advance what would happen, but rather that the event took place *so that* Scripture might be fulfilled. Whose intention was it to fulfill Scripture through this event? It was not the intent of the soldiers, but the intent of God, the primary cause of their decision.

The Gospels tell us over and over again that things happen so that Scripture may be fulfilled. Many of those events involve free decisions of human beings (see, e.g., Matt. 1:20–23; 2:14–15, 22–23; 4:12–16). In some cases, human beings (such as Jesus himself in 4:12–16) may have consciously intended to fulfill Scripture. In other cases, they either had no such intention or did not even know they were fulfilling Scripture (e.g., Matt. 21:1–5; 26:55–56; Acts 13:27–29). In any case, Scripture must be fulfilled (Mark 14:49).[19]

The picture given to us by this large group of passages is that God's purpose stands behind the free decisions of human beings. Often God tells us, sometimes long before the event, what a human being will freely decide to do. But the point is not merely that God has advance knowledge of an event, but that he is fulfilling his own purpose through that event. That divine purpose imparts a certain necessity (Gk. *dei*, as in, e.g., Matt. 16:21; 24:6; Mark 8:31; 9:11; 13:7, 10, 14; Luke 9:22; 17:25; 24:26) to the human decision to bring about the predicted event.[20] We shall, of course, have to discuss later how this necessity is compatible with human freedom.

SINS

This section raises even more serious difficulties than the last. If it is hard for us to accept God's foreordination of human decisions and actions in gen-

---

19. In this passage, Jesus says Scripture was fulfilled both in the failure of his enemies to arrest him in the temple courts and in their decision to arrest him in the garden. Both, of course, were their free decisions.

20. The nature of "fulfillment" in reference to prophecy is rather complex. Sometimes, as in Deut. 18:21–22 and Dan. 7:1–28, prophecy straightforwardly predicts future events and is fulfilled when those events take place. At other times, as in Matt. 2:14–15, the relationship between prophecy and fulfillment is not as evident. When Matthew quotes Hos. 11:1, "Out of Egypt I called my son," he is not claiming that Hosea predicted the Messiah's sojourn in Egypt, but rather, I think, that that sojourn was symbolically appropriate to Je-

eral, it is even harder to accept his foreordination of our sinful decisions and actions in particular. The former raises questions about human freedom and responsibility; the latter raises questions about God's own goodness. For how can a holy God bring about sin?

We shall deal with that problem in chapter 9. But for now, it is important to see that God does in fact bring about the sinful behavior of human beings, whatever problems that may create in our understanding. However we answer the notorious "problem of evil,"[21] we must do so in accord with Scripture, and therefore in accord with the many passages that affirm God's foreordination of everything, even including sin. Many attempts to solve the problem of evil deny this premise, but it cannot be denied by any attempt to solve the problem scripturally.

We have already seen that God controls the free decisions of human beings, particularly by controlling the heart, the center of human existence. But the hearts of fallen people are sinful, as God says through Jeremiah:

> The heart is deceitful above all things
> and beyond cure.
> Who can understand it? (Jer. 17:9)

People freely choose to do evil, but for that they are no less under God's control.

So we saw that God sent Joseph into Egypt to preserve his family in a time of famine, accomplishing that by means of the sinful actions of Joseph's brothers, who sold him into slavery. Between the time of Joseph and the time of Moses, the pharaohs turned against Israel. The psalmist does not hesitate to attribute the Egyptians' hatred to God:

> The LORD made his people very fruitful;
> he made them too numerous for their foes,
> whose hearts he turned to hate his people,
> to conspire against his servants. (Ps. 105:24)

---

sus' role as the faithful remnant of Israel. In each case, the text suggests that God was bringing about an event that in one way or another (literally, allusively, or symbolically) brought out the depth of meaning in the prophecy. In these fulfillment passages, there is always a sense of divine necessity.

21. The problem of evil concerns both *natural* evil (events that bring human suffering) and *moral* evil (sinful actions of rational creatures). Certainly God is sovereign over natural evil, for as we have seen, he manifests his judgments in history. He often deals with human sin by bringing disaster and death. See, e.g., Eccl. 7:14; Isa. 54:16; Amos 3:6. In Christian theology, natural evil is God's judgment upon moral evil (Gen. 3:14–19), so moral evil has the primacy. Moral evil, therefore, is the more serious problem, both because it stands behind all other evil, and because it raises questions about God's own character.

When God spoke with Moses about delivering Israel from Egypt, he told
him in advance that Pharaoh would not let Israel go unless he was compelled by "a mighty hand" (Ex. 3:19). Then God hardened the heart of
Pharaoh to create that unwillingness (4:21; 7:3, 13; 9:12; 10:1, 20, 27; 11:10;
14:4, 8).[22] Note the sustained emphasis on God's agency. It is also true that
Pharaoh hardened his own heart (8:15), but in the narrative God's hardening of him is clearly prior and receives greater emphasis. To harden one's
heart is to refuse God's commands, even refusing to listen to them or take
them seriously. Clearly it is a sin. God warns against it (see Ps. 95:7–8).
But in this case God made it happen, for his own specific purpose (Rom.
9:17). Having discussed God's dealings with Pharaoh, Paul summarizes:
"Therefore God has mercy on whom he wants to have mercy, and he hardens whom he wants to harden" (Rom. 9:18).[23]

No doubt Pharaoh was a wicked man before this time, and God's hardening of him could be seen from a human point of view as a natural ex-
tension of Pharaoh's previous attitudes, or even as a divine punishment for
previous sin. (When we probe more deeply, however, we have to ask how
God was previously involved with Pharaoh's heredity, environment, character, and decisions.) That is true of all the hardening passages in Scripture; God does not harden people who have been good and faithful to him.
Nevertheless, the hardening comes from God. He does deal with sinners
by causing them to become more sinful.[24]

Pharaoh is by no means the only example of hardening in Scripture. Si-
hon, king of Heshbon, would not allow Israel to pass through his land on
the way to Canaan, because "the LORD your God has made his spirit stub-
born and his heart obstinate in order to give him into your hands, as he
has now done" (Deut. 2:30; cf. Josh. 11:18–20; 1 Sam. 2:25; 2 Chron. 25:20).
Similarly, God sent "an evil spirit" upon Saul to torment him (1 Sam.
16:14). Later, God sent another spirit, who caused the false prophets to lie,
in order to lead wicked King Ahab to the battle in which he would die
(1 Kings 22:20–23).[25]

22. Compare 14:17–18, where God hardens the hearts of the Egyptian soldiers, so that
they might know that he is Yahweh.
23. In this context, Paul also quotes Ex. 33:19, one of the passages we mentioned earlier that defines the meaning of yahweh: "I will have mercy on whom I have mercy, and I
will have compassion on whom I have compassion" (Rom. 9:15). In hardening Pharaoh,
God sovereignly withheld his mercy.
24. Rom. 1:24–32 describes how God "gave up" sinners so that they would commit greater
sins.
25. On the theme of God sending evil or deceitful spirits, compare Judg. 9:23; 2 Kings
19:5–7. In 2 Thess. 2:11–12, we are told that before the coming of Christ, Satan will work

God hardened the people of Israel as well as their evil kings. This was the mission of Isaiah the prophet:

> Go and tell this people:
> "Be ever hearing, but never understanding;
>   be ever seeing, but never perceiving."
> Make the heart of this people calloused;
>   make their ears dull
>   and close their eyes.
> Otherwise they might see with their eyes,
>   hear with their ears,
>   understand with their hearts,
> and turn and be healed. (Isa. 6:9–10)

Later, Isaiah asks,

> Why, O LORD, do you make us wander from your ways
>   and harden our hearts so we do not revere you? (Isa. 63:17)

Then he complains:

> No one calls on your name
>   or strives to lay hold of you;
> for you have hidden your face from us
>   and made us waste away because of our sins. (Isa. 64:7)

Other nations, too, are objects of God's hardening. His prophets sometimes foretell that nations and individuals will rebel against God. As we have seen, Isaiah prophesies that God will send the Assyrians to plunder and trample Israel (Isa. 10:5–11). The Assyrian comes to do vile things, but he comes, says God, because "I send him" (v. 6). Similarly, the Lord promises to bring the army of Gog against Israel, "so that the nations may know me when I show myself holy through you before their eyes" (Ezek. 38:16). The prophecy indicates God's purpose: to bring about the sin of the people (vv. 10–13), in order to glorify himself in the way he deals with it.

Sometimes, without mention of prophecy, Scripture indicates that God has brought about a sinful action. Samson sought out a Philistine woman to be his wife, although God had forbidden his people to marry people from the surrounding nations. His parents were properly indignant, but they "did not know that this was from the LORD, who was seeking an occasion to con-

---

counterfeit miracles to deceive the wicked, and "God sends them a powerful delusion so that they will believe the lie and so that all will be condemned who have not believed the truth but have delighted in wickedness."

front the Philistines" (Judg. 14:4). Similarly, in 2 Samuel 24, the Lord in-cites David to conduct a census, for which God later judges him and for which David repents.

Several times in the Old Testament, God prevents certain people from following wise counsel. Absalom, the rebellious son of David, would not listen to the wise counselor Ahithophel, "for the LORD had determined to frustrate the good advice of Ahithophel in order to bring disaster on Ab-salom" (2 Sam. 17:14). Later, King Solomon's son and successor, Re-hoboam, also ignored wise counselors and the pleas of the people, and sought to establish himself as a fearsome despot, which led to the secession of the northern tribes. He did not listen to wiser men "for this turn of events was from the LORD, to fulfill the word the LORD had spoken to Jeroboam son of Nebat through Ahijah the Shilonite" (1 Kings 12:15). God also pre-vented Amaziah, king of Judah, from obeying wise counsel, since he in-tended to bring judgment on him (2 Chron. 25:20).

In the New Testament, Jesus quotes Isaiah 6 in Matthew 13:14–15 to explain why he uses parables: to enlighten the disciples, but also to harden the wicked. This passage is also mentioned in John 12:40 to explain why the Jews disbelieved despite miraculous signs. So when God's word brought a response of unbelief and rebellion, it did not fail. God's word never fails to achieve its purpose (Isa. 55:11). Rather, in these cases the word was ac-complishing precisely what God intended, difficult as that may be for us to accept.

Jesus, too, mentions sinful actions necessitated by prophecy. In John 13:18 (quoting Ps. 41:9), he excludes his betrayer from his blessing:

> I am not referring to all of you; I know those I have chosen. But this is to fulfill the scripture: "He who shares my bread has lifted up his heel against me."

Jesus knows who the betrayer is before the betrayal. He indicates that God, through Scripture, has made betrayal necessary. In John 15:25, Jesus ex-plains why the Jews unreasonably disbelieved in him despite many signs and wonders: "This is to fulfill what is written in their Law: 'They hated me without reason.' "

Paul speaks of the apostles' ministry in the same way as Isaiah 6 (2 Cor. 2:15–16), as does Peter (1 Peter 2:6–8).[26] In Scripture, God's word typi-cally brings light and salvation. But in some cases it brings hardening: dark-ness and unbelief.

Paul regards God's hardening as the reason for the unbelief of the Jews:

---

26. Peter adds, about unbelievers, that their disobedience is "what they were destined for."

What Israel sought so earnestly it did not obtain, but the elect did.
The others were hardened, as it is written:
"God gave them a spirit of stupor,
  eyes so that they could not see
  and ears so that they could not hear,
to this very day." (Rom. 11:7–8, quoting Isa. 29:10)

Paul argues in the context (chaps. 9–11) that God had to bring about the unbelief of Israel in order to accomplish the ingathering of the Gentiles (see 9:22–26 and 11:11–16, 25–32), followed by Paul's great hymn to the incomprehensible purposes of God (11:33–36).

Preceding Israel's hardening, however, was God's hardening of the Gentiles. God had revealed himself plainly to all nations through the creation (Rom. 1:19–20), but the nations had rejected God's revelation, refused to glorify him, worshiped idols, and exchanged the truth for a lie (vv. 21–25). God's response was to harden them:

> Therefore God gave them over in the sinful desires of their hearts to sexual impurity. . . . Because of this, God gave them over to shameful lusts. . . . He gave them over to a depraved mind. (vv. 24–28)

God's sovereignty over human sin culminates in his foreordination of what John Murray called "the arch crime of history," the murder of the Son of God. As we have seen, Judas's betrayal,[27] the Jews' murderous hatred of Jesus, and the horrible injustice of the Romans, were all due to "God's set purpose and foreknowledge" (Acts 2:23). These people did what God's "power and will had decided beforehand should happen" (4:28; cf. 13:27; Luke 22:22). The crucifixion of Jesus could not have happened without sin, for he did not deserve death. For God to foreordain the Crucifixion, he had to foreordain sinful actions to bring it about.

Finally, in the book of Revelation, when the evil beast sets up his satanic rule among the nations of the world, we read that "God has put it into their hearts to accomplish his purpose by agreeing to give the beast their power to rule, until God's words are fulfilled" (Rev. 17:17).

In summary, the teacher of wisdom says:

> The LORD works out everything for his own ends—
>   even the wicked for a day of disaster. (Prov. 16:4)[28]

---

27. The parallel with Joseph's betrayal by his brothers is significant.

28. As often in Scripture, however, this verse about God's control of wickedness precedes another that emphasizes the responsibility of the wicked for their own actions: "The LORD detests all the proud of heart. Be sure of this: They will not go unpunished" (v. 5).

FAITH AND SALVATION

In some ways, this section will be much happier than the last, for it deals with the positive side of God's sovereignty, rather than the negative. But we should remember that the two sides are quite inseparable; they reinforce one another. If saving faith is a gift of God, then the lack of saving faith, sinful unbelief, comes from God's withholding that blessing.[29] Thus, this section will reinforce the previous one.

Nevertheless, we should rejoice that "salvation comes from the LORD" (Jonah 2:9). We saw in our discussion of the history of redemption that God sovereignly rescues his people from sin and its consequences. And we saw in our earlier discussion of irresistible grace that God breaks down our resistance to bring us into his fellowship.

Without God's salvation, we were all once without hope, "dead in [our] transgressions and sins" (Eph. 2:1), "by nature objects of wrath" (2:3). But, says Paul,

> because of his great love for us, God, who is rich in mercy, made us alive with Christ even when we were dead in transgressions—it is by grace you have been saved. And God raised us up with Christ and seated us with him in the heavenly realms in Christ Jesus, in order that in the coming ages he might show the incomparable riches of his grace, expressed in his kindness to us in Christ Jesus. For it is by grace you have been saved, through faith—and this not from yourselves, it is the gift of God—not by works, so that no one can boast. For we are God's workmanship, created in Christ Jesus to do good works, which God prepared in advance for us to do. (Eph. 2:4–10)

This is the gospel, the central message of Scripture, that God came in Christ to reconcile us to himself by grace—by God's unmerited favor to those who deserve wrath. As we see, grace is opposed to works. Salvation comes, not through what we do, but through what God does for us. We have nothing to boast about. We are guilty sinners, whose only hope is God's mercy.

So salvation is God's work—not only in its broad historical outlines, as we saw earlier, but also for each of us as individuals. It is an exercise of God's sovereign control over his world and his creatures. That control began before we were conceived—indeed, before the world was made. For Paul tells us that

29. Note Deut. 29:4, "But to this day the LORD has not given you a mind that understands or eyes that see or ears that hear."

> [God] chose us in [Christ] before the creation of the world to be holy and blameless in his sight. In love he predestined us to be adopted as his sons through Jesus Christ, in accordance with his pleasure and will—to the praise of his glorious grace, which he has freely given us in the One he loves. (Eph. 1:4–6)

Paul also tells us that

> [God] has saved us and called us to a holy life—not because of anything we have done but because of his own purpose and grace. This grace was given us in Christ Jesus before the beginning of time. (2 Tim. 1:9)

Here we learn of God's choice (*election* is the theological term) of a people for himself, before the foundation of the world. We shall consider election in more detail, under the topic of God's decrees, in chapter 16. For now it is enough to recognize that election is a biblical truth, and that salvation is therefore ultimately by divine appointment, divine choice (cf. Acts 13:48; 1 Thess. 1:4; 5:9; 2 Thess. 2:13–14).

Certainly there is also a human choice, a choice to receive Christ, to believe in him (John 1:12; 3:15–16; 6:29, 40; 11:26).[30] Without this choice, there is no salvation (John 3:36). There are also human decisions to follow Jesus, to obey his commandments—decisions that Scripture continually urges us to make (e.g., John 14:15, 21, 23). But which choice comes first? Does God choose us for salvation and then move us to respond, or do we first choose him and thereby motivate him to choose us for salvation?

The second alternative is quite impossible, since it violates the very idea of grace. If our choosing of God moves him to save us, then salvation is based on a work of ours, and we have something to boast about.[31]

Furthermore, God's choosing took place in eternity past, before anyone was even conceived. Before we began to exist, God's plan for us was fully

---

30. Some Calvinists have used John 15:16, "You did not choose me, but I chose you," to prove that there is no human choice at all. That claim is clearly wrong in the light of the many passages that indicate the importance of human decision in our relationship to Jesus. In John 15:16, Jesus is not saying that the disciples made no decision to follow him; rather, he is indicating that his choice, not theirs, marked the beginning of their relationship to him as disciples and apostles.

31. The Arminian response to this argument is to deny that faith is a work. It is true that faith has no merit that would move God to save us. That is true of anything and everything we do. But the Arminian wants to have it both ways. He wants to say that faith has no merit, but he also wants to say that our faith somehow motivates God to save us, that God chooses us on the basis of our choosing him. But if our faith motivates God to save us, then it must have merit in his eyes.

formulated. We can no more change God's decision than we can change our grandparents.

Arminian theology, nevertheless, asserts that God chooses us because he knows in advance that we will choose to believe in him. On this view, our choice is the cause, and God's choice is the effect. We are the first cause, and God is the second. Some have supported this understanding by appealing to Romans 8:29 and 1 Peter 1:2, which say that election is based on "foreknowledge." But the foreknowledge in these passages is not God's foreknowledge that we will choose him. Often in the biblical languages, as in English, when the verb *know* has a noun rather than a fact-clause as its object,[32] it refers to a personal relationship, not a knowledge of information. In Psalm 1:6, for example, we learn that "the Lord watches over [Heb. *knows*] the way of the righteous." This does not simply mean that God knows what the righteous are doing, which would be rather obvious, but that he guards and keeps them. Compare Amos 3:2:

> You only have I chosen [Heb. *known*]
> of all the families of the earth;
> therefore I will punish you
> for all your sins.

The NIV's translation, "chosen," is correct. God is not confessing ignorance of all the families of the earth other than Israel. Rather, he is claiming a special covenant relationship with Israel. (Cf. Hos. 13:4; Matt. 25:12; John 10:14; Rom. 11:2 ["foreknew"]; 1 Cor. 8:3; 1 Thess. 5:12 [where *know* is translated "respect"]; 1 Peter 1:20 [where *foreknown* is again translated "chosen"].) So in Romans 8:29, when Paul says that God "foreknew" believers, this means that he established a personal relationship with them (from all eternity, according to Eph. 1:4–5). The Greek word translated "foreknew" could also be translated "befriended" or even "chose" or "elected."

So Scripture teaches all believers, as Jesus taught his disciples, "You did not choose me, but I chose you and appointed you to go and bear fruit— fruit that will last" (John 15:16). God's choice precedes our choice, our response, our faith. How could it be otherwise, considering everything we have already observed about God's sovereignty throughout nature, history, and human life in general? Can the choice to believe in Christ be the one choice that is beyond God's control? Is salvation the one area in which we should *not* give God the praise?[33]

---

32. This is the difference between "knowing him" and "knowing that." For example, consider the difference between "I know Bill" and "I know that Bill is forty-three years old."

33. Thanks to Vern Poythress for suggesting to me this profound question.

Many passages explicitly teach that our response is God's gift. Jesus teaches that "all that the Father gives me will come to me" (John 6:37), that "no one can come to me unless the Father who sent me draws him, and I will raise him up at the last day" (6:44),[34] and that "no one can come to me unless the Father has enabled him" (6:65). It is only by the Spirit that we call upon God as *Abba,* Father (Rom. 8:15).

When Paul and Silas first brought the gospel to the city of Philippi, one of their listeners was a woman named Lydia. "The Lord opened her heart to respond to Paul's message," whereupon she and her household were baptized (Acts 16:14–15). This language is quite straightforward: her faith came from God. Earlier, in Pisidian Antioch, a number of Gentiles came to faith in Christ, and "all who were appointed for eternal life believed" (13:48).[35] The divine appointment came first; belief (faith) was the result.[36] Therefore, people believe when God's hand is with the apostles (11:21); their conversion is evidence of God's grace (v. 23). In 18:27, also, converts are those "who by grace had believed." (Cf. Rom. 12:3; 1 Cor. 2:5; 12:9; Eph. 6:23; Phil. 1:29; 1 Thess. 1:4–5.)

Repentance, too, is the work of God in us. It is the opposite side of faith. Faith is turning to Christ; repentance is turning away from sin. You cannot have one without the other. As with faith, it is God who grants repentance. We noticed earlier that God sometimes hardens hearts, in effect keeping them from repentance. God also acts positively to give the spirit of repentance. In a passage vividly anticipating the sufferings of Christ, God announces through Zechariah:

---

34. "Draw" (*helkō*) is a strong word, sometimes translated "drag." The one dragged may resist, but not successfully. See John 18:10; 21:6, 11; Acts 16:19; 21:30; James 2:6. Arminian theologians point out that in John 12:32, Jesus promises to "draw all men" to himself. Here too, the drawing is efficacious. But in the context (especially vv. 20–22), he is promising to draw people of all nations, not only Jews—a regular theme in John's gospel (1:13; 10:16; 11:51). First Tim. 2:1–6 is a possible parallel, but I will later present a somewhat different understanding of that passage. At any rate, in John 12:32 Jesus is not promising to draw every single human being to himself.

35. This principle throws light on John 10:26, where Jesus tells the Jews, "You do not believe because you are not my sheep." To be Jesus' sheep is to be elect, to be appointed for eternal life. "I give them eternal life, and they shall never perish; no one can snatch them out of my hand" (v. 28). Again, election precedes believing. Note the same relationship in John 17, where Jesus speaks of the disciples as those whom the Father has given to him (vv. 2, 6). He tells the Father that he has taught these elect people, and as a result they have believed (vv. 6–8).

36. So we can understand why God tells Paul to remain at Corinth despite persecution: "because I have many people in this city" (18:10). God is not speaking of people who have already believed, but of those who will believe through Paul's eighteen-month ministry there. The people already belong to God, and they will come to believe through Paul's preaching.

> I will pour out on the house of David and the inhabitants of Jerusalem a spirit of grace and supplication. They will look on me, the one they have pierced, and they will mourn for him as one mourns for an only child, and grieve bitterly for him as one grieves for a firstborn son. (Zech. 12:10)

So Jesus is exalted from the cross to God's right hand "as Prince and Savior that he might give repentance and forgiveness of sins to Israel" (Acts 5:31). Later, Jewish Christians give thanks that "God has granted even the Gentiles repentance unto life" (11:18; cf. also 2 Tim. 2:25).

Many biblical teachings underscore the sovereignty of God in salvation. We will not be able to look at them in detail, since this book is not intended to be a complete systematic theology. But we should mention them. There is the doctrine of effectual calling, by which God efficaciously summons people into union with Christ (Rom. 1:6–7; 8:30; 11:29; 1 Cor. 1:2, 9, 24, 26; 2 Thess. 2:13–14; Heb. 3:1; 2 Peter 1:10). *Calling* does not always refer to effectual calling; it does not in Matthew 22:14 (and 20:16 KJV), where "many are invited [Gr. *called*], but few are chosen." Here the word refers to the universal offer of salvation through Christ, an offer that many refuse. But in the passages mentioned earlier, the "called" are those whom God has sovereignly brought from death to life.

There is also the doctrine of regeneration, the new birth. The new birth, like effectual calling, is an act of God, not something that we can bring about.[37] In the classic passage, John 3, Jesus tells Nicodemus that to be born again is to be born by the Spirit of God (vv. 5–6). In bringing about the new birth, the Spirit works as he pleases, invisibly, like the wind (v. 8).[38] How is the new birth a birth? It is the beginning of new spiritual life. We recall Paul telling us that by nature we are "dead in [our] transgressions and sins" (Eph. 2:1). The new birth brings life out of that death. Without this new birth, we cannot even see the kingdom of God (John 3:3), because our spiritual eyes are dead. Paul teaches in Romans 1 that sinners suppress the truth and exchange it for a lie. So the new birth marks the beginning of spiritual understanding, as well as the beginning of obedient discipleship.

Other passages also emphasize that our spiritual understanding is a gift of God. In Matthew 11:25–27, we learn that God the Father and God the Son both hide spiritual insight from some and reveal it to others. "No one

---

37. This is part of the thrust of the birth metaphor. Clearly we had no part in bringing about our physical birth. Our physical life came from others. Similarly, the new life comes from another, by divine grace.

38. Other passages emphasizing divine sovereignty in regeneration: John 1:13; 1 John 2:29; 3:9; 4:7; 5:1, 4, 18.

knows the Father," says Jesus, "except the Son and those to whom the Son chooses to reveal him." John tells us that "the Son of God has come and has given us understanding" (1 John 5:20); compare his words about the anointing of the Spirit (2:20–21, 27). Paul talks about the wisdom of Christ, hidden for a time, "that God destined for our glory before time began" (1 Cor. 2:7). He goes on to say that no one can understand the wisdom of Christ without God's Spirit (vv. 12–16). And when Paul speaks about the power of his preaching to bring faith, he regularly ascribes that persuasive power to God's Spirit (1 Cor. 2:4–5; 1 Thess. 1:5; 2 Thess. 2:14).[39] Unless God has given us a mind to understand, we will not appreciate his message (Deut. 29:4; cf. Isa. 6:9–10, discussed previously). So we ask God for wisdom, knowing that for Jesus' sake he is willing to give it, and that he is the only ultimate source of spiritual knowledge (James 1:5; cf. Eph. 1:17–19; Col. 1:9).[40]

Scripture also employs other ways of describing how God brings us from death and ignorance to life and spiritual perception: God circumcises our heart (Deut. 30:6), writes his law on our heart (Jer. 31:31–34), gives us a new heart (Ezek. 11:19; 36:26), gives us a heart to know him (Jer. 24:7), washes and renews us (Titus 3:4–7), creates us anew (2 Cor. 5:17), shines his light into our darkness (2 Cor. 4:6),[41] raises us from the dead with Christ to new life (Rom. 6:4), and begins a good work in us (Phil. 1:6). These expressions do not always refer to initial regeneration, the very beginnings of spiritual life, but they do refer to our spiritual life and knowledge as the work of God.

So our continuing life with God is like its beginning: we are constantly dependent on the Lord for the resources to live obediently. Without him, we can do nothing (John 15:5). We saw earlier that God is sovereign over the free decisions of people, including decisions to commit sin. And in the outworkings of saving grace, it is God who motivates his people to obey him. Sanctification, as well as regeneration, is his work, although of course we are responsible for what we do.

---

39. On the internal testimony of the Spirit, see John Murray, "The Attestation of Scripture," in *The Infallible Word,* ed. Ned Stonehouse and Paul Woolley (Grand Rapids: Eerdmans, 1946), 40–52; John M. Frame, "The Spirit and the Scriptures," in *Hermeneutics, Authority, and Canon,* ed. D. A. Carson and John Woodbridge (Grand Rapids: Zondervan, 1986).

40. So knowledge of God is part of the new life in Christ. This knowledge is not merely intellectual, but its intellectual aspect is part of an overall covenantal relation. "The fear of the LORD is the beginning of wisdom" (Ps. 111:10; cf. Deut. 4:6; Prov. 1:7; 9:10; 15:33; Isa. 33:6). See *DKG* for the implications of this for a Christian theory of knowledge.

41. Paul here draws a parallel with the original creation of light in Gen. 1:3. There is light, when before there was only darkness.

So we recall Ephesians 2, where verse 10 teaches, "We are God's workmanship, created in Christ Jesus to do good works, which God prepared in advance for us to do." We know that without God's grace, we are dead in sin (v. 1; Rom. 7:18; 8:6–8). We cannot do anything good on our own. So as we work out our salvation, we know that "it is God who works in you to will and to act according to his good purpose" (Phil. 2:13). It is the Lord who sanctifies, who makes his people holy (Lev. 20:8). He is the one who makes his people willing to work for him (Hag. 1:14), who stirs them up to generous giving and devotion to the Lord's work (1 Chron. 29:14–19; cf. 1 Kings 8:5–8). Although we are not sinlessly perfect in this life (1 John 1:8–10), he is working to perfect in us the image of Christ (Jer. 32:39–40; Eph. 5:25–27). So we pray that God will enable us to please him, for we know that that is his will, and that only he can make that happen (Col. 1:10–12).

God is also the source of any success we may have in proclaiming his word. Paul admits that his confidence in his ministry is not based on anything in him: "Not that we are competent in ourselves to claim anything for ourselves, but our competence comes from God" (2 Cor. 3:5). And "we have this treasure in jars of clay to show that this all-surpassing power is from God and not from us" (4:7; cf. 10:17). God uses us to minister to others, by means of his gifts (Rom. 12:3–8; 1 Cor. 4:7; 12:1–11; Eph. 4:1–13). These passages emphasize over and over that these are gifts of God, in Christ, by the Spirit.

So God's grace is the source of every blessing that we have as Christians. Truly, as Jesus said, "apart from me you can do nothing" (John 15:5). We have nothing that we have not received (1 Cor. 4:7). Even our response to his grace is given by grace. When God saves us, he takes away every possible ground of boasting (Eph. 2:9; 1 Cor. 1:29). All the praise and glory belongs to him.

SUMMARY PASSAGES

I do not apologize for including a large number of Scripture passages in this chapter. Nothing is more important, especially at this point in the history of theology, than for God's people to be firmly convinced that Scripture teaches God's universal control over the world, and teaches it over and over again. Scripture mentions and implies this control in many different historical and doctrinal contexts and applies it to our own life with God in a great number of ways. This sheer quantity and variety of teaching on the subject is a major point of this chapter.

I have listed these passages with little comment, for they speak for themselves. Today there are large theological movements that would deny the full extent of God's control over the universe, particularly over the free decisions of men. I have briefly mentioned a few of the arguments of these thinkers and will discuss their position further at later points in the book. But it ought to be evident now that even if there are interpretive difficulties in some of these passages, it is quite impossible to escape the cumulative force of all of them. As B. B. Warfield said with regard to biblical inspiration, the total evidence for it is like an all-devouring avalanche. One may deftly avoid a few rocks, but one cannot escape them all.

This pervasive scriptural witness sets the context in which we should consider the relatively few passages that explicitly state that God controls everything that comes to pass. In view of what we have seen, we should not expect these passages to be limited in their application. We have already shown that everything that happens in this world—both major events and tiny details—is under God's sovereign control. The passages that explicitly teach universal foreordination only summarize, with the helpful redundancy that is characteristic of Scripture, this large quantity of biblical data.

Let us now look at four passages that explicitly teach the universality of God's control over the world. First, let us note Lamentations 3:37–38:

> Who can speak and have it happen
>   if the Lord has not decreed it?
> Is it not from the mouth of the Most High
>   that both calamities and good things come?

Here the scope of God's decree is said to be universal: it covers all calamities and all good things. Nobody can make anything happen unless God has decreed that it will happen.

Next, observe what Paul teaches in Romans 8:28:

> And we know that in all things God works for the good of those who love him, who have been called according to his purpose.

Paul has been talking about the sufferings that Christians must endure in hope of the glory to come. These sufferings have a cosmic dimension: "The whole creation has been groaning as in the pains of childbirth right up to the present time" (v. 22). In view, therefore, are not only persecutions for the sake of Christ, but all the sufferings introduced into the creation by the fall of Adam: the pain of childbirth and the thorns and thistles in the world (Gen. 3:14–19). These sufferings "are not worth comparing with the glory that will be revealed in us" (Rom. 8:18), but for the moment they are difficult to bear. The good news is that Jesus' atonement has cosmic dimensions: in time, it will counteract all the effects of the Fall, as well as sin itself, so that "the creation itself will be liberated from its bondage to decay and brought into the glorious freedom of the children of God" (v. 21). Therefore, God is now working in all things, not only when we suffer for the gospel, to bring about that which is good for those who have been effectually called into fellowship with Christ. For our purposes, the conclusion is that every event is part of God's great plan to richly bless his people. We often do not see how the sufferings of this world will enhance the joy to come, but we trust that God is bringing about that result, since he works in, and therefore controls, all things.

This confidence that God is working in *all things* leads to a great hymn of confidence, which ends:

> For I am convinced that neither death nor life, neither angels nor demons, neither the present nor the future, nor any powers, neither height nor depth, nor anything else in all creation, will be able to separate us from the love of God that is in Christ Jesus our Lord. (vv. 38–39)

Let us look now at Ephesians 1:11, which reads:

> In [Christ] we were also chosen, having been predestined according to the plan of him who works out everything in conformity with the purpose of his will.

This is not the first reference in this chapter to God's sovereign predestination. Verse 4 mentions election, and verse 5 mentions predestination to adoption as sons. The first part of verse 11 ("chosen," "predestined") recapitulates the teaching of the earlier verses. But the reference to "the plan of him who works out everything" must go beyond that recapitulation. It is unlikely that Paul would have said repetitively that we have been elected and predestined according to the plan of him who elects and predestines. Rather, Paul is saying that God's saving election and predestination are part of a larger program. Salvation is part of God's overall control of the world he has made. Salvation will certainly be consummated, because the Savior is the one who controls all things.

Finally, we return to Romans. Paul teaches in Romans 9–11 that God has hardened the hearts of many Jews, in order to open the door of blessing to Gentiles. After all that is said, much remains mysterious. Paul's response is not to question God's fairness or love. He answers such complaints with the analogy of the potter and the clay (9:21–24): what right has the clay to question the prerogatives of the potter? But obviously much mystery remains. Overwhelmed, Paul praises God's very incomprehensibility:

Oh, the depth of the riches of the wisdom and knowledge of God!
    How unsearchable his judgments,
    and his paths beyond tracing out!
"Who has known the mind of the Lord?
    Or who has been his counselor?"
"Who has ever given to God,
    that God should repay him?"
For from him and through him and to him are all things.
    To him be the glory forever! Amen. (11:33–36, quoting Isa.
        40:13 and Job 41:11)

Verse 36 ascribes everything in creation to God. These "things" are not just material objects, but also events: the "judgments" and "paths" of verse 33, including God's judgment of Israel and his blessing of the Gentiles. God's involvement with his world is threefold: as its Creator ("from him"), its governor ("through him"), and the ultimate purpose ("unto him") of the whole world. God controls all things.

GOD:

CREATOR   FROM HIM

GOVERNOR   THROUGH HIM

THE ULTIMATE PURPOSE   UNTO HIM

CHAPTER 5

The Lordship Attributes: Authority

In chapter 8, we shall look at the obvious problem associated with the doctrine of divine control, namely, the relationship of this control to human responsibility. But in order to deal with that issue biblically, we should first define the other two lordship attributes, namely, authority (here) and covenant presence (chap. 6). In chapter 7, we shall consider the concepts of transcendence and immanence that emerge from the concept of divine lordship.

THE CONCEPT OF DIVINE AUTHORITY

The relationship between control and authority is one between might and right. Control means that God has the power to direct the whole course of nature and history as he pleases. Authority means that he has the right to do that. From our standpoint as creatures, God's authority is his right to command, his right to tell us what we ought to do. When he issues commands, he is supremely right in doing so. Thus, his word creates for us an obligation to obey. When he makes promises, we can trust them without question, for they are infallibly right and true.

And when he tells us to believe in the truth of his word, we must do so, both because his word can never prove false and because we have a moral obligation to believe it.[1] Therefore, God is the supreme interpreter of both

---

1. Thus, I emphasized in *DKG* that epistemology is part of ethics, that human knowledge, like everything else in human life, is governed by God's commands.

himself and the universe he has made. The world is what he says it is. His word can never prove false (John 17:17), because (1) he is omniscient (Heb. 4:12–13), (2) he never lies (Titus 1:2), (3) his word governs all creation, and—what particularly concerns us here—(4) he has the authority to declare what is the case.

Control and authority are not synonyms, but they imply one another. Since God created and governs all things, he is the original interpreter of creation, the one who understands the world in all its depths—not only its material nature, but also its ultimate meaning and purpose.[2] God, therefore, has the ultimate viewpoint on the world—the broadest, deepest understanding of it. His word about himself or about the world, therefore, is more credible than any other word or any other means of knowing. It obligates belief, trust, and obedience.

Because God is the supreme controller of the world, he is its supreme evaluator. When God created the world, he evaluated it: after saying "Let there be light" (Gen. 1:3), he "saw that the light was good" (v. 4)—and so on through the creation week. He has established the purpose of everything, and he therefore knows whether and to what degree each created thing measures up to its purpose. God judges rightly what is good or bad about it, what is right or wrong. Ultimately, his judgments, like all his purposes, will prevail. So control implies authority.

God distinguishes between himself and the false gods in that he is able to foretell the future (Isa. 41:21–29). He has authority to do so because he is in control of everything in heaven and on earth (Isa. 40:1–41:20; cf. also 43:8–13).

Control implies authority also because the Lord's creation and government establish him as the owner of all things.

> To the LORD your God belong the heavens, even the highest heavens, the earth and everything in it. (Deut. 10:14; cf. Ex. 19:5)

> Who has a claim against me that I must pay?
>   Everything under heaven belongs to me. (Job 41:11; cf. Rom. 11:35)

> The earth is the LORD's, and everything in it,
>   the world, and all who live in it;
> for he founded it upon the seas
>   and established it upon the waters. (Ps. 24:1–2)[3]

---

2. I shall offer more argument to this effect in our later discussion of God's omniscience.
3. On God's ownership of his creation, see also 1 Chron. 29:11; Pss. 82:8.; 89:11.

The owner of all, then, sets forth his standards of human conduct:

> Who may ascend the hill of the LORD?
>   Who may stand in his holy place?
> He who has clean hands and a pure heart,
>   who does not lift up his soul to an idol
>   or swear by what is false. (Ps. 24:3–4)

If God sets the standards, we may not argue with him. For us to debate with God is as ridiculous as for clay to debate with the potter:

> Woe to him who quarrels with his Maker,
>   to him who is but a potsherd among the potsherds on the ground.
> Does the clay say to the potter,
>   "What are you making?"
> Does your work say,
>   "He has no hands"?
> Woe to him who says to his father,
>   "What have you begotten?"
> or to his mother,
>   "What have you brought to birth?"

> This is what the LORD says—
>   the Holy One of Israel, and its Maker:
> Concerning things to come,
>   do you question me about my children,
>   or give me orders about the work of my hands? (Isa. 45:9–11)

God made us and therefore owns us; we may not quarrel with him. When the landowner in Jesus' parable hires servants at different times of the day to work in his vineyard, he will not submit to the workers' complaints of unfairness. He keeps his promises, but beyond that he maintains the right to do as he wants with his own money (Matt. 20:1–16). He sets the standards and will not be subject to the standards of others.[4]

So God's ownership of the world, his right to do as he wants with his own (recall the potter-clay analogy), serves as a logical link between his control and his authority.[5]

---

4. Compare the longer discussion in AGG, 171–79. These texts give us an important perspective on the problem of evil.

5. Does this relationship between control and authority imply that might makes right, at least for God? I trust the reader will see that the argument in this section for a link between control and authority is more subtle than that. Nevertheless, there is a sense in which this slogan is true at the divine level, though not at the human. For God's "might" amounts

God's authority also implies his control. For God's authority to command his creatures extends through the whole universe. He has the right to tell every creature what to do, even the inanimate ones. So he controls the storms by his command (Ps. 147:15–18), and by his word he commands all things to exist (Gen. 1; Ps. 33:6–9; John 1:3; Heb. 11:3). God exercises control by his authoritative word.

AUTHORITY AS AN ASPECT OF LORDSHIP

In chapter 3, I listed a number of passages in which Scripture defines and expounds the meaning of the mysterious name Yahweh. We saw that many of those passages stress God's control, his mighty power over the whole course of nature and history. Another prominent emphasis of these passages is the authority of the Lord. In all of them, the Lord comes to his people speaking a word that they must obey, demanding their belief and obedience.

The various interpretations of "I AM WHO I AM," listed earlier, all seem to imply, not only God's control over who he is, but also his right to define himself authoritatively. He alone will reveal his nature. He will not submit to any merely human judgments as to who he is. Moses asks for his name, a revelation of his nature. God replies mysteriously but informatively, as we have seen, in a way that maintains his sovereignty over his self-revelation. He alone will name himself, and, through his mighty acts in history, he alone will illumine the meaning of his name. He retains full authority to reveal himself as he is.

When God tells Moses his name, he also gives him a message. The name itself is a message, a prophecy, a word to Israel. Moses is to tell Israel that "I AM has sent me to you" (Ex. 3:14). So Moses becomes the prophet of Yahweh (and Aaron becomes Moses' prophet, Ex. 4:14–17). A prophet is one who speaks God's own words in God's own name.[6] When the true

---

to sovereignty over every aspect of reality, including the conceptual, the intellectual, the interpretive, and the ethical. No human being has that kind of might, either in degree or in extent. God's kind of might actually embraces right. God's might includes authority over interpretation. But his right also embraces his might, since it includes his right to command the natural world. So within God, might and right coalesce. Neither exists without the other. They are mutually perspectival.

6. That definition of a prophet is found in the promise of Deut. 18:18–19: "I will raise up for them a prophet like you [like Moses] from among their brothers; I will put my words in his mouth, and he will tell them everything I command him. If anyone does not listen to my words that the prophet speaks in my name, I myself will call him to account." Cf. Ex. 4:14–16; Jer. 1:7–12. The prophet's words are God's, and disbelieving or disobeying the prophet's words is the same as disbelieving or disobeying God's own words.

prophet speaks, God is speaking through him. So God will teach Moses what to say (Ex. 4:12). Moses is to bring God's message to Pharaoh, a message that sharply contradicts the Egyptians' image of their own invincibility, a message they will hate and resist, but one that comes with an authority that far transcends that of Pharaoh. God's power vindicates that authority, and he defeats Egypt. Yahweh is the one who gives an authoritative message, backed up by all his power.

When Yahweh appears before Israel at Mount Sinai to initiate his covenant (and therefore to expound his covenant lordship), he presents himself as Israel's lawgiver, Israel's supreme authority:

> I am the LORD your God, who brought you out of Egypt, out of the
> land of slavery.
> You shall have no other gods before me. (Ex. 20:2–3)

As in the suzerainty treaty form, the Lord announces his name, describes his mighty deliverance, and then lays down the law. He declares his name, proclaims his control, and then asserts his authority.

Throughout the Pentateuch, Yahweh is the lawgiver. Because he has re-deemed Israel, he calls them again and again to obedience.[7] In Leviticus 18, for example, God tells Israel not to imitate the practices of the wicked Canaanites. Rather:

> You must obey my laws and be careful to follow my decrees. I am
> the LORD your God. Keep my decrees and laws, for the man who
> obeys them will live by them. I am the LORD. (vv. 4–5)

God is the Lord, Yahweh, and therefore his people must obey. If God is Yahweh, he is the supreme authority. Throughout Leviticus 18 and 19, "I am the LORD" appears as a refrain, motivating Israel to keep God's laws (see 18:6, 21, 29; 19:3–4, 10, 12, 14, 16, 30–32, 34, 37).

In Deuteronomy 6, the Shema, Israel's fundamental confession of God's lordship, is followed by a powerful admonition to keep his commands. The connection is unmistakable:

> Hear, O Israel: The LORD our God, the LORD is one. Love the LORD
> your God with all your heart and with all your soul and with all
> your strength. These commandments that I give you today are to
> be upon your hearts. Impress them on your children. Talk about
> them when you sit at home and when you walk along the road,
> when you lie down and when you get up. Tie them as symbols on

---

7. In the covenant, grace precedes law, and grace provides the motivation for obedience.

ie Redemption / DELIVERANCE

your hands and bind them on your foreheads. Write them on the doorframes of your houses and on your gates. (Deut. 6:4–9)

Here the fundamental confession of Yahweh as Lord is followed by a command to love him.[8] Then there is an extended appeal to Israel to keep all of God's commandments. That appeal is found not only here, but often in Deuteronomy; it is one of the book's major themes. Yahweh is the one who commands and deserves complete obedience.

Isaiah 43:11–12 (following the *'ani hu'*, "I am he," of v. 10) reads:

> "I, even I, am the LORD,
>   and apart from me there is no savior.
> I have revealed and saved and proclaimed—
>   I, and not some foreign god among you.
> You are my witnesses," declares the LORD, "that I am God."

Here again, Scripture defines God's lordship in terms of authoritative revelation. God reveals himself, saves his people, and then reveals himself again to proclaim his mighty deeds.

So Jesus identifies himself as the Lord, not only by the power of his miracles, but also by the authority with which he speaks. To him, lordship is meaningless unless it conveys authority: "Why do you call me, 'Lord, Lord,' and do not do what I say?" (Luke 6:46; cf. Matt. 7:21–29). The twofold repetition of "Lord" adds to our impression that to Jesus authority is a defining feature of lordship. We may confirm this impression by noting the large number of passages that connect love for Jesus with obedience.[9] This relationship between obedience and love reminds us of the suzerainty treaty form in which the general law of the covenant (love, that is, exclusive covenant loyalty) is spelled out in specific areas of response (the commandments). So again Jesus stands in the place of Yahweh as the great king, the head of his covenant people. As Lord, he commands and expects obedience.

His teaching also comes with an authority far transcending (and sometimes contradicting) that of the scribes (Matt. 7:29). Even more remarkably, he commands the evil spirits (Luke 4:36). A Roman centurion compares the authority of Jesus to heal at a distance with his own military authority: as the commander tells his troops what to do, so Jesus, even from

---

8. In the suzerainty treaty form, the commandments were first general (exclusive obedience or "love") and then particular (the specific ways in which the vassal was to show love). Here, too, "love" refers to exclusive covenant loyalty.

9. See John 14:21, 23; 15:10, 14; 1 John 2:3–6; 3:22, 24; 5:3; 2 John 6. In Rev. 12:17 and 14:12, Jesus' disciples are those who "obey God's commandments."

a distance, can tell diseases to leave a person (Matt. 8:5–13).[10] Even the wind and the sea obey Jesus' word, eliciting amazement (Mark 4:35–41), for, in the Old Testament, only Yahweh had control of the winds and the waves. But what brings most amazement—and opposition—is Jesus' claim that he has the authority also to forgive sins. His authoritative word to the paralytic, "Get up, take your mat and go home" (Matt. 9:6), vindicates his authority to say "Take heart, son; your sins are forgiven" (v. 2). "Who can forgive sins but God alone?" (Mark 2:7) ask his detractors, not knowing that they are implicitly confessing Jesus' very nature. The crowd, observing these events, responds with less irony, but appropriately: "They were filled with awe; and they praised God, who had given such authority to men" (Matt. 9:8).

ABSOLUTE AUTHORITY

We have seen that God's authority is beyond that of any creature. We may describe it as *absolute* in the following ways:

1. *It cannot be questioned.* God will not be tested, as if there were an authority higher than himself. His word is not subject to evaluation by human standards. It is not doubtful or disputable. As we have seen, the clay may not dispute the intentions of the potter.

We may, to be sure, ask for evidence to verify that a word is truly God's. Deuteronomy 18:20–22 subjects would-be prophets to two tests: they are false prophets if they speak in the name of other gods, or if their prophecies turn out to be false. Acts 17:11 commends the noble Bereans for testing Paul's words against the Scriptures.

It is also true that God permits his prophets to argue with him in one sense: they sometimes ask him to turn back from his announced intentions. Abraham pleads with God not to destroy Sodom, the city in which his nephew Lot chose to live (Gen. 18:22–33). Moses intercedes for disobedient Israel, and God "relents" from his announced plan of rejecting Israel (Ex. 32:9–14). We shall discuss in a later chapter what it means for God to relent. For now, let me simply observe that neither Abraham nor Moses finds any fault with God's standards or his assessment of the situation. Nei-

---

10. Jesus commends the faith of the Roman centurion as greater than any he has seen in Israel (vv. 10–12)—a sign of the Gentiles' election and Israel's rejection. The centurion's faith is special, because it is faith in the divine authority of Jesus' word. His request to Jesus can be literally translated "Speak by a word," a redundant expression emphasizing that Jesus' word is the instrument of healing. The irony is that Israel, God's own people, is not willing to listen obediently to that wonderful word.

ther questions God's authority; indeed, that authority is the presupposition of these conversations. Abraham says:

> Far be it from you to do such a thing—to kill the righteous with the wicked, treating the righteous and the wicked alike. Far be it from you! Will not the Judge of all the earth do right? (Gen. 18:25)

God is the Judge of all the earth, the supreme authority, who cannot do wrong. So Abraham and Moses appeal to God's own justice and mercy. The dialogue actually reveals those standards in a fuller way and enables us to marvel at the rightness of God's dealings with us. And for both Abraham and Moses, God has the last word; at that point the discussion ends.

Having made these qualifications, we can state the principle thus: When we know that God has truly spoken and that he has announced his ulti- ✱ mate intentions, we have no right to question him. When he tells us something, we have no right to demand evidence over and above God's own word. Paul commends Abraham because he believed in God's promise, even though other evidence seemed to contradict it:

> [Abraham] is the father of us all. As it is written: "I have made you a father of many nations." He is our father in the sight of God, in whom he believed—the God who gives life to the dead and calls things that are not as though they were.
>
> Against all hope, Abraham in hope believed and so became the father of many nations, just as it had been said to him, "So shall your offspring be." Without weakening in his faith, he faced the fact that his body was as good as dead—since he was about a hundred years old—and that Sarah's womb was also dead. Yet he did not waver through unbelief regarding the promise of God, but was strengthened in his faith and gave glory to God, being fully persuaded that God had power to do what he had promised. That is why "it was credited to him as righteousness." (Rom. 4:16–22)

Abraham is a model of Christian faith—the faith that justifies—because he trusted in God's promise without reservation. Certainly empirical investigation of the natural possibilities would have concluded that Abraham and Sarah were too old to produce a son. But Abraham trusted God's word *rather than* the empirical evidence. Indeed, this kind of faith was characteristic of Abraham's life. He left his home in Ur to go to a country quite unknown to him. He was even willing to sacrifice Isaac, the son of the promise, on the authority of God's word. (In accepting both God's promise and God's command to sacrifice Isaac, Abraham indicated his faith that God could raise the dead—see Heb. 11:19.) His faith lapsed, to be sure, in

Egypt (Gen. 12:10–20) and in Gerar (20:1–18); he was not sinless. But Scripture commends the remarkable instances in his life when he believed God despite temptations to doubt.

Even righteous Job had to learn this lesson. He had asked for an interview with God, in which he could demand an answer from him, a reason why God had allowed him to suffer, a vindication of divine justice (Job 23:1–7; 31:35–37). But when God did appear, it was God who asked the questions and brought accusations. Job meekly submitted:

> The LORD said to Job:
> "Will the one who contends with the Almighty correct him?
>   Let him who accuses God answer him!"
> Then Job answered the LORD:
> "I am unworthy—how can I reply to you?
>   I put my hand over my mouth.
> I spoke once, but I have no answer—
>   twice, but I will say no more." (40:1–5; cf. 38:1–3; 42:1–4)

2. God's authority is also absolute in the sense that *his covenant transcends all other loyalties*. We are to have no other gods before the Lord (Ex. 20:3). We are to love him with *all* our heart; there should be no competing loyalties (Deut. 6:4–5; Matt. 22:37). The Lord is the head of the covenant, and he forbids us to grant lordship to anyone else.

Jesus strikingly claims deity by demanding the same kind of exclusive loyalty for himself. "Honor your father and your mother" (Ex. 20:12) is one of the fundamental commandments of the law, one which Jesus fully honors and urges against those who would dilute its force (Matt. 15:1–9). Nevertheless, Jesus demands of his disciples a loyalty that transcends the loyalty we owe to our parents. In Matthew 8:19–22 and 10:34–38, he teaches that the demands of discipleship take priority over duties to our parents. Only God can legitimately make such a demand. Jesus here speaks as Yahweh, the head of the new covenant in his blood. So it is not surprising that Paul can say:

> But whatever was to my profit I now consider loss for the sake of Christ. What is more, I consider everything a loss compared to the surpassing greatness of knowing Christ Jesus my Lord, for whose sake I have lost all things. I consider them rubbish, that I may gain Christ. (Phil. 3:7–8)

The principle of *sola Scriptura* follows from this teaching. No other authority may compete with God's own words. No words may be added to God's or be put on the same level of authority (Deut. 4:2; 12:32; Isa. 29:13;

Matt. 15:8–9). It is wrong to bind the consciences of God's people with merely human traditions. Only the Word of God has ultimate authority.

3. God's authority is absolute in the sense that *it covers all areas of life*. The law of Moses governed every aspect of the lives of the Israelites: not only their religious life, narrowly considered, but also their calendar, diet, politics, economics, law, marriage, divorce, sexuality, war, and many other things. It is sometimes assumed that the New Testament is less demanding, that it tells us to look to Christ and forget about rules and regulations. But Jesus did say, "If you love me, you will obey what I command" (John 14:15).[11] If anything, the New Testament is even more explicit than the Old about the application of God's Word to all areas of life:

> So whether you eat or drink or whatever you do, do it all for the glory of God. (1 Cor. 10:31)

> But the man who has doubts is condemned if he eats, because his eating is not from faith; and everything that does not come from faith is sin. (Rom. 14:23)[12]

> And whatever you do, whether in word or deed, do it all in the name of the Lord Jesus, giving thanks to God the Father through him. (Col. 3:17; cf. v. 24)

> We demolish arguments and every pretension that sets itself up against the knowledge of God, and we take captive every thought to make it obedient to Christ. (2 Cor. 10:5)

Note the universal language in these verses: *whatever, all, everything, every*. The Lord's authority extends to every aspect of human life.

To reflect a moment on recent controversy, we can see that it is wrong to try to restrict the infallible authority of God's word in Scripture to some narrowly defined religious area, or to "matters of salvation" as opposed to other matters. Certainly Scripture centers on Christ and redemption, but its applicability is not limited to the preaching of the fundamental gospel. Having created and redeemed us as our covenant Lord, God claims the authority to direct all our thinking and all our decisions. The Lord is totalitarian, as only he has a right to be.[13]

---

11. Note the many verses to this effect in the Johannine literature, mentioned earlier. This is one of the major themes of John's writings.

12. Given the references to eating and drinking in these two passages, it is not quite true that the New Testament contains no dietary laws.

13. Remember that it is God's totalitarian authority that frees us from bondage to human authorities.

DIVINE AUTHORITY IN
THE HISTORY OF REDEMPTION

One way to summarize the Bible is to say that it is a story of God's word to human beings and their response to that word in belief or unbelief, obedience or disobedience, acceptance or rejection. At each point in the biblical history, the word of God is the thing at issue. That word may take many forms: command, promise, divine name, covenant, law, gospel, prophecy, song, history, epistle, preaching, teaching. But whatever form it takes, man's response to it (under God's providence) has eternal consequences.

The first recorded human experience is that of hearing God's words, words that defined the purpose of human life:

> God blessed them and said to them, "Be fruitful and increase in number; fill the earth and subdue it. Rule over the fish of the sea and the birds of the air and over every living creature that moves on the ground." (Gen. 1:28)

God's word also comes to Adam, commanding him to work and care for the garden (2:15), and forbidding him to eat from the tree of the knowledge of good and evil, while permitting him to eat from the other trees (2:16–17). At this time, God's word alone is the issue. Adam has no independent means to determine the consequences of eating the forbidden fruit. Like Abraham later, Adam has to make his decision on the basis of God's word alone.

Then the serpent comes to Eve, essentially substituting his word for God's word, pitting his own authority against the authority of the Lord. "You will not surely die," he says (3:4). In the contest between one word and another, Eve chooses that of a talking animal over that of her gracious Creator. Unlike Abraham, she follows the enticing evidence of her senses and her unaided reason (v. 6a). Adam joins her in eating, rather than exercising godly authority over her (v. 6b). From that sin follow the curse and all the miseries of life here and hereafter (vv. 14–19).

So God's word of curse is also powerful and authoritative. Hidden in the curses, however, is a promise of life. Women will have pain in childbearing, but one child will crush the serpent's head (3:15–16). So God is merciful and does not carry out the death sentence our race deserves. God's word comes again, and man takes that word upon his lips in faith (Gen. 3:20; 4:1, 26).

Sin again prevails, and God sends his word through Noah, a preacher of righteousness. Noah obeys God's word and brings it to others (Matt. 24:32–44; Heb. 11:7; 2 Peter 2:5). Again it is God's word that is at issue, for there is no other way to know whether a flood is coming. Man's response to God's word is literally a matter of life and death.

The same thing is true for Abraham, as we have seen, who places his entire hope for life and death in a seemingly impossible promise of God. But no word of God can be void of power (Gen. 18:14, literally translated), and God gives to Abraham a son of promise.

As we have seen, Moses is the bearer of God's word, both to the Egyptians and also to Israel. All later prophets are like him (Deut. 18:18), with God's words in their mouths, demanding obedience to everything that comes from God's mouth (Deut. 8:3; cf. Matt. 4:4).

Greater than Abraham and Moses, Jesus also comes bearing a word of God. He affirms the Law and the Prophets (Matt. 5:17–20), but he also does what Scripture forbids mere men to do: he adds words of his own. He speaks often of the authority of God's word, both in the Old Testament and on his own lips (Matt. 7:24–29; Mark 8:21, 38; John 8:47; 12:47–50; 14:15, 21, 23–24; 15:7, 10, 14; 17:6, 17). Concerning Jesus' own words from God, Peter cries out, "Lord, to whom shall we go? You have the words of eternal life" (John 6:68).

Obeying Jesus' commandments is the test of love (John 14:15, etc.), the criterion of discipleship. The same is true of the word that Jesus gives to his disciples by the Spirit (John 14:16, 26; 15:26; 16:13). Obeying their word, too, is the test of godliness (Rom. 2:16; 1 Cor. 14:37; Gal. 1:8–9; 1 Thess. 4:2; 2 Thess. 3:14).

God gives his word in different ways. Sometimes he speaks it in a rather direct way, as on Mount Sinai. Sometimes he speaks through prophets and apostles. Sometimes he gives his people a written word, as when he gave tablets of stone to Moses. These forms of communication all have the same authority. The theophany on Mount Sinai was more immediately impressive than our humble biblical text. But the Bible, too, is "holy" (2 Tim. 3:15). As the stone tablets rested by the holy ark of the covenant, so the Bible brings to us the very voice of the holy God. When Deuteronomy tells us not to turn to the left or the right of God's commands, it is referring to the written Word. When the psalmist speaks about the perfections of God's word over and over again (Ps. 119), it is primarily to the written Word that he refers. The written Word is the covenant constitution of the people of God, and its authority is absolute, because the authority of its author is absolute.[14]

Without authoritative words from God, there would be no story of re-

---

14. As emphasized in chapter 2, the great king is the author of the suzerainty treaty. In the covenant document, the great king always speaks in the first person. It is his covenant; he sovereignly sets the terms. He is, therefore, the author. I hope to expand the above discussion and say much more on this subject in *The Doctrine of the Word of God*.

demption. Everything we know about salvation comes through such words. The law that we have broken to deserve hell is a divine word. The gospel that promises forgiveness to those who trust Jesus is also a divine word. And we prove our love by obeying Jesus' commands—again, divine words.

So without authoritative, divine words, it is quite meaningless to claim that Jesus is our Lord and Savior. As our Lord, he speaks words that we must obey. And as our Savior, he brings a reliable promise, without which we cannot be saved. Without words from God of absolute authority, there can be no gospel and no Christianity.

Absolute authority entails infallibility. A word of ultimate authority is beyond human criticism. We may never judge it to have failed or to have been mistaken. So God's word in Scripture, as all his other words, must be judged to be infallible and inerrant.[15]

Theologians who try to play down the importance of God's authority—whether to avoid "patriarchalism," to promote the freedom of human thought and choice, to allow greater latitude to science and philosophy, or whatever—have lost something that is central to the biblical revelation. *Everything* in Scripture comes to us as authoritative communication. Pervasively, Scripture claims our thoughts and decisions. To miss that is in one sense to miss everything, for it is to miss the lordship of Yahweh and the lordship of Christ.

THE UNIVERSALITY OF DIVINE AUTHORITY

Like the Lord's control, his authority is universal, for he is Lord of heaven and earth, Lord of all. And as for Jesus:

> Then Jesus came to them and said, "All authority in heaven and on earth has been given to me. Therefore go and make disciples of all nations, baptizing them in the name of the Father and of the Son and of the Holy Spirit, and teaching them to obey everything I have commanded you. And surely I am with you always, to the very end of the age." (Matt. 28:18–20)

> Therefore God exalted him to the highest place
> and gave him the name that is above every name,

---

15. Again, I hope to say more about this elsewhere in the Theology of Lordship series. There is, for example, much to be said also about the *human* authorship of Scripture. But it should be plain that we may not construe that human authorship in any way that detracts from the *divine* authority of the written document.

that at the name of Jesus every knee should bow,
in heaven and on earth and under the earth,
and every tongue confess that Jesus Christ is Lord,
to the glory of God the Father. (Phil. 2:9–10)

These passages should put to rest any talk of pluralism. As there is one Lord, so there is one way, one truth, one life. Nobody comes to the Father except through Jesus (John 14:6), for Jesus is himself the one Lord, God the Son, to whom all authority belongs.

CHAPTER 6

The Lordship Attributes:
Covenant Presence

We have seen that Yahweh is the supreme controller of nature and history and the supreme authority over all his creatures. In this chapter, we will see that he is also the one who calls people into fellowship with himself and therefore becomes intimately present to them.

The presence of God is a consequence of his control and authority. When we speak of God's presence, we are not referring to a physical presence, for God is incorporeal.[1] What we mean, rather, is that he is able to act on and in the creation and to evaluate all that is happening in the creation. Since God controls and evaluates all things, he is therefore present everywhere—as present as an incorporeal being can be.

But God is not merely present in the world; he is *covenantally* present. He is *with* his creatures to bless and to judge them in accordance with the terms of his covenant. It is God's covenantal presence that we will explore in this chapter.

We will recall the suzerainty treaty form, in which:

1. The Lord announces his name.
2. He describes his mighty deliverances in the past.
3. He sets forth his law, which the people should obey out of gratefulness for their deliverance.
4. He sets forth the sanctions of that law: blessings for obedience and curses for disobedience.

---

1. I shall discuss divine incorporeality in chapter 25.

5. He declares how the covenant is to be kept and enforced in the future.

Point number 2 describes the lordship attribute of *control*, and point number 3 describes that of *authority*. Now we come to point number 4, which shows that the Lord is not an absentee landlord, but continues to be with his people, both to bless them for their faithfulness and to judge them for their disobedience.

We recall also the commonly accepted interpretation of the divine name Yahweh, that he is the God who "is there," present to deliver his people from Egypt. As Peter Toon puts it, "Yahweh is God-with-his-people."[2]

The texts we have cited that shed light on the name Yahweh focus on his commitment to his people, his solidarity with them, his intention to be with them. In Exodus 3, before giving his name in verse 14, God answers a question from Moses:

> But Moses said to God, "Who am I, that I should go to Pharaoh and bring the Israelites out of Egypt?"
> And God said, "I will be with you." (Ex. 3:11–12)

Moses asks God who Moses is, before he asks in verse 13 who God is. God's answer to the first question is similar to his answer to the second. The second answer, as we have seen, is *'ehyeh 'asher 'ehyeh*, "I AM WHO I AM." The first answer is *'ehyeh 'immak*, "I will be with you," or "I am with you." We might think that "I will be with you" does not really answer Moses' question, "Who am I?" Moses asks about himself, but God replies by speaking about himself. But of course, God more than answers Moses' question. Who is Moses? He is the man with whom God is. God has covenanted to stand with Moses in his confrontation with Pharaoh. So Moses is Yahweh's man; that's who he is.

Then, in verse 13, Moses asks God what his name is, so he can report it to Israel. The "I AM" in verse 14 connects God to Israel in the same way that it connects God to Moses in verse 12. God is with Israel to deliver them.

God with us! Immanuel (Isa. 7:14; Matt. 1:23)! This is one of the most precious concepts in Scripture. The essence of the covenant is that God is *our* God and we are *his* people. To Abraham, God said:

2. Peter Toon, *Our Triune God* (Wheaton, Ill.: Victor Books, 1996), 89.

> I will establish my covenant as an everlasting covenant between
> me and you and your descendants after you for the generations to
> come, to be your God and the God of your descendants after you.
> (Gen. 17:7)

At the end of redemptive history, this purpose will be fulfilled:

> And I heard a loud voice from the throne saying, "Now the dwelling
> of God is with men, and he will live with them. They will be his
> people, and God himself will be with them and be their God. He
> will wipe every tear from their eyes. There will be no more death
> or mourning or crying or pain, for the old order of things has passed
> away." (Rev. 21:3–4)

In the meantime, God dwells with Israel in the tabernacle and in the
temple, and supremely in Jesus—God living with his people in the tabernacle of flesh (John 1:14; 2:21), Immanuel. Through Christ, God's
people themselves are his temple, the dwelling of his Spirit (1 Cor.
6:19).

All of these images reinforce the truth that God is committed to his people, that he will aid and deliver them, that he will be with them. This is a
frequent theme in God's relationship to Abraham, Isaac, and Jacob. King
Abimelech seeks a treaty with Abraham, recognizing that "God is with you
in everything you do" (Gen. 21:22). Another Abimelech says to Abraham's
son Isaac, "We saw clearly that the LORD was with you" (26:28). With Isaac's
son Jacob, God renews the covenant in the same terms as he has presented
it to Abraham and Isaac, concluding:

> I am with you and will watch over you wherever you go, and I will
> bring you back to this land. I will not leave you until I have done
> what I have promised you. (28:15; cf. 31:3, 5, 42)

Jacob's son Joseph also receives the testimony of a pagan master, this time
as a slave in Egypt:

> When his master saw that the LORD was with him and that the
> LORD gave him success in everything he did, Joseph found favor
> in his eyes and became his attendant. (39:3–4)

Covenant presence, then, means that God commits himself to us, to
be our God and to make us his people. He delivers us by his grace and
rules us by his law, and he rules not only from above, but also with us and
within us.

PRESENCE IN TIME

God's covenant presence has a number of dimensions that we ought to explore, focusing again on those texts that expound the name Yahweh. In the first place, God's presence is temporal; he is present "now." We shall see later in the book that God transcends time in important ways. But it is also important to note that God interacts with persons and events in time. God's relation to time is not only transcendent, but also immanent.

In a number of the Yahweh texts, time is problematic. In the first chapters of Exodus, Israel has been in Egypt for about four hundred years. Most likely, there has been no word from Yahweh since the time of Joseph. The people are in bondage, and they cry out to the Lord (2:23), but some must have raised a question: God has not dealt directly with us for four hundred years. Does he still exist? Is his covenant with Abraham still in force? Does he still care about Jacob's children? Here is the answer:

> God heard their groaning and he remembered his covenant with Abraham, with Isaac and with Jacob. So God looked on the Israelites and was concerned about them. (2:24–25)

In 3:6, God identifies himself to Moses as "the God of your father, the God of Abraham, the God of Isaac and the God of Jacob." Here Yahweh establishes an identity between himself and the God of long ago. The covenant he made then still holds firm, despite the four-hundred-year interval. Then, in verse 14, he identifies himself as Yahweh. The message Yahweh sends to Israel is this:

> God also said to Moses, "Say to the Israelites, 'The LORD [*yahweh*], the God of your fathers—the God of Abraham, the God of Isaac and the God of Jacob—has sent me to you.' This is my name forever, the name by which I am to be remembered from generation to generation." (v. 15)

In the past, God covenanted with the patriarchs. In the present, God has sent Moses to Israel. And in the future, God will be remembered for all generations by his "memorial" name.

In this context, the name I AM surely refers, among other things, to Yahweh's constancy over time. He is the same God that he was in Abraham's time, and he will be the same God forever. He is always present, always remembering his covenant.

As in Exodus 3, the three patriarchs appear in Exodus 6 in connection with the name Yahweh. In verse 3, God speaks of his revelation to Abraham as God Almighty, but not as Yahweh. Even in that earlier period of revelation, God was faithful to establish his covenant with Abraham (v. 4). Will God not surely also hear the groanings of Israel, to whom he has given a greater name, a greater revelation (v. 5)? So, yes, he will redeem:

> Therefore, say to the Israelites: "I am the LORD ['ani yahweh], and I will bring you out from under the yoke of the Egyptians. I will free you from being slaves to them, and I will redeem you with an outstretched arm and with mighty acts of judgment. I will take you as my own people, and I will be your God. Then you will know that I am the LORD [yahweh] your God, who brought you out from under the yoke of the Egyptians. And I will bring you to the land I swore with uplifted hand to give to Abraham, to Isaac and to Jacob. I will give it to you as a possession. I am the LORD." (vv. 6–8)

Note here the Immanuel principle: God will be with them, to be their God and to make them his people. Specifically here, the emphasis is on the continuity between God's relationship with the patriarchs and his relationship with Israel.

Other passages that emphasize and expound the meaning of yahweh are also concerned with temporal relationships. Exploring the 'ani hu' passages, we note that in Deuteronomy 32, the Song of Moses, Yahweh declares his past victories (vv. 7–35), telling the people to "remember the days of old" (v. 7). He proclaims that he is "he," the same God who ruled past ages (v. 39), and he declares how he will execute his blessings and judgments in the future (vv. 36–43). In Isaiah 41:4, Yahweh is "with the first of them, and with the last." In Isaiah 43:10, he reminds Israel that there was no god formed either before or after him, and in verse 13 he declares, "Yes, and from ancient days I am he." Other passages remind Israel of his mighty deeds in the past (Hos. 12:4–9; 13:4–8) and his eternal nature (Ps. 135:13; Isa. 26:4–8; Mal. 3:6).

John 8:31–59 is also concerned with a temporal problematic. As roughly four hundred years had passed between Joseph and Moses, so another four hundred years had passed between Malachi and Jesus. Again, Israel had been without God's immediate word for many years, and again the nation was under the dominion of a foreign power. Doubtless many asked again whether God was still alive and his covenants still in force. Again, Abraham's name enters the discussion. The Jews claim to be children of Abraham and therefore of God. Jesus tells them that Satan, not God or Abraham, is their father. They are slaves of sin and need Jesus to set them free. "Are you greater than our father Abraham?" they ask. "He died, and so did the prophets. Who do you think you are?" (v. 53).

Amazingly, Jesus announces that his significance closes the gap between Abraham's time and his own:

"Your father Abraham rejoiced at the thought of seeing my day; he saw it, and was glad."

"You are not yet fifty years old," the Jews said to him, "and you have seen Abraham!"

"I tell you the truth," Jesus answered, "before Abraham was born, I am!" At this, they picked up stones to stone him, but Jesus hid himself, slipping away from the temple grounds. (vv. 56–59)

Jesus does not say, "Before Abraham was born, I was," but rather, "Before Abraham was born, I *am*." Clearly, Jesus is claiming not merely a long past existence, but the divine name for himself. The Jews' response indicates that they understood it that way. Since they believed the claim to be false, they took it as blasphemy.

Much can be said about the deity of Christ from this passage. My present point, however, is that I AM here again indicates the continuity of the Lord's presence over time. Jesus was present to Abraham and present to all times. He is the I AM. Although God's people may wait long for him, he is always there, always ready to bless his people and judge his enemies.

PRESENCE IN PLACE

So God is "now." And he is also "here." God is present in space as well as in time. God meets Moses in a particular place: at a burning bush that is not consumed. He is within the bush (Ex. 3:2), and the area around the bush therefore becomes holy ground (3:5). God promises that he will also be with Israel. The sign of his presence is this: "When you have brought the people out of Egypt, you will worship God on this mountain" (v. 12). And when Israel does later approach Mount Sinai, the mountain is Yahweh's sanctuary. The priests who approach it must consecrate themselves, "or the LORD will break out against them" (Ex. 19:22).

Now of course God transcends space, just as he transcends time. In dedicating the temple, Solomon recognizes that "the heavens, even the highest heaven, cannot contain you. How much less this temple I have built!" (1 Kings 8:27). Nevertheless, the temple, like the tabernacle before it and Mount Sinai before that, was a place where God was specially present, so that it was in a real sense God's earthly dwelling place. This is an important principle in the history of redemption, for, as we pointed out earlier, Jesus himself is God's tabernacle (John 1:14) and his temple (2:21), and so believers, by virtue of the Spirit's indwelling, are themselves temples of God. God's presence in Jesus is not exactly the same as his presence in the temple or in believers. Jesus is the one in whom God dwells without measure. But God's presence among us in all its forms is an aspect of his overall covenant presence, and it conveys the intimate fellowship of the covenant: that he is our God and we are his people.

When Israel worshiped the golden calf, Moses interceded for them, and God agreed not to destroy them entirely (Ex. 32:9–14), but he did punish them with executions (vv. 27–29) and a plague (v. 35). In chapter 33, God agrees to bring the remaining Israelites into the Promised Land, but he denies them his presence:

> Go up to the land flowing with milk and honey. But I will not go with you, because you are a stiff-necked people and I might destroy you on the way. (v. 3)

Moses' response is significant:

> If your Presence does not go with us, do not send us up from here. How will anyone know that you are pleased with me and with your people unless you go with us? What else will distinguish me and your people from all the other people on the face of the earth? (v. 15)

The Lord relents, and sends his "Presence" with the people. Without God's presence, his people are like all the other nations. The Promised Land is of no value without the Lord. The chief blessing of the covenant is fellowship with the Lord himself.

PRESENCE IN BLESSING AND JUDGMENT

The covenant is two-sided. When God's people are faithful and obedient, he is present to bless; when they disobey, he brings judgment and disaster. When God gives his name to Moses, it connotes blessing for Israel, but judgment upon Pharaoh and the Egyptians. The Exodus accomplishes both.

So the Yahweh passages stress God's mercy and judgment:

> I will cause all my goodness to pass in front of you, and I will proclaim my name, the LORD [yahweh], in your presence. I will have mercy on whom I will have mercy, and I will have compassion on whom I will have compassion. (Ex. 33:19)

> And he passed in front of Moses, proclaiming, "The LORD, the LORD [yahweh, yahweh], the compassionate and gracious God,

slow to anger, abounding in love and faithfulness, maintaining love to thousands, and forgiving wickedness, rebellion and sin. Yet he does not leave the guilty unpunished; he punishes the children and their children for the sin of the fathers to the third and fourth generation." (Ex. 34:6–7)[3]

Some might say that we cannot take comfort in these passages, because they not only speak of blessing and forgiveness, but also warn of judgment and curse. Who of us deserves the blessing of the covenant? Do not our sins place us under the curse (Rom. 6:23)? But thanks be to God that in Christ, the true temple, believers have all the richness of God's covenant blessings. In Christ we experience his compassion, his grace, his slowness to anger, his love, his faithfulness, his forgiveness. The covenant name Yahweh, which Jesus makes his own, means all of these things to us.

THE LORD'S PRESENCE IN ALL CREATION

So far, we have been speaking only of God's presence among his covenant people. There is also a sense in which God's covenant presence is universal, just like his control and authority.

As we mentioned before, universal control and authority imply universal presence. And David draws the same conclusion from God's covenant presence in Psalm 139. As God's covenant servant, David knows that God has searched him and known him, inside and out. The implication is that God can find him anywhere:

Where can I go from your Spirit?
    Where can I flee from your presence?
If I go up to the heavens, you are there;
    if I make my bed in the depths, you are there.
If I rise on the wings of the dawn,
    if I settle on the far side of the sea,
even there your hand will guide me,
    your right hand will hold me fast. (vv. 7–10)

Since God is present with his covenant servant, he will be everywhere David goes. Covenant presence, therefore, entails universal presence.

---

3. This is an especially important passage for defining the divine nature. It is echoed often in Scripture, as in Num. 14:18; Pss. 86:15; 103:8; 111:4; 116:5; 145:8; Jonah 4:2; James 5:11.

And, as I indicated earlier, all human beings, not just Israelites and Christians, are related to God covenantally. Creation itself is a covenant, in which God delivers the world from darkness and the deep waters, commands the elements of the world to appear, and makes his temple to dwell in the midst of his creation.[4] The Spirit of God dwells with the creation from the beginning (Gen. 1:2), indicating God's commitment to be present in and with the world he has made. The covenant between God and Adam includes the whole human race (Rom. 5:12–21). We are all breakers of the Adamic covenant, but members of it nonetheless. And we are also members of God's covenant with Noah's family (Gen. 8:20–9:17), in which God pledges his presence to maintain the seasons and to delay the final judgment. The Noachic covenant is made not only with Noah's family, the human race, but also with "every living creature on earth" (9:10).

So the Lord is present everywhere and to everyone, as the one who blesses and curses according to his covenant. He is unavoidable, closer to us than anyone else. We cannot escape from him. As his control and authority are absolute, so is his presence. By "absolute presence" we mean that without him there could be no meaning, no significance, no purpose in anything. We also mean that he is the one with whom we have most to do. Therefore, the most important thing in life is to have a good relationship with God, to be his obedient covenant servants, his faithful friends, his body and bride.

---

4. For parallels between Creation and the Exodus in terms of covenant, see, for example, Meredith G. Kline, *Images of the Spirit* (Grand Rapids: Baker, 1980), 13–34.

CHAPTER 7

Transcendence and Immanence

Having discussed the three lordship attributes—control, authority, and covenant presence—we are now in a good position to consider the distinction between God's transcendence and his immanence. This twofold distinction is a traditional way of describing God's relationship to the world—somewhat different from, but also somewhat similar to, the three lordship attributes that determine the structure of the present volume. So I am asking readers in effect to replace the traditional twofold distinction with my threefold distinction. I am not generally opposed to the use of the terms *transcendence* and *immanence*, and I will occasionally use them myself, but I do believe that some cautions are in order.

The transcendence-immanence distinction has often been considered central to discussions of the doctrine of God. Stanley J. Grenz and Roger E. Olson use this distinction as the main theme of their analysis of twentieth-century theology, and they lament the "instability introduced when transcendence and immanence are not properly balanced."[1]

TRANSCENDENCE AND IMMANENCE IN SCRIPTURE

Transcendence and *immanence*, however, are not biblical terms, and so we must exercise some care in relating them to the teachings of Scripture.

1. Stanley J. Grenz and Roger E. Olson, *Twentieth-Century Theology* (Downers Grove, Ill.: InterVarsity Press, 1992), 12.

Further, there are some ambiguities in these terms as they have been used by theologians. So we should not simply take them for granted or assume that their meaning is obvious.

Transcendence invokes the biblical language of God's majesty and holiness.[2] It often represents metaphors of height as well: the Lord is God "in heaven above" (Deut. 4:39). He has set his glory "above the heavens" (Ps. 8:1). He is "enthroned on high" (Ps. 113:5). We are to exalt him, to attribute to him the highest status:

> For you, O LORD, are the Most High over all the earth;
>   you are exalted far above all gods. (Ps. 97:9)

> Be exalted, O God, above the heavens,
>   let your glory be over all the earth. (Ps. 57:5)

> God is in heaven
>   and you are on earth. (Eccl. 5:2)

Immanence refers to God's nearness, his presence on the earth, especially with his people. It stresses his involvement with human affairs. Many texts emphasizing transcendence describe God's immanence in the same context:

> Acknowledge and take to heart this day that the LORD is God in heaven above and on the earth below. (Deut. 4:39)

> To the LORD your God belong the heavens, even the highest heavens, the earth and everything in it. Yet the LORD set his affection on your forefathers and loved them, and he chose you, their descendants, above all the nations, as it is today. (Deut. 10:14–15)

> The LORD your God is God in heaven above and on the earth below. (Josh. 2:11)

> For this is what the high and lofty One says—
>   he who lives forever, whose name is holy:
> "I live in a high and holy place,
>   but also with him who is contrite and lowly in spirit,
> to revive the spirit of the lowly
>   and to revive the heart of the contrite." (Isa. 57:15)

> There is . . . one God and Father of all, who is over all and through all and in all. (Eph. 4:4–6)

---

2. Refer again to the discussion of God's holiness and his covenant headship in chapter 2.

Immanence, then, is basically equivalent to what I called in the last chapter "covenant presence." *Transcendence*, however, is harder to define. It refers to God as "the Most High," the one who dwells "above." But since God is not a physical being, except through incarnation, and since he is omnipresent, it is metaphorical to speak of him as living in any place, or in any particular direction from where we are. Scripture does refer to a real place called "heaven," in which the presence of God is found at its greatest intensity,[3] and because that place is not on earth, it is properly represented as "above," since all directions away from earth are "above." But God's presence cannot be limited to that place. As Solomon said, "The heavens, even the highest heaven, cannot contain you" (1 Kings 8:27).[4] Further, the idea that God lives in a different place, far away from man, would not in itself justify the religious awe that accompanies the exaltation language.

It is not biblical, therefore, to interpret God's transcendence to mean merely that he is located somewhere far away, in heaven. That may be part of the thrust of the terms "Most High," "exalted," and "lifted up," but there must be more to it. What is that additional content?

We should, I think, see these expressions primarily as describing God's royal dignity. He is "exalted," not mainly as someone living far beyond the earth, but as one who sits on a throne. The expressions of transcendence refer to God's rule, his kingship, his lordship. Often this meaning is explicit in texts that use transcendence language:

> Who is like the LORD our God,
>   the One who sits enthroned on high,
> who stoops down to look
>   on the heavens and the earth? (Ps. 113:5–6)

> I lift up my eyes to you,
>   to you whose throne is in heaven. (Ps. 123:1)

---

3. Compare the language in Hebrews about the "true tabernacle" (8:2), the "greater and more perfect tabernacle that is not man-made, that is to say, not a part of this creation" (9:11). That sanctuary is identified with heaven itself in 9:24. Heaven is evidently like a tabernacle; or rather, Israel's tabernacle was like heaven. It is a "dwelling" of God in that it is a holy place, a place where God makes his presence known in the most intense way. But we cannot say that he is there, rather than anywhere else.

4. Should we then define transcendence as God's existence beyond all space? I believe that God does transcend space, but, as we will see, I think that God's transcendence as the *king* is a more central concept in Scripture, and indeed that that is our best starting point for understanding other kinds of transcendence, such as his transcendence over time and space. I shall discuss these other forms of transcendence in later chapters, especially 24 and 25.

> But the LORD Almighty will be exalted by his justice,
>   and the holy God will show himself holy by his righteousness.
>   (Isa. 5:16)

In John's gospel, Jesus frequently says that he has come "from heaven" or "from above." This means that he has been with God from eternity (1:1), and that he has been sent to earth to testify concerning what he has seen of God (3:13). So there is a reference to locality in these expressions. But coming from above also means that his words have supreme authority (3:31–34). And when Jesus ascends again to heaven, he ascends to God's throne, to "the Majesty in heaven" (Heb. 1:3). He sits at "the right hand of the Mighty One" (Matt. 26:64), fulfilling the prophecy of Psalm 110:1–2:

> The LORD says to my Lord:
>   "Sit at my right hand
> until I make your enemies
>   a footstool for your feet."
> The LORD will extend your mighty scepter from Zion;
>   you will rule in the midst of your enemies. (cf. Acts 2:33–34;
>   7:55–56)

At God's right hand, Jesus intercedes for his people and calls on his Father to act with royal power (Rom. 8:34).

So the transcendence of God is best understood, not primarily as a spatial concept, but as a reference to God's kingship. God's transcendence means that he is sovereign over his creatures. And, as we have seen, God's kingship can be further analyzed into the three lordship attributes. If, therefore, we are to use the language of transcendence and immanence, it would be best to use *transcendence* for God's royal control and authority, and *immanence* for his covenant presence.

On this basis, there is no contradiction, nor even much of a tension,[5] between divine transcendence and immanence, for there is no tension between the Lord's control and authority and his covenant presence. As we have seen, the three lordship attributes imply one another. As such, they serve as three perspectives on God's lordship.[6]

---

5. "Tension," of course, is a psychological concept, relative to individual human minds. Different people feel tense about different things.

6. See *DKG* on "perspectival" relationships, especially pp. 191–94.

TRANSCENDENCE AND IMMANENCE
IN THEOLOGY   *KEY SECTION*

But other concepts of transcendence and immanence have appeared in the history of doctrine, and this is one area in which Greek philosophy has done a disservice to Christian theology.

Greek philosophy began as a revolt against popular religion, particularly against its anthropomorphic aspects. The philosophers were skeptical about claims to know the gods, and they insisted that most likely the gods were vastly different from any persons or things on earth. Note the following fragments of Xenophanes (around 530 B.C.):

> 1. There is one god, supreme among gods and men; resembling mortals neither in form nor in mind.
> 5. But mortals fancy gods are born, and wear clothes, and have voice and form like themselves.
> 6. Yet if oxen and lions had hands, and could paint with their hands, and fashion images, as men do, they would make the pictures and images of their gods in their own likeness; horses would make them like horses, oxen like oxen.
> D. 16. Aethiopians make their gods black and snub-nosed; Thracians give theirs blue eyes and red hair.
> 7. Homer and Hesiod have ascribed to the gods all deeds that are a shame and a disgrace among men: thieving, adultery, fraud.[7]

Much of this is true, even reminiscent of Scripture's scorn of idolatry. But Xenophanes did not acknowledge any revelation of God:

> 14. There never was, nor ever will be, any man who knows with certainty the things about the gods and about all things which I tell of. For even if he does happen to get most things right, still he himself does not know it. But mere opinions all may have.[8]

So most of Xenophanes' statements about God were negative. God is not like an ox, or a lion, or an Ethiopian, or a Thracian. He "resembles mortals neither in form nor in mind." Xenophanes' own "mere opinions" leaned in a pantheistic direction, and he affirmed the simplicity and unchangeability of God.[9]

---

7. Charles M. Bakewell, *Source Book in Ancient Philosophy* (New York: Gordian Press, 1973), 8–9.
8. Ibid., 9.
9. See fragments 2 and 4, quoted ibid., 8.

The Epicurean Lucretius (96–55 B.C.) pressed this negative theology in a deistic direction:

> For the nature of gods must ever in itself of necessity enjoy immortality together with supreme repose, far removed and withdrawn from our concerns; since exempt from every pain, exempt from all dangers, strong in its own resources, not wanting aught of us, it is neither gained by favors nor moved by anger.[10]

Lucretius and Xenophanes agreed, however, that God is very different from anything on earth and therefore cannot be clearly known by human beings. Since we cannot identify him with anything in our experience, we cannot regard him as taking a definite part in the historical process. This means that if we allow any place at all in our thinking for God or gods, he or they must either be the process itself (Xenophanes) or being(s) far above the process, who never enter it (Lucretius).

The sophist Protagoras (around 440 B.C.) said:

> With regard to the gods I know not whether they exist or not, or what they are like. Many things prevent our knowing; the subject is obscure and brief is the span of our mortal life.[11]

In the *Timaeus* of Plato (428–348 B.C.), the title figure also expresses some skepticism about finding out "the father and maker of all this universe."[12] Of the divine form of the Good in his *Republic*, he says,

> It is the cause of knowledge and truth; and so, while you may think of it as an object of knowledge, you will do well to regard it as something beyond truth and knowledge and, precious as these are, of still higher worth . . . and Goodness is not the same thing as being, but even beyond being, surpassing it in dignity and power.[13]

Notice the pattern: skepticism about the nature of God leads to a theology of negation: God is not this, not that. This negation expresses a kind of transcendence: God is unlike anything in the world, because he transcends the world. He is too high and lofty to be compared to things in our experience. When, inconsistently, positive statements are made about him, they lean toward a pantheistic or deistic conception.

---

10. Ibid., 309.
11. Ibid., 67.
12. *Plato's Timaeus* (New York: Liberal Arts Press, 1949), 12 (Stephanus, p. 28).
13. *The Republic of Plato* (New York: Oxford University Press, 1945, 1958), 220 (VI, 508). Compare Herman Bavinck's discussion of divine incomprehensibility in *DG*, 19–20.

Bavinck summarizes the later Neoplatonic development:

> Plotinus is even more radical. Plato ascribed many attributes to
> God. Philo complemented his negative theology with a positive
> in which he defines God as a personal, perfect, omnipotent Be-
> ing. But according to Plotinus nothing can be said of God which
> is not negative. God is an absolute unity, raised above all plu-
> rality. Accordingly, he cannot be defined in terms of thought,
> goodness, or being, for all these descriptive terms imply a cer-
> tain plurality. God, as pure unity, is indeed the *cause* of thought,
> being, goodness, etc., but is himself distinct from any of these
> and transcends them all. He is unlimited, infinite, without form
> and so entirely different from every creature that even activity,
> life, thought, consciousness, and being cannot be ascribed to him.
> Our thought and language cannot attain to him. We cannot say
> what he *is*, but we can only say what he *is not*. Even the terms
> "the One" and "the Good," of which Plotinus makes much use,
> are not to be construed as descriptions of God's being, but only
> as indicative of his relation to creatures, and suggestive of his
> absolute causality.[14]

The Gnostic religions that infected some of the early Christian churches
with heresy shared a similar view of God:

> For the creature the highest God was absolutely unknowable and
> unattainable. He was "unknown depth, ineffable, eternal silence."[15]

Bavinck mentions in passing that this pattern of thought is typical of
non-Christian religions, such as Hinduism and Islam. But despite its non-
Christian character, as Bavinck points out, this way of thinking about
God's transcendence influenced the church fathers:

> Justin Martyr calls God inexpressible, immovable, nameless. The
> words Father, God, Lord, are not real names "but appellations
> drawn from his good deeds and functions." God cannot appear,
> cannot go about, cannot be seen, etc. . . . Among many also Ire-
> naeus presents the false and partly gnostic antithesis between the
> Father: hidden, invisible, unknowable; and the Son, who re-
> vealed him.[16]

14. DG, 20. Plotinus lived A.D. 205–70.
15. Ibid.
16. Ibid., 21.

Bavinck also refers to Clement of Alexandria, Origen, Eusebius, and others. Augustine taught that God is "being" (his understanding of *yahweh*), "the name that indicates what he is in himself." All other names are "names which indicate what he is for us." Augustine also insisted that "it is easier for us to say what he is not than what he *is*." Bavinck carries the history of this conception through John of Damascus, pseudo-Dionysius, and John Scotus Erigena. The major scholastics (Anselm, Albert the Great, Thomas Aquinas) were not as radical. But they distinguished between God's essential being and his attributes and actions, and they denied that we could have any knowledge of God's essential being.[17] So the modern liberal tradition that emphasizes agnosticism about God's "metaphysical" nature (Ritschl, Harnack), or stresses that God is "wholly other" than anything in the world (Barth, Bultmann), can claim some precedent in the church's tradition.

Nevertheless, in these writings, both ancient and modern, we find a concept of transcendence that is very different from the lordship attributes of control and authority. "Transcendence" to these theologians means that God is so far above us, so very different from anything on earth, that we can say nothing, at least nothing positive, about him. He transcends our language, so anything we say about him is utterly inadequate. In modern theology, this concept leads to a skepticism about the adequacy of Scripture itself as a revelation of God and about the ability of human beings to say anything about God with real assurance.

Scripture does teach that God is incomprehensible in a sense, and I shall discuss that in chapter 11. But it never denies God's knowability. Scripture never suggests that the human mind is incapable of knowing God or that human language is incapable of speaking truly about him. Nor does it distinguish one aspect of God (his inner essence) from other aspects (his attributes and acts) and deny us knowledge of the former. Indeed, the covenant presence of God implies that we cannot escape knowing him, for we cannot know anything else apart from him. Thus Paul in Romans 1:20 tells us:

> For since the creation of the world God's invisible qualities—his eternal power and divine nature—have been clearly seen, being understood from what has been made, so that men are without excuse.

We should also note that in the history of philosophy and theology, views of divine immanence have developed that are very different from the biblical concept of covenant presence. There has been some tendency to deny divine immanence altogether (as in the deism of Lucretius and

17. Ibid., 21–24.

of some seventeenth- and eighteenth-century rationalists like John Toland, Anthony Collins, Matthew Tindal, and Thomas Paine). But abolishing God's involvement in history grants sovereignty to finite forces, deifying them. Man's intellect becomes the ultimate authority in determining truth, and natural law becomes the ultimate cause of events in nature and history. So even the deists acknowledge an immanent god, an immanent absolute, but one different from the God of Scripture.

Another alternative is pantheism, as we have seen in Xenophanes, a view we could trace through Spinoza, Hegel, and others. In this view, God is the world, taken as a whole, and the world is God. Divine immanence for such thinkers means that the world is divine. So the world is its own ultimate cause and the ultimate authority for thought. The immanence of God means that God has given his power and authority over to the world. Divine immanence on this view implies the autonomy of creatures. Pantheism and deism thus agree on the existence and importance of human autonomy.

Modern process theology claims to have a position distinct from both deism and pantheism, namely "panentheism." Pantheism says that the world is God and God is the world. Panentheism says that the world is "in" God. But of course there are different ways in which creatures can be "in" God. Paul, on Mars Hill in Athens, quotes the Greek poet Epimenides as saying that "in him we live and move and have our being" (Acts 17:28). In his letters, Paul often speaks of believers as being "in Christ." These expressions represent, I believe, various forms of God's covenant presence and of our consequent presence to him. But, in the process view, we are ourselves constituents of God's "consequent nature," and we therefore influence his nature, decisions, and actions.[18] This view denies transcendence in the biblical sense, and its view of immanence gives powers to creatures that Scripture ascribes to God alone.

Philosophers and theologians have often tried to achieve balance between the false concepts of transcendence and immanence that I have described. For example, in Gnosticism, as I mentioned earlier, God is considered to be beyond all human thought and language; nevertheless, the primary worldview of Gnosticism is monistic: God and the world are aspects of one reality, related to one another on a continuum, so that the world is divine, albeit with a lower degree of divinity.[19] In Scripture, of course, there are no degrees of divinity. God is divine; the world is not divine, and that is that. But for Gnosticism, a completely transcendent God can be brought

---

18. See, for example, John B. Cobb and David Ray Griffin, *Process Theology: An Introductory Exposition* (Philadelphia: Westminster Press, 1976), 41–62.
19. Peter Jones, *Spirit Wars* (Escondido, Calif.: Main Entry Editions, 1997), 170–71.

into contact with the world only through a continuum. Obviously, this kind of thinking generates contradictions that church fathers like Irenaeus, despite the difficulties of their own formulations, were quick to notice.

For Immanuel Kant (1724–1804), God, the human soul, and the world (as a unified whole) are "noumenal," beyond any possible human experience and therefore unknowable. In the "phenomenal" world, we can gain knowledge on the basis of our experience. But the basic features of the phenomenal world—space, time, the "categories of the understanding" such as causality, unity, and plurality—are the product of the human mind, as is the moral law. In many ways, in Kant's philosophy, man replaces God as both the ultimate source and the ultimate interpreter of reality.

Much theology since Kant has been Kantian in its structure. In Barth, for example, God is both "wholly other" (wholly hidden) and "wholly revealed."[20] God is not revealed through the definite words and sentences of the Bible, but through ineffable divine actions that theologians struggle to interpret however they will. Barth's theological concern in all of this, as stated often in his writings, is to avoid any human attempt to "possess," "control," or "manipulate" God. He wants a doctrine of transcendence that makes it impossible for human beings to control the deity in any way; so he makes God wholly hidden. It would have been better if Barth had solved the problem differently, by focusing on God's sovereignty rather than his hiddenness. It is God's control, not his absence from the world, that keeps us from controlling him.

Some more recent theologians have identified God's transcendence with the "future." Jürgen Moltmann developed this view extensively in his *Theology of Hope*,[21] emphasizing that God is not transcendent in the sense of being "up there" in a different realm; rather, he is transcendent to us as the future is transcendent to the present. The future brings all our experience to us, but it is not under our control. Moltmann, however, does not hold that the future is already written in God's plan, but that it is open and undetermined. As with Bultmann, the open future is the arena of human freedom. So, as with the Gnostics, transcendence implies ineffability. But in theological futurism, there is also a sense in which transcendence and immanence coincide. Indeed, there are hints in Moltmann and other futurists, influenced as they are by Hegel and process thought, that the divine nature is incomplete, that God becomes what he will be as he responds to the flow of the historical process, much of which is determined by autonomous human choice.

20. See CVT, 353–69, and Cornelius Van Til, *Christianity and Barthianism* (Philadelphia: Presbyterian and Reformed, 1962).

21. New York: Harper and Row, 1965. He cites Rudolf Bultmann as a source for his view that "Spirit may be called the power of futurity," 212.

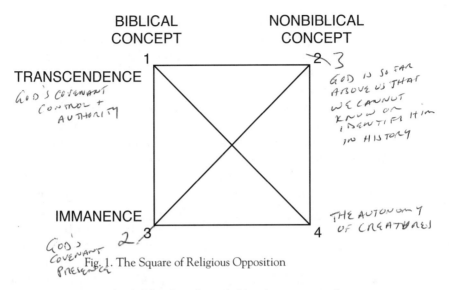

BIBLICAL CONCEPT

NONBIBLICAL CONCEPT

1

2 3 GOD IS SO FAR ABOVE US THAT WE CANNOT KNOW OR IDENTIFY HIM IN HISTORY

TRANSCENDENCE *GOD'S COVENANT CONTROL + AUTHORITY*

IMMANENCE *GOD'S COVENANT PRESENCE* *2 3*

4 *THE AUTONOMY OF CREATURES*

Fig. 1. The Square of Religious Opposition

Figure 1 summarizes the biblical and nonbiblical concepts of transcendence and immanence that we have surveyed. The left side of the rectangle represents the biblical views of transcendence and immanence that we have discussed. View 1 is biblical transcendence: God's covenant control and authority. View 2 is biblical immanence: God's covenant presence. The right side of the rectangle represents the unbiblical views we have surveyed. View 3 is nonbiblical transcendence: God is so far "above" us (wholly hidden) that we cannot know him or identify him in history. View 4 is nonbiblical immanence: the immanence of God is in effect the autonomy of creatures (wholly revealed).

The diagonal lines are lines of opposition. Views 1 and 4 are contradictory, for to say that creatures are autonomous is to contradict the assertion that God is the supreme controller of, and the authority over, the world. Views 2 and 3 are opposed, because to insist that God cannot be identified in history, that he is unknowable and unspeakable, contradicts the biblical teaching concerning God's covenant presence.

The vertical lines draw our attention to the relative consistency of the two approaches. The biblical view is consistent and without tension. Indeed, as we have seen, control, authority, and presence imply one another. The nonbiblical view is full of tension, for how can God be both ineffable and identical with the world, as in Gnosticism? How can he be both wholly hidden and wholly revealed, as in Barth? But although this system is contradictory, we can understand how this view of transcendence generates this particular view of immanence, and vice versa. If God is the nameless beyond, then necessarily we are left as masters of our own destiny, for practically speaking, he cannot rule us. We cannot take account of such a being in our values, our decisions, or our worldviews. But we cannot live without ultimate values, so we become gods ourselves. The universe cannot exist without ultimate powers of causation, so it becomes its own cause. Removing God from the world generates human autonomy. And, conversely, if our goal is to be autonomous,[22] then we must either deny God's existence altogether[23] or convince ourselves that he is too far beyond us to have any practical influence in our lives. So views 3 and 4 require one another in a sense, even though bringing them together creates tension and paradox.

The horizontal lines lead us to consider the similarity of the two ways of thinking at the verbal level. Both views of transcendence appeal to the biblical language of God's exaltation and height. Both views of immanence describe his involvement in all things. But beneath the verbal similarity, there are enormous conceptual differences, indeed contradictions, as we have seen, between the two systems. The verbal similarities indicate why the nonbiblical positions have attracted many Christians. But these issues are so important that we must penetrate beneath the surface similarities to recognize the antithesis between these two ways of thinking.

The God of the Bible is not a nameless, unknowable Absolute, removed from the course of human history. Nor is he one who gives his power and authority over to the world he has made. He dwells everywhere with us as the covenant Lord.

The important thing about the discussion of transcendence and immanence in modern theology is not that theologians have differed over the *degree of emphasis* to be placed on transcendence or immanence.[24] It is rather that modern theologians have adopted *views* of both transcendence and immanence that are sharply opposed to those of the Bible.

A RELIGIOUS ANTITHESIS

The two concepts of transcendence and immanence are not mere differences of opinion. The views identified above as views 3 and 4 constitute the fundamental worldview of unbelief. One who rejects the God of

22. Remember that Scripture teaches that autonomy is always the goal of fallen man. So it is not arbitrary to ascribe this sort of thinking ultimately to human rebellion against God.

23. Atheism is an extreme version of nonbiblical transcendence. It asserts that God is so far from the real world in which we live that he should not even be counted among real beings.

24. As Grenz and Olson often seem to suppose, in the volume cited at the beginning of this chapter.

the Bible necessarily believes the opposite of biblical theism. One cannot be neutral on this question: you are either for God or against him.

If you deny God's transcendence, his control and authority, then you must believe that ultimate control and authority are vested in the finite world—that is, that the finite world is divine. This is view 4. If you deny the covenant presence of God in creation, then you must believe that God is absent. That is view 3.

Each of these two worldviews implies an epistemology. One who believes that God is absent will question the possibility of rational thought, for he will doubt whether there is any rational structure or meaning to the world at all. He will be an irrationalist. But one who believes that the finite world is divine will believe that something in the finite world, maybe the human mind itself, constitutes the supreme authority for human knowledge. He will be a rationalist.

Cornelius Van Til pointed out that the rationalist/irrationalist tension began in the Garden of Eden. Eve would not take God's word as her ultimate authority; she looked at God's speech, Satan's, and her own, as if the three were equal. But that is to imply that there is no final truth about anything—irrationalism. Nevertheless, when required to choose, Eve claimed the right to decide for herself, over against God—autonomous rationalism.

We shall explore further the epistemological implications of biblical theism in chapter 11,[25] as we did to some extent in chapter 6. My present point is that the non-Christian views of transcendence and immanence—the non-Christian metaphysics—imply a non-Christian epistemology as well.

But even more fundamentally, the difference is religious. We must choose whether to recognize God as Lord or not. Those who do not recognize him as Lord exchange the truth for a lie (Rom. 1:25), and they lose the basis for finding truth. Although they know many things, they gain knowledge only by borrowing principles from Christian theism.

So we are not talking here about mere differences of opinion, but about spiritual warfare. These two opposite worldviews are contending today for the hearts of all people.

---

25. And of course *DKG* discusses this epistemology at great length.

PART TWO

SOME PROBLEM AREAS

CHAPTER 8

Human Responsibility and Freedom

The doctrine that God controls all things, including human decisions, typically raises for us the question, "How, then, can we be responsible for our actions?" Answering this question has been a major preoccupation of theologians who write about the doctrine of God.

The term *responsibility* is not often found in English translations of the Bible, so if we are to use the term, we need to link it to some biblical concepts and teachings. Let us distinguish first between two concepts of responsibility: (1) *accountability* to a higher authority and (2) *liability* for the consequences of our actions. We shall consider these in turn.[1]

RESPONSIBILITY AS ACCOUNTABILITY

In Scripture, human beings are clearly responsible in the first sense, since they are accountable to God as the supreme evaluator of human conduct. Human responsibility in this sense, therefore, is a consequence of God's authority. God has made us according to his plan and for his purpose. That purpose is to glorify him, to please him. The fundamental standard of human conduct is that we should reflect God's own nature. Since he has made us in his image (Gen. 1:27–28), we should behave in a way that images

---

1. There is a third sense, in which *responsibility* refers to a quality of character, as in "Joe is a responsible businessman." The responsibility in view here is integrity or honesty. I will not be discussing that concept here. For those who may be interested, the three senses form a triad: accountability is normative, liability is situational, and integrity is existential.

119

him: "Be holy," he says, "because I, the LORD your God, am holy" (Lev. 19:1; cf. 11:44; Matt. 5:48; 1 Peter 1:15–16).

God reveals the nature of holiness in his Word. His Word definitively reveals human obligations and therefore what we would call human responsibilities. Human responsibility (accountability) means that human beings are subject to God's evaluation and are therefore under obligation to obey his commands and observe his standards. It presupposes that God is the judge, the supreme evaluator, of our conduct, whether for covenant blessing or cursing.

To ask about the relationship between divine sovereignty and human responsibility in this sense, then, is initially to ask about the relationship between two lordship attributes, God's control and his authority. But, at the end of this chapter, we will also see the need to consider the third lordship attribute, covenant presence, to gain a fuller perspective.

Now although theologians take great interest in the "problem" of divine sovereignty and human responsibility, it is not one of the main concerns of the biblical writers, although they are aware of it. Just as it is plain to them that God controls everything, so it is plain to them that he is the supreme authority. Therefore, to the biblical writers, we are answerable to God for our attitudes, thoughts, words, and actions. Everything we think and do—indeed, everything we are—brings God's commendation or condemnation. Even actions like eating and drinking, which we might consider to be ethically neutral or "adiaphora," must be done to God's glory (1 Cor. 10:31). Whatever we do should be done thankfully, in Jesus' name (Col. 3:17), with all our heart (v. 23). Everything that does not come from faith is sin (Rom. 14:23). Practically every page of Scripture displays God's sovereign evaluations of human attitudes, thoughts, words, and deeds.

Indeed, we are even responsible for our moral nature. Comparing bad trees to bad people, Jesus says that the bad trees will bring forth bad fruit and will therefore be cut down and thrown into the fire (Matt. 7:15–20; cf. Luke 6:43–45). Paul teaches that because of Adam's sin, his descendants were made sinners (Rom. 5:19), and that natural sinfulness, with which we are born, leads to our condemnation (vv. 15–18) if God does not bless us with saving grace. We are responsible for what we are. We did not individually make ourselves evil by nature, but we are responsible for that evil anyway.[2] Our inheritance from Adam is not the result of our individual choice, but we must bear the guilt of it.[3]

---

2. Thus, the biblical understanding of human responsibility is at this point diminished by the view that we are responsible only for what we freely choose.

3. For a full account of the doctrine of the imputation of Adam's sin to his descendants,

Furthermore, we are responsible to seek salvation. We must make a decision to serve the Lord (Josh. 24:15–24). We must receive Christ (John 1:12); we must believe in him (John 3:16; 6:40); we must repent, believe, and be baptized (Acts 2:38). As we have seen, God chooses us before we choose him; his choice brings ours about. But we must choose, nevertheless; and if we do not make the right choice, we will not be saved.

So we are responsible for everything we are and do. On the whole, the biblical writers see no problem in affirming both total divine sovereignty and complete human responsibility. In Romans 9, Paul does cite an imaginary objector who questions the justice of God (v. 14) and says, "Why does God still blame us? For who resists his will?" (v. 19). But Paul replies, "But who are you, O man, to talk back to God? 'Shall what is formed say to him who formed it, "Why did you make me like this?" ' Does not the potter have the right to make out of the same lump of clay some pottery for noble purposes and some for common use?" (vv. 20–21). Earlier, Paul quoted Exodus 33:19: God will have mercy on whom he will have mercy.[4] But such debates in Scripture are rare. For the most part, the Bible sets forth God's involvement in everything and affirms the responsibility of all moral agents, without suggesting that there is any conflict between these two teachings.

It is significant that Scripture often affirms both divine sovereignty and human responsibility in the same passage. As we saw, Genesis 50:20 rebukes the wicked intent of Joseph's brothers, but also mentions the good intention of God in bringing about Joseph's ministry in Egypt. We also discussed Isaiah 10:5–15, where God uses the Assyrian king as his tool to punish Israel; nevertheless, the Assyrian is wicked, and he must take responsibility: "When the Lord has finished all his work against Mount Zion and Jerusalem, he will say, 'I will punish the king of Assyria for the willful pride of his heart and the haughty look in his eyes' " (v. 12). Note the parallel in Proverbs:

> The LORD works out everything for his own ends—
>   even the wicked for a day of disaster.
> The LORD detests all the proud of heart.
>   Be sure of this: They will not go unpunished. (Prov. 16:4–5)

God raises up the wicked for the day of disaster, but they are nonetheless responsible for their wickedness and shall not go unpunished.

───────────   *READ*

see John Murray, *The Imputation of Adam's Sin* (Grand Rapids: Eerdmans, 1959). Paul's argument draws a parallel between this imputation and the imputation of Christ's righteousness to his people. So if we deny the first, we have no basis for affirming the second.

4. See discussion of this and other texts in AGG, 149–90, and in chapter 9 of this book.

In 1 Kings 8:58, Solomon prays that God will "turn our hearts to him, to walk in all his ways." Then he exhorts Israel, "But your hearts must be fully committed to the LORD our God, to live by his decrees and obey his commands, as at this time" (v. 61; cf. Jer. 29:10–14).

Jesus also shows us both sides of the matter: "All that the Father gives me will come to me, and whoever comes to me I will never drive away" (John 6:37). Notice also the balance in John 1 between verse 12 and verse 13:

> Yet to all who received him, to those who believed in his name, he gave the right to become children of God—children born not of natural descent, nor of human decision or a husband's will, but born of God.

It is God who gives new birth, but those who are born of God accept the responsibility to receive Christ and believe in his name.

Scripture curses the wicked men who betrayed and crucified Jesus, but it also traces their actions to the decree of God (Luke 22:22; Acts 2:23; 4:27–28).

The evangelistic work of the early church was the work of God, but it was also the product of human preaching. Acts 13:48, as we saw earlier, mentions that "all who were appointed for eternal life believed," but 14:1 attributes faith to the preaching of Paul and Barnabas: "There they spoke so effectively that a great number of Jews and Gentiles believed."[5] In Romans 9, Paul attributes the unbelief of Israel to God's sovereign working, but in chapter 10 he attributes it to Israel's unwillingness to respond to the preaching of the gospel (vv. 14–21, especially v. 21). Paul does not hesitate, indeed, to say that it is his responsibility to "win as many as possible" (1 Cor. 9:19; cf. vv. 20–22), and even that "I have become all things to all men so that by all possible means I might save some" (v. 22). As post-Reformation Christians, we tend to be uncomfortable with such language. We want to say, "No, it's God who saves, not human preachers." But elsewhere Paul asks, "How can they hear without someone preaching to them?" (Rom. 10:14). Human preachers must seek nothing less than the salvation

---

[5] In our contemporary discussions of church growth, it is important both to remember that evangelism is God's work and to consider what human means will be most effective. Many Calvinists are embarrassed to use this language, which seems at first glance to detract from God's sovereignty in salvation. But since this language is in the Bible, this embarrassment will have to be traced to hyper-Calvinism, rather than to genuine Calvinism. We should never argue, for example, that since God is the one who persuades men of the truth, we should never seek in our preaching to persuade—or that since God is the one who reaches the heart, we should never seek in our ministry to reach the hearts of people.

of the lost, recognizing all the time that no one will be saved unless God works through them.[6]

Throughout Paul's missionary labors, God's sovereignty governs what happens, but Paul gives himself to the most rigorous exertions (2 Cor. 4:7–12; 11:23–33). In Acts 27, during Paul's journey to Rome as a prisoner, he prophesies danger to the ship (v. 10). During the storm, he says on God's authority (v. 24) that no one on the ship will die (cf. v. 34). But when sailors try to escape in a lifeboat, Paul says that "unless these men stay with the ship, you cannot be saved" (v. 31). So God has determined that all will live, yet the sailors must take responsibility for this deliverance.

The Christian life is the work of God in us, but it is also our effort to withstand temptation and obey the Lord: "Continue to work out your salvation with fear and trembling, for it is God who works in you to will and to act according to his good pleasure" (Phil. 2:12–13). In this passage, Paul not only brings the two emphases together, but shows their relationship to each other. We work *because* God works in us.

The New Testament often presents the Christian life in terms of an indicative and an imperative. The indicative emphasizes the sovereign work of God, and the imperative emphasizes our obligation, our responsibility. For example, in Colossians 3:1–3, we read:

> Since, then, you have been raised with Christ, set your hearts on things above, where Christ is seated at the right hand of God. Set your minds on things above, not on earthly things. For you died, and your life is now hidden with Christ in God.

"You have been raised" is the indicative; "set your hearts on things above" is the imperative. God raised us; we could not have raised ourselves. But Paul expects us to make a decision to give priority in our hearts and minds to the affairs of God. The Christian life is a wonderful gift of God, but it is also a spiritual battle that warrants great exertions.[7] As in Philippians 2:12–13,

---

6. I have heard Calvinists say that our goal in preaching should be only to spread the word, not to bring conversion, since that is God's work. The result is often a kind of preaching that covers biblical content, but unbiblically fails to plead with sinners to repent and believe. Let us be clear on this point: the goal of evangelistic preaching is conversion. And the goal of all preaching is a sincere response of repentance and faith. Hyper-Calvinism actually dishonors God's sovereignty, because it suggests (1) that vigorous, goal-directed human effort negates God's sovereign grace, and (2) that such vigorous effort cannot be God's chosen means of bringing people to salvation. God's sovereign purpose is to save people through the witness of other people.

7. Note the motif of athletic competition in 1 Cor. 9:24–27 and the warfare motif in Eph. 6:10–20. The Christian is to be active as he lives for Jesus. The Christian life is not a passive "letting go and letting God."

the sovereign gift of God motivates our exertions. Never in Scripture is there any hint that God's sovereignty should encourage passivity or sloth.

The book of Revelation shows over and over the wrath of God poured out upon Satan and his hosts. Satan is responsible for what he does. Nevertheless, God is on the throne. He anticipates what Satan does and limits it according to his plan.

Why do the biblical writers find it so natural to bring these themes together, a conjunction that seems so paradoxical to modern readers? Why does Paul in Philippians 2:12–13 actually appeal to God's sovereign working in order to motivate our responsible activity? Here are some suggestions as to why this linkage makes sense in the context of a biblical worldview:

1. As we saw in chapter 5, God's sovereignty involves not only his control over everything, but also his authority, his evaluation of everything. He is the supreme standard, the source of all value. Control and evaluation are two aspects of lordship, mutually implicative. It is therefore not at all surprising that they should be conjoined in Scripture. By his control, God foreordains our actions; by his authority, he evaluates them. Because of that authority, we are answerable to him, responsible. Far from being inconsistent with God's lordship, therefore, our responsibility is based upon it.

2. God's promises of success motivate believers to act in accord with those promises. Theoretically, of course, someone might respond to such a promise by relaxing and waiting passively for God to do it all. Two opposite responses to the certainty of God's promises, then, are theoretically possible. But taking action to further God's goals is not an irrational response to revelation, and it is eminently rational when we consider that our obedience is not only commanded, but also a tool by which God accomplishes his purposes. Those who obey have the joy of being God's instruments—and of reaping his rewards.

3. When we are most aware of God's providential control over us, we are most aware of the necessity to live responsibly before him. When we are overwhelmed by his grace and love—or by his wrath and judgment—we are powerfully impressed with our need to repent and believe. When we are amazed at God's work within us, we are motivated to work out our own salvation. Note that in Philippians 2:12–13, we are to work out our salvation with "fear and trembling." "Fear and trembling" in Scripture is worship, the typical response of a human being to the presence of God. The presence of God with us and in us motivates us to take responsibility. In the presence of the great king, we dare not refuse his commands.[8]

---

8. This consideration shows the relevance of the third lordship attribute, covenant presence, to the questions we are considering.

4. Without God's control over the universe, there could be no human responsibility. We live in a theistic universe, governed by a person, not by impersonal forces. Since God has planned, made, and governed all of nature and history, he has evaluated every event according to his perfect standards. If God did not exist, however, there would be no moral standards. Matter, motion, time, and space alone do not impose obligations.[9] And if God did not control everything that happens, then he would not be the ultimate interpreter, the ultimate valuer, of everything. The value of some things would then be independent of God, which is to say that they would have no value. Our responsibility, then, would be confused by two or more sources of value, possibly by two or more equally ultimate standards. Or we would be morally responsible in some areas of life, but not in others. But in Scripture there is one standard; we are to do everything for God's glory.

5. Scripture is therefore not nearly as concerned as we are to promote our self-esteem. We would like to believe that the meaning and significance of our lives depend on what we do for ourselves, without any outside influences or constraints. In Scripture, however, the goal of human life is to glorify God. Our dignity is to be found not in what we do, but in what God has done for us and in us. Our meaning and significance are to be found in the fact that God has created us in his image and redeemed us by the blood of his Son. The biblical writers, therefore, are not horrified, as modern writers tend to be, by the thought that we may be under the control of another. If the other is God, and he has made us for his glory, then we could not possibly ask for a more meaningful existence.

RESPONSIBILITY AS LIABILITY

According to the concept of responsibility set forth above, we are responsible for everything we are, think, say, or do. But we sometimes use the term *responsibility* in a somewhat different way, in the second sense noted at the beginning of this chapter, namely, to indicate our *liability* for a state of affairs. In the first sense of *responsibility*, we are always responsible and totally responsible. There is no distinction of degree, no distinction between being more or less responsible. But in the second sense, there is a difference in degree. If Bill and Joe share a plate of cookies, each is partly responsible for the emptiness of the plate. Responsibility in the sense of lia-

---

9. Compare the argument for God's existence in *AGG*, 93–118, and my debate with Paul Kurtz, "Without a Supreme Being, Everything is Permitted," *Free Inquiry* 16 (spring 1996): 4–7.

bility has to do with the *results* of our actions. But the results of our actions are never entirely the results of our own decisions. Events in the world have multiple causes, and of course none of us causes anything by his free decision alone. So courts must often ascertain the degree of liability for a crime or injury, and that judgment amounts to assigning partial responsibility. Responsibility in this second sense determines the degree of guilt that one bears as the result of wrongdoing, and the nature of the punishment.

In what follows, I shall be thinking of responsibility in the second sense. We should not, however, forget the first sense. It is important to remember that in that sense we are exhaustively responsible for everything in our lives.

RESPONSIBILITY AND ABILITY

So far, I have analyzed human responsibility without mentioning freedom. Many have claimed that freedom, defined in one way or another, is a condition of human responsibility, so that we are responsible (that is, liable) only for what we do freely.

Certainly there are cases in which that claim is credible. We might initially be appalled that eleven-year-old Billy covered the school door with graffiti. But when we learn that he did it unwillingly, under the threat of bodily harm by eighteen-year-old Mike, we tend to be far more sympathetic to Billy, and, of course, indignant toward Mike. We say that Billy should not be held responsible, because he did what he did under duress. His act was not a "free" act. He "could not have done otherwise."

Now Billy was fully responsible, in the sense that he was accountable to God for everything he did. But none of us would say that Billy is responsible in the sense of being liable for the damage done to the door. So we can see how freedom and responsibility (in the second sense) are linked to ability. In judging someone's action, we should take into consideration whether he was *able* to act in a different way. So ability, to some extent, limits responsibility.

This principle is often helpful in making judgments about other people. We may believe that Christians should attend church (Heb. 10:25), but if Aunt Martha is bedridden, we understand; she cannot help missing the service. Her inability removes her responsibility in this particular case.

Is this a biblical principle? Yes, up to a point. In Scripture, certain *kinds* of inability do limit responsibility *in some degree*. The case laws of the Pentateuch often take ability into account in prescribing penalties for lawbreaking. For instance, the law treats accidental killing differently from intentional killing in Exodus 21:12–14. One who kills intentionally is able to do otherwise, because the chief factor in the murder is his own willful decision. To the degree that a killing is accidental, it is not avoidable; indeed, "God lets it happen" (v. 13).[10]

If a thief breaks into the house of an Israelite at night, the homeowner has the right to defend himself and his household. If he kills the intruder, he is "not guilty of bloodshed" (Ex. 22:2). But if he kills such an intruder after sunrise, he is guilty. Evidently, the law presumes that in the dark of night the homeowner is less able to summon help or to determine proportionate means of defense. His inability limits his responsibility. I assume that judges in Israel would have recognized intermediate cases between the dead-of-night case and the daylight case. What if burglars break in during the day, but the homeowner cannot speak and therefore cannot summon help? What if he lives alone, far from his neighbors, and is confronted by three strong men who seek his life? In these cases, the judges would have to determine the penalty partly by deciding what alternatives were available to him, to what extent he was able to act otherwise.

Ignorance is a form of inability, and it does limit responsibility in some cases. Exodus 21:28–32 presents cases dealing with bulls that gore people to death. If the bull had the habit of attacking people, and the owner had been warned but did not confine the animal, he was punished severely. But if he had no such warning, "the owner of the bull will not be held responsible" (v. 28).

Jesus similarly teaches that knowledge is an important factor:

> That servant who knows his master's will and does not get ready or does not do what his master wants will be beaten with many blows. But the one who does not know and does things deserving punishment will be beaten with few blows. From everyone who has been given much, much will be demanded; and from the one who has been entrusted with much, much more will be asked. (Luke 12:47–48)

Again, ignorance limits responsibility, but in this case does not eliminate it. Why must the ignorant servant be punished "with few blows"? In typical cases, this kind of ignorance amounts to negligence. Servants normally have a responsibility to find out what the master expects of them. So ig-

---

10. In this passage, however, the unintentional killing of verse 13 is not entirely accidental. The passage assumes some degree of negligence on the part of the striker and therefore prescribes a penalty (cf. Num. 35:10–34). That penalty, however, is different from the penalty for murder, because the killing was less avoidable.

norance itself can be a punishable offense. But it is also a mitigating circumstance in judgments about more serious offenses.

Jesus' teaching in Luke 12:47–48 is a parable in which the master represents God. Paul also teaches that human ignorance of God's reality and his demands is culpable, because willful:

> For although they knew God, they neither glorified him as God nor gave thanks to him, but their thinking became futile and their foolish hearts were darkened. Although they claimed to be wise, they became fools and exchanged the glory of the immortal God for images made to look like mortal man and birds and animals and reptiles. (Rom. 1:21–23)

These unbelievers received a clear revelation of God's nature and power (vv. 18–20) and of his will (v. 32), but they repressed that knowledge, exchanging it for a lie (v. 25), and thus became ignorant. The result is that though they continue to have some knowledge of God, by virtue of his clear revelation, they have willfully suppressed that knowledge (1 Cor. 1:21).[11]

Leviticus 4:13–26 deals with unintentional sins of the whole community and of community leaders, prescribing sacrifices. Verse 13 reads,

> If the whole Israelite community sins unintentionally and does what is forbidden in any of the LORD's commands, even though the community is unaware of the matter, they are guilty.

Verse 22 speaks similarly about the leader's sin. Here there is an objective guilt that must be atoned for by the shedding of blood. Why is the community responsible for evils of which it was ignorant? Scripture emphasizes that we think and act, not only as individuals, but also as families and fellow citizens. What we do affects one another, and we do have responsibility for one another. When Adam sinned, his descendants inherited his guilt, as we have seen. Fathers after Adam do not communicate guilt to their children in the same way. We do not die for the sins of our parents (Ezek. 18:1–32), but for our own sin. The sins of parents, however, do tend to influence children to sin, and in that way the sins of parents can lead to the condemnation of their children.[12] Similarly (and this principle is

---

11. For more discussion of the unbeliever's knowledge and ignorance of God, see *DKG*, 49–61, and *CVT*, 187–213.

12. I take this to be the meaning of Ex. 20:5, where God says, "I, the LORD your God, am a jealous God, punishing the children for the sins of the fathers to the third and fourth generation of those who hate me." Note that the third and fourth generations are not innocent children being punished for the sins of ungodly parents. Rather, they are themselves "generations of those who hate me."

important in our time), a society that condones and even encourages sin must answer to God for sins committed in its midst, even sins of which it is largely ignorant.

Ability, therefore (of which knowledge is one kind), does limit responsibility in some cases, but usually does not eliminate it.

It is also the case that an increase in ability often brings an increase in responsibility. Isaiah 5:1–7 presents God's grace to Israel in the image of a man planting a vineyard, doing everything he can to make it produce fruit, but harvesting only bad grapes. He gives them more than he gives to the other nations, but they betray him. From those to whom much is given, much will be demanded (Luke 12:48). So Israel's unique revelation and its experience of God's deliverance and providence increase the severity of its judgment. Thus Amos 3:2 says:

> You only have I chosen
> of all the families of the earth;
> therefore I will punish you
> for all your sins.

The miracles of Jesus increase the responsibility of the disbelieving cities (Matt. 11:20–24). If the people of Sodom had seen the miracles Jesus wrought in Korazin and Bethsaida, they would have repented. So it will be worse for Korazin and Bethsaida. Listen to Jesus weeping over Jerusalem:

> O Jerusalem, Jerusalem, you who kill the prophets and stone those sent to you, how often I have longed to gather your children together, as a hen gathers her chicks under her wings, but you were not willing. Look, your house is left to you desolate. For I tell you, you will not see me again until you say, "Blessed is he who comes in the name of the Lord." (Matt. 23:37–39; cf. Luke 19:41–44)

Jesus gave special love to Jerusalem, only to be rejected. Few cities could boast that the Son of God himself had called them to repentance. But that advantage increases the judgment upon them.

We have seen in various ways how ability is proportionate to responsibility. But in Scripture, inability rarely eliminates all guilt. Exodus 21:28 and 22:2 are two cases where inability removes civil punishment. But in most cases, inabilities do not completely absolve one of responsibility, because they are balanced by abilities. For example, ignorance is a disability, but we often have the ability to avoid it.

In our relationship with God, we are never disabled in such a way as to be innocent before him. Our inabilities are combined with abilities, so that we are convicted as willful sinners. Everything we do, apart from divine grace, is sinful in that sense. Therefore, even in the second sense of *responsible*, we are totally responsible before the ultimate judge of liability. We can see now that the distinction between the two senses breaks down when we are speaking of God's final judgment. God judges all our actions by his perfect standard and finds them wanting. He knows what consequences are truly the results of our actions, and he declares us liable for those results. So when we stand before God, accountability and liability coincide. We distinguish them only on the human level, for human judges are not always able to assess liability precisely.[13]

Returning to our discussion of liability, there are some kinds of inability that do not mitigate it at all. One is our inability to avoid events that are divinely foreordained. As we saw in chapter 4, everything happens according to God's plan. Many events are predicted by God's prophets and so in one sense are inevitable. Human sins, too, are foreordained. Sometimes, indeed, as we have seen, Scripture describes God specifically as "hardening" people, that is, making them more sinful. When God brings about sin, that sin is in one sense unavoidable.

The Assyrian warriors in Isaiah 10:5–11 cannot avoid being God's tool of judgment. Nevertheless, they are fully responsible, and they themselves are under God's judgment (vv. 15–19). Jesus predicted in advance that Judas would betray him, and several texts include this betrayal under the decree of God (Luke 22:22; Acts 2:23; 4:27–28). But Judas is still fully responsible for betraying Jesus.

Certainly, from the point of view of human ability, Judas could have avoided his sinful act. He was physically able to do otherwise, and was mentally able to understand his action and to judge its moral and religious significance. He may well have known its consequences.[14] He did not act in ignorance. Nor was he forced to betray Jesus. He did what he wanted to do. So, as biblical law assesses guilt, Judas was guilty. He was able to do otherwise. His condemnation was appropriate. But in a higher and mysterious sense, his action was not avoidable, because he could not overcome the divine decree.

Another kind of inability that does not limit responsibility is *moral inability*. This disability, of course, also pertains to Judas. Indeed, it pertains to all of us. As we saw earlier, we are "made sinners" through the sin of Adam (Rom. 5:19). We are by nature hostile to God (Rom. 3:9–18). So:

13. So the triad I mentioned in an earlier footnote—accountability, liability, and integrity—form a *perspectival* triad. To have one of these qualities is to have them all. Of course, to view these terms perspectivally, we must recognize that integrity can be integrity in righteousness or in sin.

14. If such knowledge seems unlikely, the reader should consider Satan, who evidently knows perfectly well the futility of his project, yet perseveres in rebellion against God.

The mind of sinful man is death, but the mind controlled by the Spirit is life and peace; the sinful mind is hostile to God. It does not submit to God's law, nor can it do so. Those controlled by the sinful nature cannot please God. (Rom. 8:6–8)

Note the words "can" and "cannot."[15] We not only sin, but cannot do otherwise. Does this moral inability mitigate our responsibility? Imagine Hitler, say, standing before God's throne and saying, "I couldn't help the evil things I did. I was morally unable to do good. I was such a rotten person that I couldn't help sinning." An earthly judge would not take such a defense seriously. Would God accept it?

Certainly not. "The wages of sin is death" (Rom 6:23). Apart from grace, we are all afflicted with moral inability. And apart from grace, we will all die in our sins. An evil nature aggravates guilt, rather than mitigating it. It marks us out as worthless pottery, fit only for destruction (Rom. 9:21–22).

So there is no simple answer to the question whether inability limits responsibility. Inability does limit liability in some cases, in various degrees, and for various reasons. Some inabilities are self-imposed (willful) and therefore themselves culpable. Only rarely does inability completely exonerate one. Moral inability and our inability to frustrate God's purpose don't mitigate guilt at all.

— key sentence

EXCURSUS ON ABILITY

This section will be something of a parenthesis in the overall argument of this chapter, but it may help to clarify the meanings of *ability, possibility, can,* and related expressions. These terms are important, not only for the discussion of human freedom, but also in many other theological debates, on such subjects as the nature of God's omnipotence (what *can* God do?), miracles (what sorts of events *can* happen?), total depravity and common grace (what *can* man do apart from saving grace?), regeneration and sanctification (what *can* believers do as the result of grace that unbelievers *cannot* do?), Christology (was Jesus *able* to sin?), and prophecy (were Jesus' bones break*able*, given the prophecy that they would not be broken?).

Let's say that Rev. Welty is an excellent preacher. We ask him, "Can you preach for us on Sunday?" "No," he answers. He has other commitments. Now, can he preach for us on Sunday or can't he? Well, he *can* in the sense

15. Cf. Matt. 7:18; John 8:43; 1 Cor. 2:14.

that he is well qualified and competent. He *can't* in the sense that he can't overcome the conflicts in his schedule.

When he is too ill to speak in public, we might say of him either that he *can* preach or that he *can't.* The *can* pertains to his general competence and qualifications; the *can't* pertains to his current (we hope temporary) physical state. Both statements are true, despite the apparent contradiction, because they refer to two different kinds of ability.

When Welty was fourteen years old, did he have the ability to preach? We might say that he did, in the sense that he had the potential to become a preacher. He had the qualities that, with training, godliness, and divine grace, could produce fine sermons. (We can imagine his pastor saying to him, "Young man, you have the ability to become a preacher.") But, of course, there are more obvious senses in which fourteen-year-old boys, no matter how great their potential, are generally not "able" to preach.

Thus, the concept of ability is complex. There are different kinds of abilities. We sometimes say to someone, "Either you can or you can't." But it's not that simple. Often one can in some respects, but can't in others.

Can always envisages a particular act or event (what someone can do) and some circumstance that might prevent that act or event. (From this point on, I will call these circumstances "preventers.") When we say that Welty can preach, the event is preaching; the preventers would normally be lack of qualifications or training. When he is ill and we say he "can't" preach, we envisage a different set of preventers: medical deficiencies rather than deficiencies of basic competence. He is homiletically able, but medically unable.

Were Jesus' bones breakable? Was it possible that Jesus' bones could be broken? (The *-able* in *breakable* and the *-ible* in *possible* are related to the term *ability*. We are asking whether anyone or anything was able to break Jesus' legs.) Well, yes, in the sense that they had the same material composition as other human bones and therefore did not have sufficient physical strength to withstand certain kinds of blows. On the other hand, God prevented the breaking of Jesus' bones in order to fulfill prophecy (John 19:36). So there is also a sense in which Jesus' bones could not be broken. Breaking them was impossible. Again, different preventers yield different kinds of ability or possibility. The breaking of Jesus' bones was physically possible, but impossible by virtue of God's decree.[16]

So the concept of possibility is also complex. We are inclined to say that every event is either possible or impossible. But we can see that some

16. Compare Calvin's discussion in *Concerning the Eternal Predestination of God* (London: James Clarke and Co., 1961), 170.

Read

events (like the breaking of Jesus' bones) are both possible and impossible in different respects.

Philosophers, therefore, have distinguished different kinds of possibility, according to the different kinds of preventers:

Logical possibility refers to the mere absence of inconsistency. In logical possibility, inconsistency[17] is the only preventer at issue. The proposition "2 + 2 = 5" is logically impossible, because it creates an inconsistency with the rest of our mathematical system. Similarly, "The Padres beat the Pirates and they did not beat the Pirates," referring to the same game and using "beat" in the same sense twice, presents a logical impossibility. On the other hand, odd as it might seem, "Welty read the book of Isaiah in thirty seconds" is logically possible, because the proposition is not logically contradictory. Normally we would not say that Welty "can" read so fast, but it is a logical possibility.

Physical possibility refers to the laws of physics. Events are physically possible if they are not prevented by the laws of physics. Miracles are sometimes said to be impossible in this sense, but see my later discussion on that subject. We also sometimes use the term *physical possibility* to refer to the capabilities of our bodies. It is not physically possible for one man to lift a ten-thousand-pound weight, even though it is logically possible.

Economic possibility refers to what is financially possible. Someone might say that he cannot run for president, even though he is well qualified, because he cannot raise the money he would need. Running for president is not logically contradictory, and it does not violate the laws of physics or the capabilities of an average healthy body. But, for many today, it is economically impossible.

Political possibility refers to what can be accomplished in politics. We are often told that it would be good to pass a certain law, but that it is "politically impossible," meaning that the votes aren't there and minds cannot be changed.

One can think of many other kinds of possibilities and abilities: legal, medical, musical, and so on. In the previous section, we referred to moral ability and to the human ability to frustrate God's plan, which we might call "metaphysical ability."[18] Plainly, an act or event can be possible in one sense, but not in other senses. Jesus' bones were physically breakable, but they could not be broken in violation of God's intention. We could, but

17. Of course, I am talking about "logical" inconsistency here. There are other types of inconsistency that introduce a kind of circularity into this discussion. But I can't take time to discuss that issue, and I think my overall point is clear enough.
18. In my view, of course, no creature has that ability.

won't, take the time to sort out Welty's various abilities and disabilities in the previous illustrations.

Could Jesus sin? Perhaps the best short answer is that yes, he was physically and mentally capable of sinning, but no, he was morally incapable of it, since he was perfectly holy. Could he struggle with temptation? He could struggle against physical obstacles, so why not against mental and spiritual ones as well? As a man, and therefore as a divine-human person, he could struggle mentally with Satan's proposals, growing in his understanding of their nature and consequences, and maturing in his ability to relate these things to his Father's will (Luke 2:40, 52). He understood, surely, how evil tempts a man—what pleasures, however fleeting, are to be found in sin. Yet he saw all of these in their true perspective and rejected them.

Can unregenerate people believe in Jesus apart from grace? Again, they are physically and mentally able, but morally unable. We should not, like some Calvinists, neglect the senses in which the unregenerate are able, for their abilities are relevant to their responsibility.[19] As we have seen, God gave to Israel extraordinary resources of knowledge and experience, so that in important senses they could have obeyed God. The fact that they chose not to do so, despite their abilities, increases their responsibility.

In distinguishing different kinds of human abilities, however, there is some danger of drawing the lines between human faculties too sharply. Distinguishing between moral, mental, and physical ability is useful, as we have seen, but in doing so, we may forget the extent to which these abilities are interdependent. Moral rebellion against God leads to foolishness and stupidity, as I have emphasized in *DKG*.[20] It can also lead to physical sickness

19. In my view, it is not wise in an evangelistic meeting to tell non-Christians, without qualification, that they "cannot" come to Christ. I am not saying it is wrong to mention their moral and spiritual inability, but when the evangelist brings up the non-Christian's inability, its moral and spiritual nature should be spelled out. He should also emphasize that, in important respects, the unbeliever *can* come to faith. In most cases, he has the physical and mental prerequisites. No one keeps him from Christ by force. If he doesn't come, he has only himself to blame.

And we must not forget that at any time during an evangelistic witness (or, for that matter, at any other time), God may intervene to give the moral ability to respond. So, when the evangelist says that the inquirer "cannot" respond, he may be denying the grace of God at work in his very ministry. To tell unbelievers that they "cannot" come may be, ironically, a denial of God's sovereignty. And, as Steve Hays writes to me, "It's precisely because the evangelist has no direct control over conversion that he shouldn't take it upon himself to assume the responsibility of screening prospective converts, as if he's otherwise at risk of overruling God's work in conversion."

20. See also the perspectival analysis of human faculties (reason, will, emotions, imagination, etc.) in *DKG*, 328–46.

(Ps. 32:3–4; 1 Cor. 11:30; James 5:14–16). If a person hates God, his mind and body will not do the things that God approves.

God sees each of us, therefore, not as a loose collection of faculties and abilities, but as a whole person, acting from the heart (the integral center of human existence)—a heart consecrated to sin or to righteousness. The distinctions I have drawn above (like my earlier distinction between accountability and liability) are not of ultimate significance. From God's ultimate, transcendent point of view, they may not exist at all. But we do not have God's exhaustive knowledge of every human heart and its connections with every other aspect of a person. So Scripture, speaking in human terms, honoring our finite perspective, urges us to inform sinners, not only of the ways in which they are unable to believe, but also of the ways in which they are able.

FREEDOM

Freedom refers to various kinds of abilities ("freedom to") and to the lack of certain inabilities ("freedom from") that I have been calling "preventers." We have spoken of logical, physical, political, legal, economic, and metaphysical abilities and possibilities. When we speak of the abilities of people, or of what is possible for people to do, we can also describe these abilities as different kinds of freedoms. Of course, it is linguistically awkward to use the word *freedom* in some of these connections. We normally don't speak of "logical freedom," for example, because it is impossible (logically, of course) even to conceive of someone having the ability to perform logically inconsistent actions.

Several kinds of freedom are particularly important in discussions of human responsibility:

Moral freedom: the freedom to do good. As we have seen, Scripture teaches that Adam's fall took away our moral freedom, so that apart from grace we cannot (in terms of moral ability) please God. Christ sets us free from this bondage:

> Jesus replied, "I tell you the truth, everyone who sins is a slave to sin. Now a slave has no permanent place in the family, but a son belongs to it forever. So if the Son sets you free, you will be free indeed." (John 8:34–36; cf. Rom. 6:15–23; 2 Cor. 3:17)

Moral freedom is the most important kind of freedom mentioned in Scripture. It is the freedom from sin given to us by the redemptive work of Christ.

However, it is not a condition of moral responsibility. Those who are en-slaved to sin are morally responsible, just like those who are free in Christ.[21]

Compatibilist freedom: the freedom to do what you want to do. Jesus says:

> The good man brings good things out of the good stored up in his heart, and the evil man brings evil things out of the evil stored up in his heart. For out of the overflow of his heart his mouth speaks. (Luke 6:45; cf. Matt. 7:15–20; 12:33–35)

We act and speak, then, according to our character. We follow the deep-est desires of our heart. To my knowledge, Scripture never refers to this moral consistency as a kind of freedom, but the concept of heart-act consistency is important in Scripture, and theologians and philosophers have often re-ferred to it as freedom. In everyday life, we regularly think of freedom as doing what we want to do. When we don't do what we want, we are either acting irrationally or being forced to act against our will by someone or some-thing outside ourselves.

This kind of freedom is sometimes called compatibilism, because it is com-patible with determinism. Determinism is the view that every event (in-cluding human actions) has a sufficient cause other than itself. Compati-bilist freedom means that even if every act we perform is caused by something outside ourselves (such as natural causes or God), we are still free, for we can still act according to our character and desires.

There are some ambiguities in this concept, because there are different levels of human desires. Consider Billy again, who is forced by Mike, the older boy, to cover the school door with graffiti. Is Billy doing what he de-sires? In one sense, obviously not. Mike is forcing him to do what he doesn't want to do. Given Mike's threat, Billy is faced with two undesirable alter-natives: defacing the door or receiving bodily harm. Between those alter-natives, he chooses the one he desires most. So, in one sense, he does act according to his strongest desire, and in another sense he does not. We must distinguish here between Billy's overall preferences and his immediate concerns, and note that for a moment the two contradict each other. If we define compatibilist freedom in terms of Billy's overall preferences, then his act is not free. If we define it in terms of his immediate desires, then it

---

21. In an earlier note, I mentioned a third sense of *responsibility*, namely *moral integrity*. In that sense, *responsible* is an honorific term, as in "Jeff is such a responsible person." In that usage, Jeff is not only subject to moral evaluation, but also receives high marks in that evaluation. In that usage, only good people are responsible. But we are using the term dif-ferently here, so that it means only that people are subject to moral evaluation. In that sense, all people are responsible, whether or not they take their responsibilities seriously.

is free. But for purposes of judging Billy's responsibility, we would normally say that his action is not free.

On the compatibilist view, then, we can say that in one sense we always act according to our strongest desire, and in another sense we do not. We always act according to our strongest desire in the here and now, according to our strongest desire in each concrete situation. We would always like to act according to our broader preferences, but we do not always do that. So, in a compatibilist concept of freedom, we are always free to follow our most immediate desires, but not always free to carry out our more general desires.

Is compatibilist freedom a condition of moral responsibility? Yes, with the same qualifications we noted earlier with respect to Scripture's use of the principle that inability limits responsibility. The difference between murder and manslaughter, for example, is one of intention. In manslaughter, the perpetrator does not desire to take life. He does, in fact, take life, but that action does not reflect his desire. Or, to put it as we usually do, he does not have a motive for murder. He does not make a free (compatibilist) choice to kill, and therefore he should not be penalized as a murderer. But he does make other free choices, which a court might judge to amount to negligence, for which he should be penalized.

We have also seen in Scripture how ignorance limits responsibility to some extent. Part of the reason is that ignorance limits our freedom in a situation. We do what we would not want to do if we had greater knowledge. On the other hand, ignorance can be willful, as we have seen. We can desire ignorance over knowledge. Suppressing the truth can be a free act. Judges assume that that is so when they use the slogan "Ignorance of the law is no excuse." That freedom is also relevant to God's judgment.

But, as I indicated earlier, ability to overcome God's decree is not a condition of moral responsibility. The alleged freedom to overcome God's decree is not compatibilist, but libertarian (see below), and therefore not relevant to responsibility.

We also saw earlier that moral inability does not remove moral responsibility. Our study of compatibilist freedom can help us to see part of the reason why. Moral inability is simply the character of unregenerate human beings. They are free in the compatibilist sense to do what they desire to do, though their desires are evil. Moral inability does not in the least lessen compatibilist freedom, and so it does not lessen responsibility.

Libertarianism. The concept of freedom most often discussed in connection with moral responsibility is libertarianism. R. K. McGregor Wright defines this view as the belief that the human will has an inherent power to choose with equal ease between alternatives. This is commonly called "the power of contrary choice" or "the liberty of indifference." This belief does not claim that there are no influences that might affect the will, but it does insist that normally the will can overcome these factors and choose in spite of them. Ultimately, the will is free from any necessary causation. In other words, it is autonomous from outside determination.[22]

Libertarianism is sometimes called incompatibilism, because it is not compatible with determinism. Thus, it is a clear alternative to compatibilism. Libertarians emphasize that our choices are not determined in advance by God. On their view, God may be the first cause of the universe in general, but in the sphere of human decisions, we are the first causes of our actions. We have a godlike independence when we make free choices.

Furthermore, as Wright's definition implies, in libertarianism our decisions must also be independent of ourselves in a certain sense, paradoxical as that may sound. On the libertarian view, our character may influence our decisions, as may our immediate desires. But we always have the freedom to choose contrary to our character and our desires, however strong.

This position assumes that there is a part of human nature that we might call the will, which is independent of every other aspect of our being, and which can, therefore, make a decision contrary to every motivation.

Libertarians maintain that only if we have this kind of radical freedom can we be held responsible for our actions. Their principle is simple enough: if our decisions are caused by anything or anyone (including our own desires), they are not properly our decisions, and we cannot be held responsible for them. To be responsible, we must be able to do otherwise. And if our actions are caused by anything other than our free will, we are not able to do otherwise, and we are therefore not responsible.

A CRITIQUE OF LIBERTARIANISM

Libertarianism has a long history in Christian theology. Most of the church fathers more or less held this position until Augustine, during the Pelagian controversy, called it into question.[23] Since then, there has been

---

22. Wright, *No Place for Sovereignty* (Downers Grove, Ill.: InterVarsity Press, 1996), 43–44.
23. Those Calvinists who place great weight on antiquity and tradition will have to concede, therefore, that the oldest extracanonical traditions do not favor their position.

a contest between the Augustinian and the Pelagian conceptions of freedom, resulting sometimes in unstable mixtures of the two. Both Luther[24] and Calvin[25] maintained an Augustinian compatibilism, but the Socinians and later the Arminians offered vigorous defenses of libertarianism. Today the libertarian view prevails in much of evangelical Christianity and among Christian philosophers.[26] Theologically, it is defended by traditional Arminians,[27] open theists,[28] process thinkers,[29] and many others. Few theologians oppose it today, except for self-conscious Calvinists, and even some thinkers in the Reformed tradition gravitate toward libertarianism[30] or speak unclearly on the subject.[31]

But libertarianism is subject to severe criticisms:

1. The biblical data cited in chapter 4 about God's sovereign control over human decisions, even human sins, are incompatible with libertarianism.

---

24. Martin Luther, *The Bondage of the Will* (London: J. Clarke and Co., 1957).

25. See many writings of John Calvin, especially the treatise *Concerning the Eternal Predestination of God* (London: James Clarke and Co., 1961). The classic Calvinist refutation of libertarianism is Jonathan Edwards, *Freedom of the Will* (New Haven: Yale University Press, 1973).

26. Many Christian philosophers believe that libertarian freedom is essential to solve the problem of evil adequately. Alvin Plantinga's argument has been especially influential in this connection. See his *God, Freedom, and Evil* (Grand Rapids: Eerdmans, 1974).

27. The most cogent and complete Arminian argument, in my view, is Jack Cottrell, *What the Bible Says About God the Ruler* (Joplin, Mo.: College Press, 1984). See also the other two books in his trilogy on the doctrine of God.

28. Clark Pinnock et al., *The Openness of God* (Downers Grove, Ill.: InterVarsity Press, 1994).

29. For example, John B. Cobb and David R. Griffin, *Process Theology: An Introductory Exposition* (Philadelphia: Westminster Press, 1976).

30. See, for example, Plantinga's influential *God, Freedom, and Evil*.

31. See, for example, Benjamin Wirt Farley, *The Providence of God in Reformed Perspective* (Grand Rapids: Baker, 1988), and my review in *WTJ* 51 (1989): 397–400 (reprinted as appendix D in this book). Richard Muller, in "Grace, Election, and Contingent Choice: Arminius's Gambit and the Reformed Response," in *The Grace of God, the Bondage of the Will*, ed. Thomas R. Schreiner and Bruce A. Ware (Grand Rapids: Baker, 1995), 2:270, says, "It was never the Reformed view that the moral acts of human beings are predetermined, any more than it was ever the Reformed view that the fall of Adam was willed by God to the exclusion of Adam's free choice to sin." I agree that Reformed theology recognizes Adam's choice as free, but only in a compatibilist sense. Contrary to Muller, Reformed theologians did teach that God ordained the Fall (otherwise, why did supralapsarians and infralapsarians debate the *place* of the Fall among God's decrees?) and therefore ordained at least one human moral decision. And Scripture mentions many more human moral decisions ordained by God, as we saw in chapter 4. In fairness to Muller, he does recommend a compatibilist formulation at the top of page 269. But compatibilist freedom does not exclude, as he suggests it does, divine predetermination of moral acts.

Scripture makes clear that our choices are governed by God's eternal plan, even though we are fully responsible for them.

2. Scripture does not explicitly teach the existence of libertarian freedom. There is no passage that can be construed to mean that the human will is independent of God's plan and of the rest of the human personality. Libertarians generally don't even try to establish their position by direct exegesis (as, for example, I tried above to establish a biblical view of human ability and compatibilist freedom). Rather, they attempt to deduce it from other biblical concepts, such as human responsibility itself and the divine commands, exhortations, and pleadings[32] that imply human responsibility. But in this attempt, they accept a rather large burden of proof, which their arguments do not bear. Libertarianism is a rather technical philosophical notion, which makes various assumptions about causality, the relationship of will to action, the relationship of will to character and desire, and the limitation of God's sovereignty. It is a huge order to try to derive all these technical concepts from the biblical view of human responsibility, and I shall try to show below that libertarians' attempts to do so have been far from successful. And if they fail to bear this burden of proof, then we must abandon either libertarianism or *sola Scriptura*.

3. Scripture never grounds human responsibility (in the sense of accountability) in libertarian freedom, or, for that matter, in any other kind of freedom. We are responsible because God has made us, owns us, and has a right to evaluate our conduct. Therefore, according to Scripture, God's authority is the necessary and sufficient ground of human responsibility. Sometimes our ability or inability is relevant to God's judgment, and therefore to our responsibility in the sense of liability, as we have seen. But Scripture never suggests that libertarian freedom has any relevance at all, even to liability.

4. Nor does Scripture indicate that God places any positive value on libertarian freedom (even granting that it exists). That is a significant point, because the freewill defense against the problem of evil (see the next chapter) argues that God places such a high value on human free choice that he gave it to creatures even at the risk that they might bring evil into the world. One would imagine, then, that Scripture would abound with statements to the effect that causeless free actions by creatures are terribly important to God, that they bring him glory. But Scripture never suggests that God honors causeless choice in any way or even recognizes its existence.

---

32. I shall discuss at a later point how God can command and plead with sinners, even though he has foreordained their responses. Essentially, the answer is to distinguish between God's decrees and his precepts (see chap. 23).

5. Indeed, on the contrary, Scripture teaches that in heaven, the consummate state of human existence, we will not be free to sin. So the highest state of human existence will be a state without libertarian freedom. KEY

6. Scripture never judges anyone's conduct by reference to his libertarian freedom. Scripture never declares someone innocent because his conduct was not free in the libertarian sense; not does it ever declare someone guilty by pointing to his libertarian freedom. We have seen that Scripture sometimes refers implicitly to freedom or ability in the compatibilist sense. But it never refers to freedom in a demonstrably incompatibilist sense.

7. Indeed, Scripture condemns some people for acts that clearly were not free in a libertarian sense. Those acts mentioned in chapter 4 under "Sins" fall into this category, such as Judas's betrayal of Jesus. Even open theist Gregory Boyd admits that Judas's betayal was not free in the libertarian sense.[33]

8. In civil courts, libertarian freedom is never assumed to be a condition of moral responsibility. Consider Hubert, the bank robber. If guilt presupposed libertarian freedom, then in order to show that Hubert is guilty, the prosecutor would have to show that his decision to rob a bank was without any cause. But what evidence could a prosecutor bring forth to show that? Proving a negative is always difficult, and it would clearly be impossible to show that Hubert's inner decision was completely independent of any divine decree, natural cause, character, or motive. The same thing would be true for any criminal prosecution. Libertarianism would make it impossible to prove the guilt of anybody at all.

9. Indeed, civil courts normally assume the opposite of libertarianism, namely, that the conduct of criminals arises from motives. Accordingly, courts often spend much time discussing whether the defendant had an adequate motive to commit the crime. If Hubert's action could be shown to be independent of motives, then he would likely be judged insane and therefore *not* responsible, rather than guilty. Indeed, if Hubert's action was completely independent of his character, desires, and motives, one could well ask in what sense this action was really Hubert's.[34] And if it was not Hubert's action, how can he be held responsible for it? We see, then, that

33. Gregory A. Boyd, *God of the Possible* (Grand Rapids: Baker, 2000), 38.
34. One libertarian reply is that the will was Hubert's, and so the action was his. But what is meant by "will" here? Does Hubert's will have a character? Does it have preferences or desires? If so, then we are back to actions controlled by one's nature, which libertarianism rejects. Does it have no character at all? Then how is it any different from a mere force that acts at random and is quite separate from anything in Hubert? On that supposition, how can it be Hubert's will?

rather than being the foundation of moral responsibility, libertarianism destroys it.[35]

10. Scripture contradicts the proposition that only uncaused decisions are morally responsible. As we saw in chapter 4, God in Scripture often brings about the free actions, and even the sinful actions, of human beings, without in the least diminishing their responsibility. In the present chapter, we have seen how God's sovereign control of human actions and man's responsibility for the same actions are often mentioned together in the same passage.

11. Scripture denies that we have the independence demanded by libertarian theory. We are not independent of God, for he controls free human actions. Nor can we choose to act independently of our own character and desire. According to Matthew 7:15–20 and Luke 6:43–45, the good tree brings forth good fruit, and the evil tree brings forth evil fruit. If one's heart is right, his actions will be right; otherwise, they will be wrong.

12. Libertarianism, therefore, violates the biblical teaching concerning the unity of human personality in the heart. Scripture teaches that human hearts, and therefore our decisions, are wicked because of the Fall, but that the work of Christ and the regenerating power of the Spirit cleanse the heart so that our actions can be good. We are fallen and renewed as whole persons. This integrity of human personality is not possible in a libertarian construction, for on that view the will must always be independent of the heart and all of our other faculties.

13. If libertarian freedom were necessary for moral responsibility, then God would not be morally responsible for his actions, since he does not have the freedom to act against his holy character.[36] Similarly, the glorified saints in heaven would not be morally responsible, since they cannot fall again into sin. If they did have libertarian freedom, then they could fall into sin, as Origen speculated, in which case the redemption accomplished by Jesus would be insufficient to deal with sin, for it could not reach the inherent waywardness of human free will.

35. Calvinists and other antilibertarians often make this point in colorful ways. James H. Thornwell says, "As well might a weather-cock be held responsible for its lawless motions as a being whose arbitrary, uncontrollable will is his only law." *Collected Writings* (Edinburgh: Banner of Truth, 1974), 2:180. R. E. Hobart, arguing a secular form of determinism, says, "In proportion as [a person's action] is undetermined, it is just as if his legs should suddenly spring up and carry him off where he did not prefer to go." See his "Free Will as Involving Determinism and Inconceivable Without It," *Mind* 43 (January 1934): 7.

36. I shall say more about God's freedom in a later chapter.

14. Libertarianism is essentially a highly abstract generalization of the principle that inability limits responsibility. Libertarians say that if our decisions are afflicted by any kind of inability, then they are not truly free and we are not truly responsible for them. We saw earlier that inability does limit responsibility to some extent, but that this principle is not always valid, that we are always afflicted by some kinds of inability, and therefore that the principle must be used with great caution. Libertarianism throws caution to the wind.

15. Libertarianism is inconsistent, not only with God's foreordination of all things, but also with his knowledge of future events. If God knew in 1930 that I would wear a green shirt on July 21, 1998,[37] then I am not free to avoid wearing such a shirt on that date. Now libertarians make the point that God can know future events without causing them. But if God in 1930 knew the events of 1998, on what basis did he know them? The Calvinist answer is that he knows them because he knew his own plan for the future. But how, on an Arminian basis, could God have known my free act sixty-eight years in advance? Are my decisions governed by a deterministic chain of finite causes and effects? Is there some force or person other than God that renders future events certain—a being whom God passively observes? (That is a scary possibility, hardly consistent with monotheism.) None of these answers, nor any other that I can think of, is consistent with libertarianism. For this reason, the open theists,[38] like the Socinian opponents of Calvin, have denied a key element in traditional Arminianism, namely, God's exhaustive foreknowledge. That is a drastic step to take, as we shall see in our later discussion of God's knowledge (chap. 22). It seems to me that they would have been wiser to reject libertarianism, rather than drastically reconstruct their theology to make it consistent with libertarianism.

16. Libertarians like Pinnock and Rice tend to make their view of free will a nonnegotiable, central truth, with which all other theological statements must be made consistent. Libertarian freedom thus takes on a kind of paradigmatic or presuppositional status. But, as we have seen, libertarianism is unscriptural. It would be bad enough merely to assert libertarianism contrary to the Bible. But making it a central truth or governing perspective is very dangerous indeed. An incidental error can be corrected

---

37. This is, of course, a manner of speaking. I shall argue later that God's knowledge is timeless in a sense. But if God knows timelessly that I will wear a green shirt on July 21, 1998, then even in 1930 it was true to say that he knew I would wear a green shirt on July 21, 1998.

38. Clark Pinnock, Richard Rice, and others. See the reference to their book, *The Openness of God*, in footnote 28.

without much trouble. But when such an error becomes a major principle, a grid through which all other doctrinal statements are filtered, then a theological system is in grave danger of shipwreck.

17. Philosophical defenses of libertarianism often appeal to intuition as the basis for believing in free will.[39] That is, whenever we are faced with a choice, we feel that we could choose either way, even against our strongest desire.[40] We are sometimes conscious, they say, of combating our strongest desires. But whatever one may say in general about an appeal to intuition,[41] it can never be the basis for a universal negative. That is to say, intuition cannot reveal to anyone that his decisions have no cause. We never have anything that might be called a feeling of lack of causation.

Nor can intuition reveal to us that all our actions do have an outside cause. If all of our actions were determined by an agency outside ourselves, we could not identify that causation by any intuition or feeling, for we would have no way of comparing a feeling of causation with a feeling of noncausation. We can identify influences that sometimes prevail over us and sometimes don't—forces that we sometimes, but not always, resist successfully. But we cannot identify forces that constantly and irresistibly determine our thoughts and behavior. So intuition never reveals to us whether or not we are determined by causes outside ourselves.[42]

18. If libertarianism is true, then God has somehow limited his sovereignty so that he does not bring all things to pass. But Scripture contains no hint that God has limited his sovereignty in any degree. God is the Lord, from Genesis 1 to Revelation 22. He is always completely sovereign. He does whatever pleases him (Ps. 115:3). He works everything out according to the counsel of his will (Eph. 1:11). Furthermore, God's very nature is to be sovereign. Sovereignty is his name,

---

39. See, for example, C. A. Campbell, "The Psychology of Effort of Will," *Proceedings of the Aristotelian Society* 40 (1939–40): 49–74.

40. There is much argument in the literature over whether we can ever choose against our strongest desire. See my earlier comments on this question. Further, it seems to me that there is some confusion here as to the different ways in which a desire can be strong. If strength refers to an emotional power, then it is plausible to argue that however strong the desire is, we can always choose against it. But if strength refers to motivational effectiveness, then of course the strongest desire is that which actually motivates, and it is nonsense to talk about choosing contrary to one's strongest desire.

41. See *DKG*, 345–46, for my account.

42. Thanks to Steve Hays for this observation. He also points out that the libertarian appeal to intuition ignores the role of the subconscious in motivating our thoughts and behavior.

the very meaning of the name Yahweh, in terms of both control and authority. If God limited his sovereignty, he would become something less than Lord of all, something less than God. And if God became something less than God, he would destroy himself. He would no longer exist. We can see that the consequences of libertarianism are serious indeed.

FREEDOM IN THE WESTMINSTER CONFESSION

Still another kind of freedom discussed in this connection is that mentioned in the WCF 9.1:

> God hath endued the will of man with that natural liberty, that it is neither forced, nor, by any absolute necessity of nature, determined to good or evil.

The confession cites as proof texts Matthew 17:12, James 1:14, and Deuteronomy 30:19, which teach that human beings do choose to do what they will, statements compatible with either libertarianism or compatibilism. The confession denies libertarianism in 5.1 and 5.4. But the confession's reference to "absolute necessity of nature" suggests something more than compatibilism: the independence of human choices from sequences of cause and effect within nature, a freedom from natural causation.

As we have seen, Scripture (and the confession at 5.1 and 5.4) affirms that God governs all human actions. At 9.1, the confession suggests that at least some human actions may have no finite cause, though of course its earlier statements imply that those actions have a divine cause. I don't know anything in Scripture that would prove the suggestion of 9.1 to be true, but nor do I know of anything that would prove it false. But the statement cautions us against assuming that all our decisions are governed, not only by God, but also by a chain of finite causes. It opens up the possibility that some events may be determined by God's will, but not by anything in creation.

I don't think the confession's concept of natural liberty has much to do with moral responsibility. But it could be used to refute certain kinds of excuses for wrong actions. For example, if somebody says that he couldn't help stealing, since he was raised in a poor neighborhood, one could reply that there is no reason to think that being raised in a poor neighborhood *necessitates* theft. The thief is not "forced, not by any absolute necessity of nature, determined to good or evil."

CREATURELY OTHERNESS, INTEGRITY, AND SIGNIFICANCE

We have seen that, according to Scripture, human beings are fully re-sponsible for their actions. We are responsible to do everything to the glory of God. Responsibility is based on the fact that the Lord is our supreme au-thority, our supreme evaluator. In the course of his evaluation, God some-times takes our ability—our freedom—into account. In many cases, but not all, more ability means higher divine expectations, and less ability means lower expectations (Luke 12:48). But some abilities (moral ability and metaphysical ability) are not relevant at all to moral evaluation. Earlier, I rejected the claim of libertarianism that its abstract, generalized view of free will is essential to responsibility.

But the discussion so far leaves some important questions unanswered. We have so far concluded that human actions are completely under God's control. We are responsible for them simply because God has the right to evaluate them and to judge us for them. This conclusion is highly distasteful to many, especially to those attracted to libertarianism. They sense that this view dishonors man and reduces human significance. They think that on a compatibilist view of freedom, human beings are mere "robots," treated as mechanical things rather than as persons. Even worse, according to lib-ertarians, this view portrays God as judging and punishing man for things that he himself is actually responsible for.

However, we cannot distort the Bible's teaching in order to make it more palatable to people today. Even if there were no more to be said, even if there were no reply to these libertarian objections, we could not accept a nonbiblical view as the price of answering those objections. It would be better to leave the questions unanswered. For the time being, at least, these questions would define a realm of mystery. But there would be noth-ing wrong with that. Our God is so great, and his thoughts are so far above our thoughts; how could there not be unresolved mysteries in our under-standing of him?

Scripture is concerned, above all, to glorify God. Sometimes glorifying God humbles man, and those who believe Scripture must be willing to ac-cept that consequence. We covet for ourselves ever more dignity, honor, and status, and we resist accepting a lower place. But Scripture assaults our pride and honors the humble. Scripture compares us, after all, not to so-phisticated robots, but to simple potter's clay.

What if it turns out that we are robots, after all—clay fashioned into mar-velous robots, rather than being left as mere clay? Should we complain to God about that? Or should we rather feel honored that our bodies and minds are fashioned so completely to fulfill our assigned roles in God's great drama? Some creatures are born as rabbits, some as cockroaches, and some as bacteria. By comparison, would it not be a privilege to be born as an intelligent robot?

Indeed, what remarkable robots we would be—capable of love and intimacy with God, and assigned to rule over all the creatures. Is it not a wonderful blessing of grace that, when we sinned in Adam, God did not simply discard us, as a potter might very well do with his clay, and as a robot operator might well do with his malfunctioning machine, but sent his only Son to die for us? Risen with him to new life, believers enjoy unimaginably wonderful fellowship with him forever.

As we meditate upon these dignities and blessings, the image of the robot becomes less and less appropriate, not because God's control over us appears less complete, but because one doesn't treat robots with such love and honor.

Some writers seem to think that the lack of "real" (that is, libertarian) freedom would invalidate all the other blessings of this life. But is that really the case? Libertarian freedom, as we have seen, amounts to the arbitrary activity of a meaningless "will." Would we really give up all the blessings of this life in order to gain experiences of random activity?

But even if we set aside the objections of libertarians, we are left with some uneasiness and many unanswered questions. Why does God lavish such attention and love upon creatures over whom he has complete control? With the psalmist, we wonder,

> What is man that you are mindful of him,
>   the son of man that you care for him? (Ps. 8:4)

The psalmist's question comes precisely out of meditation on God's majesty and sovereignty. God has "ordained praise" from the lips of children to silence his enemies (v. 2). Why should such a God, who can simply ordain praise to himself whenever he wants, even from stones (Luke 19:40), give to man the lavish care and high authority described in the later verses of this psalm?

It is evident that God's relationship to his creatures, even though it involves complete "control," is far more than what we usually think of as control. And it is more, too, than what we usually think of as authority. So far in this chapter, we have focused on the first two lordship attributes. Now we must see how the third might help us.   CONTROL + AUTHORITY

Covenant presence means that God cares for his world. He does not set it in motion and leave it to run on its own. He remains with and in the world, to control it, to evaluate it, to bless and to judge it. He is the pot-

ter and the world is his clay, but it is not merely clay. The potter-clay analogy is a good image of God's prerogatives over us, and indeed it is literally
true that we are made of dust (Gen. 2:7). But other biblical images and
metaphors, such as "the image of God" in which man is made (Gen.
1:27–28), indicate that we are very special dust. And the dust itself, the
material creation, is, as we have seen, the object of God's wise providence.

Why should the world matter to God? Why is it significant and important to him? Some have argued that it can have no meaning if God has
complete control over it. But Scripture says that the world is meaningful
and significant *because* it is God's creation and the subject of his providence.
But what is its significance, apart from the significance of God himself?

At this point, we need to consider in more detail the relationship between Creator and creature. First, as we have seen, it is wrong to say that
because God is present, the world is God and God is the world. Covenant
presence is quite inconsistent with pantheism, for covenant presence presupposes that God and the world are different from one another. It distinguishes the world from the God who is present in and with it. He is present as the sovereign Lord, as the controller and authority. So the world is
significant, a "significant other" to God.

God's decrees foreordain, and his creative act brings into actuality, beings other than himself. Creation marks the beginning, then, of nondivine
"otherness." Of course, otherness does exist eternally within the triune divine nature. But creation is the beginning of something new: a *nondivine*
otherness, a *creaturely* otherness. Creatures are the work of God, fully
planned by him, dependent on him, and under his control. But they are
not God, not extensions of his nature.

Creaturely otherness is linked to a number of Christian mysteries and
controversies. We shall discuss later the doctrine of creation "out of nothing," the divine act that brings the creaturely other into being. How can
anything come out of nothing? And granted that God has the power to
create, how can the creation be anything other than God, since prior to
creation only God exists?

There is also some mystery about the integrity of creaturely otherness.
By *integrity*, I mean the ability of things to exist and function on their own
terms, to be distinct from other objects, to play their own distinct roles in
history. The integrity of creatures is not simply the integrity of God's nature, although creatures are certainly dependent on God ("contingent")
for their existence and functioning. God's own integrity certainly sustains
the existence and functioning of creatures. But since God has ordained creatures to be different from him, he has given them natures and functions
different from his own. When a man dies, for example, God does not die.

The man dies because that is his individual destiny. Each item in creation has its own role to play in God's wise plan. Its role is different in some way from the roles of other created things, and certainly very different from God's own role.

Therefore, if the words *independence* and *autonomy* were not so often attached to unbiblical notions like libertarianism, it might be possible to use them to describe the integrity of creaturely otherness. The human life you live has its own significance, surely granted by God, but different from God's own significance and in that sense independent of it. Of course, that life is also *dependent* on God's plan for history and his providential rule. Once God formulates his plan and creates the world, created individuals have stable, historical roles that are distinct from God himself and sometimes even opposed to him. And once God grants these roles to creatures, he will not take them away, for to do so would violate his own plan.

If God has ordained that Bill will live to be eighty years old, he will not change his mind and take Bill's life at sixty. God's plan is eternal and unchangeable. It is consistent with itself. Just as God keeps his promises, so he also sees to it that his decree is fulfilled.[43] But that means that Bill has the power to live until age eighty, and that not even God can change that, for not even God can violate his own decree.

Does God, then, limit his sovereignty? Yes and no. No, because this creaturely integrity is itself part of God's decree. At no point does God relinquish control over his world.

But I stress again that God's decree is not irrational or inconsistent with itself. In that sense, as Reformed theologians have always said, God cannot simply do anything. He cannot do something that contradicts his nature. And he cannot include one thing in his plan that contradicts another. In that sense, God is limited by the consistency of his own plan.

And that limitation has something to do with the nature of creaturely otherness. For God to be consistent with himself, he must also be consistent with Bill. God knows that, according to his plan, Bill will die at eighty. That is a fact about God's plan; it is also a fact that God foreknows about Bill. All other things that God ordains for Bill must be consistent with this reality.

We can picture God planning the universe as a man puts together a jigsaw puzzle. The individual pieces must fit with one another and with the whole. The shape of one piece determines what piece may fit next to it.

---

43. In our discussion of God's will (chap. 23), we shall consider the distinction between God's decrees and his precepts, or between his "decretive will" and his "preceptive will." In general, God's decrees represent his control, and his precepts represent his authority.

ETERNAL FOREKNOWLEDGE
AND
ETERNAL FOREORDINATION

The analogy is imperfect, of course, because God is not faced, as puzzle solvers are, with pieces made by somebody else. He makes all the pieces, and he fully controls each part as well as the whole. But he does plan the universe both as a whole and in its individual parts.[44] So because he is a wise God, he must, like the puzzle solver, fit the pieces together in a consistent, meaningful, and rational way.[45]

One can say, then, that God's plan is limited by what he knows about Bill. He foreordains according to his foreknowledge.[46] But it would be equally true to say that in this case one part of God's plan simply furnishes a logical limit to another part of it.

Arminians say that God's foreordination is based on his foreknowledge. The Calvinist need not deny that this is the case. But he should go on, then, and point out to the Arminian that that foreknowledge itself is in turn based upon foreordination!

There is in God's mind a reciprocity between foreknowledge and foreordination. Neither is simply "prior" to the other. Both are eternal. And, logically, God's knowledge is based on what he foreordains. But his foreordination is not an ignorant foreordination. He does not foreordain at random a set of circumstances and then look upon those circumstances with surprise. His plan is a wise one, formulated according to knowledge.[47]

Here we may reflect a bit on the concept of God's "middle knowledge,"

44. Recall, for example, that individual believers are chosen in Christ before the foundation of the world (Eph. 1:4).

45. In our discussion of God's omnipotence (chap. 23), we shall discuss how God is and is not limited by logic and by his own nature. In general, God cannot do anything that contradicts who he is. He cannot, therefore, be other than wise, and therefore logical. But his logic is not necessarily identical with that of any human logical system.

46. Note how the WCF describes God's providence: "God the great Creator of all things doth uphold, direct, dispose, and govern all creatures, actions, and things . . . by His most wise and holy providence, *according to His infallible foreknowledge,* and the free and immutable counsel of His own will" (5.1) (emphasis added). Here "foreknowledge," I think, refers to God's prescience, his knowledge of the future, rather than (as sometimes in Scripture and Calvinist theology) to God's eternal decree of salvation, for it is joined to the word "infallible" and is followed by a statement of the eternal decree. So God governs the world both by his eternal decree and by his infallible foreknowledge.

47. I am always suspicious of the idea of priorities within the mind of God. God's mind is eternal and simple. There is not in his mind a process in which one thought leads to another, nor is there a contest in which ideas strive to supplant one another. Everything in God's mind takes everything else into consideration. So his foreordination and his foreknowledge are eternally in perfect accord. There is no process by which the one produces the other or gets reconciled to the other. (Of course, God's settled purpose does contain priorities in the sense that it establishes certain events as more important than others, some as instrumental to others, and so on.)

KEY

[handwritten: THE DIVINE SIMPLICITY ie GOD'S KNOWLEDGE AND WILL ARE IDENTICAL IN THE DIVINE SIMPLICITY. GODS KNOWLEDGE + WILL ARE EACH A PERSPECTIVE ON GOD'S NATURE + PLAN.]

Human Responsibility and Freedom   151

as it has developed in the history of theology.[48] Middle knowledge is God's knowledge of what takes place under various conditions. His "necessary knowledge" is of everything possible, while his "free knowledge" is of everything actual. "Middle knowledge" is of things hypothetical and their results. To Molina, who first formulated the concept, middle knowledge is based, not upon God's nature or plan, but upon his perceptions of the independent (in the bad sense!) behavior of possible creatures in possible circumstances. Molina held, in other words, to a radical libertarianism. Reformed theology, of course, denies this. But Reformed theology does not deny that God has knowledge of hypothetical matters. He knows what will happen, for example, if David stays at Keilah and if he leaves Keilah.[49]

So God knows that if Bill is fatally shot at sixty, he cannot live to be eighty. Therefore, as part of his eternal plan, God prevents Bill from being fatally shot at sixty. God's will is formulated according to knowledge, including his foreknowledge of creatures; but his knowledge is also dependent upon the decisions of his will.

God does not limit his sovereignty, but his eternal plan does take creaturely integrity into account. God does not want to make creatures who have no integrity. Thus, he makes beings who are fitted to carry out their distinctive purposes, and the other elements in his plan respect those purposes. *[handwritten margin: See Bottom of Page 148]*

While this position is clearly Reformed, rather than Arminian, it does provide us with some talking points in discussions with Arminians. When they argue on behalf of free will and limited divine sovereignty, they may be erroneously groping for a genuinely scriptural point, namely, the reality of creaturely otherness and its integrity.

Indeed, we can tell the Arminian that God does take human nature into account when he formulates his eternal plan for us. But that is only one perspective! The other perspective is that God's knowledge of our nature is itself dependent upon his plan to make us in a particular way. God's will is based on his knowledge, and his knowledge is based on his will. Ultimately, all the attributes, including knowledge and will, are identical in the divine simplicity. But each attribute is a perspective on his nature and plan. The problem with the Arminian, then, is not so much what he affirms, but what he denies. His problem may also be described as monoper-

48. For a thorough discussion of middle knowledge, see chapter 22, where I will give reasons for rejecting the concept as used by Molina, Suarez, Arminius, and such modern writers as William L. Craig and Alvin Plantinga.

49. In 1 Sam. 23:9–13, God reveals to David what the men of Keilah will do to him if he stays there. So he leaves Keilah, and of course what God revealed to him does not take place. This passage indicates that God knows what will happen in any hypothetical situation, even those that never take place.

spectivalism—an insistence on looking at the problem from only one perspective.[50]

Another way to understand what I am saying is to take into account the
third lordship attribute, God's covenant presence. God not only controls
us and speaks to us with authority, but also grants to us a role to play in his
great plan. In one sense, we are tools in his hand to accomplish his vast
purpose for the universe. But, in another sense, the universe is his tool for
accomplishing his purpose in each of us. His vast power controls us, but
he always acts in full knowledge of who we are and in profound commitment to accomplish his individual purpose for each of us. Everything that
happens furthers that commitment. Therefore, Paul can say, "And we
know that in all things God works for the good of those who love him, who
have been called according to his purpose" (Rom. 8:28). Paul is speaking
here of believers, but we recall that God also raises up the wicked for the
day of disaster.

In this sense, we can say reverently that human beings (more precisely,
God's foreknowledge of each of us) influence God's eternal plan.[51] God's
sovereign plan includes a covenant commitment to every creature, to fulfill the role of that creature. That truth should be a central element in our
view of human freedom, responsibility, and significance. To feel free is to
feel that one has a significant role to play in the world, and that is true of
all of us. To feel responsible is to affirm for ourselves the purpose for which
God has made us. To feel significant is to recognize that God has given each
of us an important role in history, and that he has arranged everything else
in the universe to be consistent with that role.

DIVINE AND HUMAN CAUSALITY

We are important, not only because we are different from God and
in covenant with him, but also because we are his image. Much about
the divine image is mysterious, because God himself is mysterious. But,

50. I might add that monoperspectivalism is also a problem in hyper-Calvinism, from
the opposite side.

51. Reformed theology has acknowledged this kind of divine-human relationship, for
example, in the doctrine of accommodation. This doctrine says that God reveals himself
in a form suited to creaturely understanding. In Scripture, for example, he uses human language, generally understandable to people with ordinary intelligence. Remember that revelation itself is the execution of a divine decree. God has decreed to reveal himself in a way
that is consistent with the nature of the creatures he has decreed to make. For other examples, see the storyteller model later in this chapter.

among other things, there does seem to be something in us that is analogous to God's creativity, and that is relevant to our freedom and significance.[52]

When God creates, he chooses to actualize one world among many possible worlds, as contemporary modal logicians like to put it. He chooses one possible world and rejects others. Human choice is also an activity of affirming one alternative and rejecting others. This aspect of choice has much to do with our intuition or feeling of freedom. Perhaps, indeed, it should be considered a fifth kind of freedom, in addition to moral agency, compatibilism, libertarianism, and the "natural liberty" of WCF 9.1. I am inclined, however, to see it as an aspect of compatibilism: we act according to our desires, and our desires move us to choose some possibilities over others.

It is an interesting philosophical question to ask what the ontological status of rejected possibilities is. They are not simply nothing, for they are objects of knowledge. As we saw in the last section, God *knows* what will happen if David remains in Keilah. God knows not only facts, but hypothetical situations, the outcomes of contrary-to-fact conditions.[53] But, in the most obvious sense, these possibilities are not "real" either.

However we respond to that question, we should note that human beings steer their lives through a thicket of possibilities, choosing again and again what direction to take, what possibility to actualize, what possibility to leave to the side. There are analogies to such choices in the animal kingdom, but the uniqueness of human rationality, power, and community gives our choices a complexity and significance far beyond the decisions of any animal.

God holds us responsible for these choices, not only because of his lordship attribute of authority, but also because he is imaged in our power of choice. That power is a wonderful gift from God—wonderful not because of any connection with libertarian freedom, but because it is truly godlike. This gift speaks not of our independence from divine causation, but of our participation in God's creativity. For our choices image the choices that God himself has made in eternity, and they serve as the means by which God actualizes and rejects possibilities in history.

This is another reason why we feel free. We often feel that we face real alternatives, that in some sense we are able to choose any of them. So, for still another reason, the robot metaphor is inappropriate.

---

52. I am indebted (with thanks) to Vern Poythress for many of the thoughts in this section.
53. So the philosophical literature sometimes speaks of "counterfactuals of freedom."

MODELS OF DIVINE AND HUMAN AGENCY

I have argued that God is completely in control of the world, and that man is nevertheless fully responsible for his own actions. I have also tried to shed some light on the mystery of how this can be so, and of how God and man can both play significant roles in the course of nature and history. But that discussion has been complicated. Are there any useful pictures or illustrations that will assist our thinking in these areas? Let us consider some proposals:[54]

Pilot and copilot. The pilot and the copilot both play roles in bringing the plane to its destination. But this is not a good picture of divine and human agency, because when the copilot is flying the plane, the pilot is not doing so. Only one of them is directing the plane at any time. But in Scripture, God's control and man's action are both involved in bringing about the same historical results: recall how God brought about the action of Joseph's brothers in sending him to Egypt.

Teacher and classroom. A good schoolteacher is in control of his class, but he does not cause every action of every student. He is in control, in that he has set boundaries that he has the power to enforce. But the students make their decisions independently of him, within those boundaries. In this picture, of course, the teacher represents God, and the students represent the creation, especially God's rational creatures. This model is favorable to a libertarian view of freedom, and it attempts to reconcile libertarianism with a significant form of divine sovereignty.

In Scripture, God certainly does set boundaries. Sometimes, as with the king of Assyria in Isaiah 10, or with the devil himself in the book of Job, God permits his creatures to do certain evil things, but sets limits. God, however, is different from even the best human teacher, in that he has the power to control every thought, word, and deed of those under his lordship. God could have prevented the king of Assyria from invading Israel, but he chose not to. So when God "permits" creatures to do things contrary to his will, it is because he intends for them to do those things.[55] This is the same as if he had explicitly brought those things to pass. So the teacher-classroom model is misleading as a picture of divine sovereignty and human freedom.

---

54. Thanks here also to Vern Poythress for suggesting a discussion along these lines and for many of the ideas of this section. I take full responsibility for them, of course!

55. How can God intend for people to do wicked things? That is the subject of the next chapter.

Primary and secondary cause. We are accustomed to thinking of nature as a complex sequence of causes and effects, in which cause A brings about effect B, which in turn serves as the cause of effect C, and so on. We may picture these relationships on a billiard table: the motion of one ball causes the motion of a second, and of a third, and so on. We sometimes describe A as the "primary" or "remote" cause of C, and B as the "secondary" or "proximate" cause of C.

This model has been common in Reformed thought. Calvin defended God against the charge of being the author of sin by pointing out that God was not the proximate, but only the remote cause of human sin.[56] Many other Reformed thinkers have followed suit.[57] But I find it unpersuasive to defend God's goodness merely by saying that his involvement with sin is indirect.[58] In legal contexts, we hold a gang leader guilty for the crimes he orders his subordinates to commit, even though the leader does not personally commit them; we may recall the infamous case of Charles Manson in this connection. This principle is scriptural. As we have seen, the owner of a bull is responsible for the damage his bull causes, even though the owner did not do the damage himself (Ex. 21:28–36).

Furthermore, as we shall see in our discussion of providence, God's involvement with creation is in some senses always direct. Not even the smallest motion of the smallest object can occur without his government, preservation, and concurrence. He operates in and with the secondary causes, as well as by them.

The model is not wrong in saying that God often works through secondary causes. It is wrong, however, in suggesting that God does not also work directly, in and with his creation. Insofar as it does, it compromises with the nonbiblical concept of transcendence that we mentioned in chapter 7.

The commander and his troops. This model brings out the fact that God exercises his control particularly through his word, illustrating the unity

56. Calvin, *Concerning the Eternal Predestination of God* (London: James Clarke and Co., 1961).

57. See, for examples, Cornelius Van Til, *The Defense of the Faith* (Philadelphia: Presbyterian and Reformed, 1975), 183–87, and Gordon H. Clark, *Religion, Reason, and Revelation* (Philadelphia: Presbyterian and Reformed, 1961), 238–40.

58. James 1:13–15, of course, tells us that God never tempts or entices us to sin; his Word always prompts us toward holiness and righteousness. But that is a different issue. Again, I refer the reader to the discussion of God's decretive and preceptive wills in chapter 23. Preceptively, God commends only goodness; decretively, he sometimes ordains evil. We shall discuss the problem of evil in the next chapter.

of his control with his authority. He performs all his works by speaking: creation, providence, judgment, redemption. He makes the world by speaking (Gen. 1:3; Ps. 33:6), directs nature by his speech (Pss. 147:15–20; 148:7–8), judges us by his law, saves us by his gospel, and draws us into his fellowship by his effectual calling. Jesus heals the centurion's servant by commanding the disease to leave him, just as the centurion commands his troops and they obey (Luke 7:1–10).

This model focuses on the lordship attribute of authority, as the previous one focused on the lordship attribute of control. This one emphasizes the personal character of God's causality. God is much less like a billiard ball in motion than he is like a general (even better, a father), who accomplishes his purposes by the personal means of speaking.

The model does need to be generalized, however, to include forms of the word of God other than commands. God also accomplishes his purposes (in Scripture, for example) by such things as making promises, expressing love, and sharing with us the poetry of his own heart.

Author and characters in a story. No analogy is a perfect description of the Creator-creature relationship, because that relationship is unique. But I do believe that the author-character model conveys significant insight. The author has complete control over his characters. But, as I indicated in my discussion of creaturely otherness, the author seeks to make the characters and events fit together in a coherent and artistic way. Once he conceives of a character, that character takes on a life of its own, as we say, and the author takes responsibility to shape the events of the story in light of the integrity of the character. And of course the reverse is also true: he shapes the character to fit with integrity into the story.

In a well-wrought story, there is a causal nexus within the world that the author creates. Events can be explained, not only by the author's intention, but also by the structure of "secondary causes" within the world of the story. When events can be explained only by the author's intention, we often use terms like *deus ex machina*. Ordinarily, the intrusion of arbitrary elements that are not explainable within the world of the story is the mark of an unskilled writer.

In Shakespeare's play *Macbeth*, Macbeth kills King Duncan for his own reasons, using resources that are available to him.[59] Duncan's death can be described entirely by causes and effects within the world of the play. But the author, Shakespeare, is the ultimate cause of everything. Furthermore,

59. I have adapted this illustration from Wayne Grudem, *Systematic Theology* (Grand Rapids: Zondervan, 1994), 321–22.

although Duncan's death can be explained by causes within the drama, the author is not just the "primary cause" who sets in motion a chain of causes and effects that unfold without his further involvement. Rather, he writes every detail of the narrative and dialogue; as author, he is involved in everything that happens. So there are two complete causal chains. Every event in *Macbeth* has two causes, two sets of necessary and sufficient conditions: the causes within the play itself, and the intentions of Shakespeare.

The reason why every event in *Macbeth* can have two complete causes without irrationality is that the two sets of causes are on different levels. In a sense, Shakespeare and his character Macbeth live in two different worlds. Shakespeare could, of course, have written into the play a character representing himself. He could have entered the drama from his side. But Macbeth cannot ascend from his position in the drama and become an author on the same level as Shakespeare.

The two worlds, then, are sufficiently distinct that the two causal chains play different roles. Perhaps it is misleading to call them both causal, though we can certainly understand why it is natural to do so.

We can see one reason why Macbeth is responsible for his actions, even though Shakespeare in one sense "made him" kill Duncan. In his world, on his level, Macbeth is the necessary and sufficient cause of Duncan's death. He is fully to blame.

So Macbeth is responsible within the plane of the story—horizontally, we might say. But is he also responsible vertically? Is he responsible to Shakespeare as we are responsible to God? Well, here the analogy bogs down a bit, but some things can be said. First, Macbeth the character has not received revelation of Shakespeare's existence, nor is he held responsible for a covenant relationship with Shakespeare, as we are for our relationship with God. But an author other than Shakespeare might take on an even more godlike role: entering the drama to reveal his own standards to the characters, provoke them in some way to respond to this revelation, and then judge their responses. So vertical responsibility is possible within the authorial model. Second, Shakespeare was probably a theist, and in the play he created a world in which characters are responsible to God, not to himself. But Shakespeare is also an authority in Macbeth's world, for he sets up the standards by which Macbeth's actions will be evaluated. Shakespeare is not a modern nihilist; the world of his plays is a world in which traditional (mainly biblical) moral standards prevail. Shakespeare invents the plot that brings Macbeth down, since the playwright judges that downfall to be appropriate. So, in an important sense, Macbeth is responsible to Shakespeare.

We can see how various elements of this analogy reflect God's relationship to us: (1) God's creativity, (2) his fitting of characters to the plot and vice versa, (3) the two complete causal structures, (4) God's complete control, (5) his involvement in every detail of the story, (6) the two distinct levels of reality, (7) the asymmetry by which God has the power in himself to become man, but we don't have any power to become God, and (8) creaturely responsibility to other creatures and to God.

The relationship between the author and his characters is analogous to the third lordship attribute, covenant presence. The author is always present in the drama, arranging it to fit the characters, and the characters to fit the drama. He blesses and judges, using his own standards of evaluation. He is committed to the world he has made. His characters take on lives of their own, lives of creaturely otherness. He does not treat them as robots, even though he has complete control over them. Rather, he interacts with them on a personal level, treating them as responsible individuals with whom he enjoys a certain communion.[60] In the sense I mentioned earlier, God's creatures influence his plan, even though he has complete control over nature and history. So between God and his creatures there is a certain give-and-take, as is characteristic of personal relationships.

This analogy is imperfect, chiefly in that the characters of a novel are fictitious, while the creatures of God are real.[61] God's creative achievement is, therefore, far greater than that of any human writer. Nevertheless, the parallels are worth our meditation.

Our model suggests exciting ways of looking at the course of nature and history. As with any story, human history is plagued by terrible difficulties that seem impossible to remedy. The Fall brings a radical change in human character. We have no resources for dealing with it. But God surprises us with the most amazing and wonderful deliverance: life from the death of his Son. This is not a *deus ex machina*, for Jesus is perfectly human as well as perfectly divine. As man, he must endure all the temptations, sorrows, and miseries of the fallen world. But he rises glorious from the dead to rule all the nations and to bring his purposes to pass. We continue to live amid sorrows that are, from the standpoint of our own resources, impenetrable. But we look forward to great surprises, as God comes to humble the proud and exalt the lowly in his grand resolution of the story.

60. Dorothy Sayers is said to have fallen in love with her fictional detective, Lord Peter Wimsey. When Ayn Rand was asked whom she most admired, she cited several heroes from her novels. Writing a novel is often a give-and-take between author and characters, similar to relations among persons. Indeed, a novelist develops his characters much like a mother raises her children, until they come to behave like real human beings.

61. Also, human authors are limited by their finite intellect and imagination, by the constraints of time, by the need to write according to acceptable genres, and so on. God's creativity transcends these limitations.

Jesus also emerges from the broader historical process in the most wonderful way. For many centuries, God has prepared Israel for the coming of Christ, through prophecies, types, shadows, and redemptive events. When he arrives, he frustrates their messianic expectations. But, with a deeper understanding of Scripture (see Luke 24:25–32), we perceive a profound organic unity between the Old Testament and Jesus' life, death, and resurrection. There is tension, but also a deeper unity between the Lord and his historical environment. Thus, Scripture bears the mark of a great drama: tension, surprise, and shock, but nevertheless with a profound sense of inevitability.

As literature alone, this story would be fascinating. What is all the more wonderful is that it is real. And as we read on excitedly through a well-crafted novel to delight in the author's creative resolutions of tensions, far more may we look at the trials of this life in the confident expectation that God will resolve the tensions in a way that will delight. Thus we are encouraged to look forward to God's complete victory over sin as the final solution of the problem of evil.

In the next chapter, we shall explore in other ways how this model may aid our consideration of the problem of evil. The model is not the final statement on the relationship between God and ourselves, but it does draw our attention to biblical emphases and encourage biblical ways of thinking.

CHAPTER 9

The Problem of Evil

The second major problem we will discuss is the relationship between evil and God's sovereign lordship. The problem of evil is probably the most difficult problem in all of theology, and for many atheists it is the Achilles' heel of the theistic worldview.[1] In a nutshell, the problem is this: How can there be any evil in the world, if God exists? Or to put it more formally:

1. If God is omnipotent, he is able to prevent evil.
2. If God is good, he wants to prevent evil.
3. But evil exists.
Conclusion: either God is not omnipotent, or he is not good.

As I have formulated it, the argument assumes that God exists. But the conclusion is often taken as a *reductio ad absurdum* of that assumption. To say that God is not omnipotent or not good is to say that the God of the Bible does not exist.

The above syllogism is sometimes called "the logical problem of evil," for it accuses the theistic worldview of logical inconsistency. The charge is that theists believe in an omnipotent, good God, but inconsistently be-

---

1. I have discussed the problem of evil in AGG, 149–90, and in CVT, 83–86. I have not changed my view in any substantive way since writing those books, so there will be some overlap between them and the present chapter. However, it would not be possible to write a book on the doctrine of God without a treatment of the problem of evil. So I will have to beg the patience of some readers as I repeat myself. Perhaps it will help them if I note that this chapter contains a few observations that are new to me.

160

lieve also that evil exists. Often, of course, the problem of evil is felt, rather than argued. "The emotional problem of evil" is simply the agony we feel when we experience tragedy in life, and we cry out, "Why, Lord?"

Another distinction that we should initially make is between natural and moral evil. The former includes anything that brings suffering, unpleasantness, or difficulty into the lives of creatures. Earthquakes, floods, diseases, injuries, and death are examples of natural evil. Moral evil is the sin of rational creatures (angels and men). According to Scripture, moral evil came first. Satan's temptations and the disobedience of Adam and Eve led to God's curse upon the earth:

> Cursed is the ground because of you;
> > through painful toil you will eat of it
> > all the days of your life.
> It will produce thorns and thistles for you,
> > and you will eat the plants of the field.
> By the sweat of your brow
> > you will eat your food
> until you return to the ground,
> > since from it you were taken;
> for dust you are,
> > and to dust you will return. (Gen. 3:17–19)

God will remove this curse only on the final day, the consummation of Jesus' redemption, when he executes his final judgment and this world is replaced by a new heaven and a new earth. In the meantime, the whole creation "has been groaning as in the pains of childbirth" (Rom. 8:22) "in eager expectation for the sons of God to be revealed" (v. 19).

Scripture, therefore, gives us an explicit answer to the problem of natural evil. Natural evil is a curse brought upon the world because of moral evil. It functions as punishment to the wicked and as a means of discipline for those who are righteous by God's grace. It also reminds us of the cosmic dimensions of sin and redemption. Sin brought death to the human race, but also to the universe over which man was to rule. God has ordained that the universe resist its human ruler until that ruler stops resisting God. So in redemption, God's purpose is no less than "to reconcile to himself all things, whether things on earth or things in heaven" (Col. 1:20). The unanswered question is the problem of moral evil: how can sin exist in a theistic universe? I shall therefore focus on moral evil for the rest of this chapter.

I will assume a strong concept of divine omnipotence, based on the discussion to appear in chapter 23 and on our previous discussion (in chap.

[handwritten: God's Omnipotence / God's Goodness / God's Righteousness]

4) of the efficacy of God's sovereign control. Granted what we have already seen about God's sovereignty, the various attempts to show that God is too weak to prevent evil[2] do not seem promising. I shall also assume the goodness of God, which is implicit in our previous discussion of holiness (chap. 2), in the exposition of *yahweh* in Exodus 34:6–7, in the terse Johannine affirmation "God is love" (1 John 4:8, 16), and in many other passages (see chaps. 20–21). Exodus 34:6–7 also teaches the righteousness of God, as does Deuteronomy 32:4, "He is the Rock, his works are perfect, and all his ways are just." He does not take pleasure in evil (Ps. 5:4). His eyes are too pure to look on evil; he cannot tolerate it (Hab. 1:13).[3] I shall expound these divine attributes at greater length later in the book, but for now, we must take them as given to us by God's own revelation. I will not consider solutions that call these attributes into question.

Common defenses[4] against the problem may be divided into three general types. The first focuses on the nature of evil, the second on the ways in which evil contributes to the overall good of the universe, and the third on God's agency with regard to evil. I shall consider these in succession.

THE NATURE OF EVIL

The Christian Science sect and some forms of Hinduism maintain that evil is an illusion. If it is, of course, then the problem of evil disappears. But this claim is easily refuted. Even if evil does not exist in the real world, it certainly exists in our own minds and feelings. Even Christian Scientists and Hindus will concede that much. If it is an illusion, it is a deeply troubling one, and the very pain of it raises the problem of evil again. How can a good and omnipotent God allow us to be troubled by such illusions? So this proposal merely shifts the problem of evil to another level and therefore fails as a solution. It also fails as a claim about the world, for illusions are, after all, themselves real evils. The fact that human beings often fail

2. As in the book by Harold Kushner, *When Bad Things Happen to Good People* (New York: Schocken, 1981), but also in the literature of process theology. See David Ray Griffin, *God, Power, and Evil* (Philadelphia: Westminster, 1976), and his *Evil Revisited* (Albany: State University of New York Press, 1991), reviewed by me in *Calvin Theological Journal* 27 (1992): 435–38, reprinted as appendix H in this volume.

3. Of course, Habakkuk brings up this principle in order to ask God why he *has* been tolerating evil. In effect, Habakkuk is raising the problem of evil.

4. Alvin Plantinga, in *God, Freedom, and Evil* (Grand Rapids: Eerdmans, 1974), makes a useful distinction between a "defense" and a "theodicy." The latter has the goal of justifying God's ways to men, of demonstrating the goodness of all his actions. The former merely seeks to show that the problem of evil does not disprove the God of the Bible.

to distinguish between illusion and reality is itself an evil that must be dealt with. So if evil is an illusion, it is not an illusion. The illusionist view refutes itself.

Another view that attempts to put evil into a shadowy metaphysical category is that evil is a privation. This view is far more widespread within Christendom than the previous one, having been advocated by Augustine, the Catholic and post-Reformation scholastic traditions, and many modern apologists and theologians. To say that evil is a privation is not to say that it is an illusion. It is rather to say that it not something positive. It is a lack, a defect in a good universe. It is an absence of good, rather than the presence of something not good. Further, it is an absence of good where good should be. We do not consider it evil that a tree is unable to see, but we do pity a human being who lacks sight. Evil is, therefore, not a mere absence of good, but a privation or deprivation.

Those who hold this view begin with the biblical premise that all being is good (Gen. 1:31; 1 Tim. 4:4). So evil is nonbeing, not a substance or object. It is a lack of being, a deprivation of being. It is "negative and accidental."[5]

Étienne Gilson, the Thomist scholar, expounds the concept as follows:

> It is very certain that all things God has made are good; and no less certain that they are not all equally good. There is the good, and the better; and, if the better, then also the less good; now in a certain sense the less good pertains to evil.[6]

Later he adds:

> But what we must especially note is that these very limitations and mutabilities for which nature is arraigned, are metaphysically inherent in the very status of a created being as such. . . . Things, in short, are created *ex nihilo*, and because created they are, and are good; but because they are *ex nihilo* they are essentially mutable. . . . [T]he possibility of change is a necessity from which God Himself could not absolve his creation; for the mere fact of being created is the ultimate root of that possibility. . . . [E]verything that exists in virtue of the creative action and endures in virtue of

---

5. Étienne Gilson, *The Spirit of Medieval Philosophy* (New York: Charles Scribner's Sons, 1940), 113. Karl Barth's view of sin and evil as "nothingness" (*das Nichtige*) is similar, except that for Barth nothingness is an aspect of *Geschichte*, that highest reality shared by God and man in Christ, in which alone God is truly God and man is truly man. See *CVT*, 359–65.

6. Gilson, *The Spirit of Medieval Philosophy*, 113.

continued creation, remains radically contingent in itself and in constant peril of lapsing back into nothingness. Because creatures are apt not to be they tend, so to speak, towards nonbeing.[7]

On Gilson's view, natural evil consists of the defects in the lesser goods that God has made in creating a many-valued universe and the "mutability" of creation, which is the tendency of all good things to "lapse back into nothingness," a kind of metaphysical entropy. Remember that Gilson equates being with goodness. Since God created all things good, everything is good insofar as it has being. But as things slip back into nonbeing, they lose their goodness as well as their being. So this metaphysical lapse means that things tend to lose their perfections unless God acts to sustain them.

What of moral evil? Gilson argues that rational beings, angels and men, are also mutable:

> The whole problem now stands on a new footing: all that needs to be made in order that it may be, is always tending to unmake itself, so much so that what now permanently threatens the work of creation is literally, and in the full rigour of the term, the possibility of its *defection*. But only a possibility, be it noted, nothing more; a possibility without real danger as far as concerns the physical order which has no control over itself, but a very real and practical danger indeed in the moral order, that is to say when men and angels are concerned; for in associating them with his own divine government, their Creator requires them also to keep watch with Him against their own possible defection.[8]

Rational beings, like other creatures, tend to slip into nonbeing, to "unmake" themselves, and therefore to become less perfect than God made them to be. The difference between rational and nonrational beings is that rational beings have some control over their own metaphysical stability. They can keep themselves from losing their perfections. Gilson goes on to explain that God gave to man free will (apparently in a libertarian sense) to maintain himself in perfection. But man used his free will wrongly and fell into sin.

> For all evil comes of the will; this will was not created evil, nor even indifferent to good or evil; it was created good, and such that it needed only an effortless continuance in good to attain to perfect beatitude. The only danger threatening such a nature lies therefore in that metaphysical contingence inseparable from the state

7. Ibid., 113–14.
8. Ibid., 114–15.

of a created being, a pure *possibility*, without the least trace of actual existence, a possibility that not only could have remained un-
actualized but ought to have done so. . . . [So] it seems we may justly
claim for Christian thought that it has done everything necessary
to reduce [evil] to the status of an avoidable accident, and to banish it to the confines of this fundamentally good universe.[9]

What is God's relation to evil in this view?

Lastly, we may proceed to this final conclusion to which we must
hold firmly, however strange it may appear: viz. The cause of evil
lies always in some good, and yet, God, who is the Cause of all good,
is not the cause of evil. For it follows clearly from the preceding
considerations, that, when evil is reducible to a defect in some act,
its cause is always a defect in the being that acts. Now in God there
is no defect, but, on the contrary, supreme perfection. The evil
caused by a defect in the acting being could not, therefore, have
God for its cause. But if we consider the evil which consists in the
corruption of certain beings, we must, on the other hand, assign
its cause to God. . . . [W]hatever being and action is observable in
a bad act, is attributable to God as to its cause, but whatever de-
fectiveness is contained in the act, is attributable to the defective
secondary cause, and not to the almighty perfection of God.

Thus, from whatever angle we approach the problem, we always
come back to the same conclusion. Evil as such is nothing. It is,
therefore, inconceivable that God could be its cause. If asked, further, what is its cause, we must reply that it reduces itself to the
tendency of certain things to return to nonbeing.[10]

To some extent, Gilson's reply to the problem of evil is a form of the
freewill defense, which I shall mention briefly later. He tries, however, to
get behind human freedom to show how a wrong use of it is grounded in a
metaphysical principle: the tendency of creatures to become less perfect.
Every creature has this tendency. Rational creatures can guard against it,
but they don't necessarily succeed. When they don't, they are responsible
for allowing themselves to become imperfect. God doesn't cause moral evil,
but he does cause the existence of corruptible beings. He creates corruptible beings because he intends for them to add to the overall perfection of
the universe. But he is not responsible for the failures of rational beings to

9. Ibid., 121–22.
10. Étienne Gilson, *The Philosophy of St. Thomas Aquinas*, tr. Edward Bullough (New York: Arno Press, 1979), 161–62.

guard against their own corruption. Evil is nonbeing, and God does not create nonbeing.

I do not find this to be a cogent response to the problem of evil, for the following reasons:

1. It seems to assume libertarian freedom, which I found reason to reject in the last chapter. Some Reformed thinkers have held the privation theory while rejecting libertarian freedom: God is the efficient cause of everything good, but only the "effectually permissive cause of evil." He "merely permits" evil, because it "has not true being at all."[11] But I don't see any real difference between effectual permission and efficient causation, and I don't know why God should be responsible for what he causes efficiently, but not for what he permits effectually. I will have more to say on this later in the chapter.

2. When someone freely chooses to allow himself to become imperfect, that choice (assuming it is libertarian) is not itself the product of metaphysical entropy. That choice itself is evidently something other than a privation of good, for on Gilson's account it is prior to the privation; it is a choice to make the privation happen. But then the privation theory is quite irrelevant, an unnecessary complication to the argument. Why not simply adopt a conventional freewill defense and say that free will itself explains moral evil, rather than free will plus privation?

3. If God cannot prevent the corruption of rational beings, then how is he able to make some creatures incorruptible (angels and glorified saints)? If he can, but chooses not to, then the problem of evil recurs at a different level: why did he choose not to prevent the Fall?

4. Should we regard evil as "nothing," a mere limitation or privation of goodness? Many seem to think it obvious that we should, but I am not persuaded. Long could be seen as the negation of short, but one could also say that short is the negation of long; the same could be said for straight and crooked. It seems to be a good general practice to regard opposites on the same ontological level. Males and females are opposites, but neither is a mere negation of the other. Both are substantial beings. Why should good and evil be any different?

It is true that good is prior to evil in some ways. First, good came first in history, as Creation preceded the Fall. Second, good has positive value in itself; evil has positive value only to the extent that it enhances good. Third, good receives God's blessing; evil receives his curse. But it is not clear that any of these require us to say that evil is nonbeing, or a mere negation or privation. Is there some other asymmetry between good and evil that re-

11. Polan, cited in RD, 143.

quires us to regard evil as nonbeing? I have not been able to find suggestions of that sort in the literature. Without them, I must assume that good and evil, though opposite, are both forms of being.[12]

5. There is no biblical reason to assert that created things by nature tend to slip into nonbeing, to lose their being, or to become corrupt.[13] Scripture says nothing of the kind, and in the absence of scriptural warrant, I know of no other reason to say such a thing. It assumes that there are degrees of being, and that created things can slip from higher degrees to lower degrees. The idea that being admits of degrees comes from the philosophy of Plato, in which the Forms or Ideas are "real," with the Form of the Good being the most real entity and others being less real entities. It also fits Aristotle's view that things in the world are combinations of form and matter, but that matter is essentially a kind of nonbeing that inhibits form in various degrees. But, in the Bible, there is no hint that some things have more being than others. God and his creations exist; everything else does not exist—and that is the end of it. God is not more real than created beings, although he is very different from them in other ways. Further, in a biblical worldview there is no reason to suppose that things have an inherent tendency to become less perfect, less good, or less real.

6. But even granting Gilson's view that evil is a lack or privation of being, a kind of nonbeing, why would that absolve God of blame for evil? As presented by Gilson, God is crudely analogous to a maker of doughnuts. The doughnut maker shapes the dough into the familiar O-shape. When someone says, "I see what ingredients you use for the doughnut, but what do you make the holes out of?" the baker takes it as a bad joke. There are no ingredients for holes. The hole is simply an emptiness in the dough that appears when the pastry is created. When the baker makes one, behold, the hole is there too! Making doughnuts is not a two-step procedure in

12. The relation between being and nonbeing has, of course, been a difficult philosophical issue since Parmenides. It is difficult to describe nonbeing, or even refer to it, without making it look like a kind of being. But if evil is not an illusion, but something real, then what other conditions must it fulfill to be regarded as being? I don't believe that question has been answered.

It may be, as one of my correspondents suggests, that Augustine's adoption of the privation theory was a reaction to his original Manichaeism. The Manichees saw good and evil as equally powerful realities, in constant warfare. When Augustine became a Christian, he saw clearly that, in God's world, good is ultimate and evil is not. But what is it? Perhaps Augustine thought he could best reject the ultimacy of evil by denying to it the status of being. I find this move understandable, but not persuasive.

13. One can of course discuss the concept of physical entropy in this connection, but the arguments for that are scientific rather than biblical, and the concept has little to do with the moral corruption we are concerned with here.

which one first makes and shapes the dough, and then makes the hole; at least, it doesn't have to be. The hole is not something one must make in addition to the solid doughnut; it is only a lack or privation of dough.

Agreed. But doughnuts do, after all, have holes. The doughnut maker could have made his dough into a solid pastry without a hole, but he chose to include a hole. Shouldn't he receive blame for a hole that is too small, too large, or misshapen, or credit for one that is just the right size? Should he not take responsibility for his choice to make doughnuts rather than solid pastries?

Similarly, if God is the Creator of all the being in the universe, is he not also the source of whatever lacks or privations or negations of being there may be in the world? We saw in chapter 4 that Scripture represents God as bringing about some sinful human actions. It does not seem to me to matter much whether we regard these sins as being or nonbeing. If they come from God, they come from God, and the problem of evil remains.

7. What is evil, on a biblical view? Natural evil is God's curse, the pains brought into the world by the Fall. Moral evil is sin, the transgression of God's law (1 John 3:4). Scripture does not speculate as to whether or not these evils are "being" or "nonbeing," or where they fit into the metaphysical structure of the world.

Indeed, from a biblical point of view, there are dangers in reducing evil to metaphysics, in reducing the righteousness-sin relation to the being-nonbeing relation.[14] Cornelius Van Til often warned against "reducing ethics to metaphysics," or "confusing sin with finitude,"[15] for such reduction depersonalizes sin. In such reduction, sin becomes a defect in creation itself (ultimately, contra Gilson, a defect in God's creative act), rather than the rebellion of created persons against their Creator. And this conception grants sinners a new excuse for their sin, the finitude and mutability with which God created them.

Further, this view encourages views of salvation in which the goal is to get rid of our finitude and become divine, rather than to become obedient. These dangers are not at all hypothetical. They represent a definite tendency in the history of thought, especially systems like those of Plotinus, the Gnostics, Medieval and Eastern Mysticism, and much modern New Age thought. As we saw in chapter 7, these systems replace the biblical Creator-creature distinction with a continuum of divinity, and salvation is viewed as ascent toward the top of the ontological continuum, toward divinity.

14. In one sense, the privation theory seeks to avoid this very problem. It tries to remove evil from the metaphysical sphere by removing it from the sphere of being. But it actually encourages the metaphysicalizing of sin.

15. These two formulations are more or less synonymous.

SOME GOOD THINGS ABOUT EVIL

Another approach to the problem of evil is to claim that the presence, or at least the possibility, of evil in the world is good, when seen from a broader perspective. Even human beings are sometimes called upon to inflict pain for a good purpose: surgery to heal, punishment of children to discipline them. So perhaps God has a good purpose in permitting evil, one which outweighs the suffering and pain—one which, in the end, makes this a better world than it would have been without the intrusion of evil. Such observations have been called "the greater-good defense" against the problem of evil.[16]

Some have argued that the possibility of evil is necessary to have an orderly universe.[17] An orderly universe, on this view, is a universe governed predictably by natural law. But natural laws are impersonal. The law of gravity, for example, takes no account of persons. If someone jumps from a high cliff, he will be hurt, whether he is righteous or wicked. If God miraculously protected everybody (or those otherwise righteous) who took foolish chances, it would be difficult to predict natural events. So if we are to have an orderly, predictable universe, so the argument goes, we must be willing to accept a certain amount of pain and suffering.

Others have argued that a certain amount of evil in the world is necessary for "soul making." For example, John Hick argues that we are born morally immature, and that we need some hard knocks to gain moral fiber.[18]

The most common form of the greater-good defense is the freewill defense, which argues that God rightly risks the possibility of evil in order to allow human beings the great benefit of libertarian freedom of choice. See the previous chapter for my negative response.

Some have noticed that there are virtues that could not exist or manifest themselves, except as responses to evil: compassion, patience, courage, seeking justice, and the redemptive love by which one dies for his friends

---

16. Steve Hays, in correspondence, suggests that it is possible to argue a parallel, but weaker thesis, namely, that evil makes *alternative* goods possible: goods that do not necessarily make the world a better place, but which make it no worse. That thesis is worth exploring, and it may be beneficial to those who cannot see evil as bringing any overall benefit. But since I hold the stronger thesis of the greater good, I will argue that here, with appropriate qualifications.

17. Ronald Nash, *Faith and Reason* (Grand Rapids: Zondervan, 1988). He cites F. R. Tennant, Michael Peterson, and Richard Swinburne as advocating this approach.

18. John Hick, *Evil and the God of Love* (London: Collins, 1966). He cites the church father Irenaeus as the source of his approach.

(John 15:13). Sometimes these have been called "second-order goods," which are dependent on "first-order evils."[19]

We can think of other positive uses of evil. In Scripture, God uses evil to test his servants (Job; 1 Peter 1:7; James 1:3), to discipline them (Heb. 12:7–11), to preserve their lives (Gen. 50:20), to teach them patience and perseverance (James 1:3–4), to redirect their attention to what is most important (Ps. 37), to enable them to comfort others (2 Cor. 1:3–7), to enable them to bear powerful witness to the truth (Acts 7), to give them greater joy when suffering is replaced by glory (1 Peter 4:13), to judge the wicked, both in history (Deut. 28:15–68) and in the life to come (Matt. 27: 41–46), to bring reward to persecuted believers (Matt. 5:10–12), and to display the work of God (John 9:3; cf. Ex. 9:16; Rom. 9:17).

The thrust of all these arguments is that although evil is to be deplored in and of itself, there are some respects in which it makes the world a better place. Some have argued, therefore, that evils contribute to a greater good. Some have even argued that this world, with all its evil, is "the best possible world." The philosopher G. W. Leibniz, for example, argued that an omnipotent, omniscient, omnibenevolent God could create no less.[20]

It is certainly true that when God brings pain and suffering upon people, he has a good purpose. "You intended to harm me," Joseph explains to his brothers, "but God intended it for good" (Gen. 50:20). And in a context dealing with the sufferings of Christians, Paul says that "in all things God works for the good of those who love him" (Rom. 8:28). Recognizing and affirming this principle is an essential element in any Christian response to the problem of evil. It is essential to realize that even though God does bring evil into the world, he does it for a good reason. Therefore, he does not *do* evil in bringing evil to pass.

I would quarrel with some of the arguments mentioned above in this connection. The idea that some human pain must be endured in any orderly universe does not take account of the biblical teachings about the pre-Fall world and about the post-Consummation heaven, in which God "will wipe every tear from their eyes. There will be no more death or mourning or crying or pain, for the old order of things has passed away" (Rev. 21:4). Certainly heaven will be an orderly place, and that order will be maintained without human suffering.

Hick's soul-making theodicy overlooks the fact that Adam was created good, not morally immature with a need to develop character through suf-

---

19. And the latter, of course, are ultimately the abuses of first-order goods.
20. G. W. Leibniz, *Theodicy* (New Haven: Yale University Press, 1952).

fering. It is true that God uses evil to sanctify us, but the true making of souls, both in old and new creations, is by divine grace.

As for Leibniz's theory, many have doubted whether there could be such a thing as a "best possible world." Given any possible universe, can we not always imagine another that includes one more good or one less evil? Indeed, Scripture tells us explicitly that the present world is inferior to the world to come. If God is able to make a world that is temporarily less than best, why can't he create a world that is never the absolute best? And is it not possible that God wants to display his grace by creating beings who are less than perfectly excellent?

Nevertheless, there is a valid insight in the greater-good defense. Scripture provides many examples of God bringing good out of evil. And we know that on the Last Day, God's justice, mercy, and righteousness will be so plain to all that nobody will accuse him of wrongdoing. Rather,

> All nations will come
> and worship before you,
> for your righteous acts have been revealed. (Rev. 15:4)

When all of God's actions are added up, it will be plain that the sum total of his works is righteous. From the evils of history he has brought unquestionable good, worthy of the highest praise.

Remember the following points, however:

1. It is important for us to define *greater good* theistically. The greater good should be seen, first of all, not as greater pleasure or comfort for us, but as greater glory for God. Certainly there are events that are hard to justify as benefits to the people involved, the chief one being eternal punishment. But God is glorified in the judgment of sinners, and that is a good thing. Nevertheless, God has promised that what brings glory to him will, in the long run, also bring benefits to believers. So Romans 8:28 says that "in all things God works for the good of those who love him, who have been called according to his purpose."

2. Unless God's standards govern our concept of goodness, there can be no talk of good or evil at all. If there is no personal Absolute, values must be based on impersonal things and forces, like matter, motion, time, and chance. But values cannot be based on any of these. They arise only in a context of personal relationships, and absolute standards presuppose an absolute person. Thus, the Christian can turn the tables on the unbeliever who raises the problem of evil: the non-Christian has a "problem of good." Without God, there is neither good nor evil.[21]

---

21. See AGG, 89–102, for a fuller treatment of this argument.

3. If we are to evaluate God's actions rightly, we must evaluate them over the full extent of human history. The Christian claim is not that the world is perfect as it is now; in fact, Scripture denies that it is. But the full goodness of God's plan will be manifest only at the end of redemptive history. For his own reasons, God has determined to "write" history as a story taking place over millennia.[22] Evil would not be such a problem if it were created and overcome supratemporally (as in Barth's *Geschichte*) or in a period of, say, three seconds. The problem is with the long wait for God's salvation.[23] But for him, of course, a thousand years are as a day (Ps. 90:4). And when we look back upon our sufferings in this world, they will seem small to us as well, "not worth comparing with the glory that will be revealed in us" (Rom. 8:18). It is then that we will see how God has worked in all things for our good (Rom. 8:28). Paul, who underwent much more suffering than most of us, even says that "our light and momentary troubles are achieving for us an eternal glory that far outweighs them all" (2 Cor. 4:17).

4. God often surprises us by the ways in which he brings good out of evil. Certainly Joseph was surprised at the means God used to lift him from being a slave and a prisoner to being Pharaoh's prime minister. Certainly the Israelites were surprised at the miracles by which God brought them out of Egypt and sustained them in the wilderness. But the chief example of God's astonishing ways is found in the cross of Jesus. The prophets promised God's judgment on Israel's disobedience, but simultaneously promised that he would forgive and bless. How could he do both? Israel's disobedience merited nothing less than death. How could God be just in dealing with their sin and still bring them his promised blessings? Certainly this problem was quite impenetrable, until Jesus died in our place. His death was at the same time judgment and grace: judgment upon Jesus for our sin, and grace to the true Israel, those of us who are elect in him. And if God acted so wonderfully and surprisingly to bring good out of evil, when it seemed most impossible, can we not trust him to bring good out of the remaining evils that we experience?

5. Since the ultimate theodicy is future, we must now deal with the problem of evil by faith. We cannot total up the present evils against the present goods and from that calculation exonerate God of blame. But our inability to do this does not require us to surrender to those who use the problem of evil to deny the existence of God. For the burden of proof is,

22. See the author-character model described in chapter 8.
23. Recall the discussion of God's "presence in time" in chapter 6, and the many texts urging patience in waiting for God's time, including Hab. 2:3; Matt. 6:34; Rom. 8:25; Phil. 4:6–7; Heb. 10:36; James 1:3–4; 5:7–11.

after all, not upon us. It is the objector who must show that the evils of this world cannot be part of an overall good plan. I have shown many ways in which God brings good out of evil, even when it seems impossible for the good to prevail. Can the objector prove that God is unable to integrate the present evils into an overall good plan? This burden of proof is a heavy one, for the objector must prove a negative: that there is *no* way for God to vindicate his justice on the Last Day. I do not believe that burden has been met.

6. Does the greater-good defense presuppose that the end justifies the means? It does say that God's good purposes justify his use of evil. When we criticize someone for holding that the end justifies the means, we mean that he thinks that a noble end will justify means that would otherwise be accounted wicked. In this case, is God's act to bring about evil normally a wicked action, which he justifies *ad hoc* because of his noble purpose? But how would we judge in this context what is "normally" the case? If God brought about moral evil in some sense, that act was quite unique. Ultimately, evil came into the world only once. Other "hardenings" of people's hearts in history are actions that only God can perform. Who are we to claim that such actions are "normally" wicked, rather than confess that they are a unique divine prerogative? When a man kills an innocent person, his act is normally murder. But when God takes human life, he acts within the proper authority of his lordship. Why should we not say the same thing about his agency in bringing evil to pass?[24] At least, we must say again that the burden of proof is on the objector.

7. Since the burden of proof is on the objector, it is not necessary for us to come up with a full theodicy, a complete justification of God's ways. In this world, we walk by faith, not by sight (2 Cor. 5:7). We shall see later that seeking a theodicy can actually be sinful when people demand of God an explanation for the ills that have befallen them.

My conclusion on the greater-good defense, then, is that God certainly does will evil for a good purpose. The good he intends will be so great, so wonderful and beautiful, that it will make present evils seem small. But we are not under any obligation to show in every case how God's past and present actions contribute to the final good, and the unbeliever has no right to demand such an explanation.

Although the greater-good defense is basically sound, it leaves us with a sense of mystery. For it is hard to imagine *how* God's good purpose justifies the evil in the world.

24. I shall argue later that the ontological difference between God and man lies behind these moral distinctions.

EVIL AND GOD'S AGENCY

We have seen that natural evil is a curse that God placed on the world in response to man's sin. We also saw earlier, in chapter 4, that God does harden hearts, and that, through his prophets, he predicts sinful human actions long in advance, indicating that he is in control of free human decisions. Now theologians have found it difficult to formulate in general terms how God acts to bring about those sinful actions. Earlier in this chapter, we saw Gilson arguing that God is not the cause of sin and evil, because evil is nonbeing and therefore has no cause. Gilson is willing to say that God is the "deficient" cause (which sounds like a contrast to "efficient" cause), meaning that he creates mutable beings, but does not determine the specific defects which constitute sin. I found his privation theory, and his view of libertarian freedom, inadequate. But the discussion brings out an issue that we all must think about. Do we want to say that God is the "cause" of evil? That language is certainly problematic, since we usually associate cause with blame. Recall Mike, from chapter 8, who made Billy put graffiti on the school door. Billy, of course, made the marks, but Mike caused him to do it. And so, most of us would agree, Mike deserves the blame. So it seems that if God causes sin and evil, he must be to blame for it.

Therefore, there has been much discussion among theologians as to what verb best describes God's agency in regard to evil. Some initial possibilities: *authors, brings about, causes, controls, creates, decrees, foreordains, incites, includes within his plan, makes happen, ordains, permits, plans, predestines, predetermines, produces, stands behind,* and *wills.* Many of these are extrascriptural terms; not one is easy to define in this context. So theologians need to consider carefully which of these terms, if any, should be affirmed, and in what sense. Words are the theologian's tools. In a situation like this, none of the possibilities is fully adequate. Each term has its advantages and disadvantages. Let us consider some of those that are most frequently discussed.

1. The term *authors* is almost universally condemned in the theological literature. It is rarely defined, but it seems to mean both that God is the efficient cause of evil and that by causing evil he actually does something wrong.[25] So the WCF says that God "neither is nor can be the author or approver of sin" (5.4). Despite this denial in a major Reformed confession, Arminians regularly charge that Reformed theology makes God the author of sin. They assume that if God brings about evil in any sense,

---

25. Lest there be confusion over language: the author-story model of God's relation to creatures, which I advocated in chapter 8, does not make God the "author of sin" in this

he must therefore approve it and deserve the blame. In their view, nothing less than libertarian freedom can absolve God from the charge of authoring sin.

But, as we saw in chapter 8, libertarian freedom is incoherent and unbiblical. And, as we saw in chapter 4, God does bring about sinful human actions. To deny this, or to charge God with wickedness on account of it, is not open to a Bible-believing Christian. Somehow, we must confess both that God has a role in bringing evil about, and that in doing so he is holy and blameless. In the last section, I tried to show how the greater-good defense, properly understood, supports this confession. God does bring sins about, but always for his own good purposes. So in bringing sin to pass, he does not himself commit sin. If that argument is sound, then a Reformed doctrine of the sovereignty of God does not imply that God is the author of sin.

2. *Causes* is another term that has led to much wrestling by theologians. As we recall, Gilson, with the Thomistic tradition, denies that God is the cause of evil[26] by defining evil as a privation. Reformed writers have also denied that God is the cause of sin. Calvin teaches, "For the proper and genuine cause of sin is not God's hidden counsel but the evident will of man,"[27] although in the context he also states that Adam's fall was "not without God's knowledge and ordination."[28] Here are some other examples:

> See that you make not God the author of sin, by charging his sacred decree with men's miscarriages, as if that were the cause or occasion of them; which we are sure that it is not, nor can be, any more than the sun can be the cause of darkness.[29]

> It is [God] who created, preserves, actuates and directs all things. But it by no means follows, from these premises, that God is therefore the cause of sin, for sin is nothing but *anomia*, illegality, want of conformity to the divine law (1 John iii. 4), a mere privation of rectitude; consequently, being itself a thing purely negative, it can

---

sense. Nothing about that model implies that God commits or approves of sin. In fact, I shall argue later that it provides us with a reason to deny that.

26. Except, of course, as a *deficient* cause.

27. Calvin, *Concerning the Eternal Predestination of God* (London: James Clarke and Co., 1961), 122. Calvin accepts the privation theory, as is evident on p. 169.

28. Ibid., 121.

29. Elisha Coles, *A Practical Discourse on God's Sovereignty* (Marshallton, Del.: National Foundation for Christian Education, 1968), 15. This is a reprint of a seventeenth-century work.

have no positive or efficient cause, but only a negative or deficient one, as several learned men have observed.[30]

According to the Canons of Dordt, "The cause or blame for this unbelief, as well as for all other sins, is not at all in God, but in man" (1.5). In these quotations, *cause* seems to take on the connotations of the term *author*. For these writers, to say that God "causes" evil is to say, or perhaps imply, that he is to blame for it. Note the phrase "cause or blame" in the Canons of Dordt, in which the terms seem to be treated as synonyms. But note above that although Calvin rejects *cause* he affirms *ordination*. God is not the "cause" of sin, but it occurs by his "ordination." For the modern reader, the distinction is not evident. To ordain is to cause, and vice versa. If causality entails blame, then ordination would seem to entail it as well; if not, then neither entails it. But evidently in the vocabulary of Calvin and his successors there was a difference between the two terms.

For us, the question is whether God can be the efficient cause of sin without being to blame for it. The older theologians denied that God was the efficient cause of sin because they held the privation theory, and also because they identified cause with authorship. But if, as I recommend, we reject the privation theory, and if, as I believe, the connection between cause and blame in modern language is no stronger than the connection between ordination and blame, then it seems to me that it is not wrong to say that God causes evil and sin. Certainly we should employ such language cautiously, however, in view of the long history of its rejection by theologians.

It is interesting that Calvin does use *cause*, referring to God's agency in bringing evil about, when he distinguishes between God as the "remote cause" and human agency as the "proximate cause." Arguing that God is not the "author of sin," he says that "the proximate cause is one thing, the remote cause another."[31] Calvin points out that when wicked men steal Job's goods, Job recognizes that "the LORD gave and the LORD has taken away; may the name of the LORD be praised" (Job 1:21). The thieves, being the proximate cause of the evil, are guilty of committing it, but Job doesn't question the motives of the Lord, the remote cause. Calvin, however, does not be-

---

30. Jerome Zanchius, *Observations on the Divine Attributes*, in *Absolute Predestination* (Marshallton, Del.: National Foundation for Christian Education, n.d.), 33. Compare the formulations of the post-Reformation dogmaticians Polan and Wolleb in *RD*, 143, and of Mastricht on p. 277. All of these base their arguments on the premise that evil is a mere privation.

31. Calvin, *Concerning the Eternal Predestination of God*, 181.

lieve that the proximate-remote distinction is sufficient to show us *why* God is guiltless:

> But how it was ordained by the foreknowledge and decree of God what man's future was without God being implicated as associate in the fault as the author and approver of transgression, is clearly a secret so much excelling the insight of the human mind, that I am not ashamed to confess ignorance.[32]

He uses the proximate-remote distinction merely to distinguish between the causality of God and that of creatures, and therefore to *state* that the former is always righteous. But he does not believe that the distinction solves the problem of evil. Indeed, it does not, for as in the Billy-Mike example (chap. 8), we have good reason in many situations to associate remote causality (Mike) with blame, sometimes to the exclusion of blame for the proximate cause (Billy). It would be wrong to generalize from the Billy-Mike example to prove that God is to blame for human sin. Certainly God's motives are very different from those of Mike in our example. But we cannot prove that God is not to blame, merely by pointing out that he is only the remote cause.

At least, the above discussion does indicate that Calvin is willing in some contexts to refer to God as a cause of sin and evil. Calvin also describes God as the sole cause of the hardening and reprobation of the wicked:

> Therefore, if we cannot assign any reason for his bestowing mercy on his people, but just that it so pleases him, neither can we have any reason for his reprobating others but his will. When God is said to visit mercy or harden whom he will, men are reminded that they are not to seek for any cause beyond his will.[33]

[handwritten margin note: NO CAUSE BEYOND HIS WILL]

3. Consider now the term *permits*. This is the preferred term in Arminian theology, in which it amounts to a denial that God causes sin. For the Arminian, God does not cause sin; he only permits it. Reformed theologians have also used the term, but they have insisted that God's permission of sin is no less efficacious than his ordination of good. Calvin denies that there is any "mere permission" in God:

> From this it is easy to conclude how foolish and frail is the support of divine justice afforded by the suggestion that evils come to be

32. Ibid., 124.
33. *Institutes*, 3.22.11; cf. 3.23.1.

not by [God's] will, but merely by his permission. Of course, so far
as they are evils, which men perpetrate with their evil mind, as I
shall show in greater detail shortly, I admit that they are not pleas-
ing to God. But it is a quite frivolous refuge to say that God otiosely
permits them, when Scripture shows Him not only willing but the
author of them.[34]

God's permission is an *efficacious* permission. Heppe describes it as *volun-
tas efficaciter permittens* and quotes J. H. Heidegger:

Nor whether He is willing or refusing is God's permission like
man's permission, which admits of an eclipse which he neither wills
nor refuses, as the LOMBARD and with him the Scholastics assert.
It is effective, mighty, and not separate from God's will at all.
Otiose permission of sin separated from God's will is repugnant both
to the nature of the First Cause and to the divine and almighty foresight, to His nature and to Scripture.[35]

If God's permission is efficacious, how does it differ from other exercises of
his will? Evidently, the Reformed use *permit* mainly as a more delicate term
than *cause*, suggesting that God brings sin about with a kind of reluctance
born of his holy hatred of it.

This usage does reflect a biblical pattern. When Satan acts, he acts, in
an obvious sense, by God's permission.[36] God allows him to take Job's family, wealth, and health. But God will not allow Satan to take Job's life (Job
2:6). So Satan is on a leash, acting only within limits set by God. In this
respect, all sinful acts are similar. The sinner can go only so far before he
meets the judgment of God.

It is appropriate, therefore, to use *permission* to refer to God's ordination of sin. But we should not assume, as Arminians do, that divine permission is anything less than sovereign ordination. What God permits or
allows to happen will happen. God could easily have prevented Satan's
attack on Job if he had intended to. That he did not prevent that attack
implies that he intended it to happen. Permission, then, is a form of ordination, a form of causation.[37] The fact that it is sometimes taken oth-

34. Calvin, *Concerning the Eternal Predestination of God*, 176. Calvin's use of the term
author raises questions. He probably means that God authors evil happenings without authoring their evil character. But the use of *author* here indicates something of the flexibil-
ity of his terminology, in contrast to the relative rigidity of his successors' terminology.
35. *RD*, 90. Compare my earlier reference to Polan in *RD*, 143.
36. In this use, and in the Reformed theological use, *permission* has no connotation of
moral approval, as it sometimes has in contemporary use.
37. Traditional Arminians agree that God is omnipotent and can prevent sinful actions.

erwise is a good argument for not using it, but perhaps not a decisive argument.

I shall not discuss other terms on my list (except *wills*, which will be discussed in chap. 23). The discussion above should be sufficient to indicate the need for caution in our choice of vocabulary, and also the need to think carefully before condemning the vocabulary of others. It is not easy to find adequate terms to describe God's ordination of evil. Our language must not compromise either God's full sovereignty or his holiness and goodness.

None of these formulations solves the problem of evil. It is not a solution to say that God ordains evil, but doesn't author or cause it (if we choose to say that). This language is not a solution to the problem, but only a way of raising it. For the problem of evil asks *how* God can ordain evil without authoring it. And, as Calvin pointed out, the distinction between remote and proximate cause is also inadequate to answer the questions before us, however useful it may be in stating who is to blame for evil. Nor is it a solution to say that God permits, rather than ordains, evil. As we have seen, God's permission is as efficacious as his ordination. The difference between the terms brings nothing to light that will solve the problem.

I should, however, say something more about the nature of God's agency with regard to evil. Recall from chapter 8 the model of the author and his story: God's relationship to free agents is like the relationship of an author to his characters. Let us consider to what extent God's relationship to human sinners is like that of Shakespeare to Macbeth, the murderer of Duncan.

I borrowed the Shakespeare-Macbeth illustration from Wayne Grudem's excellent *Systematic Theology*.[38] But I do disagree with Grudem on one point. He says that we could say that either Macbeth or Shakespeare killed King Duncan. I agree, of course, that both Macbeth and Shakespeare are responsible, at different levels of reality, for the death of Duncan. But as I analyze the language that we typically use in such contexts, it seems clear to me that we would not normally say that Shakespeare killed Duncan.

So we wonder how they can object to this argument. If God could prevent sin, but chooses not to, must we not say that he has ordained it to happen? Some more recent Arminians have claimed that God created the world without even knowing that evil would occur. But doesn't this representation make God, in the words of one of my correspondents, a kind of "mad scientist," who "throws together a potentially dangerous combination of chemicals, not knowing if it will result in a hazardous and uncontrollable reaction"? Does this view not make God guilty of reckless endangerment?

38. Grand Rapids: Zondervan, 1994, pp. 321–22.

Shakespeare wrote the murder into his play. But the murder took place in the world of the play, not the real world of the author. Macbeth did it, not Shakespeare. We sense the rightness of Macbeth paying for his crime. But we would certainly consider it very unjust if Shakespeare were tried and put to death for killing Duncan.[39] And no one suggests that there is any problem in reconciling Shakespeare's benevolence with his omnipotence over the world of the drama. Indeed, there is reason for us to praise Shakespeare for raising up this character, Macbeth, to show us the consequences of sin.[40]

The difference between levels, then, may have moral, as well as metaphysical, significance.[41] It may explain why the biblical writers, who do not hesitate to say that God brings about sin and evil, do not accuse him of wrongdoing. The relationship between God and us, of course, is different in some respects from that between an author and his characters. Most significantly, we are real and Macbeth is not. But between God and us there is a vast difference in the kind of reality and in relative status. God is the absolute controller of, and authority over, nature and history. He is the lawgiver, and we receive his laws. He is the head of the covenant; we are the servants. He has devised the creation for his own glory; we seek his glory, rather than our own. He makes us as the potter makes pots, for his own purposes. He has many rights and prerogatives we don't have. Do these differences not put God in a different moral category as well?

The transcendence of God plays a significant role in biblical responses to the problem of evil. Because God is who he is, the covenant Lord, he is not required to defend himself against charges of injustice. He is the judge, not we. Very often in Scripture, when something happens that calls God's goodness into question, he pointedly refrains from explaining. Indeed, he often rebukes those people who question him. Job demanded an interview

39. Think how many writers of TV programs would be taken from us if writing a murder scene were a criminal act. No further comment is necessary.

40. As my friend Steve Hays points out in correspondence, the dark aspects of Shakespeare's dramas also add to his stature as an artist. Our admiration of Shakespeare is based partly on his understanding of the sin of the human soul and partly on his ability to expose and deal with that sin in ways that surprise us and deepen our understanding.

41. The metaphysical difference between the Creator and the world of which evil is a part may indicate the true connection between the ethical and the metaphysical, as opposed to the false connection posited by the chain-of-being thinkers mentioned earlier in this chapter. It may also indicate that there is a grain of truth in the privation theory: there is a metaphysical difference between good and evil, but it is not the difference between being and nonbeing; instead, it is the difference between uncreated being and created being.

with God, so that he could ask God the reasons for his sufferings (Job 23:1–7; 31:35–37). But when he met God, God asked the questions: "Brace yourself like a man; I will question you, and you shall answer me" (38:3). The questions mostly revealed Job's ignorance about God's creation: if Job doesn't understand the ways of the animals, how can he presume to call God's motives into question? He doesn't even understand earthly things; how can he presume to debate heavenly things? God is not subject to the ignorant evaluations of his creatures.[42]

It is significant that the potter-clay image appears in the one place in Scripture where the problem of evil is explicitly addressed.[43] In Romans 9:19–21, Paul appeals specifically to the difference in metaphysical level and status between the Creator and the creature:

> One of you will say to me, "Then why does God still blame us? For who resists his will?" But who are you, O man, to talk back to God? "Shall what is formed say to him who formed it, 'Why did you make me like this?'" Does not the potter have the right to make out of the same lump of clay some pottery for noble purposes and some for common use?

This answer to the problem of evil turns entirely on God's sovereignty. It is as far as could be imagined from a freewill defense. It brings to our attention the fact that his prerogatives are far greater than ours, as does the author-character model.

One might object that this model makes God the author of evil. But that objection confuses two senses of the word *author*. As we have seen, the phrase *author of evil* connotes not only causality of evil, but also blame for it. To author evil is to do it. But in saying that God is related to the world as an author to a story, we actually provide a way of seeing that God is *not* to be blamed for the sin of his creatures.

This is, of course, not the only biblical response to the problem of evil.

---

42. To say this is not to adopt the view of Gordon H. Clark, who argued that God, being above the moral law, is not subject to it. See his *Religion, Reason, and Revelation* (Philadelphia: Presbyterian and Reformed, 1961). Certainly God has some prerogatives that he forbids to us, such as the freedom to take human life. But, for the most part, the moral laws that God imposes upon us are grounded in his own character. See Ex. 20:11; Lev. 11:44–45; Matt. 5:45; 1 Peter 1:15–16. God will not violate his own character. What Scripture denies is that man has sufficient understanding of God's character and his eternal plan (not to mention sufficient authority) to bring accusations against him.

43. The problem is raised, of course, in the book of Job and in many other places in Scripture. But to my knowledge, Rom. 9 is the only passage in which a biblical writer gives an explicit answer to it. Job never learns why he has suffered.

Sometimes God does not respond by silencing us, as above, but by showing us in some measure how evil contributes to his plan—what I have called the greater-good defense. The greater-good defense refers particularly to God's lordship attribute of control—that he is sovereign over evil, and uses it for good. The Romans 9 response refers particularly to God's lordship attribute of authority. And his attribute of covenant presence addresses the emotional problem of evil, comforting us with the promises of God and the love of Jesus, from which no evil can separate us (Rom. 8:35–39).

PART THREE

A PHILOSOPHY OF LORDSHIP

CHAPTER 10

Ethics

The next part of the book will deal with some issues that are generally described as philosophical. In an earlier book, I defined philosophy as "an attempt to understand the world in its broadest, most general features."[1] I rejected any sharp distinction between philosophy and theology. Theology is the application of Scripture,[2] and Christian philosophy applies Scripture to philosophical questions. So philosophy may be considered a subdivision of theology. This view of philosophy is, of course, rather different from that taken by most secular and many Christian thinkers. Too often in the history of thought, particularly thought about God, autonomous philosophy has dictated the presuppositions of theology, thus muting the voice of Scripture. We have already seen examples of philosophy introducing distortions into theology: false concepts of divine transcendence and immanence, libertarian freedom, evil as privation, and confusion of sin with finitude.

In theological treatments of the doctrine of God, there have usually been a lot of philosophical prolegomena: discussions of univocal and analogical knowledge, the analogy of being, God's *esse* and existence, the relation of his being to his attributes, his nature as "pure form" and "pure act," the absence in him of anything potential, and so on. The scholastic tradition has developed very elaborate views on these subjects. I have avoided discussing

1. *DKG,* 85.
2. Ibid., 81–85.

these topics until now, for I consider it far more important at the outset of our study to be clear on the basic biblical teaching about God's covenant lordship. Besides, I question the value of much of the scholastic philosophizing, anyway. Nevertheless, students of this subject should be aware of these philosophical issues and should learn to evaluate them from Scripture. We need to ask what, if anything, Scripture says on these matters, and which of these theories, if any, is consistent with a biblical worldview.

We also need to ask if the covenantal perspective that we have developed in this book has anything to say about these philosophical issues. What happens to these questions when they are approached from the standpoint of a distinctively Christian philosophy—one governed by the Bible? And what alternatives does the covenantal worldview present to us that were not available to the Scholastics and are not available to most philosophers today?

Philosophy is often divided into metaphysics (the theory of being),[3] epistemology (the theory of knowledge), and value theory (which includes ethics, aesthetics, and perhaps some other disciplines; I shall focus on ethics here). I will use that triad as my principle of organization in this part of the book. It might seem natural to students of philosophy for me to start with metaphysics and move on to epistemology and ethics. After all, one might suppose, we must know what exists in reality (metaphysics) before we can determine how to know it and value it. But of course other orders are equally plausible, when you think about it: we must know how to *know* reality (epistemology) before we can know what reality and value are, and we must know how we *ought* to think (ethics) before we can rightly know the world and describe reality. In my vocabulary, then, the relationship between ethics, epistemology, and metaphysics is "perspectival." That is, each involves the others, so that you cannot do one without doing the other two.

This perspectival relationship suggests that we can start anywhere in the triad and work back to the other two members. Where, then, do we begin? In chapter 1, I promised to invert some traditional orders in this book, for various reasons, and I shall do that here, beginning with ethics and moving on to epistemology and metaphysics. It is fairly obvious, I think, how metaphysics determines epistemology and ethics. It is less obvious how ethics determines epistemology and then metaphysics. So I shall try here to bring these less obvious relationships into prominence. The covenantal worldview of Scripture encourages us to see lordship as an ethical rela-

---

3. In my vocabulary, *metaphysics* and *ontology* are more or less synonymous.

tionship that has epistemological and metaphysical implications, although it permits other perspectives as well.

In this chapter, then, we begin with ethics.[4] I shall indicate the distinctive values of a biblical, covenantal perspective, in terms of God's lordship attributes of control, authority, and presence.

Rather than discussing specific ethical problems, I will be discussing metaethics, which deals with general methods for approaching ethical problems. The method I consider biblical does not provide a simple, automatic solution for all our ethical dilemmas; indeed, part of its value is that it shows us why ethical problems are often so difficult. Still, it does provide us with some Christian guidelines that we need to follow if we are to make any progress in finding solutions. I have presented the most basic features of this metaethic in my *Medical Ethics: Principles, Persons and Problems*.[5] I have also alluded to it in *DKG*, which applies the same general scheme to epistemology. Although I published my epistemology before my ethics, I developed the threefold scheme in ethics before applying it to epistemology. Ethics is its natural home, and I think the ethical applications of it are more easily understood than the applications to epistemological theory. Indeed, the point of my epistemology is that it can be fruitfully understood as a subdivision of ethics and thus can be fruitfully analyzed by the use of my metaethic. I intend here to present that metaethic in more detail than in *Medical Ethics*, with some additional comparisons and ramifications. In particular, I would like to compare this approach with the approaches taken in secular philosophical systems.

The history of secular philosophical ethics presents us with three metaethical tendencies. I say "tendencies," rather than "positions," because most writers on ethics reflect more than one; rarely does anyone seek to be a pure representative of one or another. Let me name them as they have sometimes been named by others: existential, teleological, and deontological ethics.

EXISTENTIAL ETHICS

Existential ethics adopts the view that ethics is essentially a matter of human inwardness, a matter of character and motive. Ethical behavior, on this view, is not motivated by external reward, which would be mercenary, or

---

4. The rest of this chapter is a revised version of chapter 3 of my book *Perspectives on the Word of God* (Eugene, Oreg.: Wipf and Stock, 1999).

5. Phillipsburg, N.J.: Presbyterian and Reformed, 1988.

by mere law, which would be drudgery. Either of these would also be hypocrisy, for in these cases people do things they would prefer not to do, for the sake of something outside themselves, masking their true character and therefore masking their true ethical state. Rather, ethical behavior is an expression of what a person *is*. One ought not to mask his nature; rather, he should act it out. He should be what he is. There is no standard outside ourselves; what values there are in this world are the results of our decisions.

The existential tendency can be found in the Greek Sophists, who denied the existence of objective truth, but sought to teach young people how to accomplish their own ambitions.[6] It is also found in the Socratic dictum "Know thyself" and in the Aristotelian-Thomistic concept of self-realization or self-actualization.[7] The Hegelians also emphasized self-realization.[8] The modern existentialist, Jean-Paul Sartre, offered a self-realization ethic without the self.[9] Since he denied the existence of any objective human nature, he argued that ethical behavior was at best an expression of human freedom, of our difference from all things with objective natures. Postmodernism, in this respect, is very existentialist. The views of postmodernists like Lyotard and Derrida[10] would be the purest philosophical form of existential ethics, but one suspects that there are many nonphilosophers who hold this sort of view—in effect, if not in word. For those who have become epistemological skeptics—or, worse, have come to despair of all objective values—no form of ethics is very plausible except existentialism.

Nonexistentialists have appreciated and sometimes appropriated the existentialist emphasis on the inner life, on good motives as the source of right action. Indeed, this emphasis echoes the biblical teaching that out

6. My comments on the history of ethics owe much to sources such as Frank Thilly and Ledger Wood, *A History of Philosophy* (New York: Holt and Co., 1951); Alasdair MacIntyre, *A Short History of Ethics* (New York: Macmillan, 1966); and Paul Edwards, ed., *The Encyclopedia of Philosophy* (New York: Macmillan, 1967). My purpose is to take standard criticisms of various secular ethicists and show that those criticisms form a pattern that invites Christian interpretation and evaluation. For that purpose, to produce original critiques of these figures would be counterproductive.

7. Aristotle, "Nicomachean Ethics," in *The Basic Works of Aristotle*, ed. R. McKeon (New York: Random House, 1941), 935–1127.

8. For example, F. H. Bradley, *Ethical Studies* (Oxford: Oxford University Press, 1876).

9. See his *Being and Nothingness*, trans. Hazel Barnes (New York: Methuen, 1957), and his summary article, "Existentialism Is a Humanism," in *Existentialism from Dostoyevsky to Sartre*, ed. W. Kaufmann (New York: Meridian, 1956).

10. Jean-François Lyotard, *The Postmodern Explained* (Minneapolis: University of Minnesota Press, 1992), and *The Postmodern Condition* (Minneapolis: University of Minnesota Press, 1984); Jacques Derrida, *Writing and Difference* (New York: Routledge and Kegan Paul, 1978).

of the heart come the issues of life (Prov. 4:23; cf. 29:13). Jesus taught that from the heart comes human speech (Matt. 12:34), true forgiveness (Matt. 18:35), true love (Mark 12:30, 33), and all other ethical good and evil (Matt. 15:19; Luke 6:45; 8:15; 16:15; Acts 5:3). But when, as in Sartre and Lyotard, the existentialist tendency reaches the point of denying objective, external value, many resist. This sort of skepticism is always self-refuting, for in it the denial of value is presented as a value, and the denial of truth as a truth. Sartre, indeed, proposes a human lifestyle that he describes as "authentic." But what is that, if it is not an objective value?

TELEOLOGICAL ETHICS

Many who cannot accept the skepticism of existential ethics are attracted to teleological ethics, which affirms the existence of objective values to some extent. The term *teleological* comes from the Greek *telos*, which means "end" or "goal." The teleologist sets forth one relatively simple, objective goal for ethics which, he thinks, no one can legitimately question. That goal is usually called "happiness" or "pleasure." The teleologist, then, seeks to evaluate all human behavior by judging what that behavior contributes to happiness or pleasure. This procedure seems to him to be practical and reflects the way many nonphilosophical people make ethical judgments.

Teleological ethics is frequently linked to an empiricist theory of knowledge. The empiricist thinks he can show by sense experience that everyone naturally seeks happiness or pleasure. Once that is granted, he presents another argument from sense experience to identify the best means of attaining happiness or pleasure.

Aristotle's ethic has teleological elements (as well as elements of the other two tendencies).[11] More consistently teleological were the Greek Cyrenaics and Epicureans.[12] The best-known modern teleologists have been the nineteenth-century utilitarians, Jeremy Bentham[13] and John Stuart Mill.[14]

11. Aristotle, "Nicomachean Ethics."

12. For readings in these schools, see T. V. Smith, ed., *Philosophers Speak for Themselves: From Aristotle to Plotinus* (Chicago: University of Chicago Press, 1934).

13. See his *An Introduction to the Principles of Morals and Legislation* (1823; reprint, New York: Hafner, 1948).

14. See his *Utilitarianism*, reprinted often, most interestingly found in a volume of the Great Books of the Western World entitled *American State Papers* (Chicago: Encyclopedia Britannica, 1952). The volume also contains the U.S. Declaration of Independence, the U.S. Constitution, and Mill's works on democracy, *On Liberty* and *Representative Government*. I may be reading too much into this, but it is interesting that Britannica has included utilitarian ethics as among the foundational principles of American politics.

Most of us, indeed, find ourselves arguing ethical issues this way at times. What legislation, we often ask, will bring the greatest good for the greatest number? That is teleological ethics. Indeed, one might say that democracy is biased in favor of teleological ethics, for people can frequently express their happiness or unhappiness in the voting booth and to pollsters. Arguments about what is right, therefore, often become arguments about what will make people happy, and that determines how they will vote or what they will tell pollsters.

Most reflective people will agree with Bentham and Mill that ethics is goal oriented, that it seeks means of attaining goals that we find valuable. Beyond that, however, many have found problems in teleological ethics. For one thing, the teleologists disagree among themselves as to what the goal is. Is it individual pleasure (Epicurus) or the pleasure of society in general (Mill)? Is pleasure to be measured by intensity (Cyrenaics, Bentham), or are there also qualitative judgments to be made (Epicurus, Mill)?

Furthermore, what basis is there for saying that pleasure is the goal of human life? This is not, contrary to many teleologists, a simple empirical question. Nietzsche, for instance, denied that human beings pursue pleasure above all other goals; he thought that power was more fundamental than pleasure as a goal of human life. How would we settle this kind of disagreement? And even if we agree with Mill that people naturally seek pleasure for themselves, what proof is there that they seek it for society in general ("the greatest pleasure for the greatest number")? And even if we grant that people do naturally seek the happiness of society, how can we prove, as the teleologist must, that they ought to do so? Teleologists have never succeeded in satisfying their critics on these points.

Indeed, some have criticized the principle of the greatest happiness for the greatest number. Might not a racist nation one day derive enormous happiness from inflicting terrible cruelties upon a despised minority?[15] Teleological ethics seems far too open to the principle that the end justifies the means.

And even if we grant happiness as a societal goal, how do we calculate the means of attaining it? To calculate that, we must determine the causes

15. I am stating this point cautiously, because I don't want to charge any nation as such with racism. But some governments were certainly racist in the last century and inflicted terrible cruelties on the people they disliked. They generally justified themselves in part on the basis of their popular support. While their claim to popular support was usually exaggerated, it was not completely implausible. There has been a large degree of public support for racist policies in many parts of the world.

3333333333

of universal happiness, for the entire future. But who knows all the effects that a human action may ever have? And there are so many different kinds of pleasure and pain!

DEONTOLOGICAL ETHICS

The third tendency is toward deontological ethics, which is an ethic of duty. Deontologists realize that objective moral standards are hard to find on either an existential or a teleological basis. They frankly admit that no such standards can be found either in human subjectivity (as in existentialism) or in empirical knowledge (as in teleological approaches). But they believe that objective ethical standards, absolute duties, can be found in some other way, and that one may define proper ethical behavior simply as the fulfillment of those duties.

In their view, a truly righteous person does not do his duty out of personal inclination (as in existentialism) or out of some calculation of happiness (as in teleological systems). Rather, a good person does his duty "for duty's sake," as Kant put it. A good person does his duty simply because it is his duty. A duty is self-attesting and supremely authoritative; it doesn't need to be recommended on the basis of some supposedly more ultimate consideration. We should not do our duty to get rewards, or to please other people, or to become happier, or to achieve self-realization, but simply because duty is duty—because it is moral law.

Plato's thoughts about ethics were probably more deontological than anything else, though not entirely so. His "Idea of the Good" is a kind of self-attesting value that transcends all others and is known in a nonempirical way.[16] More consistent, though less profound, were the ethical systems of the Cynics and the Stoics, who both urged their hearers to renounce the supremacy of pleasure.[17] In more recent times, Immanuel Kant has been the most famous deontologist,[18] flanked by David Hume[19]

16. See various Platonic dialogues dealing with ethical matters, such as *Gorgias*, *Euthyphro*, and *The Republic*, especially chapter 23 of the latter. See, e.g., Edith Hamilton and Huntington Cairns, eds., *The Collected Dialogues of Plato* (Princeton: Princeton University Press, 1961).

17. See Smith, *Philosophers Speak for Themselves*, for readings in these movements.

18. See his *Foundations of the Metaphysics of Morals*, reproduced in *Kant on the Foundations of Morality*, ed. Brendan Liddell (Bloomington: Indiana University Press, 1970).

19. See especially the last paragraph of part 1, sect. 2, of his *Treatise of Human Nature*, vol. 3, in *Hume's Moral and Political Philosophy*, ed. H. D. Aiken (New York: Hafner, 1948). I link Hume to deontology mainly because of his discussion of what Moore calls "the naturalistic fallacy." But in his systematic treatment of ethics, there is also a large existential component.

and G. E. Moore,[20] who developed influential arguments against teleological ethics, specifically against trying to prove moral principles empir-
ically. Hume argued that "you cannot reason from 'is' to 'ought' "—that
is, from a factual state of affairs to an ethical value or obligation. Moore
called this sort of argument "the naturalistic fallacy." And if teleological
ethics is guilty of the naturalistic fallacy, and existentialist ethics is otherwise objectionable, it would then seem that we should choose a deontological alternative.

Most writers since Moore have accepted, in general, his account of the
naturalistic fallacy. The broader concern of deontological ethics, to develop
a system of absolute duties, is also appreciated by many of those who are
seeking to get beyond the popular relativism and ethics-by-opinion-poll
mentality of our present day. There is, especially since C. S. Lewis's influential article, "The Humanitarian Theory of Punishment,"[21] a greater willingness among ethical thinkers to consider certain actions intrinsically
wrong and others intrinsically praiseworthy, apart from judgments about
the general happiness of society. Christians especially can appreciate this
affirmation of moral absolutes.

However, there is a major problem in deontological ethics, namely, the
problem of identifying the absolute, self-attesting moral principles. Plato
attempted to do it by means of his general arguments for the existence of
the world of Forms. But even granting those controversial assertions, we
must note that Plato's "Good" was at best an abstraction, a generality incapable of prescribing human duties in concrete situations. Kant tried to
establish a catalogue of duties by logically analyzing ethical concepts. An
action is obligatory, he said, when it can be prescribed for all persons
equally, without logical contradiction. But few today would agree that
logic alone can distinguish between good and evil in the absence of any
empirical or subjective premises.[22]

MIXED APPROACHES

The three approaches described above are the only substantial alternatives available to non-Christian ethicists. Most of their ethical systems will
boil down to one of these three, or some combination of them.

20. G. E. Moore, *Principia Ethica* (Cambridge: Cambridge University Press, 1903).
21. In C. S. Lewis, *God in the Dock: Essays on Theology and Ethics* (Grand Rapids: Eerdmans, 1970), 287–300.
22. See, for example, MacIntyre, *A Short History of Ethics*, for a critique of "the logical
emptiness" of Kant's criterion of the categorical imperative.

It is sometimes thought that while a purely deontological, teleological, or existential ethics will not work, some combination of these approaches may be adequate. Certainly we must have some initial sympathy for this project, for, as I shall argue later, the biblical approach is multiperspectival. So why not have a secular multiperspectivalism?

The greatest ethical thinkers—those best understanding the problematics of the "pure" positions—have generally held mixed positions. I have mentioned that Plato, who is generally deontological, includes some elements of existentialism. His Forms are derived from self-knowledge, the Socratic "Know thyself." Similarly, Kant's moral law is essentially existential in origin: the moral self telling itself what to do. For Kant, as for Hegel, the good will is the only unconditionally good thing in the world. But how, then, does Kant avoid the problems of existentialism? Why should I obey the voice of the moral law, which is essentially my own voice? Is there really an objective moral law after all? I doubt that there is any adequate answer in Kant to this sort of question.

Then there is the case of Henry Sidgwick, the nineteenth-century thinker who, despite his utilitarianism, recognized that a pure utilitarianism could lead to the slaughter of minorities and to other evils. So he supplemented his utilitarianism with a "principle of justice." Not only should we seek "the greatest good for the greatest number," but we should also seek an equal distribution of happiness. But why? At this point, Sidgwick resorts to deontology—a kind of intuition of what is right. But that introduces the problems of deontological ethics and robs us of the apparent simplicity and practicality of utilitarianism.[23]

G. E. Moore, who baptized the "naturalistic fallacy," believed that the ends or goals of ethics had to be learned along deontological lines—nonempirically, by way of what Moore called "intuition." But what are the means to those ends or goals? Here Moore was evidently satisfied with utilitarianism, teaching that one simply seeks the most efficient means of reaching the deontological goal. Others, however, argued that this combination of deontological and teleological ethics is unworkable, since it reintroduces the problem of the end justifying the means. These critics of Moore sought to be more consistent deontologists, but they failed to escape the problems of consistently deontological ethics.[24]

Certainly I have not given an exhaustive survey of ethical options, but

23. Sidgwick, *The Methods of Ethics* (New York: Dover, 1966).
24. One such critic was H. A. Prichard. See his *Moral Obligation* (Oxford: Oxford University Press, 1949).

I have presented the general lines of a critique that will prove plausible to those who are acquainted with this literature. It will apply to most, if not all, non-Christian ethical systems. I have presented fairly standard criticisms of these systems. But when we put all these criticisms together, they suggest that a radical departure is needed, not merely a reworking or recombining of the same ideas.

CHRISTIAN ETHICS

Before I present a positive Christian alternative, let me try to diagnose, from a Christian point of view, the reason why secular ethics is regularly led down blind alleys. The main problem is not conceptual confusion, a lack of logical skill, or ignorance of facts, although such problems do exist in both Christian and non-Christian ethical systems. The chief problem is rather unbelief itself. Secular ethics, like secular epistemology, seeks to find an absolute somewhere other than in the Word of God. It therefore seeks its ethical standard in the most probable locations: human subjectivity (existentialism), the empirical world (teleology), or logic or reason (deontology). Seeking truth in those areas is not entirely wrong; as we shall see, one who looks faithfully in those places will find the word of God, which is an adequate ethical standard. And there is some truth in secular ethics because, despite its metaethic, it has encountered God's word in the self, in the world, and in the realm of norms (Rom. 1:32).

But the secularist is forced to reconcile what he finds in these three realms with his fundamental atheism, and here the difficulties begin. For if God does not exist, what assurance do we have that the self, the world, and law will tell us the same things? From a theistic point of view, God creates the human self and the world to exist together in harmony, and he reveals his law as that by which the self and the world will find fulfillment. But on a nontheistic basis, there is no reason to suppose that the self, the world, and law will peacefully coexist—or that ethical judgments derived from one source will necessarily cohere with ethical judgments derived from the other two. Indeed, on such a basis, there is every reason to think that these supposed sources of ethical knowledge will not be mutually consistent, and therefore that one must choose one of the three to accept unconditionally. Those who reject God, in other words, must find an alternate source of absolute truth, a substitute god, an idol. But different people prefer different idols. Hence all the confusion.

My positive Christian alternative should be evident by now. A fully

Christian ethic accepts only God's word as final. That word is found pre-eminently in Scripture, the covenant constitution of the people of God (Deut. 6:6–9; Matt. 5:17–20; 2 Tim. 3:15–17; 2 Peter 1:21), but is also re-vealed in the world (Ps. 19:1ff.; Rom. 1:18ff.) and in the self (Gen. 1:27ff.; 9:6; Eph. 4:24; Col. 3:10). A Christian will study these three realms, pre-supposing their coherence and therefore seeking at each point to integrate each source of knowledge with the other two.[25]

The existential perspective. A Christian ethical study of the self will proceed in the light of Scripture and with a recognition of the world as our God-created environment. A Christian will, like the existential tradition, seek an ethic that realizes human nature and human freedom at their best. But, through Scripture, he will be able to judge what in human nature is the result of sin and what expresses God's image. This sort of ethical study I describe as coming from "the existential per-spective." It is existential in focus, but it does not seek to isolate the self from other sources of God's revelation. Rather, it treats the self as a perspective, a vantage point or angle of vision, from which to view the full range of ethical norms and data. It does justice to the subjec-tive side of human life, particularly our sense of the direct presence of God in his Holy Spirit, re-creating us to know and to reflect his holi-ness. But it does not result in skepticism, because it is anchored in the objectivity of God's Word.

The situational perspective. Similarly, a Christian may study the created world, observing the patterns of cause and effect that produce pleasures and pains of different sorts. He cannot be blind to that, for Christ calls him to love others as himself. He cares whether people are in pain or hav-ing pleasure. But he will carry out this study in the light of scriptural norms (thus escaping the problems of the naturalistic fallacy and of cruelty to minorities, which trap the secular utilitarians) and of his own subjectiv-ity. This sort of study I describe as being from "the situational perspec-tive": it studies the situation as the milieu in which God's norms are to be applied.

The normative perspective. And of course a Christian may study God's law in a more direct way, focusing on Scripture itself. But to determine what Scripture says about a particular ethical problem, we must know more than the text of Scripture. To know what Scripture says about abor-

25. See *DKG*, 62–75, on the integration of revelation from these three sources.

tion, we must know something about abortion. To know what Scripture says about nuclear weapons, we must know something about nuclear weapons. So, odd as it may sound, we cannot know what Scripture says without knowing at the same time something of God's revelation outside of Scripture. This sort of study I call "the normative perspective." Even when we study the Bible, we don't just study the Bible, but we seek to relate the biblical texts to situations and to human subjectivity. We may call this a "Christian deontology" if we like, but it does not face the difficulties of a secular deontology. Rather than arbitrarily postulating moral rules or trying futilely to derive them from logical analysis, a Christian ethic accepts God's moral law as an aspect of God's revelation, doing so for the same reasons that he accepts that revelation as God's word.

In each perspective, then, we study all the data available, all the revelation of God. It is not that we study some under the existential perspective, other data under the situational, and still something else under the normative. Rather, in each case we study everything, but with a particular emphasis or focus. The term *perspective* describes this concept of emphasizing or focusing.

Put in more practical terms, this means that when we face an ethical problem, or when we are counseling someone else, we need to ask three questions: (1) What is the problem? (the situational perspective). (2) What does Scripture say about it? (the normative perspective). (3) What changes are needed to do the right thing? (the existential perspective). Each of these questions must be asked and answered seriously and carefully. And it should be evident that none of them can be fully answered unless we have some answer to the others.

SOME APPLICATIONS

Put this way, this scheme sounds simple enough. And yet it also helps us to understand why ethical questions often become difficult. For ethical judgments involve exegetical, empirical, and psychological knowledge, which in turn involves logical and other skills. Since different Christians have different gifts, we need to work together. Not only professional theologians, but Christians of all walks of life, need to help in the ethical enterprise. There is much to do and, unlike the situation in secular ethics, much hope for success.

Thus, the Scriptures provide us with a metaethic that avoids the traps of the various secular ethical positions. This fact has obvious apologetic significance. Not only philosophers, but nonphilosophers as well, are searching today for ethical stability. We are living at a time when ethical issues are widely discussed. When they discuss ethical problems, Christians can easily get a hearing from people who otherwise have no interest in Christian theology. But most people have little idea how ethical decisions ought to be made; they flounder around with half-baked versions of existentialism, teleology, and deontology. And many fear that beneath all this debate there may not be any basis for ethical certainty. We can show them that in this matter, as well as others, the treasures of wisdom and knowledge are found in Christ.

Our metaethic also has value within the Christian community, as we seek to edify one another in the Lord. Christians, too, need a better understanding of the basis for ethical certainty. Some would admit to having no consistent view of ethics at all; and among those who think they have a consistent view, there is disagreement over what that view should be. Those in the Reformed tradition, especially the theonomic wing, tend to see the law of God in Scripture as the one source of ethical knowledge. Dispensationalists, charismatics, and others (I realize these are strange bedfellows) fear that an emphasis on law will lead to legalism, and thus they tend to develop dangerously subjective notions of divine guidance. Two other groups find the source of ethical certainty in the historical situation: (1) those oriented toward "biblical theology" or "redemptive history," some of whom find their authority not so much in Scripture itself as in the events that Scripture describes, and (2) those who seek to find God's leading in present-day events (one extreme variety of this tendency being liberation theology).

The view that I am presenting, however, has ecumenical implications, for it helps us to listen to one another and to see both the insights and the limitations of the common views. Yes, the scriptural word is primary as the covenant constitution of the people of God. Yes, we cannot properly use the Scriptures without the subjective illumination of God's Spirit. Yes, Scripture is meaningless unless it is applicable to situations, so we must indeed understand the times in which we are living. No, none of these perspectives, rightly understood, takes precedence over the other two, because each includes the other two.

The three perspectives reflect the lordship attributes of God. The situational perspective reflects his control, for our situation is always the result of his universal creation and providence. The normative perspective reflects God's authority. He reveals himself authoritatively in all his works, but particularly in his written word, the covenant constitution of the people of God. And the existential perspective reflects God's covenant presence, as he bears witness to himself in our inmost being. So the metaethic developed in this chapter is an ethic of lordship.

So, as we saw in our discussion of the problem of evil, when ethical issues arise in theology, specifically with respect to the doctrine of God, we may not assume the validity of secular methods to determine what is right and wrong, or good and evil. Indeed, we should challenge secular ethics itself by the Word of God, insisting that ethical systems that reject Scripture are unable to determine what is right and what is wrong.

AN ETHIC OF LORDSHIP

ETHIC	LORDSHIP ATTRIBUTE
SITUATIONAL PERSPECTIVE	CONTROL
NORMATIVE "	AUTHORITY
EXISTENTIAL "	COVENANT PRESENCE

CHAPTER 11

Epistemology

In this chapter, I shall attempt to show how divine lordship bears upon human knowledge—particularly upon our knowledge of God, but then in turn upon all knowledge. As Calvin said, we know God in knowing ourselves, and ourselves in knowing God.[1] We know God by knowing his works, and we understand his works fully only when we understand their relationship to him. So although God is distinct from his creation, our knowledge of him is not distinct from our knowledge of the creation. We always know both at the same time.

So there is a Christian epistemology, just as there is a Christian ethic.[2] Indeed, the Christian ethic implies a Christian epistemology. For the Christian ethic calls upon us to do everything for God's glory. Seeking to know God and the world is one of those things we must do for God's glory. So Scripture distinguishes sharply between true wisdom and knowledge, which begin with the fear of the Lord (Ps. 111:10; Prov. 1:7; 9:10; 15:33), and the false wisdom of unbelief. It urges us not to be taken captive by the wisdom of the world, which is so foolish in the eyes of God (1 Cor. 1:18–3:22), but rather to bring every thought captive to Christ (2 Cor. 10:5). True wisdom differs from false wisdom not only in content, but also in method. The wise man hears and obeys the words that God has revealed to his prophets and

---

1. *Institutes*, 1.1.
2. This is not to say that the Bible answers all the questions discussed in the epistemological literature. But it does provide a general framework within which such answers are to be found.

apostles (1 Cor. 2:6–16); the foolish man will not accept the things of the
Spirit of God (1 Cor. 2:14).

In *DKG*, I formulated a Christian epistemology at some length, based
on the concept of God's covenant lordship. In this chapter, I will summarize some of the points made in that book that are especially relevant to
our present task, contrasting them with some alternative approaches to the
knowledge of God. Obviously, if we are to describe God accurately, we must
use methods of which he approves.

INCOMPREHENSIBILITY AND KNOWABILITY

Scripture teaches that God has made himself known to man. This revelation is universal and clear. As we have seen, man's ignorance of God is
a culpable ignorance. As Paul says,

> What may be known about God is plain to them, because God has
> made it plain to them. For since the creation of the world God's
> invisible qualities—his eternal power and divine nature—have
> been clearly seen, being understood from what has been made, so
> that men are without excuse. (Rom. 1:19–20)

And, beyond this revelation through nature, God has revealed himself
through prophets, apostles, and biblical writers, creating a definitive written revelation, the covenant constitution of the people of God.

At the same time, the biblical writers express wonder and astonishment
before God, confessing how little they understand:

> Many, O LORD my God,
>   are the wonders you have done.
> The things you planned for us
>   no one can recount to you;
> were I to speak and tell of them,
>   they would be too many to declare. (Ps. 40:5)

> Such knowledge [God's knowledge of us!] is too wonderful for me,
>   too lofty for me to attain. (Ps. 139:6)

> Great is the LORD and most worthy of praise;
>   his greatness no one can fathom. (Ps. 145:3)

> "For my thoughts are not your thoughts,
>   neither are your ways my ways,"
>   declares the LORD.

"As the heavens are higher than the earth,
   so are my ways higher than your ways
   and my thoughts than your thoughts." (Isa. 55:8–9)

Oh, the depth of the riches of the wisdom and knowledge of God!
   How unsearchable his judgments,
   and his paths beyond tracing out!
"Who has known the mind of the Lord?
   Or who has been his counselor?" (Rom. 11:33–34, quoting Isa.
    40:13)

So God is knowable and known, and yet mysterious, wondrous, and incomprehensible. How can God be both knowable and incomprehensible? Like the problems discussed earlier—divine sovereignty and human responsibility, and the problem of evil—the biblical writers don't treat this as a problem. Indeed, most believers have no trouble rejoicing in what God has revealed of himself, while worshiping in awe and wonder.

Scripture sometimes distinguishes between things that are hidden and others that are revealed:

> The secret things belong to the Lord our God, but the things revealed belong to us and to our children forever, that we may follow all the words of this law. (Deut. 29:29)

Scripture also distinguishes between things that once were hidden and later are revealed (1 Cor. 2:9; 1 Tim. 3:16). Here, mystery is located in what God has not revealed.

Sometimes, however, Scripture notes a mysteriousness also in the things that have been revealed. Paul's great hymn to God's incomprehensibility, quoted above (Rom. 11:33–36), follows the most systematic account in Scripture of God's plan of salvation, election and reprobation, and the relation of Israel to the Gentiles. One might expect Paul to complete that discussion by claiming that now everything is clear and plain. Instead, he expresses awe and wonder.[3]

Paul also prays that the Christians at Ephesus "may have power, together with all the saints, to grasp how wide and long and high and deep is the love of Christ, and to know this love that surpasses knowledge" (Eph. 3:18–19). Even after we have grasped the dimensions of Jesus' love, it still

---

3. Note also 1 Tim. 6:16, where God's invisibility is due to his "unapproachable light." In one sense, there is *too much* revelation for humans to bear. Walter Chalmers Smith captures the idea in his hymn, "Immortal, Invisible, God Only Wise": "'Tis only the splendor of light hideth thee!"

surpasses our knowledge. So God is incomprehensible even in his revelation. When God reveals himself to us, he does not thereby decrease his incomprehensibility.[4] Mature believers understand this principle well. The more deeply one understands the love of God, the wisdom of his plan, and his mighty power, the more amazed one is.

Scripture also represents God as incomparable (Ex. 15:11; 1 Kings 8:23; Isa. 40:18, 25; 46:5, 9), over against the false gods and the creatures that image them. Of course, there is a sense in which anything can be compared with anything else, positively or negatively, and these passages themselves amount to negative comparisons. Jesus' parables also provide comparisons between God's actions and those of human beings. Further, these passages should not be taken to imply that God cannot have an image, for man himself is the image of God (Gen. 1:27–28), and Christ is the image of God *par excellence* (Col. 1:15; Heb. 1:3). So the incomparability of God is limited by the comparisons that he himself has given to us in his revelation. The point of Exodus 15:11 and similar passages is that (1) God is unique, (2) we must not presume to compare him with created beings, except on the basis of his revelation, and (3) when we come to know God, we are in awe, overwhelmed; we find in him a greatness that dwarfs all other actual and potential objects of knowledge.

So the biblical writers never see the incomprehensibility of God as detracting from the reliability or authority of his revelation. The mysteriousness of God is never the basis of a general agnosticism. God's revelation is mysterious, but it is a genuine revelation.

Theologians, however, have found it difficult to formulate the precise distinction between God's incomprehensibility and his knowability. We discussed in chapter 7 the church fathers who described God (particularly the Father) as "nameless" and "inexpressible," perhaps under the influence of Hellenistic Judaism and Greek philosophy. Later thinkers emphasized that we cannot know what God is, but only what he is not.[5] But if God is literally inexpressible, then he cannot be known. Certainly these writers were not consistent with these extreme formulations, for they spoke very freely of what God has revealed of himself. But their formulations brought difficulty to later generations.

---

4. Norman Shepherd in a class lecture drew a circle on the board representing our knowledge of God. The circumference represented our exposure to the mystery outside the circle. He then increased the size of the circle to represent an increase in our knowledge of God. But when the circle got larger, so did the circumference, and so did, therefore, our exposure to the mystery. The more we know, the more we become aware of what we don't know.

5. See the survey of theologians in *DG*, 21–24.

Thomas Aquinas recommended the "way of remotion," sometimes called the *via negationis* or the *via negativa*, which allows us to speak of what God is not. He explains:

> Now, in considering the divine substance, we should especially make use of the method of remotion. For, by its immensity, the divine substance surpasses every form that our intellect reaches. Thus we are unable to apprehend it by knowing *what it is*. Yet we are able to have some knowledge of it by knowing *what it is not*.[6]

In the context, Aquinas has just proved the existence of God to his satisfaction. So in the paragraph quoted, he is not denying that we have any positive knowledge of God. He has just shown that God exists, that he is the first mover, and that he is the governor of the world, who enables all the parts of the world to work together toward a common end.[7]

The important point for Aquinas here is that we cannot in this life know God by his essence—that divine substance that "surpasses every form that our intellect reaches." So even if some knowledge of God is positive in character, it is essentially a knowledge of his effects, rather than knowledge of his essence. God far surpasses his effects, and so our knowledge of him is sharply limited. We will be able to know the essence of God in the heavenly consummation, but then only by God's gracious illumination,[8] and even then not exhaustively.[9] Aquinas argues that God's essence is "infinitely knowable," and "no created intellect can know God infinitely."[10] Furthermore, since in this life our intellects are bound to understanding material things, we cannot know the essence of God, which is immaterial, although we can know God through his effects in the material world.[11]

Calvin says that God in Scripture "speaks sparingly of his essence,"[12] and Calvin himself says far less about it than does Aquinas. Ursinus says, simply, that "we are ignorant of [God's] essence."[13] Bavinck says that our

---

6. *SCG*, 1.14.2.
7. Ibid., 1.13.35.
8. *ST*, 1.12.1.
9. Ibid., 1.12.7.
10. Ibid.
11. Ibid.
12. *Institutes*, 1.13.1.
13. Zacharias Ursinus, *Commentary on the Heidelberg Catechism* (1852 edition; reprint, Phillipsburg, N.J.: Presbyterian and Reformed, n.d.), 123.

knowledge has "for its object not God himself according to his unknowable essence, but God in his revelation to us."[14]

What is this "unknowable essence"? We shall consider essence more systematically in chapter 12. But for now we can say that *essence* usually refers
to the defining characteristics of something, those qualities that make
something what it is. For Aquinas, God's essence is his act of existing, since,
as we saw in chapter 2, he takes Exodus 3:14 to mean that God's proper
name is Being. His essence is to be, to exist. For Aquinas, God does possess other perfections and excellences within that simple act of existence.[15]
Since some creatures know that simple act of existence without knowing
it exhaustively, knowing it is a matter of degree. Glorified saints can have
partial knowledge of a simple essence.

Whatever philosophers can make of this, it certainly roams far from the
biblical text. As we saw earlier, Exodus 3:14 cannot be pressed to say that
God is Being in some metaphysical sense. But if God is not Being, then
what is he? What is his essence?

The defining qualities of God are the qualities that make him God, that
distinguish him from all other beings. If we are going to use the word
essence, it is best to understand it as comprising all the divine attributes revealed in Scripture. That God has many defining features does not compromise his simplicity, if we maintain that those attributes are inseparably
one in God.[16] But then we can state what his essence is, and we can do it

---

14. *DG*, 98. Bavinck denies that we can know God "as he is in himself" (p. 32) or that
we can have an "adequate" knowledge of him (pp. 33, 35). In my judgment, these are more
or less equivalent to "knowing God by his essence." Interestingly, much later in the book,
he distinguishes his discussion of the Trinity from his discussion of God's decrees by saying,
"Thus far we have dealt with God's being as it exists in itself" (p. 337), indicating, as he
does in the context, that we can know God as he is in himself insofar as he has revealed
that in Scripture. The barrier to knowing God as he is in himself is not our finitude, but
God's decision to withhold some of that knowledge from us. Perhaps there are some things
about God in himself that we cannot know because we are finite, but there are other things
about God in himself that he can reveal to creatures and has revealed to us.

Bavinck's use of the word *adequate* seems to be based on an older use of the term than
is common today. Philosophers sometimes spoke of "the adequation of thought and being,"
referring to perfect knowledge. In this sense, Bavinck denies that we have adequate knowledge of God. But in the modern sense of *adequate* knowledge, namely, knowledge suited to
its proper purposes, Bavinck would no doubt have affirmed that we have it.

Compare also the statements of Reformed dogmaticians to the effect that God cannot
be defined, and that "what is finite cannot express the infinite" (*RD*, 52). Among these
quotations, Cocceius uses *adequate* in the way Bavinck does.

15. Thomas Aquinas, *On Being and Essence* (Toronto: Pontifical Institute of Mediaeval Studies, 1949), 51. For more discussion of Aquinas's metaphysical formulations, see chapter 12.

16. See the discussion of simplicity in the following chapter.

in many ways: control, authority, presence, holiness, eternity, goodness, and so on. (More will be said on these subjects in the next chapter.)

Is God's essence, then, knowable? Yes and no. Yes, in that Scripture tells us about some qualities that define God as distinct from other beings, some of which we have already discussed in this book. And when Scripture describes God, it describes him as he really and truly is. So its definitions of God enable us to know him, indeed, to know his essence.

No, God's essence is not knowable, in that our knowledge of God is certainly not exhaustive. We don't know everything that can be known about God's holiness, wisdom, goodness, etc., nor how all his attributes are unified within the complete divine being. To have a perfect knowledge of that, we would have to be God. Such knowledge is impossible for the creature. The best formulation, then, is that God's essence is knowable, but not exhaustively.

We should not adopt a mental picture or model of God in which his real identity or essence is hidden in darkness, while his revealed nature is a kind of periphery around that darkness. In that picture, the darkness conceals what God really and truly is; his revealed nature is something less than his real being. On the contrary: God's names and revealed attributes tell us what he truly is, at the heart of his being. There is nothing more fundamental about him that could call his revealed nature into question. Such biblical terms as *holiness, goodness, and eternity* express God's essence. They tell us what he really is, for Scripture is true. They define him, because through them God has defined himself.[17]

My approach rejects the broad assertions of agnosticism that are often found in theological works. Such agnosticism is the epistemological correlate of the false concept of transcendence described in chapter 7. We should not press the way of remotion, as did pseudo-Dionysius and John Scotus Erigena (but not Aquinas), to say that we can know only what God is not, not what he is. Negative statements by themselves are useless: for example, one can know a thousand things that a Siberian husky is not, without having any useful knowledge of what he is.

Nor should we accept the claims of more recent thinkers who have de-

17. Historically, the objection to defining God is that God cannot be assigned to any genus or species. He does not, in other words, belong to a larger class of objects. So he cannot be defined as a member of that class and then be differentiated from other members of that class. Scripture, however, does describe God as belonging to the class of beings that are holy, good, wise, etc., and also describes his differences from other beings in those classes. Certainly God is different from all other beings in important ways, for he is Lord. But Scripture does not infer from God's uniqueness that he cannot be described in the same categories as finite beings. There is more on this subject in my discussion of analogy, below.

scribed God as "wholly hidden" or "wholly other." This kind of general agnosticism is foreign to Scripture. The Lord of Scripture is not wholly hidden. He is knowable and known to all through nature, and his revelation in Scripture is perfectly adequate to its purpose. Contrary to Barth, to say this does not make God a possession of man, or claim that God is subject to our control or manipulation. As we have seen, Scripture tells us that God is the ultimate controller, and that we are his possession, not the other way around. The more we meditate on this clear revelation, the more it rebukes our pride, our claims to self-sufficiency. It is those who deny this revelation, preferring to think of God autonomously, who seek dominance over their Creator. Nor is clear revelation opposed to grace. Rather, it is itself a gift of grace, and it sets forth consistently the message that we have nothing and are nothing, except for God's grace.

Theologians who make much of the "wholly otherness" of God are not in the least restrained in their writing and speaking about God. Typically, they have gone ahead to write great tomes, developing elaborate theories about God's nature and existence, his attributes, and the relations among the persons of the Trinity, as if they had entirely forgotten their initial agnosticism. And these tomes typically stray far from biblical teaching. It is as if their general agnosticism has given them license to speculate at will, perhaps thinking that since no human thought about God can really be true, there is no need to be careful about truth in theological writing, or careful to distinguish between what we actually know about God and what we don't.[18] Thus, again we see a false view of transcendence leading to a false view of immanence. The "wholly other" allows man to do theology autonomously, becoming his own ultimate authority, that is to say, his own god.

It is wiser, in my view, not to make general claims of ignorance about God, but rather to carefully restrict our dogmatic claims to the teaching of Scripture, and to be honest about those questions that Scripture does not resolve. God's transcendence is not a wholly otherness, but his control and authority over the creation. His immanence, therefore, as his covenant presence, does not confer his ultimate wisdom on the theologian, but provides a revelation that governs and limits our thinking and speech.[19]

18. For example, Elizabeth Johnson says that since "the reality of God is mystery beyond all imagining," "historically new attempts at articulation are to be expected and even welcomed" (*She Who Is* [New York: Crossroad, 1996], 7). The new attempt at articulation that she proposes is to speak of God exclusively in feminine terms.

19. In this discussion, the term *incomprehensibility* is being used rather differently than it was used in the conflict between Cornelius Van Til and Gordon H. Clark in the Orthodox Presbyterian Church during the late 1940s. In that controversy, *incomprehensibility* was used (somewhat inaccurately) to refer to a relationship between God's thoughts and man's

We should think of God's incomprehensibility, then, not as a "wholly otherness," but as the result of transcendence in the biblical sense: God has control and authority over creaturely knowledge. So his thoughts are not our thoughts, and his mystery permeates our knowledge.[20] This kind of incomprehensibility does not compromise God's knowability. Rather, God's incomprehensible nature becomes immanent in his revelation of himself.

ANALOGY

We should not accept the related claim that God's incomprehensibility relativizes all human language about God, including that of Scripture. We have seen that advocates of transcendence in the unbiblical sense have often claimed that God is nameless, that no human language properly applies to God.

The high scholasticism of Aquinas does not go that far. Aquinas grants that some terms apply properly to God alone, such as *highest good* and *the first being*.[21] But even these terms are "defective," he says, "as to the mode of signification."[22] By that he means that "our intellect, taking the origin of its knowledge from the senses, does not transcend the mode which is found in sensible things."[23] This discussion is difficult; but I take it that for Aquinas a word like *good* inevitably connotes for us something finite, something partly material. We can negate that connotation of finitude by using compound terms like *eternal goodness, infinite goodness,* or *highest good.*

---

thoughts. The specific question was whether a man's idea of something (say, a rose) can be identical with God's idea of the same thing. For discussion of that issue, see *DKG*, 21–40, and *CVT*, 97–113. I affirm that God's and man's ideas are different in certain respects. For example, (1) God's mind is identical with his being, (2) God and man experience different thought processes, and (3) God's ideas create and authoritatively define the realities they conceive. But God's and man's ideas may be identical in that (1) both can affirm the same truth, and (2) both may be about the same thing and therefore have the same object.

20. So incomprehensibility, obviously a mode of God's transcendence, is a mode of his immanence as well. Because God made all things, we cannot know anything fully apart from him. So all our knowledge is mysterious. God's incomprehensibility is immanent in all our knowledge of him and his world. Like holiness, which also marks God's transcendence (chap. 2), incomprehensibility reflects his immanence as well. And as God's holiness creates areas of creation that share his holiness, making the rest of the world profane by comparison, he brings his incomprehensible wisdom to his people, making the wisdom of the world foolish (1 Cor. 1:18–2:16; 3:18–23).

21. *SCG*, 1.30.2.

22. Ibid., 1.30.3.

23. Ibid.

But terms of human language must always be modified in such a way before they can properly apply to God.

Aquinas concludes, then, that words like *good* cannot apply to God "univocally," that is, in the same sense in which they apply to creatures. God's goodness, unlike man's, is identical with his essence. However, Aquinas also denies that the senses are "equivocal," that is, having nothing in common, as when we use *race* for both a contest and an ethnic group. Rather, *good* applies to God "analogously." He mentions various types of analogies, but defines the theological analogy as one

> according as one thing is proportioned to another (thus, *healthy* is said of medicine and an animal, since medicine is the cause of health in the animal body). And in this way some things are said of God and creatures analogously. . . . For we can name God only from creatures.[24]

Aquinas does not mean to say that God's goodness is nothing more than the cause of goodness in creatures. For him, the cause has some real resemblance to the effect (or, more precisely, vice versa). So God is really good. But we use the term *good* of God without knowing what that resemblance consists of, by an analogy based on the causal relation.

Aquinas avoids the global agnosticism we discussed earlier. However, his analogism is somewhat inconsistent. The negative and relational terms that generate phrases like *eternal goodness* and *highest good* need to be univocal if they are to do their job in Aquinas's system. And if *goodness* applies to God analogously by a causal relation, what about the word *cause?* Does that require another analogous relation, and another, *ad infinitum?* Somewhere, it would seem, we must be able to say something about God univocally, for there must be some univocal attribute on which to hang the analogies, whether that be *cause, being,* or something else. But if *cause* can be univocal, why can't *goodness* be?

This inconsistency can be pressed either toward global agnosticism or toward some level of literal knowledge about God. The problem, as I see it, is in Aquinas's statement that "we can name God only from creatures." According to Scripture, there is never a time in which we know creatures, but don't know God. As we have seen, God is as clearly revealed to us, as clearly known to us, as any created thing. We know him, not only by means of creatures, but also in and with creatures (as we shall see in our discussion of providence in chap. 14). And, in one sense, we know him prior to knowing creatures, for our knowledge of creatures depends on our

24. *ST*, 1.13.5.

knowledge of God. So it is as true to say that we know creatures by way of God as it is to say that we know God by way of creatures.

Human language is given to us, not only to represent finite things, but most importantly to be a means of communication with God. God is a part of our experience, and he designed human language to refer to him. So the language we use about God is not an analogous extrapolation from language about creatures. We do not first learn to speak about creatures and then force that language, via analogy and qualification, to refer to God. Rather, some human language very naturally refers to God. For example, since we were created in his image, rather than vice versa, the application of *lord* to men is an analogous extrapolation of its application to God.[25] The process of analogizing can go either way: from God to the world or vice versa.

We need not be afraid of saying that some of our language about God is univocal or literal. God has given us language that literally applies to him. When one says negatively that "God is not a liar," no word in that sentence is analogous or figurative. The sentence distinguishes God from literal liars, not analogous ones. Similarly, the statement that "God is good" uses the term *good* univocally. God's goodness is, of course, different from ours in important ways. But goodness on either the divine or the human level can be defined by such concepts as justice, mercy, and kindness. The differences between God's nature and ours do not require that we use the term *good* in different senses.[26]

More recent thinkers have also appealed to divine transcendence to show that there is something inappropriate about using human language to refer to God. Such claims often have the force of relativizing the truth of all human language about God, including that of Scripture. For example, Karl Barth says:

> God does not belong to the world. Therefore he does not belong to the series of objects for which we have categories and words by

---

25. This is not a statement about the etymology of *lord*, or about the history of its use, but only about how we *should* regard the term.

26. In rejecting Aquinas's doctrine of analogy, I am not intending to reject Cornelius Van Til's similar-sounding, but actually very different, doctrine of "analogous knowledge." By that phrase, Van Til says not that terms must be applied to God in nonliteral ways, but that in all our thought, we must seek to "think God's thoughts after him," recognizing his revelation as the source and authority for all human knowledge. That is in fact the fundamental point I wish to make about epistemology, as it was Van Til's fundamental point. See my *CVT*, 89–95. Note also my discussion there of whether there may be a continuum between literal and figurative. I would say, however, that to use the word "analogy" as Van Til does is confusing, since the word has most often been used very differently in the history of theology.

means of which we draw the attention of others to them, and bring them into relation with them. Of God it is impossible to speak, because he is neither a natural nor a spiritual object. If we *speak* of him, we are no longer speaking of *him*.[27]

How, then, can we preach or teach about God? Ott paraphrases Barth's answer:

> Barth's solution is that in our own strength and with our own possibilities it is impossible for *us* to speak of God. The fact that we speak about him and yet are unable to do so is a fault which God *himself* forgives, and in doing so he takes our human words and concepts which in themselves are inappropriate and transforms them into a fitting witness to himself.[28]

How can they be a fitting witness if they are in themselves inappropriate? If "God is good" is inappropriate in itself, what does God do to that phrase—or to us—to make it appropriate? This claim should be related to Barth's well-known view that revelation is not the communication of propositions or information, but a nonpropositional communication of God himself to us. What is communicated is God's power, love, and salvation, but not verbal content. Like Aquinas, Barth is not entirely consistent in this view. One wonders what value there is in the many volumes of Barth's *Church Dogmatics* if indeed all its words and sentences are inappropriate. Would it not be less expensive to seek God's will in a cheaper, but also inappropriate source, such as a telephone directory?

Certainly God's grace plays an important role in our preaching and teaching. But it does not change the meanings of our words from false to true. It often moves us to abandon false words and to substitute words that are true to God's Word. But nothing in Scripture suggests that God takes a false sentence and makes it true by sheer grace.

Nor does Scripture ever suggest that human words are in some general sense inappropriate to refer to God. Rather, it claims over and over that its own words, and other words that truly convey its content, are entirely appropriate and should never be disobeyed or disbelieved. It is wrong, therefore, to say that human language is defective as an instrument of divine-human communication.[29]

---

27. *ChD*, 1.2.750.

28. Heinrich Ott, *God* (Atlanta: John Knox Press, 1971), 99–100.

29. I discuss some other challenges to theological language, including the logical positivist challenge, in "God and Biblical Language: Transcendence and Immanence," in *God's Inerrant Word*, ed. John W. Montgomery (Minneapolis: Bethany Fellowship, 1974), 159–77.

However, analogy does play an important role in our knowledge of God. There are a number of areas of theology where the divine mystery is so impenetrable that we can only get a small glimpse of the truth. Often that glimpse comes through analogies. We have already seen in our discussions of human responsibility and the problem of evil that some theological problems elude our attempts at precise solutions. In those areas, I have suggested some analogies (the storyteller model, the greater-good defense) that point in the direction of better understanding, but do not remove all difficulty. We shall see that the doctrine of creation *ex nihilo* (chap. 15) and the doctrine of the Trinity (chaps. 27–29) also resist our attempts at precise, literal formulation. But theology has accepted *ex nihilo* (a phrase very difficult to define) as a suitable analogy of creation. And Scripture itself provides the names Father, Son, and Spirit, as suitable analogies for the Trinitarian persons.

LORDSHIP AND KNOWLEDGE

A biblical view of knowledge begins, not with a general agnosticism, but with God's lordship. It is the fear of the Lord that is the beginning of knowledge. He has made us to think according to his standards. Therefore, there is an ethics of knowledge. We are under obligation to believe what God reveals to us, including the legitimate implications and applications of his revelation. God also calls upon us to seek knowledge with a love for him and others, lest it be of no value (1 Cor. 8:1–3; 13). As Calvin emphasizes early in his *Institutes*, knowledge and piety are inseparable.

Among the biblical norms are some principles concerning the methods of knowledge. In chapter 10, I surveyed three tendencies in secular ethical philosophy: (1) existential ethics, focusing on motive, (2) teleological ethics, focusing on the goal of human action, and (3) deontological ethics, focusing on duties or norms. I indicated that a biblical ethic recognizes all three of these factors without absolutizing one of them over against the others. Christian ethics is triperspectival, recognizing the importance of motive, goal, and standard. Ethical discussion can focus on motive (the existential perspective), goal (the situational perspective), or standard (the normative perspective). These are perspectives, because not one can be done without the other two. Each describes the whole of ethics from one perspective. This threefold distinction arises from the lordship attributes: the existential perspective reflects God's presence in blessing and judgment, the situational perspective reflects his control, and the normative perspective reflects his authority.

In *DKG*,[30] I surveyed three similar tendencies in the field of secular epistemology: (1) subjectivism, in which there is no universal or objective truth, but only "truth for me," (2) empiricism, in which the final arbiter of truth is sense experience, and (3) rationalism, in which the final arbiter of truth is the laws of thought, logic, and other *a priori* principles. I tried to show how these approaches to knowledge, and various combinations of them, were inadequate.

Indeed, these approaches are inadequate for religious reasons. As Van Til taught us, unbelief is both rationalistic and irrationalistic at once: rationalistic in claiming to be able to ascertain the truth autonomously, apart from revelation, and irrationalistic in denying God, the only possible ground of a meaningful universe correlated with the rationality of our minds. Unbelieving irrationalism is the epistemological correlate of unbiblical transcendence, in which God is too far from us to play a role in human thought. Unbelieving rationalism is the epistemological correlate of a false immanence, in which human beings claim for themselves the supreme authority to declare what is true.

Scripture establishes as the believer's presupposition the revelation of God. That revelation takes three forms: (1) the illumination of the Holy Spirit,[31] (2) God's revelation in nature and history (that is, "natural revelation"), and (3) God's revelation by word (that is, "special revelation": direct utterance,[32] the speaking of prophets and apostles, and the Scriptures). These three forms of revelation must be taken together. Illumination is nothing in itself, being only a witness to natural and special revelation. Natural revelation must be seen through "the spectacles of Scripture," illumined by the Spirit. Special revelation makes no impact apart from illumination or apart from its application to the reader's situation and the course of nature and history.

So each of these three forms of revelation is incomplete without the others. To do justice to any one of them, we must look at the others. There-

---

30. Pp. 109–22.

31. Some may object to thinking of illumination as a form of revelation. It is true that many recent theologians, including Barth and Brunner, have misconceived the relationship between the inspiration of the biblical writers and the illumination of the reader, virtually replacing the former with the latter. Nevertheless, illumination is called "revelation" in Eph. 1:17, and Matt. 11:27 uses the word *reveal* in the sense of illumination. Illumination does not add anything new to the biblical canon, but it is genuine revelation in that it brings *knowledge* to those who receive it. It is by illumination that we understand and come to believe from the heart the message of Scripture. For an extended discussion of these three forms of revelation, see my forthcoming *Doctrine of the Word of God*.

32. Examples of direct utterance: God's speaking to Israel from Mount Sinai, and the voice from heaven at Jesus' baptism and transfiguration.

fore, in an important sense, each includes the others. Each is a perspective on the whole organism of revelation.

Describing the three forms of revelation as perspectives, we can use the same terminology we used for the ethical perspectives. (1) The existential perspective is the method of listening to the Holy Spirit's internal witness. But the Spirit directs us to the Word and to the applications of the Word in the world. (2) The situational perspective is the method of studying the course of nature and history—human experience in the broadest sense. But God's Word is a central fact of experience, one which determines our interpretations of experience, and that Word must be illumined by the Spirit. (3) The normative perspective is the method of reading the Bible to determine what God wants us to believe and do. But we cannot rightly understand or apply Scripture apart from the Spirit's work, and we cannot apply it to our own lives without some knowledge of our own life-situations, gained from general revelation.

The three perspectives, therefore, ultimately coincide. Knowledge is a unity. We cannot discover anything under one perspective that we cannot discover under the other two. The three do not cover different subject matters, but the same subject matter from different viewpoints.

Like the ethical perspectives, the epistemological perspectives reflect the three lordship attributes. The situational perspective reflects God's control, because it focuses on the whole course of nature and history, in which God works in all things according to the good pleasure of his will. The normative perspective focuses on God's authority, addressed to all creatures in his powerful Word. The existential perspective focuses on God's covenant presence, now in the person of the Spirit, to drive the truth into our hearts.

CHAPTER 12

Metaphysics

Metaphysics, or ontology,[1] examines the most basic and pervasive features of the universe. It is concerned to understand being itself and the chief distinctions within being. Thus, it seeks to formulate a general view of the world. There is, therefore, considerable overlap between metaphysics and theology. Scripture also presents a general view of the world: God as Creator, and the world as his creation. Historically, Christian theologians, especially those writing on the doctrine of God, have been in vigorous dialogue with metaphysical philosophers—sometimes attacking them, sometimes borrowing their concepts. So it is important that we examine the relationships between metaphysics and the doctrine of God and consider the possibility of a distinctively biblical metaphysics.

In the history of thought, we live in a distinctly antimetaphysical age. The philosopher Immanuel Kant (1724–1804) provided a powerful impetus toward metaphysical skepticism, as he tried to show that traditional metaphysics, whether philosophical or theological, was all speculation that went beyond the proper limits of human thought. Logical positivists in the 1920s and 1930s argued that metaphysical language was cognitively meaningless, since it could not be verified or falsified by scientific means. At about the same time, existentialists despaired of finding any objective, meaningful structure in the universe. Other forms of philosophy, such as idealism, process philosophy, and later forms of lan-

---

1. I treat these two terms interchangeably.

214

guage analysis, have been more hospitable toward metaphysics, and it appears that tolerance for metaphysics is becoming more prevalent as we begin the twenty-first century.

But the earlier atmosphere of metaphysical skepticism moved liberal theologians like Ritschl and Harnack to abandon any talk of the metaphysical nature of God or of the persons of the Trinity. In the period of neoorthodoxy (Barth, Brunner), existential theology (Bultmann), and *Heilsgeschichte* (Cullmann, Wright), it was fashionable to disparage talk of God's nature in favor of speaking of "the acts of God" or "the event of new self-understanding." In Bultmann and in secular theologies, we heard about the need to translate affirmations about God into affirmations about man. And today, in the theologies of Moltmann and Pannenberg, as we have seen, God is transcendent, not as a metaphysical absolute transcends the world, but as the future transcends the present, although both of these theologians have developed rather elaborate metaphysical systems of their own.

In orthodox Protestant theology, there is a suspicion, not so much of metaphysics as such, as of the scholastic philosophy of being, which had a large influence on the traditional formulations of the doctrine of God.

This chapter, then, will be a response to these developments, as well as an attempt to formulate a biblical metaphysic or worldview. It is not possible for biblical Christians to avoid metaphysical questions altogether. The theologians who have tried to avoid them have merely substituted one metaphysic for another: natural law for divine law, "events" for "being," "transcendent future" for "transcendent being." Furthermore, Scripture speaks, as we have seen, not only of what God does, but of what he *is*, and what we are in relation to him.

Nor is it possible to describe God only in terms of his roles or functions, avoiding discussion of his nature. As we have seen, God's role in our history is that of covenant Lord. But God does not take on that role arbitrarily, as if he could take on a completely different relationship to his creatures. And certainly it would not have been possible for you or me to take on the same role. Only God can be the covenant Lord, for that role is appropriate only for him. And why is it appropriate? Because he is our Creator, owner, and ruler. He deserves the role of Lord, because he is different in nature from all his creatures.

Not everyone can control all the events of nature and history—only one with a unique nature. Not everyone can speak with absolute authority—only one who is such a being that he has the right to be obeyed. Not everyone can be covenantally present to the whole universe, remaining distinct from it. To perform these functions, one must be different from all other beings, possessing a distinct nature.

Scripture doesn't use typical metaphysical terminology very often, but in Galatians 4:8–9, Paul reminds and exhorts the church:

> Formerly, when you did not know God, you were slaves to those who by nature are not gods. But now that you know God—or rather are known by God—how is it that you are turning back to those weak and miserable principles?

The false gods are those who "by nature" are not gods. Our object of worship must have a distinctive nature. The false gods don't have it; only the true God does. It is that distinctive nature that makes him worthy of worship. The same emphasis, without the philosophical terms, can be found in the Old Testament's denunciation of idolatry. God says through Isaiah (e.g., in 44:9–20) that idols are worthless, because they do not have the kind of nature that deserves worship.

Indeed, worship leads believers to make metaphysical assertions about God. As we shall see in our discussion of the divine attributes, we recognize God's transcendence, his aseity, his omnipotence, and so on, as we praise him for his wonderful works, as in the Psalms. So we should not despise metaphysical terminology, as if it necessarily arises out of a spiritually barren intellectualism. Sometimes it does, but the main motivation for Christian metaphysics is liturgical and therefore practical.

We discover God's distinctive nature through his actions in nature and history, as the praises of the Psalms attest. But his nature is not to be equated with his actions. His nature is his unique quality of being by which alone he performs those actions.

THE GREAT CHAIN OF BEING[2]

In this book, we have distinguished between two ways of understanding divine transcendence. The unbiblical concept sees God's transcendence in terms of divine distance and human ignorance. God is so far beyond or above us, on this view, that we cannot know him or speak truly about him. In Plotinus's Neoplatonism and in Gnosticism, the unknowable One brings about lesser beings by "emanation," as light from a lamp. These beings are more or less divine as they are near or far from the source. And there are degrees of being: more divinity means more being; less divinity means less

---

2. This heading alludes to a book by Arthur O. Lovejoy, *The Great Chain of Being* (Cambridge, Mass.: Harvard University Press, 1964), which remains a useful introduction to "continuum" metaphysics.

being. There is, then, a continuum of being between the One at the top of the scale and the material universe at the bottom.

This worldview is pantheistic, or monistic, in that everything is essentially divine. Yet, to the emanations, the One is "wholly other," and so these systems also employ at times a deistic or dualistic vocabulary. In fact, as the church father Irenaeus pointed out, there is a large amount of confusion in this scheme: God is wholly other than we are, and yet we are essentially identical with him, once we penetrate the illusions brought about by material existence.

In these systems, then, there is not only an unbiblical concept of transcendence, but also an unbiblical concept of immanence. Somewhat parallel to Barth's paradox, God is both wholly other to and wholly identical with the world. We are absolutely ignorant of him, but also (if we use the techniques of Neoplatonic philosophy or gain the Gnostic knowledge) perfectly able to know him by mystical union, if not by propositional understanding.

The biblical metaphysic, on the contrary, makes a clear distinction between the Creator and the world, his "creaturely other." God is the Lord; the universe serves him. God is entitled by nature to be Lord; we are not. His lordship extends to everything that he has made. So there is no continuum between God and creation. There are no degrees of divinity: God is divine, and we are not. There are no degrees of reality, either. God is real, and we are real.

There are, of course, two very different *levels* of reality, the Creator's and the creature's.[3] Cornelius Van Til often drew two circles on the blackboard: a larger one above, and a smaller one below. The upper circle represented God; the lower circle represented the creation. Van Til emphasized that these are distinct, not on a continuum. Often he cited the Chalcedon Declaration of 451 to show that even in the person of Christ, where there is the most intimate communion imaginable between deity and humanity, there is no "confusion" or "change" of the two.[4] Even in the person of Christ, the Creator-creature distinction holds. The two circles, in Van Til's view, emphasize the most important feature of the biblical worldview. Nonbiblical thought, he taught, is always "one-circle" thinking, putting the Creator and the creature on the same level. Neoplatonism was one of Van Til's main examples of one-circle thinking.

---

3. Reality may, of course, be divided in different ways: mental and material, possible and actual, timeless and temporal, potential and actual, etc. But these levels represent the most fundamental metaphysical division. It is God who expresses or determines (i.e., who originates, either by his nature or by his actions) all metaphysical distinctions.

4. Nor, of course, "division" or "separation."

As there are two different kinds of reality, so there are different kinds of goodness, justice, wisdom, and knowledge: those of God and those of creatures. God's knowledge, for example, is not only more extensive than ours, but also different in character. God's knowledge is essentially self-knowledge, based on his intentions and actions, which control all things. Our knowledge must have a reference point beyond ourselves, namely God's authoritative revelation in nature and Scripture. God's knowledge is the knowledge of the Creator, knowledge that creates the things it knows. It is the knowledge of the Lord, who controls the objects of his knowledge, interprets them with supreme authority, and is always present with them to act in accord with that interpretation. Our knowledge is the knowledge of creatures, which receives the reality and interpretation of its objects from God. There is no continuum between God's knowledge and ours. There is no midpoint, no ladder to heaven for us to ascend to gain a knowledge that is increasingly divine.

It is true, of course, that God knows more things than we do, so we cannot rule out entirely the language of degree, or, to that extent, continuum. God's ways are higher than ours (Isa. 55:9), and his might is greater than our powers. But to say that is not to indicate the deepest level of difference between our powers and his.[5] Similarly, we can certainly say that God is far more merciful, gracious, just, and good than we are, using the language of continuum. But is God more good than, say, unfallen Adam or the glorified saints? Surely, both unfallen Adam and the glorified saints should be considered good, and good without defect. But even their goodness is different from God's, for God's goodness is the supreme standard and example for ours—a perspective (to anticipate later discussion) on his infinite being. God's goodness is the goodness of the Creator, the Lord. Ours, at its very best, even perfected by grace, is the goodness of creatures.

Recall that when we discussed the problem of evil (in chap. 9), I mentioned the scholastic view that God created the world good, but defective. Part of what the scholastics meant, of course, is that God created a world with higher and lesser goods, and that is true. But lesser goods should not be thought of as defective. The world as God made it was not defective. It was good, but its goodness was the goodness of the creature, rather than the Creator. The language of "defect" assumes a continuum of goodness, which in turn presupposes an unbiblical view of transcendence. This view

---

5. This is the main reason why Cornelius Van Til contended so strongly for the non-identity of God's thought with ours. I fault some of the details of his argument with Gordon H. Clark on this subject, but in this controversy Van Til had a far deeper view of the Creator-creature distinction than did Clark. See CVT, 97–113.

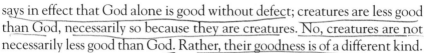

says in effect that God alone is good without defect; creatures are less good than God, necessarily so because they are creatures. No, creatures are not necessarily less good than God. Rather, their goodness is of a different kind.

The difference, of course, is not so radical as to make us wholly ignorant of it, as in the unbiblical concept of transcendence. It is possible to explain in some measure (but not exhaustively) the relevant differences between God's qualities and ours, as I have tried to do above. And of course God's attributes are imaged in creatures. We are made to be like him, and we are called to be more like him (Lev. 19:2; Matt. 5:43–48; 1 Peter 1:16). God calls us to love one another as he has loved us in Christ (John 13:34–35). But even here the difference is evident: his love is the model, and ours is the image. Or, as Abraham Kuyper and Herman Bavinck used to say, God's love is the archetype, and ours is the ectype.

So we have here, fundamentally, not a continuum, but a distinction between everything divine and everything creaturely. We are not fallen because we are finite and therefore nondivine. We are fallen because Adam failed to be the godly creature he was meant to be. And salvation does not change us into God. Rather, it makes us the best creatures we can be.[6] In heaven, too, the Creator-creature distinction will continue intact, contrary to the suggestions of some mystics. We will never transcend the status of servants. Our eternal life is and will be a life of joyful praise and service to God.

Let us return briefly to the discussion of epistemology in the previous chapter: We can now see more clearly the reason why we stand in awe of God's incomprehensibility, even though Scripture does not forbid us to speak words about him that are literally true. Everything in God is different from everything in the world. God is the source and standard of everything in the world; his attributes are the sources and standards of the world's corresponding attributes. His love, for example, is the source and standard of our love, so it is never completely the same as ours, though it is truly love. The same thing could be said of his wisdom, his knowledge, and his power.[7]

And, as we shall see, everything in God is inseparable from everything else. His attributes have divine attributes: his love is eternal and wise, his eternity is that of a loving and wise being, and so on. Everything in God

---

6. To "participate in the divine nature" (2 Peter 1:4) is not to be God. The context is ethical rather than metaphysical. Peter is saying that through God's power and promises, we have the resources for life and godliness (v. 3), specifically for overcoming lust.

7. As he is the source and standard, so he is also the ultimate ~~presence~~—the one who accompanies everything that happens in the world, and without whom nothing could take place. See my discussion of concurrence in chapter 14.

is perfectly divine and not creaturely. In the world, nothing is divine and everything is creaturely.

We cannot imagine what it is like to be God. The sheer greatness of God, and of all his qualities, greatly exceeds our power to understand. His love is beyond measure (Eph. 3:17–19), as are his wisdom, grace, power, and eternity.

THE SCHOLASTIC PHILOSOPHY OF BEING

In chapter 3, I noted Aquinas's view that in Exodus 3:14 the name I AM means that God is Being. This text, plus a number of premises from Platonic (especially Neoplatonic) and Aristotelian philosophy, forms the basis for a rather complicated metaphysical theory of the divine being that has influenced many theological discussions of the doctrine of God. The relationship of this theory to Scripture is rather tenuous, especially if we reject, as I think we should, Aquinas's interpretation of Exodus 3:14. So one could argue that a book like the present volume, that seeks to expound the biblical teachings, could well omit discussion of the scholastic theory. Indeed, those who are reading primarily for edification may omit this discussion without much loss. But those who are called to teach the doctrine of God should be at least somewhat aware of the technical language that has developed in the scholastic movement, and they should know to what extent these ideas have influenced our doctrinal formulations. Furthermore, the scholastic doctrine is not entirely wrong. There are some biblical motives behind it and some biblical truth in it that we should note.

First, some definitions are in order:

1. *Essence* is

> . . . what necessarily belongs to a thing and most intimately constitutes it, determining its particular character both statically and dynamically; without its essence, a thing would not be what it is.[8]

The essence of anything is the feature or features of it that make it what it is. *Essence* is more or less equivalent to *nature*. In finite things, the essence is stated in a definition.[9] God, however, in Aquinas's view, cannot be defined by human language, since God is not a member of a genus. So, for Aquinas, God's essence cannot be known by creatures.

---

8. Johann Baptist Lotz, "Essence," in *Encyclopedia of Theology*, ed. Karl Rahner (New York: Seabury Press, 1975), 439.
9. I am referring, of course, to a "real definition," not merely a stipulative one.

2. *Substance* is the being that *has* the essence.[10] In Aristotelian philosophy, substances are the subjects of predication, things that bear qualities. As such they are capable, as qualities are not, of independent existence. They can exist "in themselves," rather than "in something else." In the world of change, substances remain constant. They are the subjects to which changes happen. The divine being, however, is an unchangeable substance.

3. *Attributes* are the predicates, properties, or qualities[11] ascribed to a substance. Those that define its nature constitute its essence. Others are *accidents*, which are properties that are not part of the essence and therefore are not necessary to its being. For Aquinas, God has no accidents. All his attributes are essential to his being, for God is, in all his being and attributes, a *necessary* being (see below).

4. *Being* is used in two senses in scholastic philosophy. First, there is the abstract property that applies to absolutely everything, "being in general." Aquinas denies that God is being in this sense, for being in general includes the being of accidents, for example, a kind of being that is certainly not divine. Furthermore, Aquinas has a deep desire to maintain the Creator-creature distinction. To say that God is being in general would imply pantheism, the identity of God with the world.

For Aquinas, God is Being in a second, more profound sense: that of *esse*, sometimes translated *existence*. The distinction between essence and existence is basically between "what" and "that." The essence of anything is *what it is*; to say that it exists is to say *that* there is a being with such an essence. The existence of something is the fact that it is, the state of its being in existence. Further, the scholastics often speak of *esse* (an infinitive verbal form used here as a noun) as an *act*: an event by which something comes to be and continues in existence. Recent thinkers in the scholastic tradition believe that the concept of *esse* is a major philosophical discovery, one that no Greek philosopher ever conceived. To say that God is Being, then, is to say that God's essence is *esse*, that his very nature is to exist. Rather than identifying him with the world, the scholastics argue, *esse* underscores the Creator-creature distinction: for of all the beings in the universe, only God is identical with his own *esse*.

5. *Form* is that element of a substance that determines what qualities it will have. All the qualities of a substance, whether essential or accidental,

---

10. As in Robert L. Dabney, *Lectures in Systematic Theology* (1878; reprint, Grand Rapids: Zondervan, 1972), 174.

11. I take these four nouns to be synonymous, although some writers make distinctions among them for their technical purposes.

exist by virtue of the form or forms in that substance.[12] This is sometimes illustrated by the process by which an acorn becomes a tree. At the beginning of the process, the acorn is not a tree in the fullest sense, but it has within it the form of treeness, and by virtue of that form, it will become a tree in the natural course of events. We would be inclined today to understand this illustration by equating the form with the tree's genetic inheritance. But in Aristotelian-scholastic philosophy, genetic inheritance is only one kind of form. All things, animate and inanimate, have forms that make them what they are. The human soul, for example, is the form of the body. Normally, forms exist together with the matter that they form, but there are exceptions. God is pure form, without matter, and the human soul can exist without the body.[13]

6. *Matter* is the element of a substance that receives form. We tend to think of matter as "stuff" that can be touched, molded, etc., and the imagery used by scholastic and Aristotelian philosophers presents matter as a kind of clay that is molded or formed into various shapes. But of course even unmolded clay has a shape already, with many other qualities. So matter in the technical philosophical sense is not like clay at all. Grenet says it is not a body, but "a pure 'out-of-which-a-body-is-to-be.' "[14] It is devoid of all qualities, for it has no form. It can have no form, because it is the receiver of forms. Since it has no qualities, it is, in one sense, nonbeing. It is a kind of nothingness, but a nothingness that must be something in order to play its metaphysical role. So it is, paradoxically, both being and nonbeing—an apparent contradiction, at least. Like the "privations" we discussed in chapter 9, this kind of nonbeing is a problem for Aristotelian and scholastic philosophy. It is, of course, important to point out that, on this view, there is no matter in God. God is pure being, with no admixture of nonbeing.

Matter differentiates beings of the same form from one another. Form differentiates different species from each other.

7. There are two kinds of *potentiality* or *potency* in scholastic philosophy. First, there is the active kind: the power to bring about effects. Second, there is the passive kind: the capacity to receive forms, to become something different, to change, to be determined by something outside oneself.[15] Pas-

12. Compare Paul Grenet, *Thomism: An Introduction*, trans. James F. Ross (New York: Harper and Row, 1967), 6–7.

13. These exceptions pose problems for scholastic philosophy. How can form exist where there is no matter to be formed?

14. Grenet, *Thomism: An Introduction*, 16.

15. See Étienne Gilson, *The Philosophy of St. Thomas Aquinas*, trans. E. Bullough (Cambridge: W. Heffer, 1925), 66.

sive potentiality is a "relative nothingness,"[16] as in the nature of matter—if indeed matter can be said to have a nature. Aquinas says that "the being whose substance has an admixture of potency is liable not to be by as much as it has potency; for that which can be, can not-be."[17] So God has active potency, but no passive potentiality. He was not brought into being by something outside himself, and he cannot be changed into something else; he is perfectly actual.

8. *Actuality* or *act* is the opposite of potentiality. Through various causes, a being that is, say, potentially a tree, becomes one actually. So there is a process by which things change from potentiality to actuality. Essentially this is the process by which matter receives form. To be "in act" is (a) to have real existence as opposed to merely potential existence, (b) to have achieved one's potential in some respect (God, of course, is "in act" in every respect), and (c) to perform actions, as opposed merely to being affected by the actions of others. Having no passive potentiality, God is "pure act," the "pure act of being."[18]

9. *Necessity* applies to what *must* be the case. A "necessary truth" in logic is one that must be true, that doesn't just happen to be true. A "necessary being" is a being that must exist, that cannot fail to exist. In contemporary modal logic, a logically necessary being is a being that exists in all logically possible worlds. A merely possible being, on the other hand, exists in only some possible worlds.[19] In scholasticism, God is a necessary being, not merely one who happens to exist. It is his very essence to exist, and so he cannot fail to exist. He cannot not be.

10. *Contingency* is the opposite of necessity. Contingent beings depend on other beings outside themselves for their existence. So they may or may not exist; they do not exist necessarily. It is possible for them not to exist.

There are other concepts in scholastic philosophy and subdivisions of the above. But the general structure should now be evident.

We might suspect continuum thinking here, because of the identification between God and Being, but we should remember that Aquinas and his followers distinguished quite sharply between divine and human being, between Being and beings. All the same, the structure seems rather univocal for a thinker, Aquinas, who elsewhere insists that all, or at least most, of our language about God is analogical.

---

16. Grenet, *Thomism: An Introduction*, 7.
17. SCG, 1.16.2.
18. It is not obvious to me why these three different concepts should be grouped together under the terms *act* and *actuality*. Indeed, I think this is a source of ambiguity in the scholastic system. Nevertheless, I shall pass over this issue here.
19. Recall, however, what I said in chapter 8 about the different kinds of possibility.

Aquinas's short early work, *On Being and Essence*,[20] attempts to define some of the terms above, especially *essence* as it applies to God and to various created things. But in this work there is no hint of any doctrine of analogy, no suggestion that terms like *essence* and *esse* apply to God in any way other than univocally. So, in Aquinas's treatment of essence, we miss the sense of divine transcendence that permeates his doctrine of analogy. The result is that essence seems like a general concept, of which God and creatures are exemplifications, even though, of course, Aquinas denies that God is a member of any genus. He even describes essence on a kind of scale: essence is found one way in composite substances, another way in God, and a third way in immaterial beings (angels and souls). Since Scripture says nothing about the nature of essence in immaterial beings, one gets the impression that Aquinas is filling in a metaphysical blank: he needs a third kind of essence to complete the scale of being.

The form/matter distinction raises other problems: the paradoxical nature of matter, which we have noted, and the possibility of beings that have form, but no matter to receive the form. In Greek philosophy, form serves the rationalistic impulse: the forms are what the intellect comes to know—autonomously, of course. But matter serves the irrationalistic impulse: since it is unformed, it is essentially beyond our understanding, and it introduces an element of unpredictability into the world.

I have no problem affirming that God is a necessary being, but on the basis of Scripture, as we shall see later, rather than on specifically Thomistic premises. If God necessarily exists, then it is not wrong to say that his *esse* is essential to his being, though I think it no more essential than his holiness, goodness, knowledge, wisdom, and so on. And if we affirm God's necessary existence, we will have to ask in what respect he is free—or are all his plans and actions also necessary?[21]

We shall, then, look again at these concepts from time to time in this book, in order to engage historical dialogues on various issues. In general, however, I regard the scholastic concepts as an unnecessary complication. Although I am not against the use of extrabiblical terminology in applying Scripture, I don't see that the scholastic concepts above say anything true or important that can't be said better, and argued more persuasively, in biblical terms.

A more serious concern is that these doctrines fall under the scholastic heading of natural reason, which in Aquinas's view is prior to faith, "for faith presupposes natural knowledge, even as grace presupposes nature and

20. Toronto: Pontifical Institute of Mediaeval Studies, 1949.
21. See my discussion of this matter later in this chapter.

perfection the perfectible."[22] It involves reasoning from God's effects to his nature, without the aid of revelation, and under the assumption that God's effects are better known to us than he is.[23] In other words, Aquinas is recommending autonomous reasoning, which is self-consciously removed from the authority of God's Word, enabling us to argue from the same premises as Plato or Aristotle.

I don't believe that Aquinas succeeds in removing biblical assumptions from his argument. Aquinas is, after all, a Christian. But that is what he tries to do. And that is a project that we must repudiate, as those who seek to think as covenant servants of God.

SIMPLICITY

We cannot really end our introduction to the scholastic doctrine of God without saying something about the doctrine of simplicity, the immediate consequence of the distinctions we have been discussing. Simplicity is the first divine attribute that Aquinas discusses after giving his proofs for God's existence in the *Summa theologiae*,[24] and it is frequently a basic premise in his later arguments. Our discussion of simplicity will illustrate my earlier comment that the truth in scholastic philosophy may more easily be ascertained, stated, and argued from a biblical standpoint than from the standpoint of Scholasticism's own natural theology.

To say that God is simple, in scholastic philosophy, is to say that there is no composition in his being. Specifically, there is no composition of physical parts, form and matter, actual and potential, genus and differentia, substance and accident, God and his essence, essence and attributes, attributes and one another, or essence and *esse*. God is not, then, in any sense made up of parts.

Granted that God is not a physical being, it is obvious that he is not made up of physical parts. Nor can he be divided into form and matter, or actu-

---

22. *ST*, 1.2.2, Reply Obj. 1.
23. Ibid., 1.2.2.
24. In *SCG*, after a discussion of the existence of God, comes an account of the importance of the way of remotion, followed by a chapter on eternity, and then a long series of chapters denying the presence in God of such things as passive potency, matter, and composition. These are all examples of the way of remotion (including eternity, which means that God has no beginning or end, and no before or after). In this series of chapters, Aquinas denies many kinds of divisions in God, and thereby establishes the divine simplicity. Indeed, even eternity is, in Aquinas's view, a form of simplicity, since it denies that God's experience of time is divided into any succession of moments.

ality and potentiality, since he has no matter or (passive) potentiality. Nor is he made up of genus and differentia, since he is not in a genus, nor is he a genus (godhood) differentiated by species (various gods). Nor is he made up of substance and accidents, because there are no accidents in him.[25] Since God has no accidents, everything in him is essential to his being. So he is, in a sense, his essence.

But the other claims require further consideration. It is not, indeed, entirely apparent what is meant by *parts* or *divisions* in a nonphysical being. In what way could a spiritual being conceivably be divided or composed? What would be the difference, specifically, between a spiritual being whose attributes are parts of him and a spiritual being whose attributes are not parts, but somehow equivalent to himself?

For Aquinas, parts are always something less than the whole, and parts can be understood and can function to some extent apart from the whole. They are in some measure independent of the whole. If they are united into a whole, they can also, because of their independence, be removed from the whole. And if they are united to a whole, this union is a process by which a potential union is caused to be actual.

There cannot be such parts in God, for several reasons. First, there can be nothing in him that is less, or less noble, than himself. Second, nothing in him can be removed from him, for nothing in him can not be. Third, the fact that he has many attributes is not something caused, for he is the first cause. Fourth, in God there can be no process of potentiality becoming actuality, because he is pure act, with no passive potentiality.[26]

So God's attributes are not parts or divisions within the Godhead in Aquinas's fairly technical sense of *parts*, but each attribute is necessary to God's being. Each is essential to him, and therefore his essence includes all of them. God cannot be God without his goodness, his wisdom, and his eternity. In other words, he is necessarily good, wise, and eternal. None of his attributes can be removed from him, and no new attribute can be added to him. Therefore, none of his attributes exists without the others. So each attribute has divine attributes; each is qualified by the others. God's wisdom is an eternal wisdom, and his goodness is a wise and (importantly) just

---

25. God does, however, enter into relationships with creatures, as we shall see. These relationships are not essential to his being, for he would be God even if he had not chosen to create the world. I am assuming, therefore, that it is possible to distinguish between God's attributes (which are essential to his being) and predications that describe God in his relationships with creatures. I shall attempt to make this distinction at various points in this book, and readers will have to judge whether the distinction is cogent.

26. These arguments are paraphrased from SCG, 1.18.

goodness. And his *esse* is a necessary existence, necessary to his essence. Granted who God is, he cannot fail to exist.

Note that these arguments do not rule out all complexity within the divine nature. Imagine a distinguishable aspect of God's nature (such as an attribute or a person of the Trinity) that is no less noble than himself, that cannot be removed from him, that necessarily belongs to him apart from any causal process, that is not the result of a movement from potentiality to actuality. It would not be inconsistent with the doctrine of simplicity for God to have many such aspects. Indeed, since simplicity in this sense does not rule out all multiplicity, it might be less confusing to use the term *necessary existence* rather than *simplicity*.

But Aquinas sometimes seems to deny any complexity at all in God. He argues, for example, that unity must always be prior to multiplicity, so that God, who is prior to everything, must have no multiplicity.[27] Elsewhere, in *Summa contra gentiles*,[28] he argues that the different names we use for God are not synonymous, although they refer to God's simple being. He denies that such names compromise God's simplicity, not by arguing that there are genuine complexities and pluralities in God, to which the different names refer, but by arguing that the plurality is in our minds: we must conceive of the simple being of God by "diverse conceptions." On this view, it is not enough to say that God's attributes, for example, are necessary to his being; rather, the multiplicity of attributes is only apparent. In reality, God is a being without any multiplicity at all, a simple being for whom any language suggesting complexity, distinctions, or multiplicity, is entirely unsuited.

That is essentially the Neoplatonic view of Plotinus, in which the best name of God is One. Even that name is inadequate, however, since God is utterly beyond the descriptive power of human language. But One is the best name we can come up with, since unity is prior to multiplicity and more noble than multiplicity.

Aquinas argues well for the necessity of God's being. But his argument for a total absence of multiplicity in God is quite inadequate. A biblical Trinitarian cannot argue, for example, that in every respect unity is prior to multiplicity. Nor can he argue that diversity in God is only apparent, existing only in our own minds. In Scripture, as we shall see, God is both one and many, and the balance of unity and diversity in God insures the balance of unity and diversity within the created world.

Aquinas does, of course, affirm the creedal statements concerning the Trinity. His analysis of the Trinity in terms of subsistent relationships, how-

27. Ibid.
28. 1.35.2.

ever (see chap. 29), plays down the distinctions between the Trinitarian persons. Thomists argue that their view of simplicity is consistent with the Trinity, because simplicity pertains not to the three persons, but to the divine nature that they all share. However, I do not believe that we can make such a neat separation between nature and persons. Certainly the persons are just as essential to God's being as any attribute. It is not evident to me why triunity should not be considered an attribute of God along with the others. Certainly it is true to say that God's being is triune.

We are left, then, with a doctrine of God's necessary existence, rather than a doctrine of simplicity as such. But if we turn away from the scholastic metaphysics and look to Scripture, we may be able to learn something more.

Consider how Scripture sometimes employs the language of divine attributes: "God is spirit" (John 4:24); "God is light" (1 John 1:5); "God is love" (1 John 4:8, 16). These expressions state what God really and truly is. In other words, they describe his essence, not merely what he happens to be on some occasions. But note that there are three of these attributions, not just one. So God's essence can be described in three different ways. I would say that these expressions describe the whole divine essence from three different perspectives.[29]

Is it likely that God's holiness, for example, is less essential to his being than spirit, light, and love? In Psalm 89:35 and Amos 4:2, God swears by his holiness. Certainly he does not swear by something lower than himself, and he can swear by nothing higher. For God to swear by his holiness can be nothing more or less than for him to swear by himself (see Heb. 6:13). He is the holy one.

Similarly, God's truth and his character as the living God distinguish him from all false gods (e.g., Jer. 10:10). So these, too, tell who he essentially is. He cannot prove false (Num. 23:19; 2 Tim. 2:13; Titus 1:2; Heb. 6:18). And, obviously, he cannot die.

Is it possible, then, that God could renounce, or be robbed of, his lordship? Could he be the same God without his control, authority, and presence? I think not. The biblical passages dealing with these and related attributes, such as his personality, goodness, loving-kindness, and so on, present them as qualities that can never fail, without which God would not be God.[30]

29. Bavinck (*DG*, 131) approaches a perspectival formulation when he says that "we are not able to conceive of the infinite fulness of God's essence unless it is revealed to us in this, then in another relation, now from this then from another angle."

30. I realize, of course, that lordship and the lordship attributes are relational attributes, which characterize God's relationship with creatures. It might be argued, therefore, that these are not part of God's essence. Had God determined not to create the world—and he

As we saw in chapter 11, God's essence is not some dark, unrevealed entity behind his revealed character. Rather, God's revelation tells us about his essence. It tells us what he really and truly is.

The above passages do not show that all of God's attributes are necessary to his being and thus perspectives on that being, but they do provide a pattern and a way of thinking about divine attributes to which it is hard to find plausible exceptions.

But does this pattern justify talk of simplicity? If the attributes are perspectives on a single reality, that reality will be simple by comparison, though also complex, as I must keep insisting. And evidently, since there are many attributes that characterize God's essence, they are not separate from one another. Indeed, all of his attributes have divine attributes! God's mercy is eternal, and his creative power is wise. So the biblical teachings about God's attributes suggest a profound unity in his nature and among the attributes that characterize his nature.

This is not to say that God's attributes are synonymous. They all refer to his essence, but they describe different aspects of it. God really is good *and* just *and* omniscient. The multiple attributes refer to genuine complexities in his essence.

But it is important to see the unity within this complexity. And to see it, we should remind ourselves that our covenant Lord is a person. What is God's "goodness"? Is it something *in* him? It would be more accurate, I think, to say that "divine goodness," though it sounds like an abstract property, is really just a way of referring to everything God is. For everything God does is good, and everything he is is good. All his attributes are good. All his decrees are good. All his actions are good. There is nothing in God that is not good.[31]

To praise God's goodness is not to praise something other than God himself. It is not to praise something less than him, or a part of him, so to speak. It is to praise him. God's goodness is not something that is intelligible in itself, apart from everything else that God is.

God's goodness is the standard for our goodness. We are to image his goodness. Does that mean that we are to image some abstract property that is

---

was free to make that choice—he would not have been Lord. This is true, but the essence of God is such that in his relationship to his creatures, he cannot be anything other than Lord. So the lordship attributes, although not necessary in themselves, are grounded in God's essential nature. We can say that lordship is an essential attribute of God in that it is the quality of his nature by which he necessarily relates to any creature.

31. Eberhard Jüngel, in *God as the Mystery of the World* (Grand Rapids: Eerdmans, 1983), 314, says strikingly that if we do not define God as love, then the essence of God is unloving, and God is a monster.

somehow attached to God or present in him somewhere? No, it means that we are to image God himself. Our moral standard is not an impersonal, abstract property.[32] It is a person, the living God. The center of biblical morality is that we should be like him. As I argued earlier in this book, covenant lordship means personalism. The personal is prior to the impersonal. God's personal goodness defines any legitimate abstract concept of goodness.

God relates to us as a whole person, not as a collection of attributes. The attributes merely describe different things about him. They are a kind of shorthand for talking about that person. Everything he says and does is good, right, true, eternal, wise, and so on.

As we shall see later, the triunity of God does not conflict with his simplicity, understood as I have described it. Each of the three persons is "in" the other two (*circumincessio*), and therefore each exhausts the divine nature, just as every attribute includes the whole divine nature.

It seems to me, therefore, that there is a legitimate biblical motive in the doctrine of simplicity. We may be surprised to find that it is not an abstract, obscure, philosophical motive, but a very practical one. Those emerging from the murky waters of scholastic speculation may be surprised to find that the doctrine of simplicity is really fairly simple. It is a biblical way of reminding us that God's relationship with us is fully personal.

So the simplicity of God, like all his attributes, sets forth his covenant lordship. It reminds us of the unity of our covenant Lord, and the unity that he brings into our lives as we seek to honor him and him alone. The Christian is not devoted to some abstract philosophical goodness, but to the living Lord of heaven and earth.

To my mind, the biblical approach to this issue is far more edifying and persuasive than scholastic natural theology. In Scripture, there is no compromise with continuum thinking, no compromise of the Trinity, and no compromise of the centrality of God's covenant lordship.

NECESSITY AND FREEDOM

As indicated earlier, I agree with Aquinas's view that God exists necessarily. He does not merely happen to exist; he must exist. His nonexistence is impossible.

32. Some have objected that the doctrine of simplicity, according to which God's attributes are identical with himself, makes God equivalent to abstract properties. But the equation can point us in the other direction: not that God is reduced to goodness, but that goodness is seen to be God himself. Of course, the equation is between God and his own goodness (divine goodness), not between God and goodness in general.

As we saw in chapter 8, however, there is more than one kind of "possibility." In which of these senses do we deny the possibility of God's nonexistence? His nonexistence is metaphysically impossible in that nothing or nobody can prevent him from existing or put him out of existence. His necessary existence, then, follows from his aseity or self-existence, which I shall discuss in a later chapter.

It is also the case that God *must* exist if there is to be any meaning to the world. In a biblical worldview, God is the basis for all reality, and therefore for all rationality, truth, goodness, and beauty. Logic itself is based on his nature, and the logical structure of the world and the human mind is based on the fact that God's rationality, his wisdom, is reflected in the creation. Without him, therefore, we could not even speak rationally. Therefore, we must presuppose his existence in all rational thought and action. When we ascribe existence to anything in the world, we must ascribe existence to God. So we must regard God's existence as more sure, more certain, than the existence of anything else.

That includes even logic; so in one sense God is *logically* necessary. This is not to say that God's existence can be proved by logical axioms alone, or that "God doesn't exist" can be shown to be contradictory (though I think it is contradictory in a sense).[33] The point, rather, is that God's existence is necessary to the very existence of logic, for he is the very source of logical truth. So there is no logically possible world in which God does not exist.

Notice here how epistemological considerations can lead to metaphysical conclusions. For human knowledge to be possible, certain metaphysical conditions (including the existence of God) must be satisfied. We have the option, of course, of denying that human knowledge is possible. But such radical skepticism cannot be advanced as a rational view. On any rational view of the matter, therefore, God exists, and exists necessarily. This is a "transcendental" argument, reasoning from the necessary conditions of human knowledge.

The necessary existence of God implies that his defining attributes also exist necessarily. For the God we are speaking of is not a conceptual blank, but a real being, with a nature, a character. He does not exist without that nature; without it, he would not be God. So if God exists necessarily, everything that he is—his nature, his character, his essential attributes—exists necessarily.

---

33. That statement is not self-contradictory, like "No dog is a dog," but there is a contradiction in saying "God doesn't exist" while at the same time purporting to make a rational statement. That would be true in most all cases.

✝ I have spoken of "defining" attributes and "essential" attributes, implying a distinction between them and nondefining or nonessential ones. *Attribute* can be used in a broad sense to indicate any predicate we ascribe to God. Thus, love and eternity are divine attributes, but also "creator of Steve Hays." But we normally would not say that "creator of Steve Hays" belongs to the *definition* or *essence* of God. So we should distinguish between attributes that define God's essence and attributes that merely describe his relationships with creatures. Of course, God's essence and his relationships with creatures cannot be completely separated. Love is certainly an essential or defining attribute of God, but it is also a relationship between God and creatures. Lordship is a relationship between God and creatures, but it is the expression of his nature, so that in any possible world, God would be related to his creatures as Lord. Nevertheless, we may distinguish attributes that define God's nature from attributes that describe only his relationships to creatures.

Clearly, for example, God's love cannot be taken away from him. It is what he is (1 John 4:8, 16). It belongs to his definition, his essence. If the supreme being were not loving, he would not be the God of the Bible. Had God chosen not to create Steve Hays, however, he would still have been God. So "creator of Steve Hays" cannot fairly be said to be part of God's definition.

Thus, "creator of Steve Hays" and "righteous" are both predicates of God, but they are rather different. Righteousness is an essential attribute of God, one without which he would not be God. His righteousness is necessary; he cannot be otherwise than righteous. But God's creation of Steve Hays seems to be optional in a way that God's righteousness is not. We are inclined to say that God would still be God, even if he had chosen not to create Steve Hays. So we say that God's creation of Hays is a *free* act, not a necessary one.

The same consideration applies equally to all of God's creative acts. Not only Hays, but the whole world is, we say, a free creation of God, not one in which he was constrained, even by his own nature. The same may be said of providence and especially redemption, for the very idea of grace seems to imply that God might have chosen to do otherwise. God's nature, it seems, does not force him to create or redeem. For if he must create or redeem, even if the necessity comes from his own nature, it would seem that he owes something to the creation, that the creation has a claim on him (contrary to his aseity; see chap. 26). Indeed, if his very deity requires him to create and redeem, then it would seem that his deity depends, in one sense, on the world.

So most Reformed theologians have thought that although God's essential attributes are necessary to his being, his decrees governing creation and his acts in the world are not necessary, but free. So we need to reflect here a bit on what kind of freedom God has (compare our discussion of human freedom in chap. 8).

At the very least, God is free in the sense that he is not constrained by anyone other than himself. He does what he pleases (Ps. 115:3), and therefore he is always free in the compatibilist sense. He is not bound to the dictates of anyone else. He does make promises, to be sure, which obligate him to do certain things, but he makes those promises voluntarily. Nobody forces him to make them. As we have seen, God himself decides the terms of his covenants with man. In that sense, of course, all of God's acts are free, and there is no special sense in which his acts of creation and redemption are free.

In the libertarian sense, God is no more free than man, for I have given reasons in chapter 8 to question the very coherence of libertarianism. Certainly the thought of God performing actions apart from any motivations, even against his own strongest desires, is biblically absurd. In all that God does, he seeks to achieve his purposes and goals. His actions are directed by his wise counsel.

But now we face a problem, for it seems as though there is no sense of freedom which distinguishes God's necessary, self-defining acts (like the eternal generation of the Son from the Father) from God's creative, providential, and redemptive acts in history. In the compatibilist sense, all of God's actions are equally free. In the libertarian sense, none of them are free.

But there are other senses of freedom, as we saw in chapter 8. Freedom is always freedom to do something (implying a power or ability) and freedom from something (implying lack of a potential barrier or "preventer"). So there are as many kinds of freedom as there are powers and preventers. Someone may be free to do something (e.g., pilot a yacht) in view of his physical condition, but not in view of his economic condition. He may be physically free, but not economically free.

When we consider God's freedom, we are asking about powers and preventers within the divine nature. His powers are unlimited in a sense, but, as we shall see in our discussion of omnipotence (chap. 23), there are things he cannot do.

Certainly some of God's choices are constrained[34] by his own nature. He

---

34. I use the term *constrain* even though it could mislead, because the only alternative seems to be *necessitate*, which seems far less personal. *Constrain* could suggest that God is made to do something involuntarily or against his will. Of course, God is never constrained in that way. To say that God is constrained by his nature to do something is simply to say that he could not do otherwise.

cannot lie (Titus 1:2), and he cannot deny himself (2 Tim. 2:13). There are, we may say, preventers in God's nature that keep him from doing such things. He cannot lie or deny himself, because he is completely true and faithful.

In asking whether, say, creation is a free act of God, we are asking (1) whether God is able to create, and (2) whether he is able not to create. In both cases, we must explore both the powers of God and potential preventers within his nature. Obviously God is able to create, because he has done so. So the question of whether creation is a free act is the question of whether God is able also not to create. Certainly he has the power not to create. But are there in his nature preventers that would exclude that option?

One might argue that God's wisdom is such a preventer. For all his works are done in wisdom, for good reasons, though he does not always reveal his reasoning to us. It would seem, therefore, that his wisdom determines all his actions. Since God created the world, we know that God's decision to create was wise (see also Ps. 104 and Prov. 8, in which creation is ascribed to God's wisdom). Then, one might argue, for God not to create would have been unwise. So the negative alternative would have been prevented by his wisdom.

But it is not necessarily the case that the opposite of a wise action is unwise. God might have chosen not to create the world, but to do something else which would have displayed his wisdom in a different way. This issue is similar to one we discussed in chapter 9, whether God is required by his nature (specifically his wisdom and goodness) to make "the best of all possible worlds." There I argued that there may be no single possible world that is "best" in all respects, and that even if there is such a possible world, God may have had good reasons for making a world that is less than best. It does not seem, therefore, that God's wisdom and goodness constrained him to make exactly this world or prevented him from making a different world. Extending that logic slightly, I know of no divine attribute that would have required him to create or that would have prevented the world's noncreation.

Furthermore, if God is required to create, even by his nature, it would seem that the world has some claim on him. Indeed, he would not have been God if he had failed to create, for in that case he would not have had a fully divine nature. His deity, then, would depend logically upon his creation of the world, and therefore, in a sense, upon the world. That is an impossible supposition, in the light of biblical teaching about God's aseity and lordship.

The same reasoning applies to redemption. Indeed, here the case for divine freedom is even stronger. For there are attributes of God that might be thought to make redemption very unlikely. God's righteousness would seem to prevent redemption altogether, for it demands punishment for sin.[35] Does God's grace require him to redeem? Certainly not. The very idea of grace is that God is not required to give it. If God is required, even by his own nature, to give grace to us, then we have a certain claim on him. But grace excludes such claims. Here redemption is parallel to creation, as it often is in Scripture (e.g., 2 Cor. 4:6). In neither case do we have any claim upon God. Furthermore, even if God were required to redeem men, it would be hard to argue that his grace requires him to save exactly the number of those who are elect. That he saves even one is amazing. Those who are lost, Scripture teaches, have no right to complain against God. So although redemption reveals God's grace vividly, that attribute does not constrain him to save anyone or any particular group of people. Besides, as with our earlier example of creation and wisdom, so far as we know, God might well have chosen not to redeem men at all, but to show his grace in another way.

So I know of nothing in God's nature that prevented him from not creating or not redeeming. To put the point positively, there is nothing in God's nature that required him to create and redeem. And there is a strong reason to believe that he was not so required, namely, the sheer graciousness of grace.

Now, of course, God's nature is incomprehensible. We do not know his nature exhaustively. Perhaps there are attributes of God that have not been revealed to us. Theoretically, one of those attributes may have required God to create and redeem, or prevented him from not doing so. But *sola Scriptura* is our rule. We must think of God as he has revealed himself. That revelation does not authorize us to teach any constraining factors in God's work in the world, and it casts grave doubt on the existence of such factors by teaching that the world has no claim on him and is not necessary to his deity.

With these explanations, then, I would say that God's essential attributes and actions[36] are *necessary*, but that his decrees and acts of creation, providence, and redemption are *free*. They are free, not merely in a compatibilist sense, nor at all in a libertarian sense, but in the sense that we

---

35. Of course, Scripture replies to this objection by showing us how God's righteousness is fulfilled in the life and atoning death of Jesus Christ. However, it would have been very hard to anticipate how God could bring about the salvation of the elect without violating his righteousness. His righteousness is a *prima facie* preventer of redemption.

36. God's essential, necessary actions would include the eternal generation and procession within the Trinity, as well as God's intra-Trinitarian love, self-knowledge, etc.

know nothing in God's nature that constrains these acts or prevents their opposites.

In the section entitled "Divine and Human Causality" in chapter 8, I described freedom as making choices between possible alternatives. Scripture makes it clear that the damnation of believers was a genuine possibility, apart from God's free grace. So God's freedom is analogous to ours: affirming and denying options that are all, in some sense, genuinely possible. I pointed out that it is choices like these that give us our sense of being free beings. I would suggest here that God has that same self-understanding.

I would also agree with most Reformed theologians in distinguishing between God's necessary will (the will by which the Father begets the Son and the Spirit proceeds from the Father and the Son eternally, the will by which God loves, knows, and communicates within the Trinity) and his free will (the will which decrees and governs the world). Similarly, I would distinguish between God's necessary knowledge (his knowledge of his own nature) and his free knowledge (his knowledge of his freely chosen decrees and of the world as determined by those decrees). I would also distinguish between God's necessary speech (the expressions of love between the persons of the Trinity) and his free speech (his decrees and self-revelation to creatures).

This discussion leaves some difficult questions unanswered. One may well ask, if God's free decisions are not determined by any of his attributes, then where do they come from? If these decisions are not libertarian random accidents, then what accounts for them? I can only reply, with Paul,

> Oh, the depth of the riches of the wisdom and knowledge of God!
> How unsearchable his judgments,
> and his paths beyond tracing out! (Rom. 11:33)

METAPHYSICAL PERSPECTIVES

In our discussions of ethics and epistemology, I have made use of "perspectives" derived from the lordship attributes. Do these perspectives help us to understand the metaphysical nature of God and creation? I think so. The lordship attributes themselves are consequences of the divine nature. God's nature is such that he is inevitably the controller, the supreme authority, and the unavoidable presence in his creation. The ethical and epistemological perspectives are derived from these elements of his nature.

We shall see later that there may be some correspondence between the lordship attributes and the persons of the Trinity. With regard to the divine nature, we shall see that all of God's attributes are forms and manifestations of his lordship. I will propose a highly tentative way of organizing the divine attributes according to my three categories: attributes of power, knowledge, and goodness. More significantly, however, all of God's attributes set forth all three aspects of lordship.

God's attributes set forth the ways in which he controls the world. For example (as I shall amplify later), his goodness indicates the goal and motive of his control. His knowledge is based on his control over all reality, and the universality of his knowledge enables him to exercise complete control over the world. His eternity reveals his control over all temporal sequences.

These attributes also indicate his authority. They tell us authoritatively who God is. They also serve as criteria or standards for creaturely properties. His love is the standard for human love (John 13:34–35), his holiness is the standard for ours (1 Peter 1:15–16), and so forth.

The attributes also indicate ways in which God is in and with his creation. As God acts among us in history, his attributes describe the sort of person he is: wise, just, holy, and loving, yet transcendent of our time, space, knowledge, and so on.

PART FOUR

THE ACTS OF THE LORD

CHAPTER 13

Miracle

In the first twelve chapters, I tried to set out the basic covenant framework for understanding the doctrine of God. God is the covenant Lord, the one who controls all things, speaks with supreme authority, and enters into a personal relationship with his creatures to bless and to judge. We must now survey the biblical literature more broadly in order to fill out the picture I have presented. In the remainder of the book, I shall be expounding many other biblical teachings about God. But we should always remember that whenever God does anything or reveals himself, he does it for his name's sake, so that people may know that he is the Lord (e.g., Ex. 6:2, 7–8, 28; 7:5, 17; 8:22; 10:2; 12:12; 14:4, 18; 16:12; Isa. 41:20; 43:11). So all of these biblical teachings will be significantly related to the control, authority, and presence of the covenant Lord.

STRUCTURAL OVERVIEW OF PARTS FOUR THROUGH SIX

The Bible presents the nature of God in three ways. First, it provides a narrative of God's *action*. Second, it provides authoritative *descriptions* of his nature and character. Third, it provides us with a glimpse of his *inner triune life*, the fellowship of the Father, Son, and Holy Spirit. I shall discuss these topics in parts 4, 5, and 6 of this book, respectively.

These three forms of teaching focus on God's control, authority, and pres-

241

ence, respectively. The narrative of God's actions shows us how God *controls* the situation to accomplish his sovereign purposes. From that narrative, we can conclude much about God. But Scripture does not leave us alone to interpret the narrative by our own wisdom. It presents authoritative descriptions of God, exhibiting in them God's own *authority*.[1] And it also presents to us, not only an account of God's involvement in our history, but also some glimpses of God's own inner life. As we observe that inner life, we learn that God is *present*, not only as the covenant Lord of his creation, but also as the one who in his very nature takes delight in other persons.

In the categories of our philosophy of lordship, the narrative of God's involvement in our history is situational, the descriptions of God are normative, and the Trinitarian reflections are existential. And indeed these are "perspectives." For in fact we cannot fully understand God's actions without Scripture's authoritative descriptions and Trinitarian reflections, or, indeed, any of the three without the others. The Bible as a whole is a narrative, an authoritative description, and a Trinitarian drama. Each includes the others; each enriches the others. They do not describe three different sections of Scripture, or three different subject matters; rather, they describe the same subject matter—the whole Bible—from three different perspectives.

I shall begin with the situational or narrative perspective, in which Scripture declares the mighty acts of the Lord. Traditional systems of theology tend to put these at the end of the book, reasoning that we need to know what God is before we can understand what he does. However, as noted above, I believe that the biblical teachings about God's acts and self-descriptions are perspectival.[2] Indeed, there is a certain biblical logic that moves from act to description, rather than, as in the traditional approach, the other way around. God saves Israel from Egypt, and because of that mighty act, Israel and Egypt come to know that he is the Lord. The act is the basis for the description. And indeed this is often the pattern in Scripture. In Psalm 8, David validates the majesty of God from his works in creation and providence. In Psalm 18, he declares that God is his rock, fortress, and deliverer, and he sets forth the narratives that have convinced him that

---

1. These authoritative descriptions include what are usually called the attributes of God, but also his names and the biblical images of him such as shepherd, king, and father.
2. This is not to say that God's nature and his acts are the same, as in Barth's attempt to identify God's nature with the event of salvation. I am making a different point, namely, that Scripture's teaching about God's nature is coextensive with its teaching about his acts, and vice versa. Therefore, our knowledge of the one is not separate from our knowledge of the other.

God deserves these titles. Because of God's deliverances, "I will sing praises to your name" (v. 49).

What, then, are God's acts? What does he do, according to Scripture? We can distinguish the following general classifications: (1) God's intra-Trinitarian actions, such as eternal generation and procession, and the acts of love and communication among the persons; (2) his plans, or decrees, for the creation; (3) the act of creation itself, by which God brings the world into being; (4) his providence, by which he governs the course of nature and history; (5) the redemption of his people (and the fallen creation) from sin and its consequences.[3] We might add, as a sixth category, the important divine act of revelation, God's speech. But the five categories mentioned exhaust everything that takes place in eternity and time. Revelation, or divine communication, is an aspect of each of them. I shall note the revelatory aspects of all God's acts as we consider them, and I shall say something about God's speech (*logos*) in this book under his attributes of knowledge. And I shall give extended attention to it (Lord willing) in my forthcoming book, *The Doctrine of the Word of God*.

We shall look at God's intra-Trinitarian actions in part 6 of this book. Here in part 4 we shall focus on those actions of God in and for the creation. In that group of actions, the decrees are normative (God's authoritative interpretation and definitive plan for the world), creation and providence are situational (bringing to pass the situation in which God's drama takes place), and redemption is existential (bringing the hearts of people to love God).[4] These interact in various ways, and one cannot draw sharp lines between them. Creation, providence, and redemption are the inevitable outworkings of the decrees. But the decrees also take the nature of creation, providence, and redemption into account.[5] Redemption fulfills God's purpose in creation and providence, removing the curse from the universe (Rom. 8:20–22), reconciling all things to God (Col. 1:20), and bringing about a new heaven and a new earth (2 Peter 3:10–13; Rev. 21:1). So redemption is a form of creation (2 Cor. 4:6; 5:17) and the ultimate in-

---

3. In theological jargon, the first category is God's *opera ad intra,* and the final four are his *opera ad extra.* The latter are works which "terminate" outside God's own being; the former do not.

4. As in *DKG,* the structure of this book involves triads within triads. "Acts of God" is, in general, a situational perspective on our knowledge of God. But among the acts of God, there are some that are relatively normative, situational, and existential. This pattern is one illustration of the interdependence of the perspectives. There is always something normative within the situational perspective, and so on. Each perspective is a microcosm.

5. See my discussion of creaturely otherness in chapter 8. Another way to put this point, of course, is that each decree takes each of the others into account.

tention of providence: for we should interpret the regularities of the seasons as the patience of God as he brings people to repentance (2 Peter 3:3–9).

This book will not contain a specific chapter, or group of chapters, on redemption. Redemption is, of course, the main theme of Scripture, so if I were writing a complete systematic theology, those chapters would be much longer than the present volume. I would then have to deal extensively with the Incarnation, the Atonement and the Resurrection, effectual calling, regeneration, justification, and so on.[6] The present volume is limited to the doctrine of God.[7] It should be plain by now, however, that my treatment of the doctrine of God tries above all to do justice to the role that God plays in the biblical story of redemption. I have structured this work as an exposition of God's covenant lordship, and I have surveyed the history of redemption already several times, in expounding the lordship attributes. Lordship is more than redemption, but it is redemptive. We learn of it in the biblical gospel, the good news of salvation. This book assumes, therefore, that it is through our knowledge of redemption that we come to know who God is.

That leaves us with God's decrees, creation, and providence to be considered in this part of the book. I will treat these in the opposite order from traditional systematic theologies, moving from history to eternity (providence, creation, decrees), rather than the other way around (decrees, creation, providence).[8] But before I get to providence, I wish to discuss another kind of divine act, miracle, which in my understanding overlaps the categories of redemption and providence. I will discuss it at this point, because it plays an important epistemological role in Scripture. Miracles are,

---

6. Were I ever to write a book specifically on salvation, it might be organized as follows:
1. Law (redemption defined—normative)
2. Redemption accomplished in history (Jesus' atonement, resurrection—situational)
   a. Jesus as the Word—normative
   b. Jesus' acts in history—situational
   c. Jesus as God and man—existential
3. Redemption applied to believers (the *ordo salutis*—effectual calling, justification, etc.—existential); all the following are aspects of union with Christ.
   a. Election—normative
   b. Effectual calling—situational
   c. Individual soteriology—existential
      i. Regeneration, sanctification, glorification—existential
      ii. Justification—normative
      iii. Adoption—situational
7. I keep having to remind myself of that.
8. For my rationale, see chapter 1, and compare my reasons earlier in this chapter for beginning with the situational perspective.

theologically speaking, God's "mighty acts," "signs," and "wonders." It is through these that people come to know that he is Lord. And as we shall see, when people experience his mighty acts, they come to see that same might and wonder in the whole creation. This movement of thought, then, is from miracle to providence. Providence, in Scripture, is therefore an analog of miracle. So it is important for us to come to a biblical understanding of miracle.

DEFINING MIRACLE

Many of the problems surrounding the doctrine of miracle begin with the question of definition. Scripture uses a number of Greek and Hebrew nouns that are translated "miracle," "sign," "wonder," "work," and so on. None of these terms corresponds perfectly in its usage to the English term *miracle*. For example, the Greek term *sēmeion*, "sign," often refers to miracles, but it also refers to events that we would not call miracles, such as circumcision (Rom. 4:11). There are also narratives of miracles in passages lacking any of the nouns designating a miracle: see, for example, 1 Kings 17:17–24[9] and Mark 7:24–30. So we should not assume that word studies of these nouns will cover the biblical data broadly enough to generate an adequate definition of miracle.

How, then, should we seek to develop a concept of miracle? Well, we start with whatever concept we already have and try to refine it on the basis of Scripture. To use an absurd example, imagine someone who thinks that miracles always involve the use of magical nonsense syllables like "abracadabra." But a brief perusal of Scripture shows that there are no events that would fit such a definition. So either the reader must reach the odd conclusion that there are no miracles in Scripture, or he must revise his understanding of what a miracle is. This process repeats itself, as we keep bringing our concepts back to Scripture for progressive refinement. Such remolding of our prejudices, backed up by prayerful appeal to God's Spirit, is the path to greater theological understanding, not only in this area, but in many others as well. This is the famous "hermeneutical circle."

As a starting point, it is sufficient to consider our use of the English term *miracle*. What events in Scripture, if any, may be suitably called by that English term? So we begin with the most obvious point: miracles are unusual

---

9. In this passage, the mother of the resurrected boy says to Elijah, "Now I know that you are a man of God and that the word of the LORD from your mouth is the truth" (v. 24). As we shall see, attesting the truth of prophecy is a major function of miracle.

events caused by God's power, so extraordinary that we would usually consider them impossible. I will call this our preliminary definition of miracle. And we note that Scripture tells us of many such events: the flood of Noah's time (Gen. 6–9), the birth of Isaac to Abraham and Sarah in their old age (Gen. 18:10–15; 21:1–7; Rom. 4:18–22), the turning of Moses' staff into a snake and back again (Ex. 4:2–5), the plagues on Egypt, Israel's crossing of the sea on dry land, and so on.

To many philosophers and theologians, however, this basic definition is inadequate. They believe that the definition should include more detail as to how a miraculous event differs from other events, how it is accomplished, and/or its theological significance. It is often debatable, of course, how much content should be made part of a definition of something and how much should be left to subsequent description. Theologians tend to be more expansive with their definitions than are students of other fields. In this case, at least, we should not take all the proposed expansions for granted. Theological definitions of miracle tend to focus on "nature" and/or "immediacy": a miracle is supernatural as opposed to natural, and/or it is accomplished by the "immediate" power of God. Theologians have also sometimes included in definitions the concept that a miracle attests God's messengers. Let us look at these attempts to make the definition more precise.

NATURAL LAW

Many have said that a miracle bears a distinctive relationship to nature. It is "a violation of the laws of nature" (David Hume),[10] "a phenomenal effect above all the powers of nature; properly the result of supernatural power" (Robert L. Dabney),[11] "a divine intervention into, or an interruption of, the regular course of the world" (Norman Geisler),[12] "an interference with Nature by supernatural power" (C. S. Lewis).[13]

Hume's term *violation* is inappropriate, since this world belongs to God.[14]

---

10. David Hume, *An Inquiry Concerning Human Understanding* (reprint, New York: Liberal Arts Press, 1955, 1957), 122.

11. Robert L. Dabney, *Lectures in Systematic Theology* (reprint, Grand Rapids: Zondervan, 1972), 283.

12. Norman Geisler, *Miracles and Modern Thought* (Grand Rapids: Zondervan, 1982), 13.

13. C. S. Lewis, *Miracles: A Preliminary Study* (New York: Macmillan, 1947), 15.

14. Hume evidently held the view, common among the deists, that God created the world to operate according to natural law, and that God would be "violating" his own ordinances

It is no violation for him to do as he wishes in his own creation. Christian authors rarely if ever use that language, but the idea of miracle as an exception to natural law, or to the general course of nature, is fairly common.

Warfield introduces a helpful clarification at this point, also mentioned by Geisler, Lewis, and some other writers:

> A miracle is not performed by or through the forces of nature or according to its laws: but is, as Mill accurately defines it, "a new effect supposed to be produced by the introduction of a new cause." It does not "violate" any law of nature that a new cause should produce a new effect. It does not "suspend" any law of nature that the intrusion of a new force should be followed by the appearance of a new result. It does not "transgress" any law of nature that the new force is productive of new effects. The mark of a miracle, in a word, is not that it is contra-natural, but that it is extra-natural and more specifically that it is super-natural. It is not conceived as a product of nature, different from and contrary to the ordinary products of nature; but as the product of a force outside of nature, and specifically above nature, intruding into the complex of natural forces and producing, therefore, in that complex, effects which could not be produced by the natural forces themselves.[15]

For example, an airplane does not violate the law of gravity when it takes off from the earth. It merely injects into the air an upward force more powerful than the downward pull of gravity. The law of gravity remains fully in force.

Nevertheless, Warfield agrees with the others that miracles are events produced, not by a powerful force within nature, but by a force "above nature," "super-natural." Miracles, then, for him, are events that natural laws cannot account for. Therefore, Warfield also regards miracles as exceptions to natural laws, in the sense that they come from principles that supersede the laws of nature. Of course, we do not say that an airplane flight is an exception to natural law, since the flight is within the natural world and fully subject to its laws. But Warfield's view is that the "new cause" in the case of miracle is *above* nature itself. A supernatural force operates supernaturally, not according to the laws of the natural world. It is not subject to them,

---

if he ever acted contrary to those laws. But Scripture gives us no reason to believe that God intended natural laws, however defined, to be without exception, and there is no other reason (granted a theistic worldview) for thinking that natural laws are absolute.

15. B. B. Warfield, "The Question of Miracles," in *Selected Shorter Writings of Benjamin B. Warfield—II* (Nutley, N.J.: Presbyterian and Reformed, 1973), 168. He cites John Stuart Mill, *Logic*, 3.25, p. 32.

and so it operates on its own terms. It freely acts upon nature in ways that would be violations of natural law if they were done by a creature. So Warfield's definition of miracle is not radically different from that of Hume. Both understand miracle as the effect produced by a supernatural agent who acts in the world contrary to the natural laws that ordinarily bind all creatures.

Now, what is natural law? I think that there are at least four different ways of understanding it:

The ultimate principles that govern the world. In a biblical worldview, these are nothing less than the decrees of God himself. In this sense, natural laws are never broken, and miracle should not be seen as any sort of exception to natural law.

The regular processes by which God usually governs creation. These are the regularities in the natural world that scientists seek to describe with formulas and theories. Theologically, they are expressions of God's covenant with Noah to keep the seasons regular "as long as the earth endures" (Gen. 8:22). The deists and Hume believed that natural laws in this sense were absolute, operating without exception. But Scripture gives us no assurance that these laws always hold. God is free to work either through or outside of these natural laws.

In many cases, miracles are exceptions to natural law in this sense, but not in every case. For example, God dried up a portion of the Red Sea by sending "a strong east wind" (Ex. 14:21). This was a natural process, although the timing of it was quite astonishing.[16] So we should observe that miracle sometimes suspends natural law in this sense. But since it sometimes does not, "suspension of natural law" in this sense should not be included in the definition of miracle.

We should also note that "usual" is a matter of degree. Events can be more or less "usual," and many obvious miracles are not entirely unique. Jesus' miracles are often similar to works of Yahweh in the Old Testament: he stills the storm, he feeds multitudes, he raises the dead. There are, indeed, enough similarities among miracle stories themselves to include them all in the genre "miracle." On the other hand, all events, whether miracles or not, are unique (and therefore unusual) in that no event is precisely identical with any other. So this definition of miracle does not yield a sharp

16. It might be argued that this timing is itself a significant departure from "God's usual ways of governing creation." But actually, to anticipate some later argument, every event is timed to accomplish God's good purposes for his people (Rom. 8:28).

distinction between miraculous and nonmiraculous events, a distinction usually important to those who propose that miracles suspend natural law.

Furthermore, *usual* generally assumes a particular vantage point. Therefore, this definition, like the third one below, is somewhat subjective. What is "usual" to a person, or to a people at a particular point in history, depends on their own past experience, which may or may not be an adequate guide to the metaphysical structure of reality.[17]

Indeed, to say that an event suspends God's usual working is only a theologically informed way of saying that miracles are extraordinary, a point made already in our preliminary definition. So this interpretation of natural law adds nothing to that definition.

Human expectations concerning the workings of nature. There are, of course, degrees of sophistication in such expectations. In science and other academic disciplines, these expectations are quantified into laws and theories. At those levels of sophistication, the second definition above describes the data of those theories, and this third definition describes the theories themselves. But of course people in biblical times were not as scientifically sophisticated as many people are today. So "expectations" in this definition should include those at all levels of sophistication.

In this sense, miracles are exceptions to natural law, but, on this definition, natural law itself is something essentially subjective. To define miracle in this way says more about the limits of human knowledge than about the objective nature of the miraculous events. Usually, however, writers who define miracle as a suspension of law think that they are making a metaphysical point, rather than a merely epistemological one. Often they use this definition to argue that miracles have ceased, for example. But there is no reason at all to think that God is no longer performing works that violate our subjective expectations. So to define miracle as an exception to natural law in this sense may not accomplish the theological purposes of those who so define it.

The basic created structure of the universe. This is hard to describe, but something like it does seem to be in the minds of most of those who regard miracle as an exception to natural law. I say that, because they clearly don't have the first definition above in mind, and the second and third definitions are too subjective to sustain the force of their conclusions. Since they

---

17. It would be theoretically possible to use *usual* in an objective sense, based on a complete calculation of the frequency of the event in question. But to make such a calculation would require omniscience.

are matters of degree, they will not support the sharp distinction between miracle and providence that is a major goal of defining natural law.

In an e-mail debate with me, philosopher Michael Martin, an atheist, puts it this way:

> But to say that God caused all events to occur could mean two quite different things. First, it could mean that God made and sustains all natural laws. All events are brought about by the working of natural laws which in turn are brought about by God. On this view God never by-passes natural laws. All events can be explained by natural laws which in turn are explained by God. Second, it could mean that although God caused and sustains natural laws, sometimes God by-passes natural laws and directly causes events in the natural world. On this view some events are not completely explained by natural laws which are in turn caused and sustained by God, but are caused in part without the mediation of natural law. It is such cases that I have in mind when I speak of God's intervening in the natural course of events. One might also say in such cases that God suspends certain natural laws and acts without their mediation. This second interpretation is, I believe, the traditional Christian view.[18]

What he calls the traditional Christian view assumes that natural laws are a kind of mechanism within the universe that normally accounts for the events of nature. Miracles occur when God suspends those laws.[19]

I must reject this view for the following reasons:

First, Scripture never defines a miracle this way, nor does it ever identify a miracle by saying that it is a suspension of natural law.

Second, I am not convinced that there are any natural laws in this sense. The idea of a mechanism between God and creation that administers the universe in the absence of divine intervention is a deistic, rather than a biblical, model. As we saw in chapter 4, Scripture ascribes the events of nature directly to God. God brings the winds and the rain, the snow and the fog. He is involved in everything that happens and, as I shall argue later, he is directly involved in everything that happens. Even when impersonal

---

18. The debate can be found in the "Library" at the Web site of "The Secular Web": http://www.infidels.org. It is also available on a link from http://www.reformed.org.

19. Martin thinks that this view denies the uniformity of natural law required by science, so he thinks that this view of miracle makes science impossible. My reply is (1) that this view of miracle is not biblical, and (2) that science does not require absolute uniformity, only relative uniformity.

forces and secondary causes are involved, these accomplish nothing unless God himself is working in them and with them.[20]

Third, even if we assume that there are natural laws in Martin's sense, none of us knows for sure what these laws are. Science, whether ancient or modern, has not reached a final, incorrigible formulation of all the laws that govern the universe. So, on this definition, the biblical writers would not have been able to identify what events are miracles. To do that, they would have had to be omniscient, to know that in all the universe there was no law that could account for the alleged miracle.

Fourth, Exodus 14:21, cited earlier, shows that in some cases an event can be explained by what we call "natural law" (in this case, "a strong east wind") while being a miracle in the fullest sense.

So I do not believe it is scriptural or helpful to define miracle in terms of natural law, even with Warfield's qualification.

IMMEDIACY

Another attempt to make the concept of miracle more precise than it is in our preliminary definition is to describe miracles as "immediate" rather than "mediate" acts of God. J. Gresham Machen describes a miracle as "an event in the external world that is wrought by the *immediate* power of God."[21] Elsewhere he explains,

> . . . in the case of other events, God uses means, . . . whereas in the case of a miracle He puts forth his creative power just as truly as in that mighty act of creation which underlies the whole process of the world.[22]

Martin, in the e-mail debate above, says something similar:

> A miracle, in the sense relevant to my discussion, is an event that can only be explained by supernatural intervention, that is where there is a supernatural cause operating directly on the event in ques-

---

20. I shall discuss this point under the category of "Concurrence" in chapter 14.

21. Machen, *What Is Christianity? and Other Addresses* (Grand Rapids: Eerdmans, 1951), 55. Except for the word "wrought" replacing "produced," this is identical to Warfield's definition in "The Question of Miracles," 178. This is the traditional definition of the "old Princeton" theologians.

22. Machen, "Is the Bible Right About Jesus?" (1927 lectures; Phillipsburg, N.J.: Committee on Christian Education, Orthodox Presbyterian Church, 1955), 30.

tion. Clearly, Christianity assumes that there are miracles in this sense, for example, the Resurrection, Jesus' cures, and so on.[23]

Note the term "directly," which corresponds to Machen's "immediate."

Now Scripture does not distinguish explicitly between some events in which God acts mediately and others in which he acts immediately. Certainly some of his actions in creation occur without created means, particularly the act of creation out of nothing. I would say that regeneration is also an immediate act of God, bringing new life to the soul. It is difficult, at least, to imagine any created means that God could use in regeneration as it is presented in John 3.

But are all miracles such immediate acts of God? Machen compares them to creation, and I suppose there is a parallel in that miracles exhibit the omnipotence of the one who made all things. But Scripture never says in so many words that miracles are immediate. Warfield says that although we do not have testimony to the immediacy of miracle, we do have testimony to events so unusual that they "must be due to the immediate efficacy of God."[24] But what is the logical connection between unusualness and immediacy? What is there about an event that requires us to refer it to the immediate power of God? The answer is obvious in the cases of creation and regeneration, but it is not so obvious in the case of Noah's flood, or Sarah's pregnancy, or Israel's crossing of the Red Sea. Exodus 14:21, again, tells us explicitly that God dried up the Red Sea by a strong east wind. Jesus fed the multitudes with loaves and fishes. He healed the blind man in John 9 by putting mud, mixed with his saliva, on the man's eyes.

An advocate of the immediacy criterion may reply that these means are not being used in their ordinary way.[25] That is certainly true. We agreed at the outset that miracles are extraordinary. The question now is not whether they are extraordinary, but whether they ever employ created means. And it appears that they do.

But the advocate may persist: miracles are certainly events that cannot be accounted for entirely by natural processes or created means. These events are so extraordinary that at some point God's own power must be active alongside and/or in the created means. At some point in the

---

23. "The Martin-Frame Debate," www.infidels.org/library/modern/michael_martin/-martin-frame/.

24. Warfield, "The Question of Miracles," 178.

25. Louis Berkhof defines miracles as events in which God "works immediately or without the mediation of second causes *in their ordinary operation,*" *Systematic Theology* (London: Banner of Truth Trust, 1939, 1941), 176 (emphasis added).

causal chain, the power of God must touch the creation directly. Again, this is true. But it raises the further question whether any event at all can be accounted for without the power of God. On a biblical world-view, God brings about everything that comes to pass. That means that nothing can be fully accounted for, apart from his agency. And that in turn implies that any causal explanation at all ultimately terminates in God's action. That is to say that every causal explanation begins with a direct or immediate contact between God and creation. Indeed, as we shall see in our discussion of concurrence in chapter 14, divine action not only begins causal chains, but also is immediately involved with every event in the chain. He is immediately involved in every event, for no event can take place without his personal permission and involvement, his concurrence.

In other words, all events are immediate acts of God in the sense that they cannot be accounted for, apart from God's direct agency. "Immediacy," therefore, in this sense, does not serve to distinguish miracles from other events.

And, as in the last section, I must also raise here an epistemological objection. If miracles are immediate acts of God, how could anybody ever identify an event as a miracle? How could the biblical writers, or anybody, know what events have no cause other than God's direct action? The burden of proof in such a negative proposition is impossible to bear. And we have no reason to believe that anyone in Scripture even tried to bear it. Immediacy plays no role in the biblical account of miracle.

Now Scripture does teach that "only God" can do wondrous works (Pss. 72:18; 86:10). Does this language imply that God performs miracles immediately or without any natural causation? I think not: the contrast in these passages is not between what God can do mediately and what he can do only immediately. It is rather between what he can do and what other agents can do. In fact, the comparatively indirect divine acts we associate with providence are also works that only God can do. In Psalm 136, the feeding of every creature (v. 25) is one of the "wonders" that only God can do (v. 4).

ATTESTING GOD'S MESSENGERS

A third proposed theological enhancement of our basic definition of miracle is that it attests or accredits God's prophets. Loraine Boettner, in the old Princeton tradition, defined a miracle as "an event in the external world, wrought by the immediate power of God, and designed to accredit a message or messenger."[26] Unlike the first two elaborations, this one is based on a genuine emphasis of Scripture. We recall the staff of Moses that turned into a snake and back again (Ex. 4:1–5). God enabled Moses to work this miracle in response to the anticipated skepticism of Israel that God had spoken to Moses (4:1). So the miracle verified Moses' status as God's prophet. We have also mentioned 1 Kings 17:24, in which the mother of the son restored to life through the word of Elijah testifies, "Now I know that you are a man of God and that the word of the LORD from your mouth is the truth." The miracle attests Elijah as a prophet of God. (See also Ex. 7:9–13; Matt. 9:6; 11:4–6; Luke 4:18–21; John 5:19–23, 36; 10:24–26, 38; 20:30–31; Acts 2:22; 14:3; Rom. 15:18–19; 2 Cor. 12;12; Heb. 2:3–4.)

There can be no doubt, then, that a major purpose of biblical miracles is to accredit prophets and apostles, and even the Son of God, as God's messengers. And since a miracle attests the prophet, it also attests his prophecy as God's truth.

In a broad sense, we may even say that all biblical miracles[27] have this function. For the purpose of Scripture in general is to bring us God's word, with the rationale of that word. God's word itself provides us with the evidence of its own truth. And miracles constitute a substantial portion of that evidence. Every miracle of Scripture serves the gospel of redemption, by reporting God's activity in support of that message.

On the other hand, this is not the only purpose of miracles in Scripture. The flood of Genesis 6–9 did accredit Noah as a prophet, certainly. But when the rain came, it was too late for that accreditation to lead anyone to faith, outside of Noah's family. Scripture does tell us that Noah was a prophet (2 Peter 2:5), but it is silent about any events that might have accredited his prophecies to his contemporaries. The main purpose of the Flood was not accreditation, but judgment.

The Incarnation was a miracle, certainly, and it accredits Jesus' words in a way. But a better perspective is to note that Jesus' words (and works) primarily verified his divine origin, rather than the other way around. The Incarnation was not primarily a means of validating a message, but rather the very means of our salvation. It, together with the Atonement and the Resurrection, is the very content of the message.

Jesus' healings attested his words, but he did not heal merely to accredit himself as a prophet. In Matthew 14:14, we read, "When Jesus landed and

---

26. Loraine Boettner, *Studies in Theology* (Grand Rapids: Eerdmans, 1953), 51.

27. Of course, we have to exclude from this generalization the "miracles" of false prophets (Deut. 13:2; 2 Thess. 2:9).

saw a large crowd, he had compassion on them and healed their sick." The
chief purpose of this miracle was to show divine compassion, to meet the
needs of people (cf. Matt. 20:34; Mark 1:41). Jesus fed the four thousand,
also, because of his compassion for the multitudes (Matt. 15:32–39). Of
course, that very compassion attested Jesus as the Messiah. In a general
sense, everything Jesus did displayed his godly character and therefore to
some extent vindicated his claims and message. But in that sense miracles
did not attest Jesus' prophetic office more than any of his other actions.

Miracles also serve to advance God's cause in the spiritual warfare of his
people. God gives them strength beyond their own, in order to give them
victory over great nations, as in the Exodus and Israel's conquest of Palestine. God opens the hearts of Gentiles supernaturally to bring the gospel
to the ends of the earth (Acts 13:48; 16:14). He overcomes opposition to
plant his church in all nations.

Should we, then, include "attestation of prophecy" in our definition
of *miracle?* Since all biblical miracles do attest God's word, at least in a
general way, it is not easy to argue against this proposal. However, there
are some disadvantages to it. We do have some freedom in choosing what
to include in a definition. Scripture says nothing explicit about how we
should define these events, and of course it does not require any specific definition of the English word *miracle*. It does not tell us what biblical content to include in the definition and what content should remain for later description. On these matters, we should weigh the
advantages and disadvantages of different proposals. Since there is no
perfect correspondence between the English *miracle* and any of the
Greek or Hebrew terms in Scripture, all proposed definitions will have
some disadvantages.

That is also true with definitions of *miracle* that include "attestation of
prophecy." Those who advocate this refinement to our minimal definition
usually construe this attestation to be roughly contemporary with the first
articulation of the prophecy. So the prophecy in view here is new special
revelation. Now obviously miracles that occurred during the writing of
Scripture were attestations of new prophecy, because that was a time in
which some prophecy was new. But to say that miracles always attest new
special revelation prejudices the question of whether God might do similar things in our own time, not to attest new special revelation, but to attest revelation given long ago, or for one or more of the other purposes of
miracle noted above. Scripture itself doesn't discuss this question, because
it was written during a time in which God was adding special revelation
to the canon.

Every event in Scripture, not only the unusual ones, attests the truth of

God's word, the truth of prophecy. That is to say, one purpose of Scripture is to accredit itself. It is self-authenticating. Every event in Scripture is part of a narrative that, as a whole, attests the credibility of God's messengers. For example, the stoning of Stephen, recorded in Acts 7, was not a miracle, but his willingness to speak boldly of Christ in the face of his murderers was a powerful witness to the truth of the gospel, a truth newly given to the church as a result of Jesus' death and resurrection. All martyrdoms in Scripture have the purpose of accrediting revelation in this way. But it would obviously be wrong to define martyrdom as an act that bears witness to the truth of new special revelation. And, of course, it would be foolish to claim that martyrdoms therefore cease when new special revelation ceases, at the end of the apostolic age.[28] Martyrdoms continue into the present as powerful witnesses to the truth of *old* special revelation, the truth delivered once for all to the saints.

Similarly, the heroism of David's mighty men (as in 2 Sam. 23:13–17) is a powerful witness to their faith in God's covenant with David. All heroism in Scripture, similarly, bears witness to prophecy, as in the examples of Hebrews 11. But it would not be right to define heroism as involving a witness to new special revelation and then to draw the conclusion that after the completion of the canon heroism ceased.

For these reasons, I am not inclined to add "attestation of prophecy" to our basic definition of *miracle*, even though it was an important aspect of miracles during the biblical period. If we do add such a qualification to the definition, we must remember that that qualification does not really address, except in a verbal way, the question of the cessation of miracles. On a definition including "attestation of new prophetic revelation," miracles do cease at the end of the apostolic period. But that fact does not rule out the possibility of subsequent divine works, which are like our narrowly defined "miracles," except that they do not bear witness to new special revelation.

SOME OTHER REFORMED VIEWS OF MIRACLE

Other theologians have advanced rather different concepts of miracle. Abraham Kuyper, for example, emphasized that miraculous powers are not distinctively divine, but were given to Adam before the Fall and have since been largely lost, though they appear occasionally in paranormal phenomena. Jesus, in Kuyper's view, worked miracles, not

28. I am assuming that the canon of special revelation is closed.

through his divine nature, but through his unfallen human nature.[29] Johann H. Diemer, building on this conception, emphasizes that God made the lower realms of creation to serve the higher, and that grace restores the proper order between man and nature broken by sin. He believes that healings similar to those of Jesus can happen today, even outside the context of Christian faith.[30] Diemer believes that the idea of supernatural intervention does injustice to the fact that natural events are also works of God.[31]

These ideas move in the opposite direction from those of the old Princeton theologians. To Kuyper and Diemer, it is wrong to draw a sharp distinction between supernatural and natural events, or between immediate and mediate acts of God.[32] To them, miracles are natural events—indeed, nature at its best.

I agree with these Dutch thinkers that the distinction between supernatural and natural events is unhelpful here. I do not, however, see the biblical basis for saying that Jesus' miracles are wholly due to his human nature, or that miracles are paranormal powers given to Adam before the Fall. These ideas are interesting, and they may even be true. But they strike me as speculative. Nevertheless, these writings are helpful in showing us that positions rather different from those of the Princetonians have been maintained by people in the Reformed tradition. So we should not assume that the concepts of natural law and of immediacy have any privileged position in determining orthodoxy in this area. It may be, in fact, that there is no biblical ground for judging between these alternatives. The definition of miracle should not prejudice these issues.

---

29. Abraham Kuyper, *You Can Do Greater Things Than Christ: Demons, Miracles, Healing, and Science*, trans. Jan H. Boer (Jos, Nigeria: Institute for Church and Society, 1991). For the Dutch original, see *Pro Rege*, I (Kampen: Kok, 1911), 143–246.

30. Johann H. Diemer, *Miracles Happen: Toward a Biblical View of Nature* (Toronto: Association for the Advancement of Christian Scholarship, n.d.); Diemer, *Nature and Miracle* (Toronto: Wedge, 1977). Diemer follows Dooyeweerd in his understanding of the world as a system of law spheres ascending from lower to higher.

31. Gordon Spykman finds this kind of supernaturalism dualistic. See his *Reformational Theology* (Grand Rapids: Eerdmans, 1992), 287–97.

32. G. C. Berkouwer is another theologian in the Dutch Reformed tradition who avoids these sharp distinctions. In *The Providence of God* (Grand Rapids: Eerdmans, 1952), 188–231, Berkouwer cites a number of Reformed sources, including Kuyper's *E Voto* and Bavinck's dogmatics. He argues that miracles are not against nature (*contra naturam*), but against sin (*contra peccatum*). *The Providence of God* is one of Berkouwer's earlier, and, in my view, more helpful books. His whole discussion here is worth consulting, although I do disagree with some of his discussion of miracles as "proofs." My discussion here is indebted to Berkouwer's.

MIRACLES AS DEMONSTRATIONS
OF GOD'S COVENANT LORDSHIP

We have seen that miracles are unusual events, brought about by God. That is our preliminary definition. I have argued that attempts to identify miracles with suspensions of natural law, or with immediate rather than mediate acts of God, are not biblically warranted. And although I grant that biblical miracles attest special revelation, I have been unwilling to make that part of the definition of miracle. Nor do I think we have biblical warrant to identify miracles entirely with God's natural working.

But now we must consider what the main emphases of Scripture's own teaching concerning miracles are. They can be summarized, I think, in the statement, "Miracles are extraordinary manifestations of God's covenant lordship." If I were asked to provide a theologically enhanced definition of miracle, that would be it.

As we saw in chapter 2, God performs his mighty acts so that people will know that he is the Lord. Thus, miracles draw our attention to those attributes that define his lordship: his control, authority, and presence. I do not base my argument on word studies, but it is interesting that these three emphases are found in the biblical terms for miracle:

- *geburah, dynamis* (power, mighty act)—control
- *'oth, sēmeion* (sign)—authority
- *mofeth, pele', teras* (wonder)—presence

As mighty acts, miracles display the great power of the Lord to control his creation. As signs, they authoritatively reveal him. As wonders, they create in the hearts of people a religious awe, as they bring people into the presence of the living God. Let us look at these aspects more closely.

Control. Miracles are, perhaps most obviously, the result of God's enormous power. After crossing the sea on dry land, Moses and the Israelites sang praises to God for his great redemptive power:

> Your right hand, O LORD,
>   was majestic in power.
> Your right hand, O LORD,
>   shattered the enemy. (Ex. 15:6)

This power worked "wonders" (v. 11). In Egypt, God won the contest of power against the magicians and against Egypt's gods (Ex. 7:8–13; 8:19; 12:12; 15:11). Israel was confident that when they reached the Promised Land, that same power would terrify the leaders of the Canaanites: "By the power of your arm they will be as still as a stone" (v. 16). Throughout Scripture, miracles are among the "mighty works" for which God's people praise him.

In Mark 5:24–34, a woman touches Jesus' garment and is immediately healed of an ailment she has had for twelve years. When this happened, "Jesus realized that power had gone out from him" (v. 30). According to Luke 5:17, on a certain occasion "the power of the Lord was present for him to heal the sick." In Luke 6:19, "the people all tried to touch him, because power was coming from him and healing them all." In Acts, the apostles also heal people, but by God's power, not their own (3:12). Simon the sorcerer is called "the Great Power" (8:10), but he must bow before a greater power (vv. 18–24).

Authority. Miracles are "signs" and therefore revelation. Revelation from God always bears his supreme authority.

By his mighty deeds, says Moses, Yahweh has "begun to show to your servant your greatness and your strong hand" (Deut. 3:24). Miracles not only accomplish great things, but also display God to us. They teach us about him. So God feeds his people in the wilderness "to teach you that man does not live on bread alone but on every word that comes from the mouth of God" (Deut. 8:3).

In Mark 2:1–11, Jesus heals a paralytic and thereby reveals that he has the authority to forgive sins. John's gospel especially focuses on the "signs" of Jesus' ministry. Toward the end, John indicates his purpose in presenting these signs:

> Jesus did many other miraculous signs in the presence of his disciples, which are not recorded in this book. But these are written that you may believe that Jesus is the Christ, the Son of God, and that by believing you may have life in his name. (20:30–31)

In the first sign, Jesus changes water into wine at Cana. John comments, "He thus revealed his glory, and his disciples put their faith in him" (2:11). The water of Jewish ceremonial washings becomes the wine of the messianic banquet. The Lord who brings the consummation of redemption has arrived on earth. Jesus' miracles often parallel the works of Yahweh in the Old Testament, such as miraculous feedings (Ex. 16; John 6:1–14), stilling a storm (Ps. 107:29; Mark 4:35–41), raising the dead (1 Kings 17:7–24; Luke 7:11–17; John 11:1–44), and healing the blind, deaf, lame, and mute (Isa. 35:5; Luke 7:18–23). In Luke 7, Jesus lists these miracles to renew the confidence of John the Baptist that he is indeed "the one who was to come." The miracles bear powerful witness to who

Jesus is. The feeding of the five thousand reveals him as the bread of life (John 6:1–70). His raising of Lazarus reveals him as the resurrection and the life (John 11:25–26).

Miracles do not simply attest revelation, but actually *are* revelation. They reveal the character of God (his power, care, and compassion), the person and work of Jesus, the blessings of redemption, and its fulfillment in the messianic banquet.

Covenant presence. As "wonders," miracles typically evoke a powerful subjective response in those who observe them. Of course, there are some who respond wrongly—persisting in their unbelief or even ascribing the miracle to Satan (Matt. 12:24–28). But the proper and usual response is one of awe.

This awe is religious awe, due to the sense that God is present. The Exodus leads to worship: the hymn of praise in Exodus 15. God's mighty acts motivate the Psalms, in which God's people express their awe, wonder, and joy in his presence.

The miraculous catch of fish in Luke 5:1–10 is very much a religious experience for the disciples. Peter's response seems odd at first, but on reflection we can see that it is entirely appropriate: "Go away from me, Lord; I am a sinful man!" (v. 8). What does a miraculous catch of fish have to do with Peter's sin? In the miracle, Peter experiences a theophany. Jesus is God in the flesh, who rules the earth and sea. And like Isaiah, when the prophet "saw the Lord" (Isa. 6:1), Peter is reminded of his unfitness to be in God's presence. Isaiah said, "Woe to me! I am ruined! For I am a man of unclean lips, and I live among a people of unclean lips, and my eyes have seen the King, the LORD Almighty" (v. 5). But, as he does with Isaiah, God gives to Peter a prophetic commission: "From now on you will catch men" (Luke 5:10). To see the miracle rightly is to recognize God's presence in the miracle.[33]

As displays of God's control, authority, and presence, miracles may be defined as extraordinary manifestations of God's lordship. On this understanding, there is no need to be concerned about the relation of miracle to natural law, or whether miracles are mediate or immediate. And this definition helps us to understand the role of miracles in attesting prophecy. That is, one way in which miracles reveal God's nature and will is by attesting prophecy.

---

33. Compare my discussion of God's holiness in chapter 2. When we encounter God's lordship, we stand on holy ground, and that forces us to face the fact of our sin.

MIRACLE AND PROVIDENCE

To some writers, it is important that miracle and providence be sharply distinguished from each other. This view may often be motivated by the desire to argue that miracles ceased at the end of the apostolic age.[34] Those who so argue must show that miracles have distinguishing characteristics, so that they can cease while providence continues. If we cannot distinguish miracles clearly from other events, we cannot explain what it is that ceases at the end of the apostolic age. As we have seen, efforts have been made to distinguish miracles as exceptions to natural law, immediate acts of God, and attestations of new special revelation.

I do not believe, however, that Scripture warrants a sharp distinction between providence and miracle. Indeed, in Scripture the language of miracle is used for providential events, and providential events have much the same significance as miracles.

Psalm 107 is a series of testimonies to the "wonders" of the Lord. Verses 4–9 arguably refer to Israel's wilderness experience, and verses 10–22 may refer to God's chastisements of his sinful people and his response to their repentance. But verses 23–43 seem to refer to God's general providence, rather than the history of redemption specifically. God rescues sailors from storms at sea, when they cry out to him (vv. 23–32). He gives water and food to his people (vv. 33–43). These are also among God's wonders.

Psalm 136 also lists "wonders" of the Lord (v. 4), including his works of creation (vv. 5–9), the events of the Exodus (vv. 10–24), and, almost as an afterthought, the fact that God "gives food to every creature" (v. 25). General providence is a wonder of God, alongside all his miraculous deeds of creation and redemption. In Psalm 145, also, God's "wonderful works" (v. 5) and "awesome works" (v. 6) include his compassion for all (v. 9).[35] The psalmist observes,

> The eyes of all look to you,
>   and you give them their food at the proper time.
> You open your hand
>   and satisfy the desires of every living thing. (vv. 15–16)

---

34. I think there is also, often, an apologetic motive. It is thought that if miracles are not distinct from providence, they cannot serve as a proof for the truth of Christianity. Miracles have to be distinctive, special events to serve that purpose. I shall discuss the apologetic significance of miracles later. But I will say here only that providence, too, is a proof of God's reality.

35. This is reinforced in verse 8 by an allusion to the exposition of the divine name in Ex. 34:6–7.

Again, providence is among God's wondrous works. (Cf. also Job 37:5–24; 42:3.)

So there is a sense in which all providence is wonderful or miraculous. The reason, of course, is that providence, too, is God's act, manifesting his control, authority, and presence, as we shall see in the next chapter. If we must distinguish between providence and miracle, we should perhaps contrast the latter as "extraordinary" manifestations of God's lordship with the former as "ordinary" manifestations of God's lordship. But even that is not quite right, for in the eyes of the psalmist, providence itself is rather extraordinary. Only one person, after all, is able to feed all living things on earth. At any rate, we should normally place miracle on the "more extraordinary" end of the spectrum. My only point at present is that there is a spectrum or a continuum of God's acts, not a sharp distinction between providence and miracle. And there is, then, a sense in which all is miracle.

HAVE MIRACLES CEASED?

I mentioned earlier that some of the more restrictive definitions of miracle may be motivated by the desire to show more easily that miracles have ceased. For this purpose, it is important to show that miracle is sharply distinguished from providence, and that miracle performs a function (attesting new special revelation) that does not continue into the present time. I have argued that miracle and providence cannot be sharply distinguished, and I have rejected the idea that miracles always attest prophecy. So, in my view, there is no biblical reason why miracles cannot occur today.

To clarify my position, however, I should say that I fully believe that the canon of special revelation is closed.[36] And I believe, somewhat less firmly, that God has removed from the church the word-gifts of tongues and prophecy,[37] although I also agree with Vern S. Poythress that those gifts are analogous to works of the Spirit in the church today.[38] Now it is sometimes assumed that those who hold to the cessation of these charismata must also hold to the cessation of all miracles after the time of the apostles. But

36. I expect to argue that point in *The Doctrine of the Word of God.*
37. Richard B. Gaffin's *Perspectives on Pentecost* (Phillipsburg, N.J.: Presbyterian and Reformed, 1979) makes a strong case for the cessation of the charismata, but not, in my estimation, a watertight one.
38. Vern S. Poythress, "Modern Spiritual Gifts as Analogous to Apostolic Gifts: Affirming Extraordinary Works of the Spirit within Cessationist Theology," *JETS* 39 (1996): 71–101.

that conclusion does not follow. Granting that tongues and prophecy are miraculous, and that they have ceased, it does not follow that *all* miracles have ceased.

At the same time, I do not believe that the more spectacular miracles (walking on water, stilling a storm by a word, healing instantly by a word) are a normal part of Christian experience today, nor do I believe that we should feel guilty if we have not experienced such wonders.

Although the Bible seems full of miracles, these events were not common during the biblical period. Of course, by definition, miracles are uncommon or "extraordinary." But even in the biblical period, in which many miracles took place, these events were not evenly distributed over time. Many centuries went by (as from Noah to Abraham, Abraham to Moses, and Malachi to Jesus) without many miracles[39] being recorded. During Abraham's lifetime, there were theophanies and the miraculous birth of Isaac. But Abraham lived many years without seeing any miracle. For most of his life, he was made to wait, anticipating the fulfillment of God's promise. That he was, for the most part, patient during this waiting period is one of the exemplary features of Abraham's faith. Similarly, Moses spent forty years in the wilderness before God appeared to him in the burning bush and inaugurated a new era of miracles. So God evidently reserves miracles for special occasions, including the attestation of his messengers, as we have seen.

Historically, it does appear that we are living in one of those times when miracles are rare. B. B. Warfield's essay, "The Cessation of the Charismata," argues cogently that historical evidence for miracles after the time of the apostles is scarce and unpersuasive.[40] There have been many claims of miracles down through the centuries from the apostles' time to ours, but it is hard to know how much credit to give to those reports. At least it is clear that miracle is rare today, compared with the times of Moses, of Elijah and Elisha, and of Jesus and the apostles. I know very few believers who claim to have experienced miracles of this sort, and I have not experienced any myself, although I have seen God's hand, God's timing, in many unusual coincidences. But I have heard reports of miracles, especially from mission fields, by people I consider reliable.

One might, therefore, describe my position as semicessationist. I believe

---

39. I am here, of course, referring to miracles in the commonsense way, as spectacular actions of God, although I have argued that in one sense all is miracle. In the following context, *miracle* will mean "spectacular miracle."

40. In B. B. Warfield, *Miracles: Yesterday and Today* (1918; reprint, Grand Rapids: Eerdmans, 1965), 1–31.

that miracle in a broad sense (that is, providence) continues, and I am not skeptical of reports from reliable witnesses of more spectacular miracles. But I do not think that spectacular miracles are a normal part of the Christian life.

Miracles are rare today because God has no sufficient reason to make them frequent. Since Jesus has accomplished redemption once for all, the next great manifestation of divine power will be seen at his return. Until then, there is no comparable reason for spectacular divine acts. And there is no reason why we should expect God to bless us with more spectacular displays of his power than were seen, for example, in the four hundred years between Joseph and Moses.

Beyond that general consideration, there is a pattern in Scripture, in which the extraordinary serves as preparation for the ordinary.[41] We often value spectacular experience over day-to-day routine. But God's priorities are different.

During the Flood, God protected Noah and his family supernaturally, by directing them to build the ark and providing their means of life. But God's intent was not for them to live in the ark forever, but to resume a normal life on land. So, following this most extraordinary event comes a covenant in which God promises regular seasons: seedtime and harvest, cold and heat, summer and winter, day and night (Gen. 8:22). When men shed blood, they will be punished, not by a supernatural flood, but by human government (9:6). The extraordinary, then, is a preparation for the ordinary.

Similarly, in Joshua 5:12, we learn that when Israel entered the Promised Land, the manna ceased. The manna was a miraculous provision of God to feed his people in the wilderness. But his intent was not for them to live on manna forever, but to set up farms, plant crops, and eat food made the normal way. The time of manna was preparation; the normal harvests were the fulfillment of God's promise.

In John 16:7, Jesus tells the disciples that it will be better for them if he leaves the earth. That is a hard saying. The disciples experienced something wonderful in the personal ministry of Jesus, not least a great number of miracles that met their needs and confirmed their faith. But when Jesus departs, he will send the Holy Spirit, who will empower his disciples and enable them to do "even greater things" than he himself did in his earthly ministry (14:12). Through the power of the Spirit, the church will spread throughout the earth. But the age of the Spirit

ponder this

---

41. In this discussion, I am greatly indebted to Norman Shepherd's lectures on the doctrine of God. Of course, I take full responsibility for my formulations.

(after the apostolic period begins it) will be a time in which spectacular miracles are scarce. Again, the extraordinary is preparation for the ordinary.

First Corinthians 13 warns us, as it did the Corinthians, against thinking too highly of the spectacular. Paul tells them that tongues and prophecy are far less important than love. The purpose of the spectacular gifts is to establish an "ordinary" one, the one that always remains—love.

The church was originally governed by the apostles, who were specifically called by Christ and given miraculous gifts of the Spirit. But in the later sections of the New Testament, we learn that the churches established by the apostles were to be governed by elders and deacons (see 1 Tim. 3:1–13; Titus 1:5–9), whose qualifications were not to be spectacular powers, but godly character and ability to teach. Again, the extraordinary prepares for the ordinary.

So in Hebrews 2:3–4, the writer tells the Hebrew Christians to hold firm to the gospel, on the basis of the signs and wonders by which God testified (past tense) to it. He does not tell them to wait for more signs, but to believe the witnesses who have told them about the past signs. Later generations were to be persuaded, not by continuing signs, but by reports of the original signs. That, by and large, is the situation in which we live today. The ordinary succeeds the extraordinary.

So we are not to lust after more and more signs (Matt. 12:38–42), nor should we assume that people need special signs in order to be persuaded of the truth of the gospel, for God's written words in Scripture are sufficient (Luke 16:19–31).

For these reasons, we should not be surprised or unhappy that God has not provided more spectacular miracles in our own time. Miracles tend to set the stage for a time of "natural" existence. With that ordinariness we should be content and thankful.

At the same time, we should not be skeptical about reports of spectacular miracles today. God may have his reasons for occasionally performing them. If we are to be semicessationists, we should also be semicontinuationists. For example, there are tribes and nations to whom the gospel is new. It may very well be that when the gospel is brought to them, as in the book of Acts, God sometimes performs wonders to accredit his missionaries, to defeat opposition to the gospel, and to put the new church on a firm footing. Whether such events take place depends on God's sovereign purposes, not our theological generalizations.

I have also heard reports of God dealing in wondrous ways with believers in Western society—especially with those who are recent converts: striking answers to prayer, healings that defy medical expectations, amazing timing of events, and so on. Again, I am not particularly skeptical about these reports.[42] Nor am I disappointed that I don't see such amazing things in my own life. When young Christians become more mature, they often wonder why such things happen to them less often or not at all. They worry that their faith has grown dim, because they don't see as many supernatural events in their lives. That may be so, but it may also be the case that in their individual lives, as often in Scripture, the extraordinary has been a preparation for the ordinary.

It is important to keep an open mind about the possibility of miracles in our time, even though their rarity should not surprise us. We have seen that the ordinary is primary. But it is also important to remember the continuities that exist between our time and that of the apostles. This is still God's world, a world directed by a person, not by impersonal "natural laws." He rules the world to bring good to his people and glory to himself, and nothing forces him to restrict his actions to "natural means," however those be defined. It is also the case that Jesus still lives, and that his Spirit is still working in awesome power. Paul prays that the Ephesians may know God's

> incomparably great power for us who believe. That power is like the working of his mighty strength, which he exerted in Christ when he raised him from the dead and seated him at his right hand in the heavenly realms. (1:19–20)

This prayer does not expire at the end of the apostolic age. Like Paul, we live in a time when the resurrection power of God is reaching out to bring salvation to the ends of the earth. And so God for us is "able to do immeasurably more than all we ask or imagine, according to his power that is at work within us" (3:20). The rarity of spectacular events does not mean the absence of divine power in the church. And the presence of divine power means that the spectacular may occasionally intrude into our lives. Let us not be so sure that we know what God is or is not going to do. A proper study of miracle should encourage intellectual and spiritual humility.

---

42. God often, though not always, seems to be especially gentle with young believers. I believe it was Vern Poythress who suggested to me (with some of the other thoughts in this section of the chapter) that the good shepherd has a special care for the little lambs in his flock: "He gathers the lambs in his arms" (Isa. 40:11). A kind parent will keep his toddler always in view, ready to grab him before he runs into the street or goes after a fierce dog. But, as the child grows, he will train him to notice dangers and to avoid them without direct and obvious supervision.

POSSIBILITY AND PROBABILITY

Are miracles possible? In the context of a Christian worldview, of course they are. Miracles are possible because the world is under God's sovereign control. It is God who, by his nature and decrees, determines what is possible. The regularities of nature are his covenantal gift to us, and they do not at all limit his ability to work in the world as he pleases.

We need not appeal to the supposed random behavior of elementary particles in order to provide a small possibility that very unusual events may take place. According to present-day science, the smallest subatomic particles behave most strangely, but there is no known path by which they communicate their strangeness to processes involving much larger bodies. The behavior of certain subatomic particles has not moved many, if any, naturalistic scientists to believe in miracles. To rest the case for miracles on the whims of photons and quarks is to trust a frail reed. Rather, miracles are possible because God exists.

Are miracles probable? Of course they are unlikely, because they are by definition extraordinary. But that fact does not reduce their probability to zero. Probability, like possibility, is determined by God. In a Christian worldview, how likely is it that God will bring about miracles? To answer that question, we must know something about God, particularly about his intentions and goals.

God announced to Noah that the course of nature would proceed in a way that is generally regular (Gen. 8:22). But God's higher intention is to redeem a people for himself, and to do that, it is appropriate for him to perform unusual works—to accomplish salvation, to apply it, and to attest it. If the world were governed by impersonal forces, there would be no reason to expect departures from the basic functions of those forces.[43] But ours is a world ruled by a person, and he seeks fellowship with us. That is sufficient reason to expect that he will identify himself in the natural order as the ruler of it. And since he has ordained miracle as a mark of his lordship and as an attestation of his revelation, we can say that miracle is significantly probable.

EVIDENCE FOR MIRACLE

In his famous essay "Of Miracles,"[44] David Hume says:

A miracle is a violation of the laws of nature; and as a firm and unalterable experience has established these laws, the proof against

43. On the other hand, there would in that case be no reason to expect regularity, either.
44. Hume, *An Inquiry Concerning Human Understanding*, 117–41.

a miracle, from the very nature of the fact, is as entire as any argument from experience can possibly be imagined.[45]

I have rejected Hume's definition of miracle and therefore consider the rest of this quotation to be irrelevant. However, even granted his definition, he begs the question when he says that "a firm and unalterable experience has established these laws." If this argument is to stand as a proof against miracle, the experience establishing the laws must be universal and without exception. Therefore, he begins his argument by saying that nobody has ever experienced an exception to these laws. But that is precisely the question that needs to be resolved.[46]

But Hume does not quite want to argue that because natural laws are universal, miracles are metaphysically impossible. At least he does not want his argument to appear to make that assumption. An argument from experience, as he explains earlier in the essay, is never absolutely certain, but is always more or less probable. We determine the level of probability by weighing one experience against another, and, importantly, one testimony against another. So the rest of Hume's argument is about the credibility of testimony. His assumption about the unvarying laws of nature leads him to say this about the level of testimony needed to establish a miracle:

> No testimony is sufficient to establish a miracle unless the testimony be of such a kind that its falsehood would be more miraculous than the fact that it endeavors to establish.[47]

Hume then argues that no report of a miracle has ever fulfilled this criterion. In no case, he thinks, has the report of a miracle come from witnesses who are absolutely trustworthy.[48] He states that reports of miracles tend to come from emotional excess and therefore are exaggerated.[49] They tend to come from "ignorant and barbarous nations,"[50] are opposed by those of different religious persuasions,[51] and even at best should be rejected because of the "absolute impossibility or miraculous nature of the events which they relate."[52]

---

45. Ibid., 122.
46. Compare the bottom of p. 122: "But it is a miracle that a dead man should come to life, because that has never been observed in any age or country." Never? Here he dismisses the accounts of such events in Scripture.
47. Ibid., 123.
48. Ibid., 124.
49. Ibid., 125–26.
50. Ibid., 126.
51. Ibid., 128.
52. Ibid., 133.

In this last quotation, Hume tips his hand. He wants us to believe that he is not begging the question by assuming at the outset that miracles are impossible. But in the last quotation, he clearly makes that assumption. In his view, there simply cannot be any "violation of the laws of nature." His argument, essentially, is that no testimony can establish a report of something that cannot happen.

Applied to the reports of miracles in Scripture, Hume's arguments are unpersuasive unless we assume *a priori* that miraculous events are impossible. There is no reason to suppose that the biblical reports of miracles stem from emotional excess or exaggeration—and shouldn't the biblical writers be considered innocent until proved guilty? Nor is biblical Israel fairly described as an "ignorant and barbarous" nation. The most that can be said is that the biblical writers lived before the advent of modern science. But they knew from experience that, under ordinary circumstances, axheads do not float, multitudes cannot be fed with a few loaves and fishes, and men do not rise from the dead. They believed that Satan counterfeits God's miracles (Ex. 7:11–12, 22; 8:7, 17–18; Deut. 13:1–3; Matt. 24:24; 2 Thess. 2:9; Rev. 13:13), and so they had a proper skepticism about such things. But they also knew that unless miracles are really unlikely, they cannot do what God intends for them to do.

And as for the contrary claims of opposing parties, we have no evidence of such claims in the Old Testament context. So far as we know, nobody questioned whether the plagues on Egypt took place, whether Elijah raised the son of the widow of Zarephath, or whether the axhead really floated. In the New Testament period, the opponents of Christianity either resorted to transparent rationalizations (e.g., that the disciples must have stolen the body of Jesus) or conceded the miracle and attributed it to Satan.

But the more fundamental criticisms of Hume's argument are epistemological:

1. He assumes a nontheistic view of the possibility and probability of miracles. For him, possibility and probability are determined entirely by autonomous human experience, without any consideration of who God is and what God's intentions are. His argument, indeed, assumes that the God of Scripture does not exist; for if God did exist, one would have to take him into account in judging the possibility and probability of miracle, as we did in the previous section.

2. Hume assumes at the outset that divine revelation plays no role in determining whether miracles have taken place. For the Christian, however, writers like Moses, Luke, John, and Paul are perfectly credible witnesses, not because they are completely unprejudiced, sophisticated, scientific, and civilized, but because they are themselves prophets of God,

inspired by God's Spirit. It is significant that, although Paul in 1 Corinthians 15 appeals to numerous witnesses of the Resurrection (including five hundred at one time, most of whom are still living—a significant evidentiary point), his main argument for belief in the Resurrection is that it is an integral part of the gospel he has preached, having received it by revelation (Gal. 1:11–12). So, if the dead do not rise, then

> our preaching is useless and so is your faith. More than that, we are then found to be false witnesses about God, for we have testified about God that he raised Christ from the dead. But he did not raise him if in fact the dead are not raised. (1 Cor. 15:14–15)

The Corinthians should believe in the Resurrection, Paul tells them, because it is a central element in the gospel revelation.

Hume does not even consider the possibility of receiving knowledge by divine revelation. Doubtless he would consider revelation, too, to be a miracle and therefore impossible and incredible. But in so dismissing the possibility of revelation, he cuts himself off from any communication from the God who is the only ground of rational discourse. If the testimony concerning miracles is the testimony of God himself, then it would fulfill his condition quoted earlier. For the falsehood of God's testimony would certainly be more miraculous (in Hume's sense) than the facts established by such testimony.

The same must be said of many, including many scholars, who study the Bible with the presupposition that miracles, including revelation, never take place. The mainstream of modern biblical criticism began with writers like Spinoza, Reimarus, and Strauss, who made precisely that assumption. They therefore routinely denied the historicity of anything in Scripture that appeared to them to be supernatural, and they sought to reconstruct the history of Israel and the story of Jesus in line with that assumption—an assumption precisely contrary to the assumptions of the biblical writers themselves[53] and logically incompatible with all the distinctive teachings of Christianity.

More recent Bible critics in the liberal tradition have sought to break away from such naturalistic assumptions, and they have been successful in various degrees. But they have not reconciled themselves to the fact that God, as covenant Lord, rules his people by a written word, the Scriptures, of which he is the author. So they, like Hume, have often operated on the assumption that the biblical writings reflect only the level of human knowledge typical of the culture in which they were written. These critics have

53. See, for example, Robert Strimple's account of the history of criticism in *The Modern Search for the Real Jesus* (Phillipsburg, N.J.: P&R Publishing, 1995).

not taken a firm stand on the Scriptures as the very *criterion* of historical truth. But that, and nothing less, is the presupposition of Christian faith, the stance of the covenant servant of God.

MIRACLE AS EVIDENCE FOR CHRISTIANITY

Are miracles an apologetic problem or an apologetic resource? In the theological and philosophical literature, they have been both. There have been arguments about whether miracles have happened (their possibility, probability, and actuality), such as we have considered above. But miracles have also been used as evidence for the truth of Christianity.

Certainly the miracles that occurred in the Bible were intended to convince. They do not merely "propose a decision,"[54] but obligate their audience to make the right decision, to recognize and believe God. We saw earlier that miracles attest prophets. That miracles warrant belief in Christ is a frequent theme in John's gospel. Jesus says:

> Do not believe me unless I do what my Father does. But if I do it, even though you do not believe me, believe the miracles, that you may know and understand that the Father is in me, and I in the Father. (John 10:37–38)

> If I had not done among them what no one else did, they would not be guilty of sin. But now they have seen these miracles, and yet they have hated both me and my Father. (John 15:24)

Many see the miracles and don't believe (John 12:37–38), yet they ought to believe on the basis of them. And many do (e.g., John 2:23; 4:53; 6:2, 14; 7:31). John's purpose in recording the signs was "that you may believe that Jesus is the Christ, the Son of God, and that by believing you may have life in his name" (20:31).

Peter addresses the Jews on the day of Pentecost, announcing that

> Jesus of Nazareth was a man accredited by God to you by miracles, wonders and signs, which God did among you through him, as you yourselves know. (Acts 2:22)

The letter to the Hebrews also cites "signs, wonders and various miracles" by which God testified to the salvation of Christ (Heb. 2:3–4). These statements clearly imply that those who experience the miracles are obli-

---

54. G. C. Berkouwer, *The Providence of God*, 225.

gated to believe in Jesus as Lord. Thus, miracles are evidence—indeed, decisive evidence—of the truth of Jesus.

The greatest miracle, the Resurrection, is particularly important as a warrant for belief. Jesus prophesied it in answer to the Jews' question, "What miraculous sign can you show us to prove your authority to do all this?" (John 2:18). On Pentecost, Peter referred to the fact of the Resurrection in calling the Jews to faith (Acts 2:24–36). If Christ is not raised, therefore, our faith is vain (1 Cor. 15:14).

Christianity is based on historical events, and God's mighty works in history warrant faith. Miracles are an embarrassment to many intelligent Buddhists, because Buddhism is not based on historical events. If Buddhism is true, it is true by virtue of its timeless wisdom, not by virtue of historical events. But Christianity differs in this respect from Buddhism, Hinduism, and many other world religions. In Scripture, God's miraculous deeds are important to our salvation and to our knowledge of salvation.

To say that miracles warrant faith is not to say that miracles automatically bring people to faith. As we have seen, many people saw the miracles of Jesus and did not believe. Some were hardened by God, as we saw in chapter 4, so that they could not see the truth (John 12:37–40).

Nor is it always legitimate for people to demand miraculous evidence. Jesus regularly rebuked the Jews' demands for more and more signs (Matt. 12:38–45; 16:1–4; John 4:48; 6:30–40; cf. 1 Cor. 1:22). In Jesus' parable, Abraham tells the rich man in hell that he should not ask someone to rise from the dead to bring his brothers to repentance: "If they do not listen to Moses and the Prophets, they will not be convinced even if someone rises from the dead" (Luke 16:31).

Miracles are revelation, but they are not the only form of revelation. All creation reveals God (Rom. 1:18–21), and Scripture ("Moses and the Prophets") is his written revelation. In these sources, there is enough revelation to make us all responsible to believe. Paul in Romans 1 exposes unbelief as willful and culpable. No one can claim that because God has not shown him a miracle, he has an excuse for unbelief. Certainly the Jewish opponents of Jesus, who had already seen many signs,[55] had no right to demand more. No one may say that he will not believe without a miracle. In that sense, miracles are epistemologically superfluous. We don't absolutely need them, but in them God gives us more evidence than we strictly need. He piles on the evidence, to underscore the cogency of his Word.

That fact is especially important to us today, because, for the most part,

---

55. Some said, "When the Christ comes, will he do more miraculous signs than this man?" (John 7:31).

in this age of semicessation, we have not directly experienced the more spec-tacular kinds of miracles. The argument from miracle is today really an ar-gument from reports of miracle, from testimony. In the earthly ministry of Jesus, his miracles and words were somewhat independent sources of knowl-edge, each attesting the other (see John 10:38; 14:11), though of course they were also interdependent and mutually interpreting. But for us, Jesus' works and words are found in the same place, the pages of Scripture. For us, Jesus' words to "doubting Thomas" are especially appropriate: "Because you have seen me, you have believed; blessed are those who have not seen and yet have believed" (John 20:29). The miracle of the Resurrection brought Thomas to faith. But no one may demand from God a similar individual miraculous attestation. Moses and the Prophets, with the New Testament, are sufficient.

My point is not that miracles themselves are irrelevant, since we are now left with only the written Word. Miracle is part of the persuasive power of the Word itself, illumined by the Spirit. The Bible is not just any old book; it is a book of miracles that accomplish and attest God's salvation. When Paul appeals to many witnesses in 1 Corinthians 15, those witnesses are part of Scripture's self-authentication. The miracles of Scripture play a sig-nificant role in persuading us that Scripture is true.

Some may find a circle here: we believe the miracles because of Scrip-ture, and Scripture because of the miracles. It is true that Scripture is our ultimate standard—the covenant constitution of the people of God. And an ultimate standard cannot be proved by any standard other than itself. But the circularity does not render the argument unpersuasive. We do not say merely that "the Bible is the Word of God because it is the Word of God," although that is strictly true. But we recognize the specific ways in which Scripture attests itself, by presenting content that is wonderfully per-suasive and cogent. And miracle is a large part of that.[56]

Reading Scripture thoughtfully, under the Spirit's illumination, we come across credible accounts of miracles that reinforce our confidence in the scrip-tural truths attested by those miracles. And we gain confidence that the mir-acles really happened, as we gain greater understanding of God's inspira-tion of the writers who report the miracles. And then, fortified with greater confidence that the miracles really happened, we gain a greater confidence in biblical inspiration. It is a spiral process, in which two realities reinforce each other, as we compare them again and again. That is the way of faith.

56. On the question of circularity, see *DKG*, 130–33; *AGG*, 9–14; *CVT*, 299–309, and my articles in *Five Views of Apologetics*, ed. Steve Cowan (Grand Rapids: Zondervan, 2000). The next to last sentence in my paragraph sets forth the distinction I have made elsewhere between a "narrow" circle and a "broad" circle.

CHAPTER 14

Providence

The term *providence* is not often found in English translations of Scripture. Nevertheless, in Reformed theology, the definition of providence is far less controversial than that of miracle. Here are some representative definitions:

> God's works of providence are, his most holy, wise, and powerful preserving and governing all his creatures, and all their actions.[1]

> God's works of providence are his most holy, wise, and powerful preserving and governing all his creatures; ordering them, and all their actions, to his own glory.[2]

> God the great Creator of all things doth uphold, direct, dispose, and govern all creatures, actions, and things, from the greatest even to the least, by His most wise and holy providence, according to His infallible foreknowledge, and the free and immutable counsel of His own will, to the praise of the glory of His wisdom, power, justice, goodness, and mercy.[3]

> The conviction that God, in his goodness and power, preserves, accompanies, and directs the entire universe.[4]

1. WSC, 11.
2. WLC, 18.
3. WCF, 5.1.
4. Benjamin Wirt Farley, *The Providence of God* (Grand Rapids: Baker, 1988), 16.

. . . that continued exercise of the divine energy whereby the Creator preserves all his creatures, is operative in all that comes to pass in the world, and directs all things to their appointed end.[5]

Note first that these definitions all emphasize the universality of providence. God's providence extends to "all things," to "the entire universe." I dealt with the universality of providence in chapter 4, under the lordship attribute of control, and so I won't expound that topic here. But we should remember that God controls all things: inanimate creatures, the detailed course of nature, events of history, human lives, free human decisions, and even human sins.

God's "extraordinary" actions are called miracles, and his "ordinary" actions are called providence—although, as we emphasized in the last chapter, those are relative terms. We saw in Psalm 136 how the psalmist gives thanks to the Lord for all of his "wonders" (v. 4), referring first to God's works of creation and in the Exodus. But, in verse 25, he adds to the list of wonders the fact that God "gives food to every creature." We see that the psalmist is not straitjacketed by overly rigid theological distinctions. He meditates on God's wonderful deeds, and then at the end it occurs to him that, after all, general providence is pretty wonderful too! Does it take any more power or wisdom to create the world than to feed all its creatures? Is God's division of the sea waters any more wonderful than his feeding of all the humans, animals, and plants on the face of the earth? Evidently, providence also is a wonder, a miracle.

It is meditation on miracle that brings the psalmist to this point. Miracle rather shakes up our mental composure, reminding us that this world does not just drift along on its own, but is the place where a great person lives and acts.[6] And that person's influence is not only local and temporary. The God who brought the plagues on Egypt and divided the sea must be no less than the God of all nature. It is thus that our minds move from miracle to providence.

The definitions quoted above distinguish three general areas of providence, which are often designated by the terms *government, preservation,* and *concurrence* (or *concursus, cooperation*). Some writers correlate these three categories with the expressions in Romans 11:36: "from him" (preservation), "through him" (concurrence), and "to him" (government) are all things.[7] This triad does not quite fit my own triadic system, but at least there

---

5. Louis Berkhof, *Systematic Theology* (Grand Rapids: Eerdmans, 1941), 166.

6. When we contemplate the regularities of nature, we are tempted to attribute them to impersonal laws. Regularities suggest analogies with machines, natural forces, and the like. Miracles, being relatively irregular, tend more easily to suggest personal causation.

7. "To him" is correlated with government because the doctrine of God's government

is some similarity. Both government and preservation, I think, fall under my general category of control, and concurrence is obviously a form of divine presence. But is there any aspect of providence that falls under the lordship attribute of authority? I am undeterred: I propose adding to the traditional categories a reference to providence as *revelation*. That leaves us, alas, with four major concepts, rather than three, but nevertheless with correspondences to all three lordship attributes.[8]

GOVERNMENT

We saw in chapters 2–4 that God is the great king of all the earth, who controls all things in his domain. As a subdivision of providence, government speaks of that rule, but emphasizes that it is *teleological*. That is to say, God governs all events for a purpose. The English word "govern" comes from the Latin *gubernare*, "to steer a ship." That dynamic emphasis on directing the motion of something toward a goal remains in the traditional theological use of the term *govern*, though it is lost in the more common use of the word today, which is usually political. Nature and history, like ships, are moving. They have a direction, a destination, and everything works toward that end. When Hebrews 1:3 speaks of Christ "sustaining all things by his powerful word," *sustain* is the Greek verb *pherō*, meaning "bear, carry." This is not a picture of Christ as a kind of Atlas, holding up the world on his shoulders ("upholding," KJV), but a dynamic image of him carrying the world from one point to another through time. There is a destination, and Christ's purpose is to bring the world process to that goal, that conclusion.

God's rule of the world, then, is distinctly personal, not mechanical or merely causal. Other passages also stress the *telos* or goal of providence. In Ephesians 1, Paul speaks of God's good pleasure,

> which he purposed in Christ, to be put into effect when the times will have reached their fulfillment—to bring all things in heaven and on earth together under one head, even Christ.

focuses on teleology, the purposefulness of providence. However, I am not completely persuaded of the first correlation. It seems to me that "from him" is more closely related to creation than to preservation.

8. I am, of course, here jesting a bit with my readers, and I've discovered that in Reformed circles I usually need to explain my jokes. It would be wrong, certainly, to adjust the definition of providence just to fill in a blank entry in an *a priori* scheme. But, as I shall indicate, I do believe that there is good scriptural ground for my addition, and I think there is also scriptural ground for seeing providence, overall, as a demonstration of God's lordship throughout the course of nature and history.

In him we were also chosen, having been predestined according to the plan of him who works out everything in conformity with the purpose of his will. (vv. 9–11)

(See also in this connection Rom. 8:18–25, 28–30.) Scripture speaks over and over of God's purpose to glorify himself, to defeat evil, and to redeem a people to give him eternal praise. It presents to us again and again the promise of final consummation.

That consummation is not only the goal that God pursues, but also the motivation for the Christian life. It is a pity that the church's teaching on eschatology, the last days, has been concerned mostly with arguments about the order of events. In Scripture itself, the primary thrust of eschatology is ethical, in several ways:

1. We live in tension between this age and the age to come. In Christ, the age to come has already arrived, but the present age, dominated by sin, will not expire until he returns. Christ has delivered us from "the present evil age" (Gal. 1:4), so in him we already have the blessings of the age to come. But sin remains in us until the present age comes to an end (1 John 1:8–10). So while we are risen with Christ, we must still seek the things that are above (Col. 3:1–4). We have died to sin (v. 3), but we must "put to death" the sins of this life (v. 5). So the Christian life is an attempt, motivated by God's grace, to live according to the principles of the age to come. We are motivated by the goal toward which God steers the ship of history.

2. Since the present age is to end, and the things of this world are to be dissolved, the Christian ought to have a set of priorities that are radically different from those of the world (2 Peter 3:11; 1 Cor. 7:26, 29). We must not be conformed to the pattern of this world (Rom. 12:2, where the Greek word for "world" is, literally, "age"). We are to "seek first" the kingdom of God[9] and his righteousness, rather than the pleasures, even the necessities, of this life (Matt. 6:33).

3. Since we "eagerly await" the return of Jesus (Phil. 3:20; 2 Peter 3:12; 1 John 3:3), we anticipate it even now by purifying ourselves as he is pure.

4. Since the resurrection of Christ has decisively established the new age,

9. The "kingdom of God" is another term by which Scripture speaks of God's goal for the creation, and it, too, "comes" over a period of time. It came in Jesus; it comes in consummate form at his return. James W. Scott argues that the kingdom (that is, Christ himself) is also "coming" at the present time, as Jesus sends the powerful Holy Spirit to bring about the triumph of God's purposes. See Scott, "The Coming of Christ," *New Horizons in the Orthodox Presbyterian Church* 20, no. 11 (December 1999):3–5, 18, available at www.opc.org/new_horizons/NH99/NH9912a.html.

we are confident that our labors for his kingdom will not be in vain, but will inevitably prevail (1 Cor. 15:58).

5. We look to the return of Christ as our deliverance from tribulation and thus as a source of hope (Luke 21:28).

6. Knowing that Christ is coming, but not knowing the day or hour, we must always be ready to meet him (Matt. 24:44; 1 Thess. 5:1–10; 1 Peter 1:7; 2 Peter 3:14).

7. The rewards that God will give his people also serve as motivation (Ps. 19:11; Matt. 5:12, 46; 6:1; 10:41–42; Rom. 14:10; 1 Cor. 3:8–15; 9:17–18, 25; 2 Cor. 5:10; Col. 3:23–25; Eph. 6:7–8; 2 Tim. 4:8; James 1:12; 1 Peter 5:4; 2 John 8; Rev. 11:18). I have engaged in some textual overkill here, because some Christians think it unseemly to consider the rewards that God offers to his faithful servants. Certainly our works do not merit the rewards of heaven, but God promises them to us, and he often uses them to motivate our service. The Christian ethic is not a Kantian deontology (see chap. 10), an ethic of duty for duty's sake, with no consideration of blessing. In Scripture, what glorifies God also glorifies man. God's best interest is also ours. Scripture calls us to sacrifice our own interests for God's and those of one another, but only in the short run. In the long run, our interests and God's coincide.

PRESERVATION

If God is to direct the creation toward his intended goal, he must, of course, preserve its existence until it reaches that goal. Preservation, therefore, is an aspect of God's government of the world and an expression of his lordship attribute of control.

There are four ways in which God's work of preservation is evident in the world:

1. Metaphysical preservation is God's act to keep the universe in being. It is more of a "good and necessary consequence" (WCF, 1.6) than an explicit teaching of Scripture, though it is implied in Colossians 1:17—"and in [Christ] all things hold together." Without God, nothing would come into existence; that is the doctrine of creation. Without God, nothing would continue to exist; that is the doctrine of metaphysical preservation. The world continues to exist by God's permission. Were he to withdraw his permission, there would be no world. So his permission here, as with evil (chap. 9), is an efficacious permission.

Unfortunately, theologians have often formulated metaphysical preservation in accordance with the theory of the continuum of being (see chap.

12, and also chaps. 7 and 9), which states that the universe "tends toward nonbeing" because it does not have as much being as God has. On this view, God's metaphysical preservation remedies this tendency. But this view, consistently developed, puts God and the world on a continuum as well: the world lacks being, because the world is less divine than God himself. This theory has roots in Gnosticism and Neoplatonism, and it blurs the biblical distinction between the Creator and creature. In Scripture, there are no degrees of being or of divinity. The universe is not divine in any degree, and it does not lack any degree of being.

Rejecting the continuum theory, however, does not entail rejecting the idea of metaphysical preservation as such. To say that God metaphysically preserves the world is simply to say that the world is radically contingent. It depends on God for everything, and without his permission it could not continue to exist. To say this is merely to be consistent with our confession that the world is completely under the control of its sovereign Lord.

2. *Redemptive-historical preservation is God's temporary preservation of the world from final judgment*, so that he can bring his people to salvation.

In Genesis 2:17, God told Adam that he should not eat the forbidden fruit, for "when you eat of it you will surely die." When Adam and Eve ate the fruit, however, they did not die immediately. Death did enter history at that point (Gen. 3:19; Rom. 5:12), as did human pain and the curse on the earth (Gen. 3:16–19). But by the standards of strict justice, Adam and Eve should have died immediately after their disobedience. The fact that God allowed them to continue living is already an indication of grace. He was already blessing them far more than they deserved. He gave them life when they deserved death.

The woman would have pain in childbearing (Gen. 3:16), but there would be children. God would not only preserve the lives of the first couple, but would give them descendants as well. And even more wonderfully, one of those descendants would crush the head of the serpent (v. 15). So immediately after the Fall, God was gracious to mankind, based on his intention to redeem his people through Christ. The man was to labor, in order to feed and therefore sustain the human family (vv. 17–19) as it awaited the coming of the deliverer. Thus began God's preservation of the world and of the human race in redemptive history. The continuation of the natural world and of human history provides the context in which the history of redemption unfolds.

Redemptive-historical preservation, however, is limited and temporary. The biblical image of this limitation is the story of the great flood in Genesis 6–9. In Genesis 4:15, God places a mark on the murderer Cain to preserve his life. But Cain's descendants abuse their preservation and fall more deeply into sin, rejoicing in their disobedience without even showing the degree of remorse that Cain displayed (4:23–24; cf. v. 13). Yet God's patience continues. Chapter 5 records a genealogy of patriarchs with very long lives. But in Genesis 6:3, in response to very serious sin,[10] God significantly reduces the life span of human beings. His patience is drawing to an end.

But man does not heed this warning. Human life reaches a peak of sinful rebellion, and "the LORD saw how great man's wickedness on the earth had become, and that every inclination of the thoughts of his heart was only evil all the time" (Gen. 6:5). So God destroys all but one family in a great flood. Now the Flood displays, as no other event, the necessity of God's preservation of the earth. In Genesis 7:11–12, we read that

> on that day all the springs of the great deep burst forth, and the floodgates of the heavens were opened. And rain fell on the earth forty days and forty nights.

We should recall that on the first three days of creation, God divided the heaven, the earth, and the sea (Gen. 1:3–13), and the water "under the expanse" from the water above it (1:7). What God divided in Genesis 1, he now brings back together. At God's word, the creation collapses in upon itself. The waters above and the waters below again meet, and God's judgment falls on all, except for the one family who "found favor in the eyes of the LORD" (6:8).

After the Flood comes God's covenant with Noah, a covenant of preservation. God says:

> Never again will I curse the ground because of man, even though every inclination of his heart is evil from childhood. And never again will I destroy all living creatures, as I have done.
>
> > As long as earth endures,
> > seedtime and harvest,
> > cold and heat,
> > summer and winter,
> > day and night
> > will never cease. (Gen. 8:21–22)

It is not that man's sin has been washed away in the Flood. Rather, the Flood proves that historical judgments alone cannot deal with sin. The indict-

---

10. I will not discuss here the nature of this sin, which is disputed. Cases have been made that the sin was (1) mixed marriage (of Cainites and Sethites), (2) sexual relations between women and angelic beings, or (3) royal polygamy. I incline toward the last hypothesis. See Meredith G. Kline, "Divine Kingship in Gen. 6:1–4," *WTJ* 24 (1962): 187–204.

ment of the inclinations of man's heart in 8:21 is essentially the same as
the terrible indictment of antediluvian mankind in 6:5. The Flood proves
that sinfulness is nothing less than human nature. It is in Noah's family as
much as in the families that were destroyed (see 9:20–24).[11] Noah's family is saved by God's grace, not by their goodness.

So God promises to preserve the earth and the regularities of the seasons. He will again be patient. But his patience is again limited. The seasons will continue "as long as the earth endures," but there is no guarantee that it will endure forever.

Now redemptive-historical preservation has two biblical reference points,
like the two foci of an ellipse. One is the Flood, and the other is the return
of Christ. Jesus taught that at the time of his return, the situation would
be "as it was in the days of Noah" (Matt. 24:37). Peter carries the comparison further, pointing out that originally

> by God's word the heavens existed and the earth was formed out
> of water and by water. By these waters also the world of that time
> was deluged and destroyed. By the same word the present heavens
> and earth are reserved for fire, being kept for the day of judgment
> and destruction of ungodly men. (2 Peter 3:5–7)

Peter goes on to say that there will be another destruction, by fire rather
than by water: "The heavens will disappear with a roar; the elements will
be destroyed by fire, and the earth and everything in it will be laid bare"
(v. 10). God's preservation of the natural order, then, is characteristic of
the time between the two great judgments: the typical judgment of the Flood
and the antitypical judgment of the final catastrophe. The time in between
is the time of God's patience.

The covenant made with Noah is sometimes called the covenant of
"common grace," God's nonsaving grace to his enemies. It is that, but it is
also, and more significantly, a provision of special grace, of salvation. For
during this period, God is preserving the world to give people time to repent of their sins and believe in Christ:

> The Lord is not slow in keeping his promise, as some understand
> slowness. He is patient with you, not wanting anyone to perish,
> but everyone to come to repentance. (2 Peter 3:9)

So Paul, in his evangelistic preaching at Lystra (Acts 14:17) and Athens
(17:25–28), points to God's providence as evidence of his patience with

---

11. Thus we get the Reformed doctrine of "total depravity" (cf. Rom. 3:10–23; 6:17;
8:5–8).

sinners.[12] The world is being preserved because God has redeeming work to do. It is Christ, the Redeemer, in whom "all things hold together" (Col. 1:17), for he intends "to reconcile to himself all things" (v. 20).

We saw that miracle is more of a redemptive-historical category in Scripture than a metaphysical one. It is a declaration of God's covenant lordship, *contra peccatum* rather than *contra naturam*. Preservation is the same. Although metaphysical preservation may be inferred from biblical teachings, redemptive-historical preservation is much more explicit, indeed pervasive, in the biblical texts. And when we think of preservation in redemptive-historical terms, we draw together more closely in our minds the concepts of providence and miracle.

The regular passing of the seasons and God's provision of food for his creatures should lead men to repent, and it should motivate Christians to sense anew the urgency of evangelism. For Christians know that God's patience again will come to an end. There will again be a time like the days of Noah, and God will come in judgment when men least expect it.

In preserving the earth, then, God displays himself powerfully as the Lord of the covenant. He controls all things so that the world will not be destroyed. During that time, he proclaims authoritatively the gospel of salvation. And he accomplishes the purpose of his lordship: to gather a people to be his, to be with them in his covenant presence.

3. *Covenant preservation* is God's preservation of believers and the church as part of his covenant blessing. Scripture often refers to this kind of preservation:

> And now, do not be distressed and do not be angry with yourselves for selling me [Joseph] here [to Egypt], because it was to save[13] lives that God sent me ahead of you. (Gen. 45:5)

> Honor your father and your mother, so that you may live long in the land the LORD your God is giving you. (Ex. 20:12)

> These are the commands, decrees and laws the LORD your God directed me [Moses] to teach you to observe in the land that you are crossing the Jordan to possess, so that you, your children, and their children after them may fear the LORD your God as long as you live

---

12. Preachers, note that there is biblical precedent for sermons using natural revelation as their texts.

13. The word is "preserve" in the KJV. Modern translations tend to avoid this word, but clearly the idea is often present. "Save" in Gen. 45:5 does not refer to eternal salvation, but to the preserving of life.

by keeping all his decrees and commands that I give you, and so that you may enjoy long life. (Deut. 6:1–2)

The LORD commanded us to obey all these decrees and to fear the LORD our God, so that we might always prosper and be kept alive, as is the case today. (Deut. 6:24)

It was the LORD our God himself who brought us and our fathers up out of Egypt, from that land of slavery, and performed those great signs before our eyes. He protected us on our entire journey and among all the nations through which we traveled. (Josh. 24:17)

Keep me safe, O God,
for in you I take refuge. (Ps. 16:1)

Love the LORD, all his saints!
The LORD preserves the faithful,
but the proud he pays back in full. (Ps. 31:23)

He has preserved our lives
and kept our feet from slipping. (Ps. 66:9)

(Cf. Pss. 37:28; 121:5–8; 138:7; 143:11.) God protects his people, as their shield (Gen. 15:1; Pss. 3:3; 5:12; 28:7). He is their refuge (Deut. 33:27; Pss. 9:9; 14:6;18:2). They rest under his everlasting arms (Deut. 33:27). He delivers them from their enemies (Deut. 33:27; Ps. 18:17). These are frequent themes in the Psalms and elsewhere (e.g., Isa. 43:2–7); I have given only a few of many examples.

Long life is a blessing of God's covenant (Ex. 20:11), and God stands with his people in this life, as well as the next, in their struggle against death and danger. Like the psalmist in Psalm 107, every believer can testify of God's loving care amidst the afflictions of this world. And even in the more comfortable times of life, God provides what we need to live. As he feeds and clothes the sparrows, he clothes us (Matt. 6:25–34; 10:28–30). Thus, he preserves our lives, and indeed the lives of all living things (Pss. 36:6; 145:15–16; 147:8–9). In him we live and move and have our being (Acts 17:28).

Covenant preservation is corporate, as well as individual. Christ builds his church on a rock "and the gates of Hades will not overcome it" (Matt. 16:18).

This kind of preservation is closely related to redemptive-historical preservation. For as God preserves the earth in order to bring the lost to himself, he preserves his people on earth as his witnesses. And he saves them from sickness, oppression, and death as a witness of his power and a display of his lordship. When he saves the lives of his people, they give him praise. So providence, like miracle, is a display of God's lordship. God proves faithful to his covenant promise.

But like redemptive-historical preservation, covenant preservation has a limit. Death is still in the world, and God has ordained that all of us will experience it (Gen. 3:19), except for a few special recipients of grace like Enoch (Gen. 5:22) and Elijah (2 Kings 2:11–12). Jesus suffered and died for our sins, and indeed, God has promised that believers will suffer persecution for Jesus' sake (2 Tim. 3:12). That has often meant martyrdom. The complete fulfillment of covenant preservation, therefore, is not in this life, but in the next. As with Jesus, God does not abandon us to the grave or let us see decay (Ps. 16:10).

For the Bible's treatment of evil, review chapter 9. Evil is not a refutation of God's good purposes for creation or of his love for his people. The evil of this world serves God's long-term purpose to glorify himself and to do good for his people. Suffering persecution is actually a privilege; believers rejoice "because they had been counted worthy of suffering disgrace for the Name" (Acts 5:41; cf. Matt. 5:12; John 15:21). God preserves his people through persecution and honors their suffering by uniting it to the sufferings of Christ (2 Cor. 1:5; 4:10; Gal. 6:17; Phil. 3:10; Col. 1:24; 1 Peter 4:13).

Covenant preservation is what most believers mean by "providence," rather than government, concurrence, or metaphysical preservation. God is Jehovah Jireh, our provider (Gen. 22:14).

4. *Eternal preservation is God's eternal salvation* of his people. When God revealed himself to Abraham in Genesis 22:14 as "The LORD Will Provide," what he provided was a ram for sacrifice, in place of Isaac, Abraham's dear son and bearer of the covenant promise. So God's ultimate provision for his people is redemption itself. And when God provides salvation for his people, he preserves them, so that they will not fall away, for all eternity. Jesus says:

> I tell you the truth, whoever hears my word and believes him who sent me has eternal life and will not be condemned; he has crossed over from death to life. (John 5:24)

Jesus is speaking about people living on earth. When one of them believes, his eternal destiny is assured. He will not be condemned at the final judgment. He has crossed over from death to life, and will not cross back again. These believers are Jesus' sheep, of whom he says:

> My sheep listen to my voice; I know them, and they follow me. I give them eternal life, and they shall never perish; no

one can snatch them out of my hand. My Father, who has given them to me, is greater than all; no one can snatch them out of my Father's hand. I and the Father are one. (John 10:27–30)

This is the Reformed doctrine of "the perseverance of the saints." This doctrine does not teach that everybody who makes a profession of faith is eternally saved. Scripture is fully aware that some professing Christians apostatize, turning away from the truth. Judas Iscariot is the paradigm case. In John, many who "believe" in Jesus later turn away (John 6:66; 8:31–59). There are solemn warnings about apostasy and apostates in Hebrews 6:4–8; 10:26–30; 1 John 2:19. Apostates, at one time, share in the life of the church, and therefore in the blessings of the Holy Spirit. Judas himself cast out evil spirits and healed diseases in Jesus' name (Matt. 10:1–4). But apostates turn from the Lord and suffer his condemnation.

Those who persevere are those in whom God begins a work of saving grace (Phil. 1:6). And they persevere, imperfectly to be sure, in faith and holiness, until in heaven they are perfected in Christ.

REVELATION

Providence also bears the lordship attribute of authority. We can see that in the fact that providence, like creation, is by God's word:

> He sends his command to the earth;
>   his word runs swiftly.
> He spreads the snow like wool
>   and scatters the frost like ashes.
> He hurls down his hail like pebbles.
>   Who can withstand his icy blast?
> He sends his word and melts them;
>   he stirs up his breezes, and the waters flow.
> He has revealed his word to Jacob,
>   his laws and decrees to Israel.
> He has done this for no other nation;
>   they do not know his laws.
> Praise the LORD. (Ps. 147:15–20; cf. 148:5–8)

The psalmist here draws a correlation between the "command" and "word" that control the course of nature and the "word" that God has revealed to

Israel. These "words" come from the same mouth. They have the same power, the same truth, and they reveal the same God.[14]

Providence also displays the wisdom of God (Ps. 104; Prov. 8:22–36). His wisdom and his word are closely related in Scripture. God's works declare the marvelous mind of God that has planned everything to happen according to his will. He understands all the animals, the weather, the plants, and the sea creatures (Job 38–42).

Providence, then, reveals God's lordship. It reveals his power and his presence in the world he has made. It also declares his wrath against sin (Rom. 1:18), clearly reveals "his eternal power and divine nature" (v. 20), and communicates "God's righteous decree that those who do such things [i.e., commit sin] deserve death" (v. 32). From God's providence, people should know that they should not worship men (Acts 14:14–17), worship God by idols (Rom. 1:23; cf. Acts 17:22–23, 29–31), or engage in sexual impurity, including homosexuality (Rom. 1:24–27).

As miracle is an extraordinary demonstration of God's lordship, providence is an ordinary demonstration of it in some respects. However, its universality and pervasiveness make it important as a form of revelation. It is the one means that many people have now to know God. And it is the revelation by which all of us are left without excuse (Rom. 1:20).

Does providence provide guidance to us? Yes, in the sense that God's providence provides some opportunities and closes others to us. Yes, in that providence, through our spiritual gifts, heredity, environment, education, temperament, and interests, suggests to us how we can best serve God. A wise person takes his environment and his own nature into account in making decisions. Providence supplies the "situation" to which the word of Scripture must be applied. We should remember, however, that providence is not a written text like the Bible. One cannot "read" providence as one reads Scripture, to find out specifically what we ought to do. The Puritan John Flavel commented, "The providence of God is like a Hebrew word—it can only be read backwards!"[15] It is much easier to see how God has used providence to lead us in the past than to figure out how he will use it to lead us in the future. And, in any case, we can rightly interpret providence only through the spectacles of Scripture.[16]

14. See a similar correlation between nature and Scripture in Ps. 19:1–11.

15. Quoted by Sinclair Ferguson in *A Heart for God* (Colorado Springs: NavPress, 1985), 145.

16. For more observations on guidance, see the discussion of God's will in chapter 23.

CONCURRENCE

We have looked at providence as government and preservation (focusing on God's control), and also as revelation (focusing on his authority). Now we will look at providence as concurrence, which focuses on God's presence in and with all his creatures.[17]

Louis Berkhof defines concurrence as "the cooperation of the divine power with all subordinate powers, according to the pre-established laws of their operation, causing them to act and to act precisely as they do."[18] This concept emerges out of a discussion of the relationship between the divine primary cause and the natural secondary causes of events in the world. The Jesuits, Socinians, and Remonstrants argued that God determines the nature of all beings and forces in the world, but does not determine the specific actions that these beings perform.[19] This theory fits well with the libertarian view of free will, which we discussed in chapter 8.

On the contrary, most Calvinists have affirmed concurrence more or less in Berkhof's sense, and I will defend that view here.

We discussed the relevant biblical data in chapter 4: passages that teach that God controls nature, history, and individuals (including their free decisions) in minute detail. Note that, according to those passages, God does not merely determine the major trends in the world, but the smallest events as well: the falling of a sparrow, the fall of a lot, and so on. And some passages, such as Romans 8–11 and Ephesians 1, teach that he controls absolutely everything.

Now let's assume, for example, that God makes a golf ball go into a hole, using a golfer as the secondary cause. But what about the golfer's swing? Scripture tells us that God brings that about, too, for he controls everything. But there are secondary causes of the golfer's swing, also: movements in the golfer's muscles, neurons, brain, and so on. The verses we have studied imply that God causes those also. We can press this analysis into the world of molecules, atoms, and subatomic particles. Are any of their movements independent of God? Certainly not.

So the doctrine of concurrence is merely an application of the general

---

17. The second, third, and fourth forms of providence also focus on God's covenant presence. Perhaps I could have written this chapter so as to make clearer correlations between the kinds of providence and the lordship attributes, but my higher goal was clarity. I am consoled by the fact that the three perspectives are, after all, perspectives, which means that anything we say about God can be said under any of the three categories.

18. Berkhof, *Systematic Theology*, 171.

19. A. A. Hodge, *Outlines of Theology* (1879; reprint, Grand Rapids: Zondervan, 1972), 271.

principle that God brings all things to pass. Concurrence teaches that God causes events on the micro level as well as on the macro level. He uses second causes, but none of the second causes works without him. He uses second causes, but he is always working in and with them.

So there is an *immediacy* to God's causality in the world. As I said in chapter 13, "immediate" does not distinguish miracles from nonmiraculous events, because every event is caused by God immediately. Nothing can be completely explained by finite causes alone. God's will explains all events, both large and small.

The main objection to concurrence is that it makes God the author of sin, since it makes him not only the remote cause, but also the proximate cause of sin. The reader should refer to our discussion in chapter 9 of the distinction between remote and proximate, and of the concept of authorship. The "author," in these discussions, is not merely a cause of sin, but a doer of sin. And, as I argued in chapter 9, it is not clear that mere causal proximity to a sinful act makes God a doer of sin. Nor is it clear that making God a "remote" cause rather than a "proximate" cause answers those who would blame him for sin.

Another objection to concurrence is that it makes second causes superfluous. God becomes the sufficient cause of each event, and the so-called second causes don't really cause anything. This brings us again to the mystery of "creaturely otherness" (chap. 8) and the author-character model, discussed in the same chapter. God has created a universe that is significantly different from him, operating on the basis of its own nature and the laws of its being. At every moment, it is dependent on God, yet it operates out of its own God-given resources. The author-character model helps us to see something more of this relationship: with a few exceptions,[20] the events in the story have two causes, divine and creaturely. The creaturely causes are genuine. They bring about the events they cause, and the events would not come about without those causes. The same, however, can be said of the divine causes. Creation is like a book written by a gifted novelist, who creates a story-world in which events have causes within the story, but in which every event is brought about by the volition of the author.

---

20. As I mentioned in chapter 13, there are some events that have no secondary cause at all, such as the Creation, the Incarnation, and God's regeneration of the hearts of human beings. There may be others, but these are all I can ascertain from Scripture.

CHAPTER 15

Creation

We have seen God's lordship displayed in his mighty acts, and in those mighty acts we have discovered the God who rules the entire course of nature and history. Now if God is the Lord, ruling over the course of events, can he be anything less than Lord at the beginning of the world? Surely the beginning can be no exception to the general principle that God works all things in conformity to the purpose of his will (Eph. 1:11). So we now turn our attention from providence to creation.

DEFINING CREATION

Theologians have held different concepts of creation. To Aquinas, creation is "the very dependency of the created act of being upon the principle for which it is produced."[1] But, as we have seen, the world depends on God at every moment, not only at the moment of its origin. So, many theologians have argued that creation is continuous, that it takes place every moment. In creation, God produces being. But, on this view, he gives being every moment, so every moment he creates anew.

Thomas Aquinas held this position, in part because he could not overcome by natural reason Aristotle's arguments for the eternity of the world. Aquinas conceded, in effect, that God's creation of the world at the first

1. SCG, 2.18.2.

moment in time could not be proved by natural reason. It had to be an article of faith.[2] But he thought that creation in the broader sense, creation as the continuous dependence of the world on God for its being, could be proved through a cosmological argument: at any point in time, the beings in the world require a first cause in God, a cause operating in the present. So Aquinas, followed by the Thomist tradition, adopted the idea of continuous dependence as his basic concept of creation, and supplemented it with the biblical teaching that God made the world at the beginning of time. Some Reformed thinkers have also regarded providence as continuous creation.[3]

More recent thinkers have found this view attractive, perhaps in part because it doesn't require an effort to locate creation in time or to reconcile it with modern science.[4]

I do not doubt, of course, that the world depends on God for every moment of its existence. But I prefer to discuss that point under the headings of metaphysical preservation and concurrence, as I did in the previous chapter. In this book, I wish to stick as closely as possible to biblical terminology. And in Scripture, *creation* generally refers to the events of Genesis 1, when God created the heavens, the earth, the sea, and all that is in them.[5] Our definition of creation should not be influenced by what can or cannot be proved by Aristotelian natural reason, or by what can or cannot be reconciled with modern science and philosophy. In Scripture, there is a beginning of all things, and that beginning occurred when God created the world (Gen. 1:1; Job 38:4; Pss. 90:2; 102:25; Isa. 40:21; 41:4; 46:10; John 1:1; Heb. 1:10; 1 John 1:1; Rev. 1:8; 3:14; 21:6; 22:13). That beginning is

---

2. *ST*, 1.46.2.

3. Heppe cites Braunius, Ursinus, and Heidegger in *RD*, 251. Farley cites Cocceius and Ames in *The Providence of God in Reformed Perspective* (Grand Rapids: Baker, 1988), 28. Jonathan Edwards developed well-known arguments for this position. See John H. Gerstner, *The Rational Biblical Theology of Jonathan Edwards* (Orlando: Ligonier Ministries, 1992), 190–202.

4. For example, Friedrich Schleiermacher, *The Christian Faith* (New York: Harper, 1963), 1:xviii; H. P. Owen, "God, Concepts of," in *The Encyclopedia of Philosophy*, ed. Paul Edwards (New York: Macmillan, 1967), 3:344–48. Howard Van Till, an opponent of "creation science," applauds Kelsey's concept of creation as metaphysical dependence in his review of *Evolution and Creation*, ed. by Ernan McMullin, in *Faith and Philosophy* 5 (1988): 104–11.

5. An exception might be Ps. 104, where the writer describes God's providence (and the continuous production of new life) in terms of creation (v. 30). But the psalm as a whole is an echo of Gen. 1, drawing important analogies between God's original creative work and his present activity in the natural world. And, as we shall see, *creation* in Scripture also refers to redemptive re-creation. But even in that usage there is always an implicit comparison with the events of Gen. 1.

a legitimate subject of theological discussion, and the doctrine of creation is the logical place to take it up.

As we look at Genesis 1, we find that we must make a distinction between the creation of the heavens and the earth in verse 1, and God's later acts of creation within that created world order (vv. 3, 6, 9, 16, 21, and 27). Theologians have traditionally described these acts of creation as *original* and *subsequent* creation, respectively. Original creation is, strictly speaking, the only creation *ex nihilo,* "out of nothing." Subsequent creation presupposes material that already exists. Genesis 1:24, for example, says that God commanded the already existing land to bring forth living creatures. Genesis 2:7 represents God as forming man from the dust.

Nevertheless, it is plain that even those beings whom God created subsequent to the event of Genesis 1:1 owe their existence entirely to his creative act. If God had not determined to create them, they would not exist. So we may bring original and subsequent creation together in the following definition: Creation is an act of God alone, by which, for his own glory, he brings into existence everything in the universe, things that have no existence prior to his creative word.

CREATION AND COVENANT LORDSHIP

God creates the world as the Lord. We saw in chapter 3 that the Lord first reveals himself as a holy being, one before whom we must bow in worship. Indeed, many references to creation in Scripture are liturgical: they present creation as a reason for worshiping God. Creation itself, including the inanimate objects, worships God (Pss. 19:1–4; 50:6; 89:5; 98:7–9; 148:1–14; Isa. 55:12). And when we think of God as the Creator, we encounter his holiness, and we are moved to worship.

Scripture presents various connections between creation and worship. God's work of the six days entitles him to consecrate the seventh day as one of holy rest for himself and to sanctify the seventh day of the human week as a day of worship (Ex. 20:11). Indeed, God made the heavens and the earth to be his temple. In Isaiah's prophecy, God compares the created world to Israel's temple:[6]

6. See the discussion of the creation as God's temple, in the image of the divine Glory-cloud theophany, in Meredith G. Kline, *Images of the Spirit* (Grand Rapids: Baker, 1980), 20–26. In *Kingdom Prologue* (Wenham, Mass.: privately published, 1991), 18, he finds temple imagery used for the creation also in Pss. 11:4; 93; 103:19;104:1–3; Isa. 40:21–23; Mic. 1:2–3; Matt. 5:34–35.

> Heaven is my throne,
>   and the earth is my footstool.
> Where is the house you will build for me?
>   Where will my resting place be? (Isa. 66:1)

In the Psalms and elsewhere in Scripture, consideration of creation leads to worship (e.g., Neh. 9:6; Pss. 8:3–9; 33:6–9; 95:3–7; 146:5–6; Rev. 14:7). Paul tells the Gentiles at Lystra and Athens that the true God has created all things, and therefore that they ought not to worship men or idols (Acts 14:15; 17:24–25). How absurd it is that men "worshiped and served created things rather than the Creator—who is forever praised. Amen" (Rom. 1:25). Creation also motivates the heavenly hymnody of Revelation (Rev. 4:11; 14:7). In worship, we thank our Creator (Ps. 136:3–9), turn to him for help (Pss. 121:2; 124:8; 146:5–6), and seek his blessing (Ps. 134:3).

God intended such worship from the beginning, which is to say that he created the world (as our definition states) for his own glory, to bring praise to himself:

> The heavens declare the glory of God;
>   the skies proclaim the work of his hands. (Ps. 19:1)

> Bring my sons from afar
>   and my daughters from the ends of the earth—
> everyone who is called by my name,
>   whom I created for my glory,
>   whom I formed and made. (Isa. 43:6–7; cf. 60:21; 61:3)[7]

> For from him and through him and to him are all things.
>   To him be glory forever! Amen. (Rom. 11:36)

(Cf. also Prov. 16:4; 1 Cor. 11:7; Rev. 4:11.)

In other ways, too, creation reveals God's lordship. It establishes his ownership of all things and therefore his lordship over all his creation (Ps. 24:1–2). Because God has created all things, he has the right to do as he wishes with his own (see chap. 5).

Creation also displays God's lordship attributes. It displays his *control*, because it establishes that he rules the world, not only throughout history,

---

7. It may be that "creation" in these verses in Isaiah refers to redemptive re-creation rather than initial creation. But of course Scripture regularly presents re-creation as analogous to creation. When God re-creates human beings to bring him glory, he redeems them to serve again the purpose for which they were originally created. See such texts as 1 Sam. 12:22; Isa. 43:6–7; 46:13; 61:3; 62:3–5; Ezek. 36:22–23; Zeph. 3:17–18; Eph. 1:11–12; 2 Thess. 1:10.

but also at the beginning of history. Scripture underscores this point by emphasizing the universal scope of creation. God created absolutely everything and therefore owns and rules it all. Scripture indicates this universality with expressions like "the heavens and the earth":

> For in six days the LORD made the heavens and the earth, the sea, and all that is in them. (Ex. 20:11)

> You alone are the LORD. You made the heavens, even the highest heavens, and all their starry host, the earth and all that is on it, the seas and all that is in them. You give life to everything, and the multitudes of heaven worship you. (Neh. 9:6)

> Blessed is he whose help is the God of Jacob,
>   whose hope is in the LORD his God,
> the Maker of heaven and earth,
>   the sea, and everything in them—
>   the LORD, who remains faithful forever. (Ps. 146:5–6)

(Cf. also Acts 14:15; 17:24; Col. 1:16; Rev. 4:11; 10:6; 14:7.) What amazing power belongs to the one who made absolutely everything in heaven, earth, and sea!

Creation also demonstrates God's lordship attribute of *authority*. God made the world merely by speaking. He said, "Let there be light," and there was light (Gen. 1:3). He is like a commander issuing orders to his servants and gaining their instant obedience. And, even more remarkably, they obey him even before they exist.[8] They spring into existence by his command. His speaking is not an incidental part of his creative work. The psalmist takes special note of this:

> By the word of the LORD were the heavens made,
>   their starry host by the breath of his mouth. . . .
> For he spoke, and it came to be;
>   he commanded, and it stood firm. (Ps. 33:6, 9)[9]

In John 1:1, the apostle identifies Jesus as "the Word" that God spoke "in the beginning" (cf. Gen. 1:1), and therefore recognizes him as the one through whom "all things were made; without him nothing was made that

---

8. I am, of course, speaking ironically here. This metaphor is, I think, implicit in the text. I am not suggesting that created things exist before they exist, except in the mind of God. My point is not metaphysical. I am making it only to underscore, as the text does, the radical authority by which God issues his commands.

9. Heb. 11:3 and 2 Peter 3:5 also emphasize that God created by speaking his word. Note allusions to this also in Isa. 48:13 and Amos 9:6.

has been made" (John 1:3; cf. Col. 1:15–16). Jesus demonstrates his lordship by uttering his powerful word to still the waves (Mark 4:35–41) and bring healing (Luke 7:1–10).

God's word also interprets his creation. After creating the light, "God called the light 'day,' and the darkness he called 'night' " (Gen. 1:5; similarly, vv. 8 and 10). Calling or naming in the ancient Near East was not merely labeling. Names were not chosen arbitrarily or merely for aesthetic reasons, as is often the case today. Those names said something about the thing that was named. For example, in giving names to his creatures, and later in bringing animals to Adam to name (2:19–20), God established a linguistic system in which the true nature of everything could be expressed. As he has, by his plan, already interpreted all things, so, in creation, he applies that interpretation to the world and makes it authoritative for all creatures. That interpretation includes evaluation. God looks on his creations and declares them good (1:4, 12, 18, 21, 31).

Since creation occurs by the speaking of God's word, it is also an expression of his wisdom (Ps. 104:24; Prov. 3:19; 8:1, 22–36; Jer. 10:12; 51:15). The wisdom of God's work is evident to the psalmist (Ps. 104:1–35), and it boggles the mind of Job (chaps. 38–42). So creation is a revelation, however mysterious, of the great mind of God. Since creation is universal, every fact of our experience reveals God to us.

So Scripture correlates God's creative word with the written word of Scripture. As the heavens consistently declare the glory of God (Ps. 19:1), so his law is perfect, restoring the soul (v. 7). As his creative word stands firm in the heavens (Ps. 119:89–90), so his laws endure and stand as our authority (v. 91, in the context of the psalm as a whole).

Creation also manifests the lordship attribute of *covenant presence*. This is perhaps less obvious than its manifestation of the other two lordship attributes, until we remind ourselves of the alternatives to creation. Recall, in this regard, the unbiblical concept of transcendence from chapter 7, the scholastic idea that the world tends toward nonbeing (chap. 9), and the supposed chain (or continuum) of being discussed in chapter 12.

In the Neoplatonic/Gnostic scheme, God is so far removed from the world that human beings cannot even speak truly of him—though creatures are also somehow essentially divine. In this scheme, God is connected to the world by a chain of semidivine mediators. He is too exalted to create a material world. The material world comes from a lesser being. (In some Gnostic representations, the material world is a mistake, the product of a clumsy aeon, rather low on the scale of being.) Later, in the fourth century, the Arian heretics, who believed that the Son of God was a created being, used a similar argument: God the Father could not have created the world by himself. He first had to create a semidivine being, the Son or Word, who, in turn, would make the world.

The church fathers responded to this cosmology by emphasizing the doctrine of creation. Irenaeus replied to the Gnostics,[10] and Athanasius to the Arians,[11] that God does not need any mediator to create the material world. He is not defiled by touching matter directly. So creation is *direct*. It is a point at which God's finger touches the world. Yes, God the Father creates together with the Son and the Spirit. But the Son and the Spirit are not inferior beings, as Arius thought. They are fully God. So creation is the work, not of an inferior being, not of a semidivine creature, but of God himself.

So in creation, God acts as Lord. He needs no helpers; he need not fear that the creation will somehow harm him. He cannot be confused with the world, for it does not emanate from his essence, but has its own distinct nature. He controls all, interprets all, and thereby enters into an intimate relationship with his world. He confronts it as one distinct being confronts another, and he embraces it as his own good world. Then, in redemption, God again makes something new and embraces it as his own. Thus, there is in Scripture a clear parallel between creation and redemption, creation and new creation.

In all of this, God shows by his creative acts that he is the Lord. Compare also Jeremiah 33:2 and Amos 4:13; 5:8; 9:6.

CREATION AND REDEMPTION

Salvation is of the Lord (Jonah 2:9). Since creation is such a vivid revelation of God's lordship, we should expect significant parallels between creation and salvation. And, of course, Scripture does not disappoint us in that expectation.

The Genesis creation narrative either reflects or anticipates God's redemption of Israel from Egypt (assuming that Moses wrote it, as I believe). As in Exodus, God commands all the forces of nature. He brings light to the earth, just as he brings darkness to Egypt (Gen. 1:3–5; Ex. 10:15). He divides the waters of the earth (Gen. 1:6–10), just as he divides the waters of the Red Sea. He causes the earth to teem with living creatures (Gen. 1:20–25), just as he later inundates Egypt with frogs, gnats, flies, and lo-

10. Irenaeus, *Against Heresies*.
11. Athanasius, *De decretis*, 3.7; *Discourse II Against the Arians*, 17.

custs (Ex. 8:1–32; 10:1–20).[12] He celebrates his creative work in a sabbath of rest (Gen. 2:3; Ex. 20:8–11), just as he calls Israel to celebrate redemption from Egypt by keeping the Sabbath day holy (Deut. 5:15). In both creation and redemption, God displays himself as the Lord of all the earth. Creation, redemption, and judgment are similar events, requiring the same sovereign power, authority, and presence (see, e.g., Isa. 42:5–6; 45:11–13).

Creation establishes God's ownership of the world and of the human race, and therefore his right and power to redeem, to buy back his creation (Isa. 43:1–7, 14–21; 44:21–28).

Creation, too, is a covenant, in which God as Lord rules the day and the night (Jer. 33:20–25). As Lord, God calls his creatures into being, establishing their function and seeing that they maintain it. He is the power behind creation, its authoritative interpreter, and its faithful maintainer. So, says Jeremiah, God will be faithful to his covenant with David. (Note also the comparison between creation and the Davidic covenant in Ps. 89.)

So Scripture often speaks of salvation in terms of creation. In Psalm 74, Asaph calls on God to deliver Israel from oppression, recalling that "you, O God, are my king from of old; you bring salvation upon the earth" (v. 12). He describes God's saving power (vv. 13–17) in terms of creation, with allusions to the Exodus. In the prophecy of Isaiah, God speaks as the one who "created" and "formed" Israel, and then describes Israel's redemption (Isa. 43:1–7, 14–15).

The fact that salvation is a new creation is a frequent theme in Paul's writings. In 2 Corinthians 4:6, he writes,

> For God, who said, "Let light shine out of darkness," made his light shine in our hearts to give us the light of the knowledge of the glory of God in the face of Christ.

Compare John's identification of Christ with the light in John 1:4, following his statement that through Christ all things were made. In both Paul and John, darkness represents sin.[13] When God illumines us to receive the truth, it is like creation *ex nihilo*, for before God's creative word, there was no light in us; we were darkness (Eph. 5:8). Indeed, we were *dead* in sin (Eph. 2:1), until by God's grace we were "created in Christ Jesus to do good works"

---

12. The plagues show God's sovereignty specifically against elements of nature that were objects of worship in Egypt. In Ex. 12:12, God proclaims his judgment, in the Passover night, against all the "gods of Egypt."

13. Paul tends to speak of "new creation" in the sorts of contexts where John speaks of new birth or regeneration. Both figures connote the immensity of change wrought by God's grace—light from darkness, life from death. Paul's figure is better suited to present personal transformation in a context of cosmic renewal.

(2:10). So, "if anyone is in Christ, he is a new creation; the old has gone, the new has come!" (2 Cor. 5:17). As God made Adam in his image (Gen. 1:27), so he re-creates believers in the image of Christ, giving them new knowledge, righteousness, and holiness (Eph. 4:24; Col. 3:10). These are not our inheritance from fallen Adam; for these, God must create us anew. As we have borne Adam's image, so we will bear the image of the second Adam, Jesus (1 Cor. 15:45–49). And the new creation establishes a new community, not divided by circumcision into Jew and Gentile, but an "Israel of God," one in Christ (Gal. 6:15–16).

The new creation is not only an ethical transformation, but also the beginning of a cosmic renewal, a renewal as comprehensive as the original creation. Our transformation by the grace of God is only the beginning of a new heavens and a new earth (Isa. 65:17–18; 66:22; 2 Peter 3:10–13; Rev. 21:1–4) in which God's righteousness dwells. Believers are the beginning of a work of Christ, by which he will eventually reconcile "all things" to himself (Col. 1:15–20). The present creation, cursed by man's fall (Gen. 3:16–19),

> waits in eager expectation for the sons of God to be revealed. For the creation was subjected to frustration, not by its own choice, but by the will of the one who subjected it, in hope that the creation itself will be liberated from its bondage to decay and brought into the glorious freedom of the children of God. (Rom. 8:19–21)

The new creation is not intended to replace an original creation that God somehow failed to keep on course. Redemption was part of God's plan before the world was created (1 Cor. 2:7; Eph. 1:5–11; 2 Tim. 1:9; Titus 1:2). The new creation represents the *telos*, the goal, of the old. Recall Romans 11:36, in which Paul, having described the course of redemption and the relationship of Israel to the Gentiles, said that "from him and through him and to him are all things." The words "from him" may refer to the original creation. But that original creation had a goal, a purpose: it was "to him." The history of redemption, then, completes the purpose of the original creation. We may perhaps even say that the new creation completes the old, even though in the end that completion will be a drastic reconstruction (2 Peter 3:12; cf. 1 Cor. 3:12–15).

So Christians would do well to meditate on creation. To trust in God's salvation is like believing in creation: "By faith we understand that the universe was formed at God's command, so that what is seen was not made out of what was visible" (Heb. 11:3). To the writer to the Hebrews, this faith in creation is, in essence, the same as the faith of Abel, Enoch, Noah, Abraham, and the other great saints of the Old Testament. The point of comparison seems to be that in each case, faith is directed to the *invisible*. By faith, one trusts God in the absence of sight (cf. 2 Cor. 5:7). Abraham trusted God, even though he did not see the fulfillment of God's promises. Similarly, by the faith of Hebrews 11:3, we trust God's statement that the world came from him. We could not, as scientists, trace the elements of the world back to some visible starting point, for there is none. The visible world has an invisible basis.

The allusion to creation *ex nihilo* is even stronger in another New Testament reference to Abraham's faith, Romans 4:17: "He is our father in the sight of God, in whom he believed—the God who gives life to the dead and calls things that are not as though they were." Paul goes on to explain how Abraham's faith, the great model for Christian faith, the faith "credited to him as righteousness" (v. 22), was a faith in God's promise, despite apparently impossible odds, a faith that God could bring life from death. God is the God of creation, who calls things that are not as though they were, who by his word brings being out of nothingness, light out of darkness. We can trust his word, his promise, therefore, even when we do not see any visible evidence of its fulfillment.

So creation reassures us of God's faithfulness to his covenant. As day and night continue, so God's promises are steadfast. Creation assures us that he will provide for our needs. Our help is in the Lord, who made heaven and earth (Pss. 121:2; 146:5–10). The one who created all things never gets weary, and he will supply new strength to his weary people (Isa. 40:26–31). The Creator is faithful to those who suffer for him (1 Peter 4:19). As his new creation endures, so will his people (Isa. 66:22).

And such reassurance should renew our own commitment to be faithful as God's covenant servants. We should "continue to do good" even in the midst of persecution (1 Peter 4:19). We should seek his wisdom, too, for that wisdom was his agent of creation (Prov. 8).

CREATION OUT OF NOTHING

Having sketched the basic thrust of the biblical doctrine of creation, we now move to some more problematic areas. First, we will consider the concept of creation *ex nihilo*, "out of nothing." But what does it mean that God created the universe out of nothing? What is "nothing," after all? Any definition or conceptualization of *nothing* will make it into something, so such definition is, strictly speaking, impossible.

Further, in trying to visualize creation out of nothing, we tend to picture God putting things into empty space. But in the doctrine of creation *ex nihilo,* space itself is created, too. Imagine making, say, a stone, when you have nothing to make it out of, and not even a place to put it![14]

Some have thought that it would be better to speak of creation *into* nothing, rather than *out of* nothing. But in my mind both expressions have advantages and disadvantages. Both ideas are important: creation is neither "out of" a preexisting material nor "into" a preexisting place. That is, we must oppose both the Aristotelian notion of an eternal "matter" and the Platonic notion of an eternal "receptacle."

Plato and Aristotle themselves understood to some extent the problems of accounting for the world by positing preexistent realities. We can account for the preexistent realities themselves only by making them, in some sense, nothing. Both Plato's "receptacle" and Aristotle's "matter" are receivers of form, and so are essentially unformed, and therefore in one sense nonbeing. Yet they must have some sort of being if they are to receive form—indeed, if we are even to speak of them.

The pre-Socratic philosopher Parmenides sensed the problem and tried to eliminate the concept of nothingness or nonbeing from his philosophical system, even to the point of eliminating the word *not* from his philosophical vocabulary. But *not* is quite indispensable to human language, and indeed to logic itself.

We saw in chapter 9 how some thinkers have considered evil to be a form of nonbeing, and how Scholasticism viewed the whole universe as "tending to nonbeing." There we encountered the idea of degrees of being, a continuum between being and nonbeing. On this view, nothingness is really something, and all somethings are partly nothing. But, as we have seen, such a view creates terrible conceptual and theological difficulties.

So when we speak of creation out of nothing, we should not think of nothing as a kind of stuff out of which God made the world. Indeed, one of the main purposes of the doctrine is to contradict that idea. To say that God created the world from nothing is to say that God created the world without any preexisting material or medium. He merely spoke and things appeared, along with space and time for them to occupy. To say that requires no definition of *nothing.* It simply denies the view that God made the world from preexistent stuff.

The doctrine also denies pantheism or monism, the view that creation is made of God's own being, a kind of emanation from him, as light from the sun, so that the creation is itself divine. It is true that creation is in a sense *de Deo* (Edwards, Gerstner), since God is the exclusive source of cre-

---

14. And, if time is a creation, you have not one moment in which to accomplish your task.

ation. I prefer not to use that language, however, because it suggests pan-theistic emanationism.

So the doctrine of creation *ex nihilo* is perhaps best understood as a neg-ative doctrine. It does not attempt, positively, to explain the process of cre-ation, but leaves that mysterious. Its whole purpose is to deny two false views: creation from preexisting reality, and emanation from the divine essence. Since there are no other possible sources for the material being of the world, we say that there is no such source, or, in other words, that the source is *nothing*—however confusing that expression may be.

Now, granted that understanding, why should we believe in creation out of nothing? There are no biblical texts that teach it in so many words. He-brews 11:3 says that God did not make "what is seen" out of "what was vis-ible." That language is certainly consistent with creation *ex nihilo* and even suggests it, but it leaves open the possibility that God might have created the world out of what was invisible—out of some invisible, preexisting ma-terial. Romans 4:17, 1 Corinthians 1:28, and 2 Corinthians 4:6 also sug-gest the idea of creation *ex nihilo*, but they don't actually teach it. In the apocryphal book 2 Maccabees 7:28, there is an expression *ouk ex ontōn*, "not from things that are," the equivalent of "from nothing." Hebrews 1:3 and other New Testament texts may allude to this passage. But the passage it-self is not part of the biblical canon.

Nevertheless, very soon after the close of the New Testament canon, the language of creation from nothing became common currency in the church. The early postapostolic work Shepherd of Hermas uses it.[15] Later in the second century, it was articulated by Theophilus of Antioch, Aristides, and Irenaeus. This doctrine was important to the church's polemic against Gnosticism. Evidently, these men thought that it was the clear teaching of Scripture. But what was the basis for that conviction?

Some have tried to derive the doctrine of creation *ex nihilo* from the mean-ing of the Hebrew *bara'*, the word translated "create" in Genesis 1:1 and elsewhere. Certainly of all the Hebrew words translated "create" or "make," *bara'* is the most appropriate to designate creation *ex nihilo*. It almost al-ways has God as its subject.[16] In Isaiah and Jeremiah, it is the normal word for God's redemptive re-creation, which, as we have seen, is parallel to the original creation. And *bara'* never takes an "accusative of material," that is, a direct object designating the material from which something else is made, as in "Mary made the dough into cookies." In Genesis 12:2, God tells

---

15. See Mand. 1, Vision 1:6.
16. An exception is Josh. 17:15, 18. But in the Qal and Niphal, the most common ac-tive and passive voices in Hebrew, God is always the subject.

Abraham, "I will make you into a great nation": Abraham is the material out of which the nation will be made. But in that verse, the word "make" is *'asah*, not *bara'*. *Bara'* is not used in such a way. So *bara'* tends to be used in sentences that make no mention of the material ingredients from which something is made, if there are such.

So *bara'* is an appropriate term—probably the most appropriate Hebrew term—to designate creation out of nothing. But it does not always refer to that. In Genesis 1:21, 27, it refers to God making sea creatures and man, respectively, and both these creations (man explicitly, Gen. 2:7) presuppose preexisting material. So *bara'* does not mean "to create out of nothing," and we cannot, therefore, derive the doctrine out of the mere use of that word.

Nevertheless, several considerations require us to affirm creation *ex nihilo* as a good and necessary inference from the biblical doctrine of creation:

1. The world had a beginning, as we have seen (Gen. 1:1; Job 38:4; Pss. 90:2; 102:25; Isa. 40:21; 41:4; 46:10; John 1:1; Heb. 1:10; 1 John 1:1; Rev. 1:8; 3:14; 21:6; 22:13). Before that beginning,[17] there was no world, only God. So there was then no material out of which the world could be made. God is, as I shall argue in chapter 25, not a material being, so there was no material in him by which he could have made the world.

2. As we have seen, creation is universal: everything in heaven, earth, and sea is God's creation. That includes, surely, all material that can be used to make other things. So all such material is itself created. None of it existed before creation. So God did not make the world out of preexisting material.

3. As we saw earlier, God creates as the Lord. He brings the world forth by his power and command. He is the Lord; the creation is his servant. So Scripture teaches a clear distinction between Creator and creature. The world is not the lower end of a continuum with God at the top. The world is not essentially divine, as in the Gnostic scheme. So creation is not an emanation of the divine essence.

Recall that the doctrine of creation *ex nihilo* is essentially a negative doctrine, denying (1) the idea of creation from preexisting substance and (2) the idea of the emanation of the world from God's essence. The first two considerations above eliminate the first idea; the third consideration elim-

---

17. I will later argue that time itself is created, so that there is literally no temporal "before." (*Before* is sometimes used in nontemporal senses, as when we say that the number one comes before the number two, or that the king stood before the crowd to address them.) But we must at times use this language (as in Ps. 90:2; Eph. 1:4, and elsewhere) to refer to God's actions in eternity. It is difficult for us to conceptualize such actions, except in temporal terms.

inates the second idea. Since Scripture denies everything that the doctrine of creation *ex nihilo* denies, we may take creation *ex nihilo* as an implication of Scripture.

Or, to put it differently, the world was made neither from a preexisting, finite substance, nor from God's being. There is no third alternative. So the world was not made from anything. It was made from nothing.

THE SIX DAYS

Genesis 1 and 2 teach that God made the world in six days and rested on the seventh. There has been much controversy in the church, especially during the last hundred years, over the length of those days, and over whether the text teaches a literal chronological sequence.

The three major views being discussed today among evangelicals are (1) the *normal day* view, that the days are about twenty-four hours each, succeeding one another chronologically,[18] (2) the *day-age* view, that the narrative gives a chronological history of God's creative acts, but that the "days" are of indefinite duration, most likely periods of many years,[19] and (3) the *framework* view, that the passage describes God's creative acts topically, and that the succession of days is a literary device for presenting those topical categories, which does not assert a chronological sequence.[20]

I have no new insight on these issues, nor even any view on the matter that I could argue with confidence. I would direct readers to the many other scholars who are producing articles and books on these subjects. Frankly, I tend to be persuaded by the last person I have listened to (Prov. 18:17!). But the following points seem to me to be important as we seek resolution of these questions:

1. This discussion concerns the interpretation of Genesis 1 and 2. The question is not whether we should abandon the teaching of these chapters

18. See, for example, Noel Weeks, *The Sufficiency of Scripture* (Edinburgh: Banner of Truth Trust, 1988), 95–118; Robert L. Reymond, *A New Systematic Theology of the Christian Faith* (Nashville: Thomas Nelson, 1998), 392–94. The best recent argument for this view is James B. Jordan, *Creation in Six Days* (Moscow, Ida.: Canon Press, 1999). Jordan deals persuasively with a broad range of recent literature on the subject.

19. See Edward J. Young, *Studies in Genesis One* (Philadelphia: Presbyterian and Reformed, 1964); Davis A. Young, *Creation and the Flood* (Grand Rapids: Baker, 1977).

20. See Henri Blocher, *In the Beginning* (Downers Grove, Ill.: InterVarsity Press, 1984); Mark D. Futato, "Because It Had Rained," *WTJ* 60 (1998): 1–21; Meredith G. Kline, "Because It Had Not Rained," *WTJ* 20 (1957–58): 146–57; Kline, "Space and Time in the Genesis Cosmogony," *Perspectives on Science and Christian Faith* 48 (1996): 2–15; N. H. Ridderbos, *Is There a Conflict Between Genesis 1 and Natural Science?* (Grand Rapids: Eerdmans, 1957).

to accommodate secular science. The question is, What does this passage actually say? It is an exegetical issue. I am convinced that the main advocates of all three views are seeking to be true to the teaching of the passage.

2. I am not denying that secular science has influenced this debate. The claims of scientists that the universe has existed for billions of years have certainly motivated theologians to go back to the text, in order to see whether these claims are consistent with Scripture, and that has meant rethinking traditional positions. In my view, that is entirely right and proper. We should not assume at the outset that the scientists are wrong. It is also possible that our interpretation of Scripture is wrong, though it is not possible for Scripture itself to be wrong. We must be humble enough and self-critical enough to reexamine these questions, even under the stimulus of scientific claims with which we may be initially unsympathetic. This is part of our apologetic mandate to bring every thought captive to Christ. In that sense, it is right for our exegesis to be "influenced" by science.

3. But there are also wrong ways of being influenced by science. In reexamining traditional views, we should not be governed by any principles of reasoning that are inconsistent with Scripture. We should not, for example, assume the absolute uniformity of natural laws, the impossibility of miraculous events, or the absolute validity of currently accepted procedures for determining dates of origin.

4. Defenders of the framework view have presented much evidence of literary devices in Genesis 1–2. Day one corresponds with day four, two with five, and three with six, by designating realms and inhabitants,[21] respectively. The presence of a literary structure, however, does not exclude chronological sequence or normal days. Scripture often uses literary devices in narratives that are clearly historical, like the "generations" of Genesis 2:4; 5:1; 6:9, and so on.[22] The use of a literary device in a historical narrative sometimes renders the narrative incomplete,[23] and there can be reasons for narrating events in nonchronological order (as sometimes happens in the Gospels).[24] But such literary devices and intentions do not exclude either completeness or chronology, for many narratives within these literary structures are chronological.

5. The broad literary structure of Genesis 1–2 proposed by the framework theory is not incompatible with a chronological sequence. There is

---

21. Or, as Kline puts it, realms and rulers.
22. The NIV uses the term *account*; the Hebrew is literally "generations."
23. Certainly this is the case in the scheme of fourteens in Matt. 1:2–17.
24. There must be nonchronological narrative in Gen. 1, Gen. 2, or both, for the order of events differs in the two chapters.

nothing absurd in the idea that God created the world in a sequence of events in which he first made the realms and then the inhabitants of those realms.

6. Framework theorists do urge other considerations against a chronological interpretation. One is that natural processes were at work during the creation week, so that the days of creation cannot have been normal days. In Genesis 2:4–7, we are told:

> When the LORD God made the earth and the heavens—and no shrub of the field had yet appeared on the earth and no plant of the field had yet sprung up, for the LORD God had not sent rain on the earth and there was no man to work the ground, but streams came up from the earth and watered the whole surface of the ground—and the LORD God formed the man . . .

According to the framework view, the watering of the earth must have occurred on day three of the creation week, when Genesis 1 says that God made plants (vv. 11–12). If the third day was a normal day, there wouldn't have been time for the plants to grow up in response to the natural process of watering. So the third day must be figurative, says the framework theory.

The framework theorists are correct to say that until day three, the prerequisites for plant growth did not exist, and that until day six, the prerequisite for cultivated grains[25]—human farmers—did not exist. But these observations do not imply that day three was long enough for all the plants to be watered and to grow up by natural processes. Rather, Genesis 1:11 gives the impression that once rain was available, the land miraculously produced mature plants at God's command, just as mature creatures were produced at his command on other days. The water didn't bring the plants into being, but it enabled them to continue growing and to reproduce.[26] Similarly, the grain most likely existed before God created man, but there were no cultivated fields.

None of this implies that the creation week included natural processes that would take many years. Even if the rain was part of the efficient cause

---

25. I recognize that the Hebrew terms translated "shrub" and "plant" in Gen. 2:5 may refer to different kinds of plants. Futato's interpretation is that the former means "wild vegetation" and the latter means "cultivated grain." See Futato, "Because It Had Rained," 10.

26. Unless one posits abiogenesis, the naturalistic development of life from nonlife, God must have performed some creative acts to produce plants. He made either the seeds or the mature plants, which then continued to grow by natural means. And the text certainly favors the latter option. Note the repetitive language in verses 11–12: God made plants with seeds in them.

of the growth of the first plants, it is not hard to imagine God miraculously accelerating that process.

Consider this parallel: Presumably, when God made the stars to light the night, he did not have to wait millions of years for their light to reach the earth. Rather, he created light waves to illumine the earth that would be replenished by a light source, the stars. Similarly, when he created plants, he created them mature and nourished, together with a source for their continued nourishment, the rain. This is the regular pattern of the creation week: mature heavenly bodies, mature plants, mature animals, and adult human beings, placed in an environment where they could continue to carry out their divinely given mandates. What Genesis 2:5 says is that at one time in the creation week, God refrained from making the mature plants, because he had not yet created the means for their continued life.

7. So I am not persuaded by arguments that the days of Genesis 1 must be nonchronological or that they must be ages long.

8. There are reasons for taking the days as normal days. First, the word *day* may not always refer to a twenty-four-hour period, but it does most often, especially when accompanied by numerals. The phrase "evening and morning" also suggests a twenty-four-hour period (see Ex. 18:13; 27:21). Second, in the fourth commandment (Ex. 20:8–11), we are told to work six days and rest one in imitation of God's creative activity. But if the creation days were not normal days, it is not clear what we should imitate. Third, the plural *days*, used in Exodus 20:11, is never used figuratively elsewhere.

9. On the other hand, I am not persuaded that figurative views should be considered heretical, for three reasons. First, although the literal view seems to be the most natural way to take Genesis 1, a figurative view cannot be excluded, especially if points 10 and 11, below, are taken seriously. Second, there have long been differences among Christians on this matter, and various views have been accepted in the church. Only recently has there been a movement to make the literal view a test of orthodoxy.[27] Third, it is not clear to me that any other doctrines rest logically upon a literal

---

27. Augustine, in *The City of God*, 11.7, expresses puzzlement as to what kind of days these were. His view was that God created everything at once. Anselm, in *Cur Deus Homo*, 18, follows Augustine. The Reformers generally held that the creation days were twenty-four hours long, but conservative American Presbyterians, including Charles and A. A. Hodge, B. B. Warfield, J. Gresham Machen, Oswald T. Allis, and Edward J. Young, have often held other views. See "Westminster Theological Seminary and the Days of Creation," a statement affirmed on June 1, 1998, by the faculty of Westminster Theological Seminary in Philadelphia, to which I am indebted for the other references in this note.

view of the days of Genesis. The figurative views under discussion do not imperil our confession of biblical inerrancy or the historicity of Genesis, for they claim to be derived precisely from the text. A figurative view of the days does not as such warrant an evolutionary view of man's ancestry. Nor does it compromise the historicity of the Fall or any of the truths concerning our new creation in Christ. Normally we do not make literal exegesis a test of orthodoxy,[28] and I do not see why the days of Genesis should be an exception.

10. In all this discussion, we should remind ourselves that God, speaking through Moses in Genesis 1–2, has a purpose, namely, to display his glory in his creative work and to provide background for the narrative of the Fall. It is not the primary purpose of the narrative to tell us precisely how God made the world, when he did it, how long it took, and how all of this relates to the theories of modern science. Of course, the narrative may answer some of these questions on the way to achieving its primary purpose. Certainly we must assume that its statements are consistent with what really happened, with a true cosmogony. But there may not be sufficient data in the passage to determine a detailed cosmogony in the language of modern science. And we should not demand that God give us more than he has given.

11. As we have seen, divine creation (both original and subsequent) is unique. It is analogous to human production of things, but it is an absolute or ultimate productivity that is impossible for human beings to emulate. This point is even more obvious if we assume, as I have argued we should, that God creates things in a mature state. The analogy as presented in Genesis 1 suggests a temporal analogy as well, that just as human production takes various periods of time, so God's productive work in creation also took time. But I think it unwise to dogmatize as to just how far to take this analogy, that is, how precisely to take the correspondence between God's workdays[29] and ours. I myself see no reason to suppose that the creation week was longer than a normal week. But I see no reason either to require that view as a test of orthodoxy.

28. Clearly, the Atonement and the Resurrection, for example, must be understood as literal events, at the price of invalidating one's confession of Christ. But there are many passages in Scripture that some interpret literally and others figuratively, concerning which mutual tolerance is the rule.

29. This language is taken from C. John Collins, "How Old Is the Earth?" *Presbyterion* 20 (1994): 109–30, and "Reading Genesis 1:1–2:3 as an Act of Communication," in *Did God Create in Six Days?* ed. Joseph Pipa, Jr., and David Hall (Oak Ridge, Tenn.: Covenant Foundation, 1999), 131–51.

THE AGE OF THE EARTH

I am even less well equipped than in the last case to deal adequately with the remaining "hot button" issues, namely, the age of the earth and evolution. I don't have much scientific training, aptitude, or knowledge.[30] Of course, I don't think that theological conclusions should be based on scientific theories. But someone who writes on the age of the earth or on evolution is entering an area of vigorous debate about scientific claims. One cannot deal with these questions in a satisfying way unless he is able to relate his exegetical conclusions to the scientific discussion. In that respect, my treatment of these issues here will be inadequate.

My exegetical position at the moment is that the earth is young, rather than old. I argued above that the creation narrative suggests a week of ordinary days, and that there is no compelling evidence against that interpretation. That week begins a series of genealogies: Adam, Seth, and their descendants, leading to Noah (Gen. 5), and the descendants of Noah's sons, leading to Abraham (Gen. 10). These genealogies may well be intentionally incomplete, as is the Matthean genealogy of Jesus (Matt. 1). But I doubt that there are enough gaps or omissions in these genealogies to allow for millions of years of human existence.

The only way that one could argue biblically for an old earth, billions of years old, given a creation week of normal days, is to posit a gap between Genesis 1:1 and 1:3. Some theologians have argued that the text permits a long period of time there, though of course it is impossible to prove the existence of such a period from the text. The trouble is that during such a period, the heavens and the earth would have existed (1:1), but there would have been no light (1:3) or heavenly bodies (1:14–19).[31] But most scientists would deny that such a situation ever existed. Therefore, the gap theory, whatever its exegetical merits, creates more problems with science than it solves.

The young earth view implies that God created the world with an appearance of age. The Genesis 1 narrative, for example, certainly indicates that God created Adam and Eve as adults. They would have appeared to have been, say, twenty years old, when they were actually fresh from the Creator's hand. Some have said that the creation of apparent age amounts to God deceiving us, but that is certainly not the case in any general way.

---

30. I do have a fairly normal layman's interest in such questions, but I do have a hard time concentrating on complicated discussions of these matters.

31. Another possibility, however, is that during the "gap" there were heavenly bodies and light, but that these were re-created in 1:3–31.

Normally, when we see adult human beings, we can estimate their age by certain physical characteristics. The creation of Adam and Eve as adults implies only that these estimates are not always true. It shows us that (as I argued in connection with miracle) the world is only generally uniform, not absolutely so. God does not tell us in natural revelation that every mature person has existed more than ten years. So he cannot be charged with lying to us when he miraculously produces an exception to this general rule.

Some have argued that God would be lying to us if, ten thousand years ago, he made stars that appear to be billions of years old. But God has never told us that the methods scientists use to calculate the age of stars are absolutely and universally valid. The stars are not a book that literally tells us their age. Rather, they are data by which scientists believe they can learn the age of bodies in many cases.[32] Reading that data requires a whole body of scientific theory and methods by which to interpret it. What scientists may learn from Genesis is that these methods do not work for objects that have been specially created. Scientists may need to read Genesis in order to refine their methods to a higher level of precision. Of course, science may not claim that its theories are without exceptions, unless it also claims divine omniscience.

Anyone who admits to any special creations at all must grant the reality of apparent age. Assume that God simply made a bunch of rocks out of nothing and left them floating in space to generate the rest of the universe: even in this case, were a geologist to look at those rocks ten minutes after the creation, he would certainly conclude that they were many years old.

Or what if God made the world by a "big bang," by the explosion of a "singularity"? Many scientists today think that we cannot get behind the Big Bang, since it was the beginning of time and space as we know them. But the tendency of science is to ask why, and that question is not easily restrained. So some today are asking, and certainly more in the future will ask, where the Big Bang came from and how it came about. To them, even the elementary particles present at the Big Bang must have an ancestry. Such scientists will pursue evidence in those particles (like the rings of the trees in Eden) that suggests a prior existence. Thus, even those particles, to those scientists, will appear "old." My point is simply that any view of

---

32. What starlight says about the age of stars depends on your perspective. On the common scientific theory, the light we see in the stars began its journey to the earth (in most cases) many years ago. So, on the scientific view, the stars we see appear more recent than they really are. So, if theology presents us with an "apparent age" theory of the stars, astronomy presents us with an "apparent novelty" theory of the stars. Thanks to Steve Hays for this observation.

origins at all implies apparent age. If there is an origin, the things at that origin will appear to be older than the origin.

There are problems with the apparent age view. One concerns astronomical events such as supernovas. Judging from the time it takes visual evidence of a supernova to reach the earth, according to astronomical calculations, these events happened long before what young earthers regard as the time of creation. Why would God make it appear as if a great event took place when, indeed, that event could not have happened in the time available since creation? Here, though, we must remind ourselves that all apparent age involves this problem. Any newly created being, whether star, plant, animal, or human being, if created mature, will contain data that in other cases would suggest events prior to its creation. If Adam and Eve were created mature, their bodies would have suggested (on the presupposition of the absolute uniformity of physical laws and processes) that they had been born of normal parents in the usual fashion. Why, then, are there apparent supernovas? From God's point of view, they may just be another twinkle in the light stream for the benefit of mankind.

If that is not a sufficient answer, we should simply accept as a general principle that God creates beings in a way that is consistent with their subsequent role in the historical process. If Adam had a navel, that navel suggested an event (his birth) that did not occur. But it also made him a normal human being, in full historical continuity with his descendants. Similarly, the starlight that God originally created would have contained the same twinkles, the same interruptions and fluctuations, that would later be caused by supernovas and other astral events.

I find such explanations satisfactory as an answer to most problems of apparent age. One problem I find more difficult to deal with is the existence of fossils that seem to antedate by millions of years any "young earth" date for creation. If God at the Creation planted fossils in rock strata, the apparent remains of organisms that never lived, why would he have done so, except to frustrate geologists and biologists?

James B. Jordan has made some observations worth considering in this respect:

> But what about dead stuff? Did the soil [during the original creation week—J.F.] have decaying organic matter in it? Well, if it was real soil, the kind that plants can grow in, it must have had. Yet the decaying matter in that original soil was simply put there by God. Soil is a living thing, and it lives through decaying matter. When Adam dug into the ground, he found pieces of dead vegetation.

This brings us to the question of "fossils" and "fossil fuels," like oil and coal. Mature creationists have no problem believing that God created birds and fish and animals and plants as living things, but we often quail at the thought that God also created "dead" birds and fish and animals and plants in the ground. But as we have just seen, there is every reason to believe that God created decaying organic matter in the soil. If this point is granted, and I don't see how it can be gainsaid, then *in principle* there is no problem with God's having put fossils in the ground as well. Such fossils are, *in principle*, no more deceptive on God's part than anything else created with the appearance of age.[33]

Jordan's comments are bound to be controversial in some circles, but I think they deserve a thoughtful hearing. Other Christians believe that the fossils can be completely accounted for by the dynamics of a worldwide flood. But at this point I must leave the discussion in the hands of scientists operating with biblical presuppositions.

This discussion may, however, send us back to reconsider the possibility of a nonliteral creation week. One possibility recently suggested to me is that God, for whom a thousand years are like a day (Ps. 90:4), could well have "speeded up" the time of creation, resulting in the apparent age of today's universe. In other words, perhaps someone viewing the universe from the outside, and holding a clock as we know it, could have witnessed hundreds of millions of years of development as occurring in short "days"—much like time-lapse photography—even though a clock within the universe would have measured it as hundreds of millions of years.[34] As I indicated, the text suggests a literal week and does not necessitate a nonliteral view. But, as I said, nonliteral views are not excluded. And, as I have argued, it is not wrong, in the face of scientific challenge, to reconsider our exegesis, though our ultimate conclusion must be governed by Scripture, not by secular science.

EVOLUTION

I reject the theory of evolution on the following grounds:
1. In Genesis 2:7, it is a special act of God (inbreathing) which makes Adam a "living creature" (*nefesh hayyah*). God did not take an already ex-

---

33. Jordan, "Creation with the Appearance of Age," *Open Book* 45 (April 1999): 2.
34. Thanks to my editor, James W. Scott, for suggesting this possibility to me.

isting living creature and make him specifically human, as in theistic evolution. Rather, he took dust and gave it life. Adam came to life by the same divine action by which he became man.[35]

2. The frequent repetition of "according to their kinds" in Genesis 1:11–12, 21, 24–25 indicates that there are divinely imposed limitations on what can result from reproduction. I do not know how broadly these "kinds" should be construed, or how they relate to modern biological classifications like family, genus, and species. But whatever a kind is, these passages evidently imply that plants and animals of one kind do not produce plants or animals of another. But that is what must happen if the theory of evolution is to be true.

3. Although I am not well equipped to judge scientific evidence, I will simply add that, as a layman, I am not convinced by the evidence presented to me for evolution. Doubtless there has been what is sometimes called microevolution: variations in the distribution of genetic characteristics within a species, due to natural selection. So, in some environments moths of a certain color become more preponderant, and in other environments those of a different color, as color proves in different ways to be an aid to survival and reproduction. But this amounts to variation within already existing genetic possibilities, rather than a process that produces a new species, that is, a new set of genetic possibilities. Nor does it come anywhere near to proving the existence of a process that could derive all present living forms from a single cell. Evidence for macroevolution, the derivation of all living organisms from the simplest by mutation and natural selection, seems to me to be sketchy at best.

4. Further, I agree with Phillip Johnson that the real persuasive power of the theory of evolution is not the evidence adduced in its favor, but rather the fact that it is the only viable alternative to theism.[36] Of course, that consideration carries no weight with me, nor should it influence any Christian to view the theory favorably. Rather, it should make us open to criticism of the theory.

I agree with Johnson and many others that the theory of evolution has brought great harm to society, leading it to deny the biblical view of human nature as the image of God, the awful nature and consequences of sin, and our need for redemption. I am encouraged that opponents

---

35. This argument is condensed from John Murray, *Collected Writings of John Murray* (Edinburgh: Banner of Truth Trust, 1977), 2:5–13.

36. Phillip Johnson, *Darwin on Trial* (Downers Grove, Ill.: InterVarsity Press, 1993); Johnson, *Reason in the Balance* (Downers Grove, Ill.: InterVarsity Press, 1995).

of Darwinism have recently been given a better hearing in academic circles than would have been possible fifty years ago. More than any other single figure, Johnson has led this new assault on evolutionary dogma, with careful argumentation and gentle prodding of the establishment, rather than with stridency and dubious hypotheses. We are all greatly in his debt.

CHAPTER 16

God's Decrees

We have seen that God acts as Lord in miracle, providence, and creation. Now according to Scripture, all of these actions are the result of thought. We have seen that God performs miracles with distinct purposes in mind, and he governs the course of nature and history with a goal in view. He created the world, also, for his own glory and according to his own wisdom. So there is thought—a plan—behind all of God's actions. Is it possible that God acts as Lord in miracle, providence, and creation, but not in the planning of these events? Certainly not. So, just as biblical logic has led us from God's lordship in miracle to his lordship in providence and creation, so now it leads us beyond history, "before" creation, to consider his lordship in the planning stages of his great historical drama.

This chapter, then, will mark a transition in our discussion from history to eternity. We have been considering God's actions in history, and in the next chapters we will consider his eternal nature. In this chapter, we will think about the decisions God makes in eternity that govern history.

So in this chapter we shall consider God's lordship with respect to his wise plan, his eternal decrees.[1] I have already discussed many matters that theologians normally include in the doctrine of the decrees. In addition to

---

1. The word *decree* can be used either in the singular or in the plural, more or less interchangeably. The singular form considers God's plan for the whole creation as a unity. The plural form focuses on the fact that within that unified plan, God has a particular plan for every individual thing and every individual event.

313

the points reviewed in the previous paragraphs, we should recall chapter 4, in which I summarized the efficacy and universality of God's control of the world. There I concluded that God controls all things and all the events of nature and history.[2] Then, in chapters 8 and 9, I expounded the author-character model of God's involvement with the world: God does not control the world merely by setting limits for its free activity, as a teacher "controls" his classroom. Rather, like the author of a well-wrought novel, he conceives and brings about every event that happens, without compromising the integrity of his "creaturely others."

Also, the doctrine of providence (chap. 14) and the doctrine of the decrees are perspectivally related. Under providence, we considered God's sovereign direction of nature and history from below: he works in and with every event to bring it about according to his purpose. Under the decrees, we consider the same data from above, focusing on the purpose for which God brings about all things. God's sovereign working is not only from above (as in deism), nor only from below (as in pantheism), but both. God directs his creation both in his transcendence and in his immanence (chap. 7). The decree is God's purpose in eternity; creation, providence, and redemption are the execution of his decree in time.[3]

It might seem that our actual chapter on the decrees could be rather short. Indeed, it will not take long now to develop the biblical concept of God's decrees, but there is much more to say about one particular decree, the decree of election, by which God chooses some to enjoy the benefits of salvation.

GOD'S PLAN

God's decrees are the wise, free, and holy acts of the counsel of his will, whereby, from all eternity, he hath, for his own glory, unchangeably foreordained whatsoever comes to pass in time, especially concerning angels and men.[4]

---

2. I decided not to include that material in the chapter on the decrees, because (1) it is equally relevant to providence, and (2) it seemed important to me to get the fundamental picture of God's lordship before the reader early in the book.

3. I shall not argue here, though I shall assume, that God's decrees are eternal in the supratemporal sense. For that, see the discussion in chapter 24 on God's eternity. But it should be obvious that God's decree "precedes" creation in some sense (Eph. 1:3). If time itself is a creation, then the decree is "before" time, that is, supratemporal.

4. WLC, 12.

The decrees of God are, his eternal purpose, according to the counsel of his will, whereby, for his own glory, he hath foreordained whatsoever comes to pass.[5]

God from all eternity, did, by the most wise and holy counsel of His own will, freely, and unchangeably ordain whatsoever comes to pass: yet so, as thereby neither is God the author of sin, nor is violence offered to the will of the creatures; nor is the liberty or contingency of second causes taken away, but rather established.[6]

Such are Reformed confessional definitions of God's decrees. The word *decree*, referring to a divine determination, is rarely found in English translations of Scripture. (Pss. 2:7 and 148:6 are two notable exceptions.[7]) But Scripture does speak much of God's "plans," "counsel," "purposes," and so on. We saw in chapter 4 that God has plans and that those plans are efficacious: what he purposes will surely come to pass. We considered many passages like this one:

But the plans of the LORD stand firm forever,
the purposes of his heart through all generations. (Ps. 33:11)

We also saw that these plans are universal: they govern all the affairs of nature, history, and individual lives, including sin and salvation:

I make known the end from the beginning,
from ancient times, what is still to come.
I say: My purpose will stand,
and I will do all that I please. (Isa. 46:10)

The efficacy of God's purpose is as universal as his knowledge, from the beginning to the end, from distant past through all the future.

In these verses, God's decree is his "plans" or "counsel" (*'etsah*), his "purposes" (*mahsheboth*), what "pleases" (*hafets*) him. The New Testament expresses this idea with terms such as *boulē* ("will, counsel"), *thelēma* ("will, intention"), *eudokia* ("pleasure"), *prothesis* ("purpose"), *proorismos* ("foreordination"), *prognōsis* ("foreknowledge" in the sense of commitment to bring about an event or a personal relationship).[8] (For a sampling of pas-

5. WSC, 7.
6. WCF, 3.1.
7. The term *decree* is certainly justifiable, because it arises from the biblical picture of God as king, as Lord. The decrees are the sovereign commands of the Lord of all.
8. See our discussion of foreknowledge in chapter 4. William F. Arndt and F. Wilbur Gingrich translate *prognōsis* in 1 Peter 1:2 as "predestination" (*A Greek-English Lexicon of the New Testament and Other Early Christian Literature* [Chicago: University of Chicago Press,

sages that speak of God's purpose in these terms, see Matt. 11:26; Acts 2:23; 4:27–28; Rom. 8:29; 9:11; Eph. 1:5, 9, 11; 3:11; 2 Tim. 1:9; Heb. 6:17; 1 Peter 1:2.)

God's plan is *eternal* (Isa. 37:26;[9] 46:9–10; Matt. 25:34; 1 Cor. 2:7; Eph. 1:4; 3:11; 2 Tim. 1:9). As we shall see, God's plans can be historical and temporal in the sense that he wills for things to happen at one time rather than another. And sometimes he ordains something to happen temporarily. But the plan by which he ordains these temporary states of affairs is nevertheless eternal. Therefore, his plan is *immutable*, unchangeable. Although he wills for things to change in history, his plan for such change cannot be changed (Ps. 33:11; Isa. 14:24; 46:10; James 1:17). In our discussion of God's eternity in chapter 24, we shall see how God does sometimes announce policies conditionally, as when he announces judgment and then withholds it upon repentance (Ex. 32:14; Jer. 18:7–10; 26:13; 36:3; Jonah 3:8–10). But the whole course of this interaction is governed by God's eternal decree.

THE DECREES AND GOD'S LORDSHIP

God's decrees display his lordship attributes. In an obvious way, they display his *control*, for they are efficacious and universal. God's intentions will certainly be fulfilled, and they will be fulfilled for everything in the created world.

They also display his *authority*, for they are meaningful thoughts—wise plans or counsels for the world. As such, they *interpret* the world; they determine the meaning and significance of everything God makes. God's interpretations, of course, are always supremely authoritative. When he declares the significance of something for his purpose, that is the significance it has. So the doctrine of the decrees implies that God has authoritatively preinterpreted everything and every event. As Van Til emphasized, the interpretation of the facts precedes the facts. Our world is a world that is ex-

---

1957], 710). Although some Greek lexicons translate the word as "foreknowledge," following the etymology of the term, the idiomatic usage often breaks with the etymological root, so that the term can simply be translated as "choice."

9. "Long ago" and "days of old" may not connote the theological concept of eternity to everybody, but this is typical Old Testament language referring to an indefinite time in the past. The important point is that God's plan is not a response to current events, or even based on short-term foresight of current events, but comes from far in the distant past. The New Testament references expand this concept, indicating that God's plan goes back before creation.

haustively meaningful, because it is the expression of God's wisdom. Among human beings, interpretation is not the work of trying to assess for the first time the significance of uninterpreted facts. Rather, ours is a work of secondary interpretation, interpreting God's interpretation.

God's decrees also manifest his *covenant presence* with his creatures. For the doctrine of the decrees means that in his mind, God has established a personal relationship with every creature, reaching back into eternity. Of course, creaturely existence always has a beginning; it is not itself eternal. But to say that God decrees the course of nature and history is to say that God knows us before we begin to exist, and that even then he established his purpose for each of us, his relationship to us.

So God says to Jeremiah,

> Before I formed you in the womb I knew you,
>   before you were born I set you apart;
>   I appointed you as a prophet to the nations. (Jer. 1:5)

Paul says in Ephesians 1:4 that God "chose us in [Christ] before the creation of the world to be holy and blameless in his sight."

HISTORICAL ELECTION

With many persons and groups, that eternal covenant presence of God takes the form of *election*. *Election* simply means "choice"; so in Ephesians 1:4, the word "chose" describes divine election. Since election is one kind of divine decree, we can add to our list of terms indicating God's purpose and intention the biblical vocabulary of divine choice: *bahar* ("choose"), *hibdil* ("set apart"), *eklegomai* ("choose"), *proetoimazō* ("prepare before"), and *prognōsis* ("foreknowledge, choice").[10]

Ephesians 1:4 describes God electing people to salvation, but he also chooses people for specific tasks, as in Jeremiah 1:5, quoted above. In Luke 6:13, Jesus "called his disciples to him and chose twelve of them, whom he also designated apostles." (See also John 6:70; 15:16, 19; Gal. 1:15–16.) God's election of people for his service does not necessarily imply that those people will finally receive the blessings of salvation. God chose Saul to be king (1 Sam. 9:17) and prophet (1 Sam. 10:5–11), but Saul disobeyed God and came to a disgraceful end. Scripture does not affirm that Saul died in fellowship with God; it leaves his personal salvation uncertain. Jesus chose Judas, the betrayer, to be an apostle, but Jesus said of him:

---

10. See the earlier discussion in this chapter.

> "Have I not chosen you, the Twelve? Yet one of you is a devil!" (He meant Judas, the son of Simon Iscariot, who, though one of the Twelve, was later to betray him.) (John 6:70–71)

> But woe to that man who betrays the Son of Man! It would be better for him if he had not been born. (Matt. 26:24)

> While I was with [the disciples], I protected them and kept them safe by that name you gave me. None has been lost except the one doomed to destruction so that Scripture would be fulfilled. (John 17:12)

Like Saul, Judas committed suicide (Matt. 27:3–5; Acts 1:18–20), and the condemnations of Scripture preclude his salvation.

God also chose the nation of Israel for his redemptive purpose. He chose Abraham out of Ur of the Chaldees (Neh. 9:7), and chose Isaac over Ishmael, and Jacob over Esau (Rom. 9:6–13). After the Exodus, Moses said to Israel:

> Because [God] loved your forefathers and chose their descendants after them, he brought you out of Egypt by his Presence and his great strength. (Deut. 4:37)[11]

> For you are a people holy to the LORD your God. The LORD your God has chosen you out of all the peoples on the face of the earth to be his people, his treasured possession. (Deut. 7:6; cf., e.g., Deut. 10:15; 14:2; Ps. 33:12; Isa. 41:8–9; 44:1; 45:4)

God's choice of Israel was by grace, not merit:

> The LORD did not set his affection on you and choose you because you were more numerous than other peoples, for you were the fewest of all peoples. But it was because the LORD loved you and kept the oath he swore to your forefathers that he brought you out with a mighty hand and redeemed you from the land of slavery, from the power of Pharaoh king of Egypt. (Deut. 7:7–8)

> After the LORD your God has driven [the Canaanite nations] out before you, do not say to yourself, "The LORD has brought me here to take possession of this land because of my righteousness." No, it is on account of the wickedness of these nations that the LORD is going to drive them out before you. . . . Understand, then, that

11. Note in this passage the Lord's authority (his loving choice), his control ("strength"), and his Presence.

it is not because of your righteousness that the LORD your God is giving you this good land to possess, for you are a stiff-necked people. (Deut. 9:4, 6)

God chose Israel to glorify his name and to be a blessing to all the nations (Gen. 12:3). Israel was the nation through whom the Redeemer would come, and from whom the message of salvation would go out to all other nations of the world. But throughout the Old Testament period, they remained "stiff-necked." They worshiped idols, they oppressed widows and orphans, and they showed contempt for God's law. So through his prophets, God threatened to bring judgment upon them. Nevertheless, he also promised grace and forgiveness.

The interchange in the prophetic writings between the theme of judgment and the theme of grace and forgiveness is remarkable. Often the prophet moves from judgment to grace with no transition, with little indication of the reason for the change. But we can understand the relationship between the two themes in general terms.

In Isaiah 1:1–17, God expresses his displeasure at Israel's rebellion. Through the prophet, he brings a covenant lawsuit against Israel for their violation of his covenant law. He compares them with Sodom and Gomorrah, the wicked cities which he thoroughly destroyed in the time of Abraham and Lot (Gen. 18:16–19:29; cf. Ezek. 16:49–58). He says that he hates their offerings and holy feasts. He will not answer their prayers. But then, in the midst of the condemnation, comes this word of forgiveness:

> "Come now, let us reason together,"
>   says the LORD.
> "Though your sins are like scarlet,
>   they shall be as white as snow;
> though they are red as crimson,
>   they shall be as wool." (Isa. 1:18)

In this case, God offers forgiveness at the price of repentance. If they will turn from their evil ways and obey the Lord, they will receive the blessings of the covenant—but if not, they will receive the curses:

> "If you are willing and obedient,
>   you will eat the best from the land;
> but if you resist and rebel,
>   you will be devoured by the sword."
>   For the mouth of the LORD has spoken.
>   (vv. 19–20)

But how likely is their repentance? Even in Exodus, God had called them "stiff-necked" (33:5). They had worshiped a golden calf while Moses was speaking with God on Mount Sinai (32:1–35). They wandered in the desert for forty years, because they had not believed God's promise of victory over the Canaanites. Again and again, God charged them with wickedness. Yet somehow God is going to "purge away your dross and remove all your impurities" (Isa. 1:25). He continues:

> "I will restore your judges as in days of old,
>   your counselors as at the beginning.
> Afterward you will be called
>   the City of Righteousness,
>   the Faithful City."
> Zion will be redeemed with justice,
>   her penitent ones with righteousness.
> But rebels and sinners will both be broken,
>   and those who forsake the LORD will perish. (vv. 26–28)

Evidently there will be "some survivors" (v. 9) from the divine judgment who will be faithful to the Lord and will be the foundation of the new City of Righteousness. The Assyrians will bring disaster, but there will be a remnant (10:20–34). The remnant will return from their exile, and they will return to the Lord (10:21). They are the real continuation of Israel; they will receive the fulfillment of the covenant promises (11:11–12:6; 41:8–12; 43:1–7; Jer. 23:3–4; 31:7–14).

The books of Ezra and Nehemiah describe the return of the exiles, the remnant, back to the Promised Land. But God's glorious promises to the remnant through Isaiah and Jeremiah are not fulfilled. The people must confess the sin of intermarrying with the pagan nations (Ezra 9:1–10:44; Neh. 13:23–27). At the end of their prayer of repentance, they say,

> Because of our sins, [the land's] abundant harvest goes to the kings you have placed over us. They rule over our bodies and our cattle as they please. We are in great distress. (Neh. 9:37)

During the intertestamental period, some in Israel rebelled against the foreign rulers, but ultimately they were unsuccessful. During the earthly ministry of Jesus, Israel was under the domination of Roman emperors, and Jesus spoke like Isaiah of the unbelief and disobedience of Israel. Those who returned from exile were not the faithful remnant. Neither the Israel of Ezra and Nehemiah, nor the first-century Israel, formed the City of Righteousness of which Isaiah spoke. Rather, they again became like Sodom and Gomorrah—and worse (Matt. 11:20–24).

Who, then, is the faithful remnant who inherits the promises made by God to Abraham, and through whom all the nations of the earth are blessed? After the remnant passage in Isaiah 10:20–34, we read:

> A shoot will come up from the stump of Jesse;
>   from his roots a Branch will bear fruit.
> The Spirit of the LORD will rest on him—
>   the Spirit of wisdom and understanding,
>   the Spirit of counsel and of power,
>   the Spirit of knowledge and of the fear of the LORD—
> and he will delight in the fear of the LORD. (11:1–3a)

The righteous Branch will rule justly for the poor and needy and will slay the wicked (vv. 3b-5). The result will be a wonderful time of peace, when the wolf will lie down with the lamb:

> They will neither harm nor destroy
>   on all my holy mountain,
> for the earth will be full of the knowledge of the LORD
>   as the waters cover the sea. (v. 9)

It is under the rule of the righteous Branch that God's people will be gathered from all the nations (vv. 12–16) and will join together in praising God for his salvation (12:1–6).

Similarly, in the remnant promises of Isaiah 41:8–20 and 43:1–7, the people do not repent out of their own moral strength. Rather, there is a new visitation of the divine presence, a redemptive re-creation, pointing to the work of the Servant of the Lord in 52:13–53:12. Of him the prophet says:

> Surely he took up our infirmities
>   and carried our sorrows,
> yet we considered him stricken by God,
>   smitten by him, and afflicted.
> But he was pierced for our transgressions,
>   he was crushed for our iniquities;
> the punishment that brought us peace was upon him,
>   and by his wounds we are healed.
> We all, like sheep, have gone astray,
>   each of us has turned to his own way;
> and the LORD has laid on him
>   the iniquity of us all. (Isa. 53:4–6)

And in Jeremiah's prophecy of the remnant, we again see the righteous Branch (23:5–6), whose name is "The LORD Our Righteousness" (v. 6).

Ultimately, then, elect Israel is Jesus Christ. He is the faithful remnant, the righteous Branch. Through him alone comes forgiveness of sins, for he bears God's judgment in the place of his people. The Old Testament gives us a perplexing picture, for the judgment theme seems inconsistent with the theme of grace and forgiveness. If God is fully just, then it seems that nobody can receive his blessing; all will be destroyed. On the other hand, if God's mercy fulfills the terms of his promises, it seems that his forgiveness of sin would have to violate his moral order. But through Jesus, God's justice and mercy meet together in wonderful harmony. Jesus bears the full judgment of God, so that through him God's mercy brings eternal life to all his people.

And in Christ, by his grace, all believers belong to the remnant (Rom. 11:1–6). This remnant includes both Jews and Gentiles, for God has "grafted" Gentiles into the tree of Israel (11:17–21), having removed some of the Jewish "natural branches." But the Gentiles should not boast:

> But they were broken off because of unbelief, and you stand by faith. Do not be arrogant, but be afraid. For if God did not spare the natural branches, he will not spare you either. (vv. 20–21)

As not all Israelites are Israel (9:6), so not all members of the Christian church are regenerate believers. Some are elect only as the unbelieving Israelites were: historically elect, rather than eternally elect. Like Saul and Judas, they are chosen only temporarily; they can become nonelect. So the election of the visible Christian church is similar to the election of Old Testament Israel. It is an election that temporarily includes some within its bounds who will never come to true faith and will never have eternal life. This parallel between the church and Israel should not be surprising, because the church and Israel are, contrary to dispensationalism, the same body. The tree of redemption is one, and God prunes it and grafts branches onto it, in accordance with his will. So the visible church participates in the election of Israel.

Now let us consider three frequently asked questions about the election of Israel:

1. Is the election of Israel the election of a corporate entity, or is it the election of individuals? I would say both. God chooses Israel as a family, a nation. But he also chooses individuals within that family. He chooses Abraham, but not his parents and brothers. He chooses Isaac, not Ishmael. He chooses Jacob, not Esau. Paul explains:

> It is not as though God's word had failed. For not all who are descended from Israel are Israel. Nor because they are his descendants

are they all Abraham's children. On the contrary, "It is through Isaac that your offspring will be reckoned." In other words, it is not the natural children who are God's children, but it is the children of the promise who are regarded as Abraham's offspring. (Rom. 9:6–8)

God also chooses the remnant, not the entire nation, to receive his blessing. And, ultimately, God's choice is of one individual, Jesus.

Jesus establishes another corporate entity, the church. The church is elect in Christ. But, as in Israel, some apostatize. They turn away from Jesus, and there is no more hope for them (Heb. 6:1–12; 10:26–31; 1 John 2:18–19). As Paul says, God sometimes breaks off even newly engrafted branches. The writer to the Hebrews warns his Jewish-Christian readers not to turn away from God, as Israel did in the wilderness (chaps. 3–4). In the New Testament, then, there is also an election within an election, and we shall discuss that further below.

2. Is Israel chosen for salvation or for service? Again, I would say both. God calls Israel as his servant (Isa. 44:1), his witnesses (Isa. 43:10, 12). But, as God's servants, Jews have great privileges:

> What advantage, then, is there in being a Jew, or what value is there in circumcision? Much in every way! First of all, they have been entrusted with the very words of God. (Rom. 3:1–2)

> Theirs is the adoption as sons; theirs the divine glory, the covenants, the receiving of the law, the temple worship and the promises. Theirs are the patriarchs, and from them is traced the human ancestry of Christ, who is God over all, forever praised! Amen. (Rom. 9:4–5)

These are all blessings of salvation, the blessings of people who have turned from worshiping idols to serve the living and true God. Not all individuals in Israel are eternally saved. But, as we have seen, the true Israel is Christ and those who are in him. Those who belong to the true Israel are indeed eternally saved. This fact is the root of the second concept of election, to be discussed in the next section.

3. Is the election of Israel based on works or grace? As we saw in Deuteronomy 7:7–8 and 9:4–6, it is not based on Israel's numbers (power, influence) or righteousness, but wholly on God's unmerited love, that is, his grace (see also Deut. 4:37; 8:17–18; 10:15; Ezek. 16:1–14). On the other hand, Israel's continued status in God's covenant depends on obedience. God tells them at Mount Sinai, during the making of the covenant:

Now if you obey me fully and keep my covenant, then out of all nations you will be my treasured possession. Although the whole earth is mine, you will be for me a kingdom of priests and a holy nation. (Ex. 19:5–6)

Jeremiah later reminds Israel, "But I gave [your forefathers] this command: Obey me, and I will be your God and you will be my people" (Jer. 7:23). The covenant relationship itself, here, is conditioned on obedience.[12]

In Hosea, God even announces that Israel as a whole is no longer elect, that Israel is "not my people" (1:9). Yet (in another strange movement from judgment to grace) he immediately adds that "in the place where it was said to them, 'You are not my people,' they will be called 'sons of the living God' " (v. 10). Israel loses its election and regains it again. God also judges many individuals in Israel, removing covenant blessings from them because of their disobedience.

This pattern does not exist only in Old Testament Israel. Christians are saved wholly by grace (Eph. 2:8–9), yet judgments come upon faithless people in the New Testament church, such as Judas (Acts 1:15–26), Ananias and Sapphira (Acts 5:1–10), and Simon the sorcerer (Acts 8:9–25). And we have seen the warnings of Hebrews against turning away from God's grace in Christ and thereby falling into condemnation.

So although the election of Israel is by grace, there is an important place for continued faithfulness. Individuals can belong to the chosen people, yet lose their elect status by faithlessness and disobedience. Branches can be broken off "because of unbelief" (Rom. 11:20).

When we consider this divine rejection, we should not argue that the discarded branches were never really elect. There is a place for such reasoning, but it pertains to a different kind of election, which we will discuss in the following section. Here, however, we are talking about historical election. And in this context, it is possible to lose one's election. The discarded branches were indeed elect at one time, for they were part of the tree of Israel. Israel as a nation was really elect, before God declared them to be "not my people," and they became elect again, when God declared them to be "sons of the living God."

The same is true of the New Testament church. It would not be right to say that Judas, or Ananias, or the apostates of Hebrews 6 and 10 were

---

12. Obviously, obedience is required for Israel to receive the blessings of the covenant, rather than its curses. But these passages say more: that obedience is the condition on which the covenant itself exists. But perhaps the difference is only perspectival. The ultimate meaning of the covenant curse is that God is not our God and we are not his people. The covenant curse is covenant excommunication.

THIS IS VERY HELPFUL TO MAKE THIS DISTINCTION
BETWEEN HISTORICAL + ETERNAL ELECTION.

God's Decrees   325

never elect in any sense. They were elect in the sense that Israel was
elect. Indeed, when Calvinists worry about the implications of Hebrews
6 and 10, it is useful for them to consider that the apostates in these
passages are very much like Old Testament Israel: they "have once been
enlightened, . . . tasted the heavenly gift, . . . shared in the Holy
Spirit, . . . tasted the goodness of the word of God and the powers of
the coming age" (Heb. 6:4–5). Israel experienced all these things
throughout Old Testament history and particularly during the earthly
ministry of Jesus. But they rejected him and joined those who crucified
the Son of God. So those church members who turn away from Christ
"are crucifying the Son of God all over again and subjecting him to public disgrace" (6:6).

Note how Hebrews 6:4–6 emerges out of the references to Israel in chapters 3 and 4. The Israelites, blessed as they were with enlightenment, the
heavenly gift, the Holy Spirit, the word of God, and the powers of the coming age, nevertheless hardened their hearts against the Lord (3:7–11, 15).
The writer therefore urges Christians to "make every effort to enter that
rest, so that no one will fall by following their example of disobedience"
(4:11).

So God continues to break branches off the tree of redemption. Even
those who have been freshly engrafted can be broken off because of
unbelief.

ETERNAL ELECTION

But in Scripture there is also an election that cannot be lost and that
is not at all conditioned on human faithfulness or works. We saw earlier
that the election of Israel is, ultimately, the election of Jesus Christ as
the faithful remnant. Although branches of the tree of redemption can
be broken off, Christ himself can never, since the Cross, lose his fellowship with the Father. He was "chosen before the creation of the world"
(1 Peter 1:20).

So those who are "in Christ," who belong to him inwardly and not
merely outwardly, who are the true Israel, can never lose their salvation.
They are elect in a stronger sense than was the nation of Israel as a whole
and in a stronger sense than is the general membership of the visible Christian church.

This kind of election, like that of Israel as a nation, is covenantal: in it
God chooses some to be his covenant people. But the covenant is different in character. In the prophecy of Jeremiah, the Lord describes it like this:

"The time is coming," declares the LORD,
"when I will make a new covenant
with the house of Israel
and with the house of Judah.
It will not be like the covenant
I made with their forefathers
when I took them by the hand
to lead them out of Egypt,
because they broke my covenant,
though I was a husband to them,"
                                    declares the LORD.
"This is the covenant I will make with the house of Israel
after that time," declares the LORD.
"I will put my law in their minds
and write it on their hearts.
I will be their God,
and they will be my people.
No longer will a man teach his neighbor,
or a man his brother, saying, 'Know the LORD,'
because they will all know me,
from the least of them to the greatest,"
                                    declares the LORD.
"For I will forgive their wickedness
and will remember their sins no more." (Jer. 31:31–34)

The writer to the Hebrews quotes this passage in 8:8–12 and 10:16–17, and indicates that the new covenant is the covenant sealed with Jesus' blood, which puts an end to all other sacrifices. (See also Isa. 42:6; Zech. 9:11; Luke 22:20; 1 Cor. 11:25; 2 Cor. 3:6.) Hebrews 9:15 summarizes:

> For this reason Christ is the mediator of a new covenant, that those who are called may receive the promised eternal inheritance—now that he has died as a ransom to set them free from the sins committed under the first covenant.

The difference between the old and new covenants is that the blood of the new covenant, the blood of Christ, actually cleanses from sin. The blood of bulls and goats under the old covenant did not actually cleanse from sin, but only symbolized the coming work of Jesus. All those in the Old Testament period who received God's forgiveness received it on the basis of Christ's atoning sacrifice, which of course to them was still future. They were saved by faith in God's promise of the Messiah. So there were new covenant believers during the Old Testament period. Abraham is an example, for, as Jesus taught, "Your father Abraham rejoiced at the thought of seeing my day; he saw it and was glad" (John 8:56).

The blessings unique to the new covenant are the forgiveness of sins and God's law being written upon one's heart. One who has the law written on his heart obeys God willingly. He wants, in the inmost center of his being, to love God and keep his commandments. God, in other words, creates a new disposition in his new covenant people, a desire to serve him. That is the new creation I described in chapter 15.

Membership in this covenant is, of course, by God's choice, God's election. Election in the new covenant is similar to election in the old, but there are differences that are appropriate to the differences between the two covenants. Most significantly, for those chosen to be "in Christ," eternal salvation is certain:

> For those God foreknew he also predestined to be conformed to the likeness of his Son, that he might be the firstborn among many brothers. And those he predestined, he also called; those he called, he also justified; those he justified, he also glorified. (Rom. 8:29–30)

The logic is inevitable. Anyone whom God savingly foreknows,[13] he predestines to be conformed to the likeness of Christ. (That is, he writes the word on his heart.) And anyone so predestined receives an effectual call from God sometime in his life, a summons into fellowship with Christ, an order he cannot decline.[14] Those whom God calls, he justifies: he declares them righteous for Jesus' sake. And those whom he justifies, he glorifies. No one who is foreknown, predestined, called, and justified can escape glorification. Final salvation is certain.

So Paul continues in verses 31–39 with a great hymn based on the theme of the certainty of salvation for those who are in Christ. If God is for us, nobody can be against us (vv. 31–32), so God will certainly give us all things. No one can bring any charge against us before God (vv. 33–34), so there can be no condemnation (cf. v. 1). No one can separate us from the love of Christ (vv. 35–39)—nothing on earth or in heaven. The elect are Jesus' sheep, of whom none can perish or be plucked from his hand (John 10:28–29).

This kind of election is also the focus of Ephesians 1:3–14. These elect people are chosen "in [Christ] before the creation of the world to be holy

---

13. I take "foreknew" in this passage to mean "befriended beforehand" or "elected." See the argumentation for this understanding in chapter 4.

14. Review the brief discussion of effectual calling in chapter 4.

and blameless in his sight" (v. 4). The elect here will inevitably become holy and blameless. God decided that they would be such, before he created the heavens and the earth. He determined to redeem them by the blood of Christ and thereby to forgive their sins (v. 7). It is inevitable that they will hear the gospel of salvation (v. 13) and believe. And:

> Having believed, you were marked in him with a seal, the promised Holy Spirit, who is a deposit guaranteeing our inheritance until the redemption of those who are God's possession—to the praise of his glory. (vv. 13–14)

God guarantees, then, the salvation of these elect. Scripture speaks of the election of individuals to salvation also in Mattew 24:22, 24, 31; Mark 13:20–22; Luke 18:7; Acts 13:48; 1 Corinthians 1:27–28; Ephesians 2:10; Colossians 3:12; 1 Thessalonians 1:4–5; 2 Thessalonians 2:13; 2 Timothy 1:9; 2:10; Titus 1:1; and James 2:5.

This kind of election is unconditional. As we saw in chapter 4, God chooses us before we choose him. Our faithful response is a gift of his grace. So election to salvation is not based on anything we do. It is entirely gracious. It is also eternal: "before the creation of the world" (Eph. 1:4), "from the beginning" (2 Thess. 2:13), "before the beginning of time" (2 Tim. 1:9).

As *election* has two different meanings, based on the distinction between the old and new covenants, so does the biblical concept of "the book of life." In Exodus 32:33, after Israel has been found worshiping a golden calf, God says to Moses, "Whoever has sinned against me I will blot out of my book."

In Psalm 69, the writer asks God to judge the wicked in Israel:

> Charge them with crime upon crime;
>   do not let them share in your salvation.
> May they be blotted out of the book of life
>   and not be listed with the righteous. (vv. 27–28)

Here the psalmist envisions a book in God's presence containing the names of those he has chosen for covenant blessing. Initially, it seems, the list contains everybody in Israel. But God will blot some of them out because of their sin, for not all who are descended from Israel are Israel.[15] The image of people being blotted out of the book of life is parallel to Paul's image of natural branches being broken off from the tree of redemption (cf. Rev. 3:5).

So the image of the book of life can be an image of historical election, the election of Israel. But, like the term *election* itself, the image can also

15. Cf. Ezek. 13:9, in which the lying prophets "will not . . . be listed in the records of the house of Israel."

represent election in a stronger sense. In Revelation 17:8, the names that are not in the book of life have been excluded from it "from the creation of the world," and, implicitly, the names that are written in it have been there from the creation. This expression precludes the notion that one could be listed in the book and later blotted out because of something that happens in history. In Revelation 17:8 (in contrast to Ps. 69:28), no one can be blotted out of the book. Revelation 13:8 should also be taken this way, as is suggested by the correlation between the writing of the book and the Lamb being slain "from the creation of the world."

So election has two senses. I call the first one historical election, because persons who are elect in that sense can become nonelect because of their unfaithfulness during human history. The second, by way of contrast, I call eternal election, because the number of the elect in that sense is fixed from eternity. This terminology may mislead some, because the first, no less than the second, is the result of an eternal decree. But in the first, God may decree that some lose their covenant status, while he decrees no such change in the second. With that understanding, I shall continue to use that language.

Historical election and eternal election are distinct, but they cannot be entirely separated. Note the following:

1. Both historical and eternal election are aspects of God's saving purpose. The election of Israel and the temporary election of individuals in history are means by which God gathers together those who will receive his final blessing.

2. As we have seen, the remnant of historical election is none other than Jesus Christ. Jesus himself is eternally elected by God (1 Peter 1:20), together with those whom God has chosen in him. So, in the end, historical and eternal election coincide.[16] In history, they do not, for historical election is a temporal process and eternal election is forever settled before creation.

All of the eternally elect are historically elect, but not vice versa. Historical election is the process in history by which God executes his decree to save the eternally elect. As God judges the reprobate through history, the difference narrows between the historically elect and the eternally elect. In the end, the outcome of historical election is the same as that of eternal election.

---

16. Note that in Rev. 20:15, those whose names are "not found written in the book of life" are thrown into the lake of fire. Is this the historical book of life, from which names can be blotted out? Or is it the eternal book of life, written before the creation? We cannot tell. For by the Day of Judgment, all blotting will be done, and the names in the historical book will be the same as the names in the eternal book.

3. As such, historical election is a mirror of eternal election. Just as God elects Israel by grace, so he elects believers eternally by grace. He promises blessings to Israel that are essentially the blessings of salvation—ultimately, the presence of the living God with them. God's covenant presence with Israel in the tabernacle and the temple is an image of his presence with eternally elect believers in Christ. The chief difference, of course, is that among the historically elect, there are some who will not be finally saved. But even the historical rejection of unbelievers from the covenant images eternal election, for it pictures the final separation between the elect and the reprobate.

4. We may think of historical election as the visible and temporal form of eternal election. We cannot see another's heart to know for sure whether he is eternally elect. But we can see whom God has led to unite with his visible body, the church. We can see who has given a credible profession of faith in Christ. By observing the process of historical election in the light of Scripture, we gain a limited knowledge of eternal election—the best knowledge possible for us today.

5. Those who join the church are historically elect, in the way that Israel was historically elect. It is possible for people in the church to apostatize, to renounce their profession. Church membership, therefore, does not guarantee membership in the new covenant. But the church is a new covenant institution in that it proclaims God's eternal election in Christ and the forgiveness of sins through Jesus' atonement. In that sense, Israel also was a new covenant institution. So the book of Hebrews reminds its Jewish-Christian readers of the new covenant to which they are called, and it also warns them not to fall away, as did Israel in the wilderness.

REPROBATION

If God has chosen some for salvation, but not everyone, then it follows that some are not elect. Since only the elect are saved, the nonelect are ultimately lost. So God's election of some implies his rejection of others. This rejection is called *reprobation*. Traditionally, theologians have distinguished, within reprobation, between *preterition*, in which God determines not to choose certain persons for salvation, and *precondemnation*, in which he determines to punish them for their sin.

This is a hard doctrine, because it seems to conflict with God's loving and merciful nature and with his desire that all be saved (Ezek. 18:23, 32; 33:11; 1 Tim. 2:4; 2 Peter 3:9). As for the apparent conflict with God's love, see chapter 9, for the problem here is ultimately the problem of evil, though arguably it is the most difficult form of that problem. See also chapter 20 on God's love and chapter 23 on his will. In those chapters, we will consider in what sense God loves the reprobate and in what sense he wills or desires to save them. I believe that there are biblical senses in which God loves and desires to save all people.

Here I will only observe that the doctrine of reprobation is scriptural. We saw in chapter 4 that God does foreordain human sin, and therefore foreordains its consequence, which is always death (Rom. 6:23). God works all things according to the counsel of his will, and the ultimate destiny of the lost is certainly among those things.

Like election, reprobation has both historical and eternal senses. Historical Israel is elect in contrast to all the other nations (Deut. 4:37; 7:6; 14:2). In choosing Israel, God rejects the others. Nevertheless, some from other nations join themselves to Israel, and ultimately God's purpose is for Israel to fulfill his promise to Abraham to be a blessing to all nations (Gen. 12:3; 22:18; 26:4). He intends to graft the wild branches of the nations into the tree of Israel. So God's rejection of the nations is temporary, though it is part of his eternal plan. So Paul writes to Gentile Christians:

> Remember that at that time you were separate from Christ, excluded from citizenship in Israel and foreigners to the covenants of the promise, without hope and without God in the world. But now in Christ Jesus you who once were far away have been brought near through the blood of Christ. (Eph. 2:12–13)

Indeed, we must remember that all believers were once rejected by God and objects of wrath (Eph. 2:1–3). That rejection was genuine; we all deserved eternal punishment. But we thank God that that rejection was only temporary, for his eternal plan was to lead us to Christ.

In addition to historical reprobation, Scripture also teaches an eternal reprobation. God has foreordained that some will not have eternal life. Scripture teaches this doctrine by implication, for if eternal life is the result of God's election, his grace, and his means of grace in history, then eternal death can only be, ultimately, the result of God's withholding of his electing grace. Surely, when he withholds grace, he is acting no less intentionally than when he gives it. The former is no less planned than the latter. And so, eternal rejection, like eternal election, is in accordance with an eternal divine plan. This is among the "all things" that God works according to the counsel of his will (Eph. 1:11).

Scripture also teaches this doctrine explicitly. As there is a book of life, so there is also a book of condemnation. Jude refers to certain men "whose condemnation was written about long ago" (v. 4).

We know that people perish because of unbelief. But people cannot believe unless God chooses them (John 8:47; 10:26; 12:39–40). God gives to some "the knowledge of the secrets of the kingdom of heaven" (Matt. 13:11), but not to others. The others' hearts are closed by God's decision. So Jesus speaks in parables to conceal the truth from those who are not chosen to know it (Matt. 13:13–14; cf. Isa. 6:9–10). God hides the truth from the wise and learned, and reveals it to his children, "for this was your good pleasure" (Matt. 11:25–26).

The central passage on reprobation is Romans 9. It deals with both historical and eternal reprobation, and that fact has confused some readers. But we must acknowledge at the outset that the primary issue that Paul faces here is that of Israel's salvation. He says:

> I have great sorrow and unceasing anguish in my heart. For I could wish that I myself were cursed and cut off from Christ for the sake of my brothers, those of my own race, the people of Israel. (vv. 2–4)[17]

In the ministries of Jesus, the apostles, and Paul himself, salvation is offered "to the Jew first, and also to the Greek" (Rom. 1:16 KJV). But most of the Jews reject the gospel, and the church becomes increasingly Gentile. Paul himself is a Jew, and he is in anguish over the unbelief of his fellow Israelites. This is no minor issue; their eternal salvation is at stake. Paul's wish that he could be cut off from Christ for the sake of Israel, if that were possible, implies that unless God acts in a new way, the Israelites themselves will be cursed and cut off from Christ. So the issue is not just that Israel will lose its historical election as God's distinctive people. That in itself is cause for rejoicing, for it means that God now calls all nations to himself. Rather, the problem is that individual Israelites will be eternally cut off from God.

Has God's word failed (9:6)? Normally, that word is "the power of God for the salvation of everyone who believes" (1:16). We should expect that as Paul and others preach the word, God's power will bring salvation to Israel. But, so far, that does not seem to be happening. Nonetheless, says Paul, the word of God does not fail.

How can the word be powerful for salvation when its hearers do not believe? Paul's answer is that not all Israelites are Israel (9:6): not all are elect (vv. 11–12).

Paul provides illustrations of election from the sphere of historical elec-

---

17. Cf. Rom. 10:1, "Brothers, my heart's desire and prayer to God for the Israelites is that they may be saved." Again, the issue is their eternal salvation.

tion. Isaac is chosen over Ishmael (vv. 7–9), and Jacob over Esau (vv. 10–13). However, we cannot say on the basis of Scripture that either Ishmael or Esau, or the national groups formed by their descendants, are eternally reprobate. Paul is not distinguishing here between historical and eternal election. Rather, he is focusing on the principles that these two forms of election have in common. In both cases, election is by grace, apart from works (v. 12). In all these cases, election is in accordance with God's purpose (v. 11) and calling (v. 12). Esau is reprobate (whether historically or eternally) before he is born (v. 11), hated by God (v. 13). It is impossible to avoid the conclusion that Paul is making the same point about the eternal election of unbelieving Israelites:[18] they reject Christ because God has not called them. They are reprobate by the sovereign decision of God.

Otherwise, the question of verse 14, "What then shall we say? Is God unjust?" makes no sense. This question arises only because, on Paul's view, Israel's unbelief is due to God's sovereign decision. If Israel's unbelief were due only to their free decision, no one could say that God was unjust to condemn them. And Paul emphasizes the point by quoting Exodus 33:19: "I will have mercy on whom I have mercy, and I will have compassion on whom I have compassion" (Rom. 9:15; cf. v. 18). And he adds, "It does not, therefore, depend on man's desire or effort, but on God's mercy" (v. 16).

Then Paul brings up the example of Pharaoh. God says he raised him up "that I might display my power in you and that my name might be proclaimed in all the earth" (v. 17).

Again a question arises:

> One of you will say to me: "Then why does God still blame us? For who resists his will?" But who are you, O man, to talk back to God? Shall what is formed say to him who formed it, "Why did you make me like this?" Does not the potter have the right to make out of the same lump of clay some pottery for noble purposes and some for common use? (vv. 19–21)

Paul might have said that God is just, because Pharaoh and the others made a free decision to reject God. That would have been true, as far as it goes. But Paul wants to present a deeper answer, because it is also his answer to the question of Israel's unbelief. His answer is that Israel's unbelief

---

18. Of course, one cannot assume that all of those Israelites who disbelieved the preaching of Paul were eternally reprobate. Paul doubtless realized that some might come to Christ at a later time. He is concerned about the great number of the Jews who have rejected the gospel. And his answer is that God has first rejected them: some perhaps temporarily, and others permanently.

comes from God's sovereign decision. In that light, we can understand also the next question: "What if God, choosing to show his wrath and make his power known, bore with great patience the objects of his wrath—prepared for destruction?" (v. 22). None of this compromises Israel's own responsibility. Paul stresses that, too, in 9:30–10:21. But then again, in 11:1–10, he emphasizes God's sovereignty. The remnant is "chosen by grace" (v. 5). The others are hardened by God, who gives them a spirit of stupor (vv. 7–10).

We should note three points about what the doctrine of reprobation does not teach:

1. The doctrine of reprobation does not prejudice the free offer of the gospel to all. We do not know who is elect and who is reprobate, so we must proclaim the gospel freely to all. And it remains entirely true that if anybody receives Christ, he will be saved (John 1:12–13; 3:16). Jesus brings together God's sovereignty and our responsibility when he says, "All that the Father gives me will come to me, and whoever comes to me I will never drive away" (John 6:37).

2. The doctrine of reprobation does not prejudice our assurance of salvation. That assurance is not based on our reading of the eternal decrees of God, which are secret unless God reveals them, but on the promises of God.

3. This doctrine does not imply that election and reprobation are parallel in every respect. They are equally ultimate in the sense that both decrees of God are ultimately efficacious.[19] However, there is an asymmetry between them. The blessings ordained by God's eternal election are received entirely by God's grace, apart from human works. But the curses ordained by God's eternal reprobation are fully deserved, because of the sins of the reprobate.[20]

THE ORDER OF THE DECREES

Many theologians have tried to establish an "order" for God's decrees. They agree that this order is not an order in time, for the decrees are all eternal. Rather, they are looking for a logical order, in some sense. These

---

19. The concept of equal ultimacy is confusing. To some writers, like G. C. Berkouwer, it appears to deny the asymmetry mentioned in the next sentence. In Van Til's writings, however, it simply means that both election and reprobation are efficacious decrees of God; they accomplish their purpose. See CVT, 86–88; see also G. C. Berkouwer, The Triumph of Grace in the Theology of Karl Barth (Grand Rapids: Eerdmans, 1956), 390; Berkouwer, Divine Election (Grand Rapids: Eerdmans, 1960), 172–217.

20. See the Canons of Dordt, 1.6.

theologians try to picture the process of God's thinking before he created the world. When human beings make plans, they plan to do A so that they can accomplish B: they fit means to ends. Some ends have a higher priority than others. So we order our plans by such principles as fitting means to ends and prioritizing things. Those arguing for an order of the decrees suppose that God planned creation and redemption in the same sort of way.

Another kind of order is that in which decree A creates the conditions for carrying out decree B. This appears to be the order that Paul follows in Romans 8:29–30:

> For those God foreknew he also predestined to be conformed to the likeness of his Son, that he might be the firstborn among many brothers. And those he predestined, he also called; those he called, he also justified; those he justified, he also glorified.

God's foreknowledge[21] created the relationship between himself and his people so that he could predestine them to be conformed to Jesus' likeness. His predestination grounds his calling of them, and so on.

It is true that God does things with goals and purposes in mind. For example, Genesis 3:22–23 says that God banished Adam and Eve from the Garden of Eden so that they would not eat from the tree of life. On that basis, thinking along the lines of the post-Reformation Reformed theologians, one might say that God's decree to prevent Adam and Eve from eating of the tree of life preceded his decree to banish them from the Garden. Here, the precedence is logical, not temporal: the decree of the means to achieve an end presupposes the decree of that end.

It is also true that God sets priorities. Not everything is equally important to him. Jesus speaks of some matters of God's law being more important than others (Matt. 23:23). In the Bible, Creation, the Fall, and redemption are far more important than anything else that happens. So those arguing for orders of decrees rightly ask us to imagine God setting priorities.

God certainly does plan event A in order to provide conditions for the realization of event B. However, I doubt that Romans 8:29–30 teaches such an order. Strictly speaking, that passage teaches only that the group of people who are foreknown is coextensive with the group that is predestined, and so on. Furthermore, Paul does not speak here of a series of divine decrees, but rather a series of divine actions. Some of these actions (foreknowing and predestining) are decrees, but the others (calling, justifying, and glorifying) occur in history. They are the results of decrees, but Paul

21. See our account of foreknowledge in chapter 4, summarized in footnote 13 of this chapter.

does not mention the decrees that govern them. His purpose is not to give us a look inside God's thought process, but to give us the assurance that all elect persons will persevere to the end, that everybody foreknown by God will be predestined, called, justified, and glorified.

From these considerations, two problems emerge in the discussion of the order of the decrees. First, there are different kinds of order: means-end order, priority order, and condition-realization order. Second, Scripture rarely, if ever, attempts to give a broad summary of the order of God's thoughts. It does present ends and means in particular cases, priorities in others, and conditions and realizations in others. But it never, to my knowledge, presents us with any general map of God's mind. We may reasonably say, on the basis of Scripture, that God's highest purpose is to glorify himself. But beyond that, I think that little can be said.

In Reformed theology, the two main views of the order of the decrees are *supralapsarianism* and *infralapsarianism*. The proposed orders are:

SUPRALAPSARIAN

1. To elect some creatable people for divine blessing.
2. To create.
3. To permit the Fall.
4. To send Christ to provide atonement.
5. To send the Spirit to apply the atonement to the hearts of believers.
6. To glorify the elect.

INFRALAPSARIAN

1. To create.
2. To permit the Fall.
3. To elect some people for divine blessing.
4. Same as supra.
5. Same as supra.
6. Same as supra.

The controversy about the order of the decrees focuses on the order of the first three decrees, and on the odd supralapsarian notion of a decree to elect "creatable" people.

For defenders of the supralapsarian view, the important point is that God's foremost concern in his decrees is to display his grace in a chosen people. Everything else is, roughly speaking, a means to that end. In order to give grace to those people, he must create them, permit the Fall, and redeem them. So decree 1 is related to the others as end to means. But decrees 2 and 3 are probably best construed as each providing the conditions necessary for the decrees after it to be accomplished. So there is no consistent pattern of order through the list. Perhaps the reason for giving priority to decree 1 over the others is that, for supralapsarians, God's care for the elect is so much more profound than his concern for the rest of creation that the other decrees are of far lesser importance.

The infralapsarian view makes no judgment as to God's foremost concern. It simply asks us to imagine the process as if God were thinking of the order in which events would occur. Here the governing principle is mostly what I have called condition-realization. It is therefore important to understand that the two lists have different concepts of order.[22]

For infralapsarians, the important point to remember is that God elects people out of the race of fallen people and conceives of them as fallen even in his planning before the Creation. The supralapsarians reply that to conceive of election this way is to make it less important in God's mind than it should be; it makes election somehow subordinate to the Creation and the Fall.

I believe that we should not take any position on the debate between infralapsarians and supralapsarians. In urging such agnosticism, I am standing with Herman Bavinck,[23] though my reasons are somewhat different from his:

1. The two positions equivocate on the meaning of *order* and therefore can't be precisely compared with one another.

2. Scripture never explicitly presents a complete and definitive order of thoughts in God's mind, in any of the relevant senses of *order*.

3. On the contrary, Scripture warns us against trying to read God's mind. His thoughts are not our thoughts (Isa. 55:8). This discussion runs great risks of engaging in speculation into matters God has kept secret. For example, to cite a principle commonly urged in the literature, do we really know that in God's decrees "the last in execution is the first in intent?"[24] But it is not necessarily true of a symphony that the most important chords are the last ones. Nor is the last scene of a novel necessarily the most important. Is the final judgment more important than Jesus' atonement? Surely, in these areas it is dangerous to presume that we can make value judgments. Why do we think we know so much about God's mind?

4. Surely, in one sense, all of God's decrees presuppose each other and exist for the sake of each other (see our discussion of "Creaturely Otherness" in chap. 8). God formulates each decree with all the others in view.

---

22. For a somewhat more elaborate account of this issue, see *DKG*, 264, in the context of the chapter.

23. *DG*, 382–94.

24. I take it that "first in intent" here means "of first importance," "of highest priority."

Each influences the others. This fact makes it very difficult to list decrees according to any of the proposed principles of order.

5. In God's mind, where the decrees take all others into account, all may be considered ends, and all may be considered means. They are all ends, because they all represent things God intends to do. And they are all means, because each decree supports the accomplishment of the others.

6. There are therefore reciprocal relationships among the purposes of God. He works miracles to attest prophecy, but he also ordains prophets to attest his mighty works. Creation provides the backdrop for redemption, but redemption restores creation. Redemption presupposes creation, but creation itself is in the image of redemption (see chap. 15).

7. I know of nothing in Scripture that settles the question whether God in eternity views the elect as "creatable" or as "created." Most likely, he views the elect both ways. He views us as creatable, because before creation we haven't been created yet, and because he might have chosen not to create us. Since our creation, viewed from eternity past, is only possible, not actual, God thinks of us as creatable. But he also views us as created, because he has in fact eternally decreed to create us, and because only after the decree of creation is accomplished can anything else happen to us. God views us in all states, actual and possible.

8. The question whether God envisions his elect as taken from a fallen humanity, or somehow existing apart from the Fall, does not make much sense. Certainly God foreordains that his elect will be redeemed from Adam's fallen race, and I can't imagine that supralapsarians would actually deny this.[25] And, equally certainly, God knows what they would be like, absent the effects of the Fall. So we should not imagine either that God thinks about the elect while somehow putting the Fall out of his mind, or that he does not have a purpose for his elect that transcends the particular pattern of history that he brings to pass. Infralapsarians are particularly concerned to avoid the first option, and supralapsarians the second. But these two concerns are not inconsistent with one another, and they should not have led to the creation of two parties in the Reformed churches.

9. Although decrees 4–6 suggest a relatively equal standing for all divine decrees, I do not deny that God has priorities. His own glory, of course, has

25. Perhaps supralapsarians fear that this understanding makes predestination dependent on God's foresight of the Fall. But recall my argument in chapter 8 that God's foreordination should not be completely separated from his knowledge, as if he foreordained things in ignorance. Furthermore, both positions correlate predestination with God's foresight in certain ways. The supralapsarians see God as decreeing creatable people, conceived as unfallen. But that is also a kind of foresight.

the highest priority. The eternal blessing of the elect in Christ is certainly an important means to that goal, and may itself be described as the goal of history. I argued in chapter 9 that the final state will be so great as to eliminate all sadness over evil. Earlier in this chapter, I argued that the goal of historical election is to manifest eternal election. So all of God's decrees are ends, but some ends are higher than others. We should honor the truth stated somewhat inchoately by the supralapsarians, namely, that the glorification of the elect in Christ, the fulfillment of the kingdom of God, is the goal of history.

10. When one tries to see the practical relevance of all of this, it seems to boil down to a question of the meaning of the Fall or, more generally, the problem of evil. The supralapsarian position is in danger of making moral evil seem tame, as a mere step upward toward the glorification of the elect. Infralapsarians better understand the horrible, inexplicable character of evil, but they find it more difficult to understand evil as part of a harmonious divine plan.[26]

11. Supralapsarians focus on the lordship attribute of control, emphasizing that even the Fall has an intelligible role to play in God's eternal plan. Infralapsarians focus more on the lordship attribute of authority, as if to say that we should not demand of God a rationale for evil, but should simply take him at his word that he is dealing with it in his own way. Both of these responses are biblical, as we saw in chapter 9. Perhaps our present need is not to debate these positions as if they were alternatives, but to ask God to cure the discomforts that create such questions—to deal with our hearts, as the Lord who is present in blessing and judgment.

---

26. Thanks to Vern Poythress for suggesting to me this observation and the next.

PART FIVE

BIBLICAL DESCRIPTIONS
OF GOD

CHAPTER 17

Names of God

As I indicated in chapter 13, Scripture reveals God to us by narrating his actions, by describing him, and by giving us a glimpse into his inner triune life. These three categories correspond roughly to our situational, normative, and existential perspectives, respectively. They are perspectivally related because they do not deal with three distinct subject matters, but the same subject matter seen from three different angles. That subject matter is the whole Bible. The whole Bible is narrative; it is also description and Trinitarian self-disclosure.

The three are also perspectivally related because a full account of each necessarily includes the others. God's actions cannot be fully understood without the descriptions and self-disclosures. Nor can we do full justice to the descriptions or to the self-disclosures without taking the other two into account. Nevertheless, they are different perspectives, emphases, or angles from which to look at the data. We cannot expound the biblical data exhaustively, even under one of the perspectives. Normally, we will pick up under one perspective something that we have missed under another. So each one adds information to the other two, and the three perspectives serve as checks and balances on one another.

In this chapter, we move from a consideration of God's actions in Scripture to the Bible's authoritative descriptions of him. Those descriptions contain another threefold distinction: names (like *yahweh* ["Lord"], *'elohim* ["God"], and *'el shadday* ["God Almighty"]), images (like shepherd, king, and rock), and attributes (like eternity, wisdom, and love). Although my threefold scheme becomes a bit arbitrary at this point, I'm inclined to re-gard God's names as existential (for they distinguish him uniquely as a per-son), his attributes as normative (for they provide the most literal and de-tailed descriptions, which necessarily therefore tend to govern our thinking about other kinds of descriptions), and his images as situational (for they describe God by analogy to finite historical realities of our experience and thereby show how he enters our experience). But we must remember that these perspectives should not be sharply separated from each another. All of these descriptions bear to some extent the qualities of the others.

Following the pattern of most systematic theologies, I shall be saying much more about the attributes than about the names and images. The rea-son is not that the attributes are more important than the others (except in the respect noted above), but because there has been more confusion and controversy about the attributes than about the other types of de-scription. The names and images, however, deserve more attention than they have received in the history of theology. Both names and images per-vade the Bible, no less than descriptions of attributes. And it is good for students of Scripture to use these names and images to focus and correct their understanding of God's attributes, as well as the other way around.

In this chapter, then, I will be considering, all too briefly, the names of God in Scripture.

NAMING AND DESCRIBING

Names are words that designate individual persons, places, or things, rather than classes of persons or things. They are "proper" nouns, there-fore, rather than "common" nouns. Since the main purpose of names is to denote or refer, their function is more denotative than connotative. That is, we use them to point out individuals, more than to describe them. Nev-ertheless, this distinction is not a sharp one. Common nouns, like *bird*, de-note a class of beings as well as describe them. And proper nouns, like Yah-weh, as we have seen, describe as well as denote.

In contemporary Western culture, names of persons tend to have little connotation, little descriptive significance. We give names to children mainly for their sound, their commonness or uncommonness, their con-nections with family members or other people, and their utility. Those con-siderations also motivated the giving of names in the ancient Near East. But in that culture, people also considered connotation more than we typ-ically do. They often chose names that expressed their hopes, confidence, fears, observations, understandings, or feelings. Adam named his wife Eve (meaning "living") "because she would become the mother of all the living" (Gen. 3:20). In naming her, he appropriated the redemptive promise of God that the human race would continue on from generation to generation and that one day a child of a woman would destroy the serpent (Gen. 3:15). Eve named her firstborn Cain (meaning "gotten" or "brought forth"), saying, "With the help of the Lord I have brought forth a man" (Gen. 4:1).

In Scripture, God often gives names to people, indicating their roles in his plan. He changes the name of Abram (meaning "exalted father") to Abraham ("father of a multitude") to memorialize his promise that Abraham's seed would become a great nation (Gen. 17:5). To Joseph, God's angel announced that Mary "will give birth to a son, and you are to give him the name Jesus, because he will save his people from their sins" (Matt. 1:21).

Similarly, God's names in Scripture are not merely denotative markers or labels. As we have seen in the case of Yahweh (the proper name of God *par excellence*), these names are full of meaning. They tell us much about their bearer. We have seen how God expounds his name to Moses in Exodus 34:6–7:

> The Lord [*yahweh*], the Lord, the compassionate and gracious God, slow to anger, abounding in love and faithfulness, maintaining love to thousands, and forgiving wickedness, rebellion and sin. Yet he does not leave the guilty unpunished; he punishes the children and their children for the sin of the fathers to the third and fourth generation.

Here and elsewhere he expounds his name by means of attributes expressed in adjectives ("compassionate" and "gracious"), phrases, and sentences. We have seen how Scripture also expounds *yahweh* in terms of the lordship attributes of control, authority, and presence, and in what we might call the "lordship images," such as king and covenant head.

God's names, then, connote attributes and images. The opposite is also true. The attribute *jealous* is a name of God in Exodus 34:14: "Do not worship any other god, for the Lord, whose name is Jealous, is a jealous God." The point is not that God is the only being who is ever jealous, but rather that his jealousy is unique and ultimate, and characterizes him in a basic way. Similarly, the attribute *holy* is used to name God by Isaiah, who regularly calls him "the Holy One of Israel." So he can be addressed by his attributes (as "O Most High" in Ps. 9:2). Images of God also function as names: "Hear us, O Shepherd of Israel" (Ps. 80:1).

The New Testament writers regularly use the word *Christ*, which was orig-

---

1. Similarly, Paul says in 1 Tim. 1:16 that only God is immortal.

CHRIST

inally a descriptive title indicating Jesus' fulfillment of messianic prophecy and his anointing with the Spirit, as a proper name. The word *lamb*, which provides an image of Jesus as an atoning sacrifice, is virtually a proper name in the book of Revelation.

So the distinction between God's names, attributes, and images is not sharp.

The fact that God reveals himself in descriptive names refutes the statements of general agnosticism that one often finds in theology.[2] It also refutes the notion that since God has many names,[3] we may freely use terms from non-Christian religions, philosophies, and experience to describe him. Elizabeth Johnson says that because God is unknowable, we need a "proliferation of names, images and concepts" to speak of him.[4] She mentions not only the variety of biblical names for God, but also those of Jewish tradition and the "ninety-nine names of Allah" in Islam,[5] as well as other names garnered from African religions.[6] At the end of her survey, she concludes that these "many names"

> are a heritage most useful to women's desire to emancipate speech about God. They shift the debate from the narrow focus on one or two patriarchal symbols to a field at once more ancient and more living. Along with biblical usage this classical legacy sketches out a place to stand in order to move speech about God into directions more sensitive to women's interpreted experience and ultimately more liberating for all creatures, human beings, and the earth.[7]

Johnson's overall purpose in the book is to commend feminine names for God, even to the exclusion of masculine names (because of past and present oppression of women). I shall say more about this project in my discussion of images. Here she says, in effect, that one cannot exclude feminine names of God, because God is really unknown, and therefore we have the right to use any name we think is appropriate, whether it comes from the Bible, Islam, African religions, or "women's interpreted experience."

But, as we have seen, Scripture does not justify any general assertion that God is unknowable. His names communicate definite content, and they

---

2. See chapters 7 and 11 for further discussion.
3. I am alluding to John Hick, *God Has Many Names* (London: Macmillan, 1980), a defense of religious pluralism.
4. Johnson, *She Who Is* (New York: Crossroad, 1996), 117. She quotes SCG, 1.31.4 in this connection.
5. Johnson, *She Who Is*, 119.
6. Ibid.
7. Ibid., 120.

GOD IS INCOMPREHENSIBLE NOT UNKNOWABLE

are part of a broader revelation that tells us about him—even his "essence" (see chap. 11)—in considerable detail. It is true that Scripture does not reveal God exhaustively. The multitude of biblical names, therefore, enables us to learn about him from many finite perspectives. But God is incomprehensible, not unknowable. He has revealed truth about himself. Thus, we are not free to roam about in non-Christian religious traditions or in general cultural experience seeking to supplement this revelation. We may use extrabiblical names for God if those terms convey authentic biblical teaching, as a means of applying biblical revelation to our times. Indeed, that happens when we translate the original languages of Scripture into modern languages. We may use new terms in order to apply revelation to our experience, evaluating that experience by Scripture, but we may not use that experience to add to or subtract from what God has revealed in his Word.

GOD'S NAME AND GOD HIMSELF

I have argued elsewhere that there is an identity between God's word and God himself, that God's word is always divine in character,[8] never merely creaturely. The same thing may be said of God's name. God's name is God himself, God in his self-revelation.

Scripture uses the term *name* to refer to individual names of God like *yahweh* and *'elohim*, and also in a more general sense, as in the expressions "how majestic is your name" (Ps. 8:1) and "call on the name of the LORD" (Ps. 116:17). It is possible that *name* in this general sense was originally an alternative to *yahweh*, since Scripture regards the revelation of the name *yahweh* as a highly significant event. Since *yahweh* is the name *par excellence*, it may be the specific name that the psalmists call upon in so many different contexts and situations. Or, *name* in the general sense may encompass all the names of God (and, by implication, all his attributes and images—all his revelation), meaning "God's revelation of himself." This would be similar to the usage in which *name* means "reputation" (as in Prov. 22:1) or "fame." For our purposes, it does not matter much whether in these cases *name* refers only to Yahweh or denotes all of God's self-revelation. For the name Yahweh, as we have seen, itself comprehends all that God reveals of himself. All that God does reveals his lordship, and, as we shall

---

8. See my *Perspectives on the Word of God* (Eugene, Oreg.: Wipf and Stock, 1999), 13–16. I hope to develop this argument at greater length in my forthcoming *Doctrine of the Word of God*. Note also chapter 22 of this volume.

see, all his attributes and self-disclosures also proclaim what he is to us, the Lord of the covenant.

So God's name is his self-revelation. *Name*, in the general sense, is a virtual synonym of *word*.[9] And, like *word*, it is a way of referring to God himself. There is an identity between God and his name, as between God and his word. As we sing praise to God, we sing praise to his name (e.g., Pss. 7:17; 9:2; 18:49); we give to him the glory due his name (29:2); we exalt his name (34:3) and fear it (61:5). God's name is an object of worship. Since in Scripture God alone is the proper object of worship, this language equates the Lord's name and the Lord himself.

Similarly, the name of God defends us (Ps. 20:1) and saves us (54:1). We trust in his name for deliverance (33:21). His name endures forever (72:17; 135:13). It "reaches to the ends of the earth" (48:10). It is holy and awesome (111:9). God guides us "for his name's sake" (23:3). In Isaiah 30:27, it is "the Name of the Lord" itself that comes to bring judgment on the nations and blessings on his people. So God's name has divine attributes and performs divine acts. In short, Scripture says about the name of God virtually everything it says about God.

So when God chooses to make his name dwell in a place (Deut. 12:5, 11, 21; 14:23–24; 1 Kings 8:29; 9:3; 2 Kings 23:27), that place becomes a location of his special presence. To say that God's name dwells in that place is to say that God himself dwells there. God's name is his glory: When Moses asks God to see his glory, he expounds his name (Ex. 33:18–19). (Also note the parallels between God's name and his glory in Ps. 102:15 and Isa. 59:19.) To say that God's name is "in" an angel is to say that the angel has the authority of God (Ex. 23:21). It is not surprising, then, that the third commandment of the Decalogue tells us not to misuse God's name (Ex. 20:7).

One of the most remarkable proofs of the deity of Christ, then, is that the New Testament uses his name just as the Old Testament uses the name *yahweh*. When the Jewish rulers ask Peter and John, "By what power or what name" they healed a crippled man, Peter replies, "It is by the name of Jesus Christ of Nazareth" (Acts 4:7–10). He concludes, "Salvation is found in no one else, for there is no other name under heaven given to men by which we must be saved" (v. 12; cf. v. 17). In Acts 5:41 we read, "The apos-

9. As I argued in *Perspectives on the Word of God*, the word of God does take written form, but the written word is not the only form of the word. The word also creates all things (Ps. 33:6) and directs the course of nature and history (Ps. 147:15–18). God's eternal decrees are words of God that govern all things. This broader use of *word* makes it even more congruent with the broader use of *name*.

tles left the Sanhedrin, rejoicing because they had been counted worthy of suffering disgrace for the Name" (cf. 9:21; 22:16). We see that *name* can be used as a substitute for *Jesus*, just as it substitutes for *yahweh* in the Old Testament, and that the name of Jesus has the same powers as the name of Yahweh. In Isaiah 45:23, Yahweh says, "Before me every knee shall bow; by me every tongue shall swear." In Romans 14:11, Paul applies this passage to God (*theos*), but in Philippians 2:10–11 he applies it to Christ:

> . . . that at the name of Jesus every knee should bow,
> in heaven and on earth and under the earth,
> and every tongue confess that Jesus Christ is Lord,
> to the glory of God the Father.

In Romans 10:13, Paul quotes Joel 2:32, "Everyone who calls on the name of the Lord will be saved." Joel speaks of the name of Yahweh; Paul speaks specifically of the name of Jesus. In Genesis 4:26, the family of Seth begins to "call on the name of the LORD," which indicates the beginnings of corporate worship. In 1 Corinthians 1:2, Paul describes the Christian church as "those everywhere who call on the name of our Lord Jesus Christ." We call on the name of Christ for salvation and to praise him. We pray for healing "in the name of the Lord" (James 5:14), referring to Jesus.

According to Matthew 28:19, we are to baptize "in the name of the Father and of the Son and of the Holy Spirit." Here is one name, threefold. *Son* and *Spirit* are on the same level as *Father*. Baptism is initiation to discipleship, and it places upon us the name that brings together Father, Son, and Spirit.

The reference to baptism indicates that we also are bearers of the holy name of God. In our case, the name is not ours by nature; it does not make us objects of worship. Rather, God's name dwells in us as it dwelled in the tabernacle. God places his name upon us, as he placed his name in the tabernacle. In the account of the Aaronic benediction, the priests, says Yahweh, "will put my name on the Israelites, and I will bless them" (Num. 6:27). Certainly the Trinitarian apostolic benediction of 2 Corinthians 13:14 has the same significance. So God's people "bear" his name (Jer. 14:9), and on this basis they pray to God for their deliverance (v. 21). We are temples of God's Spirit and thus bearers of his name.[10]

In a still broader sense, all creation bears the name of the Lord. As we saw earlier, God's covenant lordship extends over all the earth. He has made the world to be his temple, and of course his name must dwell in his temple. I believe that Jesus implies the presence of God's name in creation in

10. Cf. Rev. 3:12; 14:1; 22:4.

Matthew 5:33–37 (cf. 23:16–22), his exposition of the third commandment. There he addresses those who try to avoid the force of oaths by not using specific names of God. Rather than swearing by Yahweh or by God, they swear by heaven, earth, Jerusalem, or even by their own head. Jesus' answer is that heaven, earth, Jerusalem, and, yes, even our heads, are subject to God's sovereignty, so that to invoke anything in creation is to invoke God himself. If we swear, "May the heavens collapse if I fail to do this," only God can bring about that collapse or prevent it. If I swear, "May my hair turn white if I am lying," only God can enforce that oath. So, when we swear by created things, we are implicitly swearing by God himself, by his own name. That means that everything in creation is a dwelling place for God's name, a place of God's presence (see chap. 6).

The unity between God's name (or God's word) and God himself reinforces the doctrine of divine simplicity that I expounded in chapter 12. The qualities designated by God's names are not parts of God or mere external attachments to his essence. They are God.

NAME AND LORDSHIP

Names in general, and God's names in particular, reflect the lordship attributes of control, authority, and presence.

CONTROL

It has been thought in many cultures of the world that to know someone's name gives power over that person. In verbal magic, names have been used in curses to bring injury, and so on. Some thoughts of this sort may have been in the mind of Jacob (Gen. 32:29) or Moses (Ex. 3:13) when they were eager to know God's name.

As with all pagan belief, this idea is parasitic on the truth. All magic aside, knowing someone's name can give one power over that person. As we have seen, names in the ancient Near East typically conveyed truth about the person named, so to know a person's name was to have some knowledge about that person. And knowledge, of course, is power. A name also gives us a means of locating the bearer of that name: we call the name, and he answers.[11] So to know a name is to have some measure of control.

11. Here I am invoking finite reflections of the lordship attributes of authority (knowledge) and presence (location) to establish control. On the finite level, as well as the divine, the lordship attributes imply one another.

It is also true that to give a name is to exercise control. The powerful give names to the weak. It is the father who names the child, the conqueror who names the captured city, and God who names his creatures.

We might expect, then, that since nobody can have control over God, he would withhold from us the knowledge of his name. In Muslim theology, God's highest and truest name is unrevealed, and, as we have seen, some theologians in the Christian tradition have said that God is nameless. These statements are intended to protect God's sovereignty. But they do not agree with Scripture, in which God freely reveals his names to us.

He reveals his names, however, in such a way as to prevent any challenge to his sovereignty. His answers to the questions of Jacob and Moses (mentioned above) are somewhat veiled, and, as we have seen, the name Yahweh, which answers Moses' question, asserts God's sovereign lordship.

But there is a sense in which the revelation of God's names gives us some control over him.[12] For God's names are covenantal. The name Yahweh denotes him as Lord of the covenant, and the other names connote different aspects of his covenant relationship to us. As we have seen, the covenant includes promises to God's people and threats of judgment against the wicked. Thus, in making a covenant, God does bind himself.[13] He empowers his people to use his name to draw on his power. We pray in his name; we claim his promises; we use his name as a ground for expecting deliverance. Through that name, ultimately the name of Jesus, we prevail. But this empowerment is always subject to his power. Prayer in God's name is prayer "according to his will" (1 John 5:14), and such prayer is itself motivated by God's Spirit (Rom. 8:26–27; Eph. 6:18).

AUTHORITY

Giving a name is also an exercise of authority, for, as noted above, it is the authority figure who names the one under his authority. When names

---

12. Note that in the context of his request for God's name, Jacob has "overcome" the divine angel in a wrestling match (Gen. 32:28)—ironically speaking, of course, and with injury to his hip. In the fight, he was seeking God's blessing. The prophet Hosea sees the wrestling as a weeping, a begging for God's favor (12:4). God's people still prevail over him as they beg for his blessings, calling on his name in prayer.

13. This doctrine may be described as "God limiting his sovereignty," but God does not limit his sovereignty as Arminians claim he does, by allowing libertarian freedom to man. The limit we are considering does not detract in the least from God's full control of every event in history. In the covenant, God binds himself to act only as he has eternally determined to act. But, as we saw in chapter 8, each part of God's eternal plan limits other parts. So when God sovereignly determines to give promises to his people, he binds himself to keep those promises.

connote meaningful content, the name is an authoritative interpretation of the one who is named. When God names people, as when he changed the name of Abram to Abraham, the given name authoritatively describes who that person is.

God's answer to Moses in Exodus 3:14 indicates that he reserves to himself the right to say who he is. But it also reveals who he is: the Lord, with all the content and implications of his lordship.

Presence

We give names also to locate persons, places, and things. Once we give a name, that label enables us to draw a map or to ask another person where something is. In the case of persons, we can call the name and expect an answer. For wherever the person is, he will respond to his name.

There is a close identity between ourselves and our names. When someone laughs at your name, or mispronounces it, you often feel slighted. This is even more true of our name in the broader sense of "reputation." To injure my good name is to injure me; to revere my name is to revere me.

As we have seen, there is a similar identity between God's name and God himself. To praise his name is to praise him. To despise his name is to despise him. The name has all of God's attributes and performs all of his acts. It is his presence in the world.

SOME NAMES OF GOD

As the name of God is equivalent to his being, his individual names connote qualities that are identical to his simple essence.[14] Since they are all names of the same person, their meanings tend to converge. Their connotations differ from one another only in rather subtle ways.

When considering the divine names, we must avoid the tendency of many theologians to try to gain meaning from etymology. Etymologies of these terms are uncertain, and even if they were certain, they would not be an adequate guide to the actual usage of the biblical writers.[15] Thus, my comments below on the most common Hebrew names for God (and some of their Greek equivalents) will be based on the actual use of these terms, rather than on etymology.

14. On this point, see the discussion of simplicity in chapter 12.
15. Like many theological errors, reliance on etymology is an instance of the genetic fallacy: judging present usage on the basis of past usage alone.

Yahweh

I have considered the Hebrew name *yahweh* at length, specifically in chapters 2–6, and more broadly by using divine lordship as the main theme of this entire book. To summarize, *yahweh* names God as holy and personal, the Lord, the head of covenants with Israel, with the nations, and with the whole creation. His lordship draws our attention particularly to his control and authority over all creatures and his presence in the created world. And, as we shall see, these lordship attributes are displayed in the many other qualities attributed to God in Scripture.

'Adon

The name *'adon* means "Lord" or "Master," stressing God's ownership of his creation. (Mal. 1:6 is a good example.) With the suffix *-ay*, it becomes *'adonay*, "my Lord." The emphasis on God's ownership of the world is already implicit in *yahweh*, as we have seen, and that ownership implies the other lordship attributes, so the meanings of the two terms are very similar.

When the Jews came to regard *yahweh* as too holy to be pronounced, they evidently substituted *'adonay* for *yahweh* in reading the Hebrew text. So the Greek translators used *kyrios* (=*'adonay*) as their translation of *yahweh*. Because of this development, what differences of nuance there may originally have been between *yahweh* and *'adonay* faded away over time. I am not convinced that there are any substantial differences between these terms as used in Scripture, when they are used of God.[16] So in this book I treat *yahweh*, *'adonay*, and *kyrios* as synonyms when they are used as divine names.

'Elohim

Unlike *'adon*, the name *'elohim* (translated by the Greek *theos* and the English *God*) does have uses somewhat distinct from those of *yahweh*. It is the general term that includes all gods, false as well as true. So *'elohim* designates the gods of the nations (e.g., Pss. 86:8; 95:3; 97:9; 135:5; Isa. 36:18; 37:12) in contrast to *yahweh*: "All the gods ['*elohim*] of the nations are idols, but the LORD [*yahweh*] made the heavens" (Ps. 96:5). *'Elohim* also occasionally designates human beings whom God has placed in positions of authority (Ps. 82:1, 6 and probably Ex. 21:6; 22:7–9). There is a close rela-

---

16. Of course, I should mention that *yahweh* is used only of God, but that *'adonay* and *kyrios* can be used of men as well.

tionship between God himself and human authority appointed by God (Ex. 4:16; 7:1; 18:15–19; 22:28; Rom. 13:1–6). But most often in Scripture, *'elohim* refers to the true God.

As the most general or generic term for God, *'elohim* tends to be prominent in contexts in which God is dealing with the creation in general or with the nations of the world apart from his covenant with Israel. It is the only divine name in Genesis 1:1–2:4a, which describes God's creation of all things. After 2:4a, the name *yahweh* enters the narrative in the compound form *yahweh 'elohim*, "the Lord God." The narrative after 2:4a begins the story of God's covenants with man, the story of the Fall and redemption; accordingly, Moses refers to *yahweh* at this point, anticipating the Exodus covenant.[17] In Ecclesiastes, Daniel, and Jonah 1:6; 3:5–10, where God is dealing generally with mankind or with the nations outside Israel, *'elohim* is prominent.

So we might be tempted to think that *'elohim* represents God outside the covenant. However, that would not be accurate. Creation itself is covenantal, as I argued in chapter 15. God's relationship with the creation is deeply analogous (though not identical) to his relationship with his covenant people. Furthermore, *'elohim* is prominent in the Flood narrative and in the covenant with Noah following the Flood (Gen. 6–9). Also, the expressions "your God" (*'elohekem*) and "our God" (*'elohenu*) are often used in parallel with *yahweh*, sometimes even without it (Ex. 3:18; 5:3; Isa. 40:1), to indicate God's special covenantal relationship with his people. And the expressions *'elohe yisra'el* ("the God of Israel") (Ex. 34:23) and *'el 'elohe yisra'el* ("God, the God of Israel") (Ezra 6:22; Pss. 68:8; 72:18) have rich covenantal associations.[18] In these phrases, God's relationship to Israel is so close that the name of Israel becomes a part of God's own name. As he has placed his name on them (Num. 6:27), he takes their name to himself.

In the New Testament, the apostle Paul uses *theos*, the Greek equivalent of *'elohim*, in contexts describing God's relationship to all the peoples

17. A cornerstone of liberal biblical criticism over the last one hundred and fifty years has been the assertion that because different divine names are used in Gen. 1:1–2:4a and 2:4b–3:24, the two passages must have been written by different authors. From this theory came the partitioning of the Pentateuch into many tiny bits, supposedly pieced together from longer documents written by four, or eight, or many more authors. The arguments supposedly proving these hypotheses are quite absurd. It is entirely sufficient to explain the use of the divine names in Gen. 1–3 by the theological distinction noted above. See Oswald T. Allis, *The Five Books of Moses* (Philadelphia: Presbyterian and Reformed, 1943), and the criticism of the documentary hypothesis by the atheist philosopher Walter Kaufmann in *Critique of Religion and Philosophy* (New York: Harper, 1958).

18. Compare "God of Abraham, Isaac, and Jacob" (Ex. 3:6, 15; 4:5; Matt. 22:32; Acts 3:13; 7:32).

of the world (Rom. 1:18–32 is a good example), following the Old Testament pattern. But he also uses *theos* in other contexts as a name for God the Father, in contrast to *kyrios* (vv. 4–6). Paul's practice does not call into question the deity of the Son. *Kyrios* is the Greek translation of the Hebrew *yahweh*, and it is certainly as much of a divine title as *theos*. This is Paul's Trinitarian terminology: *theos, kyrios, and pneuma* ("Spirit"). In this Trinitarian usage, *theos* (=*'elohim*) is God the Father of our Lord Jesus Christ, and so our Father by faith in Jesus. The Trinitarian use of *theos*, therefore, is profoundly covenantal.

So the distinction between *'elohim* and *yahweh* is one of nuance and emphasis, rather than a difference of substantive content. Everything that can be said using *yahweh* can also be said using *'elohim*, and vice versa. That fact should not be surprising, for both are names of the same infinite person.

'Elohim is a plural noun in Hebrew, but it regularly takes singular verbs. It is not a plural of majesty (as when kings and queens refer to themselves as "we"), for there is no evidence of such a use of the plural during the biblical period. Nor is there any evidence to indicate that this form is a remnant of polytheism. Christians are often inclined to take this plural as evidence of the Trinity, especially when God refers to himself with plural pronouns and verbs, as in Genesis 1:26, "Let us make man in our image."

I regard the word initially as a plural of abstraction, that is, "a more or less intensive focusing of the characteristics inherent in the idea of the stem . . . rendered in English by forms in *-hood, -ness, -ship*."[19] As I mentioned above, *'elohim* is a generic term, and thus can be used to refer to false gods and human godlike authorities, as well as the true God. Hebrew uses the plural form for abstract nouns such as *youth, old age, maidenhood,* and *life*. It may also (or alternatively) carry some force as a plural of amplification. Usually found in poetry, this plural is an emphatic statement of the root idea, as *might* (Isa. 40:26) and *counsel* (Deut. 32:28).[20] Certainly such a plural would be appropriate to designate the Trinity, for the Trinity is both an abstraction,[21] as the totality of three persons, and an amplification, as the threefold repetition of the divine nature. But it would not be possible to prove from the plurality of *'elohim* that God is triune, or even that he is a plurality of persons with a single nature. The plural utterances, as in Gen-

---

19. A. E. Cowley, *Gesenius' Hebrew Grammar* (Oxford: Clarendon Press, 1910), 396.

20. For other examples and references, see ibid., 397.

21. I am using *abstraction* to correlate with grammatical abstraction. The Trinity is abstract in the sense that it includes the three persons as three particulars. But *abstract* often connotes impersonality, and the triune God is supremely personal. Also, *abstract* might suggest that there are other Trinitarian beings, though the triune God is unique. In these respects, the term *abstract* is inappropriate.

esis 1:26, may refer to an engagement of the heavenly hosts, the "divine council."[22]

'EL

'El is another name for God that seems to connote might and power, but what name of God does not connote these attributes? Its relation to 'elohim is uncertain. It may be a short form of 'elohim (as yah is a short form of yahweh in Ps. 68:4), or it may have another derivation.

'EL SHADDAY

'El shadday is the name that God gives to himself in the covenant with Abraham:

> When Abram was ninety-nine years old, the LORD appeared to him and said, "I am God Almighty ['el shadday]; walk before me and be blameless. I will confirm my covenant between me and you and will greatly increase your numbers." (Gen. 17:1–2)

In Exodus 6:3, God says to Moses:

> I appeared to Abraham, to Isaac and to Jacob as God Almighty ['el shadday], but by my name the LORD [yahweh] I did not make myself known to them.

This statement should not be taken to mean that the name yahweh was unknown in the patriarchal period. It is common in the Genesis narrative,[23] and it is found in people's names of that time. The point of Exodus 6:3 is that 'el shadday was the name taken by God as the covenant head over Abraham and his family, and it took on the connotations of that covenant; yahweh served a similar function for God's covenant with Moses and Israel. Yahweh brings to mind all the promises, deliverances, laws, and judgments of the Mosaic covenant. God did not make himself known to the patriarchs in these specific ways. Rather, as 'el shadday, he reminded them of the Abrahamic promises and blessings.

The use of 'el shadday (or simply shadday) reinforces its connection with the Abrahamic covenant. It is used six times in Genesis, in Exodus 6:3, and

---

22. See Meredith G. Kline, *Images of the Spirit* (Grand Rapids: Baker, 1980).

23. That may, of course, be anachronistic, granted Mosaic authorship. Moses may simply have taken the prerogative of using the name for God most familiar to his readers of the post-Exodus era.

elsewhere in the Pentateuch only in Numbers 24:4 (the Balaam prophecy). It is found twice in Ruth (Naomi's lament),[24] rarely in the Psalms and Prophets, but quite often in Job. The references in Job are one reason why many scholars believe that the book of Job reflects the patriarchal period. The Greek equivalent, *pantokratōr*, is found rarely through most of the New Testament: never in the Gospels, and in Paul's epistles only in 2 Corinthians 6:18, an Old Testament quotation. But in the book of Revelation, it returns as a frequent name of God. There it is regularly used in phrases like "Lord God Almighty" (*kyrios ho theos ho pantokratōr*, Rev. 4:8), suggesting that in the consummation of history, we will praise God in all his covenant names, including *yahweh*, *'elohim*, and *shadday*. In Jesus, all of God's covenant promises converge; in him, all are "Yes" and "Amen" (2 Cor. 1:20).

Like the other divine names, *shadday* connotes might and power,[25] but it takes its specific meaning from the covenant history of the time of Abraham, Isaac, and Jacob. This covenant history is a perpetual aspect of Israel's community memory: Yahweh's immediate self-identification, first to Moses (Ex. 3:6) and then to Israel (v. 15), is that he is the God of Abraham, Isaac, and Jacob.[26] The God of Moses is the same God as the God of Abraham. *Shadday* reminds the Israelites of God's dealings with their pre-Exodus ancestors; *yahweh* reminds them especially of the Exodus deliverance and beyond.

So *'el shadday* is the God who promises to make Abraham a great nation, through which all the peoples of the earth will be blessed (Gen. 12:2–3). He is the God who fulfills these promises even when their fulfillment is greatly delayed and seems laughable (Gen. 18:12–15; 21:6). He is the one who can bring life out of death (Rom. 4:17, 19). It is Jesus, therefore, who fulfills the promise of *'el shadday*.

Compound Names

We have seen that Scripture often combines the names of God into phrases like *Lord God* and *Lord God Almighty*. We also find these names as-

---

24. Balaam was a Moabite, and Naomi was a Jew living in Moab. Moab himself, the founder of that nation, was Lot's son by his older daughter (Gen. 19:37). So in these two references there is also a patriarchal connection. Both Balaam and Naomi were wanderers in pagan territory, like Abraham. They knew God, but were not settled among God's people. Balaam came to a bad end, but Naomi received divine blessing.

25. It does not, precisely speaking, refer to divine omnipotence, but to God's supremacy over all others, his universal rule. See chapter 23.

26. And of Moses' own father (v. 6), and so, by implication, of all the generations between Jacob and Moses.

sociated closely with certain adjectives, nouns, or verbs. One that occurs rather often, beginning in 1 Samuel (but only in the Old Testament), is *yahweh tseva'oth* (often transliterated *sabbaoth*), "Lord of hosts."[27] A host is a multitude. In Scripture, it refers to the heavenly bodies (Gen. 2:1; Deut. 4:19) and to multitudes of people, especially armies (Gen. 21:22; Ex. 14:4). *Lord of hosts*, therefore, has sometimes been understood to mean "the Lord of the heavenly bodies," and, by other interpreters, "the Lord of the armies of Israel." In 1 Samuel 17:45, young David uses the phrase in apposition to "the God of the armies of Israel," as he approaches Goliath.

However, the phrase, like other divine names, tends to indicate God's vast power, more than enough to overcome any human opposition. If he were *merely* "Lord of the armies of Israel," his power would be the power of a human force. But the power implied by *Lord of hosts* is supernatural: in Isaiah 9:6–7, the child who is "Wonderful Counselor" will reign on David's throne forever, establishing an everlasting kingdom of justice and peace. The prophet says, "The zeal of the LORD Almighty [*yahweh tseva'oth*] will accomplish this." But this great redemptive consummation will not be accomplished by earthly armies.

The key to the meaning of this phrase can be found in Joshua 5:14, where Joshua, the captain of Israel's armies, meets a supernatural being who introduces himself as "commander of the army of the LORD." That this being is an appearance of God himself is evident in verse 15, where, as in Moses' meeting with God in Exodus 3, he asks Joshua to remove his shoes, honoring the "holy" place where he stands. Earlier, in Genesis 32:2, Jacob saw the angels of God arrayed as an army. And in 2 Kings 6:16–17, God opens the eyes of Elisha's servant to see heavenly horses and chariots around Elisha, indicating that "those who are with us are more than those who are with them [i.e., the Aramean invaders]."

Lord of hosts, then, speaks of God as the commander of the angelic armies. These armies fight on Israel's side when Israel is faithful to God. Note that, in Deuteronomy 20, all of Israel's wars are holy wars, to be won, not by superior manpower (note all the draft exemptions!), but by the Lord's blessing. So God's covenant provides that Israel's army will include the angelic armies when they fight according to God's law. Otherwise (as in Josh. 7), they will fight in their own strength and lose.

There is a connection, then, between the heavenly armies and the

27. The NIV translates this as "Lord Almighty," which causes some confusion with *shadday* and robs the reader of a significant image. Certainly *tseva'oth* does connote God's might, as do virtually all the names of God; however, this name also provides us with a remarkable picture of his might, namely, the heavenly armies under his command.

armies of Israel. We do not need to choose between them. But the supernatural power implicit in the phrase comes from its reference to the heavenly armies. In 1 Samuel 17:45, the phrase *Lord of hosts* may mean "God of the armies of Israel," in the larger sense including the angelic hosts, or it may refer only to the angelic hosts as the source of Israel's military power.

'*El 'elyon* (sometimes just '*elyon*), translated "Most High God," is the divine name associated with Melchizedek in Genesis 14:18–22. The Moabite prophet Balaam also uses this name in Numbers 24:16, so one gets the impression that this was an old name for God, known even before the calling of Abraham. It is also used in Deuteronomy 32:8, which speaks of "the Most High" giving the nations their inheritance. The phrase also occurs often in Daniel, the language of which frequently reflects its Babylonian setting. But we find frequent use of the phrase also in the Psalms, so there is no doubt that Israel understood it as referring to Yahweh, the one true God.

Using the Greek equivalent *hypsistos*, the New Testament speaks of God dwelling "in the highest" (Matt. 21:9; Luke 2:14) and being "the Most High" (Luke 1:32, 35, 76; 6:35). The term also occurs in references to the Old Testament (Acts 7:48; Heb. 7:1) and, interestingly, in the speech of demons (Luke 8:28; Acts 16:17).

'*Elyon* simply means "high," and it can refer to the position of objects (as in Gen. 40:17) or to the exaltation of kings and nations (as in Deut. 28:1). In chapter 7, I argued that although God may be said to dwell in a literal place (the "true temple," a consummate manifestation of his special presence) higher than the earth, the main thrust of Scripture's teaching about God's transcendence is metaphorical. The metaphor of height refers to the reality of God's control and authority. He is exalted as the king. Certainly the biblical use of '*elyon* confirms this judgment. God is "high," not merely as an object is high, but as a king or nation is exalted: by his dominion over all things.

Scripture also mentions a number of compound names with *yahweh* that commemorate particular events in the history of redemption. These serve sometimes as names of altars and places, and at other times merely as significant descriptions. They are not repeated frequently in Scripture, as are the names we have previously discussed; rather, they tend to be associated closely with one narrative or prophecy. Nevertheless, God presents them with a kind of formality, which suggests that they have a continuing importance and should be remembered.

Among these is *yahweh yir'eh* ("Jehovah Jireh," "The Lord Will Provide"), which in Genesis 22:14 names the place where God provided a ram as a sacrifice. The ram was a substitute for Isaac, Abraham's son. Isaac fulfilled

God's promise that he would give a son to Abraham and Sarah who would become a great nation. But in Genesis 22, God tells Abraham to sacrifice Isaac. The ram shows that God provides the means to give us life in place of the death that we deserve at his hand. So it speaks of Christ in his substitutionary death for our sins, God's ultimate provision.

In Exodus 15:25–26, God sweetens bitter water and promises that if Israel heeds his law, none of the diseases that he brought on the Egyptians will come upon them. He concludes, "For I am the LORD, who heals you [yahweh rof'eka]." The Messiah, in prophecy (Isa. 35:5–6) and in history (Matt. 15:30; Luke 7:22), heals diseases. Disease in Scripture is the result of sin;[28] so healing is part of redemption. In the resurrection of our bodies, God will heal all our diseases, because he has healed our sin, in Christ.

In Exodus 17, Israel prevails against Amalek as long as Moses' hands are raised. They win the battle because Aaron and Hur hold up Moses' hands until victory comes. The raising of hands is, here and elsewhere in Scripture, an appeal to God. So,

> Moses built an altar and called it The LORD is my Banner [yahweh nissi]. He said, "For hands were lifted up to the throne of the LORD. The LORD will be at war with the Amalekites from generation to generation." (vv. 15–16)

Rather than holding up a banner extolling Israel's glory, Moses held up his hands to God. The Lord was his banner. Israel prevailed only by God's grace. The war with Amalek was a spiritual battle against a people seeking to destroy God's kingdom. In such a battle, only the armor of God will prevail (Eph. 6:10–20), but that is the armor with which God himself fights our battles (Isa. 59:15–17). Jesus has worn the armor to bring in God's kingdom against all opposition.

In several passages in the Law, God reminds Israel that "I am the LORD, who makes you holy [yahweh meqaddishekem]" (Ex. 31:13; Lev. 20:8; cf. Ezek. 37:28). Compare "Be holy, because I am holy" (Lev. 11:44; 19:2; 20:7; 21:8; 1 Peter 1:15–16). God in Christ makes his people a holy nation, because he, the holy one, is their God. He separates them from all the nations of the world to be his own, and he requires their behavior to image his.

When Gideon was afraid that he would die after seeing the angel of the Lord face-to-face, the Lord reassured him, "Peace! Do not be afraid. You are not going to die" (Judg. 6:23). So Gideon built an altar, named "The LORD is Peace" (yahweh shalom) (v. 24). Scripture teaches us that Jesus is

---

28. As I did in chapter 9, I should note that this is a general proposition. I do not intend to say that each illness is the result of specific sins committed by the sick person.

the Prince of Peace, who reconciles us to God, so that we may enter his presence without dying in his wrath.

The Messiah is also called, in Jeremiah 23:6, "The LORD Our Righteousness" (*yahweh tsidqenu*), for he will bring righteous rule to his people. Here the "branch" of David, David's descendant, is divine (*yahweh*) as well as human. And his own righteousness becomes our righteousness, a remarkable Old Testament picture of our justification by God's grace (see Rom. 3:20–24; 4:18–25; 2 Cor. 5:21).

The last verse of Ezekiel's prophecy (48:35) names the city, the new Jerusalem in which God consummates the redemption of his people. The name is "THE LORD IS THERE" (*yahweh shammah*). This name describes the ultimate and inseparable relationship between God and his people, the fulfillment of God's covenant presence, Immanuel, Jesus. Our ultimate blessing in glory is not the streets of gold or the endless banquet, but the presence of the Lord himself, the God who is there.

The *yahweh* compounds, then, all speak of redemption, from a number of perspectives. They tell us that God is so intent on redeeming his people from sin and all its effects, that he names himself in many words as their Savior. We should think of him as provider, healer, war banner, sanctifier, peace, righteousness, and presence, and we should find all of these in Jesus.

yahweh yir'eh	The Lord will provide	Christ our substitute
yahweh rof'eka	The Lord our healer	Christ – healer of our sin + at our glorification; the healer of all our diseases
yahweh nissi	The Lord our banner	Christ our victory
yahweh meqaddisheken	The Lord who makes us holy	Christ our sanctifier makes us holy
yahweh shalom	The Lord is peace	Christ our reconciler
yahweh tsidqenu	The Lord our righteousness	Christ our righteousness who justifies us
yahweh shammah	The Lord is there	Christ who is always present

CHAPTER 18

Images of God

In the last chapter, I distinguished three kinds of authoritative descriptions of God that are revealed in Scripture: names, images, and attributes. Having looked briefly at the divine names, we now proceed to biblical images of God.

Images tend to be more concrete than names or attributes. In an image, the biblical writer presents a vivid picture, comparing God to some person or thing in human experience, such as a king, a father, a shepherd, a light, or a shield. Literary images are powerful teaching devices, especially for those of us who learn best from what we visualize.

For example, God's unchangeability can be hard for us to conceptualize. But Psalm 102:25–27 helps us by presenting an image:

> In the beginning you laid the foundations of the earth,
>   and the heavens are the work of your hands.
> They will perish, but you remain;
>   they will all wear out like a garment.
> Like clothing you will change them
>   and they will be discarded.
> But you remain the same,
>   and your years will never end.[1]

---

1. I owe this illustration to John W. Sanderson, *Mirrors of His Glory: Images of God from Scripture* (Phillipsburg, N.J.: Presbyterian and Reformed, 1991), an excellent book on biblical imagery of God.

We sometimes say that a picture is worth a thousand words. Biblical images of God are pictures in words, so the adage is not directly applicable. But the truth in it helps us to see the special value and importance of imagery in Scripture. "The LORD is my shepherd" (Ps. 23:1) teaches us a great many things about God at once, without stretching our powers of abstract conceptualization.

Of course, like everything in Scripture, imagery is subject to interpretation. The reader must consider how God is like a shepherd. Shepherds shear wool from their sheep; does God do something analogous to that? To understand images, then, we must look at other biblical teaching about God, including divine acts, names, attributes, and Trinitarian self-expressions. In this way, Scripture interprets itself.

Despite its need for interpretation, the imagery of Scripture has generated surprisingly little interpretive controversy. Many theological battles have been fought over God's attributes and actions, but very few over God's names and images. "The Lord is my shepherd" seems to many of us to be a simple and obvious truth, but "[God] works out everything in conformity with the purpose of his will" seems very difficult and controversial. Perhaps the reason is that images and names do not convey as much theological detail as descriptions of acts and attributes do. Or perhaps the names and images are more pedagogically efficient, communicating truth concisely and vividly, leaving us little opportunity to argue and debate.

I will not contend for the primacy of any of these forms of revelation over the others.[2] They interpret one another, as we have seen. Furthermore, it is not always easy to distinguish them. *Yahweh tseva'oth* ("Lord of hosts") is both a name and an image, as are all of the compound names of God. *'El shadday* ("God Almighty") names God by referring to an attribute. When an attribute or image is used, often as a way of addressing God, it takes on the qualities of a name. "Father" is an image, but also a name, at least in the New Testament. As we have seen, God's names in Scripture have both denotation and connotation, and their connotations can be spelled out in terms of divine attributes, acts, and images. And God's images can be transformed easily (though with literary awkwardness) into

---

2. The unsigned article "God," in *DBI*, 332, says, "Though it is right and proper to explore the person and work of God in each of these ways [names, attributes, and roles], it is primarily through images that God opens up to us and reveals something of his divine nature, purposes, character and activities." The author offers no evidence for this extreme assertion, and, enthusiastic as I am about biblical imagery, I see no reason to accept it. Compare a similar statement on p. 335, claiming that images are "more basic" than concepts of God and that images, therefore, "are the foundation on which all other thinking about God takes place."

attributes: God is fatherly, kingly, shepherdly, illuminative, lionlike (leonine), etc.

Names, images, and attributes, then, are perspectivally related: they tell us the same truths about God in different ways. The whole Bible may be seen as a literary image of God's nature and action. God's actions in history present images of him. I find it interesting that the *Dictionary of Biblical Imagery* regularly converts divine acts into images. Since Psalm 139:13–16 speaks of God knitting us together in our mother's womb, the *DBI* writer speaks of an image of God as "knitter."[3] On this basis, any description of God's acts presents an image. I confess that I find this a trifle amusing, but certainly not wrong. When God creates, he is an artisan; when he heals, he is a physician. So the whole Bible consists of divine images. But we have seen that the whole Bible is also an exposition of God's name, so that we may all know that he is the Lord.[4] And it is also, in its entirety, a conceptual description of God's nature, his lordship attributes, and all the qualities included in them.

THE THEOLOGICAL POSSIBILITY OF IMAGES

But how are images of God possible? As we have seen, God is transcendent (chap. 7) and incomprehensible (chap. 11). Indeed, between God and creatures there is no identity without difference. God's love is not the same as human love, for it is the source and standard of all other love. The same can be said of all God's qualities. Since God's attributes are identical to himself (see chap. 12), they are not identical to the attributes of any creature. Everything in God is different from everything in creation. How, then, is it possible for creatures to picture God?

Indeed, God specifically forbids certain kinds of images. The second commandment forbids the making of idols, which are images used as objects of worship (Ex. 20:4–6), and God's hatred of idolatry is a major biblical theme. Against the idolaters, God asks,

> To whom, then, will you compare God?
> What image will you compare him to? (Isa. 40:18; cf. 46:5)

The Bible, however, leaves no doubt that there are legitimate images of God. Man himself is God's image and likeness (Gen. 1:26–27; 5:1; 9:6; 1 Cor. 11:7; James 3:9). The Second Adam, Jesus Christ, is the image (like-

---

3. "God," in *DBI*, 334.
4. See chapters 2 and 3.

ness, form) of God in an even stronger sense, befitting his divine nature and his perfect humanity (2 Cor. 4:4; Phil. 2:6; Col. 1:15; Heb. 1:3). In him, God renews us in the divine image (Rom. 8:29; 1 Cor. 15:49; Col. 3:10).

The nonhuman creation also reflects and reveals God, though Scripture does not directly designate it as an image of God:[5]

> The heavens declare the glory of God;
>   the skies proclaim the work of his hands. (Ps. 19:1)

Through creation, "God's invisible qualities—his eternal power and divine nature—have been clearly seen, being understood from what has been made," by all people (Rom. 1:20). Note the visual language here: invisible things are clearly seen. Creation is a visual representation, an image, of God.[6]

And, as we have seen, Scripture abounds in images that compare God with human beings and other creatures.

But how can this be, if God is transcendent, incomprehensible, and indeed incomparable to anything in the world? In chapter 7, I argued that God's transcendence is not distance or absence; rather, he is present, as Lord. In chapter 11, I emphasized that the incomprehensibility of God is not opposed to his knowability or even to the literal truth of God's revelation. God arouses our awe, our amazement, our confessions of ignorance, even when he is best known to us.

Furthermore, when God through Isaiah speaks of his incomparability, it is in a context of worship. The specific question is whether we should see idols as legitimate competitors of God for human adoration. And of course the answer is no. The discrepancy between God and his rivals is so great that idols and their makers amount to "nothing" and are even "less than nothing" (Isa. 41:24, 29; 44:10). God is not here relegating the idols and the idol makers to a realm of metaphysical non-being; he is making the point that idolatrous worship is worthless. Similarly, God is not incomparable in a general metaphysical-epistemological sense, so that we are forbidden to compare him to anything. Rather, he is so much greater than the idols that the pretensions of the false religions are utterly ridiculous.[7]

Nor does the second commandment make the claim that God cannot

---

5. Adam and Christ, with all humanity in Adam and in Christ, are *the* image of God, the image *par excellence*. But this fact does not prevent the rest of creation from imaging God in various respects. A man images God in many more ways than does a rock. But the rock still reveals its maker.

6. For a profound discussion of creation as an image of God, see Meredith G. Kline, *Images of the Spirit* (Grand Rapids: Baker, 1980).

7. Notice the satire of idolatry in Isa. 44:12–20.

be imaged. Rather, it forbids Israel to worship him by means of images made by man. The reason is not that God cannot be imaged at all. Rather, according to Deuteronomy 4:15, God gave them the commandment because "you saw no form [temunah] of any kind the day the LORD spoke to you at Horeb[8] out of the fire." The lack of any "form" meant that Israel's worship was not to be directed toward any visible object. But the text does not say that God has no form. Indeed, Numbers 12:8 says that Moses, unlike Israel in general, was granted a vision of God's form (temunah). I think the best way to understand this aspect of Israel's worship is this: Israel was to await, not anticipate, the revelation of God's form. The form was yet to come, in the person of Jesus Christ, who exists in the form of God (Phil. 2:6).

Nor does the radical metaphysical difference between Creator and creature make comparisons impossible. As we have seen, between God and the creation there is no similarity without difference. God's attributes differ from ours in that they are the source and the standards of ours. God loves, knows, and creates as Lord; we do these things as creatures, and therefore very differently. But the fact that God's nature is the source and standard of ours does not prohibit, but rather makes possible, comparisons between God and ourselves. The creaturely effect resembles its divine cause, for everything in it comes from the cause. The qualities of creatures resemble their divine standard in various degrees and ways, for the standard is a perfect person rather than an abstract concept.

As there is between God and ourselves no similarity without difference, so there is also no difference without similarity. Even human sin reflects God's nature, for sin in its very essence is coveting God's prerogatives, trying to be "like God" in the wrong way (Gen. 3:5).

ANTHROPOMORPHISMS

The above discussion helps us in understanding the anthropomorphic language used with reference to God in Scripture. The Bible often speaks of God as if he were a man, not only by using images that describe him as a king, a shepherd, a father, and a judge, but also by speaking of God as walking (Gen. 3:8), smelling an aroma (Gen. 8:21), etc. Scripture also ascribes body parts to God, including arms (Num. 11:23), hands (Ps. 111:7), a mouth (Deut. 8:3), and eyes (Deut. 11:12).

8. Horeb is another name for Mount Sinai, so the reference is to the initial giving of the law, described in Ex. 19–20.

The *DBI* writer rightly indicates that the problem of anthropomorphism is a specific case of the broader question of cosmomorphism.[9] Scripture describes God not only as a man, but also as animals and inanimate objects. But as we have seen, all created images reflect God's nature. So the use of such language is not necessarily inappropriate. We may speak anthropomorphically of God, because he has theomorphized man.

In one sense, as Herman Bavinck puts it, *"all* Scripture is anthropomorphic."[10] All Scripture is written in human language, not some divine language. God's revelation is "accommodated," as Calvin liked to say, to human understanding. Scripture takes abstract attributes of God, no less than concrete images of him, from human life—words that have uses in our conversation about earthly things. This is the only kind of revelation there is. The purpose of revelation is communication, and so the very purpose of revelation is to get God's message into human terms. So Bavinck adds, "Whosoever, therefore, objects to anthropomorphisms, thereby in principle denies the possibility of a revelation of God in his creatures."[11] But we should not object to these, because there are genuine resemblances, amid great differences, between Creator and creature.

Does this mean that God has hands, eyes, and feet? Well, he is certainly able to do everything that we do with our hands, eyes, and feet, and much better than we can do them. But we should draw some distinction between literal[12] and figurative language, even if that distinction is not a sharp one. Granted that God is not a physical being (as I shall argue later), we are rightly inclined to say that he does not really have hands, though human hands appropriately symbolize the means of God's workmanship. We distinguish between the literal and the figurative by employing sound methods of biblical interpretation, particularly interpreting Scripture by Scripture.

These exegetical decisions are not always easy. I will later discuss questions about God's anger, his "relenting" from announced policies, his "grief," and so on. One thing we must not do, however, is to deny the truth of this language simply because it is taken from human life.

All human language is taken from human life. But all human language is also God's creation, given to us not only to communicate earthly realities, but also to reveal God to us. As I indicated in chapter 11, we should

9. "God," in *DBI*, 334.
10. *DG*, 86.
11. Ibid., 91.
12. Recall chapter 11, where I argued that at least some biblical language about God is literal.

not think of human language as if it were wholly concerned with the creation and therefore has to be twisted, qualified, or taken figuratively in order to refer to God. All human language is anthropomorphic; but more fundamentally it is, like the creation itself, theomorphic. God is really involved in human life, and so our language naturally refers to him, as well as to created referents.

SOME BIBLICAL IMAGES OF GOD

The reader will not be surprised to hear that, in my view, the fundamental image of God in Scripture is that of lordship, which can be explained as covenant headship. God is the head of covenants—covenants made with creation in general, with the human race in Adam and Noah, and with specific families in Abraham, Moses, David, and Christ. In those relationships, he is the supreme controller, the supreme authority, and the inescapable presence. See chapters 2–7 for extensive analysis of this image. The concept of God as Lord provides, as we have seen, not only an image of God, but also the chief name of God in Scripture (*yahweh, kyrios*) and the central source of divine attributes. As we shall see, all the attributes of God describe and confirm his lordship. So, the term *Lord* combines an image, a name, and attributes all at once.

Very close to the image of God as Lord is the image of him as King.[13] The Hebrew and Greek words for *king* occur over 2,800 times in Scripture. Add to those the references to *kingdom*, the corresponding verbs, and re-

---

13. The *DBI* writer cited earlier denies that *king* is a "root metaphor." For him, root metaphors are "so intrinsic to what they are communicating that they are literally indispensable" ("God," 336), and they are to be distinguished from other metaphors "that are significant or secondary." (Is "significant" the right word here?) *Father*, however, is indeed in his view a root metaphor. *Father* is irreplaceable, but *king* can be replaced by *governor* without much loss. He objects that "while king pictures someone more exalted [than *governor*], it also depicts a more unapproachable and hierarchical figure." However, *king* is a far more pervasive image in Scripture than *father*. The latter is rarely found in the Old Testament, while the former pervades both testaments. (Another *DBI* writer says, "There is scarcely a grander or more widespread image used in the Bible than king" ("King, Kingship," 476.) Furthermore, the unapproachability of God is not biblically dispensable, though of course the cross of Christ enables believers to approach God's throne boldly. Moreover, the notion that hierarchy is biblically dispensable is absurd. It brings to mind the writers I noted in chapter 2 who object to the very idea of divine lordship. The Lord has control and authority over his people, and therefore there is hierarchy. So kingship is not theologically dispensable (unless its replacement is lordship itself), and it should not be denied the status of "root metaphor" on the definition given.

lated forms, and we can see that the idea of kingship is indeed pervasive in Scripture.[14] These references, of course, include references to human kings as well as to the divine one. But, as images, human kingship and divine kingship influence one another. Human kingship is to some extent an image of the divine. But God's kingship also stands in contrast to the corruption and tyranny of earthly kings.

That God is King is a major theme of Scripture, from Exodus 15:18 onward. The Psalms speak often of the rule of God. Psalms 93–99, especially, provide concentrated reflection on the fact that God reigns over all. He is especially the king of Israel (Isa. 41:21), and he rules over Israel's human king (Pss. 5:2; 145:1). When Israel asks Samuel to appoint them a king "such as all the other nations have" (1 Sam. 8:5), the Lord tells Samuel, "It is not you they have rejected, but they have rejected me as their king" (v. 7).

Recall from chapter 2 that the covenant relationship is between a great king and a lesser king. So God rules Israel by virtue of his covenant. In this context, *King* and *Lord* are close synonyms. God's throne is the ark of the covenant, between the cherubim and beside the book of the covenant (1 Sam. 4:4; Ps. 99:1; cf. Isa. 6:1–5). As the Lord, the King controls his realm and speaks with authority. He also stands with his people, to protect and defend them, to provide justice and mercy.

But God is king, not only of Israel, but of all the nations—indeed, of the whole earth (Ex. 15:18; Pss. 22:28; 96–99; 145). God rules all, because he is God and brings all things to pass, but also, as I indicated in chapter 2, because he is related to the whole creation by covenant.

His kingdom is eternal (Ex. 15:18; Ps. 93:2), but also historical and temporal. Just as I distinguished in chapter 16 between eternal and historical election, so I must do the same here with divine kingship. God is king eternally by virtue of his divine nature. But the narrative of Scripture is a history of "the coming of the kingdom." Vos defines the historical sense of "kingdom" as follows:

> To him [Jesus], the kingdom exists there, where not merely God is supreme, for that is true at all times and under all circumstances, but where God supernaturally carries through his supremacy against all opposing powers and brings man to the willing recognition of the same.[15]

14. *DBI*, 477. Much of the information in this chapter is taken from DBI, but I take full responsibility for the formulations.

15. Geerhardus Vos, *The Teaching of Jesus Concerning the Kingdom of God and the Church* (Nutley, N.J.: Presbyterian and Reformed, 1972), 50.

God advances his kingdom by choosing the families of Noah, Abraham, Isaac, and Jacob as his special people, through whom all the nations of the earth will be blessed and will come to know that he is Lord. So in the Psalms, the earthly king, David, advances the work of Yahweh, the King over him. But David must also confess his sin (Pss. 32; 51). He looks forward to a greater King, one who is both his son and his Lord (Ps. 110:1). God is to set his King upon his holy hill, to rule all the nations (Pss. 2; 45; 72).

Jesus confounds the Pharisees by asking them how the messianic son of David could also be David's Lord (Matt. 22:41–46). It is evident that Jesus is the son of David, yet greater than David because he is God himself, who has come to rule his people. So, following John the Baptist (Matt. 3:2), Jesus begins his preaching ministry by proclaiming that "the kingdom of heaven is near" (4:17). It is he who carries through God's "supremacy against all opposing powers and brings man to the willing recognition of the same."[16] To him is given all authority in heaven and on earth (Matt. 28:18). He is King of kings and Lord of lords (Rev. 19:16; cf. 17:14).

God is not an absentee king. He is also the warrior who defends Israel against his and their enemies (Ex. 15:3; cf. Deut. 33:26; Ps. 68:5). He is the Lord of hosts, as we have seen, the Lord of the angelic armies. When Israel is faithful to the Lord, they do not need to worry about their own military resources (Deut. 20; Judg. 7:1–8). God fights for them, often with no effort on their part (as in 1 Sam. 7:10–13). Israel's victories are notable mainly for the supernatural assistance given to them. Similarly, spiritual warfare is fought by using "the full armor of God" (Eph. 6:11, 13), consisting of faith, God's Word, righteousness, peace, salvation, and especially prayer. God himself wore this armor (Isa. 59:15–17) because there was no man who could deliver Israel from her sins. So Jesus, who delivers men from sin, is the rider on the white horse, called Faithful and True, who "judges and makes war" (Rev. 19:11).

The reference to God's judgment calls to mind another frequent image, that of God as Judge. When Abraham intercedes for his nephew Lot, he asks the rhetorical question, "Will not the Judge of all the earth do right?" (Gen. 18:25). This image emphasizes the lordship attribute of authority. God is the one who evaluates all his creatures and gives to each what is due. He rightly punishes the wicked, but justifies those who are righteous in Christ. He judges the false gods as well (Isa. 41:21), exposing their futility, as when he curses the Nile and the other natural objects sacred to

---

16. Ibid.

the Egyptians, or when he makes the Philistine god Dagon bow down before the ark (1 Sam. 5:1–5).

As the Judge of all, God is the divine bookkeeper, who keeps a record of all the works of his creatures. Some judgment takes place immediately, but most takes place at the end of history, when the books are opened.[17]

God is also a lawyer. He is the prosecuting attorney, who, through his prophets, brings a covenant lawsuit against his people for their covenant violations. See, for example, Genesis 3:16–19 and 4:10–16. This is a major theme of the prophetic literature (e.g., Isa. 1–3; Rev. 2:1–3:22). And, in the person of Christ and the Spirit, God is also the defense attorney or advocate for his people (1 John 2:1; cf. John 14:16, 26; 15:26).

Finally, in the area of governance, God is the legislator, the one who sets forth the law. Israel is to obey the law because "I am the LORD your God" (Ex. 20:2; Lev. 18:2). He has the authority to makes laws for his people.[18]

Another major area of biblical images of God is that of the family, in which God is preeminently pictured as the father. The line between political and family images in Scripture is not sharp. The human race began as a family, with the father or patriarch playing the roles of prophet, priest, and king. As the human race increased in numbers, these roles became more differentiated. When the family of Israel became a nation, Moses, on the advice of Jethro, his father-in-law, set up a system of judges over "thousands, hundreds, fifties and tens" (Ex. 18:21), with himself at the top of the hierarchy.[19] So civil government in Scripture is an expansion of family government. And, appropriately, Scripture uses *father* as a metaphor for civil and military rule (Gen. 45:8; 2 Kings 5:13; Isa. 49:23; cf. Judg. 5:7, "a mother in Israel"![20]). Indeed, the metaphor extends to prophets, teachers of wisdom, and church leaders (2 Kings 2:12; 13:14; Ps. 34:11; Prov. 1:8, 10, 15; 1 Cor. 4:15; Gal. 4:19 [mother, again].) Paul presses the analogy to say that a man should not be an elder in the church if he is not a good father (1 Tim. 3:4–5; Titus 1:6). So the Westminster Catechisms understand the fifth commandment, "Honor your father and your mother," as a principle applying to all human relationships.[21]

---

17. See Sanderson, *Mirrors of His Glory*, 146–53, on the image of God as bookkeeper. See also my discussion of the book of life in chapter 16.

18. Our obligation to keep the law comes from God's authority as such. But our motivation to keep it, as sinners saved by grace, is God's redemption. See Ex. 20:2 ("who brought you out of Egypt, out of the land of slavery"); John 13:34–35; Col. 3:1–3; 1 John 3:16; 4:8–10.

19. See Frame, "Toward a Theology of the State," *WTJ* 51 (1989): 199–226.

20. See a later section in this chapter, dealing with gender.

21. WLC, 123–33; WSC, 63–66.

In Scripture, God's fatherhood is not sharply distinguished from his lordship. Sometimes the main thought is that God is Creator, as in Deuteronomy 32:6, where God rebukes Israel for its corruption:

> Is this the way you repay the LORD,
>   O foolish and unwise people?
> Is he not your Father, your Creator,
>   Who made you and formed you?

Compare Malachi 2:10. Similarly, in Acts 17:28, Paul quotes the words of the pagan Aratus, "We are his offspring." God is Father of all by virtue of creation.

But God exercises a special kind of fatherhood toward his chosen people by virtue of his covenants with them. In such contexts, Scripture emphasizes more specifically the qualities of a good family head: the father as protector, provider, and guide (Deut. 1:31), showing compassion to his children (Ps. 103:13), especially toward the fatherless (Ps. 68:5). As Father, God is the Redeemer of his people (Isa. 63:16).[22] He reaches out with joy to the returning prodigal (Luke 15:11–32). Discipline, too, is important (Prov. 3:11–12; Heb. 12:4–11). Although sometimes painful, it is evidence of our Father's love. Indeed, without it, we would not be children of God at all, but illegitimate (Heb. 12:8). As our Father, God requires the honor mentioned by the fifth commandment: "If I am a father," he asks, "where is the honor due me?" (Mal. 1:6; cf. Jer. 3:4–5, 19).

The father image, applied to God, is somewhat rare in the Old Testament, but it becomes quite central to the New, because of Jesus' teaching and because of his special relationship to God.[23] He regularly refers to God as "the Father" and "my Father," and to himself as "Son." Jesus is uniquely the "Son of God," which can only be understood in terms of the Trinity.[24] In the case of Jesus, the Son of God is no less than God.

But, remarkably, Jesus also teaches his disciples to address God as Father, as in the Lord's Prayer: "Our Father in heaven" (Matt. 6:9). God is not our Father in the same sense that he is the Father of Jesus; we are not God. Jesus delicately distinguishes the two fatherhoods of God when he speaks with Mary Magdalene after his resurrection: "I am returning to my Father and your Father, to my God and your God" (John 20:17). Elsewhere in the New

---

22. But, in the context of Isa. 63:16, the prophet knows that redemption has not yet been accomplished. He calls upon God to cease withholding his tenderness and compassion.

23. Of course, the concept of adoption, of God taking a people to bear his name, is not foreign to the Old Testament, as we saw in the last chapter. In the New Testament, however, the image of God's fatherhood describes this relationship far more often.

24. See chapter 28.

Testament, the term *adoption* is used to describe our relationship to the Father (Rom. 8:15, 23; 9:4; Gal. 4:5; Eph. 1:5). Jesus is the Son by nature; we are sons[25] by adoption. Jesus is the eternal Son, but God confers sonship upon us in time (cf. John 1:12–13). But the distinction is not a total separation. We are "coheirs with Christ," for "we share in his sufferings in order that we may also share in his glory" (Rom. 8:17).

We are sons for Jesus' sake, because of him and in him. He has redeemed us, so that we might receive the rights of sons (Gal. 4:5). All believers in Christ, therefore, are equally the sons of God. The Gentiles are coheirs with the Jews (Gal. 4:7).

To know God as Father is a special privilege of God's family, of those who know Christ. A special sign of this relationship is the intimate Aramaic word *abba*, sometimes described as a child's word for "daddy," which was used by the early Christians. Jesus used the term (Mark 14:36), and Paul teaches that God has sent upon us the Spirit of his Son, of Jesus, enabling us also to address God in that way (Gal. 4:6; cf. Rom. 8:15). So the Christian church is the family of God. Through Christ, our Father "sets the lonely in families" (Ps. 68:6).

God is also related to his people as a husband.[26] To the barren woman, deserted by her husband, Isaiah says that "your Maker is your husband— the LORD Almighty is his name" (Isa. 54:5). God is the one who found Israel "kicking about in your blood" (Ezek. 16:6), abandoned. He said to her, "Live!" He saved her life, caused her to grow up, and then married her (vv. 7–8). But she was unfaithful (v. 15). Adultery images idolatry, and in Hosea 1–3 the prophet himself becomes the image, marrying a prostitute, taking her back despite her unfaithfulness. In the New Testament, Christ is the bridegroom, and the church is the bride:

> Husbands, love your wives, just as Christ loved the church and gave himself up for her, to make her holy, cleansing her by the washing with water through the word, and to present her to himself as a radiant church; without stain or wrinkle or any other blemish, but holy and blameless. (Eph. 5:25–27)

Closely related to the images of God as father and husband is the image of God as Redeemer.[27] To redeem is to rescue or deliver from bondage

---

25. Of course, we are "sons" in a generic sense, including daughters.

26. God is pictured both as a father and as a husband. Biblical teachings are always consistent with one another, but biblical images are not necessarily so.

27. *Savior* is also an important title of God in Scripture, and, of course, of Jesus. I will take it as roughly synonymous with *Redeemer* and will not discuss it separately.

by paying a price. In Leviticus 25:47–53, a poor man may sell himself into slavery when he is unable to pay a debt. If he later prospers, he may redeem himself (v. 49). But he may also be redeemed by "an uncle or a cousin or any blood relative in his clan" (v. 49). So this is another in our series of family images. Interpreters often translate the Hebrew *go'el* as "kinsman-redeemer."[28] The book of Ruth illustrates the principle: Boaz, the kin of Ruth's father-in-law, purchases her dead husband's property and marries Ruth.

The word *go'el* often refers to God (Job 19:25; Pss. 19:14; 78:35; Prov. 23; often in Isa. 41–66). Exodus 6:6 uses the corresponding verb *ga'al* to indicate that God is redeeming his people from bondage in Egypt. In the New Testament, the price of deliverance is central: the shed blood of Christ (Eph. 1:7; Col. 1:14; Titus 2:14; Heb. 9:12, 15). Jesus, as our Redeemer, is our kinsman, fully man as well as fully God. He is our brother (Heb. 2:11–12, 17).

The image of God as a shepherd might seem to come from an entirely different realm of human experience. But this image actually overlaps those that we have already considered. As there is a close analogy between fatherhood and civic rule, so there is one between the ruler and the shepherd. The patriarchs Abraham, Isaac, and Jacob owned flocks and herds (Gen. 24:35), and Israel's greatest leaders, Moses and David, spent years of their lives as shepherds. God led the people in the wilderness "like a flock by the hand of Moses and Aaron" (Ps. 77:20). Before his death, Moses asked God to appoint a successor to him, "so the LORD's people will not be like sheep without a shepherd" (Num. 27:17). Psalm 78:70–72 draws on the life of David to indicate the parallel between shepherding and leading people.

So the role of a shepherd became a regular metaphor for the leaders of God's people. Even the wicked leaders are shepherds, but God will destroy them (Jer. 25:34–36). These shepherds take care of themselves, not of the flock:

> You eat the curds, clothe yourselves with the wool and slaughter the choice animals, but you do not take care of the flock. You have not strengthened the weak or healed the sick or bound up the injured. You have not brought back the strays or searched for the lost. You have ruled them harshly and brutally. So they were scattered because there was no shepherd, and when they were scattered they

---

28. *Padah* is another Hebrew word often translated "redeem." It does not seem to have as sharp a focus on the kinsman-redeemer provision of the law, but it is a fairly close synonym of *ga'al*, the verb root of the participle *go'el*.

became food for all the wild animals. (Ezek. 34:3–5; cf. Zech. 10:2–3; 11:15–17)

God will judge the wicked shepherds, and he himself will become the shepherd of his people:

> For this is what the Sovereign LORD says: I myself will search for my sheep and look after them. As a shepherd looks after his scattered flock when he is with them, so will I look after my sheep. I will rescue them from all the places where they were scattered on a day of clouds and darkness. I will bring them out from the nations. . . . I will bind up the injured and strengthen the weak, but the sleek and the strong I will destroy. I will shepherd the flock with justice. (Ezek. 34:11–16)

The polemic against wicked shepherds continues into the New Testament. Jesus speaks of some Jewish leaders as thieves, robbers, and hired hands, who care about the flock only as a means of their own enrichment. In contrast, "I am the good shepherd. The good shepherd lays down his life for the sheep" (John 10:11). Jesus is the shepherd who leaves the ninety-nine sheep in the open country and goes after the one that was lost (Luke 15:1–7). Literally, Jesus seeks out the tax collectors and "sinners" to bring them to repentance (v. 1).

So God is the shepherd of his people (Gen. 49:24; Ps. 80:1). He rules them by his rod and staff. The image of a shepherd, like the images of a king and a father, is, in the final analysis, an image of rule. But the shepherd rules not only by his power and authority, but by his nurturing care for the flock, his healing mercy, and his passion to find and rescue those that are lost. So the believer can take great comfort from John 10 and Psalm 23. When God is our shepherd, we have need of nothing. He leads us, restores us, and directs us into the right paths. His presence assuages our fears, even of death itself. He invites us to feast and to receive his anointing, even before he defeats our enemies. His goodness and mercy follow us forever.

So the images of government, family, and shepherding reveal, in different ways, the aspects of God's lordship that we noted earlier in the book: control, authority, and presence to bless and judge.

These are the major images of God in Scripture that are based on persons. There are others, such as the image of a potter (Isa. 64:8; Jer. 18–19; Rom. 9:19–22),[29] a farmer (Isa. 5; Matt. 13:3–8), a refiner (Ps. 12:6; Prov. 17:3; Mal. 3:2), a landowner (Matt. 20:1–16), even an unjust judge (Luke

---

29. We considered this image in connection with divine sovereignty in chapter 4.

18:1–8), and, of course, a knitter (Ps. 139:13). These, too, express various aspects of God's control, authority, and redeeming presence, as do the various references to human body parts that we noted under "Anthropomorphisms."

Personal images of God are, of course, the most adequate, since God is personal, not impersonal, and since man is *the* image of God. But, as we have seen, everything in creation declares God's glory in some way. So Scripture also draws images of God from the animal, plant, and inanimate realms. God is a moth to Ephraim, who will eat their garments in judgment (Hos. 5:12). He is like a lion, a leopard, or a bear, who will devour his wicked people (Hos. 13:7–8). The image of a lion becomes a powerful picture of triumph in Revelation 5:5, where Jesus is "the Lion of the tribe of Judah" who "has triumphed." (In the same context, of course, he is the Lamb who has been slain to take away the sin of the world.) God is the horn of a wild ox, a symbol of brute strength.[30] He is "the horn of my salvation" (Ps. 18:2; cf. Luke 1:68–69); Jesus as the lamb has ten horns in Revelation 5:6. He is an eagle, who carries his people on his wings (Ex. 19:4; Deut. 32:11–12), a bird who protects them under the shadow of his wings (Ps. 17:8).[31]

In the inanimate world, light is the most common and the most theologically important image of God. John virtually defines God when he says, "God is light; in him there is no darkness at all" (1 John 1:5). Light was God's first creation in the work of the six days (Gen. 1:3), and throughout Scripture God divides light from darkness, and overcomes darkness by light. The appearances of God to men are always accompanied by a great light, sometimes identified with his "glory," as when the pillar of fire and the fiery cloud led Israel through the wilderness (Ex. 13:21–22). There is a light of God's countenance that shines from his face (Pss. 4:6; 44:3; 89:15; 90:8). We glorify God by reflecting that light and making him known to others, thus spreading his light throughout the dark world.

Metaphorically, the contrast between light and darkness is that between truth and error, good and evil, righteousness and wickedness (Pss. 36:9; 37:6; 43:3; 119:130; Prov. 4:18; 6:23; 13:9). The Lord is our light and salvation (Ps. 27:1). In sin, we are darkness,[32] but in Christ we are light (Eph. 5:8). Christ is "the true light that gives light to every man" (John 1:8) who came

30. Sanderson, *Mirrors of His Glory,* 121–25.
31. Recall Jesus' image of himself as the hen who would have gathered her chicks under her wings (Matt. 23:37).
32. This is a powerful description of total depravity, as is Paul's earlier expression, "dead in your transgressions and sins" (Eph. 2:1).

into the world. He is the light of the world (John 8:12), and he appoints and enables his disciples to be bearers of that light, so that they too are the light of the world (Matt. 5:14–16). As God first commanded the light to shine out of darkness, so he "made his light shine in our hearts to give us the light of the knowledge of the glory of God in the face of Christ" (2 Cor. 4:6). This church is called, then, to turn men "from darkness to light" (Acts 26:18). So in Jesus, light is an image of the fullness of salvation: enlightenment of the mind and turning of the heart to serve God.

The image of a rock also comes from the inanimate world. It is an image of strength, protection, and unchangeable perfection. Several times, as Israel wandered in the wilderness, God dealt with them in connection with a rock. In Exodus 17, the people complain that they have no water, putting the Lord to the test. God tells Moses, "I will stand there before you by the rock at Horeb" (v. 6). On God's order, Moses smites the rock, and water comes out for the people to drink (v. 6). Edmund P. Clowney has shown that in smiting the rock, Moses in effect smote God.[33] God accepted the blow due to Israel for their grumbling, anticipating the sacrifice of Christ.

The rock also appears in Exodus 33:21–23, where God grants Moses a partial revelation of his glory. In Numbers 20:1–13, the Israelites grumble again about the lack of water, and again Moses brings them water from the rock. But this time God does not tell him to smite the rock, only to speak to it. Moses smites the rock anyway, and does so twice. For his disobedience, God will not permit him to enter the Promised Land.

Deuteronomy 32:4 says that "[God] is the Rock, his works are perfect." He is "the Rock [Jeshurun's] savior" (v. 15; cf. vv. 18, 30–31; 1 Sam. 2:2; 2 Sam. 22:2–3, 32, 47; Ps. 18:2, 31, 46, and often in the Psalms and Prophets). Clearly the "Rock" that accompanied Israel in the wilderness was an image of God, or more. Paul describes the wilderness wanderings like this:

> They all ate the same spiritual food and drank the same spiritual drink; for they drank from the spiritual rock that accompanied them, and that rock was Christ. (1 Cor. 10:4)

So the wise man who builds the house of his life upon a rock, rather than on shifting sand, is the man who hears the words of Jesus and does them (Matt. 7:24). He builds his life on Christ.

Other inanimate objects that are used as images of God (with fairly obvious meaning) are the tower or refuge (Ps. 46:11), the shield (Ps. 3:3), the

---

33. See Edmund P. Clowney, *The Unfolding Mystery* (Colorado Springs: NavPress, 1988), 123–26.

consuming fire (Ex. 13:21; 24:17; Heb. 12:29) that destroys those who dishonor God's holiness, and the water of life (Ps. 36:9; Jer. 2:13; John 4:1–15; Rev. 21:6; 22:1, 17) that quenches spiritual thirst. Like all the images, these view God's lordship from various perspectives.

Other images, such as that of a lamb, pertain especially to Jesus, and should be expounded in connection with Christology. We have already seen a remarkable identity between the names and images of God and those given in Scripture to Jesus Christ. In my view, this identity is a powerful proof of Jesus' deity.

GOD AND GENDER

Much recent theology has focused on the appropriateness of feminine language for God. The late evangelical theologian Paul K. Jewett made this question central to his *God, Creation, and Revelation*.[34] Although he denied in his preface that "I have any thought of accommodating the exposition of the Christian faith to the canons of modernity,"[35] he sometimes used "she" for God[36] and gave much space to the defense of feminist arguments. Elizabeth Johnson's *She Who Is*,[37] a comprehensive treatise on the doctrine of God, has as its main thesis the necessity of using feminine language (more or less exclusively, for the time being)[38] with reference to God. These titles are typical of many.

This question is certainly not a major concern of Scripture itself, nor is it a high priority of the present volume. But since theology is application, it is important for us to apply biblical principles to issues of concern to contemporary people. And there certainly are biblical principles that are relevant to this question.

What Would a Female God Be Like?

First, we should be clear that this question is about *imagery*. No one argues that God is literally male or female, since Christians generally agree that God is incorporeal (as the Bible teaches).[39] Elizabeth Johnson does

34. Paul K. Jewett, *God, Creation, and Revelation* (Grand Rapids: Eerdmans, 1991).
35. Ibid., xvi.
36. Ibid., 336–47.
37. Elizabeth Johnson, *She Who Is* (New York: Crossroad Publishing, 1996). I will interact with some of her arguments in this section.
38. Ibid., 54.
39. See my discussion of God's incorporeality in chapter 25.

believe that God is physical in the panentheistic sense: God's body is the world.[40] But even she does not base her argument for the femininity of God upon physical characteristics.

Further, although Scripture sometimes represents God anthropomorphically by using images of body parts, those parts never include sexual organs.[41] So sexuality as such is not part of Scripture's visual imagery. The issues with regard to feminine images of God, therefore, are subtle. They have to do with analogies between God's status, character, personality, and actions, and those we associate with women.

The very nature of this question raises problems for feminism. Are there traits of character or personality that are distinctive to women in some degree? Sometimes feminists have said no. In their view, all human character and personality traits are common to men and women, and to think otherwise is to engage in stereotypes. At other times, they have recognized that there are differences (in degree, at least), but have wanted society to give greater honor to those traits associated with women.

Johnson and some others want to have it both ways. She insists that our notion of the feminine (and therefore the feminine God) should include "intellectual, artistic," and "public leadership," and even "pride and anger."[42] She praises the religion of Ishtar (in the Old Testament, Astarte or Ashtoreth, the wife of Baal, Judg. 2:13; 10:6; 1 Sam. 7:3–4; 12:10) for finding in their goddess "a source of divine power and sovereignty embodied in female form," who wages war and exercises judgment.[43] On this basis, male and female traits are essentially the same. What society needs to understand is that they can be found in women as well as men.[44]

This emphasis conflicts, however, with Johnson's distaste for the notions of "power-over,"[45] and rule and submission.[46] She sees these as typically male characteristics that feminist theology should avoid ascribing to God. Is

---

40. Johnson, *She Who Is*, 230–33. She introduces her panentheism toward the end of the book. Her main arguments don't depend on it in any obvious way.

41. The Hebrew verb *raham* ("have compassion") is related to the noun *rehem*, "womb." So some have thought that there is an allusion to God's "womb" in Ps. 103:13 and Jer. 31:20. The same argument has been made with regard to the corresponding New Testament term, *splanchnizomai*. However, this term and its cognate forms never clearly refer to a womb in the New Testament. This argument presses etymology much too far.

42. Johnson, *She Who Is*, 53. Cf. pp. 181–85, 256–59.

43. Ibid., 55–56. Johnson frequently appeals to non-Christian religions to commend their theology of gender. That practice raises legitimate questions about the biblical integrity of her theology.

44. Note also her critique of stereotypes, ibid., 47–54.

45. Ibid., 21, 69, 269–71.

46. Ibid., 69.

"power-over" a male trait that feminist theology would displace in favor of female traits? Or is it a trait that feminists should embrace as properly feminine and find in a female deity?

It is not clear, therefore, what kind of god a female deity would be. Would she be far more nurturing, kind, hospitable, and friendly than the male deity of patriarchal theology? Or would she be just as powerful, dominant, and aggressive as any male, yet nevertheless somehow female? Johnson usually seems to favor the latter alternative, with some inconsistency, as we have seen. But then, what is distinctively female about this deity? If her femininity is not physical, we can judge her gender only by traits of character and personality. But on Johnson's description, the goddess's traits are common to males and females. So it is hard to judge what Johnson really means to assert when she says that God is female.

Feminine Images of God in Scripture

Nevertheless, we should proceed to look at the biblical data. It should be agreed that although God is the Creator and therefore the exemplar of both "masculine" and "feminine" virtues (however these be defined), the biblical images of God, insofar as gender is relevant to them, are predominately masculine. The pronouns and verbs referring to God in Scripture are always masculine, and the images used of him (Lord, King, Judge, Father, husband, etc.) are typically masculine.[47]

There are, however, some feminine images of God in the Bible. In Deuteronomy 32:18, God, through Moses, rebukes Israel, saying:

> You deserted the Rock, who fathered you;
>   you forgot the God who gave you birth.

In this image, God plays both male and female roles in Israel's origin. In Numbers 11:12, Moses, frustrated by the grumbling of the Israelites, denies before God that he (Moses) conceived these people and brought them forth. So he asks, "Why do you tell me to carry them in my arms, as a nurse carries an infant?" Perhaps the thought expressed in Deuteronomy 32:18 lies behind Moses' words: God conceived Israel and gave her birth, and so God should be her nursemaid. These two passages are often mentioned in the feminist literature, but the female imagery is very brief. In the context, nothing much is made of the fact that God gives birth or might be a nursemaid. The imagery here is less striking than that of Galatians 4:19, where the apostle Paul describes himself in the pains of childbirth for the church, and

---

47. There is one female judge, however: Deborah (Judg. 4–5).

1 Thessalonians 2:7, where he says that he and his colaborers were "gentle among you, like a mother caring for her little children." No one ever suggests on the basis of these passages that we should regard Paul as female. Nor do Numbers 11:12 and Deuteronomy 32:18 require us to rethink God's gender.[48]

In Isaiah 42:14–15, God declares impending judgment:

> For a long time I have kept silent,
>   I have been quiet and held myself back.
> But now, like a woman in childbirth,
>   I cry out, I gasp and pant.
> I will lay waste the mountains and hills
>   and dry up all their vegetation.

Feminist writers often mention this passage as presenting a feminine image of God. The image here is certainly feminine. An expectant mother may spend many months in modest quietness, but when her time comes to give birth, she will scream! Similarly, God delays his judgment, but when the right time comes, he will certainly make his presence known. Of course, Scripture often mentions the pain of childbirth as God's curse (Gen. 3:16) and, proverbially, the worst pain imaginable. So, as metaphor, it applies naturally and frequently to both men and women. Psalm 48:4–6 reads:

> When the kings joined forces,
>   when they advanced together,
> they saw her [Zion] and were astounded;
>   they fled in terror.
> Trembling seized them there,
>   pain like that of a woman in labor.

These kings are male, but they tremble like a woman giving birth (cf. Isa. 13:8; 21:3; 26:17; Jer. 4:31; 6:24; Mic. 4:9). So while Scripture does use this feminine metaphor for God, it gives us no more encouragement to think

---

48. Nor, even more obviously, should we draw such a conclusion from Isa. 46:3. That passage mentions Israel's conception and birth, but does not suggest that God conceived and bore the nation. Of course, he did, in a sense, and the passage may recall Deut. 32:18. However, Isa. 46:3 certainly does nothing to strengthen the theological case for a feminine God. The same should be said of Isa. 49:15, which is often mentioned in the feminist literature. In this passage, God places his love for his people far above and beyond the love of a mother for her baby. There is a resemblance between God and the mother, but the note of contrast is more predominant. God claims, not to be a mother, but to be far greater than any mother. And, in Isa. 66, it is Zion who is in labor (v. 8) and who will nurse (vv. 11–12). God's only motherly function in the passage is to comfort (v. 13).

of God as female than it gives us to think of these kings as female. The feminine imagery used for God in Isaiah 42:14–15 is common in Scripture, and is often used for male persons.

In Luke 15:8–10, Jesus tells a parable about a woman who lights a lamp, sweeps the house, and searches carefully to find a lost coin. When she finds it, she calls her friends together to rejoice. Some believe that the woman represents God, perhaps Jesus specifically, as do the shepherd and the father in the other two parables in Luke 15. However, the parable focuses more on the rejoicing of the friends (i.e., the angels, v. 10) than on the homemaker's efforts. In Matthew 23:37, Jesus compares himself to a hen who gathers her chicks under her wings. This is certainly a feminine metaphor, but certainly not one that calls into question the gender of Jesus.

Beyond these specific passages, there are some broader biblical ideas thought by some to presuppose a feminine element of some kind in God. One is the use of *raham* and *splanchnizomai* for divine compassion, a use I discussed briefly in an earlier footnote. See chapter 20 for more discussion.

Another is the use of the word *Spirit* (Heb. *ruah*, Gr. *pneuma*). *Ruah* is a feminine noun, and Genesis 1:2 may picture the Spirit "brooding" as a mother bird. Scripture also represents the Spirit as the giver of life (Ps. 104:30), particularly new birth (John 3:5–6).

Not much can be derived from this grammatical point, however. Feminine nouns do not necessarily denote female persons,[49] and the corresponding Greek term *pneuma* is neuter. Furthermore, "hover" is also a possible interpretation of the word *rahaf* in Genesis 1:2. And in John 3, the word translated "born" (*gennaō*) can mean "beget" as well as "bear," so it may refer to the male role in procreation. Nevertheless, the interpretation "bear" is preferable in John 3:5 because of Nicodemus's response in verse 4. I would conclude that there may well be a couple of feminine images of the Spirit in Scripture, but that hardly suggests that the Spirit is a feminine person of the Trinity.[50] If the group of images we discussed earlier is insufficient to justify talk of divine femininity, certainly these two images are not sufficient to prove the femininity of the Spirit.

Another concept under discussion is that of wisdom (Heb. *hokmah*, Gr. *sophia*). Both the Greek and the Hebrew terms are feminine nouns, and, in Proverbs, wisdom is personified as a woman (7:4; 8:1–9:18). Wisdom is

49. Since examples can sometimes help to get us out of the habit of relying too much on grammatical form, I would point out here that the Latin *uterus* ("womb," as in English) is masculine.

50. See Johnson, *She Who Is*, 50–54, for some references. Johnson herself prefers not to limit the femininity of God to the person of the Spirit, although she discusses the Spirit extensively (pp. 124–49).

a divine figure in Proverbs 8:22–31, and the New Testament identifies it with Christ (1 Cor. 1:24, 30; Col. 2:3; cf. Isa. 11:2; Jer. 23:5), as it also uses the closely related term *Word* (John 1:1–18). So some have concluded that the second person of the Trinity is feminine.[51]

But that is a poor argument. For one thing, Jesus is unquestionably male. Therefore, the suggestion that wisdom requires female embodiment is simply wrong. As for the female personification of wisdom in Proverbs, there is a perfectly obvious reason for that, one that has nothing to do with a female element in the Godhead. Proverbs 1–9 presents the reader with two women, sometimes called "Lady Wisdom" and "Lady Folly." Lady Folly is the harlot who entices a young man to immorality. Lady Wisdom also cries out to men in the city (8:1–4), urging them to lead a godly life. Wisdom is a lady, not because the writer wants to assert a feminine element in the Godhead, but simply as a literary device presenting a positive alternative to the female prostitute.

My conclusion from these biblical references is that there are a few feminine images of God in Scripture, but they do not suggest any sexual ambivalence in the divine nature. They do not justify, let alone necessitate, the use of "Mother" or feminine pronouns for God. Nor do they justify attempts to suppress the overwhelmingly masculine images and pronouns used with reference to God.

The Theological Importance of Masculine Imagery

But the feminist might reply here that since God is not literally male, and Scripture contains some female imagery, as well as male imagery, we should be free to speak of God in either male or female terms. Johnson asks, "If it is not meant that God is male when masculine imagery is used, why the objection when feminine images are introduced?"[52]

This reply would be cogent if the preponderance of male imagery in the Bible were theologically unimportant. So feminists often argue that Scripture places little importance on the maleness of Jesus or on the importance of speaking of God in masculine terms. The masculine imagery, they argue, is understandable in view of the patriarchalism of ancient culture, but it makes no difference to the essential message of Scripture.

There are, however, a number of reasons to think that the overwhelming preponderance of masculine imagery has some theological importance:

1. As we have seen, God's names are of great theological importance.

51. Ibid., 150–69.
52. Ibid., 34.

They reveal him. There is no reason to assume that the proportions of male and female imagery are not part of this revelation of his nature. As Johnson and others insist, a change in the balance of sexual imagery is not theologically neutral; it does change our concept of God.[53] Do we have the right to change the biblical concept of God?

2. To underscore the last point, it is also important to recognize that in Scripture God names himself. His names, attributes, and images are not the result of human speculation or imagination, but of revelation.[54] He has not authorized any change in the balance of male and female imagery, and we should not presume to make such changes on our own authority.[55]

3. Female deities were well known to the biblical writers. Ashtoreth (Judg. 10:6; 1 Sam. 7:4; 12:10) was worshiped by the Canaanites as the wife of Baal. The coupling of male and female deities was an important aspect of pagan fertility worship. So, in writing about Yahweh, the Old Testament writers did not choose masculine language unthinkingly, unaware of any alternative. They were not influenced by a unanimous cultural consensus. Rather, they distinctly rejected any worship of a goddess or of a divine couple.

4. As we saw in chapter 15, creation is a divine act that produces a reality outside of God himself, a "creaturely other." The world is not divine, nor an emanation from his essence. Nor does God create by "making room 'within' himself for the nondivine."[56] As a metaphor for this biblical view of creation, the male role in procreation is more suitable than the female.

5. In Scripture, the most central name for God is Lord, which indicates his headship of the covenants between himself and his creatures. In Scripture, rule in the covenant community is typically a male prerogative. Kings, priests, and prophets are nearly always male. Authority in the church is

---

53. So they really do not believe, though they sometimes claim to, that sexual imagery concerning God is unimportant.

54. Johnson's view is different. In her view, God is a great mystery and no language is entirely appropriate to describe him (see *She Who Is*, 6–7, 44–45, 104–12). He has "many names" (117–20), so we should be as open to feminine as to masculine names for him. Here I see the nonbiblical concept of transcendence that I opposed in chapters 7 and 11. God has revealed himself in language that is appropriate to his nature.

55. I am not suggesting that we must reproduce the emphasis of Scripture with mathematical precision. Theology and preaching always change the emphasis of Scripture, for they apply biblical truth to people, rather than simply reading the Bible. But it would not be good application to speak of God regularly as "she," or to raise the level of feminine imagery to, say, 80 percent of our references to God.

56. Johnson, *She Who Is*, 234. She is quoting William Hill, *The Three-Personed God* (Washington: Catholic University of America Press, 1982), 76, n. 53. This is the panentheistic model of God's relationship to the world.

given to male elders (1 Cor. 14:35; 1 Tim. 2:11–15).[57] The husband is the head of the covenant formed by marriage.[58] A switch to feminine imagery for God would certainly dilute the strong emphasis on covenant authority that is central to the biblical doctrine of God. This is one reason why, as I indicated in chapter 2, some feminist theologians, including Johnson, actually oppose the idea of God's lordship.

6. As we saw earlier in this chapter, God relates to his people as husband to wife. Clearly this profound image would be obscured, were we to regard God as female. This is important, not only for the doctrine of God, but also for the doctrine of man (theological anthropology). It is important for both male and female Christians to know, and to meditate deeply on the fact, that in relation to God they are female—wives called to submit in love to their gracious husband. It is the church, not God, that is feminine in its spiritual nature.[59]

7. One frequent suggestion of compromise is that we eliminate all sexually distinctive language, either male or female, in referring to God. Instead of calling God our Father, we would speak of our Parent or Creator.[60] Unisex language, however, inevitably suggests that God is impersonal, and that is completely unacceptable from a biblical standpoint.[61] Certainly to

57. I cannot, of course, begin here to enter the controversy surrounding this point. I do believe there is room for debate about whether, and in what circumstances, a woman may "speak in church," and whether women may be deacons. But it seems to me obvious from these passages that women are not admitted to that office that makes the final decisions on the affairs of the church. See Susan Foh, *Women and the Word of God* (Phillipsburg, N.J.: Presbyterian and Reformed, 1979); James B. Hurley, *Man and Woman in Biblical Perspective* (Grand Rapids: Zondervan, 1981); "Report of the Committee on Women in Office," in *Minutes of the Fifty-fifth General Assembly* (Philadelphia: Orthodox Presbyterian Church, 1988), 310–73; John Piper and Wayne Grudem, eds., *Recovering Biblical Manhood and Womanhood* (Wheaton, Ill.: Crossway Books, 1991); Mil Am Yi, *Women and the Church: A Biblical Perspective* (Columbus, Ga.: Brentwood Christian Press, 1990), for sound discussions of these issues.

58. Marriage is a covenant in Scripture (Ezek. 16:8, 59; Mal. 2:14), strongly analogous to the covenants between God and man. In marriage, the husband is head of the wife (1 Cor. 11:3; Eph. 5:23). Feminists sometimes argue that "head" means "source" and has no connotations of authority. But see Wayne Grudem's strong argument to the contrary, "The Meaning of *Kephalē*," in *Recovering Biblical Manhood and Womanhood*, ed. Piper and Grudem, 425–68. In any case, Scripture asserts the authority of the husband over the wife in many places, even when the word *head* is not used. See Num. 30:6–16; Eph. 5:22; Col. 3:18; 1 Tim. 3:12–13; Titus 2:5.

59. Thanks to Jim Jordan (in correspondence) for this observation.

60. Some have suggested that we refer to the persons of the Trinity as Creator, Redeemer, and Sanctifier, or the like. But this proposal reduces the ontological Trinity (the eternal persons, Father, Son, and Spirit) to the economic Trinity (the actions of these persons in and for the world). It also ignores the *circumincessio*, the involvement of each person in every act of the others.

61. Even more obvious is the impersonalism that would result if we substitute neuter for

eliminate *Father* in favor of more abstract terms would be to eliminate something very precious to Christians.[62]

8. Has the use of preponderantly male imagery for God resulted in the oppression of women?[63] There is a deep divide between feminist and non-feminist Christians as to what constitutes oppression. In traditional Christianity, it is not degrading for a woman to be submissive to her husband and excluded from the ruling offices in the church. Often, in the view of feminist writers, it is degrading for anybody to be subject to the authority of anyone else, even God. But submission to the authority of others is unavoidable in human life, for both men and women; this is one of the hardest lessons that fallen human beings have to learn. Much more can be said on this issue. Certainly men have abused women throughout history. And certainly both men and women have sometimes justified this abuse by a misunderstanding of male headship. But it would be hard to show that a better understanding of God, or a more wholesome relationship between the sexes, would result from the substitution of female or impersonal imagery for male imagery for God.

My conclusion, then, is that we should follow the biblical pattern and use predominantly male imagery for God, with an occasional female image. I would not object to a preacher occasionally saying that God is the "mother" of the church. As in Deuteronomy 32:18, we can observe that although our physical birth comes from two sources, our spiritual birth comes from only one: Yahweh, who is both mother and father to us. Nor is it wrong to use childbirth, homemaking, mother birds, and even extra-biblical female images as images of God and illustrations of his actions. And, as we shall see, I think much more should be made of the submission of the persons of the Trinity to one another, as the archetype of the godly wife's submission to her husband. But there is no biblical justification for using predominantly female imagery for God or representing him with female pronouns.

---

masculine pronouns. But something must be done with the pronouns if our goal is to eliminate sexually distinctive language for God. Or do we try the impossibly awkward course of avoiding pronouns altogether?

62. One author (I apologize for not remembering who) comments that we do not, after all, address our own parents as "Parent." Indeed, the connotations of such an address would be entirely inappropriate to the relationship.

63. Johnson says, "Wittingly or not, it undermines women's human dignity as equally created in the image of God" (*She Who Is*, 5). Note her examples on pp. 23–28, 34–38. She wants to argue that the use of feminine language for God is actually truer than the alternative, for it conveys the biblical truth that women are not to be oppressed. That truth is indeed important, but it should be expounded by biblical texts that are actually relevant to the issue, not by distorted renderings of the biblical imagery for God.

CHAPTER 19

God's Attributes

Having looked briefly at God's names and images in Scripture, we shall now give more extended attention to his attributes—although, as we have seen, names, images, and attributes cannot be sharply distinguished from one another, but are perspectivally related. The relatively greater emphasis on attributes is common in theological writings. The reason is not that attributes are more important or informative than names or images, but rather that they have proven in some cases to be more difficult and controversial.

REVIEW OF THE DIVINE ATTRIBUTES

As discussed in chapter 12, an attribute is a concept expressed by an adjective (as *eternal*) or a noun (as *eternity*),[1] used to describe a person or thing. The Bible uses many of these terms, like *love, righteousness, holiness, grace, knowledge, truth,* and *eternity* to describe God, and there are others not specifically mentioned in Scripture (such as *immensity, aseity,* and *personality*) that can be deduced from biblical teachings. The defining or essential attributes of God are those without which he would not be God; they belong to him necessarily, rather than contingently. Therefore, the attributes, like the names and images, tell us who God really and truly is.

---

1. Of course, phrases can also serve as attributes, as when we speak of God's slowness to anger (Ex. 34:6).

In chapter 12, I argued that the defining or essential attributes of God should not be considered parts of him, but rather are perspectives on his whole being, that is, his essence. In that sense, God is "simple." He is also complex, but each attribute describes God's entire complexity, not just a part of it. So no attribute is separable from the others. Each attribute has all the attributes: God's love is eternal, just, and wise. His eternity is the eternal existence of a just and wise person. Nevertheless, each attribute presents God's essence from a different perspective, so that the collection of them gives us some insight into the complexities of his being.

Does God's simplicity, then, mean that his eternity is the same as his love, or that his knowledge and justice are identical? The attributes do differ in perspective and emphasis, but they ultimately coalesce. Yes, God's eternity is the same as his love, for his eternity is the eternal existence of a loving person, and his love is the love of that eternal person. That is to say, eternity and love are not abstract qualities that characterize many beings including God, and that exist in him alongside many other abstract qualities. Rather, they are God himself. Our standard of love is not something in God, alongside other things, but God himself. And to find what eternity is, we should not search among abstract "eternal objects" like numbers and the properties of creatures; rather, we should simply look to God himself.

Ultimately, then, the rather abstruse notion of divine simplicity, which identifies God's attributes as his essence, reduces to divine personalism. That is, God is a person, not a collection of abstract qualities. It is tempting to think of God as a collection of abstract qualities when we consider the divine attributes, but we must keep reminding ourselves that God is a person, and that the divine attributes represent his powers and character traits.

So God's attributes are unique to him, even though they can be imaged in the creation.

GOD'S ATTRIBUTES AND HIS LORDSHIP

The following points are important in relating God's attributes to his lordship:

God's lordship is grounded in his eternal nature, and therefore in his attributes. God's covenant lordship, as we've seen, is a relationship between God and creatures in history. But his lordship in history should help us understand his lordship in eternity. In chapters 13 and 14, we discussed God's acts in time (miracle and providence) as the Lord. We saw that since God is the Lord throughout the course of history, he cannot be less than Lord at the beginning of history, which makes him the Creator (chap. 15). And if he acts as Lord in the creation of the world, then surely he acts as Lord in the planning of creation and history, that is, in his eternal decrees (chap. 16). Now, we can carry this argument a step further. If God acts as Lord, that is no accident. His actions as Lord reveal what he is; they reveal his nature. Thus, we move from a consideration of history to the beginning of history, to God's eternal plan for history, to God's own eternal existence. Similarly, the biblical writers often derive God's attributes from his actions in nature, history, and eternity.[2]

The false gods, Paul tells us, are those "who by nature are not gods" (Gal. 4:8). They are "weak" and "miserable" (v. 9)—that is, they have attributes inconsistent with deity. The true God, by contrast, has a nature that entitles him to be revered as Lord. He is simply the kind of being that deserves worship.

So lordship is not just a "relative" attribute, an attribute describing a relation and nothing more. Rather, God's lordship is grounded in his nature. He acts as Lord because it is his nature to act that way with his creatures. Indeed, he would not be God if he did not control everything he made, rule it with supreme authority, and pervade all creation with his presence. So, in a certain sense, lordship is an essential attribute of God's nature. Or, perhaps it would be better to say that God's lordship is grounded in essential attributes of his nature. The covenant relationship, manifest in history, is eternally appropriate. That is to say, God's nature is such that he necessarily relates to creatures as the Lord.

So, when we describe God as Lord, we are describing him "in himself," not only as he relates to us. Reformed thinkers have been somewhat ambivalent about whether we can know God in himself. Part of the problem is that the phrase "in himself" is ambiguous. Herman Bavinck says at one point, echoing Calvin, that "there is no knowledge of God as he is in himself."[3] But later on, when he moves from discussing the divine attributes to discussing the divine counsel (decrees), he says, "Thus far we have dealt with God's being as it exists in itself."[4] Certainly we cannot know God in himself, if that means to know him as he knows himself, or to know him

2. Some examples: Pss. 68:32–35; 107:1–43; 118:29; 136:1–26; Rom. 11:33–36. The attributes describe both God's acts and his essence, contrary to some theologians.
3. *DG*, 32. Here Bavinck seems to endorse some language based on the nonbiblical form of transcendence (chap. 7), in setting forth what the editor calls the "truth contained in agnosticism." Plainly, however, his overall position is one of biblical transcendence.
4. Ibid., 337.

without any human interpretation, or to know him apart from his revelation to us. But if that means to know God as he is revealed, and therefore as he really and truly is, then we can and should know God in himself. God's revelation tells us his very nature.[5]

We should think about God's attributes as servants, within the covenant relationship. These distinctions should remind us of other implications of God's lordship for our present task. Even though we are here discussing God as he is in himself, we will still be doing so as his covenant servants.[6] We will be thinking and speaking of him as creatures, in creaturely language, and therefore by way of accommodation, as we have seen. And we will be thinking and speaking of him on the basis of his revelation, not our own speculation and imagination. Therefore, we will be thinking and speaking of him from the standpoint of our own needs and concerns, seeking applications of his revealed Word.

So in considering God's eternal nature, his essence, from various attributive perspectives, we will in one sense be thinking beyond the scope of the covenant relationship. But, in another sense, we will still be thinking within that relationship, for we can never extricate ourselves from it. Some students may experience psychological and spiritual tension in maintaining these two perspectives simultaneously. But there is no contradiction here. For example, as creatures, we say "God is love," because God says it of himself (1 John 4:8). We say it, as he has said it, in creaturely language, language given to us by God, accommodated to our understanding, and provided to meet our needs as sinners saved by grace. So this language has a significant relationship to us as covenant servants. Nevertheless, it is also true; it tells us what God really and truly is. It is objective. God would be love if he had never made man. But our understanding, thought, and speech about his love is relative to our status as covenant servants.

The attributes describe God's lordship from various perspectives. As we saw in chapter 2, God reveals himself so that all might know that he is Lord. So God gives us all forms of revelation, in nature, historical events, the written Word, and indeed his own Son, to declare his lordship. We have seen how this is true of miracle, providence, redemption, creation, and God's names and images. Clearly, the same is true of God's attributes. We learned his lordship attributes from an analysis of the biblical use of his covenant

---

5. For more discussion of this issue, see *DKG*, 32–33. See also our discussion in chapter 11 of whether language about God can be literally true.

6. I intended *DKG* to be an account of what servant thinking is like and how it is done.

name, Yahweh. Those attributes declare in a very direct way the lordship of God. Scripture presents other attributes, too, as expositions of God's covenant name. For example:

> Then Moses said, "Now show me your glory."
>
> And the LORD said, "I will cause all my goodness to pass in front of you, and I will proclaim my name, the LORD, in your presence. I will have mercy on whom I will have mercy, and I will have compassion on whom I will have compassion." (Ex. 33:18–19)

> Then the LORD came down in the cloud and stood there with him and proclaimed his name, the LORD. And he passed in front of Moses, proclaiming, "The LORD, the LORD, the compassionate and gracious God, slow to anger, abounding in love and faithfulness, maintaining love to thousands, and forgiving wickedness, rebellion and sin. Yet he does not leave the guilty unpunished; he punishes the children and their children for the sin of the fathers to the third and fourth generation." (Ex. 34:5–7)

Both of these passages expound God's name,[7] the first in terms of his sovereign mercy and compassion, the second in terms of his compassionate, forgiving love as well as his wrath. Indeed, Scripture presents all the attributes of God as the responses of God's people to God's revelation in history, and that revelation, as we have seen, is always a revelation of the Lord. In the Psalms and passages like Romans 11:33–36, the attributes appear in contexts of praise, when the writer meditates on the works of the Lord in creation and redemption.

So we should expect, as we study the attributes, that they will manifest God's lordship in various ways—his control, authority, and presence. Indeed, I shall try to show that each of the attributes in fact manifests his lordship, and that this fact is crucial to our understanding of the attributes. I shall try to show that each attribute (1) displays God's sovereign *control* over some aspect of creation, (2) presents God's *authoritative standard* for some aspect of creation, and (3) shows a quality of God's own character, so that the attribute is *present* in God's own nature and characterizes his *presence* in the world. God's love, for example, is (1) a sovereign love, by which he controls the drama of redemption (1 John 4:10, 19), (2) a love that sets the standard for our love (John 13:34–35; 1 John 3:16; 4:19), and

---

7. This is perhaps questionable in the case of 33:18–19, but I cannot understand the function of the passage in context unless it anticipates the revelation of 34:6–7. Certainly the two passages are thoroughly consistent.

(3) a love that characterizes his essence (1 John 4:8, 16) and therefore all his dealings with creatures.

DOES GOD HAVE A FUNDAMENTAL ATTRIBUTE?

Some theologians have tried to show that one attribute of God (or a group of attributes) uniquely describes his essence and therefore is more fundamental than the others. In some cases, they have tried to deduce some or all of the other attributes from the fundamental attribute. As we recall from chapter 3, for Aquinas the proper name of God is Being. So Aquinas deduces many, perhaps all, of God's attributes from the premise that God's essence is identical to his being (*esse*, "existence"). Bavinck usefully surveys other such attempts in the history of theology: for Duns Scotus, God's fundamental attribute was infinity; for some Reformed theologians, aseity;[8] for Cornelius Jansenius, veracity; for Saint-Cyran, omnipotence; for the Socinians, will; for Hegel, reason; for Jacobi, Lotze, Dorner, and others, absolute personality; for Ritschl, love.[9] Among theologians since Bavinck's day, we can note Barth's emphasis on "love in freedom,"[10] Buber's and Brunner's "person,"[11] and Moltmann's "futurity."[12]

For example, it is certainly tempting to say that love is God's fundamental attribute, because 1 John 4:8, 16 says that "God is love," and because a love that imitates God's love is central in biblical ethics (John 13:34–35; Phil. 2:1–11; 1 John 3:16; 4:10). But does "God is love" describe anything more fundamental to God than "God is light" (1 John 1:5) or "God is spirit" (John 4:24)? Or does it describe God's nature more perfectly than the exposition of God's name (in terms of both love and wrath) in Exodus 34:6–7? What about "the LORD, whose name is Jealous" in Exodus 34:14 (cf. 20:5), or "Holy One of Israel" (Pss. 71:22; 78:41; 89:18; Isa. 1:4 and often in Isaiah; cf. Isa. 6:3), or almightiness, the attribute given to God in the patriarchal name *'el shaddai* (see chap. 17)?

8. Gordon H. Clark proposes a logical deduction of all God's attributes from the attribute of aseity. See his "Attributes, the Divine," in *Baker's Dictionary of Theology*, ed. Everett F. Harrison (Grand Rapids: Baker, 1960), 78–79.

9. *DG*, 114–20. Love is also the central attribute of God for the open theists of today. Richard Rice says, "From a Christian perspective, *love* is the first and last word in the biblical portrait of God," in Clark Pinnock et al., *The Openness of God* (Downers Grove, Ill.: InterVarsity Press, 1994), 18.

10. *ChD*, 2.1–2.

11. Martin Buber, *I and Thou* (Edinburgh: T. and T. Clark, 1937); Emil Brunner, *Dogmatics*, vol. 1: *The Christian Doctrine of God* (London: Lutterworth Press, 1949).

12. Jürgen Moltmann, *The Theology of Hope* (New York: Harper and Row, 1965).

Of course, I am tempted to make lordship the fundamental attribute. Certainly, Lord is the fundamental name of God in Scripture, and all biblical revelation expounds it. It is the attribute most often mentioned in the Scriptures, by the constant use of *yahweh* and *kyrios*. For pedagogical purposes, and for purposes of edification, it makes good sense to start where Scripture starts and emphasize what Scripture emphasizes, especially since lordship leads so easily to a consideration of other topics. Yet I would not want to say that lordship is metaphysically central to God's nature in a way that holiness, love, eternity, and righteousness are not. These other concepts can also be central in specific biblical contexts. They can also name God, even define him, as in 1 John 1:5 and 4:8.

So instead of yielding to the temptation to make lordship fundamental, I yield to my other temptation, namely, to make all the attributes perspectival. That is the implication of the doctrine of simplicity, as we saw in chapter 12 and earlier in this chapter. That conclusion is confirmed by the attempts of theologians, often very persuasively, to make this or that attribute fundamental. Perhaps they are all correct in seeing their favorite attribute as the essence of God and trying to derive the others from it. Perhaps all of God's attributes can be derived from his holiness, aseity, love, jealousy, omnipotence, or any number of others. If all of the attributes describe God's simple essence from various perspectives, then any of them can be taken as fundamental in a given context. All of them, after all, involve all the others. Ultimately, all of them, identical to God's simple essence, are identical also to each other.

But these theologians are wrong to think that the centrality of their favorite attribute excludes the centrality of others. These writers are (as is often the case among theologians) right in what they assert, but wrong in what they deny. Ritschl is right to say that love is God's essence, but wrong to deny that holiness is. And that kind of error is sometimes linked to other errors. Often, when a theologian makes God's love central, he intends to cast doubt on the reality or intensity of God's wrath and judgment—contrary to Scripture. That was the case with Ritschl and is the case with some modern evangelicals.[13]

I am not saying that all attributes are equally important. We may recall from chapter 18 the comment by one writer that God is a "knitter" in Psalm 139. Well, I suppose that on that basis we should recognize "knitting capacity" as a divine attribute. But of course that would not be as important as love or omnipotence. It would be a perspective on all of God's attributes,

13. See the excellent critique of these by Robert A. Peterson, *Hell on Trial* (Phillipsburg, N.J.: P&R Publishing, 1995).

for all of God's work is the knitting of a tapestry to set forth his glory. But it is not the most important perspective in Scripture.

Sometimes it is possible to derive divine attributes from others by means of logic. In general, it is appropriate to derive the implications of biblical teaching "by good and necessary consequence."[14] Scripture itself often does this (as in the apostle Paul's frequent "therefore's"), and it is part of our mandate to apply the Scriptures to human life.[15] In the realm of attributes, certainly God's aseity entails his immortality, his truth entails his justice, and so on. But of course all attempts at logical deduction depend on accurate definitions and formulations of premises. These cannot be derived from the science of logic alone. So we must keep going back to Scripture to get the premises for such arguments, to understand the meanings of these premises, and to test the conclusions derived from the arguments. In other words, logic cannot be a substitute for exegesis. Logical argument, in this area, depends on biblical exegesis, just as exegesis depends on logic.

And if no attribute is fundamental in an absolute or exclusive sense, then there may be no single path for logical deductions. One may deduce lordship from aseity, or aseity from lordship. One may deduce justice from truth, or truth from justice. So we may use any defining attribute of God, if we understand it well enough, as a premise for the deduction of any other.[16]

CLASSIFYING GOD'S ATTRIBUTES

A study of the divine attributes must begin and end somewhere, and the progress from beginning to end ought to follow a pattern that is edifying and memorable. There are many attributes of God, and they are difficult to grasp individually or as a whole, unless they are presented systematically, with larger categories and subcategories.

Scripture, however, does not present the attributes of God in any particular order. God declares his attributes, in contexts like Exodus 34:6–7, to show the motivation for his mighty acts of deliverance and judgment. In the Psalms, the writers respond to these acts in somewhat impromptu fashion, inferring from God's actions the personal qualities of the God whom they worship. If one or more of God's attributes were fundamental to the

14. WCF, 1.6.

15. For an extensive argument advocating the use of logic in theology, and an attempt to define its limits in this task, see *DKG*, 242–301.

16. This point reflects my general aversion to the concept of logical order. See chapter 16 and *DKG*, 260–70.

others, that would give us some guidance as to the order of presentation. But we have seen reason to doubt that there are such fundamental attributes.

Writers on this subject have chosen various schemes, arrangements, and orders in which to present the divine attributes. Many of these are based on the distinction between transcendence and immanence. Theologians have often thought that there is a natural division between attributes reflecting God's transcendence (such as aseity, eternity, and immensity) and others reflecting his immanence (such as justice, love, and grace). Various terms have been used to express this broad duality, such as absolute/relative,[17] natural/moral, greatness/goodness, immanent/emanant,[18] formal/material, metaphysical/moral, passive/active,[19] negative/positive,[20] God in himself[21]/God in relation to the world, absoluteness/personality,[22] and incommunicable/communicable.

In the footnotes, I have dealt with some of the problems that modern readers encounter in trying to understand this terminology. But it is also important to note that these distinctions are often misleading, even for those who do understand them. One problem is that, as means of classifying attributes, transcendence and immanence are not sharply separable. The attributes of transcendence are immanent in that they are revealed in cre-

17. Trying to understand this in the best sense, we should avoid using *relative* in such a way as to compromise the absoluteness of all of God's attributes. What seems to be meant is that in the attributes of immanence, God establishes relations with creatures. But even then this duality is problematic. By his decrees, creation, and providence, God as a person (not just some of his attributes) establishes relationships with creatures. In establishing them, his attributes of transcendence are as important as his attributes of immanence.

18. Here the meaning of *immanent* is almost opposite to the way we have so far used the term. In the immanent/emanant contrast, immanent attributes are those that remain in God (immanent in him) and do not go out of him (emanate) to creatures. Others (mainly Lutheran writers) make the same point using terms like quiescent/operative or indwelling/outgoing.

19. In one sense, of course, God is never passive; that is, his essence and decrees never change due to the influences of creatures. But Shedd, who mentions this distinction, sees God's "passive" attributes as more or less what God *is* as opposed to what he *does*, that is, how God finds himself. See W. G. T. Shedd, *Dogmatic Theology* (Grand Rapids: Zondervan, 1950), 1:334.

20. This terminology comes from the view that the attributes of transcendence are expressed by a *via negativa* (see chap. 11); that is, that God is the negation of certain elements of our experience (such as dependent being, time, and space).

21. Recall the ambiguity of this phrase, noted earlier in this chapter.

22. If I were to adopt a twofold distinction, based on the transcendence/immanence duality, I would choose this one. It reflects the point I made in chapter 2, that the biblical God, unlike the gods of other religions and philosophies, is both personal and absolute. The weaknesses of this distinction, however, are its suggestion that the "personality" attributes of God are something other than absolute, and the difficulty of assigning divine attributes exclusively to each category—the same problem we see in the other twofold classifications.

ation (Rom. 1:20), are relevant to creatures (as eternity in Ps. 90), and have implications for our piety (as aseity in Acts 17:25). Furthermore, the attributes of immanence are certainly transcendent. For example, God's love is absolute (1 John 4:8), a measure of his greatness (Eph. 3:18), and metaphysical (it belongs to his being; see the next section).

Reformed theologians have often used the classification incommunicable/communicable.[23] In this terminology, some attributes (the attributes of transcendence, such as aseity, eternity, and immensity) cannot be shared by God and man, while others (the attributes of immanence, such as love, knowledge, and power) can be. But this classification also breaks down. In one sense, all divine attributes are incommunicable. Our love, at its best, is an image of God's love, but it is not divine. God's love is identical to his very essence, and therefore radically distinct from ours, even from our love at its best.

In another sense, all divine attributes are communicable. Man is the image of God. We are not merely the image of some divine attributes; we image God himself, who is inseparable from all his attributes.[24] Our creaturely otherness and integrity (chap. 8) image God's aseity, for our created integrity enables us to think, act, and speak of our own desires and motives. Our very relationship to God is an image of his eternity[25] and immensity, for in him we have access to the knowledge, power, and love of one who transcends time and space.[26] When we hear and believe God's Word, we see reality from his supratemporal and supraspatial viewpoint. And he has also given us memory, imagination, and science, through which, to a degree impossible for lower creatures, we are able to know the past, plan for the future, and communicate and travel over vast reaches of space.

There is a larger problem with all classifications based on the transcendence/immanence distinction. The concept of transcendence underlying these distinctions appears to be more like the unbiblical concept than the biblical one (recall our discussion of these in chap. 7). In these dualities, God's transcendence is a kind of distance from the world. That distance is epistemic as well as ontological: our language is incapable of expressing God's transcendence. So transcendence represents God's incomprehensi-

23. See, for example, *DG*, 113–251. Heppe says the Lutherans objected to this distinction because they insisted that all divine attributes are communicated to the human nature of Christ. See *RD*, 62.

24. Note again our larger emphasis, that we relate to God as a person, not to attributes as impersonal, abstract entities.

25. Hence, in Scripture, life in fellowship with God is eternal life.

26. For some other ways in which we image God's transcendence, particularly his self-attestation, omniscience, and creativity, see *DKG*, 25–29.

bility or mystery, a negation of creaturely experience and language. On this basis, God is so far away from us that we cannot speak of him truly.

When this kind of transcendence is applied to the divine attributes, the conclusion is that God is "beyond" the world in the sense of being beyond created being (aseity), beyond time (eternity), beyond space (immensity), etc. These concepts put God beyond the world of our experience and therefore in a realm about which we know little, if anything. But, this view continues, we can know God's love, justice, and wisdom, since God demonstrates these in our world. This picture lies behind some of the confusions I noted earlier, such as the notion that we image only some divine attributes (the others being too far beyond us), or the notion that only some divine attributes establish relationships between God and creatures.

But we saw in chapter 7 that although God is "high above" us, that height pertains primarily not to distance or incomprehensibility, but to royal status. I argued then that we should not define transcendence as God's distance from us, but as his royal control and authority over his world. His immanence, then, is his covenant presence; it represents the fact that God's control and authority are inescapable in the world he has made. On this basis, it would be impossible to distinguish attributes of transcendence from attributes of immanence. All of God's attributes describe his control and authority, and all equally describe his presence in the world. When God acts as Lord, in his control, authority, and presence, he acts as one person, not as a group of attributes that might be opposed to another group. A theology of lordship is intensely personalistic.

What kind of order or structure of the divine attributes, then, is appropriate to a theology of lordship? Well, many orders are possible. The theology of lordship, you may recall, tends to be flexible on questions of order. My inclination, of course, is to choose an order that somehow reflects the control/authority/presence distinction. But that is difficult, for, as I argued earlier in this chapter, all divine attributes reflect all three lordship attributes.

I have decided to group the attributes around the general concepts of power, knowledge, and goodness, which have a certain affinity to the lordship attributes, but aren't quite the same.[27] So all the attributes of God display the lordship attributes, but some are more conveniently described as powers, others as forms of knowledge, and others as forms of goodness. This scheme is not particularly profound, but the attributes do seem to cluster

27. This distinction recalls the distinction in philosophy between metaphysics, epistemology, and ethics. However, I resist the notion of a metaphysical attribute, for reasons mentioned below.

into these general categories. They do indicate the shape of biblical teaching, and they are unlikely to create the confusion that we have noted in the traditional distinctions.

The main difficulty with this threefold scheme pertains to the attributes traditionally associated with transcendence: aseity, eternity (including unchangeability), immensity, and incorporeality (including invisibility), to which I would add holiness and incomprehensibility. These don't fit obviously or easily into any of my three categories. But the problem may be a lingering effect of the unbiblical concept of transcendence. For example, what does it really mean to say that God is eternal? Where does Scripture authorize us to say that God is outside or above time? Is there a "supratime" around time, in which God exists? Is there a "supraspace" around space, in which he is located, so that he can be "beyond space" (the common definition of *immense*)? These issues are difficult and widely discussed today. As we shall see, I favor the view that God is supratemporal and supraspatial, but the burden of Scripture's own doctrines of eternity and immensity is not to propound spatial or supraspatial metaphors, but rather to insist that God is Lord of time and space. He is in control of them, has authority over them, and is present throughout them.

So I shall describe God's eternity as a form of his power (implausible as that may seem at first): in this case, as his power over time itself and every aspect of the temporal sequence. I shall similarly describe the other attributes of transcendence.

DISTINCTIONS WITHIN ATTRIBUTE GROUPS

Within the three groups of attributes, I will make a few other distinctions. In each group, I will distinguish some attributes that seem to focus particularly on the defining characteristic of that group (control, authority, or presence). I use the word *focus* advisedly. Each attribute refers to all the lordship attributes, not only one. But there do seem to be some differences of degree or focus.

The attributes that focus on control seem to be more dynamic. That is, they draw much of their meaning from God's actions in history. Those that emphasize authority seem to be more static,[28] in that they denote con-

---

28. The term *static* is usually a derogatory term in modern theology. To many theologians, God is in every respect dynamic, never static. I dissent from this view. The God of Scripture is both active and unchangeable, as we shall see. Both his mighty deeds and his constant reliability deserve our highest praise.

	Goodness	Knowledge	Power
Control Dynamic; Content	Goodness Love Grace Mercy Patience Compassion Jealousy Wrath	Speech Incomprehensiblity	Eternity Immensity Incorporeality Will Power Existence (*esse*)
Authority Static; Form, Structure	Justice Righteousness	Truth	Aseity Simplicity Essence
Presence Integrity; Involvement	Joy Blessedness Beauty Perfection Holiness	Knowledge Wisdom Mind Knowability	Glory Spirituality Omnipresence

Fig. 2. The Attributes of God

stancies in God's nature, a structure that defines the limits of his possible actions. God's authority, his standards of right and truth, remain constant throughout time and eternity. The distinction between control and authority also seems to me to be somewhat analogous to the traditional distinction between content and form, or content and structure.

The third group of attributes emphasizes God's presence. These attributes are present in God; they indwell him, and therefore constitute his character (integrity). They are also present in all his dealings with creatures (involvement). Perhaps we may say that they represent a synthesis between the dynamic and the static, between content and form, being God's attributes in their concreteness.

To present all these relationships, I have placed the more important attributes in figure 2. I certainly am not dogmatic about the position of any attribute on this chart, or even about the usefulness of the chart itself. It is almost certainly too schematic to represent in more than a rough way the rich, complex interrelationships of the divine attributes. None of the attributes can really be contained in any single cell of the chart; they break out of the scheme with frustrating frequency. Nonetheless, the chart may be suggestive. It may help readers to see why I discuss the attributes in the order I do within the three major groupings, although I will not always follow the order indicated on the chart.

STARTING WITH GOODNESS

Where, then, do we start? With power, knowledge, or goodness? Usually, systematic theologians have started with power, particularly with those attributes traditionally associated with transcendence. But, as the reader may have noticed, this volume has often varied the traditional order of topics; see chapter 1 for some of the reasons. In general, this book moves from history to eternity, rather than the other way around.[29] We have looked at the divine acts before the divine attributes, and we have looked at those acts in the opposite order from which they are usually considered, starting with God's acts in history, moving toward the beginning of history, and then to eternity.

Similarly, my discussion of the attributes will begin with goodness, and then move on to knowledge and power. The traditional order was popular in the past because students of theology tended then to have a background in philosophy. Traditional philosophy usually started with metaphysics (being, time, space) before moving on to epistemology and ethics. Today, however, we cannot assume that students have much background (or interest) in philosophy. It may be better these days to start with the ethical attributes and move on to the epistemological and metaphysical—that is, to start with what students know best and then show them gradually why the metaphysical attributes are also important.

The traditional order has also been encouraged by the false assumption that the attributes of power or transcendence are more fundamental to God's nature than the others. The term *metaphysical* suggests that view, as if these attributes represent God's being in a more basic way than the other attributes. But, as we have seen, no attribute is metaphysically basic in this sense; all the essential attributes denote God's entire being. For that reason, I resist using the term *metaphysical* for the power-attributes, however attractive that term may be from other considerations.

For these reasons, pedagogical and substantive, I prefer to begin with the ethical attributes, or, as I call them, the attributes of divine goodness. Scripture, as we have seen, never suggests that God's eternity or aseity is more fundamental to his nature than his love or justice. Indeed, those passages of Scripture that sound most like definitions of God tend to focus on his attributes of goodness, not his attributes of knowledge or power. As we have seen, this is true of Exodus 33:19 and 34:6–7 (expositions of the divine name). Other passages, such as Psalm 103:8–10, allude to Exodus

---

29. But, as I emphasized in chapter 1, this book is, in the language of modern theologians, a theology "from above" rather than "from below."

34:6–7 in describing God's fundamental nature. Exodus 34:14 tells us that his "name is Jealous" (I shall argue that God's jealousy is a form of his love). "God is love" (1 John 4:8, 16) is another example, as is "God is light" (1 John 1:5), for, as we saw in chapter 18, light speaks of God's truth and righteousness.[30] God's holiness, so definitive of God in the prophecy of Isaiah, also has a profoundly ethical meaning (see chap. 2).

In Scripture, too, it is much easier to find clear references to God's attributes of goodness than to his attributes of power (especially those focused on metaphysics or transcendence). Aseity, eternity (in the sense of supratemporality), immensity, and incorporeality are deduced from Scripture, not explicitly taught in it. But love, justice, and mercy are taught explicitly and pervasively. This emphasis is understandable, for Scripture is a book about redemption from sin. Contrary to many false religions and philosophies, our problem is sin, not finitude. So the prominent terminology about God tends to be ethical rather than metaphysical. Pedagogically, then, it makes sense to start with what is most prominent and explicit in Scripture before moving to what is less so.

The suzerainty treaty pattern in biblical covenants between God and man (see chap. 2) also stresses ethics. God reveals his name and then his past blessings (grace), our obligations (justice), and his sanctions (blessing and curse). So God's ethical attributes are central to his covenant lordship.

So love is no less fundamental to the nature of God than his aseity or eternity. God's love is bedrock. There is nothing more basic to his nature. When we know that God is love and understand what that means, then we know what God really and truly is.

1 GOD IS LOVE
2 GOD IS LIGHT
3 GOD IS SPIRIT

30. The third Johannine statement of equivalence, "God is spirit" (John 4:24), focuses, as I shall argue, on the coming of the Spirit at Pentecost, and on the necessity of worship in the Spirit, that is, in his power and according to the truth he has revealed. It is difficult, therefore, to decide what category of attributes to put "spirituality" in. Power and truth (knowledge) are involved, but also our ethical obligation to worship God according to his will.

CHAPTER 20

God's Goodness

We now begin a systematic study of God's attributes. I have already dealt with some of them: holiness and personality (chap. 2), the lordship attributes (therefore sovereignty) (chaps. 3–6), transcendence and immanence (chap. 7), incomprehensibility and knowability (chap. 11), necessity and freedom (chap. 12), simplicity (chap. 12), and the attributes implicit in God's names and images (chaps. 17 and 18). I shall not repeat all of these studies in what follows, but I will occasionally review the past material so as to show how the previously discussed attributes relate to those we discuss here.

In this chapter, we shall begin our discussion with the first major group of divine attributes, those I call the attributes of goodness. These include goodness, perfection, love, grace, patience, faithfulness, mercy, justice, righteousness, jealousy, wrath, beauty, joy, and blessedness.[1] Naturally, I begin with goodness itself.

GOODNESS AS PERFECTION

Good is, first of all, a general term of commendation. We describe as good any kind of excellence, including beauty, economic value, usefulness, or

---

1. Holiness (chap. 2) is also part of this group, representing the radical difference between God and creation and his moral antithesis to sin. It has affinities to the power group as well, since it evokes awe and threatens judgment on those who take God lightly.

skillfulness—indeed, anything that evokes a favorable response. In theology, we tend to focus on moral goodness, but there are many other kinds of goodness as well. We may describe someone as a "good plumber" or a "good pianist," even though he is morally wretched.[2] A dinner, or computer, or hammer can be good, even though inanimate objects are not subject to moral evaluation. So, in Scripture, God says that light is good (Gen. 1:4), together with all other created things (vv. 10, 12, 18, 21, 25; cf. 1 Tim. 4:4).

Theologians have sometimes understood God's goodness as including both moral goodness and other kinds of excellencies (or "perfections"). I don't know of any Scripture passage in which *good* or *goodness* refers to divine perfections generally, but it is a common usage in theology, and we should take a brief look at it. Scripture does use the term *perfect*, and we should examine that.

For Thomas Aquinas, as we have seen, God's fundamental nature is Being. And, in his view:

> Goodness and being are really the same, and differ only in idea. . . . The essence of goodness consists in this, that it is in some way desirable. . . . Now it is clear that a thing is desirable only in so far as it is perfect, for all desire their own perfection. But everything is perfect so far as it is actual.[3]

So, for Aquinas, God's goodness includes all the qualities of a perfectly actual being, indeed all perfections. When a being becomes perfectly actual, that is, when it achieves the end or goal implicit in its own nature, then it becomes perfect. So the more being, the more goodness.

Scripture rarely uses *perfect* as a divine attribute. Matthew 5:48 is the only passage I know that applies the adjective *perfect* (*teleios*) to God. There Jesus tells his disciples, "Be perfect, therefore, as your heavenly Father is perfect." But the Hebrew equivalent, *tamim*, occurs in Deuteronomy 32:4, 2 Samuel 22:31, and Psalm 18:30, referring to God's ways.

Tam and *tamim* mean "complete," "without defect." Their most common

---

2. Of course, this issue is more complicated than I am able to present it here. Moral wretchedness does corrupt our thoughts, words, and deeds in many ways. For its effects on thinking and reasoning, see *DKG*. Satan has "good" powers of reason and strength, but his overall goal of trying to defeat God makes him a pathetically stupid figure, a paradigm of irrationality. Paul says the same of Satan's followers, declaring that although they know God, they do not worship him, and they exchange the truth for a lie (Rom. 1:21, 25). Nevertheless, as a matter of linguistic usage, *good* can describe beings who are not morally upright.

3. *ST*, 1; see also *SCG*, 1. Recall that, for the Thomist, evil is not being, but a privation of being (chap. 9).

use is to designate sacrifices as perfect or unblemished. *Teleios* inherits these meanings as well as the idea of maturity (reaching one's *telos*, "end" or "goal"). The respect in which someone or something is complete or mature depends on the context. Applied to human beings, these terms refer to a general moral uprightness or spiritual maturity, implicitly comparing one person with others. Since, according to Scripture, sinless perfection is impossible in this life (1 John 1:8–10), the "perfect" man is not wholly without sin, but is "blameless" (as was Noah "among the people of his time," Gen. 6:9). So "perfection" in human beings is usually a relative perfection, not an absolute one. In three passages, however, *teleios* is used absolutely, referring to a goal that cannot be achieved in this life (Matt. 5:48; 19:21; James 3:2).

This absolute use is also found, of course, when these terms are applied to God as grounds for worship (Deut. 32:4) or as a supreme ideal for man (Matt. 5:48). They apply to God's nature (Matt. 5:48) and to his plans and actions ("ways" in Deut. 32:4; 2 Sam. 22:31; Ps. 18:30).

Whatever may be said about this terminology as such, it is plain that in Scripture every attribute ascribed to God is supremely excellent. As we shall see, this is true of all of his goodness, knowledge, and power. So it is right to ascribe to God the highest perfections in all his attributes. The name given to God by Anselm of Canterbury, therefore, is appropriate: God is "a being than which nothing greater can be conceived."[4]

Thomas Morris has advocated a theological method that he calls "perfect being theology," modeled after Anselm.[5] In this method, we determine the nature of God by asking what attributes or qualities a perfect or maximally great being would have. This method is legitimate, but the concept of perfection is somewhat problematic. People have often disagreed about what qualities constitute perfections. Orthodox Protestants say that unchangeability is a perfection in God, but modern process thinkers and open theists believe that unchangeability is a defect in a person. On their view, a person is more perfect if he can change, adapting to new situations as they come along. Medieval theologians believed that God's existence is a perfection, but Buddhists believe that a form of nothingness is superior to existence. So it is important for us to go to Scripture for our concept of perfection. We cannot use the concept of perfection with confidence unless God tells

4. Anselm, *Proslogium*, chap. 2, in *Saint Anselm: Basic Writings*, ed. S. N. Deane (La Salle, Ill.: Open Court, 1962), 7. Greatness, of course, consists of perfections.
5. In *Our Idea of God: An Introduction to Philosophical Theology* (Notre Dame: University of Notre Dame Press, 1991) and elsewhere.

us what perfection is. He is perfect, but according to his own standard of perfection.

THE EUTHYPHRO PROBLEM

Here, however, we come to a problem that emerges with many of the attributes. In chapter 19, I said that each attribute (1) describes God's control over some aspect of reality, (2) serves as the authoritative standard for all creaturely images of that attribute, and (3) describes qualities present in God himself and therefore in all his dealings with us. Some philosophers have raised questions about the relationship between the second and the third points. When we ascribe an attribute to God and also make him the standard for identifying and evaluating that quality, the two statements generate a kind of circularity.

If I say that Bach's music is the greatest ever written, I make a meaningful, if disputable claim. But if someone asks my criteria for greatness in music, and I reply, "likeness to Bach's," then the significance of my claim seems to be reduced. Bach's superiority then becomes tautological and trivial, for of course, of all composers, Bach's music is most like Bach's. An admirer of Mozart, or even of Lawrence Welk, could use the same circular argument, and it would be equally unconvincing. Or imagine me claiming to be the world's greatest basketball player, and then defining basketball greatness as whatever I do on the court. On that definition, my apparently audacious claim becomes true, but utterly uninteresting.

Similarly, some have argued that if we say "God is good," but then make God the standard or criterion of goodness, we make the initial claim meaningless. If we say both "God is good" and "Good is whatever God is," then God's "goodness" could be anything at all. When we make God our standard of goodness, he could hate the righteous, reward wickedness, and betray his friends, but those actions would be good, simply because God did them.

So Plato, in *Euthyphro,* poses the question of whether piety is what the gods say it is, or whether the gods command piety because of its intrinsic nature, apart from their own wishes. In Plato's mind, the former makes the nature of piety arbitrary, one that could be changed on the whim of a god. But the second alternative, which Plato certainly prefers, means that piety is independent of the will of the gods, something to which the gods' opinions are subject. So either piety is arbitrary or the gods are subject to something higher than themselves.

Some philosophers have identified a similar problem in biblical theism:

406   BIBLICAL DESCRIPTIONS OF GOD

if good is what God says, then goodness is subject to the arbitrary whims of a personal deity.[6] But if goodness is independent of God, then he is subordinate to the abstract concept of goodness. The same problem would arise with righteousness, truth, wisdom, beauty, or any attribute that serves as a model or criterion for the same attributes imaged in creation.

In my view, this problem arises from the inability of Plato and other philosophers to see goodness as something personal. Many of them never seem to question the view that goodness, truth, etc., are impersonal.[7] They reason that since goodness is an abstract entity, it cannot be identical with a person.

I question this assumption. It is plausible to argue this way on the human level, for human goodness is shared by many and thus should not be identified absolutely with any one of us. And of course the behavior of one human being cannot define goodness.[8] Since goodness is not a human person, some conclude, it must be something impersonal, an abstract object.

But when we think of goodness as an attribute of God, we must surely think differently. Remember from chapter 19 that not one of God's attributes is strictly communicable. In that sense, God's goodness is strictly his own. It is not shared by anybody else, but God has imaged it in the creation. Before creation, only God existed, and his goodness was not shared with anyone but the persons of the Trinity. Indeed, it was nothing less than God's own nature (see chap. 12). So God's goodness is God, and therefore personal.

So goodness is the behavior and self-revelation of a person, not a general or abstract concept. Certainly it would be wrong to regard the behavior of any mere human being as the criterion of goodness. But of course God is unique.

6. See Stephen Evans, *Philosophy of Religion* (Downers Grove, Ill.: InterVarsity Press, 1985), 68–96; R. W. Hepburn, *Christianity and Paradox* (New York: Pegasus, 1958), 128–54; C. B. Martin, "The Perfect Good," in *New Essays in Philosophical Theology*, ed. Antony Flew and Alasdair C. MacIntyre (London: SCM, 1955), 212–26. See also the literature on the "divine command theory" of ethics, such as Robert Adams, *The Virtue of Faith* (Oxford: Oxford University Press, 1987); Paul Helm, ed., *Divine Commands and Morality* (Oxford: Oxford University Press, 1981).

7. Similarly, many scientists and philosophers of science assume that the impersonal aspects of the universe are more fundamental than the personal aspects. So they tend to believe that explanations of phenomena in terms of impersonal realities (matter, motion, time, space) are more basic than explanations in terms of personal choice. On this assumption, scientists prefer theories that reduce the personal to the impersonal. This explains the objectively implausible preference for naturalistic evolution over creation as an explanation for the forms of living beings.

8. I am not here denying the sinlessness of Jesus. But we can appreciate his sinlessness more if we understand how audacious it is to claim that any man is sinless.

So the good is not, as in Plato's view, an abstract form superior to God. Is the good, then, what God says it is? Yes, but God's word is not arbitrary. God commends goodness to us because he is himself supremely good. His commands to us are based on what he himself is.[9] So it is true to say that goodness is what God says it is, and it is also true to say that God commends the good because it is good.

A mere human being cannot be the standard of goodness, because his nature is not perfect. His commands would indeed be subject to the suspicion of arbitrariness. As a finite and fallen creature, he might indeed declare what is good today to be bad tomorrow. People like Adolf Hitler, Josef Stalin, and Jim Jones, who have demanded absolute allegiance from their followers, have typically led them into sin, error, and death. But God's word cannot be arbitrary in this way, for God is supremely and unchangeably good.

A form of circularity here is unavoidable. When we say that God is good, we evaluate God's conduct on the basis of his own revelation. God is both supremely good and the ultimate standard of goodness. Does this circularity fall prey to the criticisms that apply to the examples I mentioned above (regarding Bach, Mozart, Welk, and myself)?

I think not, for these reasons:

1. Whatever may be said for their music, Bach, Mozart, and Welk are human beings. None is fit to be the absolute criterion of musical excellence. To make Bach the ultimate standard of musicality is to ignore the fact that musical excellence occurs in types of music very different from Bach's. So there are objections to using human beings as ultimate criteria, entirely apart from questions of circularity—objections that do not apply to God.

2. This circularity is very similar to the circularity of presuppositional apologetics that I have discussed elsewhere.[10] There is always a kind of circularity when we are dealing with an ultimate standard. If one's standard of truth is human reason, one can argue for that standard only by a rational argument, an argument that presupposes the truth of its conclusion. Similarly, if God is the supreme standard of truth and rationality, one may argue for that standard only by presupposing it. For if the conclusion is true,

---

9. Obviously, there are differences between what is good for God and what is good for man. For example, God has the right to take human life for his own purposes; we do not. We have an obligation to worship a being other than ourselves; God does not. God's prerogatives, his "rights," are different from ours. But the differences as well as the similarities between God's ethics and ours are based on his nature. Both the uniqueness of God's nature and the resemblances between God and his creaturely images are important to ethics.

10. *DKG*, 130–33; *AGG*, 9–14; *CVT*, 299–309. See also my contributions to *Five Views on Apologetics*, ed. Steven B. Cowan (Grand Rapids: Zondervan, 2000).

this is the only kind of argument permissible. Likewise, when we argue that God is good, we must appeal to the only true standard of goodness that there is, namely, God. We have no other choice.

The same circularity is present in any attempt, Christian or non-Christian, to establish a criterion of goodness. Let's say that someone tries to prove that goodness is an abstract form, without any personal exemplification. He must then somehow derive specific ethical content from that form.[11] But then it becomes his task to show that these ethical principles are in fact good. If his abstract form is indeed the supreme standard, then he must show the content of the abstract form to be good by reference to the abstract form. That argument is circular, too. So if theistic reasoning is circular at this point, its circularity is shared by all other forms of reasoning.

3. Some might argue that circularity still presents a problem, despite the above observations. For even though this circularity is shared by all religions and philosophies, they might say, it is still circularity and therefore objectionable. But if it is, the whole enterprise of reason is invalidated, and we are forced into radical skepticism. But that sort of objection is self-refuting. If the circularity of reason invalidates reason itself, then it invalidates the objection as well. Besides, skepticism itself is a self-refuting position. To argue it, or even to assert it, is to deny it.[12]

4. Our subjective uneasiness with this circularity stems in part from our tendency to reduce the differences between God and man (see the first point, above) and in part from our failure to understand concretely how we actually learn about God's goodness. The biblical writers never say that God is good because he says he is good, and that he says he is good because he is good. That would be narrow circularity.[13] Rather, they describe and praise God's mighty acts of deliverance, his kindness in providence, and his grace in salvation. These are big, bold, obvious evidences of goodness.

---

11. As we saw in chapter 10, this is a very difficult problem for non-Christian deontologists like Plato and Kant. How can you derive ethical principles from an abstract concept, without falling victim to the naturalistic fallacy? Plato, by the way, recognized that the so-called problem of self-predication was a difficult one for his philosophy: how can the form of goodness be good, the form of truth be true, and the form of manhood be human, when these are all impersonal abstractions? And if goodness must be defined by an abstract form, how about the goodness of that abstract form? Does that require another abstract form, *ad infinitum*? This is sometimes called the "third man" argument, from its application to the form of manhood. (If the form of manhood is human, does that humanness require another form to account for it? Then man presupposes the form man, which presupposes another form man, etc.)

12. See *DKG*, 360–63.

13. Compare the distinction between broad and narrow circularity in my writings on circularity mentioned in footnote 10.

They overwhelm believing readers and call from us almost involuntarily the confession that God is good. At this stage of our thinking, there may seem to be no circularity at all.

But as we think more deeply, we realize that, of course, we learn of these evidences from God himself. We learn them from God's Word, and the biblical writers themselves learn them from God's inspiration. There is also general revelation: God reveals his goodness through his actions in the course of nature and history, both in the experience of the biblical writers and in our own. So everything we know about God's goodness comes from him. God's revelation is both our ultimate criterion of truth and our sole source of knowledge about God's goodness. We believe that God is good, then, because God tells us that he is good. So the circularity is present. But it is a broad circularity, not a narrow one. It is a circularity loaded with content, full of evidence, and richly persuasive. We are literally surrounded by evidence of God's goodness.

So when someone says that for God to be his own standard allows him to be an arbitrary despot, declaring what is good today to be evil tomorrow, the critic is not dealing with the reality of God's revelation. The God who reveals himself in all creation is simply not that kind of person. We do not know him as an arbitrary despot. We have heard of arbitrary despots, but our God is not like them.

God has made us to hear his voice, as obedient children listen to a loving father. We know him because he knows us and addresses us. He declares his goodness, and he demonstrates it richly. We don't merely know the bare fact that God is good; we know *him*. We learn to trust someone by observing his or her behavior. With God, there is far more evidence than that, for all creation presents to us his actions and his love.

God's goodness is not always obvious on the surface, especially when we experience injustice or suffering. But in the end we shall see that even that injustice and suffering manifests the goodness of God.[14] Then believers will see his wrath as justice and our sufferings as his fatherly discipline (Heb. 12:4–12).

GOODNESS AS BENEVOLENCE

As we have seen, *goodness* has a broad range of meaning. It can apply even to inanimate objects. With respect to persons, *goodness* sometimes refers to character and behavior that is in accord with God's standards. In

14. See chapter 9 for a discussion of the problem of evil.

this usage, it is more or less synonymous with *righteousness*, which we will consider later. (E.g., Gen. 3:5; Lev. 5:4; Num. 24:13; 1 Sam. 12:23; 2 Sam. 14:17; Ps. 25:8; Rom. 2:10; 3:12; 7:18; 2 Cor. 5:10.)[15]

But by far the most common meaning of *goodness* in Scripture (Hebrew *tov*, Greek *agathos, kalos*) is "benevolence." A good person is one who acts to benefit others. Benevolence is part of righteousness, but a part that Scripture often singles out. God is the chief example of goodness. Consider these passages:

> You intended to harm me, but God intended it for good to accomplish what is now being done, the saving of many lives. (Gen. 50:20)

> Now Moses said to Hobab son of Reuel the Midianite, Moses' father-in-law, "We are setting out for the place about which the LORD said, 'I will give it to you.' Come with us and we will treat you well, for the LORD has promised good things to Israel." (Num. 10:29)

> He will bring you to the land that belonged to your fathers, and you will take possession of it. He will make you more prosperous [lit., do you good] and numerous than your fathers. (Deut. 30:5)

(See also Josh. 24:20; Judg. 17:13; 2 Sam. 16:12; Mark 3:4; John 10:11; Acts 14:17.) God is the source of all blessings (Ps. 34:8–10; James 1:17). Truly, he is good to Israel (Ps. 73:1). From the righteous, God withholds no good thing (Pss. 84:11; 85:12; 103:5; Matt. 7:11). One important blessing is God's mercy, which is often paired with goodness in the Psalms (Pss. 100:5; 106:1; 107:1; 109:21; 118:1; 136:1). And God's good mercies include the forgiveness of sins (Ps. 86:5).

OBJECTS OF GOD'S GOODNESS

To whom is God good? Certainly to Israel, his covenant people (Ps. 73:1). After the account of Israel's conquest of the Promised Land under Joshua, we read, "Not one of all the LORD's good promises to the house of Israel failed; every one was fulfilled" (Josh. 21:45; cf. Ps. 119:65, 68). In such contexts, goodness is a covenantal category. God's goodness means that he gives blessings in accordance with his covenant promises. Goodness is a form of God's covenant lordship. Recall the references to mercy and grace in the

15. In some of these texts, however, there is some reference to goodness as benevolence, which I take up in the next paragraph.

exposition of the name Yahweh (Ex. 34:6–7). And as God's goodness is covenantal, it is also redemptive: God's goodness to his people is the blessing of heaven itself for the sake of Christ. Paul is confident that "he who began a good work in you will carry it on to completion until the day of Christ Jesus" (Phil. 1:6). In Christ, we have "good hope" (2 Thess. 2:16). Because he is our high priest, good things are coming (Heb. 9:11; 10:1).

However, God does not do good only to those who obey him. He blesses his people before there is any inclination in their hearts to obey. His blessing begins before time (Eph. 1:4). And he blesses us in time, not only as a reward for faithfulness (Deut. 4:1), but before we are faithful. God's grace initiates the covenant. We obey him because he has delivered us (Ex. 20:2; 1 John 4:10). So God has been good to us even when we have hated him and rebelled against him. It was while we were yet sinners that Christ died for us (Rom. 5:8).

And God blesses many who never do come to love and serve him. His goodness is not restricted to those who are eternally elect. The nation of Israel inherited the Promised Land, but many of the Israelites fell into the worship of other gods. God was good to them, but they did not respond in trust and obedience, and so failed to receive God's ultimate blessing. God is good to his enemies (Matt. 5:45), sending the rain and sunshine on the just and the unjust. For some, these good blessings lead to repentance (Acts 14:17; 17:24–34; Rom. 2:4; cf. 2 Peter 3:9), but many remain in their sins, despite God's kindness.

Indeed, God's goodness extends universally:

> The LORD is good to all;
> he has compassion on all he has made. (Ps. 145:9)

The psalmist goes on to specify some of God's universal compassions:

> The LORD is faithful to all his promises
> and loving toward all he has made.
> The LORD upholds all those who fall
> and lifts up all who are bowed down.
> The eyes of all look to you,
> and you give them their food at the proper time.
> You open your hand
> and satisfy the desires of every living thing. (vv. 13–16)

Compare Matthew 5:45 and Acts 14:17. All rain and sunshine, and all crops and food, are blessings of God upon all his creatures.

These universal blessings are not exceptions to the covenantal nature of God's goodness. They are very much a part of it. Notice that in Psalm

145:8 (preceding the passage quoted above), the psalmist recalls the exposition of the divine name in Exodus 34:6–7:

> The LORD is gracious and compassionate,
>   slow to anger and rich in love.

The following verses (10–13) speak of Yahweh's kingdom, mighty acts, and
everlasting dominion—typical covenantal language. But the passage refers,
not to Israel specifically, but to the whole creation. Compare Psalm 36:5–9.
We see here, as I mentioned in chapter 2, that the whole earth is God's
temple; he relates to the entire creation as the Lord.[16]

So God is good to all creatures and to all men, giving them blessings
of his covenant lordship. This is not to say, however, that he gives to all
the blessings of salvation in Christ. Whatever role the animals, rocks, and
trees of the earth may play in the world to come, they are not guilty of
sin as human beings are, and so they are not granted the blessings of forgiveness in Christ. Of course, the lower creation is affected by sin and redemption. God placed a curse on the creation because of human sin (Gen.
3:17–19), and now it is "groaning as in the pains of childbirth" (Rom.
8:22), awaiting the redemption of the children of God. But the creation
itself is not saved in the sense that God's elect people are saved. Yet creation does receive blessings that flow from God's covenant lordship. Everything in creation is blessed in accordance with its nature and the role it
plays in God's cosmic drama (recall the author-character model discussed
in chaps. 8 and 9).

Therefore, human beings do not all receive the same blessings of God's
goodness. Those who are eternally elect receive the fullness of eternal life.
Those who are eternally reprobate receive blessings only in this life. Those
blessings should not be disparaged. The nonelect experience the goodness
of God in a profound way (Acts 14:17), sufficient to convince them of their
need to repent (Rom. 2:4). They have no valid complaint that God has
not been good to them. Indeed, God has given them (as to all of us) many
more blessings than they deserve.

Is God good to the lost in hell? The question isn't settled by Psalm
145:9; most likely, the damned are not included in the psalmist's universe
of discourse.[17] And the fact that goodness is an attribute of God does not

---

16. Note also chapters 13 and 14, in which I draw a close connection between miracle
and providence. Miracle is clearly a redemptive covenantal category: Yahweh does mighty
works to save his people. But providence is not sharply distinct from miracle.

17. The doctrine of the future life is not as clearly set forth in the Psalms as it is elsewhere in Scripture.

imply that all creatures everywhere are the recipients of that goodness. There is no logical problem with the possibility that God is good only to those people who are not condemned to hell, and that the condemnation of the wicked is itself a benevolence of God directed to the other people: God establishes his justice and, for the sake of his people, exiles those who would turn the cosmos into chaos.

There may be some ways, however, in which God is good even to the lost. Perhaps he is as good to them as he can possibly be, given their hatred of him and the demands of his justice. And if there are degrees of punishment in hell (as suggested by Luke 12:47–48), then, even in hell, God may exercise his benevolence by mitigating punishments. It may also be worth considering that in their very punishment in hell, God is giving a privilege to the lost—the privilege of displaying his justice and his victory in the spiritual war (cf. Rom. 9:17). Those who find no benevolence in this privilege might be advised to consider whether their standards of goodness are sufficiently theocentric.

But such thoughts are somewhat speculative. Certainly it is hard for us to think of eternal punishment as divine benevolence. A somewhat more satisfying answer to the question is that God is good to creatures in different ways and at different times, depending on their natures and their roles in God's plan for history. His goodness does not obligate him to give the same blessings to all, or to give the same blessings to any creature throughout his existence. If the lost in hell are now receiving no blessings at all, they cannot complain that God was never good to them. During this life, they were surrounded by God's goodness, just like all other creatures. Furthermore, as Scripture often represents it, the wicked typically prosper in this life and oppress the righteous. In the next life, these roles are reversed (Luke 16:19–31).[18] So even the reprobate should confess that God has been good to them, far more than they deserved.

The elect experience suffering in this life and glory in the next (Rom. 8:18; 1 Peter 1:3–9). But suffering has its value, and at the Last Day none will charge God with being less than benevolent (cf. chap. 9). On the contrary, but similarly, the nonelect experience God's blessing in this life, but his wrath in the life to come. As we do with the elect, we must consider their lives as a whole, not only in terms of their final destination. When we do that, we cannot deny, nor can they, that they have had a rich experience of God's goodness.

18. Also compare the many statements about how God's salvation humbles the proud and exalts the humble (as 1 Sam. 2:1–10; 2 Sam. 22:28; Job 40:12; Ps. 75:7; Isa. 2:12; 13:11; 14:4–23; 40:3; Matt. 23:12; Luke 1:46–55).

GOD'S GOODNESS AND HIS LORDSHIP

We have seen that God's goodness reflects his sovereign *control*, for it is his decision to bestow blessings on the world he has made. Earlier, we saw that God is the *authority* over goodness, for he defines what goodness is. As for his *presence*, we have seen that goodness characterizes God in all his dealings with creatures.

GOD'S LOVE

The concepts of goodness and love overlap considerably in Scripture. Goodness, as we have seen, is a very broad concept, but love is more narrowly focused on benevolence. But though love is narrower, it is also theologically richer. God's love is at the heart of the biblical story, especially precious to the hearts of God's people.

Jack Cottrell offers an excellent definition of God's love: "his self-giving affection for his image-bearing creatures and his unselfish concern for their well-being, that leads him to act on their behalf and for their happiness and welfare."[19] We note that although goodness applies to the creation generally, love is distinctly a relationship between persons. This definition also brings out well that God's love includes both affection and action, both feelings and deeds. The biblical emphasis is upon God's deeds. But the terms for compassion, pity, and mercy (especially *raham, hamal, splanchnizomai,* and *oiktirō*), as aspects of God's love, connote strong emotion, as do the parallels between God's love and human marriage (Ezek. 16:1–63; Hos. 1:2–11; 3:1–5). These emotions are, to be sure, emotions of jealousy (leading to wrath) as well as tenderness.

I will not make much of the differences between the various Hebrew and Greek words for love. Much has been said about the differences between the Greek terms *eros* (erotic love—not used in the New Testament), *philia* (friendship), and *agapē* (the New Testament word normally used to express the love of God and love between believers).[20] There may be some intentional wordplay between the verbs *phileō* and *agapaō* in John 21:15–17, but if there is, the force of it isn't entirely clear to me. Otherwise, the New Tes-

---

19. Jack Cottrell, *What the Bible Says About God the Redeemer* (Joplin, Mo.: College Press, 1987), 336.

20. See, for example, C. S. Lewis, *The Four Loves* (London: Geoffrey Bles, 1960), and the more technical study, Anders Nygren, *Agape and Eros*, trans. Philip Watson (London: SPCK, 1953).

tament does not make much of the differences between these terms, although it uses *agapaō* regularly for redemptive love.

Of course, both *philia* and *agapē* are sharply different from *eros*, simply because *eros* is distinctly sensual. So theologians have said much about how *eros* is acquisitive, egocentric, desiring something from its object, and how *agapē* by contrast is spontaneous, unmotivated, indifferent to the present value of the object, and self-giving. There is some truth in this contrast. Clearly, *eros* would have been inappropriate to designate God's love, and certainly the love of God is self-giving.[21] But the self-giving nature of God's love is not found so much in the word *agapē* as in the teaching of Scripture about God's love.[22] The main reason, I think, that the New Testament writers chose the unusual word *agapē* to refer to God's love is that the Septuagint translators used this word to translate the Hebrew *'ahavah*.[23] Therefore, the New Testament use of *agapē* reiterates and expands the concept of the love of God in the Old Testament. Its nuances, therefore, are best discovered through Bible study, rather than a study of Greek lexical stock.[24]

Related to the recent discussions of *eros* and *agapē* is the traditional theological distinction in God's love between benevolence, beneficence, and complacency. Francis Turretin explains:

> A threefold love of God is commonly held; or rather there are three degrees of one and the same love. First, there is the love of benevolence by which God willed good to the creature from eternity; second, the love of beneficence by which he does good to the creature in time according to his good will; third, the love of complacency by which he delights himself in the creature on account of the rays of his image seen in them. The two former precede every act of the creature; the latter follows (not as an effect its cause, but as a consequent its antecedent). By the love of benev-

21. I am not convinced that it is in every sense "unmotivated" and "indifferent to the present value of the object."

22. This is a good example of what James Barr has identified as a confusion between words, concepts, and teachings. See Barr, *The Semantics of Biblical Language* (Oxford: Oxford University Press, 1961).

23. Perhaps the translators were moved in part by the fact that these two terms sound somewhat alike. But the more significant reason may have been that when the Septuagint was translated, "*agapan* was becoming the standard verb for 'to love' because *philein* had acquired the meaning 'to kiss'" (Moisés Silva, *Biblical Words and Their Meaning* [Grand Rapids: Zondervan, 1983], 96).

24. In 2 Sam. 13:15, the Septuagint uses *agapē* to refer to an incestuous rape. This is within the range of the term, considered simply as a Greek word. It is the nature of God's love that leads the biblical writers to use the term mostly for noble affections.

olence, he loved us before we were; by the love of beneficence, he loves us as we are; and by the love of complacency, he loves us when we are (viz., renewed after his image). By the first, he elects us; by the second, he redeems and sanctifies us; but by the third, he gratuitously rewards us as holy and just. John 3:16 refers to the first; Eph. 5:25 and Rev. 1:5 to the second; Is. 62:3 and Heb. 11:6 to the third.[25]

Not all of Turretin's references use the word *love*, but the distinction reflects a genuine variation of scriptural usage. The references to divine complacency show that God's love is not always "indifferent to the qualities of its objects." God loves the righteous, according to Psalms 37:28 and 146:8. Certainly, in these passages, the fact that these people are righteous motivates his love. Israel's obedience motivates God's love for them in Deuteronomy 7:13, although God also loved them before they were obedient and in spite of their disobedience (Deut. 9:4–6). So in Proverbs 8:17, God's wisdom says, "I love those who love me," even though 1 John 4:19 says, "We love because he first loved us" (compare the broader context in vv. 7–21). For more examples of God's love of complacency, see John 14:21, 23. An adequate understanding of God's love must deal with all three aspects of it. Bringing them together, we may say that God loves us first (benevolence and beneficence), and then loves us because of his work in us (complacency), including our response of obedience.

OBJECTS OF GOD'S LOVE

GOD'S SELF-LOVE

Love is God's nature, a fundamental characterization of his Trinitarian being (1 John 4:8, 16; Ex. 34:6–7). It binds the Father and the Son to one another: the Father loves the Son (Matt. 3:17; 17:5; John 3:36; 5:20; 10:17; 17:24, 26 [eternally]; Col. 1:13); the Son loves the Father (John 14:31). The love between the persons of the Trinity is eternal. And since God does not exist without his three persons, the love among those persons is *necessary* to his nature.

So God's love is first of all directed toward himself, but even his self-love is self-giving. In divine self-love, each person of the Trinity embraces the others and glorifies the others.

25. Francis Turretin, *Institutes of Elenctic Theology* (Phillipsburg, N.J.: P&R Publishing, 1992), 1.242.

God's love for creatures, on the other hand, is *free*.[26] He is not constrained to create the world in order to have someone to love. His love has fully interpersonal relationships apart from creation. In creating the world, therefore, he freely chose to direct his love outside his own triune being. He loves the creation voluntarily.

Scripture defines God's love, therefore, by the relationships among the Father, the Son, and the Spirit, not by his relationships with the world. Trinitarianism, therefore, guards God's aseity, his independence from the world. (My discussion of aseity is found in chap. 26.) God does not need the world in order to love. He is not relative to the world. Thus, his love is fully sovereign. He loves us as the Lord.

God's Universal Love

God's love for the creation is universal, as is his goodness. If God is good to all, as we have seen, then surely he loves all. For both goodness and love in these contexts refer to God's benevolence, his seeking the welfare of others. If God is good to all, then surely that benevolence is no accident. It is motivated by a self-giving affection and concern for his creatures' well-being, that is, by love.

In Matthew 5:43–48, Jesus commands his disciples to love their enemies, and he refers to God the Father as his example:

> But I tell you: Love your enemies and pray for those who persecute you, that you may be sons of your Father in heaven. He causes his sun to rise on the evil and the good, and sends rain on the righteous and the unrighteous. . . . Be perfect, therefore, as your heavenly Father is perfect. (Matt. 5:44, 48)

The disciples should love their enemies, Jesus says, because God loves his enemies. God's love for his enemies is universal, for the sunshine and the rain are universal. This passage is parallel to the references we saw earlier that refer to God's universal goodness in providence.

Besides the universal love of God in providence, there is another kind of divine universal love, which has a specifically redemptive purpose: "For God so loved the world that he gave his one and only Son, that whoever believes in him shall not perish but have eternal life" (John 3:16). In the Johannine literature, *world* often has a moral connotation (e.g., John 7:7; 8:23; 12:25, 31; 14:17). It is the creation, cursed by human unbelief and disobedience to God. As such, it is the arena of the Incarnation: Jesus came

26. On God's necessity and freedom in general, see chapter 12.

down from heaven into the world (e.g., John 1:9–10; 3:19; 6:14; 7:4). Since all people who are apart from Christ are cursed for their unbelief and disobedience (John 3:36), *world* includes everybody apart from grace. It is a universal term. But in John's writings, the world is also the object of salvation, not only in 3:16, but also in 1:29; 3:17; 4:42; 6:33, 51; 8:12; 9:5; 12:47; 17:21, 23.

This usage does not imply universal salvation. John makes it perfectly clear that not everyone in the world will be saved, but only those who believe in Christ. When Christ comes to save the world, it is only "whoever believes in him" who will not perish (cf. 1:12; 3:17–21, 36). After John 3:16–17, the evangelist adds, "Whoever believes in him is not condemned, but whoever does not believe stands condemned already because he has not believed in the name of God's one and only Son" (v. 18; see also vv. 19–21). So before his death, he prays for his disciples, and specifically not for the world: "I pray for them. I am not praying for the world, but for those you have given me, for they are yours" (John 17:9).

My conclusion is that God sent his Son, motivated by his love for the whole world. Jesus comes as "Savior of the world" (John 4:42; 1 John 4:14), but not every individual in the world will be saved. Through Christ, God will lift the curse from the creation, and the creation will again be under the dominion of those who love God. God will banish those who serve Satan, "the prince of this world" (John 12:31; 14:30; 16:11; cf. Eph. 2:2), from the world to come.

Does the coming of Christ benefit the reprobate? Certainly the general cultural benefits of Christianity benefit all. To the providential benevolence of God to all people, we should add that God blesses all human beings by the coming of Jesus and the Spirit. And the reprobate are also blessed by the fact that God gives them an opportunity to turn from their wickedness and believe in Christ. These benefits are not accidental. God intends them for good, and so they come from God's love.

To be sure, all of these benefits (both providential and redemptive-historical), on the Last Day, bring greater condemnation on the reprobate, on those who never do believe. Some Calvinists conclude that these benefits, therefore, have nothing to do with God's love, but only with his wrath. But, as we have seen, divine attributes are not easily separated.[27] And it is important for us to take history seriously. Before they come to faith, believers are under the wrath of God—real wrath (Eph. 2:3). Similarly, in the time before the Last Judgment, unbelievers, even the reprobate, experience the love of God—real love. God's grand historical novel (see chaps.

27. We shall look more closely at God's wrath at a later point.

8–9) is not concerned only with endings, but also with beginnings and middles. His love for the reprobate is real love, even though it leads later to wrath. God judges the wicked because they have despised "the riches of his kindness" (Rom. 2:4). That kindness must be real kindness if it is to be a valid ground for their condemnation.

Some Calvinists hesitate to say to unbelievers, "God loves you," for they think that God loves only the elect, and it is impossible to know whether any particular unbeliever is elect. Obviously, such a phrase can be misunderstood. But in Deuteronomy 7, Moses tells the people of Israel that God "set his affection on" them (v. 7) and "loved" them (v. 8; cf. 4:37; 10:15; 23:5; 33:3; Ps. 44:3; Jer. 31:3; Hos. 11:1; Mal. 1:2), even though there have been, are, and will be unbelievers within Israel. His covenant with them is a "covenant of love" (v. 12). The prophets tell the people about God's love in order to motivate their faithfulness.[28]

And Paul tells unbelievers about God's kindness to them in Acts 14:17, as well as implicitly in Acts 17:26–30 and Romans 2:4. We certainly are well within the limits of Scripture when we point out to non-Christians that God has loved them in many ways, by giving them life, health, and various measures of prosperity. And we can add, as I shall explain later (chap. 23), that God desires their salvation (Ezek. 18:23; 33:11; 1 Tim. 2:4; 2 Peter 3:9). In his patience, he has allowed time for repentance (2 Peter 3:9; Rev. 2:21). These kindnesses should motivate unbelievers to turn to the Lord.

On the basis of John 3:16, we can also say, "God loves you, because you are his handiwork, his image. God sent his Son to die, to redeem a people from this fallen world. So he gave you a priceless opportunity: if you believe, you will be saved. If you do believe, you will enjoy the fullness of God's blessing. If you do not, you have only yourself to blame." I grant that such an appeal "sounds Arminian." It appears to say that God sent Jesus only to make salvation hypothetically possible for all, but that the final determination is made by man. But the appeal does not say that at all. The final determination is by God; but here, as in many other cases (see chap. 8), God's sovereignty does not negate human responsibility; rather, it makes it all the more important. God makes the final determination as to who is saved, but one may not be saved unless one believes (John 1:12; 3:15–16, 36; 5:24; 20:31), and those who disbelieve die for their own sins.

The full story is this: God sent his Son with both hypothetical and categorical intentions. Categorically, Christ died only for his elect—what is

28. Thanks to Norman Shepherd for suggesting this point to me.

called "limited atonement."[29] Hypothetically, he died so that *if* anyone at all should believe, he would be saved. His death makes that hypothetical statement true.[30] So Christ died to guarantee salvation to the elect and to provide the opportunity of salvation for all.[31]

Some may say that this "opportunity" is meaningless for the nonelect, for God has predetermined that they will never avail themselves of it. But that is to think unhistorically. As we saw earlier, when God sends rain and sunshine upon the unjust (including the reprobate), these are genuine benefits, even though in the end it increases their condemnation. The rain and sunshine are not curses, but in the cases of the reprobate they become so, because they are blessings spurned. These must be genuine blessings if they are indeed to increase the sinner's condemnation.

God's natural blessings are means by which he calls sinners to repent and believe (Acts 14:14–18; Rom. 2:4). The opportunity to believe in Christ is also a genuine blessing of God that should motivate repentance and faith. It, too, must be a genuine blessing if the rejection of it increases the condemnation of the nonelect. And it is: God's free offer of the gospel is entirely sincere and true: if anyone believes in Jesus, he will certainly be saved.[32]

GOD'S SAVING LOVE

So there are various ways in which God loves everyone, whether elect or nonelect. But the form of divine love most central to Scripture's message is the love of God in saving sinners. This is the gospel of Christ, the

29. I cannot take the space here to defend this controversial doctrine. That has been done well by John Murray in *Redemption Accomplished and Applied* (Grand Rapids: Eerdmans, 1955). The telling point is that the atonement must be limited because it is efficacious. If Christ died for someone, that person is saved. Scripture teaches that even in some of the apparently universalist texts. For example, in 2 Cor. 5:15, Paul says that Jesus "died for all." But he died for them so that "those who live should no longer live for themselves but for him who died for them and was raised again." So the range of "all" must be limited to those whose lives are changed by God's grace.

30. For more on the argument that the atonement brought salvation both categorically for the elect and hypothetically for all, see my review of *Calvinism and the Amyraut Heresy*, by Brian Armstrong, in *WTJ* 34 (1972): 186–92.

31. I am assuming the common Reformed view that the atonement is efficient for the elect, but sufficient for all. As my friend Mark Horne points out, it would be bizarre to imagine that Jesus could have saved a few more people if he had suffered a bit longer or more intensely. His sacrifice was perfect.

32. I shall discuss "the free offer of the gospel" in my discussion of the will of God in chapter 23.

good news. We have already seen that it is the Father's love for the world that sent Jesus to save sinners (John 3:16). Here we focus on God's special love for the people whom Jesus came to save.

Throughout Scripture, redemption comes from God's love. As we saw in the previous section, God chose Israel because he loved her,[33] not because she was more numerous than other peoples (Deut. 7:7–8) or because she was more righteous (9:4–6). That love began with the oath he swore to Abraham (7:8). God's love sovereignly instituted the covenant relationship, and so it preceded any love that man offered God. In the Old Testament, as in the New, "we love because he first loved us" (1 John 4:19). And God's sovereign love motivates our response of obedience, which leads to more divine love:

> If you pay attention to these laws and are careful to follow them, then the LORD your God will keep his covenant of love with you, as he swore to your forefathers. He will love you and bless you. (Deut. 7:12–13)

So God's love both initiates the covenant and continues as his people respond in obedience. It initiates the covenant unconditionally, but its continuance is conditioned on human obedience.

For believers, of course, all conditions are met by Jesus, which guarantees salvation for them and motivates their continued obedience. The Old Testament could not, in the nature of things, focus as sharply on the Cross as could the New. But in the Old Testament also, redemption is the motivation for obedience. Israel is to keep the Ten Commandments because God delivered them from the land of Egypt, the house of bondage (Ex. 20:2), and Israel is to imitate God's redemptive activity. Just as God freed Israel from Egypt, so Israelites are to give rest to their servants (Deut. 5:12–15). And when Israel fails to obey, she must bring a sacrifice and look to the coming sacrifice of the Messiah (Isa. 52:13–53:12).

The New Testament typically defines love (both the love of God and the love required of believers) by reference to the cross of Christ. We have already seen this in John 3:16. "God so loved" means that God loved the world in this particular way; by sending his Son, God shows the very nature of his love for us. Note also:

---

33. Note the correlation between love and choice (i.e., election), here and in 4:37; 10:15. The reference here is to historical election. But Paul correlates God's love also with eternal election in Eph. 1:4. This relationship underscores the sovereignty of God's love.

Greater love has no one than this, that he lay down his life for his friends. You are my friends if you do what I command. (John 15:13–14)[34]

But God demonstrates his own love for us in this: While we were still sinners, Christ died for us. (Rom. 5:8)

The life I live in the body, I live by faith in the Son of God, who loved me and gave himself for me. (Gal. 2:20)

Live a life of love, just as Christ loved us and gave himself up for us as a fragrant offering and sacrifice to God. (Eph. 5:2)

Husbands, love your wives, just as Christ loved the church and gave himself up for her. (Eph. 5:25)

This is how we know what love is: Jesus Christ laid down his life for us. And we ought to lay down our lives for our brothers. (1 John 3:16)

This is how God showed his love among us: He sent his one and only Son into the world that we might live through him. This is love: not that we loved God, but that he loved us and sent his Son as an atoning sacrifice for our sins. (1 John 4:9–10, following the "God is love" of v. 8).

To him who loves us and has freed us from our sins by his blood . . . (Rev. 1:5)

In Romans 8:35, the love of Christ, from which nobody can separate us, is the love of him who "did not spare his own Son, but gave him up for us all" (v. 32). In Ephesians 2:4, God's "great love for us" is salvation from sin, particularly his shed blood (v. 13). Compare other passages where Jesus' atonement is a model for our behavior toward one another: Matthew 20:25–28; 2 Corinthians 5:14–15; Philippians 2:1–11; 1 Peter 2:21–25.

So God's expectation of us is to imitate him—to image him. We might respond by saying that of all God's acts, Jesus' atonement is the one we are least able to imitate, and in a way that is true. The Cross as a model for human ethics shows us how very far from God's standards we still are. But by faith and through God's Spirit, we can make a start. My present point, however, is simply that the Atonement is a profound representation of God's very nature. "God is love" implies that God will go to the uttermost to bless

---

34. In terms of Turretin's distinctions, verse 13 represents beneficence, and verse 14 represents complacency.

his people. He will give himself to the greatest extent. And if the Cross represents God's character in such profundity, it cannot help but be the standard for our own lives.

But God's saving love for us did not begin at the Cross. As we have seen, it was the love of God that sent Jesus to earth. And, even before the Incarnation, God's love for us reaches back to eternity (Eph. 1:4–5). So God's saving love motivates even the eternal election of God's people.[35] Then it reaches out to us in time, through the Atonement, bringing us into God's family: "How great is the love the Father has lavished on us, that we should be called children of God!" (1 John 3:1; cf. Eph. 1:5).

So Paul waxes eloquent, praising the vastness of God's love, its incomprehensibility:

> And I pray that you, being rooted and established in love, may have power, together with all the saints, to grasp how wide and long and high and deep is the love of Christ, and to know this love that surpasses knowledge—that you may be filled to the measure of all the fullness of God. (Eph. 3:17–19)

God's love is great, because God is. To know God's love is to be filled with his very fullness.

People sometimes ask whether God's love is "unconditional." In one sense, God's love is conditional, for God declares conditions that must be met by those who are seeking his blessings. Some don't meet those conditions and receive eternal punishment. But when God loves someone in Christ before the foundation of the world, God himself meets the conditions, so that that person will certainly be saved eternally. To those who belong to Christ, there are no further conditions. Nothing can separate us from his love. In that sense, God's saving love is utterly unconditional.

GOD'S LOVE AND HIS LORDSHIP

We have therefore seen various ways in which God's love is a covenantal concept. It is God's love that initiates his covenant with Israel, and, indeed, all his covenants with men. His love chooses us for salvation before the foundation of the world. So his love is *controlling*, sovereign.

Process theologians and open theists object to the idea that God's love

---

35. This is also true of historical election (recall the distinction between historical and eternal election made in chap. 16). Note the parallels between God's love and his choice of Israel in Deut. 4:37; 7:6–7; 10:15.

controls people. They argue that love never controls, that it works "persuasively" rather than "coercively." God's love does certainly coerce some people. God coerces his enemies when he judges them for the sake of his beloved. Thus, God's love acts in wrath. It is also possible to see coercion sometimes in the conversion of sinners. The vision of Christ on the road to Damascus blinded Saul.

But the issue is most clearly focused in this question: Does God violate our free will in converting us? Yes and no. He makes us believe in him, something we resist apart from grace. In that sense, he forces us to believe against our will. But when we believe, surely, we are doing something we want to do, for God's grace also changes our wants. In that sense, we believe willingly. In conversion, then, God brings us to act contrary to our depraved will, and in accord with a new will given by grace.

So *coercion* is not the best word to describe what happens in conversion. The problem is not that *coercion* connotes too much divine control, but rather that it connotes too little. God does not need to coerce, for he has control of our hearts and thus makes us believe without any sense of being forced. So control and coercion are not the same thing, as is implicit in our earlier discussion of free will (see chap. 8).

What about persuasion? Well, God does persuade us to believe, in the sense that he makes us want to believe. But in doing this, he works changes in us that are far deeper than the term *persuasion* suggests. He creates in us a new heart.

God's love is also the *authoritative* norm for our behavior, for we are to image God's very redemptive love in Christ. And it is his love that leads him to be *present* with us.

GOD'S GRACE

Grace in Scripture refers to God's benevolence, as do *goodness* and *love*, but with different perspectives and nuances.

The KJV translates the Hebrew *hen* (verb: *hanan*) as "grace"; the NIV often translates it as "favor," sometimes as "mercy," and in other ways. Often in human relationships, the question arises about one person's attitude toward another: will he welcome me; be open to a request; be friend or foe? A positive attitude is called favor. Typically in the Old Testament, the word occurs in the phrases like "find favor in his eyes." For example, Laban says to Jacob, "If I have found favor in your eyes, please stay. I have learned by divination that the LORD has blessed me because of you" (Gen. 30:27; cf., e.g., 32:6; 33:8, 10, 15; 34:11).

When used to describe human favor, *hen* does not presuppose any details about why the favor is needed or granted. The use of the term does not determine whether the favor is merited or not, or what motivates the one who gives it. We must search the context for that additional information, if it is available.

Weighty theological issues enter the picture, however, when God is the one who shows *hen*. Since man is fallen and cursed, any favor shown by God to him is surprising. This is especially true with regard to the first reference in Scripture to God's *hen*. Prior to the Flood, the wickedness of man had become very great, so that "every inclination of the thoughts of his heart was only evil all the time" (Gen. 6:5).[36] But amazingly we read in verse 8 that "Noah found favor [*hen*] in the eyes of the LORD." Here it is plain, not from the general use of *hen*, but from the context of Genesis 6, that this favor of God was not based on Noah's goodness. Surely God included Noah in the terrible judgment of verse 5. For his own reasons, God was favorable to Noah. But those reasons did not include Noah's merit. Although he was more godly than other men (v. 9), his godliness did not entitle him to deliverance. But God gave him a warning, and he responded in faith (Heb. 11:7).

In Genesis 33:11, Jacob tells his brother Esau that God has been "gracious" to him, so that he can present his brother with lavish gifts. The soteriological meaning of grace is not as evident here as in Genesis 6 and Hebrews 11, but the term summarizes the way in which God has fulfilled his promises to Abraham, Isaac, and Jacob, enabling them to prosper in the land of promise. Jacob was a schemer; he did not deserve God's blessing, but he received it by grace. When Jacob's son Joseph sees his beloved brother Benjamin after many years apart, he is overcome with joy, but is unable to reveal his true identity. So he pronounces upon Benjamin a benediction: "God be gracious to you, my son" (Gen. 43:29).

The next reference to divine grace is in Exodus 33:12–17, where Moses asks God to teach him and to be present with Israel (cf. 34:8). He bases his plea on the fact that God knows him by name and that he has "found favor" (v. 12) with God, and he makes his request so that God will show him continued favor (v. 13). God must be present with Israel so the world will know that God is "pleased" (*hen* again) with Moses and with Israel (v. 16).

36. This verse is a powerful statement of the total depravity of man. Note the universal indications: "every," "only," "all the time." And not only man's actions are wicked, but also his thoughts, and even the inclinations of his thoughts. His thoughts reveal the quality of his heart. And lest anyone think that the Flood solved the problem of human sin, Gen. 8:21 speaks the same way of man after the Flood: "Every inclination of his heart is evil from childhood." That is God's post-Flood assessment of Noah's family.

The Lord grants the request, because "I am pleased with you and I know you by name" (v. 17). Then God displays his glory to Moses, and promises to proclaim his name, Yahweh, to him. He follows with the phrases we have looked at before as a central exposition of the divine name: "I will have mercy [hanan] on whom I will have mercy, and I will have compassion [raham] on whom I will have compassion" (v. 19). In Romans 9:15, as we have seen, Paul quotes this passage to indicate God's absolute sovereignty in redemption.

God's grace is also prominent in the next biblical exposition of the name Yahweh, in Exodus 34:6: "The LORD, the LORD, the compassionate [rahum] and gracious [hannun] God, slow to anger, abounding in love and faithfulness."

In these passages, as in Genesis, God chooses people (here, Moses individually and Israel as a nation) in order to show them favor. Like Noah, Jacob, and Benjamin, Israel is undeserving. She is "stiff-necked." Exodus 33 and 34 follow Israel's disobedience with the golden calf, a disobedience that continues (with periodic revivals) throughout Israel's history. God's favor to Israel, therefore, is not based on Israel's righteousness, as God later explains:

> After the LORD your God has driven them [the Canaanite tribes] out before you, do not say to yourself, "The LORD has brought me here to take possession of this land because of my righteousness." No, it is on account of the wickedness of these nations that the LORD is going to drive them out before you. It is not because of your righteousness or your integrity that you are going in to take possession of their land; but on account of the wickedness of these nations, the LORD your God will drive them out before you, to accomplish what he swore to your fathers, to Abraham, Isaac and Jacob. Understand, then, that it is not because of your righteousness that the LORD your God is giving you this good land to possess, for you are a stiff-necked people. (Deut. 9:4–6)

If this passage seems repetitious, we should conclude that the point is important, and that God took special pains to communicate it to a stiff-necked people.

God's grace to men, then, appears in spite of man's unrighteousness, and by God's utterly sovereign decision ("I will have mercy on whom I will have mercy"). It is legitimate, therefore (though not implicit in the hanan vocabulary as such),[37] to define God's grace theologically as his "sovereign, unmerited favor, given to those who deserve his wrath."

---

37. For example, Luke 2:40 tells us that Jesus increased in "favor" (charis, the New Testament equivalent of hen) with God and man. But clearly we should not assume that Jesus did not deserve God's favor.

We can also see from these references that God's grace, like his love, is *covenantal*. It is implicit in the covenant name of God. Yahweh initiates the covenant by choosing undeserving people to bear his name: Noah, Abraham, Isaac, Jacob, Moses, Israel as a nation. That is grace. Then God shows more grace to his chosen people, based on his covenant promises to Noah, Abraham, and the others. But if God's grace is not based on human merit, then what is the reason for it? Is it arbitrary? No; as I said in connection with Genesis 6, God has his own reasons, but they are not based on human merit. Rather, they are based on his decision to save men from sin by way of covenants, by making promises and fulfilling them. This is the basic shape of God's historical drama (chaps. 8 and 9).

[margin handwritten note: PONDER]

[margin handwritten note: AND THIS is TO THE PRAISE OF HIS GLORY (HIS ULTIMATE REASON)]

So the priestly benediction, in which Aaron and his sons "put my name on the Israelites" (Num. 6:27), invokes God's grace:

> The LORD bless you
> and keep you;
> the LORD make his face shine upon you
> and be gracious [*hanan*] to you;
> the LORD turn his face toward you
> and give you peace. (Num. 6:24–26)

Israel bears God's name; he is her Lord, Yahweh, present with her. So he shows favor, not because of Israel's righteousness, but because he is her covenant Lord. Grace, therefore, is utterly *personal*. It is the Lord's own attitude of favor toward his people.

In the New Testament, the vocabulary of grace (the Greek *charis*[38] and variants) appears rarely in the Gospels, though John emphasizes the point that grace and truth come through Jesus Christ (John 1:14–17). In the book of Acts, the term appears at 4:33, indicating the divine influence that moved the church to care sacrificially for its poor. Here grace is not only an attitude of favor on God's part, as in the Old Testament, but also an active power, enabling people to do the works of God.

When many Gentiles believe in Christ at Antioch, Barnabas arrives and sees "the evidence of the grace of God" (11:23). Here again, God's grace is his power, bringing about faith. God favors these Gentiles and therefore enables them to believe. Compare Acts 18:27, which says that Apollos "was a great help to those who by grace had believed." As we saw in chapter 4, faith is a gift of God's grace.

So "the grace of God" in 13:43 refers to the gospel. Paul and Barnabas

---

38. This term translates *hen* in the Septuagint, and also *hesed,* which we shall consider later.

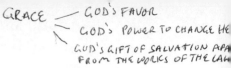

GRACE — GOD'S FAVOR
— GOD'S POWER TO CHANGE HE[ARTS]
GOD'S GIFT OF SALVATION APA[RT]
FROM THE WORKS OF THE LAW

urge their hearers "to continue in the grace of God." So the gospel is "the word of his grace" (20:32; 14:3), "the gospel of the grace of God" (20:24).

In Acts 15, the concept of grace enters the polemics between the Christians, on the one hand, and the Jews and Judaizers, on the other. Some Christians of Pharisaic background have insisted that the Gentile converts "must be circumcised and required to obey the law of Moses" (15:5); that is, that the Gentiles must become Jews in order to become Christians. Peter advises otherwise: God brought the Gentiles to faith, making no distinction between them and the Jewish Christians (compare Peter's vision and his experience with Cornelius in Acts 10 and 11):

> Now then, why do you try to test God by putting on the necks of the disciples a yoke that neither we nor our fathers have been able to bear? No! We believe it is through the grace of our Lord Jesus that we are saved, just as they are. (15:10–11)

From this point on in the New Testament, grace is not only God's favor, and not only God's power to change hearts, but also the gift of salvation apart from the works of the law. Such is Paul's emphasis:

> But now a righteousness from God, apart from law, has been made known, to which the Law and the Prophets testify. This righteousness from God comes through faith in Jesus Christ to all who believe. There is no difference, for all have sinned and fall short of the glory of God, and are justified freely by his grace through the redemption that came by Christ Jesus. (Rom. 3:21–24; cf. 4:4, 16; 11:6; Gal. 2:21)

Paul contrasts grace not only with obedience to the Law of Moses, but with any reliance on our own works as a means of salvation:

> For it is by grace you have been saved, through faith—and this not from yourselves, it is the gift of God—not by works, so that no one can boast. (Eph. 2:8–9)

> [God] has saved us and called us to a holy life—not because of anything we have done but because of his own purpose and grace. This grace was given us in Christ Jesus before the beginning of time. (2 Tim. 1:9)

In 2 Timothy 1:9, God gives us his grace in our eternal election (see chap. 16).[39] So his grace cannot possibly be based on our works. Rather, it gives

---

39. Compare Rom. 11:5, in which the remnant is chosen (elected) by grace.

us the power to do good works (2 Cor. 9:8; Eph. 2:10). Indeed, it is God's grace that gives us the abilities we need to preach the gospel and to do his will (Rom. 12:3, 6; 1 Cor. 3:10; 15:10; 2 Cor. 8:7; Gal. 2:9; Eph. 3:7–8; 4:7). So, as in the Old Testament, God's saving grace is unmerited. It is given to us for God's reasons, not because of anything good in us.[40]

Also, as in the Old Testament, grace appears in the benediction, the blessing of God. The apostolic greetings (e.g., Rom. 1:7; 1 Cor. 1:3) and benedictions (Rom. 16:20, 24; 1 Cor. 16:23; and especially 2 Cor. 13:14) always emphasize grace. In Numbers 6:24–26, Aaron's sons declare God's grace by putting his name on the people. In 2 Corinthians 13:14, Paul does the same thing as he places God's threefold name upon the church: "May the grace of the Lord Jesus Christ, and the love of God, and the fellowship of the Holy Spirit be with you all."

So all the blessings of God come to us by God's sovereign grace. Without his grace, we are nothing. By grace comes the forgiveness of our sins, the power to do good works, and the ability to serve the people of God. And all of these come from the most amazing grace of all:

> For you know the grace of our Lord Jesus Christ, that though he was rich, yet for your sakes he became poor, so that you through his poverty might become rich. (2 Cor. 8:9)

COMMON GRACE AND GOD'S PATIENCE

We have seen that although God directs his goodness and love especially to believers, there are also senses in which God's goodness and love are universal. "The LORD is good to all" (Ps. 145:9), and he loves even his enemies by sending them rain and sunshine (Matt. 5:44–45). So many have thought that the same may be said of grace, that there are forms of divine grace that God gives to the nonelect.

To my knowledge, Scripture never uses *hen* or *charis* to refer to his blessings on creation generally or on nonelect humanity. So it would perhaps be better to speak of God's common goodness, or common love, rather than

---

40. However, once we are saved, God continues to give gifts and blessings. These too are grace, and they are certainly not merited, but they do sometimes take into account the previous works of God in us. James 4:6 and 1 Peter 5:5 (quoting Prov. 3:34) say, "God opposes the proud but gives grace to the humble." God gives additional gifts of grace to those to whom he has first given the grace of humility. We saw earlier that God loves his people unconditionally, but he also loves them more and more, in response to their obedience. The same may be said of grace.

his common grace. The word *grace* in Scripture tends to be more narrowly focused on redemption than *goodness* and *love*, although the latter terms also have rich redemptive associations.

But we should not quarrel over words at this point. As I said in the last section, a redemptive focus is not necessarily or always a part of the use of *hen* and *charis*. Certainly in Luke 2:52, where Jesus grows in *charis* with God and man, the term does not imply redemption from sin. *Hen* and *charis* simply refer to God's favor, and obviously his goodness and love are forms of his favor. So if God's goodness and love apply universally in some senses, the same is true of God's favor, his grace.

Also, Scripture teaches us about God's grace even in some places where *hen* and *charis* are absent. Clearly the parable of the prodigal son (Luke 15:11–31) is about grace, although the specific terms for grace are missing from the passage.

The use of the term *grace* in this connection, rather than *goodness* or *love*, may be related to the tendency of some Reformed writers to restrict common grace to the beneficial effects of the gospel upon society, or at least to place their major focus there. But the broader discussion of the concept, in the writings of Calvin[41] and the later monumental treatment by Abraham Kuyper,[42] sees it more broadly.[43] Murray defines common grace as *"every favour of whatever kind or degree, falling short of salvation, which this undeserving and sin-cursed world enjoys at the hand of God."*[44] The words *"favour," "undeserving,"* and *"sin-cursed"* show the relationship that Murray sees between these common blessings and the grace of God.

Within this general definition, theologians have distinguished various aspects of common grace:

God Restrains Sin

God prevents fallen men from doing all the wrong they could do. He places a mark on Cain, so that others will not take his life (Gen. 4:15). He confuses the languages of men during the building of the tower of Babel,

---

41. See *Institutes*, 2.2.16; 2.3.4. Other references are in Herman Kuiper, *Calvin on Common Grace* (Grand Rapids: Smitter Book Co., 1928).

42. Abraham Kuyper, *De Gemeene Gratie* (Kampen: Kok, 1945).

43. The narrower view can be found in Charles Hodge, *Systematic Theology*, 2.654, and in A. A. Hodge, *Outlines of Theology* (Grand Rapids: Zondervan, 1972), chap. 28, sec. 13. John Murray discusses this issue in the excellent article "Common Grace," in his *Collected Writings of John Murray* (Edinburgh: Banner of Truth Trust, 1977), 2.93–119.

44. Murray, "Common Grace," 96 (italics his). Much of what follows is dependent on Murray's treatment.

lest "nothing they plan to do will be impossible for them" (Gen. 11:6). He prevents Abimelech, the king of Gerar, from sexual sin with Abraham's wife, Sarah (Gen. 20:6). He restrains Egypt's oppression of Israel by sending plagues on Egypt and delivering his people (Ex. 1–15). He prevents King Sennacherib of Assyria from doing all the harm to Israel that he has planned (2 Kings 19:27–28). He protects his Son Jesus from harm until his hour comes. He restrains "the secret power of lawlessness" (2 Thess. 2:7).[45] These examples can be multiplied almost indefinitely. Common grace in this sense pervades biblical history and our own experience. Satan himself is on a leash: God allows him to go only so far, and no farther (see Job 1:12; 2:6). So God keeps wickedness under tight control. He allows it to advance only as far as will serve his purposes (cf. chaps. 8–9).

Sometimes, however, that advance is dramatic. Paul says in Romans 1 that God "gave over" the idolatrous heathen to worse and worse sins (vv. 24–32). Human sin grew worse and worse before the Flood, until God was grieved that he had made man (Gen. 6:5). The inhabitants of Canaan became worse and worse until God judged them by giving their land to Israel (Gen. 15:16). But God always sets a limit to what sinners can do.

God Restrains His Wrath

The fact that human beings receive any blessings at all is surprising. God would have acted justly if he had destroyed the human race after the Fall. But instead he allowed human life to continue, promising redemption by the offspring of the woman (Gen. 3:15). And throughout Scripture we see that God does not give people the awesome punishment they deserve. Murray points out that God restrains the painful effects of the curse: of the thorns and thistles (Gen. 3:17) and of the wild beasts (Gen. 9:2, 5).[46] God sometimes "overlooks" disobedience (Acts 17:30; cf. 14:16; Rom. 3:25). In the Old Testament period, he permitted divorce because of Israel's hardness of heart (Matt. 19:8), even though he hates divorce (Mal. 2:16).

One day, all wrongs will be righted. God will punish all sin, either by punishing the offender or by placing his sins on Jesus. But the final judgment is yet future. That, too, is a restraint on God's wrath. And that, too, is grace, for God postpones judgment in order to give people an opportunity[47] to repent: "He is patient with you, not wanting

---

45. I have no new wisdom on this difficult text, but at least that much is clear to me.
46. Murray, "Common Grace," 102.
47. Recall our reference to the gospel as "the opportunity to believe," in connection with God's love.

anyone to perish, but everyone to come to repentance" (2 Peter 3:9; cf. Rev. 2:21).

God's patience (*'erek 'af, makrothymia*),[48] often rendered "longsuffering" in the KJV, is an important divine attribute. We find it in the exposition of the divine name in Exodus 34:6 and in later biblical recollections of that passage (Num. 14:18; Ps. 86:5; Rom. 2:4). There are many other references to it throughout Scripture, and it occurs regularly in New Testament lists of Christian virtues (e.g., Rom. 5:3; 2 Cor. 6:6; Gal. 5:22; Eph. 4:2; Col. 1:11; 3:12; 1 Thess. 1:3; 2 Tim. 3:10; cf. 1 Cor. 13:4, making it a quality of love). When Paul, in defending his apostleship, sets forth "signs, wonders and miracles" as "the things that mark an apostle" (2 Cor. 12:12), he adds, interestingly, that these "were done among you with great perseverance [*hypomonē*]." A true apostle is, among other things, one who does not expect instant results (even with spectacular divine attestations), but sticks to the work that God has given him, patiently waiting for the fruit of his labors.

So God is a God who waits. He can accomplish his will instantly. He can bring final judgment on the wicked immediately. But he chooses not to do so. He has chosen to write a drama and spread it out in temporal sequence (see chap. 8). So he tolerates evil for a time (see chap. 9), waiting until later to judge it fully. Now we learn that God's decision to wait is not arbitrary, nor is it mainly in the interest of creating a more interesting story. Rather, it is a function of his love and grace. So he gives people time for repentance. Peter says, "Bear in mind that our Lord's patience means salvation" (2 Peter 3:15).

We might ask why God's patience shows his love, rather than an arbitrary decision in his eternal decree to arrange the temporal sequence in one way rather than another. As I indicated in chapter 8, when God formulates his eternal decree, he takes into account all the creatures he intends to make. His decree takes into account his knowledge of creatures, just as his knowledge of creatures takes into account his decree. So his decree to lengthen the temporal sequence genuinely reflects his knowledge of, and love for, those he intends to create.

God's patience is a model for our own. We, too, should not expect or demand instant results from our labors or exhortations, or instant answers to prayer. In carrying out our goals, we must remember the importance of others' needs and priorities, and we must be willing to adjust our schedules to serve them. And our plans must especially respect God's priorities—his timing. We should await God's time, as he first awaited ours.

---

48. *Hypomonē* is also found often in the New Testament, but not as an attribute of God.

God Gives Temporal Blessings to All

Here we may consider all the blessings mentioned earlier as God's goodness and love: rain and sunshine, food for all living things (Pss. 65:5–13; 104; 136:25; 145:9, 15–16). We should recall that these also call people to faith and repentance (Acts. 14:17). God also gives civil government for "good" (Rom. 13:4), so that "we may live peaceful and quiet lives in all godliness and holiness" (1 Tim. 2:2; cf. 1 Peter 2:14).

We should mention here the blessings that are specifically connected with the advance of the gospel, which are emphasized by those who define common grace more narrowly. The gospel has not only brought many to faith, but has also brought about improvements in society, in the condition of the poor, in marriage and families, in political and economic freedom, in justice, in education, in the work ethic, and so on.

Scripture says specifically that such blessings come upon the unbelieving and reprobate: "The Lord blessed the household of the Egyptian [Potiphar] because of Joseph" (Gen. 39:5).[49] Jesus says in a parable that Lazarus's rich tormenter received "good things" in his earthly life (Luke 16:25).

As we saw earlier in this chapter, these blessings reveal the kindness of God, his attitude of favor to the recipients of his blessings. Some object to saying that God shows "favor" to the reprobate. Gary North insists that God gives "favors" to the reprobate, but not "favor."[50] But certainly, as we have seen, God gives these gifts intentionally. They reveal his motives. God "blessed" Potiphar's house. God gave good things to the rich man because he intended to give him good things. He filled the heathen's hearts "with joy" (Acts 14:17) because he wanted them to be joyful. God gives favors, because he is favorable. But of course he will not be favorable to unrepentant men forever. Again, let us take history seriously. God's wrath on the wicked at the end of history will be real wrath, but his kindness to them before the end is also real kindness. As we have seen, it is goodness and love. So it is also grace and favor.

The term *favor* may be subject to some misunderstanding. It can refer to a kindly disposition or to advocacy, as in "I favor the Republican candidates." God never favors the wicked in the sense of advocating their purposes or desiring them to accomplish their goals. But he does have a kindly disposition to all his creatures. Psalm 145:9, Matthew 5:43–48, and other

---

49. Note that the passage does not say only that God blessed Joseph, but that God blessed Potiphar's house for the sake of Joseph. So the blessing was on Potiphar's house.

50. Gary North, *Dominion and Common Grace* (Tyler, Tex.: Institute for Christian Economics, 1987), 20.

passages refer not only to the gifts, but also to the divine disposition underlying these gifts.[51]

UNREGENERATE PEOPLE DO GOOD

In one sense, no one can do good apart from the saving grace of God. We have seen that man is depraved (Gen. 6:5; 8:21; Rom. 3:9–18). "Those controlled by the sinful nature cannot please God" (Rom. 8:8). The "good" that I have in mind here is that which is good in the highest sense: good works done for the glory of God, obedient to the Word of God, and motivated by faith and love for God.

But Scripture attributes good, in lesser senses, to the unregenerate. King Jehu was an idolater (2 Kings 10:29, 31), but God said to him, "Because you have done well in accomplishing what is right in my eyes and have done to the house of Ahab all I had in mind to do, your descendants will sit on the throne of Israel to the fourth generation" (v. 30). Similarly, King Joash came to a bad end, but Scripture says that he "did what was right in the eyes of the LORD all the years Jehoiada the priest instructed him" (2 Kings 12:2). Jesus says that even the wicked do good to those who do good to them (Luke 6:33).

So, although one cannot do good in the fullest sense without the blessings of God's saving grace, one can carry out the commandments of God in an external and temporary fashion, as did the Pharisees during Jesus' earthly ministry. One can also choose to commit sins that are relatively less wicked than others. These "good works" may be beneficial to society, and so they are sometimes called "civic righteousness." Compare WCF, 16.7:

> Works done by unregenerate men, although for the matter of them they may be things which God commands; and of good use both to themselves and others: yet, because they proceed not from an heart purified by faith; nor are done in a right manner, according to the Word; nor to a right end, the glory of God, they are therefore sinful, and cannot please God, or make a man meet to receive grace from God: and yet, their neglect of them is more sinful and displeasing unto God.

51. This paragraph summarizes a discussion in *CVT*, 229. See the chapter in that book on common grace for discussion of Van Til's view and the views of some of his critics (pp. 215–30).

Murray adds, "The ploughing of the wicked is sin, but it is more sinful for the wicked not to plough."[52]

UNREGENERATE PEOPLE KNOW TRUTH

Here we should make a distinction strictly parallel to the fourth point above, because, as I indicated in *DKG*, knowledge is an aspect of ethics. Scripture draws an antithesis between the wisdom of God, of which the fear of the Lord is the beginning (Ps. 111:10; Prov. 1:7), and the wisdom of the world (1 Cor. 1:18–2:15; 3:18–23). In terms of this antithesis, unbelievers have no true knowledge. But Scripture attributes knowledge to them in lesser senses. They know God from natural revelation, although they repress that knowledge (Rom. 1:18–21). The Pharisees are able in some measure to teach correctly (Matt. 23:2–3), although people should not imitate their behavior.

This knowledge is paradoxical, a knowledge that is fundamentally stupid and irrational. Satan doubtless knows more facts about God and his purposes than most of us, but he persists in his utterly futile project to unseat God from his throne.

Christians can learn things from unbelievers. But they should always look at the teachings of unbelievers with an especially critical eye, for sin distorts the understanding of God and therefore of his world.

UNREGENERATE PEOPLE EXPERIENCE SOME BLESSINGS OF THE HOLY SPIRIT

Murray puts it this way: "*Unregenerate people receive operations and influences of the Spirit in connection with the administration of the gospel, influences that result in experience of the power and glory of the gospel, yet influences which do not issue in genuine and lasting conversion and are finally withdrawn.*"[53] In the Old Testament, it sometimes happens that a person otherwise not noted for his godliness experiences the inspiration of God's Spirit. Examples are Balaam (Num. 22:1–24:25 [note 22:7; 24:1]; 2 Peter 2:15; Rev. 2:14) and King Saul (1 Sam. 10:9–11). Judas Iscariot, the disciple who betrayed Jesus, is condemned by Scripture in strong terms, yet he was one who preached the coming of the kingdom, healed the sick, raised the dead, and drove out demons (Matt. 10:5–8).

These individual cases illustrate a larger pattern in Scripture. Israel as a

---

52. Murray, "Common Grace," 107n.
53. Ibid., 109 (italics his).

nation experienced extraordinary blessings of God's Spirit. God did mighty works to deliver the Israelites from Egypt, to feed them in the wilderness, and to save them from their enemies. But, as a nation, God cast them into exile, and then rejected them as his people.

To whom much is given, from him much is required. So Korazin, Bethsaida, and Capernaum will be judged more harshly than Sodom and Gomorrah, Tyre, and Sidon (Matt. 11:21–23; Luke 10:13–15). They saw great miracles, mighty works of God's Spirit, but they did not turn to Christ.

There are those who join the Christian church, experience the work of the Spirit there, and yet turn away in apostasy. Jesus speaks of the seed of the Word of God falling on bad soil, growing up for a while, and then dying off (Matt. 13:1–9), indicating that some apparent conversions will prove to be only temporary. So the writer of Hebrews tells us:

> It is impossible for those who have once been enlightened, who have tasted the heavenly gift, who have shared in the Holy Spirit, who have tasted the goodness of the word of God and the powers of the coming age, if they fall away, to be brought back to repentance, because to their loss they are crucifying the Son of God all over again and subjecting him to public disgrace. (Heb. 6:4–6)

This is a troubling passage. It is hard to see how the description could fit someone who is unregenerate. But all these descriptions fit Balaam and Saul, national Israel and Judas Iscariot. We also read of such apostates in Hebrews 10:26–29, 2 Peter 2:20–22, and 1 John 2:19.

Much can be said about the issues raised by these passages. They do not call into question the doctrine of the perseverance of the saints, for that doctrine tells us that all regenerate people will persevere, not that all professing Christians will do so. But these passages do make it difficult for us to distinguish between those who are regenerate and those who are unregenerate church members. We can be thankful that we do not have to read people's hearts. Elders of churches admit people to membership on the basis of a profession of faith in Christ that is not evidently inconsistent with their lives. If it later appears that the person does not believe, then the church should excommunicate him (Matt. 18:15–20; 1 Cor. 5:1–12).

But for our present purposes, the main point to notice is that some of the blessings of God's common grace look very much like the blessings of salvation itself. Certainly it is a blessing, even for a reprobate, to be part of a Christian community, to receive the wisdom and experience the love of that community. Of course, hearing the Word of God will increase his condemnation, and receiving the sacraments unworthily can lead to sickness and death (1 Cor. 11:17–34). But God will sometimes use a counterfeit Christian to exhort his people or evangelize the lost. *These works are works of God.*

It can be discouraging to God's people when such a one finally leaves the body, especially to those who were helped spiritually by his ministry. We should not assume that God does not work through such people. God uses Satan himself to accomplish his good purposes. But in time, God's judgment will make clear the differences between the elect and the reprobate.

The doctrine of common grace, like the doctrines of creation, providence, and the decrees, encourage us to see God's blessings everywhere. Every bit of food, every bit of rain and sunshine, comes from the goodness of our heavenly Father. God really does love us; he seeks our good. And while the Last Judgment tarries, God seeks the good of the reprobate as well. Thus, we should praise his name.

GOD'S COVENANT LOVE

The Hebrew term *hesed* is difficult to translate into English. The usual renderings have included "mercy" (KJV), "lovingkindness" (ASV), and "steadfast love" (RSV). The NIV uses "kindness" and "love" in various contexts. In Exodus 34:6, the KJV translates it as "goodness." The Septuagint translates it as *eleos*, "mercy," which enters the New Testament in passages employing the *hesed* concept. *Eleos*, however, also seems to be used in a more general sense, like our English word *mercy*: "God's goodness toward those who are in misery."[54] I have often felt that "loyalty" and "faithfulness" are sometimes good translations for *hesed*, although those terms overlap considerably with *'emeth* and *'emunah*, which are often found together with *hesed*.

Despite the difficulty of translation, *hesed* represents one of the most important divine attributes, found in about 245 verses of Scripture. Over and over, God's people praise him, "for his [*hesed*] endures forever" (1 Chron. 16:34, 41; 2 Chron. 7:3, 6; 20:21; Pss. 107; 118; 136). Like other attributes of goodness, *hesed* is part of the definitive exposition of the name of Yahweh in Exodus 34:6.

The key to the meaning of *hesed* is the concept of covenant that we have often explored in this book (see especially chaps. 2 and 3). In Deuteronomy 7:9, 12, Moses exhorts Israel:

> Know therefore that the Lord your God is God; he is the faithful
> God, keeping his covenant of love to a thousand generations of

54. *DG*, 206.

those who love him and keep his commands. . . . If you pay attention to these laws and are careful to follow them, then the LORD your God will keep his covenant of love with you, as he swore to your forefathers.

In the phrase "covenant of love," the word "love" is *hesed*, in a Hebrew phrase that closely identifies *hesed* with the covenant itself. Similarly in 1 Samuel 20:8, David says to Jonathan, "As for you, show kindness [*hesed*] to your servant, for you have brought him into a covenant with you before the LORD."[55] Compare also Nehemiah 1:5 and 9:32. Notice also the close connection between *hesed* and God's promises to Jacob and Abraham in Micah 7:20 ("as you pledged on oath to our fathers") and the connection of *hesed* with David (Ps. 18:50; Isa. 55:3).[56] God made covenants with Abraham (including Isaac and Jacob) and David that included promises of *hesed*.

In chapter 3, we discussed the suzerainty treaty form that underlies the biblical covenants:

1. Name of the great king
2. Historical prologue (past blessings of the great king toward the vassal)
3. Stipulations (laws, vassal's obligations)
   a. General: exclusive loyalty
   b. Specific, detailed
4. Sanctions
5. Continuity

In this model, the general stipulation of exclusive loyalty was sometimes called "love."[57] Covenant loyalty may seem to us to be a political concept of love, which does not capture the rich emotional meaning of the term. But, of course, when we are covenantally loyal to God, we consecrate to him everything we are, loving him with heart, soul, strength, and mind

---

55. Sometimes *hesed* appears in the context of personal relationships, as in the one between David and Jonathan, without mention of a formal covenant. For example, 2 Sam. 10:2 says, "David thought, 'I will show kindness (*hesed*) to Hanun son of Nahash, just as his father showed kindness (*hesed*) to me.'" Cf. 1 Kings 2:7; 1 Chron. 19:2; 2 Chron. 24:22. If these loyalties and reciprocities are not formally covenantal, there is nevertheless a strong analogy between them and covenantal relationships.

56. Note that three times in Matthew, people cry out to Jesus as the Son of David to have "mercy" on them (Matt. 9:27; 15:22; 20:30).

57. Note that on this model, there is no opposition between love and law, since love is part of the law. Nor is there any antithesis between grace and law, since obedience to the law is the vassal's response to the grace described in the historical prologue.

(Deut. 6:5; Matt. 22:37)—including, of course, all our emotion. It is not surprising, then, that Scripture regards marriage as a covenant (Ezek. 16:8; Mal. 2:14), and that marriage is an image of the relationship between God and his people (Hos. 1–3; Ezek. 16; Eph. 5:22–33).

Hesed refers to this covenant loyalty in Scripture, both in covenants on the human level (e.g., the covenant between David and Jonathan in 1 Sam. 20:8) and in covenants between God and man. But *hesed* also refers to God's covenant loyalty—the commitment of the Lord to the covenant relationship.

For God to show *hesed* is for him to keep the promises of his covenant. So Scripture often couples the term with *'emeth* ("truth, faithfulness") (e.g., Gen. 24:27, 49; 47:29; Ex. 34:6; Josh. 2:14; Ps. 26:3) or *'emunah* ("faithfulness") (Deut. 7:9; Pss. 89:2; 92:2). These terms interpret one another, becoming virtually one concept together. *Hesed* is God's faithfulness to his covenant promise, his truthfulness to his word, the fact that he will bless his people as he says he will. So to plead God's "mercies" (*hesed*) is to plead the promises of the covenant (Pss. 6:4; 31:16; 69:16).

On rare occasion, however, *hesed* refers to curses rather than blessings. "Kindness" may be a misleading translation of *hesed* in 1 Samuel 20:8. In the context, David suggests that Jonathan's *hesed* might lead him to kill David, if indeed David has been unfaithful to him and to Saul.[58] Covenants in Scripture are often two-sided: they include blessings for those who obey the covenant law, but curses for those who disobey. *Hesed* requires the fulfillment of both kinds of sanction.

Now we saw earlier in this chapter that the love of God sovereignly initiates his covenants. The word *'ahavah* refers to this love in Deuteronomy 7:8. *Hesed* (as in 7:9) typically refers, not to the love of God that initiates a covenant, but to a divine love that presupposes a covenant's present existence. God's *'ahavah* creates the relationship; his *hesed* fulfills and completes it.[59] So of the two terms, *'ahavah* tends to be more closely equivalent to "grace": it is not a response to human obedience.[60] But *hesed* does frequently presuppose human obedience to the covenant stipulations.[61] Note in Deuteronomy 7:9 that God keeps his covenant of *hesed* "to a thousand generations of

---

58. Compare 2 Tim. 2:11–13, which extols the faithfulness of the Lord, but includes the warning, "If we disown him, he will also disown us" (v. 12).

59. Compare the relationship between *'ahavah* and *hesed* in Jer. 31:3: "I have loved you with an everlasting love (*'ahavah*); I have drawn you with loving-kindness (*hesed*)."

60. In the suzerainty treaty formula, *'ahavah* would be found at points 1 and 2.

61. This is the case in the quasi-covenantal uses of *hesed* within relationships on the human level, as we saw earlier in 2 Sam. 10:2 and other verses.

those who love him and keep his commandments." Hesed can be God's response to repentance (Deut. 4:30–31; Ps. 51:1).[62] Note also these verses:

> To the faithful [hasid, from the hesed root] you show yourself faithful,
>   to the blameless [tamim] you show yourself blameless. (2 Sam.
>   22:26; cf. Ps. 18:25)

> All the ways of the LORD are loving [hesed] and faithful
>   for those who keep the demands of his covenant. (Ps. 25:10)

> . . . and that you, O Lord, are loving [hesed].
> Surely you will reward each person
>   according to what he has done. (Ps. 62:12)

Hesed, then, is typically conditional, in a way that 'ahavah is not.

Normally, then, God's hesed is given to those who obey him. This fact should not, however, be used to justify a doctrine that we are saved by works. As we have seen, God's sovereign love ('ahavah) initiates the covenant relationship, and hesed is based on God's promises. As R. T. France puts it, "It is love (ahabah) that launches a marriage, but it is chesed that makes a go of it."[63] So God's love pervades our covenant life, from beginning to fulfillment.

The intensely covenantal context of hesed suggests that it might be limited to the covenant people of God, without the more general applications that we have made of the concepts of goodness, love, and grace. Even hesed, however, describes God's love to his creation as a whole. In Psalm 36, the psalmist contrasts the wickedness of men (vv. 1–4) with the hesed of God (vv. 5 and 10):

> Your love [hesed], O LORD, reaches to the heavens,
>   your faithfulness to the skies.
> Your righteousness is like the mighty mountains,
>   your justice like the great deep.
> O LORD, you preserve both man and beast.
>   How priceless is your unfailing love [hesed]!
> Both high and low among men
>   find refuge in the shadow of your wings.
> They feast on the abundance of your house;
>   you give them to drink from your river of delights.
> For with you is the fountain of life;
>   in your light we see light. (vv. 5–9)

This passage, like the other hesed passages we have examined, is full of covenantal language. Again we see the coupling of hesed with 'emunah in

---

62. Compare Ps. 103:3–4, where hesed follows forgiveness, healing, and redemption.
63. R. T. France, The Living God (London: Inter-Varsity Press, 1970), 90.

verse 5, and with *righteousness* and *justice* in verse 6. The "house" of the Lord (v. 8) is often the temple in Scripture, or more broadly the people of God. The pictures of feasting and drinking (v. 8) typically refer to God's appointed feasts and to the blessings of fellowship with the Lord. But here the reference is not merely to Israel, but to animals (v. 6) and "high and low among men."

Since creation itself is covenantal (chap. 15), a temple of God, and since the preservation of the earth is promised in God's covenant with Noah (Gen. 8:21–22), I take it that his providential preservation of life is his *hesed*.[64] Or perhaps the psalmist is thinking specifically of God's *hesed* to Israel, and he sees that *hesed* in God's providential preservation of life throughout the earth. In any case, God's blessings to all his creatures are expressions of his *hesed*. So God loves Israel, but in loving Israel, he loves the whole world. The purpose of God's covenant with Abraham, after all, was to bless all the nations in him (Gen. 12:3). So there is common *hesed*, as there is common goodness, love, and grace.

GOD'S COMPASSION

"Compassion" is perhaps the best general way to translate *raham, hamal, splanchnizomai, oiktirō,* and *metriopatheō*[65] as used in Scripture. *Hamal* is sometimes translated "pity" or "love," and *raham* as "be merciful." These words indicate a sympathetic view of another's distress, motivating helpful action. *Raham* and *splanchnizomai* relate etymologically to the inner body, particularly to the womb. Perhaps for that reason they often have strongly emotional connotations. I will argue later that God does have emotions, although they are not physically based. Call them attitudes rather than emotions, if you prefer, but these terms convey well the intensity of God's love and concern.

Raham is the "mercy" of Exodus 33:19 and 34:6, which I have identified as significant expositions of the divine name. So "merciful and gracious" (34:6) ("gracious" is *hannun*, related to *hen*) resounds through Scripture as a basic characterization of God (see Neh. 9:17, 31; 2 Chron. 30:9; Pss. 86:15; 103:8; 111:4; 112:4; 145:8; Joel 2:13; Jonah 4:2). Since "compassion" expounds his covenant name, we are not surprised to find him showing compassion for the sake of his covenant (2 Kings 13:23).

---

64. Thanks to Mark Futato for this suggestion. Of course, I take responsibility for the formulation here.

65. This word is used only once in Scripture, at Heb. 5:2, where it describes Jesus' ability as a man to sympathize with his people.

God often shows compassion for his people after they have rebelled and he has judged their sin (as in Deut. 13:17; 30:3). So compassion motivates him to forgive their sins (Ps. 78:38).

Matthew tells us that on several occasions Jesus was moved by compassion for people to heal and feed them (Matt. 9:6; 14:14; 15:32; 20:34). Readers familiar with the Old Testament find in these references the compassion of Yahweh.

So, like the other attributes of God that we have discussed, God's compassion is a model for ours: "If anyone has material possessions and sees his brother in need but has no pity [*splangchna*] on him, how can the love of God be in him?" (1 John 3:17). It is very wicked to be forgiven a great debt, and then to have no compassion on someone who owes us a small debt (Matt. 18:21–35). Compassion is a necessary ingredient of the love of Christ (see also 1 Peter 3:8; Jude 22).

OTHER FORMS OF GOD'S GOODNESS

God's gentleness, meekness, or humility ('*anah, prautēs, epieikeia*) is mentioned in 2 Samuel 22:36 and Psalm 18:35, and Scripture often commends this virtue in human beings. (See Num. 12:3; Pss. 22:26; 25:9; 2 Cor. 10:1, where Paul mentions "the meekness and gentleness" of Christ to those who have criticized him as meek in their presence, but bold when away; Gal. 5:22; 1 Thess. 2:7; 2 Tim. 2:24; Titus 3:2; James 3:17.)

It may be a bit surprising to find the Bible occasionally referring to God as meek or gentle. But this language is important, both theologically and for the Christian life. In Matthew 20:20–26, Jesus explains the nature of leadership in his kingdom: not being served, but serving; being great by being a slave. And he presents himself as the example: "just as the Son of Man did not come to be served, but to serve, and to give his life as a ransom for many" (v. 28). As we saw in our discussion of love, the love of Christ is the standard for the Christian life. Now we see that such love involves humility, a self-abasement that does not destroy us, but fulfills what God meant us to be.

There is something mysterious here, but as I grope for words, I would conclude that Jesus' self-abasement reveals something about the very lordship of God.[66] For all his mighty power, he is the Lord who serves his people. This divine service does not compromise his power or authority; rather,

---

66. It also reveals something about the relationships between the persons of the Trinity: see chapter 29.

it is the form that his power takes. He makes all things work for good—not only his own good, but the good of those who love him (Rom. 8:28). My perception is that gentleness and humility are among the virtues least practiced by Christians today. If God himself can serve his creatures, surely we, who can boast of nothing except the cross, should be able to serve without seeking constantly to maintain or improve our own status and reputation.

There are a few references to the "beauty" (*no'am*) of the Lord (Pss. 27:4; 90:17), and others to the "beauty of holiness" (*hadarah*) (1 Chron. 16:29; 2 Chron. 20:21; Ps. 29:2). God designed the temple to be a beautiful place, and, as we have seen, the temple is itself an image of the heavenly temple, the theophany itself. So God's image is found in aesthetic as well as ethical ways. The beauties of the earth and of human art are significantly analogous to the beauty of the Creator of all. The vast riches of creation are far too great to be ascribed merely to utilitarian purposes. God's intentions (as in the author/novel model we explored in chaps. 8 and 9) are aesthetic as well as ethical. And, of course, as with all attributes, God's beauty serves as a norm for ours.[67]

God "rejoices" (*samah*) in the creation (Ps. 104:31) and in people (*ratsah*, Ps. 149:4). We often read about what does and does not "delight" (*hafets*) him. We will look again at this concept under the category of God's will, with which his "pleasure" is partly synonymous. But it is refreshing to know that joy is a divine attribute and that when the Spirit plants joy in us (Gal. 5:22), we are becoming more like God. We should not think of God, or the ideal Christian, as constantly disapproving or dour.

"Peace" (*shalom, eirēnē*) in Scripture refers mostly to a quality of human life given by God as a blessing of salvation. But by implication it is also a divine attribute. God is called "the God of peace" in Romans 15:33 and 16:20, 2 Corinthians 13:11, and Hebrews 13:20. In chapter 17, we noted the compound name *yahweh shalom* in Judges 6:24: "The LORD is Peace." The Messiah is the Prince of Peace in Isaiah 9:6, and "of the increase of his government and peace there will be no end" (v. 7).

Peace is a very common term in Scripture. "Peace be to you" (expressed variously in Judg. 6:23; 19:20; Ps. 122:8; Luke 10:5; 24:36) is the common Hebrew greeting, and "go in peace" is the common farewell (Luke 8:48). Theologically, it represents the fullness of the blessings of salvation: peace as opposed to war, but also completeness, wholeness, and prosperity. The Lord promises peace to his redeemed people (Pss. 4:8; 29:11; 37:11; 119:165;

67. How it serves as a norm is a difficult question. But at least, insofar as art conveys a message, that message ought to be consistent with God's revelation.

Isa. 26:3; Luke 2:14; John 14:27; Rom. 5:1). The gospel is the message of peace (Acts 10:36). So the Aaronic benediction pronounces the blessing of peace upon God's people (Num. 6:26), and the apostolic greetings and benedictions in the New Testament regularly include "peace" along with "grace" (Rom. 1:7; 2 Cor. 1:2; Gal. 1:3; 6:16). These phrases may bring together the Old Testament emphasis on peace with the New Testament emphasis on grace.

Peace comes from God alone, since the Fall has made us prone to wars and fighting (James 4:1–3). Peace, like all blessings of salvation, makes us like God. So, like all blessings of salvation and Christian virtues, peace among men is a reflection of God's own nature; it is a divine attribute. God is completely at peace with himself. We often experience struggles between contradictory impulses within us. God, on the contrary, is completely in harmony with himself. His three persons glorify and serve one another willingly and cheerfully. He is whole, well, and prosperous—blessed and happy.

Blessedness appears in expressions like "God be blessed" (*eulogetos*, expressed variously, e.g., in Rom. 1:25; 9:5; 2 Cor. 1:3), and "blessed" (*makarios*) is a divine attribute in 1 Timothy 1:11 and 6:15. We can easily understand what it means for God to bless us, but what does it mean for us to bless God?

Although God has no needs, as we shall see, creation nevertheless benefits him by displaying his attributes (grace, goodness, wisdom, power, and so on), glorifying his name (as people recognize him as Lord), and eliciting the praises of his creatures. *Eulogētos* can be translated "praised," so that to "bless" God is to "praise" him. In Psalm 103:1, the KJV translates *barak* as "bless," the Septuagint *eulogeō*, the NIV "praise."

But there may be more to God's blessedness than the praises of his creatures. *Makarios* is often found in beatitudes (teaching that begins with "blessed is," as in Ps. 1:1; Matt. 5:3–11; James 1:12; Rev. 14:13). It is sometimes translated "happy," although in modern English *happy* tends to refer merely to emotional satisfaction. Happiness in Aristotle, for example, is overall good fortune, a good life in every sense. The beatitudes of Scripture indicate the components of such happiness, as well as the happiness that is a consequence of such behavior.

God is supremely blessed, because he is the full embodiment, indeed the archetype, of the virtues described in the beatitudes and elsewhere in Scripture. Those virtues bring about the best life possible, including supreme satisfaction, and that satisfaction belongs to God.

Of course, as we shall see, God is grieved by the works of Satan and human sin. But, as he sees the end from the beginning, he is able to see the course of history in its full context, from its widest perspective. So while he grieves about particular evils, he rejoices that his overall plan is wonderful, that it achieves all his purposes.

God's blessedness shows us that the greatest possible happiness is to be found only by imaging the blessedness of God himself. We can see this image perfectly in the life of Jesus.

We began this chapter by looking at perfection, and we now come full circle, ending with blessedness, that quality of life possessed by one who embodies all perfections. What a wonderful God we have!

CHAPTER 21

God's Righteousness and Wrath

In this chapter, we continue our discussion of God's attributes of goodness—his attributes in the general sphere of ethics. God's righteousness is a form of his goodness. But righteousness raises different issues and requires us to explore other themes. And then our consideration of both goodness and righteousness will force us to ask some serious questions about the wrath of God, his jealousy, and even his hatred.

If you review the chart of the attributes hesitantly proposed in chapter 19, you will notice that when we move from goodness to righteousness, we are moving from a "control" cell to an "authority" cell. The main idea of divine righteousness is that God acts according to a perfect internal standard of right and wrong. All his actions are within the limits (if we can use that term reverently) of that standard. So God's righteousness is the form or structure of his goodness, and his goodness is the concrete, active embodiment of his righteousness.

The chart, however, exaggerates the difference between goodness and righteousness, which is part of the reason for my hesitation in proposing the chart. To say that God is good implies that he is righteous. So goodness includes righteousness, rather than being separate from it. And Scripture often presents God's righteousness, as we shall see, not merely as an authoritative standard, but also as an active power bringing salvation. In other words, righteousness, like goodness, can itself be an active, dynamic benevolence, not just the static structure of benevolence. Recall also from the previous chapter that God's goodness, like his righteousness, is an au-

446

thoritative standard for the corresponding human virtues. Love also, particularly as we see it in Christ, is a standard for our conduct, indeed, the very mark of the Christian (John 13:34–35). So goodness and righteousness are not separable in God's actual being and action. Both describe his dynamic actions to save his people, and both serve as standards of conduct.

We should remind ourselves again that all these divine attributes are just different ways of describing a person. When this person does mighty works in our history and experience, all his attributes come with him. Whatever he does, he simultaneously reveals his benevolence and his authoritative standards.

The Hebrew *tsedeq* and the Greek *dikaiosunē* are translated "righteousness, rightness, justice, lawfulness." The terms are therefore in the forensic sphere, the sphere of law and the courtroom, the sphere in which one advocates or defends behavior. This is why I put righteousness where I did in figure 2 of chapter 19. Because God's covenant contains law (the "stipulations," chap. 2), God's relationship to us inevitably has a forensic side. Our God makes demands of us; he expects us to act according to his standards, and therefore to be righteous. Liberal theologians have sometimes sought to eliminate law from this relationship, thinking that it conflicts with the biblical emphasis on love. But law and righteousness permeate the Scriptures, and, as we have seen, love itself requires us to keep God's commandments (1 John 5:3).

Note that the same terms in the original languages can be translated either "righteousness" or "justice." In English, there is some difference between these two terms. *Righteousness* comes from a German root (*Recht*), *justice* from a Latin one (*justitia*). In English, *right* and *righteous* tend to apply more often to individuals, and *just* and *justice* to institutions, societies, and rulers, though that generalization has many exceptions. Both can refer either to persons or to actions.[1] The Hebrew and Greek terms can include any of these nuances, depending on the context. The Hebrew *mishpat*, "judgment," however, can sometimes be translated "justice," but rarely (if ever) "righteousness."

The older theologians made a number of distinctions within God's righteousness that can be presented in a Ramist[2] outline:

1. In general, ethical predications pertain to persons, actions, and attitudes. I'm not aware of places in Scripture where righteousness pertains to attitudes.
2. Petrus Ramus (1515–72) was an influential French Protestant philosopher. He believed that the proper method in studying a subject was to divide it into two parts, and each of those parts into two parts, until one reaches the supposedly ultimate elements of the subject matter. Of course, we now know that he was incorrect. The proper method in theology is not to divide everything into twos, but rather into threes!

1. Internal (God's moral excellence)
2. External (the rectitude of his conduct)
   a. Rectoral or legislative (promulgating just laws for his creatures)
   b. Distributive (administering rewards and punishments)
      i. Remunerative (distributing reward)
      ii. Retributive (distributing punishment)

Scripture nowhere specifies these distinctions in so many words, and its actual way of presenting God's righteousness is quite different, as we shall see. Still, this outline does list a number of genuinely biblical uses of the concept. My own triadic approach would look more like this:

1. Existential perspective: God's moral excellence, the quality of his character and actions (1 on the Ramist outline)
2. Normative perspective: God's standards for himself and creation (including, but going beyond, 2a on the Ramist outline)
3. Situational perspective: God's actions, by which he makes his righteousness prevail (including 2b on the Ramist outline)[3]

The first point essentially equates God's righteousness with his goodness, so I will not add further discussion of it here, although I will be stressing that the other two points arise from God's own character. The other two categories also overlap with goodness, but in those areas I would like to present more biblical data.

GOD'S RIGHTEOUS STANDARDS

God reveals his standards to us in his deeds and in his personal self-revelation, but most explicitly in his revealed law. His law is not arbitrary, but is based on his own nature. The moral law is not something above him, that has authority over him. Nor is it something he has created, as if (as nominalism would have it) he could change it at will (making adultery to be virtuous, for example). Rather, his moral standard is simply himself, his person, his nature. His acts are righteous because he is a righteous God. Righteousness, therefore, is his desire, his pleasure. So, as I mentioned in

---

3. This, like the normative perspective, may go beyond the Ramist outline, for it would include necessary acts of God (acts of God within his Trinitarian self-existence), which don't refer to the creation. But this area is mysterious, and I have no biblical guidance here as to what sorts of acts these might be. Still, I believe that God in his essence is active, and that he always acts righteously. Those statements would be true of his eternal existence, as well as his actions in time.

chapter 12 (under "simplicity"), the standard for our moral behavior is not an abstract concept, but an infinite person, God himself.

Of course, God has certain rights that we do not have: the right to take human life as he sees fit, the right to act autonomously without honoring someone higher than himself, and so on. But, for the most part, his law instructs us to imitate his character and conduct. He made us in his image, to be like him. When we sinned in Adam, he called us back to imitate him. The main principle of the Mosaic Law is, "Be holy because I, the LORD your God, am holy" (Lev. 19:1). The Ten Commandments call Israel to a lifestyle that is a suitable response to God's great deliverance: "I am the LORD your God, who brought you out of Egypt, out of the land of slavery" (Ex. 20:2). As God worked for six days and rested on the Sabbath, so Israel is to do the same (vv. 8–11). As God gave Israel rest from their bondage, they are to give rest to their families, servants, and animals (Deut. 5:15). The same principle exists in the New Testament. Jesus tells his disciples, "Be perfect, therefore, as your heavenly Father is perfect" (Matt. 5:48), and Peter applies Leviticus 19:1 directly to the church in 1 Peter 1:15–16.

Imitating God implies imitating Christ.[4] The Christian life arises from our renewal in the image of Christ (Eph. 4:22–24; Col. 3:10). As we have seen, this imitation of God includes loving one another as Christ loved us (John 13:34–35; 15:12; Eph. 5:2; 1 John 4:10–11).

So the righteousness that God expects from us is essentially to image his own ethical character—his love, his holiness, his righteousness.

We can find the basic standards of God's righteousness, making allowance for those areas of discontinuity between God's rights and our own, in the laws of Scripture. What he commands of us is what he himself is and does. God seeks his own glory, so he forbids us to worship other gods (Ex. 20:3), to make idols (vv. 4–6), or to misuse his name (v. 7). He has chosen to act in a historical pattern of work and rest, so he instructs us to imitate that pattern (vv. 8–11). He makes covenants and respects their terms, including structures of authority (v. 12). He loves life (v. 13) and fidelity (v. 14). He demands respect for his ownership of the world and for the secondary ownership he confers upon us (v. 15). He loves truth (v. 16) and purity of heart (v. 17). The other laws in Scripture spell out the meanings of the Ten Commandments more fully and apply them to various specific situations. God intended some of those secondary laws, like the require-

---

4. Notice how virtually everything we say about God can be said about Christ as well. Thus, the biblical doctrine of God supplies pervasive and comprehensive proof of the deity of Christ. I shall make note of this fact later, but the reader should notice these references as we go along and let the depth of Scripture's testimony to the deity of Christ overwhelm him.

ments of animal sacrifice, for the specific situation existing before the coming of Christ. They are no longer literally binding after the final sacrifice of Jesus. But they continue to instruct us about God's character, telling us what things are of great concern to him.

The penalties given in the laws also teach us about God's righteousness. The chief principle governing them is set forth in Obadiah 15:

> As you have done, it will be done to you;
>   your deeds will return upon your own head.

Compare Jeremiah 50:29; Habakkuk 2:8; Joel 3:4, 7; and the *lex talionis* in Exodus 21:24: "eye for eye, tooth for tooth."[5] The death penalty for murder is similar: "Whoever sheds the blood of man, by man shall his blood be shed" (Gen. 9:6). (See also Matt. 7:2; Rev. 16:6; 18:6–7.)

One theme of the wisdom of God in Proverbs is that the wicked fall into the snares they set for the righteous:[6]

> These men lie in wait for their own blood;
>   they waylay only themselves!
> Such is the end of all who go after ill-gotten gain;
>   it takes away the lives of those who get it. (Prov. 1:18–19)

> If a man digs a pit, he will fall into it;
>   if a man rolls a stone, it will roll back on him. (Prov. 26:27)

(Cf. Prov. 1:31; 10:16; 11:8; 28:10; 29:6; Pss. 35:8; 141:10.) There is a "poetic justice" to God's providence. It doesn't happen with mechanical regularity, for at times the wicked prosper and the righteous seem forsaken. But the schemes of the wicked, in the end, will be seen to have heaped up judgment upon the wicked themselves. As they have done, it shall be done to them. On the Last Day, God will right all wrongs, and, as we saw in chapter 8, there will be no more complaints against his justice.

So righteousness is a kind of elemental fairness. As we sow, so shall we reap. As we want others to do to us, we should do to them. This principle "sums up the Law and the Prophets" (Matt. 7:12).[7]

God's own judgments are fair in the most perfect way. In pleading for

---

5. The law of talion was never intended as an excuse for personal vengeance, but was, as Vern Poythress puts it, "a directive to judges making decisions regarding penalties in cases of injury." See Poythress, *The Shadow of Christ in the Law of Moses* (Brentwood, Tenn.: Wolgemuth and Hyatt, 1991), 123. This book is an excellent analysis of biblical law, to which I am indebted for much of the information in the present discussion.

6. One can hardly think about this principle today without reference to the cartoon figure Wyl E. Coyote, whose schemes to trap the Roadrunner inevitably backfire on him.

7. This passage, often called "the Golden Rule," is therefore equivalent to the two great-

his nephew Lot, Abraham asks rhetorically, "Will not the Judge of all the earth do right?" (Gen. 18:25). Scripture proclaims:

> He is the Rock, his ways are perfect,
>   and all his ways are just. (Deut. 32:4; cf. Ps. 92:15)

> The LORD is righteous in all his ways
>   and loving toward all he has made. (Ps. 145:17)

All his judgments are righteous (Pss. 9:8; 50:4–6; 51:4; 96:10, 13; 98:9), as is his law, the standard by which his judgments are made (Deut. 4:8; Pss. 19:7–9; 119:138, 142; Isa. 42:21). The fact that he judges all things in heaven and on earth implies that his standards are the highest standards of righteousness.

GOD'S RIGHTEOUS DEEDS

We may well expect, then, when we move from the normative to the situational perspective, that God's actions in history will apply his righteous standards and insure their triumph. That is indeed the case, as indicated in the passages I cited on God's judgment. But under the situational perspective, we note something else as well, which gives us a much richer picture of God's righteousness.

Righteousness in Scripture is not only a standard governing conduct, but also a means of salvation. In 1 Samuel 12:6–11, Samuel enumerates God's "righteous acts" (v. 7) as his deliverances, both from Egypt and during the time of the judges. This use of *righteous* is a bit surprising. We can understand how the deliverance of God's people from Egypt (the Old Testament paradigm of redemption) was an act of God's grace, or his love. And certainly this deliverance was righteous, in the sense that it was in accordance with his perfect standards ("You have kept your promise because you are righteous" [Neh. 9:8]). But how did this deliverance accord with God's standards? Israel was a sinful, disobedient people. Surely she didn't deserve to be saved. Indeed, as we saw in the previous chapter, God didn't choose Israel because of her numbers or her righteousness. So why does this deliverance provide evidence of God's righteousness in particular? Does it not, indeed, pose a problem for God's righteousness, calling it into question?

In Psalm 9:7–8, the psalmist reflects on God's rule:

---

est commandments of the law, the commandments to love God and to love our neighbor as ourselves. Jesus teaches that these, too, sum up the law (Matt. 22:34–40).

> The LORD reigns forever;
>> he has established his throne for judgment.
> He will judge the world in righteousness;
>> he will govern the peoples with justice.

Then he adds,

> The LORD is a refuge for the oppressed,
>> a stronghold in times of trouble. (v. 9)

Here we want to ask, does verse 9 simply change the subject, moving from the forensic sphere to that of divine protection—or is there a connection between these topics?

Even more striking is Isaiah 46:12–13:

> Listen to me, you stubborn-hearted,
>> you who are far from righteousness.
> I am bringing my righteousness near,
>> it is not far away;
>> and my salvation will not be delayed.
> I will grant salvation to Zion,
>> my splendor to Israel.

Here God brings his righteousness and his salvation to bear on Israel in the same event. He saves Israel by bringing his righteousness near. And he does this in a context that fully acknowledges Israel's unrighteousness. Righteousness and salvation are parallel concepts also in Psalms 40:10; 85:9–10; 98:2–3; and Isaiah 45:8; 51:5.

God's righteousness even brings forgiveness of sins. We learn in 1 John 1:9, "If we confess our sins, he is faithful *and just* and will forgive our sins and purify us from all unrighteousness" (italics mine). Again, forgiveness comes through God's righteousness. But why righteousness, rather than grace or love, which would seem more appropriate here?

The background of this usage can be found in the biblical teaching that God rescues the righteous from their oppressors. In Psalm 34:15–22, we read:

> The eyes of the LORD are on the righteous
>> and his ears are attentive to their cry;
> the face of the LORD is against those who do evil,
>> to cut off the memory of them from the earth.
> The righteous cry out, and the LORD hears them;
>> he delivers them from all their troubles.
> The LORD is close to the brokenhearted
>> and saves those who are crushed in spirit.

A righteous man may have many troubles,
>   but the LORD delivers him from them all;
he protects all his bones;
>   not one of them will be broken.
Evil will slay the wicked;
>   the foes of the righteous will be condemned.
The LORD redeems his servants;
>   no one will be condemned who takes refuge in him.

The "righteous" here are not sinlessly perfect, but relatively perfect or upright (*tamim*, see chap. 20). They are "in the right" over against their enemies, who would seek to destroy them. But they cannot rescue themselves, so they cry out to God. God then acts to vindicate the cause of the righteous, over against the wicked. These divine acts are not only acts of goodness, grace, and love, but also the righteousness of God.

In other passages, those here called righteous are called afflicted, oppressed, weak, poor, or needy. In Psalm 72, the writer prays for the messianic king:

Endow the king with your justice, O God,
>   the royal son with your righteousness.
He will judge your people in righteousness,
>   your afflicted ones with justice.
The mountains will bring prosperity to the people,
>   the hills the fruit of righteousness.
He will defend the afflicted among the people
and save the children of the needy;
>   he will crush the oppressor. (vv. 1–4)

(Cf. Pss. 10:14; 35:10; 68:5; 82:3; 113:7; 140:12; 146:7–9; Jer. 22:16.) Note the emphasis on righteousness and the king's righteous judgment for the afflicted over against their oppressors. In Psalm 82, God berates human rulers because they show partiality to the wicked. He tells them:

Defend the cause of the weak and fatherless;
>   maintain the rights of the poor and oppressed.
Rescue the weak and needy;
>   deliver them from the hand of the wicked. (vv. 3–4)

The Messiah obeys the Lord:

He will not judge by what he sees with his eyes,
>   or decide by what he hears with his ears;
but with righteousness he will judge the needy,
>   with justice he will give decisions for the poor of the earth.

He will strike the earth with the rod of his mouth;
    with the breath of his lips he will slay the wicked.
Righteousness will be his belt
    and faithfulness the sash around his waist. (Isa. 11:3–5; cf. Pss.
        7:6–13, 17; 143:1–4, 11)

When Jesus, the Messiah, comes into the world, his coming is good news for the poor, for he is to exalt the lowly and bring down the proud (Isa. 40:4; Luke 1:51–53;[8] 4:18–19).

God's righteousness saves the afflicted from their powerful oppressors. The Lord is particularly concerned with those who have the least power in society: widows, orphans, and aliens. In Exodus 22:22, God commands, "Do not take advantage of a widow or an orphan." Deuteronomy 10:18 says of God, "He defends the cause of the fatherless and the widow, and loves the alien, giving him food and clothing."[9] Israel is to be compassionate towards them:

When you are harvesting in your field and you overlook a sheaf, do not go back to get it. Leave it for the alien, the fatherless and the widow, so that the LORD your God may bless you in all the work of your hands. (Deut. 24:19; cf. 26:12–13)

Isaiah 1:16–17 adds:

Stop doing wrong,
    learn to do right!
Seek justice,
    encourage the oppressed.
Defend the cause of the fatherless,
    plead the case of the widow.

Lacking earthly power and opposed by those who should be defending them, the afflicted turn to the Lord:

"Because of the oppression of the weak
    and the groaning of the needy,
I will now arise," says the LORD.
    "I will protect them from those who malign them." (Ps. 12:5)

Yet I am poor and needy;
    may the Lord think of me.

8. Compare the prayer of Hannah in 1 Sam. 2, especially verses 3–8.
9. In modern society, the clearest application of this principle is to the unborn, who have no voice, and who are being murdered by the millions every year.

You are my help and my deliverer;
  O my God, do not delay. (Ps. 40:17)

We are reminded of the situation facing the nation of Israel before the Exodus. They were enslaved, in severe pain and suffering, oppressed by the most powerful ruler of the time. Humanly speaking, they had no hope of escaping that oppression. So they cried out to the Lord, who heard them and delivered them, triumphing over Pharaoh, his soldiers, and his gods. This salvation was not only grace, but also righteousness. God vindicated his righteous people against their wicked oppressors.

But, later in their history, some Israelites themselves became oppressors. God intervened against them to save his afflicted ones, who could do nothing but cry out to him for mercy. In time, the oppressors grew more numerous, the afflicted less so. But the afflicted were the true remnant (see chap. 16), God's elect within the larger nation.

Although the cause of the afflicted is righteous, compared to that of their oppressors, God delivers them, not because of their own good works, but because they cry out to God for mercy. They are, therefore, justified by faith in God's righteousness, not their own. In Isaiah 45:24, they confess that "in the LORD alone are righteousness and strength."

Liberation theology has made much of this biblical theme, saying that God is on the side of the poor.[10] But liberation theologians tend to take *poor* in a largely economic sense. Certainly it is true that widows, orphans, and aliens tend to be economically destitute in Scripture. It is also true that the oppression condemned in Scripture was often economic oppression. Scripture calls God's people in many ways to care for the poor.[11]

But God doesn't deliver people merely because they have a low level of income or wealth. The "sluggards" of Proverbs (6:6, 9; 10:26; 13:4; 20:4; 26:16), the lazy people who won't work for their living, are not the recipients of God's deliverance. And, of course, God delivers some who are eco-

---

10. Gustavo Gutierrez, *A Theology of Liberation* (Maryknoll, N.Y.: Orbis, 1973).

11. This was a central concern of the apostles, for example (Acts 6:1–4; Gal. 2:10), and of the early church as a whole (Acts 2:44–45; 4:32–35). The Old Testament mandated care for the poor through (1) protection of private property (Ex. 20:15; 22:1–15)—not its abolition, as in the Marxist agendas of liberation theologians, (2) allowing the poor to glean in the fields (Lev. 19:9–10; Deut. 24:19–22), (3) immediate payment of wages (Lev. 19:13), (4) willing, compassionate lending (Ex. 22:25–27; Deut. 15:7–11), (5) fairness in economic dealings (Ex. 22:22–24), (6) impartiality in the courts (Ex. 23:6–9), (7) Hebrew slavery— actually a kind of household service for those who could not pay their debts (Ex. 21:1–11; Lev. 25:39–55; Deut. 15:12–18), (8) giving rest to servants on the Sabbath (Ex. 20:10; 23:12), (9) allowing the poor to take freely from the fields during the sabbatical year (Ex. 23:10–11; Lev. 25:1–7), (10) remitting debts in the sabbatical year (Deut. 15:1–6), and (11) returning sold property in the year of Jubilee (Lev. 25:13–17).

nomically wealthy: Abraham, Moses, and David.[12] God delivers "the poor" because they are unjustly oppressed, whether economically or otherwise, and they turn to God, trusting and hoping in him alone.

God tells judges not to be on the side of the poor, but to be impartial:

> Do not pervert justice; do not show partiality to the poor or favoritism to the great, but judge your neighbor fairly. (Lev. 19:15; cf. Deut. 1:16–17; 16:18–20; 25:1)

But of course the problem in Israel was not that judges tended to favor the poor, but that they tended to favor the rich. So God emphasizes justice to the poor:

> Do not deny justice to your poor people in their lawsuits. Have nothing to do with a false charge and do not put an innocent or honest person to death, for I will not acquit the guilty. (Ex. 23:6)

God is impartial and just, not a respecter of persons (Rom. 2:11; Eph. 6:9; Col. 3:25; 1 Peter 1:17). He will certainly "bring about justice for his chosen ones, who cry out to him day and night" (Luke 18:7).

So God's righteous salvation is covenantal, given to the elect remnant who trust in his promises. Scripture never suggests that God's righteousness requires an equal distribution of wealth in society, as on the Marxist and liberationist accounts. Rather, it requires equality of all people before the law and fairness in our dealings with one another.

God's righteousness, as the salvation of the afflicted, is the background for Paul's doctrine of justification. In Romans 1:17, Paul indicates why he is "not ashamed of the gospel" (v. 16):

> For in the gospel a righteousness from God is revealed, a righteousness that is by faith from first to last, just as it is written: "The righteous will live by faith."

To Martin Luther, this verse posed a problem. As a Roman Catholic monk, he was accustomed to thinking of God's righteousness only as the divine standard of judgment. God's righteousness, therefore, was a fearsome thing. How could the revelation of God's righteousness be "good news" (gospel)? Even more perplexing, how could it be "the power of God for the salvation of everyone who believes" (v. 16)? Luther eventually concluded that God's "righteousness" here is not the righteousness by which he judges men

---

12. David identifies himself as "poor and needy" in Ps. 40:17. David endured suffering, indeed oppression, at different times in his life, but, so far as we know, that oppression was never focused on his material wealth.

on the Last Day, but the righteousness he *gives* us, *imputes to us, in this life,* by grace through faith. This meaning is clear in Romans 3:21–22:

> But now a righteousness from God, apart from law, has been made known,[13] to which the Law and the Prophets testify. This righteousness from God comes through faith in Jesus Christ to all who believe.

Just as our sin and condemnation come through Adam, so our righteousness, justification, and life come through Jesus (Rom. 5:12–19). Righteousness comes not through our works, but only through God's free gift, his grace (3:24). Christ has "become for us . . . righteousness" (1 Cor. 1:30). And "God made him who had no sin to be sin for us, so that in him we might become the righteousness of God" (2 Cor. 5:21).

Although this gift of righteousness is free to us, it is not free to God. An awful price has been paid, the sacrifice of God's only Son:

> God presented him as a sacrifice of atonement, through faith in his blood. He did this to demonstrate his justice, because in his forbearance he had left the sins committed beforehand unpunished— he did it to demonstrate his justice at the present time, so as to be just and the one who justifies those who have faith in Jesus. (Rom. 3:25–26)

So we see now why the gospel of Christ is a revelation of God's righteousness, not only of his goodness, grace, and love. The gospel tells us what God has done so that he can declare us righteous, not because of our works, but because of the sacrifice of Christ.

But it also vindicates God's own righteousness (Rom. 3:26). How could God declare sinners to be righteous? Is it not a perversion of justice to clear the guilty? Is that not, indeed, a violation of his own name (Ex. 34:7)? But the perfect sacrifice of Jesus is the basis of our righteousness, and when God clears our guilt for Jesus' sake, he is acting justly. Through Christ, God is able both to justify the ungodly (us) and to defend himself against any charge of injustice.

So, like the salvation of the poor and needy in the Old Testament, our salvation in Christ is by God's righteousness. Jesus himself is the ultimate remnant, the poor and needy one, oppressed, crying out to God alone. Although Father and Son are estranged for a time, God hears his prayer and raises him gloriously from the dead. And when God raises Jesus, he raises us in him (Rom. 6:3–14).

13. Note the parallel here with 1:17.

Now we understand why God is not only faithful, but also just, to forgive our sins (1 John 1:9). And we understand that the righteousness of God is gospel as well as law. It is not only a standard of conduct, but the power of God for salvation.

Like his goodness, love, and grace, therefore, God's righteousness has both general and particular aspects. In the sense of fairness, God treats all creatures in righteousness. He never violates his standards of conduct. But in the active, redemptive sense, God's righteousness saves only those who are righteous by faith.

And like his holiness (see chap. 2), his righteousness is both fearsome and loving, both a forbidding transcendence and a redemptive immanence.

GOD'S JEALOUSY

In the rest of this chapter, I will be considering some divine attributes that, in the view of some, conflict with God's goodness, love, grace, and righteousness. We will be looking at God's jealousy, hatred, and wrath.

Jealousy (Heb. qin'ah, Gk. zēlos) is a passionate zeal to guard the exclusiveness of a marriage relationship, leading to anger against an unfaithful spouse. In Numbers 5:11–31, Moses describes "a grain offering for jealousy" (v. 15) and a test of fidelity to be given when a man suspects his wife of unfaithfulness. To my knowledge, Scripture never presents jealousy as a negative trait. It may seem so in Song of Solomon 8:6 in the KJV ("jealousy is cruel as the grave"), but that text takes on a different appearance in the more accurate NIV rendering. In context, the NIV reads,

> For love is as strong as death,
>   its jealousy unyielding as the grave.
> It burns like blazing fire,
>   like a mighty flame.

Here, fiery jealousy is part of love, the prerogative of love that is as strong as death. It is the proper attitude of a man toward his wife (cf. Prov. 6:34). It is entirely right for him to be zealous for her purity and for the exclusiveness of her love for him. Qana' can be used (as jealousy in modern English) for the sin of envy (Gen. 26:14; 30:1; Ps. 37:1), but Scripture treats jealousy and envy as distinct concepts.

Jealousy is an important attribute of God:

> You shall not make for yourself an idol in the form of anything in heaven above or on the earth beneath or in the waters below. You

shall not bow down to them or worship them; for I, the LORD your God, am a jealous God, punishing the children for the sins of the fathers to the third and fourth generation of those who hate me, but showing love to a thousand generations of those who love me and keep my commandments. (Ex. 20:4–6; cf. Deut. 5:8–10)

The reason for the prohibition of idolatry (and possibly for the first commandment as well) is that God is jealous. God's jealousy is always directed against idolatry (see Deut. 32:16, 21; Josh. 24:19–20). But note the close connection between God's jealousy and his name. In Exodus 34:14, Yahweh says, "Do not worship any other god, for the LORD, whose name is Jealous, is a jealous God." Earlier, in verse 7, in what I have argued is a definitive exposition of the name Yahweh, we find the same language of jealousy as in 20:5, "He does not leave the guilty unpunished; he punishes the children and their children for the sins of the fathers to the third and fourth generation." God is jealous for his great name in Ezekiel 39:25. For his name's sake, he will not give his glory to another (Isa. 42:8; 48:11).

So jealousy is an attribute of God, a description of the divine nature. By nature, he deserves and demands exclusive worship and allegiance.

In the Bible's emphasis on God's jealousy, we see that there is a profound analogy between God's covenant and the marriage relationship. Idolatry is like adultery. The same attitude of covenant disloyalty lies behind both sins. Husbands should love their wives as Christ loves the church (Eph. 5:25). That love is exclusive in both cases. So God's jealousy clearly manifests his lordship.

As in the above passages, God's jealousy is closely connected to his wrath and judgment. Moses associates God's jealousy with the figure of "consuming fire" (Deut. 4:24; cf. Heb. 12:29) and the burning of his anger (Deut. 6:15).

From this discussion we can see that God's jealousy is not inconsistent with his love or goodness. On the contrary, his jealousy is one aspect of his love. Although God has some love for all of his creatures, as we have seen, he has an exclusive love for his own people, and he demands the same of them. When they violate that love, he behaves like a godly husband—he becomes jealous. There is nothing wrong with that jealousy. It reflects the intensity of his love. When a man's beloved wife turns away and loves another man, he is rightly jealous. If he were not, that would be evidence that he does not care for her. In Scripture, adultery is serious business: a capital crime in the Old Testament (Lev. 20:10) and a ground for divorce in the New (Matt. 19:9). Idolatry is similarly a capital crime in the Old Testament (Deut. 13:1–5).

GOD'S HATRED

More difficult to reconcile with God's love and goodness is his hatred (Heb. *sane'*, Gk. *miseō*).[14] Proverbs 10:12 contrasts hate and love:

> Hatred stirs up dissension,
>> but love covers over all wrongs.

Since the law of love, as we have seen, is the norm of human conduct, Leviticus 19:17 urges, "Do not hate your brother in your heart."[15] Scripture often urges us, however, to hate evil (Pss. 97:10; 101:3; 119:104, 128, 163; Amos 5:15; Jude 23; Rev. 2:6). And godly hatred is directed not only against evil deeds, but also against some people: "I hate double-minded men, but I love your law" (Ps. 119:113).[16] The psalmist asks:

> Do I not hate those who hate you, O Lᴏʀᴅ,
>> and abhor those who rise up against you?
> I have nothing but hatred for them;
>> I count them my enemies. (Ps. 139:21–22)

Scripture, then, seems to recommend hatred in some contexts, but to deplore it in others. So we must look more closely to see if there are different kinds of hatred, or different situations in which it is and is not appropriate. First, let us note that *hate* in Scripture does not always refer to hostility. Jacob loved Rachel, but hated Leah (Gen. 29:31, in Hebrew; NIV says "not loved"). His love for Rachel was, of course, an erotic love (vv. 17–18), and that kind of love was probably what he lacked for Leah; the term *hate* doesn't need to be taken any more strongly than that. Verse 30 says simply that "he loved Rachel more than Leah." If there was also hostility between Jacob and Leah, it would be hard to prove it from the passage.

Similarly, Jesus calls us to hate our family and even our own lives in comparison to our love for him (Matt. 10:37; Luke 14:26; John 12:25), even though he strongly endorses the fifth commandment ("Honor your father

---

14. Some passages, like Prov. 11:20, also speak of God "detesting" something or regarding something as an abomination (*to'evah*). *Quts* is "abhor" in Lev. 20:23 and elsewhere.

15. Significantly, the verse adds, "Rebuke your neighbor frankly so you will not share in his guilt." A frank airing of differences guards love, rather than destroying it. So the New Testament encourages the swift and open discussion of differences, leading to reconciliation (Matt. 5:23–26; 18:15–20; Eph. 4:26). When we do not seek the quick resolution of differences, we tend to harbor grudges, and that turns love into hate.

16. It is not, therefore, true in every sense that we are to "hate the sin, but love the sinner." In some senses, God expects us to hate sinners.

and your mother") in Matt. 15:3–9. Here *hate* and *love* measure relative priorities: we are to love Jesus far more than anyone here on earth.

Furthermore, even when hatred includes hostility, that hostility should be understood essentially as a policy of opposition. Just as love in Scripture is more act than feeling (though the latter is often involved), so it is with hatred. To hate someone is to oppose their goals and to take action, if possible, to prevent them from succeeding. This hatred may include emotional revulsion, of course. Indeed, we should be emotionally disgusted with wickedness. But one may hate the wicked in the sense of opposing (intellectually, volitionally, and emotionally) their policies and plans, without feeling emotional disgust for them personally. (Similarly, one may love another person by seeking to help meet the person's needs, without feeling emotional passion for that person.) Hatred may also include desiring the worst for someone else, but it does not necessarily mean that.

The meaning of *hate*, therefore, like the meaning of *love*, varies in different biblical contexts. Emotional disgust, practical opposition, relative priorities, lack of romantic attraction, and seeking the worst for somebody may be involved in hatred in different proportions in different contexts. In some contexts, hatred excludes love (which also has various senses); in others, it does not.

So, although Proverbs 10:12 contrasts love and hate (and certainly they should be contrasted in most contexts!), the two are not always or in every respect incompatible. If love is a disposition to seek the good of someone else, and hate is opposition to the values and plans of someone, then it is certainly possible both to love and to hate the same person.[17] For example, it is possible to hate some vicious despot (Hitler, Stalin, Idi Amin, Pol Pot, Slobodan Milosevic) in the sense of opposing his plans and calling upon God to judge him, and indeed being emotionally disgusted by his character and actions, while at the same time desiring his conversion. We should always keep that qualification in mind when we pray the imprecatory psalms, which call down judgments on the enemies of God and of the psalmist.

God also hates wickedness and the wicked themselves (Lev. 20:23; Deut. 25:16; 5:5; 11:5; Prov. 6:16–19; 11:20; 16:5; 17:15; Jer. 12:8; Hos. 9:15; Zech. 8:17; Rev. 2:6, 15). His hatred has awful consequences, of course. Ultimately, God will destroy his enemies and send them to hell. But God's present enmity is not always his final word. All of us were once "by nature objects of wrath" (Eph. 2:3) because of sin. As I argued in chapter 20, God's wrath

---

17. This point is similar to the one I made about the ambiguity of favor in my discussion of common grace in chapter 20.

upon us then was genuine wrath. We were wicked, and God really hated us. We were headed for hell. But God loved us in Christ (Eph. 2:4). Since that love went back before the creation of the world (1:4), there must have been a period of time when God loved and hated us simultaneously. Before an elect person is converted, God both loves and hates him: God opposes him and prevents him in the long term from achieving his wicked purposes, but God also has glorious blessings in store for him.

Now in Romans 9:13 (quoting Mal. 1:3) we read, "Jacob I loved, but Esau I hated." Paul traces God's attitudes toward the two men back before their birth, "in order that God's purpose in election might stand" (v. 11). As I said in chapter 16, it is difficult to interpret this passage, because it uses illustrations from God's historical election of Israel to teach us about God's eternal election. I don't believe we can determine from this passage whether or not Esau was ultimately a saved man. Historically, however, God chose Jacob, not Esau, to inherit the promises given to Abraham. Jacob receives God's special covenant love, his *hesed*, as God separates his family from all the nations and promises special blessings to him and to his seed. God does not give that particular kind of love to Esau, and he never intended to. God planned before Esau's birth that he would not have it. In this sense, Esau is "hated."

It is important for Paul's readers to know that God discriminates between people before they are born. It is not necessarily a discrimination between eternal salvation and eternal punishment. In Esau's case, I have no reason to think that it was. But it is, in other cases. Paul teaches that God's eternal discrimination explains the unbelief of Israel. If the unbelief of many Jews continues until their death, we must conclude that God's sovereign discrimination explains their eternal condemnation. In that case, God's hatred for them would have more serious consequences than his hatred for Esau.

What, then, should we conclude about God's love? His hate and his love do not exclude one another in every respect. The attribute of hatred does not in itself compromise Scripture's teaching that "God is love." God does love and hate some people at the same time, in different respects.

There are some, of course, who eventually receive no love from God: the devil and his angels, and the lost in hell. But the fact that "God is love" does not require that his love be distributed equally to everybody and everything in creation. God's punishment of Satan and his followers shows the greatness of his love to the saved: to rid their world of evil and to establish his justice. Indeed, in all that he does, he advances the purposes of his love.

But this point raises a further question: Can we also say that God is hate?

Is hate, like love, a defining attribute of God, and therefore a way of describing his essence?

We could perhaps answer this question simply by denying that God's hate is a defining or essential attribute. (See the distinction in chap. 12.) Certainly Scripture does not emphasize his hatred in the way it emphasizes his love. And it is certainly difficult to imagine how there could be any hatred in God, apart from the creation. There are no enmities in the Trinity, only love between the persons. So perhaps hatred is only an accidental or relational attribute, an attribute arising from God's relationship to the creation.[18]

But this solution to the problem misses some nuances. God cannot love goodness without hating evil. The two are opposite sides of the same coin, positive and negative ways of describing the same virtue. In the mind of God before creation, evil existed only as an idea in his mind, only as a possibility. But surely God regarded that possibility with hostility. Even though he intended to bring evil into existence (see chap. 9), he regarded it as something to be overcome, rather than as something to be honored.

"God is love," then, implies that from eternity past, God has had an implacable hatred of evil. That hatred is not separable from his perfect nature. It is a necessary and defining attribute, not a merely accidental or relational one. "God hates evil" gives us a profound description of his character. "God is hate," however, is not a helpful way of making this point, since it creates terrible confusion. But once we specify the objects of God's hate, we can state clearly that it is a divine attribute.

As we have seen, "God is love" can also be misunderstood by people who don't know the objects of God's love and the type of love in view. But the apostle John accepted that risk in 1 John 4:8. There are greater risks, I think, in speaking of God's hatred. But we need to accept those as well, in order to communicate the full teaching of God's Word on this important matter.

In the final analysis, then, it is biblical and edifying to say that God by nature is throughout eternity passionately opposed to evil. This hatred pervades all his thoughts and actions. God is the supreme hater of wickedness.

GOD'S WRATH

The biblical vocabulary for God's wrath is extensive: in Hebrew, *'af*, *'ebrah*, *haron*, *qetsef*, *hemah*; in Greek, *orgē* and *thymos*, in various forms. These words are also translated "anger," "fury," and so on.

---

18. We might be tempted to say the same thing about God's jealousy, if the Old Testament were not so emphatic in identifying jealousy with God's own name.

Jesus teaches that being angry with one's brother violates the sixth commandment:

> You have heard that it was said to the people long ago, "Do not murder, and anyone who murders will be subject to judgment." But I tell you that anyone who is angry with his brother will be subject to judgment. (Matt. 5:21–22)

Accordingly, anger is included in a number of New Testament lists of sins (Gal. 5:20; Eph. 4:31; Col. 3:8; 1 Tim. 2:8; James 1:19–20). On the other hand, Ephesians 4:26–27 says:

> "In your anger do not sin": Do not let the sun go down while you are still angry, and do not give the devil a foothold.

Paul suggests that the sin is not so much in the anger itself as in our tendency to nurse that anger rather than seeking reconciliation. Jesus displayed anger (*zēlos*, from the vocabulary of jealously we considered earlier) when he cleansed the temple of money changers (John 2:17). We can assume, I believe, that anger, like hatred, is appropriate when directed against God's enemies. Jeremiah tells his hearers that he is "full of the wrath of the LORD, and I cannot hold it in" (6:11).

So Scripture speaks often of the wrath of God as his response to sin. Wrath differs from jealousy and hatred, in that jealousy is more focused on the specific sin of idolatry, while wrath opposes our sin in general. Also, jealousy and hatred are motives for wrath, while wrath actually executes punishments.

It is interesting to note that many Bible texts simply speak of "wrath," without mentioning God as the source of it. For example:

> The Levites, however, are to set up their tents around the tabernacle of the Testimony so that wrath will not fall on the Israelite community. The Levites are to be responsible for the care of the tabernacle of the Testimony. (Num. 1:53)

(Cf. Num. 18:5; Josh. 9:20; 22:20; 1 Chron. 27:24; 2 Chron. 19:10; 24:18; Matt. 3:7; Luke 21:33; Rom. 4:15; 5:9; 9:22; 13:4–5; Eph. 2:3; 1 Thess. 1:10; 2:16; 5:9.)[19] In Leviticus 10:6, Numbers 16:46, and Romans 2:8, *wrath* is also used somewhat impersonally, although the divine source is mentioned in the context.

19. In some of these passages, the NIV and other modern translations supply a name of God or a pronoun to indicate the source of the wrath. I am following the original languages here.

C. H. Dodd, in his commentary on Romans,[20] argues that for Paul, wrath is a kind of impersonal force, or a natural law by which transgressions automatically receive their consequences. Dodd evidently thinks that this view mitigates the problem of evil somewhat and enables us to think more consistently of God as love. But his view exaggerates the implications of these data:

1. There is no shortage of verses that ascribe wrath directly to God, such as Numbers 11:33; 2 Kings 22:13; John 3:36; Romans 1:18; Ephesians 5:6; Colossians 3:6; Hebrews 3:11; 4:3; and Revelation 14:10, 19; 15:1, 7; 16:1; 19:15. Note also the striking, ironic phrase, "the wrath of the Lamb," in Revelation 6:16. The biblical writers are not in doubt about whose wrath it is.

2. When Scripture describes the actual course of God's wrath in history, it speaks very personally of God's action. Dodd finds in Romans a number of impersonal formulations, but these refer back to "the wrath of God" in 1:18. Then Romans 1 describes God's wrathful actions against those who suppress his truth: he "gives them over" to greater sin (vv. 24, 26, 28). At each point, God takes personal initiative. Indeed, as we have seen, the process of reprobation depends on God's very personal hatred (9:12). Paul leaves no doubt that the salvation and judgment of men are based on God's personal decisions.

3. As I indicated in chapters 13–14, Scripture does not teach that God runs the universe by a system of impersonal "natural laws" that are somehow independent of his immediate action. Indeed, nothing happens without God's personal ordination (chap. 4). Dodd's construction, on the contrary, is essentially deist.

4. As I argued in chapter 9, we should not try to solve or mitigate the problem of evil by compromising God's causation of all things.

5. There is a better way to understand the relatively impersonal references to wrath. God can be terrifying:[21] "It is a dreadful thing to fall into

---

20. C. H. Dodd, *The Epistle of St. Paul to the Romans* (New York: Harper, 1932), 21–23, and elsewhere. See, on the contrary, Leon Morris, *The Cross in the New Testament* (Grand Rapids: Eerdmans, 1965), 189.

21. Jesus does take away that terror from his people, since he has torn in two the veil of the temple (Matt. 27:51) and has called us to enter boldly into the Most Holy Place (Heb. 10:19). This does not, of course, relieve us of the need to show "reverence and awe" in God's presence (12:28). But the wrath of God in Scripture is against those who are not trusting in Jesus, and in the book of Hebrews it is threatened against those who renounce Christ and return to Judaism. For these, "no sacrifice for sin is left, but only a fearful expectation of judgment" (Heb. 10:26–27). It is in this context that the author affirms the dread of falling into the hands of God (v. 31). So the wrath of God is still terrifying to those who experience it, and when believers contemplate it, they should recognize that dimension of it.

the hands of the living God" (Heb. 10:31). God's wrath can come on men in surprising and sudden ways, although he reveals them to us in retrospect as righteous and wise. After God appointed Moses to be Israel's deliverer, "the LORD met Moses and was about to kill him" (Ex. 4:24) because he had failed to circumcise his son. After God delivered Israel from Egypt, he met them at Mount Sinai. These were the people he had chosen in love (Deut. 7:8), yet he warned them not to ascend the mountain "or he [Yahweh] will break out against them" (Ex. 19:24). Like C. S. Lewis's Aslan, God is good, but he is not tame. There is something wild, mysterious, and threatening about God's wrath, which is not always easy to reconcile with what we know of God's love.

The Jews were sparing in their use of divine names in any case, and the biblical writers naturally tended to use abbreviated terms so as not to dwell too much on the perplexing, mysterious, and frightening aspects of God's nature. But they were not consistent in this pattern. We should confess honestly that we do the same. Although Scripture abounds in references to God's wrath and in teaching about the final judgment, we tend to abbreviate it. In our teaching, the proportion of our references to God's love and to his wrath is not nearly the same as the proportion in Scripture. I include myself in this generalization. I don't think this is necessarily wrong; we do, after all, have some biblical precedent, in the brusque references to "the wrath." In this usage, we can feel the writer cringe and look away. And that teaches us something about how terrible the wrath of God really is. "Our 'God is a consuming fire'" (Heb. 12:29; cf. Ex. 24:17; Lev. 10:2; Deut. 4:24; 9:3; Ps. 97:3; Isa. 33:14; 2 Thess. 1:7).

God's wrath is terrible, but, in the course of history, the Lord is eager to defer that anger, to forgive those who turn from sin. We have seen in the last chapter that he is patient ('arek), and we note now that he is 'erek 'af, "slow to anger" (Ps. 103:8; Joel 2:13; Jonah 4:2). He gives sinners many opportunities to repent (2 Peter 3:9). As we shall see in our discussion of God's will, he does not desire the death of the wicked. His love postpones his wrath. This patience is part of his name in Exodus 34:6–7, and God tells us through Isaiah,

> For my own name's sake I delay my wrath;
> > for the sake of my praise I hold it back from you,
> > so as not to cut you off. (Isa. 48:9)

So God delays his wrath for the sake of his love. But there remain serious questions about how God's wrath is related to his love, and to his other attributes. How can God be love at all, if he ever brings his wrath against his creatures?

[handwritten margin annotations: "God's Love", "Righteousness Jealousy", "God's Wrath"]

The relationship between God's love and his wrath can best be seen by considering two intermediate concepts, God's righteousness and his jealousy.

We have seen that God's love always observes the boundaries of his righteousness. Even in redemption, God takes enormous pains, so that, in showing love, he may be just (Rom. 3:26). The sacrifice of Christ insures that God's redemption is both loving and righteous, so that Scripture can even appeal to God's righteousness as a ground for the forgiveness of sins, and thus God's righteousness becomes a form of his love. But it is also God's righteousness that insures the final punishment of those who reject his love—that is, his wrath against them. Without the wrath of God against those who finally disbelieve, God's love is no longer righteous. So God's righteousness binds together his love and his wrath. God's righteous love must be wrathful, if at the end of history there remain any unrepentant people.

We can also move from God's love to his wrath by means of his jealousy. God's love is covenantal. It creates a special relationship between God and his creatures—a marriage, in effect. So when people reject him, he is filled with holy jealousy, and the result is wrath. When we see God's love, not as a mere sentimental affection, but as a covenant commitment, we see it as a jealous love that leads to wrath when it is abused.

So God's love and his wrath are not at odds with one another. If we think they are, we have not understood God's love. Perhaps it is unnecessarily paradoxical to say that God's wrath is a form of his love. Some theologians have said that sort of thing in order to suggest that God's wrath may not be as severe as the church has historically believed. I have no such intention. God's wrath is terrible to contemplate. It is no doubt worse than we might imagine from the biblical figures of fire and worm.[22]

Some have also argued that God's anger is a mere moment in the course of his love, based on passages like Psalm 30:5—

> For his anger lasts only a moment,
> > but his favor lasts a lifetime;
> weeping may remain for a night,
> > but rejoicing comes in the morning.

---

22. I cannot here enter into a defense of the biblical teaching concerning eternal punishment. I reject annihilationism, conditional immortality, universalism, and the other alternatives offered by theologians. Scripture is plain in teaching that the consequences of unbelief are severe (2 Thess. 1:7–9). Sin is terrible, a violation of infinite holiness, justice, and love; what punishment less than eternal torment could possibly be appropriate? As thorough studies of this matter, I recommend Robert A. Peterson, *Hell on Trial* (Phillipsburg, N.J.: P&R Publishing, 1995); Robert A. Morey, *Death and the Afterlife* (Minneapolis: Bethany House, 1984); John H. Gerstner, *Repent or Perish* (Ligonier, Pa.: Soli Deo Gloria Publications, 1990).

But the psalmist here speaks explicitly to God's saints:

> Sing to the LORD, you saints of his;
> praise his holy name. (v. 4)

Sadly, for those who are not saints, Scripture makes it clear that it is weeping, not rejoicing, that will come in the morning (Matt. 8:12; 22:13; 24:51; 25:30), and God's favor will remain only for a night (recall our discussion of common grace in chap. 20).

But God's wrath is nevertheless an outworking of his love. Once we understand God's love, we know it as a tough love, one that respects his standards of righteousness and burns in jealousy against those who betray it. God's wrath serves the purposes of his love, and his love is the richer for it: it bestows on his beloved the ultimate blessing of a sin-free world.[23]

---

23. "God is wrath," of course, is as misleading as "God is hatred." But Deut. 4:24; 9:3 and Heb. 12:29 identify God with the "consuming fire" of Ex. 24:17 (cf. Num. 11:1–3; Ps. 97:3; Isa. 33:14; 2 Thess. 1:7).

CHAPTER 22

God's Knowledge

We shall now consider another group of attributes, those concerned with God's knowledge and knowability, sometimes called the intellectual or epistemological attributes. On the chart in chapter 19, I arranged seven attributes in this category, two of which we have already considered. In chapter 11, I argued that God's *incomprehensibility* represents his transcendence (control and authority) over all creaturely knowledge. Because of that transcendence, his thoughts are not our thoughts, and his mystery permeates even the revelation he gives us. His incomprehensibility, however, never compromises his *knowability*. We know God really and truly through his revelation. Such knowledge is impossible on a view of incomprehensibility generated by an unbiblical notion of transcendence (chap. 7), a concept typical of both scholastic and liberal theology. But genuine knowledge of God is always affirmed by Scripture.

In this chapter, we shall deal with the other five epistemological attributes. God's *speech* is his dynamic communication, by which he brings all things to pass and interprets them for his hearers. His *truth* is the constant structure or "limit" of his speech, as righteousness is the structure or limit of his goodness. His *knowledge, wisdom,* and *mind* represent the integration of these in his own being, and therefore in his presence with us. To say that God has all knowledge and wisdom, and to say that he is a fully rational mind, is to say that all of his speech (to himself and to the world) has the quality of truth.

GOD'S SPEECH

God's ability to communicate is not a frequent topic in theological treatments of the divine attributes. But it would be hard to find a subject more frequent in Scripture than the word of God. Again and again we read that the word of the Lord came to a prophet. Hundreds of times the prophets proclaim, "Thus says the Lord."

God's speaking is certainly one of his important actions. As I indicated in chapter 13, I considered including a chapter on God's speech in part 4 of this book. But there is so much to be said about God's speaking, his word, that the topic requires a separate volume, and I expect to provide that in my *Doctrine of the Word of God*.[1] In the present volume, I have stressed the element of revelation (that is, divine speech) in all the acts of God described in chapters 13–16, by emphasizing how these acts express God's lordship attribute of authority, together with the other lordship attributes. All these actions reveal him, for through them we know that he is the Lord. They communicate his truth authoritatively.

So God's words are among his mighty acts, and his mighty acts convey his word. But in Scripture there is also a kind of alternation between word and act, which suggests that God's words deserve separate treatment. God's words announce what he will do, then he acts, and then by further words he interprets what he has done and announces further actions. For example, in Genesis 6:9–21, God tells Noah of the coming Flood. In 7:1–8:19, the Flood comes and subsides. Then in 8:20–9:28, God interprets the implications of the Flood, initiates a new covenant, and declares future events. This alternation is in fact the macrostructure of Scripture. The Old Testament announces the coming of Christ to redeem his people. The Gospels narrate the fulfillment of that announcement. The rest of the New Testament interprets that event and announces further events to come.

Of course, God's words and acts are also related perspectivally. For all his acts reveal his word or plan, all his words are themselves acts, and we know about God's acts entirely and exclusively through his word. Thus, for us to know God's words and to know his acts are the same thing. The alternation model may mislead us concerning the full relationship between word and act, but it does help us to see the value of looking at history from both perspectives, rather than from only one.

I shall discuss these matters and many more at length in the forthcoming volume. For now, I would like to explore briefly the question of whether

---

1. For a preview of that work, see my little book, *Perspectives on the Word of God* (Eugene, Oreg.: Wipf and Stock, 1999).

we should consider God's speech as a divine attribute. I answer in the affirmative.

God's word (Heb. *davar*, Gk. *logos*, *rhēma*),[2] according to Scripture, is his self-expression. Scripture itself is God's word in this sense (2 Tim. 3:16),[3] but the speech of God is not limited to written revelation. In Genesis 1, God creates all things by speaking, a fact that arouses the awe and praise of later biblical writers:

> By the word of the LORD were the heavens made,
> > their starry host by the breath of his mouth.
> He gathers the waters of the sea into jars;
> > he puts the deep into storehouses.
> Let all the earth fear the LORD;
> > let all the people of the world revere him.
> For he spoke, and it came to be;
> > he commanded, and it stood firm. (Ps. 33:6–9)

(Cf. also Ps. 148:5; Prov. 8:22–30;[4] John 1:1–3, 10; Heb. 1:2; 11:3; 2 Peter 3:5–7.)

God's word also directs the course of providence. God not only brings the world out of nothing by his word, but also commands its course of action after that (Gen. 1:9, 11, 22; 8:22). So,

> He sends his command to the earth;
> > his word runs swiftly.
> He spreads the snow like wool
> > and scatters the frost like ashes.
> He hurls down his hail like pebbles.
> > Who can withstand his icy blast?
> He sends his word and melts them;
> > He stirs up his breezes, and the waters flow. (Ps. 147:15–18)

(Cf. Job 37:12;[5] Pss. 18:15; 29:3–9; 148:6–7; Matt. 8:26–27; Heb. 1:3; 2 Peter 3:5–7.)

2. Of course, we also find this concept in the many words in both languages meaning "speak," "command," etc., as well as in the rich redundancy of terms in Ps. 119 and elsewhere that refer to God's testimonies, statutes, laws, ordinances, ways, precepts, decrees, commands, etc.

3. The Greek term *theopneustos* here means "breathed out by God," in other words, "spoken by God."

4. Here the subject is personified Wisdom, not the word as such. But wisdom and word are closely related in Scripture. So the writer of Prov. 8 alludes to the creation by God's word in Gen. 1 to underscore his point that all God's works are done in wisdom.

5. To be sure, this is part of a speech by Elihu, one of Job's friends, who do not speak truly of him. However, Job's friends usually do speak truth, but not about Job. They utter

The word is living (Heb. 4:12), and active also in judgment (e.g., Gen. 3:17–19; 6:7; 11:6–7) and in grace. It is his word that heals, saves, and delivers us. Note the emphasis on the word when Jesus heals the centurion's son in Luke 7:1–10[6] (cf. Ps. 107:20). Scripture describes God's saving acts as words of God, speeches of God. Salvation begins when God speaks his decree before time. He executes that decree by sending the living Word, Jesus (John 1:1–14; 1 John 1:1–3). He draws us to himself by the word of effectual calling (Isa. 43:1; see chap. 4) and by the gospel. Paul says:

> I am not ashamed of the gospel, because it is the power of God for the salvation of everyone who believes: first for the Jew, then for the Gentile. (Rom. 1:16; cf. Phil. 2:16; 1 Thess. 1:5; 2:13; 2 Tim. 1:10)

He calls us by a new name (Isa. 62:2; 65:15).

God's word, then, is involved in everything that he does—in his decrees, creation, providence, redemption, and judgment, not only in revelation narrowly defined. He performs all his acts by his speech.

Further, God and his word are always present together. Where God is, his word is, and vice versa. Note the many biblical correlations between God's word and his Spirit:[7] Genesis 1:2–3; Psalm 33:6 (cf. 104:30); Isaiah 34:16; 59:21; John 6:63; 16:13; Acts 2:1–4 (the coming of the Spirit leads to Spirit-empowered words); 1 Thessalonians 1:5; 2 Thessalonians 2:2; 2 Timothy 3:16 (the scriptural word is *theopneustos*, coming from the divine breath or spirit); 2 Peter 1:21 (the breath or Spirit of God carries the biblical writers along). The nearness of God is the nearness of the word (Deut. 4:5–8; 30:11–14), and that nearness is the nearness of Christ (Rom. 10:6–8).

So in the word of God we see all of God's lordship attributes represented. We see his *control* in the word's powerful actions,[8] his *authority* in his words

---

truths about God, but they wrongly apply those truths to Job. That I think is the intention of the author. So I don't think it wrong to quote Elihu in this connection, especially since his words are corroborated by many other texts.

6. In verse 7, the centurion, through his friends, asks Jesus to "speak by a word (*eipe logō*)" to heal his servant. "Speak" would have been sufficient, but the friend adds "by a word," a redundancy giving special emphasis to the centurion's faith that Jesus, like only Yahweh, is able to heal simply by speaking. Then comes the comparison between Jesus and the centurion himself: Jesus has authority to command disease, just as the centurion is able to command his soldiers. Jesus commends the centurion's faith as greater than any he has found in Israel. This faith is specifically faith in the word of Jesus.

7. "Spirit" in Scripture translates *ruah* (Heb.) and *pneuma* (Gk.). Both of these terms can also mean "breath" or "wind." The image is that when one person speaks to another, his breath carries the words to the other person. So the word and the Spirit must be joined if we are to receive God's revelation.

8. The *power* of the word is a major theme in Scripture: see Isa. 55:11; Rom. 1:16; 1 Thess. 1:5; Heb. 4:12, and many of the other passages listed in this section. In Jer. 1:9–12, God's

addressed to us, and his *presence* in the inseparability of his word and Spirit.

We have reason, then, to see God's speech as an essential attribute of his nature. Note also:

1. Scripture distinguishes the true God from all the false ones, because he speaks; he is not dumb like the idols (Hab. 2:18–20; 1 Kings 18:24–46; Pss. 115:5–8; 135:15–18; 1 Cor. 12:2).

2. One biblical picture of the Trinity is that the Father is the speaker (see the references above), the Son is the word he speaks (John 1:1–14; Rom. 10:6–8 [alluding to Deut. 30:11–14]; 2 Cor. 1:20; Heb. 1:1–3; 1 John 1:1–3; Rev. 19:13), and the Spirit is the breath that carries that word to its destination (Ps. 33:6; see footnote 7).

3. The speech of God has divine attributes: righteousness (Ps. 119:7), faithfulness (119:86), wonderfulness (119:142), truth (John 17:17; Ps. 119:142), eternity (Ps. 119:89, 160), omnipotence (Gen. 18:14; Luke 1:37; Isa. 55:11), and perfection (Ps. 19:7–11).

4. God's word is an object of worship (Pss. 56:4, 10; 119:120, 161–62; Isa. 66:5). Many times Scripture calls us to praise "the name" of the Lord (e.g., Pss. 9:2; 34:3; 68:4; 138:2). As we saw in chapter 17, there is a close relation between God's name, his word, and his being.

5. God's word is God,[9] and therefore it is his "self-expression" in the very highest sense. This must be so if God's word is to be an object of worship, or to have divine attributes, or to model the Trinity, or to distinguish God from idols. And John 1:1 says this in so many words.[10] In point 2 above, I listed a number of verses equating Christ with the word of God. In John 1:1, however, the word of God is not only Christ, but also the word by which God created the heavens and the earth. "In the beginning" (v. 1) clearly alludes to Genesis 1:1, and the reference to creation in verse 3 again recalls the creation narrative in which God creates by his word. By implication, all the words by which God decrees, creates, provides, judges, and saves, are divine.[11]

---

word in the prophet's mouth gives him power "over nations and kingdoms to uproot and tear down, to destroy and overthrow, to build and to plant." But the word is not a bare power or brute force; it is also *meaning*. It always says something intelligible, contrary to many liberal and neoorthodox theologians. God not only creates the world by his word, but also interprets it, giving names and evaluations (Gen. 1:5, 8, 10, 12, etc.). So God's words express his authority, as well as his power and presence.

9. There is some Jewish precedent for this identification. *Memra* ("word") in the Targums is one of many terms that the Jews of the time used to avoid direct use of the divine name.

10. For more discussion of this passage, focusing on its implications for the deity of Christ, see chapter 28.

11. Another important passage identifying God and his word is Hebrews 4:12–13. In verse 12, we learn that the word is living and active, judging the human heart. Verse 13 refers to God's omniscience. In the NIV there appears to be a change of subject between these two

John 1:1 also distinguishes God's word from God: "The Word was *with* God." Here we find ourselves in the midst of Trinitarian mystery. The same paradox exists in the Bible's teaching concerning Jesus. Jesus is the Word, so the Jesus-Word is God, but is also distinct from God. God is one, but he exists, as we shall see, in three persons.

So sometimes we read that the word and God are the same, and sometimes we read that the word is God's tool, as in "By the word of the LORD were the heavens made" (Ps. 33:6). We have seen this unity and complexity of God's nature in other contexts (see chap. 12). As with the persons of the Trinity, God's attributes are both identified with him and distinguished from him in Scripture.

We should also distinguish God's necessary words from his free words, as in chapter 12 we distinguished his necessary acts from his free acts. His necessary words are the eternal communications between Father, Son, and Spirit, expressing their mutual love. His free words are his words (both among the Trinitarian persons and to the creation) concerning the creation. His necessary words are necessary to his very being as God; his free words are not.

For now, however, the important point is that by his very nature God is a speaking God. In chapter 2, I indicated that only in biblical religion is there such a thing as a personal absolute. The same may be said of God's speech, an aspect of his personality. Only in biblical religion is there a God who is absolute and who also speaks to his creatures. And in his speech he brings himself to us.

So the word of God is a great treasure. We should rejoice that our God is not dumb, like the gods of the nations, but has shared with us his laws, his wisdom, and his love.[12] And God is always with and in his word. When we read his written word, we encounter him; when we encounter him, we hear his word.

It is also good to know that God not only speaks to us, but also speaks to himself, since he is word by nature. The Father, Son, and Spirit search one another's hearts (1 Cor. 2:10–11). They express love and glorify one another eternally (John 17:24). God knows himself exhaustively. We creatures do not have perfect self-knowledge. In our hearts, souls, and bodies there are hidden depths that we do not understand. Often our thoughts and actions (to say nothing of our physical conditions) surprise us; often they reveal things about ourselves that we had not known and

---

verses: the word in verse 12, God in verse 13. But in the Greek, there is no change of subject. The word is the omniscience of God himself.

12. For perspective buffs, law is normative, wisdom is situational, and love is existential.

would perhaps just as soon not have known. But there are no unexplored depths in God's nature. He does not surprise himself. He is word. His word exhaustively expresses his being to himself, among the persons of the Trinity. Our God has perfect knowledge of who he is and of what he does.

I conclude that God's word, his speech, is an essential attribute, inseparable from God's being. It is particularly identical to the second person of the Trinity,[13] but all three persons are involved in God's speech, and the word of God exists wherever God is.

GOD'S TRUTH

All God's words are true. His Word is truth (John 17:17; cf. 2 Sam. 7:28; 1 Kings 17:24; Ps. 119:43, 89–90, 142, 151). So, as on the chart in chapter 19, truth is the internal standard that governs God's speech.

Herman Bavinck distinguishes three different meanings of *truth* (Heb. *'emeth, 'emunah*, Gk. *alētheia*)[14] in Scripture: metaphysical, logical (I would say, epistemological or propositional), and ethical.[15] In the metaphysical sense, to say that something is true is to say that it is "all that it is supposed to be."[16] True gold is the genuine article, as opposed to fool's gold. In Scripture, God is the true God, as opposed to the idols. God says through Jeremiah:

> Hammered silver is brought from Tarshish
>   and gold from Uphaz.
> What the craftsman and goldsmith have made
>   is then dressed in blue and purple—
> all made by skilled workers.

13. There is no scriptural reason why it cannot be identical both to the whole Godhead and to one of the three persons. Spirit is both a particular person of the Trinity and a characterization of the whole divine nature (John 4:24). Father is the name of the first person of the Trinity, but Scripture also teaches that the whole triune God bears a fatherly relation to his people (chap. 18).

14. The Septuagint sometimes uses *pistos*, "faithful," to translate the Hebrew terms. The KJV translates *pistos* as "true" in 2 Cor. 1:18, but more recent translations do not follow it here. But, as we shall see, *faithful* and *true* are closely related terms in Scripture.

15. *DG*, 201–2.

16. Ibid., 201. Thus, Thomas Aquinas equated Being and Truth, developing his equation between God and Being (see chap. 3). For him, being, unity, truth, beauty, and goodness (see chap. 9) are all ultimately the same, both in God and in the creation. These are the "transcendental" concepts that frequently enter his theology.

> But the LORD is the true God;
>   he is the living God, the eternal King.
> When he is angry, the earth trembles;
>   the nations cannot endure his wrath. (Jer. 10:9–10)

And God says through Paul: "They tell how [the Thessalonians] turned to God from idols to serve the living and true God" (1 Thess. 1:9). Jesus says that eternal life is "that they may know you, the only true God, and Jesus Christ, whom you have sent" (John 17:3).

We may also describe as metaphysical a somewhat different, but related usage, in which *truth* denotes what is ultimate in comparison with other realities. John Murray says:

> We should bear in mind that 'the true' in the usage of John is not so much the true in contrast with the false, or the real in contrast with the fictitious. It is the absolute as contrasted with the relative, the ultimate as contrasted with the derived, the eternal as contrasted with the temporal, the permanent as contrasted with the temporary, the complete in contrast with the partial, the substantial in contrast with the shadowy.[17]

Like the other divine attributes, metaphysical truth pertains not only to God the Father, but also to his Son, Jesus Christ. Jesus says, "I am the way and the truth and the life. No one comes to the Father except through me" (John 14:6). As in the contrast between the true God and the idols, Jesus here sets aside all the other religions of the world and presents himself as the only genuine mediator between God and man (cf. 1 Tim. 2:5). First John 5:20 identifies the Son and the Father by means of the attribute of truth:

> We know also that the Son of God has come and has given us understanding, so that we may know him who is true. And we are in him who is true—even in his Son Jesus Christ. He is the true God and eternal life.[18]

The Spirit is also "the truth" in 1 John 5:6.

---

17. Murray, *Principles of Conduct* (Grand Rapids: Eerdmans, 1957), 123. He points out that in John 1:17, "The law was given through Moses; grace and truth came through Jesus Christ," John is not saying that the law is false or untrue; rather, it is incomplete, compared to the fullness of God's revelation in Christ. So Christ is the true light (John 1:9). Other examples of this use of *true* and *truth*: John 6:32, 35; 15:1; 17:3; Heb. 8:21. In this sense, *true* approaches *perfect*, on which see chapter 20.

18. Clearly, the antecedent of "he" in the last sentence is Jesus Christ. So this verse clearly teaches the full deity of Christ. See the discussion of this passage in chapter 28. The emphasis on metaphysical truth makes this identification all the more emphatic.

Epistemological or propositional truth can be seen as an implication of metaphysical truth.[19] It is a property of language, rather than reality in general. But true language is language that rightly represents reality, that expresses the way something "really is." Truth in this sense is the proper correlation between language and reality. A true statement is one on which we can rely; it will not mislead us. The same can be said of commands (Ps. 119:142, 151) and promises (2 Sam. 7:28; Heb. 10:23).[20] So in the verses cited at the beginning of this section, God's words are truth.[21] God cannot lie (Num. 23:19; Titus 1:2; Heb. 6:18), nor can he be in error (Heb. 4:12–13). So he is true, though every man is a liar (Rom. 3:4).

His truth, like all his attributes, is of the highest perfection. So in his lordship attribute of authority, he is the very standard of truth for his creatures. Like goodness and righteousness (chaps. 20 and 21), truth is what God is and therefore what he says. There is no higher standard than God against which his truth may be measured. So God's metaphysical ultimacy implies that he is the standard of propositional truth.

There are times when God in judgment sends upon men "a lying spirit" (1 Kings 22:22) or "a powerful delusion" (2 Thess. 2:11). Such is the mystery of evil (chap. 9). And it is at least arguable that he does not condemn lying in defense of human life, as in the case of the Hebrew midwives (Ex. 1) and Rahab (Josh. 2). Such is the difficulty of living in a fallen world. However, there is no case in Scripture of God's own word ever proving false.[22]

The importance of propositional truth in Scripture cannot be denied. Since its beginnings in the seventeenth century, liberal theology has de-

---

19. It is not always easy to distinguish whether a particular Scripture passage is speaking of metaphysical or propositional truth. Rev. 3:7 and 6:10 refer to Jesus as the one who is "true," probably both in the metaphysical sense and in the sense that what he says is always reliable. The same is true for the reference to the Spirit in 1 John 5:6. First John 5:20 combines and connects these meanings.

20. Modern philosophers sometimes distinguish propositions, commands, promises, questions, etc., as different "speech acts," among which only propositions, strictly speaking, can be true or false. On this view, only propositions make truth claims, and so only propositions may be judged as to their truth. But of course other sorts of speech acts often presuppose truth claims, and they often communicate propositional knowledge alongside their other functions. "Johnny, put the dog down" is a command, but it assumes that there is a dog, that Johnny is carrying him, etc.

21. See also Deut. 17:4; 1 Kings 10:6; Eph. 4:24.

22. There are cases, as in the book of Jonah, in which God announces judgment, but retracts that announcement later upon repentance. I shall discuss these later under the topic of God's unchangeability. For now, I will simply say that when God announced the judgment against Nineveh, the announcement was true; the Ninevites really were under God's judgment, as indeed we all were, before we received the grace of God.

nied the possibility of propositional revelation—revelation in which God reveals words and sentences that agree with reality. The older liberalism (through the time of Herrmann and Harnack) simply denied the divine authority of Scripture, treating the Bible as a collection of merely human religious writings. Thus they were able to maintain the autonomy of their own thought, denying the need to place their scholarship under the authority of God's Word. The neoorthodoxy of Barth and Brunner said much about the authority of the Word, but they conceived of God's Word as a kind of gracious divine power that did not convey any propositional truth.[23] So the neoorthodox, like the older liberals, justified autonomous human thought and acknowledged the freedom of Bible critics from any divine constraints.

But God clearly reveals himself in the Bible, not only through personal confrontations and events in history, but also through words, which he speaks directly to his people (Ex. 20:1–17; Deut. 4:12; Matt. 3:17; 17:5) and through prophets who bear his full authority (Deut. 18:17–22;[24] Jer. 1:10–12; John 16:13; 1 Cor. 14:37). And, as we saw in the last section, God also provides written words given by the Spirit. These words are among those that have the quality of divine truth. Is the Bible inerrant, then? It certainly is, if *inerrant* means "true" in the propositional sense.

The third kind of truth, ethical truth, emerges naturally from the other two. Metaphysical truth is genuineness; epistemological truth faithfully represents what is genuine; ethical truth is faithfulness in all areas of life. We represent the truth, not only in words, but in the language of our actions. Our deeds tell the world what we really believe to be true. So God calls upon us not only to speak the truth, but also to live it. One who lives, walks in (2 John 4), or does (1 John 1:6) the truth, in whom the truth exists (1 John 2:4), is reliable, trustworthy, and faithful—first to God and therefore to reality. He does not lie (1 John 1:6; 2:21, 27) or deceive himself (1 John 1:8). And he also keeps God's commandments in other areas (1 John 2:4). Jesus said that if we love him, we must keep his commands (John 14:15); so, to be faithful, we must be obedient. Love must also be true: "Dear children, let us not love with words or tongue but with actions and in truth" (1 John 3:18).[25]

God is true also in the ethical sense. As we saw in chapter 20, *'emeth* is

---

23. The older liberals were concerned with truth, but they did not see it as divinely revealed. The neoorthodox were concerned with revelation, but they did not see it as conveying propositional truth. So the liberals believed in *alētheia* without *logos*, and the neoorthodox believed in *logos* without *alētheia*.

24. The test of a prophet in verse 22 is whether or not his prophecy comes true.

25. Other examples: Neh. 9:33; Pss. 15:2; 25:5; 26:3; 51:6; 86:11; Ezek. 18:9; Hos. 4:1; John 3:20–21; Gal. 5:7.

a close synonym and frequent companion to *hesed*, "covenant love" or "faithfulness." *'Emunah* is also closely related:

> Know therefore that the LORD your God is God; he is the faithful ['*emunah*] God; keeping his covenant of love to a thousand generations of those who love him and keep his commandments. (Deut. 7:9; cf. 4:31; 2 Sam. 17:28; Ps. 40:11; Hos. 12:1)

By nature, he is "a faithful God" (Deut. 32:4; cf. 1 Cor. 1:9; 10:13; 1 Thess. 5:24; 2 Thess. 3:3; Heb. 10:23; 11:11; 1 John 1:9). He is reliable, dependable, the "Rock" (1 Sam. 2:2; Pss. 18:2; 62:2; Isa. 26:4). As Bavinck says, "He is a perfectly reliable refuge for all his people, Ps. 31:6, 36:5."[26]

I have indicated how propositional truth arises out of metaphysical truth, and ethical truth out of propositional truth.[27] But there are also relationships in the other direction. One's ethical reliability requires one to seek and speak propositional truth, and one's view of propositional truth dictates one's view of what is. The three kinds of truth are perspectivally related in the sense that none can exist without the others, and each determines how we view the others. So the three kinds of truth coalesce in God's being, with one another, and with the other divine attributes.

GOD'S KNOWLEDGE

Many philosophers have defined *knowledge* as "justified, true belief." Although some have found problems with this definition,[28] it is still the starting point for many philosophical discussions. There is, however, no consensus among philosophers as to what constitutes "justification" in this definition, so knowledge remains somewhat mysterious to epistemologists.[29] The question of justification is, of course, the question of what norms should properly govern and evaluate claims to knowledge. So knowledge has an ethical dimension: items of knowledge are not only beliefs, but

26. *DG*, 200.
27. Gordon H. Clark derives metaphysical and ethical truth from propositional truth in *Baker's Dictionary of Theology*, ed. Everett F. Harrison (Grand Rapids: Baker, 1960), 532–33, reinforcing his generally intellectualist approach to theology. But he does not consider the possibility that similar deductions can be made in the opposite direction or that these varieties of truth may be mutually dependent.
28. Edmund Gettier, in "Is Justified True Belief Knowledge?" *Analysis* 23 (1963):121–23, began the recent discussion. See, for example, John Pollock, *Contemporary Theories of Knowledge* (Totowa, N.J.: Rowman and Littlefield, 1986), 180–93.
29. For my thoughts, see *DKG*, 104–68, and my "Christianity and Contemporary Epistemology," *WTJ* 52 (1990): 131–41.

beliefs we ought to have. But the ethical dimension of knowledge shows that knowledge cannot be grounded only in finite reality. It must presuppose God, who is the only adequate source of norms.[30]

Another problem with the definition of knowledge as justified, true belief, is that this definition is suited only to the knowledge of propositions— items of information ("knowing that"). What about the knowledge of skills ("knowing how") or of persons? Knowing how to do something cannot be reduced to a knowledge of propositions. One may memorize thousands of truths about playing football, but that knowledge, in itself, will not make someone a skilled quarterback. Similarly, knowing a friend is not merely knowing propositions about him.[31] I may know more true propositions about the President of the United States than about the boy who delivers my newspaper. But I may yet truthfully claim that I know the newsboy, and not the President.[32]

In the view of Scripture, the most important kind of knowledge is the knowledge of God. Knowing God is the key to all other knowledge: "The fear of the LORD is the beginning of knowledge" (Prov. 1:7). So knowledge is fundamentally knowledge of a person. It is also covenantal, since the personal God is our covenant Lord. He calls upon us to seek knowledge as his obedient servants.[33]

God made and preinterpreted all things in the universe, as we saw in chapter 15. Our task in knowing the world is to think God's thoughts after him. Therefore, propositional knowledge is based on knowledge of a person. He supplies the norms, the justifications, that are missing in secular

---

30. See my *Perspectives on the Word of God*, 39–56, for an argument to this effect; see also the "moral argument" in *AGG*, 93–102, and the argument on pages 102–4 that rationality itself is value-based. In *DKG*, I present the larger epistemological perspective warranting these arguments. I am glad that some recent thinkers are discussing the question of normativity in knowledge. See especially Alvin Plantinga, *Warrant: The Current Debate* (New York: Oxford University Press, 1993) and *Warrant and Proper Function* (New York: Oxford University Press, 1993). The third volume in Plantinga's trilogy will deal with the relationship of epistemic warrant to God.

31. On the other hand, factual knowledge about a friend does not necessarily decrease the existential quality of a friendship. Normally it is beneficial, contrary to Emil Brunner, *Truth as Encounter* (Philadelphia: Westminster Press, 1964). On the knowledge of persons, compare the scriptural usage in which knowledge refers to sexual intercourse, as in Gen. 4:1.

32. Although these three kinds of knowledge are not reducible to one another, it is still true that each depends on the other two. You cannot know propositions unless you have the skill to achieve knowledge, and unless you know the divine person who understands all things. Similarly for the other two; so, in one sense, the three are perspectivally related. Propositions are, perhaps, normative; skills, situational; personal knowledge, existential.

33. Note the correlations between obedience and knowledge in many passages of Scripture. In Jer. 22:16, the two are virtual synonyms. See *DKG*, 43–45.

accounts of knowledge, as well as the truths that we are to believe and the mental capacity for us to come to knowledge.[34] God also enables us to learn skills: "Praise be to the LORD my Rock, who trains my hands for war, my fingers for battle" (Ps. 144:1).

Knowledge (Heb. *da'ath*, Gk. *gnōsis, epignōsis*)[35] is also a divine attribute:

> The LORD is a God who knows,
>   and by him deeds are weighed. (1 Sam. 2:3)

> Does he who teaches man lack knowledge? (Ps. 94:10)

If human knowledge is dependent on God, then God's own knowledge depends on God. That is, it is self-attesting, self-referential, and self-sufficient.[36] His knowledge is the ultimate "justified, true belief." He is the ultimate *justification* of knowledge, the standard for creaturely knowledge and his own knowledge.[37] He is the ultimate *truth:* the truth is what he is and what he has decreed to be. And this justification and this truth are enclosed in God's ultimate mind, ultimate subjectivity, ultimate *belief.* So, as many theologians have taught, God's knowledge depends only on himself. God knows all things by knowing himself and knowing his plan for the universe.

Since both of these objects of thought are eternal, God's knowledge is eternal:

> I make known the end from the beginning,
>   from ancient times, what is still to come.
> I say: My purpose will stand,
>   and I will do all that I please. (Isa. 46:10)

GOD'S KNOWLEDGE AND HIS LORDSHIP

Scripture draws a number of connections between God's knowledge and his lordship. We saw in chapters 4 and 16 that God's knowledge of people often refers, not to propositional knowledge, not to knowledge about them,

---

34. So the triad "justified, true belief" is triperspectival. Justification is normative, truth is situational (the facts as they really are), and belief (a subjective state) is existential. See *DKG* for elaboration.

35. I will also refer to some verses employing the Hebrew root *bin*, often rendered "to understand." The Greek *eidenai*, along with *ginōskō* (the root of *gnōsis*) is also translated "to know."

36. This is God's aseity, his self-existence and self-sufficiency, with respect to knowledge. I shall later discuss aseity in more general terms.

37. On the circularity implicit in this formulation, see chapter 20.

but rather to his choice, his election of them as his covenant servants. Here "knowledge" is like "befriending." In Amos 3:2, God says to Israel, "You only have I chosen [NIV; in Heb., literally, *known*] of all the families of the earth." Clearly, God is not here expressing ignorance of the nations other than Israel. But his special covenant relation with Israel is here called knowledge.

If, as I have argued, God is the covenant Lord (in different ways, to be sure) to everything in creation, then he knows everything covenantally. He has, in other words, chosen everything for his own purposes. And this purposeful choice implies propositional knowledge. If God creates and directs the whole course of nature and history, and if that creation and direction presuppose his wise purpose, then God knows everything: himself and everything in creation.

So Scripture connects God's knowledge with his *control* over creation and providence:

> Who has measured the waters in the hollow of his hand,
>   or with the breadth of his hand marked off the heavens?
> Who has held the dust of the earth in a basket,
>   or weighed the mountains on the scales
>   and the hills in a balance?
> Who has understood the mind of the LORD,
>   or instructed him as his counselor?
> Whom did the LORD consult to enlighten him,
>   and who taught him the right way?
> Who was it that taught him knowledge
>   or showed him the path of understanding? (Isa. 40:12–14)

These are, of course, rhetorical questions. Those in verse 12 have as their answer "only the Lord," and those in verses 13–14, "no one." Since God has created all things, he has all knowledge of them. That knowledge is self-contained; he did not learn it from anyone. Compare also Psalm 139:1–24. God made the world by his wisdom (Ps. 104:24; Prov. 3:19; 8:27; Jer. 10:12; 51:15).[38]

The lordship attribute of *authority* can be seen in the way Scripture connects God's knowledge with his judgments. As D. A. Carson puts it,

> Yahweh can well judge all men and nations (Ps. 67.5), for not only is he all-powerful, he is all-knowing. His omniscience is not in-

---

38. For more references to God's knowledge exhibited in creation and providence, review chapters 4, 14, and 15. In Ps. 104, note all the details of the course of nature ascribed to God's wisdom.

frequently associated with the certainty and exhaustive nature of his impending judgment (e.g. Isa. 29.15f; Jer. 16.16–18; Ezek. 11.2, 5; Ps. 139.1ff; Prov. 5.21; 24.2).[39]

God knows exhaustively what sinners do, and he evaluates their actions rightly. His evaluations are the very standard of truth; they cannot be wrong. He is the teacher, and we are always the pupils. So "does he who teaches man lack knowledge" (Ps. 94:10)? Certainly not. The fullness and accuracy of his knowledge cannot be questioned.

Both God's control and his authority are found in his decrees and plans for the universe, as in Isaiah 46:10, quoted earlier. Since God will certainly accomplish his purpose, and since that purpose encompasses all of time, the end from the beginning, he is able to make known whatever will come to pass. Such revelation, of course, presupposes knowledge.

God's knowledge also emerges, obviously, from his lordship attribute of *presence*. Because God is everywhere, no one can hide from him (2 Chron. 16:9; Ps. 139:1–24; Prov. 5:21; 15:3; Jer. 23:24; Acts 17:24–28; Heb. 4:13). He knows everything we do, including our secret sins (2 Kings 6:12; Pss. 10:10–14; 33:13–15; 90:8; Prov. 24:12; Ezek. 8:12; Hos. 5:3). Indeed, he knows our hearts and our thoughts (1 Sam. 16:7; 1 Kings 6:12; 8:39; Pss. 94:11; 139:2, 23–24; Prov. 15:11; 21:2; Jer. 17:10; 20:12; Ezek. 11:5; Luke 16:15; John 2:25; Acts 1:24; Rom. 8:27; 1 Cor. 4:5; 1 Thess. 2:4; Heb. 4:12–13; 1 John 3:20; Rev. 2:23).[40]

OMNISCIENCE

It should now be obvious that the extent of God's knowledge is universal. God controls the whole course of nature and history (see above and chaps. 4, 14, and 15) and controls everything by a wise plan (chap. 16). He is the "author" of the text of history (chap. 8). His wise plan constitutes knowledge—knowledge of everything, omniscience.[41] His knowledge is just as extensive as his lordship. As we saw in the last section, his

39. D. A. Carson, *Divine Sovereignty and Human Responsibility* (Atlanta: John Knox Press, 1981), 25. Other passages that correlate omniscience with judgment are 1 Thess. 2:4 and Heb. 4:12–13.

40. Note that John 2:25 and Rev. 2:23 ascribe this same knowledge to Jesus. Note also that a number of these references also deal with the lordship attribute of authority, as they refer to God's sovereign judgment against sin.

41. More formally, God's omniscience may be defined as his knowledge of all actual and possible states of affairs, and/or of the truth value of all propositions. (I shall discuss his knowledge of possibilities in a later section.) We should not say that God asserts or utters all true

control, authority, and presence are universal and therefore presuppose universal knowledge.

Our confession of God's omniscience is not based only on the above arguments. Scripture states it quite explicitly and often:

> Great is our Lord, and mighty in power;
> his understanding has no limit. (Ps. 147:5)

> [Peter] said, "Lord, you know all things; you know that I love you." (John 21:17; cf. 2:24–25)

> For the word of God is living and active. Sharper than any double-edged sword, it penetrates even to dividing soul and spirit, joints and marrow; it judges the thoughts and attitudes of the heart. Nothing in all creation is hidden from God's sight. Everything is uncovered and laid bare before the eyes of him to whom we must give account. (Heb. 4:12–13)

> For God is greater than our hearts, and he knows everything. (1 John 3:20)

God knows all about the starry heavens (Gen. 15:5; Ps. 147:4; Isa. 40:26; Jer. 33:22) and the tiniest details as well (Pss. 50:10–11; 56:8; Matt. 10:30). "God knows" is an oathlike utterance (2 Cor. 11:11; 12:2–3). It certifies the truth of human words, because it presupposes that God's knowledge is exhaustive, universal, and infallible. God's knowledge is absolute knowledge, a perfection, and so it elicits religious praise (Ps. 139:17–18; Isa. 40:28; Rom. 11:33–36).

Wicked people often think that God will not notice what they do, but they will find that God does know, and that he will certainly condemn their sin (Pss. 10:11; 11:4; 73:11; 94:7; Isa. 29:15; 40:27; 47:10; Jer. 16:17–18; Ezek. 8:12). To the righteous, however, God's knowledge is a blessing of the covenant (Ex. 2:23–25; 3:7–9; 1 Kings 18:27; 2 Chron. 16:9; Pss. 33:18–20; 34:15–16; 38:9; 145:20; Matt. 6:32). He knows what is happening to them, he hears their prayer, and he will certainly answer.

---

propositions. When Joe Smith says "I am a sinner," he expresses a true proposition. God knows that that proposition, spoken by Joe, is true, and he knows the state of affairs of which Joe speaks. But God does not assert that proposition in so many words, because he is not Joe, and he is not a sinner. A point like this should be obvious, but it has actually generated considerable philosophical discussion. For instance, some have said that God cannot know that "Today is Tuesday" (uttered by Joe on Tuesday) if he is supratemporal. They have argued that point as a refutation of God's supratemporality. More will be said on this issue at a later point.

GOD'S KNOWLEDGE OF THE FUTURE

Does God's omniscience include knowledge of the future? Certainly it does, in the view of Scripture. We have seen that God foreordains the whole course of history by his eternal plan. If he plans and foreordains all things, surely he knows them, *a fortiori*.

But some professing Christians have expressed doubts that God has exhaustive knowledge of the future. Lelio and Fausto Socinus (uncle and nephew), together with their followers, are best known for their denials of the deity of Christ and of substitutionary atonement. But they also "held to a heretical doctrine of God."[42] Robert Strimple explains:

> The Socinian doctrine can be stated very briefly, and it must be contrasted with both Calvinism and Arminianism. Calvinism (or Augustinianism) teaches that the sovereign God has *foreordained* whatsoever comes to pass, and therefore He *foreknows* whatsoever comes to pass. Arminianism denies that God has foreordained whatsoever comes to pass but wishes nevertheless to affirm God's foreknowledge of whatsoever comes to pass. Against the Arminians, the Socinians insisted that logically the Calvinists were quite correct in insisting that the only real basis for believing that God *knows* what you are going to do next is to believe that he has *foreordained* what you are going to do next. How else could God know ahead of time what your decision will be? Like the Arminians, however, the Socinians insisted that it was a contradiction of human freedom to believe in the sovereign foreordination of God. So they went "all the way" (logically) and denied not only that God has foreordained the free decisions of free agents but also that God foreknows what those decisions will be.[43]

Although contemporary freewill theists[44] or open theists claim to be Arminian in their theology, they have in fact become Socinian[45] in their

---

42. Robert B. Strimple, "What Does God Know?" in *The Coming Evangelical Crisis*, ed. John H. Armstrong (Chicago: Moody Press, 1996), 140.

43. Ibid., 140–41.

44. For examples of this type of theology, see Richard Rice, *God's Foreknowledge and Man's Free Will* (Minneapolis: Bethany House, 1985); Clark Pinnock et al., *The Openness of God* (Downers Grove, Ill.: InterVarsity Press, 1994). See my critique in *No Other God* (Phillipsburg, N.J.: P&R Publishing, 2001).

45. As Strimple points out ("What Does God Know?" 141), one of the "selling points" of open theism is that it is a new position. But in fact it is an old heresy, rejected by the church four hundred years ago.

view of God's knowledge.[46] For Arminians, God's foreknowledge plays a
very important role, because it is central to their attempt to maintain a doctrine of divine sovereignty together with their doctrine of libertarian free
will.[47] Open theists abandon this attempt, holding that God does not have
exhaustive knowledge of the future. They argue that if God knows the future completely, the future must be fixed, and man cannot be really free
(that is, free in the libertarian sense).

Much of the open theists' argument depends on the libertarian view of
human freedom. To those who, like myself, reject that position, the open
theists' argument from Scripture is not very persuasive. Nevertheless,
since there is quite a bit of controversy over this matter today, I should
give some broad attention to the Scripture teaching on the subject of God's
foreknowledge.[48]

God's Knowledge of the Future in General

God's knowledge of the future is important in Scripture, both as an aspect of his sovereignty, as we have discussed, and as a foundation for
prophecy. Note the test of a true prophet in Deuteronomy 18:21–22:

> You may say to yourselves, "How can we know when a message has
> not been spoken by the LORD?" If what a prophet proclaims in the
> name of the LORD does not take place or come true, that is a mes-
> sage the LORD has not spoken. That prophet has spoken pre-
> sumptuously. Do not be afraid of him.

46. The same is true of the "moral government theology" of Gordon C. Olson and others. See E. Calvin Beisner, *Evangelical Heathenism* (Moscow, Ida.: Canon Press, 1996).

47. On libertarianism, see chapter 8.

48. In chapter 4 and earlier in this chapter, I argued that when Scripture refers to knowledge, it often has personal relationships in view, not knowledge of facts. The same can be
said of God's foreknowledge of men in Rom. 8:29 and 11:2 and 1 Peter 1:2. These verses
don't speak primarily of God knowing facts in advance, but of his establishing relationships
with people before the world was made. Nevertheless, foreknowledge in this sense entails
knowing facts in advance. So I believe that these verses are relevant to our present concerns, as they were to earlier topics of discussion. In this section, I shall use *foreknowledge*
in the more common sense, to mean *knowledge beforehand*, the present focus of our attention.

There is another problem in the use of the term *foreknowledge*. Some would argue that
since God is timelessly eternal, the word *foreknowledge* is inappropriate. God's knowledge,
on this view, is timeless, and therefore not "before" anything. I shall discuss God's relationship
to time under the topic of eternity. For now, let us just say that the term *foreknowledge* simply means that before any event transpires, God knows it will occur. On this reading, the
timelessness of God's knowledge warrants the use of *foreknowledge*, rather than calling that
term into question.

A true prophet has God's words on his lips (vv. 18–20). When his prophecies predict future events, God's word gives him supernatural knowledge. If the event does not happen, the prophet is proved false. Deuteronomy 18 does not consider the possibility that God himself may have been in error, and that the prophet faithfully proclaimed the divine errors to the people. Moses presupposes that God himself is omniscient and cannot err in foretelling the future. The text banishes from the outset any consideration that God might be wrong. In the language of chapter 12, God is necessarily right. And this passage shows us that his omniscience extends to future events.[49]

Knowledge of the future is not only the test of a true prophet. It is also the test of a true God. In the contest between Yahweh and the false gods of the ancient Near East, a major issue is which God knows the future. This is a frequent theme in Isaiah 40–49, a passage that focuses on the sovereignty of Yahweh over against the absurd pretensions of the false gods:

> "Present your case," says the LORD.
> "Set forth your arguments," says Jacob's King.
> "Bring in your idols to tell us
> what is going to happen.
> Tell us what the former things were,
> so that we may consider them
> and know their final outcome.
> Or declare to us the things to come,
> tell us what the future holds,
> so we may know that you are gods. (Isa. 41:21–23; cf. 42:9;
> 43:9–12; 44:7; 45:21; 46:10; 48:3–7)

Prediction of future events is not the only aspect of prophecy. Prophets also interpret history, exhort to repentance and faithfulness, and proclaim God's standards and promises. As we shall see in a later discussion of God's unchangeability, some prophecies that apparently predict the future are actually conditional. God announces the destruction of Nineveh, for example, but then retracts that announcement when the Ninevites repent (Jonah 3:4, 10; see also 4:1–2, alluding to Ex. 34:6–7; cf. Jer. 18:7–9).

Nevertheless, amid the diverse elements of prophecy, one crucial element is prediction of the future. Knowledge of the future is a defining mark of

---

49. There is an interesting confirmation of this point in the story of Micaiah and Ahab in 1 Kings 22:1–28. Micaiah's final word sums up the teaching of the passage on the nature of prophecy: "If you [Ahab] ever return safely, the LORD has not spoken through me" (v. 28). See also Dan. 2:22; Amos 3:7.

the true God and of his true prophets. Prophecies often indicate in general terms the coming of God's judgment, as:

> See, the day of the LORD is coming—
>   a cruel day, with wrath and fierce anger—
> to make the land desolate
>   and destroy the sinners within it. (Isa. 13:9)

They describe the coming of the Messiah (Isa. 9:6–7; 11:1–9) and the coming of Gentiles to seek the Lord (Acts 15:15–18). But sometimes prophets describe the future in even more specific terms. The prophet Samuel tells young King Saul that he will meet two men who will tell him that his lost donkeys have been found. Then he will meet three men going to Bethel carrying three goats, three loaves of bread, and a skin of wine. Then he will meet a procession of prophets near Gibeah, and so on (1 Sam. 10:1–8). These events take place exactly as the prophet indicated (vv. 9–11).

In the New Testament, the writers emphasize over and over again that various events take place so that the Scripture might be fulfilled (e.g., Matt. 2:15, 17; 3:3; 8:17; 12:17). In some cases, these fulfillments may involve Jesus' deliberate intention to fulfill prophecy. In other cases, the fulfillment may be a mere parallel between an event in the history of Israel and an event in Jesus' life (as Matt. 2:15)—a literary device intended to underscore the evangelist's assertion that Jesus is the true remnant of Israel. But, in many cases, the gospel writers clearly intend to ascribe to the Old Testament prophets a supernatural knowledge of the future, as when Micah predicted that the Messiah would be born in Bethlehem (Mic. 5:2; Matt. 2:6).

GOD'S FOREKNOWLEDGE OF FREE HUMAN DECISIONS AND ACTIONS

Now the open theists do not deny the reality or importance of predictive prophecy. But they believe that when God reveals future events, he is either (1) announcing his own intentions, (2) speaking in general terms that could be fulfilled in many ways, (3) announcing events that are necessary (or highly probable?) consequences of past and present states of affairs, or (4) announcing what will take place if certain conditions obtain.[50] What the open theists deny, however, is that God foreknows the free decisions of human beings. On the open theists' libertarian view, such divine foreknowledge destroys human freedom.

---

50. See Richard Rice, "Biblical Support for a New Perspective," in *The Openness of God*, by Pinnock et al., 50–53.

As Robert Strimple points out, however, to deny that God knows the free decisions of men in advance is no small reduction in the church's traditional view of God's knowledge. It is not a modest or limited proposal, as Pinnock and Rice seem to think:

> Either they are disingenuous, or they have not thought through sufficiently the implications of their position.
>
> Think about it. Just how "limited" is the part of the world's ongoing history that we are asked to see as not under God's control, nor even within his present knowledge? How many truly significant occurrences in our world are *not* the actions of human beings or the consequences of such actions? Pinnock and Rice give us surprisingly few specific examples of such occurrences—preferring to speak vaguely of "divine actions that are not dependent upon circumstances in the creaturely world." Perhaps the fact that the sun will shine on my picnic tomorrow would be one such event. But even a "natural" phenomenon such as whether or not tomorrow will be sunny in Southern California may well be determined by how much smog has been produced by how many automobiles whose drivers decided to turn on the ignition key in the past several days. And, of course, at a global level, how could God know it as absolutely certain that someone would not have made this planet uninhabitable before tomorrow by recklessly unleashing a nuclear holocaust?[51]

In the following discussion, I shall mention some passages that in my opinion cannot be understood in terms of the above four categories[52] and that show God's absolute foreknowledge of free human acts. In my list must be included the passages in chapter 4 that show God foreordaining free acts of human beings. If he foreordains, again, he must foreknow.[53] But note also the following.

---

51. Strimple, "What Does God Know," 143. In a footnote he points out that Pinnock denies that God has preordained, or even permitted, "evil events in our lives, such as destructive earthquakes or ravaging floods." So, Strimple says, "It is not clear how Pinnock can even affirm that God controls all purely 'natural' events."

52. Of course, in one sense every predictive prophecy falls under category 1. The free actions of men are under God's control, so that his knowledge of free human actions is also a knowledge of his own action. However, I am here expounding my own position, not that of the open theists. They presume a sharp distinction between God's knowledge of his own actions and his knowledge of men's actions. In this section, I assume that distinction for the sake of argument and show that God foreknows actions of men which, on the libertarian view, are not caused by divine actions.

53. And, of course, foreknowledge proves foreordination. This is why Isaiah invokes divine foreknowledge to prove God's sovereignty, in contrast to the false gods.

In Genesis 9:24–27, Noah, speaking as a prophet of God, indicates the future of two sons and a grandson. Clearly, the prophecy is intended to describe, not the earthly lives of these individuals, but the history of their descendants. The grandson, Canaan, is to be a slave of Noah's sons Shem and Japheth. Yahweh is to be blessed as "the God of Shem," and Japheth will live in the tents of Shem. This prophecy is important in Moses' history because it indicates that Israel (as Shemites) will conquer Canaan and that all the nations (Japhethites) will be blessed through Shem (cf. Gen. 12:3). This prophecy does not begin to be fulfilled until Israel's conquest of Canaan many centuries later, and the specific form of the blessing to Japheth does not become evident until Jesus sends out his disciples to take the gospel to "all nations" (Matt. 28:19).

So the prophecy of Noah predicts events many centuries in advance. But it also anticipates free actions of human beings. The prophecy cannot be fulfilled unless the family of Shem develops into a nation capable of defeating the family of Canaan in battle. For that to happen, countless marriages and births must take place, much cultural development must occur, geopolitical events must put Israel and Canaan into proximity, hostility between them must develop, military power must grow in Israel, and, above all, Israel must put its faith in the true God.[54] Similarly, the blessing on Japheth presupposes that the Japhethites will hear of the God of Israel and will freely put their trust in him. So the fulfillment of Noah's prophecy requires millions of free human decisions. In giving Noah those words, God foreknew that those free decisions would take place.

God's covenant with Abraham also anticipates free human decisions:

> Then the LORD said to him, "Know for certain that your descendants will be strangers in a country not their own, and they will be enslaved and mistreated four hundred years. . . . In the fourth generation your descendants will come back here." (Gen. 15:13–16)

As we learn from later narratives in Genesis, Abraham's descendants, several centuries later, become "strangers" in Egypt, because of the betrayal of Joseph by his brothers, Joseph's walk with God that elevates him to a position of authority, Jacob's decision to move to Egypt, and the rise of a Pharaoh who is hostile to the Jews. All these events take place through

---

54. As we have seen, of course, faith is God's gift. But when God gives faith, he foreordains that we will freely believe. The divine gift precedes the human response, but there is a human response and human responsibility (chap. 8). So, in this section, I shall assume that when God or his prophet foretells that someone will believe, he is foretelling a free human act.

the free decisions of human beings: of Joseph, his brothers, Jacob, the Pharaohs. The return of Israel to Canaan is also a complicated story about free human decisions, a story written by the hand of God (Gen. 45:5–8; 50:20). When God predicts these events, he is also predicting the free human decisions that are necessary to bring these events about.

The same analysis would apply to the prophecies of Isaac (Gen. 27:27–29, 39–40) and Jacob (who gathers his children "so I can tell you what will happen to you in days to come" [Gen. 49:1]), the Balaam oracles (Num. 23–24), the Song of Moses (Deut. 32:1–43), and the blessing of Moses on the tribes of Israel (Deut. 33:1–29).

First Samuel 10:1–7 is Samuel's prophecy of specific events, as we saw earlier. Note now that these events cannot occur unless free human decisions are made. Samuel says that Saul will meet two men near Rachel's tomb (v. 2)—not three, not one. Evidently, each man made a free decision to travel that road, and the two freely agreed to walk together. They also freely decided what to say to Saul, but Samuel knew in advance what they would say. Then Samuel identifies the next group that will meet Saul—exactly how many men there will be, exactly what they will be carrying, and what Saul will do in response. Again, Samuel knows in advance (because the Lord knows in advance) what free decisions these people will make.

In 1 Samuel 23:11, God tells David that if he stays in Keilah, the citizens will turn him over to Saul. Presumably, the decision of the inhabitants of Keilah is a free one. But God knows what that free decision would be. Now this is a conditional prophecy, and thus might be thought to be in the open theists' category 4.[55] David's betrayal will occur only on the condition that he stays in Keilah. But God is not here saying what he, God, will do on that condition; rather, he is saying what the Keilahites will do, what their free decision will be. God's knowledge, even conditional knowledge, of free human acts, does not cohere with the system of open theism.

In 1 Kings 13:1–4, an unnamed prophet from the southern kingdom of Judah comes to Jeroboam, ruler of the northern kingdom of Israel, and rebukes his false worship:

> O altar, altar! This is what the LORD says: "A son named Josiah will be born to the house of David. On you he will sacrifice the priests of the high places who now make offerings here, and human bones will be burned on you."

---

55. As events develop, the condition is not fulfilled. David does not stay in Keilah, and so the people of Keilah do not deliver him up.

Jeroboam reigned approximately 931–910 B.C., Josiah 639–609; so the prophecy foretells an event three hundred years in the future, mentioning Josiah by name, foretelling his actions. The prophecy also implies much about Josiah's values. He is to be a champion of the true worship of Yahweh. The prophecy anticipates many free human decisions: the marriages, conceptions, and births that lead to Josiah, the name given to him, the plot that elevates him to the kingship (2 Kings 21:23–24), his training and character, his decision to repair the temple (22:1–7), his response to the rediscovery of the law (vv. 11–20), and his renewal of the covenant (23:1–3).

In 2 Kings 8:12, the prophet Elisha sadly tells Hazael, the future king of Syria, that he will do great harm to Israel: "You will set fire to their fortified places, kill their young men with the sword, dash their little children to the ground, and rip open their pregnant women." These are to be Hazael's free decisions, foreknown by God. Hazael himself considers them unlikely (v. 13). Perhaps the open theist will object that any Syrian king would do these things, granted the historical circumstances, so that this passage would fall under category 3 (human decisions rendered necessary by historical situations). However, if the open theist takes this option, he thereby concedes that Hazael's decisions were not free in the libertarian sense, and therefore that Hazael was not morally responsible for his heinous actions. One would hope that open theists are not so generous to more recent practitioners of genocide. But this passage illustrates well a dilemma facing the open theist: he must conclude from this passage either that God foreknew Hazael's free decision, or that Hazael was not a free agent. Neither conclusion is consistent with the theory of open theism.

According to Psalm 139:4, God knows our words "completely" before they are on our tongue. Also,

> All the days ordained for me
>   were written in your book
>   before one of them came to be. (v. 16)

Does this mean that God foreknows all the events of the days of our lives, or only that he knows the number of days allotted to us? Even if the psalmist intends only the latter in this passage, he is attributing to God a profound foreknowledge of free human decisions. Length of life depends on a great many human decisions: decisions of our parents and caregivers during our childhood, our decisions affecting health and diet, decisions to become involved in dangerous activities, decisions creating friendships and enmities, decisions of friends to rescue us from danger, decisions of enemies to pursue aggression, and, most of all, decisions as to our values, for divine wisdom brings length of life (Prov. 3:2).

We saw that 1 Kings 13:1–4 refers to Josiah by name, three hundred years before his birth. Similarly, Isaiah 44:28–45:13 (and most likely 46:11) refers to Cyrus, the Persian king who authorized the return of Israel from exile to Canaan. Isaiah prophesied in Judah during the reigns of Uzziah, Jotham, and Hezekiah (1:1), in the eighth and seventh centuries B.C. Cyrus conquered Babylon around 539 B.C. and ruled it until around 530. So Isaiah's prophecy anticipated Cyrus's birth, name, conquest, rule, character, and numerous free decisions, over a century in advance.

In Jeremiah 1:5, Yahweh says that he knew the prophet before his conception and appointed him as a prophet. So God knew that of all the marriages in Israel, and all the various combinations of sperm and egg, one would produce a specific individual named Jeremiah, equipped in advance to be a prophet. Many free human decisions led to the conception of Jeremiah in his mother's womb, and God knew all those decisions in advance.

Jeremiah himself, in 37:6–11, reports in advance the free decisions of the Egyptian and Babylonian military leaders, opposing the predictions of rival pundits (vv. 9–10).[56] For similar prophecies, see 25:9 and 39:15–18. In 25:11, Jeremiah says that Judah's captivity will last seventy years. Ezekiel also sets forth some future actions of the king of Babylon in great detail (Ezek. 21:18–23; 26:1–14; 30:10). And Daniel's predictions of the history of empires (Dan. 2; 9; 11) anticipate innumerable free decisions by rulers, soldiers, and peoples, giving timetables for sequences of historical events centuries in advance.

In the New Testament, Jesus teaches that his Father knows the day and the hour of his coming (Mark 13:32). But that day, we learn, will not come until after other events have taken place—events that depend upon free human decisions (13:1–30). So God knows in advance that those decisions will be made, and he knows when they will have been made. Compare Jesus' prophecy of the destruction of the temple in Matthew 24:2. He knew in advance that some people would freely decide to destroy God's house.

Jesus also knew in advance who would betray him (Matt. 26:24). The open theist may not respond that Judas's acts were determined by existing conditions known by Jesus, since Jesus makes it clear in the passage that Judas was responsible for his action. According to open theism, then, Judas's act must have been free and therefore unpredictable. But in fact Jesus predicted it (cf. John 6:64; 13:18–19). In John 13:38, Jesus also pre-

56. Again, the open theist has the option of regarding these military decisions as historically determined and the prophecy as based on God's knowledge of the determining conditions. But, as I noted before, it would be ironic to find freewill theists resorting to determinist explanations of human behavior in order to validate their theory.

dicts Peter's threefold denial, an act for which Peter later takes full responsibility.

In Acts 2:23, Peter ascribes the events of Jesus' death to "God's set purpose and foreknowledge," noting also the responsibility of "wicked men" (cf. Acts 4:27–28).

Jesus knows in advance what kind of death Peter will die (John 21:18–19). Before his death, Peter will be dressed and led somewhere against his will. So, again, Jesus indicates his foreknowledge of free human actions.

Passages Alleged to Teach Divine Ignorance

There really is a great amount of evidence in Scripture that God knows in advance the free decisions of human beings. Indeed, one wonders how the open theists, in the face of so much biblical data, can maintain their position. One of their main arguments is philosophical rather than exegetical: they maintain that the future is inherently unknowable, because it is not a proper object of knowledge. On this view, statements about the future are either false or neither true nor false.[57] The argument is that the future is not presently real, and therefore cannot be an object of knowledge. There is, I think, some truth in this assertion.[58] But the same is true of the past, since we are not directly acquainted with it. So if true statements can refer only to what is presently real, statements about the past are in the same boat as statements about the future.

And the argument also applies to what we call the present. Some have understood the present as a knife-edge between the past and the future, which vanishes before we can conceptualize it. In that case, no statement can be strictly a statement about the present. Usually we think of "the present" as the recent past. But then our statements about the present are as problematic as those about the past, which are in turn as problematic as those about the future. So, the argument that purports to show the unknowability of the future entails the unknowability of the past and the present as well—that is, the unknowability of everything.

The discussion can get very technical and complicated, but, as I see it, those who argue for the unknowability of the future are mainly interested

---

57. This assertion, of course, violates our usual understanding of statements about the future. If I say that the San Diego Padres will win the pennant, and later they do, normally my statement would be considered true, otherwise false. One must be strongly committed to a libertarian metaphysic to abandon this commonsense understanding.

58. Future states of affairs are not real in the present, but God's plan for the future is a reality today. Statements about the future are statements (either true or false) about the nature of God's plan for the future.

in finding a view of knowledge that is consistent with libertarian freedom, which I have given reason to reject. I doubt if any theist who rejects libertarian freedom has ever been tempted to think of the future as unknowable. In any case, this position is certainly unscriptural, for, as we have seen, according to the Bible, God does know the future.

Open theists, however, do propose biblical arguments as well. Without giving much consideration to the many passages we have looked at, both above and in chapters 4 and 14, they point out some texts that, in their view, suggest divine ignorance.

In Genesis 3:9, after Adam and Eve have eaten the forbidden fruit, God calls to Adam, "Where are you?" Does this question indicate that God could not locate Adam's hiding place (v. 8)? If so, the passage would prove too much from an open theist perspective, for it would show that God is ignorant, not only of the future, but of some events in the past and present. In fact, however, the passage does not teach God's ignorance of anything. "Where are you?" is the first of God's four questions for Adam and Eve (the other three are in vv. 11 and 13). He intends for them to admit their wrongdoing by answering his questions. His probing questions reveal ignorance no more than do the questions of any skillful prosecuting attorney.[59]

The same is true of Genesis 11:5, which states that "the LORD came down to see" the tower that sinful men were building in defiance of his will. Was the Lord ignorant of the tower before he came down? If so, why did he come down at that particular place? And, in that case, God is ignorant of the present; the passage says nothing about any divine ignorance of the future. But in fact there is no divine ignorance here. As in Genesis 3:9, God is visiting sinful men in preparation for judgment. When God "draws near" to men in Scripture, it is for blessing and/or judgment. In this case, the Lord creates confusion of language, dooming the tower project to failure and scattering the people over the face of the earth.

Genesis 18:20–21 speaks of another time when God drew near to judge—in this case, the cities of Sodom and Gomorrah. Here, however, a somewhat stronger case can be made for divine ignorance than in Genesis 3:9 and 11:5. God says,

> I will go down and see if what they have done is as bad as the outcry that has reached me. If not, I will know. (v. 21)

Does God here admit that his visit to Sodom will help him gain information that he did not already possess? Several points need to be made here:

---

59. Recall our earlier discussion of the relationship between God's knowledge and his judgments. He is omniscient because he is the ultimate judge of all.

1. As before, this passage concerns God's knowledge of the present, not of the future.

2. As in the two earlier passages, the emphasis is not on God gaining information to complete his own understanding of the situation, but rather on God as prosecutor gathering evidence to present an indictment. Chapter 19 vindicates God's judgment, for the two angels not only know about the wickedness of Sodom, but actually experience it. The evidence is very specific and concrete. In that sense, the divine visit adds to the knowledge that is relevant to the judgment.

3. Nevertheless, when taken literally,[60] the verse does describe an increase in God's knowledge. Traditionally, this description has been understood as an anthropomorphism (see chap. 18): a description of divine knowledge in terms literally appropriate only to human knowledge. On this view, God does not gain knowledge by his visit to Sodom, but only appears to gain it. Anthropomorphisms in descriptions of God are appropriate, as we have seen,.

Thus, the tradition accommodates the language of Genesis 18:20–21 to the broader biblical teaching about God's omniscience. The alternative, of course, is to take passages like this one literally and to accommodate the broader teaching to this one (and to the few passages like it), regarding the omniscience texts as somewhat hyperbolic.[61] But the latter alternative is unwarranted. For one thing, the sheer number of omniscience texts is vastly greater than the number of apparent ignorance texts. For another thing, God's omniscience, as we have seen, is a fundamental ground for the confidence of God's people in the Lord's power and promises. If God is not literally omniscient, then that ground of confidence becomes null and void. Furthermore, in the theophanic context of this passage, there are good reasons for taking the text anthropomorphically. When God appears as a man, he has special reason to describe his knowledge in human terms.

4. But there may be something more than anthropomorphism here. In the theophany of Genesis 18, there is an anticipation of the greater the-

---

60. Of course, nobody takes the passage literally in every respect. A perfectly literal reading, as Douglas Wilson points out, would leave us with a God "who has to walk to get places" (vv. 2–3), who gets his feet dirty (v. 4), who gets tired (v. 4), etc. See Wilson, *Knowledge, Foreknowledge, and the Gospel* (Moscow, Ida.: Canon Press, 1997), 30. Such a conclusion would be the result of saying that God must be limited in all the ways he appears to be limited by his theophanic form. But if God transcends that form in some ways, why not in all ways? (Note the parallel discussed below between incarnation and theophany. Christ's divine nature transcended his material form, without compromising his true humanity.)

61. This discussion reflects Paul Helm's structuring of the problem in *The Providence of God* (Leicester: InterVarsity Press, 1993), 51–52. See appendix E of this volume.

ophany of God in Jesus Christ. Orthodox Christians believe that the incarnate Son of God has two natures, divine and human. According to his divine nature, he is fully omniscient. According to his human nature, he "grew in wisdom and stature" (Luke 2:52). As we have seen, Jesus was omniscient during his days on earth (John 16:30). But he also gained knowledge by asking people questions, by having new experiences. At times he was amazed at what took place (as in Luke 7:9). The theophanic incarnation of Genesis 18 also presents us with a being who is divine in some ways and human in others. There may be significant analogies between this theophany and Christ. It is best for us to be cautious in attempting to conceptualize the theophany.

5. Considerations 3 and 4 may be grounded in a still broader principle. In chapters 6 and 7, we saw that God is not only transcendent, but also fully present in space and time. God's presence in time does not detract from his transcendence or his omniscience. Nevertheless, he always knows what time it is. As he is with me now while I write, he experiences with me the transition from 11:09 to 11:10 a.m. And he is aware of how the world at 11:10 is different from the way it was at 11:09. In other words, the immanent God does experience change,[62] though he himself is unchanging. And since every change brings something new, God experiences newness (as the angels experienced the wickedness of Sodom; recall comment 2 above). This divine experience is evidently similar in these ways to our experience of learning new things. God knows the end from the beginning, but he also understands what it is like to experience something that hasn't happened before.

PONDER THIS

I would conclude, therefore, that God's immanence in time necessitates that his knowledge-in-immanence be significantly analogous to human knowledge, however difficult that fact may be for us to describe. Our difficulties in describing it are similar to the difficulties we have describing the knowledge of Christ (see comment 4, above). The language of God learning new things is, therefore, anthropomorphic, but not merely anthropomorphic (see comment 3, above). In this case, the anthropomorphism reveals a genuine resemblance between human knowledge and God's knowledge in his immanence.

In Genesis 22:12, God tells Abraham, "Now I know that you fear God, because you have not withheld from me your son, your only son." Abraham was willing to sacrifice his son Isaac at God's command, but God provided a ram as a substitute (v. 13). Before this test, was God ignorant about what Abraham would do? I think not, because of the many texts that teach

---

62. I shall discuss this assertion at greater length in chapter 24, under the topic of God's eternity and unchangeability.

divine omniscience. The reference to an apparent increase in God's knowledge may be accounted for by the previously stated principles. First, the issue is more judicial than epistemological. God is looking for evidence of Abraham's faithfulness, his fear of God. So James says that Abraham was "considered righteous for what he did [KJV: "justified by works"] when he offered his son Isaac on the altar" (2:21). Second, it is legitimate for us to speak of anthropomorphism here. But that anthropomorphism is grounded in the nature of God's involvement in the temporal sequence.

The same considerations bear on Deuteronomy 13:3, "The LORD your God is testing you to find out whether you love him with all your heart and with all your soul." Note how often the language of "finding out" appears in the context of testing. This is the case also in the Psalms, where God is said to "search" his people (44:21; 139:1, 23). He knows how the test, the search, will come out, but that does not make the actual test superfluous. In chapter 8, I stressed the importance of both divine sovereignty and human responsibility. In some senses, as I indicated there, God responds to our responses to him. So our responses to tests are important to God. The gospel itself is such a test, and our response to it is crucial to our relationship with God.

In Jeremiah 26:2–3, the Lord tells Jeremiah to preach his word to the temple worshipers and then adds, "Perhaps they will listen and each will return from his evil way. Then I will relent and not bring on them the disaster I was planning because of the evil they have done." I shall discuss the divine "relenting" under the topic of God's unchangeability.[63] Here let us simply note that God sometimes announces judgment, not for the purpose of describing his eternal plan, but to test the response of people. That test is not complete, of course, until the response actually takes place. Positive and negative responses are still possible.[64] So there is an element of uncertainty that God here expresses by saying "perhaps." That term should be understood similarly in Ezekiel 12:3. This principle also accounts for the legitimacy of the questions raised by the king of Nineveh in response to Jonah's preaching: "Who knows? God may yet relent and with compassion turn from his fierce anger so that we will not perish" (Jonah 3:9).

---

63. The word *perhaps* (Heb. *'ulay*) often occurs in texts where people are hoping uncertainly that God will bring them some benefit (e.g., Gen. 18:24–30; Ex. 32:30; Isa. 37:4). The present passage may be construed anthropomorphically as God taking their way of speaking on his own lips.

64. Recall our discussion of possibility in chapter 8. In one sense, only one response is possible, the response that God has foreordained. But given other perspectives, other abilities and preventers, we may speak of things being possible that are contrary to God's eternal plan. It is, for example, logically possible that Christ would not have died for sinners. But that possibility was excluded by God's plan.

There are also a number of passages that speak of God remembering (Gen. 9:15–16; Ex. 6:5) or forgetting (Pss. 9:18; 13:1; Jer. 23:39). "Remember" in these texts simply means that God fulfills his covenant promises. Human beings are prone to think that God has forgotten his promises when their fulfillments are delayed. So when the fulfillment comes, it is as when (note the anthropomorphism) a man remembers something he has forgotten. But Scripture makes it clear that God never actually forgets his covenant.[65] "Forgetting," then, is the temporary delay as seen from a human point of view. Forgetting can also be, as in Jeremiah 23:39, God casting someone out of the covenant fellowship.[66]

Among those passages that supposedly support a doctrine of divine ignorance, we are left with only one closely parallel group: Jeremiah 7:31, 19:5, and 32:35, where God says,

> They [the people of Israel and Judah] built high places for Baal in the Valley of Beth Hinnom to sacrifice their sons and daughters to Molech, though I never commanded, nor did it enter my mind, that they should do such a detestable thing and so make Judah sin.

Does the phrase "nor did it enter my mind" attribute ignorance to God? "Mind" here is *lev,* meaning "heart." Heart is a frequent word in Scripture, but only rarely does it refer to God. In reference to men, phrases with *lev* that are translated "come into the mind" or "come into the heart" indicate not just the presence of an idea in the mind, but an intention or desire of the heart, as in 2 Chronicles 7:11 and Nehemiah 7:5. In Jeremiah 32:35, "nor did it enter my mind" is parallel to "I never commanded." So these passages do not assert divine ignorance, but rather deny in the most emphatic terms that human sacrifice was God's intention or the desire of his heart.[67]

Indeed, Leviticus 18:21 and Deuteronomy 18:10 make it obvious that the thought of human sacrifice did enter God's mind as an item of knowledge. Also in God's mind was the knowledge that Israel might engage in such a horrid practice and therefore needed to be warned against it.

I conclude, then, that although these passages raise interesting issues and

---

65. Wilson comments on Gen. 8:1, "God remembered Noah": "Does God smack his forehead in this passage? 'Oh, yeah! *Noah!*' Or in Exodus 6:5: 'Man, that was close! I almost forgot. The *covenant!*'" (*Knowledge, Foreknowledge, and the Gospel,* 39).

66. Since *knowing* can mean inclusion in covenant fellowship (as in Amos 3:2), *forgetting* can mean exclusion.

67. Of course, this interpretation raises the question of how God could decree, or even allow to happen, a practice contrary to his intention and desire. The answer is to be found in the distinction between his decretive and preceptive wills, which we shall consider in chapter 24.

suggest new perspectives about God's knowledge-in-immanence, they do not teach divine ignorance of any sort. Our earlier conclusion stands: God is omniscient, and his omniscience includes exhaustive knowledge of the future.

GOD'S KNOWLEDGE OF POSSIBILITIES

God knows not only what is actual in the past, present, and future, but also what is only possible. He knows not only what is, but also what is not, but could be. And of course he also knows what could not be. In Jeremiah 26:3 ("Perhaps they will listen and each will turn from his evil way"), considered in the last section, "perhaps" indicates a possibility that may or may not become actual. As we saw in chapter 8, there is a sense in which nothing "can" happen unless God has eternally planned to make it happen. But there are other kinds of possibility, based on different kinds of abilities and preventers, so that there are senses in which states of affairs are possible even though God has sovereignly determined not to bring them about. Many events, for example, are logically possible, even though God has ordained that they will not occur. Similarly, events can be physically possible, economically possible, politically possible, and so on, even though they are impossible from the standpoint of God's decree. God has determined, by his nature and his creative activity, all the things, properties, and relationships that govern possibility in these senses, and so of course he knows what is possible and what is not.

God's knowledge of what is possible is sometimes called his *necessary knowledge*, *natural knowledge*, or *knowledge of intellect*, as opposed to his *free knowledge* or *knowledge of vision*. Ultimately, what is possible is what is compatible with God's own nature. Since God knows his nature necessarily, he knows possibilities necessarily.[68] This is true of what we might call "metaphysical" possibility, in which the only preventer is incompatibility with the divine nature. But of course the other kinds of possibility— physical, economic, legal, and so on—depend, not only on God's nature, but also on his decisions to create the world in a certain way. Physical possibility, for example, is not merely what is consistent with the divine nature, but what is consistent with the laws of physics (or, alternatively, consistent with the capabilities of the human body). Physical possibility, then, presupposes God's decision to create the world in a certain way. Metaphysical possibility, therefore, is the kind of possibility that theologians have in mind when they speak of God's necessary knowledge of possibility.

---

68. For the distinction between necessity and freedom in God, see chapter 12.

Free knowledge and *knowledge of vision* refer to God's knowledge of actualities, the things he has decided to actualize at some point in the history of the creation. It is called free because, as we saw in chapter 12, creation is a free act of God, not a necessary act. God has knowledge of the world because he freely decided to create the world.

The distinction between intellect and vision draws an analogy between divine and human knowledge. On some accounts of human knowledge, the intellect knows what is merely possible (for example, logical and mathematical relationships), and our sense perception (including vision) tells us what actually exists. For example, the intellect tells us that if we have only three pencils, we have less than four. But sense perception tells us whether or not we actually have three pencils. This distinction between intellect and sensation is, however, somewhat oversimplified. I have argued in *DKG* that even in human knowledge, intellect and sensation are mutually dependent. It would certainly be unwise to make a sharp distinction between what God knows by his intellect and what he knows by his senses. For one thing, literally speaking, God has no sense organs.

In Reformed theology, God knows what is possible by knowing his nature. He knows created actuality by knowing his eternal decree. Knowledge of his nature is necessary; knowledge of his decree is free, because the decree itself is free.

GOD'S KNOWLEDGE OF CONTINGENCIES: "MIDDLE KNOWLEDGE"

Between necessary and free knowledge, some theologians have defined a third category of divine knowledge, which they have called "middle." William Lane Craig distinguishes the three forms of divine knowledge as follows:

1. *Natural Knowledge:* God's knowledge of all possible worlds. The content of this knowledge is essential to God.
2. *Middle Knowledge:* God's knowledge of what every possible free creature would do under any possible set of circumstances and, hence, knowledge of those possible worlds which God can make actual. The content of this knowledge is not essential to God. . . .
3. *Free Knowledge:* God's knowledge of the actual world. The content of this knowledge is not essential to God.[69]

69. William Lane Craig, *The Only Wise God* (Grand Rapids: Baker, 1987), 131.

These distinctions were first developed by the Spanish Jesuit Luis Molina (1535–1600), and were adopted by other Jesuits, Socinians, Arminians, some Lutherans, and the Amyraldian Calvinists of Saumur. Thomists and mainstream Reformed theologians have generally rejected the notion. In recent years, a number of Christian philosophers have adopted the concept, such as Craig and Alvin Plantinga.[70]

Given Craig's definition, it is difficult to see at first why Reformed theologians have objected to the concept. Certainly, God does know what every free creature would do in every possible circumstance.[71] The most frequently cited biblical examples are appropriate. In 1 Samuel 23:7–13, David is staying in a town called Keilah, when Saul comes seeking his life. He asks the Lord whether, if he stays in Keilah, the inhabitants will deliver him to Saul. God answers, "They will" (v. 12), and so David leaves. Here God expresses knowledge, not of what will actually happen (for the Keilahites never get the opportunity to betray David), but of what *would* happen under other circumstances. So God knows what the Keilahites would do under circumstances other than the actual ones. As philosophers sometimes put it, he knows the truth of a contrary-to-fact conditional: *If David stays, the Keilahites will betray him.*

The other text often cited in this connection is Matthew 11:20–24. Here Jesus says that if the inhabitants of Tyre, Sidon, and Sodom had seen the miracles of Jesus, they would have repented.[72] In fact, they did not see the miracles of Jesus and did not, therefore, have that opportunity to repent. But Jesus knows what they *would* have done in other circumstances. So Jesus here expresses knowledge of a contrary-to-fact conditional truth.

These passages, of course, are not intended to make technical theological points about God's eternal knowledge. Perhaps we should not insist upon precisely literal interpretations. But granting the previous arguments of this book, it is plain that God, governing all things by his eternal decree, knows what each thing is capable of and what would result from any alteration of his plan.

Indeed, God in Scripture often speaks of what would happen in conditions other than those that actually occur. God says over and over again in different ways that if Israel is faithful, she will receive all of God's blessings in the land of promise. That statement is true; but it is a contrary-to-

70. Plantinga, *The Nature of Necessity* (Oxford: Clarendon Press, 1974), 169–80.
71. Heppe notes Gomarus, Walaeus, Crocius, and Alsted as Reformed theologians who held to middle knowledge in this sense. See *RD*, 79. See also *DG*, 192.
72. They are being compared with the inhabitants of the cities of Korazin, Bethsaida, and Capernaum, who saw the works of Jesus, but still did not believe.

fact conditional. In fact, Israel never displays that faithfulness (except, of course, in the remnant, Jesus Christ). It is also true that if Paul, say, had not repented and believed in Christ, he would have been lost. Scripture often pictures contrary-to-fact possibilities in order to display the grace and justice of God.[73]

From a Reformed point of view, however, it is difficult to see why this kind of divine knowledge must be isolated as a third kind of knowledge, alongside necessary and free knowledge. Note that in Craig's definition, necessary knowledge is a "knowledge of all possible worlds," and middle knowledge is a "knowledge of those possible worlds which God can make actual." What is the difference between these? Are there worlds that are genuinely possible, but which God cannot make actual? What is a "possible world" if it is not a world that God can make actual?

And why should we not include the possible actions of free creatures (in definition 2) as ingredients of the possible worlds of definition 1? When God knows possible worlds, does he not also, by virtue of that knowledge, also know all possible free creatures and their possible actions? So, from a Reformed point of view, there is no reason why we shouldn't regard God's knowledge of contingencies under the category of necessary knowledge.

So we should reject Craig's assertion that this knowledge is "not essential to God." It does, of course, deal with creatures, and creatures are not necessary to God. But it deals with possible creatures, not actual ones, and with their actions under possible circumstances, not actual ones. So it does not depend on God's decree to create the actual world. God knows what creatures and what creaturely actions are possible, simply because he knows himself. He knows what he can bring about. God knows these possibilities simply by knowing his own nature. And his knowledge of his own nature is necessary.

But this approach to God's knowledge of contingencies was not satisfactory to Molina or to other exponents of middle knowledge. To understand why, we should note that the term *free* in Craig's definition 2 refers to libertarian freedom. And, indeed, most all the defenders of middle knowledge as a distinct theological category have held libertarian views. Indeed, much of their enthusiasm for middle knowledge has been that it provides a vocabulary for speaking about God's knowledge of creaturely actions that are free in the libertarian sense.

Now if libertarianism is true, then middle knowledge is indeed distinct

---

73. It may also be possible to infer from Scripture what would have happened to mankind if Adam and Eve had not sinned; hence, there have been many theological discussions of that contrary-to-fact conditional.

from God's necessary knowledge. For, on this view, God does not know the possible free actions of creatures merely by knowing himself. Since he does not cause their free actions, he cannot know their free actions, or their possible free actions, without knowing the creatures themselves.

error

I argued in chapter 8 that libertarianism is false—and even incoherent. Here, I should add that libertarianism brings incoherence into this discussion as well. To see this, let us follow Craig's argument further:

> By his middle knowledge God knows all the various possible worlds which he could create and what every free creature would do in all the various circumstances of these possible worlds. For example, God knew that Peter, if he were to exist and be placed in certain circumstances, would deny Christ three times. By a free decision of his will, God then chose to create one of those possible worlds. . . . Thus, God is able to know future free acts on the basis of his middle knowledge and his creative will.[74]

On Craig's view, God considers all possible worlds by his middle knowledge, and then chooses to create one of them. In the world he chooses to create, someone named Peter exists, who, in these created circumstances, will deny Christ three times. Note that I said "will," not "could" or "might." Once God creates a world (including a world history) that includes Peter's denial, that denial is inevitable.

So what room is there in this scenario for libertarian freedom? Once Peter is created, his denial is inevitable—determined, one might say. Craig has employed the concept of middle knowledge in order to maintain libertarian freedom together with divine foreknowledge. But at the moment of Peter's terrible decision, how can he be said to have libertarian freedom? Rather, he can only deny Jesus because he is living in a world in which that denial is an ingredient. God determined before Peter was born that he would betray Jesus.

Craig doesn't see it this way. He believes that God has decided to create this world, based on his knowledge of what creatable Peter would freely (in the libertarian sense) choose, and on his knowledge of other creatable creatures in this creatable world. But how can Peter make a libertarian free choice when he is part of a world in which the events of his life, including his denial of Jesus, have been decided before his birth?

Indeed, when God "chose to create one of those possible worlds," was he not foreordaining everything that would come to pass in that world? Craig may say that God's choice was motivated by his knowledge of Pe-

74. Craig, *The Only Wise God*, 133.

ter's libertarian free choices, but God's choice itself necessarily limited Peter's freedom, so that he would no longer have that kind of free will.

Libertarian free choices, as we saw in chapter 8, are choices with absolutely no preventers. Defenders of libertarianism often fail to understand the diversity that exists among the kinds of freedom, depending on different kinds of goals, abilities, and preventers. They tend to think that the only alternatives are "some prevention" and "no prevention." Craig here fails to realize that God's creation of a possible world is in fact a preventer to the libertarian free choices of the creatures. If God has chosen to make the world a certain way, no creature can thereafter freely choose to make the world different. There may be other preventers that are missing from Peter's situation, but God's foreordination of a particular world in fact prevents him from making any decisions other than the ones he does make.

Craig would like to believe that middle knowledge reconciles divine sovereignty with libertarian freedom.[75] In fact, it does not. If divine creation on the basis of middle knowledge means anything, it means that libertarianism is excluded. Craig is inconsistent to affirm both libertarianism and the divine act of actualizing a complete, possible world, including all creaturely choices.

If we abandon libertarianism, we abandon the traditional meaning of middle knowledge, and then, as I said earlier, there is no reason to distinguish God's knowledge of contingencies from his necessary knowledge of himself. It is still important, however, that we affirm God's knowledge of the possible actions of possible and actual creatures, of what they will or would do in all circumstances. In chapter 8, I suggested that this knowledge is indeed part of the rationale of creation. God creates the world according to his eternal plan, but that plan presupposes his knowledge of creatable, possible worlds, and, indeed, his foreknowledge of the actual world. God foreordains everything that comes to pass, but he does not foreordain in ignorance. He knows and understands what he foreordains and what he chooses not to foreordain. Therefore, the integrity of creatures (chap. 8, again) is part of God's plan from the beginning.

GOD'S WISDOM

Wisdom (Heb. *hokmah*, Gk. *sophia*; *phronimos* is also translated "wise" in the New Testament) is a kind of heightened knowledge, a knowledge that penetrates to deep significance and practical relevance. We are some-

75. Ibid., 133–38.

times encouraged to think of wisdom as "knowledge put into practice," but knowledge itself can also be practical, and wisdom can be theoretical. Bavinck probably separates the two too sharply when he says:

> Wisdom and knowledge are rooted in different capacities of the soul. The source of *knowledge* is study; of *wisdom*, discernment. *Knowledge* is discursive; *wisdom* intuitive. *Knowledge* is theoretical; *wisdom* practical, teleological; it makes knowledge subservient to an end. *Knowledge* is a matter of the mind apart from the will; *wisdom* is a matter of the mind made subservient to the will. *Knowledge* is often very unpractical; i.e., not adapted to the common affairs of life, *wisdom* is adapted to life; it is ethical in character; it is the art of proper living; it characterizes the man who rightly employs his greater store of knowledge, and who chooses the best end and the best means for reaching that end.[76]

There is some truth here, but wisdom can involve study, knowledge can involve discernment, and so on. And when we consider wisdom as a divine attribute, we should not separate it sharply from other divine attributes, such as knowledge.

In Scripture, we first hear of God giving wisdom to human beings in Exodus 28:3; 31:3, 6, etc., where the wisdom amounts to skill in craftsmanship for the building of the tabernacle and its furnishings (cf. 1 Kings 7:14). Note here that wisdom involves "knowing how," not just "knowing that." It is a knowledge of skills as well as facts. God also gives wisdom to rulers as judges (Deut. 34:9; 1 Kings 3:28; Prov. 1:3). But wisdom also includes many other forms of knowledge. Solomon, the Old Testament paradigm of wisdom,

> spoke three thousand proverbs and his songs numbered a thousand and five. He described plant life, from the cedar of Lebanon to the hyssop that grows out of walls. He also taught about animals and birds, reptiles and fish. (1 Kings 4:32–33)

Praising the wisdom of God, Daniel speaks about the "deep and hidden things" that God reveals (as, in context, the nature and interpretation of Nebuchadnezzar's dream) (Dan. 2:22). So wisdom can include revealed secrets.

But most often in Scripture, *wisdom* has an ethical meaning. "I guide you in the way of wisdom and lead you along straight paths," says the teacher of wisdom in Proverbs 4:11, calling his son to forsake wickedness. God pro-

---

76. *DG*, 195–96.

claims the wisdom of the laws he gives to Israel in Deuteronomy 4:6–8 (cf. Ps. 19:7). James asks:

> Who is wise and understanding among you? Let him show it by his good life, by deeds done in the humility[77] that comes from wisdom. But if you harbor bitter envy and selfish ambition in your hearts, do not boast about it or deny the truth. Such "wisdom" does not come down from heaven but is earthly, unspiritual, of the devil. For where you have envy and selfish ambition, there you find disorder and every evil practice.
>
> But the wisdom that comes from heaven is first of all pure; then peace-loving, considerate, submissive, full of mercy and good fruit, impartial and sincere. Peacemakers who sow in peace raise a harvest of righteousness. (James 3:13–18)

Here, as in Proverbs and Ecclesiastes, wisdom is the skill of godly living. Wisdom walks "in the way of righteousness, along the paths of justice" (Prov. 8:20). Those who live wisely, then, reap the covenant blessing of prosperity, for wisdom will be "bestowing wealth on those who love me and making their treasuries full" (v. 21).

Wisdom is also God's way of salvation. When Stephen bore witness to Christ, his hearers "could not stand up against his wisdom or the Spirit by whom he spoke" (Acts 6:10). The gospel is the wisdom of God, foolish to the world, but the power of God for salvation (Rom. 1:16; 1 Cor. 1:18–2:16; 3:18–23; 8:1–3). Ultimately, God's wisdom is Christ (1 Cor. 1:30; Col. 2:3; cf. Isa. 11:2).

So wisdom is exceedingly precious—more precious than gold or silver (Ps. 19:10; Prov. 16:16).

In all these passages, wisdom is God's gift. It was God's Spirit who came upon the tabernacle artisans and upon Joshua when he succeeded Moses as Israel's leader. Solomon asked God for wisdom and he received it, together with riches and long life. It was God who revealed secrets to Daniel. Stephen spoke with wisdom by the Spirit. To James, true wisdom comes from above. James also reminds us that if we lack wisdom, we "should ask God, who gives generously to all without finding fault" (1:5), and he promises that such prayers will be answered. The gospel of Christ is "God's secret wisdom" (1 Cor. 2:7), which Paul spoke, "not in words taught us by human wisdom but in words taught by the Spirit, expressing spiritual truths

---

77. Note the emphasis on humility in this passage, a virtue not always present in those who claim wisdom. Cf. Prov. 11:2.

in spiritual words" (v. 13). That is the most important thing to know about true human wisdom.

So "the fear of the LORD is the beginning of wisdom" (Ps. 111:10; cf. Prov. 9:10; 15:33)—and the beginning of knowledge, too (Prov. 1:7). Wisdom can be found in God's Word, and we are wise when we obey God's teaching (Ps. 119:98–100; Eccl. 12:13; Col. 3:16; 2 Tim. 3:15).

Scripture refers also to the wise men of other countries, the pagan teachers of wisdom. Sometimes it recognizes their genuine insight. First Kings 4:31 presents Solomon's wisdom as greater than that of several wise men of the nations of his time. The language here is not antithetical; the difference is one of degree. But when the pagan wise men compete with God, their efforts are pitiful (Gen. 41:8; Ex. 7:11; Jer. 8:9; 10:7).

Taken as a whole, the body of ungodly wisdom is indeed antithetical to the wisdom of God's Word. God proclaims against "the wise" of unfaithful Israel, "The wisdom of the wise will perish, the intelligence of the intelligent will vanish" (Isa. 29:14). Paul says of unbelievers, "Although they claimed to be wise, they became fools" (Rom. 1:22). And in 1 Corinthians 1:18–2:16; 3:18–23; 8:1–3, he shows the sharp opposition between the wisdom of the world and the wisdom of God. If the fear of the Lord is the beginning of wisdom, then wisdom that rejects the Lord is not wisdom at all, but foolishness. In the passage from James quoted above, false wisdom is said to be "of the devil."

The above discussion can help us understand the nature of wisdom as a divine attribute. God's wisdom is the source of his words and laws. It is the source and standard for all the world's knowledge and skills, for godly living, and for the way of salvation in Christ. All of God's work in creation and providence reveals his wisdom (Pss. 104:24; 136:5; Prov. 3:19; Jer. 10:12; 51:15), reinforcing what we said in chapter 16, that everything in nature and history happens according to God's wise plan, his decree. God's wisdom not only inspires crafsmen, but is a craftsman (Prov. 8:30).

Proverbs 8–9 personifies God's wisdom, anticipating the New Testament identification of wisdom with Christ.[78] Much of what the passage says about wisdom applies to Christ, as it is ascribed to him elsewhere in Scripture. Proverbs 9:1–4 compares interestingly with Matthew 11:28, where Jesus, in the wisdom tradition, calls all who are weary and burdened to learn of him and to bear his gentle yoke. One problem with this identification,

78. Wisdom and word are closely related concepts in Scripture, as we have seen. God's word is also the craftsman who makes the world and governs the course of nature and history. In John 1 and elsewhere, Jesus is identified as the Word, in a context dealing with the creation. So Jesus as *logos* reinforces the identification of Jesus as *sophia*.

however, is Proverbs 8:22, "The LORD brought me [wisdom] forth as the first of his works, before his deeds of old." The expression "brought forth" (*qanah* in Hebrew) has been taken to mean "created" or "gave birth." The Arian heretics of the fourth century used this verse as a proof text to teach that the Son of God was a created being. However, *qanah* need not bear this meaning. It is the same word translated "get" when the wisdom teacher advises his son to "get wisdom" in 4:5, 7; 16:16; 17:16. Proverbs 8:22 simply means that when God began his creative work, he did what he advises men to do: he "got wisdom." Of course, unlike the human beings addressed elsewhere in Proverbs, God "got wisdom" from his own nature, summoning forth that wisdom to the task of creation. The role of wisdom here, as the first work of God, is similar to what other passages tell us when they point to God's speaking as the beginning of creation (Gen. 1:3; Ps. 33:6).

Meditation on God's wisdom drives his people to praise him. In Romans 11:33–36, the apostle Paul, having surveyed the history of salvation, falls down in amazement at all that God has done and the wisdom revealed in it:

> Oh, the depth of the riches of the wisdom and knowledge of God!
>> How unsearchable his judgments,
>> and his paths beyond tracing out!
> "Who has known the mind of the Lord?
>> Or who has been his counselor?"
> "Who has ever given to God,
>> that God should repay him?"
> For from him and through him and to him are all things.
>> To him be the glory forever! Amen.

GOD'S MIND

Theologians, especially in the scholastic tradition, are fond of talking about God's intellect or reason, but these terms are rare or nonexistent in English translations of Scripture. These translations do use the term *mind* occasionally of God, representing a wide variety of Hebrew and Greek expressions: *peh* ("mouth," Lev. 24:12), *nefesh* ("soul," 1 Sam. 2:35), *lev* ("heart," Jer. 19:5; 32:35; 44:21), *phronēma* ("thoughts, purposes," Rom. 8:27), *nous* (the usual Greek word for "mind," Rom. 11:34; 1 Cor. 2:16). The Bible certainly has no interest in isolating a divine faculty called "the intellect" and discussing its relation to other divine faculties like "will" or "imagination," in the manner of scholastic philosophy. The use of *soul* and *heart* to describe the location of God's thoughts indicates that thought belongs to his whole self, his whole being, rather than to some faculty within him, distinguished from other faculties. Certainly that is what the doctrine of simplicity (chap. 12) would suggest.[79]

The passages that refer to God's mind are more concerned with his thoughts and expressions than with the faculty that produces them. That is the case in all the passages cited above. As we shall see, this data is similar to the biblical data about God's will. Of course, Scripture speaks of God's will much more often than it speaks of his mind. But in both cases it is concerned with contents and expressions, rather than their source in some inner faculty. God's will consists of his decrees and precepts. God's mind is his thoughts. If we are to speak of some mental or volitional faculty in God, that faculty can be nothing less than his whole being. God is a willing God and a thinking God. So it is proper to deal with these concepts under the category of divine attributes.

Even though biblical references to God's mind are somewhat scarce, there is no doubt that God thinks. As we have seen, everything in the world happens in accordance with a divine plan. Planning is a form of thinking. Speech, knowledge, and wisdom, which we have considered in this chapter, all presuppose thought. So does God's justice, for it requires precise evaluation of creaturely action. And his faithfulness presupposes that he remembers his covenant and acts in accordance with it. God's thought permeates the creation, and it fills his revealed Word. It amazes us, driving us to praise (Rom. 11:33–36). It is incomprehensible (chap. 11). God's thoughts are not ours (Isa. 55:8).

Is God's thought rational or logical? Certainly it is both. Logic involves two things: the validity of arguments and consistency between propositions. God often presents arguments to people in Scripture, giving them reasons to obey him. "Since, then, you have been raised with Christ, set your hearts on things above" (Col. 3:1). So God imposes on us the responsibility to think logically, to think consistently with his revelation.[80] And of course that responsibility images God's own nature.

God also speaks and acts consistently. We see this in his eternal plan, as he arranges the objects and events of the universe in a consistent narrative. We see it in his speech,[81] for his word is always true. Truth is always

---

79. See *DKG*, 328–46, for a similar treatment of human faculties.

80. Thus, logic may be considered a subdivision of ethics. See *DKG* for a development of this idea.

81. I would not translate *logos* as "logic" in John 1:1, as Gordon Clark recommends in *The Johannine Logos* (Nutley, N.J.: Presbyterian and Reformed, 1972), 19. In John 1 (as opposed to some of the philosophical sources Clark mentions), the emphasis is on communication, rather than rationality or logic as such. But there is no doubt that God's *logos* is

consistent with itself; it always excludes falsehood. God's righteousness entails that he will be consistent in his judgments and impartial. His faithfulness means that he will speak and act consistently with his covenant promises. And his knowledge is logically consistent, for knowledge is true belief, excluding all falsehood.

So God acts and thinks in accordance with the laws of logic. This does not mean that he is bound by these laws, as though they were something "above" him that had authority over him. The laws of logic and rationality are simply the attributes of his own nature. As he is righteous, so he is logical. To be logical is his natural desire and pleasure. Nor does he create the laws of logic, as if they were something he could change at will. Rather, they are necessary attributes, inalienable qualities of all his thinking and acting.

To say this is not to say that God's revelation is necessarily in accord with some particular human system of logic. Systems of logic are developed by human beings in an effort to catalogue and describe the factors that generate validity and invalidity, consistency and inconsistency. They recommend methods for testing validity and consistency and for constructing valid arguments and consistent sets of propositions. But because these systems are human, they are fallible. Just as one generation of scientists tries to improve on the knowledge of previous generations, so logicians try to improve on previous systems of logic. For example, Bertrand Russell thought that he had discovered some faults in Aristotle's system of logic, and his work led to systems of greater sophistication and complexity. But future logicians may find fault with Russell's system, just as future scientists may find fault with contemporary quantum theory. No human system of logic, then, necessarily measures up to the mind of God. God's logic is perfect, the standard for all human logic.

Therefore, it is at least possible that something in God's revelation may appear contradictory, according to the best current logical systems, and yet be quite consistent in terms of the ultimate nature of logical truth.[82]

---

meaningful and intelligible. It is not a numinous, ineffable power that comes upon men, as in some modern theologies.

82. If the Bible's teaching about God did not stretch our minds, we would be tempted to doubt its truthfulness. How can the Lord of all creation be perfectly understandable to us? But we need to be more humble, recognizing how small our minds really are. I heard an interesting illustration: imagine a tribe of two-dimensional people living on a flat surface. A cube intersects the plane of their existence, so that it appears to the tribe as a square with four corners. But then a revelation comes to them that the figure actually has eight corners, and what appear to be corners on the plane aren't really corners at all. The people would surely accept that revelation, if they did accept it, as a challenge to their very rationality. But the difference between God and man is much greater than the difference between three-dimensional and two-dimensional reality.

It is also the case, as I emphasize in *DKG* (pp. 242–301), that some of God's revelation may seem inconsistent to us, not because of defects in our logical system, but because we fail in some measure to understand what God has revealed. Someone may think, for example, that God is being inconsistent in telling the Jews under Joshua to kill the Canaanites, while telling New Testament believers to love their enemies. But this apparent inconsistency is resolved when we understand the difference between Joshua's situation and ours, and the differences between the duties of armies and those of private individuals.

The doctrines that are most often described as "apparently contradictory" are divine sovereignty and human freedom, the problem of evil, and the Trinity. Cornelius Van Til believed that these doctrines involve "apparent contradictions" that can never be reconciled by the human mind.[83] However, I don't think Scripture tells us which apparent contradictions are reconcilable by men and which ones are not. On the three doctrinal issues mentioned above, I have tried in this book to state them nonparadoxically, in ways that remove the appearance of contradiction, while preserving, of course, the mystery of God's relationship to the world. I may have succeeded or failed. But I see no reason why we should stop trying. Some apparent contradictions can be removed by careful study of God's Word. Others, perhaps, await future increases in our Bible knowledge, or even, perhaps, future developments in the science of logic itself. Others, perhaps, await the vastly increased knowledge of God (1 Cor. 13:8–12; 1 John 3:2) that we will gain when we meet him in glory. And still others may be such that creaturely minds can never reconcile them.

If there are some apparent contradictions that we cannot reconcile (now, or in the future, or ever), we should simply try to hold both sides of the paradox, as best we can, and walk by faith. If divine sovereignty and human responsibility seem contradictory to us, we may and should, nevertheless, both continue to regard God as sovereign and accept responsibility for our thoughts and actions. And in that case, we should be careful not to adopt any apparently logical inferences from divine sovereignty that compromise human responsibility, or vice versa.

Our faith does not depend on our being able to reconcile all apparent contradictions. Rather, it rests on the solid foundation of God's revelation of himself—in creation, in Scripture, and in Christ. So we walk by faith, rather than by sight.

---

83. See CVT, 151–60.

CHAPTER 23

God's Power

We shall now consider the attributes of power, sometimes called "metaphysical" attributes (but note my objections to that phrase in chap. 19). On the chart in chapter 19, we are moving ahead to the third column.

In chapter 17, I noted that all of the names of God focus to some degree on God's power. Certainly the immensity of God's power made a huge impression on believers during the biblical period. Consider:

> Lift up your heads, O you gates;
> >be lifted up, you ancient doors,
> >that the King of glory may come in.
> Who is this King of glory?
> >The LORD strong and mighty,
> >the LORD mighty in battle. (Ps. 24:7–8)

> I pray also that the eyes of your heart may be enlightened in order that you may know the hope to which he has called you, the riches of his glorious inheritance in the saints, and his incomparably great power for us who believe. That power is like the working of his mighty strength, which he exerted in Christ when he raised him from the dead and set him at his right hand in the heavenly realms, far above all rule and authority, power and dominion, and every title that can be given, not only in the present age but also in the one to come. And God placed all things under his feet and appointed him to be head over everything for the church, which is his body, the fullness of him who fills everything in every way. (Eph. 1:18–23)

Now to him who is able to do immeasurably more than all we ask or imagine, according to his power that is at work within us, to him be glory in the church and in Christ Jesus throughout all generations, for ever and ever! Amen. (Eph. 3:20–21)

In chapter 4, I discussed God's control as an attribute of his lordship. There we looked at many passages indicating the efficacy and universality of God's control over creation. God's control of all things—in creation, providence, and redemption—displays his wisdom, as we have seen, and also his mighty power. That he does all these things astounds and overwhelms human beings. Such power drives us to worship. No one else has nearly as much power as God. This is also an important element in the biblical teaching concerning miracle: in his mighty works, God displays his power—his lordship as control (chap. 13).

Nobody can frustrate him:

O LORD, God of our fathers, are you not the God who is in heaven? You rule over all the kingdoms of the nations. Power and might are in your hand, and no one can withstand you. (2 Chron. 20:6)

But he stands alone, and who can oppose him?
   He does whatever he pleases. (Job 23:13)

There is no wisdom, no insight, no plan
   that can succeed against the LORD. (Prov. 21:30)

   Yes, and from ancient days I am he.
No one can deliver out of my hand.
   When I act, who can reverse it? (Isa. 43:13)

All the peoples of the earth
   are regarded as nothing.
He does as he pleases
   with the powers of heaven
   and the peoples of the earth.
No one can hold back his hand
   or say to him: "What have you done?" (Dan. 4:35)

He can subdue anybody who resists him, and eventually he will. On the way to the cross, Jesus said to his captors:

Do you think I cannot call on my Father, and he will at once put at my disposal more than twelve legions of angels? (Matt. 26:53)

Paul speaks of God,

> who, by the power that enables him to bring everything under his control, will transform our lowly bodies so that they will be like his glorious body. (Phil. 3:21)

He does things that are proverbially impossible: raising from the stones children for Abraham (Matt. 3:9), bringing what is out of what is not (Heb. 11:3). He makes *all* things work together for the good of those who love him (Rom. 8:28).

So his name is not only "the Holy One of Israel" (e.g., Isa. 1:4), but also "the Mighty One of Israel" (Isa. 1:24; cf. 49:26, 60:16). He is *'el shadday, pantokratōr,* God Almighty.

There is in Scripture, therefore, a pervasive emphasis on God's mighty power, contrary to the modern theologians (mentioned in chap. 2) who object to the notion of a God who has power over others.

GOD'S OMNIPOTENCE

The greatness of God's power is ground for religious praise, as we saw in the passages quoted from the Psalms, Ephesians, and elsewhere. False gods are weak and beggarly (Gal. 4:9). In such praise, the believer regards God's power as an absolute, the very standard of power. (As often, metaphysical assertions grow out of the stance of worship, not out of mere rational analysis.) To attribute weakness to God is incompatible with the stance of worship. God is always powerful, always competent.

Thus arises the doctrine of omnipotence. The term *omnipotence* is not in Scripture, but the term is appropriate to refer to two biblical ideas, closely related to one another:

GOD CAN DO ANYTHING HE PLEASES

> But he stands alone, and who can oppose him?
>   He does whatever he pleases. (Job 23:13)

> Our God is in heaven;
>   he does whatever pleases him. (Ps. 115:3)

> The LORD does whatever pleases him,
>   in the heavens and on the earth,
>   in the seas and all their depths. (Ps. 135:6)

The LORD Almighty has sworn,
"Surely, as I have planned, so it will be,
    and as I have purposed, so it will stand.
I will crush the Assyrian in my land;
    on my mountains I will trample him down.
His yoke will be taken from my people,
    and his burden removed from their shoulders."
This is the plan determined for the whole world;
    this is the hand stretched out over all nations.
For the LORD Almighty has purposed, and who can thwart him?
    His hand is stretched out, and who can turn it back? (Isa.
        14:24–27)

So is my word that goes out from my mouth:
    It will not return to me empty,
but will accomplish what I desire
    and achieve the purpose for which I sent it. (Isa. 55:11)[1]

All the peoples of the earth
    are regarded as nothing.
He does as he pleases
    with the powers of heaven
    and the peoples of the earth.
No one can hold back his hand
    or say to him: "What have you done?" (Dan. 4:35)[2]

See also the section of chapter 4 dealing with the efficacy of God's control.

NOTHING IS TOO HARD FOR GOD

The difference between this idea and the previous one is that this one explicitly describes what God can do in universal terms: not only can he do what he wants to do, but *nothing* is too hard for him—or, conversely, all things are possible for him. Note:

Is anything too hard for the LORD? I will return to you at the appointed time next year and Sarah will have a son. (Gen. 18:14)

---

1. Note that here the divine omnipotence is the omnipotence of his word. Compare the discussion of God's word in the preceding chapter. We shall see other passages that link omnipotence to the fulfillment of God's word. Note the discussion of Luke 7 in the preceding chapter. Jesus' word is as effective over disease as the centurion's orders are over his men.
2. These are the words of Nebuchadnezzar, king of Babylon. But it is evident in context that here he is telling the truth, having been humbled by the Lord.

The angel who announces to Mary the coming birth of Jesus echoes this language: "For nothing is impossible with God" (Luke 1:37).

In Numbers 11:23, God says to Moses, "Is the LORD's arm too short? You will now see whether or not what I say will come true for you." Again, God gives a promise that seems impossible: he will provide meat in the desert. But, of course, Israel should not measure the probability of God's word coming true over against the unlikelihood of the event. God's word is supremely authoritative, and they should trust it as the very standard of truth. So the question "Is the LORD's arm too short?" is rhetorical. Ascribing weakness to God contradicts the very nature of lordship and the authority of his word. So of course this task is not too hard for the Lord.

Face-to-face with God, having been brought to the end of himself, first by his sufferings and then by God's amazing knowledge and power, Job admits, "I know that you can do all things; no plan of yours can be thwarted" (Job 42:2). God can do *all things*.

The prophet Jeremiah prays to God, "Ah, Sovereign LORD, you have made the heavens and the earth by your great power and outstretched arm. Nothing is too hard for you" (Jer. 32:17). Then the Lord replies, "I am the LORD, the God of all mankind. Is anything too hard for me?" (v. 27). To Zechariah, God discloses a coming wonder, and says, " 'It may seem marvelous to the remnant of this people at that time, but will it seem marvelous to me?' declares the LORD Almighty" (Zech. 8:6).

When Jesus' disciples asked who can be saved, if salvation is nearly impossible even for the rich, he replied, "With man this is impossible, but with God all things are possible" (Matt. 19:26; cf. Mark 10:27; Luke 18:27). And before his death on the cross, he prayed:

> "*Abba*, Father," he said, "everything is possible for you. Take this cup from me. Yet not what I will, but what you will." (Mark 14:36)

We should not exaggerate the difference between the first and the second lists. Even the passages in the second list (with the significant exception of Mark 14:36) refer in context to actions that God actually carries out. But in the second list of passages, the believers' confidence is based on a universal premise: God can fulfill his promise to me, because he can do *anything*. So, in these passages, "God can do all things" is a normative premise that should govern the thinking of his people. When God promises something that seems impossible, God's people should be thinking, not only that "God's word is always true," but also that "God can do all things." So the realm of possibility for God is wider than the realm of actuality. God *can* do things that he does not actually do. We should never restrict our view of God's power only to what he does, or has done, in history. God does not exhaust his power in his work of creation and providence.

We might be tempted to equate possibility with actuality on the basis of the doctrine of the divine decree. For there is a sense in which it is impossible for anything to happen that God has not decreed to happen. Here is a sense of possibility in which God's decree is the preventer: *x* is impossible because God has not decreed it; *y* is possible because either *y* is God or *y* is decreed by God. But we learned in chapter 8 that there are many kinds of possibility, with different kinds of preventers. When Scripture speaks of God being "able to do all things," of "all things being possible" with God, it is presupposing a different concept of possibility than that in which God's decree is the preventer. Rather, it is assuming a sense in which some things are possible that God has not decreed. Logical possibility is one such sense. God did not decree that my birthday should be in September, but such a state of affairs is logically possible, and God *could* have ordained it. To be consistent with the texts we have mentioned, we must say that in some sense God is able to do "all things," not just the things he has ordained.

WHAT GOD CANNOT DO

The "all things," however, requires some interpretation. The problem of defining it has engendered much controversy. The reason is that there are clearly some things that God can't do, such as lying, stealing, making another God, making a square circle, making a stone so big he cannot lift it, and so on. Therefore, philosophers and theologians have tried in one way or another to qualify the "all" in "God can do all things"—to find an alternative way of defining the concept, or reject it altogether.

Let us look at six kinds of actions that God cannot perform:

1. *Logically contradictory actions*, such as ultimately saving and condemning the same individual, making a round square (i.e., an object that is both square and not square at the same time and in the same respect), or making a rope with only one end.[3] As we saw in the previous chapter, God is a logical, rational being, though he does not necessarily conform to the laws of any human system of logic. The laws of logic are an aspect of his own character. Being logical is his nature and his pleasure. So the fact that he cannot be illogical is not a weakness. It may not fairly be described as a lack of power. Indeed, it is a mark of his great power that he always

3. Assuming that it is logically impossible to generate an actually infinite object out of finite material parts.

acts and thinks consistently, that he can never be pushed into the inconsistencies that plague human life.

We note here, as we shall with other "qualifications of omnipotence," that there are problems of language here. Not every "inability" is a lack of power; indeed, some inabilities are marks of extraordinary power. Imagine a baseball player who hits a home run whenever he comes to the plate. Someone might say of him, "He can't hit singles or doubles." That sounds like a weakness, until you look at the broader context.

Remember also my analysis of abilities, possibilities, and "cans" in chapter 8. In considering these issues, it is important to understand the relevant preventers. In the case of God's inability to be illogical, his illogicality is prevented by his righteousness, faithfulness, truth, rational speech, knowledge, and wisdom. God's incapacity here is not due to illness, injury, lack of strength, a crowded schedule, and so on. It is due to traits that are wholly admirable. This sort of reasoning will help us to see how alleged divine inabilities are really strengths. The term *inability*, therefore, is misleading in this context, though it is literally applicable. *Inability* is usually a pejorative, but in this case there is nothing deserving of criticism.

2. *Immoral actions*, like lying, stealing, coveting, and breaking his promises. God is *apseudēs* (Titus 1:2), "nonlying":[4]

> God is not a man, that he should lie,
>   nor a son of man, that he should change his mind.
> Does he speak and then not act?
> Does he promise and not fulfill? (Num. 23:19)

Balaam's questions in this passage are obviously rhetorical. It is unthinkable that God should lie or fail to keep his promise. He "cannot disown himself" (2 Tim. 2:13). He "cannot be tempted by evil" (James 1:13). God does, of course, have some moral prerogatives that human beings do not have, such as the right to take human life for his own reasons. But, for the most part, human morality is an imaging of God: "Be holy, because I am holy" (1 Peter 1:16; cf. Lev. 11:44–45; 19:2; 20:7; Matt. 5:48). God is the standard for human morality, so he cannot be less than perfect in his holiness, goodness, and righteousness.

Again, we may speak of God's inability here, but we are really talking about something admirable—moral excellence and consistency. These are

---

4. One can argue whether this means "one who cannot lie" (so KJV) or merely "one who does not lie" (so NIV). But clearly *apseudēs* characterizes all of God's actions. A god who lies is not the God of the Bible. So I take *apseudēs* as an essential attribute. Thus, the KJV translation is appropriate.

the only qualities that "prevent" him from immoral actions. So, again, the term *inability* is misleading.

3. *Actions appropriate only to finite creatures*, like buying shoes, celebrating one's birthday, or taking medicine for a cough. Again, God's inability to do these things is not due to any lack of power. He is quite capable of taking on human form and doing all these things. His "inability" exists only in his nonincarnate state, and in that state, the reasons he "cannot" do these things pertain to his strengths, not to his weaknesses.

4. *Actions denying his own nature as God*, such as making another god equal to himself, abandoning his divine attributes, or absorbing the universe into his own being. God necessarily exists as the one true God. If he were to perform any of these actions, he would no longer exist as the one true God. The world would then no longer be a theistic universe, but rather a chaos. But in fact there could be no such world. So these actions are impossible. Even God cannot perform them. But that fact is good for everybody. It does not deserve the pejorative label *inability*.

5. *Changing his eternal plan*. God's eternal plan is unchangeable (see chap. 16). There has been some discussion as to whether or not God can change the past. I prefer to deal with this issue without getting into the complications of current scientific theories about time. The most relevant point is simply that just as God's eternal plan has determined what will happen in the future (to us), so it determined what would happen in the past (to us). Since that plan does not change, God cannot change the past or the future.

6. *Making a stone so large that he cannot lift it*. This is the famous "paradox of the stone," loved by philosophers.[5] We are at first inclined to say that this is a logically contradictory action, like making a round square. What gives us pause, however, is that the description is not formally contradictory in any obvious way, and this is in fact an action that some human beings can perform. There is no incoherence in the idea of a human being making an object too big to lift. People do it all the time. So why should this action be incoherent in the case of God? And is this a case in which human beings can do something that God cannot do?

But we have just seen (in class 3, above) that there are many acts that are appropriate only to finite beings. The act in question here is, I think,

---

5. Some of the significant essays in the recent discussion, by George I. Mavrodes, Harry G. Frankfurt, C. Wade Savage, and others, are gathered in Linwood Urban and Douglas N. Walton, *The Power of God* (New York: Oxford University Press, 1978), 131–68. The same considerations mentioned here bear also on the question of whether God can "make a chair not made by God," and similar examples. This action is coherent and possible for human beings, but it is not appropriate for God. Were he to perform it, it would compromise his nature as God.

one of those. I mentioned earlier that when God takes on human form, he can do any number of these things, and that is also true in this case. Indeed, Jesus himself, during his days as a carpenter, might have made an object (say a house) that, as a man, he was unable to lift. The question is really whether God could do this in his nonincarnate state.

So, what keeps God from making the stone is his infinity—not a weakness, but a strength. But the issues raised by the actions in classes 1 and 4 enter here, too. For God to make an object so large that he cannot lift it would involve either a contradiction of his omnipotence (class 1) or an abandonment of it (class 4). For God is omnipotent, which certainly means that he can lift any stone of any weight. So the preventer here is his infinity, together with his logical nature or his power itself. These are all, of course, strengths, rather than weaknesses. Perhaps what makes this puzzle so fascinating is that the three issues of power, logic, and infinitude need to be sorted out before a satisfying solution can be found.

DEFINITIONS OF OMNIPOTENCE

But how, then, shall we define *omnipotence*, granted all these qualifications? Some philosophers have decided that because of the above complications, *omnipotence* cannot be defined. It must either be denied or be replaced by a different concept.[6]

We may be tempted to say that the omnipotence of God means that he can do anything, except for the six classes of actions listed in the previous section. But that would be a rather unwieldy definition, and it certainly would not express clearly that insight into God's power that drove the biblical saints to worship.

Anthony Kenny[7] discusses some of the alternative definitions available in the philosophical literature. Here is my own list with comments, influenced somewhat by his, but avoiding too much technical complication:

1. *God is able to do whatever he wants*. But this is also true of the elect angels and glorified saints, who are not omnipotent.

2. *God is able to do anything that is logically possible*. But some of the actions excluded in the previous discussion are logically possible.

3. *God can do whatever is possible*. This definition would incorporate different kinds of possibility, other than logical possibility. But for whom are these actions possible? Not creatures, because God's omnipotence includes

---

6. See, for example, Anthony Kenny, *The God of the Philosophers* (Oxford: Clarendon Press, 1979), 95–96.
7. Ibid., 91–99.

actions that are impossible for creatures. If by "possible" we mean "possible for God," our definition is tautological: God can do whatever God can do. That definition would be true, but not informative.[8]

4. God has infinite power. "Infinite power" requires further definition, if it is not to include power to perform the actions excluded earlier. So this phrase doesn't help us.

5. God has power over all things. Certainly he does have this power, according to Scripture. He is supreme, in control, the Lord of all. But this attempted definition changes the subject. We want to know what God can do, in the course of exerting his power.

6. God has more power than anyone. This is also scriptural, but it poses the same problem as definition 5.

7. God can do anything that is compatible with his attributes. This is Kenny's solution,[9] and I think it is the best one that is available at present. There is a problem here, however, and that is that all of God's attributes can be construed as powers, as I illustrate in this volume.[10] So this definition (like definition 3 on the second interpretation) lands in tautology, telling us that God can do what he can do.

This, however, is the same kind of circularity that we considered in chapter 20, in the section dealing with the problem posed by Plato in *Euthyphro*. There we saw that God's goodness, for example, is defined by his whole nature (the doctrine of simplicity), and also that God's whole nature is good. Good is what he is, says, and does, but what he is, says, and does is good. Here we are saying the same thing about God's power. His power is defined by his whole nature, as in Kenny's proposal. But his whole nature should be defined as power, for power is not ultimately something abstract, but a concrete divine person. God's power is everything that he is; all his attributes manifest his power.

The reason for this problem is that there is no one or no thing higher

---

8. Alvin Plantinga illustrates this problem by reference to Mr. McEar, who is capable only of scratching his ear. If omnipotence means that someone can do anything possible for him to do, then McEar is omnipotent. See Plantinga, *God and Other Minds* (Ithaca: Cornell University Press, 1967), 170.

9. My formulation is, of course, a simplified paraphrase. Kenny's version: "the possession of all logically possible powers which it is logically possible for a being with the attributes of God to possess" (*The God of the Philosophers*, 98). I consider logic itself to be an attribute of God, so the references to logical possibility are superfluous.

10. Kenny says, in parentheses, "If the definition is not to be empty 'attributes' must here be taken to mean those properties of Godhead which are not themselves powers: properties such as immutability and goodness" (ibid., 98). But isn't immutability God's power to remain the same despite change in the world, and isn't goodness his power to do good and avoid evil?

than God by which to define his attributes. Nor are his attributes really separable from one another; each is a perspective on his whole nature.

So, in one sense, our definition boils down to "God can do what he can do." The definition is circular, as all definitions of divine attributes ultimately are. But the circle need not be a narrow one (see chap. 20, again), since we learn of God's nature through his revelation, which is rich in content. For example, God's righteousness is everything he is, but it is also his mighty acts to redeem his people from unjust oppression. Similarly, God's power is everything he is, but it is also his marvelous work of creation, providence, and redemption, as well as his ability to conceptualize and bring into being possibilities beyond the actual world.

In the end, we cannot define precisely what God is able to do. But we are confident that he can do everything Scripture describes him as doing, and much more. And we know that the only preventers are his own truth, righteousness, faithfulness, and so on. That fact should assure us that God is entirely competent to accomplish all his righteous, loving purposes.

ABSOLUTE AND ORDINATE POWER

The nominalistic tradition in theology, of which William of Occam is the most famous representative, developed a distinction between God's absolute power and his ordinate power. As I indicated earlier, Scripture teaches that God's power is not exhausted in history, that God is able to do many things that he does not choose to do. As we have seen, however, it is not easy to define the full scope of God's power.

Some nominalists took the most extreme position: that absolute power is the power to do absolutely anything. On their view, God has the power to do logically contradictory things, even to change the laws of logic themselves. As Bavinck puts it, on the nominalist view,

> God was able to sin, to go astray, to suffer, to die, to be changed into a stone or into an animal, to change bread into the body of Christ, to effect contradictions, to undo the past, to make false what was true and true what was false, etc. God is pure indifference or arbitrariness, absolute potency, without content: he *is* nothing but may *become* anything.[11]

Such is *absolute* power, as some nominalists conceived of it.[12] God is, on their view, *ex lex*, above the laws of rationality, truth, and morality, free to

11. DG, 243.
12. Occam himself, however, was more moderate. He did not include logically con-

act against them or change them as he wishes. God's power to do what he chooses to do they called *ordinate*. Others, however, denied that God had absolute power, so defined, and insisted that God's power is limited to what he chooses to do.[13]

We have seen that, according to Scripture, there are some things that God cannot do. The nominalist view of absolute power described by Bavinck contradicts this biblical teaching. And, as Bavinck says, it leaves us with a god who has no definite nature—only a kind of libertarian freedom that allows him to do anything at all. His nature is not righteous or good; rather, he merely chooses to act in accord with these qualities, until he decides to act otherwise. Apart from this libertarian free choice, he is nothing—or a monster. He is not good, or loving, or righteous, or wise. So such nominalism radically contradicts the biblical doctrine of God.

On the other hand, we have also seen that God's power extends beyond his actual choices. So of the two groups Bavinck mentions, neither is correct.

Charles Hodge, who also rejects the nominalistic view of God's absolute power, redefines the distinction between absolute and ordinate power in this way:

> A distinction is commonly made between the *potentia absoluta* and the *potentia ordinata* of God. By the latter is meant the efficiency of God, as exercised uniformly in the ordered operation of second causes; by the former, his efficiency, as exercised without the intervention of second causes. Creation, miracles, immediate revelation, inspiration, and regeneration, are to be referred to the *potentia absoluta* of God; all his works of providence to the *potentia ordinata*.[14]

His version of the distinction, certainly very different from the nominalist version, was also the teaching of his son, A. A. Hodge, and their successors at Princeton Theological Seminary in the late nineteenth and early twentieth centuries.

These definitions do avoid the problems generated by the nominalistic

---

tradictory actions in the category of "absolute power." For him, God is not able to perform such actions. Rather, God's absolute power is his power to do anything he wishes. His absolute power establishes a structure of regularities, and in his relations to creation he works only within the limits of that structure. God's power operating within those limits is called "ordinate power." See Occam, Quodlibetal Questions 6, q. 1, in *Opera Philosophica et Theologica*, vol. 9 (New York: St. Bonaventure Publications, 1966), 585.14–586.24. Concerning this "structure," however, see my comments on the fourth concept of natural law in chapter 13.

13. Among these, Bavinck cites Spinoza, Schleiermacher, and Strauss, among others.
14. Charles Hodge, *Systematic Theology* (Grand Rapids: Eerdmans, n.d.), 1:410.

ones described by Bavinck. However, they deal with different issues from the ones arising out of the nominalist discussion. Therefore, it is rather confusing to use the terms *absolute* and *ordinate* this way. Furthermore, Scripture says very little about the distinction on which Hodge places such great weight (see "Miracles and Immediacy" in chap. 13). Hodge's view of absolute and ordinate power serves, for example, as a basis for his view of miracle as "immediate" divine activity. But I believe that that view of miracle is not scriptural.

Can anything be salvaged from the discussion of absolute versus ordinate power? Of course, we are not under any biblical obligation to use these terms. If we do choose to give them some positive meaning in accord with Scripture, we may define God's ordinate power as the power exerted in the things he chooses to do. Absolute power, then, would be God's power to do things other than those he actually chooses to do. We should admit that we cannot precisely delimit the range of God's absolute power. It is not without limit, as we have seen, and for that reason the term *absolute* may be confusing in this context. We do not know the full extent to which God's attributes may limit what he can do. But God does have power to do things he chooses not to do, and it may be useful to find some new terminology by which to express this idea.[15]

OMNIPOTENCE AND REDEMPTION

All the controversy about omnipotence may distract us from the actual purposes of God in revealing his power to his people. God does not reveal his omnipotence merely so that we can engage in philosophical speculation on what he can or cannot do. As with all his revelation, God wants the doctrine of omnipotence to edify his people (2 Tim. 3:16–17).

As I said earlier, God's power drives his people to worship. It also warns us against governing our lives by our own expectations of what is possible, leaving God out of account. For example, we may, like the disciples, wonder how certain classes of people could be saved: the very rich (as in Luke 18:23–27), hardened criminals, persecutors of Christians, and so on. So we may be tempted to ignore such people in the course of our gospel witness, focusing only on those who, from our human perspective,

---

15. I'm sorry, but all the terms that occur to me have drawbacks of their own, such as *hypothetical* power, *extradecretal* power, *potential* power, *dormant* power, *middle* power (between God's necessary will and his free will; see below), and *contingent* power. Maybe a reader can suggest a better one.

we deem to be "winnable." But the words of the Lord Jesus would turn us from such despair and favoritism: "What is impossible with men is possible with God" (v. 27).

Redemption itself contradicts all human expectations. It is God's mighty power entering a situation that, from a human viewpoint, is hopeless. God comes to Abraham, who is over a hundred years old, and to Sarah, far beyond the age of childbearing, and he promises them a natural son. Sarah laughs. But God asks, "Is anything too hard for the LORD?" (Gen. 18:14). God's omnipotence intervenes, and Isaac is born. The omnipotence is the power of God's covenant promise. The Hebrew text literally reads, "Is any word of God void of power?" God's powerful word comes into our world of sin and death and promises salvation. Isaac will continue the covenant, and from him, in God's time, will come the Messiah, who will save his people from their sins. When the Messiah comes, he will be born, not to a barren woman like Sarah, but to a virgin—an even greater manifestation of God's omnipotence. So to Mary the angel echoes God's promise to Abraham: "Nothing is impossible with God" (Luke 1:36).

So God's word never returns to him void (Isa. 55:11). It is his omnipotence, doing for us what we could never do for ourselves. Apart from God's power, we could expect only death and eternal condemnation. But he brings life in the place of death. So the resurrection of Christ becomes a paradigm of divine power in Ephesians 1:19–23, cited earlier. A God who can raise people from the dead can do anything. He is a God who is worthy of trust.

POWER AND WEAKNESS

I have so far emphasized, as Scripture does, the obvious forms of divine power as seen in creation, providence, and miracle. But by focusing on such spectacular exhibits of God's power, we may tend to think of it as a kind of brute strength that can overpower any obstacle by sheer force. As Paul Helm says,

> It is tempting to think of God as a Herculean figure, able to out-lift and out-throw and outrun all his opponents. Such a theology would be one of physical or metaphysical power; whatever his enemies can do God can do it better or more efficiently than they.[16]

16. Paul Helm, *The Providence of God* (Leicester: InterVarsity Press, 1993), 224. Much of my discussion in this section is based on Helm's, with thanks.

But, he adds, we should resist this temptation, "for the Christian view of providence reveals not only the power of God, but his weakness also."[17] How is God weak? Paul says in 1 Corinthians 1:25 that "the weakness of God is stronger than man's strength." He is thinking here of the cross of Christ (see 1:18, 23–24). Jesus was delivered up to death by wicked men, so that God would raise him up in glory, having made him an offering for the sins of his people (Acts 2:23).

Jesus refuses to be an earthly ruler, or to bring in his kingdom by the sword. Rather than kill his enemies, he dies at their hand. All of this gives every appearance of weakness. But Paul says that the cross is "the power of God and the wisdom of God" (1 Cor. 1:24). Clearly, God used this time of weakness to accomplish his most amazing—indeed, his most powerful—work, bringing life from death and defeating Satan and all his hosts.

So also, in our own time, the most powerful work of God, the gathering of people out of Satan's clutches into Christ's kingdom, is accomplished not through warfare or politics, not through the influence of money or fame, but "through the foolishness of what was preached" (1 Cor. 1:21). Jesus sends his people throughout the world, to all nations, bearing only his word (Matt. 28:18–20). But that word is "the power of God for the salvation of everyone who believes" (Rom. 1:16). God's power lies in the humble medium of preaching, and indeed in the suffering of his people (1 Peter 2:13–3:22; 4:12–19). They defeat Satan through the armor that God supplies: truth, righteousness, the gospel of peace, faith, salvation, the word of God, and prayer (Eph. 6:10–20). Thus we are "strong in the Lord and in his mighty power" (v. 10).

Some writers today believe that God is weak, in the sense that he is unable to do what he would like to do. On this view, he cannot eradicate evil, though he would like to, and he cannot make any progress without our help.[18] Scripture does not teach the weakness of God in this sense. Indeed, such a view of God contradicts a vast amount of biblical teaching on God's sovereignty, control, and power.

But it is important for us to recognize that God's sovereign, controlling power appears, not only in spectacular displays like the miracles of Jesus, but also in events in which people perceive him as weak. As I indicated in chapter 13, spectacular things in Scripture are typically preparation for the ordinary things. But God is at work in the ordinary, as much as in the extraordinary. He often works behind the scenes, and he often does his most

---

17. Ibid.

18. For examples of this view, see the references to Harold Kushner and the process theologians in chapter 9.

wonderful works through apparent defeats. So he tells Paul, "My power is made perfect in weakness" (2 Cor. 12:9). And Paul says,

> I will boast all the more gladly about my weaknesses, so that Christ's power may rest on me. That is why, for Christ's sake, I delight in weaknesses, in insults, in hardships, in persecutions, in difficulties. For when I am weak, then I am strong. (2 Cor. 12:9–10)

GOD'S WILL

God's power works according to his will. Theologians tend to regard God's will as his faculty for making decisions, as they regard his mind as his faculty of thought. But, as we saw in the preceding chapter, Scripture rarely, if ever, speaks of a divine faculty of thought distinct from the thoughts themselves, or distinct from other faculties, such as his will. Similarly, although Scripture often refers to God's will (much more often than to God's mind), it does not typically speak of his will as some metaphysical or psychological entity in God that enables him to make decisions and exercise power. Rather, God's will consists of the decisions themselves. The decision maker, as we would expect from the doctrine of simplicity, is not some part of God, or some faculty within God, but God himself, the person. God is the one who acts; his will is what he decides.

Although God's will has many dimensions, as we shall see, a simple but accurate definition would be this: God's will is anything he wants to happen.

Old Testament English translations rarely use the term *will* in reference to God, though *ratson* ("pleasure, delight, favor") is so translated in Psalms 40:8 and 143:10. In the New Testament, *thelēma* ("wish, will") is used fairly often in this way, but *boulē* and *boulēma* ("counsel") much less so. However, the concept is often expressed by the term *pleasure* (or *good pleasure*), which usually translates the Hebrew root *hafets* (as in Isa. 44:28; 46:10) and the Greek *eudokeō* (as in Eph. 1:5, 9; Phil. 2:13). God's will is what pleases him. The words *thinking* and *planning* (Hebrew *hashav*) and *choosing* (Hebrew *bahar*) are also relevant. And *way* (Heb. *derek*, Gk. *hodos*) is found many times in Scripture referring to God's will (almost always in the preceptive sense; see below). In the preceptive sense, *will* and *way* are often interchangeable (though not entirely synonymous) with the broad vocabulary of revelation: *ordinances, testimonies, laws, statutes, commandments, words*, etc.

These terms are used more or less interchangeably. The differences of nuance between the terms are not, I think, of doctrinal importance. One could not argue, for example, that one term more typically denotes God's will as decree and another term God's will as precept. If this distinction is legitimate (see below), both sides of it are expressed by each of the biblical terms.

Given these definitions of God's will (what he wants to happen, what pleases him), it is not wrong to say that God wills his own being (his necessary will) and also wills everything in creation (his free will). I don't know any passage of Scripture that makes this distinction explicitly, but I have given reasons to distinguish between necessity and freedom in God (in chap. 12), and we have also discussed necessity and freedom with regard to God's speech and knowledge (in chap. 22). God's necessary will includes his willing of the intra-Trinitarian relations: The Father willingly begets the Son, and the Father and Son willingly bring forth the Spirit, who proceeds from them. See our later discussion of the Trinity for more details of these relationships.

ANTECEDENT AND CONSEQUENT WILLS

Among human beings, there are many different kinds of wants and pleasures, and of course we tend to arrange them in priorities. Some things we want more than other things. Some we cannot achieve, so we settle for others. We postpone fulfilling some desires until others are realized. Sometimes one must be realized before another. Some are not compatible with others, and so we must choose between them. For these reasons, some of our desires are unfulfilled, temporarily or permanently.

You may recall the illustration in chapter 8 of Mike, who forces Billy to vandalize the schoolhouse. We saw there the ambiguity of the phrase *strongest desire*. Faced with Mike's threats, Billy's strongest desire in the short term was to do Mike's bidding. But in the long term, he wanted Mike to leave him alone.

Often our prioritizing of desires is due to our weakness, as in the above case, but sometimes not. Someone might desire an ice-cream cone and have easy access to one, but voluntarily postpone fulfilling that desire until finishing a piece of work. He might value finishing the job more than eating the ice-cream cone, or perhaps not. Maybe he actually values the ice cream more, but believes he will get more enjoyment from it after the job is done. So, our decision-making process is often complicated. The relationships between our many desires, and between the various means of achieving them, are complex.

Here we see some analogy to the complexities of God's will. God also has many desires, variously valued and prioritized. Some of God's desires he achieves immediately. But since he has determined to create a world in time and has given to that world a history and a goal, some of his desires, by virtue of his own eternal plan, must await the passing of time. Further, there are some good things that, by virtue of the nature of God's plan, will never be realized. I indicated in chapter 8 that God's plan is consistent with itself, respecting the integrity of creatures. If God has ordained that Joe will have exactly three children, that excludes the possibility that he will have five, even though two more children might be a good thing. And, as we saw in chapter 9, God's broad intentions for history may exclude the blessing of a world existing without any history of evil.

So theologians have made various distinctions within the larger concept of the will of God. God's will is, of course, one; but since it is complex, some have distinguished different aspects of it—different "wills." We should be careful with this language, but it does make it easier for us to consider the complications of our topic.

One distinction is between God's antecedent and consequent wills. God's general valuation of some things as good we may call his *antecedent* will; his specific choices among those good things (in view of the overall nature of the world he intends to make) may be called his *consequent* will. That distinction is legitimate, since God's eternal plan respects the integrity of the beings he intends to create and takes them into account. Again, God may genuinely value many states of affairs that are simply not compatible with the "story" he has chosen to tell (chaps. 8–9).

God's thinking, of course, is not a temporal process. All his thoughts are simultaneous, as we shall see in the following chapter. Nevertheless, it is helpful to represent God's thought *as if* it occurred in two stages: first, God evaluates every possible state of affairs; second, God chooses among these values, rejecting some and accepting others for the sake of his historical drama.

However, Roman Catholic, Lutheran, and Arminian theologians have used the antecedent-consequent distinction to make room for libertarian freedom. On their view, God's antecedent will includes the salvation of all men. His consequent will, however, awaits the (libertarian) free decisions of human beings. Those who choose to believe, God blesses; those who do not, he condemns to eternal punishment. These blessings and curses come by his consequent will.

In my view, these theologians are right in saying that God antecedently wants everyone to be saved. We shall look more closely at this question later, but universal salvation is certainly a good thing, a desirable state of affairs. They are also right to claim that, in view of the actual historical situation, God does not bring that result to pass. There is no harm in calling this second volition "consequent." In his eternal plan, God does determine not to achieve certain good things, at least partly because of the nature of the creatures he intends to create.

The Roman Catholic, Lutheran, and Arminian theologians are wrong, however, in saying that God's consequent will is dependent on the (libertarian) free decisions of man. I have given many reasons for denying the truth of libertarianism.

DECRETIVE AND PRECEPTIVE WILLS

Reformed theologians have often rejected the antecedent-consequent distinction, because of its association with libertarian freedom. But they have adopted a rather similar distinction, between God's decretive and preceptive wills. God's *decretive* will is simply what in chapter 16 we called God's decree. It is his eternal purpose, by which he foreordains everything that comes to pass. God's *preceptive* will is his valuations, particularly as revealed to us in his Word (his "precepts"). The decretive will focuses on God's lordship attribute of control, the preceptive will on the lordship attribute of authority. God's decretive will cannot be successfully opposed; what God has decreed will certainly take place. It is possible, however, for creatures to disobey God's preceptive will—and they often do so.

The decretive will is sometimes called "the will of God's good pleasure" (*beneplacitum*). This is somewhat misleading, because Scripture speaks of God's "pleasure" in both decretive and preceptive senses: for example, decretive in Psalm 51:18 and Isaiah 46:10, and preceptive in Psalms 5:4 and 103:21. Some have also called the decretive will God's hidden or secret will, but that too is misleading, since God reveals some of his decrees through his Word.

For that reason, I hesitate also to call the preceptive will the revealed will (*signum*, "signified will"), though that language has often been used for this concept. *Preceptive* is also somewhat misleading, for it does not always have to do with literal precepts (God's laws, commandments). Sometimes God's preceptive will refers not to precepts, but to states of affairs that God sees as desirable, but which he chooses not to bring about (as in Ezek. 18:23; 2 Peter 3:9). Still I will use *preceptive* because of customary usage, and because I don't know of any better term.

How does this distinction compare with the antecedent-consequent distinction? God's preceptive will, like the antecedent will, consists of his valuation of every possible and actual state of affairs. His decretive will, like the consequent will, determines what will actually happen. The difference is that the concept of a decretive will excludes libertarianism. God's decision as to what will actually happen is not based on his foreknowledge of the libertarian free choices of men. It is based instead on his decision to write his historical drama in a certain way.

It is therefore disingenuous for Arminians to criticize Calvinists for teaching "two wills" in God. Arminianism—indeed, all theologies—recognize some complexity in God's will (though confessing its ultimate unity), and theologians of all persuasions have sometimes talked about multiple wills in God. Arminians and even open theists also like to distinguish God's "will of permission," concerning which Paul Helm says,

> Suppose . . . there are areas of human action (including human evil action) which God not only does not will, but which he does not know will happen until the events occur. Nevertheless, the events in these areas are *permitted* by God, albeit in a very loose and weak sense. For if God did not allow them, and in some sense support them, then they would not occur. . . . God then wills (permits) what he does not will (command). . . . So it is not an advantage of that view that it avoids having to think of God having two "wills."[19]

Does Scripture warrant this distinction? Here are some passages that use the words *thought, intent, pleasure, purpose, counsel,* and *will* to refer to God's decretive will:

> You intended to harm me, but God intended it for good to accomplish what is now being done, the saving of many lives. (Gen. 50:20)

> At that time Jesus said, "I praise you, Father, Lord of heaven and earth, because you have hidden these things from the wise and learned, and revealed them to little children. Yes, Father, for this was your good pleasure." (Matt. 11:25–26)

---

19. Helm, *The Providence of God*, 132. The Arminian exegete I. Howard Marshall admits that there is a duality within the will of God, in "Universal Grace and Atonement in the Pastoral Epistles," in *The Grace of God and the Will of Man*, ed. Clark Pinnock (Grand Rapids: Zondervan, 1989), 56: "We must certainly distinguish between what God would like to happen and what he actually does will to happen, and both of these things can be spoken of as God's will."

This man was handed over to you by God's set purpose and fore-knowledge; and you, with the help of wicked men, put him to death by nailing him to the cross. (Acts 2:23)

Therefore God has mercy on whom he wants to have mercy, and he hardens whom he wants to harden.

　　One of you will say to me: "Then why does God still blame us? For who resists his will?" (Rom. 9:18–19)

In him we were also chosen, having been predestined according to the plan of him who works out everything in conformity with the purpose of his will. (Eph. 1:11)

(Cf. Pss. 51:18; 115:3; Isa. 46:10; Jer. 49:20; 50:45; Dan. 4:17; James 1:18; Rev. 4:11.) I would say that God's "paths" in Romans 11:33 should also be taken in the decretive sense, although elsewhere the term is almost always preceptive.

　　Here are some passages in which these terms are used in a preceptive sense:

Not everyone who says to me, "Lord, Lord," will enter the king-dom of heaven, but only he who does the will of my Father who is in heaven. (Matt. 7:21)

Therefore do not be foolish, but understand what the Lord's will is. (Eph. 5:17; cf. 6:6)[20]

(Cf. Pss. 5:4; 103:21; Matt. 12:50; John 4:34; 7:17; Rom. 12:2; 1 Thess. 4:3; 5:18; Heb. 13:21; 1 Peter 4:2.) These passages refer literally to precepts of God.

　　The following passages refer, not to precepts as such, but to desirable (and thus preceptive) states of affairs that God does not ordain:

Do I take any pleasure in the death of the wicked? declares the Sov-ereign LORD. Rather, am I not pleased when they turn from their ways and live? (Ezek. 18:23)

The Lord is not slow in keeping his promise, as some understand slowness. He is patient with you, not wanting anyone to perish, but everyone to come to repentance. (2 Peter 3:9)

There are other passages in which God expresses a desire for repentance from human beings, which may or may not be forthcoming: Isaiah 30:18; 65:2; Lamentations 3:31–36; Ezekiel 33:11; Hosea 11:7–8.

---

20. *Will* here is *thelēma*, which in 1:11 is clearly decretive.

DOES GOD DESIRE THE SALVATION OF ALL?

If God desires people to repent of sin, then certainly he desires them to be saved, for salvation is the fruit of such repentance. Some Calvinists, however, have denied this conclusion, reasoning that God cannot possibly desire something that never takes place. But I have dealt with that objection already. Scripture often represents God as desiring things that never take place. As we have seen, he wants all people to repent of sin, yet we know that many people never repent. And there are many other examples. God desires all people to turn from false gods and idols, hold his name in reverence, remember the Sabbath, honor their parents, and so on. But those desires are not always fulfilled.

The reason is that God's "desires" in this sense are expressions of his preceptive will, not his decretive will. His decretive desires always come to pass; his preceptive desires are not always fulfilled. So there is nothing contrary to Calvinistic theology in the assertion that God wants everyone to be saved.

Furthermore, there are specific passages that lead to this conclusion. We saw in chapter 20 that in some senses God is gracious and loving to all his creatures, including those that are unrighteous (Matt. 5:44–48).[21] God sends rain and fruitful seasons to everybody and even "fills [their] hearts with joy" (Acts 14:17). God desires the best for his creatures, and the very best for them, of course, is salvation in Christ.

In Deuteronomy 5:29, God expresses his desire in passionate terms:

> Oh, that their hearts would be inclined to fear me and keep all my commands always, so that it might go well with them and their children forever! (cf. Deut. 32:29; Ps. 81:13–14; Isa. 48:18)

In these passages, God expresses an intense desire, not only for obedience, but also for the consequence of obedience, namely, the covenant blessing (cf. Ex. 20:12) of long life and prosperity. Ultimately, the covenant blessing is nothing less than heaven itself—eternal fellowship with God.

Divine passion is even more obvious in Matthew 23:37 (Luke 13:34), where Jesus weeps over Jerusalem, saying,

> O Jerusalem, Jerusalem, you who kill the prophets and stone those sent to you, how often I have longed to gather your children to-

21. For further discussion of these passages, see John Murray, "The Free Offer of the Gospel," in *Collected Writings of John Murray* (Edinburgh: Banner of Truth Trust, 1982), 4:113–32. In this section I am much indebted to Murray's article.

gether, as a hen gathers her chicks under her wings, but you were not willing.

The gathering here certainly includes the blessings of salvation. Jesus wants the people of Jerusalem to be gathered to him.

In the prophecy of Ezekiel, God's desire for human repentance is also a desire that the repentant one will have life. *Life* is often a biblical summary of God's salvation that brings us out of death (as in Eph. 2:1–7). Through Ezekiel, God says:

> Do I take any pleasure in the death of the wicked? declares the Sovereign Lord. Rather, am I not pleased when they turn from their ways and live? (Ezek. 18:23)

> Rid yourselves of all the offenses you have committed, and get a new heart and a new spirit. Why will you die, O house of Israel? For I take no pleasure in the death of anyone, declares the Sovereign Lord. Repent and live! (vv. 31–32)

> Say to them, "As surely as I live, declares the Sovereign Lord, I take no pleasure in the death of the wicked, but rather that they turn from their ways and live. Turn! Turn from your evil ways! Why will you die, O house of Israel?" (33:11)

In Isaiah 45:22, God again cries out:

> Turn to me and be saved,
> all you ends of the earth;
> for I am God, and there is no other.

Murray argues that the range of this plea is not universal in a merely ethnic sense (all nations, but not all individuals), but embraces all individuals.[22] Part of his argument is based on the fact that the verse (and the context) emphasizes the uniqueness of the true God and his prerogatives over his entire creation. His plea must be as broad as his lordship authority.

Second Peter 3:9 teaches the same desire on the part of God:

> The Lord is not slow in keeping his promise, as some understand slowness. He is patient with you, not wanting anyone to perish, but everyone to come to repentance.

Those who want to limit the reference of this passage to the elect sometimes focus on "you," suggesting that this limits the reference to believers.

22. Ibid., 126–27.

Like other New Testament letters, this one is written to the church, and it presumes faith on the part of its readers. Yet, also like other letters, this one recognizes that professing believers are subject to many temptations in this life and that some do fall away. When they fall away permanently, they thereby show that they never had real faith. So, in addressing believers, Peter is not assuming that all his readers are among the elect. And "patience" (*makrothymei*) here is an attitude that, according to other passages, God shows to the reprobate (Rom. 2:4; 9:22). The passage itself makes no distinction between elect and reprobate.

So, Peter may be expressing God's desire that everyone in the church will come to repentance, but if his focus is thus on the church, he is not distinguishing between elect and reprobate within the church. My own view, however, is that his thought in this verse goes beyond the church: "anyone" and "everyone" are not necessarily included among "you." So, after describing God's patience with his people in the church, Peter looks beyond them, asserting God's desire for universal human repentance.

Murray does not deal with 1 Timothy 2:4, but it is much discussed in this connection. That verse says that God "wants all men to be saved and to come to a knowledge of the truth." It is certainly plausible to take "all" here to refer to ethnic universalism[23] (see the discussion of Isaiah 45:22, above), especially since verses 1 and 2 urge prayer "for everyone—for kings and all those in authority, that we may live peaceful and quiet lives in all godliness and holiness." Reformed commentators typically insist that verses 1–2 cannot be universal except in the sense "all sorts." They then draw the conclusion that God desires the salvation of "all men without distinction of rank, race, or nationality,"[24] but not the salvation of every individual.

But the parallel between the language here and that of passages like Isaiah 45:22 might lead us to question this interpretation. And, in my view, verses 1–2 do not have to be taken only as a universalism of classes of people. To pray for a king is at the same time to pray for his people as individuals. Hendriksen thinks it impossible that in verses 1–2 Paul could be asking prayer for every person on earth. There is no time, he thinks, to do this in more than a "very vague and global way."[25] But it would also be impossible to pray specifically for every king and magistrate on the face of the earth. In any case, Paul's desire is simply that we pray for the nations in

23. Of course, there are many passages of Scripture in which "all" does not refer to every human being. "All" is often limited by its context, as in Mark 1:37; 5:20; 11:32; Luke 3:15; John 3:26; Rom. 5:18; 1 Cor. 15:22; Titus 2:11.

24. William Hendriksen, A Commentary on the Epistles to Timothy and Titus (London: Banner of Truth, 1960), 95.

25. Ibid., 94.

the spirit of God's blessing to Abraham, that God's grace will be applied to all people throughout the world and produce peace.

The real barrier to taking 2:4 in a way similar to the other passages we have discussed is not verses 1–2, but verses 5–6:

> For there is one God and one mediator between God and men, the man Christ Jesus, who gave himself as a ransom for all men—the testimony given in its proper time.

If we see verse 4 as indicating God's desire for the salvation of every individual, must we not then take Jesus' "ransom" also in a universalistic sense, contrary to the Reformed doctrine of limited atonement? But the point of verses 5–6, in my view, is very similar to the point made in Isaiah 45:22 and its context. Notice how in both Isaiah 45:22 and 1 Timothy 2:4–6, the thought moves from God's desire that all be saved to the exclusiveness of God's prerogatives and saving power. My own inclination is to take verses 5–6 not as enumerating those for whom atonement is made, but as describing the *exclusiveness* of God's saving work in Christ. His ransom is for all men in the sense that there is no other.

If we read the passage this way, there is no reason, dogmatic or exegetical, why we should not take verse 4 (which is so like the other verses we have explored) to indicate God's desire for the salvation of everyone. I am inclined to take this position, though I don't regard the question as fully closed. My main point, however, is that we should not allow our exegesis of this passage to be prejudiced by the dogmatic view that God cannot desire the salvation of all. If this passage does not teach such a desire, many other passages do.

WHICH IS THE REAL WILL OF GOD?

Bavinck says:

> Roman Catholics, Lutherans, Remonstrants, etc., proceed from the "expressed or signified will" [i.e., preceptive will]; they regard this as God's real will consisting in this: that God does not will sin but merely permits it; that he wills the salvation of all men; that he offers grace to all; etc.; then, after man has decided, God conforms himself to that decision and determines what he wills, namely, salvation for those who believe, perdition for those who don't believe. The "consequent will" follows man's decision and is not the real, essential will of God; it is the act of God which is occasioned by

man's deportment. The Reformed, on the other hand, proceeded from "the will of God's good pleasure" [i.e., his decretive will]; they regarded this as the real, the essential will of God. That will is always fulfilled; it always effects its object; it is eternal and immutable. The "expressed" or "signified" will [i.e., the preceptive will], on the contrary, is God's precept revealed in the Law and in the Gospel; it is for us the rule of life.[26]

Bavinck here presents an adequate summary of the differences between the Reformed and their major opponents. I cite him only to dissent from both parties in their desire to identify one will of God as the "real" will.

God's decrees and his precepts both represent divine values. It is true that the decrees always take effect, whereas the precepts do not necessarily do so. That seems to give special honor to the decrees above the precepts. But one can also argue the other way: God's precepts represent his ideals, which describe states of affairs that are often far more excellent than the world as it has been decreed. God's precepts, for example, demand a world in which everyone honors the true God, in which everyone honors his parents, in which there is no murder or even murderous anger, etc. Would not such a world be better than the one in which we live?[27]

God's precepts also express goals, to which his decrees are means. The new heaven and the new earth are a place where righteousness dwells (2 Peter 3:13; cf. Matt. 6:33). So one could argue that God's preceptive will is his "real" will, the one he seeks to achieve in this world through the history of redemption.[28]

But I will not argue that point. Rather, I will insist that Scripture does not value one will above another, or compare one unfavorably to the other. The fact is that both these precepts and these decrees are divine desires and should be given the highest honor. God's precepts are an object of worship in the Psalms (56:4, 10) and are worthy of the most profound meditation (Ps. 1) and obedience (Ps. 119). God's decrees represent his control, and his precepts represent his authority. We honor both equally as we honor the Lord.

---

26. DG, 238.
27. See chapter 9 for an argument that this is not necessarily "the best of all possible worlds."
28. I have argued in previous chapters that God's decision to make a world in time lies behind some of the more difficult problems of theology. See chapter 9 on the relevance of this consideration to the problem of evil. So here we should note that the temporality of creation has some bearing on the problem of understanding the duality of will in God.

A THIRD WILL?

Christians have often spoken of "God's will" in ways that seem to escape the classifications "preceptive" and "decretive." A typical case is when a church member asks his pastor how he can find "God's will for my life." In answering this question, the pastor would be rather unkind to talk about God's decretive will ("God's will for your life is whatever happens"). And to refer to God's preceptive will seems to miss the point ("God's will for you is found entirely in the Bible, *sola Scriptura*"). The church member is not asking for God's law or the gospel. He is asking whether and how he can get guidance from God in making practical decisions: whether or whom to marry, what to study in school, what field of work to enter, and so on. So, is "God's will for my life" a third aspect of God's will, coordinate with the other two?

This kind of question has opened the door to dangerous subjectivism. Christians have sometimes been told that the will of God in this sense comes through as a strong feeling given by God. Feelings do play an important role in human knowledge, both of Scripture and of other things.[29] But *sola Scriptura* means that Scripture alone is the complete transcript of God's words to us. Emotions (together with reason, imagination, sense percep- tion, etc.) can help us understand and apply Scripture to our circumstances, but they cannot add anything to the words of God in the Bible. That is, emotions can sometimes make us aware of considerations that are relevant to a decision. But apart from Scripture, they cannot obligate us to make one decision rather than another. Only Scripture provides divine norms, norms establishing an ultimate obligation.

Further, Scripture itself never advises God's people to expect God to lead them through feelings apart from his Word. To walk in God's ways is to walk according to his testimonies, his ordinances, his words.

It would be wrong, however, to tell an inquirer that God does not guide his people in making specific decisions in life. Scripture has much to say about wisdom, which God gives liberally to his people (James 1:5). As we saw in the preceding chapter, wisdom begins with the fear of the Lord (Ps. 111:10) and the following of his precepts. A godly person seeks, through wisdom given by the Spirit, to *apply* the precepts of the Lord to the circumstances of life.[30]

Sometimes wisdom dictates or rules out a particular course of action. For example, a wise person will not fail to worship the true God, and he will

---

29. See *DKG*, 152–64, 335–40.
30. For discussion of the concept of application, see *DKG*, 81–85, 93–98.

not commit adultery. But sometimes wisdom leaves open a range of options. It calls for a man to support his family (1 Tim. 5:8), but it does not dictate precisely what kind of shelter, clothing, or food to provide. One reason for the confusion about "God's will for my life" is that the phrase suggests only one possible course of action. We might think that if we have a choice between living in San Diego or living in Philadelphia, then God wants us to live in one city, but not the other. But, as a matter of fact, either choice might well be acceptable to God. If our motives are right and neither move would involve us in conflict with God's law, then we can assume that either decision is within the will of God.

But that choice may need some refinement. For example, my choice to live in Philadelphia may not conflict with God's Word in any big, obvious ways. But, after prayerful meditation, it may become evident that I could make much better use of my gifts in San Diego. Or it may be that the situation in Philadelphia would offer more temptations to sin, which, knowing myself, I would be best off avoiding. Or it may be that there are better opportunities for Christian growth or service in one place or the other. All of these must be weighed in the decision, and there might be several pluses and minuses on each side.

Wisdom is more than insight in obeying Scripture in the big, obvious ways. According to Proverbs, it is also intelligence, knowledge, skills, understanding circumstances (including their likely consequences), self-knowledge, and understanding other people. It is a discernment that comes through reading Scripture, but a reading that arises out of spiritual maturity and experience.[31] Thus, it is the ability to weigh the pluses and minuses of the alternatives before us. This, too, involves obeying Scripture, for Scripture requires us to be wise, to redeem opportunities.[32]

God wants us, then, to make our decisions as wisely as possible. This is his preceptive will. In the example given above, taking into account all the pluses and minuses of moving to Philadelphia or San Diego, it may well be that one decision is wiser than the other—although neither choice may be wiser. When I choose one cabbage over another in the supermarket, it usually is the case that neither choice is wiser than the other. But if one decision is wiser than the other, then it is correct to say that that choice is the will of God, in the preceptive sense. For God's preceptive will in-

31. See such passages as Rom. 12:1–2; Eph. 5:8–10; Phil. 1:9–10; Heb. 5:12–14, in which knowledge of God's will comes through regeneration, sanctification, and testing. I discuss this in DKG, 153–55.

32. For more helpful discussion of the ways in which God leads us to make such choices, see Edmund P. Clowney, Called to the Ministry (Philadelphia: Westminster Theological Seminary, 1964); James C. Petty, Step by Step (Phillipsburg, N.J.: P&R Publishing, 1999).

cludes not only the words of Scripture itself, but the good and necessary consequences of Scripture.[33] When one choice is wiser than the other, God's preceptive will tells me to make the wiser choice. On the other hand, if the two possible decisions are indistinguishable in terms of wisdom, then either decision is within God's will.

God guides his people, then, through Spirit-given wisdom, based on Scripture—wisdom that enables us to understand what is at stake in our choices and to evaluate those circumstances in a godly way. Through such guidance, God reveals to us our vocation, to invoke a good Reformation term.

Therefore, we do not absolutely need a third category of God's will, in addition to his decretive and preceptive wills. But we should not oversimplify our understanding of God's preceptive will. It includes, not only the explicit words of Scripture, but the words of Scripture applied to each of us, using the God-given gifts of intelligence, spiritual discernment, and so on.

However, a third category of God's will might be helpful. We do, after all, have some leeway as to how to divide the pie of biblical teaching. Strictly speaking, of course, only one category is needed: God's "wants" or "desires." But, as we have seen, God has many different kinds of desires, so that some analysis is helpful. Scripture does not explicitly distinguish between decrees and precepts, but, as we look at Scripture, we see that it speaks of God's will in these two ways. So, to help us make sense of scriptural teaching, we distinguish between God's decretive will and his preceptive will. Perhaps it would be helpful to make wisdom or vocation a third category, in order to avoid misunderstandings. After all, it would be wrong, as we have seen, to tell an inquirer that God's will includes only his decrees and the Bible, as if to imply that God does not guide us in specific ways.

So I would suggest the following teaching for such inquirers: God guides us through his decrees, his written Word, and Spirit-given wisdom. By his decrees, he opens doors and closes them, giving us some opportunities and withholding others, but those circumstances of our lives do not in themselves tell us how to behave. By Scripture, he tells us what he wants us to do, showing us how to respond to these circumstances. By Spirit-given wisdom, God enables us to apply Scripture to circumstances.

Scripture speaks of "God's will" to describe the outcome of using wisdom to apply Scripture in our lives in Romans 12:2 and Ephesians 5:10 (cf. Phil. 1:9–10; Heb. 5:14). God certainly knows what kind of life we would live if all our decisions were as wise as possible. We should not hesitate, then, to describe that life as God's will. This is not to say that if we make

33. WCF, 1.6. On the inclusion of applications among these consequences, see *DKG*, 84.

an unwise decision, we have missed out forever on God's will for our lives. After we make an unwise decision, we should turn to God's wisdom again, confident that it will lead us in the path of blessing.

These three categories—decree, precept, and wisdom—are perspectivally related. God decrees to act according to his precepts and his wisdom. His precepts include the teaching that we should bow before God's sovereign decrees and seek his wisdom. And his wisdom is displayed both in his decrees and in his Word. In terms of the overall triadic structure of my theology of lordship, the decree is situational, the precept is normative, and wisdom is existential.

CHAPTER 24

Lord of Time

In this chapter, I shall continue my discussion of God's attributes of power. Here we shall look at his attributes of infinity, eternity, temporal omnipresence, and unchangeability. These (especially the last three) have to do with God's relationships to time. Theologians do not generally refer to these as attributes of power, but as metaphysical attributes (God's relations to the metaphysical structure of creation), incommunicable attributes (since none of these can be predicated of creatures), attributes of transcendence (since they indicate God's transcendence over time), and so on. See chapter 19 for my objections to these classifications. I prefer to call them attributes of power, because I reject certain assumptions of the other classifications, and because I see God's transcendence, not as his absence from the space-time world, but as his presence as the Lord. Eternity, for example, as I shall explain it, does not primarily mean that God is "outside" time (though it is better to say that he is "outside" than that he is "inside"), but rather that he is present in time as the Lord, with full control over the temporal sequence.

GOD'S INFINITY

I shall say little about God's *infinity*, for the word is almost never used in Scripture, and what can be said about it is best said under other headings. Only Psalm 147:5, in certain translations (e.g., KJV and NASB), can be said to regard infinity as a divine attribute, and there it is specifically his "understanding" that is described as infinite. On that, see our discussion of omniscience in chapter 22.

To Plato and some other Greek writers, infinity (*apeiron*, a term not used in Scripture) is a negative quality. To them, being is indistinguishable from nothingness until it takes on distinct characteristics (*perata*), which "limit" it. So for Plato and Aristotle, matter is nothing until limited by form. Plotinus, however, recognized a positive sense of infinity as well as a negative sense. Like Plato, Plotinus taught that matter is infinite in the bad sense. But the divine being, Plotinus's One, is infinite in the sense of being "above" and "beyond" all distinct characteristics.[1]

Neither of these concepts of infinity is really appropriate to the God of Scripture. Obviously, God is not like the matter of Plato and Aristotle, lacking definite characteristics. Nor, as we have seen, is he "above" or "beyond" all of these. As I indicated in chapter 7, God is not transcendent in the sense of being beyond human predication. He is transcendent as the Lord.

As Lord, he has distinct characteristics. He even has limits in one sense, as we saw in our discussion of omnipotence in the preceding chapter. There we saw that God cannot simply do anything in the way the nominalists imagined. He can do only what is consistent with his other attributes: what is wise, loving, righteous, and so on. Any positive attribute is a delimitation in one sense, for it excludes what is contrary to that attribute; it excludes some divine modes of being that would otherwise be possible. But God is limited only by his own nature, only by himself, not by anything in creation. No creature may determine what God is, or keep him from doing what he wants to do. If we choose to use the term *infinity*, we should use it primarily in that way, simply to indicate that no creature can place any limits on God. *Infinite*, then, will simply be the opposite of *finite*—another way of expressing the biblical Creator-creature distinction.

More specific knowledge of God's infinity is best reserved for the discussion of other attributes. Our discussions of omnipotence and omniscience have shown what might be meant by "infinite power" and "infinite knowledge." When we speak of infinity in relation to other attributes, the term comes very close to meaning "perfection" (see chap. 20). In this chapter, we will consider some attributes often described as infinite. As Bavinck says, "Infinity applied to time is eternity," and "infinity applied to space is omnipresence" (or immensity, as I would prefer).[2] So we will explore God's infinity as we discuss his other perfections.

1. See H. P. Owen, "Infinity in Theology, Metaphysics," in *The Encyclopedia of Philosophy*, ed. Paul Edwards (New York: Macmillan and Free Press, 1967), 190–93.
2. DG, 154, 157.

Accordingly, we should understand God's infinity in either or both of these ways: (1) No creature can place limits on God, and/or (2) God's attributes are supremely perfect, without any flaw.[3]

GOD'S ETERNITY

The terms *eternity* and *eternal* in Scripture represent several Hebrew (*'ad, 'olam, qedem*) and Greek (*aidios, aiōn, aiōnios*) terms. These terms can refer to long periods of time or even to endless duration through time. Whether they can also refer to a radical transcendence of time itself is a possibility that we will explore below. *Aiōn*, when not used to refer to a finite period of time, tends to be found as the genitive *tōn aiōnōn* ("of the ages"), the adjective *aiōnios*, or in phrases such as *eis ton aiōna* ("to the age"), *eis tous aiōnas*, and *eis tous aiōnas tōn aiōnōn* ("to the ages of the ages").

In the Bible, *eternal* usually refers, not to God's nature, but to the quality of life or punishment that awaits human beings: eternal life or eternal death. But here are some of the rare uses of these terms as divine attributes, or referring to God's other attributes or decrees:

> Abraham planted a tamarisk tree in Beersheba, and there he called upon the name of the LORD, the Eternal ['*olam*] God. (Gen. 21:33)

> The eternal [*qedem*] God is your refuge, and underneath are the everlasting arms. (Deut. 33:27)

> For since the creation of the world God's invisible qualities—his eternal [*aidios*] power and divine nature—have been clearly seen, being understood from what has been made, so that men are without excuse. (Rom. 1:20)

> . . . according to his eternal [*tōn aiōnōn*] purpose which he accomplished in Christ Jesus our Lord. (Eph. 3:11)

Compare also 1 Timothy 1:17 ("the King eternal") and Hebrews 9:14 ("the eternal Spirit").

Now there has been a long debate as to the definition of eternity as a divine attribute. The Greek philosophers Parmenides, Plato, and Plotinus understood "eternal" reality to be timeless—beyond or outside time. For Parmenides' Being, Plato's Forms, and Plotinus's One, there is no change, no before or after.

---

3. Neither of these concepts has much to do with mathematical infinity. Introducing that concept into discussions of God's nature is usually unhelpful, in my view.

Christian theologians have also spoken of God as timeless, as existing before time,[4] and so on. This language became especially common during the Arian controversy of the fourth century, when orthodox theologians opposed the Arian contention that there was "a time when the Son was not."[5] No, they replied, both the Father and the Son existed before time. Time is their creation. So they themselves are essentially timeless.[6] Augustine says to God in his *Confessions*,

> Thy present day does not give way to tomorrow, nor indeed, does it take the place of yesterday. Thy present day is eternity.[7]

The classic statement of God's atemporal eternity is found in Boethius's *Consolation of Philosophy*, 5.6. There he defines God's eternity as "the simultaneous and perfect possession of infinite life." This definition held sway in the church for many centuries. We can find its equivalent in Anselm[8] and Aquinas[9] (but not in Duns Scotus and William of Occam), and in the major post-Reformation theologies.[10]

The Socinians opposed this view. They held that God's eternity means merely that he has no beginning nor end, not that he is above or outside of time itself. On their view, God experiences temporal succession as we do. Their position was a necessary implication of their denial of exhaustive divine foreknowledge, which I discussed in chapter 22.

---

4. Strictly speaking it is improper to speak of something occurring before time, because *before* is primarily a temporal expression. Without time, there is no before or after. However, it is convenient for those who believe that time is part of the creation to refer to God's eternal nature apart from creation by the phrase *before time*. There are spatial uses of *before* as well, as in "stand before the king," and perhaps we can think of God "standing before time" in that sort of way, though even that is a metaphor.

5. More precisely, the Arians asserted a "when" (*pote*) when the Son was not, rather than a "time" (*chronos*). The difference, in my judgment, is rhetorical rather than substantial.

6. Hilary of Poitiers is a particularly strong example. In *On the Trinity*, 8.40, he says, "Again, let him who holds the Son to have become Son in time and by His Incarnation, learn that through Him are all things and we through Him, and that His timeless Infinity was creating all things before time was."

7. Augustine, *Confessions*, 11.3.

8. Anselm, *Proslogium*, chap. 19, and *Monologium*, chap. 22, in *St. Anselm: Basic Writings*, ed. S. N. Deane (La Salle, Ill.: Open Court, 1962), 25, 78–81.

9. SCG, 1. He says (sec. 3), "There is, therefore, no *before* or *after* in Him; He does not have being after non-being, nor non-being after being, nor can any succession be found in his being."

10. Luther and Calvin themselves did not concern themselves much with the definition of eternity, or in general with defining divine attributes. But their successors resumed the discussion, generally following the Boethian-Augustinian approach. See *RD*, 65. Francis Turretin's discussion is representative, in *Institutes of Elenctic Theology* (Phillipsburg, N.J.: P&R Publishing, 1992), 1:202–4.

In the nineteenth century, some conservative Reformed theologians questioned the Boethian-Augustinian view. James H. Thornwell seemed to be of two minds on the subject. He more or less affirmed the Boethian tradition, but at the same time he commented that "these are abortive efforts to realize in thought what transcends the conditions of our consciousness."[11] The traditional formula, in his view, is a mere negation; it tells us nothing positive about God's eternity, which remains a mystery.

Charles Hodge affirmed that all "external events" are

> ever present to the mind of God. . . . He sees how they succeed each other in time, as we see a passing pageant, all of which we may take in in one view.[12]

But he was agnostic "concerning the relation of succession to the thoughts and acts of God."[13] He wondered if God can be truly personal if there is no temporal succession among his thoughts. Nevertheless, he believed that even in human life there are temporal anomalies in our thought processes, as when someone recalls, on his death bed, a language he had spoken long ago, but had seemingly forgotten, and he granted that there could be even more temporal oddities in the thought of God.[14]

Even more skeptical of the tradition was the twentieth-century Presbyterian theologian James Oliver Buswell, who argued that if God is timeless, it is meaningless to say that the elect are predestined before the foundation of the world, and that if the past is not past for God, we are yet in our sins.[15]

Oscar Cullmann argued that "primitive Christianity knows nothing of a timeless God."[16] One argument arises from his study of the term *aiōn* in its various forms. He says that since *aiōn* is used for both a limited and an unlimited duration ("eternity"), eternity must be similar to a limited duration, rather than something drastically different. So eternity is not timelessness, but rather a period of time of unlimited duration. *Aiōnes*, the plural form often used in expressions for eternity, represents "the linking of an unlimited series of limited world periods."[17]

---

11. *The Collected Works of James Henley Thornwell* (Edinburgh: Banner of Truth, 1974), 1:192.
12. Charles Hodge, *Systematic Theology* (Grand Rapids: Eerdmans, n.d.), 1:388.
13. Ibid.
14. Ibid., 388–89.
15. James Oliver Buswell, *A Systematic Theology of the Christian Religion* (Grand Rapids: Zondervan, 1962), 42–47.
16. Oscar Cullmann, *Christ and Time* (Philadelphia: Westminster Press, 1950), 65.
17. Ibid., 46.

James Barr, however, took issue with Cullmann, arguing that plurals need not be "akin" to singulars in the way and to the degree that Cullmann thought necessary.[18]

A new phase of the discussion began with Nicholas Wolterstorff's article, "God Everlasting."[19] He argued, first, that productive acts (like creation, providence, and redemption) occurring in time presuppose a temporal cause (in this case, a temporal God). Second, God's redemptive actions in Scripture are temporally successive, indicating that the biblical writers "regard God as having a time-strand of his own."[20] Third, Wolterstorff argued that unless God is temporal, he cannot know propositions like "event A is happening now," for only a temporal being can know propositions that are temporally "indexed." These arguments, with others, have been accepted by many. So at present one may speak of a consensus among theistic philosophers that God is in time. Joining this consensus are the process theologians and the open theists.[21] One vigorous, thorough, and cogent philosophical dissent from this consensus, however, has been written Paul Helm.[22]

As with the denial of exhaustive divine foreknowledge (chap. 22), the strongest motive for this consensus, in my opinion, is the desire of these thinkers to make room for libertarian freedom. If God is timelessly eternal, it is difficult to argue that he is ignorant of what to us is future, for he sees all times equally from his eternal vantage point. And if God knows exhaustively what to us is future, then he knows the free acts of human beings before they take place.[23] And if he knows these actions in advance, it is hard to argue that they are free in a libertarian sense.

ARGUMENTS AGAINST DIVINE ATEMPORALITY

Here I shall look at some of the philosophical and theological arguments. We shall look at the biblical data in a later section. The philosophical debates are more complicated than what I present here. I am trying to sim-

18. James Barr, *Biblical Words for Time* (Naperville, Ill.: Alec R. Allenson, 1969), 67–85.
19. In *God and the Good,* ed. Clifton Orlebeke and Lewis Smedes (Grand Rapids: Eerdmans, 1975), 181–203.
20. Ibid., 193.
21. Another philosophical movement, earlier in the twentieth century, that affirmed divine temporality, was the "Boston personalist" movement of Edgar Sheffield Brightman and others. Brightman says that "the divine eternity means God's endless duration," in *The Finding of God* (New York: Abingdon Press, 1931), 131.
22. Paul Helm, *Eternal God: A Study of God Without Time* (Oxford: Clarendon Press, 1988).
23. The "before" is, of course, from our temporal point of view.

plify and compress, to present the gist of the arguments in each case with a summary evaluation.

I shall argue later that God is indeed temporal in his immanence, but that he is (most likely) atemporal in his transcendence. He exists in time as he exists throughout creation. But he also (I say with some reservations) exists beyond time, as he exists beyond creation. So in this section we will consider arguments to the effect that God is *merely* temporal, with no supratemporal existence. That is the position I will refer to as "temporalism."

1. Wolterstorff's first argument above does not persuade me. It is not obvious that an atemporal being could not bring about a series of events in a time sequence without himself being part of the sequence. The author-character model we explored in chapters 8 and 9 is a suitable analogy of such causation. Wolterstorff's first argument also suggests that every event presupposes a chain of temporal causes without beginning, an idea that falls prey to the standard criticisms of an "actual infinite." If the chain of causes has no first member, then it has no ultimate cause.

2. Passing over Wolterstorff's second argument for the moment, let us consider his third argument. We discussed that, in effect, in chapters 22 and 23. In my discussion of omnipotence, I argued that there are some acts that God cannot do, because they are not appropriate to him for one reason or other. These include not only lying and stealing, but also actions like paying taxes, eating dinner, or making a stone too big for him to lift. These "inabilities" do not cast any doubt upon his might and power. Similarly, in the discussion of omniscience, we saw that there are some kinds of knowledge (as of "what time it is now") that presuppose a finite, temporal point of view. But God's "ignorance" of these propositions does not lead us to reconsider his omniscience, because (1) he knows all the facts that are expressed by these propositions, from his own transcendent point of view, (2) he can know these facts from a human point of view by becoming incarnate, and (3) in one sense, he always knows facts from every finite point of view, because of his immanence in the world.

3. Some have said, further, that if God is supratemporal, then time must be unreal.[24] But surely that does not follow. God is the Creator; the world is his creature. The creature is radically different from the Creator. But it is not thereby unreal. God's handiwork is as real as it can be. If God is atemporal, but made time as part of his creation, then time is very much part

24. Clark Pinnock, "God Limits His Knowledge," in *Predestination and Free Will*, ed. David Basinger and Randall Basinger (Downers Grove, Ill.: InterVarsity Press, 1986), 156. See also Helm's discussion of Norman Kretzmann's position in "Timelessness and Foreknowledge," *Mind* 84 (1975): 515–27.

of the creaturely reality, though not part of the eternal divine reality. This consideration also answers Buswell's argument. The Atonement is really past in the historical sequence that God has made, and the return of Christ is really future, relative to our place in that history.[25] From God's atemporal perspective, our sins are eternally forgiven for Jesus' sake.

4. Another argument is that if God is supratemporal, then all events are simultaneous with each other. Richard Swinburne argues:

> God's timelessness is said to consist in his existing at all moments of human time—simultaneously. Thus he is said to be simultaneously present at (and a witness of) what I did yesterday, what I am doing today, and what I will do tomorrow. But if t1 is simultaneous with t2 and t2 with t3, then t1 is simultaneous with t3. So if the instant at which God knows these things were simultaneous with both yesterday, today and tomorrow, then these days would be simultaneous with each other. So yesterday would be the same day as today and as tomorrow—which is clearly nonsense.[26]

But Helm points out that *simultaneous* is itself a temporal expression. If God is atemporal, then his consciousness is not simultaneous with anything.[27] Swinburne even speaks of "the instant at which God knows these things." But *instant* is also a temporal expression. If God is atemporal, there is no "instant" at which he gains an item of knowledge. He has that knowledge always, from our point of view, and timelessly from his. He looks down on history from his eternal vantage point and sees t1, t2, and t3 as what they are—three different points in the historical sequence.

All of these arguments for God's mere temporality are equally strong as arguments for God's mere spatiality.[28] We could, as in Wolterstorff's first argument, argue that a spaceless, immaterial being cannot create items in spatial relation to one another without himself being in spatial relation to them. Or we could argue that God cannot know that something is "here" without himself having spatial location. Or we could argue that if God is nonspatial, then space must be unreal. If God is aware of locations s1, s2,

---

25. When Buswell says that, on the atemporal view, God cannot elect people "before" the foundation of the world, atemporalists appropriately reply that "before" here is strictly incorrect, but almost a necessity of language. See my justification for the use of the term in footnote 4.

26. Swinburne, *The Coherence of Theism* (Oxford: Clarendon Press, 1977), 220–21.

27. Helm, *Eternal God* (Oxford: Clarendon Press, 1988), 26–27. He also points out some more complicated issues in this connection, which I must pass by in the present discussion.

28. See Helm, "God and Spacelessness," *Philosophy* 55 (March 1980): 211–21.

and s3, we could argue that these locations must be identical with one another. Although many theologians and philosophers want to assert God's mere temporality, relatively few of them (mainly pantheists and panentheists) want to assert his mere spatiality. Perhaps consideration of the similarity of the temporalist arguments with the spatialist arguments will help some to see faults in both.

ARGUMENTS FOR DIVINE ATEMPORALITY

Again, I remind the reader that the issue here is not whether God is immanent in time, but whether in addition to this immanence he is also transcendent over time, in the sense of having an atemporal existence.[29] The following arguments contend that he does.

1. Aquinas argued that God is atemporal as a consequence of his unchangeability: "Now in a thing lacking movement, and which is always the same, there is no before and after."[30] Since God is unchangeable, then, he is atemporal. Aquinas is assuming Aristotle's definition that time is "the number of motion." Where there is no change to measure, there is thus no time, and therefore no sequence. But Aristotle's definition can be questioned. Sometimes we measure motion by time, but sometimes the reverse, as with a clock.

If, as with modern science, we regard time as an objective reality, then it is not obvious that a changeless object must be outside of time. Hard as it is to conceive, it is not logically impossible that there is a rock somewhere that remains ever the same, but in time. I do believe that atemporality entails unchangeability, but I do not see any reason to believe the reverse.

2. Augustine argued that if God were temporal, he would increase in knowledge and therefore be less than omniscient.[31] It seems that at each moment, a temporal God would learn a new fact, namely that a moment of time has changed from future to present, and another from present to past. But the argument gives no reason why God would not anticipate these events, or, indeed, that he could not have perfect knowledge of every future event (and therefore of the transitions of events from future to pres-

---

29. This is, of course, my way of formulating the issue. Some of the writers I refer to below would not be comfortable with the view that God has a temporal existence along with his atemporal existence.

30. *ST,* 1.10.1; cf. *SCG,* 1.15.3. Aquinas presents other arguments for divine eternity, but they apply mainly to the conclusion that God is without beginning or end, which is granted by both atemporalists and temporalists.

31. Augustine, *The City of God,* 11.21.

ent to past). So it is not evident that divine temporality would compromise omniscience in this way.

3. The definition of Boethius suggests that if God were temporal, he would not possess his entire life all at once. Some of his life experience would be lost to the past, and some would not yet be attainable because it remains in the future. Thus, God would experience lack, contradicting his aseity. And a temporal God would also have his life divided into temporal parts, contrary to the doctrine of simplicity. But these considerations seem to me to be rather speculative. It is not obvious that Scripture attributes to God the "simultaneous" enjoyment of his entire life, or that any lack of that would be an imperfection. There is no reason why a temporal God would not be able to remember the past and anticipate the future perfectly. Would that not be a sufficient "possession of infinite life"? If God is temporal, should the temporal pieces of his experience be considered "parts of him"? I am not convinced that they should be.

4. Some have claimed that a God who exists in time, without beginning or end, would embody an "actual infinite," that is, an infinity of actual events in temporal sequence, past and future. If God is temporal, then time is not created. If time is not created, then it extends infinitely far into the past. In that case, an infinity of days would have elapsed before God's creation of the world. But if an infinity of days elapsed before creation, then creation never took place. But since creation did take place, God must not embody an actual infinite, and so he exists outside of time. I cannot detect a flaw in this argument, but I would hesitate to give it doctrinal weight, in the absence of biblical teaching.[32]

5. Some have suggested scientific arguments for divine atemporality. W. Norris Clarke argues:

> For if, according to Einstein, there is no one time-framework for the whole cosmos—there is no one "now" for the whole cosmos at once, but many different "nows," according to one's perspective from within the physical system—then which time-framework is God in? If one says that he is present to each thing even in its own immediate time-framework, then how does he coordinate them all into a unity of consciousness, as he must clearly do? Would not such a coordination be precisely in some sense a knowledge *transcending* at least all forms of our time, since the latter by nature simply

cannot be synthesized in its own terms but is intrinsically and irredeemably multiple?[33]

If time and space are relative, then what is past from one perspective will be future from another. So if God combines all perspectives in one vision, he has knowledge of the future, contrary to the temporalist view.

This type of argument seems promising, but I am not really competent to evaluate it. I will leave this one to people better trained in science. I do think it is generally unwise, however, to base theological doctrines on current scientific theories.

I conclude that the philosophical and scientific arguments on either side are insufficient to establish as doctrine either God's mere temporality or his atemporality. Of these arguments, I find the fourth atemporalist argument to be the most persuasive. In any case, we should conclude that the atemporalist position should not be simply dismissed as a remnant of Greek philosophy.

SCRIPTURE ON GOD AND TIME

As with all theological questions, only Scripture can ultimately resolve the question of the nature of God's eternity.

I agree on the whole with Barr's critique of Cullmann's arguments about *aiōn* in its various forms. One cannot derive a temporalist view of God from this language. Indeed, nothing much can be learned on this matter from the *aiōn* vocabulary, though a study of its use may suggest the temporality of God to some readers. The frequent use of *aiōnios* to refer to the eternal life of God's people should not be taken in an atemporal way. Nothing in Scripture suggests that human beings will ever transcend time.[34] "Eternal" life is life without end, in fellowship with the eternal God. So one would naturally think that the term has the same meaning when applied to God.

---

33. W. Norris Clarke, "Christian Theism and Whiteheadian Process Philosophy: Are They Compatible?" in *Process Theology*, ed. Ronald Nash (Grand Rapids: Baker, 1987), 241–42. He also mentions some speculative arguments from the fields of parapsychology and quantum mechanics, from physicist David Bohm and brain researcher Karl Pribham. For a similar argument, see Royce Gruenler's article in the same volume, "Reflections on a Journey in Process," 348–50, and at much greater length in his book *The Inexhaustible God* (Grand Rapids: Baker, 1983), 75–100.

34. Some have taken Rev. 10:6 ("there should be time no longer," KJV) to indicate a nontemporal existence for the creation. But the context speaks rather of impending judgment, so I think the NIV is correct to translate it as "there will be no more delay." That is the only verse I know that has been used to suggest that our eternal life is nontemporal.

A number of passages speak of God as having no beginning or end (Deut. 32:40; Pss. 33:11; 93:2; 102:24, 27; 145:13; 146:10), and in the absence of other evidence it would seem best to say only that God is *everlasting*—persisting through time, rather than transcending it.

We should remember, of course, that the biblical writers did not have in mind our modern, scientific concept of time, or even (most likely) the Platonic philosophical distinction between time and eternity. Their understanding of time was more immediate and practical. They understood that God gives us a certain number of years of life before we die, but that his years never fail. There is no reason to suppose that they thought much about the "nature" or "essence" of time, or the relations sustained to time (so defined) by God and man.[35] Certainly they didn't see time primarily as a kind of "box" that a person can be either inside or outside of.

So perhaps we should back away a bit from the original terms of our question. It may not be possible to derive from Scripture an explicit answer to the question of whether God is merely temporal or indeed supratemporal. But I do think there is biblical reason to conclude that God's relationship to time is very different from our own. For the biblical God transcends a number of limitations associated with our experience of temporality:

The limitation of beginning and end. In the passages cited above, Scripture teaches that God has no beginning or end. Temporalists and atemporalists agree on that proposition. But it is also significant that the world has a beginning, and that God exists "before" that beginning. Genesis begins with "the beginning" (*re'shith, archē*), and many other passages refer to the initial creation as the beginning (e.g., Isa. 40:21; 41:4, 26; 46:10; Matt. 19:4; Heb. 1:10). But the Creator precedes the creation. John 1:1 says that the

---

There are other passages that speak of our sharing eternal fellowship with God and indeed sharing something of his mode of existence, as we will one day join him in his heavenly dwelling (1 Cor. 14:42–54; Rev. 21:1–4). But these do not suggest that our existence then becomes supratemporal. Rather, it is life in a spatial-temporal place called heaven, the place of God's definitive theophany, where Jesus lives forever in his resurrection body and we live with him in bodies like his.

35. Ludwig Wittgenstein begins his *Philosophical Investigations* with a quotation from Augustine on the subject. Platonist that he was, Augustine admitted difficulty in defining time: "If nobody asks me, I know; but if somebody asks me, I don't know." Wittgenstein took this as an example of how philosophical problems arise. We use words like *time* very naturally, without perplexity, until somebody asks us for its definition or essence. Then we are bewildered, and find it necessary to consult philosophers. Wittgenstein's own suggestion is that if we are able to use the word *time* in its everyday settings, then we understand it sufficiently. It may not be possible to define it, to reduce all of its uses to one essence. Nouns are not always amenable to the description of their essence. See Wittgenstein, *Philosophical Investigations* (New York: Macmillan, 1968), 1.

creative Word existed before the beginning, not only at the beginning. One translation that brings out the durative force of the verb reads, "When all things began, the Word already was."

James Barr argues, contrary to Cullmann, that this beginning can be taken as the beginning of time itself:

> In general there is a considerable likelihood that the early Christians understood the Genesis creation story to imply that the beginning of time was simultaneous with the beginning of the creation of the world, especially since the chronological scheme takes its departure from that date.[36]

This "chronological scheme" includes, not only the six days of creation ✓ (however they are to be understood), but also the establishment of day and night (Gen. 1:5) and the creation of the heavenly bodies "to separate the day from the night, and let them serve as signs to mark seasons and days and years" (v. 14).

This argument does not prove absolutely from Scripture that time itself had a beginning. It would be possible, certainly, for time to exist in the absence of days and nights demarcated by the movements of heavenly bodies. But certainly the biblical writers saw God as having his own existence beyond and prior to the history of the material creation and the human race. And it is problematic to try to imagine what role time would have played prior to the creation, when there were no bodies in motion, but only the unchanging God. What we know as time, measured by the heavens, affecting our practical lives, certainly began with the creation. If God experienced time before the creation, his experience of it was certainly very different from ours today.

The limitation of change. I have chosen to discuss God's unchangeability in a separate section below. But clearly God is unchangeable in some respects (Mal. 3:6), and however one interprets it, his unchangeability gives him an experience of time that is different from ours.

The limitation of ignorance. Over time, our memories of the past grow dim, and our anticipation of the future is always highly fallible. But, as I argued in chapter 22, God knows perfectly what to us are the past, the present, and the future—seeing them, in effect, with equal vividness. This does not mean that all times are indistinguishable for him. He knows that one event happened on Monday and another on Tuesday, and he understands the

36. Barr, *Biblical Words for Time*, 75.

process by which one event flows into the next. Thus, it is misleading to say that there is no succession of moments in God's consciousness.[37] But he does see all events laid out before him, as one can see an entire procession from a high vantage point.

The procession analogy is a frequent illustration of an atemporal consciousness.[38] An atemporal being would see all events equally vividly. Since God can do this, his experience of time, in still another sense, is very different from ours. Indeed, his relationship to time is quite unique.

The limitation of temporal frustration. To us, time often seems to pass too slowly or too fast. It passes too slowly as we wait for something to happen, but too fast when we face a deadline. For God, however, time never passes too slowly:

> For a thousand years in your sight
>   are like a day that has just gone by,
>   or like a watch in the night. (Ps. 90:4)

But neither does time pass too quickly for God: "With the Lord a day is like a thousand years, and a thousand years are like a day" (2 Peter 3:8). I am not here trying to make a point about time traveling at multiple speeds in God's consciousness. I doubt if these passages have in mind anything so abstruse. Rather, the point is that God is so completely in control of the temporal sequence that he is able to accomplish precisely what he wants.

The same point can be made by reflecting on "when the fulness of the time was come" in Galatians 4:4 (KJV; "when the time had fully come," NIV). God has carefully structured the whole history of the world to accomplish his own specific purposes. (See chaps. 4 and 16 for more biblical evidence of God's divine control in the accomplishment of his eternal purpose.)

Again, we must conclude that God's experience of time is very different from ours. He looks at time as his tool in accomplishing his purposes; we look at it as a limit on our choices. He is the Lord of time. "By his own authority" he sets "the times or dates" (Acts 1:7; cf. 17:26; Mark 13:32).

What conclusion follows from these four ways in which God transcends

37. God does not sense one moment of his own transcendent consciousness flowing into another. However, he fully understands the process by which time flows in the creaturely world.

38. One could also use the analogy of a movie film. When you watch the film projected onto the screen, you see one frame at a time, each moving into the next. But if you could look at the film itself (only short ones, I gather, are suitable for this illustration), stretched out before your field of vision, you could see all the frames at once, and therefore events at all different times in the film simultaneously.

the limitations associated with time? Shall we say that God is merely "in" time, or is he in some way "outside of" time?[39] Well, try to imagine what it would be like to have a consciousness without beginning and end, without change, with perfect knowledge of all times, and with complete sovereignty over temporal relationships. What would that feel like?

When we talk about ourselves being "in time," part of what we mean is that to us time is a limit. It is a sort of box that we cannot get out of; it limits our knowledge and our choices. To God, time is clearly not that sort of box. A much better metaphor is the atemporalist one, that he looks down on time from a lofty height. So it seems to me that God's experience of time, as Scripture presents it, is more like the atemporalist model than like the temporalist one.

I cannot present a watertight argument for divine atemporality. However, it seems to me that once we deny the existence of libertarian freedom, all the relevant considerations favor atemporality, and none favor temporality.

More important than the question of temporality, however, is God's lordship over time. Since chapter 7, I have argued that God's transcendence is not his being outside or beyond history, but rather his being Lord and King, in control of all things and speaking with authority over all things. So God's special relation to time, whether temporal or atemporal, should not be defined first in terms of temporality, but in terms of lordship.

Some temporalists have used the phrase "Lord of time" as an alternative to calling God atemporal.[40] But temporalists who espouse libertarian freedom (that is, most temporalists) need to ask how libertarianism can possibly be consistent with divine lordship as Scripture presents it.

GOD'S TEMPORAL OMNIPRESENCE

We have not exhausted the biblical teaching on God's relationship to temporal reality. So far, we have focused on the nature of God's transcendence in relation to time. Now we must look at his temporal immanence.

Here I return to Wolterstorff's second argument, which I passed over earlier, that God's redemptive actions in Scripture are temporally successive,

39. Later I shall argue that God is immanent in time (chap. 7). Here, however, I am concerned with the nature of his transcendence with respect to time, his eternity. Does that transcendence imply that he is outside of time in some sense, or not?

40. Cullmann, *Christ and Time*, 69; Wolterstorff, "God Everlasting," 203; Otto Weber, *Foundations of Dogmatics* (Grand Rapids: Eerdmans, 1983), 2:456–58.

and that the biblical writers regard God as having a time strand of his own. This is certainly right. I mentioned earlier that God accomplishes his purposes in the fullness of time. That fact is a testimony to his sovereignty, but also to the importance of temporal relationships in the divinely ordained course of history.

The biblical narrative relates a historical succession of events—events of creation, fall, and redemption. As Oscar Cullmann, Geerhardus Vos, and others have pointed out, the New Testament tells us of two ages: the old age and the new age. The old age is the age of fallen humanity, running from the Fall to the Last Judgment. The new age is the age of salvation, beginning with the coming of Christ and running forever into the future. We now live in the time when the two ages overlap. So history is a linear pattern of events, beginning at creation, reaching a climax in the work of Christ, continuing on to the Last Judgment, and concluding in the eternal state.

The work of Christ took place once for all. Its *pastness* is important to the New Testament writers. The *presentness* of the time of decision is also important: "I tell you, now is the time of God's favor, now is the day of salvation" (2 Cor. 6:2). And the *futurity* of the consummation is important: suffering now will be followed by glory later (1 Peter 1:3–7).

All these events are God's works, and so he works in a temporally successive pattern. The sequence is foreordained by God's decree, but he brings it to pass in time. Now Wolterstorff takes this temporal pattern to imply that God has "a time-strand of his own," and therefore that God is temporal.

In one sense, Wolterstorff is correct. We saw in chapters 6 and 7 that covenant presence is an important element of God's lordship. And that means both that God is *here* and that he is here *now*. Israel needed to learn in Egypt that God was present, not only to the patriarchs four hundred years before, but to them as well, in their current experience. God not only *works* in time, but is also *present* in time, at all times.

Too little attention has been paid to God's temporal omnipresence in the discussion of his relationship to time. Much of what some writers want to gain by a temporalist view (other than, of course, libertarian freedom) can be as easily secured through sufficient recognition of God's temporal covenant presence. For example, a covenantally present God, like a temporalist God, can know (and assert) temporally indexed expressions like "the sun is rising now." He can feel with human beings the flow of time from one moment to the next. He can react to events in a significant sense (events which, to be sure, he has foreordained). He can mourn one moment and rejoice the next. He can hear and respond to prayer in time. Since

God dwells in time, therefore, there is give-and-take between him and human beings.[41]

As I indicated in chapter 14, God's providence operates on the world both from above (government) and from below (concurrence). And in the incarnation of Jesus Christ, we see again how the eternal God entered time. In Christ, God entered, not a world that is otherwise strange to him, but a world in which he had been dwelling all along.

But God's temporal immanence does not contradict his lordship over time or the exhaustiveness of his decree. These temporal categories are merely aspects of God's general transcendence and immanence as the Lord. The give-and-take between God and the creation requires, not a reduced, but an enhanced, view of his sovereignty. God is the Lord *in* time as well as the Lord *above* time.

So God is temporal after all, but not merely temporal. He really exists in time, but he also transcends time in such a way as to exist outside it. He is both inside and outside of the temporal box—a box that can neither confine him nor keep him out. This is the model that does the most justice to the biblical data.

GOD'S UNCHANGEABILITY

Another attribute describing God's relationship to time is his unchangeability or immutability. Whether we think of change as the measure of time or time as the measure of change, the two are closely related.

The earliest Greek philosophers struggled in their attempt to understand change. How does one thing change into something else? Thales evidently thought that all things come from water, but what is the mechanism that makes water change into other things? To Anaximenes, who taught that everything comes from air, the mechanism is condensation and rarefaction. But the very idea of change bewildered Parmenides. For him, change always implies something appearing out of what it is not. But something cannot come from nothing. So Parmenides taught that there is no change. Change is an illusion; the world is really unchanging. But then, where does the illusion of change come from? Are the illusions of change illusions of illusions? And on it goes, *ad infinitum*.

Heraclitus began with the proposition that everything changes. But if everything changes, how can we identify something long enough to talk about it? If something is constantly undergoing change, how can one talk

---

41. There is more on this interaction in the next section.

meaningfully about it? Heraclitus answered that although everything changes, it does so according to a rational pattern, which he called the *logos*, which is accessible by the human mind. But does the *logos* change? Evidently not; it is a bit of constancy in a changing world, a rock from which we can view the restless ocean of universal change.

After Heraclitus, philosophers generally tried to identify something constant, something unchanging in the world of change. For Plato, it was the world of Forms. For Aristotle, it was both the formal aspect of substance and his god, the great Unmoved Mover. For Plotinus, it was the One. In modern times, there have been various kinds of gods (Descartes, Spinoza, Leibniz, Locke, Berkeley), absolutes (Hegel), changeless ways of attaining truth (rationalism, empiricism, Kantian transcendentalism), and unchanging abstract objects (process philosophy).[42] Some have denied the existence of a changeless reality, but for them the price has been a radical loss of meaning (Nietzsche, existentialism, postmodernism).

It does seem necessary for human thought, if it is to have real knowledge, to have access to something unchanging, a vantage point by which we gain a rational understanding of the changing world. In Christian thought, the ultimate vantage point has always been God.[43]

Scripture refers to God as unchanging:

> In the beginning you laid the foundations of the earth,
>   and the heavens are the work of your hands.
> They will perish, but you remain;
>   they will all wear out like a garment.
> Like clothing you will change them
>   and they will be discarded.
> But you remain the same,
>   and your years will never end. (Ps. 102:25–27)

> I the LORD do not change. So you, O descendants of Jacob, are not destroyed. (Mal. 3:6)

> Every good and perfect gift is from above, coming down from the Father of the heavenly lights, who does not change like shifting shadows. (James 1:17)

---

42. Of course, for process philosophers the eternal objects have no actual existence, only potential. So process thought arguably belongs among the systems of thought that have lost all coherent meaning.

43. Cornelius Van Til and others have argued that only the Christian God, as absolute person, is able to provide the presuppositions of meaningful experience. See *CVT*, 51–78, 311–22; *AGG*, 57–147.

One particular emphasis is that God does not break his word or change his mind:

> God is not a man, that he should lie,
>   nor a son of man, that he should change his mind.
> Does he speak and then not act?
>   Does he promise and not fulfill? (Num. 23:19)

> He who is the Glory of Israel does not lie or change his mind; for he is not a man, that he should change his mind. (1 Sam. 15:29)

In other passages, God says in specific cases that he will not change his mind (Ps. 110:4, quoted in Heb. 7:21; Jer. 4:28; 20:16; Ezek. 24:14). So, as we have seen in earlier chapters, God's counsel stands firm; his purpose will certainly come to pass (e.g., Deut. 32:39; Ps. 33:11; Isa. 43:13). The image of the rock (see chap. 18) underscores Yahweh's stability, the sureness of his purposes.

A GOD WHO RELENTS

Nevertheless, there are a number of problems that arise in discussions of God's unchangeability. First, there are many passages of Scripture in which God does appear to change his mind. For example, in Exodus 32:9–10, God announces judgment against Israel for their false worship:

> "I have seen these people," the LORD said to Moses, "and they are a stiff-necked people. Now leave me alone so that my anger may burn against them and that I may destroy them. Then I will make you into a great nation."

But Moses seeks God's favor, calling on him to "relent" (v. 12). "Relent" here translates *naham*, the same word translated "change his mind" in Numbers 23:19 and 1 Samuel 15:29 (KJV: "repent").[44] And God does relent: "Then the LORD relented and did not bring on his people the disaster he had threatened" (Ex. 32:14).

Six verses after 1 Samuel 15:29, which denies that God relents, we read:

> Until the day Samuel died, he did not go to see Saul again, though Samuel mourned for him. And the LORD was grieved that he had made Saul king over Israel. (v. 35)

---

44. When used of God, *naham* of course cannot mean to repent of sin, so the King James translation is misleading here. It can mean "relent," "change one's mind," or "be grieved" (usually referring to an intense grieving).

"Was grieved" translates *naham*. So in this passage we learn that God does not "change his mind" (v. 29) yet he "was grieved" that he had made Saul king (v. 35). These verses appear to be contradictory. Similarly, before the Flood, God "was grieved [*naham*] that he had made man on the earth" (Gen. 6:6). It seems again that God has changed his mind: from joy in creating man to grief.

The prophet Joel calls on Israel to repent:

> Rend your heart
>   and not your garments.
> Return to the LORD your God,
>   for he is gracious and compassionate,
> slow to anger and abounding in love,
>   and he relents from sending calamity.
> Who knows? He may turn and have pity
>   and leave behind a blessing—
> grain offerings and drink offerings
>   for the LORD your God. (Joel 2:13–14)

This passage is especially interesting because it quotes the exposition of the divine name Yahweh in Exodus 34:6–7, but adds to this exposition that the Lord is one who "relents" (*naham*). (This is evidently an inference from the emphasis on forgiveness in Ex. 34.) So relenting is part of his very nature as the Lord. He is the Lord who relents.

The prophet Amos records a dialogue between himself and the Lord:

> This is what the Sovereign LORD showed me: He was preparing swarms of locusts after the king's share had been harvested and just as the second crop was coming up. When they had stripped the land clean, I cried out, "Sovereign LORD, forgive! How can Jacob survive? He is so small!"
>
> So the LORD relented.
>
> "This will not happen," the LORD said.
>
> This is what the Sovereign LORD showed me: The Sovereign LORD was calling for judgment by fire; it dried up the great deep and devoured the land. Then I cried out, "Sovereign LORD, I beg you, stop! How can Jacob survive? He is so small!"
>
> So the LORD relented.
>
> "This will not happen either," the Sovereign LORD said. (Amos 7:1–6)

We are reminded here of Abraham's intercession for Lot in Sodom (Gen. 18:16–33) and Moses' calling on God to spare Israel (Ex. 32:9–14). In both passages, the intercessor gets his way. The Lord relents; he retreats from the judgment he originally announced.

When Jonah arrives at Nineveh, he announces, "Forty more days and Nineveh will be overturned" (Jonah 3:4). This is God's word, given through his prophet. But Nineveh is not overturned. God relents from his purpose. Jonah is not surprised, however:

> But Jonah was greatly displeased and became angry. He prayed to the LORD, "O LORD, is this not what I said when I was still at home? That is why I was so quick to flee to Tarshish. I knew that you are a gracious and compassionate God, slow to anger and abounding in love, a God who relents from sending calamity." (4:1–2)[45]

Like Joel, Jonah quotes Exodus 34:6–7, drawing from that passage the conclusion that God relents. This connection with the name Yahweh again suggests that relenting belongs to God's very nature: he is "a God who relents." Relenting is a divine attribute.

But how can this be, in the face of passages like 1 Samuel 15:29, which appear to deny that God relents?

In the light of Joel 2:13–14 and Jonah 4:1–2, it is not a mere game with words to say that relenting is part of God's unchangeable nature. In Jeremiah 18:5–10, God indicates that such relenting is part of his general way of working:

> Then the word of the LORD came to me: "O house of Israel, can I not do with you as this potter does?" declares the LORD. "Like clay in the hand of the potter, so are you in my hand, O house of Israel. If at any time I announce that a nation or kingdom is to be uprooted, torn down and destroyed, and if that nation I warned repents of its evil, then I will relent and not inflict on it the disaster I had planned. And if at another time I announce that a nation or kingdom is to be built up and planted, and if it does evil in my sight and does not obey me, then I will reconsider the good I had intended to do for it."

Compare Jeremiah 26:3, 13, 19 (referring to Isa. 38:1–5); 42:10. Here the Lord states that many prophecies of judgment and blessing are *conditional*. God reserves the right to cancel them or reverse them, depending on people's response to the prophet. As Calvin puts it, speaking of Jonah's prophecy:

---

45. Cf. also 1 Chron. 21:15.

Who now does not see that it pleased the Lord by such threats to arouse to repentance those whom he was terrifying, that they might escape the judgment they deserved for their sins? If that is true, the nature of the circumstances leads us to recognize a tacit condition in the simple intimation.[46]

Some prophecies, then, may appear to be straightforward predictions, but they are, according to the principle of Jeremiah 18:5–10, really warnings, with tacit conditions attached.

Sometimes, as in the passages from Jeremiah, Joel, and Jonah, those tacit conditions have to do with obedience or disobedience, repentance or complacency. Sometimes, as in Genesis 18:16–33, Exodus 32:9–14, and Amos 7:1–6, prayer is such a condition. When the prophet intercedes for his people, God relents from the judgment he has announced. The prophet stands before the throne of God himself and pleads for God's people, and God answers by relenting.

How is all of this compatible with the sovereignty of God? Note the following points:

1. Jeremiah 18:5–10 follows a passage (vv. 1–4) in which God compares himself to a potter and Israel to clay—a radical image of God's sovereignty. God's relenting is his sovereign decision. His right to withdraw his announced judgments and blessings is part of his sovereignty.

2. If we interpret these passages (as did Jonah) according to the principle of Jeremiah 18, we are interpreting them as expressions of his preceptive will, rather than his decretive will (chap. 23): as warnings, not as predictions of what will certainly happen. So there is no question of his decretive will failing. His preceptive will, of course, unlike the decretive, can be disobeyed, though at great cost.

3. As I indicated in chapters 8–9 and elsewhere, even God's decretive will, his eternal plan, takes human actions and prayers into account. God's decretive will in the book of Jonah is not to judge Nineveh at that time. But he has eternally determined to accomplish his purposes through Jonah's prophecy and the repentance of the Ninevites.[47] It is God's eternal intention to forgive Israel in the situation of Amos 7:1–6. But he does this through the power of Amos's intercession, and not without it.

But how is all this compatible with the authority of the prophetic word? In Jonah 3:4, God through his prophet announces something that does not

---

46. *Institutes*, 1.17.14.
47. This is an example of what I mentioned earlier in the chapter: the give-and-take between human beings and God in his temporal immanence.

take place, the destruction of Nineveh. Yet Deuteronomy 18:21–22 says that the test of a true prophet is this:

> You may say to yourselves, "How can we know when a message has not been spoken by the Lord?" If what a prophet proclaims in the name of the Lord does not take place or come true, that is a message the Lord has not spoken. That prophet has spoken presumptuously. Do not be afraid of him.

On this criterion, should not Jonah have been denounced as a false prophet? No, because God had revealed that such prophecies have tacit conditions. What Jonah said to Nineveh really was, "Yet forty days and Nineveh will be destroyed, *unless* you repent of your sins and turn to the Lord." Jonah himself understood that God might forgive Nineveh (Jonah 4:2), despite the apparently categorical language of the prophecy. The Ninevites understood it, too. Their king said, "Who knows? God may yet relent and with compassion turn from his fierce anger so that we will not perish" (3:9). Jonah was a true prophet, announcing God's judgment with tacit conditions. His words were God's words; his tacit conditions were God's tacit conditions.

But then does Deuteronomy 18:21–22 become a dead letter? Not at all. Not all prophecies are conditional. Sometimes prophets do make straightforward predictions of events to come. Obviously in 1 Samuel 10:1–7, for example, there is no conditionality. Samuel simply tells Saul a number of events that will take place in the immediate future, and they happen exactly as Samuel said. (For other examples, see the general treatment of predestination in chap. 4 and the discussion of divine foreknowledge in chap. 22.) We must determine from the context which principle is operative: straightforward prediction or conditional proclamation.

Some prophecies, moreover, are qualified by assurances. In Jeremiah 7:15, God says that exile is certain—so certain that the prophet is not even to pray for the people, "for I will not listen to you" (v. 16). Here God makes known his decretive will. What he has predicted will certainly come to pass. In Amos 1:3, 6, 9, 13; 2:1, 4, 6, God announces future judgments and says that these will certainly come to pass; he will not turn back his wrath. For other examples, see Isaiah 45:23; Jeremiah 4:28; 23:20; 30:24; Ezekiel 24:14; and Zechariah 8:14. Sometimes God even takes an oath to indicate the certainty of the predicted events (Ps. 110:4; Isa. 14:24; 54:9; 62:8; Jer. 44:26; 49:13; 51:14; Amos 4:2; 6:8; 8:7). Sometimes the phrase "as surely as I live" pledges the unconditional truth of the prophecy (Ezek. 5:11; 14:16, 18, 20; 20:3, 31,

33; 33:27; 35:6, 11). In these examples, God declares his unchangeable decretive will.[48]

We are likely to find tacit conditions in prophecies of blessing and judgment, according to Jeremiah 18:5–10. To be sure, some such prophecies are unconditional, as we saw in the previous paragraph. But most of them are conditional, and most conditional prophecies are prophecies of blessing and judgment. Blessing and judgment are the twin sanctions of God's covenants. Often the prophet serves as the prosecuting attorney for God's "covenant lawsuit." In the covenant, God offers two alternatives: blessing for obedience and cursing for disobedience (see chap. 2). It is the prophet's job to hold out both alternatives. Prophecies of blessing and judgment are often conditional because they are proclamations of God's covenant. So it should not surprise us either to find that "relenting" is part of God's covenant name.

To say that a lot of prophecy is conditional is not to say that "anything can happen" following a prophecy. Even conditional prophecy limits what can and cannot happen. The covenant itself is sealed by God's oath, and so its curses and blessings will certainly come to pass, granted the relevant conditions. The result will not be neutral; it will be either curse or blessing. Most of these prophecies are imprecise, to be sure; they don't describe exactly what kind of blessing or curse is coming, or precisely when. But they speak the truth.[49]

How Is God Unchanging?

We have seen that *unchanging* needs some definition beyond the obvious, since Scripture attributes to God some kinds of changes, even changes of mind. There are also philosophical questions that arise. Say that Susan becomes a Christian on May 1, 1999. Before that date, we could not say of God that he was "believed in by Susan," but after that date we could say that. A change has taken place, one that could be interpreted as a change in God.

Philosophers sometimes call these "Cambridge changes,"[50] to distin-

---

48. The fact that many passages have these explicit assurances suggests that prophecies without them may not have this unconditional character. So these passages, too, reinforce our impression that many prophecies in Scripture are conditional.

49. In this section, I am greatly indebted to Richard Pratt's important article, "Historical Contingencies and Biblical Predictions," available at www.thirdmill.org. Pratt distinguishes (1) prophecies qualified by conditions, (2) prophecies qualified by assurances, and (3) predictions without qualifications, and he analyzes each group most helpfully.

50. It evidently means that there are some kinds of events that only subtle philosophers would regard as changes.

guish them from "real changes." On the human level, consider that Mary has the property of being taller than her son Justin on January 1, 1998, but loses that property on January 1, 1999. She has remained the same height, but Justin has grown taller. Normally we would say that Mary has not changed in this respect, but that Justin has. If we are in a philosophical frame of mind, however, we can formulate the event as a change in Mary, by saying that she has lost and/or gained a property. We might call this a Cambridge change as opposed to a real change.

It is not easy in some cases to distinguish between the two,[51] but most of us would grant intuitively that there is a distinction to be made. Hence, theologians have often said that God does not change "in himself," but does change "in his relations to creatures." So Bavinck says, "Whatever change there is, is wholly in the creature."[52] When God changes his attitude from wrath to favor, it is because the creature has moved from the sphere of Satan to the sphere of Christ.

Some "changes" in God can be understood in this way, but it would be wrong, I think, to understand all of them according to this model. For one thing, Reformed theology insists that when a person moves from the sphere of wrath to that of grace, it is because God has moved him there. God's change in this context (from wrath to grace) is not the product of creaturely change; rather, the creaturely changes come at God's initiative. Pannenberg says that medieval theologians reasoned like this:

> Because of God's immutability any change in God's attitude to sinners has to begin with a change on our side. This was the main impulse behind the development of the Scholastic doctrine of a *gratia creata*. Only when the soul in its creaturely reality is adorned with this grace can the unchanging God have a different attitude toward it.[53]

Certainly the biblical doctrine of God's unchangeability is not intended to lead to such conclusions. But how do we avoid them?

I will not take up here the difficult and probably unedifying task of distinguishing Cambridge changes from real changes. If such a distinction turns out to be impossible, then it won't hurt us to concede that God does indeed change in some of these relational ways, just as we have conceded that

51. See, for example, Helm, *Eternal God*, 45.
52. DG, 148.
53. Wolfhart Pannenberg, *Systematic Theology* (Grand Rapids: Eerdmans, 1988), 1:437. He refers to J. Auer, *Die Entwicklung der Gnadenlehre in der Hochscholastik*, vol. 1: *Das Wesen der Gnade* (1942).

God changes his mind in some senses. But Scripture does clearly teach that God is immutable in some important ways. So we need to spend some time thinking about what specific changes Scripture intends to exclude when it speaks of God's unchangeability. As I see it, they fall into four categories:

1. God is unchanging *in his essential attributes*. WSC's answer to question 4 says that "God is a Spirit, infinite, eternal, and unchangeable, in his being, wisdom, power, holiness, justice, goodness, and truth." Hebrews 13:8 (speaking specifically of Christ) and James 1:17 speak in general terms of God being unchangeable. Notice also Hebrews 1:10–12 (quoting Ps. 102:25–27):

> He also says,
> "In the beginning, O Lord, you laid the foundations of the earth,
>   and the heavens are the work of your hands.
> They will perish, but you remain;
>   they will all wear out like a garment.
> You will roll them up like a robe;
>   like a garment they will be changed.
> But you remain the same,
>   and your years will never end."

Here the writer underscores the fundamental contrast between the Creator and the creature: creatures change, but God does not. The passage does not merely say that God is without end, though that is true. Rather, it says that God, unlike nature (which is worn out from one season to the next), always remains the same. And, remarkably, the author applies this teaching, not specifically to God the Father, but to Christ. Then in 5:8 he says of Christ, "Although he was a son, he learned obedience from what he suffered." Note the word "although" (*kaiper*). The writer considers it somewhat anomalous that the Son of God should actually suffer and increase in knowledge. (The church deals with that anomaly, of course by distinguishing between Jesus' divine and human natures.) The author's main conception, therefore, is that God (Father or Son) does not change.

God's wisdom and knowledge are unchanging because, as we saw in chapter 22, they are exhaustive. Since God knows all things in all times, from all eternity, his knowledge neither increases nor decreases. Nor does his power change, for, as we saw in chapter 23, God is omnipotent, and there are no degrees of omnipotence. The same must surely be said of God's goodness and truth, for, as we have seen, God is supremely perfect in these attributes—indeed, he is the standard for the corresponding attributes in human beings.

2. God is unchanging *in his decretive will*. Psalm 33:11 reads:

But the plans of the LORD stand firm forever,
　　the purposes of his heart through all generations.

As we saw in chapters 4, 8–9, and 14–16, God governs all things by the story he has written, his eternal decree that governs the entire course of nature and history. That story has already been written; it cannot and will not be changed.

　　3. God is unchanging in his covenant faithfulness. When God says, "I the LORD do not change. So you, O descendants of Jacob, are not destroyed" (Mal. 3:6),[54] he is telling them that he will surely fulfill his covenant promises, despite Israel's disobedience. He is the Lord of the covenant, and he will not forsake his people. In Micah 7:19–20, the prophet says to God:

> You will again have compassion on us;
> 　　you will tread our sins underfoot
> 　　and hurl all our iniquities into the depths of the sea.
> You will be true to Jacob,
> 　　and show mercy to Abraham,
> as you pledged on oath to our fathers
> 　　in days long ago.

The covenant continues through time. As we saw in chapter 6, this is an important biblical theme. God is present with his covenant people through many generations, despite the people's temptation to relegate the covenant to a past age. So God says, in Psalm 89:34–37:

> I will not violate my covenant
> 　　or alter what my lips have uttered.
> Once for all, I have sworn by my holiness—
> 　　and I will not lie to David—
> that his line will continue forever
> 　　and his throne endure before me like the sun;
> it will be established forever like the moon,
> 　　the faithful witness in the sky.

And God says in Isaiah 54:10,

> "Though the mountains be shaken
> 　　and the hills be removed,
> yet my unfailing love for you will not be shaken

---

54. This verse may also refer to the unchanging nature of God's being. Lordship, as we have seen, is not only a description of God's relationship to creatures, but also a key to his own nature.

nor my covenant of peace be removed,"
says the LORD, who has compassion on you.

In these contexts, the unchanging character of God's covenant is vitally
important to the biblical doctrine of salvation. It is this covenantal immutability that comforts us, that reassures us that as God was with Abraham, Isaac, and Jacob, so he will be with us in Christ. So Jesus is the same,
yesterday, today, and forever (Heb. 13:8).

The writer to the Hebrews does say that God's covenant with Israel is
"obsolete." Of the new covenant, he says, "By calling this covenant 'new,'
he has made the first one obsolete; and what is obsolete and aging will soon
disappear" (Heb. 8:13). Does God's covenant, then, change after all? No,
the first covenant is obsolete, not because God will violate its terms, but
because he will fulfill those terms in a far more glorious manner than the
Jews imagined. God's promises endure; through Jesus, all the nations of the
earth are blessed:

> Because God wanted to make the unchanging nature of his pur-
> pose very clear to the heirs of what was promised, he confirmed it
> with an oath. God did this so that, by two unchangeable things in
> which it is impossible for God to lie, we who have fled to take hold
> of the hope offered to us may be greatly encouraged. We have this
> hope as an anchor for the soul, firm and secure. It enters the inner
> sanctuary behind the curtain, where Jesus, who went before us, has
> entered on our behalf. He has become a high priest forever, in the
> order of Melchizedek. (Heb. 6:17–20)

4. God is unchanging *in the truth of his revelation.* What God declares to
be true was true from the beginning and always will be (Isa. 40:21; 41:4;
43:12; 46:10). So his ancient words remain our infallible guide, despite the
passing of time and the changes in human culture (Rom. 15:4; 2 Tim.
3:16–17).

UNCHANGEABILITY AND TEMPORAL OMNIPRESENCE[55]

Obviously, God is unchangeable in his atemporal or supratemporal existence. But when he is present in our world of time, he looks at his creation from within and shares the perspectives of his creatures. As God is
with me on Monday, he views the events of Sunday as in the past, and the

---

55. Thanks to Vern Poythress for suggesting to me many of the ideas of this section. I
take full responsibility for the formulations.

events of Tuesday (which, to be sure, he has foreordained) as future. He continues to be with me as Monday turns into Tuesday. So he views the passing of time as a process, just as we do.

Theologians have sometimes described God's relenting as "anthropomorphic." There is some truth in that description, for divine relenting is part of the interaction between God and his people in history, an interaction in which God's activity is closely analogous to human behavior. For example, in the exchange between God and Amos in Amos 7:1–6, God engages in a conversation with a man, as an actor in history. The author of history has written himself into the play as the lead character, and he interacts with other characters, doing what they do.

That is one perspective on the situation. The other is the atemporal perspective: God has eternally decreed that he will forgive Israel, by means of Amos's intercession. This decree never changes.

History involves constant change, and so, as an agent in history, God himself changes. On Monday he wants a certain thing to happen, and on Tuesday he wants something else to happen. He is grieved one day and pleased the next. In my view, this is more than just anthropomorphic description. In these accounts, God is not merely *like* an agent in time; he really is *in* time, changing as others change. And we should not say that his atemporal, changeless existence is more real than his changing existence in time, as the term *anthropomorphic* might suggest. Both are real.

Neither form of existence contradicts the other. God's transcendence never compromises his immanence, nor do his control and authority compromise his covenant presence. God stirs up "one from the east" to subdue nations and kings (Isa. 41:2). This is God as a historical agent. But the prophecy concludes in verse 4:

> Who has done this and carried it through,
>   calling forth the generations from the beginning?
> I, the LORD—with the first of them
>   and with the last—I am he.

God has planned from the beginning that the eastern scourge would devastate Palestine. That is God as an atemporal agent, controlling everything by his decree.

The difference between God's atemporal and historical existences begins, not with the creation of man, but with creation itself. In Genesis 1, God creates light and darkness, and then names them "day" and "night" (v. 5). Here, God is acting in a sequence. Then, on the second day, he makes the expanse to divide the waters, and names it "sky" (v. 8). On the third day, he gathers the sea and lets dry land appear, defining "land" and "seas"—

"and God saw that it was good" (v. 10). That last phrase is especially interesting. God acts and then evaluates his own work. He acts and then responds to his own act.[56]

God's historical novel, remember, is a logical, temporal sequence, in which one event arises naturally out of the one before. When God himself becomes an actor in the drama, he acts in accordance with that sequence. He sends the rains and then brings the harvest. At one time, his interest is producing rain; at another, harvest. Thus do his interests change over time, according to his unchanging plan.

SOME MODERN VIEWS

PROCESS THEOLOGY

My approach bears a superficial resemblance to process theology, which also recognizes two modes of existence in God, transcendent and immanent, sometimes called the "primordial" and "consequent" natures of God. John B. Cobb and David Ray Griffin explain the process view as follows:

> For Charles Hartshorne, the two "poles" or aspects of God are the abstract essence of God, on the one hand, and God's concrete actuality on the other. The abstract essence [which Whitehead called God's primordial nature—JF] is eternal, absolute, independent, unchangeable. It includes those abstract attributes of deity which characterize the divine essence at every moment. For example, to say that God is omniscient means that in every moment of the divine life God knows everything which is knowable at that time. The concrete actuality [or consequent nature—JF] is temporal, relative, dependent, and constantly changing. In each moment of God's life there are new, unforeseen happenings in the world which only then have become knowable. Hence, God's concrete knowledge is dependent upon the decisions made by the worldly actualities. God's knowledge is always relativized by, in the sense of internally related to, the world.[57]

This position is deeply unscriptural, and it should not be confused with the position taken in this book. Note the following differences:

56. If we take a nonchronological view of the days of Gen. 1, we must still recognize that God's creative work precedes his rest in chronological sequence.

57. John B. Cobb and David Ray Griffin, *Process Theology: An Introductory Exposition* (Philadelphia: Westminster Press, 1976), 47–48.

1. For Hartshorne, God's primordial nature is abstract. In my view, God exists atemporally as a concrete person.

2. For Hartshorne, even God's primordial nature is temporal. In the above definition, God's primordial omniscience is defined by what he knows "in every moment of the divine life." In my view, God transcends time.

3. In process thought, God in his consequent nature is relative to the world and dependent on it. But I maintain that God is self-contained and sovereign, both as transcendent and as immanent.

4. Process theologians teach that God does not have exhaustive knowledge of the future. Scripture says that he does (see chap. 22).

5. In process thought, there is no unchanging standpoint from which change can be identified and measured. Since the "eternal objects" (equivalent to God's primordial nature) are abstract, rather than concrete, and possible, rather than actual, they cannot serve as such a standpoint. But in Scripture, God, as concrete actuality, stands exalted as the unchanging Lord of time.

There are many problems in process theology, besides its manifest unscripturality, that I cannot take time here to discuss. I will say that process theology does not teach a credible doctrine of divine transcendence. For these thinkers, God as primordial is a mere abstraction, not a concrete actuality. To say that God is primordial or transcendent, on this view, is simply to say that every possible universe will include some kind of process deity. On the other hand, God as consequent, in process thought, is not clearly distinct from the world and is relative to it. Although process thought seeks to distinguish itself from pantheism (it prefers to be called panentheism: all is in God), it is not clear to me what there is in this God that is not also in the world. So in this view there is no meaningful Creator-creature distinction and no sovereign Lord.

FUTURISM

Most thinkers who limit God to the temporal process limit him (as human beings are limited) to existence in the present. Some theologians, however, impressed by the eschatological dimension of Scripture, think of his existence as primarily future. For them, God is transcendent, not as one who lives in a realm above us, nor (as I have maintained) as one who rules the world as Lord, but as future time which inevitably overwhelms the present. This is not to say that the future has a fixed character; for these writers, the future is open; this is part of the reason for its transcendence. We cannot predict it or control it; we can only receive it as blessing or judgment.

This position was set forth in some detail by Jürgen Moltmann in *Theology of Hope*.[58] In a later work, he said simply that God is "the power of the future."[59] He finds some anticipations of his view in Rudolf Bultmann,[60] who also emphasizes the openness of the future and speaks of the future as the nature of God. Similarly, Wolfhart Pannenberg says that "an existent being acting with omnipotence and omniscience would make freedom impossible,"[61] and so makes this suggestion:

> The future seems to offer an alternative to an understanding of reality which is concentrated upon what is existing. For what belongs to the future is not yet existent and yet it already determines present existence.[62]

Stanley Grenz, an evangelical with some sympathy for this position, says,

> The future orientation suggested by thinkers such as Pannenberg and Moltmann provides a promising starting point for conceiving of the divine reality. God is best conceived not as standing behind us or above us, but in front of us. For systematic theology, this basic outlook means that we no longer seek to answer theological questions from the perspective of the past—from the decisions God made before the creation of the world. Rather we engage in the theological enterprise by viewing reality from the perspective of the future—from God's ultimate goal for creation.[63]

Scripture does teach that God is the "coming one," and it puts major emphasis on the future. But that future is not a perfectly open future, as at least Bultmann and Moltmann believe, but a future conceived in God's eternal plan. Furthermore, it is simply unbiblical to identify God with the future, as over against the present and the past, and as opposed to an atemporal existence. God rules the past, the present, and the future, and he exists independently of all three. He is the Beginning and the End, the Alpha and the Omega. Scripture looks back on God's mighty works of the past, praises him as the one who is with us today, and looks forward to the certain fulfillment of his promises in the future. Thus, biblical faith honors

58. Jürgen Moltmann, *Theology of Hope* (New York: Harper, 1967).
59. Jürgen Moltmann, *The Experiment Hope* (Philadelphia: Fortress, 1975), 51.
60. Moltmann, *Theology of Hope*, 190, 212, 283.
61. Wolfhart Pannenberg, *The Idea of God and Human Freedom* (Philadelphia: Westminster Press, 1973), 109.
62. Ibid., 110.
63. Stanley Grenz, *Theology for the Community of God* (Nashville: Broadman and Holman, 1994), 104–5.

God as the chief agent in history and as the one who stands above history. Contrary to futurism, as expounded by Grenz, we should seek to answer theological questions multiperspectivally, both from the standpoint of the future and from the standpoints of the past and the present—and from the standpoint of the decisions that God made before the creation of the world, such as that mentioned in Ephesians 1:4.

Futurism also raises serious questions about the very existence of God in the present. If God is not an "existent being acting with omnipotence and omniscience" in the present, but one who is coming to be in the future, then it is simply the case that in the world as we know it God does not exist.[64] That perspective is entirely contrary to that of Scripture.

Pannenberg and Moltmann have not, in my opinion, maintained this sort of view consistently, especially in their later works, though they continue to hint at it. They often speak of God as existing in the past and present. The qualifications they have made on their general futurist position are too complicated to go into here. But insofar as they make God a temporal being, insist on an open future, promote libertarian views of freedom, and question the full reality of God's atemporal, past, and present existence, they have turned far from the biblical doctrine of God.

64. Pannenberg is deeply influenced by Hegel, for whom God is the absolute reality, coming to self-consciousness in the world.

CHAPTER 25

Lord of Space, Matter, Light, and Breath

In the preceding chapter, we saw that there are analogies between God's relationship to time and his relationship to space. I maintained there that the arguments against divine atemporality are analogous to arguments that might be used to show that God is spatial. In this chapter, I shall discuss specifically the question of God's relationship to space (immensity, spatial omnipresence), along with the related questions of his relationship to matter (incorporeality), light (invisibility, glory), and breath (spirituality).

GOD'S IMMENSITY

God's immensity is to space what his atemporal eternity is to time. This does not mean merely that God is omnipresent in space, but that he transcends space altogether. As in the preceding chapter I argued that God is both atemporal and omnipresent in time, so I will here maintain that he is both nonspatial (immense) and omnipresent in space.[1] We can establish God's immensity from the following considerations:

EXPLICIT SCRIPTURE TEXTS

Unlike *eternity, immensity* is not a biblical term. But it has enjoyed much use in theology to express God's spatial transcendence. Theologians have

---

1. Some theologians have equated immensity with omnipresence; others have distinguished them. See *RD*, 66. I believe the distinction indicated between these terms is a useful one.

576

derived the concept from several texts. For example, at the dedication of the temple, King Solomon asks,

> But will God really dwell on earth? The heavens, even the highest heaven, cannot contain you. How much less this temple I have built! (1 Kings 8:27; cf. 2 Chron. 2:6)

Solomon implies that God not only fills the heavens and the earth, but also transcends them altogether. The totality of the heavens and the earth constitutes the totality of space. So no space can contain God. Similarly, God says through Isaiah:

> This is what the LORD says:
> "Heaven is my throne,
>   and the earth is my footstool.
> Where is the house you will build for me?
>   Where will my resting place be?
> Has not my hand made all these things,
>   and so they came into being?"
>   declares the LORD. (Isa. 66:1–2)

Heaven is God's throne, but the king is greater than the throne he sits on. Again, if heaven and earth exhaust what we call space, God is greater than space—beyond it, immense.

An Ethical Focus

The metaphysical point of God's immensity is closely related to an ethical one, each implying the other. Israel was often tempted to believe that God's presence in the temple made them immune to invasion or conquest. Some thought that God was bound to help them, no matter how wicked they were, because the temple was his home. He was bound to the temple and therefore to the people of Israel, they thought:

> Her leaders judge for a bribe,
>   her priests teach for a price,
>   and her prophets tell fortunes for money.
> Yet they lean upon the LORD and say,
>   "Is not the LORD among us?
>   No disaster will come upon us." (Mic. 3:11)

There was some truth in this supposition. Israel was, after all, God's covenant people. The covenant was indeed a bond between them. But the covenant contained curses for disobedience as well as blessings for obedience. At the very making of the covenant in Exodus 19–20, God made it plain that he was not bound to take Israel's side if they forsook him. To those who would worship idols, he declared:

> . . . for I, the LORD your God, am a jealous God, punishing the children for the sin of the fathers to the third and fourth generation of those who hate me, but showing love to a thousand generations of those who love me and keep my commandments. (Ex. 20:5–6)

In Amos 3:2, God invokes the covenantal bond as the basis for his punishments:

> You only have I chosen
>   of all the families of the earth;
> therefore I will punish you
>   for all your sins.

On another occasion, God tells Jeremiah to stand near the temple and say,

> Hear the word of the LORD, all you people of Judah who come through these gates to worship the LORD. This is what the LORD Almighty, the God of Israel, says: Reform your ways and your actions, and I will let you live in this place. Do not trust in deceptive words and say, "This is the temple of the LORD, the temple of the LORD, the temple of the LORD!" If you really change your ways and your actions and deal with each other justly, if you do not oppress the alien, the fatherless or the widow and do not shed innocent blood in this place, and if you do not follow other gods to your own harm, then I will let you live in this place, in the land I gave your forefathers for ever and ever. (Jer. 7:2–7)

The people thought they were safe (v. 10) to do things God detests. He reminds them that he destroyed a previous "dwelling for my name" at Shiloh (v. 12) and will do the same to the existing temple (v. 14). Similarly, in Acts 7:49–51, Stephen quotes Isaiah 66:1–2, followed by this indictment: "You stiff-necked people, with uncircumcised hearts and ears! You are just like your fathers: You always resist the Holy Spirit!"

So it is important to say that although God manifests his presence in a special way in various places, even to the point that a place can be called his dwelling, he is not bound to any place. He cannot be confined. He is greater than any place where he may be said to dwell, including the heavens and the earth themselves.

BIBLICAL PERSONALISM

Another consideration invokes the principle of biblical personalism, which, as we saw in chapter 12, is the ground of divine simplicity. God is with his creatures in space and time. But if he is extended through space, he cannot be present as a whole person to every creature. Rather, he would have to be divided into parts, so that part of him is present to one person, and another part to another person. That is not the biblical doctrine of God's omnipresence. In Scripture, God is present as a whole person to all. This implies that he is as fully present at one point in space as at any other. But if God is fully present at every point in space, he cannot be spatially extended. "He is *totus* in all *res*, *totus* in single things, *totus* in himself."[2]

LORDSHIP AND SPACE

We can think about God's immensity in the same way we thought about his atemporal eternity. Clearly, God's relationship to space is different from ours. We are limited by our bodies to a certain portion of space; God is not. The time, expense, and effort of travel limit our ability to visit different places. That is not true of God. We are not sovereign over the material universe. We are subject to many things beyond our control, like weather, earthquakes, soil conditions, and pollution. These limitations are in part due to our finitude, and in part due to the curse brought by God upon the world and upon ourselves after the fall of Adam. But God is not subject to any of these limits. He created the world and completely controls it. Past, present, and future are written in his eternal plan.

So God is sovereign over spatial reality, the Lord of space. That is the primary biblical meaning of immensity as God's aspatiality. As we shall see, the point is not that God is excluded from space, but rather that he sovereignly controls it. He is not in space as if space were a kind of box confining him.

GOD'S SPATIAL OMNIPRESENCE

In chapters 6 and 7, I expounded covenant presence, or immanence, as a lordship attribute of God. As we saw there, God is present both now and here, with all his creatures at all times and places. In chapter 24, I described

2. Salomon Van Til, quoted by Heppe in *RD*, 64.

God's presence in time as his temporal omnipresence. In this chapter, we focus on his corresponding presence in space—spatial omnipresence.

If, as I shall argue, God is not a corporeal being, spatial omnipresence cannot mean that God is a physical substance spread throughout the material universe. What it means, rather, is that God's power, knowledge, and ability to act in the finite world are universal.[3] God can instantly act at any place; he knows everything that happens, and he personally governs and directs everything in the universe (from above and from below, as we saw in chap. 14). So omnipresence is a direct implication of God's lordship, in his control and authority, as well as his covenant presence. We discussed the universality of his power, knowledge, and involvement with his world in other contexts, and so nothing more really needs to be said to establish the doctrine of divine omnipresence.

But we should note some Bible texts that teach the doctrine explicitly. For example, David says to the Lord:

Where can I go from your Spirit?
Where can I flee from your presence?
If I go up to the heavens, you are there;
if I make my bed in the depths, you are there.
If I rise on the wings of the dawn,
if I settle on the far side of the sea,
even there your hand will guide me,
your right hand will hold me fast. (Ps. 139:7–10)

David is not saying that God just happens to be wherever David chooses to go. Rather, David understands that the very nature of God as Lord makes him inescapable. The one who made and controls heaven and earth is necessarily present everywhere in the world he has made.

Similarly, Paul says to the Athenian philosophers:

"For in him we live and move and have our being." As some of your own poets have said, "We are his offspring." (Acts 17:28)

For Paul, as for David, God's omnipresence is an implication of his lordship. God created everything and determined the course of history so that he would be available to all:

The God who made the world and everything in it is the Lord of heaven and earth and does not live in temples built by hands.[4] And

3. Note that this triad corresponds to the lordship attributes.
4. Note the allusion to 1 Kings 8:27, which we considered under the topic of immensity.

he is not served by human hands, as if he needed anything, because he himself gives all men life and breath and everything else. From one man he made every nation of men, that they should inhabit the whole earth; and he determined the times set for them and the exact places where they should live. God did this so that men would seek him and perhaps reach out for him and find him, though he is not far from each one of us. (vv. 24–27)

God is present everywhere, because he is the source of everything and of every person on the earth, and because he is the controller of nature and history. And he has controlled history in such a way that he is inevitably present to all.

However, Scripture does sometimes speak of God as being absent from, or far from, some people. So we must again make some distinctions. God's presence can mean several things:

1. It can mean that God is present at every place, which is the doctrine of omnipresence proper, as in the above texts.

2. It can refer to God's presence in special holy places (chap. 2), like the burning bush (Ex. 3:5–6), Mount Sinai (Ex. 19:10–13, 20–23), the tabernacle, and the temple. Jesus is, of course, the fulfillment of these holy places (as in John 1:14; 2:21), the true temple. And through him, God's people become temples of the Holy Spirit (1 Cor. 6:19),[5] for they are members of Christ himself (6:15).[6] Compare Ephesians 3:17 and Colossians 1:27.

Heaven is a place in which God's presence is localized supremely. Scripture sometimes represents God as in heaven, looking down on the earth (Deut. 26:15; Pss. 11:4; 33:13–14; 115:3). The risen Jesus, still man as well as God, is in heaven now at God's right hand. In that sense, he is absent from us now and will return on the Last Day. But in the Spirit he is with us always (Matt. 28:20).

This language does not mean that God's power, knowledge, and freedom to act are greater in the holy places than elsewhere on earth. But we might say that in these places his presence is more intense and more intimate, and the penalties for disobedience are more severe. When God makes his dwelling in a place, that place becomes his throne. We show special deference to him there, and we become more aware of his power to bless or curse.

---

5. There are also references in the Old Testament to God indwelling his people. See Isa. 63:11 and Hag. 2:5. The Old Testament, however, does not distinguish explicitly between God's corporate dwelling with Israel (in the tabernacle and temple) and his dwelling in believers as individuals.

6. Compare Eph. 1:22–23, which combines the idea of Christ's special dwelling in his people with the idea of him filling all things.

3. God's presence also has an ethical meaning in Scripture. This meaning is related to the previous one, but it is more general. God is present with the righteous and absent from the wicked:

> But your iniquities have separated
> you from your God;
> your sins have hidden his face from you,
> so that he will not hear. (Isa. 59:2)

So:

> The LORD is far from the wicked
> but he hears the prayer of the righteous. (Prov. 15:29)

God calls upon the wicked to "come near" to him, by repenting of their sin (James 4:8), and he calls upon the righteous to draw near to him in worship and obedience (Ps. 73:28; Heb. 10:22). In this sense, God is absent from the wicked and present with the righteous. His presence is proportional to our ethical kinship with him.

God can also be said to be present with the wicked—in judgment. This is not a contradiction, just similar language making different points. The consequences for the wicked are the same:

> Though they dig down to the depths of the grave,
> from there my hand will take them.
> Though they climb up to the heavens,
> from there I will bring them down.
> Though they hide themselves on the top of Carmel,
> there I will hunt them down and seize them.
> Though they hide from me at the bottom of the sea,
> there I will command the serpent to bite them. (Amos 9:2–3;
> cf. Jer. 23:23–24)

Note the interesting parallels with Psalm 139:7–10, quoted earlier. In Psalm 139, God's presence was a blessing to David (though also a caution). Here God's presence means judgment to the wicked.

But, in a special way, God dwells with those with a contrite heart:

> For this is what the high and lofty One says—
> he who lives forever, whose name is holy:
> "I live in a high and holy place,
> but also with him who is contrite and lowly in spirit,
> to revive the spirit of the lowly
> and to revive the heart of the contrite." (Isa. 57:15)

God's special presence with the righteous is a blessing that entails his special providences in their earthly lives and his gift of eternal life. Therefore, to the righteous, God is "an ever-present help in trouble" (Ps. 46:1). The only way human beings can be righteous, of course, is through the grace of Jesus Christ. Those who are in Christ can never be separated from God's love (Rom. 8:39; cf. Ps. 16:11; John 14:23; Rom. 8:9–10; 2 Cor. 3:17).

GOD'S INCORPOREALITY

I don't know of any Scripture verse that actually says that God is incorporeal or immaterial. Perhaps there is some hint of it in the resurrection appearance of Jesus in Luke 24:36–40:

> While they were still talking about this, Jesus himself stood among them and said to them, "Peace be with you." They were startled and frightened, thinking they saw a ghost. He said to them, "Why are you troubled, and why do doubts rise in your minds? Look at my hands and my feet. It is I myself! Touch me and see; a ghost does not have flesh and bones, as you see I have." When he had said this, he showed them his hands and feet.

The word "ghost" here is *pneuma,* "spirit," and this passage may be seen to contrast spirit with corporeality. So when John 4:24 tells us that "God is spirit," we may deduce that God is not a body. On the other hand, I'm inclined to think the NIV is right to see in Luke 24 a reference to ghostliness, not spirituality as such. And, as I will indicate later, the point of John 4:24 is not God's immateriality, but his possession of the qualities of the Holy Spirit. So perhaps it would not be wise for us to try to prove God's incorporeality from John 4:24 and Luke 24:36–40.

Nevertheless, God's incorporeality is clearly a good and necessary consequence of biblical teachings that we have already considered. Certainly God in his atemporal and/or nonspatial existence cannot be a physical being.

But what of God as immanent, as omnipresent in space and time? It may be helpful to consider more specifically what it means to have a body. Jonathan Harrison formulated "five things which I am saying when I say that this body is my body."[7] Richard Swinburne summarized them like this:

> The first is that disturbances in it [my body—JF] cause me pains, aches, tingles, etc.; whereas disturbances in the table or the body over there are unfelt. The second and related thing is that I feel

---

7. Richard Swinburne, *The Coherence of Theism* (Oxford: Clarendon Press, 1977), 102.

the inside of this body. I feel the emptiness of the stomach and the position of these limbs. The third thing is that I can move directly many parts of this body—whereas I can move parts of some other body or thing by moving parts of this body. . . . The fourth thing is that I look out on the world from where this body is. It is things around this body which I see well, things further away which I see less well. I learn about other things in the world by their effects on this body (i.e. on the sense-organs of this body). The fifth thing is that my thoughts and feelings are affected by goings-on in this body. Getting alcohol into this body makes me see double.[8]

This description of having a body, which seems to me to be pretty accurate, is clearly not a description of God's transcendent (atemporal and nonspatial) existence. There is no physical body (including the entire universe) that has such relationships to God in his transcendence.

Nevertheless, the question does arise as to whether God, as immanent in time and space, has qualities analogous to those of physical bodies. Consider Harrison's five categories: First, we would not want to say that states of affairs in the universe cause states of affairs in God. God, after all, is the ultimate cause of all states of affairs. But, as omnipresent in time and space, God is fully aware of what is happening in every location. He "feels" (see the later discussion of impassibility) what is going on. That is at least somewhat analogous to Harrison's first category.

Second, God feels directly everything that is going on in the universe he inhabits as the omnipresent one. Third, God can move "directly" any object in the universe. Fourth, as omnipresent in time and space, God "looks out from" every location. Fifth, God's thoughts are not "affected" by happenings in the world, but he certainly perceives them and responds appropriately (see chap. 24) to the events of the world.

I would draw these conclusions:

1. God is not to be identified with any physical being, for he is transcendent over space and time.

2. If God is simple (chap. 12), it is hard to imagine how he can be physical. If he has a body, then he, like any other physical being, can be divided into parts.

3. If he is omnipresent in space and time, he cannot be a particular physical being, for no such being could inhabit all times and places equally.

4. If God had a physical existence, his body would have to be the entire universe. But we must not identify him with the universe. That would be

---

8. Ibid., 102–3.

pantheism, and we have seen good reasons to disavow that view. In Scripture, Creator and creature are distinct. God is not the creation; he is the Creator, the Lord of creation. We should not forget that God, as omnipresent, is at the same time transcendent.

5. Nor, for the same reason, should we think of the world as part of God's being (panentheism, all is in God). Everything in the world is created by God, and so nothing in the world is divine.

6. Nevertheless, God is present in the world he has made. In his immanent temporal and spatial omnipresence, God experiences the world in ways similar to the ways we do. His experience of the world is analogous to what it would be if the universe were his body. Indeed, we can say more than this. God experiences the world, not only from his transcendent perspective and from the perspective of the whole universe, but also from every particular perspective within the universe. Since he is with me, he experiences the world from my perspective, as well as from the perspective of every other being in the universe. True omniscience must include a knowledge of every such perspective.[9]

We should not be surprised that there are significant analogies between God's experiences of the world and our own. Scripture tells us that we were made in his image.

THEOPHANY AND INCARNATION

The above discussion provides useful background in considering Scripture's teachings about theophany and incarnation. We have seen that God is capable of viewing the world from finite perspectives, in ways analogous to the experiences of finite beings. The doctrines of theophany and incarnation show us that God is able to take on a physical form. In that physical form, his relationship to the world is more closely analogous to Harrison's categories than in his general omnipresence.

A theophany is a visible manifestation of God to human beings. God may appear in the form of an angel (Gen. 32:22–32, especially v. 30), or of a man (Gen. 18:16–33). Most often he appears as the Glory-cloud, the fiery cloud that led Israel through the wilderness and settled on the sanctuary. Meredith G. Kline explains:

> When the inner reality veiled within the theophanic cloud is revealed, we behold God in his heaven. The world of the Glory the-

---

9. Compare my discussion in chapter 22 of passages alleged to teach divine ignorance.

ophany is a dimensional realm normally invisible to man, where God reveals his presence as the King of glory enthroned in the midst of myriads of heavenly beings.[10] It is the realm into which the glorified Christ, disappearing from human view, entered to assume his place on the throne of God. It is the invisible (or "third") heaven brought into cloud-veiled visibility.[11]

Kline finds this theophany in Genesis 1:2, the brooding of the Spirit over the waters, and in other texts dealing with the Spirit. So he identifies the Spirit with the Glory-cloud as well.

We saw earlier that although God is everywhere, he sometimes reveals himself in particular holy places where his presence is especially intense. The theophany is this kind of holy space. So, appropriately, the theophanic Glory-cloud descends upon the tabernacle, and the bright "cloud" envelops Jesus, Moses, Elijah, and the disciples on the Mount of Transfiguration (Matt. 17:5).

Insofar as the glory is God's "address" or geographical location, we can understand better the texts we noted earlier in which God "looks down from heaven" on the sons of men. That he inhabits heaven in a unique sense implies that heaven is a privileged perspective from which he views the creation. But since God's heavenly dwelling does not contradict his general omnipresence, his heavenly perspective does not cancel out the fact that he views the world from all other perspectives as well.

The incarnation of the Son of God in Jesus Christ is, of course, unique in human history. Jesus is a theophany (as Jesus tells Philip, "Anyone who has seen me has seen the Father" [John 14:9]), but much more. Only in the case of Jesus did God become flesh permanently, being conceived in the body of a woman, experiencing a human infancy and growth, and increasing in wisdom and stature, subject to the sufferings of this life and to death itself.

There is great mystery here. Jesus never abandons his divine attributes. He is omniscient, omnipotent, and omnipresent.[12] Yet he suffers and thirsts and displays ignorance. Christians have understood these facts in terms of the two natures of Christ, as defined by the Council of Chalcedon in 451.

---

10. Kline refers in a footnote to Ezek. 1:1ff.; 3:12ff.; 10:1ff.; 11:22ff.; 43:2ff. He says these are "a good place to start, but once it is determined that the Glory is a revelational modality of heaven, every biblical unveiling of the scene of the heavenly throne and the divine council becomes a source for our envisaging of the divine presence within the cloud-theophany." Meredith G. Kline, *Images of the Spirit* (Grand Rapids: Baker, 1980), 17n. The theophany of Isaiah's famous vision in Isa. 6:1–13 and the visions of John in Revelation also display these features.

11. Ibid., 17.

12. "Kenosis" Christologies maintain that when the Son of God became man, he set aside

Jesus has a complete divine nature and a complete human nature. The two natures are distinct, not mixed or turned into one another (for the Creator-creature distinction must be affirmed even in Christ, in which the Creator and the creature are most intimately joined); but neither are they separated or divided in their functions.

But the two natures are united in one person. That person is a divine person, the very Son of God in human flesh. In Christ, God "has been tempted in every way, just as we are—yet was without sin," so he can "sympathize with our weaknesses" (Heb. 4:15). In Christ, God certainly perceives the world not only from his transcendent perspective, not only from all creaturely perspectives, but uniquely from one particular creaturely perspective. The body of Jesus is God's body in Harrison's sense. But at the very same time, God (the Son, as well as the Father and the Spirit) has an existence that transcends all physical limitation.

God is not, therefore, to be defined as a physical being. (Even the incarnate Son of God had a divine sovereignty over space and time.) But as Lord of all things that are material and physical, he is supremely able to understand the world from the perspective of every physical being, to reveal himself in any physical form that he chooses, and even to take human flesh, so that he has his own body, without abandoning his transcendent existence.

I argued that it is perhaps better to say that God is Lord of time and Lord of space than to say merely that God is atemporal and nonspatial. Although he does have atemporal and nonspatial existence, he is also temporally and spatially omnipresent. His sovereignty does not mean that he is excluded from time and space; rather, it means that he acts toward them as Lord, not as one who is limited by them. The same point can be made about God's incorporeality. This doctrine does not exclude God from physical reality. Rather, it teaches that he relates himself to physical reality as the Lord, transcending it and using it as he chooses.

GOD'S INVISIBILITY

The same approach will help us to understand better the biblical teaching concerning God's invisibility. To say that God is invisible is not to exclude God from the realm of the visible, but to regard him as the Lord of visibility, the Lord of light.

---

some or all of his divine attributes. But God cannot be God, as we have seen, without his attributes. If the incarnate Christ lacked any essential divine attribute, then he was not God in the flesh.

Several biblical texts speak of God as invisible (Greek *aoratos*) (Rom. 1:20; Col. 1:15; 1 Tim. 1:17; Heb. 11:27). The Johannine literature says in a number of places that no one has ever seen God (John 1:18; 5:37; 6:46; 1 John 4:12, 20).

As we have seen, however, God has revealed himself by theophany and incarnation, both of which are highly visible means. In a real sense, to see the theophany or the incarnate Christ is to see God.

In the presence of theophany, the question is not whether God can be seen, but rather whether any human being can survive after seeing him. In Exodus 33, Moses asks to see God's "glory" (v. 18). God promises Moses an experience of his "goodness" and an exposition of his "name" (v. 19). "But," he adds, "you cannot see my face, for no one may see me and live" (v. 20). Typically, God's people are terrified to look upon God (Ex. 3:6; Job 13:11; Isa. 6:5).

But some do in fact see God, and amazingly their lives are preserved. Hagar, cast out of Abraham's house by Sarah after the birth of Ishmael, meets God and responds to him:

> She gave this name to the LORD who spoke to her: "You are the God who sees me," for she said, "I have now seen the One who sees me." (Gen. 16:13)

Jacob, having wrestled with the theophanic angel of the Lord, names the place of his encounter Peniel, saying, "It is because I saw God face [*panim*] to face, and yet my life was spared" (Gen. 32:30). Manoah and his wife, the parents of Samson, experience a theophany and exclaim, "We are doomed to die! . . . We have seen God!" (Judg. 13:22), but they do not die. After the Exodus and the giving of the law, God asked the priests and elders of Israel to "come up to the LORD" (Ex. 24:1). They went up "and saw the God of Israel" (v. 10). Verse 10 significantly adds, "But God did not raise his hand against these leaders of the Israelites; they saw God, and they ate and drank." Isaiah (Isa. 6:1) and Amos (Amos 9:1) also "saw the Lord."

From the cleft of a rock, God grants to Moses an image of his "back," but "my face [*panim*] must not be seen" (Ex. 33:23). We wonder, did God reveal his *panim* to Jacob, but not to Moses? And if so, why the apparent difference? And what is the difference between merely seeing God and seeing his face? The mystery concerning Moses' experience of God includes the use of the term *temunah*. In Deuteronomy 4:15, God speaks to Israel through Moses and grounds the prohibition of idolatry in the fact that "you saw no form [*temunah*] of any kind the day the LORD spoke to you at Horeb out of the fire." Yet in Numbers 12:8, when Miriam and Aaron are contesting Moses' primacy over them as a prophet, God says,

With [Moses] I speak face to face [*peh*, "mouth"; not *panim*],
   clearly and not in riddles;
   he sees the form [*temunah*] of the Lord.
Why then were you not afraid
   to speak against my servant Moses?"

So Moses saw God's *temunah*, but Israel did not see it.[13] Apparently, too, Moses received revelation by *peh*, but not *panim*, though Jacob actually saw God's *panim*.

The language of divine visibility is often applied to the incarnate Christ in the New Testament. The apostle John insists that although no one has ever seen God, Jesus has made him known (John 1:18). And Jesus makes God known in highly visible ways. To Philip, Jesus says, "Anyone who has seen me has seen the Father" (14:9). John's first letter glories in the visibility and tangibility of the revelation of Jesus:

> That which was from the beginning, which we have heard, which we have seen with our eyes, which we have looked at and our hands have touched—this we proclaim concerning the Word of life. The life appeared; we have seen it and testify to it, and we proclaim to you the eternal life, which was with the Father and has appeared to us. (1 John 1:1–2)

Compare Acts 1:3, 1 Corinthians 15:3–8, and 2 Peter 1:16–18, which emphasize the visibility of Christ in his transfiguration and resurrection. New Testament writers appeal to "eyewitnesses" to vindicate the gospel (Luke 1:21; 2 Peter 1:16).

We do not now literally see Jesus, since his ascension to the Father's right hand. But, evidently reminiscing about the visibility of Jesus' earthly ministry, the writer to the Hebrews speaks about how we "see" him:

> But we see Jesus, who was made a little lower than the angels, now crowned with glory and honor because he suffered death, so that by the grace of God he might taste death for everyone. (2:9)

---

13. I disagree with Bavinck's statement (in *DG*, 175) that God is "unpicturable, Ex. 20:4; Deut. 5:8; since he is without form, Deut. 4:12, 15." Deuteronomy does not say that God is without form; it only says that God did not display his form to Israel on Mount Sinai. And God is certainly not unpicturable in any straightforward sense. He images himself in theophany, Christ is his image *par excellence* (Col. 1:15; Heb. 1:3), and man is his image as well (Gen. 1:27). God prohibits worship by images, not because he cannot be pictured, but because the old covenant was founded on the revelation of God in his invisibility, and because he intends to assert his exclusive right to make images of himself.

These biblical emphases, both on God's invisibility and on his visibility, sometimes come together, forming paradoxes:

> So we fix our eyes not on what is seen, but on what is unseen. For what is seen is temporary, but what is unseen is eternal. (2 Cor. 4:18)

> By faith [Moses] left Egypt, not fearing the king's anger; he persevered because he saw him who is invisible. (Heb. 11:27)

It is a bit difficult to know how to bring these biblical data together into a precise theological formulation. I am not able to unravel the distinctions between *panim, peh,* and *temunah.* Nor can I determine the precise nature of the visual revelation given to Jacob, Moses, Miriam, Aaron, the elders of Israel, the nation of Israel, Isaiah, and others, and how these revelations differed from one another. But on some points we can be fairly confident:

1. God is *essentially invisible.* This means, not that he can never be seen under any circumstances, but rather that, as Lord, he sovereignly chooses when, where, and to whom to make himself visible. He controls all the matter and light in the universe, so that he alone determines whether and how he will be visible to his creatures. So his relationship to visibility (to light and matter) is similar to his relationship to time and space.

2. God has often made himself visible, in theophany and in the incarnate Christ, so that human beings may on occasion truly say that they have "seen God." The Glory-cloud theophany (see the preceding section) is a permanent, visible revelation of God, located in heaven, but sometimes visible from earth. And at God's right hand in heaven is Jesus, who remains both God and man and therefore a permanently visible divine person.

3. "No one has ever seen God" (John 1:18a) means that no one has ever seen God apart from his voluntary theophanic-incarnational revelation. "God the One and Only, who is at the Father's side, has made him known" (v. 18b).

4. It is right to be terrified in the presence of theophany. The theophany is always holy ground. In the vicinity of theophany, God will judge severely any lack of proper reverence. And, as with Adam and Eve in the garden, God often comes to us for the purpose of judging sin. But, as we have seen, some people do see God without losing their lives. So we see the grace of God, preserving life, though we have forfeited the right to live.[14] When God hides Moses in "a cleft in the rock" so Moses can see

---

14. So God's warning, "Man shall not see my face and live," is like the conditional prophecies we examined in chapter 24. Although God prescribes death to sinners who look upon him, he reserves the right to extend the grace of forgiveness.

his "back" (Gen. 33:22–23), the difference between back and face is somewhat obscure. But in the cleft of the rock the church is right to see an anticipation of Christ.

5. There is a rather notable difference in this respect between the inauguration of God's covenant with Moses and the beginning of the new covenant in Christ. In the former instance, God stresses that the people saw no form (*temunah*). The reason is not that there was no *temunah* to be seen, for Moses saw God's *temunah*, according to Numbers 12:8. Rather, although the Sinai revelation included many visible phenomena, God withheld from Israel the intimate vision he granted to Moses, the vision of God's *temunah*. But the New Testament writers positively exult over the visibility of Jesus' coming. The incarnate Christ is as emphatically visible (as in 1 John 1:1–3) as Yahweh in the Mosaic covenant was emphatically invisible. The new covenant begins with a revelation of profound visibility.

6. The visibility of God often has an eschatological thrust in Scripture. The new covenant, with its highly visible revelation of God, is the beginning of "the age to come," in which God sets all things right. This new age overlaps the old age of sin's dominion until the second coming of Jesus and the final judgment. Then the old age ("this age") ends, and God consummates "the age to come." The visibility of Jesus is the beginning of the end, in which God will be profoundly visible in theophany and incarnation. So the theophanies throughout Scripture anticipate our heavenly fellowship with God. Note the following:

Blessed are the pure in heart,
    for they will see God. (Matt. 5:8)

Now we see but a poor reflection as in a mirror; then we shall see face to face. Now I know in part; then I shall know fully, even as I am fully known. (1 Cor. 13:12)

Dear friends, now we are children of God, and what we will be has not yet been made known. But we know that when he appears, we shall be like him, for we shall see him as he is. (1 John 3:2)

Look, he is coming with the clouds, and every eye will see him, even those who pierced him; and all the peoples of the earth will mourn because of him. So shall it be! Amen. (Rev. 1:7; cf. Zech. 12:10)

GOD'S GLORY

We have seen that although God is essentially invisible, there are important ways in which he makes himself visible. God's glory, as a divine attribute, is related to his visibility, so it is appropriate here to discuss it.

Glory, with the verb *glorify* and adjective *glorious*, is one of the most common terms in the Christian vocabulary, but one of the hardest to define precisely. What does it actually mean to "glorify" God or to "seek God's glory"?

Glory and its related forms represent several different words in Hebrew (*kavod, tif'arah, hod, hadar*) and Greek (*doxa, timē, eulogia*). *Kavod* and *doxa* are the most common of these. *Kavod* is also translated "wealth" or "riches," as is the Greek *timē*. Both terms can be translated "reputation," "splendor," or "honor."[15]

THE GLORY-THEOPHANY

To see how these meanings fit together, we can perhaps start with the idea of a great light shining from God's theophanic presence. As we saw in the above discussion of theophany, the cloud that led Israel through the wilderness and settled on the tabernacle is called the "glory." One of the earliest references to the glory of the Lord occurs in Exodus 16, when the Israelites, newly released from Egypt, begin to grumble about the lack of food. God promises manna, and then we read:

> So Moses and Aaron said to all the Israelites, "In the evening you will know that it was the Lord who brought you out of Egypt, and in the morning you will see the glory of the Lord, because he has heard your grumbling against him. Who are we, that you should grumble against us?" Moses also said, "You will know that it was the Lord when he gives you meat to eat in the evening and all the bread you want in the morning, because he has heard your grumbling against him. Who are we? You are not grumbling against us, but against the Lord."
> Then Moses told Aaron, "Say to the entire Israelite community, 'Come before the Lord, for he has heard your grumbling.' "
> While Aaron was speaking to the whole Israelite community, they looked toward the desert, and there was the glory of the Lord appearing in the cloud. (vv. 6–10)

The "glory" here is certainly the bright theophany in the cloud. As we have seen, Kline calls this theophany the Glory-cloud.

---

15. There is also the verb *kauchaomai*, often translated "glory" in the KJV, but better translated "boast," as in the NIV.

GLORY AS GOD'S PRESENCE

In many passages, "glory" is simply the created light that emerges from the theophany. One could argue from these passages that glory is something that accompanies God, rather than a divine attribute as such. In the Glory-cloud, however, God is with his people, immanent and covenantally present. So *glory* can refer, not only to the created light surrounding God in the theophany, but to God himself, present with his people. So it appears regularly in contexts of praise:

> Yours, O LORD, is the greatness and the power
>   and the glory and the majesty and the splendor,
>   for everything in heaven and earth is yours.
> Yours, O LORD, is the kingdom;
>   you are exalted as head over all. (1 Chron. 29:11)

> Lift up your heads, O you gates;
>   be lifted up, you ancient doors,
>   that the King of glory may come in. (Ps. 24:7)

> . . . to the praise of his glorious grace, which he has freely given us in the One he loves. (Eph. 1:6)

Jesus (the fulfillment of the tabernacle and the temple) shares the very glory of God, which is a remarkable testimony to his deity. He says, "And now, Father, glorify me in your presence with the glory I had with you before the world began" (John 17:5; cf. 17:22, 24; Matt. 25:31; John 1:14; 2:11). He is called "the Lord of glory" in 1 Corinthians 2:8 and James 2:1. He is particularly glorious in what would seem least glorious, his death for sin. Referring to his coming death, he says, "The hour has come for the Son of Man to be glorified" (John 12:23), and, "Now is the Son of Man glorified and God is glorified in him" (John 13:31; cf. Rev. 5:11–12; 7:9–12). In his death, of course, and for most of his earthly life, he did not emit a visible light. (The Transfiguration, however, was a literal glorification.) The death of Christ was glorious in that, like the glory-theophany, it revealed one who is supremely worthy of praise.

GOD'S GLORY IN CREATION

So the glory is God himself, covenantally present. But God's presence glorifies the creation, too. Creation is not divine, but it is his finite glory-light. God has made the world to be his temple, so it declares his glory (Ps. 19:1). Adam is not only the image of God, but the glory of God as well (Ps. 8:5; 1 Cor. 11:7).

In these passages, glory is not a literal light. The created qualities of the universe and of human beings may not have literally glowed, but the world was something splendid, a product that enhanced God's reputation.

Adam's sin, however, marred his glory, as it marred the image of God in which he was made. But redemption restores that glory, both in this life—"And we, who with unveiled faces all reflect the Lord's glory, are being transformed into his likeness with ever-increasing glory, which comes from the Lord, who is the Spirit" (2 Cor. 3:18)—and especially in the life to come (Rom. 8:18; 1 Cor. 2:7; 2 Cor. 4:6, 17; Heb. 2:10).

It is God's intention for the creation to return glory back to him. When our lives image the attributes of God, others see the glory of God's presence in us as his temple. So we bring God's glorious reputation to the eyes of others. Thus we ourselves are part of the light that goes forth from God over the earth.

In this ethical sense, Scripture calls on us to glorify God. In one sense, of course, we cannot increase God's glory. But when we speak truly of him and obey his Word, we enhance his reputation on earth (and among the angels [Eph. 3:10]), and we ourselves become part of the created light by which people come to know God's presence. So Jesus says that his disciples are "the light of the world" (Matt. 5:14), as he is (John 8:12; cf. Matt. 4:14–16).

We can also understand glorifying God as giving praise to him. *Doxa* is sometimes translated "glory" and sometimes "praise." The two ideas are closely related. Our words and our lives bring praise to God, which shows his glory-light to the world. To glorify God, then, is simply to obey him, and therefore to proclaim his greatness by our words and deeds.

GLORY AND THE TRINITY

We have seen how God glorifies his creation and the human race, and how creation, in turn, glorifies God. The circle of glorification, however, does not begin with creation. There is also a circle of glorification within the Trinity itself.[16] The Father glorifies the Son (John 8:50, 54; 13:32; 14:13; 17:1, 5), and the Son glorifies the Father (John 7:18; 13:31; 17:4). The Spirit glorifies the Son (John 16:14), and therefore glorifies the Father through the Son. In this context, we learn also that Christian believers glorify Christ (John 17:10), and he gives glory to believers: "I have given them the glory that you gave me, that they may be one as we are one" (v. 22).

There is great mystery here as we gain a glimpse of the intra-Trinitarian

---

16. Thanks to Jeff Meyers for drawing my attention to this pattern.

being of God. More discussion of the Trinity, and of this mutual glorification, will come in chapter 29. At least we can say that in the Trinity there is a mutual glorification, in which each person glorifies the others. As we explore the mysterious inwardness of the Godhead, we are no longer talking about a glory-light in a literal sense. Rather, each member of the Trinity speaks and acts in such a way as to enhance the reputations of the other two, to bring praise and honor to the other persons. There is here a mutual deference, a willingness to serve one another. That is the mind of Christ (Phil. 2:5) that motivated the Son of God to become a sacrifice for the sins of men.

The Father does glorify himself (John 12:28), but he does this by glorifying the Son and the Spirit and by glorifying his people. Although he deserves all glory and praise, he serves others and thereby attracts even more glory to himself.

Jesus prays in John 17:22 that his people may be "one as we are one." How can the church possibly be one as God himself is one? The church is not divine, and so it can never achieve the perfect oneness of the Father, Son, and Spirit. But the passage does help the church to set some goals to achieve with God's help. One way toward a oneness that reflects the Trinity is for us to glorify one another as do the persons of the Trinity. That means loving one another, serving one another, praising one another, honoring one another. If we really sought to glorify one another, we would seek, even across denominational and traditional lines, to make one another look good, to enhance one another's reputations, rather than to make ourselves look good at everyone else's expense.[17]

GOD'S SPIRITUALITY

We will have much more to say later about the Holy Spirit as the third person of the Trinity. But in this section I am interested in spirit or spirituality as an attribute of God, as in John 4:24, where Jesus says, "God is spirit, and his worshipers must worship in spirit and in truth." Here Jesus is probably not referring specifically to the Holy Spirit, but to spirituality as an attribute of the triune God. We shall see, however, that there is a close relationship between the qualities of the Holy Spirit and the spirituality of the triune God.

Theologians have sometimes defined spirituality negatively as incorpo-

17. For more on this subject and the applications of John 17, see my essay "Walking Together," available at www.thirdmill.org.

reality and/or invisibility. Bavinck does this, although he adds a more positive definition.[18] Scripture does hint that spirit is immaterial, in Isaiah 31:3 and Luke 24:36–43, which I discussed earlier under the topic of incorporeality. But spirit is more than just incorporeality or invisibility.

As we have seen, Scripture identifies the glory-theophany with the Spirit of God. Kline says:

> There is indeed a considerable amount of biblical data that identify the Glory-cloud as particularly a manifestation of the Spirit of God. Here we will cite only a few passages where the functions performed by the Glory-cloud are attributed to the Spirit—Nehemiah 9:19, 20; Isaiah 63:11–14; and Haggai 2:5—and mention the correspondence of the work of the Holy Spirit at Pentecost to the functioning of the Glory-cloud at the exodus and at the erection of the tabernacle.[19]

Note that Kline says that the Glory-cloud is "a manifestation" of the Spirit. Kline's association of the Spirit with the cloud is helpful, and it implies that everything I said earlier about the Glory-cloud pertains to the Spirit as well. Of course, Scripture also refers to the working of the Spirit in the absence of a theophany.

The Glory-cloud provides a model for the broader and less literal senses of *glory*. God's glory is an "outshining" from him, not only of literal light, but also of creative power and ethical qualities. Thus, the Glory-cloud provides a model that helps us understand the work of the Spirit in other contexts. As the Glory-cloud rested upon the tabernacle and entered the temple, so the Spirit indwells believers, who are temples of the Holy Spirit (1 Cor. 6:19). As God's presence in the cloud empowered his people, gave them direction, and accompanied them with blessing and judgment, so the Spirit acts throughout Scripture.

In general, God's Spirit is his presence in the world, performing his work as Lord. Later we will see that Spirit, like God's Word (John 1:14) and God's fatherhood, is both a divine attribute and a person of the Trinity. But for now let us focus on the ways in which *spirit* describes God's actions in the world.

---

18. *DG*, 179. Bavinck's positive definition is that as spirit, God is "the hidden, incomposed (uncompounded, simple), absolute ground of all creaturely, somatic and pneumatic, essence." I'm not sure what this means or how it can be derived from the biblical data concerning spirit.

19. Kline, *Images of the Spirit*, 15. He cites also Meredith M. Kline, "The Holy Spirit as Covenant Witness" (Th.M. thesis, Westminster Theological Seminary, 1972), and his own *Structure of Biblical Authority* (Grand Rapids: Eerdmans, 1975).

The words in Hebrew (*ruah*) and Greek (*pneuma*) that are translated "spirit" can also mean "wind" or "breath," which are regular biblical metaphors for the work of the Spirit. As wind blows invisibly and unpredictably, so the Spirit gives new birth (John 3:5–8). As words cannot be communicated without breath, so the Spirit regularly accompanies the word of God to its destination (2 Sam. 23:2; Isa. 59:21; John 6:63; 1 Thess. 1:5; 2 Tim. 3:16; 1 Peter 1:12; 2 Peter 1:21). This is true, not only of prophecy, but of creation as well:

> By the word of the LORD were the heavens made,
>   their starry host by the breath of his mouth. (Ps. 33:6)

For pedagogical purposes, it is convenient to distinguish the connotations of *spirit* along the lines of the lordship attributes: power, authority, and presence in blessing and judgment. I shall then say a bit about the role of God's Spirit in redemptive history.

POWER

Like a mighty, rushing wind, the Spirit exerts the great power of God. The prophet Micah says:

> But as for me, I am filled with power,
>   with the Spirit of the LORD,
>   and with justice and might,
> to declare to Jacob his transgression,
>   to Israel his sin. (Mic. 3:8)

We have seen the Spirit's involvement in the great work of creation (Gen. 1:2; see also Pss. 33:6; 104:30). The *ruah* is also the power behind the cherubim (Ezek. 1:12, 20) and the power behind the unusual strength of Samson (Judg. 13:25) and others (Judg. 14:6, 19; 15:14). The Spirit lifts people up and carries them away (2 Kings 2:16; Ezek. 3:12, 14; 8:3; 11:1, 24; 37:1; 43:5; Acts 8:39–40; and figuratively, 2 Peter 1:21). The Spirit gives power to preaching (Luke 4:14; Rom. 15:19; 1 Cor. 2:4; 1 Thess. 1:5).

AUTHORITY

As already suggested, it is the Spirit who appoints prophets and brings the word of God to them. The Spirit is the breath behind the word. Among the many passages connecting the Spirit with prophecy, see Genesis 41:38; Numbers 24:2; 1 Samuel 10:6, 10; 2 Kings 2:9, 15–16; Nehemiah 9:30; Isaiah 61:1; Ezekiel 2:2; 3:24; Joel 2:28; Luke 1:17; and 1 Peter 1:11. It is also the Spirit who speaks through Jesus, his apostles, and the New Testament prophets, bringing the new covenant revelation (Matt. 10:20; Luke 4:14; John 3:34; 14:16–17; 15:26; 16:13; Acts 2:4; 6:10; 1 Cor. 2:4, 10–14; 7:40; 12:3; 1 Thess. 1:5; Rev. 2:7; 19:10).

It is the Spirit who gives wisdom (see chap. 22)—both practical skills and ethical understanding (Ex. 28:3; 31:3; 35:31; Deut. 34:9). The Spirit raises up men with the wisdom to rule and win battles (Num. 11:17, 25–29; Judg. 3:10; 6:34; 11:29; 14:6, 19; 15:14; 1 Sam. 11:6; 16:13). He gives gifts to the church to edify the body (1 Cor. 12:1–11).

The anointing of prophets, priests, and kings with oil symbolized their investiture by the Spirit. Kline writes about the garments of the priests as replicating the Glory-Spirit[20] and about "the Prophet as Image of the Glory-Spirit."[21] Jesus, the Messiah (the anointed one), the ultimate prophet, priest, and king, is therefore richly endued with the Spirit (Isa. 11:2; 42:1; Matt. 3:6; 4:1; 12:18; Luke 4:16–21, fulfilling Isa. 61:1–2).

PRESENCE IN BLESSING AND JUDGMENT

The Spirit is also God with us. David asks,

> Where can I go from your Spirit?
> Where can I flee from your presence? (Ps. 139:7)

In Israel, the Spirit made his home in the tabernacle and the temple. Christians are temples of the Spirit, and therefore have the Spirit dwelling within them (1 Cor. 3:16; Gal. 4:6; 5:16–26; 1 Peter 1:2). As the "breath" of God gave life to Adam (Gen. 2:7), so the Spirit gives new spiritual life (John 3:5–8; 6:63; 1 Cor. 15:45; 2 Cor. 3:6; 1 Peter 3:18; 4:6). And the Spirit enables the believer to grow in righteousness (Rom. 8:1–17).

So the Spirit is present to bless God's people. But, as is less widely acknowledged, the Spirit is active in judgment as well. Kline argues, rightly I think, that *ruah hayyom* in Genesis 3:8 should not be translated "cool of the day," but as "Spirit of the day," where "day" is a kind of anticipation of the Day of Judgment. Kline finds this use of *spirit* also in Isaiah 11:1–4, 2 Thessalonians 2:8, and 1 Peter 4:13–16.[22]

20. Kline, *Images of the Spirit*, 35–56.
21. Ibid., 57–96.
22. Ibid., 97–131.

The Spirit in Redemptive History

As we have seen, the Spirit has never been absent from the world or from God's people. But the Spirit's presence is not merely a constant feature of the world's landscape. Rather, as always with the immanent God, the Spirit acts in different ways at different times. He is active in all the developments that take place throughout the history of redemption. The major development in the New Testament period is the Spirit's "coming" on the Day of Pentecost (Acts 2), empowering the church to bring the gospel of Christ to Jerusalem, Judea, Samaria, and "the ends of the earth" (Acts 1:8).

This special presence of the Spirit is always in the forefront of the New Testament writings. So when Jesus declares in John 4:24, "God is spirit, and his worshipers must worship in spirit and in truth," he is not saying merely that God is invisible and incorporeal. Nor is the point of the verse that in worship we should focus on immaterial things. Rather, Jesus is speaking of the great coming event ("a time is coming" [v. 23]) when, at his behest, the Spirit comes with power upon the church. When the Spirit comes, worship, like evangelism, will be "in Spirit." The great power of the Spirit will motivate the prayer and praise of God's people.

That worship will also be "in truth." In context, I think that this "truth" is not merely truth in general as opposed to falsehood. The worship of the old covenant, as God ordained it, was not false. Jesus here refers to the truth he came to bring: the truth of salvation through the blood of his cross, the gospel of grace. Therefore, worship in Spirit is Christ-centered. The Spirit bears witness to Christ, and he motivates God's people to sing the praises of Jesus.

To say that "God is Spirit," then, is to say that true worship of God is directed to the Son by the Spirit. God identifies himself with the Spirit and tells us here that the qualities and acts of the Spirit are indeed the qualities and acts of God. God's spirituality, then, means not only that God is invisible and immaterial, but that he bears all the characteristics of the Spirit who dwells with his people.

CHAPTER 26

The Self-Contained God

In this chapter I shall explore two closely related attributes of God, his aseity and his impassibility.

GOD'S ASEITY

The term *aseity* comes from the Latin phrase *a se,* meaning "from or by himself." Bavinck defines it by saying that God "is whatever he is by his own self or of his own self."[1] He derives this attribute from the "I AM" of Exodus 3:14, which he takes in the sense "I WILL BE THAT I WILL BE."[2] This is the first divine attribute that Bavinck discusses, and he considers it central: "All other attributes were derived from this one."[3] It is "commonly viewed as the first of the attributes."[4]

---

1. *DG,* 144.
2. Ibid. (emphasis his). Of course, I take Ex. 3:14 somewhat differently, as setting forth the control, authority, and presence of the covenant Lord (chaps. 2–6). But, as we shall see, that lordship implies aseity.
3. Ibid. Bavinck agrees that the other attributes are included in this one because "by it they are all ascribed to God in an absolute sense; i.e., by this description God is recognized as God in *all* his perfections" (pp. 126–27). He adds that we cannot derive these attributes by means of logic, but only by revelation. But note Gordon H. Clark's attempt to derive them by logic, using biblical premises, in "Attributes, The Divine," in *Baker's Dictionary of Theology,* ed. Everett F. Harrison (Grand Rapids: Baker, 1960), 78–79. Since God's thought is logical (chap. 22), we should not see revelation and logic as a simple antithesis. But it is right to insist that arguments of this sort be based on biblical premises.
4. *DG,* 145. Earlier Bavinck said that aseity, or absoluteness, is the concept we need "to

600

Nevertheless, Bavinck prefers the term ~~independence~~ to the term *aseity*. He says:

> Among the Reformed this divine perfection receives even greater emphasis, even though the word "aseity" soon gives place to the better term "independence." "Aseity" merely expresses the fact that God is self-sufficient in his *existence;* but "independence" has a broader connotation, and indicates that God is self-sufficient in *everything:* in his existence, in his attributes, in his decrees, and in his works.[5]

I am unable to verify this distinction between aseity and independence. One could argue that aseity is the better term, because it refers to God "as he is in himself," apart from creation, while independence presupposes a created world (at least in God's plan) from which he is independent. On that account, aseity is more fundamental. God is independent of the world because in himself he is *a se*. And, contrary to Bavinck, I don't think that aseity need be limited to existence; like independence, it can be freely applied to everything God is and does, to his attributes, decrees, and works. For practical purposes, then, I would consider the two terms interchangeable, noting that aseity takes the concept to a deeper level.

We can therefore use these words as synonyms for *aseity: independence, self-existence, self-sufficiency,* and *self-containment*.[6] The term *self-caused* (*causa sui*), sometimes used as another synonym, is misleading. Since efficient causation requires some priority of the cause to the effect, it is impossible to bring about one's own existence in a literal sense. Taken nonliterally, however, the term means that God is uncaused and has within himself sufficient reasons or grounds for his existence. *Absolute* is another term I shall sometimes use as a synonym for *a se*, although with certain divine attributes it can also mean "infinite" or "unqualified." When I spoke of God as "absolute personality" in chapter 2, "absolute" had the sense of "*a se*."

In chapter 2, I suggested that the phrase "absolute personality" was useful in defining the biblical God over against the gods of pagan religions and

---

designate God as *God,* and to distinguish him from all that is not God" (p. 125), and that in this respect "aseity (absolute essence) may be called the primary attribute of God's being" (p. 127).

5. Ibid., 144–45.

6. Cornelius Van Til liked to refer to God as self-contained, meaning "that God is in no sense correlative to or dependent upon anything besides his own being." *Defense of the Faith* (Philadelphia: Presbyterian and Reformed, 1963), 9. Van Til agreed with Bavinck's estimate of the centrality of aseity and with Bavinck's view that all the other divine attributes are included in aseity. See Van Til, *An Introduction to Systematic Theology* (Nutley, N.J.: Presbyterian and Reformed, 1974), 206.

secular philosophies. Non-Christian thought often acknowledges personal gods that are not absolute, or absolute principles that are not personal. Only Scripture presents consistently the reality of a God who is both personal and absolute.[7] It is appropriate that we discussed God's personality toward the beginning of the book, and now we look at his absoluteness toward the end of our discussion of the divine attributes. Everything in between has shown the interaction of these. We have seen that all of God's other attributes are absolute—that he is self-sufficient in his goodness, righteousness, wisdom, relations to time and space, and so on. But all of these attributes also characterize him as a person. They are not abstract, impersonal principles. Rather, God's righteousness is everything he is and does as a person, and similarly for his other attributes.

Theologians have usually treated aseity as a metaphysical attribute, that is, one that focuses on the independence of God's being over against other beings. It seems to me, however, that the same basic concept is equally important in the epistemological and ethical areas. That is to say, God is not only self-existent, but also self-attesting and self-justifying. He not only exists without receiving existence from something else, but also gains his knowledge only from himself (his nature and his plan) and serves as his own criterion of truth. And his righteousness is self-justifying, based on the righteousness of his own nature and on his status as the ultimate criterion of rightness.[8]

So I agree with Bavinck and others that aseity is a very important attribute (although, for reasons mentioned in previous chapters, I hesitate to call it the central attribute). But though Reformed writers agree on the importance of divine aseity, they have often failed to offer substantial and precise biblical support for the doctrine. Bavinck lists a great many texts to show God's independence from the world,[9] but he offers no argument to show that that independence is an absolute independence, or that God is absolutely self-existent and self-sufficient in all things.

As we work our way toward such an argument, we should recall the emphasis of this book on God's lordship and therefore upon his absolute control, authority, and presence in blessing and judgment. As we have seen, God's control is such that every event takes place at his initiative; he is never moved to act by anything outside himself. His authority is the ultimate standard of truth and right; he looks to nobody outside himself to de-

---

7. I owe this insight to Van Til. See my CVT, 51–61.

8. For discussion of the issue of circularity raised by this formulation, see chapters 20, 22, and 23.

9. DG, 142–43.

fine that standard. And he is present in all the world that he has made; nobody can shut him out.

God's control is absolute in that both his atemporal decree and his concurrent working in time (chaps. 14 and 24) govern the world exhaustively, so that even within time and space he is the one on whom everything else depends. He determines the course of history before anything is created, so his decree is not dependent on the world. That decree is unchangeable, not subject to the influence of creatures.[10]

His authority is absolute in that he is self-sufficient in his goodness, righteousness, truth, wisdom, and knowledge—the unchanging standard of all the corresponding creaturely virtues. Creaturely truth, for example, would be meaningless without his truth, but his truth does not depend on the world he has made. He knows all things through himself, by knowing his nature and his eternal plan, and he creates the truth about the actual world by his creation and providence. Our knowledge depends on his (Ps. 36:9), but his does not depend on anything except himself.

His presence is absolute, in that he acts as a whole person at all times and places. The creation cannot continue to exist without God's continued preservation and concurrent providence in the smallest details of nature and history. But he can exist in all his perfections without the world.

The specific texts used to support the general concept of divine aseity can be brought into an argument as follows:

1. *As Lord, God owns all things*. He is "possessor of heaven and earth" (Gen. 14:19, 22 KJV).[11] Similarly:

> The earth is the LORD's, and everything in it,
>   the world, and all who live in it. (Ps. 24:1)

> For every animal of the forest is mine,
>   and the cattle on a thousand hills.
> I know every bird in the mountains,
>   and the creatures of the field are mine.
> If I were hungry I would not tell you,
>   for the world is mine, and all that is in it. (Ps. 50:10–12)

(Cf. Ex. 19:5; Deut. 10:14; Job 41:3; Pss. 82:8; 89:11; 1 Chron. 29:11.)

2. *Everything possessed by creatures comes from God*. Scripture emphasizes

---

10. Remember, however, what I said before about how God's knowledge of creatable persons influences his plan (chaps. 8, 16, 22). But here one part of God's plan influences another part; it is not that creatures modify God's plan on their own initiative.

11. The NIV translates "Creator," but "possess" is the more frequent meaning of *qanah*, while other words are far more commonly translated "create."

the universality of creation, as we saw in chapter 15. God has created everything in the heavens, on the earth, and in the sea (e.g., Ex. 20:11; Neh. 9:6; Ps. 146:5–6). Thus, "every good and perfect gift is from above" (James 1:17).

3. *When we give something back to God, we give him only what he has first given us.* This follows from the previous point. We are "stewards" of God's land (Luke 12:42; 16:1–8; Titus 1:7), accountable to use these blessings to his glory. Everything in creation remains his, even after he has given it to us, so even our own possessions are his.

4. *When we give something back to God, he is not obligated to recompense us.*

> So you also, when you have done everything you were told to do, should say, "We are unworthy servants; we have only done our duty." (Luke 17:10)

5. *So God owes nothing to any creature.*

> Who has a claim against me that I must pay?
> Everything under heaven belongs to me. (Job 41:11)

And Paul later quotes Job:

> "Who has ever given to God,
>   that God should repay him?"
> For from him and through him and to him are all things.
>   To him be the glory forever! Amen. (Rom. 11:35–36)

Now of course, as we have seen, God does put himself under obligation to creatures by making covenants and promises, and by displaying to them the constancies of his nature. But these obligations, based on his nature and his voluntary covenants, are self-imposed, not forced on him by creatures. Paul tells us that God is not only the first cause, but also the first giver. He does recompense people for their obedient service. But he has first given them the privilege of serving him and receiving that reward.

6. *So God has no needs.* God gives to us, not so that we will help him repair some lack in his being and life, but because he is the first giver. He is not dependent on us, for then he would owe his existence or his well-being to us. This truth has important relevance to the worship of God's people. Look at a bit more of Psalm 50, which I began to quote above:

> I do not rebuke you for your sacrifices
>   or your burnt offerings, which are ever before me.
> I have no need of a bull from your stall

> or of goats from your pens,
> for every animal of the forest is mine,
>   and the cattle on a thousand hills.
> I know every bird in the mountains,
>   and the creatures of the field are mine.
> If I were hungry I would not tell you,
>   for the world is mine, and all that is in it.
> Do I eat the flesh of bulls
>   or drink the blood of goats?
> Sacrifice thank offerings to God,
>   fulfill your vows to the Most High,
> and call upon me in the day of trouble;
>   I will deliver you, and you will honor me. (vv. 8–15)

Biblical worship, unlike much pagan worship, is not intended to meet the needs of God. The purpose of animal sacrifice in the Old Testament was not to satiate God's hunger, but symbolically to atone for human sin. As verses 14 and 15 make clear, in worship we offer our thanks for the fact that God has met our needs. Through vows we incur our obligations to him. And we will call upon him to meet our needs in the future.

So God speaks against idolatry through Isaiah's satiric wit:

> As for an idol, a craftsman casts it,
>   and a goldsmith overlays it with gold
>   and fashions silver chains for it.
> A man too poor to present such an offering
>   selects wood that will not rot.
> He looks for a skilled craftsman
>   to set up an idol that will not topple. (Isa. 40:19–20; cf. 41:7;
>   46:6; Jer. 10:3–5; Hab. 2:18–20)

And in Isaiah 44:15–17, we read of a carpenter who cuts down some wood:

> It is man's fuel for burning;
>   some of it he takes and warms himself,
>   he kindles a fire and bakes bread.
> But he also fashions a god and worships it;
>   he makes an idol and bows down to it.
> Half of the wood he burns in the fire;
>   over it he prepares his meal,
>   he roasts his meat and eats his fill.
> He also warms himself and says,
>   "Ah! I am warm; I see the fire."

> From the rest he makes a god, his idol;
>> he bows down to it and worships.
> He prays to it and says,
>> "Save me; you are my god."

The idol is dependent on man. Therefore, it is ridiculous that a man should worship it. To make an idol, you must be skillful. You must know what wood to use, because you don't want your god to rot on you. You must make it carefully, because you don't want your god to topple over. And, of course, it is your choice as to what wood you burn and what wood you worship. You are the one who saves the god from flaming destruction. In this way, the Lord mocks worship in which the god is dependent on the worshiper, in which the worshiper meets the god's needs.

When Paul encounters idolatry in Athens, he describes true worship:

> The God who made the world and everything in it is the Lord of heaven and earth and does not live in temples built by hands. And he is not served by human hands, as if he needed anything, because he himself gives all men life and breath and everything else. From one man he made every nation of men, that they should inhabit the whole earth; and he determined the times set for them and the exact places where they should live. God did this so that men would seek him and perhaps reach out for him and find him, though he is not far from each one of us. "For in him we live and move and have our being." As some of your own poets have said, "We are his offspring."
>
> Therefore since we are God's offspring, we should not think that the divine being is like gold or silver or stone—an image made by man's design and skill. In the past God overlooked such ignorance, but now he commands all people everywhere to repent. (Acts 17:24–30)

God is not worshiped by men's hands, "as if he needed [*prosdeomai*] anything." He is worshiped by men's hands, but the hands are raised in praise and thanksgiving, not to supply the needs of God. He is the one who has given us everything: life, breath, times, and places. It is in him that we live and move and have our being. We depend utterly on him; he does not depend at all on us.

7. *So God is by nature* a se. A being with no needs is an extraordinary being, to say the least. Here, as elsewhere in the doctrine of God, we are forced to draw metaphysical conclusions from the nature of worship. If worship

is what Scripture says it is, then the object of worship must be utterly without any needs and independent of his worshipers.

Scripture rarely uses metaphysical language, but in Galatians 4:8–9, Paul says:

> Formerly, when you did not know God, you were slaves to those who by nature are not gods. But now that you know God—or rather are known by God—how is it that you are turning back to those weak and miserable principles? Do you wish to be enslaved by them all over again?

Note the phrase "who by nature are not gods" (*tois physei mē ousin theois*). Paul agrees with our previous statement that a being worthy of worship must have a nature worthy of worship. But the false gods are "weak" (*asthenē*), and "miserable" (*ptōcha*, "poor, begging"). A god who depends on his worshipers to remedy his weaknesses and poverty does not deserve worship. So the true God is one who is not weak in any respect, nor is he poor. He is God by nature: self-existent and self-sufficient, *a se*.

Although aseity is a metaphysical idea, our knowledge of it is, like all other divine attributes, grounded in the practical reality of God as covenant Lord. We confess his aseity, because such a confession is implicit in the very act of worship, in the reverence that the worshiper has for his Lord.

With this background, we can understand how Paul's praise to God in Romans 11:36 entails the metaphysical claim that God is self-existent, self-sufficient, *a se*:

> For from him and through him and to him are all things.
> To him be the glory forever! Amen.

He has created and provided all things ("from him"); nothing happens without his power ("through him"); he receives everything back ("to him"). He has no needs; he is self-sufficient.

In all traditions of thought, secular as well as religious, there has been a search for something *a se*: an ultimate cause of being, an ultimate standard of truth, an ultimate justification of right. In the realm of being (metaphysics), it may be a deity, a system of abstract forms, or natural law. In the realm of knowledge (epistemology), the standard may be a religious or secular authority, human subjectivity, sense experience, reason, or some combination of these (see *DKG*). In the realm of ethics, it may be a system of duties, a calculation of consequences, or human inwardness (see chap. 10). Ideally, the metaphysical absolute, the epistemological norm, and the ethical norm should all be grounded in one being, since these three are correlative to one another. But non-Christian thought has usually found it impossible to locate all of these ultimates in a single principle. Part of the problem is that non-Christian thought is determined that its absolute be impersonal. But an impersonal being cannot serve as a norm for knowledge and ethics, nor can it be a credible first cause. So, many non-Christians have given up the quest for an absolute, preferring to embrace meaninglessness and chaos. The non-Christian substitutes for God have failed, just as the idols of Psalm 50 and Isaiah 40 have failed. Only the *a se* God of Scripture can give unity and meaning to human thought and experience.

So aseity is essential to a credible doctrine of God, not a mere bit of abstract theorizing. It is also important to note that aseity does not isolate God's being from the world, but rather enables God to enter our history without confusing his being with the being of the world. If God entered the world out of need, then he would be dependent on the world; then there would be no clear distinction between Creator and creature. But he enters our world, not out of need, but as the *a se* Lord of all.

DOES GOD HAVE FEELINGS?

Theological literature has sometimes ascribed to God the attribute of *impassibility*. This concept has been used to deny that God has emotions or feelings and to deny that God suffers. These two issues are related to one another in various ways, but I would like to discuss them sequentially: the question of emotion here, and the question of suffering in the next section.

The aseity of God enters into both questions, because it has been argued that both emotions and suffering are inappropriate to one who is utterly self-sufficient, independent, and autonomous, not to mention unchangeable.

With regard to divine emotions, we have seen that Scripture ascribes many attitudes to God that are generally regarded as emotions. In previous chapters, we have discussed biblical references to God's compassion, tender mercy, patience, rejoicing, delight, pleasure, pity, love,[12] wrath, and jealousy. I noted in chapter 24 that *naham* is sometimes properly translated "be grieved" (as of God in Genesis 6:6), and Ephesians 4:30 tells us not to "grieve" the Holy Spirit of God.

Beyond all of that, we should note that God, speaking in Scripture, regularly expresses emotion and appeals to the emotions of his hearers. There is passion in God's words when he addresses Israel: "Turn! Turn from your

12. Love is not merely emotional, but it certainly has an emotional component to it.

evil ways! Why will you die, O house of Israel?" (Ezek. 33:11), or when Paul turns from his logical exposition of God's plan of salvation and bursts forth in praise (as, e.g., in Rom. 8:31–39 and 11:33–36).

But emotion is present even in language that is relatively calm. That is true of both divine and human language. Calmness itself is an emotion. And even a matter-of-fact statement like "In the beginning God created the heavens and the earth" (Gen. 1:1) is intended, not only to inform us, but to give us a certain feeling about the event described. Indeed, it may not be possible to distinguish the intellectual force of language from its emotional force. Intellectual communication intends to give the hearer, among other things, a feeling of "cognitive rest,"[13] an inner satisfaction that the communication is true.

Scripture does not distinguish "the emotions" as a part of the mind that is radically different from the intellect and the will. As I said in chapters 22 and 23, Scripture does not speak of God's mind and will as "faculties" interacting in various ways, only of the thoughts and decisions God makes. The same may be said of God's emotions. Scripture refers to God's individual emotions, but it doesn't specify any metaphysical or categorical difference between these, on the one hand, and his thoughts and decisions, on the other.

Nevertheless, some theologians have drawn a sharp line between emotions and other kinds of mental content, and they have put biblical references to God's emotions into the category of anthropomorphisms. On this view, for example, when Scripture says that God knows his people, he really does know them, but when it says that God is angry, he is not "really" angry.

Why is it that theologians have sometimes thought that emotions are unworthy of God? D. A. Carson comments:

> In the final analysis, we have to do with the influence of certain strands of Greek metaphysical thought, strands which insist that emotion is dangerous, treacherous, and often evil. Reason must be set against emotion, and vulnerability is a sign of weakness. One may trace this line from Aristotle's "unmoved mover" through platonic and neo-platonic writings to the Stoics. The conclusion must be that "God is sensible, omnipotent, compassionate, *passionless;* for it is better to be these than not to be" (so Anselm in *Proslogium,* chap. 6).[14]

13. See *DKG,* 152–53, in the context of pp. 149–62, and also pp. 335–40.
14. D. A. Carson, *Divine Sovereignty and Human Responsibility* (Atlanta: John Knox Press, 1981), 215.

I think that Carson is right, and that these strands of Greek metaphysical thought are not biblical. So they provide no basis for denying the existence of divine emotions. A few more observations may help to clarify the issue:

1. Emotions in human beings often have physical accompaniments and symptoms: tears, a queasy stomach, an adrenaline flow, etc. Since God is incorporeal (chap. 25), his emotions are not like ours in that respect. Of course, we should not forget that God did become incarnate in Christ, and that Jesus really did weep (Luke 19:41; John 11:35). But God's incorporeality gives us no reason to deny in some general way that God has emotions. In human beings, thinking is also a physical process, involving the brain. But we would never dream of denying that God can think, simply because he is incorporeal.

2. Doctrines like God's eternal decree, his immutability, and his aseity sometimes lead us to think that he cannot truly respond to what happens in the world. Responding seems to assume passivity and change in God. Now emotions are usually responses to events. They are, indeed, sometimes called "passions," a term that suggests passivity. This consideration is one reason why theologians have resisted ascribing emotions to God.

But although God's eternal decree does not change, it does ordain change. It ordains a historical series of events, each of which receives God's evaluation. God evaluates different events in different ways. Those evaluations themselves are fixed in God's eternal plan. But they are genuine evaluations of the events. It is not wrong to describe them as responses to these events.[15]

Furthermore, we have seen that God is not only transcendent beyond time and space, but also immanent in all times and spaces. From these immanent perspectives, God views each event from within history. As he does, he evaluates each event appropriately, when it happens. Such evaluations are, in the most obvious sense, responses.

Does such responsiveness imply passivity in God? To say so would be highly misleading. God responds (both transcendently and immanently) only to what he has himself ordained.[16] He has chosen to create a world that will often grieve him. So ultimately he is active, rather than passive. Some may want to use the term *impassible* to indicate that fact.

3. As suggested in the second observation, much of what we are inclined

15. Recall again the role I have ascribed to God's knowledge in the very formulation of his eternal plan (chap. 8). God knows what he plans, and each element of his plan takes the others into account. So his eternal plan itself includes his response to each element of that plan.

16. Recall the discussion of God's temporal omnipresence in chapter 24. In Gen. 1, even before man is created, God responds to his own creative actions.

The fact that emotions exist in man and man is made in the image of God and all that is somehow reflects God's glory — implies that God in some respect has emotions although perfect in their expression.

to call "emotion" in God is his evaluation of what happens in history. He rejoices in the good and grieves over the evil. There should be no doubt that God, as our supreme authority, is the ultimate and exhaustive evaluator of everything that happens in nature and history. His evaluations are always true and appropriate.

Now sometimes, in order to be appropriate, an evaluation must include some superlatives, some exciting language.[17] For example, it is not enough to say merely that God rules; to express the full truth of the matter, we need expressions like "King of kings and Lord of lords." When we find such colorful expressions, we are inclined to say that they express emotion, that they have emotional content. Indeed, they are emotional expressions, but they are also the sober truth. They represent an infallible evaluation of the facts. Again we see a kind of coalescence between emotion and intellect, and an argument in favor of asserting that God has emotions: without emotions, God would lack intellectual capacity, and he would be unable to speak the full truth about himself and the world.

4. Of course, there are emotions that are inappropriate for God. God is never homesick, anxious about tomorrow, inwardly troubled by divided intentions, compulsive, or addicted. He is not like human beings, who are often overcome by waves of passion, who make decisions on the basis of momentary feelings, and whose passions lead them to make false judgments. God doesn't have such kinds of emotions, but that doesn't mean that he lacks the emotions ascribed to him in Scripture.

CAN GOD SUFFER?

Recently, a number of theologians have questioned the traditional Christian view that God is unable to suffer.[18] Richard Bauckham summarizes Jür-

---

17. I wish this point were better understood by young preachers. Too often they try to convey truth without passion, which often means making it uninteresting. Sometimes they defend this by saying that they want to convey the "objective" truth, not mixing it up with "subjective" emotion. But they fail to realize that a dispassionate exposition of God's Word often falsifies it. We do not rightly expound Rom. 11:33–36, for example, unless we convey to our hearers Paul's sense of amazement and wonder. The same point applies to commentators and theologians.

18. Of seminal importance is Kayoh Kitamori, *Theology of the Pain of God* (Richmond: John Knox Press, 1965), followed closely by Jürgen Moltmann, *The Crucified God* (London: SCM Press, 1974). Compare Eberhard Jüngel, *God as the Mystery of the World* (Grand Rapids: Eerdmans, 1983), which emphasizes "the identification of God and the crucified Jesus." Feminist theology generally supports this paradigm: e.g., Elizabeth Johnson, *She Who Is* (New York: Crossroad, 1996), 246–72. For recent statements of the tra-

gen Moltmann's "three reasons for speaking of God's suffering."[19] The first is the passion of Christ. Moltmann sees his argument as following the tradition of Luther's "theology of the cross," which "makes the cross, for all its stark negativity, the basis and criterion of Christian theology."[20] Moltmann believes that the doctrine of impassibility in the church fathers was based on Greek philosophy rather than on trying to "understand the being of God from the event of the cross."[21]

Moltmann's second reason for attributing suffering to God is the nature of love. In Moltmann's view, divine love entails "reciprocity" between God and creation. It must be possible for him to be "affected by the objects of his love." So God must be vulnerable to suffering. This argument is based, not on a mere analogy between divine and human love, but upon the nature of divine love revealed in the Cross.[22]

Thirdly, Moltmann appeals to the problem of human suffering.[23] He finds no adequate answer to the problem of evil, except to say that God suffers with suffering human beings. Again, he does not argue merely from human suffering to divine suffering, but rather from God's suffering with Jesus on the cross. This event has soteriological implications: "all suffering becomes God's *so that he may overcome it.*"[24]

I have argued earlier in this chapter that God experiences grief and other negative emotions, not only in the incarnate Christ, but in his non-incarnate being as well. Isaiah expresses God's grief in terms of distress or affliction (*tsar*):

> In all their distress he too was distressed,
>   and the angel of his presence saved them.
> In his love and mercy he redeemed them;
>   he lifted them up and carried them
>   all the days of old. (Isa. 63:9)

---

ditional view, see Richard Creel, *Divine Impassibility* (Cambridge: Cambridge University Press, 1986); Millard Erickson, *God the Father Almighty* (Grand Rapids: Baker, 1998); Thomas G. Weinandy, *Does God Suffer?* (Notre Dame, Ind.: University of Notre Dame Press, 2000).

19. Bauckham, "In Defence of *The Crucified God*," in *The Power and Weakness of God*, ed. Nigel M. de S. Cameron (Edinburgh: Rutherford House Books, 1990), 93.

20. Ibid., 94.

21. Ibid., 95. The traditional view is that Jesus suffered on the cross as man, but not as God, and that no suffering should be attributed to God the Father. The tradition rejected the idea that God the Father suffered, the position called patripassianism.

22. Ibid., 95–96.

23. Ibid., 96–99.

24. Bauckham quotes Moltmann, *The Crucified God*, 246.

God is the compassionate God, who knows the agonies of his people, not only as the transcendent author of history, but as the immanent one who is with them here and now. In the incarnate Jesus, he draws yet nearer, to be "made like his brothers in every way," in order to be "a merciful and faithful high priest" (Heb. 2:17). Thus, the Son of God empathizes with us:

> For we do not have a high priest who is unable to sympathize with our weaknesses, but we have one who has been tempted in every way, just as we are—yet was without sin. (Heb. 4:15)

This emotional empathy can be called "suffering," although that is perhaps a misleading term. There is no reason in these passages to suppose that God suffers any injury or loss. The same is true of the biblical references to God's weakness (see my discussion of that in chap. 23).

But is there any sense in which God suffers injury or loss? Certainly Jesus suffered injury and loss on the cross. And I agree with Moltmann that Christ's sufferings are the sufferings of God. The Council of Chalcedon (451), which defined orthodox Christology, said that Jesus has two complete *natures*, divine and human, united in one *person*. We may say that Jesus suffered and died on the cross "according to his human nature," but what suffered was not a "nature," but the person of Jesus. And the person of Jesus is nothing less than the second person of the Trinity, who has taken to himself a human nature. His experiences as a man are truly his experiences, the experiences of God.

Are these experiences only of the Son, and not of the Father? The persons of the Trinity are not divided; rather, the Son is in the Father, and the Father is in the Son (John 10:38; 14:10–11, 20; 17:21). Theologians have called this mutual indwelling *circumcessio* or *circumincessio*.

However, the Father does not have exactly the same experiences of suffering and death that the Son has. Although they dwell in one another, the Father and the Son play different roles in the history of redemption. The Son was baptized by John; the Father was the voice from heaven at his baptism. The Son was crucified; the Father was not. Indeed, during the Crucifixion, the Father forsook the Son as he bore the sins of his people (Matt. 27:46). Was the Father, nevertheless, still "in" the Son at that moment of separation? What exactly does it mean for the Father to be "in" the Son when he addressed the Son from heaven? These are difficult questions, and I have not heard any persuasive answers to them. But we must do justice to both the continuity and the discontinuity between the persons of the Trinity. Certainly the Father empathized, agonized, and grieved over the death of his Son, but he did not experience death in the same way that the Son did.

Paul, in Romans 8:32 says, "He who did not spare his own Son, but delivered him up for us all—how shall he not also, along with him, graciously give us all things?" Here Paul states the cost of our salvation to God the Father. Surely this is loss to the Father. We cannot imagine how much. The Father did not die, but he gave up his own Son.

But God the Son did die, and of course he rose again. So in his incarnate existence, God suffered and even died—yet his death did not leave us with a godless universe. Beyond that, I think we are largely ignorant, and we should admit that ignorance.

To summarize, let us distinguish, as we did earlier, between four modes of divine existence:

1. In his atemporal and nonspatial transcendent existence, God ordains grievous events and evaluates them appropriately. He grieves in that sense, but does not suffer injury or loss.

2. In his temporal and spatial omnipresence, he grieves with his creatures, and he undergoes temporary defeats on his way to the complete victory he has foreordained.

3. In his theophanic presence, he is distressed when his people are distressed (Isa. 63:9), but he promises complete victory and vindication both for himself and for his faithful ones.

4. In the Incarnation, the Son suffers injury and loss: physical pain, deprivation, and death. The Father knows this agony, including the agony of his own separation from his Son. He regards this event as the unique and awful tragedy that it is, but also as his foreordained means of salvation. What precise feelings does he experience? We do not know, and we would be wise not to speculate.

Moltmann is right to find divine suffering in the cross in the senses mentioned above. But he is wrong to conclude that the doctrine of God's impassibility is merely a remnant of Greek philosophy. As we have seen, the doctrine of impassibility should not be used to deny that God has emotions, or to deny that God the Son suffered real injury and death on the cross. But God in his transcendent nature cannot be harmed in any way, nor can he suffer loss to his being. In his eternal existence, "suffering loss" could only mean losing some attribute, being defeated in his war with Satan, or otherwise failing to accomplish his eternal plan. Scripture assures us that none of these things will happen, and so they cannot happen. In this sense, God is impassible.

In conclusion, I will offer some comments on Moltmann's three points noted above. As we will recall from Bauckham's summary, Moltmann's view comes from a particular methodology, his application of Luther's "theology of the cross." Certainly our theology should be centered on the redemption accomplished by Christ. As Paul says, in one sense we should "know nothing . . . except Jesus Christ and him crucified" (1 Cor. 2:2). We should proclaim Jesus' atonement and victory in all our theological work. However, as we have seen, Jesus' death is in many ways mysterious, especially in regard to the relationships between the Son and the Father. What Moltmann does, I fear, is to insist very dogmatically on one dubious interpretation of this mystery (namely, that the Father suffers metaphysical loss in the death of Jesus) and to use that as a paradigm for interpreting everything else in the Bible, even to the point of denying some other biblical teachings. I do not think such a procedure can properly claim justification in the theology of the cross.

As to Moltmann's second point, I would agree that love involves reciprocity. God's love, both in the eternal fellowship of the Trinity and in the world of creatures, is responsive in the ways I have indicated previously. However, love does not require "vulnerability" in the sense of susceptibility to injury and loss. Is it really impossible to love someone who cannot be ultimately harmed? Millions of Christian believers over the centuries would affirm that it is possible. The psalmists typically express their love for God as their strength and deliverance (Pss. 18:1; 31:23; 116:1); it doesn't occur to them to say they love God because he is vulnerable. Paul praises the omnipotence of God's love: it is such a powerful love that nothing can separate us from it (Rom. 8:35–39).

Moltmann's third point, that God shares our sufferings in order to overcome them, is correct—in Jesus:

> He was despised and rejected by men,
>   a man of sorrows, and familiar with suffering.
> Like one from whom men hide their faces
>   he was despised, and we esteemed him not.
> Surely he took up our infirmities
>   and carried our sorrows,
> yet we considered him stricken by God,
>   smitten by him, and afflicted. (Isa. 53:3–4)

As we have seen from Hebrews, Christ was made like us so that he could be a merciful and faithful high priest, empathizing with our infirmities. He takes away sin, the cause of those infirmities, and he hears our prayers with understanding. But this principle should not be magnified into a metaphysical assertion about God's vulnerability, for, as we have seen, God's eternal nature is invulnerable, and that invulnerability is also precious to the believer.

God's suffering love in Christ, therefore, does not cast doubt upon his aseity and unchangeability. It is, however, ground for rejoicing. I close with words from a sermon on Philippians 2:5–8 by B. B. Warfield:

> We have a God who is capable of self-sacrifice for us. . . . Now, herein is a wonderful thing. Men tell us that God is, by very necessity of His nature, incapable of passion, incapable of being moved by inducement from without; that he dwells in holy calm and unchangeable blessedness, untouched by human sufferings or human sorrows for ever,—haunting
>
> > The lucid interspace of world and world,
> > Where never creeps a cloud, nor moves a wind,
> > Nor ever falls the least white star of snow,
> > Nor ever lowest roll of thunder moans,
> > Nor sound of human sorrow mounts to mar
> > His sacred, everlasting calm.
>
> Let us bless our God that it is not true. God can feel; God does love. We have Scriptural warrant for believing, as it has been perhaps somewhat inadequately but not misleadingly phrased, that moral heroism has a place within the sphere of the divine nature: we have Scriptural warrant for believing that, like the hero of Zurich, God has reached out loving arms and gathered to his own bosom that forest of spears which otherwise had pierced ours.
>
> But is not this gross anthropomorphism? We are careless of names: it is the truth of God. And we decline to yield up the God of the Bible and the God of our hearts to any philosophical abstraction. We have and we must have an ethical God; a God whom we can love, in whom we can trust.[25]

---

25. B. B. Warfield, "Imitating the Incarnation," in *The Person and Work of Christ* (Philadelphia: Presbyterian and Reformed, 1950), 570–71. Thanks to Jeff Meyers for drawing my attention to this passage.

PART SIX

THE TRIUNE GOD

CHAPTER 27

God, Three in One

Earlier, I indicated that Scripture reveals God to us (1) by declaring his acts, (2) by giving us authoritative descriptions of him, and (3) by giving us a glimpse of his inner, triune life. These forms of revelation correspond to the situational, normative, and existential categories, respectively. We now move on to consider the third of these.

The third category is not radically distinct from the second. Contrary to some writers, it is not necessarily wrong to think of God's triunity as an attribute (and therefore as God's nature). Also, God's triunity is related to his acts (the first category), for within the Godhead[1] are the acts of eternal generation and procession, as well as acts of love and communication among the three persons. But we can almost sense that when we discuss the Trinity, we are reaching a new level of depth in our understanding of God. Gerald Bray writes:

> The revelation of the Trinity, as opposed to the implied unitarianism of Judaism, can be explained only by the transformation of perspective brought about by Jesus. The Trinity belongs to the inner life of God, and can be known only by those who share in that life. As long as we look at God on the outside, we shall never see beyond his unity; for, as the Cappadocian Fathers and Augustine realized, the external works of the Trinity are undivided (*opera Trini-*

---

1. *Godhead* is an old term for "divine being" or "divine nature," often used especially when one wishes to contrast the one divine nature with the three persons.

tatis ad extra sunt indivisa). This means that an outside observer will never detect the inner reality of God, and will never enter the communion with him which is promised to us in Christ. Jews may recognize God's existence and know his law, but without Christ they cannot penetrate the mystery of that divine fellowship which Christians call the Holy Trinity.[2]

We must, of course, distinguish between Judaism on the one hand and God's Old Testament revelation on the other. Unlike Judaism, the Old Testament should not be charged with implied unitarianism; Old Testament revelation certainly does not teach the sufficiency of knowing God's existence and his law. Despite the veil of the temple, God invited his people in the Old Testament into an intimate relationship with him: "I will take you as my own people, and I will be your God" (Ex. 6:7). "The LORD is my shepherd, I shall not be in want" (Ps. 23:1). "I have loved you with an everlasting love; I have drawn you with loving-kindness" (Jer. 31:3).

Yet Bray is right to emphasize that something new appears in the New Testament revelation. The tearing of the temple veil through the atoning work of Christ certainly brings us to a greater level of fellowship with God: "And God raised us up with Christ and seated us with him in the heavenly realms in Christ Jesus" (Eph. 2:6). As we stand before the Father in the Son, we enjoy a knowledge of God's intra-Trinitarian fellowship that was not available to the Old Testament saints. The Old Testament anticipates the doctrine of the Trinity in many ways, and its teaching is fully compatible with that doctrine. Indeed, it provides much useful material for the study of the Trinity, as we shall see. But to understand this theme in the Old Testament, we must read it from a New Testament vantage point.[3]

2. Gerald Bray, *The Doctrine of God* (Downers Grove, Ill.: InterVarsity Press, 1993).

3. Otto Weber, in *Foundations of Dogmatics* (Grand Rapids: Eerdmans, 1981), 1:349–53, offers some valid warnings to theologians like myself who deal with the being and attributes of God before discussing the Trinity (the fairly traditional order of discussion). Certainly this procedure entails the danger of developing a doctrine of God based on philosophical abstractions rather than on God's relationship to us in Christ. However, as Weber admits, his preference for discussing the Trinity first may not be made into an absolute requirement. To make it such would be to invalidate the order of Scripture itself, which presents God in the Old Testament primarily (though not exclusively) as a singular being, and only in the New Testament as an explicitly Trinitarian one. My focus on God as covenant Lord has, I believe, answered Weber's concerns and prepared the way, as does the Old Testament doctrine of covenant lordship, to discuss Christ and the Spirit as Yahweh. In any case, as I indicated in chapter 1, it is unwise to take too seriously questions about the order in which theological topics should be discussed. So I disagree with Paul K. Jewett's statement that "the location of the Trinity in the table of contents tells the discerning student more about a treatise on systematics than anything short of reading the book itself," in *God,*

In this part of the book, I shall explore the biblical glimpse into God's inner life and therefore into the life that believers share with him. We should remind ourselves from time to time that it is only a glimpse. God has withheld much in this area that we would like to know. The mysteries before us here are especially intractable. But this study can be enormously rewarding. In sharing with us even a little of his triune existence, God has given the church a great blessing.

As Sinclair Ferguson points out, it is before Jesus goes to the cross that he has the most to say to his disciples about the Trinity, about his relationship to the Father and to the Spirit (John 13–17).[4] It is the cross that enables us to share the unity and love that exists eternally between the Father and the Son (John 17:11, 22–26). It is the cross, resurrection, and ascension of Christ that bring to us the full power and knowledge of the Holy Spirit (John 14:16–17, 26; 15:26; 16:13). Such are the blessings we learn of when we study the doctrine of the Trinity. The study can at times seem technical and dry, but the rewards are great.

TRINITARIAN BASICS

Far from being an abstruse philosophical speculation, the doctrine of the Trinity attempts to describe and account for something biblically obvious and quite fundamental to the gospel. That fact is this: Scripture testifies from beginning to end that God is one, but it also presents three persons who are God: the Father, the Son, and the Holy Spirit. As we shall see, there is no legitimate argument against the deity of these three persons. Their deity pervades Scripture and assures us that our salvation is from beginning to end a divine salvation, the work of God himself. Nor can it be debated whether the biblical God is one. Indeed, his oneness is also important to our salvation. He is God alone; there is none beside him. So none can prevent him from bringing eternal salvation to his people.

So God is one, but somehow also three. This fact is difficult to understand, but it is quite unavoidable in Scripture and central to the gospel. The doctrine of the Trinity attempts to account for this fact and to exclude heresies that have arisen on the subject. Its basic assertions are these: (1) God is one. (2) God is three. (3) The three persons are each fully God. (4)

Creation, and Revelation (Grand Rapids: Eerdmans, 1991), 265. There and on p. 266, Jewett suggests that to put the discussion of the Trinity toward the end of a systematic theology is to go the way of Schleiermacher. I plead innocent.

4. Sinclair B. Ferguson, *A Heart for God* (Colorado Springs: NavPress, 1985), 18–37.

Each of the persons is distinct from the others. (5) The three persons are related to one another eternally as Father, Son, and Holy Spirit. I shall discuss these assertions in order.

GOD IS ONE

The doctrine of the Trinity teaches both God's threeness and his oneness. The adjective *triune* refers to God as both three (*tri*) and one (*une*). We shall begin our study of the Trinity by focusing on God's oneness. This is the order followed in Scripture itself: the Old Testament emphasizes God's oneness; the New Testament focuses far more clearly on the personal distinctions within God's being.

Theologians speak of God's unity in several senses: (1) his simplicity, which I discussed in chapter 12, (2) the unity of the persons within the Trinity, (3) the uniqueness of God's nature, sometimes called his generic unity, and (4) God's numerical oneness: the fact that there is only one of him. I will be discussing the second sense in later contexts. The third and fourth senses seem to me to coalesce. When Scripture says that there is only one God, it clearly has in mind a very definite kind of God. To say that God is numerically one is to say that there is only one being with that unique nature.[5] In this section, therefore, I shall discuss God's unity in this sense.

In chapter 2, I mentioned the Shema of Deuteronomy 6:4–5, the fundamental Old Testament confession of God's covenant lordship:

> Hear, O Israel: The LORD our God, the LORD is one. Love the LORD your God with all your heart and with all your soul and with all your strength.

Note here that verse 4 is also a confession of God's oneness. That oneness is important to the covenant. There is only one covenant Lord. This passage brings together the third and fourth senses of God's unity listed above. God is one being (quantitatively) because there is only one Lord (qualitatively). The Lord's acts reveal his uniqueness:

> Ask now about the former days, long before your time, from the day God created man on the earth; ask from one end of the heav-

---

5. I reject the view of Paul K. Jewett, among others, that "numeric oneness" is an unwarranted addition to "generic oneness" (*God, Creation, and Revelation*, 295), and the view of Jürgen Moltmann that "the unity of the divine tri-unity lies in the *union* of the Father, the Son and the Spirit, not in their numerical unity" (*The Trinity and the Kingdom* [San Francisco: HarperSanFrancisco, 1991], 95).

ens to the other. Has anything so great as this ever happened, or has anything like it ever been heard of? Has any other people heard the voice of God speaking out of fire, as you have, and lived? Has any god ever tried to take for himself one nation out of another nation, by testings, by miraculous signs and wonders, by war, by a mighty hand and an outstretched arm, or by great and awesome deeds, like all the things the LORD your God did for you in Egypt before your very eyes?

You were shown these things so that you might know that the LORD is God; besides him there is no other. (Deut. 4:32–35; cf. v. 39)

This passage also reveals God's unity, both numerically ("there is no other") and generically (God did uniquely great and awesome deeds). Similarly, Deuteronomy 32:39 declares:

See now that I myself am He!
   There is no god besides me.
I put to death and I bring to life,
   I have wounded and I will heal,
   and no one can deliver out of my hand.

God's oneness is related to all his lordship attributes. Only one being can be fully in *control* of all other beings, so that no one can deliver out of his hand. He is the God of all things in heaven, on earth, and in the sea (Deut. 4:39; 2 Kings 19:15), because he created them all (Neh. 9:6; Mal. 2:10). The same is true with respect to the lordship attribute of *authority*:

This is what the LORD says—
   Israel's King and Redeemer, the LORD Almighty:
I am the first and I am the last;
   apart from me there is no God.
Who then is like me? Let him proclaim it.
   Let him declare and lay out before me
what has happened since I established my ancient people,
   and what is yet to come—
   yes, let him foretell what will come.
Do not tremble, do not be afraid.
   Did I not proclaim this and foretell it long ago?
You are my witnesses. Is there any God besides me?
   No, there is no other Rock; I know not one. (Isa. 44:6–8; cf. 45:21)

Only God speaks authoritatively of the past and the future. And he is the one ultimate lawgiver and judge (James 4:12).

God also is unique as Lord in his *presence* with human beings:

> I am the LORD, and there is no other;
>   apart from me there is no God.
> I will strengthen you,
>   though you have not acknowledged me,
> so that from the rising of the sun
>   to the place of its setting
> men may know there is none besides me.
>   I am the LORD, and there is no other. (Isa. 45:5–6)

So God is the only Savior:

> Turn to me and be saved,
>   all you ends of the earth;
>   for I am God, and there is no other. (Isa. 45:22)[6]

Much New Testament reflection on the unity of God focuses on the fact that he is the God of both Jews and Gentiles, the only Savior of men, the only one who can truly bless all the nations, as he promised Abraham. (See Rom. 3:29–30; Gal. 3:20;[7] 1 Tim. 2:5; cf. Isa. 37:16.) All nations are to know that he alone is God (2 Kings 19:19).

Besides the Lord, there is "no one else" (cf. 2 Sam. 7:22; 1 Kings 8:60; Isa. 46:9; 1 Cor. 8:4). There is "none like him" (Ps. 86:8). He "alone" is God (2 Sam. 22:32; 2 Kings 19:19; Pss. 18:31; 86:10; Isa. 37:16). He is the only one who does wondrous works (Ps. 72:18), the "only true God" (Jer. 10:10; John 17:3; 1 Thess. 1:9), the "only wise God" (Rom. 16:27; 1 Tim. 1:17; Jude 25), the only true Father (Matt. 25:9), the only one who is good (Mark 10:18), the only source of spiritual gifts (1 Cor. 12:4–6; Eph. 4:4–6).[8]

From our previous study of the doctrine of God, it is not difficult to see that all of his attributes imply his unity. Only one being can be the stan-

---

6. Cf. Zech. 14:9; Acts 9–10. All these passages teach that since there is only one God, he is the God of all the nations.

7. This is a difficult passage, but I take it to mean that God worked through mediators to bring the law to Israel, conditioning blessings on Israel's response—but that in the covenant with Abraham, he worked alone, unilaterally promising to bless all nations in Abraham's seed.

8. These are Trinitarian passages, distinguishing the three persons of the Godhead as the source of spiritual gifts. Note how these Trinitarian distinctions appear in passages that stress the unity of God. It is remarkable that the New Testament writers do not see the Trinitarian distinctions as compromising God's unity, but as reinforcing it.

dard of perfection, goodness, love, knowledge, truth, and so on. Only one being can be the owner of all things (e.g., Gen. 14:19, 22; Ps. 24:1). All of God's attributes are unique. For example, his love is not the same as creaturely love, for it is the source and standard of all creaturely love. And all his actions are uniquely his own: only one being could be the Creator of all and the one who governs the whole course of nature and history. Only one being could govern all things by his own eternal decree.

Remarkably, Jesus Christ, God the Son, also is a divine unity, the one and only Savior and Lord. He is the way, the truth, and the life (John 14:6), the only name by which we must be saved (Acts 4:12). Eternal life is "that they may know you, the only true God, and Jesus Christ, whom you have sent" (John 17:3).[9]

The unity of God profoundly affects the religious life of the believer. The nature of the covenant is that the vassal be exclusively loyal to one Lord. The first and second commandments of the Decalogue proscribe worship of anyone other than Yahweh, or worship of Yahweh by the use of idols. We are to worship him alone (Ex. 22:20; Isa. 42:8–9), serve him only (1 Sam. 7:3), trust him alone (2 Kings 19:19; Ps. 71:16), and seek honor from him alone (John 5:44). God's unity, therefore, is not merely a numerical fact, but a central concern of piety. Before God's presence we confess that he alone is God.

GOD AND THE GODS

Scripture does sometimes refer to "gods" other than Yahweh. For example,

> Who among the gods is like you, O Lord?
> Who is like you—
>> majestic in holiness,
>> awesome in glory,
>> working wonders? (Ex. 15:11)

(Cf. Ex. 18:11; 20:3, 23; 23:13; Deut. 29:26; Judg. 11:24; 1 Sam. 26:19; 2 Kings 5;[10] Pss. 82:1, 6; 96:4–5; 1 Cor. 8:5.) On the basis of such passages,

---

9. Note again how the Trinitarian distinction does not compromise John's emphasis on the singularity of the source of eternal life.

10. I list this passage among the others, but I really cannot understand why some writers think it teaches henotheism. Naaman does receive some kind of indulgence with regard to his (slight and forced) participation in Rimmon worship (vv. 18–19). But the real climax of the story is Naaman's repudiation of henotheism in verse 15: "Now I know that there is no God in all the world except in Israel." He takes Israelite soil back home to Aram

some writers have claimed that there are in Scripture traces of henotheism or monolatry: acknowledging the existence of many gods, but worshiping only one of them.[11]

Significantly, these writers claim only that there are traces of henotheism in Scripture. Clearly, the pervasive doctrine of Scripture, as we saw in the preceding section, is that there is only one true God who rules all things. But are there a few exceptions to this pervasive emphasis? I think not. The following points are decisive:

1. If the doctrine of God's oneness means that only one being has ever been called God, or that only one being has ever been worshiped, then of course it is false, as these passages indicate. But, as we have seen, the numerical oneness of God is also a qualitative oneness: there is only one supreme being and therefore only one being who truly deserves worship. In that sense, all of Scripture bears consistent witness to God's oneness.

2. The passages that refer to "gods" make this very point: God is far greater than the "gods," and he is sovereign over them. This is true even in Judges 11:24, where Jephthah seems to acknowledge that the god Chemosh gave certain lands to the Ammonites. In verse 27, Jephthah commits the dispute to the judgment of Yahweh, and Yahweh's victory is devastating to Ammon (vv. 32–33).

The term *gods* in these passages clearly refers, not to beings that have the same nature as the true God, but to beings that are far less. If *God*, therefore, refers to a being that is truly supreme in his attributes and powers, then these passages, like those presented in the preceding section, teach that there is only one God.

3. The actual ontological status of these "gods" is not always clear.[12] Does Chemosh actually exist, according to Judges 11:24? Or is Jephthah speaking ironically or by way of concession to the Ammonite way of thinking? When Elijah challenges the priests of Baal on Mount Carmel, he refers to Baal sarcastically:

(v. 17), not because of a henotheistic belief that God's presence is limited to the land of Israel, but because he believes, correctly, that there is a special presence of God in the Holy Land and therefore that the Holy Land is the proper place to offer sacrifice. Furthermore, even if the writer of 2 Kings does represent Naaman as a henotheist, he certainly does not represent God as a henotheistic deity. The chapter begins with the affirmation that Yahweh, not Rimmon, has given victory to Aram (v. 1).

11. For example, Heinz R. Schlette, "Monotheism," in *Sacramentum Mundi: An Encyclopedia of Theology*, ed. Karl Rahner et al. (New York: Herder and Herder, 1970), 979–81. See also Otto Weber, *Foundations of Dogmatics*, 1:355.

12. Note also that in Ps. 82:1, 6 *'elohim* evidently refers to human beings in positions of authority. In that sense, of course, there are many gods, but that is not the sense used here.

At noon Elijah began to taunt them. "Shout louder!" he said. "Surely he is a god! Perhaps he is deep in thought, or busy, or traveling. Maybe he is sleeping and must be awakened." (1 Kings 18:27)

Clearly we should not derive any ontological conclusions from such humor. Many of these "gods" may simply be fictional. However, we cannot assume that that is always the case. Paul equates false gods with demons in 1 Corinthians 10:20. The important thing is that we recognize that these beings, fictitious or real, are those who "by nature are not gods" (Gal. 4:8). Although they are called "gods" by men (1 Cor. 8:5), they do not deserve that name and do not deserve worship.

4. Every part of Scripture opposes the view that there are other beings who are somehow equal to God. In Genesis, God is the sole Creator of all things, the one who alone destroys the earth in a flood, the one who promises to bless all the families of the earth through Abraham (Gen. 12:3), and who works all things for good (Gen. 50:20) for the redemption of his people. Exodus narrates a contest between Yahweh and the "gods" of Egypt (12:12) and declares Yahweh to be incomparable (Ex. 15:11). The same is true of the narratives of conquest in Joshua and Judges and of God's dealing with Israel and the nations throughout Scripture. Jesus is King of kings and Lord of lords (Rev. 19:16).

CONTEMPORARY CRITIQUES OF MONOTHEISM

Most dictionaries define *monotheism* somewhat as follows: "the doctrine or belief in the existence of only one God." In its primary use of the term *God*, Scripture is clearly monotheistic in this sense.

Nevertheless, Jürgen Moltmann has written "A Criticism of Christian Monotheism."[13] He defines *monotheism*, however, rather differently from our dictionary definition. He equates this term with the Greek expression *monarchia* and explains:

> But monotheism and monarchianism are only the names for two sides of the same thing: the One is the principle and point of integration for the Many. The One is the measure of the Many. The

13. Moltmann, *The Trinity and the Kingdom*, 129–50. Cf. Weber, *Foundations of Dogmatics*, 1:353–55. Wolfhart Pannenberg takes issue with Moltmann's polemic against monotheism, saying that he is "guilty of a wrong terminological decision," in *Systematic Theology* (Grand Rapids: Eerdmans, 1988), 1:336n.

One God has always been appealed to and comprehended in the context of the unity of the world.[14]

So Moltmann takes *monotheism* to designate an attempt to join the God of Scripture "with the monarchical concept of Greek philosophy."[15] Later he says:

> Strict monotheism has to be theoretically conceived and implemented, as Islam proves. But once it is introduced into the doctrine and worship of the Christian church, faith in Christ is threatened: Christ must either recede into the series of the prophets, giving way to the One God, or he must disappear into the One God as one of his manifestations. The strict notion of the One God really makes theological christology impossible, for the One can neither be parted or imparted. It is ineffable. The Christian church was therefore right to see monotheism as the severest inner danger, even though it tried on the other hand to take on the monarchical notion of the divine Lordship.
>
> Strict monotheism obliges us to think of God without Christ, and consequently to think of Christ without God as well.[16]

Here Moltmann equates monotheism, or "strict" monotheism, with the philosophical "One" of Plotinus or Gnosticism, adopted to some extent in Muslim theology.[17] Certainly he is right to oppose such views. In this book, I have described this philosophical concept of oneness as a false concept of transcendence (chap. 7). The Bible does not teach that God is one in the sense of having no plurality or complexity (chap. 12). Nor is God "ineffable" in the sense of being unknowable or indescribable (chap. 11). I have argued that this kind of philosophical oneness (reflected, unfortunately, in some theological accounts of divine simplicity) is inconsistent with biblical Trinitarianism (chap. 12). And, contrary to some Greek philosophers, Scripture does not teach that oneness is in every respect prior to plurality. Since God is both one and many, as I shall argue later, unity and plurality are equally ultimate in God and in the world he has made.

So I agree with Moltmann that this philosophical view of divine one-

---

14. Moltmann, *The Trinity and the Kingdom*, 130.

15. Ibid., 131.

16. Ibid.

17. I would put greater distance initially between the One of the philosophers and the Allah of Mohammed. However, to the extent that Muslim theology rigorously excludes any distinctions or complexities within God and denies that God can be truly known, it approaches the philosophical concept.

ness makes Christology impossible. But it is rather odd that Moltmann takes over a perfectly good term, *monotheism*, and gives it such a pejorative definition. Perhaps, however, we can find a hint of his motivation in the quotation above, where he speaks about "the monarchical notion of divine Lordship." And later in the book he has more to say about divine lordship or rule:

> The idea of the almighty ruler of the universe everywhere requires abject servitude, because it points to complete dependency in all spheres of life.
>
> The doctrine of the Trinity which evolves out of the surmounting of monotheism for Christ's sake, must therefore also overcome this monarchism, which legitimates dependency, helplessness and servitude. The doctrine of the Trinity must be developed as the true theological doctrine of freedom. Religiously motivated political monotheism has always been used in order to legitimate domination, from the emperor cults of the ancient world, Byzantium and the absolute ideologies of the seventeenth century, down to the dictatorships of the twentieth. The doctrine of the Trinity which, on the contrary, is developed as a theological doctrine of freedom must for its part point towards a community of men and women without supremacy and without subjection.[18]

From this quotation we can see that Moltmann's opposition to "monotheism" includes opposition to the idea of God as "the almighty ruler of the universe" and the ideas of divine supremacy and human subjection. But this criticism is not really a criticism of the Greek philosophical concepts. For Plotinus and the Gnostics, the One does not really rule in any meaningful sense. Their One is not a personal being who issues commands; rather, it is an impersonal principle, at the same time the substance of all reality and dualistically opposed to the world. This view is, of course, subject to criticism of many sorts; but it does not encourage servitude in any meaningful sense. This philosophical god cannot demand service and has no right to demand it.

Moltmann's critique at this point, then, is not really aimed at Greek philosophy. His real target is certain views of divine rule that have appeared in the history of Christian theology. Here his use of *monotheism* refers specifically to these views. Moltmann evidently believes that these views are identical to, or deeply influenced by, the Greek philosophical concept of unity. But that belief is not self-evident.

18. Moltmann, *The Trinity and the Kingdom*, 192.

Shall we accept Moltmann's critique of traditional notions of divine rule? Like too many theologians, Moltmann here brings together in one concept things that should be discussed separately.[19] I would not want to defend the idea that the biblical God requires "abject servitude." *Abject* connotes passive, perhaps grudging or fatalistic, acceptance of duty, with no joy or anticipated benefit. That is not the service required by the biblical God. But "complete dependency" is something else entirely. Yes, indeed, creatures are completely dependent on God, as we have seen over and over again. He supplies everything that sustains us, every good gift, everything that we need for eternal blessing. And it is difficult to believe that a professing Christian theologian would object to the idea of God as "the almighty ruler of the universe." Is it not obvious in Scripture that God is precisely that?

I do, of course, oppose the governmental tyrannies on Moltmann's list. But his alternative, his ideal "community of men and women without supremacy and without subjection," raises red flags. First, the biblical teaching about God's lordship and our subjection to him gives no encouragement whatever to human dictatorships. Indeed, Samuel Rutherford in 1644 appealed to God's supreme rule over everything precisely to oppose the absolute claims of human monarchs.[20] Second, Moltmann's radical egalitarianism and feminism are unscriptural (see chap. 18).

So Moltmann begins his critique of monotheism by rightly rejecting the false "One" of Greek speculation. But then he tries to relate this false oneness to other views: God as almighty ruler, our complete dependence on him, abject servitude, political despotism, and domination. Some of these views deserve criticism; some do not. But Moltmann does not show why all of them must be treated the same, or how all of them are based on Greek speculation. His odd use of the term *monotheism* is, I think, a verbal attempt to connect Greek speculation with the Christian positions he doesn't like, wrapping them all up in one conceptual bundle. So he creates in the reader's mind a feeling of connection between these ideas, even though he has not shown that such a connection actually exists.

But the worst part of Moltmann's discussion is the fact that he objects not so much to monotheism as to divine lordship itself. Compare the similar arguments against divine "rule," "monarchy," and "power over" made by Johnson and Pinnock that I discussed in chapter 2.

Contrary to Moltmann, we should affirm monotheism in its biblical

---

19. Compare my comments in chapter 2 on Elizabeth Johnson and Clark Pinnock.

20. Samuel Rutherford, *Lex, Rex* (reprint, Harrisonburg, Va.: Sprinkle Publications, 1980).

sense: there is one God who is Lord of all. He is the sole object of worship, the sole controller of the world, the ultimate authority to whom we must be subject, and the only Savior and Judge. To reject the oneness of God in this sense is to reject his lordship.

GOD IS THREE

Alongside monotheism is another biblical theme, which stresses that God is not a *mere* oneness. He is not like the One of Plotinus, who lacks any complexity at all. Although God is numerically one and simple (chap. 12), he has many attributes, thinks a vast number of thoughts, and performs innumerable actions. His attributes are one, but that oneness can be characterized in many ways. His thoughts are one, but they pertain to innumerable objects. His actions are one, but they have vast numbers of effects in the world. His life is the ultimate in richness and fullness. Scripture expresses this richness in various ways, eventually bringing its specifically Trinitarian character into focus.

We shall begin with phenomena found mostly in the Old Testament, and then move on to see the fulfillment of this incipient Trinitarianism in the New Testament. Warfield's comment about the nature of the Old Testament testimony is valuable:

> The Old Testament may be likened to a chamber richly furnished but dimly lighted; the introduction of light brings into it nothing which was not in it before; but it brings out into clearer view much of what is in it but was only dimly or even not at all perceived before. The mystery of the Trinity is not revealed in the Old Testament; but the mystery of the Trinity underlies the Old Testament revelation, and here and there almost comes into view. Thus the Old Testament revelation is not corrected by the fuller revelation which follows it, but only perfected, extended and enlarged.[21]

PLURALS

The very greatness of God, the richness of his inner life, entails some kind of plurality within him. Perhaps that multifaceted greatness, the sheer vastness of his power and wisdom, has something to do with the use of plu-

21. Benjamin Breckinridge Warfield, "The Biblical Doctrine of the Trinity," in his *Biblical Doctrines* (Grand Rapids: Baker, 1981), 141–42. This is an enormously helpful article, of which I have made much use in writing this section.

ral nouns for him in the Old Testament. In chapter 17, I analyzed the plural form of *'elohim* in terms of abstraction and amplification: *'elohim* refers to God as generic deity, but also, perhaps, as the supreme, rich being. *'Elohim* usually takes a singular verb, but it takes plural verbs in Genesis 20:13; 35:7; Exodus 32:4; Nehemiah 9:18; and Isaiah 16:6. Note also the plural form of *'adon* in Malachi 1:6, of two Hebrew terms for *creator* in Psalm 149:2 and Ecclesiastes 12:1, and of *ba'al* (referring to God as husband) in Isaiah 54:5. The "seven spirits" of Revelation 1:4; 3:1; 4:5; 5:6 are evidently an intensive reference to the Holy Spirit.

God also sometimes speaks in the plural, as in "Let us make man in our image" (Gen. 1:26; cf. 3:22; 11:7). Perhaps we are to understand this language as a consultation of the heavenly council, the Glory-cloud we discussed in chapter 25. But even that is to underscore the fact that when God appeared to people in the Old Testament, he appeared as a rich diversity of form, movement, and sound, interacting dynamically with the heavenly beings and with his spatio-temporal creation.

We should not try to derive any precise doctrinal content from these grammatical peculiarities. In every language, plural forms sometimes denote singular realities (like *pants* in English). I do think it significant, however, that the writers and characters of the Old Testament, emphatic monotheists that they were, do not object to these plural forms or try to avoid them, even though the language offered them alternatives. In the text, there is no evident embarrassment. That suggests that they regarded God, not as a bare unity, but as a unity of many things.

HYPOSTATIZATIONS

The Old Testament refers to a number of beings that are somehow identical to, yet distinguished from, God. These are sometimes described as *hypostatizations* or *personifications* of divine attributes.

The *word* of God is certainly divine (see chap. 22), being an object of praise (Ps. 56:4, 10). Yet it is also God's tool in his making and governing of the world: by the word of the Lord were the heavens made (Ps. 33:6). He "sends" his word (Ps. 147:18; cf. 107:20; 148:8). His word "goes out" of his mouth to accomplish his purposes (Isa. 55:11). So the Old Testament establishes a unity and a difference between God and his word. In intertestamental and Hellenistic Judaism, "Word" becomes a kind of intermediary between God and the world, a link in the "great chain of being" (chap. 12). But the New Testament restores it to the fully divine status it deserves, identifying the Word with Christ (John 1:1–14). So the Old Testament hypostatization is fulfilled in New Testament Trinitarianism.

In Scripture, there is a close relationship between God's word and his *wisdom*. The Old Testament also hypostatizes God's wisdom in Proverbs 3:19, "By wisdom the LORD laid the earth's foundations, by understanding he set the heavens in place." Wisdom is a divine attribute, but it is also that by which God made the world. Also, in Proverbs 8:1–9:12, God's wisdom takes the form of a lady (see chap. 18), calling men to fear the Lord and hate evil (cf. also Job 28:37; Jer. 10:12; 51:15). As with the Word, the New Testament identifies wisdom with Christ (1 Cor. 1:30). Once again, hypostatization anticipates somewhat the doctrine of the Trinity.

God's *name* is another example of this phenomenon. The name of God is God himself (see chap. 17), but he saves us by his name (Isa. 54:1), guides us for his name's sake (Ps. 23:3), and makes his name to dwell in a place (Deut. 12:5). Jesus is the fulfillment of God's name, the name to which every knee shall bow (Phil. 2:10).

God's *glory*, as we saw in chapter 25, is a divine attribute, but also a visible form by which he manifests himself to creatures. God exists above time and space, but his glory resides in heaven and also in earthly places of his choosing (Deut. 26:15; Ezek. 43:4–7).

DIVINE PERSONS IN THE OLD TESTAMENT

God's *Spirit* is closely related to his glory, as we saw in chapter 25. Clearly the Spirit is divine; he is God at work in the world. But the Old Testament also makes a distinction between God and the Spirit, as in Genesis 1:2, where God creates and the Spirit hovers over the waters. The Spirit is the breath (*ruah*) by which God's word accomplished its creative purpose (Ps. 33:6). God creates by his Spirit (Job 26:13). As with his word, God sends the Spirit to do his bidding (Ps. 104:30). The Spirit enters the prophets so that they can hear and speak God's word (2 Sam. 23:2; Ezek. 2:2; cf. Zech. 7:12). This use of *Spirit* finds its fulfillment in New Testament Trinitarianism, as the Spirit comes upon the church from the Father and the Son.

The phrases *angel of the Lord* and *angel of God* (even, sometimes, simply *angel*) often refer to a divine being. Not every angel in Scripture is divine: in Revelation 19:10 and 22:9, an angel refuses worship and tells John to worship God instead.[22] But in many cases the angel is God. Appearing to

---

22. However, my list of passages in which the angel is a divine being would be somewhat longer than Bavinck's in *DG*, 257. I am not as certain as he is that "an ordinary angel is meant" in 2 Sam. 24:16, 1 Kings 19:5–7, and other passages. In 2 Sam. 24:16, to be sure, God tells the angel to cease his destruction, but that is not inconsistent with a relationship between God and a divine angel.

Hagar, the angel speaks as God, making covenant with her and her children (Gen. 16:6–13; 21:17–20). In Genesis 22:11–12, the angel tells Abraham that "you have not withheld from me your son, your only son," where "me" must be God (v. 2). In Genesis 31:11–13, the angel identifies himself as "the God of Bethel." In 32:30, Jacob says of the man (called an "angel" in Hosea 12:4) who wrestled with him that "I saw God face to face, and yet my life was spared." (See also Gen. 48:15–16; Ex. 3:2–22; 13:21 [cf. 14:19; 32:34]; 23:20–23; Num. 20:16; Isa. 63:8–9; Zech. 1:8–12; Mal. 3:1.) But in Exodus 23:20 and 32:34, God distinguishes himself from the divine angel. The angel is one whom God is "sending" (23:20).

The *Messiah* is a human deliverer, a son of David, but also God. He is the servant of the Lord who suffers to bear the sins of his people (Isa. 52:13–53:12). But, in the final analysis, no mere human can save Israel from its sins. Only God's own arm can bring salvation (Isa. 59:15–20; cf. 43:3, 11; 45:15, 21; 49:26; 60:16; 63:8). Salvation is of the Lord (Jonah 2:9). So the coming king is called God in Psalm 45:6, but is distinguished from God in verse 7. And in Psalm 110:1, a verse applied to Christ several times in the New Testament, David's messianic Son is also his Lord:

> The LORD says to my Lord:
> "Sit at my right hand
> until I make your enemies
> a footstool for your feet."

TRIADS IN THE OLD TESTAMENT

So far, we have considered various attributes and personal beings in the Old Testament that are divine, yet distinguished from God. But the number three, which is essential to the doctrine of the Trinity, has not yet entered the discussion.

There is something mysteriously captivating to the human mind about the number three. Threefold repetitions and distinctions abound in human life and speech, both in Scripture and outside it. I have a file containing hundreds of these, including not only theological triads (e.g., prophet, priest, and king), but also physical ones (e.g., solid, liquid, and vapor) and mental ones (e.g., Augustine's memory, understanding, and will), not to mention, of course, the lordship attributes (control, authority, presence) and my three perspectives (normative, situational, and existential). For more, see appendix A.

I'm not sure how all this is related to the doctrine of the Trinity, but I would be surprised if there were no significant connection at all. I will explore later some of the connections that I consider valid and helpful. Nevertheless, as we survey some of the triads in the Old Testament, it would not be wise for us to take all of them simply as adumbrations of the Trinity. To some extent, these triads are like the plural forms we discussed earlier: they serve to amplify what is being said, to raise the language to a level worthy of deity. The threefold formulation suggests completeness and fulfillment. We sense fulfillment when manifoldness (two) terminates in completeness (three).

But of course that amplification, that completeness, itself finds its fulfillment in the doctrine of the Trinity. God is the threefold God, life at its greatest amplification, its greatest fulfillment. God's full nature and attributes are best displayed in the unity of love, knowledge, and power among the three persons.

Earlier we considered some Old Testament divine attributes and personal theophanies that find fulfillment in New Testament Trinitarianism. From a New Testament vantage point, we can align these with the Father, the Son, and the Spirit: clearly *Word* and *Messiah* should be identified with the Son, and *Spirit* with the Spirit. But *glory* surely pertains to all three persons, as does *wisdom*. In any case, the Old Testament does not place these attributes and personal theophanies into a distinctly triadic order.

Nevertheless, we can find triads of various sorts in the Old Testament. As with the other Old Testament texts we have considered, these do not imply a precise or detailed doctrine of the Trinity, but they are important for what they contribute to the full Trinitarian doctrine of the New Testament.

The Aaronic benediction, by which God places his name on Israel, is threefold:

> The Lord bless you
>   and keep you;
> the Lord make his face shine upon you
>   and be gracious to you;
> the Lord turn his face toward you
>   and give you peace. (Num. 6:24–26)

Note the threefold repetition of "Lord."[23] This passage may be the model for the explicitly Trinitarian apostolic benediction: "May the grace of the Lord Jesus Christ, and the love of God, and the fellowship of the Holy Spirit be with you all" (2 Cor. 13:14).

---

23. Note also that "grace" in the second clause and "peace" in the third anticipate the typical New Testament apostolic blessing: "Grace be to you and peace."

In Isaiah 6:3, the angels sing, "Holy, holy, holy is the Lord Almighty." The threefold repetition amplifies God's holiness, indicating that it is vast, far beyond any creaturely holiness.

In Isaiah 33:22, the prophet says:

> For the Lord is our judge,
>   the Lord is our lawgiver,
>   the Lord is our king;
>   it is he who will save us.

This is a threefold repetition of "Lord," ascribing to him three offices that, interestingly, correlate with the three functions of modern governments.[24] His government of the world is all-encompassing. For other threefold references to God, see Jeremiah 33:2 and Daniel 9:19. Compare Revelation 1:4–5; 4:8.

Old Testament Triads of Divine Beings

We saw earlier that the word of God and the wisdom of God are divine, yet somehow distinct from God. So God is able to "send forth" his word or to create the world "by" his wisdom. God and his word are one, but also two. Similarly, God and his wisdom are one, but also two. But there are also passages where three such divine beings are brought together. These passages anticipate the doctrine of the Trinity in a special way.

First, in Psalm 33:6, we read:

> By the word of the Lord were the heavens made,
>   their starry host by the breath of his mouth.

Here we find together the Lord, his word, and his breath (*ruah*, "Spirit"). This is what I have sometimes called the linguistic model of the Trinity. The Father is the speaker, the Son is the word (cf. John 1:1–14), and the Spirit is the breath that carries the word to the hearer.

Second, Isaiah 48:16 reads:

> Come near me and listen to this:
> "From the first announcement I have not spoken in secret;
>   at the time it happens, I am there."
> And now the Sovereign Lord has sent me,
>   with his Spirit.

---

24. They also correlate with the lordship attributes: king = control, lawgiver = authority, judge = present in blessing and judgment.

The speaker is Yahweh, as the preceding context indicates. But the verse says that Yahweh has been sent by someone else, called "the Sovereign LORD," together with another called "his Spirit." From a New Testament vantage point, we can see this as a Trinitarian passage. Interestingly, the following verse adds, "This is what the LORD says—your Redeemer, the Holy One of Israel," a threefold self-description corresponding somewhat to the Trinitarian persons (cf. 44:6).

Third, in Isaiah 63:9–10, we read:

> In all their distress he too was distressed,
>   and the angel of his presence saved them.
> In his love and mercy he redeemed them;
>   he lifted them up and carried them
>   all the days of old.
> Yet they rebelled
>   and grieved his Holy Spirit.
> So he turned and became their enemy
>   and he himself fought against them.

Here we read of Yahweh, the angel of his presence, and his Holy Spirit. The angel, of course, is the divine being who, we noted earlier, led Israel through the wilderness.

Fourth, in Haggai 2:5–7, Yahweh says:

> "This is what I covenanted with you when you came out of Egypt. And my Spirit remains among you. Do not fear."
> This is what the LORD Almighty says: "In a little while I will once more shake the heavens and the earth, the sea and the dry land. I will shake all nations, and the desired of all nations will come, and I will fill this house with glory," says the LORD Almighty.

Here the Lord affirms that his Spirit remains in Israel and that the "desired of all nations," the Messiah, will come, bringing glory to the temple. The Lord, the Messiah, and the Spirit correspond to the three persons of the Trinity in the New Testament.

THE DIVINE PERSONS OF THE NEW TESTAMENT

For all the adumbrations of the Trinity in the Old Testament, much therein remains unclear. For example, from the data of the Old Testament alone, it would be difficult, if not impossible, to determine how many divine beings there are. One might well ask if *Word, wisdom, name, glory, angel, Messiah,* and *Spirit* designate seven distinct divine beings, and, if not, what the relationships among them are. Is the triad *Lord, Word, breath* (Ps. 33:6) the same as the triad *Lord, angel, Spirit* (Isa. 63:9–10)?

In the New Testament, however, the writers are clearly settled on the existence of three divine persons, called Father, Son, and Spirit. To the Son applies what the Old Testament ascribed to God's word, his wisdom, his name, the Messiah, and, most likely, the divine angel. So the New Testament brings much more clarity into our understanding of these persons. In that way, the New Testament is very different from the Old. Yet, as Warfield points out, the New Testament writers sense no tension between their teaching and that of the Old Testament:

> To their own apprehension they worshipped and proclaimed just the God of Israel; and they laid no less stress than the Old Testament itself upon His unity (John 17:3, 1 Cor. 8:4, 1 Tim. 2:5).[25] They do not, then, place two new gods by the side of Jehovah as alike with him to be served and worshipped; they conceive Jehovah as at once Father, Son, and Spirit. In presenting this one Jehovah as Father, Son, and Spirit, they do not even betray any lurking feeling that they are making innovations. Without apparent misgiving they take over Old Testament passages and apply them to Father, Son, and Spirit indifferently.[26]

There is, then, no controversy in the New Testament that its Trinitarianism is consistent with the Old Testament. Indeed, for the New Testament writers, as Warfield also points out, the Trinity is settled doctrine:

> If they betray no sense of novelty in so speaking [of God as a Trinity], this is undoubtedly in part because it was no longer a novelty so to speak of Him. It is clear, in other words, that, as we read the New Testament, we are not witnessing the birth of a new conception of God. What we meet within its pages is a firmly established conception of God underlying and giving tone to the entire fabric. It is not in a text here and there that the New Testament bears its testimony to the doctrine of the Trinity. The whole book

25. I would note, though Warfield doesn't do so here, the remarkable fact that these passages, which stress divine unity, also distinguish between two or more persons of the Trinity (note vv. 5–6 after 1 Cor. 8:4; cf. also Eph. 4:3 6). One might have thought that the biblical writers would have avoided making Trinitarian distinctions when writing about God's oneness, lest they obscure the point being made. Evidently, the New Testament writers not only think that Trinitarianism is consistent with divine unity, but also think that God's threeness somehow *underscores* his unity. Perhaps the thought is that we can see the oneness of God even more clearly when we see him as three persons working in perfect harmony.

26. Warfield, "The Biblical Doctrine of the Trinity," 142.

is Trinitarian to the core; all its teaching is built on the assumption of the Trinity; and its allusions to the Trinity are frequent, cursory, easy and confident. It is with a view to the cursoriness of the allusions to it in the New Testament that it has been remarked that "the doctrine of the Trinity is not so much heard as overheard in the statements of Scripture." It would be more exact to say that it is not so much inculcated as presupposed. The doctrine of the Trinity does not appear in the New Testament in the making, but as already made.[27]

In the New Testament, there is no systematic, point-by-point exposition of the doctrine of the Trinity, like the exposition of justification in Romans 3–5. The New Testament gives systematic attention to doctrines that were controversial in the early church. Evidently the Trinity was not in dispute. It appears there "in full completeness,"[28] accepted by all.

So something remarkable happened between the completion of the Old Testament and the first writings of the New. What was vaguely intimated in the Old Testament became a clear, settled doctrine in the New, needing no elaborate definition or defense. Of course, what happened was that the Son of God became flesh, and the Holy Spirit came upon the church with power. The events of Christmas and Pentecost changed everything. Jesus "came from the Father" (John 16:28), and he sent the Spirit from the Father (John 15:26). All the blessings of salvation come through those three persons. Jesus died for sinners, rose again, and ascended to glory. The Spirit empowered the church for its universal mission. It was these epochal events that brought all the Old Testament divine attributes, hypostatizations, triads, and persons together in Father, Son, and Spirit. So the church naturally came to praise, thank, and worship these three. And its teaching about salvation continually revolved around the work of the Father, the Son, and the Spirit.

So everything in the New Testament is about the Father, the Son, and the Spirit.[29] In the birth narratives, Jesus is conceived by the Holy Spirit (Matt. 1:18, 20; Luke 1:35) and thus comes to be "God with us" (Matt. 1:23), "the Son of God" (Luke 1:35). At his baptism, the three persons are present: Jesus, the Spirit descending as a dove (Matt. 3:16; Luke 3:22), and

---

27. Ibid., 143.
28. Ibid., 143, quoting Gunkel.
29. I can only scratch the surface in this survey of New Testament Trinitarian teaching. I will enter into more depth later in my discussions of the deity of Christ and the Holy Spirit and of other Trinitarian issues (chaps. 28–29).

the Father speaking from heaven, "This is my Son, whom I love; with him I am well pleased" (Matt. 3:17; cf. 17:5; Luke 3:22).

In Matthew 4 and Luke 4, the Spirit leads Jesus into the wilderness, where Satan tempts him. The temptation is essentially an invitation to Jesus (as to Adam in Gen. 3) to serve Satan rather than the Father (see Matt. 4:4, 7, 10). Jesus then returns to Galilee "in the power of the Spirit" (Luke 4:14) and announces in the synagogue that he fulfills Isaiah 61:1–2: The Spirit of the Lord is upon him (Luke 4:18) to proclaim the year of the Lord's (the Father's) favor (v. 19). He casts out devils by the Spirit of God (Matt. 12:28) to show that the kingdom of God (the Father) has come. Compare Acts 10:38, where Peter speaks of "how God anointed Jesus of Nazareth with the Holy Spirit and power, and how he went around doing good."

The richest Trinitarian teaching in the Gospels is in the Johannine discourses preceding Jesus' atoning death. Here Jesus expresses eternal intimacy with the Father (John 17, especially vv. 5, 10–11, 22, 26) and promises to send upon the church the Holy Spirit from the Father (and to come to them himself in the Spirit) (14:16–18, 26; 15:26; 16:13–15; 20:21–22).

After his resurrection, Jesus commissions his disciples to make disciples and baptize them "in the name of the Father and of the Son and of the Holy Spirit" (Matt. 28:19). One name is here applied to three divine beings, coordinate with each other. Remember that baptism in the New Testament is into the name of God, not into the name of any creature (1 Cor. 1:14–15).

In Acts 2, Jesus fulfills his promise:

> Exalted to the right hand of God, he has received from the Father the promised Holy Spirit and has poured out what you now see and hear. (v. 33)

So Peter urges the people:

> Repent and be baptized, every one of you, in the name of Jesus Christ for the forgiveness of your sins. And you will receive the gift of the Holy Spirit. The promise is for you and for your children and for all who are far off—for all whom the Lord our God will call. (vv. 38–39)

The Father offers the Holy Spirit to all who embrace the Son in faith. Compare also Acts 9:17–20 (in the conversion of Saul).

Paul makes a rich use of Trinitarian formulations. It is helpful to remember that in his usual vocabulary, *theos* ("God") represents the Father, *kyrios*

("Lord") or *huios* ("Son") the Son, and *pneuma* ("Spirit") the Spirit. So a passage like 1 Corinthians 12:4–6 or Ephesians 4:4–6, which distinguishes "one Spirit . . . one Lord . . . one God," is deeply Trinitarian.[30]

The first part of Paul's letter to the Romans may be said to have a Trinitarian structure: the judgment of God the Father upon sin (1:18–3:20), the atoning work of the Son, by which God justifies and sanctifies the ungodly (3:21–7:25), and the freedom and assurance of the Spirit (8:1–39). Paul mentions the three persons together in 1:1–4; 5:1–5; 6:4;[31] 8:1–4, 8–9, 11, 14–17; 15:16, 30. (See also 1 Cor. 6:11; 8:6; 12:4–6; 2 Cor. 1:21–22; 3:3–4; 5:5–8; 13:14;[32] Gal. 4:6;[33] Eph. 1:3–14;[34] 2:18, 22; 3:2–5, 14–17; 4:4–6; 5:18–20; Phil. 3:3; Col. 1:6–7; 3:16–17; 1 Thess. 1:2–6; 5:18–19; 2 Thess. 2:13–14; 1 Tim. 3:15–16; Titus 3:4–6.)

Other New Testament writers also bring together the persons of the Trinity in their account of God's salvation (see Heb. 2:3–4; 6:4–6; 9:14; 10:29–31; 1 Peter 1:2; 4:13–19; 1 John 4:2, 13–14; 5:6–12; Jude 20–21; Rev. 1:4–5).[35] Notice also in Revelation 13 a Satanic counterfeit of the Trinity: (1) a dragon, (2) a beast (healed of a fatal wound) who receives great power and authority from the dragon (vv. 2–3), and (3) a second beast (vv. 11–18) who makes everyone worship the first beast, and who works miraculous signs.

The New Testament also contains many passages in which two of the three persons appear as the common source of blessing: Father and Son

---

30. This vocabulary explains why Paul distinguishes Jesus from *theos* ("God"). Paul does this, not to cast any doubt on the full deity of Christ, but simply to distinguish the Son from the Father. Indeed, he does sometimes use *theos* for Christ (see Rom. 9:5; 2 Thess. 1:12; Titus 2:13), but his general practice is not to do so. Nevertheless, the term he typically applies to Christ, *kyrios*, is as strong a divine title as *theos*—and perhaps even more so, in the light of its connection with *yahweh* in the Septuagint. See the later discussion of the deity of Christ.

31. Here Paul uses *glory* rather than *Spirit*, but, as we have seen, these concepts are closely related.

32. Here is a benediction, threefold as in Num. 6:24–26, coordinating the three persons as the ultimate source of all spiritual blessings.

33. The NIV gives 3:26–4:7 the title "Sons of God"; 5:1–15, "Freedom in Christ"; and 5:16–26, "Life by the Spirit." These titles are appropriate. The intervening sections, 4:8–20 ("Paul's Concern for the Galatians") and 4:21–31 ("Hagar and Sarah"), are arguably subdivisions of 3:26–4:31, all of which could be labeled "Sons of God."

34. Note the focus on the Father's election in verses 3–6 (recapitulated in vv. 11–12), the work of Christ in verses 7–10, and the seal of the Spirit in verses 13–14.

35. This passage presents several intensive triadic structures: a threefold reference to the Father as he "who is, and who was, and who is to come," an intensively plural reference to the Holy Spirit as "the seven spirits before his throne," and a threefold reference to Jesus, "the faithful witness, the firstborn from the dead, and the ruler of the kings of the earth."

(Rom. 6:4; 1 Cor. 15:24–28), and Christ and the Spirit (John 14:16, 18, 23; Acts 16:7; Rom. 8:2, 9; 2 Cor. 3:17; Gal. 4:6; Phil. 1:19; 1 Peter 1:10; cf. Gal. 3:3; 5:16, 25). Note the apostolic greetings and benedictions in 1 Corinthians 1:3; 2 Corinthians 1:2; Galatians 1:3; Ephesians 1:3; 6:23–24; 1 Thessalonians 1:1; 2 Thessalonians 1:2; 1 Timothy 1:2; 2 Timothy 1:2; Titus 1:4, which are always from God our Father and our Lord Jesus Christ. And in 2 Corinthians 13:14, Paul names all three persons.

In the following chapter, I shall take a closer look at the biblical teaching on the deity of Christ and the Spirit, and that study will reinforce the pervasiveness of Trinitarian teaching in the Scriptures. I shall also examine the distinct ministries of the persons and their unity in these ministries. But it should be evident already that the New Testament holds a profoundly Trinitarian view of God.

The main thrust of these passages is that all three persons bring us salvation and equally deserve our praise and thanks. They are together in the ministry of the prophets and in Jesus: in his words and miracles, his resurrection from the dead, and in the Spirit's work of illumination, conviction, adoption, sanctification, and glorification. As Warfield points out, these passages are not formal teaching about the Trinity. Rather, they teach about other matters, but almost subconsciously take on a Trinitarian form. So the doctrine of the Trinity is "overheard." Let us take one passage as an example. In 1 Corinthians 12:4–6, Paul says:

> There are different kinds of gifts, but the same Spirit. There are different kinds of service, but the same Lord. There are different kinds of working (*energēmatōn*), but the same God works all of them in all men.

Warfield comments:

> It may be thought that there is a measure of what might be called artificiality in assigning the endowments of the church, as they are graces to the Spirit, as they are services to Christ, and as they are energizings to God. But thus there is only more strikingly revealed the underlying Trinitarian conception as dominating the structure of the clauses: Paul clearly so writes, not because "gifts," "workings," "operations," stand out in his thought as greatly diverse things, but because God, the Lord, and the Spirit lie in the back of his mind constantly suggesting a threefold causality behind every manifestation of grace. The Trinity is alluded to rather than asserted; but it is so alluded to as to show that it con-

stitutes the determining basis of all Paul's thought of the God of redemption.[36]

The full proof of the proposition that "God is three" awaits our study of the deity of Christ and the Spirit, to which we now proceed. But from our present study, we should expect to find a common status for the Father, the Son, and the Spirit. All three stand together as Creator and Savior. Scripture joins them together in contexts of praise and thanksgiving. They are the ultimate object of the believer's trust and hope. What else can they possibly be, other than one, somehow threefold God?

---

36. Warfield, "The Biblical Doctrine of the Trinity," 159. Concerning 2 Cor. 13:14, he comments: "[Paul] does not say, as he might just as well have said, 'The grace and love and communion of God be with you all,' but 'The grace of the Lord Jesus Christ, and the love of God, and the communion of the Holy Spirit, be with you all.' Thus he bears, almost unconsciously but most richly, witness to the trinal composition of the Godhead as conceived by him" (p. 160).

CHAPTER 28

The Three Are God

We shall now consider the third of the five propositions by which I summarized the doctrine of the Trinity in the preceding chapter. We have seen that God is one, and that God is three. Now we must focus more closely on the deity of the three persons.[1] Of course, this discussion will overlap that of the second proposition. To show the threeness of God, it is necessary to show that the beings mentioned in the triads are actually divine. I began to show that in the previous chapter by citing texts showing that all the works of creation and salvation, which are distinctively works of God, have a threefold source. But there are many other texts that undergird this conclusion, and we should look at them here at least in a summary way.

Summary is the appropriate term. I cannot begin, in one chapter, to duplicate or surpass the thoroughness of B. B. Warfield's *The Lord of Glory*[2] or Robert Reymond's *Jesus, Divine Messiah*.[3] Because of these and other com-

---

1. The deity of the Father may, of course, be taken for granted, so our discussion will focus on the deity of the Son and the Spirit. In considering the deity of the Son, we will focus on the New Testament data concerning the incarnate Christ, for that is where we learn most about the person of the eternal Son.

2. Benjamin B. Warfield, *The Lord of Glory* (1907; reprint, Grand Rapids: Baker, 1974).

3. Robert L. Reymond, *Jesus, Divine Messiah* (Phillipsburg, N.J.: P&R Publishing, 1990). In this masterful volume, Reymond not only exegetes relevant passages, but also interacts with recent critical scholarship to establish the authenticity of those New Testament texts to which he appeals. He shows that even on the assumptions of skeptical biblical critics, it is possible to derive from the New Testament a high Christology—indeed, a full doctrine of Jesus' deity. I will not enter into those arguments here, but rather will simply presuppose,

prehensive studies of the deity of Christ, I believe that a summary here will be sufficient.

These volumes also support the main point I want to make here, which is that the deity of the divine persons is a *pervasive* teaching of the New Testament (supported in important ways by the Old). The deity of Christ, for example, is not to be found only in a handful of controversial verses. It is found in one way or another on nearly every page of the New Testament. Even a book-length treatment is scarcely sufficient to do justice to the evidence. Christians do injustice to the subject when they focus exclusively on the relatively few (but very significant) passages in the New Testament where Jesus is called *theos*, "God." These passages are only the tip of the iceberg.

In the preceding chapter, we noted Warfield's point that the doctrine of the Trinity in the New Testament is "not so much inculcated as presupposed." The New Testament writers have no need to prove the Trinity; the coming of Christ and the coming of the Spirit for our salvation proved the doctrine of the Trinity adequately for both the writers and the original readers of the New Testament. So for us modern readers, the doctrine is "not so much heard as overheard." But we overhear it everywhere. In that sense, it is pervasive. Warfield makes the same point in regard to the deity of Christ. He notes:

> The late Dr. R. W. Dale found the most impressive proofs that the Apostles themselves and the primitive churches believed that Jesus was one with God, rather in the way this seems everywhere taken for granted, than in the texts in which it is positively asserted.[4]

The same point holds true in this case, because the deity of Christ and the deity of the Spirit are of course essential to the doctrine of the Trinity. So, like the overall doctrine of the Trinity, the doctrines of the deity of Christ and the deity of the Spirit were not controversial among first-century Christians. The New Testament writers rarely, if ever, try to prove them. But they mention and imply them again and again. They presuppose them—and, as Cornelius Van Til used to say in another connection, presupposition is often the best proof.

---

as I have throughout this volume, the truth of Scripture as God's word. That assumption, of course, immediately opens up to us all the New Testament data, regardless of the critics' evaluation of them. But I do regard Reymond's discussions as very valuable, and I commend them to the reader.

4. Warfield, *The Lord of Glory*, 1.

FUNCTIONAL AND ONTOLOGICAL CHRISTOLOGIES

I shall not give much space to the often-discussed question of whether New Testament Christology is "functional" or "ontological."[5] The issue here is whether Scripture ascribes to Jesus only divine *functions* (roles, actions, relationships with creatures) or whether it also ascribes to him a divine *being*—regarding him as the Creator, rather than merely a creature.[6] I am content to make the following observations:

1. Applied to the New Testament, the functional-ontological antithesis is rather artificial. Scripture never makes such a distinction explicitly in regard to Christ, and it would be hard to find any implicit distinction of this sort. Carson cites T. E. Pollard as saying that "it is questionable whether St. John gave any thought to the ontological nature of the Sonship," to which Carson replies that "it is doubtful whether St. John gave any thought to the functional nature of the Sonship."[7] Certainly, the view that Jesus' deity is functional, but not ontological, would never have occurred to any biblical writer; this sort of distinction was not in their conceptual vocabulary.

2. Reymond correctly says:

> It is as psychologically impossible for modern men as it was for the men of New Testament times to be satisfied with an interest only in Jesus' functional significance and never question or address the ontological issue that His functional significance forces upon them.[8]

He cites Matthew 8:27 (cf. Mark 4:41), in which Jesus' lordship over the winds and waves leads the disciples to ask, "What kind of man [*potapos*] is this? Even the winds and the waves obey him!" He also cites Matthew 16:13–17, where Jesus asks the disciples who he is and receives an ontological answer.

3. As we have seen in this volume, the biblical writers are interested in the ontological nature of God—his names and attributes—as well as his ac-

---

5. For excellent surveys and evaluations of the literature of this discussion, see Reymond, *Jesus, Divine Messiah*, 1–43, especially pp. 11–15, and (focusing on Johannine studies) D. A. Carson, *Divine Sovereignty and Human Responsibility* (Atlanta: John Knox Press, 1981), 149–62.

6. Christ, of course, is creature as well. He has a perfect human nature as well as a perfect divine nature. This chapter, however, is concerned with the doctrine of the Trinity, not Christology. So I will be focusing on Jesus' deity rather than his humanity. But none of this discussion should be taken to imply any disparagement of Jesus' full humanity.

7. Carson, *Divine Sovereignty and Human Responsibility*, 149–50. He quotes T. E. Pollard, *Johannine Christology and the Early Church* (London: Cambridge University Press, 1970), 17.

8. Reymond, *Jesus, Divine Messiah*, 12–13 (emphasis his).

tions. It is God's unique ontological status that distinguishes him from all creatures and entitles him to their worship. God is radically different from creatures, making it sinful to worship any creature or to worship God by the use of idols. It would be most strange if the New Testament writers had no interest in the ontological status of their own object of worship, Jesus Christ.

4. We shall see that many of Jesus' functions (his actions, roles, and relationships with creatures) are uniquely divine: actions that only God can take, roles that only God can perform, relationships that only God can sustain to his creatures. But one who performs uniquely divine functions must be God.

5. As we shall see below, Scripture sometimes speaks quite directly of Jesus' divine nature, over and above the many inferences of his deity that we may draw from its teachings about Jesus' functions. Of course, as I mentioned earlier, the bulk of its teaching is indirect, "overheard." That indirectness has, perhaps, been the main reason why some have found functional Christologies to be plausible. But when we look carefully at Scripture's indirect references to Jesus' deity, we discover that they bear witness, just as much as direct statements, to a fully ontological Christology. That this Christology is presupposed in Scripture, rather than merely stated, makes it all the more certain.

TAKING JESUS' DEITY FOR GRANTED

Here are some examples from the New Testament in which the deity of Christ is taken for granted, rather than positively asserted.

1. Jesus' teaching in the Gospels is remarkably egocentric. In the Sermon on the Mount, the last beatitude describes the blessedness of those persecuted "because of me" (Matt. 5:11). This persecution is like the persecution of the Old Testament prophets because of Yahweh (v. 12). In the comparison, the apostles are prophets, and Jesus is Yahweh.

In verse 17, Jesus denies that he has come "to abolish the Law or the Prophets." But what human teacher might even be suspected of doing that? Only God could abolish them. The question does not even arise unless Jesus is God. In fact, he does not abolish them, but he does speak with astonishing authority (7:28–29), contradicting the traditions of the elders and claiming that his own words represent the foundation of human life (7:24–27). He says that he has the right to determine who enters the kingdom of heaven (7:21–23). He determines who will know the Father (11:27). He demands that people be willing to lose all in order to follow him (16:25). He speaks of "his angels" (13:41; 16:27; 24:31). It is he who will reward and punish the deeds of men (16:27–28; 25:31–46), and the basis of the judgment will be the relationship of men to him.

Jesus' egocentrism is even more obvious in the gospel of John. There he draws attention to himself over and over. "I am," he claims, the bread of life (6:48), the light of the world (8:12), the resurrection and the life (11:25), the way, the truth, and the life (14:6), and so on. We shall consider later the relation of these statements to Exodus 3:14.

Over and over again, Jesus tells people to "follow me" (Matt. 4:19; 8:22; 9:9; 16:24; 19:21; John 10:27; 12:26; 13:36; 21:19, 22). In most of these passages, Jesus' call comes to men who are to be his special followers, but sometimes it is a general command to all who would believe in him (Matt. 16:24; John 10:27; 12:26).

In Matthew 19:16–21, Jesus assumes, for the sake of argument, that the rich young man has kept the commandments of the Decalogue that deal with his responsibility to other human beings. But the young man still lacks something. Instead of referring him to the first four commandments, which deal with his duty to God, Jesus tells him to sell his goods, give to the poor, and then "come, follow me" (v. 21). Jesus here calls on the young man to follow him, when we might have expected Jesus to exhort him to worship God. The two here are functionally equivalent.

No Old Testament prophet ever drew attention to himself in this way, claiming to be the source of all divine blessing and the standard of all divine judgment. Godly teachers typically turn attention away from themselves and point people to God. If Jesus is not God, his egocentric teaching is prideful—even blasphemous. Only if he is God is it admirable.

Jesus places loyalty to himself even above family loyalty. In Matthew 10:37, Jesus announces:

> Anyone who loves his father or mother more than me is not worthy of me; anyone who loves his son or daughter more than me is not worthy of me.

In Luke 14:26, he puts it even more strongly:

> If anyone comes to me and does not hate his father and mother, his wife and children, his brothers and sisters—yes, even his own life—he cannot be my disciple.[9]

Family loyalty is a very high value in Scripture, enshrined in the fifth commandment, "Honor your father and your mother," and later in the apos-

9. Recall, however, our discussion of hatred in chapter 21. It does not necessarily involve hostility, and it can be a relative expression.

tolic injunction: "If anyone does not provide for his relatives, and especially for his immediate family, he has denied the faith and is worse than an unbeliever" (1 Tim. 5:8). Jesus himself rebuked the Pharisees and the teachers of the law because they allowed people to dishonor their parents by making special gifts to God (Mark 7:11). Nevertheless, of course, there is certainly a sense in which God deserves greater honor than parents. But this is true only of God—certainly not any human teacher. But in Matthew 10:37, Jesus claims an honor due only to God. So believers do all things (including suffering) for the name of Jesus (Acts 9:16; Rom. 15:30; 2 Cor. 12:10; 3 John 7).

In none of these passages does Jesus teach that he is God. He simply assumes divine status, functions, and prerogatives.

2. As D. James Kennedy points out, Jesus in the Gospels never withdraws or modifies a statement, never apologizes or repents (though among human beings such is a mark of greatness), never seeks advice, and never asks for prayer for himself.[10] He sometimes behaves strangely—sleeping in a boat during a storm (Matt. 8:24) and allowing Lazarus to die (John 11:37)—without explaining his actions. Such behavior can be considered virtuous only in God himself. Once again, these texts do not teach Jesus' deity; they presuppose it.

3. In Galatians 1, Paul defends his apostleship against Judaistic critics. He identifies himself as "Paul, an apostle—sent not from men nor by man, but by Jesus Christ and God the Father, who raised him from the dead" (1:1). Here Paul is vitally concerned with the Creator-creature distinction. His apostolic call comes, emphatically, from God and not from men. Note, however, that in the context of this sharp distinction, Paul places Christ on the side of the Creator: Paul is an apostle sent, not by a man, but by *Jesus Christ*. Jesus is on the side of the Creator. Jesus is the sending God.[11]

Of course, Paul does not intend to deny the humanity of Jesus. He stresses it emphatically elsewhere (e.g., 1 Tim. 2:5). Indeed, he might have said even here that he had been sent, not by an ordinary man, but by that most extraordinary man, Jesus Christ. But in this passage he sets Jesus sharply over against any human source of his apostleship. So Jesus is God. Paul makes the same contrast in verses 10 and 12:

> Am I now trying to win the approval of men, or of God? Or am I trying to please men? If I were still trying to please men, I would

10. D. James Kennedy, *Truths That Transform* (Old Tappan, N.J.: Fleming H. Revell, 1974), 57.

11. On this point, see J. Gresham Machen, *Machen's Notes on Galatians* (Nutley, N.J.: Presbyterian and Reformed, 1972), 202.

not be a servant of Christ . . . I did not receive [the gospel] from any man, nor was I taught it; rather, I received it by revelation from Jesus Christ.

Christ is a man, to be sure. But Paul serves Christ, receives his gospel from Christ, rather than any man. In this passage, Paul is not expressly teaching the doctrine of the deity of Christ. That doctrine is not a point of disagreement between himself and his detractors. Paul assumes that doctrine as something conceded by all sides. It is taken for granted.

4. The salutations and benedictions we noted in the last chapter (as, "Grace and peace to you from God our Father and from the Lord Jesus Christ" [Rom. 1:7]) are easy to overlook, since they occur so frequently. But they assume nothing less than a divine role for Jesus. In Romans 1:7, grace and peace represent all the benefits of salvation, benefits that come only from God.[12] But, as we saw in the preceding chapter, these benefits have a twofold (and threefold in 2 Cor. 13:14) source. Only God is the Savior (Isa. 43:11), but Father and Son are both the saving God.

CHRIST, THE COVENANT LORD

The most fundamental biblical datum, in my view, is the way in which Jesus stands in the place of Yahweh as the Lord of the covenant. In the early chapters of this book, we saw that covenant lordship is crucial to the biblical doctrine of God. Yahweh, Lord, is the name by which God wishes his people to know him. The Lord is the one who controls all things, speaks with absolute authority, and enters creation to draw creatures into covenant relation with him. The most concise, and arguably most fundamental, summary of Old Testament teaching is "Yahweh is Lord." But the New Testament, over and over again, represents Jesus as Lord in the same way that the Old Testament represents Yahweh as Lord. The most fundamental summary of New Testament teaching is, "Jesus Christ is Lord" (Rom. 10:9; 1 Cor. 12:3; Phil. 2:11).

Jesus' blood is "my blood of the covenant, which is poured out for many for the forgiveness of sins" (Matt. 26:28), represented by the wine of communion. The cup, he says, is "the new covenant in my blood" (1 Cor. 11:25). This alludes to God's promise of a new covenant in Jeremiah 31:31. The

12. Grace (charis) resembles a Greek greeting; peace (eirēnē) is the equivalent of the Hebrew shalom. So these terms summarize the benefits of salvation and also welcome both Greeks and Jews who believe in Jesus.

letter to the Hebrews speaks of Jesus as the "mediator" of the new covenant (8:8, 13; 12:24). As the God-man, he is the mediator. But he is more than the mediator; he is the Lord of the covenant.

So we focus on the New Testament use of *kyrios*, "Lord." *Kyrios* is the most common title of Christ in the New Testament. In some passages, it may be a polite form of address or an acknowledgment of his status as a teacher (Matt. 8:21; 15:27; 17:15; 18:21).[13] But more passages by far employ the term as a divine title, identifying Jesus with Yahweh, the Lord of the Old Testament.

The Septuagint regularly uses *kyrios* to translate both the name *yahweh* and the term *'adon*, "Lord." Some have argued that this use of *kyrios* occurs only in copies of the Septuagint from Christian sources. It is true that the only copies from demonstrably non-Christian sources use the Hebrew tetragrammaton YHWH, rather than *kyrios*, for *yahweh*. This fact, of course, does nothing to refute the thesis that *kyrios* was the normal Greek rendering of *yahweh*, or to support the thesis that this use of *kyrios* represents a Christian distortion of the Old Testament text. In the non-Christian sources, *yahweh* is left untranslated, rather than given a translation other than *kyrios*. So the question remains open as to how the writers of those copies of the Septuagint referred to Yahweh in Greek. And other linguistic evidence certainly affirms the use of *kyrios* for *yahweh*. Carl F. H. Henry says:

> Yet it must be granted that not only Philo and Josephus, but also apocryphal Old Testament books like Wisdom of Solomon use KURIOS for YAHWEH, an identification that was also made in Greek-speaking synagogues. Christians acquainted with Greek-speaking Jewry therefore would readily use the term KURIOS to include the connotation of God Almighty.[14]

Some have claimed that the pagan use of *kyrios* in the mystery religions and/or the emperor cult also influenced the New Testament. That *kyrios* was accepted by many in the ancient world as, in some contexts, a divine title, certainly aided the Christian proclamation of Jesus as Lord, though of

13. However, I am not willing to concede all vocative uses of *kyrios* to this polite usage, as does David F. Wells in *The Person of Christ* (Westchester, Ill.: Crossway, 1984), 75. It seems to me, for example, that in Matt. 8:8, the extraordinary faith of the centurion, who believes that Jesus can heal by a mere word, may well have included an extraordinary understanding of Jesus' lordship. And our view of the disciples' use of *kyrie* depends somewhat on our assessment of the maturity of their understanding.

14. Carl F. H. Henry, *God, Revelation and Authority* (Waco: Word, 1976), 2:236. Cf. I. Howard Marshall, *The Origins of New Testament Christology* (Downers Grove, Ill.: InterVarsity Press, 1976), 99.

course Christian evangelists had to distinguish their concept of lordship from that of the general culture. In this respect, *kyrios* played a role similar to *theos*.

But the main influence on the New Testament use of *kyrios* was clearly the Old Testament. That was such an overwhelming influence that there is no need to look for any other, and it yields a concept of divine lordship incompatible with any pagan notion. As Christopher Kaiser says of the confession "Jesus is Lord" (1 Cor. 12:3),

> The form of this confession may have been designed as a direct counter-statement to the civic confession, "Caesar is Lord" (*kurios kaisar*), but the content is clearly Hebraic in its allusion to Yahweh, the Lord of the Old Testament.[15]

The Old Testament looks forward to a deliverer who is distinct from Yahweh, yet also bears the title of Lord. In Psalm 110:1, David declares,

> The LORD says to my Lord:
>   "Sit at my right hand
> until I make your enemies
>   a footstool for your feet."

In Jeremiah 23:5–6, Yahweh promises:

> "The days are coming," declares the LORD,
>   "when I will raise up to David a righteous Branch,
> a King who will reign wisely
>   and do what is just and right in the land.
> In his days Judah will be saved
>   and Israel will live in safety.
> This is the name by which he will be called:
>   The LORD Our Righteousness.

To the New Testament writers, "the Lord our Righteousness" is Jesus. They clearly equate the lordship of Jesus with that of Yahweh. They frequently cite Old Testament passages that speak of Yahweh and refer those to Jesus. In Matthew 3:3, for example, the writer cites Isaiah 40:3 in reference to John the Baptist:

> This is he who was spoken of through the prophet Isaiah: "A voice of one calling in the desert, 'Prepare the way for the Lord [*kyrios*], make straight paths for him.'"

---

15. Christopher B. Kaiser, *The Doctrine of God* (Westchester, Ill.: Crossway, 1982), 29. In a note, he refers to the discussion of "Jesus is Lord" in J. N. D. Kelly, *Early Christian Creeds* (London: Longman, 1972), 14–15.

"Lord" in Isaiah 40:3 is *yahweh*, but in Matthew 3:3 (cf. Mark 1:3; Luke 1:76; John 1:23) the word refers to the one for whom John paved the way (by his own admission, Matt. 3:11–17), namely, Jesus. In Matthew 21:16, Jesus cites Psalm 8:2 to defend the praises of the children directed to him. But in Psalm 8 (see v. 1), the praises are directed to Yahweh. Compare also:

- Isaiah 6:1–10 and Matthew 13:14–15; John 12:37–41
- Psalm 110:1 and Matthew 22:44–45
- Malachi 3:1 and Luke 1:76
- Psalm 23:1 and John 10:11
- Isaiah 8:14 and Romans 9:32–33
- Joel 2:32 and Romans 10:9–13
- Isaiah 45:23 and Romans 14:11; Philippians 2:16
- Jeremiah 9:24 and 1 Corinthians 1:31
- Isaiah 40:13 and 1 Corinthians 2:16
- Psalm 68:18 and Ephesians 4:8–10
- Isaiah 2:10, 19, 21; 66:15 and 2 Thessalonians 1:7–9
- Psalm 130:8 and Titus 2:13
- Psalm 102:25–26 and Hebrews 1:10
- Isaiah 51:6 and Hebrews 1:11
- Psalm 34:8 and 1 Peter 2:3
- Isaiah 8:13 and 1 Peter 3:15
- Zechariah 12:10 and Revelation 1:7
- Jeremiah 17:10 and Revelation 2:23
- Psalm 62:12 and Revelation 22:12
- Isaiah 40:10 and Revelation 22:12

So the New Testament writers regularly use *kyrios* as a divine title of Christ.[16] That usage antedates even the birth of Jesus. When Mary, the mother of Jesus, visits Elizabeth, the mother of John, in Luke 1:43–44, Elizabeth asks:

> But why am I so favored, that the mother of my Lord [*kyrios*] should come to me? As soon as the sound of your greeting reached my ears, the baby in my womb leaped for joy.

Surely the leaping of baby John was a supernaturally evoked response, appropriate to a divine visitation; Elizabeth's use of *Lord* should be taken in a similarly exalted sense. Then the angel announces to the shepherds in

16. They also use *kyrios*, as in the Old Testament, to refer to God the Father, which provides further confirmation that they regarded the term as a divine title. See Matt. 1:20; 9:38; 11:25; Acts 17:24; Rev. 4:11.

the field, "Today in the town of David a Savior has been born to you; he is Christ the Lord" (Luke 2:11). The angel announces that the long-expected Messiah, Christ, has been born, and that he is the Lord.

So the Baptist comes to "prepare the way for the Lord" (Mark 1:3, quoting Isa. 40:3). In Isaiah, the verse announces the coming of Yahweh; John applies it to Jesus.

In Mark 2:28, Jesus claims to be "Lord [*kyrios*] even of the Sabbath." This is an astonishing claim. In the Old Testament, the Sabbath is the day that Yahweh claims for himself, over against all human interests: "Six days you shall labor and do all your work, but the seventh day is a Sabbath to the LORD your God" (Ex. 20:9–10). It is holy to him (vv. 8, 11). So through Isaiah, God chastises the people for "doing as you please on my holy day" (Isa. 58:13). The Sabbath belongs to the Lord alone and not to any man. But in Mark 2:28, Jesus claims lordship over it. Clearly this use of *kyrios* is a claim to deity.

The Sabbath is God's dwelling in time; the temple is his dwelling in space. Just as he is greater than the Sabbath, so Jesus is greater than the temple, the dwelling place of God (Matt. 12:6). It is his house, as the Sabbath is his day (Matt. 21:12–13). He is the Lord himself, come to his temple to purge it (Mal. 3:1). In the theology of the New Testament, believers are a temple "in the Lord" (Eph. 2:21), and in the end the final temple is the Lord God Almighty himself and the Lamb (Rev. 21:22).

In Mark 5, the gospel writer identifies *kyrios* with deity more subtly. Jesus tells the healed demoniac, "Go home to your family and tell them how much the Lord has done for you, and how he has had mercy on you" (v. 19). This is language from the Psalms and elsewhere that is typically used of divine blessings. But the demoniac "went away and began to tell in the Decapolis how much Jesus had done for him" (v. 20). Notice how "Jesus" in verse 20 replaces the clearly divine "Lord" (*kyrios*) in verse 19.

Following the miraculous catch of fish, Peter "fell at Jesus' knees and said, 'Go away from me, Lord; I am a sinful man!' " (Luke 5:8). This is the response of a sinner before the holy God, like Isaiah's:

> "Woe to me!" I cried. "I am ruined! For I am a man of unclean lips, and I live among a people of unclean lips, and my eyes have seen the King, the LORD Almighty." (Isa. 6:5)

Later Jesus teaches that the title *kyrios* grants him such authority that disobedience to him is unthinkable: "Why do you call me, 'Lord, Lord,' and do not do what I say?" (Luke 6:46). As with Yahweh in the Old Testament, authority is a lordship attribute of Jesus. When he speaks, people are amazed at his authority, which is far beyond that of any earthly teacher (Matt. 7:28–29; cf. 13:54; 22:33; Mark 1:22; 6:2; Luke 4:32; John 7:46).[17]

The climax of the Gospels' use of *kyrios* comes in Matthew 22:43–46 (cf. Mark 12:35–37; Luke 20:41–44), where Jesus silences his Jewish critics by quoting Psalm 110:1,

> The LORD says to my Lord:
> "Sit at my right hand
> until I make your enemies
> a footstool for your feet."

Jesus then asks them how the Christ, the Messiah, the Son of David, could also be David's Lord. The *kyrios* here is the covenant Lord even over David; he takes the place of Yahweh, to the amazement and scandal of Jesus' enemies.

Similarly significant are those passages that present Jesus, as *kyrios*, as the judge of all on the Last Day (Matt. 7:21–23; 25:37, 44), and the remarkable confession of Thomas (see below) that Jesus is "My Lord and my God!" (John 20:28).[18] Peter preaches to Cornelius's household that Jesus is "Lord of all" (Acts 10:36; cf. Rom. 10:12).

For Paul, as we saw in the preceding chapter, *kyrios* is the distinctive name of the second person of the Trinity, as in 1 Corinthians 8:6; 12:4–6; 2 Corinthians. 13:14; Ephesians 4:4–6. So Paul's occasional contrast between *theos* and *kyrios* does not make *kyrios* less than God; it simply distinguishes the Father from the Son as two persons in the Godhead. So for Paul, the fundamental Christian confession is *kyrios Iesous*, "Jesus is Lord" (Rom. 10:9; 1 Cor. 12:3; Phil. 2:11). He is the Lord on whom we call for salvation (Rom. 10:12–13; cf. Joel 2:32; Acts 2:21), whose message brings faith (v. 17). He is, indeed, "the Lord of glory" (1 Cor. 2:8; cf. James 2:1). So Paul is *doulos*, a bondservant of Christ, his Lord (Rom. 1:1; Gal. 1:10). Christians are "called to belong to Jesus Christ" (Rom. 1:6).

Jesus' resurrection marks a change in the nature of his lordship. In the terms of traditional Reformed theology (see WSC, 27–28), the Resur-

---

17. In Matt. 7:28–29, the reference to Jesus' authority introduces two events in which Jesus heals by his mere word. The faith of the centurion in Matt. 8:5–13 is great because he believes that Jesus can "just say the word" (note the redundant expressions in the Greek) and bring healing, just as the centurion himself can command soldiers to do his bidding. Similar contexts can be found for the other references to the authority of Jesus' teaching.

18. See a later section in this chapter for the use of *theos* in this verse. The presence of both *theos* and *kyrios* here requires us to take *kyrios* as a divine title.

rection marks the end of Jesus' "state of humiliation" and the beginning of his "state of exaltation," in which he exercises his sovereign authority from the courts of heaven. In his exalted state, he has gained title to all the kingdoms of the earth, not only by virtue of his deity, but also by virtue of his victory in history over Satan, sin, and death. So although Jesus is always Lord, there is a sense in which he also receives lordship in a higher sense, as a gift from the Father upon completion of redemption. So the risen Christ tells his disciples, "All authority in heaven and on earth has been given to me" (Matt. 28:18). Paul in Romans 1:4 speaks of him being "declared with power to be the Son of God by his resurrection from the dead." And in 14:9 he says, "For this very reason, Christ died and returned to life so that he might be the Lord of both the dead and the living." And a yet higher form of lordship awaits Jesus. He now sits at the right hand of God, his priestly work completed, waiting for his enemies to be made his footstool (Heb. 10:12–13; cf. 1 Cor. 15:25–28).

When Scripture talks of Jesus' lordship during his earthly ministry, it is not always clear whether it speaks of his lordship as God incarnate, or whether it speaks by anticipation of his coming lordship in redemptive history. In my view, the biblical writers do not always clearly distinguish between these. For some purposes, the distinction is unimportant; divine lordship is divine lordship. In any case, it is important to remember that the historical process by which Jesus acquires power over the world does not detract at all from the eternal lordship that he holds by virtue of being God. The former represents his immanence; the latter represents his transcendence. As God incarnate, Jesus experiences change that includes increased power and authority. As eternal and transcendent God, Jesus is always the sovereign Lord.

Besides its use of *kyrios* and *doulos*, the New Testament speaks of Christ's covenant lordship by making even more direct allusion to Exodus 3:14, where God reveals his name to Moses as "I AM." This is the source for the name Yahweh, and therefore of the concept of covenant lordship.

In the gospel of John, Jesus often takes the name I AM on his lips. Sometimes he uses it with significant predicates: "I am the bread of life" (6:35), "I am the light of the world" (8:12; cf. 10:7–11; 11:25; 14:6; 15:1). Even more significantly, he uses I AM without predicate to indicate (as in Ex. 3:14) his presence to bless and judge. To the woman of Samaria, he says, "I who speak to you am he" (4:26). But there is no "he" in the Greek, which reads literally, "I am [*egō eimi*], who speaks to you." It is not wrong to supply the "he," though its absence is significant. And even the phrase "I am he" recalls Exodus 3:14 by way of the "I am he" (*'ani hu'*) passages in Deuteronomy 32:39–40, Isaiah 41:4, 43:10–13, etc. (see chap. 2).

In John 8:24, Jesus tells the Jews, "I told you that you would die in your sins; if you do not believe that I am *the one I claim to be,* you will indeed die in your sins." The italicized phrase has been added by the NIV translators. The original reads, "If you do not believe that I am, you will indeed die in your sins." Again, it is not necessarily wrong to complete the phrase so as to read "I am he" or "I am the Messiah." But the simple *egō eimi* indicates already that the claim Jesus makes is momentous indeed. He is no ordinary Messiah. Similar constructions are present in John 8:28 and 13:19. We are even more impressed at the momentousness of these statements in 18:5–6 (cf. v. 8):

> "Jesus of Nazareth," they replied.
> "I am he" [literally, "I am"], Jesus said. . . . When Jesus said, "I am he," they drew back and fell to the ground.

Here (and therefore implicitly in the earlier instances), "I am" is a powerful word that repels the Lord's enemies.

The climax of the "I am" theme in John is found at the end of the eighth chapter:

> "Your father Abraham rejoiced at the thought of seeing my day; he saw it and was glad."
> "You are not yet fifty years old," the Jews said to him, "and you have seen Abraham!"
> "I tell you the truth," Jesus answered, "before Abraham was born, I am!" (vv. 56–58)

Abraham came into being (*ginomai*); Jesus simply is. In context, the passage speaks of Jesus' transcendence over time: Abraham looked forward to him, and he existed before Abraham. But the emphasis here is not merely on preexistence, which could have been expressed as "before Abraham was born, I was." The "I am," especially in the light of other such references in John, clearly identifies Jesus with the I AM of Exodus 3:14, with Yahweh himself. The Jews understand: in verse 59 they pick up stones to kill him. From their point of view, this statement was blasphemy. From the Christian standpoint, it can be nothing less than a claim to deity in the fullest sense.[19]

Jesus is no less than the covenant Lord, Yahweh come in the flesh.

19. For more on this, refer to my earlier discussion in chapter 3, which incorporates some New Testament references to Jesus.

CHRIST, THE SON OF GOD

Like the other divine titles of Christ,[20] *Son of God* can also be used for finite beings: angels (Job 1:6; 2:1, and most likely Pss. 29:1; 89:6), kings (2 Sam. 7:14; Pss. 2:7; 89:26–27), priests (Mal. 1:6; cf. Heb. 5:5–6), Israel (Deut. 14:1; Isa. 63:9; Jer. 31:9, 20; Hos. 1:10; 11:1), Adam (Luke 3:38), and Christian believers (Matt. 5:9; John 1:12; Rom. 8:14–16, 19, 23; Gal. 3:26–4:7; Eph. 1:5; 1 John 3:1–2; Rev. 21:7). Acts 17:28 also implies that God is the Father over all people by virtue of creation. In these passages, *son* (*huios* or *teknon*) connotes various facts about the nature, function, origin, and inheritance of the persons in view.

But Scripture calls Jesus the Son of God in a unique sense. Of course, Jesus fulfills the sonships of Adam, Israel, and its officers in important ways, and his sonship reveals facts about his nature, function, origin, and inheritance. But his sonship is of a different order from that of anyone else. He is *the* Son of God (Luke 1:31–32; John 1:34; 1 John 5:20). He is God's *own* Son (Rom. 8:3, 32), and God is his *own* Father (John 5:18). He speaks of God as "my Father" (Matt. 25:34; 26:29; Luke 24:49; John 14:23), and in other passages he speaks of his Father in ways that indicate the uniqueness of this relationship:

> If anyone is ashamed of me and my words in this adulterous and sinful generation, the Son of Man will be ashamed of him when he comes in his Father's glory with the holy angels. (Mark 8:38; cf. 13:32; 14:36)

Jesus taught his disciples to pray, "Our Father" (Matt. 6:9), but he did not join in that prayer with them. He never uses the word *our* to identify his relationship to God with that of the disciples. Indeed, after his resurrection, he informs them that "I am returning to my Father and your Father, to my God and your God" (John 20:17). Here he distinguishes between his own relationship to God and theirs, between his sonship and theirs. Of course, there is a strong analogy between the two. Jesus' intimate "*Abba*, Father" (Mark 14:36) becomes part of the piety of the early church as well (Rom. 8:15; Gal. 4:6), for the Spirit of Jesus himself moves the disciples to speak to God this way.

Jesus' sonship, indeed, is prior to ours. We can become sons of God only if he gives us authority to do so (John 1:12; cf. 14:6; 17:26). And, as we

---

20. We have seen how *kyrios* can be a form of polite address. Even *theos* (=*'elohim*) refers to human judges in Ex. 21:6; 22:7–9; Ps. 82:1, 6; John 10:34.

saw above, we cry out *"Abba,* Father," because the Spirit of Jesus moves us to pray as he did (Rom. 8:15).

The terms "only begotten [*monogenēs*]²¹ Son" (John 1:14, 18; 3:16, 18; 1 John 4:9) and "beloved [*agapētos*] Son" (Matt. 3:17; 7:5; Mark 1:11; 9:7; 12:6) also indicate the uniqueness of Jesus' sonship, as do other passages that display the intimate relationship of the two divine persons. Matthew 11:25–27 is one of these:

> At that time Jesus said, "I praise you, Father, Lord of heaven and earth, because you have hidden these things from the wise and learned, and revealed them to little children. Yes, Father, for this was your good pleasure. All things have been committed to me by my Father. No one knows the Son except the Father, and no one knows the Father except the Son and those to whom the Son chooses to reveal him."

Even more remarkable is Jesus' so-called high priestly prayer in John 17, which begins:

> After Jesus said this, he looked toward heaven and prayed:
> "Father, the time has come. Glorify your Son, that your Son may glorify you. For you granted him authority over all people that he might give eternal life to all those you have given him. Now this is eternal life: that they may know you, the only true God, and Jesus Christ, whom you have sent. I have brought you glory on earth by completing the work you gave me to do. And now, Father, glorify me in your presence with the glory I had with you before the world began." (vv. 1–5)

Here we get a glimpse of the eternal fellowship between the Father and the Son: their mutual knowledge, mutual love, and mutual glorification. We see here the obedience of the Son in the unique work of redemption, assigned to him by the Father. And in John 5:18–23 we read:

> For this reason the Jews tried all the harder to kill him; not only was he breaking the Sabbath, but he was even calling God his own Father, making himself equal with God.

---

21. Most scholars today have concluded that *monogenēs* comes from *genos* ("kind") rather than *gennaō* ("beget, bear"), and thus should be translated "only" or "unique," rather than "only begotten," as in the older translations. I am not convinced of this conclusion. For example, it seems to me that the translation "God the One and Only" in John 1:18 (NIV) doesn't make much sense. See my discussion of this term in chapter 29, in the section on the eternal generation of the Son.

Jesus gave them this answer: "I tell you the truth, the Son can do nothing by himself; he can do only what he sees his Father doing, because whatever the Father does the Son also does. For the Father loves the Son and shows him all he does. Yes, to your amazement he will show him even greater things than these. For just as the Father raises the dead and gives them life, even so the Son gives life to whom he is pleased to give it. Moreover, the Father judges no one, but has entrusted all judgment to the Son, that all may honor the Son just as they honor the Father. He who does not honor the Son does not honor the Father, who sent him."

Here the fellowship between the Father and the Son implies that the Son shares his Father's knowledge, love, powers, and prerogatives.

Compare also John 1:18, in which the only begotten God is "at the Father's side,"[22] and John 10:15, which expresses the exhaustive mutual knowledge of the Father and the Son.

Clearly, Jesus' unique sonship implies his ontological deity. To Jews, a "son of" someone (or figuratively of something) shares the nature of his parent. And we have seen that Jesus and his Father share distinctively divine love, knowledge, powers ("the Father . . . shows him all he does," including the power to raise the dead), and prerogatives (to judge the world, to receive divine honor) (cf. Matt. 28:18). New Testament references to Jesus' sonship typically emphasize his equality with the Father, as in the above texts and John 3:35; 10:37–38. His sonship is above that of the angels (Heb. 1:5).[23]

The Jews of Jesus' day understood that his claim to divine sonship implied equality with God (John 5:18; 10:31). It was this claim that led to the Jews' charge of blasphemy against him (Matt. 26:63–66), which led to his crucifixion. Jesus never denied this claim or its meaning; indeed, he affirmed it before his accusers (Matt. 26:64).

Like his lordship, Jesus' sonship has various historical dimensions. As he became Lord in a higher sense by virtue of his resurrection, so he is "de-

22. Compare also Christ's being "with God" in John 1:1.
23. The writer to the Hebrews is interested in showing the superiority of Christ to all other beings, and therefore the superiority of the Christian gospel to Old Testament Judaism. Note 5:8, "Although he was a son, he learned obedience from what he suffered." The concessive "although" (kaiper) suggests that, unlike earthly sons, there is something anomalous about the Son of God having to learn obedience through suffering. Clearly, in the mind of the writer, Jesus' sonship implies divine attributes that are prima facie inconsistent with learning obedience through suffering. The anomaly, of course, arises from the nature of the Incarnation. Thanks to Dennis Johnson for this insight.

clared with power to be the Son of God by his resurrection from the dead" (Rom. 1:4). God's statement of Psalm 2:7, "You are my Son; today I have become your Father," is applied to the day of resurrection in Acts 13:33. But Scripture also calls him Son of God by virtue of his supernatural birth in Luke 1:35. Like his lordship, Jesus' sonship describes his eternal nature, revealed progressively through the events of redemptive history. Jesus was the Son before he was sent into the world (John 3:17; 17:5; Gal. 4:4; Rom. 8:3; Col. 1:3–17; Heb. 5:5–6).

Like his lordship, Jesus' sonship is prominent in the confessional passages of the New Testament. Peter's confession is that Jesus is "the Christ, the Son of the living God" (Matt. 16:16). (Cf. John 11:27; 20:31; Acts 8:37; Heb. 4:14; 1 John 2:23; 4:15; 5:5.) See also Jesus' own confession before the Sanhedrin in Matthew 26:63–64, and the Father's confession of his Son from heaven in Mark 1:11; 9:7.

There is considerable overlap between the concepts of Lord and Son. Both indicate Jesus' rule over his covenant people (as Son, he is the covenant king of Ps. 2:7). Both indicate Jesus' powers and prerogatives as God, especially over God's people: in other words, divine control, authority, and presence. We can describe the difference between them as perspectival: *Son* emphasizes Jesus' relationship to his Father, while *Lord* emphasizes his relationship to his people. But each encompasses the emphasis of the other. Lordship presupposes sonship, and sonship implies lordship.

JESUS, THE CHRIST

Christ or *Messiah* means "anointed one." In the Old Testament, prophets (1 Kings 19:10), priests (Ex. 29:7; 30:30–33), and kings (1 Sam. 10:1; 16:13; 24:10) were anointed with oil as they assumed office. The Jewish messianic expectation at the time of Jesus' earthly ministry focused on a royal figure, a descendant of David (Matt. 22:46), who would liberate Israel from Rome and reestablish Israel as a great power.

But the Old Testament itself anticipates the coming of one who is far more than a political deliverer. It rarely uses the term *Messiah* (Ps. 2:2 and Dan. 9:25–26), but it does speak often of a coming king who would be far greater than David. The sons of Korah sing of the coming king, addressing him thus:

> Your throne, O God, will last for ever and ever;
>   a scepter of justice will be the scepter of your kingdom. (Ps. 45:6)

Through Isaiah, God characterizes the coming Savior:

> For to us a child is born,
>> to us a son is given,
>> and the government will be on his shoulders.
> And he will be called
>> Wonderful Counselor, Mighty God,
>> Everlasting Father, Prince of Peace. (Isa. 9:6)

And through Micah, God says:

> But you, Bethlehem Ephrathah,
>> though you are small among the clans of Judah,
> out of you will come for me
>> one who will be ruler over Israel,
> whose origins are from of old, from ancient times. (Mic. 5:2)

Through Zechariah (2:8–11), God speaks of himself both as one sending and one sent to live with his people.

Earlier we noted Psalm 110:1, in which the Davidic king is also David's Lord.[24]

The coming of the Messiah, therefore, is also the coming of God. The Old Testament often looks forward to a day of the Lord, when Yahweh will come to set things right. In Isaiah, again, we read:

> Truth is nowhere to be found,
>> and whoever shuns evil becomes a prey.
> The LORD looked and was displeased
>> that there was no justice.
> He saw that there was no one,
>> he was appalled that there was no one to intervene;
> so his own arm worked salvation for him,
>> and his own righteousness sustained him.
> He put on righteousness as his breastplate,
>> and the helmet of salvation on his head;
> he put on the garments of vengeance
>> and wrapped himself in zeal as in a cloak. (59:15–17)

---

24. I will not enter into the exegetical controversies surrounding these passages, controversies that have been vigorous. For any Bible believer, however, it is plain that (1) in the New Testament, Christ is a divine figure, and (2) the New Testament writers found in the Old Testament a divine Messiah. Clearly, for example, the writer of Heb. 1:8 read Ps. 45:6 as teaching that the Messiah is God.

Paul's "full armor of God" (Eph. 6:10–18) was first the armor worn by God himself. No one but God can institute justice on earth and bring salvation from all the effects of sin.

We have seen how Old Testament passages about the lordship of God refer to Jesus in the New Testament. So quite literally the coming of Christ is the coming of Yahweh. As Zechariah foresaw, the humble king riding on a donkey brings with him all the power of the sovereign Lord to bring peace and judgment (9:9–17).

At a number of points in the Gospels, Jesus directly claims to be the Messiah (Matt. 16:16–17; Mark 14:62; John 4:25–26; 11:25–27).[25] His messiahship is, along with his divine sonship, the focus of Peter's confession in Matthew 16:16, and that of Martha in John 11:27. Note in 1 John 2:22 the condemnation of those who deny that Jesus is the Christ, and in 5:1 the identification of those who are born of God with those who believe that Jesus is the Christ. John has written his gospel "that you may believe that Jesus is the Christ, the Son of God, and that by believing you may have life in his name" (John 20:31).

In much of the New Testament, "Jesus Christ" becomes a proper name, in which his title is attached almost inseparably to his given name. Central to the biblical gospel is the affirmation that Jesus is the Messiah.

As Christ, Jesus fulfills all the Old Testament expectations of deliverance. He is the son of David and the Son of God—the final prophet, priest, and king. Once the Old Testament expectation and man's true need are rightly understood, it is plain that *Christ*, like *Lord* and *Son*, is a divine title.

JESUS CHRIST IS GOD

There are about ten passages in which the New Testament directly identifies Jesus as God (*theos, morphē theou, theotēs*). These have been contested exegetically, but I think these disputes have been due less to genuine difficulties in the texts than to theological resistance to Jesus' claims. So the followers of Arius in the fourth century and many others down to the Jehovah's Witnesses and some liberal theologians of our time have sought to minimize the teaching of these passages. Their effort, in my view, is not difficult to refute, and in any case it is futile, for countless other passages

---

25. Robert Reymond also notes other passages in which the claim is made "obliquely": Matt. 22:42–45; 23:10; 24:5; Mark 9:41; 12:35–37; 13:21–22; Luke 24:44–46; John 10:24–25. See his *Jesus, Divine Messiah*.

give Jesus a divine title, and others we shall consider later teach his deity in other ways. The deity of Christ is a pervasive teaching of Scripture.

The identification of the Messiah with *theos* begins in the Old Testament, where the Messiah is *'elohim* (Ps. 45:6; cf. Heb. 1:8), *'immanu 'el* (Isa. 7:14; cf. Matt. 1:23), and *'el gibbor* (Isa. 9:6). But let us now consider the New Testament data:

JOHN 1:1

This verse is the most famous and most hotly disputed of the passages we shall consider. For convenience of discussion, I shall number its three clauses:

(1) In the beginning was the Word,
(2) and the Word was with God,
(3) and the Word was God.

Clearly, "Word" here refers to the preincarnate Christ, since verse 14 says that "the Word became flesh and made his dwelling with us." Thus, the passage identifies Jesus as "the Word" by which God created the heavens and the earth (v. 3).[26]

At the very least, then, the passage teaches that Jesus existed before creation. The verb "was" in the first clause (Greek *ēn*) is in the imperfect tense, which indicates a duration before the "beginning." So the first clause might be translated, "When all things began, the Word was already in existence." The second clause, therefore, teaches that before creation (in timeless eternity, as I argued in chap. 24), Jesus the Word was "with God" (*pros ton theon*), in eternal fellowship with him.

Even without looking at the third clause, we can discern clear evidence of Jesus' deity here. The biblical cosmology recognizes the Creator and the creature, with nothing in between. The Word in this passage is not a creature, but the Creator. It is the divine Word that existed before creation, by whom all things were made (v. 3). Indeed, the divine Word is, as we saw in chapter 22, an attribute of God, a perspective on the whole divine nature, and therefore fully divine.

We must, however, look more closely at the third clause. In the Greek, the subject and predicate are in reverse order: literally, "God was the Word." But the English translations are correct. Greek often places the subject of a sentence after the predicate, and in this case "Word" is clearly the

---

26. "In the beginning" draws our attention back to Gen. 1:1, and verse 3 indicates that the Word was the agent of creation. God made the world by speaking. Cf. Ps. 33:6, 9.

subject, as indicated by parallels with the other clauses and also by the definite article, which precedes "Word," but not "God." Thus, clause three reverses the order of clause two, which places the subject before the predicate.

Why the reversal? Some have argued that the reverse order emphasizes the predicate, *God*, in the third clause: the Word was *God!* This point is correct, I think, but it is part of a larger pattern. Clauses two and three form a chiasm. Chiasm is a device found often in Hebrew writing and in other writing influenced by Hebrew, in which ideas, concepts, words, or themes are structured in the order A B B A, or A B C C B A, etc. Here the two clauses form an A B B A chiasm, featuring the nouns (in order) *Word, God, God, Word*. The chiastic structure emphasizes the middle term, in this case *God*. A major intent of the verse, therefore, is to set forth the relationship of the Word to God.

The absence of the definite article from "God" in the third clause, however, has led some to argue that it does not entail deity in the fullest sense, but only divine or godlike qualities, so that *theos* should be translated "a god" or "divine" (in a loose sense). But that conclusion does not follow, for the following reasons:

1. The absence of the article may be "a purely grammatical phenomenon."[27] When, as here, a Greek sentence uses "to be" to connect a subject and a predicate noun, the predicate noun normally lacks the article, even when it is definite. So the absence of an article implies nothing about the precise sense of *theos*.

2. This argument is even stronger in passages like ours, where the predicate precedes the subject. The "Colwell Rule" states that in such a sentence, the predicate noun usually lacks an article, even though it is definite, but that the subject of the sentence, if definite, will employ the definite article.[28] So again the phenomenon has a grammatical explanation and does not presuppose any change of meaning between "God" in clause two and "God" in clause three.

3. As we have seen, in such constructions the predicate noun usually or normally lacks the article. Following that normal practice here may have also served the author's purpose to draw additional attention to the term *God*, the center of the chiasm. Dropping the article focuses on the noun

27. C. H. Dodd, "NT Translation Problems II," *The Bible Translator* 28 (January 1977): 103.

28. For a recent discussion of this grammatical point, see Lane C. McGaughy, *Toward a Descriptive Analysis of EINAI as a Linking Verb in the New Testament*, SBLDS 6 (Missoula, Mont.: SBL, 1972), esp. pp. 49–53, 73–77.

itself, and it brings the two occurrences of *theos* closer together in the chiasm. This consideration weakens further the need for further explanation of the construction.

4. In similar verses, where *theos* is a predicate noun lacking the definite article, a reference to God in the fullest sense is indisputable (see Mark 12:27; Luke 20:38; John 8:54; Rom. 8:33; Phil. 2:13; Heb. 11:16).

5. There are many other verses, some in the same first chapter of John, in which *theos* lacks a definite article, but in which the reference to God in the fullest sense is indisputable. Nobody would claim a reduced meaning of *theos*, for example, in 1:6, 13, or 18.

6. Even if we grant that *theos* without the definite article puts some emphasis on the qualities of God rather than his person, this supposition does not entail that *theos* in the third clause has a reduced sense. To prove otherwise, one must show that the qualities in view are something other than the essential attributes of God. If the qualities are essential qualities, then the third clause identifies the Word with God in the highest sense.

7. A very strong argument is needed to prove that the meaning of *theos* changes between clause two and clause three. That burden of proof has certainly not been met.

JOHN 1:18

Our next passage reads, "No one has ever seen God, but God the One and Only [or, better, "the only begotten God"], who is at the Father's side, has made him known."

Here the question is what textual tradition we should follow. Some ancient Greek manuscripts read *huios* instead of *theos:* "only begotten Son," rather than "only begotten God." But the manuscripts usually considered to be of higher quality (Aleph and B) and many citations from church fathers read *theos*. Internal evidence confirms this conclusion. In textual criticism, one principle often followed is that the most difficult reading should be preferred, since a scribe is more likely to soften the reading than to make it more difficult.[29] Here the more difficult reading is certainly *monogenēs theos;* we can understand how a scribe would be tempted to replace it with the more usual and more understandable *monogenēs huios*. So both the manuscript tradition and the principle of difficulty favor the reading *monogenēs theos*, "only begotten God."

If that reading is correct, this verse teaches that no one has seen God

---

29. My experience in proofreading my own work does not consistently bear out this principle, for whatever that observation may be worth.

(presumably, the Father), but that the only begotten God (in context, the Word or the Son) has made him known. Here again, Jesus is called God.

JOHN 20:28

In this verse, Thomas, having just seen the risen Christ, cries out, "My Lord and my God!" Some have interpreted this as an oathlike expression of surprise, as profane people today sometimes say "my God!" But this interpretation is quite impossible. It is not a vocative expression. And clearly, in context, the author's intent is to present a cogent confession of faith by one of the first witnesses of the Resurrection. Three verses later, John tells us that "these [signs] are written that you may believe that Jesus is the Christ, the Son of God, and that by believing you may have life in his name" (v. 31). So the point of verse 28 is that Thomas now discerns who Jesus really is; he believes that Jesus is the Christ, the Son of God.

ACTS 20:28

Here Paul exhorts the elders of the church of Ephesus:

> Keep watch over yourselves and all the flock of which the Holy Spirit has made you overseers. Be shepherds of the church of God, which he bought with his own blood.

The antecedent of "he" is "God"; but "he" clearly refers to Jesus, who bought the church with his own blood.

ROMANS 9:5

In the context of this verse, Paul mourns the unbelief of Israel. Reflecting on God's former blessings to them, he says, "Theirs are the patriarchs, and from them is traced the human ancestry of Christ, who is God over all, forever praised! Amen." Some have wanted to read "Christ, the one who is over all. May God be forever praised! Amen." On the second translation, Christ is not called God, although "over all" does grant his messianic dominion. On that reading, Paul pauses in his discussion to utter a doxology.

However, in a doxology, one would expect "praised" (*eulogētos*) to precede "God" (*theos*), as in 2 Corinthians 1:3 and Ephesians 1:3, rather than to follow it, as here. Furthermore, the first (NIV) translation fits better in the context. There, Paul speaks of the human ancestry of Christ, followed naturally by a reflection on his divine nature. So there seems no reason except theological prejudice to adopt the doxological interpretation.

To be sure, it is unusual for Paul to refer to Jesus as *theos*. As I mentioned earlier, Paul usually restricts *theos* to the Father and uses *kyrios, huios,* or *Christos* for the Son. But the contrast between Jesus' human origin and his divine nature in this passage makes the exception logical at this point. Certainly Paul believed in the deity of Christ; that is evident in his use of *kyrios*. So it is not contrary to his theology, though it is somewhat contrary to his usual vocabulary, to speak of Jesus as *theos*.[30]

1 Timothy 3:15–16

Here, Paul says:

> . . . if I am delayed, you will know how people ought to conduct themselves in God's household, which is the church of the living God, the pillar and foundation of the truth. Beyond all question, the mystery of godliness is great:

> He appeared in a body,
>   was vindicated by the Spirit,
> was seen by angels,
>   was preached among the nations,
> was believed on in the world,
>   was taken up in glory.

The nearest antecedent of "He" in verse 16 is "God" in verse 15. But verse 16 clearly describes the incarnate life of Christ.

2 Thessalonians 1:12; Titus 2:13; 2 Peter 1:1

In Titus 2:13, Paul exhorts his readers to live godly lives, "while we wait for the blessed hope—the glorious appearing of our great God and Savior, Jesus Christ." On this translation, Jesus Christ is called God. The alternative translation is "the great God and our Savior Jesus Christ," which identifies Jesus as Savior, but not as God.

As with John 1:1, a rule of Greek grammar, in this case the Granville Sharp Rule, is relevant:

> When the copulative *kai* connects two nouns of the same case, if the article *ho* or any of its cases precedes the first of the said nouns

---

30. See Bruce Metzger, "The Punctuation of Rom. 9:5," in *Christ and Spirit in the New Testament,* ed. B. Lindars and S. Smalley (Cambridge: Cambridge University Press, 1973), 95–112. See also the commentaries on Romans by Cranfield, Fitzmyer, and others.

or participles, and is not repeated before the second noun or participle, the latter always relates to the same person that is expressed or described by the first noun or participle, i.e. it denotes a farther description of the first-named person.[31]

This rule fits Titus 2:13, in which the definite article precedes *theos*, is not repeated before *sōtēr*, and the two nouns are joined by *kai*. So we should conclude that *theos* and *sōtēr*, "God" and "Savior," denote the same person, Jesus Christ.

In confirmation of this view, the passage speaks of the "appearing" (*epiphaneia*). In the New Testament, this term is used only of Christ, not of God the Father. The other uses, all pertaining to Christ, are found in 2 Thessalonians 2:8; 1 Timothy 6:14; and 2 Timothy 1:10; 4:1, 8. So the appearing here, too, is that of Christ, who is God, not of God and Christ. Here too, then, *theos* refers to Christ.

The Granville Sharp rule also makes *theos* refer to Christ in 2 Peter 1:1, which refers to "the righteousness of our God and Savior Jesus Christ." Note the parallel with "Lord and Savior Jesus Christ" in verse 11.

For the same reason, 2 Thessalonians 1:12, which refers to "the grace of our God and the Lord Jesus Christ" (in the NIV), should perhaps better be translated "the grace of our God and Lord Jesus Christ."

HEBREWS 1:8

This verse quotes Psalm 45:6 and applies it to Christ to show that he is greater than the angels:

> But about the Son he says,
> "Your throne, O God [*theos*], will last for ever and ever,
>   and righteousness will be the scepter of your kingdom."

Clearly, the writer to the Hebrews believes that *theos* here refers to Jesus.

1 JOHN 5:20

John tells his readers:

> We know also that the Son of God has come and has given us understanding, so that we may know him who is true. And we are in

31. H. E. Dana and Julius R. Mantey, *A Manual Grammar of the Greek New Testament* (New York: Macmillan Co., 1955), 147. Others favoring this interpretation of these verses: Nigel Turner, *Grammatical Insights into the New Testament* (Edinburgh: T. and T. Clark, 1977), 15–16; Murray J. Harris, *Jesus as God* (Grand Rapids: Baker, 1992), 174–85; the commentaries by I. Howard Marshall, Michael Green, Douglas Moo, and Gordon H. Clark.

him who is true—even in his Son Jesus Christ. He is the true God and eternal life.

Although commentators differ, I believe that the most likely antecedent of "he" in the third sentence of this verse is "his Son Jesus Christ," not "him who is true." Normally we should choose the closest possible antecedent, and here that is "his Son Jesus Christ." Furthermore, the Greek word translated "he" is *houtos*, a demonstrative pronoun literally meaning "this one." A demonstrative pronoun most naturally refers to the one to whom the most attention has been drawn in the context, and here that would be Jesus, who is named three times. Right after referring to Jesus Christ, John adds, in effect, "*This* is the one who is the true God and eternal life." But even if "he" refers specifically to the Father, rather than the Son, the relationship between the two is very close. To be in Jesus is to be in God. And, as in John 14:6 and 17:3, Jesus is the way to eternal life with the Father.

PHILIPPIANS 2:6

We should also look briefly at two texts that do not use *theos* to refer directly to Christ, but use forms of the term in such a way as to clearly affirm Jesus' deity. In Philippians 2:1–11, Paul exhorts the church to have the mind of Christ: an attitude of humility, putting others ahead of oneself. He uses the example of Christ, who humbled himself by leaving the divine glory and suffering death for human beings. In verse 6, Paul indicates the essential nature of Jesus and therefore his right to full divine honor: "Who, being in very nature God, did not consider equality with God something to be grasped." The NIV correctly translates *en morphē theou hyparchōn* as "being in very nature God." There is some dispute over the meaning of the phrase *morphē theou*, often translated "form of God." Most interpreters have agreed with M. R. Vincent that *morphē* here is "that expression of being which is identified with the essential nature and character of God, and which reveals it."[32] More recent writers have sought to read *morphē theou* either as "image of God" or "glory of God," but the linguistic case for these options is weak.[33] The parallel between *morphē theou* and *morphē doulou* in verse 7 forces us to take *morphē* in the sense of "essential qualities." So Paul

32. M. R. Vincent, *A Critical and Exegetical Commentary on the Epistles to the Philippians and to Philemon*, International Critical Commentary (New York: Scribner, 1897), 57–58.

33. See David F. Wells, *The Person of Christ*, 63–64, for a brief rebuttal of these positions.

is teaching that Jesus was fully God, but humbled himself to the point of death to save us from sin.[34]

COLOSSIANS 2:9

In this text, Paul affirms that "in Christ all the fullness of the Deity (*to plērōma tēs theotētos*) lives in bodily form." Paul may use the word *plērōma* ("fullness") in response to the gnostics, for whom the *plērōma* was a system of many deities that were somehow emanations of one supreme being. Paul affirms that Jesus is not one of these emanations, but contains in himself the fullness of deity. This text, then, teaches the deity of Christ in the strongest possible sense. "Fullness" rules out any weakening of the meaning of "Deity." This language is even stronger than the texts that apply the term *theos* to Jesus, if that were possible.

EPILOGUE

Someone might ask why references to Christ as God in the New Testament are so few and so often controversial. As for the controversy, it is not surprising that people want to find ways to reject the stupendous claim that Jesus is God. His deity has long been a stumbling block for unbelievers.

Nevertheless, we might well wish that these references were more frequent in the New Testament. Ignatius, bishop of Antioch (d. 110–115), refers to Jesus as God fourteen times in his seven letters, so that usage seems well established in the postapostolic generation. But it may surprise us that the New Testament writers themselves seem to take so little notice of the astounding fact that a man was God.

We should remember, however, that *theos*, "God," is not the only term that indicates the deity of Christ. As I have mentioned, Paul uses *theos* rarely of Christ, because he prefers the divine title *kyrios*. If anything, *kyrios* is actually the stronger term. *Theos* is more or less the New Testament equiv-

---

34. The controversy over the "emptying" (*kenōsis*) of verse 7 belongs to a study of the Incarnation rather than to the question of the deity of Christ as such. However, if Jesus, in his incarnation, divested himself of any essential divine attributes, as the "kenosis theory" requires, then during his incarnate state (which continues eternally) he was and is not God at all. As we have seen, God cannot be God without his essential attributes. But the idea that Jesus was not God when he was in the flesh contradicts a vast amount of biblical data, as we have seen. The nature of the *kenōsis* can be understood perfectly well as the self-humbling of God's servant, expressed, for example, in the Servant Songs of Isaiah. See R. B. Strimple, "Some Exegetical Considerations on Phil. 2:5–11 in Recent Studies," *WTJ* 41 (1979): 247–68.

alent of *'elohim*, and *kyrios* the New Testament equivalent of *yahweh*. And *yahweh* not only names God, but focuses on his relationship to his people as Lord of the covenant. Thus, we should not be surprised that Jesus is called *kyrios* in the New Testament far more often than he is called *theos*.

We should also remember that the New Testament is more interested in redemption than in ontology *per se*. *Yahweh* and *kyrios* are divine names, but they focus particularly on God's redemptive covenant, rather than the divine nature as such. It is certainly remarkable that Jewish monotheists like the apostles came to believe that a man was God. But for them it was even more astonishing that in this God-man, all the redemptive promises of God had been fulfilled. This wonderful fulfillment of redemption is better expressed by the *yahweh-kyrios* vocabulary than by *'elohim-theos*.

The New Testament also witnesses to the deity of Christ by calling him Son and Christ, as well as in other ways to be discussed below, reinforcing the conclusion that the deity of Christ is a pervasive doctrine of Scripture.

OTHER TITLES OF CHRIST

1. *Son of Man* is the title that Jesus uses most often of himself. Others use it of him only in Acts 7:56 and Revelation 1:13; 14:14. In general, a "son of man" is a man, just as the "son of God" (in the unique sense noted earlier) is God. So *son of man* is the regular phrase by which God addresses the prophet Ezekiel.[35] But there is much more to be said about the New Testament usage, which regularly alludes to Daniel 7. In that passage, Daniel sees God, "the Ancient of Days," on his throne of judgment, surrounded by thousands of attendants. Then:

> In my vision at night I looked, and there before me was one like a son of man, coming with the clouds of heaven. He approached the Ancient of Days and was led into his presence. He was given authority, glory and sovereign power; all peoples, nations and men of every language worshiped him. His dominion is an everlasting dominion that will not pass away, and his kingdom is one that will never be destroyed. (vv. 13–14)

Who is this being who is "like a son of man"? The interpretation of the vision equates this son of man with "the saints":

---

35. So also in Ps. 8:4–8. But note here, as in the Christological usage, the emphasis on the dominion and authority of the son of man over all other creatures. Similarly, Ps. 80:17.

> The four great beasts are four kingdoms that will rise from the earth.
> But the saints of the Most High will receive the kingdom and will
> possess it forever—yes, for ever and ever. (vv. 17–18)

They possess the kingdom because the Ancient of Days pronounces judgment in their favor (v. 22).

Jesus' self-designation as the Son of Man, however, certainly distinguishes him from other men, even from "the saints." For in the New Testament passages, the Son of Man is not the church as a whole, but an individual who rules both the church and the world. *Son of Man* is equivalent
to other Christological titles: the Son of Man is Christ, the Son of God
(Matt. 16:13–16), and Lord (even of the Sabbath) (Matt. 12:8; Mark
2:28). When the Son of Man is lifted up in crucifixion, says Jesus, "then
you will know that I am" (John 8:28, a verse that, as we have seen, may
contain an allusion to the "I AM" of Exodus 3:14).

In a broader biblico-theological context, we may understand that the Son
of Man is related to the saints as their representative. He is the Second
Adam (1 Cor. 15:22, 45–49). Because of his perfection, God pronounces,
as in Daniel 7:22, a judgment in favor of the saints, rather than against them.
As Son of Man, he has the power to forgive sins (Mark 2:5–10; Luke
5:20–24; 7:47–49; Acts 5:31). Appropriately, it is the Son of Man who
"gathers his elect" when he returns in glory (Mark 13:27), for he is the one
who planted them as "good seed" on the earth (Matt. 13:37).

He is perfect, not only in his character, but also in that he lays down his
life as a perfect sacrifice for sin. So Jesus often calls himself the Son of Man
when discussing his sufferings (Matt. 8:20), death (Mark 8:31; 9:12, 31;
10:33, 45; 14:21, 41; John 3:14–15; 8:28), burial (Matt. 12:40), resurrection (Mark 8:31; 9:9, 31; 10:34), and glorious return (Matt. 16:27; 24:44;
25:31; 26:64; Mark 8:38; 13:26; 14:62; Luke 19:10; John 6:62). The references to the return of the Son of Man on the clouds bring us back full circle to the picture in Daniel 7:13–14. So, like Daniel's son of man, Jesus receives power and authority, participating in the final judgment (Mark
8:38). He has authority to judge because he is the Son of Man (John 5:27).

Son of Man, therefore, refers in the first instance to Jesus' humanity as the
representative of God's elect, who saves them from sin. But, as we have seen,
only God can save (Jonah 2:10). The Son of Man is a transcendent, heavenly figure, as in Daniel 7, who, like Yahweh, "comes with the clouds" (recall
our earlier discussion of the divine Glory-cloud in chap. 25) and rules with
power and authority. He is Lord of all things human, including the Sabbath
day (Matt. 12:8; Mark 2:28). So Jesus, as the Son of Man, is human, but not
merely human. As the Son of Man, he shares divine powers and prerogatives.

2. *Word* is a title of Christ in John 1:1–14 (which we considered earlier) and Revelation 19:13. It is implicit in Colossians 1:15–18, which describes Jesus as the agent of creation, the Old Testament role of God's word (Gen. 1; Ps. 33:6, 9), and in Hebrews 1:2–4, in which Jesus is the final revelation of God. As we saw in chapter 22, Word is an attribute of God, and from our earlier discussion of John 1 it is evident that Word is there a divine title.[36]

3. *Image of God* applies, of course, to all human beings (Gen. 1:27), but, like other titles that we have considered, it applies to Jesus in a higher sense. He is the light of God that no sinner has in himself; all of us need to see his glory if we are to be saved (2 Cor. 4:4). He is *the* image of God, and thus he has special prerogatives over the world—prerogatives of God, not of a mere man. He is the Creator, the one in whom all things hold together, supreme over all (Col. 1:15–20). He is "the radiance of God's glory and the exact representation of his being, sustaining all things by his powerful word" (Heb. 1:3). The writer to the Hebrews describes Jesus in these ways to show that he is higher than the angels.

4. *Savior* (similarly *Redeemer, Deliverer*) is a term we often associate with Jesus' mission on earth. But it is also a divine title in the Old Testament. It is associated also with human deliverers (Judg. 3:9, 15; 6:36; Isa. 19:20), but in one sense salvation is exclusively divine. Only God can save us from our worst predicament: "I, even I, am the LORD, and apart from me there is no savior" (Isa. 43:11; cf. 45:15, 21; 47:4; 49:26; 60:16; 63:1–8; Hos. 13:4; Luke 1:47; 1 Tim. 2:3; 4:10; Titus 1:3; 3:4; Rev. 19:1).

The New Testament makes it clear that Jesus is the Savior in this highest sense. When the angel announces the birth of Jesus to the shepherds, he speaks of a "Savior" who is "Christ the Lord" (Luke 2:11). The Samaritans confess that Jesus "really is the Savior of the world" (John 4:42). Peter announces that "God exalted [Jesus] to his own right hand as Prince and Savior that he might give repentance and forgiveness of sins to Israel" (Acts 5:31). In such contexts, Jesus is *the* Savior, the one who brings the final deliverance from sin. (Cf., e.g., Acts 13:23; Eph. 5:23; Phil. 3:29; 2 Tim. 1:10; Titus 1:4.)[37]

5. *Holy One* is a divine title in the Old Testament (as 2 Kings 19:22; Pss. 71:22; 73:41; 89:18–19, often in Isaiah and later prophets). In the New Tes-

---

36. The use of *Word* as a divine title can also be found in extrabiblical Jewish literature. See the Onkelos Targum on Gen. 3:8, 10, 24, which describes the voice of the Word (*memra*) walking in the garden; also in Deuteronomy 33:27.

37. Note the alternation between "God our Savior" in Titus 1:3 and "Christ Jesus our Savior" in 1:4. Both phrases are common in the later books of the New Testament, and they are virtually interchangeable.

tament, the demons themselves bear witness that Jesus is "the Holy One of God" (Mark 1:24; Luke 4:34). He is the Holy One of Psalm 16:10, who cannot see corruption (Acts 2:27; 13:35). Although all of God's people are holy, the term applied to Jesus is certainly singular and distinct. He is *the* Holy One. Similar points can be made about the title *Righteous One* (Acts 3:14; 7:52; 22:14).

6. *The Alpha and the Omega, the First and the Last,* and *the Beginning and the End* are also divine titles. In Isaiah 44:6, God says, "I am the first and I am the last; apart from me there is no God." There can be only one "first and last," and that one can only be God. Compare Revelation 1:8. But the book of Revelation often applies these phrases to Jesus, even putting them on the lips of the risen Christ himself (see Rev. 1:17–18; 2:8; 22:13).

7. Recall also our discussions of images of God in chapter 18, where I indicated that Scripture applies to Jesus many of the images that are applied to God, like *shepherd, rock, king, judge, bridegroom, lion,* and *light.* As these images apply to God in distinctive ways, so they apply to Jesus in closely related ways.

DIVINE ATTRIBUTES OF JESUS

I must be briefer in listing other biblical grounds for our confession of Jesus' deity. The evidence presented is already overwhelming; I can only indicate briefly some biblical resources for a more comprehensive treatment of the subject.

As the biblical images of God apply in a distinctive way to Jesus, so do the divine attributes, as I have often indicated in chapters 19–26. Scripture defines God's love by the cross of Christ, where he laid down his life for his friends (John 15:13–14; Eph. 5:2, 25; 1 John 3:16; Rev. 1:5). Jesus' compassion uniquely reflects that of Yahweh (Matt. 9:6; 14:14). The Messiah is God's Prince of peace (Isa. 9:6). He is the righteous one (Acts 3:14; 7:52; 22:14; James 5:6), and the holy one (Luke 1:35; 4:34; John 10:36; Acts 3:14; 4:27, 30; Heb. 7:26). Even God's wrath is "the wrath of the Lamb" (Rev. 6:16).

Scripture epitomizes Jesus' ethical qualities by telling us that he is sinless (John 8:46; 2 Cor. 5:21; Heb. 4:15; 7:26; 1 Peter 2:22; 1 John 3:5). Satan had no hold on him (John 14:30). Scripture presents Jesus' sinlessness more as a quality of his perfect human nature than a mark of his deity. His sinless life enabled him to be the perfect lamb of God, the spotless sacrifice for sin. But it is also relevant to a discussion of his deity, for even the slightest sin would be impossible in a divine being.

It is quite amazing that a man's closest acquaintances (enemies as well as friends—Luke 4:34; 23:4) would come to the conclusion that he was without sin. None of us will ever deserve that sort of testimony. Even the greatest figures of Scripture, like Abraham, Moses, and David, were guilty of sin. Scripture is realistic about the worst faults in the best of us. But it records no negative testimony, and supreme positive testimony, about the character of Jesus.

Jesus is God's truth (John 14:6), the one who is true, full of truth (John 1:14), even "the true God" (1 John 5:20). Like God, Jesus knows all things (Matt. 11:25–27; John 2:24–25; 16:30; 21:17; Col. 2:3). There is no record of his ever having made an error or mistake. He has a supernatural knowledge of events and facts (John 4:16–19, 29). He knows the thoughts, even the hearts, of human beings (Matt. 9:4; 12:25; Mark 2:8; Luke 6:8; 9:47; John 1:47; 2:24–25; 21:17; Rev. 2:23). He knows the future. He knows that he must die at the hands of sinners (Matt. 16:21; Mark 8:31; Luke 9:22). He knows in advance who will betray him (Matt. 26:24), Peter's denial (John 13:38), the kind of death Peter will die (John 21:18–19), and the future of the kingdom (Matt. 8:11). He knows the Father as the Father knows him, and he is sovereign in revealing the Father to human beings (Matt. 11:25–27; Luke 10:22; John 10:15). Jesus is the wisdom of God (1 Cor. 1:24, 30; Col. 2:3).

It is true that, as a man, Jesus grows in wisdom and knowledge (Luke 2:52). Even as an adult, he receives information from others and responds as others do—for example, concerning Lazarus (John 11:1–3).[38] But, in the Lazarus narrative, Jesus also shows extraordinary, divine knowledge (vv. 4, 11, 14). But note Mark 13:32. It is hard to understand how in Jesus there can coexist a limited human knowledge and an unlimited divine knowledge, but biblical Christology (summarized by the Council of Chalcedon in the formula "one person, two natures") presses us to affirm this fact. So, in some mysterious way, Jesus during his earthly life expresses ignorance concerning the time of his return (Mark 13:32). He has yet more instruction to receive from his Father. In this respect, his knowledge is like his power. He can do all things, but on earth he does only what his Father shows him and tells him to do. Similarly, he knows all things, but on earth he is subject to his Father, and as man he comes to know only what the Father has taught him.

Jesus is the almighty *power* of God, made manifest in weakness (1 Cor.

---

38. In chapter 22, we noted that God in the Old Testament also responds to information in this sort of way. He asks questions to which he already knows the answers, but he responds to the answers he elicits from human beings. Such give-and-take is part of his immanence in time and space, as we saw in chapters 24 and 25.

1:18, 23–25; Phil. 3:21). The winds and sea obey him, prompting the disciples to ask what kind of man he is (Matt. 8:26–27), for in the Old Testament only Yahweh rules the storms (Pss. 65:7; 89:9; 107:29). The miracle narratives in the New Testament present Jesus as doing wonders by his own power, rather than merely allowing God to work through him. Compare Matthew 14:19 and John 2:1–11. To Jesus, appropriately, God gives all *authority* (Matt. 28:18; Eph. 1:22; Col. 2:10; Rev. 1:18). And, to complete the triad of lordship attributes, Jesus is *omnipresent,* with his creatures everywhere (Matt. 18:20; 28:18–20; Eph. 1:21–23).

Jesus also shares the Father's eternity. He existed with the Father before his incarnation (John 1:1, "with God"). The Father sent him; he "came from heaven" (John 3:13; 5:36–38; 6:29–42; 7:28–29; cf. Phil. 2:5–7; 2 Cor. 8:9). The Father, of course, is eternal, but he cannot be an eternal Father without an eternal Son. If *Father* is an ontological title of God, then *Son* must be as well. And John 8:58, in which Jesus directly evokes the "I AM" of Exodus 3:14, attributes to Jesus the same transcendence over time that Scripture ascribes to Yahweh. The book of Revelation speaks of Jesus as "the Alpha and the Omega," "the Beginning and the End" (22:13; cf. 1:17; 2:8). Like Yahweh, Jesus is the living one (Rev. 1:18).

So Jesus is immutable: "Jesus Christ is the same yesterday and today and forever" (Heb. 13:8). The writer to the Hebrews attributes to Jesus the unchangeability that Psalm 102 ascribes to Yahweh (Heb. 1:8, 10, 12).

As the Father is glorious, so also is the Son. The New Testament refers often to the glory of Christ, and this glory can be no less than what Scripture attributes to God the Father. We have seen the importance of the Glory-cloud, by which Yahweh manifests himself to human beings. He is the glory in the midst of Israel (Zech. 2:5). But that glory is also the glory of the Messiah. In Isaiah 4:2, the branch of Yahweh, the Messiah, is glorious. And John tells us that when Isaiah saw a vision of Yahweh's glory in Isaiah 6, he was in fact seeing the glory of Jesus (John 12:41). So the New Testament writers marvel that they, too, have seen Jesus' glory (John 1:14; cf. Luke 13:17; John 2:11; 14:9; 17:24; Acts 26:13; 1 Tim. 1:11; Heb. 1:3). He is nothing less than "the Lord of glory" (1 Cor. 2:8), "our glorious Lord Jesus Christ" (James 2:1). So he is the divine source of our glorification (Rom. 8:21; Eph. 5:27).

DIVINE ACTS OF JESUS

Jesus does everything the Father does (John 5:19), and therefore he does things that only God can do. He works together with his Father in every act of God. So he is the Creator (John 1:1–3; Heb. 1:2–3; Col. 1:15–16). Creation is an act of God alone (Isa. 40:26; 44:24; 45:7, 12). In the biblical cosmology, as we have seen, there are two levels of reality: that of the Creator, and that of the creature. By virtue of incarnation, Jesus is a creature, but by virtue of his creative work, he is the Creator, and therefore divine.[39]

Jesus is also the author of providence. He is "sustaining all things by his powerful word" (Heb. 1:3). "In him all things hold together" (Col. 1:17). But this, too, is exclusively the work of God, who preserves all things (Ps. 36:6–9) and governs all as the great king (Pss. 22:28; 47:2).

As we saw in the previous section, Jesus works miracles by his own inherent power, as Yahweh in the Old Testament. Miracles introduce us to the redemptive sphere: so Jesus is not only the author of the old creation, but of the new creation as well. He is the source of all spiritual blessings, "everything we need for life and godliness" (2 Peter 1:3). As we saw in the preceding chapter, the Father, the Son, and the Spirit are the common source of all the blessings of salvation. Jesus is "the way and the truth and the life" (John 14:6).

Most pointedly in the gospel accounts, Jesus forgives sins, not only by proclaiming the Father's forgiveness, but in his own right. Forgiving sins is something that only God can do (Isa. 43:25; 44:22), and therefore is an act that arouses godly fear (Ps. 130:4).[40] Jesus assumes that divine prerogative and proves his right to it by performing miracles (Mark 2:5–7; Luke 7:48), which provokes a charge of blasphemy from his opponents (cf. Matt. 9:3; Luke 5:21). The martyr Stephen asks Jesus to forgive the sins of his murderers (Acts 7:60), and the apostles proclaim forgiveness in Jesus' name (Acts 5:31; 13:38; Col. 3:13).

Jesus also shares with his Father the work of final judgment (Matt. 7:21–23; John 5:22; Acts 17:31; 1 Cor. 4:4; 11:32; 1 Thess. 4:6; 2 Thess. 1:8–9; 2 Tim. 4:8; Rev. 2:23; 19:11). He is the ultimate authority, the final evaluator, of the universe.

---

39. The two natures of Christ do not make him a kind of divine-human hybrid. As the Council of Chalcedon stated, his two natures are "unconfused and unchanged," as well as "undivided and unseparated." So even in the person of Christ, where divinity and humanity are most intimately related, the two are distinct. Creator remains Creator, and creature remains creature. Jesus is fully God and fully man, not some kind of intermediate being.

40. I can forgive sins committed against me, but I cannot forgive someone for his sins against a third party, least of all against God. But Jesus presumed the right to forgive all the sins of human beings.

JESUS, OBJECT OF FAITH AND WORSHIP

Scripture does not shrink from the remarkable conclusion that we should worship Jesus as God. Idolatry, the worship of anything other than the true God, is a terrible sin in the Bible. But to worship Jesus is not idolatrous; rather, it is the very heart of believing piety.

We saw in the preceding chapter how the Father, the Son, and the Spirit appear together in apostolic blessings and doxologies. Jesus himself taught that the Father had committed all judgment to him,

> that all may honor the Son just as they honor the Father. He who does not honor the Son does not honor the Father, who sent him. (John 5:23)

We read often in the Gospels about people bowing down (*proskyneō*, often translated "worship" in the KJV) before Jesus (Matt. 2:2, 11; 9:18; 14:33; John 9:38). It is hard to know how much significance to attach to this expression of deep respect. The term can be used for religious worship, but it is hard to know the exact meaning of the bowing in all these cases.

Peter, however, rebukes someone who bowed down to him in a similar context (Acts 10:25–26), so we should judge it inappropriate when directed to a mere man, or even an angel (Rev. 19:10; 22:8–9). But Jesus never rejects this worship, and certainly the practice is consistent with the worship given to him by the apostolic church. In Matthew 28:9, 17, and John 9:35–38, certainly nothing less than the highest religious adoration is in view. All are to bow before the name of Jesus (Phil. 2:10). According to Hebrews 1:6, the angels themselves worship him. The hymns of Revelation are about Jesus (Rev. 5:11–12; 7:10).

The disciples "call on the name" of Jesus (1 Cor. 1:2), echoing language regularly used in Scripture for the worship of God (going back as far as Gen. 4:26). Indeed, Paul tells them to do "all" things in the name of Jesus (Col. 3:17).

In Acts, the disciples pray to Jesus (1:24; 7:59–60), as does Paul (2 Cor. 12:8). Jesus himself promised to answer prayers offered in his name (John 14:13–14; cf. Rom. 10:12).

As J. Gresham Machen argued so eloquently against the theological liberalism of his day,[41] Scripture presents Jesus, not primarily as a model or example of faith, but as the object of faith. We believe in Jesus for salvation (John 3:15–16; 6:29; 8:24; 16:9; 17:20; Acts 3:16; 10:43; 16:31; 1 John 3:23; 5:13; 3 John 7), and to believe in him is to believe in God

---

41. J. Gresham Machen, *Christianity and Liberalism* (New York: Macmillan, 1923).

(John 12:44; 14:1). There is no other name by which we must be saved (Acts 4:12).

So faith in Christ involves total commitment, taking precedence over our family (Matt. 10:35–37) and even our own life, as we take up the cross (Matt. 16:24–26). God alone is an appropriate object of such commitment.

David Wells points out about thirty instances in Paul's writings where there is

> a complete linguistic identification of Christ with Yahweh. If Yahweh is our sanctifier (Ex. 31:13), is omnipresent (Ps. 139:7–10), is our peace (Judg. 6:24), is our righteousness (Jer. 23:6), is our victory (Ex. 17:8–16), and is our healer (Ex. 15:26), then so is Christ all of these things (1 Cor. 1:30; Col. 1:27; Eph. 2:14).[42]

He goes on to show the identity between Christ and God in regard to the gospel, the church, the kingdom, divine love, the Word, peace, the Day of Judgment, grace, salvation, and God's will. Paul is a slave to God and to Christ, lives for the glory of God and of Christ, places his faith in God and in Christ, and knows God and Christ for salvation. To Wells's list we can add parallels from other parts of the New Testament. Both God and Christ are "the Alpha and the Omega" (Rev. 1:8; 21:5–7; 22:13); both possess the divine throne (Rev. 22:3) and divine titles (Rev. 1:17; 19:11, 13, 16; 22:12).

The commitment of the biblical writers to Christ as the ultimate object of faith and worship led them often to speak of Christ and the Father in interchangeable terms (though not neglecting the distinction between the two persons). So we see again the pervasiveness of the biblical teaching concerning the deity of Christ.

ALLEGED PROBLEM PASSAGES

This pervasiveness places a heavy burden of proof upon those who would find in Scripture any denials of Jesus' deity. But critics of this doctrine have found very few passages on which to base their claims. We have already noted the implausibility of their treatment of John 1 and other passages. Their case is no more persuasive in regard to the passages listed below.

42. Wells, *The Person of Christ*, 64–65.

PROVERBS 8:22

In this verse, God's wisdom says, according to the NIV, "The LORD brought me forth as the first of his works, before his deeds of old." As we have seen, Scripture identifies Christ with the wisdom of God (as in 1 Cor. 1:30). So some have argued that Proverbs 8:22 regards wisdom, and therefore Christ, as a created being, rather than as an uncreated person of the Godhead.

The verb "brought forth" in the NIV represents the Hebrew *qanah*. The Septuagint renders *qanah* here as *ktizō*, "create," and that translation seems to have generated the debate before us. But the Hebrew word that describes the initial creation in Genesis 1 is *bara'*, not *qanah*. *Qanah* need not mean "create," but can also mean "get, possess"; accordingly, the KJV and the ASV translate "The Lord possessed me." A few observations:

1. The relationship of wisdom to Christ should not be pressed in this passage. Trinitarian theology is not an emphasis of the chapter, and its language is highly metaphorical. So we should not look here for precise descriptions of the relationship between the Father and the Son.

2. Even if God's wisdom is a creation in some sense, it may yet, like other created things, serve as a fit title of the uncreated Christ.

3. Nevertheless, I believe it is quite impossible to make this text teach that God somehow created his own wisdom. That notion contradicts much biblical teaching elsewhere, and it is essentially unintelligible. God's essential attributes, as we have seen, are eternal and necessary, and certainly wisdom is one of these. And if God did create his own wisdom, what was he like before he created it? Unwise? Is wisdom itself somehow an unwise creation, an unwise work of God? But Scripture testifies that all of God's works are done in wisdom (Ps. 104:24).

4. The actual meaning of *qanah*, I think, can be discerned from other uses of this verb in Proverbs. A major exhortation in this book is to "get" wisdom, and "get" represents *qanah* (4:5, 7; 16:16; 17:16; 19:8; 23:23). What Proverbs 8:22 says is that God is the archetype of the wise man. As human beings should "get" wisdom, so God also "got" wisdom for his works of creation and providence. The verse doesn't tell us where God went to "get" his wisdom. From elsewhere in Scripture, however, we know that God got his wisdom out of his own being, not from anything outside himself. So the passage is consistent with biblical Christology, though it is not primarily a Christological passage.

5. There is natal imagery in verses 24–25, but this is clearly part of the metaphorical structure of the passage. Even as metaphor, bearing is very different from creation, and it is a remarkably appropriate metaphor for the idea of God "getting" wisdom out of his own being.

MARK 10:18

Here, a man has addressed Jesus as "good teacher," and he replies, "Why do you call me good? . . . No one is good—except God alone." It is sometimes alleged that Jesus here denies his own goodness (and therefore his deity), but that view is utterly inconsistent with the common teaching of the New Testament (discussed above) that Jesus was sinless. Jesus' point is that the man needs to think harder about goodness. If Jesus is good in the highest sense, then he must be more than a good teacher; he must be God. So this passage bears witness to, not against, the deity of Jesus.

JOHN 14:28; 1 CORINTHIANS 11:3; 15:28

In John 14:28, Jesus tells his disciples, "You heard me say, 'I am going away and I am coming back to you.' If you loved me, you would be glad that I am going to the Father, for the Father is greater than I." Some have argued that the word "greater" (Greek *meizōn*) proves that Jesus is essentially inferior to the Father and therefore by nature something less than God, a mere creature.

But there are many ways in which the Father is "greater" than the incarnate Christ that have nothing to do with inferiority of nature:

1. Jesus utters these words in what the Westminster Catechisms call his "state of humiliation" (WLC, 42–57; WSC, 23–28). In John 14, he faces the cross itself. But throughout his earthly ministry, he lives in subjection to his Father. As perfect man, he obeys God, seeks God's blessing in prayer, and does the works the Father shows him. He cannot act by himself, but only in subjection to the Father (John 5:30). He treats the Father, in other words, as any covenant servant should: as his superior, as the one who is greater. And, as Jesus remains both human and divine through all eternity, he will, as human servant, always be subject to the Father in these ways.

2. Furthermore (and this is an important context for John 14:28), Jesus' ascension into heaven is the occasion on which the Father's power comes in even greater fullness, through the Holy Spirit. Because Jesus is "going to the Father," believers will do "even greater things" than the works performed by Jesus in the flesh (John 14:12). In this regard, too, the Father's work will be greater than Jesus' own. And of course the Son himself, then, will be given a more exalted status. (As explained earlier in this chapter, Jesus received at the Resurrection an additional title to divine sonship and lordship.)

3. As I shall indicate in the next chapter, theologians have sometimes described the Father as "the fountain of deity," ascribing to him a sort of

primacy within the Trinity itself, by which he is fitly described as the "first" person of the Godhead. Theologians maintaining that proposition often insist that the Father's primacy is not one of nature, but one of eternal role. That primacy takes nothing away from the identity of nature or essence between the Father and the Son.

4. In any case, it is plain that this passage deals with the economic, rather than the ontological, relations between the Father and the Son,[43] for Jesus speaks of an event in history in which he is "going to" the Father. So the verse cannot be made to teach that the Son is ontologically less than the Father.

I'm inclined to think that the second consideration above comes closest to the thought of Jesus in John 14:28. But, in any case, it should be evident that it is foolish to jump from the word "greater" in this verse to the conclusion that Jesus is by nature inferior to the Father.

The case is similar in regard to 1 Corinthians 11:3 ("the head of Christ is God") and 15:28 ("then the Son himself will be made subject to him who put everything under him, so that God may be all in all"), where I think the first consideration above is determinative. As the servant of God, who remains eternally man as well as God, Jesus demonstrates his obedience by subjecting himself and his kingdom to the headship of God the Father.

John 17:3

Here Jesus prays to the Father, "Now this is eternal life: that they may know you, the only true God, and Jesus Christ, whom you have sent." Some have claimed that in this verse there is a contrast between "the only true God" and "Jesus Christ," so that Jesus Christ cannot be the only true God.

But Jesus does not use "the only true God" in contrast to himself. Rather, as any Jew of the time would have understood, "the only true God" is in contrast to the false gods, the idols of the world. Indeed, in this verse, Jesus stresses his unity with the Father, for the disciple's saving knowledge is a knowledge both of the Father and of the Son. "The only true God" and "Jesus Christ" are parallel objects of saving knowledge. Indeed, 1 John 5:20, which echoes John 17:3, identifies Jesus himself as "the true God," by whom saving knowledge comes:

---

43. See the following chapter for a discussion of this distinction. With respect to the Trinity, *ontological* refers to the inherent nature of the three persons (where there is equality), and *economic* refers to their roles in relation to the creation (where there is subordination).

We know also that the Son of God has come and has given us understanding, so that we may know him who is true. And we are in him who is true—even in his Son Jesus Christ. He is the true God and eternal life.

1 Corinthians 8:6

Here Paul writes that, although pagans worship many gods and lords, "yet for us there is but one God, the Father, from whom all things came and for whom we live; and there is but one Lord, Jesus Christ, through whom all things came and through whom we live." As with John 17:3, some have claimed that this verse limits deity to the Father, in contrast to the Lord Jesus Christ. But, as we saw earlier, we do not have here a contrast between deity ("God") and nondeity ("Lord"), but rather a distinction between two divine persons.

Note also that in this passage both the Father and the Son are, in the context, objects of Christian worship. Both are also agents of creation and authors of the redeemed life. So both are fully divine.

Colossians 1:15–18

Here Paul writes of Jesus:

> He is the image of the invisible God, the firstborn over all creation. For by him all things were created: things in heaven and on earth, visible and invisible, whether thrones or powers or rulers or authorities; all things were created by him and for him. He is before all things, and in him all things hold together. And he is the head of the body, the church; he is the beginning and the firstborn from among the dead, so that in everything he might have the supremacy.

The term *firstborn* (*prōtotokos*) has led some people to claim that Christ had a beginning, a birth. He was, they say, born before the creation of everything else, but he is nevertheless a creature.

However, in Scripture, *prōtotokos* focuses more on status and authority than on time of birth. In Psalm 89:27, God promises to make David his firstborn, even though he was one of the younger sons in his family. The point is that God will give David a preeminence. Clearly, too, making David God's "firstborn" in Psalm 89:27 is not bringing him into existence; to the psalmist, David already exists.

The term is similar to *archē* ("beginning, ruler") in Revelation 3:14: "These are the words of the Amen, the faithful and true witness, the ruler [*archē*] of God's creation." *Archē* here emphasizes preeminence and does not in the least suggest that the ruler is himself a created being with a beginning. Compare the use of *alpha and omega* in Revelation 21:6 and 22:13.

Indeed, Paul emphasizes in Colossians 1 that Jesus created "all things" (v. 16), placing him "before" all of them (v. 17). Logically, if he literally created everything, he cannot himself be a creature, for he could not have created himself. But, more importantly, note the emphasis on preeminence: his primacy, both in creation and in the church, his rule over them. So even his status as "the firstborn from among the dead" is directed toward his supremacy. It does not make him equal to other resurrected souls. We should similarly understand his status as "the firstborn of all creation."

There is another possible interpretation of these references to Christ as "the firstborn." Early Christian preaching connected Psalm 2:7, "You are my Son; today I have become your Father," with the resurrection of Jesus (Acts 13:33), and the idea of Jesus as the "firstborn" of resurrected people seems to have caught on in the church as a standard title of Christ. See Romans 8:29, Hebrews 1:6 and 12:23, and Revelation 1:5, and note the related idea of Jesus as the "firstfruits" of the resurrection in 1 Corinthians 15:20, 23. Compare also Paul's observation that Jesus was "the first to rise from the dead" in Acts 26:23. Perhaps, then, we should understand that Jesus was "the firstborn from among the dead" (Col. 1:18) as the first person raised to resurrection life, and that his resurrection authority (see Rom. 1:4; Matt. 28:18), extended to the whole universe by his exaltation to the right hand of God (Acts 2:32–36; Phil. 2:9–11), made him "the firstborn over all creation" (Col. 1:15). This interpretation does acknowledge a temporal precedence in the term "firstborn," but it is Jesus' precedence in the Resurrection, not as a first creature. And this approach underscores the emphasis of the passage on Jesus' preeminence.[44]

THE DEITY OF THE HOLY SPIRIT

Some have argued against the full deity of the Holy Spirit. The ancient Arians, followed by modern cultists, made the Son by nature less than God, and the Spirit less than the Son. But it is not difficult to show that Scripture regards the Spirit, like the Son, as fully God. My treatment of this issue will be parallel to my treatment of the deity of Christ, but briefer, because the biblical references are fewer, and because the arguments here closely parallel arguments already made.

44. Thanks to James W. Scott for this suggestion.

We have already seen that in the Trinitarian texts, the Spirit stands alongside the Father and the Son (Matt. 28:19; Rom. 15:19; 2 Cor. 13:14; Eph. 2:21–22; 4:4–6; Phil. 3:3; Rev. 1:4–5; 2:7). It is inconceivable that in these texts, which identify the divine name, specify the ultimate source of spiritual blessing, and speak of God in worshipful terms, one of the three members should lack full divine status. There are also a number of texts that mention two members of the Trinity. We saw earlier that some texts mention the Father and the Son, but there are also several that mention the Son and the Spirit as equal partners.[45] (See Acts 9:31; Rom. 15:30; 1 Cor. 6:11; Phil. 2:1; Heb. 10:29; Rev. 2:18, 29, where both the Son and the Spirit speak God's words to the churches.) In these passages as well, it is impossible that one partner should be divine and the other less than divine.

Furthermore, New Testament writers often refer to Old Testament texts dealing with Yahweh and apply them to the Holy Spirit. For example, words ascribed to Yahweh in Jeremiah 31:33–34 are ascribed to the Spirit in Hebrews 10:15–17. Similar parallels are found in Exodus 25:1 and Hebrews 9:8, in Psalm 95:7–11 and Hebrews 3:7–11, in Isaiah 6:9–10 and Acts 28:25–28, and in Isaiah 64:4 and 1 Corinthians 2:9.

Scripture actually refers to the Spirit as God in Acts 5:3–4. Ananias lied to the Holy Spirit (v. 3); therefore he has lied to God (v. 4). In 1 Corinthians 3:16–17, Paul says that believers are the temple of God, because the Spirit of God dwells in them (cf. 6:19–20).

In Mark 3:28–29, Jesus speaks of a blasphemy "against the Holy Spirit," but in Scripture blasphemy is always against God.

Like Jesus, the Spirit has divine attributes. The Messiah's own divine qualities can be represented as due to the Spirit's endowment:

> The Spirit of the LORD will rest on him—
> the Spirit of wisdom and of understanding,
> the Spirit of counsel and of power,
> the Spirit of knowledge and of the fear of the LORD. (Isa. 11:2)

The Spirit is the grace and love of God given to man, motivating believers to godliness (Rom. 5:5; 15:30; 2 Cor. 6:6; Gal. 5:16–17; Phil. 2:1; Col. 1:8). As such, he is the living water, the fullness of divine blessing (Luke 11:13; John 4:10; 7:38–39; Rev. 22:1, 17). He is the power of God (Judg. 14:6; 1 Sam. 11:6–7; Isa. 11:2; 40:6–7; Mic. 3:8; Luke 1:35; Acts 1:8; 10:38; Rom. 15:13, 19).

---

45. I don't know of any passages where the Father and the Spirit are mentioned without the Son. The reason for this may be that the Son and the Spirit have a very close relationship: the Spirit comes to bear witness to the Son (John 14:26; 15:26; 16:13).

Like the Father and the Son, the Spirit is eternal (Heb. 9:14), omniscient (Isa. 40:13; 1 Cor. 2:10–11), wise (Isa. 11:2), omnipresent (Ps. 139:7–10; Acts 1:8), and incomprehensible (Isa. 40:13). Scripture calls him holy nearly one hundred times, and clearly his holiness is the holiness of God, not the derivative holiness of a creature.

Like the Son, the Spirit performs all the acts of God. He is the agent of creation (Gen. 1:2; Pss. 33:6;[46] 104:30), and therefore is not a creature. Like the Father and the Son, he judges creatures (John 16:8–11). He is the giver of life, both physical and spiritual (Gen. 2:7; Job 33:4; Ps. 104:30; John 3:5–8; 6:63; Rom. 8:11; 1 Cor. 15:45; 2 Cor. 3:6; cf. earlier references to the living water and the water of life). He makes us aware of our adoption by God (Rom. 8:15). Through him, we are washed, sanctified, and justified (1 Cor. 6:11). The Spirit confers gifts on God's people, so they can serve him in many ways (Judg. 3:10; 6:34; 11:29; 1 Cor. 12:6, 11). He is the Paraclete, the believer's advocate (John 14:16, 26; 15:26; 16:7). He is "another" advocate, for Jesus himself is the original. The Spirit, then, shares in the work of Jesus, standing to defend God's people.

He is also the teacher of the church, the one who speaks the word of God.[47] Regularly in the Old Testament, the Spirit comes upon prophets, enabling them to speak God's words (Num. 11:25; 24:2; 1 Sam. 10:10; 18:10; 19:23; 2 Kings 2:9; 2 Chron. 18:23; 24:20; Isa. 61:1; Ezek. 2:2; Mic. 3:8). So to Paul the Scriptures of the Old Testament are *theopneustos,* "breathed out by God's Spirit [*pneuma*]" (2 Tim. 3:16). Jesus promises his disciples that the Spirit will give his words to them (Matt. 10:20; Luke 12:12). So when the Spirit comes upon the apostles in the book of Acts, they speak of Jesus. John even says that because of the anointing of the Spirit, God's people need no human teachers (1 John 2:27).[48]

So we see that God is one, but that he is also three persons, each of them fully divine.

---

46. Recall that in Hebrew "breath" and "spirit" are the same word, *ruah.* The Spirit is the powerful breath of God that accomplishes God's purposes, although, as we shall see, he is also personal.

47. The Trinitarian picture here is that the Father is the speaker, the Son is the word, and the Spirit is the powerful breath that carries the word to its hearers and brings about their response.

48. I presume that John is speaking of the basic teachings of the gospel, which, as he says, his readers already know. Elsewhere, the New Testament does make provision for human teachers in the church and instructs Christians to listen to them (e.g., Heb. 13:7, 17).

CHAPTER 29

Father, Son, and Spirit

In chapter 27, I presented a summary formulation of the doctrine of the Trinity: (1) God is one. (2) God is three. (3) The three persons are each fully God. (4) Each of the persons is distinct from the others. (5) The three are related to one another eternally as Father, Son, and Holy Spirit. Chapter 27 introduced the subject and developed theses 1 and 2. Chapter 28 defended thesis 3. In this chapter, I will deal with theses 4 and 5, focusing on the distinctions and relations among the three persons.

In this chapter, I shall give more attention than before to the church's creedal formulations and to the history of theological reflection on these subjects, since that tradition has raised and answered important questions about the Trinity that pertain especially to theses 4 and 5. I shall therefore be giving more consideration here to the technical terminology by which the Trinitarian distinctions have been expressed.

THE DISTINCTNESS OF THE PERSONS

Some theologians, impressed with the biblical emphasis on the unity of God, have minimized the distinctions between the Father, the Son, and the Spirit. Bavinck explains:

> The precursors of Sabellianism in the second and third centuries A. D. were Noetus, Praxeas, Epigonus, and Cleomenes, who taught

that in Christ, the Father himself was born, suffered, and died; that the names Father and Son indicate one and the same person in different relations; namely, before and during the period of his incarnation *per se* and in his historical manifestations; or that Christ's divine nature is the Father and that his human nature is the Son. In the third century this monarchianism, patripassianism,[1] or modalism was advocated and developed by Sabellius. Father, Son, and Spirit are three names for one and the same God, one and the same being. He calls this being *"Huiopatōr,"*[2] and applies this name successively to its three consecutive energies or modes. God existed first in the person, manifestation, or mode of the Father, as Creator and Lawgiver; then in the person or prosopon[3] of the Son, as Redeemer, from the time of the incarnation to the moment of the ascension; finally, in the person or prosopon of the Holy Spirit as Giver of Life.[4]

This position holds that God is one person, with three masks (*prosōpa*), playing three roles. For Sabellius, the roles were historically successive, but for some modalists they are simultaneous, each a kind of aspect or revelation of God. For modalists, as with Gnostics and Arians, the divine nature itself is hidden from us, because it is transcendent. We know God only through various roles that he plays in history, but none of these roles presents us with God as he really is. (Recall my critique of this view in chap. 7.)[5]

Thus, the doctrine of the Trinity is related to the doctrines of God's transcendence and immanence, and, in turn, to the doctrines of divine lordship and revelation. If God's transcendence removes him from our knowledge, then of course we have no rational basis for making Trinitarian distinctions within his being. But if God is transcendent as the Lord, involved in our history and revealing himself in his Word, then we can make the distinctions that he himself has revealed to us.

We can understand, then, why modalism appealed especially to later thinkers such as Erigena, Abelard, Joachim of Floris, Servetus, Boehme,

---

1. Literally, "Father-suffering," expressing the belief that the Father suffered on the cross.

2. Literally, "Son-Father."

3. Literally, "mask." But the church later used this term to express the orthodox concept of a divine "person."

4. *DG,* 287.

5. Compare the discussion in Helmut Thielicke, *The Evangelical Faith* (Grand Rapids: Eerdmans, 1977), 2:146–49, and Otto Weber, *Foundations of Dogmatics* (Grand Rapids: Eerdmans, 1981), 1:366–71.

Swedenborg, Kant, Schleiermacher, Schelling, and Hegel, whose thought was governed more by speculation than by Scripture.[6] Apart from revelation, the human mind would never conceive of the Trinity.[7] Apart from revelation, God would be an unknown, a mystery, about which nothing more could be said. If there were differentiations or distinctions to be made within such a being, we could not know them. We would therefore be shut up either to modalism or to a view like Arianism, in which all "divine distinctions" are actually within the creaturely realm.

In Scripture, however, as we have seen, the Father, the Son, and the Spirit are all divine, and they are distinct from one another. That should be obvious from all the personal transactions between them. The Father appoints the Son to a place of honor (Pss. 2:7; 110:1). The Father and the Son know each another (Matt. 11:27), but the Son is somehow ignorant of something the Father knows (Mark 13:32). The Word is with God, as well as being God (John 1:1–2). The Father gave his Son to die for sinners (John 3:16; Gal. 4:6). Jesus prays to the Father (e.g., Mark 14:36; John 17), making requests, giving thanks, expressing love.[8] He teaches the disciples to pray to the Father in the name of Jesus (John 16:23). Jesus asks the Father to send the Spirit, who is "another" counselor, distinct from Jesus himself (John 14:16). The Father speaks from heaven, testifying to the Son (Matt. 17:5). Jesus ascends to the Father (John 20:17) and sits down with him on his throne (Rev. 3:21). The angelic chorus ascribes salvation to God and to the Lamb (Rev. 7:10). None of this makes sense on a modalistic basis. The members of the Godhead are distinct persons.

---

6. Karl Barth has often been accused of modalism, because he objects to the idea that God has three "centers of consciousness," and he interprets the Trinity merely as an expression of the freedom of God as Lord "to become wholly different from Himself and then to return to Himself": see Cornelius Van Til, The New Modernism (Philadelphia: Presbyterian and Reformed, 1946), 222; cf. pp. 221–30, 145–59. See also Leonard Hodgson, The Doctrine of the Trinity (New York: Scribner's, 1944), 229. Barth rejected this criticism, however. See ChD, 4.4.19–23.

7. However, there have been some modalists of evangelical background, such as the "Jesus only" Pentecostals, who have attempted the impossible task of defending this position from Scripture. See, for example, John Miller, Is God a Trinity? (Hazelwood, Mo.: Word Aflame Press, 1975). But Miller, like the liberal rationalists, frequently argues that orthodox Trinitarianism contradicts reason.

8. Modalists sometimes reply that in his prayers, Jesus' human nature (the Son) is conversing with his divine nature (the Father). However, natures are not personal beings. They do not converse with one another. Only persons enter into personal transactions. So Jesus is either two persons (the heresy ascribed to Nestorius) or one person distinct from the person of the Father.

THE DISTINCT PERSONALITY OF THE SPIRIT

Clearly, then, the Father and the Son are distinct persons.[9] But questions have been raised as to whether the Spirit is a third person coordinate with the Father and the Son, or a kind of impersonal force or power associated with God.

We are often inclined to equate "spirit" with the nonmaterial realm, so that it amounts to a force that animates matter. But spirits in Scripture, human as well as divine, are persons, not impersonal forces. And as I indicated in chapter 25, God's spirituality is not merely power, but the personal qualities of the Holy Spirit.

Scripture does certainly connect the Spirit closely with the power of God (see Mic. 3:8; Zech. 4:6; Luke 1:17, 35; 4:14; Acts 1:8; 10:38; Rom. 1:4; 15:13, 19; 1 Cor. 2:4; 1 Thess. 1:5; 2 Tim. 1:7). But the power of God is never impersonal. It is a power directed by God's intelligent plan to accomplish his purposes. The Spirit, therefore, represents not only God's power, but also his wisdom (Ex. 28:3; 31:3; 35:31; Deut. 34:9; Isa. 11:2; Dan. 5:11, 14; Luke 1:17; 2:40; Acts 6:10; 1 Cor. 2:4; 12:8; Eph. 1:17). The Spirit has a "mind" (Rom. 8:27). Often it is quite impossible to substitute *power* for *spirit* (see, e.g., Acts 10:38; Rom. 15:13; 1 Cor. 2:4). The Holy Spirit is not a mere power; he is the *personal bearer* of divine power.

Pneuma ("spirit") is a neuter word in Greek (although the corresponding Hebrew term, *ruah*, is feminine). However, the biblical writers sometimes use masculine pronouns with it, emphasizing the personality of the Spirit. In John 14:17, Jesus speaks of

> the Spirit of truth. The world cannot accept him, because it neither sees him nor knows him. But you know him, for he lives with you and will be in you.

(Cf. John 14:26; 16:14; 1 Cor. 12:11.) The Spirit speaks, using the first person "I," in Acts 10:19–20; 13:2.

The Spirit performs acts that only persons perform: comforting, revealing, inspiring, speaking, witnessing, hearing, sending, knowing, teaching, guiding, striving, interceding.

As we have seen, the Spirit is divine, coordinate with the Father and the Son as a bearer of the divine name (Matt. 28:19; 2 Cor. 13:14). So he cannot be different from them in nature. But for the same reason, he must be distinct from them, as the Father and the Son are distinct from each another.

9. For the technical definition of *person* in this context, see later discussion.

Second Corinthians 3:17–18 has sometimes been thought to compromise the distinction between the Spirit and Christ. Paul says there:

> Now the Lord is the Spirit, and where the Spirit of the Lord is, there is freedom. And we, who with unveiled faces all reflect the Lord's glory, are being transformed into his likeness with ever-increasing glory, which comes from the Lord, who is the Spirit.

Here Paul alludes to Exodus 34:34, where Moses removes a veil from his face when he enters the presence of the Lord (that is, Yahweh). In the Exodus passage, the Lord to whom we turn (v. 16) is Yahweh, without explicit Trinitarian distinction. Yahweh is, as we have seen, Father, Son, and Spirit in one. The Lord *is* the Father, *is* the Son, and also *is* the Spirit. So to cite here an identity between the Lord and the Spirit causes no Trinitarian confusion. Paul identifies Yahweh specifically with the Spirit here because he is talking about the Spirit's ministry of giving life, as opposed to the law's ministry of death (v. 6). When we turn to the Lord, Yahweh, we are turning to the Spirit. The Lord (Yahweh) is Spirit (cf. John 4:24), not law, so he opens our hearts (v. 15) and gives spiritual life (v. 6), freedom (v. 17), and glory (v. 18).

The problem in 2 Corinthians 3:17–18 arises because "Lord" (*kyrios*) is also, as we have seen, Paul's normal term for Jesus Christ, and in his application of Exodus 34, "turning to the Lord" is "turning to Jesus." This application is appropriate, because of course Yahweh is Jesus; to turn to Yahweh is to turn to Jesus. "The Lord" in 2 Corinthians 3:17–18, I would say, refers primarily to Yahweh, but there is certainly some connotation here of Christ as Lord, especially since the passage deals with the contrast between law and grace. And since Yahweh is the Spirit, and Jesus is Yahweh, in one sense Jesus is the Spirit.

This creates some awkwardness with the standard Trinitarian language,[10] but Paul is not concerned here to make precise Trinitarian distinctions, nor certainly to repudiate distinctions he makes elsewhere between the three persons.

We do see here some of the mystery of the Trinity. Although the doctrine is not irrational, there are aspects of it that are very difficult to understand. Generally, we say that things which are identical to the same thing (here, Jesus and the Spirit to Yahweh) are identical to each other (so the Lord is the Spirit). In 2 Corinthians 3:17–18, that logical inference is al-

---

10. I recall the traditional Sunday school illustration: The Father is God, the Son is God, the Spirit is God; but the Father is not the Son, nor the Son the Spirit, nor the Spirit the Father.

lowed. But we know from other Scriptures that that is not the whole story, and the identity here is not an identity in every sense, but an identity of nature or essence.[11]

Of course, this passage does imply a very close relationship between Christ and the Spirit in ways other than commonness of nature, as we see elsewhere in biblical phrases like "Spirit of Christ." Christ accomplishes his work by a special endowment of the Spirit (Isa. 61:1; Matt. 3:16; 12:18; Luke 4:18), and the work of the Spirit is to bear witness to Christ (John 15:26). But these phrases themselves reflect a distinction between Christ and the Spirit, as does the phrase "Spirit of the Lord" here in verse 17.

The passage recalls 1 Corinthians 15:45, where Jesus, as the Second Adam, is made "a life-giving spirit." In their function of giving life, the Son and the Spirit are both so intimately involved that they are scarcely distinguishable. Another passage that intertwines references to Christ and the Spirit in their life-giving work is Romans 8:9–11:

> You, however, are controlled not by the sinful nature but by the Spirit, if the Spirit of God lives in you. And if anyone does not have the Spirit of Christ, he does not belong to Christ. But if Christ is in you, your body is dead because of sin, yet your spirit is alive because of righteousness. And if the Spirit of him who raised Jesus from the dead is living in you, he who raised Christ from the dead will also give life to your mortal bodies through his Spirit, who lives in you.

But of course this fact doesn't prevent biblical writers in other contexts from making distinctions between the Son and the Spirit, as we saw above, just as biblical writers make personal distinctions within the being of Yahweh. Jesus prays that the Father will send the Spirit (John 14:16), another counselor, and he will not come in power until Jesus ascends to the Father.

CIRCUMINCESSIO

Scripture, therefore, presents a delicate balance between the distinctness of the persons of the Trinity and their mutual involvement, and I must now say more about the latter. *Circumincessio, circumcessio, circumcession, perichoresis*, and *coinherence* are technical terms for the mutual indwelling of the persons: the Father in the Son, and the Son in him (John 10:38;

---

11. Later in this chapter, I shall discuss Vern Poythress's Trinitarian use of logic, which bears on this question.

14:10–11, 20; 17:21); both in the Spirit, and the Spirit in them (Rom. 8:9). To see Jesus is to see the Father (John 14:9), for he and the Father are one (10:30). After Jesus departs from the earth, he will "come" in the Spirit to be with his people (14:18).[12]

All three persons are involved in all the works of God in and for creation.[13] As we have seen, the Father (Gen. 1), the Son (John 1:3; Col. 1:16), and the Spirit (Gen. 1:2; Ps. 104:30) are involved in the work of creation. The same is true of providence, and, in many ways, redemption and judgment. This is not to say that the three persons play identical roles in these events. The Father, not the Son, sent Jesus into the world to redeem his people; the Son, not the Father or the Spirit, became incarnate to die on the cross for our sins. At the moment of death, indeed, he was, in some mysterious way, even estranged from his Father (Mark 15:34). The Spirit, not the Father or the Son, came on the church with power on the day of Pentecost (having been sent by the Father and the Son [John 14:15–21]), although the Son comes to us in and by the Spirit.

According to 1 Peter 1:1–2, the Father is the one who foreknows, the Son is the one who sprinkles blood, and the Spirit is the one who sanctifies. This is a useful generalization about the distinctive roles of the divine persons: the Father plans, the Son executes, and the Spirit applies. But of course Peter is not here describing a precise division of labor. He knows that all of these events require the concurrence of all three persons.

MUTUAL GLORIFICATION

The concurrence of the three persons of the Trinity in all that they do is a profound indication of their unity. There is no conflict in the Trinity. The three persons are perfectly agreed on what they should do and how their plan should be executed.[14] They support one another, assist one an-

12. Remarkably, Jesus also compares the mutual indwelling of the members of the Trinity with (1) the dwelling of the divine persons in believers, and (2) the unity of believers with one another (John 17:21–23). These, of course, are analogies, not identities, for we cannot be one exactly as God is one. But we are to support one another, indeed to glorify one another, as the members of the Trinity do. For more applications of this principle to the Christian life, see my "Walking Together," available at www.thirdmill.org, Online Magazine 1:17–18 (June 21 and 28 and July 4, 1999).

13. These are the *opera ad extra* in the traditional terminology, the works of God that terminate outside himself. There are also acts that God performs within his own being (*opera ad intra*) in which only one person is involved, such as the Father's begetting of the Son. I shall discuss these later.

14. As a man, Jesus prays to the Father that he will not have to drink the cup of the Fa-

other, and promote one another's purposes. This intra-Trinitarian "defer-ence," this "disposability"[15] of each to the others, may be called "mutual glorification."[16]

In the gospel of John, the Father glorifies the Son (John 8:50, 54; 12:23; 17:1) and the Son glorifies the Father (7:18; 17:4). The Spirit glorifies the Son (16:14), who in turn glorifies the Father.

To my knowledge, no text says precisely that the Father or the Son glorifies the Spirit, but the Father and the Son do honor the Spirit in his particular work. In John 16:7, Jesus tells his disciples:

> It is for your good that I am going away. Unless I go away, the Counselor will not come to you; but if I go, I will send him to you.

The Spirit, the Counselor, has his special work, which is different from that of the Son. The Spirit can do that work only after the Son has ascended to the Father. So the Son defers to the Spirit. He "goes away," so that the Spirit may come. Jesus testifies, indeed, that after he has gone and the Spirit has come, the disciples will do "greater" works than those that Jesus performed on earth (John 14:12). So Jesus pays honor to the Spirit: he rejoices that in one sense the Spirit's ministry will be greater than his own. So the Father and the Son glorify the Spirit by giving him a distinctive and important role in the work of redemption.

The mutual deference of the persons of the Trinity is a major theme in the gospel of John. The Son is always subject to the Father (5:30; 6:38; 7:18; 9:4; 10:18), but the Father defers to the Son by answering his prayers, granting him authority, and testifying on his behalf (3:35; 5:22–23, 26–27; 6:37, 43–44; 11:41–42; 12:26; 14:10; 15:2, 8).

Jesus is disposable to believers as well: see, e.g., John 6:49–51, 55–56; 10:7–9. He lays down his life for them. Amazingly, the Lord is their servant (John 13:1–17; cf. Matt. 20:26–28), and this servanthood is to be a

---

ther's wrath (Matt. 26:39). Does this desire express a disagreement within the Godhead? I think not. His request is legitimate, as the Father surely recognizes, for to drink the cup of wrath is something anyone should shrink from. And Jesus also recognizes that if the cup cannot be avoided, he must accept it (v. 42); the Father's will must be done. There is a mysterious tension between the Father and the Son in this prayer, anticipating the Father's estrangement from Jesus at the cross, but there is no disagreement between them as to what must happen. In this time of prayer, the eternal agreement of Father and Son becomes a temporal process, in which the elements of agreement come together in time.

15. Royce Gordon Gruenler, *The Trinity in the Gospel of John* (Grand Rapids: Baker, 1986), 21 and passim.

16. In this section, I am indebted to personal correspondence with Peter Leithart and Jeffrey Meyers, in addition to Gruenler and others.

model for relationships among believers in the church. Those in authority are not to rule for their own benefit, as the "lords" of the Gentiles; rather, they are to serve those who are under their authority, as Jesus served them. So the mutual disposability of the members of the Trinity for one another carries over into their relationships with human beings and serves as a model for their own behavior.

Certainly there are senses in which believers can never be one as the persons of the Trinity are one, and yet Jesus calls us into the oneness of the Father and the Son (John 17:22). Clearly Jesus does not intend to erase the distinction between the Creator and the creature. But the concept of mutual glorification suggests an important way in which Christians can be like the members of the Trinity: we, too, are called to defer to one another in this way, to glorify one another, to be disposable to one another's purposes—that is, to love one another as God loved us.

SUBSTANCE AND PERSONS

The main outlines of the biblical doctrine are now before us. But we must also look at various questions about this doctrine that have arisen in church history and that are still with us. One of these asks us to define ontologically or metaphysically what it means to be a member of the Trinity. How are the Father, the Son, and the Spirit to be distinguished or identified with the one true God? Or, to put it differently, when we say that God is one and that God is three, what is it that is one, and what is three?

We should be cautious in discussing such questions, to avoid speculation that goes beyond Scripture. Scripture itself does not use technical terms for God's oneness and threeness, and, as we saw for example in our discussion of 2 Corinthians 3:17, it is not always concerned with terminological precision in describing the relations of the three persons. It is important, however, to think about these matters, if only to avoid unbiblical formulations like those of Sabellianism and Arianism, and so that we can benefit from the important reflections on this subject by theologians of the past.

As it struggled to define the doctrine of the Trinity precisely, the church came to adopt specialized terminology for God's oneness and threeness (see fig. 3). In general, these terms have served the church well. But they have also raised additional questions and caused some misunderstandings. A number of points need to be made, therefore, to promote clarity, and to describe further the circumstances in which the church came to adopt this language.

	GREEK	LATIN	ENGLISH
One	*ousia, physis*	*substantia, essentia*	being, substance, essence, nature
Three	*hypostaseis, prosopa*	*personae*	persons, subsistences, modes of subsistence

Fig. 3. Terms Expressing God's Oneness and Threeness

1. These are not biblical terms, but are taken from various secular uses—philosophical, legal, and otherwise. We should not, therefore, take them as sacrosanct. I doubt that we will find better terms at this juncture in history, but we should not cringe at the thought that these terms may be problematic to some people.

Many important Christian thinkers have expressed reservations about this language. Augustine said, "The answer 'three persons' is given, not that something should be said, but so as not to remain wholly silent."[17] Calvin observed:

> Where names have not been invented rashly, we must beware lest we become chargeable with arrogance and rashness in rejecting them. I wish, indeed, that such names were buried, provided all would concur in the belief that the Father, Son, and Spirit, are one God, and yet that the Son is not the Father, nor the Spirit the Son, but that each has his peculiar subsistence. I am not so minutely precise as to fight furiously for mere words. For I observe, that the writers of the ancient Church, while they uniformly spoke with great reverence on these matters, neither agreed with each other, nor were always consistent with themselves.[18]

Calvin goes on to note inconsistencies in terminology between Jerome, Hilary, and other writers.

2. At the same time, we should not be unwilling to use extrabiblical terms

17. Augustine, *On the Trinity*, 5.9.10 (cf. 7.4.9); translation from David Brown, "Trinitarian Personhood and Individuality," in *Trinity, Incarnation, and Atonement*, ed. Ronald J. Feenstra and Cornelius Plantinga (Notre Dame: University of Notre Dame Press, 1989), 48.
18. *Institutes*, 1.13.5.

when they are theologically helpful. The work of theology is not to repeat the language of Scripture, but to apply the language of Scripture to our thought and life.[19]

3. In the Greek language prior to the Trinitarian use of these terms, and even in early Christian theology, *ousia* and *hypostasis* were not clearly or consistently distinguished. Christopher Kaiser says that "*hypostasis* and *ousia* were originally synonyms in patristic thought and remained so well into the fourth century."[20] Indeed, the original Nicene Creed anathematizes those who say that "he, the Son of God, is of a different *hypostasis* or *ousia*" (from the Father).[21] But later discussions, particularly the work of the Cappadocian fathers, led to a distinction between these two terms, and it became orthodox to say that the Father and the Son were different *hypostaseis*, but not different *ousiai*. To some extent, this decision was arbitrary. Theologians needed a term for the divine unity, and they picked *ousia*; they needed a different term for the divine plurality, and they picked *hypostasis*. There was nothing in the nature of these terms themselves that required the church to use *ousia* for the unity, and *hypostasis* for the plurality, of God.

Gordon Clark, after citing an instance in which he believes Augustine identifies person and substance,[22] says:

> In spite of all the linguistic confusion, . . . [Augustine] made it quite clear that the Godhead was one in one sense and three in a different sense. Whether this difference be called *person* or *substance* is inconsequential. . . . Although it is not familiar to our ears, one could say that God is one person and three substances. In fact, translate *substance* back into Greek and it is most orthodox to say that the Godhead is three substances. It makes no difference what term one uses, provided that he clearly states that they are not synonymous. God is one and three in different senses.[23]

Elizabeth Johnson carries this line of thought a bit further:

---

19. See my discussion of "theology as application" in *DKG*, esp. pp. 76–85. Compare *DG*, 294: "Scripture was not given to us in order that we should merely repeat its exact words in parrot-like fashion but in order that we should digest it in our own minds and express it in our own words."

20. Christopher B. Kaiser, *The Doctrine of God* (Westchester, Ill.: Crossway, 1982), 66. Cf. *DG*, 295.

21. From the original version of the Creed (A.D. 325). The more familiar version was ratified by the Council of Constantinople in 381 and does not contain these anathemas.

22. I read the Augustine passage somewhat differently from Clark.

23. Gordon H. Clark, *The Trinity* (Jefferson, Md.: Trinity Foundation, 1985), 52–53.

In explaining Augustine's point, Edmund Hill suggests that we try referring to the persons as three *x*'s in God, or as A, B, C, so unknown is the threesomeness to which the term refers. Centuries later Anselm of Canterbury will even speak of "three something-or-other," "three I know not what" (*tres nescio quid*).[24]

I agree with Anselm that when we use terms like *substance* and *person* to refer to God, we do not entirely understand what we are talking about, but we should not embrace total agnosticism on this matter. We should avoid deductions based only on the extrabiblical philosophical uses of these terms. Use of the terms is legitimate, but only as markers to be filled with biblical content. To say that God is three *persons* does not add anything to what we learn in Scripture about the Father, the Son, and the Spirit. Rather, the term *person* should include all and only the content of the biblical teachings. *Person* is simply a label for the ways in which the Father, the Son, and the Spirit are alike, in distinction from the Godhead as a whole.

It would be wrong for us to think that a careful historical study of the uses of these terms would yield the essence of the relationships between the one triune God and the three persons thereof. What we know about these relationships (and in this area we often know less than we think we do) comes not from a study of these technical terms, but from the teachings of Scripture. The terms serve merely to label the concepts that we derive from the Bible.

4. By etymology and use, the Greek *hypostasis* and the Latin *substantia* were more or less equivalent. But the Greeks used *hypostasis* for the plurality of God, and the Latins used *substantia* for God's oneness. This fact led to much misunderstanding, and all the more so, because the Latin "one substance" sounded Sabellian to the Greeks: for it seemed that what the Greeks numbered as three, the Latins numbered as one. And similarly, the Greek "three hypostaseis" sounded Arian or even tritheistic to the Latins— as if the Latins believed in one divine substance, one God, and the Greeks believed in three.[25] These suspicions were even more encouraged by the fact that Sabellianism was predominantly a Western (Latin) heresy, and Arianism was predominately an Eastern (Greek) heresy. And the Latins preferred *persona* (originally, "mask") to denote the threeness of God, a term

---

24. Elizabeth Johnson, *She Who Is* (New York: Crossroad, 1996), 203. She refers to Edmund Hill, *The Mystery of the Trinity* (London: Chapman, 1985), 59–60, and Anselm, *Monologium*, 78, quoted in *St. Anselm: Basic Writings*, ed. S. N. Deane (La Salle: Open Court, 1974), 142.

25. Partly for this reason, Augustine preferred the term *essentia* to *substantia*. But in Augustine's time, *essentia* was a new term, not generally used in Latin.

with a significant history in Sabellianism. Understandable as these suspicions were, most scholars would agree that it was possible to express orthodox Trinitarianism using either the Greek or the Latin terminology, and indeed many writers did. The confusion warns us against pursuing theological controversy based wholly on the individual words people employ, and it provides further ground for a limited agnosticism concerning the precise meanings of these terms.

✝   5. *Substance, nature, being,* or *essence,* in this context, is simply what God is—everything he is. Mueller defines *ousia* and *essentia* as "the divine nature with all its attributes."[26] Understood thus, it is evident that there can be only one divine substance, for there can be only one God.

6. The term *person* has had many meanings over the centuries, and there has been much theological controversy over what it ought to mean. Johnson says that *hypostasis* is

> a philosophical term that is virtually untranslatable into modern English. Its approximate meaning connotes a firm base from which an existing thing stands forth and develops; or a full-stop to a nature; or the fundamental subsistence of a thing.[27]

As noted earlier, the Latin term *persona* (equivalent to the Greek *prosōpon*) could mean "mask" or "role," a meaning congenial to Sabellianism. It was also used to refer to a legal entity, a being with rights and obligations. Sometimes writers used the term in the way modern writers speak of persons. That was natural, since Scripture pictures the members of the Trinity as having personal interactions with one another. But not until Boethius (475–524) defined *persona* as "an individual substance of a rational nature"[28] did a "modern" definition of *person* become generally accepted. Boethius himself, however, recognized a difficulty here: If the persons of the Trinity are "individual substances," how can it also be said, as in the traditional Latin vocabulary, that God is "one substance"?[29] And some modern writers have argued that this concept of *person,* applied to the Trinity, is trithe-

---

26. J. Theodore Mueller, *Christian Dogmatics* (St. Louis: Concordia, 1934), 153. In Aristotle's philosophy, substance is what "exists in itself" as the bearer of attributes.

27. Johnson, *She Who Is,* 203. *Subsistence* refers to a way in which something exists.

28. Boethius, *A Treatise Against Eutyches and Nestorius,* 3, in *Boethius: The Theological Treatises,* ed. and trans. H. F. Stewart and E. K. Rand (Cambridge, Mass.: Harvard University Press, 1926), 85.

29. Edmund J. Fortman points out some further inconsistencies and hesitations in Boethius's own use of *substantia,* both for God's oneness and for his threeness. See Fortman, *The Triune God* (Grand Rapids: Baker, 1972), 163–64. Thomas Aquinas substituted the term *subsistence* for the term *substance* in this definition, in *ST,* 1.29.1.

istic.[30] Nevertheless, as we shall see later, many today advocate something like the Boethian definition in their defense of "social Trinitarianism."

7. Many writers have defined *person* as a relation within God. This definition seeks to avoid tritheism, but it poses difficulties of understanding. Gerald Bray finds this to be "a basic concept in Augustine's trinitarianism,"[31] and it becomes quite central to the understanding of Thomas Aquinas, who says:

> Distinction in the Godhead occurs only through relations of origin [paternity, filiation, procession]. . . . But a relation in the Godhead is not like an accident inhering in a subject. Instead, it is the divine essence itself. For that reason it is subsistent, just as the divine essence subsists. Therefore, just as deity is God, so divine paternity is God the Father, who is a divine person. 'Divine person', therefore, signifies a relation as subsisting.[32]

Cornelius Plantinga notes that Thomas also presents the persons as "real persons, just as they are in the Gospel of John."[33] But he finds Aquinas's "relation" doctrine to be inconsistent with his Johannine realism. Aquinas does, to be sure, indicate that the relations are different from one another: paternity is different from filiation, etc. But, says Plantinga,

> Thomas simplifies things so aggressively that even that difference is eventually washed out. For each person is identical with his relation: the Father just is paternity; the Son just is filiation; the Spirit just is procession. Further, these relations themselves, Thomas explicitly says, are all really the same thing as the divine essence. They differ from it only in intelligibility, only in perception, only notionally, not ontologically. For everything in the universe that is not the divine essence is a creature.[34]

As we saw in chapter 12, the doctrine of divine simplicity plays a large role in Aquinas's thought. Nothing in God is distinct from the divine essence—neither his attributes nor his Trinitarian persons. But if the persons are just

---

30. Fortman refers to Barth (*The Triune God*, 261), Rahner (p. 299), and others who oppose the idea of three "centers of consciousness" in God and consider it tritheistic. Compare also Johnson, *She Who Is*, 203. For Barth, see *ChD*, 4.1.204–5.

31. Gerald Bray, *The Doctrine of God* (Downers Grove, Ill.: InterVarsity Press, 1993), 173.

32. *ST*, 1.29.4c; cf. 1.32.2–3.

33. Cornelius Plantinga, "The Threeness/Oneness Problem of the Trinity," *Calvin Theological Journal* 23 (1988): 47.

34. Ibid. Thanks to Ralph A. Smith for his excellent critical summary of Plantinga's argument in *Paradox and Truth* (Tokyo: Covenant Worldview Institute, 2000).

alternative names of the divine essence, Plantinga objects, Aquinas's view is indistinguishable from modalism. And when we take *Father, Son,* and *Spirit* as names of relations (paternity, filiation, spiration), are we not reducing concrete persons to abstract ideas, denying the real personalism of the biblical accounts?

I agree with Plantinga that we should reject Aquinas's view that the three persons are distinct only notionally, only in our minds. That position is, in my view, indistinguishable from Sabellianism. There is real distinction, real complexity, in God, as I discussed in chapter 12. There I argued that God is not simple in the sense of lacking all complexity, but in the sense that each of his necessary attributes exhausts his being. We saw that each necessary attribute is a way of looking at God's complete nature. Each attribute, indeed, includes all the others: his love is eternal, his mercy is just, etc. But this kind of mutual perspectivalism does not exclude, but rather presupposes, complexity in the Godhead, for it is true to say that God is merciful, just, and eternal. His being is so complex that these and all his other attributes truly characterize him.

So now we can take a similar approach to the persons of the Trinity. Each exhausts the divine being; each bears all the divine attributes; indeed, each is in the other two (*circumincessio*). So when we encounter one person, we are encountering the triune God. But when we learn that the divine being contains everything described by the divine attributes, and everything in the three persons as well, we are impressed with the wonderfully rich complexity that is God. There is a real difference between the Son, praying in the garden to his Father, and the Father, hearing him in heaven. But both Son and Father belong to the rich complexity that is the divine essence, and both exhaust that essence.

Like Plantinga, I question Aquinas's definition of the persons of the Trinity as the relations of paternity, filiation, and spiration within the Godhead. Aquinas's concept of a "subsistent relation" is most odd. Relations do not subsist on their own, apart from the things they relate. Paternity doesn't exist by itself, apart from the persons (Father, Son) related to one another by paternity. And to suggest that *relation* is somehow a better term than *person* to designate the members of the Trinity is, I think, wrong. The persons are not "really" relations, rather than true persons. They are persons standing in relation.

Unlike Plantinga, I believe in a doctrine of divine simplicity that is sufficient to justify the identity of the persons and their relations to the whole divine nature. We may say, then, that the persons are identical to their relations; but, on my view, it is also true to say that the relations are identical to the persons. The doctrine of simplicity should not entail reductionism. The persons are identical to their relations, but they are not reducible to their relations; they are not mere relations. The persons are no more reducible to relations than the relations are reducible to the persons. The persons and the relations exist together; both categories exhaust the divine nature, and both express the complexity of the divine nature.

Plantinga argues that to define persons as relations implies reducing concrete personal beings to impersonal abstractions like paternity. My proposal, however, is that both persons and relations can be defined in terms of one another, belonging as they do to the fullness of the Godhead. Both ultimately encompass the whole Godhead, and the whole Godhead is concrete and personal, not abstract and impersonal. So the ultimate identity of persons and relations means not that persons are really abstractions, but that the abstractions are really personal.[35] Paternity, for example, is simply the Father, standing in relation to the Son.

8. So we can see that there are important relations between the persons of the Trinity and the personality of the Godhead (recall our discussion in chap. 2), though there are important distinctions to be made between them. Some theologians have maintained that in a sense the whole triune God is one person. B. B. Warfield, for example, argues that in the Old Testament (which contains only hints of the Trinitarian distinctions), "the great thing to be taught the ancient people of God was that the God of all the earth is one person."[36] A full account of the Trinity would have confused the ancient Hebrews, Warfield says, in the great battle between monotheism and polytheistic idolatry.

Cornelius Van Til says:

> It is sometimes asserted that we can prove to men that we are not asserting anything that they ought to consider irrational, inasmuch as we say that God is one in essence and three in person. We therefore claim that we have not asserted unity and trinity of exactly the same being.
>
> Yet this is not the whole truth of the matter. We do assert that God, that is, the whole Godhead, is one person.[37]

35. Recall that I made the same point in chapter 12 with regard to the divine attributes. To identify God with his attributes is not to say that he is an abstraction or a collection of abstract qualities. It is, rather, to insist that his attributes are fully personal. Interestingly, the argument that divine simplicity implies an abstract God was made by Cornelius Plantinga's brother, philosopher Alvin Plantinga, in *Does God Have a Nature?* (Milwaukee: Marquette University Press, 1980).

36. Benjamin Breckinridge Warfield, "The Spirit of God in the Old Testament," in *Biblical and Theological Studies* (Philadelphia: Presbyterian and Reformed, 1952), 153.

37. Cornelius Van Til, *An Introduction to Systematic Theology* (Nutley, N.J.: Presbyterian

704   THE TRIUNE GOD

Van Til is not teaching here the contradictory position that God is one person and three persons in the same sense of *person*, although Gordon Clark accused him of that.[38] In the quoted passage, Van Til's "we" joins him to those who "claim that we have not asserted unity and trinity of exactly the same being." He only wishes to say that "this is not the whole truth of the matter." And indeed it is not, if only because the whole truth is beyond human understanding.

As I said in chapter 2, we should not deny that personality is an attribute of God. That God is personal, rather than impersonal, is a central teaching of Scripture, over against nonbiblical religions and philosophies. And if God is personal, and God is one, then surely in a sense he is one person. Indeed, through most of the Old Testament, except for some Trinitarian adumbrations, God acts as a single person: planning, creating, governing, speaking, redeeming, and judging.

When we speak of God as a person, or as personal, we are using *person* in a sense that is different from its Trinitarian use. The personality of the Godhead does not add a fourth person to the three, nor another relation, in the technical sense. However, the two senses are related, especially if we interpret the Trinitarian concept of person in a somewhat Boethian sense. For each of these persons exhausts the Godhead, and each person is in and with the other two. The Godhead is personal, because it is tripersonal. Being three persons, the Godhead cannot help but be personal, rather than impersonal, in character.

9. Since God's substance is personal, the Trinitarian persons are also substantival. They are each a subject of predication. They are distinct from one another, and each has some property that distinguishes it from the others. In the traditional vocabulary, these properties are unbegottenness (the Father), begottenness (the Son), and passive spiration (the Spirit).[39] Theologians have taken care to call these personal properties rather than attributes of God. Attributes, in the usual theological vocabulary, belong to

---

and Reformed, 1974), 229. See my discussion of this passage in *CVT*, 65–71. Aquinas also says (in a rather obscure discussion of number) that in one sense God is one person: see *ST*, 1.30.3. And of course more recent thinkers like Barth and Rahner, who object to the idea of three "centers of consciousness" in God, would agree. See *ChD*, 1.1.400, 414–15; Weber, *Foundations of Dogmatics*, 1:377.

38. Clark's criticism was presented in a taped lecture. See the formulation of John Robbins, Clark's disciple, in *Cornelius Van Til: The Man and the Myth* (Jefferson, Md.: Trinity Foundation, 1986), 20—a booklet that I do not recommend as an analysis or critique of Van Til.

39. For more discussion of these personal properties, see below.

the whole divine nature and to all three persons, while personal properties belong to only one of the persons.

But the personal properties are attributes grammatically and metaphysically. Certainly the Father, the Son, and the Spirit are beings, subjects of predication, as is the Godhead as a whole. The persons are, in the Greek terminology, *hypostaseis*. Boethius was not unreasonable (though he was terminologically awkward) in calling them *substances*. And the personal properties are predicates of those substantival subjects, attributes of the persons. And since each person exhausts the divine nature, the personal properties are predicates of the divine nature, attributes of God. God is a Father (Mal. 1:6; John 5:18; 1 John 3:1), a Son (John 1:1, 14, 18), and a Spirit (John 4:24).

But how can the three persons be distinct from each other when each is coterminous with the whole divine being? I believe that my account of divine simplicity, in which the identity of everything divine with the divine being indicates (rather than negates) the complexity of this being, is of some help. Simplicity embraces distinctness, rather than canceling it out. That God is a Father, a Son, and a Spirit indicates real complexity in God's nature, a nature that encompasses real distinctions. *Father, Son, and Spirit* are not synonyms. Each says something different, something distinct, about God. And each refers to something different about God. But we do not know the precise nature of that complexity-in-unity.

Again, we must acknowledge our ignorance of the precise distinction between substance and person in God and of the precise interactions between these. God has given us, in Scripture, a glimpse into his inner life, but only a glimpse.[40] The Trinity is not an irrational doctrine, but it is highly mysterious. It is not contradictory, but we do not always see clearly how apparent contradictions can be resolved.

Theologians have too often made global statements about God's ineffability, his "wholly otherness," but in the details of their theology have claimed micro- and macroscopic knowledge of the divine being. I prefer that we make no global statements about God's unknowability, but that we be more modest in admitting, concretely and specifically, what we do not know. This warning is especially needed when we come to Trinitarian theology.

---

40. Vern S. Poythress puts it better, perhaps, by saying that these concepts should be used "analogically," in "Reforming Ontology and Logic in the Light of the Trinity," *WTJ* 57 (1995): 216. I shall describe this article and Poythress's concept of analogy later in this chapter.

THE ONTOLOGICAL AND ECONOMIC TRINITIES

The *ontological* Trinity (sometimes called the immanent[41] Trinity) is the Trinity as it exists necessarily and eternally, apart from creation. It is, like God's attributes, what God necessarily is. The *economic* Trinity is the Trinity in its relation to creation, including the specific roles played by the Trinitarian persons throughout the history of creation, providence, and redemption. These are roles that the persons of the Trinity have freely entered into; they are not necessary to their being.[42]

Sabellianism denies that the Trinity is ontological; for the modalist, Father, Son, and Spirit are not the nature of God, but only roles that God assumes in history. Arianism, similarly, teaches that the three persons are not necessary to the being of God, for the Son and the Spirit are creations of the one true God, the Father, who is monopersonal. But the biblical position is that God is a Trinity both ontologically (eternally and necessarily) and economically (as he relates to creatures).

Many recent theologians, such as Barth and Rahner, have argued that the ontological/economic distinction is faulty, creating too large a separation between God's nature and his revelation of himself in history. There are three principles that they particularly wish to guard by this critique. First, God reveals himself as he really and truly is. His economic dealings with us, particularly his revelation in Scripture, do not distort his true nature. Second, the incarnate life of Jesus is itself an aspect of the life of the eternal Son of God. The actions and experiences of Jesus in time are actions and experiences of God. Third, the economic roles played by the three persons must be appropriate to their natures. That the Son, rather than the Father or the Spirit, became incarnate, was a decision made freely by the persons of the Trinity, but not an arbitrary one.

I believe, however, that it is too much to say, with Rahner, that "the 'economic' Trinity is the 'immanent' Trinity and the 'immanent' Trinity is the

---

41. Do not confuse this use of *immanent* with the immanence of God, discussed in chapter 7. The two concepts are nearly opposite to one another. The immanent Trinity is the Trinity apart from creation; the immanence of God as a lordship attribute is God's involvement with his creatures. Trinitarian immanence is the presence of God with himself, rather than with creation, although of course the immanent Trinity does enter into relations with creation. In entering into these relations, it does not become anything other than it is immanently or ontologically.

42. Compare our discussion of necessity and freedom in chapter 12, and of the distinctions between God's necessary attributes and his free attributes (necessary and free will, knowledge, speech) in other chapters.

'economic' Trinity."[43] There is a difference between what God is necessarily and what he freely chooses to do in his plan for creation.

ETERNAL GENERATION

In human life, a child's existence begins in an event called begetting or generation. The same was true of the incarnate Christ: Jesus was begotten in the womb of Mary by the power of the Holy Spirit. Now many theologians have asked if there is an analogous event in the eternal realm. As we have seen, Jesus is the Son of God, not only in his earthly life, but also eternally. His sonship is ontological, not merely economic. The begetting of Jesus in the womb of his mother was a historical event, an economic event. Can we also speak of an ontological begetting, an eternal generation, to which he owes his eternal sonship?

Many have dismissed this question (and the answers to it) as speculative, and there is some truth in this criticism. But we should give attention to this discussion because of its prominence in the history of doctrine, and also because it deals with real concerns of faith.

Our faith moves us to worship Jesus as the Son of God, in the power of the Spirit. So it is legitimate for us to ask what it means for Jesus to be the Son, and for the Spirit to be the Spirit. As we have seen, these titles, understood biblically, imply that both persons are divine. But do they teach us anything more than that?

The divine Son and Spirit are analogous to human sonship and spirituality. But how far does the analogy reach? Human sons are younger than their fathers, but this is not true of the divine Son, who exists in eternity alongside his father. Human sons are born weak, ignorant, and sinful, but not the divine Son, who shares his Father's perfections through all eternity. So our concept of divine sonship must be refined, purged of connotations that are inappropriate to an infinite being. But after all the refining, what is left? Does Jesus' sonship have anything in common with ours?

A common answer has been that both divine and human sonship are the result of *generation*, of *begetting*. Thus, the Nicene Creed (revised in 381) confesses faith in "one Lord Jesus Christ, the only begotten Son of God, begotten from the Father before all time, Light from Light, true God from true God, begotten not created." But what is this begetting? The idea of begetting, like the idea of sonship, must be refined, if it is to refer to God. Among human beings, begetting normally occurs in a sexual relationship.

43. Karl Rahner, *The Trinity* (New York: Seabury Press, 1974), 22. Cf. *ChD*, 1.1.8–15, 358.

It occurs in time, so that a human being who did not exist at one time comes into existence at a later time. But eternal begetting is surely neither sexual nor temporal, nor does it bring into existence someone who otherwise would not have existed, for God is a necessary being, and all three divine persons share the attribute of necessary existence. .

After we have refined the concept, then, what is left of the idea of eternal begetting? Or should we discard that idea as part of our refining of the term *Son?*

Some have described eternal generation as the "origin" or "cause" of the Son.[44] But that notion poses serious problems.[45] God has no origin or cause, and if the Son is fully God, then he has no origin or cause either. He is *a se.* He has within himself the complete ground of his existence. Is begetting the cause of the Son in the sense of the divine act that *maintains his existence, so that he constantly depends on the Father?*[46] But this idea would imply that the Son's existence is contingent, rather than necessary; it, too, would compromise the aseity of the Son.

Most insist that eternal causality or origin must be distinguished from causes and origins in the finite world, by not being temporal. It is not by the Father's choice or will, but by his nature—or by his necessary will, rather than his free will.

Certainly creation *ex nihilo* is inappropriate within the Godhead, as the church insisted over against the Arians. But then what is it that eternal generation generates? If eternal generation does not confer existence on the Son, what does it confer? Some have claimed that by it, the Father communicates the divine nature to the Son. Zacharias Ursinus wrote, "The Son is the second person, because the Deity is

---

44. *RD,* 115: "This intrapersonal relationship results in the distinction of the divine persons according to origin, order and operation. . . . As therefore the Son has his existence from the Father, and the H. Spirit His from the Father and from the Son, so too in divine action the Father's will takes precedence." Likewise, the Eastern Orthodox theologian Vladimir Lossky, quoted in Fortman, *The Triune God,* 280, says, "The Father is called the cause of the Persons of the Son and the Holy Spirit," although, Lossky adds, "this unique cause is not prior to his effects. . . . He is not superior to his effects." These are, Lossky says, "relations of origin." Olin Curtis even says, "The Father is the causal ground of the Son's existence," in *The Christian Faith* (Grand Rapids: Kregel, 1971).

45. Speaking of the Cappadocian theology, Gerald Bray says, "It is difficult to see what 'cause' can mean when speaking of an eternal person, and all too easy to reflect that the word represents a lingering trace of pre-Nicene subordinationism, which held that there was a time when the Son (and the Spirit) did not exist" (*The Doctrine of God,* 159).

46. This idea would be similar to the idea of creation as a continuous process; see chapter 15.

communicated to him of the Father by eternal generation."[47] Calvin, however, attacked that position, arguing that "whosoever says that the Son has been given his essence from the Father denies that he has being from himself."[48] If the Son's deity is derived,[49] then, says Calvin, the Son is not *a se*. But if he is not *a se, autotheos,* God in himself, he cannot be divine.

But then what is it that the Father confers upon the Son in eternal generation? According to Calvin, what the Son receives from the Father is not his divine essence, but his personhood:

> Therefore we say that deity in an absolute sense exists of itself; whence likewise we confess that the Son since he is God, exists of himself, but not in relation to his Person; indeed, since he is the Son, we say that he exists from the Father.[50]

Calvin is apparently saying that the Son receives his sonship from the Father, but neither his existence nor his divine nature. He is the Son because the Father has made him the Son. But what does that mean? It could be taken to mean merely that *Father* and *Son* are reciprocal terms. A person cannot be a son unless he has a father. And since the reverse is also true, we could say that just as the Son receives his sonship from the Father, so the Father receives his fatherhood from the Son. That would be a clear understanding of the relationship, and rather obvious, but trivial. Certainly it does not suggest anything closely analogous to human begetting.

But Calvin and others in the Reformed tradition seem to have a more unidirectional concept in mind: the Father is the origin of the Father-Son relationship, in some way that the Son is not. But what does it mean to be the originator or creator of a relationship in which one stands necessarily and eternally? Certainly we should not imagine that a unitarian God, by executing some eternal process, became triune. Nor should we imagine that the Father, existing eternally with two other unnamed beings, somehow acted to make them his Son and his Spirit, respectively.

The terms *Father* and *Son* bring to our minds the idea of generation. But when we try to apply that idea to the divine being, words fail us. When we try to refine it, to make it appropriate to the divine being, its meaning seems to slip away from us. Can Scripture help us to formulate a clearer concept

---

47. Ursinus, *Commentary on the Heidelberg Catechism* (Cincinnati: T. P. Bucher, 1851), 135.

48. *Institutes,* 1.13.23. Compare B. B. Warfield's discussion in *Biblical Doctrines* (Edinburgh: Banner of Truth, 1988), 171.

49. The notion of derived deity is oxymoronic.

50. *Institutes,* 1.13.25.

of eternal generation? Let us explore some of the biblical data used by theologians to prove and explain the doctrine.

1. Many have emphasized, as I did in the preceding chapter, that Jesus' sonship is eternal and ontological, not merely temporal. So, they have concluded, he must have been begotten, not only temporally, but eternally as well. But what does *begetting* mean in this context? If it is merely a verbal form of the noun *Son*, taking *Son* to mean "one begotten," then the conclusion follows trivially. Eternal sonship implies eternal begetting, because that is what sonship means. But this reasoning doesn't tell us anything about eternal begetting beyond what we already know about sonship. On this basis, sonship and begetting are simply alternate ways of saying the same thing: to be a Son is to be begotten, and to be begotten is to be a Son. The doctrine of eternal generation on this basis is verbally superfluous.

On the other hand, if begetting is an event prior to sonship, one that brings sonship into being, then the conclusion does not follow at all. The fact that Jesus' incarnate sonship is due to an act of begetting (Luke 1:35) does not imply that Jesus' eternal sonship is also the result of begetting. Obviously there are major differences between the origin of Jesus' earthly sonship and the origin of his eternal sonship. As I indicated earlier, the concept of sonship is subject to theological refinement. For example, no one would argue that since Jesus' earthly sonship began in the womb of a woman, his eternal sonship must also have begun there (or in some analogous place). The idea of begetting is, *prima facie*, also inappropriate to God. Should it not also be dropped in the interest of theological refinement? Apart from other biblical data, there is no reason to conclude that begetting is more appropriate to the ontological Trinity than gestation in the womb.

2. Some have argued from the term *monogenēs*, which Scripture applies to Christ (e.g., John 1:14, 18; 3:16), that the Son is eternally begotten. The KJV translates this term "only begotten." Recent translations, however, have preferred such translations as "only," "unique," or "one and only." The debate concerns both etymology and usage. The etymological question is whether the *genēs* in *monogenēs* comes from *gennaō* ("beget") or from *genos* ("kind, genus"). In my view, a good case can still be made for the former view of the etymology.[51] On the question of usage, I agree with Lee Irons[52]

51. See Lee Irons, "The Eternal Generation of the Son," available at http://members.aol.com/ironslee/private/Monogenes.htm. As Irons points out, however, the usage of the term is far more important than the etymology in determining meaning—a point definitively argued by James Barr in *The Semantics of Biblical Language* (Oxford: Oxford University Press, 1961).

52. Irons, "The Eternal Generation of the Son."

and John V. Dahms[53] that the uses of *monogenēs* in John should be taken in the traditional way, based on considerations of context and intelligibility. On John 1:18, "the only begotten God, who is in the Father's bosom, has made him known" (Irons' translation), Irons comments:

> The NIV completely misses the point ("God the One and Only . . . has made him known"), for it is not the fact that the Son is the only God (as opposed to another god) but the fact that he is begotten of God (and thus truly God) which enables him to make God known.[54]

The other *monogenēs* texts, in my view, are also consistent with this understanding of the term.

These considerations, then, justify the language of eternal generation.[55] But, in my judgment, the *monogenēs* texts tell us very little about the nature of that generation. "Begotten" is little more than a synonym for "Son." If it suggests or presupposes an event prior to Christ's sonship, by which he became the Son, it certainly does not describe that event. "Only begotten" stresses the unique status of this Son over against all creatures, over against any other being that might be called a son of God,[56] but "only" adds nothing to our understanding of the nature of divine begetting. Certainly the texts employing *monogenēs* will not enable us to decide whether the generation is of existence, divine essence, or personhood, or what a communication of personhood, if that is the nature of eternal generation, might mean.

3. A third consideration, only hinted at in the literature, is this: Although it is improper to assume an exact correspondence between human sonship and divine sonship, nevertheless the former ought to be similar to the latter. That the Son, rather than the Father or Spirit, became incarnate, was not arbitrarily decided by God. There must have been some reason why it was more appropriate for the Son to become incarnate than for the Father or the Spirit to do so.

---

53. John V. Dahms, "The Johannine Use of *Monogenēs* Reconsidered," *New Testament Studies* 29 (1983): 222–32. F. F. Bruce, also, in *The Gospel of John* (Grand Rapids: Eerdmans, 1984), 65, n. 26, says that the evangelist may himself have associated (informally, not as an expert on etymology) *monogenēs* with *gennaō*, drawing parallels with our new begetting or birth from God.

54. Irons, "The Eternal Generation of the Son."

55. However, the understanding of *monogenēs* underlying this argument is controversial. So I do not believe that the doctrine should be made a test of orthodoxy on the basis of this argument.

56. This stress, of course, is shared by the interpretation of *monogenēs* that derives it from *genos*.

Thus, the fact that Jesus was begotten and born in history does give us some hints as to his eternal nature. His earthly begetting images something of his eternal relationship to the Father. I would suggest that perhaps the phrase "eternal generation" could be taken to designate that parallel. To say that the Son is eternally generated from the Father is to say that something about his eternal nature makes it appropriate for him to be begotten in time.

As we thus meditate on the nature of Jesus' eternal sonship, we should not confine our attention to his begetting. As Pannenberg says:

> Relations among the three persons that are defined as mutual self-distinction cannot be reduced to relations of origin in the traditional sense. The Father does not merely beget the Son. He also hands over his Kingdom to him and receives it back from him. The Son is not merely begotten of the Father. He is also obedient to him and he thereby glorifies him as the one God. The Spirit is not just breathed. He also fills the Son and glorifies him in his obedience to the Father, thereby glorifying the Father himself. In so doing he leads into all truth (John 16:13) and searches out the deep things of Godhead (1 Cor. 2:10–11).[57]

Along with the Son's eternal generation, then, we can speak of his eternal obedience and eternal glorification of the Father. But these assertions (including the assertion of eternal generation) should not be the subject of microscopic analysis and rigid enforcement as tests of orthodoxy. They are biblical hints as to the nature of the eternal relationship between the Father and the Son.

To summarize: the biblical data authorize us to speak of the eternal generation of the Son, and it is certainly appropriate for the church to confess the statements of the Nicene Creed quoted earlier. But they do not describe this eternal relationship in any detail. We know at least that *Son* is not an arbitrary title; the eternal Son is analogous to human sons in some way. Negatively, we should reject the idea that the Father gives existence to the Son by a creative act and the idea that the Father confers divine essence upon the Son, giving him a derived deity. Whether we confess that the Father confers sonship upon the Son should await further clarification of the idea.

A certain amount of reverent agnosticism is appropriate here. There is much that the Bible does not reveal about the relationship of the Son to the Father. Charles Hodge says:

---

57. Wolfhart Pannenberg, *Systematic Theology* (Grand Rapids: Eerdmans, 1991), 320.

The relation, therefore, of the Second Person to the First is that of filiation or sonship. But what is meant by the term, neither the Bible nor the ancient creeds explain. It may be sameness of nature; as a son is of the same nature as his father. It may be likeness, and the term Son be equivalent to *eikōn, apaugasma, charaktēr,* or *logos,* or revealer. It may be derivation of essence, as a son, in one sense, is derived from his father. Or, it may be something altogether inscrutable and to us incomprehensible.[58]

And Robert Dabney says:

[This doctrine] seems to me rather a rational explanation of revealed facts, than a revealed fact itself. On such a subject, therefore, none should dogmatize.[59]

Earlier, Dabney expresses his concerns more strongly:

The discussions and definitions of the more formal and scholastic Theologians, concerning the personal distinctions in the Godhead, have always seemed to me to present a striking instance of the reluctance of the human mind to confess its own weakness. For, let any read them with the closest attention, and he will perceive that he has acquired little more than a set of terms, whose abstruseness serves to conceal from him their practical lack of meaning.[60]

What the Bible reveals is that there is one God in three persons, persons related to one another as Father, Son, and Spirit. Much of the rest of Trinitarian theology, one suspects, is an attempt to get beyond this fundamental truth by multiplying forms of *Father, Son,* and *Spirit.* When we are told, for example, that there are four "relations" in the Godhead, namely *paternity, filiation,* and *active and passive spiration (procession),* we get the impression that we are being taught something beyond the meaning conveyed by *Father, Son,* and *Spirit.* But is that impression correct? Does *eternal generation* mean anything more than that the Father is eternally Father and the Son is eternally Son? Do we know anything more about eternal gen-

58. Charles Hodge, *Systematic Theology* (reprint, Grand Rapids: Eerdmans, n.d.), 1:468. He adds, "The Nicene fathers, instead of leaving the matter where the Scriptures leave it, undertake to explain what is meant by sonship, and teach that it means derivation of essence."

59. Robert L. Dabney, *Lectures in Systematic Theology* (reprint, Grand Rapids: Zondervan, 1972), 205.

60. Ibid., 202.

eration than that? Much of this reflection, it seems to me, really amounts to putting the names of the three persons into different forms, without any increase in knowledge or edification. I have tried to treat these discussions with respect and to point out what I think can be gained from them. But I confess that I cannot escape the notion that at least some of this discussion amounts to playing with words.

ETERNAL PROCESSION

The same question arises in the case of the Holy Spirit. The Father and the Son send the Spirit to earth (on Pentecost and other occasions), so that he *proceeds* from them. The names of the Spirit in the original languages, *ruah* and *pneuma*, suggest the image of divine breath: the Spirit proceeds from God as our breath proceeds from our mouths. Now the question arises: is there an eternal procession of the Spirit from the Father and the Son (or just from the Father, as held by the Eastern church) analogous to his processions in history?

The church has used the word *procession* (*ekporeusis, emanatio*), rather than *generation or begetting*, as in the case of the Son, to designate the Spirit's eternal "relation of origin." These different words are used because *begetting* obviously pertains to the Son (especially as *monogenēs*), but not to the Spirit, and because *procession* corresponds somewhat to the biblical ideas of sending and breathing. *Procession* is a somewhat broader term than *generation*, conveying less specific imagery. But many theologians have expressed ignorance as to how procession differs from generation. Heppe quotes Sohnius as saying,

> What the property (procession) is and, as it were, the formal distinction between generation and procession . . . the doctors of the Early Church *Augustine* and the *Damascene* and others admit their ignorance since it has not been expressly defined in God's Word.[61]

Alting adds, "*Ekporeusis* is distinguished from generation. But how, we don't know."[62]

As with the eternal generation of the Son, questions arise about the meaning of the eternal procession of the Spirit. Does it refer to a derivation of existence? Of deity? Of personhood? And if so, what does that mean? These questions have not been discussed as much in regard to the Spirit

---

61. *RD*, 130. See also *DG*, 312–13.
62. *RD*, 130.

as in regard to the Son, but they are equally difficult in the present discussion, and they lead to similar conclusions. My discussion of them would essentially repeat my treatment of eternal generation, so I will not say more on these topics here.

What is the biblical evidence for the eternal procession of the Spirit? That, too, is parallel to that of the previous section:

1. It would be odd if Scripture presented generation as the relationship between the Father and the Son, but said nothing about the relationship between them and the Spirit. So we should expect to find some relationship involving the Spirit in Scripture, such as the theological tradition calls *procession*. Of course, we must see what we actually do find, and not just look for what we expect to find.

2. The term *Spirit* and the primary biblical model of the Spirit (that is, breath) suggest derivation. But, as with *Son*, this does not tell us anything specific about that derivation. As with the Son's generation, we want to ask what is being derived: existence? deity? spirithood? And we want to know the meanings of these things. But Scripture doesn't tell us much, if anything, that enables us to describe the nature of procession, beyond the fact itself.

3. Although there is no biblical term applied to the Spirit comparable to *monogenēs*, there is one biblical text that has often been thought to teach the Spirit's eternal procession, namely, John 15:26, where Jesus says:

> When the Counselor comes, whom I will send to you from the Father, the Spirit of truth who goes out from the Father, he will testify about me.

The "sending" here is, of course, temporal rather than eternal. But "goes out" is the Greek *ekporeuetai*, which is often translated "proceeds." This verb is in the present tense, so it does not refer to the future sending (at Pentecost) of the previous clause. Many writers, therefore, have understood this verse to teach the eternal procession of the Spirit. That interpretation, however, is by no means obvious. In my view, the Spirit's present procession may simply be the regular way in which the Spirit enters the world to do God's business. Jesus is saying that he will send the Spirit, whom the Father regularly sends into the world (upon prophets, kings, and Jesus himself), on a special future occasion to bear witness to him. As the Spirit has gone out from the Father to rest on Jesus, so the Spirit will come to the apostles at Jesus' behest. On this interpretation, John 15:26 does not explicitly teach the eternal procession of the Spirit.

4. However, I would suggest here that the historical processions of the Spirit from the Father are *appropriate* to the Spirit's eternal relationship

within the Godhead. The Spirit is the member of the Trinity whom the Father and the Son send, over and over again, to do their business on earth. Unlike the Son, he is not generated or born as a human being. He comes like breath or wind (John 3), invisibly, but with an intimate relationship to creatures. He transforms them from within. We should regard this sort of ministry as appropriate to the Spirit, as generation is appropriate to the Son. It is not an accident, not an arbitrary divine choice, that the Spirit is regularly the one who *is sent*, who *descends*, who *comes* into our world from the Father and the Son. So perhaps there is value in defining eternal procession as that quality of the Spirit which makes it appropriate for him to receive these missions from the Father and the Son and to proceed as he does into the temporal world.[63]

But, as with generation, Scripture does not give us any detailed information about the nature of the Spirit's eternal procession. Again, exhortations to theological modesty are in order.

FILIOQUE

The Nicene Creed, as reformulated at the Council of Constantinople in 381, confesses faith in "the Holy Spirit, the Lord and life-giver, who proceeds from the Father." John Leith notes:

> In the West the original text "who proceeds from the Father" was altered to read "from the Father and the Son [*filioque*]." This alteration is rooted in the theology of the Western Church, in particular the theology of Augustine. The procession from the Son was vigorously affirmed by the Council at Toledo in 589 and gradually was added to the creed, though it was not accepted as part of the creed at Rome until a number of centuries had passed.[64]

The Eastern church did not look with favor upon this change and thought it arrogant of the Western churches to alter an ecumenical statement of faith without consulting their Eastern brothers. This doctrinal issue was one of the main causes of the schism between the Eastern and Western churches that occurred in 1054 and continues to the present.

I am inclined to agree with the Eastern Christians that the Western church

---

63. The reader should review the quote from Pannenberg in the last section: the Spirit's distinctive property is not only procession, but also filling and glorifying the Son, leading into all truth, etc.

64. John Leith, *Creeds of the Churches* (Richmond: John Knox Press, 1973), 32.

should not have modified the creed without the consent of the whole church. But in this book, I am, of course, concerned with doctrinal issues rather than church polity. So I shall consider what the Bible has to say about whether the Spirit proceeds from the Father only, or from the Father and the Son.

The East, following the lead of the Cappadocian fathers, focuses on the Father as "the fountain of deity" and then asks how the other persons are related to him. The West, following Augustine, focuses more on the whole Godhead, the simple divine nature, and then asks how there can be three persons within that simple nature and how those persons are related to one another. As we have seen, the Western tradition has been tempted in a Sabellian direction, to reduce the concrete persons to "relations." But the West has sometimes charged the East with subordinationism (as in Calvin's critique of the notion of "derived deity").

Western thinkers have wanted to see everything in God in relation to everything else in God, emphasizing the *circumincessio* (which, to be sure, is also affirmed in the East). So for them, at least as the East sees it, the existence of the Son and the Spirit is due primarily to their necessary existence as God, not to a particular act of the Father, although Western theologians also frequently affirm that the Father is "the fountain of deity."

Eastern theologians tend to see the Western position as compromising the concreteness and integrity of the three divine persons, as if the Spirit's existence comes, not from the Father or the Son or both, as concrete persons, but from the divine nature generally.

I shall have more to say later about the two Trinitarian models that here confront one another. In general, my view is that both are legitimate, and that neither, as a model, resolves the specific question before us. But these models are important to the controversy, for they indicate why some of the more specific arguments weigh more heavily in Eastern theology and others in Western theology. Let us consider some of the more specific arguments:

1. Eastern theologians claim that John 15:26 refers the Spirit's procession (*ekporeuetai*) exclusively to the Father. But Western theologians point out that in that very verse, it is Jesus who sends the Spirit to the disciples. I have argued that the reference of *ekporeuetai* to eternal procession has not been established. If my understanding is correct, then both the procession and the sending mentioned in the verse take place in history. Now that understanding does not make the verse irrelevant to the doctrine of eternal procession, for, as we have seen, it is legitimate to find an analogy between the historical and the eternal relationships among the persons of the Trinity. But if both the procession and the sending of John 15:26 take place in time, that would support, by analogy, the Western view that the Spirit's eternal procession is from both the Father and the Son.

718 THE TRIUNE GOD

2. Some Western theologians claim that the Eastern view separates the Spirit from Christ. If the Spirit proceeds only from the Father, rather than from Jesus, they say, then we can come to the Father by the Spirit apart from Jesus, leading to a kind of mysticism rather than a cross-centered piety. Some Eastern theologians, in turn, charge that it is the West that encourages mysticism, for Western theology ascribes eternal procession, in the end, to a vague, abstract "Godhead," rather than to the concrete person of the Father. However, I find little evidence to support any of these charges. Mysticism has arisen in both the East and the West, regardless of their views on eternal procession. Contrary to Western charges, Eastern Christians do make Jesus a central object of devotion. Practically speaking, there is no reason to think that they approach God apart from Christ. Furthermore, Eastern theologians have been willing to say that the Spirit proceeds from the Father *through* the Son, or from the Father *to rest on* Christ (after the model of Jesus' baptism).[65] Both of these models, it seems to me, encourage Christ-centered piety. Finally, contrary to Eastern claims, Western theology, despite its particular concern for the unity of the Godhead, does not teach that the Spirit proceeds from the Godhead, but rather from the Father and the Son.

3. Western thinkers have sometimes criticized the Eastern view as subordinationist, for in the procession of the Spirit, the Father and the Son are not equal. However, it is surely not subordinationist merely to draw a distinction between the activities of the Father and the Son. Why, then, does this particular distinction indicate subordinationism? Even on the Western view, the roles of the persons in generation and procession are not identical to one another.

4. The analogy between the eternal and temporal proceedings of the Spirit favors the Western view. As we have seen, both the Father and the Son send the Spirit into the world, and Scripture frequently refers to the Spirit both as "the Spirit of God" and as "the Spirit of Christ." It refers once to "the Spirit of your Father" (Matt. 10:20). The mission of the Spirit is to testify about Christ (John 15:26).

5. But it is dangerous to develop doctrines only on the basis of analogy. And even if John 15:26 does constitute a proof text for one position or the other, the church has usually not seen fit to create tests of orthodoxy on the basis of only one proof text. Although I somewhat prefer the Western formulation, I think both the East and the West were unwise to divide over this issue. Neither view should have been made a test of orthodoxy.

6. We should remember that Scripture gives us no precise definition of

65. See, for example, Bray, *The Doctrine of God*, 157.

person or *substance*, or of *generation* or *procession*. The best arguments for eternal generation and procession are based on analogy, rather than explicit biblical teaching or logical inference from explicit teaching. These considerations should moderate our advocacy of either position. Again, theological humility is in order. God has given us a glimpse of his inner life, not a map or a treatise.

SUBORDINATION

The fourth-century battle in the church over the Trinity focused mostly on the subordinationism of the Arian party. The Arians taught that the Son and the Spirit were creatures and thus were not of the same nature (*homoousios*) as the Father, but subordinate beings. Orthodox, Nicene Trinitarianism denied that the Son and the Spirit were ontologically subordinate, insisting that they were divine in the same sense as the Father— equal to him in glory, sharing with him the divine nature with all the divine attributes.

But although the church has officially denied the *ontological* subordination of Arianism, it has affirmed *economic* subordination among the persons of the Trinity. That is, the persons of the Trinity voluntarily subordinate themselves to one another in the roles they perform in respect to creation. As we have seen, the Father sends the Son into the world, and the Son joyfully obeys his Father's will. On earth, the Son does only what his Father gives him to do (and even knows only what the Father gives him to know [Matt. 24:36]). In the end, he delivers up the kingdom to his Father (1 Cor. 15:24) and himself becomes one of the subjects in his Father's kingdom (v. 28). When the Spirit enters the world, he does not speak of himself (John 16:13), but only what he hears (presumably from the Father and the Son). And, as I pointed out in the section on "mutual glorification," the Father also defers to the Son and the Spirit in various ways.

So we may summarize by saying that biblical Trinitarianism denies ontological subordination, but affirms economic subordination of various kinds. But there is a third kind of subordination that has been debated for many centuries and has been much discussed in recent literature. That might be called eternal subordination of *role*.

Both Eastern and Western thinkers have regularly affirmed that God the Father has some sort of primacy over the other two persons. Theologians have used phrases like *fons deitatis* ("fountain of deity") and *fons trinitatis* ("fountain of the Trinity") to describe the Father's distinct role in the Trinity.[66] That the Father has some sort of primacy is implicit in the name Father, and of course the doctrines of eternal generation and procession suggest that the Father has some sort of unique "originative" role. So the church has generally spoken of the Father as the "first" person of the Trinity, and the Son and the Spirit as the "second" and "third" persons, respectively. Furthermore, if, as I have claimed, the economic activities of the persons are analogous to their eternal relationships, then the forms of economic subordination mentioned above suggest a pattern. The Son and the Spirit are voluntarily subordinate to the commands of the Father, because that kind of subordination is appropriate to their eternal nature as persons. (But, we should recall, the Father defers to the Son and the Spirit, honoring and glorifying them as they honor and glorify him.)

This kind of subordination is not the ontological subordination of Arius. Nor is it merely economic, for it has to do with the eternal nature of the persons, the personal properties that distinguish each one from the others. Dahms calls it "essential and eternal,"[67] but perhaps "essential" is misleading in this context, since it suggests a difference in nature, whereas orthodoxy teaches that the three persons have the same nature, essence, and being. But it is right to describe this difference of role as eternal. We may put it this way: There is no subordination within the divine nature that is shared among the persons: the three are equally God. However, there is a subordination of role among the persons, which constitutes part of the distinctiveness of each. Because of that subordination of role, the persons subordinate themselves to one another in their economic relationships with creation.

But how can one person be subordinate to another in his eternal role while being equal to the other in his divine nature? Or, to put it differently, how can subordination of role be compatible with divinity? Does not the very idea of divinity exclude this sort of subordination?

The biblical answer, I think, is no. Scripture presents God, even the Father, as one who serves, who accepts affliction for his people. See my discussion of God's power in weakness (in chap. 23), of his suffering love (in chap. 26), and of mutual glorification (earlier in this chapter). Even more obviously, the incarnate Son comes into the world as the Lord, but not as the lords of the Gentiles (Matt. 20:25–28). He is the servant-king, who rules for the benefit of his people, and who calls the rulers of his church to

---

66. This is a central point in the theology of the Cappadocian fathers. See, for example, Fortman, *The Triune God*, 76. Among Reformation thinkers, see Ursinus, *Commentary on the Heidelberg Catechism*, 135.

67. John V. Dahms, "The Subordination of the Son," *JETS* 37 (1994): 351–64.

do the same. Subordination, in the sense of serving others in love, is clearly a divine attribute, one that serves as an explicit model for our behavior. Such service does not compromise the full deity of the Son and the Spirit; rather, it manifests their deity.

This eternal hierarchy of role may account for some of the language in Scripture about the Father being "greater" than the Son (John 14:28), about the Son being able to do nothing of himself (John 5:19), and so on. See my discussion of these passages in the preceding chapter.

Subordination of role has become an important topic in recent evangelical theological discussion, largely in relation to feminism. Some have argued that there is no subordination of any sort within the Godhead, and therefore that the Trinity is a completely egalitarian society. The Trinity supposedly thus provides a model for an egalitarian human society, in which gender, for example, plays no part in determining a person's role in family, church, or society.[68] Advocates of this view insist that any distinction of role based on gender demeans those in subordinate roles.

In reply, other writers have made a case for the "eternal subordination" of the Son and the Spirit, as I have done above.[69] They argue that there is a hierarchy of role within the Trinity, and that that hierarchy does not compromise the equality of nature, glory, and honor among the persons. Accordingly, hierarchies of role in human society, even those based on gender, do not demean those who are subordinate to higher authorities.

Again, we should be careful of trying to derive too much by way of analogy between the historical appearances of the Trinitarian persons and their eternal relations. But I do think that analogy at least suggests eternal roles of submission within the Trinity, which do not detract in the least from the intrinsic deity of each person.

Should we regard this Trinitarian hierarchy as a model for human society? Scripture does teach that human beings were created in the image of God and ought to be like God in their conduct. It also calls us, as in Matthew 20:25–28 and John 13:1–17, to be like Jesus in serving one another. I hesitate to place much ethical weight on the intra-Trinitarian role relationships, however, since what we know of them is based only on biblical analogy. But certainly we have plenty of direct biblical teaching that

---

68. For this argument, see Gilbert Bilezikian, *Beyond Sex Roles* (Grand Rapids: Baker, 1985), and particularly Bilezikian's "Hermeneutical Bungee-Jumping: Subordination in the Godhead," *JETS* 40 (1997): 57–68.

69. See Stephen D. Kovach and Peter R. Schemm, Jr., "A Defense of the Eternal Subordination of the Son," *JETS* 42 (1999): 461–76, and Dahms, "The Subordination of the Son." For other titles and a brief summary of the debate, see Wayne Grudem, *Systematic Theology* (Grand Rapids: Zondervan, 1994), 251.

we should follow the example of Jesus in history. And that example is, I believe, a reflection of his intra-Trinitarian life.

The notion that subordination to authority demeans a person is absurd on the face of it. All of us are subordinate to some authorities beyond ourselves: government, employers, church governments, etc. Even "absolute" monarchs must please their subjects, if only to protect themselves against coups and assassinations. Ultimately, we are all under the authority of God. To rebel against submission as such is to rebel against God himself. He places us under authority, not to oppress us, but so that we can fulfill our callings. We should not be at all surprised to find that such submission reflects the very life of the Trinity.

TRINITARIAN MODELS

I have said that God gives us only a glimpse of his inner Trinitarian life. But, as we have seen, it has proved difficult for theologians to be satisfied with a mere glimpse. A certain amount of sheer curiosity, plus the laudable desire to make the mystery of the Trinity as clear as possible, within the limitations of revelation, has led theologians to illustrate the Trinity in different ways. There have been many attempts to illustrate the Trinity, but in this section I shall consider the two main historical models that have been used to describe the nature and relationships of the persons.

The first is the nature of the human mind; the second is the nature of human social relationships. The first type of model, often called *psychological Trinitarianism,* is especially connected with the name of Augustine, who expounded it at great length in *On the Trinity.* He finds oneness and three-ness in the faculties of the mind: intellect, memory, and will. He also explores the phenomena of self-knowledge, in which we find the unitary person functioning in three ways: the knower, the known, and the knowledge. He also considers the nature of self-love: the lover, the beloved, and the love between them. So, although he often speaks of the three persons as different centers of consciousness, as persons in the modern sense, he tends, when he wishes to define the nature of the Trinity theologically, to picture God as a single mind, and the persons as if they were aspects of that mind, like memory, imagination, and will.

Thomas Aquinas, although he insists that the Trinity is a matter of faith, not natural knowledge, nevertheless makes the above concepts of self-knowledge and self-love into a virtual *proof* of the Trinity, starting with the data of natural reason. He tries to prove from natural theology that God exists and that he has the attributes (among others) of knowledge and love.

But then he argues that God's knowledge and love both require adequate objects and that these can be no less than divine persons, or, as he describes them, subsistent relations.[70] And because God's intellectual activity consists entirely of knowledge and love, there can be only two persons in addition to the Father.

The problem with these models, of course, is that they do not account for the New Testament data, in which the persons of the Trinity are actual centers of consciousness, entering into various transactions with one another: the Father sends the Son, the Son prays to the Father, the Father answers the prayers of the Son, the Father and the Son together send the Spirit. Indeed, the Augustinian-Aquinas type of model veers toward Sabellianism.[71] Augustine and Aquinas were quite aware of that danger and sought to avoid it by making various distinctions. But when you stand back and look at their big picture, the dangers are apparent.

The difficulty is to get sufficient distinction into a model based upon the individual human mind. If you try to emend the model to include such distinction, you might consider the pathology of multiple personality in human psychology. In these cases, there do seem to be distinct persons living in one body. The different personalities may have different talents, different levels of knowledge, different levels of maturity, and they may behave very differently. Some of them may be ignorant of the existence of the others. Yet in some situations these have been eventually "integrated" into one personality.

Of course, in many respects, multiple personality is a very poor analogy of the Trinity. For example, the mutual ignorance among the multiple personalities, and indeed their frequent hostility to one another, are very different from the harmony of Father, Son, and Spirit. But if we consider a situation in which there are distinct personalities, which are entirely conscious of one another and in complete harmony, we might have a promising illustration.

We all display different "faces" to the world. We use different vocabularies with different people; we write in different styles. Our sense of humor often varies, depending on whom we are with. This is not just play-

---

70. The argument, in effect, is that the Father's self-knowledge is so perfect that it constitutes another person exactly like him (the Son). (Similarly with love and the Spirit.) The thought is intriguing. But what about the Son's equally perfect self-knowledge? Does that generate still another person? And what about the Son's perfect knowledge of the Father? Does that generate another Father? I think this sort of reasoning is another example of what Dabney called "the reluctance of the human mind to recognize its own weakness."

71. Recall that I indicated the same danger with regard to the Western teaching that equates the persons with "subsistent relations."

acting (as on a fully Sabellian analogy). In these variations, we display different real aspects of ourselves.

Indeed, there are various situations in which we hold internal conversations—conversations that are not redundant, but actually informative. Consider situations in which we try to conjure up memories of things. The memory is part of us, but it is also something for which we search. Consider the phenomenon of dreaming: part of us creates the dream; another part observes, and is sometimes surprised by what transpired. In the experience of dream reading, one part of the mind creates a text, and another part reads it. And there are, we are told, various transactions that take place between our right brain and our left brain. Sometimes (often, to be sure, in pathological cases) one part of the brain hears a voice produced by another part. Again, conceive of a mind that has infinitely more complexity than the human mind, but which is perfectly harmonious and self-aware. Perhaps then you will have something approaching an adequate analogy of the Trinity.

The second type of model is taken from interpersonal relationships on the human level. This is often called *social Trinitarianism*. Social Trinitarians cite as their theological mentors, not Augustine, but the Cappadocian fathers—Basil of Caesarea, Gregory Nazianzen, and Gregory of Nyssa. Augustine began with the unity of God and tried to find pluralities within that unity; the Cappadocians, on the other hand, started from the three persons and sought to describe various kinds of unity among them. They began by describing the Father (the *fons deitatis*) and his various motives for eternally begetting the Son and sending forth the Spirit. The Boethian definition of *person* as an "individual substance of a rational nature" (to say nothing of the biblical picture itself) might have led to a more social view of the Trinity in the West, but in its formal theological definitions, Western theology retained, for many centuries, the Augustinian psychological model as its main point of reference. One significant exception was Richard of St. Victor (d. 1173), who departed from medieval Augustinian formulations and set forth a kind of social Trinitarian doctrine.

But there has been a resurgence in social Trinitarianism, particularly in the past thirty or forty years. Earlier in the century, we may recall, both Barth and Rahner denied emphatically that there were three "centers of consciousness" in God. But more recently the pendulum has swung almost entirely to the other side. Leonard Hodgson's pioneering work[72] has been followed by similar formulations by Jürgen Moltmann,[73] Wolfhart Pan-

---

72. Hodgson, *The Doctrine of the Trinity*.
73. Jürgen Moltmann, *The Trinity and the Kingdom* (San Francisco: Harper and Row, 1981).

nenberg,[74] Colin Gunton,[75] Cornelius Plantinga,[76] Royce Gruenler,[77] and many others. Some have used the social model in the interest of open theism,[78] an approach rejected earlier in this volume; but Gruenler and others have used the social model without evident sympathies for open theism.

The great strength of social Trinitarianism is the weakness of psychological Trinitarianism: its harmony with the portrayal of transactions between the divine persons in the Scriptures. The New Testament, especially the gospel of John, presents the Trinity, not as three aspects of a single mind, but as three real persons, conversing, loving, sending, and so on. The weakness of the social model, however, is the difficulty of finding adequate unity among the persons to justify a confession of monotheism. As Sabellianism was a danger to Western theologians, so tritheism (particularly in its Arian form) was a danger to Eastern theologians.[79]

Here, as with the psychological model, I think that godly speculation can have an edifying function. For it may be that among human beings there is more unity than appears on the surface. One could infer from extrasensory experiences and certain scientic theories (supposedly based on subatomic physics) that all minds may be united at a deep level. But, more significantly, we should reflect on the solidarity of the human race in Adam and of the elect in Christ. Certainly this solidarity is federal and representative. But is that all? The representative model has always been troubled by the specter of arbitrariness. Certainly God has a right to appoint Adam as my representative, but does that appointment have any basis in God's justice and wisdom? I suspect that representation is rooted in something deeper than itself. I am not impressed with attempts to base this solidarity in a kind of Platonic realism, or to draw metaphysical conclusions from our seminal presence in Adam's loins. But I can't avoid the conclu-

74. Pannenberg, *Systematic Theology*, 259–336.

75. Colin Gunton, *The Promise of Trinitarian Theology* (Edinburgh: T. and T. Clark, 1991).

76. Cornelius Plantinga, "The Threeness/Oneness Problem of the Trinity," *Calvin Theological Journal* 23 (1988): 38–52; id., "Social Trinity and Tritheism," in *Trinity, Incarnation, and Atonement*, ed. Ronald J. Feenstra and Cornelius Plantinga (Notre Dame, Ind.: University of Notre Dame Press, 1989), 21–47. Note his popular treatment, "The Perfect Family," in *Christianity Today*, March 4, 1988, 24–27.

77. Gruenler, *The Trinity in the Gospel of John*.

78. Clark Pinnock, "Systematic Theology," in *The Openness of God*, by Clark Pinnock et al. (Downers Grove, Ill.: InterVarsity Press, 1994), 107–9.

79. Indeed, as we saw earlier, their very terminology suggested these dangers. The Western theologians, saying that God had one substance (*substantia*) and three persons (*personae*, originally "masks"), sounded Sabellian to Eastern theologians, who said God had one being (*ousia*) and three substances (*hypostaseis*), which sounded tritheistic or Arian to Western theologians.

sion that at some level the human race (and its successor, the Christian church) is far more "one" than might appear on the surface.[80]

And it may be even more unified in the future. When we are in heaven, no doubt we will retain our individual characteristics. But the earthly family will be transcended by the people of God, so that there will be no more marrying or giving in marriage. And the evident unity among that family will be greater than that of the earthly family: a union that will take away any potential grief over the loss of sexuality. No doubt we will share knowledge and talents on a scale unprecedented in this life. Could such a social system be an adequate analogy of the Trinity? It does seem to me to point in that direction.

Both of these two models, the psychological and the social, contain some important biblical truth, and they may both glimpse parts or aspects of what we may one day see more clearly. Certainly, in Scripture, God does often behave as a single individual, as I indicated in my discussion of *person*. This is the predominant Old Testament perspective, although it does hint at personal distinctions in the Godhead. The predominant New Testament picture is social, although it does reaffirm that God is one. We should not expect, certainly in this life, to reduce this mysterious biblical teaching to the confines of a single model. But both of these pictures help us somewhat to focus our glimpse.

TRINITARIAN ANALOGIES

In addition to using these general models, theologians have tried to illustrate the Trinity with triadic structures found in nature, history, and philosophy. These illustrations are sometimes called *vestigia trinitatis*, vestiges, images, or evidences of the Trinity in the created world.

If all of creation reflects God's invisible nature, his power and glory, is there any way in which creation reflects the Trinity as such? Karl Barth emphatically denied the existence of *vestigia trinitatis*, as part of his critique of natural theology, and Aquinas, too, insisted that one could know the Trinity only by revelation. But we saw above that Aquinas was not entirely consistent in this claim.

I know of nothing in Scripture that rules out the possibility of *vestigia trinitatis*. We have seen that the world as a whole reflects God's glory, and that glory is the glory of the triune God. So the whole creation is a *ves-*

---

80. But, of course, we are not "one" in such a way as to compromise the antithesis between believers and unbelievers and ultimately between the elect and the nonelect.

tigium trinitatis. But are there specific analogies or evidences of the Trinity in the world?

Certainly there are various phenomena that are three in one sense and one in another (or, more broadly, one and many). Saint Patrick's shamrock is as good an example as any. But are there phenomena that can be more specifically related, in edifying ways, to the Trinitarian unity and diversity?[81]

The number three seems omnipresent in Scripture, nature, philosophy, and religion. I have catalogued hundreds of triads, including many that might be thought to reflect the Trinity in one way or another.[82] Some of the parallels, to be sure, are far-fetched. But in order to evaluate these analogies, we should recall the general roles played by the three persons in the economy of creation and redemption. Although all three persons are involved in all acts of God, we saw that there was a general division of labor as follows: the Father plans, the Son accomplishes, the Spirit applies.

The persons of the Trinity also correspond roughly to the three main events of the biblical story: creation (in which the emphasis is on the Father), redemption accomplished (the Son's incarnation, perfect life, atonement, and resurrection), and redemption applied (the Spirit's application to our hearts of the Son's redemptive work).

These roles suggest a correspondence between the persons of the Trinity and the "lordship attributes" expounded in this book. The Father is the *authority*; the Son *controls* all things, obedient to the Father's authoritative plan; the Spirit represents God's *presence* with the world as the divine plan unfolds.

Or should we say, rather, that the Father is the controller, the Son is the authority (because he is the Word), and the Spirit is the presence? I am somewhat torn between the two models, but I now prefer the first, since it better fits the patterns of mutual glorification and the eternal subordination of roles that we have seen in the Trinity. But the choice between these two alternatives is not terribly important, since all persons of the Trinity have all the lordship attributes, and each person is "in" the other two (*circumincessio*), so that the location of the lordship attributes is only a question of emphasis. Also, most importantly, all the lordship attributes presuppose the Trinity. God's control is the control by which each person

---

81. Everything, of course, reflects God's glory and therefore his triune nature in a general way. Thus, as we shall see, Van Til relates the Trinity to the overall unity and diversity of the created world. But I am asking here whether there are any particular phenomena that offer instructive analogies to the Trinity.

82. In appendix A, I have collected about one hundred of these.

AUTHORITY   CONTROL   PRESENCE   ·

sovereignly employs the creation to glorify the others. His authority is that ②
of a speaker (the Father) uttering a word (the Son) and carrying it to his
hearers by his powerful breath (the Spirit). And God's presence is the
presence of the Father, in the Son, by the Spirit.   ③
The lordship attributes also include one another. God exercises his control by speaking with authority in the presence of his creation. His authority
controls all things in his presence, and he is present in authoritative blessing and judgment that ultimately determines the creature's destiny.

All of God's activities in the world, therefore, are Trinitarian—the result of the complex interplay between the three persons. And all the
covenantal triads I have employed in the Theology of Lordship books[83] arise
out of the unity and complexity of God's Trinitarian being, such as the history, law, and sanctions of the suzerainty treaties; knowledge of world, law,
and self in *DKG*;[84] the situational, normative, and existential perspectives,
and so on.[85]

So the covenant structure of Scripture reveals many analogies of the Trinity. I believe that we can also find analogies of the Trinity elsewhere in Scripture and outside it, especially (1) where beginning moves to accomplishment and then to application and consummation, (2) where categories in
a group (especially a group of three) coinhere, (3) where there are significant analogies to the lordship attributes or the three perspectives that
emerge out of them, (4) when three categories exhaust their universe of
discourse, or (5) when there seems to be an emphatic, intentional repeat-
ing of the number three, as in biblical law, narrative, and theology.

I think that one or more of these principles apply to the *vestigia* noted
in appendix A. The reader might profitably look through that appendix
for examples.

PHILOSOPHICAL ANALOGIES

Philosophers, too, have found it hard to resist threefold formulations.
Hegel and other idealist philosophers are famous for their triadic understanding of reality as dialectical (self-negating and consummating): (1) an
idea or state of affairs exists, then (2) negates itself, and then (3) reinte-
grates with its negation, bringing the process to a higher level. When I have
an idea, for example, I often on reflection find truth in its negation. But

83. So far, the two volumes in the series are *DKG* and this one.
84. *DKG*, 62–73.
85. For a more complete list, see appendix A.

when I find a way to combine the truth of the original idea with the truth of the negation, I see more of the truth than I saw before.[86] Hegel believed that both human thought and human history follow this pattern. In history, one social order succumbs to another, but civilization rises to a higher level when a culture incorporates values from both the original order and its negation. Hegel saw this process as the true meaning of the reality for which the Trinity is a symbol.

Hegel's understanding is far from that of Scripture. What Scripture presents as a triune God, Hegel presents as a triadic structure in reality in general. I also resist Hegel's notion that the Son negates the Father (though it can at least be said that the Son is *not* the Father), to be rejoined by the consummating Spirit. In the biblical view, all three persons contrast with one another, and all three are united by a common nature, including a mutual love.

Cornélius Van Til regarded all the world as a *vestigium trinitatis*, in its remarkable diversity in unity, which has baffled philosophers through the years. Realists have thought that the reality of the world is its oneness, for we know the world by bringing things together under concepts. The concepts are what is rational, not the particular things. On the other hand, nominalists have thought that what is real are particular things (sometimes even little particles of things), and that concepts are mental constructions. Realists reduce particulars to universal concepts; nominalists do the reverse. But in fact it is impossible to think of particular things apart from universal qualities, or to justify assertions about universals without reference to particulars.

So unbelieving philosophers will always fail in their attempt to gain an exhaustive knowledge of the world by reducing it to some dimension that they think their reason can handle. The universe is irreducibly both one and many. The one cannot be understood without reference to the many, and vice versa. The universe is both one and many because God is also one and many. He has made the world in his triune image. So the doctrine of the Trinity serves as a rebuke to would-be autonomous epistemology.[87]

Vern S. Poythress carries this argument still further. He finds a Trini-

---

86. Plato's thought is also called dialectical, usually for the simple reason that Plato wrote dialogues rather than treatises. But there is a kinship between Plato and Hegel here. Plato evidently believed that dialogue was not a mere form, but a valuable tool in gaining truth. In dialogue, one character argues a thesis, another (usually Socrates) refutes it, and then they try to reach a greater understanding based on the progress of the argument: thesis, antithesis, synthesis.

87. For a longer account of Van Til's use of the Trinity to solve "the one and many problem," see my CVT, 71–78.

tarian analogy in physical science in the triad of particle, wave, and field, and in linguistics in Kenneth Pike's concepts of feature mode, manifestation mode, and distribution mode.[88] Poythress adopts the terminology of contrast, variation, and distribution: to find meaning, we seek to find how a linguistic unit is distinctive, differing from others (contrast), how it may vary in sound and form while remaining the same word (variation), and the contexts in which it functions (distribution). (In my terms, these are the normative, existential, and situational perspectives, respectively.)

More recently, Poythress has written "Reforming Ontology and Logic in the Light of the Trinity: An Application of Van Til's Idea of Analogy."[89] Here he ascribes to the persons of the Trinity three aspects: the instantiational, the associational, and the classificational, which he explains as follows:

> Each Person of the Godhead is particular. Let us call this particularity the *instantiational* aspect. Each person is an instantiation of God. Second, God exists in fellowship and communion. The Persons of the Godhead exist in association with other Persons, in context of fellowship with other Persons. We may call this aspect the *associational* aspect. Third, the Persons of the Godhead are all God. They are classified using the category "God." We may call this aspect the *classificational* aspect.
>
> The *classificational* aspect expresses the fact that the three Persons share common attributes and are all God. Thus it is closely related to the unity of the three Persons in one God. The *instantiational* aspect expresses the particularity of each Person, and in this way is closely related to the *plurality* of Persons in the Godhead. But of course each Person is one Person, with unity. And this God is three Persons, with diversity. Unity and diversity are "equally ultimate" as Van Til reminds us. . . .
>
> . . . The classificational aspect reflects the character of God the Father, who is the same through all the dynamicity of God's historical actions. The instantiational aspect reflects the character of God the Son, who became flesh for us. The associational aspect of

88. Vern S. Poythress, *Philosophy, Science and the Sovereignty of God* (Nutley, N.J.: Presbyterian and Reformed, 1976), 123–24; id., "A Framework for Discourse Analysis," *Semiotica* 38–3/4 (1982): 289–90. Kenneth Pike, *Language in Relation to a Unified Theory of the Structure of Human Behavior* (The Hague: Mouton, 1967), 84–93; id., *Linguistic Concepts: An Introduction to Tagmemics* (Lincoln: University of Nebraska Press, 1982), 41–65.

89. *WTJ* 57 (1995): 187–219.

mutual fellowship and indwelling reflects the character of God the Holy Spirit, who indwells us.[90]

He stresses, however, that the three persons coinhere, each existing in and with the others; so none of these aspects is limited to any one person.

Since creation reflects the Trinity, human language, thought, communication, and logic also have these aspects. Poythress reiterates Van Til's critique of realism and nominalism by showing that realism (both Platonic and Aristotelian) exalts the classificational aspect above the others, trying to find "pure categories" untainted by particular instantiations and contextual associations. Empiricism absolutizes the instantiational; subjectivism absolutizes the associational. These types of reductionism are plausible, because the aspects coinhere: each encompasses the other two. But in fact there are no pure universals, pure particulars, or pure relationships. Trying to reduce knowledge to one aspect is idolatrous. It is trying to find an absolute starting point in creation, rather than in God's triune existence.

Poythress analyzes communication similarly, into expressive, informational, and productive aspects, a triad that intersects the former one, so that we can ask, for example, "how the classificational aspect displays the expressive, informational, and productive purposes of God."[91] Nevertheless, this triad also corresponds to the persons of the Trinity:

> In sum, we may say that the eternal Word is the archetypal speech of God. This archetypal speech enjoys three aspects: in its *expressive* aspect, it is the speech of God the Father; in its *informational* aspect, its specific content is God the Son; in its *productive* aspect, it is "searched" and carried into effect in God the Holy Spirit. By analogy, God's speech to us displays these three aspects. It is expressive of who God is, and in it we meet God himself; it is informational and contains specific statements and commands; it is productive in us in blessing and curse—in sanctification, or in punishment, or in judgment. These three aspects are coinherent and presuppose one another, as we would expect. Each is a perspective on the whole. Together they form a perspectival triad analogically related to the Trinitarian character of God.[92]

Now logical syllogisms are usually said to depend for their validity on the univocal use of terms: a term must have the same sense in premises and

90. Ibid., 190–92. He cites Cornelius Van Til, *Defense of the Faith* (Philadelphia: Presbyterian and Reformed, 1963), 25.
91. "Reforming Ontology and Logic," 202.
92. Ibid., 201.

conclusion. For practical purposes, many logical syllogisms have sufficient continuity of meaning to generate valid conclusions. But, says Poythress, there is no such thing as a univocal term. All terms are analogical. That is to say that, as in the Trinity, there is no pure instantiation apart from association and classification. Consider this syllogism:

1. Whatever the Father does, the Son also does. (John 5:19)
2. The Father begets the Son.
Conclusion: The Son begets the Son.

The syllogism would appear to follow the rules of logic, but the instantiation of premise two as a particular case of premise one is not appropriate. Such instantiation must take account of the distinctive nature of the associations and classifications within the persons of the Trinity. Similarly, instantiation in logical reasoning about earthly matters cannot involve merely mechanical substitutions of concepts, but must take into account the distinctive nature of those concepts and their association with other realities in the world.[93] Logic requires the activity of a person, relating his premises and conclusions to his entire range of experience and knowledge.[94] Those who claim that there are logical contradictions in Scripture (including the doctrine of the Trinity itself), Poythress argues, fail to understand the terms they use in proper scriptural senses, determined by all the biblical data.[95] Biblical use of logic is "conditioned by redemptive history."[96] All of this suggests a conclusion bearing on all reasoning: In a Trinitarian universe, only God himself, by his revelation, can give us the stability of meaning by which we reason logically.

Poythress also discusses logical circularity, alternative views of logic, the use of logic in apologetics, and implications for linguistics and other sciences. His proposal is a powerful one, with implications for all of human life.

TRINITY AND THE LORDSHIP OF GOD

Does the doctrine of the Trinity have anything to do with the main theme of this book, the lordship of God? Yes, a large part of the significance of this doctrine is its relationship to God's lordship. The doctrine of the Trin-

93. Ibid., 200–207.
94. Ibid., 210–11.
95. Ibid., 211–13.
96. Ibid., 214–15.

ity is not given to relieve our curiosity. It is given to make us better covenant servants and children of God's family.

The battle for the Trinity during the fourth century was about the lordship of Jesus. The question was whether Jesus was fully Lord, as much entitled to that designation as God the Father.

The real passion of that battle was not over metaphysics or technical language. It was over the practical religious realities of worship and salvation. Should we worship Jesus? Is he the Lord who comes to save his people? Worship is our chief duty as creatures, and salvation is our chief blessing as sinners saved by grace. In both of these areas, the doctrine of the Trinity plays a major role.

Worship. Athanasius, the great defender of Nicene orthodoxy, put the question of worship very pointedly: if the Arians are right, then for centuries Christians have been worshiping a creature, and worshiping a creature is idolatry. Scripture agrees with Athanasius, not only with his doctrine, but also with his focus on worship. As we have seen, much of the Trinitarian language of Scripture appears in liturgical texts: the baptismal formula of Matthew 28:19, the apostolic greetings and benedictions (Rom. 16:27; 2 Cor. 13:14), a polemic against idolatry (1 Cor. 8:4–6), and a call to prayer (Rom. 15:30).

Salvation. Athanasius also made the point that if Jesus was a mere creature, as on the Arian view, then we are not saved. Only the Lord can save. As we have seen, *Savior* is an exclusively divine title in Isaiah (e.g., 43:11; 45:21). Once again, Athanasius tapped into a major concern of Scripture itself. For much of the Trinitarian teaching in the New Testament comes in contexts where the writers wish to enumerate the richness of the blessings of salvation (see, e.g., John 17:3; 1 Cor. 12:4–6; Eph. 3:5–7; 4:4–6; 2 Thess. 2:13–14; 1 Peter 1:2; 1 John 5:5–6). Can it be eternal life to know a mere creature (John 17:3)? Can the gifts of salvation be the gifts of mere creatures (1 Cor. 12:4–6; Eph. 4:4–6)?

As we meditate on the different, but unified roles of the three persons in saving us, we are driven back to worship. We are saved by the eternal purpose of the Father, by the atoning work of the Son, through the power and wisdom of the Spirit. We grow in our understanding of God's grace as we see how each person of the Trinity interacts with the others to bring us out of darkness and into the light.

So the doctrine of the Trinity powerfully supports the lordship of Jesus, the eternal Son. But it also supports the lordship of the Father and of the Spirit. To see this more clearly, let us look again at the lordship attributes:

Control. The Arians wanted to worship a big God, a God who was truly transcendent, beyond our knowing. But in the end, their God was dependent on the world. For, they reasoned, if God were to come into direct contact with the world, his deity would be threatened. Therefore, God had to create and redeem the world through semidivine mediators like the Son and the Spirit. That was God's weakness: the world was capable of threatening his deity.

On the contrary, in biblical Trinitarianism, God has nothing to fear from the world. God is the Lord, who can create the world with his own finger. He needs no finite associates, only his own Son and Spirit, who are themselves fully divine. So Trinitarianism reinforces the lordship attribute of sovereign control.

Authority. The doctrine of the Trinity reminds us that God is the one who authoritatively defines himself. We might imagine that God's love, for example, is defined as a relationship between himself and the world. But then a divine attribute would be dependent on the world. God would have needed the world in order to have an adequate object for his love. But Trinitarianism teaches us that God's love is defined, not by the world, but by the eternal love between the Father and the Son.[97] God would have been a loving God even if he had chosen not to create the world. So God is sovereign in defining his own nature.[98] And he is sovereign, not only in defining his love, but in exercising it. He loves the world, not because he must, but because he chooses freely to do so.

The important corollary is that we must think of God, not on the basis of our own autonomous philosophies, but on the basis of his revelation of himself. Matthew 11:25–27, an important passage for understanding the relationship of the Son to the Father, teaches us that we can know the Father only through the Son's revelation of him. First Corinthians 2:10–15 says the same thing about the Spirit. Since God himself determines what he is (by his nature and by his free decisions), his words about himself must constrain our thoughts about him. He is the authoritative Lord.

Presence. I mentioned that the doctrine of the Trinity is connected to a view of the Creator-creature relationship: God is not forced to relate to the

---

97. See how important it is that the Son be fully God.

98. A similar point could be made about God's knowledge. God's knowledge is first of all his intra-Trinitarian knowledge of himself. He knows the world by knowing himself and knowing his plan. So his knowledge is not dependent on the world, but rather is fully sovereign.

world through semidivine mediators. He can and does touch the world directly—in creation, providence, redemption, and judgment.

And the persons of the Trinity do indeed enter our history in all these ways. They reveal themselves in the world so clearly that they can be models for us. So Jesus exhorts us to be holy as the Father is holy (Matt. 5:48). We are to love one another as Christ has loved us (John 13:34–35). We are to be fit dwellings of the Holy Spirit, his temples (1 Cor. 6:19).

Even more remarkably, the persons of the Trinity relate to us in ways that are analogous to the ways in which they relate to one another. Remarkably, God is not only the Father of Jesus, but also the Father of believers (Matt. 6:9; John 20:17). We become one with the Father "as" the Son and the Father are one (John 17:11, 21–23). We become spiritual as we are indwelt by the divine Spirit (1 Cor. 2:15–16; Gal. 6:1).

So the doctrine of the Trinity is quite integral to the doctrine of divine lordship. It reinforces God's sovereign control, his aseity, the sovereignty of his love and knowledge, the authority of his Word, the intimacy of his relationship to the creation, the richness of salvation. The doctrine of the Trinity is not an incidental addition to the doctrine of God; rather, it is the doctrine of God as a whole, in which God gives us a glimpse of his own inner life.

CHAPTER 30

Summary and Conclusion

[handwritten annotation: EXCELLENT SUMMARY OF THE BOOK. WHAT HE (FRAME) PRESENTED ABOUT GOD AND HOW THAT RELATE TO HIS DIVINE LORDSHIP: THE CONTROLLER, THE SUPREME AUTHORITY AND HIS INESCAPABLE PRESENCE]

Who, then, is God? He is Yahweh, the Lord, the controller of all nature and history, the supreme authority for all his creation, the one who is inescapably present to all creatures for blessing and/or cursing. He is *transcendent*, not in the sense of being far from the creation or inaccessible to the human mind, but in the sense that he rules all things. Therefore, there is no contradiction between his transcendence and his immanence. For his universal rule brings his power, knowledge, and goodness to bear everywhere, at every time, to every creature.

Human beings are *free*, not in the sense of being undetermined or free of divine control, but in the sense that they are (1) accountable to God, (2) able to act according to their nature and desires, and (3) able to act according to the integrity of their nature as beings distinct from God. Like God, they are able to choose among possible courses of action. Even evil and sin are under God's sovereignty. He controls evil in such a way as to bring from it a greater good, although that greater good is often mysterious to us in the present life.

God calls us to think about ethics, epistemology, and metaphysics in accordance with his revelation. Christian *ethics* follows the standard of God's revelation, which teaches that human actions should seek the glory of God and be motivated by faith and love. Thus, Christians are able to think about ethical problems from three perspectives: duty, goal, and motivation, in contrast with non-Christian ethical systems, which separate these perspectives from one another and from God.

Epistemology can be understood as a subdivision of ethics in the sense that the human activity of knowing, like other human activities, must be subject to God's standards, must seek his glory, and must be motivated by faith and love. When we come to know God himself, we must bow before his incomprehensibility, but affirm confidently what he has revealed of himself.

Christian *metaphysics* should be founded on the Creator-creature distinction, rejecting any suggestion of a continuum of being between God and the world. God is simple, not in the sense of lacking complexity, but in the sense that all his attributes, and his Trinitarian persons, bear the whole divine essence. That essence, in turn, includes all the rich variety of his attributes and personal distinctions. God's nature is necessary in that it could not be otherwise. But God is free to act or not to act in the world, as he chooses.

God reveals himself in Scripture by presenting his acts, by describing himself in words, and by giving a glimpse of his inner Trinitarian being. We considered these in an order nearly opposite to the usual order, for Scripture often begins where we are, in time and space, reflecting on God's acts in history, and finding in them reason to affirm God's attributes and Trinitarian persons.

Miracle is an extraordinary manifestation of divine lordship, and *providence* is the relatively ordinary manifestation of God's lordship in his everyday rule of the world. That rule includes governing, preserving, revealing himself, and concurring in the actions of secondary causes. *Creation* shows us God's lordship at the beginning of history, when he brings the world out of nothing—an apt picture of salvation in Christ, by which God brings life from utter death. The *decrees* of God show us that God's lordship over us precedes even creation, that his plan for history is eternal. Thus, salvation and judgment are entirely in his hands.

God's verbal descriptions of himself include his names, his images, and his attributes. God *names* himself, and his self-naming displays his lordship. He alone names himself, indicating that he is fully in *control* of his own nature, that he identifies himself with supreme *authority*, and that he wills to be *present* in history by giving to creatures names by which they can call on him.

Scripture uses various *images* to refer to God. I discussed a number of these, giving special attention to recent discussions of God and gender. I concluded that our primary imagery for God should be masculine, as is that of Scripture, but that we should also imitate Scripture in its occasional use of feminine images.

The *attributes* of God describe God's lordship from different perspectives and as exercised in different situations. They show God's *control* over various aspects of creation, his *authority* as the standard for his creatures (in goodness, knowledge, power, etc.), and the modes of his *presence* in our world—the ways he acts in history. But they also describe his inner nature, the ways in which the persons of the Trinity relate to one another.

God *is good* to all creatures, but not always in the same way or in the same degree. He gives to all of us more than we deserve, and to his elect (elect sinners) he gives the incredible blessing of eternal fellowship with himself. His goodness never conflicts with his *righteousness*, for his standards always prevail against challenge. But righteousness is not only God's standard, but also his action to bring about his kingdom in history. So God's righteousness is his salvation, and also his wrath in the destruction of the wicked.

God's *knowledge* is the knowledge of the Lord, and therefore it is the criterion of all creaturely knowledge, given to creatures by grace. It is the knowledge that governs the whole course of nature and history. Therefore, there can be nothing of which God is ignorant. Scripture also testifies abundantly, contrary to much current theology, that God knows the future exhaustively, since the future is the outworking of his own eternal plan.

God's *power* is the power of the Lord, governing all things. He cannot do things that are contrary to his nature (sin, contradict himself, etc.), but his power is sufficient to accomplish everything he purposes to do, and more. Mysteriously, however, he often chooses to accomplish his purposes, not by displays of brute strength, but by manifesting his power in weakness. God's *will* consists of his decrees, his precepts, and the wisdom he gives to his creatures.

God is *the Lord of time*, in that he arranges and uses the temporal sequence for his own purposes. Time never slows him down, limits his knowledge, or keeps him from accomplishing his purposes. So the model of God "above" time is more appropriate than the model of God "in" time. Nevertheless, God is not only transcendent, but also immanent, with respect to time. He is present at all times, as in all space.

God is also both transcendent (*immense*) and immanent (*omnipresent*) with respect to space. Therefore, he has sovereign control over his visible manifestations. But his presence in space (together with his presence in time) enables him to share the creature's perspective, giving him full access to creaturely perspectives.

God is also *self-contained* (*a se*). His existence is not dependent on anything outside himself, nor does he have needs that must be met by others. Far from keeping God away from creation, this doctrine enables him to relate to the world without losing his own nature as Lord. If he came into the world as a suppliant, needing something from us, he would not be distinguishable from a creature. It is God's aseity that enables him to enter relations with the world *as Lord*. God's aseity is not incompatible with his emotional life, or even with divine grief and suffering. God cannot suffer metaphysical loss, but God the Son really experiences death, and God the Father the loss of his Son.

When we move on to discuss *the Trinity*, we must regularly remind ourselves that God has given us only a glimpse of his triune life, not a full and detailed view. Nevertheless, he has clearly revealed (1) that he is one, (2) that he is three, (3) that the three are God, (4) that the three are distinct from one another, and (5) that they are related to one another eternally as Father, Son, and Spirit. These points can be made with various technical terms that have been developed during the history of the church. There is value in these technical formulations, but in the end they don't take us beyond these five fundamental assertions.

The doctrine of the Trinity further reinforces our emphasis on divine lordship. (1) The Trinity is the root of the lordship attributes and the threefold distinctions springing from them. (2) The Trinity emphasizes that God's attributes, even his interpersonal qualities, are defined by virtue of his own nature, not by his relationships to the creation. (3) God's actions in the world, such as creation, providence, and redemption, are Trinitarian, so that even his associates in these works are divine rather than created. (4) God's Trinitarian being enables him to model for us, not only individual perfections, but interpersonal ones as well.

DOES GOD EXIST?

I considered including a chapter on the existence of God, but I have dealt with that subject elsewhere,[1] and this book is already too large. But I shall say a few words here about how the subject bears on the reflections of this book.

Theologians usually deal with the existence of God at the beginning of their treatises, thinking, perhaps, that there is not much point in discussing God unless we can first assure ourselves that he exists. On the other hand, there is also a good argument for including this subject at the end: for if we are going to ask about God's existence, we must first ask what kind of God we are talking about. And surely the nature of anything determines

1. AGG, 89–118; CVT, 239–336; "Presuppositional Apologetics," in *Five Views of Apologetics*, ed. Steven Cowan (Grand Rapids: Zondervan, 2000), 207–31.

how we should go about establishing its existence. We do not verify the presence of a dog on the street in the same way that we verify the existence of quarks or goodness or unicorns.

In this book, I have written at great length about the God of the Bible. How does all of this description bear upon the question of his existence? Certainly we are not to prove God's existence in the same way that we prove the existence of rabbits in the garden. God is not a corporeal being, and he does not manifest himself visibly or tangibly on demand. Indeed, if we are to come to know him, it must be at his sovereign initiative.

Nevertheless, Scripture does say that God is clearly revealed in the world (Ps. 19:1–4; Rom. 1:18–20). God has taken the initiative to reveal himself, although Paul in Romans also says that sinful human beings repress that truth in unrighteousness.

So, as I have said, epistemology is inseparable from ethics. If we are going to acknowledge God's clear revelation, he must remove from us that sinful suppression of the truth. This means that we will never be thoroughly persuaded of God's existence until his grace in Jesus renews our hearts. There are arguments for God's existence—ontological, cosmological, teleological, moral, epistemological, etc.—that are of some value. Even the unregenerate sometimes confess the existence of God on the basis of argument, experience, or feeling. But they do not live for him. Such tentative beliefs are not sufficient to produce a God-centered life. And in the worldview of an unbeliever, there is a profound skepticism that mitigates the force of any theistic commitment. That skepticism implies that the God of the Bible cannot exist. Thus, "non-Christian theism" is always in some way inconsistent with itself.

The traditional arguments can also be helpful to believers. But the believer's confidence is actually based elsewhere. Faith comes from the sovereign work of the Spirit, who gives us a belief in God that is not merely tentative or theoretical, but life-changing.

The Spirit works in and with the Word. All that we know about God from Scripture forms our basis of faith. Now Scripture, as we've seen, makes God central to everything. He is not only the Creator, Provider, and Redeemer, but also the supreme authority for all of human thought. His attributes, as we have seen, provide standards for our thought. We are to think God's thoughts after him, or presuppose his Word in all our thought and life.

The Spirit, therefore, gives the regenerate person a new mind, the mind of Christ. He enables the Christian to think in a new way, as part of the renewed life. That new way is to think biblically. As we have seen, Scripture contains a distinctive epistemology. Knowing is not autonomous.

Belief in God on His terms, not ours - Lordship

It is not merely the manipulation of empirical data, logical principles, and human experience. It is submitting our thinking to God's revelation in Scripture and in the world, and letting Scripture govern our interpretation of the world. And Scripture must take precedence in our thought over the reasoning of scientists, philosophers, psychologists, Bible critics, or historians.

Now to someone who thinks biblically, the existence of God is obvious. God revealed his name clearly to Israel. Apart from his creation and providence, nothing could exist. Without his eternal decree, the world would be utter chaos. God is the standard of goodness, justice, and truth. Time and space themselves are his servants. So unless he exists, nothing else could exist. Unless God exists, there could be no rational order in the world, no goodness, justice, or truth, no time or space. No fact could be what it is without God; so every fact reveals God.

Thus, God's existence is certain, not tentative or merely probable, as traditional apologetics often suggests. Indeed, God is the very criterion of certainty, because he is the criterion of truth and rationality.

So everything in this book has apologetic force. The biblical doctrine of God (as everything else in Scripture) presents a way of looking at everything that makes the existence of God not only plausible, but utterly persuasive. It presents a worldview in which every fact bears witness to God. In the biblical worldview, nothing makes sense apart from the presupposition of God's reality.

As you read or reread this book, consider the biblical worldview afresh. See if it doesn't account for the meaningfulness of the created world in a way that no non-Christian philosophy or religion can do. And then consider that that worldview depends on the biblical God. That is the ultimate proof that God exists.

So God's lordship is not only the key to understanding his nature, but also the key by which we may come to believe in him. If we are to believe in God with confidence and assurance, we must come to believe in him as the Lord. And that means believing in him on his terms, not ours.

His terms are these: "Believe in the Lord Jesus, and you will be saved—you and your household" (Acts 16:31). He calls upon us to admit that we are sinners in his sight (Rom. 3:23), to accept (by grace) the sacrifice of Jesus as God's payment for sin (Mark 10:45), and to trust Jesus as Lord and Savior (John 1:12–13; Eph. 2:8–10). *Gospel*

Believing in Christ opens you to all the riches of life with God. The covenant becomes your covenant, and the Lord becomes your Lord. All that God is becomes yours, for he has said, "I will take you as my own people, and I will be your God" (Ex. 6:7; cf. Rev. 21:3, 7). You will live under his standards, which will bring you good (Deut. 10:13; Matt. 6:33). God will renew your relations with others, as you enter his family, his body. Yes, all this will come with suffering, but with joy in the end.

Jesus said, "I tell you the truth, no one who has left home or brothers or sisters or mother or father or children or fields for me and the gospel will fail to receive a hundred times as much in this present age (homes, brothers, sisters, mothers, children and fields—and with them, persecutions) and in the age to come, eternal life" (Mark 10:29–30; cf. 1 Peter 1:3–9).

The biblical doctrine of God describes and offers you a new life. And everything in that new life confirms that he is real, that he loves you, and that nothing can separate you from his love (Rom. 8:35–38).

MORE TRIADS

I will present here a list of triads (longer than the list in chap. 29) that have sometimes been thought to reflect or illumine the Trinity in some way. I will offer a few comments, but normally will present them without comment.

I have tried to weed out those that seem to me to be obviously arbitrary, contrived, or uninteresting, but readers should not assume my evaluation of any of these. I do not place any theological weight on these examples—nor do I urge readers to do so. All I would claim is that these triads are of some interest and that they may in some measure reflect, illumine, or provide evidence for the doctrine of the Trinity. I do not rest my faith in the Trinity on any of these triads (except for the first one).

Some are taken from other sources, but I will not be able to provide adequate documentation in many cases. I have been building this list for many years, and I have lost track of many sources, for which I apologize to the authors.[1] Chapter numbers refer to the present volume.

SCRIPTURE AND CHRISTIAN THEOLOGY

1. Texts anticipating, reflecting, or explicitly teaching the Trinity (chaps. 27–29).

2. Divine act, covenant making, and period of application.

3. History, law, and sanctions, as elements of the suzerainty treaty.

---

1. Nathan Wood, *The Trinity in the Universe* (Grand Rapids: Kregel, 1984) has an even longer list of *vestigia*.

4. God's word as powerful, meaningful, and self-expressive.[2]

5. Events, words, and persons as media of God's word.[3]

6. Prophet, priest, and king.

7. Revelation, inspiration, and illumination.

8. Revelation: general, special, and existential.[4]

9. Control, authority, and presence, as God's lordship attributes (discussed throughout this volume).

10. God's oneness as unity, equality, and concord (Augustine).

11. Goodness, knowledge, and power, as classifications of divine attributes (as in this volume). Omnipotence, omniscience, and omnipresence, as exemplifications of these.

12. The theological account of God's holiness as *mysterium tremendum et fascinans* (mystery arousing fear and fascination) (Rudolph Otto).

13. The threefold repetition of "holy" in Isaiah 6:3.

14. God as life (John 14:6), light (1 John 1:5), and love (1 John 4:8, 16).

15. God's righteousness as standards, actions, and moral excellence (chap. 21).

16. God's will as decree, precept, and wisdom (chap. 23).

17. God's spirituality as control, authority, and presence (chap. 25).

18. God's acts, attributes, and persons (as in this volume).

19. Miracles as signs, wonders, and powers (see chap. 13).

20. Creation of heaven, earth, and sea (the three-layered universe).

21. The sun, moon, and stars.

22. Providence as government, revelation, and concurrence.

23. God's decrees, creation-providence, and redemption.

24. Law, redemption accomplished, and redemption applied (chap. 13).

25. Jesus as the Word, his acts in history, and his nature as God and man (chap. 13).

26. Election, effectual calling, and individual soteriology (chap. 13).

27. Biblical history: the old covenant period, from the Incarnation to the Resurrection, Pentecost to the consummation.

28. The three parts of the Old Testament in the Hebrew Bible: the Law, the Prophets, and the Writings.

29. Many triads in Bible stories and laws: three stories in Noah's ark, three sendings of birds after the Flood, three sons of Noah, three visitors to Abraham, three patriarchs, three divisions of the tabernacle, three feast periods, three offerings. The cleansing of a leper by blood, water, and oil on

2. See my *Perspectives on the Word of God* (Eugene, Oreg.: Wipf and Stock, 1999), 9–16.
3. Ibid., 17–35.
4. Ibid., 31–32.

the ear, thumb, and toe (Lev. 14:1–20). Three years in Jesus' ministry, three temptations, and three crosses.

30. Grain, wine, and oil as chief staples, elements of offerings, sacraments, and rites.

31. Creation, redemption accomplished, and redemption applied.

32. Man as image of God: in Meredith Kline's view, the image consists of physical, judicial, and moral qualities (in my terms, situational, normative, and existential qualities).[5]

33. Human responsibility as accountability, liability, and integrity (chap. 8).

34. Justification, adoption, and regeneration-sanctification as the major benefits of redemption (chap. 13).

35. The grounds of assurance of salvation: the promises of God, the fruit of salvation in one's life, and the internal witness of the Spirit (normative, situational, and existential). See WCF, 18.2.

36. Sanctification: definitive, progressive, and final (at the consummation).

Non-Christian Religion

37. A. A. Hodge says that the doctrine of the Trinity captures and balances the truth in deism, pantheism, and mythology, by its teaching about the Father, Spirit, and Son, respectively.[6]

38. Triadic polytheisms: (a) Brahma, Vishnu, and Siva in Hinduism; (b) Osiris, Isis, and Horus in Egyptian religion; (c) Sin, Shamash, and Ishtar (Babylon); (d) Anu, Elish, and Ea (Sumer); (e) Uranos, Kronos, and Zeus (Greece); Odin, Thor, and Loki (Norse).

39. Raimundo Panikkar: everyone has three aspects: divine, anthropic, and cosmic (normative, existential, and situational).

40. In mysticism: cogitation, meditation, and contemplation.

41. In mysticism: purification, illumination, and ecstasy.

Ontology

42. Predicables, cases, and exemplifications, like wisdom, Socrates' wisdom, and Socrates. I see these as normative, situational, and existential, respectively.[7]

5. Meredith G. Kline, *Images of the Spirit* (Grand Rapids: Baker, 1980).
6. See his interesting discussion in A. A. Hodge, *Evangelical Theology* (Edinburgh: Banner of Truth, 1976), 107–10.
7. See Nicholas Wolterstorff, *On Universals* (Chicago: University of Chicago Press, 1970), 133.

43. Thales is said to have believed that every object has three dimensions: physical, living, and divine.

44. Hegel's being, nothing, and becoming, and other triads on the pattern of thesis, antithesis, and synthesis.

45. Many twofold distinctions can be construed as triads, for the two terms are related in an important way, producing a unity that brings them together,[8] similar to Hegel's dialectic. Thus: subject/object, naïve/theoretical, free/determined, one/many, form/matter, etc.[9]

46. Instantiation, association, and classification (Vern Poythress, described in chap. 29; other threefold distinctions in his writings: particle, wave, field; expressive, informational, productive).

47. Beginning, middle, and end.

48. Good, true, and beautiful, seen as convertible in scholastic philosophy. But being, unity, and particularity are also among the convertible "transcendentals."

EPISTEMOLOGY

49. Object, subject, and law (*DKG*).

50. The situational, normative, and existential perspectives.

51. In logic: major premise, minor premise, and conclusion.

52. Dooyeweerd: the Archimedean point, by which we see the world rightly, must not be separated from our selfhood, divine law, or the totality of the meaning of the cosmos. (I see these as existential, normative, and situational, respectively.)

53. Rationalist, empiricist, and subjectivist approaches of secular philosophy (*DKG*).

54. Knowledge as justified, true belief (see chaps. 11 and 22).

ETHICS

55. Faith, hope, and love, as virtues that abide (1 Cor. 13:13).

56. Three lusts (1 John 2:16).

57. Teleological, deontological, and existential schools of secular ethics.[10]

58. Great commandments: love God, love yourself, and love your neighbor.

59. The world, the flesh, and the devil.

---

8. Thanks to my correspondent Daniel Davis (henceforth DCD) for this observation.
9. DCD.
10. Wolterstorff, *On Universals*, 40–50.

60. Goal (glory of God), motive (love, faith), and standard (Word of God).

61. Good works seek the goal of God's glory, on the basis of the cross of Christ, in the power of the Spirit.

LANGUAGE

62. Contrast, variation, and distribution (Poythress: see chap. 29).

63. Expressive, informational, and productive (Poythress: see chap. 29).

64. Locution, illocution, and perlocution: locution is a piece of language; illocution is what is done in the language (command, question, statement, etc.); perlocution is what is done through the language (educate, mislead, annoy, amuse, etc.).[11]

65. Three grammatical persons: I, you, and he.

66. Theories of meaning, locating meaning in the author's intention, the hearer's understanding, and the text itself.

EDUCATION

67. Grammar, rhetoric, and dialectic—the classic *trivium*.

MATHEMATICS

68. Theories of mathematics: formalism (determined by inner consistency), constructivism (based on the structure of the human mind), and Platonism (mathematical objects and relations belong to the ontology of the world).

THE PHYSICAL WORLD

69. Field, wave, and particle (see chap. 29).

70. Red, green, and blue (the primary colors of the cathode ray tube), or red, blue, and yellow (the primary painters' colors), from which other colors can be made. I have said (rather tongue-in-cheek) of the first triad that blue is the sky (normative), green is the earth (situational), and red is the interior of the body (existential).

71. Yolk, white, and shell.

72. Liquid, solid, and gas.

---

11. See J. L. Austin, *How to Do Things with Words* (Cambridge, Mass.: Harvard University Press, 1975).

73. Height, width, and length. (Each constitutes all of space, yet they are distinct.)

74. Outside, inside, and above. (Also used as three viewpoints: "from outside," etc.)

75. Number, space, and time (yielding arithmetic, geometry, and calculus).

76. Past, present, and future.

77. Matter, energy, and meaning. David Bohm, a disciple of Einstein, believed that each of these replicates the other two. Each is a basic manifestation of reality.

78. The nine dimensions of some recent theories: a trinity of trinities.

79. Root, trunk, and branches.

80. The sun brings light, heat, and life.

The Human Body

81. Circulation, respiration, and nervous system.

The Human Mind, Personality

82. Mind, knowledge, and love.

83. Memory, understanding, and will. (Numbers 82–85 are important to Augustine's discussion of the Trinity.)

84. Being, knowing, and willing.

85. In self-knowledge: the self as subject, object, and knowledge.

86. In self-love: the self as lover, beloved, and love.

87. Thought, word, and deed.

88. Intention, action, and response (especially within the same person).

89. We form our selfhood in our relations to others.

90. Unity and plurality in the human mind and in the human race (chap. 29).

91. Some people are normativists, always seeking justice. Others are situationalists, wanting to be committed to a cause or activity beyond themselves. And some are existentialists, focused on their own feelings. In families, the oldest child is often normativist, and the other children sort out the other two roles. These are aspects of all of us, but we differ in focus.

Human Society, Culture

92. Husband, wife, and child.

93. Physician, pharmacist, and patient. (Normative, situational, and

existential, respectively, if you take this triad from the patient's point of view.)[12]

94. Think, work, and serve (the motto of Tennessee State University).[13]

95. Gödel, Escher, and Bach (relatively normative, situational, and existential).[14]

THE CHURCH

96. Piety, doctrine, and social action, seen as varying emphases among (especially Reformed) Christians. In truth, each requires the others.

ART, MUSIC, AND LITERATURE

97. I, IV, and V, the three primary chords, defined by triads of tones.

98. Root position and two inversions of triadic chords.

99. Tonic, tierce, and quint.

100. Melody, harmony, and rhythm (the music as composed).

101. Timbre, volume, and harmony (the music as presented).

102. The threefold structure of the twelve-bar blues.

103. The threefold structure of many classical forms: theme, development, and recapitulation; fast, slow, and fast movements in sonatas and concerti; the *da capo* aria.

104. Themes with variations, in which the variations correspond one-to-one with the theme, but are widely different from each other.

105. Composer's conception, the score, and the performance (any of these can be called "the piece").[15]

106. Beauty as integrity, proportion, and splendor.

107. Aesthetic theories: formal (locating beauty in qualities inherent in objects), emotional (locating it in the response of the perceiver), and relational (finding beauty in the capacity of objects to arouse responses). I see these as normative, existential, and situational, respectively.[16]

108. "Unity without monotony" as an aesthetic criterion.[17]

109. Jesus' parable of the talents (Matt. 25:14–30) describes three stew-

---

12. Taken from an ad for Women's International Pharmacy, placing each term at one point on a triangle. Anything is fair game for theology!

13. DCD.

14. See Douglas R. Hofstadter, *Gödel, Escher, Bach* (New York: Random House Basic Books, 1980).

15. Thanks to Steve Hays for this suggestion.

16. DCD.

17. DCD.

ards: one increased the Lord's investment, then a second did, but the third did not. As in many jokes,[18] two people would seem to be too few, and four too many. The first sets up a pattern, the second establishes it as a continuing pattern, and the third consummates the pattern, driving home its significance. This is not essentially different from the work of the persons of the Trinity: initiation, accomplishment, and application.[19]

110. The *chiasm* is a frequent literary device in Scripture, especially in the Psalms, but also in prophecy, prose narratives, etc. It is essentially an A-B-A form in which one idea, theme, image, or motif gives rise to another, then returns to the first with some level of enrichment. The chiasm can become more complicated, when the text includes chiasms within chiasms: so, A-B-A, B-C-B, C-D-C creates the total structure as A-B-C-D-C-B-A. Often the central item (D in our example) receives the emphasis. But the overall structure can be understood as triadic: theme, additional theme, return.

111. The chiasm exists implicitly in all literature. A story begins in a situation and encounters a problem that brings the situation to a different state: thesis, antithesis, and synthesis-consummation (as in the "quest" genre: a journey from comfort to ordeal to enlightenment; stasis, katabasis, anabasis). In Scripture: Jesus' preincarnate glory, his state of humiliation, and his resurrection and ascension to an even greater acknowledgement of his lordship; or creation, fall, redemption.

HISTORY

112. Confrontation, consolidation, and continuation: stages of major cultural movements (reformations in the church and political change).

---

18. I recall watching on TV a discussion among several comedians about "three guys" jokes (as, "An atheist, a priest, and a rabbi were going past a bar. . . ."). They agreed that there was something unique about the number three that was crucial to that form of humor.

19. We should, of course, not see a rigid or unvarying pattern here. There are also important twofold distinctions in Scripture (e.g., Old and New Covenants, Creator and creature, double restitution for theft in the Mosaic law, law and gospel), as well as fourfold, sevenfold, tenfold, etc. But the threefold distinctions are strangely pervasive, and they hold special interest for our present discussion.

MARK KARLBERG ON
The Doctrine of the Knowledge of God

In 1989, Mark W. Karlberg published in *JETS* a review article in critique of my *DKG*.[1] I thought at the time, and still do think, that it is incompetent.[2] Karlberg is a historian who has no credentials or particular accomplishments (beyond M.Div.–level courses) in the fields relevant to an analysis and evaluation of *DKG*: epistemology, philosophy, and apologetics.[3] And

---

1. Mark W. Karlberg, "On the Theological Correlation of Divine and Human Language: A Review Article," *JETS* 32 (1989): 99–105.

2. Since I often express myself in nontraditional ways, I seem to attract criticism from people who don't like the *sound* of what I am saying, but can't or won't take the trouble to seriously analyze and evaluate my argumentation. Another example is Richard Horner's review of *CVT* in *New Horizons* 17, no. 4 (April 1996): 24. See my reply (drastically abridged by the editor) in the issue of July 1996, p. 22. Frankly, I feel that there has been in recent years something of an epidemic of this sort of thing in Reformed circles. But I certainly do not write off all criticism of my work as incompetent. I have been helped (though not necessarily swayed) by such highly competent critics as Harold A. Netland ("Apologetics, Worldviews, and the Problem of Neutral Criteria," in *The Gospel and Contemporary Perspectives*, ed. Douglas Moo [Grand Rapids: Kregel, 1997], 138–52), and my four coauthors of the book *Five Views of Apologetics*, edited by Steven Cowan (Grand Rapids: Zondervan, 2000).

3. I have elsewhere complained about the recent tendency of scholars trained primarily in history to presume to speak dogmatically on other matters. See my "In Defense of Something Close to Biblicism," *WTJ* 59 (1997): 269–318, with replies by David F. Wells and Richard A. Muller, and a closing statement from me. The article is reprinted in my *Contemporary Worship Music* (Phillipsburg, N.J.: P&R Publishing, 1997), 175–201, without the interchange. See also my paper "Traditionalism," available at www.thirdmill.org. Karlberg is a rather extreme example of this general trend.

751

the review shows very little understanding of the issues with which I deal in the book.[4]

The editor of *JETS* did not permit replies to reviews or review articles,[5] and I probably would not have replied at the time, even if I had been permitted to do so. In general, I think it best to let sleeping dogs lie, and I feared that an interchange would not be of much benefit to my readers or to Karlberg. I had hoped that the article would be deservedly forgotten, and that Karlberg and I could go on to other things.

However, in recent years I have gotten a number of communications from people who have asked for my response to Karlberg's article, and a number of people seem even to be taking Karlberg's position for granted. The sleeping dog doesn't seem to want to lie still. The last straw, which finally provoked the present response, was the endorsement of Karlberg's article by Robert Reymond in *A New Systematic Theology of the Christian Religion*.[6] I have great respect for Dr. Reymond's work, and the fact that he recommends Karlberg's article indicates that I ought to take it more seriously. If a man of Reymond's stature was unable to see the flaws in Karlberg's attack, then others may also need help in identifying them. However, Reymond has not persuaded me to evaluate Karlberg's article more favorably.

Karlberg begins with my assertion that "meaning is application," and comments:

> Rather than locating the truth in God himself, as Reformed dogmaticians have uniformly done, Frame rests meaning in human language—language that is itself informed by the language of God in Scripture.[7]

4. Indeed, I can't understand why the editor of *JETS* accepted it for publication. When someone submits for publication a radically negative attack on a book outside his own field, I should think that would be a red flag—a signal for an editor to get some advice from people in that field, or otherwise to reject the article outright. The editor should have suspected (as I do) that the article is motivated in part by personal and/or ideological hostility.

5. I don't quarrel with this general policy. Debates have to end somewhere, although sometimes there is a legitimate academic purpose in permitting some give-and-take on an issue. But in cases like this, when an article raises so many red flags, an exception to the general rule is necessary to insure fairness. I am grateful to the editors of *Mid-America Journal of Theology*, who invited me to reply ("Reply to Mark W. Karlberg," in vol. 9, no. 2 [fall 1993]: 297–308) to another Karlberg attack (see appendix C).

6. Robert L. Reymond, *A New Systematic Theology of the Christian Religion* (Nashville: Thomas Nelson, 1998), 103. I consider the endorsement of Karlberg's position to be an unfortunate blot on a very fine book.

7. Karlberg, "Theological Correlation," 100.

Here he implies that for me there is no sense in which truth or meaning[8] is located in God. That is, of course, a total distortion of my position. In *DKG* and all my other writings, I have said over and over again that truth is an attribute of God, and that God is the origin of all truth. In *DKG*, I say that "truth, like knowledge and wisdom, comes by grace, by Trinitarian communication, by Word and by Spirit."[9] And then I list twenty-three Scripture references to support the point. As for meaning, Karlberg himself quotes my statement that meaning is "that *use* of language *that is authorized by God.*"[10]

So meaning, like everything else, comes from God. It does not "rest" in human language, in the sense that human language is autonomous. But, of course, human language is meaningful because God has made it so. And it is certainly proper for Christian thinkers to investigate how human language can be meaningful, that is, how God makes it meaningful. Has any Reformed dogmatician ever denied this? I very much doubt it. If Karlberg denies it, then he simply doesn't understand the question.

Karlberg also seems to be rather confused on the relationship between the content of Scripture and that of other human knowledge. First, he complains that I make too sharp a distinction between Scripture and extrascriptural theology. Is there no theology in the Bible? he asks.[11] But then he argues that I do not distinguish sufficiently between Scripture and other human knowledge. He quotes me:

> We have seen that knowledge of God involves (and is involved in) knowledge of His law, the world, and ourselves. It is also important to see that the latter three forms of knowledge are involved in one another because of their mutual coordination in God's plan.[12]

---

8. I am not clear as to how Karlberg intends to relate truth and meaning. These are not synonymous, but Karlberg jumps rapidly from one to the other without explaining the move, except to say that my question, "What is meaning?" is "similar" to Pilate's question, "What is truth?" (ibid.). Does he have anything to say on these issues, except that Frame is somehow guilty by association with Pilate?

9. *DKG*, 49.

10. Karlberg, "Theological Correlation," 100, quoting *DKG*, 33. I have added some italics.

11. Karlberg, "Theological Correlation," 100. My answer, by the way, is "Yes, there is." The biblical writers *apply* that portion of the word of God that has been revealed to them at their particular point in redemptive history and thereby do theology. "Scripture" and "application" are not mutually exclusive categories. But once the canon is completed, there is a substantial difference between inspired Scripture and the postcanonical application of it.

12. Ibid., quoting *DKG*, 65.

He comments, "The author also speaks of these three perspectives as correlative and coextensive." Then:

> What this does is to place Scripture on a par with the human situation (including both the situational and existential factors). For Frame there are merely differences of emphasis among these three.[13]

Karlberg here evidently thinks that I equate Scripture with the normative perspective. That is a misunderstanding. The normative perspective, like the other two perspectives, is a perspective on all reality, not a synonym for "Scripture." In saying this, I make the point that everything is normative in one way or another,[14] just as everything is part of our situation, and everything is part of our subjective experience. Scripture is not identical to the normative perspective, for (1) it is found in the other two perspectives as well, as the fact that illumines all other facts (situational) and the element of our subjectivity that illumines all others (existential), and (2) because there are divine norms other than Scripture.[15]

Now the statements that "everything is normative," and that "there are divine norms other than Scripture" might seem to be playing into Karlberg's hands. Do these statements not make Scripture correlative to, or identical to, extrascriptural data? Not in the least. These statements merely reiterate the unanimous conviction of Reformed theology that there is general revelation as well as special revelation. Everything reveals God (Ps. 19:1–2; Rom. 1:18–21), and all revelation is authoritative. Natural revelation informs us of the existence of God, his "eternal power and divine nature" (Rom. 1:20), and his moral law, that is, his norms (Rom. 1:32). Paul teaches that this revelation is absolutely authoritative—just as authoritative as Scripture, for it is the standard by which men will be judged.

In this very traditional understanding, therefore, there are divine norms (general revelation) other than Scripture, and everything is normative (for general revelation includes everything that God has made). Scripture and general revelation do not differ in their degree of authority, for they are both the revelation of God. Are they, then, equal in every way? No. Scripture plays a very special role within the "hierarchy of divine norms."[16] It is "the treaty of the great king," the written constitution of the covenant people of God.[17] It is the ultimate criterion of truth, the standard against

---

13. Karlberg, "Theological Correlation," 100, citing a reference to *DKG*, 141.
14. *DKG*, 137–38.
15. That is, some divine norms can be discovered outside of Scripture. But I do not believe that there are divine norms other than those derivable from Scripture.
16. *DKG*, 137–38.
17. Ibid., 40–41, especially footnote 35.

which all truth-claims must be measured, as I make clear in my discussion of "normative justification."[18]

Sin distorts our understanding of general revelation, as Paul teaches in Romans 1, and as Reformed theology has always affirmed. God has given us Scripture, so that the gospel of Christ will overcome our sin and enable us to use general revelation as God intended. The Scriptures are the "spectacles" (Calvin) that we need to view general revelation correctly. Is it fair for Karlberg, then, to say that this account "strikes at the very heart of the Reformed tradition"?[19]

Now after Karlberg has said that for me Scripture and natural revelation are identical, he quotes me as drawing an important distinction between them:

> There is, in other words, an important difference between the Scriptures on the one hand and the reasoning by which we determine applications of Scripture on the other. We discover the applications through fallible means, but of course that is true with regard to all exegesis, all understanding of Scripture. But once we discover a true application of Scripture, that application is unconditionally binding.[20]

Then he comments:

> The author misconstrues the element of human subjectivity in theological discourse, jeopardizing the authority and self-sufficiency of Scripture. In Frame's theological method, how can the fallible process of Scriptural application result in "unconditionally binding" obligation to law—that is, Scripture? Has not Frame blurred the distinction he claims to make between the infallible Scriptures and fallible Christian theology?[21]

Karlberg has not carefully read the statement he quotes. The word "true" in the last sentence is important. I'm not saying that all our theological assertions are unconditionally binding, but just the true ones, the scriptural ones. Can anyone doubt that teachings expressing the truth of Scripture are binding? If a pastor proclaims true interpretations of the Word, are those

---

18. Ibid., 123–39. I expect to say much more on this subject in my forthcoming *Doctrine of the Word of God*.

19. Karlberg, "Theological Correlation," 100.

20. Ibid., 101, quoting *DKG*, 68.

21. Karlberg, "Theological Correlation," 101. Karlberg's equation here between "law" and "Scripture" may reflect another misunderstanding. In *DKG*, I do not equate these. "Law" includes the norms of natural revelation (Rom. 1:32) as well as Scripture.

interpretations not unconditionally binding? Certainly they are. He may preface them with "Thus saith the Lord!" This is what the Second Helvetic Confession means when it says, "The preaching of the Word of God is the Word of God."[22] The Confession is not ascribing to preachers a general infallibility. It is saying that when they present biblical truth, that truth is no less authoritative on their lips than it is on the pages of Scripture itself. The same is the case in *true* theology.[23]

Karlberg says that my method tends "to undermine the authority of Scripture"[24]—a very drastic criticism for which he gives not a shred of evidence. And he also says that my method

> challenges Scripture's attribute of perspicuity. Frame castigates traditional dogmatics for expounding what he calls "precise statements of doctrine" free of all subjective influences—that is, statements of truth that are objectively and eternally valid.[25]

This is an absurd distortion of my position. I have never criticized dogmatics for expounding precise statements of doctrine. I have only argued that, since Scripture itself is not always perfectly precise, we should not always prefer precision to imprecision. We should not seek to be maximally precise in our theology, but rather to be just as precise as Scripture is—no more, no less.[26] I also deny that any interpretation can be free from subjective in-

---

22. Chapter 1.

23. There is a remaining problem, of course. We cannot always be absolutely sure that our theological claims are true. So what right do we have to preface them with "Thus saith the Lord"? But this has been a continuing problem in Reformed theology. I suspect the authors of the Second Helvetic Confession felt the same tension, and I doubt if Karlberg has any definitive resolution of the problem. In practice, the answer is to claim certainty only where God gives us certainty (recognizing that even those claims are fallible), and to acknowledge where we lack that certainty. There are many biblical doctrines that are so certain that we must build all our life and thought (including our criteria of certainty!) upon them. Concerning those, we cannot help but say, "Thus saith the Lord," for God's Word is our only basis for certainty. See *DKG*, 134–36.

Karlberg himself says that "to the extent that our interpretation of Scripture . . . corresponds to God's revelation in nature and Scripture it provides a metaphysically ultimate and true analysis of the world" ("Theological Correlation," 104). I'm not sure what he means by "metaphysically ultimate," but he seems to be making, in even stronger terms, the point he criticizes me for making. Yet he makes it in such a way as to make the reader think that I would disagree with it!

24. Karlberg, "Theological Correlation," 102.

25. Ibid., referring to *DKG*, 307.

26. The doctrine of perspicuity says that Scripture is clear, not that it is precise. Evangelicals commonly point out, for example, that round numbers in Scripture do not constitute errors, because Scripture normally doesn't claim to use absolutely precise numbers. See *DKG*, 215–41. It is in this sense, and not in any other, that I say Scripture is sometimes

fluences, because every interpreter is a human subject. But subjective influence does not make it impossible to discover truth, indeed, truth that is "objectively and eternally valid."

When Karlberg equates doctrinal statements that are "free of all subjective influences" with "statements of truth that are objectively and eternally valid," he drastically distorts my position. I have never made that equation, and I reject it out of hand. One of the main emphases of *DKG* is that objectivity and subjectivity, understood biblically, are not enemies of one another. All knowledge involves both an object and a subject.[27] That is certainly the first lesson in any epistemology. Karlberg apparently doesn't understand this,[28] yet he presumes to write about epistemology as if he were an expert. That combination of ignorance and arrogance is what leads me to question his basic competence to evaluate a book like *DKG*.

Karlberg disagrees with my contention that it is not necessarily sinful to make a theological error.[29] Actually, what I say is that although unfallen Adam "could not have made a mistake about his present duty before God," he could have made theological mistakes of other kinds.[30] (Karlberg, as usual, fails to note my qualification.) This is a difficult question, and I am open to discussion about it. But I don't think it is as obvious as Karlberg does that Adam would have sinned if he had harbored in his mind, say, the wrong view of the *filioque*. And Karlberg's alternative view, that Adam could have made mistakes about nontheological matters, but not about theological ones, strikes me as absurd. "Limited inerrantists" claim to be able to draw a sharp line between theological and nontheological content, but inerrantist evangelicals, especially the Reformed, have always opposed this kind of dichotomy. As Van Til emphasized, nothing can be fully understood apart from God, so there is a theological component in all knowledge.

Then Karlberg attacks my critique of the notion of theology as a progressive accumulation of facts. He misleadingly paraphrases what I oppose as "reorganizing and developing the system of doctrine contained in the Scriptures,"[31] and he provides no reference in *DKG* for his account of my

---

"vague," much as that language seems to distress Karlberg ("Theological Correlation," 102). Furthermore, I never (in *DKG* or anywhere else) express opposition to the use of technical terms *per se* in theology, as Karlberg says I do (p. 102), although I do suggest some cautions in using them (as Karlberg himself does in this context).

27. And, to complete the triad, all knowledge involves a norm.
28. This same elementary confusion exists also in his review of my *CVT*. See appendix C.
29. Karlberg, "Theological Correlation," 103.
30. *DKG*, 21.
31. Karlberg, "Theological Correlation," 103.

[handwritten note: All knowledge involves an object, subject and a norm.]

view. In fact, I have no objection to anyone reorganizing and developing the biblical system of doctrine; I only present reasons for not making these activities the fundamental *definition* of theology. Karlberg, as usual, does not present these reasons or offer any argument for his own position. He simply states his distorted understanding of my view and expects the reader to agree with him. Karlberg, certainly, is open to the same charge he makes against me, that I show "little willingness to listen sympathetically to [my] critics and instead [am] too ready to misinterpret [my] opponents."[32]

The same goes for his statement that I err on "the Van Til/Clark debate . . . , theonomy . . . , the doctrine of the decrees, the *ordo salutis*, and faith as the sole instrument of justification."[33] That list covers a lot of territory, especially considering that Karlberg doesn't even bother to document or describe my views on these matters, let alone provide arguments against them.[34] These are very serious charges, as are his earlier comments that my views "strike at the very heart of the Reformed tradition"[35] and that they "undermine the authority of Scripture."[36] He speaks repeatedly of my "serious errors" and "grave deficiencies."[37]

When we are compelled to make such serious charges, we have an obligation to interpret our opponent with great care and to show by cogent argument why he is in error and why those errors are of fundamental importance. That Karlberg has not done these things indicates either intellectual incompetence or a recklessness that disregards the good name of a brother.[38]

---

32. Ibid. The reader will have to judge whether Karlberg's charge against me is true. He has not documented in his article any place where I misinterpret an opponent or critic. His review doesn't discuss my treatment of opponents.

33. Ibid., 104.

34. My doctrine of soteriological justification is not even discussed in *DKG*, and I do not recall ever publishing anything that systematically discusses justification by faith alone. I have no idea where Karlberg gets his information about me, but what he says here is slanderous. In fact, I affirm all the statements of the Reformed confessions on the doctrine of justification.

35. Karlberg, "Theological Correlation," 100.

36. Ibid., 102.

37. Ibid., 104.

38. See WLC, 144.

MARK KARLBERG ON
Cornelius Van Til: An Analysis of His Thought

In addition to his review article of *DKG* (see appendix B), Mark W. Karl-berg also reviewed my *Cornelius Van Til: An Analysis of His Thought*.[1] The review appeared in the *Mid-America Journal of Theology*.[2] When the editors received Karlberg's review, they noted how thoroughly negative it was and graciously invited me to respond in the same issue. The following is my reply, with some revision. Although the subject is somewhat removed from the subject of the present volume, I think it will be of some use for readers to have access in one volume to both of my replies to Karlberg. The reader should notice that I have similar objections to the two reviews.

Negative reviews can be helpful to an author. I recently received such a review of my Van Til book from Michael Butler, who, following up some concerns of the late Greg Bahnsen, criticized my account of Van Til's transcendental argument. Butler was gracious enough to forward his review to me by e-mail before it was to be published. Although I disagreed with Butler, I found the exchange useful, because Butler made a serious case for his position. Thinking through that argument and responding to it was a stimulating experience. Perhaps, in the course of time, this exchange will motivate me to further thought and improved formulations, if not retractions.

1. Phillipsburg, N.J.: P&R Publishing, 1995.
2. Vol. 9, no. 2 (fall 1993): 297–308. This issue of the journal was actually published in 1998.

DISAGREEMENT WITHOUT ARGUMENT

Karlberg's review is quite different. He attacks my positions on a great number of matters, but almost never (I say "almost" only because I may have missed something) presents any argument for his position. He simply states dogmatically what the truth is, in his view, and how I fall short of it.

My first example: Karlberg faults me for not stressing the importance of covenant theology and the influence of Geerhardus Vos on Van Til's thought. He says that covenant theology is "the warp and woof of [Van Til's] apologetic theology." Well, that's something we could have discussed. In the book, I do mention Van Til's friendship with Vos and some Vossian influences in Van Til's writing (pp. 20–21). The appendix by Edmund P. Clowney mentions biblical-theological emphases in Van Til's preaching. In writing the book, I was certainly open to finding also in Van Til's apologetic system a major covenantal, redemptive-historical emphasis.

But in fact Van Til does not say much about distinctively redemptive-historical issues. He says nothing about dispensationalism. In eschatology, he never gets much beyond the basics of eternal life and divine judgment. He never addresses questions about the relations of law and grace in the various historical covenants. He never presents distinctively Christocentric interpretations of Old Testament texts, except in his sermons. He even says that "theology is primarily God centered rather than Christ centered."[3] He does discuss common grace in a redemptive-historical framework, and my book treats that in detail. He emphasizes "direct revelation in history" over against Karl Barth. He also uses phrases like "the Christian story," which indicate his familiarity with the redemptive-historical approach to Scripture. But he doesn't elucidate these phrases, nor do they play any substantive role in the development of his apologetic argument. Doubtless Van Til would have *said* that redemptive history is vitally important.[4] But in fact, contrary to Karlberg and William Dennison, he rarely dealt with it in his apologetic writing.

Now it is possible that I have missed something important here. This

---

3. Van Til, *An Introduction to Systematic Theology* (Privately printed, 1971), 2. That contrast sounds terrible, I know, to biblical theologians, but that is Van Til's own phraseology.

4. It is not difficult to construe Van Til's approach in terms of covenantal categories. Thus, in my *DKG*, I develop a Van Tillian epistemology in terms of God's covenant lordship. Certainly his thinking is admirably fitted to this kind of treatment. But it is interesting and curious that Van Til never did this himself.

discussion would have been profitable to me if Karlberg had given some examples of the "centrality of covenant theology" in Van Til's writing that I had missed. But Karlberg offers none. Rather, he seems to assume that everybody knows he is right. So all that remains to be done is for Karlberg to denounce my "serious and glaring omission." He seems to want me to repent of an error simply on his say-so.

Another example of Karlberg's dogmatism: I spent four chapters of the book dealing with Van Til's treatment of the history of apologetics. My conclusions about the apologetic tradition are much more favorable than Van Til's. I would have found it helpful if Karlberg, who is himself a historian, had entered the discussion to show me where in this analysis I am wrong and Van Til is right. He does not do this. He merely faults me because "in each of these cases . . . it is Van Til who loses out to his theological disputants." In other words, I am wrong simply because I reach a different conclusion from Van Til and Karlberg.

The same thing is true on the issue of the antithesis between the believer and the unbeliever in knowledge. Van Til himself admitted that this is a "difficult point."[5] I spend one chapter trying to sort out five of the different ways in which Van Til tries to formulate this antithesis. It was not an easy chapter to write, and I would still be happy to receive additional help in understanding these issues. The best Karlberg can do, however, is to fault me for claiming that unbelievers know some "truths." Oddly, he admits that Van Til himself attributes truths to the unbeliever, as "merely borrowed capital from Christianity." Does Karlberg think that I regard the unbeliever's knowledge as anything other than borrowed capital? If so, what did I say that gave him that idea? (Had he shown me any such passage in my book, I would have retracted it in this response.) But again, he presents no argument, just a lot of rhetoric about my "rationalistic evidentialism."

On the Clark controversy, Karlberg objects to my conclusion that Van Til misunderstood or misrepresented Clark. Again, I ask, what was wrong with my argument? And again, Karlberg doesn't say. My crime, evidently, is simply that I disagreed with Van Til to some extent (even, I must add, in the course of *defending* Van Til's general view of God's incomprehensibility).

Similarly, Karlberg dogmatically rejects my account of God's decrees and of the problem of evil. He accuses me of misreading Aquinas, Butler, Carnell, and Clark, but provides not one specific instance. He attacks my view of creedal doctrinal detail without specifying how comprehensive and de-

5. Van Til, *An Introduction to Systematic Theology*, 26.

tailed *he* thinks creeds should be,[6] and certainly without defending any alternative view against mine. He merely expects his readers to accept these judgments on Mark Karlberg's say-so.

Who is Mark Karlberg, to demand such instant acquiescence on the part of his readers? A writer in historical theology, as I mentioned before. To my knowledge, he has neither credentials nor expertise in apologetics or epistemology beyond the courses he took in seminary.[7] Certainly he hasn't shown any such expertise in the present review. Why, then, did he write it? My most charitable interpretation is that Karlberg is what I call in the book a "movement Van Tillian." He is unwilling to admit any failing of substance in Van Til (or in Machen or Kline, his other heroes). He has bought into a party line that says Van Til was almost (?) always right and his opponents almost always wrong. One of my most prominent motives in writing the book was to combat that kind of thinking. Karlberg perceives, therefore, that he and others who think like him are among the major targets of the criticisms of my book, and he feels the need for somebody to strike back. Frame doesn't buy the party line, so Karlberg must stand in the breach, come to the rescue: Karlberg *Defensor Fidei*. He does this even though he is tongue-tied when it comes to serious interaction. All he can say is (to employ a phrase Van Til uses in a different connection) "You are wrong, and I am right."

If readers find this kind of approach credible, I don't know what more I can say. But for those capable of some critical distance from movement thinking, I add this: I take the movement mentality to be the exact antithesis of Christian scholarship, the chief rule of which is that we may not idolize men. I love and admire Van Til enough, as Karlberg points out, to call him "perhaps the most important Christian thinker since Calvin." But I do not think we do Van Til—or even Calvin—a service by treating them as deuterocanonical. Godly scholars assume the existence of finitude and sin in every thinker, including themselves, and they insist on testing everything by God's Word alone. The best honor we can do for Van Til is to treat him critically, for only thus can we be serious in determining how to build on his foundation.

---

6. It is logically possible to argue that creeds should be as exhaustive as Scripture. I presume that that is not Karlberg's position. So where does he draw the line?

7. I confess that my problem here is not only with Karlberg, but with the editorial policies by which such writing is accepted for publication. Beyond the present instance, I am still bewildered after several years as to why editor Ronald Youngblood accepted his review of my *DKG* (entitled "On the Theological Correlation of Divine and Human Language") for publication in *JETS* 32 (1989): 99–105 (see appendix B).

IS FRAME A VAN TILLIAN?

Karlberg might reply that his real intent in writing his review was to expose me to the Reformed public: to show that I was not the Van Tillian that I pretended to be.[8] In the book, I myself raised that issue (pp. 17–18, 391). I was quite forthright, from the introductory chapters onward, in saying that my approach to Van Til would be one of critical analysis, not slavish defense. I told my readers that they would have to be the judges of whether or not I was a "pure" Van Tillian.

But, as a matter of fact, that question is of little interest to me. I want above all to hold a scriptural position. If that turns out also to be Van Tillian, so be it. If it turns out to be evidentialist, or Clarkian, or Plantingan, or something else, that won't bother me very much. Historical schools of thought are useful categories for analysis, but poor guides for thought. Christian thinkers should be far more concerned about what God's Word says than about what historical party they are associating with.[9]

At the same time, I wish to emphasize here that I am not nearly as critical of Van Til as Karlberg's review makes me appear. From Karlberg's account, the reader would never guess that I defend enthusiastically Van Til's distinctive positions on God's aseity and absolute personality, the ontological Trinity as the eternal one-and-many,[10] the universal scope of divine foreordination, the equal ultimacy of election and reprobation,[11] analogi-

8. We gather from his italics that Karlberg intends us to feel aghast when he writes that "Frame's work, in my judgment, marks a *decisive departure* from Van Tilian presuppositionalism."

9. This is one reason I did not take the course of discussing Van Til's Dutch forebears, as Karlberg thinks I should have. Doubtless if he had written such a book, he would simply have taken Van Til's ideas for granted and then inserted them into their historical context. But my intent was to critically analyze Van Til's thought to determine its truth, not simply to accept his position and inquire where his ideas came from. One cannot resolve issues of truth by historical description; attempts to do so are called "genetic fallacies." The only way to resolve controversial issues is through exegesis and argument, not historical description. That is, perhaps, one of my differences with Karlberg, for, as we have seen, Karlberg oddly seems to think he can resolve these questions without argument. He thinks he can refute me merely by showing that I depart in some measure from a historically defined tradition. For my response to this kind of methodology, see my "Traditionalism," available at www.thirdmill.org.

Even for my purposes, of course, it might have been useful to compare Van Til with earlier Reformed thinkers, but the book was already a long one, and I still think my choice of subjects was wise.

10. This includes his rather controversial view that God is (paradoxically) in one sense *one* person.

11. Naturally I reject as absurd Karlberg's talk about a "wedding" in my book "between Arminianism and Calvinism."

cal knowledge, divine incomprehensibility,[12] the necessity, authority, clarity, and sufficiency of both natural and special revelation, the necessity of presupposing God's Word in all of our reasoning, the relation of intellect, emotions, and will, the place of logic and paradox, the role of evidence, the nature of common grace and antithesis,[13] the necessity of circular and transcendental argument, and many, many other specific points. Nor would a reader of Karlberg's review suspect that I had (or even could have) included as an appendix a 22-page refutation of the traditional evidentialism of John Gerstner and R. C. Sproul. The main thrust of my 463-page book is defensive and affirmative. The critical observations are intended only to clarify, sharpen, and improve Van Til's own methodology.

The chief function of a review is to give readers an idea of what is in a book and what its general thrust is. In that respect, Karlberg's review is a failure.

SOME OTHER ISSUES

Some may think I was too harsh earlier when I questioned Karlberg's expertise in apologetics and epistemology. But that judgment was a considered one, based not only on Karlberg's apparent inability to argue his positions, but also upon a number of places in the review where he clearly misunderstands the issues he discusses.[14] Examples:

1. When I described Van Til as "isolated," I did not intend that, as Karlberg thinks I did, as a criticism *per se*.[15] Indeed, I indicated (p. 37) that "such isolation may sometimes be necessary for the free development of important and controversial theological ideas." My point was (and it should have been obvious) that such isolation creates problems for a thinker that may need to be remedied by his successors.[16]

---

12. When Karlberg quotes me as rejecting one of Van Til's arguments against Clark as "preposterous," he is referring to a discussion of a subpoint of a subpoint. Any fair-minded reader would recognize that the overall thrust of my discussion aims to defend *every* theological point of importance to Van Til in the controversy with Clark.

13. As Karlberg says, I do question some of Van Til's formulations of the antithesis. I believe that some of them are unbiblical as well as inconsistent with one another. But the formulations I recommend, following this analysis, are Van Til's own. I have had to choose some of Van Til's formulations and reject others.

14. My judgment is also based upon Karlberg's quite incompetent review of my *DKG* (to which I offer a reply here in appendix B).

15. Nor did I intend as a criticism my statement that the Orthodox Presbyterian Church was a "tiny" denomination. That was simply a statement of fact to underscore the degree of Van Til's isolation. The size of a Christian body is never in itself ground for criticism, though the reasons for its size (whether the size be great or small) may be.

16. As for Karlberg's gratuitous personal remarks about my own isolation, I grant that

2. I do not see a "tension" between Van Til's "winsome manner" and his "vigorous apologetic defense . . . and thoroughgoing critique," as Karlberg thinks I do. I do see a tension between Van Til's winsomeness and his sometimes unfair criticisms of his opponents.

3. Karlberg cites my threefold analysis of reformations (confrontation, consolidation, and continuation) and points out that Van Til's career included all these aspects. I agree; indeed, I said that the three phases could not be sharply distinguished. Karlberg then warns that we shouldn't "reduce" the "individual labors" of Van Til and others to "mere confrontation." Did it perhaps escape Karlberg's notice that I align Van Til primarily *not* with "confrontation," but with "consolidation"?

4. Karlberg descends to personal criticism rather often in this review, the main thrust of it being that I am more interested in promoting my own positions than in analyzing Van Til. Certainly my analysis of Van Til is from my own point of view; no writer (certainly not Karlberg) can write from any point of view other than his own. But I certainly disavow any intention to distort Van Til's teaching to make him sound like me, or to criticize Van Til's work merely to enhance my own reputation. If Karlberg is going to make such accusations, which I deeply resent, let him produce some evidence. It is usually considered bad manners to raise such issues in a scholarly discussion.

And it is even worse to distort what a writer says in a way that smears his character. That's what Karlberg does when he says, "[Frame] believes that his work probes 'more deeply into Van Til's thought than have either his traditional friends or foes.' " This quote (from p. ix) makes me sound hugely egotistical. But Karlberg has left out some significant parts of the context. The complete paragraph reads:

> This is not the last word on Van Til. I hope herein to further a genuine dialogue on his work, a dialogue that has heretofore been hindered by misinformation and poorly reasoned arguments for and against him. I am trying to go more deeply into Van Til's thought than have either his traditional friends or foes. If I have not succeeded, I pray that this book will provoke one or more successful alternative accounts with the same ambitions.

Note here the first and last sentences and the word "trying," which Karlberg leaves out of the sentence he quotes. By this distortion, Karlberg makes it look as if I am on an ego trip. In any case, what he says is false. I

---

they are largely true, though I doubt that that admission has much relevance to our discussion. Karlberg needs to be reminded that the *tu quoque* argument is a fallacy.

do not "believe" that my work probes more deeply than anyone else's. That depth has been my goal. Whether I have achieved it, others must judge.

5. He says that according to my interpretation of election and reprobation, " 'particular people' though under the wrath of God are neither elect nor reprobate. They *become* elect or reprobate in time." As usual, he does not present any quotes or evidence that this is my view. I simply deny it. I haven't the foggiest notion why he thinks I hold such a position. There is, of course, such a thing as historical election (Israel was God's elect, but later became *lo ammi*), but there is also the eternal election and reprobation of God, forever settled in the divine decree, which I defend in chapter 6 of my book.

6. He rejects my definition of a presupposition as "the fundamental religious direction of a person's thought" and says that herein I "substitute human subjectivism for the objective revelation of God." Nonsense. *Presupposition* does sometimes refer to something objective (i.e., to what is presupposed), but far more often it refers to the basic commitment of a human person, something subjective. That is how both Van Til and I use the term. To so define the word is not subjectivist, however, because in our view a person's basic subjective commitment must be to the objective revelation of God.

Or does Karlberg imagine that even to discuss the subjective act of presupposing necessarily compromises God's objective revelation? The most elementary fact about human knowledge is that it involves both a subject and an object.[17] Therefore, epistemology must discuss both the subjective and the objective aspects of knowledge. Van Til understood this well. If Karlberg doesn't understand it, he should not participate in this discussion.

7. At the end of his review, Karlberg calls upon us to "abandon all pretense regarding the use of rational argument to justify, validate, or corroborate the thoughts and ways of the Creator to the creature." Is he denying the value of rational arguments in apologetics, asking us, as the earlier part of the paragraph suggests, to substitute proclamation for argument? That would be characteristic of Karlberg's practice in this review, but it would be very much opposed to Van Til's own conception of apologetics. Van Til eschewed fideism and insisted that Christianity was rationally defensible. He said that a testimony that is not an argument is not a testimony, and vice versa.[18] Those who interpret Van Til fideistically play into the hands of his evidentialist critics, who find that a most damaging admission.

17. And a norm, to complete my triad. See *DKG*.
18. Van Til, "Why I Believe in God" (Philadelphia: Committee on Christian Education, Orthodox Presbyterian Church, n.d.), 16.

Or is Karlberg merely condemning *some kinds of* rational arguments? If so, he has confused us by not telling us which ones he has in mind. Or is he merely saying that rational arguments are less important in Christian witness than the Word of God and the Holy Spirit? Certainly that is true, both for Van Til and for me, but I fail to see how that bears upon anything we have been discussing.

8. Finally, I should say a bit about perspectivalism, which Karlberg finds at the root of all my errors. As usual, Karlberg gets it wrong. He quotes as my "definition" of perspectivalism a passage which is not a definition at all, but a description of one implication of it. A better definition: perspectivalism is the recognition that because we are finite, sinful, and therefore fallible, we need to guard against error by looking at the truth from many angles or perspectives. Scripture recognizes this fact in giving us four gospels, rather than one: four perspectives on the same events. Similarly, it gives us both Kings and Chronicles, and both Jude and 2 Peter 2. It narrates the Exodus, and then presents it poetically in Exodus 15 and many Psalms.

The first page of Calvin's *Institutes* tells us that we cannot know ourselves without knowing God, and that we cannot know God without knowing ourselves. Interestingly, Calvin adds, "I don't know which comes first." His point is that knowing God and knowing ourselves are simultaneous and inseparable. Knowing God and knowing oneself are really one single act of knowledge, viewed from different perspectives. To say this is not to identify self and God, but it is to identify *knowing* self with *knowing* God.

This implies that to know God's Word, we must also know how the Word applies to ourselves. To miss the applications is to miss something crucially important about the Word. God gives us his Word for the purpose of application (2 Tim. 3:16–17). So one cannot understand the Bible without understanding how it applies to his life. We cannot, like the Pharisees, claim to know the "meaning" of Scripture without understanding its bearing on our lives. Interpretation and application are one.

Karlberg rejects this formulation in favor of the more traditional maxim that doctrine precedes application. Why? Again, he gives no argument. He mentions the influence of Wittgenstein on me;[19] I do not deny that I have read Wittgenstein with some profit. But that is not an argument against the truth of my view, unless we assume that we can learn nothing at all from non-Christian thinkers.[20] Without argument, he says that my equa-

19. Another genetic fallacy.
20. Karlberg, of course, may be assuming that, since he rejects my criticisms of Van Til's "extreme antithetical language." But I argue in my book that this notion is unbiblical and not representative of Van Til at his best.

[handwritten: INTERPRETATIONS AND APPLICATION (IS OBEDIENCE A SEPERATE ISSUE?)]

tion between interpretation and application "compromises Scripture's own authority" and even "obscures the Creator/creature distinction." I absolutely deny these charges, and I am quite bewildered by them. I really have no idea how he gets from my texts to his conclusions. But if anyone is confused about my position, let me put it this way: interpretation and application are one, but they are interpretations and applications of Scripture, the infallible, inerrant, supremely authoritative, and sufficient Word of the Creator God.

I suspect that part of the problem that Karlberg and others have with my view at this point is that they equate God's Word with "doctrine." So when I say that doctrine is not prior to life, they think I am saying that God's Word is not prior to life. I, however, follow the biblical usage in which "doctrine" (*didachē, didaskalia*) is the human activity of *communicating* the Word of God. As such, doctrine, like all human activities, is part of life, and subject to Scripture. So the important thing is not to make doctrine prior to life, but to make both doctrine and life subject to Scripture.[21] *[handwritten: KEY]*

[handwritten in margin: KEY]

As for my argument that Van Til is implicitly perspectival, it should surprise nobody. He is a disciple of Calvin and Kuyper, and he has a rich sense of the organic unity of God's creation, of how everything is profoundly related to everything else through the unity of God's eternal plan. My book discusses that at length. Would that Karlberg had paid a small amount of attention to that discussion.

What perspectivalism does is to recognize the unity of human experience under the supreme authority of God's revelation. It removes from us the temptation of idolizing some element of human experience, whether traditional or contemporary, and it frees us to judge our experiences by God's Word alone, *sola Scriptura*.[22] So the thrust of perspectivalism is precisely opposite to what Karlberg thinks it is. And, incidentally, it therefore sets us free from the kind of blind traditionalism and party spirit that characterizes Karlberg's review. Perhaps that is why Karlberg is so strongly bent on opposing it. I can only ask readers to go back and read what I have actually written, testing it by God's Word. I have provided extensive scriptural support for my positions, and I can only ask that that support be examined seriously.

---

21. There are some biblical senses in which life is prior to doctrine: regeneration is prior to faith and spiritual understanding (John 3:3); nonconformity to the world precedes our ability to test and approve God's will (Rom. 12:2). For more on these subjects, see *DKG*.

22. See my "In Defense of Something Close to Biblicism," *WTJ* 59 (1997): 269–318, with replies from David F. Wells and Richard A. Muller. My article, without the interaction, is reprinted in my *Contemporary Worship Music* (Phillipsburg, N.J.: P&R Publishing, 1997), 175–201.

REVIEW OF BENJAMIN WIRT FARLEY,
The Providence of God[1]

This review was originally published in the *Westminster Theological Journal.*[2] In it I tried to expose some confusions, especially about predestination, that exist, not only in Farley's work, but also in other recent theological writers in the Reformed tradition. I thought that readers of this volume might find it profitable to observe this interchange.

Divine providence is, I think, one of the more neglected doctrines in today's theologies, and I am pleased to find in this book evidence of some concentrated thought on the subject. There are, however, many weaknesses in it, so many that its chief value may be to stimulate others to develop better treatments of the subject.

The book tries to cover many bases: biblical teaching, Greek philosophical concepts, the history of Christian doctrine, the impact of modern science, modern theological discussions of "acts of God," the "challenge of process theology." Obviously, a book of this size cannot deal in depth with so many topics. The book is like a great big theological dictionary article, presenting the basic facts plus some very concise personal observations, usually summarizing "common wisdom" on the various issues. Those

---

1. Grand Rapids: Baker, 1988.
2. *WTJ* 51 (1989): 397–400.

who have need for such a summarized treatment should buy the book. However, those who, like me, pick up books with such titles hoping to find some new insights into difficult problems (such as, in this case, evil, freedom, and predestination) will be disappointed.

Farley has three degrees from Union Theological Seminary of Richmond, Virginia (including doctoral work under John Leith), and now teaches Bible, Religion, and Philosophy at Erskine College. He identifies his theological position as Reformed, and he is interested in other traditions mainly for the contributions they can make toward a Reformed understanding. In general, Farley's position within the Reformed camp is conservative; he greatly respects the classical formulations. His own formulations are more in debt to Louis Berkhof than to anyone else. However, Farley has the annoying habit of routinely referring to Barth and Brunner as "modern proponents of a Reformed perspective" (p. 229; cf. pp. 19, 23, 24, 27, 31, etc.), without any awareness of the great gulf between them and Calvin as shown, e.g., by Van Til in *Christianity and Barthianism*.[3] Similarly, he welcomes Reinhold Niebuhr to the Reformed tradition (p. 107).

Farley's own views also raise questions here about the meaning for him of "Reformed." He affirms the Reformation's *sola Scriptura*, but his formulation of it is disappointing: he says that it forbids principles which "might actually repudiate, contradict, or compromise the central motifs of the Bible" (p. 17).[4] Only the central motifs? And I shall discuss later the question of Farley's view of divine sovereignty; that, too, raises some questions about his actual relation to the Reformed tradition.

The book begins with some basic distinctions. Farley argues first that providence is "a doctrine of faith" rather than "a postulate of reason." He notes here some interesting biblical connections between providence and faith, but he never quite explains what view he is opposing. Is he simply affirming *sola Scriptura* as above? Is he saying that providence is not part of general revelation? Then what of Acts 14:17; 17:24–28; etc.? Is he saying that we repress this truth apart from faith? But is that not the case with all of God's truth? Is he opposing philosophical attempts to prove divine providence? What kind of philosophical attempts? Christian? Non-Christian? All? In any case, much more must be said about Christian epistemology.

Then he argues that providence is importantly related to the doctrine of election. His dependence on Barth and Brunner here is a bit disconcerting, and the precise relationship of the two doctrines somewhat eludes

---

3. Philadelphia: Presbyterian and Reformed, 1962.

4. Even if he had made his definition broader, to include everything in Scripture, this formulation defines, not the sufficiency of Scripture, but its authority.

his descriptions. Evidently he doesn't want "to subsume, as completely as Barth does, the preservation of human life under the rubric of salvation or election" (p. 36). But this question is not a question of degree ("as completely as"), but a question of precisely what relation is in view. Also, Farley seems to feel that this emphasis gives us more of a "christological accent" (p. 25) and makes our formulations "less authoritarian, speculative, and deductive" than the "older Reformed dogmatics" (ibid.). This point seems to me neither clear nor obvious, especially in view of the fact that it suggests supralapsarianism, a view which is often portrayed as the very source of much "authoritarian, speculative, and deductive" thinking in the post-Reformation period.

He then argues in a fairly traditional way, though again in dialogue with Barth, that providence is not "continuous creation" (pp. 27ff.) and expounds the basic Reformed view in terms of preservation, cooperation ("concurrence"), and government (pp. 31–46). Nothing new here; as a summary it is fine.

Similarly for the historical survey that occupies the next six chapters and the bulk of the book. Through this section he intersperses some analysis with the descriptive material, but one will not find here, for example, any notable contributions to interpretive controversies about Plato or Aquinas. Farley's evaluations are very sketchy. He seems to feel that he must say something positive and something negative about everybody; so for example he tells us that Plato's god has "high moral and rational attributes" (p. 58), but "yet" he is forced to admit that this god is only "a myth which functions in a metaphorical way to attest to the phenomenon of the power and possibility of an ideal Good" (ibid.). In my view, it would have been less misleading to weight the criticism in a more strongly negative direction. What good are God's moral and rational attributes if, in the final analysis, he is only a myth? Well, I may be carping here. The real problem is that Farley's analyses are so sketchy that he is never able to develop an argument yielding fresh insight. When I read such books I am tempted to carp.

Farley attempts to deal with all major thinkers only through Schleiermacher. His treatment of the impact of science ends with Darwin, though some later developments are mentioned. Among twentieth-century thinkers, he deals only with G. Ernest Wright, Rudolf Bultmann, Gordon Kaufman, the process thinkers (mainly Cobb and Griffin, *Process Theology*, with an exposition of Gilkey's reply in *Reaping the Whirlwind*), and of course Barth and Brunner. Again, this is good theological dictionary material; but when one considers the enormous impact of twentieth-century sciences, philosophies, and theologies upon people's views of providence, one wishes that Farley had done much more to bring his discussion up to date. Nothing, really, is said about Heisenberg or Einstein (not to mention "chaos theory"), or philosophers of science like Kuhn. We miss also any significant treatment of existentialism, analytic philosophical discussions of determinism, or even significant theological views like those of Pannenberg or the liberation theologians.

We should not, however, exaggerate the importance of the problems I have noted above. Most of these problems derive from the format of the book, in which Farley is forced to deal with many things in a very short space. Since the length of a book is often determined by the publisher rather than the author, the format problem may not be entirely of Farley's making. And in any case, the overconciseness does not prevent the book from being a useful survey of basic facts for those who need to have them.

I do have, however, a more serious criticism, a substantive one which goes beyond format problems. That is the author's confusion on that most basic issue, the sovereignty of God.

Farley is a Calvin scholar and has edited and translated Calvin's *Sermons on the Ten Commandments* and *Treatises Against the Anabaptists and the Libertines*. He notes in the preface to *The Providence of God* that in working through the second Calvin volume, especially chapters 13–16 of the *Treatise Against the Libertines,* he "was struck by the clarity and simplicity of Calvin's argument against the Libertines' pantheistic and deterministic interpretation of nature and history" (p. 11). These chapters "proved Calvin's theology to be far less deterministic than I had previously thought it to be" (ibid.). More specifically, he says, Calvin rejected "the notion that God is the unqualified cause of all causes" (p. 154; cf. pp. 219, 235). Farley then resolved, in writing *The Providence of God*, to keep in view "Calvin's own approach as a sort of guiding norm" (ibid.).

In the present volume, then, Farley seeks to develop a Reformed position which is not "deterministic" in the way that he thinks, for example, Zwingli's position was (pp. 143–50). He makes a distinction between "hard" and "soft" determinism. So far as I can tell, he never defines "hard" determinism, though he associates it with fatalism, the idea that "regardless of what we do, the outcome will be the same" (p. 69, quoting Adolf Grunbaum). "Soft" determinism means that "Rules for managing individuals and nations can be based only on causal laws which tell us that *if* such and such is done, it is likely that the outcome will be thus and so" (ibid., again quoting Grunbaum). Not having access to Grunbaum's article, I won't try to explain Grunbaum's meaning here. Farley, however, takes this principle to mean that "events are rightly the results of antecedent causes, but not necessarily the results of unalterable, predetermined *causae*" (ibid. I confess I don't understand this very well. He seems to be saying in the first clause that all (?) events are caused; but in the second clause he says that these causes are not unalterable, nor are they themselves predetermined. If they are not predetermined, then evidently they are uncaused. But that would mean that not all events are caused, contrary to the impression left by the first clause.

At any rate, it is fairly clear to me (not entirely) that Farley is here opening a door to "free will" in the sense of philosophical libertarianism and theological Arminianism. See especially pp. 75, 78f., 91, 149, 166. His "soft determinism" seems not to be determinism at all in any conventional philosophical sense. It is, rather, an indeterminism. It is possible that I have misunderstood him here. It certainly would have improved communication if Farley had offered some comparison between his view of freedom and that of Calvin's opponent Pighius, or between his and that of Arminius, who brought grief to later Calvinists. But Farley seems almost intentionally vague in this area.

Another confusing thing is that Farley leaves out a very significant alternative. That is the view that although all events including human decisions are foreordained (by God in the theological context), free human choices are still important because (a) they are not coerced and (b) they are necessary means to the preordained end. That is, incidentally, the view which is *usually* called "soft determinism" by philosophers. William James had it in mind when he first developed the hard/soft distinction in his "The Dilemma of Determinism." Paul Edwards, in "Hard and Soft Determinism" associates this view also with Hume, Mill, and Schlick. I would say too that this is the position of the Westminster Confession of Faith, 9.1, and of Calvinists generally.

Including Calvin. Farley's book did stimulate me to study closely Calvin's *Treatise Against the Libertines*, 13–16 (in Farley's edition!), and I certainly did not find what he thinks is there. On Farley's own account, Calvin is here criticizing a *pantheistic* determinism. His opponents were maintaining that no distinction can be drawn between God's acts and ours and that therefore "it is not lawful to condemn anything" (p. 255). Calvin replies by emphasizing that God does no sin and that men are responsible before him. But to support those points he does not resort to any kind of libertarianism. On the contrary, he begins by saying, "We do not deny that whatever comes to pass does so by the will of God" (p. 242). Providence is universal, and "what pagans and the illiterate attribute to fortune we must assign to the providence of God" (p. 244). Creatures "who constitute secondary [*inferieurs*] causes are only means by which [God] fulfils his will . . ." (pp. 244, 245). But, "when we say that God works in evildoers, that does not prevent them from working also in their own behalf" (p. 245); and "(Scripture) attributes to them the work which they have done by the ordinance of God" (ibid.). At no time does Calvin here say what Farley attributes to him, namely, that God is not "the unqualified cause of all causes." There is not a hint of libertarianism here. (And even if there were, what would Farley do with all the apparent "determinism" of Calvin's other writings? Farley's reliance upon four chapters of the *Treatise* is a frail reed indeed.) Calvin is a soft determinist in the sense of my definition, not Farley's.

So: buy the book to get a concise factual history of the concept of providence, but not to seek new or deep insight. Above all, try to ignore what he says about determinism and freedom, which in my opinion will only produce confusion.

All events, including human decisions, are foreordained by God; free human choices are still important because (a) they are not coerced and (b) they are necessary means to the preordained end.

Human liberty does not consist in the capacity to perform uncaused actions, but in the capacity to act according to one's own desires; a capacity which is "compatible" with the divine foreordination of those desires and actions.

REVIEW OF PAUL HELM,
The Providence of God[1]

I include this review[2] to draw readers' attention to a very fine Reformed work, somewhat popular in style, but very insightful. Helm responds to what we now call open theism. I take issue with a few things, but the book has taught me much.

Over the last twenty years, there has been a revival of religious, and especially Christian, influence upon philosophy. When I majored in philosophy at Princeton from 1957 to 1961, a student would have been laughed out of a seminar for even tentatively suggesting a theistic response to a philosophical question. Today, however, a great number of well-respected philosophical thinkers are arguing historic Christian positions. With this movement we may associate names like Plantinga, Wolterstorff, Alston, Mavrodes, Adams, Swinburne, Hasker, Craig, Stump, Zagzebski, Morris, Willard, Kreeft. Paul Helm, professor of the history and philosophy of religion at King's College of the University of London, has been very much a part of this, but also more.

While there is much to applaud in this movement, I confess that I have been disappointed that certain views are almost universally shared among

---

1. Leicester: InterVarsity Press, 1993.
2. Originally published in *WTJ* 56 (1994): 438–42.

these thinkers, especially (1) weak views of biblical authority, (2) the conviction that divine supratemporality must be jettisoned for philosophical reasons, and (3) the idea that the problem of evil and the nature of human moral responsibility require us to adopt an indeterminist concept of human freedom such as was advocated by Pelagius, Molina, and Arminius.

On all three of these matters, Helm diverges from the consensus. Once an associate editor of *The Banner of Truth*, Helm has worked in the history of doctrine as well as philosophy. He is a Calvinist, and one who does not hesitate to argue the philosophical cogency of historic Reformed positions. He recognizes the central, indeed sufficient, role of Scripture in doctrinal formulation, and he has argued the timelessness of God in his book *Eternal God*. In previous books, but especially in the present volume, he has also articulated and defended a historic Reformed view of divine sovereignty. To me, therefore, his writing is enormously refreshing, and all the more so because he does his work so very well. The present volume itself is excellently done on the whole with, of course, a few imperfections.

The Providence of God seeks to set forth the biblical doctrine of providence, discussing both philosophical and practical issues related to it. That may be a bit much to try to include in a volume of this size. You will not find here the kind of in-depth exegesis characteristic of Bavinck or Murray. For the most part, Helm sticks with exegetical points which are fairly obvious, however neglected by our Arminian friends. An exception would be pp. 224–28, where his interesting discussion of the "weakness of God" gets beyond the scope of traditional Reformed exegesis. The philosophical and more broadly theological argumentation is more satisfying than the Scripture exegesis as such, although I wished at a number of points (especially pp. 168ff., 177ff., 189ff., and 224ff.) that Helm had taken more space (or been permitted more space by his editors) to give more adequate development to his thoughts.

While I'm mentioning formal weaknesses of the volume, I would also observe that on a number of matters (such as prayer, pp. 78ff., 145ff.; efficacious grace, pp. 119f., 189f.; voluntarism, pp. 165ff., 183f.; fatalism, pp. 137ff., 218ff., 232ff.; two divine "wills," pp. 47ff., 131ff.), Helm sketches a position, breaks off the discussion, and then resumes it later in the book. This creates some repetition as well as some separation between matters that should perhaps have been discussed together. Later discussions sometimes contain material that would have been helpful for a reader to have at the earlier point. For example, the discussion of modeling on pp. 31ff. would have been more helpful had it been placed beside the actual description of providential models on pp. 168ff. Some case could be made for this "resumptive" approach, but I find it something of a hindrance to comprehension.

On the whole, however, the book is very clearly written and contains cogent arguments on important issues, which I will summarize here, with some evaluation.

Helm identifies his Calvinistic position as a "no-risk" view of providence, as over against various views of Arminian, Socinian, and "process" thinkers, in which God "takes risks." For Helm, God takes no risks, because he has foreordained all the events of nature and history. Helm expounds the no-risk view in three interrelated contexts: the course of nature and history, the history of redemption, and the experience of the individual Christian (in my vocabulary: situational, normative, and existential, respectively).

Methodologically, he insists that a Christian doctrine of providence must be derived from Scripture (p. 27), but not by way of deduction from some master-concept, nor by development of a quasi-scientific "theory" which could be tested by events. He not only rejects the analogy between theology and scientific explanation, but also with "personal explanation," on the ground that God's intentions (as opposed to the intentions of finite agents) are known only as he reveals them. But isn't that true of finite agents as well, making possible the kind of analogy he himself develops on p. 36? Here again, I wish he had expounded his argument at greater length.

Positively, he urges the use of "models" by which the scriptural data can be drawn together coherently and false inferences discouraged. His fundamental model is that of biblical divine sovereignty and the resulting "compatibilist" view of human freedom (pp. 66ff., 174ff.). That is, human liberty does not consist in the capacity to perform uncaused actions, as in "risky" views of providence (otherwise called indeterminism, libertarianism, Arminianism), but in the capacity to act according to one's own desires, a capacity which is "compatible" with the divine foreordination of those desires and actions.

Helm supplements this basic model with others on pp. 168ff.: that of evil as a "privation," divine "permission" of evil, specific "permission" (not the Arminian *nuda permissio*), and a distinction between "levels" (divine and creaturely) of causality. All of these, I think, deserve more thorough discussion than he presents. I'm not as convinced as he is of the value of the first two. As to the fourth, he remarks that, on the model of dual "causal levels," "it is hard to see that there can be two separate sets of necessary and sufficient conditions for the same action" (p. 182), and leaves the matter there. But he might have explored further submodels, like the relation between an author and the characters in a novel, in which that same duality of necessary and sufficient conditions obtains.

But doesn't Scripture sometimes represent God as "taking risks," being ignorant, changing his mind, giving people the power to resist his will? Granted that Scripture also includes affirmations of God's foreordination of all things, should we accommodate the latter expressions to the former, or vice versa? Helm responds to this question by pointing out the theological costs and benefits of the two alternatives. In the final analysis, the risk language must be accommodated to the no-risk teaching; else we would have to deny clear biblical teachings about God's omniscience, will, and efficacious grace. That would be a "theological reductionism in which God is distilled to human proportions" (p. 52). He explains the "risk" language in terms of Calvin's doctrine of accommodation, but with an insight of his own: God must represent his actions as temporal in order to demand a human response in space and time. This is a rather profound point, correct in my estimation, and one which, again, I wish he had been able to expound at greater length.

Today it is popular among philosophers to use the concept of divine "middle knowledge" (knowledge of what will happen granted any possible set of conditions) in order to reconcile divine sovereignty with indeterminist human freedom. Helm points out quite rightly that if people have such indeterminist freedom, God cannot have "middle knowledge" of what they will do granted previous conditions. For the conditions, on this view, never determine human free actions. Thus indeterminism excludes divine middle knowledge. Helm is absolutely right here, and I can't understand why so many other sophisticated philosophers have failed to see this point.

Helm recognizes that it is not possible to make these matters perfectly transparent to reason, but he is also (I think wisely) reluctant to state *a priori* what can and cannot be understood by reason: see the discussion of antinomy on pp. 61–66.

His discussions of pantheism, panentheism, deism, and theism are illuminating, although I am not entirely clear as to a couple matters: (1) Helm argues that pantheism and panentheism exclude any interaction between Creator and creature, because "it is impossible for one thing to interact with itself" (p. 73). True; but if the pantheist (unlike Parmenides) permits some degree of complexity within his monistic reality, it is not clear why there could not be some interaction between God and his aspects/parts, as indeed finite persons interact with their own bodies, qualities, and thoughts. (2) Helm thinks the idea of creation in time is conducive to deism (p. 79), but I am not persuaded by his very sketchy argument for this assertion.

Helm's account of providence in the history of redemption will be fa-

miliar ground to students of Reformed theology, but probably not to n
customers of InterVarsity Press. He discusses creation, the Fall, covenant,
miracle and prophecy, the Incarnation, and the important (though sometimes neglected) matter of the attitudes toward providence shown by
Old and New Testament saints. He rightly rejects as unbiblical the rather
technical, philosophical definitions of miracle in terms of a natural/
supernatural distinction or in relation to laws of nature (p. 106). Here he
departs from many philosophical accounts and from the typical representations of the Old Princeton theologians.

He presents a solidly biblical doctrine of guidance (pp. 121ff.) based on
the commands, rather than the decretive will, of God. He points out that
even "risk" views of providence must allow for a distinction between these
two "wills" of God (I would prefer a distinction between two senses of "will"
when that term is applied to God). Fatalism is rejected because God foreordains means as well as ends (pp. 137ff.). Therefore our actions and decisions have significant effects upon the course of history. Petitionary prayer
is a special case of this principle (pp. 153ff.).

Helm points out helpfully that divine foreordination is compatible with
the view that some events in the world lack physical causes (pp. 142ff.).

His discussion of the problem of evil is also both orthodox and insightful. He rejects the nominalist/voluntarist idea that God is above moral predication *ex lex* (pp. 163ff., 183ff.). As we have seen earlier, he also rejects
the traditional free-will defense, while giving some support to "privation"
and "permission" models.

His main defensive strategy, however, is a form of the "greater good defense," that God permits evil in order to bring about important goods not
otherwise realizable. His particular emphasis: that the specific blessings of
the heavenly glory "cannot be properly understood except in terms that
presuppose sin and suffering" (p. 203). Some have regarded evil as reme-
dial (e.g., the Irenaean view that evil produces maturity of character), and
others have regarded it as necessary for justice, to display and maintain the
moral order in the universe. On Helm's view, these two principles unite in
the cross of Christ, through which is accomplished both God's vindication
of God's justice and his renewal of the creation.

The final chapter contains some practical suggestions for applying the
doctrine of providence to the Christian life. The most interesting suggestion here is that we need to recognize the fact that God's power in providence is not a "raw power" which immediately accomplishes its every purpose by sheer force. Rather, the nature of God's power, like his purpose for
evil, is best seen at the cross of Christ. God's power is displayed in weakness and suffering, in patience, often in the delay of judgment and the sal-

vation of sinners. Yet herein is a strength greater than any mere army or weapons of war. Thus it is wrong for us to try to identify God's providence directly with any human political program.

In sum, the book has a few weaknesses, but it is in general a very good introduction to the doctrine of providence and a reliable guide through many important problem areas.

REVIEW OF FREDERICK SONTAG AND
M. DARROL BRYANT (EDS.),
God: The Contemporary Discussion[1]

I include this review[2] of a book that well illustrates the confusion in contemporary theology about the doctrine of God. It is an especially clear statement of what I have described in this volume as "nonbiblical views of transcendence and immanence." The book is so confused that I often find it amusing, and I hope you will too.

In December 1981 a group of scholars met on the island of Maui, Hawaii, to discuss the subject of God. The conference was sponsored by the New Ecumenical Research Association, a project of the Unification Theological Seminary, itself a project of the Unification Church, which follows the teachings of the Rev. Sun Myung Moon. This conference was billed as the "first annual" conference of this sort; whether one was held in 1982 or later I do not know.

Evidently it was not difficult to get the scholars to come to Maui: 164 attended, 24 of whom contributed essays to this volume. Among the more well-known essayists: Heinrich Ott, John Macquarrie, John Hick, J. N. Findlay, Robert P. Scharlemann, William Johnston, S.J., Ninian Smart. Others who attended, but who are not represented by published essays here,

---

1. Barrytown, N.Y.: Unification Theological Seminary (Rose of Sharon Press), 1982.
2. Originally published in *WTJ* 46 (1984): 198–205.

include Colin Brown, Donald Dayton, Tom Driver, Frederick Ferré, Anthony Flew, George Mavrodes, Peter Munz, Nelson Pike, Richard Quebedeaux, James Robinson, Richard Rubinstein, James Deotis Roberts. The essayists represent all the major religious traditions and philosophical schools (except for evangelical Christianity!). They discuss a wide variety of issues. The quality of thought is generally high, although a few of the essays (Bilaniuk on Eastern Orthodoxy, Dhirasekera on Buddhism, Kwak on Unificationism) are simple expositions of well-known views.

The Unificationists themselves keep a fairly low profile in this volume. Two essays represent their viewpoint. The one by Kwak, mentioned above, is a simple, straightforward exposition of their teachings; it does not even mention the Rev. Moon. The other, by Young Oon Kim, relates Unification theology to other viewpoints with which it has some initial affinity. Kim draws some interesting parallels and distinctions between Unificationism and process theology, also with Swedenborgianism. This essay has some importance: the Unification Church has become an influential body lately because of its financial and political strength, even apart from its religious system. Yet it is a bit amusing to view the seriousness with which Kim compares Moon's bizarre theology to the views of Whitehead, invoking names like Eliade and Moltmann. One almost expects another essay comparing Heidegger with Ernest Angeley, or Karl Rahner with the Flying Nun. Kim says nothing about Moon's alleged messianic pretensions. The only essayist to reflect on those claims is J. N. Findlay, who expresses thanks that those coming to the conference were not required to express "the slightest acceptance" of those claims (p. 195). Findlay himself thinks that "Messiahs are necessarily many, and of varying charisma" and thus declines "to pass judgment on any genuine Messiah or to grade him favorably or unfavorably in relation to others, any more than I would do in relation to my dearest friends" (p. 196). Diplomatic of him.

An information sheet which I received with the book explains that this volume intends to respond "to the growing call for a world theology." I missed that call; it must have come while I was out of the room. Seriously, I doubt that anyone has uttered such a call, except for a group of academics unrepresentative of their religious communities. Still, within that group of academics, at least within the group that met on Maui, there are some indications of a developing consensus which transcends the differences of religious tradition. While not all of the essayists endorse every detail of this consensus, there does seem to be a substantial and surprising unity of mind on many significant issues.

1. First, there is consensus on the nature of divine *transcendence*. Huston Smith in his brief opening remarks to the conference announces (with

the apparent assurance that he is saying nothing controversial: this is part of the "shared discernment that we have in common") that the "sacred" is something "completely beyond us" (p. 3). To Ott, the great mystery of religion ("whether we call this mystery 'God,' 'Dhamma,' 'Brahman,' or whatever") is "fundamentally inexpressible" (p. 9, cf. p. 11). It is (in Ott's terms) "wholly-other" (p. 12). It (sometimes called "he," sometimes "she") should not be regarded as "a" being among others (Macquarrie on Heidegger, pp. 157f., 163; Scharlemann, pp. 266, 270ff.; Kadowaki on Zen, p. 375). It is not an "object" (Murti on Hinduism, pp. 29ff.; Kadowaki, p. 384). Thus this mystery cannot be known by objective means, the means by which we come to know the things around us. Its name is "mystery" (Ott, pp. 9ff.). The object of religious awareness is "utterly disproportionate to the human perceivers" (Hick, p. 176). "The Truth in itself is inexpressible" (Tiwari on Hinduism, p. 248), "indefinable . . . indescribable" (ibid., p. 256). God is "wholly other than our thinking and other than the being of the world or of *Dasein*" (Scharlemann, p. 267; *Dasein* = human nature). According to Scharlemann, the most adequate thought about God conceives him "as other than God" (p. 270), an otherness best symbolized by the crucified Christ. Johnston reminds us of the apophatic Christian mystics who taught that "God can be loved but that he cannot be conceptually known" (p. 365). The "term of transcendence" is "nameless undefinable mystery" (Kadowaki, p. 384). Since God is transcendent, "the cosmos necessarily is a kind of veil" (Smart, pp. 397f.), a veil which "here and there, so to speak, is removed so that God can be seen through it. God unveils herself [*sic*]."

Thus our authors have no sympathy for any rational "proofs" of God's existence (pp. 104, 163, 249, 255, 297ff., 363ff., 391, 395ff.). It is possible to speak about revelation, as long as we remember that "in his revelation, in the incarnation of the *logos,* he does not cease to be mystery, he does not make himself into a seizable and comprehendible object. . . . [Before him] silent adoration is finally the only adequate attitude. . . . [Language] grows out of silence and opens into silence, and even as language it still remains penetrated by silence" (Ott, p. 14). For such reasons, the Hindu Murti concludes that revelation comes only through myths (p. 26). Smart insists that any revelation in words can be interpreted in various ways and thus, by its very nature, will fail to communicate unambiguously (pp. 398ff.); thus revelation cannot be said to communicate "knowledge," though it does "stir creativity in us" by its "character of strange openness."

2. This consensus on divine transcendence leads to a further consensus regarding *transreligious ecumenism*. If God is really nameless, inexpressible, beyond all description, then all the would-be describers of God (including

writers of scriptures) must admit their fallibility and inadequacy. Thus Ott warns us that "a Christian, for example, may not enter into such dialogue [with those of other religions—JF] with any prefixed judgments about the truth of the other religion" (p. 7). Dialogue, he says, is necessarily an "open situation"; it involves "risk." It demands "rejection of presuppositions" (p. 9). We must, of course, be faithful to our own religious convictions (p. 8); but those convictions, rightly understood (as under #1 above) will not lead a Christian or anyone else into a dogmatic stance. If we properly understand the mysteriousness of God, we will not claim for our religion any *exclusive* truth to which we must bear witness (p. 16). Thus we can sympathize with the Hindu conviction that the different religions represent different paths to God (pp. 34f.); we will not seek to convert others (p. 39). We can commend the Anlo people of Africa for their pluralism (p. 148). On such assumptions, Hick's thesis becomes interesting: that God's personal character (*persona*) is the sum total of his interactions with human communities, so that he has one *persona* in Hinduism, another in Buddhism, etc. (p. 175; cf. Scharlemann, p. 270ff.). (The fact that some forms of Buddhism are atheistic is irrelevant; "nothingness" can be another name for the nameless absolute.) And we are not surprised to hear from Johnston that Christian apophatic mysticism has much in common with Zen (p. 372), or from Kadowaki that Zenists may be counted among Rahner's "anonymous Christians" (p. 383). If God is "transcendent" as in #1, then it does not seem to be important whether we call him God, Dhamma, or Brahman, nor must we require the diplomatic Findlay to give grades to his various Messiah-friends.

The ecumenical spirit of the conference was not only theoretical; it was evident also in the wide variety of views presented for serious consideration. Not only did the delegates sit still (we assume) for Kim's learned comparison between Whitehead and the Rev. Moon; in itself that would have been mere good manners, since the Unificationists hosted the conference. But we also have in this volume a highly sympathetic account of popular Filipino religion by V. R. Gorospe, S.J. Roman Catholicism is the majority religion in the Philippines; but among the less-educated majority, this Catholicism is mingled with influences from older Eastern religions, with animistic beliefs and practices, and with thaumaturgy (faith healing, possession trances, ecstatic preaching, etc.). Gorospe generally commends this mixture, noting that such religion can teach us much about respect for the earth (pp. 104f.), about the need to overcome the "separation of the sacred and the profane" in modern life (pp. 120f.). Gorospe finds something good in every popular superstition. His defense of flagellation rituals is worth the price of the book (p. 124):

Penitential flagellations have been regarded in the past as signs of perversion, exhibitionism, sadomasochism, fanaticism, or anti-clericalism and are now being exploited by the tourism industry. But these penitential rites can be sacramentalized by bringing in the Sacraments of Reconciliation and the Eucharist and by harmonizing the reading of the Passion with these flagellation penances. They can become "signals of transcendence" for ascetic renewal and self-denying love. . . . The value of the flagellation rite can be defended by relating it to a primary principle of Christian asceticism, the need for self-discipline.

The Jesuit talent for syncretism is not dead in our time! Similarly, Christian R. Gaba expounds the religious beliefs and practices of the Anlo people of west Africa. They worship God through the mediation of ancestors and lesser deities. While it appears that these lesser deities crowd God out of the picture at times, Gaba reassures us that it only appears so because of the nature of the formal ritual which "leads to a permissible exaggeration of the functions of these spirit beings" (p. 133). (My guess is that if the priests of Baal had used such an argument on Elijah, they would not have had great success.) Gaba tells us that to the Anlos sin is not a "state" but "life-negating" acts (p. 140), and that for them salvation is by works (p. 144). He commends them (as Gorospe commended the Filipinos) for having a good perspective on the "sacred dimension of life" (p. 146).

3. Thus the consensus moves from transcendence to ecumenism. Is there any place, though, for divine *immanence* in this scheme? Certainly, but again in a special sense. If God is beyond all words, then all words about him must be judged by autonomous human reason, as we have seen. But to say this is to say that in practice we are to regard our autonomous judgments as divine. Findlay uses this very argument: since God is the source of values, and since we must assume (as Kant) the right of human beings to choose their values autonomously, therefore God *is* the capacity for autonomous choice (p. 190). He is "in some sense the inmost nature of all persons." Ott comes at the same conclusion in a different way: we note that unfathomable mystery is to be found, not only in God, but also in ourselves. But if mystery is as such divine, then "the essence of human being participates in the mystery of God" (p. 13). All of this ties in with the Hindu equation of Brahman (God) with Atman (the human soul; Murti, pp. 28ff.). In deep meditation, "we know God or our Deepest Self not externally through representation, but by being it entirely. . . . We become identical with the real" (p. 27). Kadowaki (comparing Zen with Christianity) quotes Rahner's words: "The term 'self-communication' is really intended to signify that God

in his own most proper reality makes himself the innermost constitutive element of man . . . man is the event of God's absolute self-communication" (p. 394). Macquarrie reminds us that for Heidegger the unity of essence and existence that theologians have attributed to God (and by which they have *defined* God) pertains also to human beings (p. 160). Love, says Tiwari, is "not the result of unity-in-diversity nor has it any outside motive; it is the experience of pure identity with the Essence which in itself is Love" (p. 256). To put it simply, "God is none other than the Self" (p. 39). From supertranscendence (God is a total mystery) we move to superimmanence (God is identical with me).

The approach of process theology is a bit different at the outset, but ends up at the same point. Process theology is mentioned a number of times in this volume, and not only as a foil to Rev. Moon. Macquarrie notes some common emphases between process thought and Heidegger (pp. 162f.), and Hick, after the manner of the Whiteheadians, tells us that God changes as the traditions about him change (p. 176). Gorospe even informs us that the popular Filipino religion "acknowledges God as Creator and His active presence without in any way denying scientific evolution and process philosophy" (p. 112). I wonder if he asked them about that. But the most extensive discussion of process thought is the article by Theodore Vitali. It is obscure, as much process theology is; and thinkers of this school are never so obscure as they are when seeking to resolve intramural disputes.

In this article, Vitali criticizes the views of fellow Whiteheadians Norris Clarke and Robert Neville. These men (to make a very long story short) find that traditional process philosophy lacks intelligibility because it lacks a clear concept of the world's origin. Since God and the world "create" one another in process thought, the God-world complex lacks any unequivocal cause and thus rests on chance. Clarke and Neville offer two different ways to remedy this problem, both returning to sort of modified, amended, revised forms of creation *ex nihilo*. Vitali doesn't like these expedients because they compromise what he deems essential to process thought—the notion that the universe produces changes in God. He thinks that the problem of intelligibility can be solved by more "traditional" process resources: Hartshorne's ontological argument which establishes God's necessary existence, which provides, in turn, a rationale for the existence of the world. (Of course, Hartshorne's argument establishes only the "primordial" nature of God, God's most abstract features. God's concreteness comes through his interaction with the world; and in my view there is still a major problem of intelligibility at that level, and thus with the process-god in general.) At any rate, Vitali makes it clear that for the process thinker, as for those mentioned in the previous paragraph, man has attributes that traditionally have been ascribed to God; and he admits that such confusion between Creator and creature leads to problems in the system.

Such is the consensus which emerges from this volume. My critique can perhaps be discerned from the tone of my exposition; but some points deserve more explicit treatment. First on the concept of *transcendence:* The statement that God is not an "object" or "a" being among others has become a kind of litany in modern theology. Everyone treats it as perfectly obvious. I confess, however, that I really don't find it obvious; I'm not even sure I know what it means. Someone without theological sophistication would probably take these statements to mean that God is not a *material* "object"—a "thing" that we can see, touch, manipulate, etc. But of course no one except cultists and Stoics would claim that God is material. Do these statements mean, then, that God is not an "object" of *discourse?* That he is not a "being" in the sense of an object of predication, something that can be thought of or spoken about? Well, all the language about God's "inexpressibility" suggests such a notion. But surely the writers in this volume do claim to speak about God. Even the statement that "God is not an object" is a statement about God. If God is *literally* inexpressible, how did these thinkers manage to produce a 419-page book about him? The Muslim theologian Gaafar Sheikh Idris, dissenting significantly from the general consensus outlined above, argues against some of his fellow Muslims who believe that only negative or metaphorical statements can be made concerning God. His arguments are good on the whole; they show that consistent "negationism" is impossible and contrary to the requirements of religious worship (pp. 279ff.). From a Christian standpoint, I must point out that Scripture does not teach anything like the doctrine of transcendence presented in the consensus. There is in the Bible a doctrine of divine incomprehensibility (Isa. 55:8f., Rom. 11:33–36): we cannot comprehend God's ways or thought. He has not revealed himself to us exhaustively; thus there is always more to him than we know. But Scripture never deduces from this fact that there is any defect in its own account of God. Although the word of the prophets, apostles, and Scriptures is not exhaustive, it is nonetheless *true.* Thus, God *is* an object of predication, and, in *that* sense, he is "a" being among others, an "object."

Second, on the subject of *transreligious ecumenism:* Just as it is self-refuting to publish a 419-page book about an "inexpressible" God, so it is self-refuting to promote an all-inclusive ecumenism. If dialogue must be totally open, without any presuppositions about the truth or falsity of another's religion, then of course one must also leave open the question of the truth of one's own convictions, including his convictions about the legitimacy of ecumenism. But in fact, the book shows very little openness to those who would deny the model of "many paths to one transcendent reality." Tiwari, indeed, does differ somewhat from the consensus at this point, indicating certain differences between Christian and Hindu conceptions and making it clear that a choice must be made (pp. 245ff.); but in general the book's authors are exceedingly dogmatic and exclusivistic in their ecumenism. Thus it is not surprising that the one religious view which is conspicuously missing here is that of evangelical Christianity; such Christianity cannot be tolerated in the ecumenical discussion, for it must necessarily challenge the consensus at every point.

Then on the consensus view of *immanence:* clearly it deifies the creature and demolishes the lordship of God over his world. In Scripture, God's transcendence is his sovereignty—his supreme power and authority. *Because* of (not in spite of) that power and authority, God is the most significant, the most prominent fact of our experience. Thus he is intimately present, immanent, clearly revealed, in his world. The consensus theology reverses this structure: therein, *man* or *creation* has supreme power, authority, divinity. God, then, if he exists, is either identical to man-creation (immanence) or totally other—absent, hidden from creation (transcendence).

Thus, we do find in this book the beginnings of a "world theology"; but it is a world theology contrary to the gospel of Jesus Christ, a world theology devised by "the prince of this world." It has no more authority or power than any other bit of academic speculation. Interestingly, Theodore Vitali, after resisting the attempts of Clarke and Neville to reintroduce creation *ex nihilo*, expresses some concern with the situation created by arguments like his own. He realizes that to oppose the Christian tradition as he has done produces a real problem, for

> the future of process philosophy will depend upon its ability to function within the Great Tradition. If process philosophers and theologians are unable to retain and enhance the formal elements in the Christian Creeds, it is my opinion that process philosophy will slip off into the wayside of Western thought. (p. 242)

Well, that is a problem, and not only for Vitali; it calls the whole conference into question. What do these people know about God anyway? They do not even claim the gift of prophecy, only academic credentials. But since when do academic credentials confer upon anyone a knowledge of God? Yet they feel perfectly free to reason autonomously, ignoring, patronizing, or attacking the "Great Traditions" of living religions, creating an artificial religion of their own. Indeed, for the most part, they are quite ignorant of *God's* theology, his way of salvation in Christ. It is symbolic that this conference was convened under the auspices of the Unification Church;

for this volume demonstrates graphically the extent to which modern theology has gone cultic: autonomous reasoning, rejection of biblical doctrine, phony tolerance, creation of a new, exclusive religious community in which Whiteheadians can converse amiably with Unificationists and Filipino animists, but from which disciples of Jesus Christ are excluded.

There *is* a true world theology. Jesus shed his blood, not for our sins only, but for those of the whole world (1 John 2:2). And he calls us to "go into all the world and teach all nations" (Matt 28:19). The gospel of Christ is not captive to the "Western mind." To the Hindu and Buddhist, it proclaims a way to overcome the suffering of life, not by escaping into nothingness, but by a new life of fullness and abundance. To the animist and idolater, it proclaims a direct path to the very presence of God, through Jesus whose death destroyed the veil in the temple. To the modern Jew, who (like Roth in our volume, pp. 345ff.) is more preoccupied by Auschwitz than by the Old Testament, the gospel presents a God who sent his son to suffer and die (crucified simply because of *who he was*) that his people might live. May God continue to rebuke the wisdom of the world with the simplicity, the foolishness of the cross.

APPENDIX G

REVIEW OF COLIN BROWN,
Miracles and the Critical Mind[1]

I include this review[2] to supplement chapter 13 of the present volume. I was greatly helped by Brown's book, but have tried to move beyond it in a few ways.

Colin Brown, professor of systematic theology at Fuller Theological Seminary, has written what is in many ways a definitive treatise on the subject of miracle. It is both a history of thought on the matter and an analysis of many important issues.

The author's historical research has been remarkably thorough, virtually exhaustive of the literature in English on the topic, and covering well some significant authors who have written in other European languages. I often felt, in fact, that Brown was trying to cover *too many* figures. I learned more than I really wanted to know about the obscurer writers of the deist period (pp. 47ff.), and about the nineteenth century "embattled orthodox" (esp. pp. 147ff.). (By the way, why are S. T. Coleridge, John Stuart Mill, F. W. Newman, Matthew Arnold, and F. D. Maurice included in a section on "Protestant orthodoxy"?) Perhaps Brown sought such completeness in order to give the book qualities of a reference text, but I think his evident

---

1. Grand Rapids: Eerdmans, 1984.
2. Originally published in *WTJ* 47 (1985): 140–46.

(occasional) desire for "total coverage" sometimes detracts from the progress of the book's substantive arguments. (He rather often describes someone's idea without any real analysis or evaluation, then leaves it without noting any clear relation to his own theses.) On the other hand, there are also some significant omissions. Dutch Reformed theology is not handled well: Brown mentions Kuyper only briefly in a footnote (p. 357), Bavinck and the cosmonomic thinkers not at all. Berkouwer, also, is omitted, though the chapter on miracle in his *The Providence of God* is one of the more helpful treatments available. Is Berkouwer's thought not at least as important as that of Thomas Chubb or Viscount Bolingbroke (p. 51)? Brown's rationale for including one figure and excluding another sometimes escapes me. Still, we must be grateful for the enormous amount of work Brown has put in on this project. The reader needs only to look through the forty-seven pages of rich, concise endnotes to recognize the presence of scholarship of a high order.

The substantive discussion of issues surrounding miracle is interspersed with the historical material and is summarized in a forty-six page "Postscript." Topics covered cluster around the issues of (1) the definition of miracle, (2) the possibility of miracle, (3) the possibility of identifying an event as miraculous, (4) the evidential value of miracles, and (5) the place of miracles in the four gospels. (These are my titles; Brown divides the material differently.) The question of whether miracles occur today also comes up in the expositions of past thinkers, but Brown offers no analysis of his own on that subject.

(1) Brown's discussions of the definition of miracle present a somewhat surprising pattern, though he himself does not seem to make very much of it. While the detractors of orthodox Christianity, such as Spinoza (pp. 30ff.) and Hume (pp. 79ff.), define miracle as a "violation of the laws of nature" and criticize the concept as such, few if any Christian thinkers have defined the term that way. Aquinas, immersed as he was in natural law and nature/grace problematics, is perhaps an exception: for him, a miracle "properly" speaking is an event beyond the power of any creature, possible only by divine agency (p. 12). That may be equivalent to Hume's definition, once all the Aristotelian apparatus is made explicit; but that is not obvious. Warfield, too, said that miracles require at some point the "immediate efficacy of God" (p. 199), but he also denied that miracle was "contranatural." (The contrast between "immediate" and "mediate" efficacy raises some problems—one of the few problem areas which Brown does not address in the book.) Warfield's idea, and possibly also that of Aquinas, was of a *new* cause entering the system of nature, leaving all the former causal patterns otherwise intact. (Cf. also C. S. Lewis, "an interference with Na-

ture by supernatural power" [p. 291]: note, an interference with *nature*, not a violation of natural law. A model similar to Warfield's seems here to be at work.)

And Christians outside the Thomistic tradition have typically endorsed much more "naive" (I would say more biblical) definitions. Augustine's (which Aquinas, interestingly, endorses) is far from any Enlightenment speculation about laws of nature: "whatever appears that is difficult or unusual above the hope and power of them who wonder" (p. 7). Brown finds similar conceptions in John Donne (p. 28), Isaac Newton (p. 75), Joseph Butler (p. 95), John Locke (p. 95), J. H. Newman (p. 138), Blondel (p. 142), Horace Bushnell (p. 164), Ian Ramsey (p. 183), Robert Young (p. 191), Douglas Erlandson (pp. 192ff.), Norman Geisler (pp. 210ff.), Louis Monden (p. 216), and Alan Richardson (pp. 225ff.), and he notes few (if any) clear examples of "violation" definitions (though he discusses R. F. Holland, who says that *some* miracles may be "violations" [pp. 174ff.]).

I wish that Brown had made some comments about this pattern, for it would seem to be significant. If Brown is right and I have interpreted him correctly, it would seem that many criticisms of the Christian doctrine would have to be at least restructured. The question, then, would not be how testimony for miracle could overcome testimony in favor of natural law (Hume), but rather what grounds we have for denying evidence for something "difficult or unusual" (Augustine), or for denying the possibility of a "new cause" entering the system (Warfield).

(2) Brown is more concerned with the possibility of adequate testimony for miracles (see [3] below) than with the possibility of miracles as such. He does, however, refute the suggestion that a basis for miracle might be found in the supposed "randomness" of the universe proposed by quantum physicists (pp. 179f., 206ff., 291), rightly pointing out that such a "basis" actually destroys miracle in the biblical sense by explaining it naturalistically. Rather, Brown argues, we should seek the ground of possibility for miracle in the reality of God and the analogy between divine and human activity: as we can initiate and terminate sequences, so can God (p. 291). Thus, when we assert the possibility of miracle, there is always an element of faith-commitment involved (p. 183 and passim). Miracle is possible because God exists.

(3) On the question of the identification of miracle, Brown discusses Hume's arguments, and the various rejoinders to them, in considerable detail. Hume argues, *a priori*, that testimony in favor of miracle can never overcome the "firm and unalterable experience" we have that things always occur by natural means; then he argues *a posteriori* that the actual testimony in favor of miracles is questionable because of the incompetence, bias, etc.

of the witnesses. Brown gathers a great many replies to these arguments, some quite useful: (a) Hume has no right to speak of a "firm and unalterable experience" without first investigating the testimony for and against miracle; yet he claims to be able to dismiss such testimony *a priori* because of that "firm and unalterable experience" (p. 92). (b) The argument against miracle is not consistent with Hume's own account of causation (p. 93). (c) Questions arise in connection with Hume's definition of miracle as a "violation of the laws of nature" (pp. 94ff.; see [1] above). (d) Hume is unfair in his criteria for the evaluation of testimony (pp. 96ff.).

This discussion leads Brown to some broader epistemological observations: "The significance of Hume's critique lies in the fact that it raises the question of the frame of reference in which any piece of historical data has to be assessed" (pp. 98f.). Hume advanced a particular frame of reference, a particular set of presuppositions for the analysis of historical data; but he advanced those presuppositions dogmatically, attempting "to foreclose discussion" on the question of what frame of reference is best. But that question will not go away: "What we call *historical facts* are not items of data that can be directly inspected but interpretation placed on data that have commanded acknowledgment" (p. 99).

This denial of brute fact is one of the pervasive themes of the book. Brown presents it not only as his own view, but as the view of most all Christian apologists and theologians throughout history. Those who know Bishop Joseph Butler only by way of Van Til's syllabus *Christian-Theistic Evidences* may be surprised to hear that Butler was a sort of "presuppositionalist" (p. 59). He believed that "all facts are theory laden" (same page). "Butler's case is built upon the presupposition of 'an intelligent Author and Governor of nature' as the necessary condition for the rationality of the universe and objective moral values" (same page). Of course, that sort of presupposition would be insufficient for Van Til, who challenges us to presuppose nothing less than the full biblical teaching. But Butler here does recognize that the facts cannot be rightly assessed apart from some faith commitment, the only question being *which* faith commitment.

Brown makes similar points about Ian Ramsey (pp. 183ff.), B. B. Warfield (!) (pp. 197ff.), John Warwick Montgomery and Norman Geisler (!!) (pp. 206ff.), Alan Richardson (pp. 225ff.); cf. his own analysis of the question (pp. 279ff.). It is illuminating to see the concessions to presuppositionalism within the "evidentialist" tradition. (Cf. in this regard my review of *Classical Apologetics,* by Sproul, Gerstner, and Lindsley, *WTJ* 47 [1985]: 279–99.) In the treatments of Ramsey and Richardson, I think that Brown is too uncritical of the rather sharp distinctions these men make between scientific and religious (or historical) reasoning. After Kuhn and Polanyi, to say nothing of Van Til and Dooyeweerd, surely we must recognize that facts are "theory laden," even "faith laden," in science as much as in theology or history. Perhaps this confusion lies behind Brown's statement toward the end that "miracles cannot be the object of scientific investigation, for science can only deal with nature as it is left to itself" (p. 292). This statement is curious, first in that it suggests a picture of an autonomous natural order ("nature . . . left to itself"), which Brown seemed to have rejected in refusing to define miracles as "violations." Second, it suggests that science can have no dealings with God, when in fact science is as dependent on faith commitments as are history and theology.

(4) The evidential value of miracles likewise turns on the question of faith presuppositions and the relation of facts to theory. Again, the reader may be surprised at how many Christian thinkers throughout history have been presuppositionalists of a sort. Comparing Brown's treatment with that of the authors of *Classical Apologetics* may convince the reader of the influence of presuppositions in historical analysis! As I said in my review of that book, I think the truth is somewhere in between the two views. Still, the frequency of assertions that miracles prove Christianity only to the eyes of faith seemed remarkable to me.

I don't understand, therefore, why Brown structures his discussion in terms of a controversy between a faith-commitment view and a "hard evidentialist" position "which regards evidential data in and of itself as sufficient proof of the conclusions to be drawn" (p. 145). In my study of this volume, I could not find a single thinker who could be classified as a "strict" evidentialist. Locke is not one of them (p. 58), nor is Butler (p. 59), nor Paley (pp. 144ff.). Nor (perhaps to the surprise of some) were Archibald Alexander (pp. 163f.), W. G. T. Shedd (pp. 166), Charles Hodge (pp. 166f.). (Brown thinks Hodge was *too much* an evidentialist, but not a consistent one, and therefore, I would judge, not a "hard" or "strict" one.) Nor Warfield, Carnell, Montgomery, Geisler (pp. 198–215). But strangely, after showing that all of these "evidentialists" conceded in effect the presuppositional point, Brown concludes: "Geisler's work may represent the end of the line of the strict evidentialist approach to the Gospel miracles. It is a line that Roman Catholic and British Protestant writers on this subject have already passed" (p. 215). Geisler a strict evidentialist? I thought Brown had just finished proving the contrary. And I honestly don't see in Brown's discussion any evidence that the Roman Catholic and British writers were any more sophisticated in these matters than the theologians of Old Princeton or modern American evangelicalism; the comparison seems quite gratuitous.

Perhaps the confusion stems from the fact that Brown regards as an "evidentialist" (however "hard" or "strict") anyone who claims that miracles "prove" Christianity. To him, that claim is incompatible with the view that knowledge of God comes by faith and that miracles themselves cannot be rightly assessed apart from faith. Although he does not say so, he seems to be trying (like many evidentialists!) to avoid circular argument in Christian apologetics. One may see miracle as part of our faith commitment, or as a proof of Christianity, he seems to be saying, but not both. Here, he could learn much from Van Til, who argues that all proof, all argument for Christianity, presupposes faith, but that this circularity is inevitable. Argument for an ultimate criterion of truth (such as the God of the Bible) must always be circular, presupposing for its own intelligibility the criterion it seeks to establish. But that fact does not detract from the argument's evidential value. God has made man's mind to reason in a theistic way. Even the unbeliever knows at some level that what this circular argument says is true; and to reiterate that argument is to press the truth upon him in the most cogent way.

(5) Brown's discussion of the place of miracle in the gospel accounts (pp. 293ff.) makes some interesting points. The works of Jesus, he argues, are not straightforward proofs of his divinity. They are works of the Father, works of the Spirit, works of the Word (*logos*). Rather than being proofs of the Christian message, therefore, the miracles are "more like the prophetic signs of the Old Testament the prophet performed to illustrate and embody his message" (p. 323). Miracles can harden as well as convince; the difference is faith (pp. 323f.). All of this reinforces Brown's position on "evidence" (see [4] above). Here, therefore, I continue to have a problem with his too-sharp contrast between proof and faith commitment.

The discussion of the roles of the Father, Word, and Spirit in miracle leads Brown to some reflections on the doctrine of the Trinity (pp. 324ff.). He wants to deny that the persons of the Trinity are each "autonomous" from the others in a tritheistic sense. Thus he repudiates the tendency in Christian thought to "relate the miracles to the exclusive personal action of Jesus and . . . treat them in isolation from the activity of the Father and the Spirit" (p. 325). I confess to some confusion here. He gives no examples of this tendency, and I really have no clear idea of what he has in mind. Further, although I too repudiate tritheism and understand that "person" originally did not designate an autonomous individual, I am unsatisfied with a mere statement to the effect that "the three persons of the Trinity are three ways in which God is God" (p. 325). Without qualification, that statement could be pressed in a Sabellian direction. As he says, "These must remain questions for other studies" (p. 325). I wish he had saved them for later, for a time when he could present them in more cogent form.

In the preface, Brown indicates his plan to write another book on miracle, focusing on exegetical questions. That is welcome news, for the chapter on Scripture in the present book is inadequate as it stands. For one thing, it deals only with the four gospels, not with the Old Testament or Acts or with miracle terminology elsewhere in the New Testament. Further, of the many substantive issues discussed in the historical portion of the book, very few of them are raised in the exegetical chapter. Only the point about "proof" and "faith" arises in a direct examination of Scripture. But many other problems cry out for exegetical study: What definitions or concepts of miracle adequately reflect the biblical data? Is there a "biblical standard of possibility" for historical events? How did the people of God in Scripture identify events as miraculous? Surely as the Christian faces these questions, his first concern must be to find answers coherent with biblical teaching.

Still, we can hardly fault Brown for including too little in this immensely rich volume! More needs to be said, to be sure, but that can wait. It will be some years before we absorb all that he has taught us here. We have gained herein much information, and also much edifying instruction about the place of faith in the Christian's knowledge of God.

APPENDIX H

REVIEW OF DAVID RAY GRIFFIN,
Evil Revisited[1]

I am reprinting this review, which originally appeared in the *Calvin Theological Journal*,[2] to supplement the discussions of process theology, free will, and the problem of evil, in the present volume.

Griffin is one of the most prominent advocates of process theology and perhaps the movement's leading spokesman on the question of theodicy, the problem of evil. In this volume, he restates the theses of his earlier book, *God, Power, and Evil: A Process Theodicy* (Philadelphia: Westminster Press, 1976), and he offers rebuttals to the critics of his earlier argument.

There is not much in this book for those of us who hold to a traditional Calvinistic position (he calls it "all-determining theism"). He brushes that position aside with quick strokes: all-determining theism makes sin meaningless and evil ultimately illusory (pp. 13–14). In this short but rather confusing discussion, he mixes up Lutheran ("God's left hand"), Reformed ("revealed" vs. "secret" will), and Roman Catholic (evil is nonbeing) motifs.

Nor is there anything much in the book for those who have *basic* questions about process theology, such as:

(1) How do we know that the world is made up of creative actual occa-

---

1. Albany: State University of New York Press, 1991.
2. 27 (1992): 435–38.

sions, without resorting to the fallacy of division—i.e., without gratuitously attributing the qualities of our experienced world to its supposed basic elements?

(2) What are the qualifications of process theologians to revise the biblical teachings about God? (They have academic credentials, yes; but those are usually considered inadequate to convey *religious* authority. Are they known for their piety, their holiness, their kindness, their prophetic mandates, their extraordinary friendships with God?)

(3) Is process theology too high a price to pay for a solution to the problem of evil? Do we really want to give up the central biblical teaching of the sovereignty of God so that we can get an intellectually satisfying answer? Or does loyalty to Jesus Christ demand that we put up with an occasional mystery?

(4) Is the process God any more than a principle of unity within the plurality of the world itself? If not, why should we call it "God"?

We can grasp at least the general direction of Griffin's thinking on these matters by his statement on p. 52:

> My position, by contrast, assumes that we have no infallible revelation. That assumption is based partly on the fact that no such revelation seems to exist, but partly on the fact that my understanding of the God-world relationship does not allow for any such revelation to occur.

The latter clause indicates the presupposition which he brings to the question of revelation: his own autonomous thought must always be the ultimate judge of any purported revelation. Therefore, the Bible, which on the contrary claims the right to rule over all human thought, must be dismissed as, in effect, fraudulent. Those who accept the Bible's claim must similarly dismiss Griffin's approach.

Who, then, can benefit from this book? Well, those of us who, for professional reasons, must keep up with the ins and outs of process theology probably cannot legitimately avoid this volume. There are a few new wrinkles here. Griffin announces in the preface that this book contains a stronger doctrine of evil, which he calls "the demonic." He also tries to answer the objection that the process God, while answering the problem of evil, enfeebles our hope by raising questions about God's ultimate triumph.

There is also an interesting discussion in which Griffin distinguishes between efficient cause and coercion (pp. 96–119): God does not coerce (he only "persuades," as the process tradition emphasizes), but he does cause efficiently. This distinction requires Griffin, of course, to redefine "efficient cause" so that it refers only to the divine gift of each occasion's "initial aim."

In my view, this redefinition does not help very much to answer the concerns which prompted the question. There is still nothing in the process system that corresponds well to the *traditional* concept of efficient cause.

The book also contains a relatively new process doctrine of the Trinity: God, the world, and creativity (pp. 188–92). Process theologians have found it notoriously difficult to formulate a functional equivalent to historic Trinitarianism compatible with their system. Their God, of course, is bi- or dipolar, not tripolar. Griffin's approach is more cogent than the alternatives, granted his premises; but it does in effect grant the charge of pantheism.

The volume will also be of interest to those whom Griffin calls "traditional free will theists" and to those with a scholarly interest in that position. Most of the critics to whom Griffin replies are of that persuasion: people who hold an Arminian-libertarian view of free will and who believe that is a sufficient answer to the problem of evil. Among them are David and Randall Basinger, Steven T. Davis, Alvin Plantinga, Nelson Pike, Bruce Reichenbach. Griffin's dialogue with these (and with some fellow process theologians) takes up most of the book.

It does seem to me that this sort of Arminianism faces a crisis today. Griffin's critique of it, like the critiques of less extreme thinkers like Richard Rice and Clark Pinnock, seems to me to be cogent in this way: if Arminians really want to say that man is fully autonomous in his choices, then they must deny the biblical teaching (Rice and Pinnock, of course, would not put it this way; nothing would prevent Griffin from doing so) that God's omniscience includes future events (cf. pp. 83–87). If God knows the future perfectly, then *some* kind of foreordination exists, either from God's will or from some other mysterious source (fate?). To eliminate this "determinism," one must eliminate divine foreknowledge or rest with mystery; but of course the hallmark of Arminianism is *not* to rest with mystery. So the Arminian is balancing on a razor's edge. The more he thinks, the more he is in danger of falling either to one side (denying scriptural teaching, or even embracing process theology itself) or the other (Calvinism, or "all-determining theism").

Griffin is an intelligent writer, whatever one may think of his presuppositions. Every now and then, he presents an insight that deserves consideration even by Calvinists. For example, on pp. 31–32, he argues that God's goodness follows from his omniscience, since his omniscience is not merely a propositional understanding but an actual "feeling" of all that is happening. Orthodox Calvinists will reject the pantheistic assumptions here; but can we deny that God not only knows the propositional truths about the universe but also, somehow, knows how every finite being feels?

To follow out the implications of this fact might help us to a better balance between intellect and emotion in our view of God and in our human epistemology.

On the whole, then, this book is a worthy sequel to *God, Power, and Evil;* but its usefulness is limited for those who reject the distinctives of Arminian and process thought.

APPENDIX I

REVIEW OF BRIAN G. ARMSTRONG,
Calvinism and the Amyraut Heresy[1]

This review is reprinted from the *Westminster Theological Journal*.[2] It enlarges my discussion of scholasticism in chapters 1–2, and of God's universal love in chapter 20 of this book.

It is a bit surprising that the name of Moise Amyraut (Latin form *Amyraldus;* hence "Amyraldianism") is not better known in a time such as ours, when so many evangelical Christians want to be known as "four point Calvinists." Many, indeed, in our time seem to want to say (a) that Christ atoned in some sense for the sins of every human being, (b) that nevertheless all men are not saved, and (c) that in the final analysis it is God, not man, who determines what persons shall be saved and which ones lost. But making these propositions work together in a scripturally and logically cogent way is a task requiring considerable subtlety of mind, and no one, to my knowledge, has ever done it better than Amyraut. Further, Amyraut wove these propositions into the context of a rather distinctive theological *approach*—a method, emphasis, and style significantly different from those of other theologians of his time (1596–1664). I suspect that the ap-

1. Madison, Milwaukee, and London: University of Wisconsin Press, 1969.
2. 34.2 (1972).

801

peal of "four point Calvinism" even today can be best understood by reference to Amyraut's general theological mentality—a mentality shared to some extent by many today who know little of Amyraut. Thus, both proponents and critics of the "four point" position can benefit from a study of Amyraut's theology and approach to theology. In such a study, Professor Armstrong's book can be enormously helpful.

In brief, Armstrong's thesis is that Amyraut's thought, style, emphasis, and method were very similar to Calvin's and very dissimilar to those of the "orthodox," "scholastic" theologians who came to dominate the Reformed churches after Calvin's time. According to Armstrong, Amyraut, like Calvin, was a "humanist" by background and thus brought to his theology a historical consciousness, an ethical concern, and a skillful textual scholarship. By contrast, the scholastics were preoccupied with formal logic, rationalistic systematizing, and speculative metaphysics more than with the history of redemption and the concrete realities of the Christian life.

Since twentieth-century theology is in a sense a series of attempts to transcend scholastic ways of thinking, it is not surprising that Armstrong's Amyraut comes out looking very much like a modern man. On every page, it seems, we see ourselves and our colleagues. Like us modern theologians, Amyraut is an ecumenist. He has a passion for the unity of the church: he works for Reformed-Lutheran union; he eschews inflammatory language in debate; he gains respect even from the Roman Catholic hierarchy; he works against schism in his own communion, even occasionally defending his opponents against unfair attack. Yet his ecumenism is not without principle: he has the militancy to polemicize sharply against Arminian and Roman views on the really crucial issues. Amyraut is as we are—or as we wish we were.

We avoid scholasticism by avoiding speculation concerning God's secret counsel; we want to limit our thought to what God has revealed; so does Amyraut. For instance, he, like Calvin and unlike the scholastics, discusses predestination, not in the context of the doctrine of God (as an aspect of God's secret counsel), but in the context of the application of redemption (as an implication of God's historical redemptive activity). Thus he makes the doctrine of predestination a comfort, not a threat. (For a moment we wondered: is this Amyraut talking, or G. C. Berkouwer?) We want to be "fearlessly anthropomorphic," recognizing that all revelation is in some sense adapted to our human understanding; so does Amyraut. We want to "think historically," viewing redemption as an unfolding historical process rather than only as an eternal decree. We want to be *"biblical* theologians" and therefore *"covenant* theologians." Amyraut does too. He senses the centrality of the covenant concept in Scripture, particularly the distinction between "absolute" covenants (such as the Noahic, providing unconditional guarantees of blessing) and "hypothetical" covenants (such as the Mosaic, where the blessing is conditioned upon human obedience to the covenant law). (Is this Amyraut talking, or Meredith G. Kline?) He is sensitive, too, to the historical distinctiveness of the new covenant in contrast with the old, and thus, according to Armstrong, was able to reaffirm the centrality of the doctrine of justification by faith, a doctrine which had been deemphasized by the scholastics. Faith itself is "central" to Amyraut, as to Calvin. Amyraut is an "existential" thinker, concerned with the needs of concrete human life. We try to be like that too.

The distinctive propositions of "Amyraldianism" arise out of Amyraut's covenant theology, specifically from his absolute/hypothetical distinction. On Amyraut's view, Jesus died in order to put one of the "hypothetical" covenants into effect. He died to establish a new covenantal order—a way by which men may be saved if they obey the covenantal command to believe. Since all men are under this new covenantal order, responsible to obey its command, recipients of its conditional promise, it may be said that Christ "died for" all men without exception; for his death puts this new covenant into force. Yet Amyraut is still a Calvinist in that he recognizes that redemption must be particularistic at some point. Man is dead in trespasses and sins, and therefore cannot of himself fulfill the conditions of any "hypothetical covenant," even that instituted by the death of Christ. This inability, he stresses, is "moral," not "natural" (we might paraphrase "sin is an ethical, not a metaphysical disability"—but would that be Amyraut talking, or Cornelius Van Til?). It is a real inability, however, keeping man from doing anything good. Thus regeneration is necessary; and the Spirit regenerates only those who from all eternity have been chosen by God for salvation. Thus on Armstrong's account, Amyraut's theology, in contrast with scholasticism, is not only "Christocentric" (because "historically oriented") but also "Pneumatocentric" (because the work of the Spirit is so decisive). Don't we want our theology to be that way too? >

The present reviewer is not an expert on Amyraut, nor on seventeenth-century theology, nor on Calvin either, for that matter; so if Armstrong has misinterpreted anyone or overlooked some relevant data, you won't learn about that here. I suspect that there are few problems of this sort; surely there are fewer prima facie omissions in Armstrong's research than, say, in Jack B. Rogers's *Scripture in the Westminster Confession* (a book otherwise remarkably similar to Armstrong's in categories, argument, and point of view). Yet (and this point is often overlooked) accuracy of interpretation and comprehensiveness of scholarship are not sufficient to establish a case.

The logic of the matter must be considered as well. Let us examine Armstrong's argument that Amyraut was "truer to Calvin" than were the "scholastic" orthodox Calvinists. Armstrong bases this conclusion (1) upon similarity of "approach," method, theological structure, etc., between Amyraut and Calvin, and (2) upon demonstrable doctrinal agreement between them. Let us look at each of these in turn:

(1) Just what degree and kind of agreement can be demonstrated by a comparison of method and structure? This is a fairly difficult question. Theologians notoriously often have their strongest disagreements with those whose approach is apparently most similar to their own. Would Calvin have condemned the method of his scholastic successors? Armstrong is fairly sure that he would have; I am not sure one way or the other. I suspect that he would have found *some* of the scholastic formulations "speculative," but I have no reason to say that he would have rejected the entire effort. Why could he not have thanked God for raising up successors with different backgrounds, interests, and skills from himself? Might he not actually have prayed for helpers skilled in logic and philosophy who could develop a tighter, more systematic formulation of the truth than he could have? Armstrong makes his feelings clear on this point but in my opinion doesn't adequately argue his view. Let us be more specific. Armstrong attaches great significance to the fact that Amyraut and Calvin did not, while the scholastics did, discuss predestination under the *locus de Deo*. Now this fact is interesting, especially so since Amyraut himself makes a point of it, explaining why he avoids this scholastic practice. This difference in method, then, clearly differentiates Amyraut from the scholastics. But does it demonstrate more than formal unity between Amyraut and Calvin? And does it demonstrate more than formal disunity between Calvin and the scholastics? Not unless we know not only Amyraut's reasons for his structuring, but also Calvin's reasons for his and the scholastics' reasons for theirs. Armstrong says nothing persuasive on these matters, nor is he especially clear. Occasionally he seems to be saying (though not very coherently) that predestination was not really very important for Calvin; but I hate to attribute this view to Armstrong since it is so patently absurd and since in any case it is implausible to advance this as the reason for Calvin's encyclopedic arrangement. It is therefore not at all clear that this point of structure joins Calvin to Amyraut and separates him from the scholastics. It is this sort of difficulty that seems to me to invalidate much of Armstrong's argumentation from method, structure, etc.

(2) But now: may we nevertheless demonstrate that Amyraut's distinctive teachings were in basic agreement with those of Calvin? Armstrong's exposition of Amyraut's covenant theology does, I think, remove one tra-

ditional objection against the assertion of such agreement. The objection is that Amyraut introduces a contradiction into the Reformed teaching which Calvin would not have tolerated: God did, and did not, intend the benefits of the atonement for all men equally. Armstrong's analysis shows that on Amyraut's view the only "benefit" of the atonement as such is the covenant arrangement by which men may be saved if they believe. This benefit is given to all men equally, with no reservation. Thus no contradiction need arise, and Amyraut need not, at this point, be accused of contradicting himself or Calvin. (Armstrong, however, does not seem to realize that no logical tension remains here—hence his rather strange treatment of logic and rationality on p. 170.) Yet the doctrinal agreement between Amyraut and Calvin can be challenged at a more basic level. Armstrong shows through various citations that Calvin, like Amyraut, believed (a) that God wants all men to be saved if they believe and (b) that the atonement of Christ carries out this desire of his. But such citations do not show that Calvin accepted the distinctive tenets of Amyraut, nor do they show that Calvin would have disapproved of the scholastic alternatives. For the scholastics themselves could easily have accepted (a) and (b), without thereby blunting their anti-Amyraldianism at all. The point at issue here is not whether God wants all men to be saved if they believe. (Of course he does! Second Peter 3:9 teaches as much!) Nor is it whether the atonement furthers this particular desire. (Of course it does! It *does* legitimize the sincere offer of salvation to anyone who believes!) No, the point at issue in the Amyraldian controversy is neither (a) nor (b) nor both, but rather (c), that the *only* purpose of the atonement is to further the divine desire named in (a). Amyraut thought that the only purpose of the atonement was to make salvation possible for men if they believe, that its only function was to establish a "hypothetical covenant." Armstrong, so far as I can see, presents no evidence that (c), the real point at issue, was held by Calvin, or even that it is compatible with Calvin's thinking. Amyraut's arguments for (c), in fact, in my view, show how far Amyraut really is from Calvin both in method and in doctrine. The bases which Amyraut offers for (c) are such as the following: an extremely rigid view of the Trinitarian economy (he held that only the Holy Spirit, not the Father or Son, could work "efficaciously"), a rigid view of the historical structure of redemption (the Spirit alone "applies" redemption, while only the Son is active in the "accomplishment" of it), and a desire to "render [God's predestinating] mercy superlatively commendable" (in this context, to Roman Catholic inquirers). Armstrong himself presents these as Amyraut's reasons for (c), but does not try to find these in Calvin; in fact it is obvious that this sort of thinking is quite foreign to Calvin and Scripture and that it amounts to a kind of rationalism as bad as any scholastic rationalism. Armstrong admits that there is a problem about Amyraut's "rationalism," particularly in connection with his view of faith. (The least cogent discussion of Armstrong's book is his attempt to show that Amyraut's *persuasio* is really much more existential than the scholastic *fiducia*.) But Armstrong seems blind to the rigid, actually unhistorical character of Amyraut's argumentation and the indefensibility of the distinctive Amyraldian thesis on the basis of anything in Calvin.

Thus we cannot accept Armstrong's explicit thesis, that Amyraut was "truer to Calvin" than his scholastic opponents. Further, we are unable to go all the way with Armstrong's implicit thesis, namely, that Amyraut is a good example for contemporary Reformed theologians to follow. There is much that is admirable about Amyraut as a man and as a thinker, and we are most grateful to Armstrong for his well-researched and compelling theological portrait. I'm not sure, though, that the book is worth $12.50 [1972 dollars]. Perhaps, however, the best lesson we can learn from this study—besides the weakness of the "four point" position!—is that escaping scholasticism is not enough, and that at least some of the conventional "escapes" from scholasticism, both of Amyraut's day and our own, may in fact lead us back into the very evils we were trying to avoid. And let us not suppose that some new theological system will arrive to banish scholasticism forever! I suspect that no particular theological method will provide a sure escape from those evils which we connect with scholasticism; developed by sinful man those evils are sins of the heart, and they can creep into any method, any kind of system, if the theologian is not on guard. The remedy for theological barrenness is not necessarily a new method, but always a prayer of repentance.

Bibliography

Anselm. *St. Anselm: Basic Writings*. Edited by S. N. Deane. LaSalle: Open Court, 1974.

Aristotle. *The Basic Works of Aristotle*. Edited by Richard McKeon. New York: Random House, 1941.

Armstrong, Brian. *Calvinism and the Amyraut Heresy: Protestant Scholasticism and Humanism in Seventeenth-Century France*. Madison, Wis.: University of Wisconsin Press, 1969.

Bakewell, Charles M. *Source Book in Ancient Philosophy*. New York: Gordian Press, 1973.

Barth, Karl. *Church Dogmatics*. Edinburgh: T. and T. Clark, 1936–60.

Bauckham, Richard. "In Defence of *The Crucified God*." In *The Power and Weakness of God: Impassibility and Orthodoxy*, edited by Nigel M. de S. Cameron, 93–118. Edinburgh: Rutherford House Books, 1990.

Bavinck, Herman. *The Doctrine of God*. Grand Rapids: Eerdmans, 1951.

Berkhof, Louis. *Systematic Theology*. Grand Rapids: Eerdmans, 1941.

Berkouwer, G. C. *The Providence of God*. Grand Rapids: Eerdmans, 1952.

Bray, Gerald. *The Doctrine of God*. Downers Grove, Ill.: InterVarsity Press, 1993.

Brown, Colin. *Miracles and the Critical Mind*. Grand Rapids: Eerdmans, 1984.

Calvin, John. *Concerning the Eternal Predestination of God*. London: James Clarke and Co., 1961.

———. *Institutes of the Christian Religion*. Edited by John T. McNeill. Translated by Ford Lewis Battles. The Library of Christian Classics. Philadelphia: Westminster Press, 1960.

Carson, D. A. *Divine Sovereignty and Human Responsibility: Biblical Perspectives in Tension.* Atlanta: John Knox Press, 1981.

Clark, Gordon H. *Religion, Reason, and Revelation.* Philadelphia: Presbyterian and Reformed, 1961.

Cobb, John B. and David Ray Griffin. *Process Theology: An Introductory Exposition.* Philadelphia: Westminster Press, 1976.

Cottrell, Jack. *What the Bible Says About God the Ruler.* Joplin, Mo.: College Press, 1984.

Cowan, Steven B., ed. *Five Views of Apologetics.* Grand Rapids: Zondervan, 2000.

Craig, William Lane. *The Only Wise God: The Compatibility of Divine Foreknowledge and Human Freedom.* Grand Rapids: Baker, 1987.

Dabney, Robert L. *Lectures in Systematic Theology.* 1878. Reprint, Grand Rapids: Zondervan, 1972.

Dooyeweerd, Herman. *In the Twilight of Western Thought.* Philadelphia: Presbyterian and Reformed, 1960.

Edwards, Jonathan. *Freedom of the Will.* New Haven: Yale University Press, 1973.

Farley, Benjamin Wirt. *The Providence of God in Reformed Perspective.* Grand Rapids: Baker, 1988.

Fortman, Edmund J. *The Triune God.* Grand Rapids: Baker, 1972.

Frame, John M. *The Amsterdam Philosophy: A Preliminary Critique.* Phillipsburg, N.J.: Harmony Press, n.d.

———. *Apologetics to the Glory of God: An Introduction.* Phillipsburg, N.J.: P&R Publishing, 1994.

———. "Christianity and Contemporary Epistemology." *WTJ* 52 (1990): 131–41.

———. *Contemporary Worship Music: A Biblical Defense.* Phillipsburg, N.J.: P&R Publishing, 1997.

———. *Cornelius Van Til: An Analysis of His Thought.* Phillipsburg, N.J.: P&R Publishing, 1995.

———. *The Doctrine of the Knowledge of God.* Phillipsburg, N.J.: P&R Publishing, 1987.

———. *Evangelical Reunion: Denominations and the One Body of Christ.* Grand Rapids: Baker, 1991.

———. "In Defense of Something Close to Biblicism." *WTJ* 59 (1997): 269–318. Also published as appendix 2 in Frame's *Contemporary Worship Music.*

———. *Medical Ethics: Principles, Persons, and Problems.* Phillipsburg, N.J.: P&R Publishing, 1988.

————. *No Other God: A Response to Open Theism*. Phillipsburg, N.J.: P&R Publishing, 2001.

————. *Perspectives on the Word of God: An Introduction to Christian Ethics*. Phillipsburg, N.J.: P&R Publishing, 1990; Eugene, Ore.: Wipf and Stock, 1999.

————. "The Spirit and the Scriptures." In *Hermeneutics, Authority, and Canon*, edited by D. A. Carson and John Woodbridge, 213–35. Grand Rapids: Zondervan, 1986.

————. "Toward a Theology of the State." *WTJ* 51 (1989): 199–226.

————. *Worship in Spirit and Truth*. Phillipsburg, N.J.: P&R Publishing, 1996.

Frame, John M. and D. G. Hart. *The Regulative Principle of Worship: Scripture, Tradition, and Culture*. Glenside, Pa.: Westminster Campus Bookstore, 1998.

Frame, John M. and Paul Kurtz. "Without a Supreme Being, Everything Is Permitted." *Free Inquiry* 16 (spring 1996): 4–7.

Gaffin, Richard B. *Perspectives on Pentecost: Studies in New Testament Teaching on the Gifts of the Holy Spirit*. Phillipsburg, N.J.: Presbyterian and Reformed, 1979.

Geisler, Norman. *Miracles and Modern Thought*. Grand Rapids: Zondervan, 1982.

Gerstner, John H. *Repent or Perish*. Ligonier, Pa.: Soli Deo Gloria Publications, 1990.

Gilson, Étienne. *The Philosophy of St. Thomas Aquinas*. Translated by Edward Bullough. New York: Arno Press, 1979.

————. *The Spirit of Medieval Philosophy*. New York: Charles Scribner's Sons, 1940.

Grenet, Paul. *Thomism: An Introduction*. Translated by James F. Ross. New York: Harper and Row, 1967.

Grenz, Stanley J. and Roger E. Olson. *Twentieth-Century Theology: God and the World in a Transitional Age*. Downers Grove, Ill.: InterVarsity Press, 1992.

Griffin, David Ray. *Evil Revisited: Responses and Reconsiderations*. Albany: State University of New York Press, 1991.

Grudem, Wayne. *Systematic Theology: An Introduction to Biblical Doctrine*. Grand Rapids: Zondervan, 1994.

Gruenler, Royce Gordon. *The Trinity in the Gospel of John: A Thematic Commentary on the Fourth Gospel*. Grand Rapids: Baker, 1986.

Helm, Paul. *Eternal God: A Study of God Without Time*. Oxford: Clarendon Press, 1988.

————. *The Providence of God*. Leicester: InterVarsity Press, 1993.

Henry, Carl F. H. *God, Revelation and Authority*. Waco, Tex.: Word Books, 1976–82.

Heppe, Heinrich. *Reformed Dogmatics*. Grand Rapids: Baker, 1950, 1978.

Hick, John. *Evil and the God of Love*. London: Collins, 1966.

Hodge, Charles. *Systematic Theology*. 1872. Reprint, Grand Rapids: Eerdmans, n.d.

Hume, David. *An Inquiry Concerning Human Understanding*. Reprint, New York: Liberal Arts Press, 1955, 1957.

Jewett, Paul. *God, Creation, and Revelation: A Neo-Evangelical Theology*. Grand Rapids: Eerdmans, 1991.

Johnson, Elizabeth A. *She Who Is: The Mystery of God in Feminist Theological Discourse*. New York: Crossroad Publishing, 1996.

Johnson, Phillip. *Reason in the Balance: The Case against Naturalism in Science, Law, and Education*. Downers Grove, Ill.: InterVarsity Press, 1995.

Jones, Peter. *Spirit Wars: Pagan Revival in Christian America*. Escondido, Calif.: Main Entry Editions, 1997.

Kaiser, Christopher B. *The Doctrine of God: A Historical Survey*. Westchester, Ill.: Crossway Books, 1982.

Kenny, Anthony. *The God of the Philosophers*. Oxford: Clarendon Press, 1979.

Kline, Meredith G. *Images of the Spirit*. Grand Rapids: Baker, 1980.

Machen, J. Gresham. *Christianity and Liberalism*. New York: Macmillan, 1923.

Moltmann, Jürgen. *The Crucified God*. London: SCM Press, 1974.

———. *Theology of Hope*. New York: Harper and Row, 1965.

———. *The Trinity and the Kingdom*. San Francisco: HarperCollins, 1981.

Morey, Robert A. *Death and the Afterlife*. Minneapolis: Bethany House, 1984.

Muller, Richard. "Grace, Election, and Contingent Choice: Arminius's Gambit and the Reformed Response." In *The Grace of God, the Bondage of the Will*, vol. 2, edited by Thomas R. Schreiner and Bruce A. Ware, 251–78. Grand Rapids: Baker, 1995.

Murray, John. "The Attestation of Scripture." In *The Infallible Word*, edited by Ned Stonehouse and Paul Woolley, 40–52. Grand Rapids: Eerdmans, 1946.

———. *Collected Writings of John Murray*. Edinburgh: Banner of Truth Trust, 1977.

———. *The Imputation of Adam's Sin*. Grand Rapids: Eerdmans, 1959.

———. *Redemption Accomplished and Applied*. Grand Rapids: Eerdmans, 1955.

Pannenberg, Wolfhart. *Systematic Theology*. Grand Rapids: Eerdmans, 1988.

Peterson, Robert A. *Hell on Trial: The Case for Eternal Punishment*. Phillipsburg, N.J.: P&R Publishing, 1995.

Pinnock, Clark, et al. *The Openness of God.* Downers Grove, Ill.: InterVarsity Press, 1994.

Piper, John and Wayne Grudem, eds. *Recovering Biblical Manhood and Womanhood: A Response to Evangelical Feminism.* Wheaton, Ill.: Crossway Books, 1991.

Plantinga, Alvin. *God, Freedom, and Evil.* Grand Rapids: Eerdmans, 1974.

Plantinga, Cornelius. "The Threeness/Oneness Problem of the Trinity." *Calvin Theological Journal* 23:1 (1988): 37–53.

Plato. *The Collected Dialogues of Plato.* Edited by Edith Hamilton and Huntington Cairns. Princeton: Princeton University Press, 1961.

Poythress, Vern S. "Modern Spiritual Gifts as Analogous to Apostolic Gifts: Affirming Extraordinary Works of the Spirit within Cessationist Theology." *JETS* 39 (1996): 71–101.

———. "Reforming Ontology and Logic in the Light of the Trinity: An Application of Van Til's Idea of Analogy." *WTJ* 57 (1995): 187–219.

———. *The Shadow of Christ in the Law of Moses.* Brentwood, Tenn.: Wolgemuth and Hyatt, 1991.

Reymond, Robert L. *Jesus, Divine Messiah: The New Testament Witness.* Phillipsburg, N.J.: P&R Publishing, 1990.

Rice, Richard. *God's Foreknowledge and Man's Free Will.* Minneapolis: Bethany House, 1985.

Ryken, Leland, James C. Wilhoit, and Tremper Longman III. *Dictionary of Biblical Imagery.* Downers Grove, Ill.: InterVarsity Press, 1998.

Sanders, John. *The God Who Risks: A Theology of Providence.* Downers Grove, Ill.: InterVarsity Press, 1998.

Sanderson, John W. *Mirrors of His Glory: Images of God from Scripture.* Phillipsburg, N.J.: Presbyterian and Reformed, 1991.

Schleiermacher, Friedrich. *The Christian Faith.* Edinburgh: T. and T. Clark, 1956.

Smith, Ralph A. *Paradox and Truth.* Tokyo: Covenant Worldview Institute, 2000.

Sontag, Frederick and M. Darrol Bryant, eds. *God: The Contemporary Discussion.* Barrytown, N.Y.: Unification Theological Seminary (Rose of Sharon Press), 1982.

Spykman, Gordon J. *Reformational Theology: A New Paradigm for Doing Dogmatics.* Grand Rapids: Eerdmans, 1992.

Strimple, Robert B. "What Does God Know?" In *The Coming Evangelical Crisis: Current Challenges to the Authority of Scripture and the Gospel,* edited by John H. Armstrong, 139–53. Chicago: Moody Press, 1996.

Thielicke, Helmut. *The Evangelical Faith.* Grand Rapids: Eerdmans, 1977.

The Third Millennium. Third Millennium Ministries, Inc. Winter Springs,

Fla. 23 Feb. 2002 <http://www.thirdmill.org>. This Web site includes articles by Richard L. Pratt Jr., John M. Frame, and others under *Magazine Online*.

Thomas Aquinas. *On Being and Essence*. Toronto: Pontifical Institute of Mediaeval Studies, 1949.

—————. *Summa contra gentiles*. 4 vols. Notre Dame, Ind.: University of Notre Dame Press, 1997.

—————. *Summa theologiae*. 5 vols. Allen, Tex.: Christian Classics, 1981.

Van Til, Cornelius. *Defense of the Faith*. Philadelphia: Presbyterian and Reformed, 1975.

—————. *An Introduction to Systematic Theology*. Nutley, N.J.: Presbyterian and Reformed, 1962.

Vos, Geerhardus. *Biblical Theology: Old and New Testaments*. Grand Rapids: Eerdmans, 1948.

Warfield, Benjamin Breckinridge. 1929. Reprint, *Biblical Doctrines*. Grand Rapids: Baker, 1981.

—————. *The Lord of Glory*. 1907. Reprint, Grand Rapids: Baker, 1974.

—————. *Miracles: Yesterday and Today*. 1918. Reprint, Grand Rapids: Eerdmans, 1965.

—————. *Selected Shorter Writings of Benjamin B. Warfield*, vol. 2. Edited by John E. Meeter. Nutley, N.J.: Presbyterian and Reformed, 1973.

Weber, Otto. *Foundations of Dogmatics*. Translated and annotated by Darrell L. Guder. 2 vols. Grand Rapids: Eerdmans, 1981.

Wells, David F. *God in the Wasteland: The Reality of Truth in a World of Fading Dreams*. Grand Rapids: Eerdmans, 1994.

—————. *The Person of Christ: A Biblical and Historical Analysis of the Incarnation*. Westchester, Ill.: Crossway, 1984.

The Westminster Standards: The Confession of Faith, The Larger Catechism, The Shorter Catechism. Suwanee, Ga.: Great Commission Publications, 1978.

Wilson, Douglas. *Knowledge, Foreknowledge, and the Gospel*. Moscow, Ida.: Canon Press, 1997.

Young, E. J. "The Call of Moses II." *WTJ* 30 (1967): 1–24.

Index of Names

Abelard, Peter, 689
Adams, Robert, 406n.6
Albert the Great, 110
Allis, Oswald T., 305n.27, 354n.17
Alsted, J. H., 502n.71
Alston, William, 13n.26, 775
Alting, J., 714
Ames, William, 290n.3
Amyraut, Moise, 6n.11, 801–6
Anaximenes, 559
Anselm, 110, 305n.27, 404, 546, 699
Aquinas, Thomas, 4–5, 38–39, 40, 188,
    203–4, 207–8, 210, 220–28, 289, 392,
    403, 475n.16, 551, 700n.29, 701–2,
    704n.37, 722, 726, 761, 771, 781–92
Aristides, 300
Aristotle, 4, 5, 6, 27, 40, 188, 189, 220,
    221, 225, 289, 299, 444, 511, 544,
    551, 560, 609, 791
Arius, 663, 719–20
Arminius, J., 151n.48, 776
Armstrong, Brian, 6n.11, 420n.30, 801–6
Arndt, William F., 315n.8
Arnold, Matthew, 790
Auer, J., 567n.53
Augustine, 110, 138–39, 163, 167n.12,
    305n.27, 546–47, 551, 554n.35, 619,

697, 698, 699, 717, 722, 724, 744,
    748, 792
Austin, J. L., 747n.11

Bahnsen, Greg, 759
Bakewell, Charles M., 107n.7
Barr, James, 415n.22, 548, 553, 555,
    710n.51
Barth, Karl, 6, 8, 22n.4, 38, 110, 112,
    163n.5, 172, 206, 209–10, 212n.31,
    215, 217, 242n.2, 392, 478, 690n.6,
    704n.37, 706, 724, 726, 760, 770
Basil of Caesarea, 724
Basinger, David, 799
Basinger, Randall, 799
Bauckham, Richard, 611, 614
Bavinck, Herman, 108n.13, 109–10,
    203–4, 219, 228n.29, 337, 367, 389,
    392, 475, 506, 523–25, 537, 544, 567,
    589n.13, 596, 600–601, 602,
    633n.22, 688, 776
Beisner, E. Calvin, 486n.46
Bentham, Jeremy, 189–90
Berkeley, G., 560
Berkhof, Louis, 252n.25, 275n.5, 287, 770
Berkouwer, G. C., 271n.54, 334n.19, 791,
    802

813

Index of Subjects

Calvinism, 485–86, 797, 799
Cambridge changes, 566–67
Canons of Dordt, 176
Cappadocian Fathers, 619, 698, 708n.45,
    717, 720n.66, 724
categorical imperative, 192n.22
Catholic theologians, 530–31
causation, 114, 155, 156, 175–77, 178
    and authorship, 176
central motifs, 8, 12, 22
certainty, 741
chain of being, 216–20
Chalcedon Declaration, 217
change, 545, 555, 559–61, 610
    in God, 566–70
character, 138
charismatics, 6
chiasm, 665, 750
choice. *See* election
Christ (title), 345–46, 661–63, 673
Christian life, 123, 277, 449
Christian Science, 162
Christology, 131, 646–47
church, 282, 283, 322–23, 385
church fathers, 109, 295, 300
church growth, 122n.5
church membership, 330
circular reasoning, 273n.56, 405, 407–9,
    522–23, 732, 795
    broad, 409
    narrow, 408–9
circumcessio, 230, 613, 693
circumincessio, 385n.60, 613, 693–94, 702
civic righteousness, 434
civil government, 371, 433
classificational aspect, 730–32
cleft in the rock, 588, 590–91
coercion, 424, 798–99
coinherence, 693
commander-troop analogy, 155–56
commandments, 528
common grace, 34, 131, 281, 429–37
communicable attributes, 14, 396
compassion, 441–42
compatibilism, 136–37, 139n.31, 145, 233,
    777
complacency (God's love), 415–16,
    422n.34

composition, 225
concurrence, 275–76, 287–88, 290, 559
conditional immortality, 467n.22
conscience, binding of, 89
consequent will, 529–31, 532, 537
consummation, 277, 558, 591
contingencies, 223, 501–5
continuum
    of being, 217–19, 278–79, 299
    in God's acts, 262
contra naturam, 257n.32, 282
contra peccatum, 257n.32, 282
control, 15–16, 40, 42, 43–46, 95, 101–2,
    155–56, 602–3, 737
    and attributes, 391, 397, 398, 514
    and authority, 80–83, 124
    and creation, 292–93
    and decrees, 316
    efficacy of, 47–50
    and evaluation, 124
    and God's acts, 242
    and God's name, 350–51
    and God's oneness, 623
    and goodness, 446
    and knowledge, 483
    and metaphysics, 236–37
    and miracles, 258–61
    and omnipresence, 580
    and problem of evil, 182
    and providence, 278
    and Son, 727
    and supralapsarianism, 339
    and Trinity, 734
    universality of, 50–53, 76–79
    and word, 473
conversion, 123n.6, 424
cosmic renewal, 297
cosmological argument, 290
cosmomorphism, 367
Council of Chalcedon, 613, 678n.39
Council of Constantinople, 698n.21, 716
counsel. *See* decrees
"counterfactuals of freedom," 153n.53
covenant, 12, 30–35, 42, 55, 94–96, 100,
    283, 323–24, 354
    Amyraut on, 803–5
    and attributes of God, 390
    blessings, 100–101

and lordship, 414
and love, 414
as personal, 406
and redemption, 411
and reprobate, 412–13
and righteous, 446–47
as universal, 411–12
by unregenerate, 434
gospel, 11, 427
government (providence), 275–78, 559
grace, 70, 76, 131, 232, 235, 279, 424–49,
    635n.23, 650n.12
as covenantal, 427
and gospel, 427
and law, 84, 428, 438n.57
and nature, 224–25
and works, 323–24
Granville Sharp Rule, 668–69
greater-good defense, 169–74, 182
Greek philosophy, 3, 7, 107, 188, 202,
    224, 553, 609–10, 628, 629, 630
guidance, 286, 539, 779
guilt, 129–31

happiness, 189–91, 193, 444
hard determinism, 772–73
hardening, in Scripture, 66–69, 73, 173
hatred, 460–63
healing, 360
heart, 62–63, 135, 142, 499, 509
heaven, 105–6, 141, 297, 577, 581, 591
Hegelians, 188
Heilsgeschichte, 215
hell, goodness in, 412–13
Hellenistic Judaism, 202
henotheism, 625n.10, 626
hermeneutical circle, 245
heroism, 256
hierarchialism, 23, 24, 721
higher creation, 257
Hinduism, 27, 109, 162, 272, 784, 785,
    789
history, 571
holiness, 120, 205, 291, 398
Holy One (title), 674–75
holy places, 581
Holy Spirit. *See* Spirit
holy wars, 358

horn of salvation, 376
hostility, 460–61
human choice, in salvation, 71–72
human conception, 59–60
human creativity, 153
human significance, 152, 153
humanism, 802
humility, 429n.40, 442–43, 507n.77
husband, 385
    God as, 373
hyper-Calvinism, 122n.5, 123n.6, 152n.50
hypostatizations, 632–33

idealism, 214
idolatry, 107, 216, 364, 373, 459, 464,
    605–6, 625, 679
ignorance, 127–28, 137
image of Christ, 297
image of God, 148, 152–53, 297, 311,
    364–65, 376, 396, 594
images of God, 343–45, 362–86
immanence, 97, 103–5, 110–11, 207, 397,
    610, 689, 785–86, 788
    in time, 497
    unbiblical views of, 110–15, 206
    See also presence
immanent Trinity. *See* ontological Trinity
Immanuel, 95–96, 98
immediacy, 251–53, 257, 288, 346
impersonal absolute, 27nn.15,16
impersonal forces, 26
imputation
    of Adam's sin, 120n.3
    of Christ's righteousness, 121n.3, 457
inability, 127, 129–31, 135, 143, 519
Incarnation, 254, 417–18, 497, 586–87,
    588, 589, 614, 660n.23, 676, 678,
    706, 707
incommunicable attributes, 14, 396, 543
incompatibilism, 138
incomprehensibility of God, 78, 108n.13,
    110, 200–207, 219, 235, 365, 398,
    469, 737
inconsistency, 133
incorporeality, 398
independence, of God. *See* aseity
independence, human, 142, 149
indeterminist freedom, 776, 777, 778

and suffering, 612, 615
as saving, 420–23
as universal, 417–19, 534–37
and wrath, 466–68
"love in freedom," 392
lower creation, 53, 257, 412
loyalty, 647–48. *See also* covenant loyalty
Lutherans, 502, 530–31

Macbeth, 156–57, 179–80
macroevolution, 311
Manichaeism, 167n.12
manna, 264
marriage, 34, 385
martyrdom, 256, 284
matter, 222–23, 576
maturity, 404
meaning, 473n.8, 753
mediation, 250
Medieval mysticism, 168
meekness, 442–43
mental ability, 134
mercy, 437, 441
Messiah, 360, 361, 634, 635, 638, 661–62
metaethics, 187, 196–98
metaphysical attributes, 400–401, 513, 543
metaphysical possibility, 500
metaphysical preservation, 278–79, 282, 290
metaphysical skepticism, 214
metaphysical truth, 475–79
metaphysics, 39, 186, 214–37, 400, 607, 736–37
    and epistemology, 231
    and miracle, 249
    and theology, 214
microevolution, 311
middle knowledge, 150–51, 501–5, 778
mind, 60n.14, 509
miracles, 129, 131, 244–73, 303, 412n.16, 737, 779, 790–96
    as apologetic, 271–73
    as attestation of prophecy, 253–55
    cessation of, 262–66
    as extraordinary, 246, 252
    and immediacy, 251–53
    and lordship, 258–60

and natural law, 246–51
and providence, 261–62, 275
and revelation, 260, 269–70, 272
modalism, 689–90, 706
monarch. *See* king, kingship
monarchianism, 627, 629, 689
monergism, 51
monism, 217, 299
monolatry, 626
monoperspectivalism, 151–52
monotheism, 627–31, 703
moral ability, 134
moral evil, 161, 168, 173. *See also* sin
moral freedom, 135–36
moral inability, 130–31, 134, 137
Mormons, 27
Moses, 83–84, 86–87, 91, 95, 97, 99–100, 254, 263, 425–26, 487, 588, 590
motivation, 736–37
motive, 211
Mount Sinai, 91, 581
multiperspectivalism. *See* perspectivalism
Muslims, 27, 787
mutable creation, 174
mutual glorification, 595, 694–97, 720, 727
mutual indwelling, 693–94
mystery, 201, 202
mysticism, 2, 718, 745

Naaman, 625–26n.10
name of God, 21, 343–45, 352–61, 383–84
    and glory, 348
    and jealousy, 459
    and lordship, 350–52
    as Word of God, 348
names, 363–64
    in Ancient Near East, 344–45
    as covenantal, 351
    as revelation, 384
narrative perspective. *See* situational perspective
natural evil, 161, 168
natural knowledge, 500, 501
natural law, 53, 111, 169, 215, 257, 303, 791, 792
    and miracle, 246–51
natural liberty, 145

Index of Scripture

3:34—429
4:5—509, 681
4:7—509, 681
4:8—376
4:11—506
4:23—188–89
5:21—483
6:6—455
6:9—455
6:16–19—461
6:23—376
6:34—458
8—234, 298, 471n.4
8–9—508
8:1—294
8:1–4—383
8:1–9:12—633
8:17—416
8:20—507
8:21—507
8:22—508–9, 681
8:22–30—471
8:22–31—382–83
8:22–36—286, 294
8:27—482
8:30—508
9:1–4—508
9:10—199, 508
10:12—460, 461
10:16—450
10:26—455
11:2—507n.77
11:8—450
11:20—460n.14, 461
12:13—508
13:4—455
13:9—376
15:3—483
15:11—483
15:29—582
15:33—199, 508
16:4—292
16:4–5—121
16:5—461
16:6—507
16:16—509, 681
16:33—52
17:3—375

17:15—461
17:16—509, 681
18:17—302
19:8—681
20:4—455
21:2—483
21:30—514
21:31—55
22:1—347
23—374
23:23—681
23:24–25—681
24:2—483
24:12—483
26:16—455
26:27—450
28:10—450
29:6—450
29:13—188–89

Ecclesiastes
5:2—104
12:1—632

Song of Solomon
8:6—458

Isaiah
1–3—371
1:1—493
1:4—28, 392, 515
1:1–17—319
1:9—320
1:16–17—454
1:18—319
1:19–20—319
1:24—515
1:25—320
1:26–28—320
2:10—653
2:12—413
2:19—653
2:21—653
4:2—677
5—375
5:1–7—129
5:16—106
5:19—28

6—677
6:1—260, 588
6:1–3—586n.10
6:1–5—369
6:1–10—653
6:3—28, 392, 636, 744
6:5—28, 260, 588, 654
6:9–10—332, 686
7:14—95, 664
8:13—653
8:14—653
9:6—443, 662, 664, 675
9:6–7—358, 488
9:7—443
10—154
10:5–11—130
10:5–12—55
10:5–15—121
10:15–19—130
10:20—28
10:20–34—320, 321
10:21—320
11:1–3—321
11:1–4—598
11:1–9—488
11:2—383, 507, 598, 686, 687
11:3–5—321, 453–54
11:9—321
11:11–12:6—320
11:12–16—321
12:1–6—321
12:6—28
13:8—381
13:9—488
13:11—413
14:4–23—413
14:24—316, 565
14:24–25—55
14:24–27—48, 515
14:26–27—55
16:6—632
17:7—28
19:20—674
21:3—381
21:22—96
26:3—443–44
26:4—479

11:3—83, 293n.9, 297–98, 300, 471, 515
11:6—416
11:7—90, 425
11:11—479
11:16—666
11:19—87
11:27—588, 590
12:4–11—372
12:4–12—409
12:7–11—170
12:8—372, 465n.21
12:23—685
12:25—49
12:28—29
12:29—377, 466, 468n.23
12:40—651
13:7—687n.48
13:8—568, 570, 677
13:17—687n.48
13:20—443
13:21—533

James
1:1—34
1:3—170
1:3–4—170, 172n.23
1:5—507, 539
1:12—278, 444
1:13—519
1:13–15—155n.58
1:14—145
1:17—316, 410, 560, 568, 604
1:18—533
1:19–20—464
2:1—655, 677
2:5—328
2:21—498
3:2—404
3:9—364
3:13–18—507
3:17—442
4:1–3—444
4:6—429n.40
4:8—582
4:12—624
4:13–16—61

5:6—675
5:7–11—172n.23
5:11—101n.3
5:14—349
5:14–16—134–35

1 Peter
1:1–2—694
1:2—315n.8, 316, 486n.48, 598, 641, 733
1:3–7—558
1:3–9—413, 742
1:7—170, 278
1:10—642
1:11—597–98
1:12—597
1:15–16—120, 181, 237, 360, 449
1:16—28, 219, 519
1:17—456
1:20—325, 329
2:3—653
2:13–3:22—527
2:14—433
2:21–25—422
2:22—675
3:8—442
3:15—653
3:18—598
4:2—533
4:12–19—527
4:13—170, 284
4:13–16—598
4:13–19—641
4:19—298
5:4—278
5:5—429n.40

2 Peter
1:1—35, 668–69
1:3—219n.6, 316, 678
1:4—219n.6
1:11—669
1:16—589
1:16–18—589
1:19–21—33
1:21—195, 472, 597
2—767

2:5—90, 254
2:15—435
2:20–22—436
3:3–9—244
3:5—293n.9, 471
3:5–7—281
3:8—556
3:9—281, 330, 411, 419, 431–32, 466, 531, 533, 535–36
3:10—281
3:10–13—243, 297
3:11—277
3:12—277, 297
3:13—538
3:14—278
3:15—432

1 John
1:1—290, 301
1:1–2—589
1:1–3—472, 473, 591
1:5—228, 376, 392, 393, 401, 744
1:6—478
1:8—478
1:8–10—277, 404
1:9—452, 458, 479
2:1—371
2:3–6—85n.9
2:4—478
2:16—746
2:18–19—323
2:19—285, 436
2:21—478
2:22—663, 789
2:23—661
2:27—478, 687
3:1—423, 705
3:1–2—658
3:2—512, 591
3:3—277
3:4—168, 175
3:5—675
3:16—371n.18, 391, 392, 422, 675
3:18—478
3:20—484